Lecture Notes in Artificial Intelligence 4130

Edited by J. G. Carbonell and J. Siekmann

Subseries of Lecture Notes in Computer Science

Ulrich Furbach   Natarajan Shankar (Eds.)

Automated Reasoning

Third International Joint Conference, IJCAR 2006
Seattle, WA, USA, August 17-20, 2006
Proceedings

 Springer

Series Editors

Jaime G. Carbonell, Carnegie Mellon University, Pittsburgh, PA, USA
Jörg Siekmann, University of Saarland, Saarbrücken, Germany

Volume Editors

Ulrich Furbach
Universität Koblenz-Landau
Fachbereich Informatik
Universitätsstrasse 1, 56070 Koblenz, Germany
E-mail: uli@furbach.de

Natarajan Shankar
Computer Science Laboratory, SRI International
Menlo Park, CA 94025, USA
E-mail: shankar@csl.sri.com

Library of Congress Control Number: Applied for

CR Subject Classification (1998): I.2.3, F.4.1, F.3, F.4, D.2.4

LNCS Sublibrary: SL 7 – Artificial Intelligence

ISSN   0302-9743
ISBN-10   3-540-37187-7 Springer Berlin Heidelberg New York
ISBN-13   978-3-540-37187-8 Springer Berlin Heidelberg New York

Springer is a part of Springer Science+Business Media

springer.com

© Springer-Verlag Berlin Heidelberg 2006
Printed in Germany

Typesetting: Camera-ready by author, data conversion by Scientific Publishing Services, Chennai, India
Printed on acid-free paper   SPIN: 11814771   06/3142   5 4 3 2 1 0

Preface

This volume contains the papers presented at the Third International Joint Conference on Automated Reasoning (IJCAR 2006) held on August 17–20, 2006, in Seattle, Washington as part of the Federated Logic Conference (FLoC 2006). The IJCAR series of conferences is aimed at unifying the different research disciplines within automated reasoning. IJCAR 2006 is the fusion of several major conferences:

- **CADE:** The International Conference on Automated Deduction
- **FroCoS:** Workshop on Frontiers of Combining Systems
- **FTP:** The International Workshop on First-Order Theorem Proving
- **TABLEAUX:** The International Conference on Automated Reasoning with Analytic Tableaux and Related Methods
- **TPHOLs:** The International Conference on Theorem Proving in Higher-Order Logics

Prior versions of IJCAR were held at Cork, Ireland in 2004 and Siena, Italy in 2001.

These proceedings contain 3 contributions by invited speakers including 1 full paper and 2 short abstracts, 41 research papers, and 8 system descriptions. It also includes a short overview of the CASC-J3 competition for automated theorem proving systems that was conducted during IJCAR 2006. In addition to the plenary CAV–IJCAR–ICLP speaker David Dill, the invited speakers included Bruno Buchberger, Adnan Darwich, and Dale Miller. The contributed papers were selected from 133 research paper submissions and 18 system description submissions. Both the number and quality of these submissions were exceptionally high. Each paper was reviewed by at least three referees, and decisions were reached after over two weeks of discussion through an electronic Program Committee meeting. The submissions, reviews, and discussion were coordinated using the EasyChair conference management system. The accepted papers spanned the entire spectrum of research in automated reasoning including formalization of mathematics, proof theory, proof search, description logics, interactive proof checking, higher-order logic, combination methods, satisfiability procedures, and rewriting.

The Herbrand Award for distinguished contributions to automated reasoning was given to Wolfgang Bibel in recognition of his far-sighted vision and leadership for the field, and his seminal technical contributions. The selection committee for the Herbrand Award included previous award winners, the IJCAR 2006 Steering Committee, the CADE Inc. trustees, and the IJCAR 2006 Program Committee. The Herbrand award ceremony and the acceptance speech were part of the conference program.

The workshops at IJCAR 2006 were coordinated by the Workshop Chair Maria Paola Bonacina, and included:

- **ACL2:** The ACL2 Theorem Prover and Its Applications
- **AFM:** Automated Formal Methods with PVS, ICS, and SAL
- **CFV:** Constraints in Formal Verification
- **DISPROVING:** Non-Theorems, Non-Validity, Non-Provability

- **ESCoR:** Empirically Successful Computerized Reasoning
- **FATES/RV:** Formal Aspects of Testing and Runtime Verification
- **LFMTP:** Logical Frameworks and Meta-Languages: Theory and Practice
- **PDPAR:** Pragmatics of Decision Procedures in Automated Reasoning
- **PLPV:** Programming Languages meets Program Verification
- **STRATEGIES:** Strategies in Automated Deduction
- **UITP:** User Interfaces for Theorem Provers
- **VERIFY:** Verification Workshop

In addition to the Program Committee and the reviewers, many people contributed to the success of IJCAR 2006. The Conference Chair John Harrison managed the physical organization of the meeting. Sergey Berezin served as the Publicity Chair. Peter Baumgartner coordinated the Woody Bledsoe student travel awards. The IJCAR 2006 Steering Committee consisted of Franz Baader, Ulrich Furbach, Reiner Hähnle, Natarajan Shankar, Toby Walsh, Peter Baumgartner, John Harrison, Tobias Nipkow, Cesare Tinelli, and Andrei Voronkov. The FLoC 2006 General Chair Moshe Vardi, the Program Co-chairs Thomas Ball and Jakob Rehof, the FLoC Workshop Chair Gopal Gupta, and the IJCAR representative Reiner Hähnle also assisted with many organizational issues and questions. Special thanks go to Andrei Voronkov and his EasyChair system, which makes many tasks of a program chair much more easier.

We would like to thank all the people involved in organizing IJCAR 2006 and FLoC 2006, as well as the sponsors of FLoC 2006, Cadence, IBM, Microsoft Research, NEC, and The John von Neumann Minerva Center for the Development of Reactive Systems.

June 2006   Ulrich Furbach
                                                              Natarajan Shankar

Conference Organization

Program Chairs

Ulrich Furbach
Natarajan Shankar

Program Committee

Alessandro Armando
Matthias Baaz
David Basin
Bernhard Beckert
Michael Beeson
Maria Paola Bonacina
Hubert Comon
Amy Felty
Martin Giese
Rajeev Gore
Tom Henzinger
Jason Hickey
Ian Horrocks
Dieter Hutter
Andrew Ireland
Deepak Kapur
Helene Kirchner

Michael Kohlhase
Chris Lynch
Michael Maher
Tom Melham
Jose Meseguer
Aart Middeldorp
Ilkka Niemelae
Christine Paulin-Mohring
Larry Paulson
Carsten Schuermann
Stephan Schulz
John Slaney
Mark Stickel
Aaron Stump
Geoff Sutcliffe
Frank Wolter
Hantao Zhang

Conference Chair

John Harrison

Workshop Chair

Maria Paola Bonacina

Publicity Chair

Sergey Berezin

Travel Awards

Peter Baumgartner

External Reviewers

Behzad Akbarpour
Carlos Areces
Serge Autexier
Arnon Avron
Emilie Balland
Peter Baumgartner
Yves Bertot
Gerd Beuster
Lars Birkedal
Frederic Blanqui
Stefan Blom
Krysia Broda
Chad Brown
Achim Brucker
Richard Bubel
Pierre Casteran
Yannick Chevalier
Agata Ciabatonni
Alessandro Cimatti
Koen Claessen
Sylvain Conchon
Pierre Corbineau
Marcello D'Agostino
Jeremy Dawson
Stephanie Delaune
Leonardo de Moura
Louise Dennis
Clare Dixon
Francesco M. Donini
Roy Dyckhoff
Mnacho Echenim
Thomas Eiter
Bill J. Ellis
Santiago Escobar
Stephan Falke
Chris Fermüller
Jean-Christophe Filliatre
Bernd Fischer
Pascal Fontaine
Lilia Georgieva
Jurgen Giesl

Birte Glimm
Isabelle Gnaedig
Sergey Goncharov
Ben Gorry
Bernardo Cuenca Grau
Alberto Griggio
Gudmund Grov
Dimitar Guelev
Elsa Gunter
James Harland
Keijo Heljanko
Joseph Hendrix
Miki Hermann
Steffen Hoelldobler
Doug Howe
Marieke Huisman
Joe Hurd
Ullrich Hustadt
Rosalie Iemhoff
Florent Jacquemard
Radha Jagadeesan
Predrag Janicic
Tommi Junttila
Yevgeny Kazakov
Florent Kirchner
Vladimir Klebanov
Boris Konev
Konstantin Korovin
Simon Kramer
Temur Kutsia
Timo Latvala
Carla Limongelli
Carsten Lutz
Jacopo Mantovani
Jia Meng
Stephan Merz
George Metcalfe
Thomas Meyer
Marius Minea
Glyn Morrill
Georg Moser

Till Mossakowski
Boris Motik
Normen Müller
Fabrice Nahon
Leonor Prensa Nieto
Robert Nieuwenhuis
Immanuel Normann
Michael Norrish
Hans J. Ohlbach
Florina Piroi
Adam Poswolsky
Florian Rabe
Silvio Ranise
Jason Reed
Greg Restall
Julian Richardson
Christophe Ringeissen
Andreas Roth
Andrey Rybalchenko
Gernot Salzer
Jeffrey Sarnat
Ralf Sasse
Uli Sattler
Steffen Schlager
Vasu Singh
Christoph Sprenger
Mark Steedman

Mark-Oliver Stehr
Gernot Stenz
Peter Stuckey
Sebastiaan Terwijn
Alwen Tiu
Ashish Tiwari
Ralf Treinen
Dmitry Tsarkov
Harvey Tuch
Anni-Yasmin Turhan
Xavier Urbain
Josef Urban
Rene Vestergaard
Luca Viganò
Laurent Vigneron
Christian Vogt
Uwe Waldmann
Toby Walsh
Tjark Weber
John Wheeler
Burkhart Wolff
Chunlai Zhou
Calogero G. Zarba
Jian Zhang
Paul Zimmermann
Evgeny Zolin

Table of Contents

Session 3. System Description 1

Session 4. Higher-Order Logic

Session 5. Proof Theory

Session 6. System Description 2

Session 7. Search

Session 8. Proof Theory

Session 12. CASC-J3

Session 13. Rewriting

Session 14. Description Logic

Mathematical Theory Exploration

Bruno Buchberger

Research Institute for Symbolic Computation
Johannes Kepler University Linz, Austria

Mathematics is characterized by its method of gaining knowledge, namely reasoning. The automation of reasoning has seen significant advances over the past decades and, thus, the expectation was that those advances would also have significant impact on the practice of doing mathematics. However, so far, this impact is small. We think that the reason for this is the fact that automated reasoning so far concentrated on the automated proof of individual theorems whereas, in the practice of mathematics, one proceeds by building up entire theories in a step-by-step process. This process of exploring mathematical theories consists of the invention of notions, the invention and proof of propositions (lemmas, theorems), the invention of problems, and the invention and verification of methods (algorithms) that solve problems. Also, in this process of mathematical theory exploration, storage and retrieval of knowledge plays an important role. The way how one proceeds in building up a mathematical theory in successive, well structured, layers has significant influence on the ease of proving individual propositions that occur in the build-up of the theory and also on the readability and explanatory power of the proofs generated. Furthermore, in the practice of mathematical theory exploration, different reasoning methods are used for different theories and, in fact, reasoning methods are expanded and changed in the process of exploring theories, whereas traditional automated reasoning systems try to get along with one reasoning method for large parts or all of mathematics.

We describe a methodology for the algorithmic support of mathematical theory exploration. Starting from any mathematical knowledge base (collection of formulae that may be axioms, definitions, propositions, lemmas, theorems, problem specifications, algorithms), in one exploration round, we introduce a few new notions by axioms or definitions and then explore the possible interactions of these notions with all existing notions as completely as possible before we proceed to the introduction of the next notions. Achieving a certain degree of completeness in the current exploration round is crucial for decreasing the complexity of proving in the subsequent exploration rounds. The invention of axioms and definitions, the invention of propositions that describe interactions between notions, the invention of problems involving the new notions, and the invention of algorithms that solve these problems is something which, typically, needs a certain degree of human intervention. However, we show that significant algorithmic support for these invention steps is possible by the use of *formula schemes*. Formula schemes are formulae with higher order variables for functions and predicates that describe fundamental properties of functions and predicates, as for example commutativity, isomorphy, etc., that have proved to be useful in the practice of mathematics.

U. Furbach and N. Shankar (Eds.): IJCAR 2006, LNAI 4130, pp. 1–2, 2006.

The application of formula schemes provides a kind of bottom-up support in the exploration of mathematical theories. A second idea is orthogonal to the use of formula schemes and provides top-down support in the exploration: We provide tools for the analysis of failing proofs. Failing proofs contain a lot of creative information. They give us hints about missing links in the systematic exploration of notions. For example, a failing induction proof of a conjecture may give us a hint about which lemmas we should try to prove before going back to the proof of the conjecture. The extraction of intermediate lemmas from failing proofs can, however, also be applied for the synthesis of algorithms.

We illustrate the interplay between the use of formula schemes, lemma extraction from failing proofs and automated reasoning (special reasoners for special theories) in a couple of examples. Our main example is the theory of Groebner bases that has found numerous applications in many different areas of mathematics (algebraic geometry, symbolic analysis, algebraic combinatorics etc.). Particular emphasis is put on a new method for the algorithm-supported synthesis of algorithms, which we call *lazy thinking method*, which combines the use of formula schemes and the extraction of conjectures from failing (automated) proofs in the following way:

- We start from a formal specification P of the problem and try out one algorithm scheme A after the other from a list of algorithm schemes. Such a scheme defines A recursively in terms of unkown subalgorithms B, C, etc.
- For the chosen scheme A, we try to prove (by an automated reasoner) the correctness theorem that states that A solves problem P. Typically, this proof will fail because nothing is known on the subalgorithms B, C, etc.
- We analyze the failing proof object and extract properties Q, R, etc. for B, C, etc. such that if B, C, etc. had these properties then the correctness proof could continue and eventually succeed. (We have a couple of heuristic rules for this extraction.)
- Properties Q, R, etc. can now be conceived as specifications for the subalgorithms B, C, etc. Now we either have suitable algorithms B, C, etc. already available in our current mathematical knowledge base (in this case we are done) or we call the lazy thinking method recursively for B, C, etc.

We demonstrate that this seemingly simple procedure has significant inventive power: It is strong enough, for example, to automatically synthesize an algorithm for the construction of Groebner bases. This is surprising because the construction of Groebner bases is a completely nontrivial problem which - in the early days of computer algebra - was even conjectured to be algorithmically unsolvable.

We also give some remarks, again in the example of Groebner bases theory, on the use of special theorem provers and the expansion and change of provers during the process of mathematical theory exploration and the implications of these facts on future reasoning systems for mathematics.

All the examples are given in our Theorema system, which tries to implement the above approach to mathematical theory exploration.

Searching While Keeping a Trace: The Evolution from Satisfiability to Knowledge Compilation

Adnan Darwiche

Computer Science Department
University of California, Los Angeles
CA 90095-1596, USA
darwiche@cs.ucla.edu

Satisfiability testing has seen significant growth over the last decade, leading to orders of magnitude improvements in performance over a relatively short period of time. State of the art algorithms for satisfiability, which are based on DPLL search, were originally meant to find a single satisfying assignment, but their scope has been extended recently to perform exhaustive searches for the purpose of counting and enumerating models. Moreover, the algorithms have been augmented with sophisticated techniques, such as component analysis and formula caching, which are critical to their performance in real–world applications. In a parallel thread of developments, work has been commencing in the area of knowledge compilation, which aims at converting knowledge bases into tractable representations that allow some hard operations to be performed in polytime on the compiled representations. Work in this area has lead to the identification of a comprehensive taxonomy of tractable languages that explicates their relative succinctness and the polytime operations they support.

In this talk, I will examine these two threads of developments in automated reasoning and show a deep connection that has evolved over the last few years. In particular, I will show that the trace of a search can be interpreted (and stored) as a propositional sentence, leading each search algorithm to define a propositional language consisting of sentences generated by all possible executions of the algorithm. I will show several matches between exhaustive search algorithms in common use today and well–known languages based on Binary Decision Diagrams (BDDs) and Decomposable Negation Normal Form (DNNF), which currently dominate the area of knowledge compilation. I will also discuss two implications of such matches: (1) a uniform and practical framework in which successful search techniques can be harnessed for the compilation of knowledge bases into various languages of interest, and (2) a new methodology whereby the hidden power and limitations of search algorithms can be unveiled by looking up the properties (tractability and succinctness) of corresponding propositional languages.

The talk will provide an exposition to many empirical studies that reflect the state of the art in exhaustive DPLL search and knowledge compilation. The talk will also show how these developments have lead to automated reasoning systems that are now forming the backbones of state of the art problem solvers in various areas, including planning (probabilistic and deterministic), state estimation and diagnosis, and probabilistic reasoning in graphical models.

U. Furbach and N. Shankar (Eds.): IJCAR 2006, LNAI 4130, p. 3, 2006.
© Springer-Verlag Berlin Heidelberg 2006

Representing and Reasoning with Operational Semantics

Dale Miller

INRIA & LIX, École Polytechnique

Abstract. The operational semantics of programming and specification languages is often presented via inference rules and these can generally be mapped into logic programming-like clauses. Such logical encodings of operational semantics can be surprisingly declarative if one uses logics that directly account for term-level bindings and for resources, such as are found in linear logic. Traditional theorem proving techniques, such as unification and backtracking search, can then be applied to animate operational semantic specifications. Of course, one wishes to go a step further than animation: using logic to encode computation should facilitate formal reasoning directly with semantic specifications. We outline an approach to reasoning about logic specifications that involves viewing logic specifications as theories in an object-logic and then using a meta-logic to reason about properties of those object-logic theories. We motivate the principal design goals of a particular meta-logic that has been built for that purpose.

1 Roles for Logic in the Specification of Computations

There are two broad approaches to using logic to specify computational systems. In the *computation-as-model* approach, computations are encoded as mathematical structures, containing such items as nodes, transitions, and state. Logic is used in an external sense to make statements *about* those structures. That is, computations are used as models for logical expressions. Intensional operators, such as the modals of temporal and dynamic logics or the triples of Hoare logic, are often employed to express propositions about the change in state. This use of logic to represent and reason about computation is probably the oldest and most broadly successful use of logic for specifying computation.

The *computation-as-deduction* approach uses pieces of logic's syntax (formulas, terms, types, and proofs) directly as elements of the specified computation. In this much more rarefied setting, there are two rather different approaches to how computation is modeled. The *proof normalization* approach views the state of a computation as a proof term and the process of computing as normalization (via β-reduction or cut-elimination). Functional programming can be explained using proof-normalization as its theoretical basis [23]. The *proof search* approach views the state of a computation as a sequent (a structured collection of formulas) and the process of computing as the search for a proof of a sequent: the changes that take place in sequents capture the dynamics of computation. Proof

U. Furbach and N. Shankar (Eds.): IJCAR 2006, LNAI 4130, pp. 4–20, 2006.

search has been used to provide a theoretical foundation for logic programming [33] and to justify the design of new logic programming languages [31].

The divisions proposed above are informal and suggestive: such a classification is helpful in pointing out different sets of concerns represented by these two broad approaches (reduction, confluence, etc, versus unification, backtracking search, etc). Of course, a real advance in computation logic might allow us merge or reorganize this classification.

This classification can help to categorize the various proof systems that have been used to reason about computation systems. For example, the computation-as-model approach usually implies that one divides the problem of reasoning about computation into two steps. In the first step, one *implements mathematics* via some set-theory or higher-order logic (for example, HOL [14], Isabelle/ZF [46], PVS [44]). In the second step, one reduces program correctness problems to mathematics. Thus, data structures, states, stacks, heaps, invariants, etc, all are represented as various kinds of mathematical objects. One then reasons directly on these objects using standard mathematical techniques (induction, primitive recursion, fixed points, well-founded orders, etc).

Researchers who specify computation using the proof-normalization approach usually first implement mathematics, but this time, in a constructive mathematics, using, for example, Martin-Löf type theory [23] and higher-order intuitionistic logic or dependent type theory (for example, Coq [9] and NuPRL [8]).

This paper describes another possibility for the construction of a prover that takes its inspiration from the proof search approach to the specification of computation.

2   The Proof Search Paradigm

As one builds cut-free proofs of sequents (in the sense of, say, Gentzen [12]), sequents change and this change, reading proofs bottom-up, is used to capture the dynamics of computation that one intends to model. The cut-rule and the cut-elimination process do not have roles to play during this simulation of computation: instead, they can play important roles in reasoning about specified computations.

While proof search can be seen as a means of giving a broad foundation to logic programming, there are a number of aspects of proof search (as computation) that have not been embraced by the general logic programming community. For example, proof search relies primarily on proof theory for new designs and analysis tools, instead of model theory as is more customarily used by logic programming researchers. Proof search generally stresses logically correct deduction even if non-logical techniques, such as dropping all occur-checks during unification and using the ! pruning or "cut" operator of Prolog, can yield more effective executions. Also, proof search design and theory also focuses on the meaning of logical connectives and quantifiers for expressiveness and for new designs. Such a focus is in contrast to, say, constraint logic programming [21].

As we highlight in the rest of this section, the proof search paradigm allows for a relatively straightforward treatments of such "intensional" aspects of computation as binders, binder mobility, and resource management.

2.1 Encoding Symbolic Expression Via λ-Tree Syntax

Most human authored and readable symbolic expressions start life as strings: such linearly organized data are full of semantically unimportant information such as white space, infix/postfix operators, and parentheses. Before processing such *concrete syntax*, one removes much of this concrete nonsense by parsing the data into a more abstract representation we call here *parse trees* (often also called *abstract syntax*).

Most parsing technology unfortunately leaves the names of bound variables in the resulting parse trees. Although binders are, of course, important aspects of the meaning of computational objects, the name of variables used to encode binders are another form of concrete nonsense. Since dealing with bindings in syntax is a well known problem, various techniques are available to help make this concrete and semantically meaningless aspect of syntax more abstract. One approach to bindings in syntax uses deBruijn numerals [5]. While such an encoding has proved its value within implementations, deBruijn numerals seem too explicit and complicated to support declarative reasoning of syntax. Other approaches involve the direct use of named variables and a version of set theory to accommodate names and renaming [11].

The *higher-order abstract syntax* (*hoas*) [47] approach to encoding syntax proposes that bindings in data should be mapped to the bindings found in whatever programming or specification language one is using. Within functional programming, term-level binders are then encoded as functional objects. While some interesting specifications have resulted [10,18], this approach has numerous semantic problems. For example, while expressions with bindings are still intended to be finite and syntactic objects, the corresponding functions yields values that are usually infinite in extension. Also, there are usually many more constructors for function spaces than simply the λ-abstraction within a functional programming setting: for example, recursive function definition.

In contrast, the proof search approach to the specification of computation allows for a different approach to hoas. In that setting, λ-terms modulo various weak subsets of λ-conversion can be used to directly encode expressions. Here, α-conversion abstracts away from the names of bindings, β_0-conversion allows for *binder mobility* [28,30], and β-conversion allows for object-level substitution. We shall use the term *λ-tree syntax* [29] to denote the proof search approach to hoas. While there is a long history of using λ-tree syntax in specifying computation, starting with Huet and Lang [20] and Miller and Nadathur [32], few computer systems actually support it directly: the λProlog [40] programming language and the Isabelle [43] and Twelf [48] specification languages are the best known exceptions.

Using meta-level application to encode object-level applications is standard practice: for example, one uses meta-level application to apply, say, *cons*, to two arguments: ($cons\ X\ L$). The λ-tree syntax approach is simply a dualizing of this practice that uses meta-level abstraction to encode object-level binders.

2.2 Encoding Computational Processes as Formula or as Terms

It seems that there are two choices one can make when encoding "active" components of a computation into proof search. Usually, these active objects, such as computation threads, automata states, etc, which we collectively call here as simply "processes", are encoded as terms. In this *process-as-term* approach, predicates are then used to state relationships between computational items. For example, we have statements such as "M has value V", "in context Γ, M has type σ", "P makes an A transition and becomes Q", etc. Given such atomic formulas, one then encodes operational semantics as compound formulas within either an intuitionistic or a classical logic. For an example of encoding the π-calculus using this process-as-term approach, see [35,54] and Section 6.

With the availability of linear logic and other sub-structural logics, it seems sensible to consider another style of encoding where processes are encoded directly as formulas. In the *process-as-formula* approach to encoding, formulas no longer denote truth values: instead they denote "resources" which can change over time. In such a setting, the combinators of a processes calculus are mapped to logical connectives and the environment of a computation thread (including, for example, memory and other threads) are modeled via a logical context (within a sequent, for example). In principle, this approach requires fewer non-logical constants than are used with the process-as-term approach. There is a large literature of specifying programming language features in this manner using linear logic [31].

While encodings using the process-as-formula approach can often capture the notion of process execution or of reachability, they fail to directly support rich notions of program or process equivalences, such as bisimulation or observational equivalence. To capture these equivalences, the process-as-term approach has provided more successes.

3 Operational Semantics as Logic Specification

A common style of operational semantics specification is presented as inference rules involving relations. We illustrate how such semantic specifications can be mapped into logical specifications.

For example, some of the rules for specifying CCS [37] are given by the following inference rules.

$$\frac{P \xrightarrow{A} R}{P + Q \xrightarrow{A} R} \qquad \frac{Q \xrightarrow{A} R}{P + Q \xrightarrow{A} R} \qquad \frac{P \xrightarrow{A} P'}{P|Q \xrightarrow{A} P'|Q} \qquad \frac{Q \xrightarrow{A} Q'}{P|Q \xrightarrow{A} P|Q'}$$

By viewing $+$ and $|$ as constructors of processes and $\cdot \longrightarrow \cdot$ as a predicate of three arguments, it is easy to write these inference rules as the following first-order Horn clauses.

$$\forall P \forall Q \forall A \forall R[P \xrightarrow{A} R \supset P+Q \xrightarrow{A} R]$$

$$\forall P \forall Q \forall A \forall R[Q \xrightarrow{A} R \supset P+Q \xrightarrow{A} R]$$

$$\forall P \forall A \forall P' \forall Q[P \xrightarrow{A} P' \supset P|Q \xrightarrow{A} P'|Q]$$

$$\forall P \forall A \forall Q' \forall Q[Q \xrightarrow{A} Q' \supset P|Q \xrightarrow{A} P|Q']$$

For a slightly more challenging specification of operational semantics, we consider a specification of call-by-name evaluation, which involves bindings and substitution (call-by-value evaluation can also be used here just as easily). Let the type *tm* denote the syntactic category of untyped λ-terms and let the two constructors *abs* of type (*tm* → *tm*) → *tm* and *app* of type *tm* → *tm* → *tm* denote abstraction and application within the untyped λ-calculus, respectively. This encoding places α-equivalence classes of untyped λ-terms in one-to-one correspondence with βη-equivalence classes of terms of type *tm*. To specify call-by-name evaluation, we use an infix binary predicate ⇓ to denote evaluation between two arguments of type *tm*. Call-by-name evaluation can be specified by the following two inference rules.

$$\frac{}{(abs\ \lambda x.S) \Downarrow (abs\ \lambda x.S)} \qquad \frac{M \Downarrow (abs\ \lambda x.S) \quad (S[x/N]) \Downarrow V}{(app\ M\ N) \Downarrow V}$$

To translate these inference rules into logic, one needs to explain carefully the proper treatment of binding (here, λx) and the definition of term-level substitution (here, $S[x/N]$). As is often observed, these details are complex and there are a number of different solutions. Furthermore, dealing with all those details does not help in understanding the essential *semantics* of such a specification rule. Fortunately, we can simply invoke the λ-tree approach to syntax to address these problems. In particular, we assume that our logic contains variables of higher-order type (in particular, of type *tm* → *tm*) and that it contains an equality of simply types that includes βη-conversion. In this way, we can simply reuse the careful specification done by, say, Church in [6], of how λ-abstraction and logic interact. Given this motivation, we can now choose to write the above specification as simply the following (higher-order) Horn clauses [41]:

$$\forall R.[(abs\ R) \Downarrow (abs\ R)]$$

$$\forall M \forall N \forall V \forall R.[M \Downarrow (abs\ R) \wedge (R\ N) \Downarrow V \supset (app\ M\ N) \Downarrow V]$$

Here, R has type *tm* → *tm* and corresponds to the expression λx.S and the substitution $S[x/N]$ is replaced by the expression (R N).

Various forms of static analysis, such a typing, can be specified using inference rules as well. Consider, for example, the specification of simple typing for the untyped λ-calculus. To specify simple typing for the untyped λ-calculus, we introduce the logic-level type *ty* to denote the syntactic category of simple type expressions and use the constructors *gnd* of type *ty* (denoting a ground, primitive type) and *arr* of type $ty \rightarrow ty \rightarrow ty$ (denoting the function type constructor). The usual rule for simple typing is given as follows:

$$\frac{\Gamma \vdash M : (\text{arr } U \ T) \qquad \Gamma \vdash N : U}{\Gamma \vdash (\text{app } M \ N) : T} \qquad \frac{\Gamma, x : T \vdash S : U}{\Gamma \vdash (\text{abs } \lambda x.S) : (\text{arr } T \ U)} (\dagger)$$

The second inference rule has the proviso ($\dagger$): x must be a new variable; that is, it is not free in T, U, nor in any of the pairs in Γ. To encode these inference rules into logic, we first pick a binary predicate *typeof*, whose arguments are of type *tm* and *ty*, respectively, to denote the colon relation above. Then the following formulas provide an elegant encoding of these typing inference rules.

$$\forall M \forall N \forall T \forall U [\textit{typeof } M \ (\text{arr } U \ T) \wedge \textit{typeof } N \ U \supset \textit{typeof } (\text{app } M \ N) \ T]$$

$$\forall R \forall T \forall U [\forall x. [\textit{typeof } x \ T \supset \textit{typeof } (R \ x) \ U] \supset \textit{typeof } (\text{abs } R) \ (\text{arr } T \ U)]$$

Notice that these formulas are no longer Horn clauses. The use of λ-tree syntax allows for dispensing with any explicit reference to bindings. The use of the implication in the body of clauses means that the explicit context Γ is being managed implicitly by logic. The term-level binding in λx can be seen as "moving" to the formula-level binding $\forall x$. During proof search, this formula-level binding will be replaced with an eigenvariable: thus, this formula-level binding will move to a proof-level binding. Such *binder mobility* gives λ-tree syntax one of its strength: a specification does not need to specify details about how binders are encode, instead, binders only need to be moved from term-level to formula-level to proof-level bindings. Details of binders need to be addressed only by implementors of the logic.

4   What Good Is a Logic Specification Anyway?

People working in programming language specification and implementation have a history of using declarative tools. For example, both lexical analyzers and parsers are often generated by special tools (e.g., lex and yacc) that work from such declarative specifications as regular expressions and context-free grammars. Similarly, operational semantics has been turned into interpreters via logic programming engines [4] and denotational semantics have been used to generate compilers [45].

Given a history of interest in declarative techniques to specify programming language systems, it seems natural to now focus on the question: why should anyone care that we have written an operational semantic specification or a typing relation declaratively? What benefits should arise from using λ-tree syntax, from using intuitionistic logic or linear logic?

One benefit arises from the fact that logic is a difficult discipline to follow: the efforts of the specifier to hammer a specification into a declarative setting that lacks, for example, side-conditions, can often lead to new ways of thinking about what one is specifying. Such rarefied and declarative settings can also allow broad results to be inferred from specifications: for example, the fact that bisimulation is a congruence can be established for process calculi (see, for example, [15,56]) or for functional programming languages [19] by checking syntactic conditions on the declarative specification of operational semantics.

Another benefit is that an implementation of logic might provide a uniform means to animate a wide range of logic specifications.

The benefit that concerns us here, however, is that a logic specification should facilitate the inferring of formal properties. While this might sound obvious, designing a "meta-logic" for reasoning about logic specifications requires some work. We motivate via some examples one particular meta-logic.

5   Example: A Subject-Reduction Theorem

Consider again the specification of evaluation and typing given in Section 3. The following theorem is usually called the *type preservation* or the *subject-reduction* theorem. The informal proof of this theorem below is taken from [24].

Theorem 1. *If P evaluates to V and P has type T then V has type T.*

Proof. We write $\vdash B$ to mean that there is a *uniform proof* of B, where uniform proofs are certain kinds of cut-free proofs that have been used to formalize the notion of goal-directed proof search [33]. Restricting to such uniform proofs in this setting does not result in a loss of completeness. We proceed by induction on the structure of a uniform proof of $P \Downarrow V$ that for all T, if $\vdash$ *typeof P T* then $\vdash$ *typeof V T*. Since $P \Downarrow V$ is atomic, its proof must end by backchaining on one of the formulas encoding evaluation. If the backchaining is on the $\Downarrow$ formula for *abs*, then P and V are both equal to *abs R*, for some R, and the consequent is immediate. If $P \Downarrow V$ is proved using the $\Downarrow$ formula for *app*, then P is of the form *app M N* and for some R, there are shorter proofs of $M \Downarrow$ (*abs R*) and (RN) $\Downarrow V$. Since $\vdash$ *typeof* (*app M N*) T, this typing relation must have been proved using backchaining and, hence, there is a U such that $\vdash$ *typeof M* (*arr U T*) and $\vdash$ *typeof N U*. Using the inductive hypothesis, we have $\vdash$ *typeof* (*abs R*) (*arr U T*). This atomic formula must have been proved by backchaining on the *typeof* formula for *abs*, and, hence, $\vdash \forall x.$[*typeof x U* $\supset$ *typeof* (*R x*) *T*]. Since our meta-language is (intuitionistic) logic, we can instantiate this quantifier with N and use cut and cut-elimination to conclude that $\vdash$ *typeof* (*R N*) *T*. (This last step is essentially a "substitution lemma" which comes for free given cut elimination and our use of λ-tree syntax.) Using the inductive hypothesis a second time yields $\vdash$ *typeof V T*.

This proof is clear and natural and we would like our meta-logic to support similarly structured proofs. This example suggests that the following features would be valuable in the meta-logic.

1. *Two distinct logics.* In the above informal proof, there are clearly two distinct logics being used. One logic is written with logical syntax and describes some relations, e.g. typability and evaluation. The second logic is written

with English text: atomic formulas of that logic are (provability) judgments about the object-logic. This use of two distinct logics – one for the specifying operational semantics and typing and one for the meta-logic – is an important aspect of our approach to reasoning about computation.

2. *Structural induction* over object-level sequent calculus proofs was used. Obviously induction over other structures (e.g., expressions, formulas) and co-induction play important roles in meta-level reasoning about computation.

3. The *instantiation of meta-level eigenvariables* was used in this proof. In particular, the variable P was instantiated in one part of the proof to $(abs\ R)$ and in another part of the proof to $(app\ M\ N)$. Notice that such instantiation of eigenvariables within a proof does not happen in proof search in conventional sequent calculi.

4. The *inversion of assumed judgment* was used in the above proof a few times, leading, for example, from the assumption $\vdash$ *typeof* $(abs\ R)$ $(arr\ U\ T)$ to the assumption $\vdash \forall x[typeof\ x\ U \supset typeof\ (R\ x)\ T]$. The specification of *typeof* allows the implication to go in the other direction, but given the structure of the specification of *typeof*, this direction can also be justified at the meta-level.

The system Twelf is capable of proving such type preservation properties along rather similar lines, except that an explicit meta-logic with an explicit induction rule is replaced by a meta-level tool that checks properties such as coverage and termination [51].

In the example above, bindings in the object-logic and object-language played a small role: they were treated only by instantiation. In the next section, we consider the π-calculus since it provides a more challenging problem for dealing with bindings in syntax and in computations.

6   Example: A π-Calculus Specification

To encode the syntax of the π-calculus, let the types p, n, and a denote the syntactic category of processes, names, and actions, respectively. A signature for the π-calculus can thus be listed as

$$0 : p, \qquad out : n \to n \to p \to p, \qquad in : n \to (n \to p) \to p,$$
$$+, \mid\ : p \to p \to p, \quad match : n \to n \to p \to p, \quad \nu : (n \to p) \to p.$$

For example, the expression $x(y).P$, where x is a name and y is a binding with scope P, can be encoded using a constructor *in* as the expression $(in\ x\ (\lambda y.P'))$. Similarly, the restriction operator $\nu x.P$ can be encoded as $\nu(\lambda x.P)$.

We next introduce three constructors for actions: τ denotes the silent action and the down arrow $\downarrow$ and up arrow $\uparrow$ encode input and output actions, resp: in particular, the expression $(\downarrow xy)$ denotes an input action on channel x of value y. Notice that the two expressions, $\lambda y.\uparrow xy$ and $\uparrow x$, denoting *abstracted actions*, are equal up to η-conversion and can be used interchangeably.

To specifying the operational semantics of the π-calculus, we use the horizontal arrow $\longrightarrow$ to relate a process with an action and a continuation (a process), and the "harpoon" ——⇀ to relate a process with an *abstracted* action and an *abstracted* continuation (of types $n \to a$ and $n \to p$, resp.).

The following three rules (named (CLOSE), (RES), (OPEN)) are part of the specification of one-step transitions for the π-calculus: the full specification using λ-tree syntax can be found in, for example, [34,36].

$$\frac{P \xrightarrow{\downarrow X} M \quad Q \xrightarrow{\uparrow X} N}{P \mid Q \xrightarrow{\tau} \nu y.(My \mid Ny)} \qquad \frac{\forall n(Nn \xrightarrow{A} Mn)}{\nu n.Nn \xrightarrow{A} \nu n.Mn} \qquad \frac{\forall y(Ny \xrightarrow{\uparrow Xy} My)}{\nu y.Ny \xrightarrow{\lambda y.\uparrow Xy} \lambda y.My}$$

The (CLOSE) rule describes how a bound input and bound output action can yield a τ step with a ν-restricted continuation. The (RES) rule illustrates how λ-tree syntax and appropriate quantification can remove the need for side conditions: since substitution in *logic* does not allow for the capture of bound variables, all instances of the premise of this rule have a horizontal arrow in which the action label does not contain the universally quantified variable free. Thus, the usual side condition for this rule is treated declaratively. There is a direct translation of such inference rules into, say, λProlog [40], in such a way that one can directly animate the operational semantics of the π-calculus.

7   Example: Bisimulation for the π-Calculus

There seems to be something questionable about the use of the universal quantifier in the premises of the operational semantics for the π-calculus above. For example, the (RES) rule says that if $Nn \xrightarrow{A} Mn$ is provable for all instances of the free variable n then the transition $\nu n.Nn \xrightarrow{A} \nu n.Mn$ is justified. This does not seem to be a completely correct sense of what is implied by the original specification rule of the π-calculus. A more correct sense of the rule should be something like: if $Nn \xrightarrow{A} Mn$ is provable for some *new* name n, then the above conclusion is justified. In a proof search setting involving only positive inference about computation (for example, judgments involving only *may* behavior of a process), such a quantifier appears only positively and is instantiated with a new (proof-level bound) variable called an *eigenvariable*. In this setting, the notion of *new* name is supported well by the universal quantifier. If, however, negative information is being inferred, as is possible with judgments involving *must* behaviors, then the universal quantifier is instantiated with any number of existing names. This seems like the wrong meaning for this rule.

To illustrate this example more concretely, note that for any name x, the process $\nu y.[x = y]\bar{x}z$ is bisimilar to 0: that is, this process can make no transitions. This fact also seems to follow from the nature of bindings: the scope of the bindings for x and for y are such that any instance of x can never equal y (a simple consequence of that fact that sound substitutions avoid variable capture). Now, proving this bisimulation fact should be equivalent to proving

$$\forall x \forall A \forall P' \neg (\nu y.[x = y]\bar{x}z \xrightarrow{A} P')$$

Using the above operational semantics, this should be equivalent to proving

$$\forall x \forall A \forall P'' \neg \forall y([x = y]\bar{x}z \xrightarrow{A} P'') \quad \text{and} \quad \forall x \forall A \forall P'' \exists y \neg ([x = y]\bar{x}z \xrightarrow{A} P'')$$

Now it seems that standard proof theory techniques will not achieve a proof: somehow we need to have additional information that for every name there exists another name that is distinct from it. Adopting such an axiom is often done in many settings, but this seems to go against the usual spirit of sequent calculus (a system usually containing *no* axioms) and against the idea that proof theory is, in fact, an ideal setting to deal with notions of bindings and scope directly.

To come up with a proof theoretic approach to address this problem with using the $\forall$-quantifier in operational semantics, Miller and Tiu [35,36] introduced the ∇-quantifier: the informal reading of $\nabla x.Bx$, in both positive and negative settings, is equivalent to Bx for a new name x. To support this new quantification, sequent calculus is extended to support a notion of "generic judgments" so that "newness" remains a (proof-level) binding and can be seen as being hypothetical. That is, the truth condition of $\nabla x.Bx$ roughly reduces to the conditional "if a new name c is created then Bc." Notice that no assumption about whether or not the domain of quantification is non-empty is made (this detail makes ∇ behave differently from the Gabbay-Pitts "newness quantifier" [11]). If one is interested only in establishing one-step transitions (and not their negation), then it is possible to use ∇ and $\forall$ in the premises of the operational semantics for the π-calculus interchangeably.

Using ∇-quantification instead of $\forall$-quantification in the premise of the (RES) rule does, in fact, allow proving the formula

$$\forall x \forall A \forall P' \neg (\nu y.[x = y]\bar{x}z \xrightarrow{A} P'),$$

since this now reduces to $\forall x \forall A \forall P'' \nabla y \neg ([x = y]\bar{x}z \xrightarrow{A} P'')$. If one follows the proof theory for ∇ carefully [36] this negation is provable because the expressions $\lambda y.x$ and $\lambda y.y$ do not unify (for free variable x). Notice that the binding of y is maintained all the way to the level of unification where, in this case, it ensures the correct failure to find an appropriate instance for x.

Using the ∇-quantifier, it is now easy and natural to specify bisimulation for the π-calculus with the equivalence displayed in Figure 1. Notice the elegant par-

$$\begin{aligned}
bisim\ P\ Q &\equiv \forall A \forall P' [P \xrightarrow{A} P' \Rightarrow \exists Q'.Q \xrightarrow{A} Q' \wedge bisim\ P'\ Q'] \wedge \\
&\quad \forall A \forall Q' [Q \xrightarrow{A} Q' \Rightarrow \exists P'.P \xrightarrow{A} P' \wedge bisim\ Q'\ P'] \wedge \\
&\quad \forall X \forall P' [P \xrightarrow{\downarrow X} P' \Rightarrow \exists Q'.Q \xrightarrow{\downarrow X} Q' \wedge \forall w.bisim\ (P'w)\ (Q'w)] \wedge \\
&\quad \forall X \forall Q' [Q \xrightarrow{\downarrow X} Q' \Rightarrow \exists P'.P \xrightarrow{\downarrow X} P' \wedge \forall w.bisim\ (Q'w)\ (P'w)] \wedge \\
&\quad \forall X \forall P' [P \xrightarrow{\uparrow X} P' \Rightarrow \exists Q'.Q \xrightarrow{\uparrow X} Q' \wedge \nabla w.bisim\ (P'w)\ (Q'w)] \wedge \\
&\quad \forall X \forall Q' [Q \xrightarrow{\uparrow X} Q' \Rightarrow \exists P'.P \xrightarrow{\uparrow X} P' \wedge \nabla w.bisim\ (Q'w)\ (P'w)]
\end{aligned}$$

Fig. 1. A specification of bisimulation for the π-calculus

allelism between using ∀ to quantify bisimulation of abstracted continuations for bound inputs and using ∇ to quantify bisimulation of abstracted continuations for bound outputs. As is shown in [54], proving this formula in intuitionistic logic yields *open bisimulation* [49]. Without an inference rule for co-induction, this equivalence is only correct for the *finite* π-calculus (a subset of the π-calculus that does not contain the replication operator ! nor recursive definition of processes). If we add the excluded-middle assumption $\forall w \forall z (w = z \lor w \neq z)$ (which is trivially true in a classical meta-theory), the resulting specification can be used to specify *late bisimulation* [38] (see [54] for the precise statements regarding this specification). A logic programming-style implementation of proof search provides an immediate *symbolic bisimulation* checker (in the sense of [17,3]) for the finite π-calculus [54,53].

8   The LINC Meta-logic

The three examples above allow us to now motivate the design of a meta-logic that can be used to state properties of object-level provability and, hence, to reason about operational semantics (via their encodings into object-logics). Our meta-logic is called LINC, an acronym coined by Tiu [52] for "lambda, induction, nabla, co-induction." This logic contains the following three key features.

First, LINC is based on the predicative and intuitionistic fragment of Church Simple Theory of Types [6] (restricted to the axioms 1 – 6). Provability for this logic can be described as being essentially Gentzen's LJ sequent calculus [12] to which is added simple typing for all variables and constants, quantification at all types (excluding the type of predicates), and an inference rule that allows βη-conversion on any formula in a sequent. This logic provides support for λ-tree syntax. Considering a classical logic extension of LINC is also of some interest, as is an extension allowing for quantification at predicate type.

Second, LINC incorporates the proof-theoretical notion of *definition*, a simple and elegant device for extending logic with the if-and-only-if closure of a logic specification (similar to the *closed-world assumption* [7]). This notion of definition was developed by Hallnäs and Schroeder-Heister [16,50] and, independently, by Girard [13]. This feature of definitions allows for the "inversion of assumed judgments" mentioned at the end of Section 5 and for the ability to capture not just *may* behavior but also *must* behavior. In particular, definitions are central to the treatment of bisimulation mentioned in Section 7 (see also [27]) and for doing model checking directly with operational semantics (see, for example, [53,55]). It also allows for certain failures of proof search to be turned into successful proofs of negations. Definitions are also a natural place to incorporate inductive and co-inductive inference rules: for full details, see paper by McDowell, Miller, Momigliano, and Tiu [25,26,35,39,52].

Third, LINC contains the ∇ quantifier, which, as we just illustrated, allows for more natural and direct reasoning about syntactic encodings based on λ-tree syntax.

As Tiu has shown in [52], under restrictions of appropriately "stratified" definitions (a restriction which rules out, for example, a predicate being defined as its own negation), the LINC logic satisfies cut-elimination. The logic $FO\lambda^{\Delta\mathbb{N}}$ of [25,26] is a subset of LINC, corresponding roughly to the fragment that results from deleting the ∇-quantifier, removing co-induction, and limiting induction to natural number induction.

The principal use of the ∇-quantifier is helping with the treatment of bindings in λ-tree syntax encodings. In fact, we know of no use of ∇ in specifications that involve only, say, first-order terms. It is also the case that ∇ is interchangeable with $\forall$ when definitions are "positive": that is, when they contain no occurrences of implications and negations. In such Horn clause-like definitions, one can interchange these two quantifiers in the body of definitions without affecting the atomic formulas that are provable [36].

9   Formal Reasoning About Logic Specifications

Figure 2 presents an architecture for organizing the various symbolic systems involved with the specification of and reasoning about computation systems. The top level contains the *many* applications about which we hope to provide formal proofs. Possible applications should include programming languages, specifications languages, security protocols, type systems, etc.

The middle layer contains a *few* object-level logics, such as Horn clauses (HC), hereditary Harrop formulas (HH) [33], and linear logic (LL). These logics all have well understood meta-theories and their operational semantics is given by proof search following the normal forms dictated by uniform proofs and backchaining [33] or focused proofs [1]. In fact, all of these logics can be seen as modularly sitting inside one single logic, namely, linear logic.

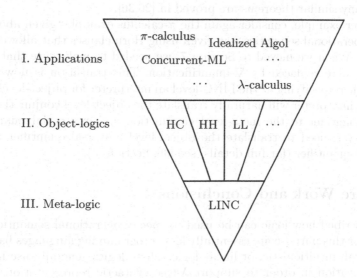

Fig. 2. A three level architecture

The bottom layer consists of the single logic LINC, where object-level provability must be encoded (as an abstracted logic programming interpreter) and important results about object-level provability (including cut-elimination) must be proved. Also, object-level logic specifications used to capture aspects of an application must also be encoded into the meta-level. Since the meta-logic and object-logic share the same application and abstraction, terms used to encode application-level objects (for example, a π-calculus expression) are the same at both levels.

To illustrate these three-levels, consider the proof of the subject-reduction theorem in Section 5. The application level contains two classes of linguistic items: untyped λ-terms (constructed using *abs* and *app*) and simple type expressions (constructed using *gnd* and *arr*). The formulas in Section 5 that specify evaluation and typing are object-level (hereditary Harrop) formulas. At the meta-level, such formulas are simply terms, where object-level predicates, such as $\Downarrow$ and *typeof*, are now binary constructor in the meta-logic and where object-level logic connectives and quantifiers are also meta-level term constructors (requiring meta-level λ-abstraction to encode quantifiers). Formulas at the LINC (meta-logic) level must now encode the notion of provability for the object-level logic as well as any other judgments that are specific to the application being considering (such as, say, bisimulation). For example, provability of hereditary Harrop formulas can be defined in LINC via a predicate, say, *seq* Γ B to describe when the object-level formula B is provable from the list of object-level formulas in Γ and the object-level formulas describing evaluation and typing (see [26, Section 4.3] for specifics on how this can be done). The meta-level formula that one wishes to prove within LINC is then

$$\forall P \forall V [seq\ nil\ (P \Downarrow V) \supset \forall T [seq\ nil\ (typeof\ P\ T) \supset seq\ nil\ (typeof\ V\ T)]]$$

This and many similar theorems are proved in [26,36].

For another example, consider again the π-calculus examples given above. In Section 6, operational semantics was given using Horn clauses that allowed $\forall$ in their bodies. When we moved to Section 7, we needed to make sure that these $\forall$-quantifiers were replaced by ∇-quantification. This transition is now easily explained: when specifying at the LINC level an interpreter for object-level Horn clauses, that interpreter will naturally translate the object-level conjunction and existential quantifier to the meta-level conjunction and existential quantifier. It will, however, need to translate the object-level universal quantifier to the meta-level ∇-quantifier (for full details, see [36, Section 6]).

10   Future Work and Conclusions

We have described how logic can be used to specify operational semantics: the logics used for this purpose are essentially logic programming languages based in either classical, intuitionistic, or linear logic. These logics generally use higher-type quantification in order to support λ-tree syntactic representation. Logic is also used to reason about specifications made in this first logic. This second logic is thus a *meta-logic* for reasoning about provability in those *object-logics*. A particular meta-logic, LINC, is based on intuitionistic logic and incorporates the ∇-quantifier and principles of induction and co-induction.

Armed with the meta-logic LINC, with several interesting examples of using it to reason about computation, and with several years of experience with implementing proof search systems involving the unification of λ-term, it is now time to build prototype theorem provers for LINC and develop larger examples. Already, we can use λProlog [40] via its Teyjus implementation [42] to animate specifications given in a number of object-logics. A simple model checking-style generalization of (part of) λProlog has also been implemented and used to verify various simple properties of, say, the π-calculus [55,53].

One of the goals of the Parsifal project at INRIA is to use this two level logic approach to reason formally about operational semantics, say, in the context of the POPLmark challenge [2]. We also hope to use this framework to reason about specification logics themselves: for example, to prove soundness of logics used to annotate programming languages for extended static checking, such as the ESC/Java2 object logic [22]. Consistency of two simpler object-logics have been proved in [26] by showing showing formally in (a subset of) LINC that cut-elimination holds for them.

Acknowledgments. I am grateful to the anonymous reviewers for their helpful comments on an earlier draft of this paper. This work has been supported in part by the INRIA "Equipes Associées" Slimmer, ACI grants GEOCAL and Rossignol, and the Information Society Technologies programme of the European Commission, Future and Emerging Technologies under the IST-2005-015905 MOBIUS project. This paper reflects only the author's views and the Community is not liable for any use that may be made of the information contained therein.

References

1. J.-M. Andreoli. Logic programming with focusing proofs in linear logic. *J. of Logic and Computation*, 2(3):297–347, 1992.
2. B. E. Aydemir, A. Bohannon, M. Fairbairn, J. N. Foster, B. C. Pierce, P. Sewell, D. Vytiniotis, G. Washburn, S. Weirich, and S. Zdancewic. Mechanized metatheory for the masses: The PoplMark challenge. In *Theorem Proving in Higher Order Logics: 18th International Conference*, LNCS, pages 50–65. Springer-Verlag, 2005.
3. M. Boreale and R. D. Nicola. A symbolic semantics for the π-calculus. *Information and Computation*, 126(1):34–52, April 1996.
4. P. Borras, D. Clément, T. Despeyroux, J. Incerpi, G. Kahn, B. Lang, and V. Pascual. Centaur: the system. In *Proceedings of SIGSOFT'88: Third Annual Symposium on Software Development Environments (SDE3)*, Boston, 1988.
5. N. Bruijn. Lambda calculus notation with namefree formulas involving symbols that represent reference transforming mappings. *Indag. Math.*, 40(3):348–356, 1979.
6. A. Church. A formulation of the simple theory of types. *J. of Symbolic Logic*, 5:56–68, 1940.

7. K. L. Clark. Negation as failure. In J. Gallaire and J. Minker, editors, *Logic and Data Bases*, pages 293–322. Plenum Press, New York, 1978.
8. R. L. Constable et al. *Implementing Mathematics with the Nuprl Proof Development System*. Prentice-Hall, 1986.
9. T. Coquand and G. Huet. The calculus of constructions. *Information and Computation*, 76(2/3):95–120, February/March 1988.
10. J. Despeyroux, A. Felty, and A. Hirschowitz. Higher-order abstract syntax in Coq. In *Second International Conference on Typed Lambda Calculi and Applications*, pages 124–138, April 1995.
11. M. J. Gabbay and A. M. Pitts. A new approach to abstract syntax with variable binding. *Formal Aspects of Computing*, 13:341–363, 2001.
12. G. Gentzen. Investigations into logical deductions. In M. E. Szabo, editor, *The Collected Papers of Gerhard Gentzen*, pages 68–131. North-Holland, Amsterdam, 1969.
13. J.-Y. Girard. A fixpoint theorem in linear logic. An email posting to the mailing list linear@cs.stanford.edu, February 1992.
14. M. Gordon. HOL: A machine oriented formulation of higher-order logic. Technical Report 68, University of Cambridge, July 1985.
15. J. F. Groote and F. Vaandrager. Structured operational semantics and bisimulation as a congruence. *Information and Computation*, 100:202–260, 1992.
16. L. Hallnäs and P. Schroeder-Heister. A proof-theoretic approach to logic programming. II. Programs as definitions. *J. of Logic and Computation*, 1(5):635–660, October 1991.
17. M. Hennessy and H. Lin. Symbolic bisimulations. *Theoretical Computer Science*, 138(2):353–389, Feb. 1995.
18. M. Hofmann. Semantical analysis of higher-order abstract syntax. In *14th Symp. on Logic in Computer Science*, pages 204–213. IEEE Computer Society Press, 1999.
19. D. J. Howe. Proving congruence of bisimulation in functional programming languages. *Information and Computation*, 124(2):103–112, 1996.
20. G. Huet and B. Lang. Proving and applying program transformations expressed with second-order patterns. *Acta Informatica*, 11:31–55, 1978.
21. J. Jaffar and J.-L. Lassez. Constraint logic programming. In *Proceedings of the 14th ACM Symposium on the Principles of Programming Languages*, 1987.
22. J. R. Kiniry, P. Chalin, and C. Hurlin. Integrating static checking and interactive verification: Supporting multiple theories and provers in verification. In *VSTTE'05, Proceedings of Verified Software: Theories, Tools, Experiements*, Zurich, Switzerland, October 2005.
23. P. Martin-Löf. Constructive mathematics and computer programming. In *Sixth International Congress for Logic, Methodology, and Philosophy of Science*, pages 153–175, Amsterdam, 1982. North-Holland.
24. R. McDowell and D. Miller. A logic for reasoning with higher-order abstract syntax. In G. Winskel, editor, *12th Symp. on Logic in Computer Science*, pages 434–445, Warsaw, Poland, July 1997. IEEE Computer Society Press.
25. R. McDowell and D. Miller. Cut-elimination for a logic with definitions and induction. *Theoretical Computer Science*, 232:91–119, 2000.
26. R. McDowell and D. Miller. Reasoning with higher-order abstract syntax in a logical framework. *ACM Trans. on Computational Logic*, 3(1):80–136, 2002.
27. R. McDowell, D. Miller, and C. Palamidessi. Encoding transition systems in sequent calculus. *Theoretical Computer Science*, 294(3):411–437, 2003.
28. D. Miller. A logic programming language with lambda-abstraction, function variables, and simple unification. *J. of Logic and Computation*, 1(4):497–536, 1991.

29. D. Miller. Abstract syntax for variable binders: An overview. In J. Lloyd and et. al., editors, *Computational Logic - CL 2000*, number 1861 in LNAI, pages 239–253. Springer, 2000.
30. D. Miller. Bindings, mobility of bindings, and the ∇-quantifier. In J. Marcinkowski and A. Tarlecki, editors, *18th International Workshop CSL 2004*, volume 3210 of *LNCS*, page 24, 2004.
31. D. Miller. Overview of linear logic programming. In T. Ehrhard, J.-Y. Girard, P. Ruet, and P. Scott, editors, *Linear Logic in Computer Science*, volume 316 of *London Mathematical Society Lecture Note*, pages 119 – 150. Cambridge University Press, 2004.
32. D. Miller and G. Nadathur. A logic programming approach to manipulating formulas and programs. In S. Haridi, editor, *IEEE Symposium on Logic Programming*, pages 379–388, San Francisco, September 1987.
33. D. Miller, G. Nadathur, F. Pfenning, and A. Scedrov. Uniform proofs as a foundation for logic programming. *Annals of Pure and Applied Logic*, 51:125–157, 1991.
34. D. Miller and C. Palamidessi. Foundational aspects of syntax. *ACM Computing Surveys*, 31, September 1999.
35. D. Miller and A. Tiu. A proof theory for generic judgments: An extended abstract. In *18th Symp. on Logic in Computer Science*, pages 118–127. IEEE, June 2003.
36. D. Miller and A. Tiu. A proof theory for generic judgments. *ACM Trans. on Computational Logic*, 6(4):749–783, Oct. 2005.
37. R. Milner. *Communication and Concurrency*. Prentice-Hall International, 1989.
38. R. Milner, J. Parrow, and D. Walker. A calculus of mobile processes, Part II. *Information and Computation*, pages 41–77, 1992.
39. A. Momigliano and A. Tiu. Induction and co-induction in sequent calculus. In M. C. Stefano Berardi and F. Damiani, editors, *Post-proceedings of TYPES 2003*, number 3085 in LNCS, pages 293 – 308, January 2003.
40. G. Nadathur and D. Miller. An Overview of λProlog. In *Fifth International Logic Programming Conference*, pages 810–827, Seattle, August 1988. MIT Press.
41. G. Nadathur and D. Miller. Higher-order Horn clauses. *Journal of the ACM*, 37(4):777–814, October 1990.
42. G. Nadathur and D. J. Mitchell. System description: Teyjus—a compiler and abstract machine based implementation of Lambda Prolog. In H. Ganzinger, editor, *Proceedings of the 16th International Conference on Automated Deduction*, pages 287–291, Trento, Italy, July 1999. Springer-Verlag LNCS.
43. T. Nipkow, L. C. Paulson, and M. Wenzel. *Isabelle/HOL: A Proof Assistant for Higher-Order Logic*. Springer, 2002. LNCS Tutorial 2283.
44. S. Owre, J. M. Rushby, , and N. Shankar. PVS: A prototype verification system. In D. Kapur, editor, *11th International Conference on Automated Deduction (CADE)*, volume 607 of *LNAI*, pages 748–752, Saratoga, NY, jun 1992. Springer-Verlag.
45. L. Paulson. Compiler Generation from Denotational Semantics. In B. Lorho, editor, *Methods and Tools for Compiler Construction*, pages 219–250. Cambridge Univ. Press, 1984.
46. L. C. Paulson and K. Grąbczewski. Mechanizing set theory: Cardinal arithmetic and the axiom of choice. *J. of Automated Deduction*, 17(3):291–323, Dec. 1996.
47. F. Pfenning and C. Elliott. Higher-order abstract syntax. In *Proceedings of the ACM-SIGPLAN Conference on Programming Language Design and Implementation*, pages 199–208. ACM Press, June 1988.
48. F. Pfenning and C. Schürmann. System description: Twelf — A meta-logical framework for deductive systems. In H. Ganzinger, editor, *16th Conference on Automated Deduction*, number 1632 in LNAI, pages 202–206, Trento, 1999. Springer.

49. D. Sangiorgi. A theory of bisimulation for the π-calculus. *Acta Informatica*, 33(1):69–97, 1996.
50. P. Schroeder-Heister. Rules of definitional reflection. In M. Vardi, editor, *Eighth Annual Symposium on Logic in Computer Science*, pages 222–232. IEEE Computer Society Press, IEEE, June 1993.
51. C. Schürmann and F. Pfenning. A coverage checking algorithm for LF. In *Theorem Proving in Higher Order Logics: 16th International Conference, TPHOLs 2003*, volume 2758 of *LNCS*, pages 120–135. Springer-Verlag, 2003.
52. A. Tiu. *A Logical Framework for Reasoning about Logical Specifications*. PhD thesis, Pennsylvania State University, May 2004.
53. A. Tiu. Model checking for π-calculus using proof search. In M. Abadi and L. de Alfaro, editors, *CONCUR*, volume 3653 of *LNCS*, pages 36–50. Springer, 2005.
54. A. Tiu and D. Miller. A proof search specification of the π-calculus. In *3rd Workshop on the Foundations of Global Ubiquitous Computing*, volume 138 of *ENTCS*, pages 79–101, Sept. 2004.
55. A. Tiu, G. Nadathur, and D. Miller. Mixing finite success and finite failure in an automated prover. In *Proceedings of ESHOL'05: Empirically Successful Automated Reasoning in Higher-Order Logics*, pages 79 – 98, December 2005.
56. A. Ziegler, D. Miller, and C. Palamidessi. A congruence format for name-passing calculi. In *Proceedings of SOS 2005: Structural Operational Semantics*, Electronic Notes in Theoretical Computer Science, Lisbon, Portugal, July 2005. Elsevier Science B.V.

Flyspeck I: Tame Graphs

Tobias Nipkow, Gertrud Bauer, and Paula Schultz[†]

Institut für Informatik, TU München

Abstract. We present a verified enumeration of tame graphs as defined in Hales' proof of the Kepler Conjecture and confirm the completeness of Hales' list of all tame graphs while reducing it from 5128 to 2771 graphs.

1 Introduction

In 1611 Kepler asserted what every cannoneer of the day must have known, that the so-called cannonball packing is a densest arrangement of 3-dimensional balls of the same size. In 1900 this assertion became part of Hilbert's 18th problem. In 1998 Thomas Hales announced the first (by now) accepted proof. It involves 3 distinct large computations. After 4 years of refereeing by a team of 12 referees, an abridged version was published only recently [5]. The referees declared that they were 99% certain of the correctness of the proof. The programs were merely given a "diagonal look". Dissatisfied with this state of affairs Hales started the informal open-to-all collaborative *flyspeck* project (www.math.pitt.edu/~thales/flyspeck) to formalize the whole proof with a theorem prover. This paper is the first definite contribution to flyspeck.

Hales' proof goes roughly like this: any potential counter example (denser packing) gives rise to a *tame* plane graph, where tameness is a very specific notion; enumerate all (finitely many) tame graphs (by computer); for each of them check (again by computer) that it cannot constitute a counter example. For modularity reasons Hales provided the *Archive*, a collection of files with (hopefully) all tame graphs.

We recast Hales' Java program for the enumeration of all tame graphs in logic (Isabelle/HOL), proved its completeness, ran it, and compared the output to Hales' Archive. It turns out that Hales was right, the Archive is complete, although redundant (there are at most 2771, not 5128 tame graphs), and that one tameness condition present in his Java program was missing from his proof text. Apart from the contribution to Hales' proof, this paper demonstrates that theorem provers can not just formalize known results but can help in establishing the validity of emerging state-of-the-art mathematical proofs.

An intrinsic feature of this proof, which it shares with Gonthier's proof of the Four Colour Theorem [3], is the need to perform massive computations involving the defined functions (§1.3, §5). Hence efficiency is a concern: during the development phase it is not very productive if, after every change, it takes a week to rerun the proof to find that the change broke it. Part of the achievement of our work is narrowing the gap between the specification of tameness and the enumeration (to simplify the proof) without compromising efficiency unduly.

U. Furbach and N. Shankar (Eds.): IJCAR 2006, LNAI 4130, pp. 21–35, 2006.

Here is one motivating glimpse of where the tame graphs come from: each one is the result of taking a cluster of balls and projecting the centers of the balls on to the surface of the ball in the center, connecting two centers if they are within a certain distance. For an eminently readable overview of Hales' proof see [4], for the details see [5], and for the full Monty read [6] and accompanying articles in the same volume. For Hales' Java program and his Archive see his web page or the online material accompanying [5]. The gory details of our own work can be found in the Isabelle theories available from the first author's home page and the *Archive of Formal Proofs* (afp.sourceforge.net). The thesis [1] also contains full details but is a precursor to the work presented here: the enumeration and the proof have changed considerably and the proof has been completed.

1.1   Related Work

Obua [10] and Zumkeller [11] work towards the verification of the remaining computational parts in Hales' proof.

Gonthier's proof of the Four Colour Theorem [3] is very much concerned with efficient data structures for various computations on plane graphs, a feature it shares with our proof. At the same time he employs *hypermaps* as a unifying representation of plane graphs. Potentially, hypermaps could play the same role in the less computational but mathematically more abstract parts of flyspeck.

1.2   Basic Notation

Isabelle/HOL [9] conforms largely to everyday mathematical notation. This section introduces further non-standard notation and in particular a few basic data types with their primitive operations.

Types. The basic types of truth values, natural numbers and integers are called *bool*, *nat*, and *int*. The space of total functions is denoted by $\Rightarrow$. Type variables are written $'a$, $'b$, etc. The notation $t::\tau$ means that term t has type τ.

Sets (type $'a$ *set*) come with their usual syntax. The pointwise image of set M under a function f is written $f \ ` M$.

Lists (type $'a$ *list*) come with the empty list [], the infix constructor $\cdot$, the infix @ that appends two lists, and the conversion function *set* from lists to sets. Function *hd* yields the head of a list, *last* the last element, and *butlast* drops the last element. Variable names ending in "s" usually stand for lists, $|xs|$ is the length of xs, *distinct xs* means that the elements of xs are all distinct. Instead of *map f xs* and *filter P xs* we frequently write $[f\,x.\ x \in xs]$ and $[x{\in}xs\ .\ P\,x]$.

1.3   Proof by Evaluation

Many theorem provers (ACL2, Coq and PVS) have the ability to evaluate functions during proof by compilation into some efficient format followed by execution. Isabelle has been able to generate ML code for some time now [2]. Recently this has been made available as an inference rule: given a term t, all functions in t are compiled to ML (provided this is possible), t is reduced to u by the ML system, and the result is turned into the theorem $t = u$. Essentially, the ML system is used as an efficient term rewriting engine. To speed things up further, *nat* and *int* are implemented by arbitrary precision ML integers.

In order to remove constructs which are not by themselves executable, code generation is preceded by a preprocessor that rewrites the term with specified lemmas. For example, the lemmas $\forall x \in set\ xs.\ P\ x \equiv list\text{-}all\ P\ xs$ and $\exists x \in set\ xs.\ P\ x \equiv list\text{-}ex\ P\ xs$ replace bounded quantifiers over lists with executable functions. This is the key to bridging the gap between specification and implementation automatically and safely.

Because lists are executable but sets are not, we sometimes phrase concepts in terms of lists rather than sets to avoid having to define the concept twice and having to provide a trivial implementation proof.

2 Plane Graphs

Following Hales we represent finite, undirected, plane graphs as lists (= finite sets) of faces and faces as lists of vertices. Note that by representing faces as lists they have an orientation. Our enumeration of plane graphs requires an additional distinction between *final* and *nonfinal* faces. This flag is attached directly to each face:

$$vertex = nat, \quad face = vertex\ list \times bool, \quad graph = face\ list$$

The projection functions for faces are called *vertices* and *final*. The *size* of a face is the length of its vertex list. Occasionally we call a list of vertices a face, too. A graph is final if all its faces are final. Function $\mathcal{F}$ returns the set of faces of a graph, i.e. is a synonym for function *set*. Function $\mathcal{V}$ returns the set of vertices in a graph, *countVertices* the number of vertices. Given a graph g and a vertex v, *facesAt g v* computes the list of faces incident to v.

For navigation around a face f we consider its list of vertices as cyclic and introduce the following notation: if v is a vertex in f then $f \cdot v$ is the vertex following v and $f^i \cdot v$ is the ith vertex following v (where i may also be -1). This description is ambiguous if there are multiple occurrences of v in f, but this cannot arise in our context.

Representing faces as lists means that we want to regard two vertex lists *us* and *vs* as equivalent if one can be obtained from the other by rotation, in which case we write $us \cong vs$. We introduce the notation

$$x \in_{\cong} M \equiv \exists y \in M.\ x \cong y, \qquad M \subseteq_{\cong} N \equiv \forall x \in M.\ x \in_{\cong} N$$

Throughout most of this paper we pretend that a graph is just a face list, but in reality it is more complicated. To avoid recomputation, *countVertices* and *facesAt* are (hidden) components of the graph.

2.1 Enumeration of Plane Graphs

Not every list of faces constitutes a plane graph. Hence we need additional means of characterizing planarity. We have chosen an operational characterization, i.e.

an executable enumeration due to Hales. The reason is that we can then view the enumeration of tame graphs as a restriction of the enumeration of plane graphs. The justification for not starting with a more abstract traditional characterization of planarity is that this is the first definite contribution to flyspeck and it is not yet clear which notion of planarity is most suitable for the rest of the project. In a nutshell, we wanted to concentrate on the new (and unchecked by referees!) enumeration of tame graphs rather than the mathematically well understood issue of planarity.

The graphs required for Hales' proof are plane graphs with at least 2 faces (including the outer one), where each face is a simple polygon of size ≥ 3. In the sequel the term *plane* refers to this class. Hales' enumeration of plane graphs proceeds inductively: you start with a seed graph with two faces, the final outer one and the (reverse) nonfinal inner one. If a graph contains a nonfinal face, it can be subdivided into a final face and any number of nonfinal ones as shown below. Final faces are grey, nonfinal ones white. The unbounded grey square indicates the unbounded outer face.

Because a face can be subdivided in many ways, this process defines a tree of graphs. By construction the leaves must be final graphs, and they are the plane graphs we are interested in: any plane graph (in the above sense) of n faces can be generated in $n-1$ steps by this process, adding one (final) face at a time.

This definition is also meant to serve as the basis of the actual enumeration. Hence we reduce its redundancy, i.e. the number of times each graph is generated, by the following means:

- The enumeration is parameterized by a natural number p which controls the maximal size of final faces in the generated graphs. The seed graph contains two $(p+3)$-gons and the final face created in each step may at most be a $(p+3)$-gon. As a result, different parameters lead to disjoint sets of graphs. Note that the nonfinal faces may (and need to be) of arbitrary size.
- In each step we subdivide only one fixed face and the new final face always shares one fixed edge with the subdivided face; which face and edge are chosen is immaterial. This does not affect the set of final graphs that can be generated but merely the order in which the final faces are created.

Formalization. Now we are ready for the top level formal specification:

PlaneGraphs $\equiv \bigcup p\ \{g \mid Seed\,p\ [next\text{-}plane\,p] \rightarrow^* g \land final\ g\}$

where $Seed_p \equiv [([0,\ldots,p+2], True), ([p+2,\ldots,0], False)]$ is the seed graph described above. Notation $g_0\ [f] \rightarrow^* g$ is simply suggestive syntax for $(g_0, g) \in$

$\{(g,\ g')\ |\ g' \in set\ (f\ g)\}^*$, i.e. we can reach g from g_0 in finitely many steps via function $f :: graph \Rightarrow graph\ list$. In our case f is $next\text{-}plane_p$ which maps a graph to a list of successor graphs:

$next\text{-}plane_p\ g \equiv$
$let\ fs = [f \in faces\ g\ .\ \neg\ final\ f]$
$in\ if\ fs = []\ then\ []$
$\quad else\ let\ f = minimalFace\ fs;\ v = minimalVertex\ g\ f$
$\qquad in\ \bigsqcup_{i \in [3..p\ +\ 3]}\ generatePolygon\ i\ v\ f\ g$

If there are only final faces, we are done. Otherwise we pick a minimal nonfinal face (in terms of size) and a minimal vertex within that face. Minimality of the vertex refers to its distance from the vertices in the seed graph. This policy favours compact graphs over stringy objects. Its implementation requires an additional (hidden) component in each graph. But since the choice of vertex (and face) is irrelevant as far as completeness of the enumeration is concerned, so is the precise implementation.

Having fixed f and v we subdivide f in all possible ways by placing an i-gon inside it (along the edge from v to its predecessor vertex in f), where i ranges from 3 to $p+3$. Function $generatePolygon$ returns a list of all possible successor graphs and the suggestive syntax $\bigsqcup_{i \in I} F\ i$ represents the concatenation of all $F\ i$ for i in I.

Function $generatePolygon$ operates and is explained in stages:

$generatePolygon\ n\ v\ f\ g \equiv$
$let\ enumeration = enumerator\ n\ |vertices\ f|;$
$\quad enumeration = [is \in enumeration\ .\ \neg\ containsDuplicateEdge\ g\ f\ v\ is];$
$\quad vertexLists = [indexToVertexList\ f\ v\ is.\ is \in enumeration]$
$in\ [subdivFace\ g\ f\ vs.\ vs \in vertexLists]$

Enumeration. We have to enumerate all possible ways of inscribing a final n-gon inside f such that it shares the edge $(f^{-1} \cdot v,\ v)$ with f (which is removed). The new n-gon can in fact share all edges with f, in which case we simply finalize f without adding any new nonfinal faces; or it can touch f only at $f^{-1} \cdot v$ and v and all of its other vertices are new; or anything in between. Following Hales one can describe each of these n-gons by a list of length n of increasing indices from the interval $\{0,\ldots,|vertices\ f| - 1\}$. Roughly speaking, index i represents vertex $f^i \cdot v$ and a pair i,j of adjacent list elements is interpreted as follows: if $i < j$ then the new polygon contains an edge from vertex $f^i \cdot v$ to $f^j \cdot v$; if $i = j$ then the new polygon contains a new vertex at that point. For example, given the face $[v_0,\ldots,v_5]$, the index list $[0,2,3,3,3,5]$ represents some face $[v_0,v_2,v_3,x,y,v_5]$ where x and y are new vertices.

The enumeration of all these index lists is the task of function $enumerator$ which returns a $nat\ list\ list$. We have proved that $enumerator\ n\ m$ returns all (not necessarily strictly) increasing lists of length n starting with 0 and ending with $m - 1$:

$set\ (enumerator\ n\ m) =$
$\{is\ |\ |is| = n \wedge hd\ is = 0 \wedge last\ is = m - 1 \wedge last\ (butlast\ is) < last\ is \wedge$
$\quad increasing\ is\}$

Condition *last (butlast is)* < *last is* excludes lists like $[\ldots,m,m]$ which would insert a new vertex behind the last element, i.e. between $f^{-1} \cdot v$ and v.

The next stage in *generatePolygon* removes those index lists which would create a duplicate edge: *containsDuplicateEdge g f v is* checks that there are no two adjacent indices $i < j$ in *is* such that $(f^i \cdot v, f^j \cdot v)$ or $(f^j \cdot v, f^i \cdot v)$ is an edge in g (unless it is an edge in f, in which case no duplicate edge is created because f is removed). Finally the index list is turned into a list of vertices as sketched above employing

$$\textbf{datatype } 'a \; option = None \mid Some \; 'a$$

to distinguish an existing vertex $Some(f^i \cdot v)$ from a new vertex *None*:

indexToVertexList f v is ≡ *hideDups* $[f^k \cdot v. \; k \in is]$
hideDups $(i \cdot is) = Some \; i \cdot hideDupsRec \; i \; is$
hideDupsRec a $[] = []$
hideDupsRec a $(b \cdot bs) =$
$(\textbf{if } a = b \textbf{ then } None \cdot hideDupsRec \; b \; bs \textbf{ else } Some \; b \cdot hideDupsRec \; b \; bs)$

The result (in *generatePolygon*) is *vertexLists* of type *vertex option list list* where each list in *vertexLists* describes one possibility of inserting a final face into f.

Subdivision. The last step in *generatePolygon* is to generate a new graph *subdivFace g f vos* for each *vos* in *vertexLists* by subdividing f as specified by *vos*. This is best visualized by an example. Given a face $f = [1,\ldots,8]$ and *vos* = [*Some 3*, *Some 3*, *None*, *Some 4*, *None*, *Some 8*] the result of inserting a face specified by *vos* into f is shown below.

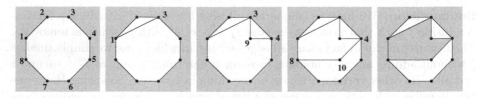

Subdividing is an iterative process where in each step we split the (remaining) face in two nonfinal faces; at the end we finalize the face. In the example we first split the face along the path $[1,3]$, then along $[3,9,4]$ and finally along $[4,10,8]$. Each splitting in two is performed by *splitFace g u v f newvs* which returns a new graph where f has been replaced by its two halves by inserting a list of new vertices *newvs* between the existing vertices u and v in f. The straightforward definition of *splitFace* is omitted.

Repeated splitting is performed by *subdivFace′ g f u n vos* where u is the vertex where splitting starts, n records how many new vertices must be inserted along the seam, and *vos* is a *vertex option list* from *vertexLists*:

subdivFace′ g f u n $[] = makeFaceFinal \; f \; g$
subdivFace′ g f u n $(vo \cdot vos) =$
$(\textbf{case } vo \textbf{ of } None \Rightarrow subdivFace′ \; g \; f \; u \; (Suc \; n) \; vos$

| *Some v* ⇒
   if f · u = v ∧ n = 0 then subdivFace' g f v 0 vos
   else let ws = [countVertices g..<countVertices g + n];
     (f₁, f₂, g') = splitFace g u v f ws
   in subdivFace' g' f₂ v 0 vos)

The definition is by recursion on *vos*. The base case simply turns *f* into a final face in *g*. If *vos* starts with *None*, no splitting takes place but *n* is incremented. If *vos* starts with *Some v* there are two possibilities. Either we have merely advanced one vertex along *f*, in which case we keep on going. Or we have skipped at least one vertex of *f*, in which case we must split *f* between *u* and *v*, inserting *n* new vertices: the term $[i..<j]$ is the list of natural numbers from and including *i* up to but excluding *j*. Function *splitFace* returns the two new faces along with the new graph. Only *f₂* is used (it is the face that is subdivided further), but returning both faces helps to state many lemmas more succinctly.

Function *subdivFace* (called from *generatePolygon*) simply starts *subdivFace'*:

$$subdivFace\ g\ f\ (Some\ u \cdot vs) \equiv subdivFace'\ g\ f\ u\ 0\ vs$$

Note that because all index lists produced by *enumerator* are nonempty, all vertex lists produced by *indexToVertexList* are nonempty and start with *Some*.

2.2 Invariants

Almost half the proof is concerned with verifying that *PlaneGraphs* satisfy certain invariants which are combined into the predicate *inv :: graph ⇒ bool*. Probably half that effort is caused by showing that the extended graph representation, primarily *facesAt*, is kept consistent. The remaining properties are: each face is of size ≥ 3 and all its vertices are distinct, there are at least two faces, the faces are distinct modulo ≅ and if the graph has more than 2 faces also modulo reversal, the edges of distinct faces are disjoint (where edges are pairs of adjacent vertices in an oriented face), and any nonfinal face is surrounded by final faces.

3 Tame Graphs

Tameness is rooted in geometric considerations but for this paper it is simply a fixed interface to the rest of Hales' proof and should be taken as God given.

3.1 Definition of Tame Graphs

The definition relies on 4 tables a :: *nat ⇒ nat*, b :: *nat ⇒ nat ⇒ nat*, c :: *nat ⇒ int*, d :: *nat ⇒ nat*. Their precise definition is immaterial for this paper and can be found elsewhere [1,5]. Like Hales (in his Java program) we have scaled all rational numbers (from the paper proof) by 1000, thus turning them into integers.

Summing over the elements of a list (below: of faces) is written $\sum x \in xs\ f\ x$. Function *faces* returns the list of faces in a graph: in our simplified model of graphs it is the identity but in the real model it is a projection.

Functions *tri* and *quad* count the number of final triangles and quadrilaterals incident to a vertex. Hales calls a face f *exceptional* if it is a pentagon or larger, i.e. if $5 \le |vertices\ f|$. Function *except* returns the number of final exceptional faces incident to a vertex. A vertex has *type* (p, q) if $p = tri\ g\ v$, $q = quad\ g\ v$ and *except* $g\ v = 0$.

A graph is *tame* if it is plane and satisfies 8 conditions:

1. The size of each face is at least 3 and at most 8:

   $tame_1\ g \equiv \forall f \in \mathcal{F}\ g.\ 3 \le |vertices\ f| \wedge |vertices\ f| \le 8$

2. Every 3-cycle is a face or the opposite of a face:

   $tame_2\ g \equiv$
   $\forall a\ b\ c.$
    $is\text{-}cycle\ g\ [a,\ b,\ c] \wedge distinct\ [a,\ b,\ c] \longrightarrow$
    $(\exists f \in \mathcal{F}\ g.\ vertices\ f \cong [a,\ b,\ c] \vee vertices\ f \cong [c,\ b,\ a])$

   where $is\text{-}cycle\ g\ vs \equiv hd\ vs \in set\ (neighbors\ g\ (last\ vs)) \wedge is\text{-}path\ g\ vs$, function *neighbors* does the obvious and

   $is\text{-}path\ g\ [] = True$
   $is\text{-}path\ g\ (u \cdot vs) =$
   $(\textbf{case}\ vs\ of\ [] \Rightarrow True \mid v \cdot ws \Rightarrow v \in set\ (neighbors\ g\ u) \wedge is\text{-}path\ g\ vs)$

3. Every 4-cycle surrounds one of the following configurations:

   The tame configurations are straightforward to describe:

   $tameConf_1\ a\ b\ c\ d \equiv [[a,\ b,\ c,\ d]]$
   $tameConf_2\ a\ b\ c\ d \equiv [[a,\ b,\ c],\ [a,\ c,\ d]]$
   $tameConf_3\ a\ b\ c\ d\ e \equiv [[a,\ b,\ e],\ [b,\ c,\ e],\ [a,\ e,\ c,\ d]]$
   $tameConf_4\ a\ b\ c\ d\ e \equiv [[a,\ b,\ e],\ [b,\ c,\ e],\ [c,\ d,\ e],\ [d,\ a,\ e]]$

   Predicate *tame-quad* formalizes that its parameters form one of the tame configurations, taking rotation into account:

   $tame\text{-}quad\ g\ a\ b\ c\ d \equiv$
   $set\ (tameConf_1\ a\ b\ c\ d) \subseteq_\cong vertices\ `\ \mathcal{F}\ g\ \vee$
   $set\ (tameConf_2\ a\ b\ c\ d) \subseteq_\cong vertices\ `\ \mathcal{F}\ g\ \vee$
   $set\ (tameConf_2\ b\ c\ d\ a) \subseteq_\cong vertices\ `\ \mathcal{F}\ g\ \vee$
   $(\exists e \in \mathcal{V}\ g - \{a,\ b,\ c,\ d\}.$
    $set\ (tameConf_3\ a\ b\ c\ d\ e) \subseteq_\cong vertices\ `\ \mathcal{F}\ g\ \vee$
    $set\ (tameConf_3\ b\ c\ d\ a\ e) \subseteq_\cong vertices\ `\ \mathcal{F}\ g\ \vee$
    $set\ (tameConf_3\ c\ d\ a\ b\ e) \subseteq_\cong vertices\ `\ \mathcal{F}\ g\ \vee$
    $set\ (tameConf_3\ d\ a\ b\ c\ e) \subseteq_\cong vertices\ `\ \mathcal{F}\ g\ \vee$
    $set\ (tameConf_4\ a\ b\ c\ d\ e) \subseteq_\cong vertices\ `\ \mathcal{F}\ g)$

Finally, $tame_3$ also takes reversal of orientation into account:

$tame_3 \ g \equiv$
$\forall a\ b\ c\ d.$
$\quad is\text{-}cycle \ g \ [a,\ b,\ c,\ d] \ \wedge \ distinct \ [a,\ b,\ c,\ d] \longrightarrow$
$\quad tame\text{-}quad \ g \ a \ b \ c \ d \ \vee \ tame\text{-}quad \ g \ d \ c \ b \ a$

4. The degree of every vertex is at most 6 and at most 5 if the vertex is contained in an exceptional face:

$tame_{45} \ g \equiv \forall v{\in}\mathcal{V} \ g. \ degree \ g \ v \leq (\textit{if except } g \ v = 0 \textit{ then } 6 \textbf{ else } 5)$

We have combined conditions 4 and 5 from [5] into one.

5. The following inequality holds:

$tame_6 \ g \equiv 8000 \leq \sum_{f{\in}faces \ g} \mathrm{c} \ |vertices \ f|$

6. There exists an admissible assignment of weights to faces of total weight less than 14800:

$tame_7 \ g \equiv \exists w. \ admissible \ w \ g \ \wedge \ \sum_{f{\in}faces \ g} w \ f < 14800$

Admissibility is quite involved and discussed below. Although this is not immediately obvious, $tame_7$ guarantees there are only finitely many tame graphs. It also is the source of most complications in the proofs because it is not straightforward to check this condition.

7. There are no two adjacent vertices of type $(4,0)$:

$tame_8 \ g \equiv \neg \ (\exists v{\in}\mathcal{V} \ g. \ type_40 \ g \ v \ \wedge \ (\exists w{\in}set \ (neighbors \ g \ v). \ type_40 \ g \ w))$

Now $tame$ is the conjunction of $tame_1$ up to $tame_8$; the numbering follows [5].

Note that $tame_8$ is missing in earlier versions of the proof, e.g. www.math.pitt.edu/~thales/kepler04/fullkepler.pdf of 13/3/2004. The second author noticed and informed Hales of this discrepancy between the proof and his Java code, where the test is present. As a result Hales added $tame_8$ in the published versions of his proof.

3.2 Admissible Weight Assignment

For $w :: face \Rightarrow nat$ to be an *admissible weight assignment* it needs to meet the following requirements:

1. $admissible_1 \ w \ g \equiv \forall f{\in}\mathcal{F} \ g. \ \mathrm{d} \ |vertices \ f| \leq w \ f$
2. $admissible_2 \ w \ g \equiv$
$\quad \forall v{\in}\mathcal{V} \ g. \ except \ g \ v = 0 \longrightarrow \mathrm{b} \ (tri \ g \ v) \ (quad \ g \ v) \leq \sum_{f{\in}facesAt \ g \ v} w \ f$
3. $admissible_3 \ w \ g \equiv$
$\quad \forall \ V. \ separated \ g \ (set \ V) \ \wedge \ set \ V \subseteq \mathcal{V} \ g \longrightarrow$
$\quad\quad \sum_{v{\in}V} \mathrm{a} \ (tri \ g \ v) \ +$
$\quad\quad \sum_{f{\in}[f{\in}faces \ g \ . \ \exists v{\in}set \ V. \ f \ \in \ set \ (facesAt \ g \ v)]} \mathrm{d} \ |vertices \ f|$
$\quad\quad \leq \sum_{f{\in}[f{\in}faces \ g \ . \ \exists v{\in}set \ V. \ f \ \in \ set \ (facesAt \ g \ v)]} w \ f$

The first two constraints express that d and b yield lower bounds for w. The last requirement yields another lower bound for w in terms of *separated* sets of vertices. Separatedness means that they are not neighbours, do not lie on a common quadrilateral, and fulfill some additional constraints:

$separated_1$ g V $\equiv$ $\forall v \in V.$ *except* g $v \neq 0$
$separated_2$ g V $\equiv$ $\forall v \in V. \forall f \in set$ *(facesAt* g v). $f \cdot v \notin V$
$separated_3$ g V $\equiv$
$\forall v \in V. \forall f \in set$ *(facesAt* g v). $|vertices\ f| \leq 4 \longrightarrow \mathcal{V} f \cap V = \{v\}$
$separated_4$ g V $\equiv$ $\forall v \in V.$ *degree* g $v = 5$

Note that Hales [5] lists 4 admissibility conditions, the third of which our work shows to be superfluous.

3.3   Enumeration of Tame Graphs

The enumeration of tame graphs is a modified enumeration of plane graphs where we remove final graphs that are definitely not tame, and cut the search tree at nonfinal graphs that cannot lead to tame graphs anymore. Note that in contrast to the enumeration of plane graphs, a specification we must trust, the enumeration of tame graphs is accompanied by a correctness theorem (Theorem 3 below), the central result of the work, stating that all tame graphs are generated. Hence it is less vital to present the tame enumeration in complete detail (except to satisfy the curiosity of the reader and allow reproduceability).

The core of the tame enumeration is a filtered version of *generatePolygon*:

$generatePolygonTame$ n v f g $=$ $[g' \in generatePolygon\ n\ v\ f\ g$. $\neg$ *notame* $g']$

In reality this is not the definition but the characteristic lemma. The actual definition replaces the repeated *enumeration* of lists of index lists in *generatePolygon* by a table lookup. This is "merely" an optimization for speed, but an important one. The filter *notame* removes all graphs that cannot lead to a tame graph:

$notame$ g $\equiv$ $\neg$ $(tame_{45}$ g $\wedge$ *is-tame*$_7$ $g)$
is-tame$_7$ g $\equiv$ *squanderLowerBound* $g < 14800$

Using $tame_{45}$ on nonfinal graphs is justified because the degree of a vertex can only increase as a graph is refined and because *except* takes only the final faces into account.[1] Function *squanderLowerBound* computes a lower bound for the total admissible weight of any final graph that can be generated from g. By $tame_7$ this lower bound must be < 14800.

$squanderLowerBound$ g $\equiv$ $\sum_{f \in finals\ g}$ d $|vertices\ f|$ $+$ *ExcessNotAt* g *None*

The lower bound consists of a d-sum over all final faces (justified by $admissible_1$ and the fact that d cannot be negative) and an error correction term *Excess-NotAt*. The definition of *ExcessNotAt* is somewhat involved and not shown.

---

[1] $tame_6$ on the other hand cannot be used to filter out nonfinal graphs because function c may return both positive and negative values, i.e. summing over it is not monotone under the addition of new faces.

Essentially we enumerate all maximal separated sets of vertices, compute the "excess" over and above the d-sum for each one (taking a and b into account as justified by $admissible_2$ and $admissible_3$), and take the maximum. Note that the number of separated sets can grow exponentially with the number of vertices.

On top of *generatePolygonTame* we have a variant of *next-plane$_p$*:

next-tame0 p g ≡
let fs = [*f* ∈ *faces g* . ¬ *final f*]
in if fs = [] *then* []
  else let f = *minimalFace fs*; *v* = *minimalVertex g f*
    in ⊔$_{i \in}$ *polysizes p g* *generatePolygonTame i v f g*

where *polysizes* restricts the possible range [*3..p* + *3*] to those sizes which can still lead to tame graphs:

polysizes p g ≡ [*n* ∈ [*3..p* + *3*] . *squanderLowerBound g* + d *n* < *14800*]

The justification is that the insertion of a new *n*-gon into *g* adds at least d *n* to *squanderLowerBound g*. Hence all these graphs would immediately be discarded again by *notame* and *polysizes* is merely an optimization, but one which happens to reduce the run time by a factor of 10.

The key correctness theorems for *squanderLowerBound* (recall *inv* from §2.2) are that it increases with *next-tame0* (in fact with *next-plane*)

Theorem 1. If *g′* ∈ *set* (*next-tame0 p g*) and *inv g* then *squanderLowerBound g* ≤ *squanderLowerBound g′*.

and for (final) tame graphs *squanderLowerBound* is a lower bound for the total weight of an admissible assignment:

Theorem 2. If *tame g* and *final g* and *inv g* and *admissible w g* and $\sum_{f \in faces\ g} w\ f$ < *14800* then *squanderLowerBound g* ≤ $\sum_{f \in faces\ g} w\ f$.

These two theorems are the main ingredients in the completeness proof of *next-tame0* w.r.t. *next-plane*: any tame graph reachable via *next-plane* is still reachable via *next-tame0*.

Now we compose *next-tame0* with a function *makeTrianglesFinal* (details omitted) which finalizes all nonfinal triangles introduced by *next-tame0*:

next-tame1 p ≡ *map makeTrianglesFinal* ∘ *next-tame0 p*

This step appears to be a trivial consequence of *tame$_2$* which says that all 3-cycles must be triangles, i.e. that one should not be allowed to subdivide a triangle further. The latter implication, however, is not completely trivial: one has to show that if one ever subdivides a triangle, that triangle cannot be re-introduced as a face later on. A lengthy proof yields completeness of *next-tame1* w.r.t. *next-tame0*. The invariants (§2.2) are absolutely essential here.

As a final step we filter out all untame final graphs:

next-tame p ≡ *filter* (λ*g*. ¬ *final g* ∨ *is-tame g*) ∘ *next-tame1 p*
is-tame g ≡ *tame$_{45}$ g* ∧ *tame$_6$ g* ∧ *tame$_8$ g* ∧ *is-tame$_7$ g* ∧ *is-tame$_3$ g*

Tameness conditions 1 and 2 are guaranteed by construction. Conditions 45, 6 and 8 are directly executable. Condition 7 has been discussed already. This leaves condition 3, the check of all possible 4-cycles:

is-tame$_3$ *g* ≡
∀ *vs*∈*set* (*find-cycles* 4 *g*).
  is-cycle g vs ∧ *distinct vs* ∧ |*vs*| = 4 ⟶ *ok4 g vs*

This implementation is interesting in that it employs a search-and-check technique: function *find-cycles* need not be verified at all because the rest of the code explicitly checks that the vertex lists are actually cycles of distinct vertices of length 4. This can at most double the execution time but reduces verification time. In fact, *find-cycles* is expressed in terms of a *while*-functional [9] which simplifies definition but would complicate verification. Function *ok4* is a straightforward implementation of *tame-quad*.

Note that this search-and-check technique is applicable only because we merely need to ensure completeness of the enumeration of tame graphs, not correctness. Otherwise we would need to verify that *find-cycles* finds all cycles.

Completeness of *next-tame* w.r.t. *next-tame1* follows from Theorem 2 together with the implementation proof of *ok4* w.r.t. *tame-quad*. Putting the three individual completeness theorems together we obtain the overall completeness of *next-tame*: all tame graphs are enumerated.

Theorem 3. If $Seed_p$ [$next\text{-}plane_p$]$\rightarrow^*$ *g* and *final g* and *tame g* then $Seed_p$ [$next\text{-}tame_p$]$\rightarrow^*$ *g*.

The set of tame graphs is defined in the obvious manner:

$TameEnum_p \equiv \{g \mid Seed_p\ [next\text{-}tame_p]\rightarrow^*\ g \land final\ g\}$
$TameEnum \equiv \bigcup_{p \le 5} TameEnum_p$

An executable version of $TameEnum_p$ is provided under the name *tameEnum*. It realizes a simple work list algorithm directly on top of *next-tame* and need not be shown or discussed, except for one detail. Being in a logic of total functions we have to apply an old trick: since we want to avoid proving termination of the enumeration process (which is bound to be quite involved), *tameEnum* takes two parameters: the usual *p* and a counter which is decremented in each step. If it reaches 0 prematurely, we return *None*, otherwise we return *Some Fs* where *Fs* is the collected list of final graphs, the result of the enumeration. When running *tameEnum* we merely need to start with a large enough counter. Because the returned graphs are all final we reduce each graph to a list of list of vertices via

fgraph g ≡ *map vertices* (*faces g*)

before including it in the result. Hence the actual return type of *tameEnum* is *vertex fgraph list* where

$$'a\ fgraph = 'a\ list\ list.$$

We merely show *tameEnum*'s correctness theorem, not the definition:

Theorem 4. If *tameEnum p n* = *Some Fs* then *set Fs* = *fgraph* ‘ $TameEnum_p$.

As a final step we need to run *tameEnum p n* with suitably large n (such that *Some* is returned) for all $p \leq 5$ [2] and compare the result with the contents of the Archive.

4 The Archives

It turned out that Hales' Archive was complete but redundant. That is, our verified enumeration produced only 2771 graphs as opposed to Hales' 5128. The reason is twofold: there are many isomorphic copies of graphs in his Archive and it contains a number of non-tame graphs (partly because for efficiency reasons he does not enforce *tame₃* completely in his Java program). The new reduced Archive can be found at the first author's web page.

The new Archive is a constant *Archive :: vertex fgraph set* in the Isabelle theories which is defined via the concatenation of 6 separate archives, one for each $p \leq 5$:

Archive $\equiv$ *set (Tri @ Quad @ Pent @ Hex @ Hept @ Oct)*

The main theorem of our work is the completeness of *Archive*:

Theorem 5. If $g \in PlaneGraphs$ and *tame g* then *fgraph g* $\in_\simeq$ *Archive*.

Relation $\simeq$ is graph isomorphism (§4.1) and $x \in_\simeq M \equiv \exists y \in M.\ x \simeq y$. This theorem is a combination of the completeness of *next-tame* (Theorem 3) and of *fgraph ' TameEnum* $\subseteq_\simeq$ *Archive* (where $M \subseteq_\simeq N \equiv \forall x \in M.\ x \in_\simeq N$). The latter is a corollary of the fact that, for each $p \leq 5$, *tameEnum p n* (for suitable n) returns *Some Fs* such that *Fs* is equivalent to the corresponding part of the Archive. Quite concretely, we have proved by evaluation (§1.3) that *same (tameEnum 0 800000) Tri*, *same (tameEnum 1 8000000) Quad*, *same (tameEnum 2 20000000) Pent*, *same (tameEnum 3 4000000) Hex*, *same (tameEnum 4 1000000) Hept*, and *same (tameEnum 5 2000000) Oct*, where *same* is an executable check of equivalence (modulo $\simeq$)[3] of two lists of *fgraphs*. Corollary *fgraph ' TameEnum* $\subseteq_\simeq$ *Archive* follows by correctness of *tameEnum* (Theorem 4).

We cannot detail the definition of *same* (or its correctness theorem) but we should point out that it is a potential bottleneck: for $p = 2$ we need to check 15000 graphs for inclusion in an archive of 1500 graphs — modulo graph iso-morphism! Although isomorphism of plane graphs can be determined in linear time [8], this algorithm is not very practical because of a large constant factor. Instead we employ a hashing scheme to home in on the isomorphic graph quickly. The graphs of each archive are stored in a search tree (a *trie*) indexed by a list of natural numbers. The index is the concatenation of a number of hash values invariant under isomorphism. The most important component is obtained by adding up, for each vertex, the size of the faces around that vertex, and then sorting the resulting list. This idea is due to Hales.

---

[2] By *tame₁* we are only interested in graphs where all faces are of size $\leq 8 = 5+3$, the *3* being added in *next-plane*.

[3] A check for $\subseteq_\simeq$ would suffice but it is nice to know that *Archive* is free of junk.

4.1 Plane Graph Isomorphisms

For lack of space we present our definition of isomorphism but not its implementation:

$is\text{-}pr\text{-}iso\ \varphi\ Fs_1\ Fs_2 \equiv is\text{-}pr\text{-}Iso\ \varphi\ (set\ Fs_1)\ (set\ Fs_2)$
$is\text{-}pr\text{-}Iso\ \varphi\ Fs_1\ Fs_2 \equiv is\text{-}Hom\ \varphi\ Fs_1\ Fs_2 \wedge inj\text{-}on\ \varphi\ (\bigcup_{F \in Fs_1} set\ F)$
$is\text{-}Hom\ \varphi\ Fs_1\ Fs_2 \equiv map\ \varphi\ `\ Fs_1\ //\ \{\cong\} = Fs_2\ //\ \{\cong\}$

Parameter φ is a function of type $vertex \Rightarrow vertex$. Predicate $is\text{-}pr\text{-}iso$ compares lists of faces (*fgraphs*), $is\text{-}pr\text{-}Iso$ sets of faces; pr stands for *proper*. Proper isomorphisms assume that the faces of both graphs have the same orientation. An isomorphism is defined as usual as an injective homomorphism. A homomorphism must turn one graph into the other, modulo rotation of faces: the infix $//$ is quotienting and the symbol $\{\cong\}$ is defined as $\{(f_1, f_2)\ |\ f_1 \cong f_2\}$.

'Improper' isomorphisms allow to reverse the orientation of all faces in one graph (*rev* reverses a list):

$is\text{-}iso\ \varphi\ Fs_1\ Fs_2 \equiv is\text{-}Iso\ \varphi\ (set\ Fs_1)\ (set\ Fs_2)$
$is\text{-}Iso\ \varphi\ Fs_1\ Fs_2 \equiv is\text{-}pr\text{-}Iso\ \varphi\ Fs_1\ Fs_2 \vee is\text{-}pr\text{-}Iso\ \varphi\ Fs_1\ (rev\ `\ Fs_2)$

Two *fgraphs* are isomorphic if there exists an isomorphism between them:

$g_1 \simeq g_2 \equiv \exists \varphi.\ is\text{-}iso\ \varphi\ g_1\ g_2$

5 Statistics

The starting point were 2200 lines of Java, the result 600 lines of executable HOL (= ML), excluding comments, debugging aids, and libraries. This reduction is primarily due to simplifications of the algorithm itself: not splitting the treatment of triangle and quadrilateral seed graphs into 17 cases, dropping all symmetry checks, dropping the special treatment of nonfinal quadrilaterals, and dropping some complicated lower bound estimates (which are all still present in [1]). The simplicity of the final solution belies the difficulty of arriving at it.

The whole formalization encompasses 17000 lines of definitions and proofs. Running the complete proof takes 165 minutes on a Xeon: the completeness proof takes 15 minutes, evaluating the enumeration 105 minutes, and comparing the resulting graphs with the Archive (modulo graph isomorphism) 45 minutes.

During execution of the enumeration, the gargantuan number of 23 million graphs are generated and examined, of which 35000 are final. The distribution of graphs over the new Archive (for $p = 0, \ldots, 5$) is (20,22,13), (923,18,12), (1545,18,13), (238,17,12), (23,16,12), and (22,15,12), where each triple gives the number of graphs, average number of faces, and average number of vertices for that group of graphs.

6 Future Work

The enumeration of plane graphs needs to be connected with some abstract notion of planarity. Hales is preparing a revised proof based on hypermaps that could serve as the glue — face lists are easily turned into hypermaps. On the other end, it needs to be shown that none of the tame graphs constitutes a counter example. The linear programming techniques for this step are in place [10], but their application is nontrivial and not well documented in Hales proof.

Finally there is the exciting prospect of modifying our proof to cover a very similar graph enumeration in the proof of the *Dodecahedral Conjecture* [7].

Acknowledgments. The first author wishes to thank: Tom Hales for generously hosting his sabbatical semester at the University of Pittsburgh and for patiently answering all questions; Jeremy and Sean for lunches and friendship; Q & U for late night entertainment.

References

1. G. Bauer. *Formalizing Plane Graph Theory — Towards a Formalized Proof of the Kepler Conjecture.* PhD thesis, Technische Universität München, 2006.
2. S. Berghofer and T. Nipkow. Executing higher order logic. In P. Callaghan, Z. Luo, J. McKinna, and R. Pollack, editors, *Types for Proofs and Programs (TYPES 2000)*, volume 2277 of *Lect. Notes in Comp. Sci.*, pages 24–40. Springer-Verlag, 2002.
3. G. Gonthier. A computer-checked proof of the four colour theorem. Available at research.microsoft.com/~gonthier/4colproof.pdf.
4. T. C. Hales. Cannonballs and honeycombs. *Notices Amer. Math. Soc.*, 47:440–449, 2000.
5. T. C. Hales. A proof of the Kepler conjecture. *Annals of Mathematics*, 162:1063–1183, 2005.
6. T. C. Hales. Sphere packings, VI. Tame graphs and linear programs. *Discrete and Computational Geometry*, 2006. To appear.
7. T. C. Hales and S. McLaughlin. A proof of the dodecahedral conjecture. E-print archive arXiv.org/abs/math.MG/9811079.
8. J. E. Hopcroft and J. K. Wong. Linear time algorithm for isomorphism of planar graphs (preliminary report). In *STOC '74: Proc. 6th ACM Symposium Theory of Computing*, pages 172–184. ACM Press, 1974.
9. T. Nipkow, L. Paulson, and M. Wenzel. *Isabelle/HOL — A Proof Assistant for Higher-Order Logic*, volume 2283 of *Lect. Notes in Comp. Sci.* Springer-Verlag, 2002. http://www.in.tum.de/~nipkow/LNCS2283/.
10. S. Obua. Proving bounds for real linear programs in Isabelle/HOL. In J. Hurd, editor, *Theorem Proving in Higher Order Logics (TPHOLs 2005)*, volume 3603 of *Lect. Notes in Comp. Sci.*, pages 227–244. Springer-Verlag, 2005.
11. R. Zumkeller. A formalization of global optimization with Taylor models. In *Automated Reasoning (IJCAR 2006)*, 2006. This volume.

Automatic Construction and Verification of Isotopy Invariants

Volker Sorge[1], Andreas Meier[2], Roy McCasland[3,*], and Simon Colton[4]

[1] School of Computer Science, University of Birmingham, UK
V.Sorge@cs.bham.ac.uk
http://www.cs.bham.ac.uk/~vxs
[2] DFKI GmbH, Saarbrücken, Germany
ameier72@web.de
http://www.ags.uni-sb.de/~ameier
[3] School of Informatics, University of Edinburgh, UK
rmccasla@inf.ed.ac.uk
http://www.inf.ed.ac.uk/~rmccasla
[4] Department of Computing, Imperial College London, UK
sgc@doc.ic.ac.uk
http://www.doc.ic.ac.uk/~sgc

Abstract. We extend our previous study of the automatic construction of isomorphic classification theorems for algebraic domains by considering the *isotopy* equivalence relation, which is of more importance than isomorphism in certain domains. This extension was not straightforward, and we had to solve two major technical problems, namely generating and verifying isotopy invariants. Concentrating on the domain of loop theory, we have developed three novel techniques for generating isotopic invariants, by using the notion of universal identities and by using constructions based on substructures. In addition, given the complexity of the theorems which verify that a conjunction of the invariants form an isotopy class, we have developed ways of simplifying the problem of proving these theorems. Our techniques employ an intricate interplay of computer algebra, model generation, theorem proving and satisfiability solving methods. To demonstrate the power of the approach, we generate an isotopic classification theorem for loops of size 6, which extends the previously known result that there are 22. This result was previously beyond the capabilities of automated reasoning techniques.

1 Introduction

The classification of abstract algebraic objects such as groups and rings has been a major driving force in pure mathematics. For the majority of algebraic domains, however, full classifications have been elusive (with notable exceptions being Abelian groups, finite simple groups and Abelian quasigroups [17]). This is partially due to the sheer number of classes in domains such as quasigroups, where the axioms are not particularly restrictive. Due to this volume of classes,

---

* The author's work was supported by EPSRC MathFIT grant GR/S31099.

U. Furbach and N. Shankar (Eds.): IJCAR 2006, LNAI 4130, pp. 36–51, 2006.

automatic techniques have much potential to add to mathematical knowledge. In particular, enumeration techniques have been used to count the instances of certain finite algebras [11] and model generating and constraint solving techniques could solve open existence problems [19]. Moreover, using first order theorem proving, McCune et. al have generated single axiom representations for numerous algebraic domains [9].

We are more interested in qualitative rather than quantitative results. To this end, we have developed a bootstrapping algorithm for the construction of classification theorems in finite algebraic domains. While it is largely generic, its power relies upon the automatic discovery of algebraic invariants which are able to discriminate between members of different classes defined by the equivalence relation under consideration. When considering isomorphism equivalences, we were able to employ machine learning techniques to generate the invariants, and this led to novel theorems which achieve classifications up to isomorphism of quasigroups and loops of small order [4]. We provide a brief overview of the bootstrapping algorithm in Sec. 2.

We present here the application of the bootstrapping algorithm to the production of classification theorems up to *isotopism*, an equivalence relation which is of greater importance than isomorphism in certain domains, in particular algebraic loop theory. Unfortunately, the machine learning approach did not suffice for this application, as finding isotopy invariants is a much more complex task. Hence, concentrating on the domain of loop theory, we have developed new methods for generating isotopy invariants, as described in Sec. 3. Firstly, using results from the literature, we show how universal identities can be used to generate invariants via an intricate interplay of model generation and theorem proving. Secondly, we present two new sets of invariants derived by systematically examining substructures of loops, and we describe their construction, which uses symbolic computation techniques.

As described in Sec. 4, it has also been a challenge to automatically verify that a conjunction of invariant properties defines an isotopy class (another important aspect of the bootstrapping algorithm). For this reason, we have developed methods for simplifying the problems with computer algebra, before providing proof via a satisfiability solver. As a by-product, these methods significantly simplify the task of generating non-isotopic models. Having solved the problems of generating and verifying isotopic invariants, we have employed the bootstrapping algorithm to generate new results. In particular, in Sec. 5, we present an isotopic classification theorem for loops of order 6, which extends the known enumeration theorem by providing a full set of classification properties.

2   Background

As described in [4], we have developed a bootstrapping algorithm for generating classification theorems in algebraic domains of pure mathematics. Moreover, we have applied this approach to constructing new classification results with respect to isomorphism mainly in the algebraic domains of quasigroups and loops. In this section, we briefly outline this method, and summarise our previous results.

The bootstrapping algorithm takes a set of properties, $\mathcal{P}$, a cardinality, n, and an equivalence relation, E, as input. It returns a decision tree that contains the classification theorem for the algebraic structures of order n that satisfy $\mathcal{P}$ with respect to E, as well as a set of representants for each equivalence class. During the construction, a set of theorems are proved, which – taken together – prove the correctness and the completeness of the classification theorem.

In detail, the method proceeds as follows. Firstly, it initialises a decision tree with root node $\mathcal{N}$ labelled with the properties $\mathcal{P}$. We denote the properties that a node is labelled by as $\mathcal{P}_{\mathcal{N}}$. The algorithm then works iteratively, starting with the root node and moving on to successive nodes in the tree. It constructs an example of an algebraic structure of order n satisfying $\mathcal{P}_{\mathcal{N}}$. When no example can be produced, the algorithm will prove that no structure of size n with properties $\mathcal{P}_{\mathcal{N}}$ can exist. When an example does exist, one of two things happen, either: (1) the process shows that the node represents an equivalence class with respect to E, i.e., it proves that all structures of order n that satisfy the properties $\mathcal{P}_{\mathcal{N}}$ are equivalent to each other under E, or (2) the process constructs another algebraic structure satisfying $\mathcal{P}_{\mathcal{N}}$, which is not equivalent to the first one. Note that cases (1) and (2) are mutually exclusive and can be performed in parallel. For case (2), the algorithm computes a discriminating property P for the two structures, such that P holds for one structure and $\neg P$ holds for the other. P is then used to further expand the decision tree by adding two new nodes $\mathcal{N}'$ and $\mathcal{N}''$ below $\mathcal{N}$, with labels $\mathcal{P}_{\mathcal{N}'} = \mathcal{P}_{\mathcal{N}} \cup \{P\}$ and $\mathcal{P}_{\mathcal{N}''} = \mathcal{P}_{\mathcal{N}} \cup \{\neg P\}$ respectively.

The algorithm then iterates over these nodes and adds to the tree accordingly. After new nodes have been created for each of these nodes, the above steps are carried out again. The algorithm terminates once no more expansions can be applied. Leaf nodes either represent equivalence classes or are empty, i.e., no structure exists with the properties given in the node. The final classification theorem comprises the disjunction of the properties which label the leaf nodes.

The bootstrapping algorithm is a framework that combines a host of reasoning techniques which play their part in achieving the overall goal. In particular, it relies on third party systems to generate algebras and discriminants, and to verify the construction of the decision tree at each step. We use the following methodologies in the different steps of the algorithm:

Generating Algebras. We use model generation to construct algebras. In the first step, the algorithm calls a model generator to return an algebra corresponding to the input axioms. Throughout the process, model generators are used to construct algebras which are not equivalent to a given algebra. For the experiments described in [4], we used the model generator Mace [10], but we have replaced this by Sem [22] and Finder [18], as they are more effective in our domain. While Sem is generally the more powerful of the two, it has weaknesses when dealing with function symbols of arity greater than 2, which can be introduced when we employ Skolemisation techniques (see [12] for details).

Generating Discriminants. The approach to constructing discriminating properties varies from equivalence relation to equivalence relation. When dealing with the isomorphism relation, we treated the generation of a discriminant for a pair of algebras as a machine learning problem, and successfully applied automated theory formation [3] and inductive logic programming [5] to such problems.

Verifying Properties. Throughout the bootstrapping procedure, all the results coming from third party systems are independently verified by first order automated theorem provers. Thus, for a given discriminant P and two algebras Q and Q', we show that (1) P is a proper discriminant for the equivalence relation E [which means that if Q and Q' differ with respect to the property, then they cannot be members of the same equivalence class], (2) P holds for Q, and (3) P does not hold for Q'. Proving these properties explicitly guarantees the overall correctness of the constructed decision tree. The proofs themselves are generally not very challenging, and we have experimented with several provers. We generally employ Spass [21] for these tasks.

Verifying Equivalence Classes. The most difficult verification problems occurring during the classification process involve showing that a given node forms an equivalence class with respect to the equivalence relation under consideration. More formally, we need to prove that, for a particular set of properties of a node, P, all algebras of cardinality n, which satisfy P, are equivalent, and every member of the equivalence class satisfies P. These types of proof are necessary to fully verify the completeness of a decision tree. Although the theorems are essentially second order, because we work in a finite domain, they can be expressed as propositional logic problems by enumerating all possible equivalence mappings for structures of cardinality n and thus made accessible to ATP systems. In our original experiments, described in [4], we used Spass for these problems, as it was the only system which coped with the massive clause normalisations required (cf. [20]). For later experiments, we replaced Spass by state of the art SAT solvers and developed a range of encoding techniques for a diverse range of systems (cf. [12]). Currently we have integrated zChaff [13] that can handle pure boolean SAT problems, the DPLLT [7] system, which can handle ground equations, and CVClite [2], which can also deal with finite quantification. While using SAT solvers increases the power of our algorithm, if translated naively, many of the proof problems would still be beyond the capabilities of state of the art systems. To enable us to solve these problems, we implemented some computer algebra algorithms in GAP [8] that exploit some mathematical domain knowledge to reduce complexity.

In our experiments with isomorphism as the equivalence relation, we mainly concentrated on the domain of quasigroups and loops. A *quasigroup* is a nonempty set G together with a binary operation $\circ$ that satisfies the property $\forall a, b \in G. (\exists x \in G. x \circ a = b) \land (\exists y \in G. a \circ y = b)$. This property is often called the Latin Square property and has the effect that every element of G appears exactly once in every row and every column of the multiplication table of $\circ$. A *loop* is a quasigroup that contains a unit element, i.e., an element e such that $\forall x \in G. x \circ e = e \circ x = x$. We generated novel isomorphism classification theorems for quasigroups of orders 3 to 5 and loops of order 4 to 6, a partial classification of loops of order 7, as well as some classification theorems for quasigroups of orders 6 and 7 with additional special properties, e.g., idempotency. The largest decision tree so far is the full isomorphism classification of quasigroups of size 5. This contains 2875 nodes and 1411 isomorphism classes, but is relatively shallow, with a maximum depth of 23. Its completion took more than four months of processing time. For more details see http://www.cs.bham.ac.uk/~vxs/quasigroups/.

3   Generating Isotopy Invariants

The isotopy equivalence relation is of considerable importance in quasigroup theory, hence we concentrate on isotopy in this paper. It is defined as follows:

Definition 1. *We say two quasigroups* $(G, \cdot)$ *and* $(H, *)$ *are* isotopic *to each other — or G is an* isotope *of H — if there are bijective mappings* α, β, γ *from G to H such that for all* $x, y \in G$, $\alpha(x) * \beta(y) = \gamma(x \cdot y)$ *holds.*

Isotopy is an equivalence relation and the classes induced by it are called isotopism classes. It is a generalisation of isomorphism, since G and H are isomorphic if $\alpha = \beta = \gamma$. In other words, while two quasigroups can be isotopic but not necessarily isomorphic to each other, all members of an isomorphism class belong to the same isotopism class. Importantly, every quasigroup is isotopic to a loop, which we call its loop-isotope [14]. Thus, in certain respects, we can restrict the classification of quasigroups to just the classification of loops.

As mentioned above, an important function of the bootstrapping algorithm is to generate invariant properties which enable us to discriminate between two algebras belonging to different equivalence classes. For instance, when dealing with the isomorphism equivalence relation, if one example of an algebra was commutative (i.e., $\forall x, y. (x*y = y*x)$) and another was not, then they could not belong to the same isomorphism class. Our machine learning approach was able to generate such properties, given background concepts including the multiplication operation. Unfortunately, such simple properties do not enable us to distinguish between members of different isotopy classes. For example, commutativity is not an isotopy invariant, as the isotopism (α, ι, ι), where ι is the identity mapping and $\alpha \neq \iota$, can map a commutative quasigroup to a non-commutative isotope. Due to the more complicated nature of isotopy invariants, initial experiments with the learning system failed to identify any suitable isotopy invariants.

In light of this failure, we developed bespoke methods for generating three types of isotopy invariants that are used while producing isotopic classifications of loops. We first describe the generation of universal identities (quasigroup isotopy invariants), which builds on a concept introduced by Falconer [6]. We describe how we obtain these invariants using an interplay of model generation and theorem proving. We also present two more types of invariants, which are based on substructures, which – to the best of our knowledge – have not been reported in the literature on loops, hence represent a novel way of characterising loops. These invariants are derived by systematically examining substructures of loops, and are constructed using symbolic computation techniques.

3.1   Universal Identities

Following Falconer [6], from a given loop identity we derive a universal identity. We first define two additional operations $\backslash$ and $/$ on a pair of elements such that:

1. $x \cdot (x\backslash y) = y$ and $x\backslash(x \cdot y) = y$ 2. $(y/x) \cdot x = y$ and $(y \cdot x)/x = y$

Note that these operations are well defined because loops are quasigroups. Given a loop identity $w_1 = w_2$, where w_1, w_2 are words of a loop, i.e., combinations of elements of a loop with respect to the loop operation $\cdot$, we can obtain a *derived* or *universal identity* $\overline{w}_1 = \overline{w}_2$ by recursively applying the following transformations:

1. if $w = x$, then $\overline{w} = x$;   2. if $w = u \cdot v$, then $\overline{w} = (\overline{u}/y) \cdot (z\backslash\overline{v})$

Here y and z are arbitrary elements of a loop, i.e., new universally quantified variables. As an example, consider the two loops below:

L_4	0	1	2	3	4	5
0	0	1	2	3	4	5
1	1	2	0	5	3	4
2	2	0	1	4	5	3
3	3	5	4	1	0	2
4	4	3	5	0	2	1
5	5	4	3	2	1	0

L_8	0	1	2	3	4	5
0	0	1	2	3	4	5
1	1	2	0	4	5	3
2	2	0	1	5	3	4
3	3	5	4	1	0	2
4	4	3	5	0	2	1
5	5	4	3	2	1	0

The following universal identity holds for L_4 but does not hold for L_8:

$$\forall x. \forall y_1. \forall y_2. (x/y_1) \cdot (((x/y_1) \cdot (y_2\backslash x)) \cdot (y_2\backslash x)) = ((x/y_1) \cdot (y_2\backslash x)) \cdot ((x/y_1) \cdot (y_2\backslash x)).$$

This universal identity was derived from the following loop identity:

$$\forall x. x \cdot ((x \cdot x) \cdot x) = (x \cdot x) \cdot (x \cdot x)$$

To generate universal identities for isotopy invariants, we have to first find an equation that holds in some loops, transform it into a derived identity, and subsequently show that this new identity is indeed a loop invariant. In order to get a large number of invariants we employ a process of interleaving model generation and first order theorem proving with intermediate transformations of the respective results. We first systematically generate identities I for which we check whether they are loop identities, by trying to generate a loop of size ≤ 8 that satisfies I using the model generator Mace. All identities for which a loop exists are then transformed into universal identities U as described above. Each U is then passed to at least one first order theorem prover in order to show that it is an isotopy invariant. We employ both Vampire [15] and E [16] for this task. Combined, these show that around 80% of the universal identities are indeed isotopy invariants. Note that for each universal identity, U, we show that it is an invariant under isotopy independently of the size of a loop. We can therefore reuse these universal identities in different classifications. Consequently, we do not have to repeat this step in every classification, but rather perform it offline and collect universal identities in a pool of confirmed isotopy invariants. To date, we have generated 54,000 confirmed loop identities, which can be translated into universal identities. From these, we have attempted to prove 8,000 to be isotopy invariants and have succeeded to show this for 6,831 using both Vampire and E.

During the classification of loops of a particular size, n, we draw on this pool by first filtering them again by using the model generator Finder to generate loops of size n that satisfy the invariant. We then extract those invariants for which at least one loop of order n exists, and we use only these as potential discriminants. Note that the filter discards any invariants which cannot solve any discrimination problem, as no loop of size n satisfies the invariant property. Then, when we need to discriminate between two loops we test whether one the invariants holds for one and not for the other, using DPLLT or CVClite. While the model generation and theorem proving stages are ran in parallel by distributing the problems on a large cluster of processors for both the generation and testing of invariants, finding a discriminant can still take a very long time. Moreover, universal identities are not necessarily sufficient to discriminate between two non-isotopic quasigroups. We therefore explore only a limited number of randomly selected invariants, and if this is not successful, we employ two different methods for generating invariants, which are based on the substructures of quasigroups, as described in Sec. 3.2 and Sec. 3.3.

3.2   Substructure Invariants

Let $(G, \cdot)$ be a quasigroup, and let A and B be non-empty subsets of G. We adopt the usual notation for the set $A \cdot B$, namely, $A \cdot B = \{a \cdot b : a \in A \wedge b \in B\}$.

Lemma 1. *Let $(G, \cdot)$ be a quasigroup and let $(H, *)$ be a quasigroup that is isotopic to $(G, \cdot)$ under the bijections (α, β, γ). Then, for any non-empty subsets A and B of G, we have $|A \cdot B| = |\alpha(A) * \beta(B)|$.*

Proof. Observe that since γ is a bijection, then $|\gamma(A \cdot B)| = |A \cdot B|$. It suffices then to show that $\gamma(A \cdot B) = \alpha(A) * \beta(B)$. But this follows immediately from the fact that for all $a \in A$ and $b \in B$, we have $\gamma(a \cdot b) = \alpha(a) * \beta(b)$.

When G is finite, one can interpret the elements of A (resp., B) as designating a subset of rows (resp., columns) in the multiplication table of G. The set $A \cdot B$ then consists of the elements where these rows and columns meet. The above result thus suggests the following notation:

Notation 1. Let $(G, \cdot)$ be a quasigroup of order n, and let i, j, k each be integers such that $1 \leq i, j, k \leq n$. Let $G(i, j, k)$ denote the set:

$$G(i, j, k) = \{(A, B) : A, B \subseteq G, |A| = i, |B| = j, |A \cdot B| = k\}.$$

Theorem 1. *Let $(G, \cdot)$ and $(H, *)$ be isotopic quasigroups of order n, and let i, j, k each be integers such that $1 \leq i, j, k \leq n$. Then $|G(i, j, k)| = |H(i, j, k)|$.*

Proof. Note that the one-to-one correspondence between the collection of ordered pairs (A, B) such that $A, B \subseteq G, |A| = i, |B| = j$, and the corresponding collection of ordered pairs of subsets of H, is preserved under isotopy. The result now follows easily from Lemma 1.

Continuing with the notation above, fix an element $(A, B) \in G(i, j, k)$, and for each $g_h \in A \cdot B$, $(1 \leq h \leq k)$, let $f(g_h) = |\{(a, b) \in A \times B : a \cdot b = g_h\}|$. In other words, $f(g_h)$ is the number of times that g_h appears in the block formed by A and B (which we will henceforth refer to as the $A \cdot B$ block). We let $F(A, B) = (f(g_1), \ldots, f(g_k))$, and call this the (un-ordered) *frequency-tuple* of (A, B). If two such frequency-tuples F and F' are the same (up to order), then we write $F \approx F'$.

Lemma 2. *Let $(G, \cdot)$ and $(H, *)$ be isotopic quasigroups (under the bijections (α, β, γ)) of order n, and let i, j, k each be integers such that $1 \leq i, j, k \leq n$. If $(A, B) \in G(i, j, k)$, then $F(A, B) \approx F(\alpha(A), \beta(B))$.*

Proof. In light of Theorem 1, it suffices to prove that, for every $g \in A \cdot B$, $f(g) = f(\gamma(g))$. But this equality follows immediately from the fact that if $a \cdot b = g$, then $\alpha(a) * \beta(b) = \gamma(g)$.

Given this latest result, we adopt the following notation:

Notation 2. Let $(G, \cdot)$ be a quasigroup of order n, let i, j, k be integers such that $1 \leq i, j, k \leq n$, and let F be a frequency-tuple for some $(C, D) \in G(i, j, k)$. Then, let $G(i, j, k, F)$ denote the set:

$$G(i, j, k, F) = \{(A, B) \in G(i, j, k) : F(A, B) \approx F\}$$

Theorem 2. *Let $(G, \cdot)$ be a quasigroup of order n, let i, j, k be integers such that $1 \leq i, j, k \leq n$, and let F be a frequency-tuple for some $(C, D) \in G(i, j, k)$. Furthermore, let $(H, *)$ be a quasigroup isotopic to $(G, \cdot)$. Then $|G(i, j, k, F)| = |H(i, j, k, F)|$.*

Proof. This is an immediate consequence of Theorem 1 and Lemma 2.

To generate isotopy invariants based on Theorems 1 and 2, we implemented an algorithm that compares the number of elements in substructures for two quasigroups $(G, \cdot)$ and $(H, *)$. This works iteratively, as follows: for $i = 2, \ldots, n - 1$, $j = 2, \ldots, n - 1$, and $k = max(i, j), \ldots, n$, if $|G(i, j, k)| \neq |H(i, j, k)|$ then return the invariant, otherwise continue. If all the possible substructures are exhausted without yielding an invariant, we perform a frequency analysis for all the $G(i, j, k)$ and $H(i, j, k)$ until we find a pair $G(i, j, k, F)$ and $H(i, j, k, F')$, such that $F \neq F'$. To keep the formulas resulting for these invariants small, we always prefer an existence argument over the actual comparison of numbers of substructures. That is, we give a preference to invariants, such that either $|G(i, j, k)| = 0$ or $|H(i, j, k)| = 0$.

As an example of such an invariant, consider property P_9 below that expresses that there exists a 2×2 substructure that contains exactly 2 distinct elements. Note the use of the unique existence quantifier for variables v_1 and v_2.

$$P_9: \quad \exists r_1, r_2 \cdot \exists c_1, c_2 \cdot \exists! v_1, v_2 \cdot r_1 \neq r_2 \wedge c_1 \neq c_2 \wedge v_1 \neq v_2 \wedge \bigwedge_{i=1}^{2} \bigwedge_{j=1}^{2} \bigvee_{k=1}^{2} (r_i \cdot c_j = v_k)$$

With respect to P_9, consider these loops:

L_{21}	0	1	2	3	4	5
0	0	1	2	3	4	5
1	1	0	4	5	2	3
2	2	3	0	1	5	4
3	3	2	5	4	0	1
4	4	5	1	0	3	2
5	5	4	3	2	1	0

Note that L_{21} satisfies property P_9, due to the boxed structure, which is a 2×2 structure with exactly 2 elements. However, P_9 does not hold for L_{23}, i.e., $|L_{23}(2,2,2)| = 0$.

L_{23}	0	1	2	3	4	5
0	2	0	1	5	3	4
1	0	1	2	3	4	5
2	1	2	0	4	5	3
3	4	3	5	0	2	1
4	5	4	3	1	0	2
5	3	5	4	2	1	0

3.3 Patterns

Given non-empty subsets A and B of a quasigroup $(G, \cdot)$, we look for patterns amongst the numbers of distinct elements within the respective sub-blocks. By this, we mean the following: Let $|A| = i$, $|B| = j$, and choose i', j' such that $1 \le i' \le i$ and $1 \le j' \le j$. Now for each k, $1 \le k \le n$, we let $AB(i', j', k) = \{(A', B') : A' \subseteq A, B' \subseteq B, |A'| = i', |B'| = j', |A' \cdot B'| = k\}$. Furthermore, let $p_k = |AB(i', j', k)|$. In other words, p_k is the number of $i' \times j'$ sub-blocks of the $A \cdot B$ block, that have precisely k distinct entries. We now let $\mathfrak{P}_{i', j'}(A, B) = (p_1, \ldots, p_n)$, and we call $\mathfrak{P}_{i', j'}(A, B)$ the $i' \times j'$ *pattern-tuple* of (A, B).

Lemma 3. *Let* $(G, \cdot)$, $(H, *)$, (α, β, γ), i, j, k, n *be as in Lemma 2, and let* i', j' *be integers such that* $1 \le i' \le i$ *and* $1 \le j' \le j$. *If* $A, B \subseteq G$ *such that* $|A| = i$ *and* $|B| = j$, *then* $\mathfrak{P}_{i', j'}(A, B) = \mathfrak{P}_{i', j'}(\alpha(A), \beta(B))$.

Proof. Note that for each k, $1 \le k \le n$, and for each $(A', B') \in AB(i', j', k)$, we have $|A' \cdot B'| = |\alpha(A') * \beta(B')|$, by Lemma 1. Now since α and β are bijections, then $(A', B') \in AB(i', j', k)$ if and only if $(\alpha(A'), \beta(B')) \in \alpha(A)\beta(B)(i', j', k)$. The result now follows in a straightforward manner.

Following similar lines as previously, we introduce the following notation:

Notation 3. Let $(G, \cdot)$ be a quasigroup of order n, and let $\mathfrak{P}_{i', j'}$ be an $i' \times j'$ pattern-tuple of (C, D) for some $C, D \subseteq G$ such that $|C| = i$ and $|D| = j$ ($1 \le i, j \le n$), where integers i', j' are such that $1 \le i' \le i$ and $1 \le j' \le j$. We let $G(i, j, \mathfrak{P}_{i', j'})$ denote the set:

$$G(i, j, \mathfrak{P}_{i', j'}) = \{(A, B) : A, B \subseteq G, |A| = i, |B| = j, \mathfrak{P}_{i', j'}(A, B) = \mathfrak{P}_{i', j'}\}$$

Theorem 3. *Let* $(G, \cdot)$ *be a quasigroup of order* n, *and let* $\mathfrak{P}_{i', j'}$ *be an* $i' \times j'$ *pattern-tuple of* (C, D) *for some* $C, D \subseteq G$ *such that* $|C| = i$ *and* $|D| = j$ *($1 \le i, j \le n$), where integers* i', j' *are such that* $1 \le i' \le i$ *and* $1 \le j' \le j$. *Furthermore, let* $(H, *)$ *be a quasigroup isotopic to* $(G, \cdot)$. *Then* $|G(i, j, \mathfrak{P}_{i', j'})| = |H(i, j, \mathfrak{P}_{i', j'})|$.

Proof. This follows immediately from Lemma 3.

In order to generate additional invariants for a given pair of quasigroups $(G, \cdot)$ and $(H, *)$, we employ Theorem 3 in a similar fashion to that used in Sec. 3.2. That is, we successively compare the number of patterns of the same size and the same number of distinct elements.

4 Simplifying Problems

The most difficult verification problems which occur during the classification process involve showing that a given node forms an isotopy class, i.e., we need to prove that a particular set of properties is indeed classifying with respect to isotopy. The opposite problem is to take a given node that doesn't form an isotopy class, and construct a representant that is not isotopic to the existing representant of the node. To solve these two problems with automated theorem provers and model generators requires considerable effort, as basic formalisations of these problems are not solvable using state of the art techniques. We therefore employ several computational methods, implemented in the computer algebra system GAP [8], for reducing the complexity of the problems to be solved. The methods we developed for isotopism problems make use of those we developed for the corresponding isomorphism problems and also exploit some known results from the isotopy theory of quasigroups. Hence, we first give a brief account of how we handled isomorphism problems (for further details see [12]), and then present their adaptation for isotopism, using theorems presented in [14].

4.1 Handling of Isomorphism Problems

In general, to prove that a particular set of properties associated with a node on the decision tree is classifying with respect to isomorphism is a higher-order problem, as it requires proving that all structures satisfying the properties are isomorphic. However, since we are concerned with finite structures, the proof problem can be reduced to first-order and even propositional logic by enumerating all (finitely many) possible isomorphic structures of the representant, Q, of the node. With all isomorphic structures available, it suffices to prove that each structure that satisfies the properties of the node equals one of the isomorphic structures. For the construction of a non-isomorphic structure, it suffices to generate a structure that satisfies the properties of the node but differs from each of the isomorphic structures.

A naive approach to enumerate all isomorphic structures considers all $n!$ possible bijective mappings for structures of cardinality n. From each of these bijective mappings, a structure can be constructed that is isomorphic to Q, and these $n!$ are all possible isomorphic structures of Q. This naive approach can be simplified by the usage of generating systems. A structure Q with binary operation $\circ$ is said to be *generated* by a set of elements $\{q_1, \ldots, q_m\} \subseteq Q$ if every element of Q can be expressed as a combination — usually called a factorisation or word — of the q_i under the operation $\circ$. We call a set of generators together with the corresponding factorisations a *generating system*. Given a generating system, we can exploit the fact that each isomorphism is uniquely determined by the images of the generators, to reduce the total number of isomorphisms that we need to consider. If n is the cardinality of the structures and m is the number of generators, then, instead of $n!$, there are only $\frac{n!}{(n-m)!}$ possible mappings and possible resulting structures to consider, since only the m generators have to be mapped explicitly.

In theory, the worst case complexity resulting from the simplification with generating systems is still $n!$, because there is no guarantee that a generating system with a small number of generators exists. In our experiments, however, the number of generators was typically only 2, so the complexity for isomorphism problems was reduced to n^2 from $n!$. This approach requires additional effort in order to compute a (minimal) generating system for Q, as well as to prove that a computed system is indeed a generating system for Q. The former task is performed by GAP, whereas the latter task results in an additional proof problem, which is trivial even for large n.

4.2   Handling of Isotopism Problems

Unfortunately, we cannot directly employ the trick of using generating systems since we now have three, instead of one, bijective mappings to consider, so the images of the generators no longer uniquely determine isotopisms. This means a naive approach to performing the isotopism proof or model construction would have to consider all $(n!)^3$ possible triples of bijective mappings to be applied to a representant Q of a node in the classification tree. As for the case of isomorphism, from the $(n!)^3$ possible triples of bijective mappings, all $(n!)^3$ structures that are isotopic to Q can be computed. With all the isotopes of Q available, an automated theorem prover can be used to show that each structure that satisfies the properties of the node equals one of the isotopes. Moreover, a model generator can be asked to compute a structure that satisfies the properties of the node but differs from each of the isotopes. However, we have found that this naive approach exceeds the abilities of state of the art systems, even for $n = 4$.

In order to simplify our problems, particularly by making use of the reduction offered by generating systems, we exploit the following known results from the isotopy theory of quasigroups (see [14] for details).

Definition 2. *A quasigroup $(G, \cdot)$ is a* principal isotope *of the quasigroup $(G, *)$ if there are permutations α, β, ι on G such that for all $x, y \in G, \alpha(x) * \beta(y) = \iota(x \cdot y)$, where ι is the identity permutation.*

Theorem 4. *If $(G, \cdot)$ and $(H, *)$ are isotopic quasigroups, then $(H, *)$ is isomorphic to some principal isotope of $(G, \cdot)$.*

Definition 3. *Let $(G, \cdot)$ be a quasigroup. Let f and g be fixed elements of G. Then the isotope $(G, *)$ such that $(x \cdot g) * (f \cdot y) = x \cdot y$ for all $x, y \in G$ is called the* fg-isotope *of $(G, \cdot)$.*

Theorem 5. *Let $(G, \cdot)$ and $(H, *)$ be quasigroups. H is isotopic to G if and only if it is isomorphic to an fg-isotope of G.*

These results show that, for our purposes, we no longer need to consider quasigroups with distinct ground sets (the set G will typically suffice). Moreover, it is easy to show that every fg-isotope is, in fact, a loop with unit element fg. Consequently, every quasigroup has a loop isotope, and hence, rather than compute all $(n!)^3$ isotopes for a structure Q, it suffices to:

1. compute the set of all fg-isotopes of Q, $\mathcal{FG}(Q)$,
2. remove structures from $\mathcal{FG}(Q)$ that are isomorphic to other structures in $\mathcal{FG}(Q)$ until the resulting set $\mathcal{FG}'(Q)$ contains no pair of isomorphic structures,

3. compute the set of all structures that are isomorphic to a structure in
$\mathcal{FG}'(Q)$. We denote this set: $\mathcal{I}_{fg}(Q)$.

For a given representant, Q, there are n^2 fg-isotopes and for each fg-isotope
there are $n!$ isomorphic structures. Hence, our simplification reduces the complexity from $(n!)^3$ structures in the naive approach to $n!n^2$ structures. Although
this is already a considerable improvement, the resulting complexity still exceeds
the capabilities of state of the art systems, even for small n. We now observe
that step 3 discusses isomorphisms only, which consequently allows us to exploit
the generating systems simplification developed for the isomorphism problems.
Hence, instead of step 3 above, we can perform the following alternative steps:

3a. compute a generating system for each structure in $\mathcal{FG}'(Q)$, respectively,
3b. for each pair of a structure in $\mathcal{FG}'(Q)$ and its generating system, compute
    the set of isomorphic structures with respect to the generating system, re-
    spectively. Then, compute the union $\mathcal{G}_{fg}(Q)$ of all resulting structures.

In theory, the worst case complexity of $\mathcal{G}_{fg}(Q)$ is still $n!n^2$. However, in our
experiments, we found that the complexity of $\mathcal{FG}'(Q)$ is typically n rather than
n^2, and the complexity resulting from the isomorphisms typically comes to n^2
instead of $n!$ when the generating system simplification is exploited. Hence, in
practise, the simplified isotopism proof and model generation formalisations typically require the consideration of just n^3 structures. Note that additional effort
is necessary to prove that two given structures are isomorphic in step 2, and
to compute and verify generating systems in step 3a. However, these additional
problems are trivial even for large problems.

5   Results

Our primary result is a new qualitative isotopy classification theorem for loops
of order 6, in the sense that it provides a full set of classifiers for the 22 known
isotopism classes and corresponding representants. The decision tree for the theorem is given in Fig. 1 (for display purposes, we have broken it up into five
parts). The entire tree consists of 43 nodes, where the doubly circled leaf nodes
represent isotopy classes. The respective classifying properties correspond to the
conjunction of discriminants given along the path from the leaves to the root.
The discriminants themselves are given below the tree in Fig. 1.
  Note that the top three discriminants are universal identities, while the remainder are substructure invariants, with the exception of P_{11}, which is a pattern invariant. The pattern invariant and four of the substructure invariants
(P_4, P_5, P_6, P_9) use an existence argument. The reason for the relatively low
number of universal identities as discriminants is that in each step we only test
100 invariants randomly selected out of the overall pool of known invariants
before testing for discriminating substructure properties. This restriction is necessary as in our current implementation, testing universal identities with respect
to discrimination still consumes a lot of search time. However, we hope that with
more advanced encoding techniques and better pre-selection criteria for universal

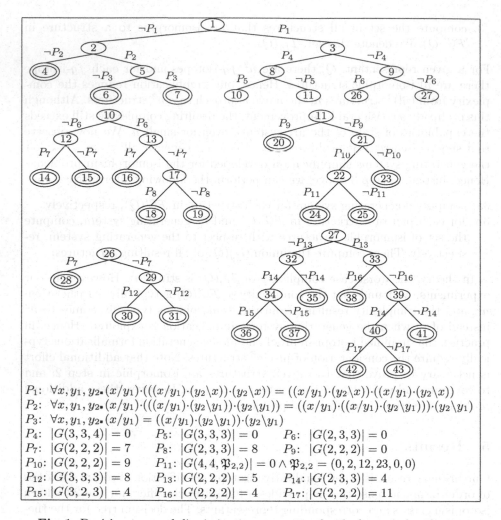

P_1: $\forall x, y_1, y_2 \bullet (x/y_1) \cdot (((x/y_1) \cdot (y_2 \backslash x)) \cdot (y_2 \backslash x)) = ((x/y_1) \cdot (y_2 \backslash x)) \cdot ((x/y_1) \cdot (y_2 \backslash x))$
P_2: $\forall x, y_1, y_2 \bullet (x/y_1) \cdot (((x/y_1) \cdot (y_2 \backslash y_1)) \cdot (y_2 \backslash y_1)) = ((x/y_1) \cdot ((x/y_1) \cdot (y_2 \backslash y_1))) \cdot (y_2 \backslash y_1)$
P_3: $\forall x, y_1, y_2 \bullet (x/y_1) = ((x/y_1) \cdot (y_2 \backslash y_1)) \cdot (y_2 \backslash y_1)$
P_4: $|G(3, 3, 4)| = 0$ P_5: $|G(3, 3, 3)| = 0$ P_6: $|G(2, 3, 3)| = 0$
P_7: $|G(2, 2, 2)| = 7$ P_8: $|G(2, 3, 3)| = 8$ P_9: $|G(2, 2, 2)| = 0$
P_{10}: $|G(2, 2, 2)| = 9$ P_{11}: $|G(4, 4, \mathfrak{P}_{2,2})| = 0 \wedge \mathfrak{P}_{2,2} = (0, 2, 12, 23, 0, 0)$
P_{12}: $|G(3, 3, 3)| = 8$ P_{13}: $|G(2, 2, 2)| = 5$ P_{14}: $|G(2, 3, 3)| = 4$
P_{15}: $|G(3, 2, 3)| = 4$ P_{16}: $|G(2, 2, 2)| = 4$ P_{17}: $|G(2, 2, 2)| = 11$

Fig. 1. Decision tree and discriminating properties for the loops 6 classification

identity invariants, we will be able to replace more substructure discriminants
in the decision tree by universal identities.

For the construction of the models in the tree, we used the Sem, Finder, and
DPLLT systems. Apart from the proof problems concerning universal identities, which were carried out by Vampire or E, the majority of the verification
proofs have been done with CVClite or DPLLT. A translation into a purely
propositional problem without equality, was prohibitive, however, as both the
number of variables and nesting depth of the quantifications led to intractably
large boolean satisfiability problems. While most properties of the tree are fully
automatically verified, we still had difficulty proving that some of the leaf nodes
are indeed isotopy classes. However, we hope to finalise this by shifting to the
new version of DPLLT in the future. Moreover, given that the number of isotopy
classes of order 6 is indeed 22 as known from the literature [11,14] and given the

proved discriminating nature of the classifying properties, the decision tree does indeed constitute a classification theorem.

We are currently working on the classification theorem for loops of order 7, for which there are 564 isotopy classes. So far, we have generated 563 nodes in the decision tree, which contains 439 substructures invariants, with an additional 7 employing frequencies, and 117 depending on pattern invariants or frequency on patterns. We suspect that the remaining isotopy class can be discriminated by extending the concept of patterns by a recursion depth. In many cases, the model generation fails to produce any results, so we re-use results from our isomorphism classification of loops of order 7, as well as enumeration results by McKay and Myrwold [11], to search for non-isotopic models. That is, we start with a set of isomorphism class representatives of order 7 loops and search amongst those for one that is non-isotopic to a given loop. Once we have finished the tree, we hope to simplify it by searching for useful universal identities.

6 Conclusions and Future Work

We have shown how the bootstrapping algorithm developed in [4] has been extended to produce isotopy classification theorems in loop theory. This involved solving two technical problems, namely the generation of isotopic invariants, and verifying that nodes in the classification tree define isotopy classes. To solve the first problem, we used the notion of universal identities to generate a pool of thousands of invariants, and we also developed new techniques for using concepts based on substructures as invariants. To solve the second problem, we combined facts from algebraic quasigroup theory in a novel computational way to extend techniques we developed in the context of isomorphism classification to isotopy problems. This not only significantly simplified the verification tasks but also made the related task of generating non-isotopic models feasible.

However, it has become clear that it will be difficult to exceed loops of size 7 or 8 with our existing techniques. In particular, the computational techniques to generate substructure invariants need to be improved in order to scale up to larger sizes. This problem can be partially overcome by using more universal identities as discriminants. To this end, it is necessary to cut down on search time by using more intelligent pre-selection of universal identity invariants, as well as producing better reformulations of problems involving universal identities to make them accessible to efficient SAT solving techniques. It is also not clear that our current set of invariants will suffice for all orders. Indeed, we have already investigated another kind of invariant – which extends the concept of frequency to patterns – but which has not been used in the context of the results presented in this paper. Finding new types of isotopy invariants for loops is certainly interesting from a mathematical viewpoint.

We plan to extract details of the bespoke invariant generation techniques developed for isotopy into more extensive background knowledge and improved production rules for the machine learning approach. We believe that it may be possible to re-instate the learning approach, thus restoring a more generic approach to invariant discovery, and possibly discovering new invariants. We also plan to undertake a detailed analysis of the decision trees, as well as a comparison of classification theorems of different sizes for particular structures. From a purely technical point of view, an efficient reimplementation of the entire bootstrapping algorithm would be desirable to overcome some limitations of the Lisp implementation and choice of data structures.

Historically, classification projects have been undertaken for algebras with relatively few classes for small orders (e.g., there are only 5 groups of size 8 up to isomorphism). However, classification of other algebras are no less valid projects, albeit ones which are possibly more suited to an automated approach, due to the large number of classes of small order (e.g., there are $106,228,849$ loops of size 8 up to isomorphism and $1,676,267$ up to isotopism). We have shown that it is possible to make progress on large classification projects, but that this requires the combination of reasoning techniques, including theorem proving, model generation, machine learning, satisfiability solving and symbolic algebra. We believe that such integrated approaches will lead the way in the application of automated reasoning to complex mathematical discovery tasks.

References

1. R. Alur and D. Peled, eds. *Proc. of CAV 2004, LNCS* 3114. Springer Verlag, 2004.
2. C. Barrett and S. Berezin. CVC Lite: A New Implementation of the Cooperating Validity Checker. In Alur and Peled [1], pages 515–518.
3. S. Colton. *Automated Theory Formation in Pure Mathematics*. Springer, 2002.
4. S. Colton, A. Meier, V. Sorge, and R. McCasland. Automatic Generation of Classification Theorems for Finite Algebras. In *Proc. of IJCAR 2004, LNAI* 3097, pages 400–414. Springer Verlag, 2004.
5. S. Colton and S. Muggleton. Mathematical Applications of Inductive Logic Programming. *Machine Learning Journal*, 2006 (forthcoming).
6. E. Falconer. Isotopy Invariants in Quasigroups. *Transactions of the American Mathematical Society*, 151(2):511–526, 1970.
7. H. Ganzinger, G. Hagen, R. Nieuwenhuis, A. Oliveras, and C. Tinelli. DPLL(T): Fast Decision Procedures. In Alur and Peled [1], pages 175–188.
8. GAP Group. *Groups, Algorithms, and Programming, v4.7*, 2002. gap-system.org.
9. W. McCune. Single axioms for groups and Abelian groups with various operations. *Journal of Automated Reasoning*, 10(1):1–13, 1993.
10. W. McCune. *Mace4 Reference Manual and Guide*. Argonne Nat. Laboratory, 2003.
11. B. McKay, A. Meynert, and W. Myrvold. Counting Small Latin Squares. In *Europ. Women in Mathematics Int. Workshop on Groups and Graphs*, pages 67–72, 2002.
12. Andreas Meier and Volker Sorge. Applying SAT Solving in Classification of Finite Algebras. *Journal of Automated Reasoning*, 34(2):34 pages, 2005.
13. M. Moskewicz, C. Madigan, Y. Zhao, L. Zhang, and S. Malik. chaff: Engineering an efficient SAT Solver. In *Proc. of DAC-2001*, pages 530–535, 2001.
14. H. Pflugfelder. *Quasigroups and Loops: Introduction*, volume 7 of *Sigma Series in Pure Mathematics*. Heldermann Verlag, Berlin, Germany, 1990.
15. A. Riazanov and A. Voronkov. Vampire 1.1. In *Proc. of IJCAR 2001, LNAI* 2083, pages 376–380. Springer Verlag, 2001.
16. S. Schulz. E: A Brainiac theorem prover. *J. of AI Comm.*, 15(2–3):111–126, 2002.
17. J. Schwenk. A classification of Abelian quasigroups. *Rendiconti di Matematica, Serie VII*, 15:161–172, 1995.

18. J. Slaney. *FINDER, Notes and Guide*. Center for Information Science Research, Australian National University, 1995.
19. J Slaney, M Fujita, and M Stickel. Automated reasoning and exhaustive search: Quasigroup existence problems. *Computers and Mathematics with Applications*, 29:115–132, 1995.
20. G. Sutcliffe. The IJCAR-2004 Automated Theorem Proving Competition. *AI Communications*, 18(1):33–40, 2005.
21. C Weidenbach, U Brahm, T Hillenbrand, E Keen, C Theobald, and D Topic. SPASS Version 2.0. In *Proc. of CADE-18, LNAI* 2392, pages 275–279. Springer, 2002.
22. J. Zhang and H. Zhang. *SEM User's Guide*. Dep. of Comp. Science, UIowa, 2001.

Pitfalls of a Full Floating-Point Proof: Example on the Formal Proof of the Veltkamp/Dekker Algorithms

Sylvie Boldo

INRIA Futurs – PCRI
LRI, Bât. 490, Université Paris Sud
91405 Orsay Cedex, France
Sylvie.Boldo@inria.fr

Abstract. Some floating-point algorithms have been used for decades and proved decades ago in radix-2, providing neither Underflow, nor Overflow occurs. This includes the Veltkamp algorithm, used to split a float into an upper part and a lower part and the Dekker algorithm, used to compute the exact error of a floating-point multiplication.

The aim of this article is to show the difficulties of a strong justification of the validity of these algorithms for a generic radix and even when Underflow or Overflow occurs. These cases are usually dismissed even if they should not: the main argument in radix 2 of the first algorithm fails in other radices. Nevertheless all results still hold here under mild assumptions. The proof path is interesting as these cases are hardly looked into and new methods and results had to be developed.

1 Introduction

Some algorithms have been known for decades and thoroughly used. They have been proved by different people using different paths. This can be seen enough for the result to be considered correct [1]. Nevertheless, examples have shown that even in this case, the proof may be wrong [2,3]. In particular, such floating-point results can reasonably be assumed to be correct in the general case (radix 2, no Underflow, no Overflow). This assumption is usually based on a pen and paper proof. In this kind of proof, the hypotheses and where they are used are well hidden: it is difficult to remove a hypothesis such as "the radix is 2" and see where the proof has to be modified. This is the reason why we use formal methods and proof assistants that give a high guarantee in the result.

Some formalizations have already been successful including both hardware-level [4,5,6] and high-level floating-point arithmetic [7,8]. We use the Coq proof assistant [9] where floating-point arithmetic has already been formalized [10]. The case study we are interested in is first the Veltkamp algorithm used to split floating-point numbers into an upper and a lower part. This algorithm was discovered at the same period both by Veltkamp who is probably the main author of [11,12] and by Dekker [13]. Both paternities are uncertain, that is why we chose to use their most common denomination.

U. Furbach and N. Shankar (Eds.): IJCAR 2006, LNAI 4130, pp. 52–66, 2006.
© Springer-Verlag Berlin Heidelberg 2006

The second case study is an algorithm by Dekker [13] that computes the exact floating point error of a multiplication: for two floating-point numbers a and b in a given format, we compute two floating-point numbers r_1 and r_2 in the same floating-point format such that r_1 is the rounding of $a \times b$ and $a \times b = r_1 + r_2$ (this is an exact mathematical equality). With other similar techniques, this allows the computation with floating-point expansions [13,14,15] to do multi-precision computations using the floating-point unit of the processor. Such methods are used in computational geometry [15] to give the correct answer to "is this point to the left or to the right of this line?" or "is this point in or out of this circle?".

This paper is organized as follows: Section 2 describes floating-point arithmetic and our formalization of it. Section 3 describes the splitting algorithm and its full proof. Section 4 describes the exact multiplication algorithm and its full proof. Section 5 gives some perspectives.

2   Floating-Point Arithmetic

Floating-point formats, numbers and operations are defined by the IEEE-754 standard for binary floating-point arithmetic [16,17], that is under revision [18], and by the IEEE-854 standard for generic radix [19]. A format is a limit on the size of the fraction and on the size of the exponent. A floating-point number is then composed of a sign, a fraction and an exponent within these limits. The value of the floating-point number is then: $(-1)^s \; 1.f \times 2^{e-B}$ where s is the sign bit, f is the fraction (the list of bits), e is the exponent and B is a known bias. For special values of the exponent, we get either smaller values that are called subnormals (their value is $(-1)^s 0.f \times 2^{1-B}$) or exceptional values such as $\pm\infty$.

As in [20], the Coq formalization of floating-point arithmetic [10] represents a floating-point number by a pair of integers. For example, the radix-2 number $1.001_2\text{E}1$ is represented as $(1001_2, -2) = (9, -2)$. The left part of a float is called the significant and the right part is the exponent. Note that the exponent is shifted compared to the exponent of the IEEE machine number. The radix is defined as 2 in the IEEE-754 standard and can be either 2 or 10 in the IEEE-854 standard. With the increasing interest in the radix 10, we set the radix β as an integer greater than 1. Therefore, a float can be interpreted as a real value as follows: $(n, e) \in \mathbb{Z}^2 \;\hookrightarrow\; n \times \beta^e \in \mathbb{R}$.

We restrict ourselves to the numbers that fit in a given floating-point format, that gives both the precision p of the format and its minimal exponent E_i. We say that a float (n, e) is bounded if and only if $|n| < \beta^p$ and $e \geq -E_i$.

The main characteristic of this formalization is that many floats (called a cohort [18]) may share the same real value: $(4, 3)_{10} =_\mathbb{R} (40, 2)_{10} =_\mathbb{R} (400, 1)_{10} =_\mathbb{R} (4000, 0)_{10}$. To retain uniqueness, we define a canonical representation corresponding to the IEEE float. The reader does not have to bother with the canonicness or not of the floats in the proof. These ponderous details are handled by the proof assistant (and the author). For a canonical float $f = (n_f, e_f)$, the ulp (unit in the last place) has a simple expression: $\text{ulp}(f) = \beta^{e_f}$.

The rounding to nearest is denoted by $\circ$. It gives the bounded float that is the closest to the real value. When in the middle, this rounding can give either of the enclosing floats. This implies that if $f = \circ(x)$, then $|x - f| \leq \mathrm{ulp}(x)/2 = \beta^{e_f}/2$. The default IEEE rounding mode is denoted by $\overset{\mathrm{even}}{\circ}$: when in the middle, it gives the float with the even mantissa (ending with a zero in radix 2).

All lemmas and theorems explained below are proved in Coq. The corresponding files `Veltkamp.v` and `Dekker.v` can be found at the following address: `http://lipforge.ens-lyon.fr/www/pff/`.

3 Splitting of Float

3.1 Algorithm and Hand-Waving Proof

Algorithm. The Veltkamp algorithm [11,12,13] splits a float x in two floats x_1 and x_2 such that $x = x_1 + x_2$ and x_1 is the result of rounding x on a smaller precision. More precisely, let s and t be two integers such that $2 \leq s \leq t - 2$.

The working precision is on t bits (or digits) and we want to have x_1 on $t - s$ bits. The remainder x_2 fits on s bits. The algorithm, described below, only contains usual floating-point operations using the working precision. The constant C can be stored beforehand so the algorithm consists of 4 operations:

Algorithm 1 (Veltkamp) *Let $C = \beta^s + 1$.*

$$p = \circ(x \times C)$$
$$q = \circ(x - p)$$
$$x_1 = \circ(p + q)$$
$$x_2 = \circ(x - x_1)$$

Hand-Waving Proof. We compute $p \approx (\beta^s + 1) \times x$ and $q \approx x - p \approx -\beta^s \times x$. Therefore p and $-q$ are very near one from another and x_1 is computed exactly.

And $p + q \approx x$ as $q \approx x - p$, but the exponent of q is about s plus the exponent of x so that all the bits of x lesser than this value are lost. So, we only have in x_1 the first $t - s$ bits of x.

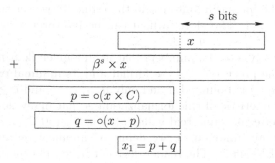

Of course, a drawing is not a proof, and especially not a formal proof. We have to deal with many cases, including the possible values of the exponent of p and x_1 and, the main point is the values of the exponent of q.

3.2   Proof

Lemma 1 (ImplyClosest). *For a bounded float f (in precision p), if we have $\beta^{e+p-1} \leq z \leq \beta^{e+p}$ and $\beta^{e+p-1} \leq f$ and $|z - f| \leq \frac{\beta^e}{2}$, then $f = \circ(z)$.*

In this lemma, e is an integer being the exponent of f. As both z and f are greater that β^{e+p-1}, we do not fall into the pitfall described below. For more on the definition of the ulp so that this pitfall does not exist, see [21].

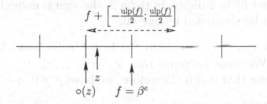

Radix-2 Assumptions. Let us move to the proof of the Veltkamp algorithm. We first assume the radix is 2 and that there is no Underflow: all floats are normal floats. We assume that the rounding is any rounding to nearest in precision t. Here are the steps taken to prove Algorithm 1:

1. $x_1 = p + q$,
2. $e_q \leq e_p \leq s + 1 + e_x$,
3. $e_q \leq s + e_x$,
4. $e_q \geq s + e_x$,
5. $x_1 = \circ_{t-s}(x)$ using Lemma 1,
6. $x = x_1 + x_2$,
7. x_2 fits on $s - 1$ bits.

All proofs will be described in the next subsection except Step 3's and 7's. As a matter of fact, these assumptions only hold in radix 2.

Lemma 2 (eqLe2). $\beta = 2 \Rightarrow e_q \leq s + e_x$.

We bound q: $|q| = \circ(|p - x|) \leq (2^s + 1)|x| + \frac{1}{2}\mathrm{ulp}(p) - |x| + \frac{1}{2}\mathrm{ulp}(q)$. Then $|q| \leq 2^s|x| + \mathrm{ulp}(p) \leq |n_x|2^{e_x+s} + 2^{s+1+e_x} = (|n_x| + 2)2^{e_x+s}$.

If $|n_x| \leq 2^t - 3$, then $|q| < 2^{t+e_x+s}$ and we deduce that $e_q \leq s + e_x$.

If not, then we either have $|n_x|$ equal to $2^t - 2$ or $2^t - 1$:

- if $|n_x| = 2^t - 1$, then $|p| = 2^{e_x+s+1}(2^{t-1} + 2^{t-s-1} - 1)$ and $|q| = 2^{e_x+s}(2^t - 2)$,
- if $|n_x| = 2^t - 2$, then $|p| = 2^{e_x+s+1}(2^{t-1} + 2^{t-s-1} - 1)$ and $|q| = 2^{e_x+s}(2^t - 2)$,

In any case, we have that $e_q \leq s + e_x$.   □

This lemma is very useful as it exactly gives the exponent of q, which is the key point of the proof in [13,15].

Here is a counter-example when $\beta = 10$, $t = 6$ and $s = 3$. For $x = 999996$, we have $x \times 1001 = 1000995996$ that is rounded into $p = 1001000000$ and $x - p = -1000000004$ therefore $q = -10000000000$ has for exponent $4 + e_x = 1 + s + e_x$. What fails in the previous proof is that we have $|q| \leq (n_x + \beta)\beta^{e_x+s}$. So instead of having 2 cases to check, we have β cases to check and when $\beta > 2$, we can find among these cases some where the result does not hold.

Lemma 3 (Veltkamp_tail2). $\beta = 2 \Rightarrow x_2$ *fits on* $s - 1$ *bits.*

It will be proved later (Lemma 13) that x_2 can be represented with a mantissa smaller or equal to $\frac{\beta^s}{2}$. As $\beta = 2$, this mantissa is smaller or equal to β^{s-1}, therefore x_2 can be represented on $s - 1$ bits. □

This fact is well-known in radix-2, but has counter-examples in greater radices, for example when $\beta = 10, t = 6$ and $s = 3$. For $x = 123456$, we have $x_1 = 123000$ and $x_2 = 456$ cannot fit in 2 digits. In radix 2, the sign is enough to compensate one bit and x_2 can be shortened by one bit.

A Proof with a Generic Radix But Still no Underflow. We assume there is no Underflow. We want to prove that $x_1 = \circ_{t-s}(x)$. By symmetry of the rounding, we assume that $x > 0$. Therefore, we have $p > 0$, $q < 0$ and $x_1 > 0$.

Lemma 4 (hxExact). $x_1 = p + q$

We use Sterbenz's lemma [22] to prove it. First, $-q = \circ(p - x) \leq \circ(p) = p$.
Second, if $f = \circ(z)$ and f is normal, then $|z| \leq |f|\left(1 + \frac{\beta^{1-t}}{2}\right)$, so

$$p = (p - x) + x \leq |q|(1 + \tfrac{\beta^{1-t}}{2}) + \frac{xC}{\beta^s+1} \leq |q|(1 + \tfrac{\beta^{1-t}}{2}) + |p|\frac{1+\frac{\beta^{1-t}}{2}}{\beta^s+1}.$$

Therefore, some computations lead to $p \leq 2|q|$. □

Lemma 5 (eqLeep, epLe). $e_q \leq e_p \leq s + 1 + e_x$

As $|q| \leq |p|$, we have $e_q \leq e_p$. As $p = \circ\left((\beta^s + 1) \times x\right) \leq \circ\left(\beta^{s+1} \times x\right)$, we have $e_p \leq s + 1 + e_x$. □

Lemma 6 (eqLe). *We either have* $e_q \leq s + e_x$ *or both* $q = -\beta^{t+s+e_x}$ *and* $|x - x_1| \leq \frac{\beta^{e_x+s}}{2}$.

The result is a disjunction: either we are in the common case (like in radix-2) where the exponent of q will be known exactly, or we are in the exceptional case corresponding to the counter-example of the previous section: then q is slightly too big to have the exponent $s + e_x$. Nevertheless, we can bound the difference between x and x_1 as if q had a smaller exponent.

$$|q| = -q = \circ(p - x) \leq p - x + \tfrac{1}{2}\text{ulp}(q) \leq (\beta^s + 1)x + \tfrac{1}{2}\text{ulp}(p) - x + \tfrac{1}{2}\text{ulp}(q).$$

Therefore, $|q| \leq \beta^s x + \text{ulp}(p) \leq n_x \beta^{e_x+s} + \beta^{s+1+e_x} \leq (n_x + \beta)\beta^{e_x+s}$.
If $n_x \leq \beta^t - \beta - 1$, then $|q| < \beta^{t+e_x+s}$ and we deduce that $e_q \leq s + e_x$.
If not, then $n_x \geq \beta^t - \beta$, so

$$x \times C \leq \beta^{e_x}\left(\beta^t - 1\right)\left(\beta^s + 1\right) < \beta^{s+1+e_x}\left(\beta^{t-1} + \beta^{t-s-1}\right)$$
$$p \leq \beta^{s+1+e_x}\left(\beta^{t-1} + \beta^{t-s-1}\right) \leq \beta^{t+s+e_x} + \beta^{t+e_x}$$

So, we have $p - x < \beta^{t+s+e_x}$ and $-q \leq \beta^{t+s+e_x}$.
If $-q < \beta^{t+s+e_x}$, the result holds. When $-q = \beta^{t+s+e_x}$, we bound $x - x_1$:

- if $p - x \leq -q$, then $-q$ is nearer to $p - x$ than $(-q)^-$, therefore the distance between $p - x$ and $-q$ is smaller than half the distance between q and its predecessor: $|x - x_1| = |(p - x) - (-q)| \leq \frac{-q - (-q)^-}{2} = \frac{\text{ulp}((-q)^-)}{2} = \frac{\beta^{e_x+s}}{2}$.

– if $p - x \geq -x$, then $|x - x_1| = |(p - x) - (-q)| = p - x + q$ so we have
$|x - x_1| \leq \beta^{t+s+e_x} + \beta^{e_x+1} - \beta^{t+s+e_x} \leq \frac{\beta^{e_x+s}}{2}$. $\qquad\square$

Lemma 7 (eqGe). $e_q \geq s + e_x$

We bound q: $|q| = \circ(p - x) \geq p - x - \frac{1}{2}\mathrm{ulp}(q) \geq \beta^s x - \frac{1}{2}\mathrm{ulp}(p) - \frac{1}{2}\mathrm{ulp}(q)$
Therefore $|q| \geq n_x \beta^{s+e_x} - \beta^{s+1+e_x} \geq (n_x - \beta)\beta^{s+e_x}$.

So if $n_x \geq \beta^{t-1} + \beta$, we have $e_q \geq s + e_x$.

If not, we may have $n_x = \beta^{t-1}$. In this case, all the computations are exact
and $-q = \beta^{s+t-1+e_x}$ has a good exponent.

The last uncovered possibility is that $\beta^{t-1} + 1 \leq n_x \leq \beta^{t-1} + \beta - 1$. Note that
in radix 2, there is only one such float. Here, we precisely bound p and q:
$$x \times C \geq \beta^{e_x}\left(\beta^{t-1} + 1\right)\left(\beta^s + 1\right) > \beta^{s+e_x}\left(\beta^{t-1} + \beta^{t-s-1} + 1\right)$$
$$p \geq \beta^{s+e_x}\left(\beta^{t-1} + \beta^{t-s-1} + 1\right) \geq \beta^{t+s-1+e_x} + \beta^{t-1+e_x} + \beta^{s+e_x}$$
$$p - x \geq \beta^{t+s-1+e_x} + \beta^{t-1+e_x} + \beta^{s+e_x} - \beta^{e_x}\left(\beta^{t-1} + \beta - 1\right) > \beta^{t+s-1+e_x}$$
$$-q \geq \beta^{t+s-1+e_x}$$
In all cases, $e_q \geq s + e_x$. $\qquad\square$

Therefore, we always have $|x - x_1| \leq \frac{\beta^{e_x+s}}{2}$! Indeed, depending on the case
of Lemma 6 and the result of Lemma 7, we either have $e_q = s + e_x$ or both
$q = -\beta^{t+s+e_x}$ and $|x - x_1| \leq \frac{\beta^{e_x+s}}{2}$. But if $e_q = s + e_x$, then we also have
$|x - x_1| = |(x - p) - q| \leq \frac{\mathrm{ulp}(q)}{2} = \frac{\beta^{e_x+s}}{2}$.

Lemma 8 (Veltkamp_aux_aux). $\beta^{t-1+e_x} \leq x_1$

If $n_x \geq \beta^{t-1} + \frac{\beta^s}{2}$, then $\beta^{t-1+e_x} \leq x - \frac{\beta^{s+e_x}}{2} \leq x - |x - x_1| \leq x_1$.

If not, then we have an integer $\varepsilon < \frac{\beta^s}{2}$ such that $n_x = \beta^{t-1} + \varepsilon$. And we can
exactly give the values of p and q using ε: $p = \beta^{s+e_x}\left(\beta^{t-1} + \beta^{t-1-s} + \varepsilon\right)$ and
$q = -\beta^{s+e_x}\left(\beta^{t-1} + \varepsilon\right)$. So $x_1 = \beta^{t-1+e_x}$. We proved these are the only possible
rounding to nearest of $x \times C$ and $x - p$ using Lemma 1. $\qquad\square$

Lemma 9 (Veltkamp_pos). $x_1 = \circ_{t-s}(x)$

Let us apply Lemma 1 with $z = x$, $f = x_1$, $p = t - s$ and $e = e_x + s$.

We first have to prove that x_1 can be represented on $t - s$ bits. We know that
$e_q = s + e_x$ and $s + e_x \leq e_p \leq s + e_x + 1$, therefore $x_1 = p + q$ can be represented
with the exponent $s + e_x$. The corresponding mantissa m is then such that:
$|m| = |x_1|\beta^{-s-e_x} \leq (|x| + |x - x_1|)\beta^{-s-e_x} < \beta^{t-s} + \frac{1}{2}$.

So $|m| \leq \beta^{t-s}$. This implies that there exists a float v bounded on $t - s$ bits
that is equal to x_1 (it has exponent $s + e_x$ and mantissa m except when $m = \beta^{t-s}$
where it has exponent $1 + s + e_x$).

We then have $\beta^{e_x+t-1} \leq x \leq \beta^{e_x+t}$ as x is normal. From Lemma 8, we have
that $\beta^{e_x+t-1} \leq x_1$. Finally, we have that $|x - x_1| \leq \beta^{e_x+s}/2$, that ends the
proof. $\qquad\square$

Why Underflow Does Not Matter Here. The reason why Underflow does
not matter here is that we only deal with floating-point additions. Indeed, multiplying x by C is only adding x and $x\beta^s$ (which is a bounded float). When you

perform a floating-point addition, you cannot lose precision due to Underflows: all the only nonzero digits will be above the Underflow threshold.

Note that the Underflow threshold on precision $t-s$ is the same as in precision t. We then artificially create a floating-point format with an Underflow threshold small enough to guarantee that all our floating-point numbers in the working precision will be normal. We put $E_i^{ext} = E_i + t - 1$.

Lemma 10 (`bimplybplusNorm`). *If f is bounded and nonzero, there exists g such that g is normal with respect to the extended format and equal to f.*

We transform our subnormal x into a normal float in the extended precision. We then have to link the rounding modes in the working and extended formats.

Lemma 11 (`Closestbplusb`). *If $f = \circ^{ext}(z)$ and f is bounded in the working format, then $f = \circ(z)$.*

Lemma 12 (`Closestbbplus`). *Let f_{ext} be a float (possibly unbounded) such that $e_{f_{ext}} \geq -E_i$. If $f = \circ(f_{ext})$, then $f = \circ^{ext}(z)$.*

When performing a floating-point addition, we are exactly in this case: the real we want to round is an integer multiplied by the Underflow threshold. Even when x is subnormal, we prove that the algorithm gives the expected result:

Theorem 1 (`Veltkamp`). *If x is a bounded float, if p, q and x_1 are computed using the Algorithm 1, then*

$$x_1 = \circ_{t-s}(x).$$

As for x_2, we first prove

Lemma 13 (`Veltkamp_tail_aux`). *The value $x - x_1$ can be represented with exponent e_x and a mantissa smaller or equal to $\frac{\beta^s}{2}$.*

When x is normal, as $x_1 \geq \beta^{t-1+e_x}$, we know that x_1 has an exponent greater than the exponent of x. When x is subnormal, its exponent is minimal, therefore the exponent of x_1 is greater. So in any case, $x - x_1$ can be represented with exponent e_x. More $|x - x_1| \leq \frac{\beta^{e_x+s}}{2}$, so the mantissa is $|x - x_1|\beta^{-e_x} \leq \frac{\beta^s}{2}$. $\square$

Lemma 14 (`Veltkamp_tail`). *$x = x_1 + x_2$ and x_2 fits on s bits.*

From Lemma 13, we know that $x - x_1$ fits on t bits. It will therefore be computed exactly. More, the lemma also states that $x_2 = x - x_1$ can be represented with a mantissa strictly smaller than β^s, therefore fits on s bits.

3.3   Special Rounding to Nearest Matters

Rounding to Nearest, Ties to Even. We now assume all the computations are done using $\overset{even}{\circ}$. The goal is to prove that $x_1 = \overset{even}{\circ}_{t-s}(x)$.

Lemma 15 (ImplyClosestStrict2). *For a bounded float f (in precision p), a real z and an integer e, if we have $\beta^{e+p-1} \leq z \leq \beta^{e+p}$ and $\beta^{e+p-1} \leq f$ and $|z - f| < \frac{\beta^e}{2}$, then $f = \circ(z)$ and f is the only possible rounding to nearest.*

The only difference with Lemma 1 is that the "less or equal to" $\frac{\beta^e}{2}$ has become a "less than" to guarantees that f is the only rounding to nearest.

Lemma 16 (ClosestImplyEven_int). *For a bounded float f and a real z, if $f = \overset{\text{even}}{\circ}(z)$ and f is positive, and there exists an integer n such that the real number $z = \beta^{e_f} \times \left(n + \frac{1}{2}\right)$, then f is even.*

We know that $|x - x_1| \leq \beta^{e_x+s}/2$. If we more have $|x - x_1| < \beta^{e_x+s}/2$, then using Lemma 15 and Lemma 9, we easily prove that $x_1 = \overset{\text{even}}{\circ}_{t-s}(x)$. The only remaining case is the tie-breaking case when $|x - x_1| = \beta^{e_x+s}/2$. We know from Theorem 1 that $x_1 = \circ_{t-s}(x)$, so we only have to prove that either x_1 is even (on $t - s$ bits) or is the only possible rounding to nearest of x.

If the radix id odd, then $|x - x_1| = \beta^{e_x+s}/2$ implies that there exists an integer m such that $2 \times m = \beta^s$. As $s \geq 2$ and β is odd, then β^s is odd, therefore $2 \times m$ is odd, which is impossible.

Let us assume the radix is even. From the proof of Lemma 9, we have two cases: x_1 either has exponent $s+e_x$ or is equal to $(\beta^{t-s-1}, 1+s+e_x)$. In the second case, x_1 is even as β is even. Let us look at the first case where $e_{x_1} = s + e_x$. Then we will prove that the bits at level $s + e_x$ of both p and q are even and the lower bits are zero. As $x_1 = p + q$, this will imply that x_1 is even.

As $s + e_x \leq e_q \leq e_p \leq s + e_x + 1$, the bits lower than $s + e_x$ are even for both p and q. Let us prove that the $s + e_x$-bits are even. As $|x - x_1| = \beta^{e_x+s}/2$, there exists $\varepsilon \in \{1, -1\}$ such that $x = x_1 + \varepsilon \beta^{e_x+s}/2$.

If $e_p = s + e_x + 1$, then the bit at level $s + e_x$ is zero. If $e_p = s + e_x$, there exists $m \in \mathbb{Z}$ such that $x \times C = \beta^{e_x+s}(m + \varepsilon/2)$. From Lemma 16, p is even.

For q, we split depending on Lemma 6. If $q = -\beta^{t+s+e_x}$, then its $s + e_x$ bit is even. In the other case, $e_q \leq s + e_x$, then there exists $m \in \mathbb{Z}$ such that $x - p = \beta^{e_x+s}(m + \varepsilon/2)$. From Lemma 16, this implies that q is even.

In all cases and for both p and q, the $s + e_x$ bits are even. So x_1 is even. $\quad\square$

Rounding to Nearest, Ties Away from Zero. An interesting fact is that this algorithm holds for rounding to nearest and rounding to nearest, ties to even, but not for rounding to nearest, ties away from zero [18]. This rounding means that, when exactly in the middle of two floating-point numbers, we choose the one with the bigger absolute value. This rounding is also known as Banker's rounding, since it is used in banking and phone bills: when in the middle of two cents, you always have to pay more. When all the operations are performed using rounding to nearest, ties away from zero, the result is not the rounding to nearest, ties away from zero of the input: for example let $\beta = 2$, $t = 6$ and $s = 3$. If $x = 100100_2$, then $p = 101001\ 000_2$ and $q = -100101\ 000_2$ so $x_1 = 100\ 000_2$, which is not the expected result ($101\ 000_2$ as the rounding is away from zero). This is a unexpected behavior as these two roundings differ in very few points.

3.4   Conclusion on Splitting

We finally proved that this algorithm is correct whatever the radix and the precision. Nevertheless, being generic with respect to the radix is difficult. It easily changes assertions as authors are trained in radix-2 properties. Being generic has a cost, and formal proofs are particularly useful here as it is hard to guess which properties will still hold and which will not when the radix changes.

The main drawback of this algorithm is that it may overflow: when computing $p = \circ(x \times C)$, an overflow may occur. It is the only place where it can occur as $|q| \leq |p|$ and the other computed values are much smaller. This algorithm does not overflow if $x \times C$ does not overflow. If M is the greatest floating-point number, in rounding to nearest, ties to even or away from zero, this exactly means that $|x| \times C < M + \frac{\text{ulp}(M)}{2}$. And in IEEE formats, $M = (2^t - 1)2^{2t-3}2^{E_i}$. We therefore need $|x| < \frac{(2^{t+1}-1)2^{E_i+2t-4}}{2^s+1}$. A sufficient assumption is $|x| \leq 2^{E_i+2t-2}$.

4   Exact Multiplication

4.1   Algorithm and Hand-Waving Proof

Algorithm. For two bounded floats x and y, the Dekker algorithm [13] computes two bounded floats r_1 and r_2 such that $r_1 = \circ(x \times y)$ and $x \times y = r_1 + r_2$.

The algorithm is described below. It only contains operations using the working precision (t bits). We use $s = \left\lceil \frac{t}{2} \right\rceil$ to split x and y in two (near-)equal parts.

Algorithm 2 (Dekker)

$$(x_1, x_2) = Split(x)$$
$$(y_1, y_2) = Split(y)$$
$$r_1 = \circ(x \times y)$$
$$t_1 = \circ(-r + \circ(x_1 \times y_1))$$
$$t_2 = \circ(t_1 + \circ(x_1 \times y_2))$$
$$t_3 = \circ(t_2 + \circ(x_2 \times y_1))$$
$$r_2 = \circ(t_3 + \circ(x_2 \times y_2))$$

Hand-Waving Proof. The idea is that there is no error in the computation of t_1, t_2, t_3 and r_2. The multiplications are exact as the multiplicands are half-size numbers. The additions are exact as they mostly cancel as we know r_2 will fit on t bits:

$r_1 = \circ(x \times y)$			
$t_1 = x_1 \times y_1 - r$			
	$t_2 = t_1 + x_1 \times y_2$		
		$t_3 = t_2 + x_2 \times y_1$	
			$r_2 = t_3 + x_2 \times y_2$

4.2 Proof

This algorithm seemed to be believed by Dekker to be correct whatever the radix [13]. Nevertheless, it was discovered later by Linnainmaa [23] that this was not the case. In fact, this algorithm perfectly works in radix-2 and works in generic radix when the precision is even (see below).

To guarantee a computation is exact, we give a possible exponent e (meaning that $f \times 2^{-e}$ is an integer) and prove that $|f| < \beta^{e+t}$. The proofs will mostly be inequalities as possible exponents will be deduced from one code line to the other.

We first assume there is no Underflow. In this case, we know that x_1 can be represented with exponent $e_x + s$, that x_2 can be represented with exponent e_x and that $|x_2| \le \beta^{s+e_x}/2$. The same properties hold for $y/y_1/y_2$. As explained before, we choose $s = \lceil t/2 \rceil$ so that x_1 and y_1 will be on $\lfloor t/2 \rfloor$ digits and x_2 and y_2 on $\lceil t/2 \rceil$ digits.

The first inequalities needed are:

- $|x_2 \times y_2| \le \beta^{2s+e_x+e_y}/4$,
- $|x_2 \times y_1| < \beta^{t+s+e_x+e_y}/2 + \beta^{2s+e_x+e_y}/4$,
- $|x_1 \times y_2| < \beta^{t+s+e_x+e_y}/2 + \beta^{2s+e_x+e_y}/4$,
- $|x \times y - r| \le \beta^{t+e_x+e_y}/2$: as $|x \times y| < (\beta^t - 1)^2 \beta^{e_x+e_y}$, we have $e_r \le t + e_x + e_y$.
- $e_r \ge t - 1 + e_x + e_y$: as x and y are normal, we have $|r| \ge \beta^{2t-2+e_x+e_y}$.

As for the multiplications of halves:

- $x_1 \times y_1$ will be computed exactly with exponent $2s + e_x + e_y$ as $2\lfloor t/2 \rfloor \le t$.
- $x_1 \times y_2$ will be computed exactly with exponent $s + e_x + e_y$ as $\lfloor t/2 \rfloor + \lceil t/2 \rceil \le t$.
- $x_2 \times y_1$ will be computed exactly with exponent $s + e_x + e_y$ as $\lfloor t/2 \rfloor + \lceil t/2 \rceil \le t$.

Therefore the t_is are computed exactly:

- t_1 can be exactly represented with exponent $t - 1 + e_x + e_y$. More,
$$| - r + x_1 \times y_1| \le |r - x \times y| + |x_1 \times y_2| + |x_2 \times y_1| + |x_2 \times y_2|$$
$$< \beta^{t+e_x+e_y}/2 + \beta^{t+s+e_x+e_y} + 3\beta^{2s+e_x+e_y}/4 < \beta^{2t-1+e_x+e_y}.$$
- t_2 can be exactly represented with exponent $s + e_x + e_y$. More,
$$|t_1 + x_1 \times y_2| = | - r + x_1 \times y_1 + x_1 \times y_2| \le |r - x \times y| + |x_2 \times y_1| + |x_2 \times y_2|$$
$$< \beta^{t+e_x+e_y}/2 + \beta^{t+s+e_x+e_y}/2 + \beta^{2s+e_x+e_y}/2 < \beta^{t+s+e_x+e_y}.$$
- t_3 can be exactly represented with exponent $s + e_x + e_y$. More,
$$|t_2 + x_2 \times y_1| = | - r + x_1 \times y_1 + x_1 \times y_2 + x_2 \times y_1| \le |r - x \times y| + |x_2 \times y_2|$$
$$\le \beta^{t+e_x+e_y}/2 + \beta^{2s+e_x+e_y}/4 < \beta^{t+s+e_x+e_y}.$$

What is left is the last computation: if $x_2 \times y_2$ is computed exactly, then r_2 will be computed exactly as r_2 would then be equal to $x \times y - \circ(x \times y)$, which is representable when no Underflow occurs. We deduce from the inequalities that:

Lemma 17 (Dekker_aux). *Provided no Underflow occurs, if $x_2 \times y_2$ is representable, then $x \times y = r_1 + r_2$.*

The problem is that $x_2 \times y_2$ fits on $2 \times \lceil t/2 \rceil$ digits and this can outbound t by 1 in some cases. There are various solutions:

- If some extra-precision is available, then it can be used just for the computation of $x_2 \times y_2$ to guarantee the exactness of the result.
- If the radix is 2, then x_2 and y_2 fit on $s - 1$ bits, therefore $x_2 \times y_2$ fits on $2 \times \lceil t/2 \rceil - 2 \leq t$ bits and the computation is exact.
- If the precision is even, then $2 \times \lceil t/2 \rceil = t$ and the computation is exact.

Theorem 2 (Dekker1). *Provided* $e_x + e_y \geq -E_i$, *if* $\beta = 2$ *or* t *is even, then* $x \times y = r_1 + r_2$.

The "no Underflow" assumption is explicit in this theorem: x and y may be subnormal, but the requirement is that the sum of their exponent is greater than the Underflow threshold. This is indeed a necessary and sufficient condition for the error term to be representable [24]. This theorem means that, if the error term can be exactly represented, it will be computed by the given algorithm.

4.3   When Underflow Happens

Underflow may happen in this algorithm and its consequences are harmful: instead of a certain mathematical equality, the only possible result is a bound on the error of the computations. Indeed, instead of all floating-point computations being exact, they may all become error-prone and each computation has to be taken care of and its error bounded.

The problem is then of the duality: if we are above the Underflow threshold for one computation, then it is exact. If we are under the Underflow threshold, then the error of the considered computation is less than $\beta^{-E_i}/2$. If we just bound the error on each computation, the error bound will be huge as exactness will not be considered. Therefore, to get an error bound that is a multiple of β^{-E_i}, we have to take a great care of the propagation of the error.

More precisely, we define an extended format where there will be no Underflow (same precision as the working format, but a small enough Underflow threshold to be sure it will not be undertaken). We then define the following property for the floating point numbers a and a' and the real numbers ε and r: $\mathtt{Underf\_Err}(a, a', r, \varepsilon)$ iff $a = \circ(r)$, a' is bounded on the extended format, $|a - a'| \leq \varepsilon \beta^{-E_i}$ and if the exponent of a' is greater than the Underflow threshold of the working precision, then $a = a'$.

We can then initialize the error computation by this lemma:

Lemma 18 (Underf_Err1). *If* a' *fits on the extended format and* $a = \circ(a')$, *then* $\mathtt{Underf\_Err}(a, a', a', 0.5)$.

Typically, the property on the computation of $x_1 \times y_2$ is: if the corresponding exact float on the extended format has a large enough exponent, then the computation is error-free; if not, the error is bounded by $\beta^{-E_i}/2$.

The most used lemma is the one corresponding to the computations of the t_is:

Lemma 19 (Underf_Err3). *Let us assume that* $\mathtt{Underf\_Err}(x, x', r_x, \varepsilon_x)$ *and that* $\mathtt{Underf\_Err}(y, y', r_y, \varepsilon_y)$. *Assume there exists a floating-point number* z' *on the extended format such that* $z' = x' - y'$ *and* $e_{z'} \leq \min(e_{x'}, e_{y'})$. *Now, let* $z = \circ(x - y)$. *Then, if* $\varepsilon_x + \varepsilon_y \leq \beta^{p-1} - 1$, *we have* $\mathtt{Underf\_Err}(z, z', x - y, \varepsilon_x + \varepsilon_y)$.

If the Underflow threshold is not undertaken, the computation is exact as it was undertaken neither for x', nor for y'. If the Underflow threshold is undertaken, then the accumulated error is the one on x, plus the one on y. There is no error in the computation of $x - y$ as both are subnormal.

The hypothesis $\varepsilon_x + \varepsilon_y \leq \beta^{p-1} - 1$ is here to guarantee that the drift is not too big. When the drift grows, it might create x and y that are greater than the smallest normal number, and then the error could no more be bounded by $\beta^{-E_i}/2$. This assumption is here easily fulfilled as the final bound is $3.5\beta^{-E_i}$:

Lemma 20 (Dekker2). *If $\beta = 2$ or t is even, then $|x \times y - (r_1 + r_2)| \leq \frac{7}{2}\beta^{-E_i}$.*

The Underflow problem has already been tackled in a recent paper by Ogita, Rump and Oishi [25] where they give a bound of $5\beta^{-E_i}$. There is no real proof of it and the authors confirm this bound is rough. The $\frac{7}{2}$ bound could probably be sharpened too. In particular, if the radix is 2, it can be reduced to 3.

Theorem 3 (Dekker)
  Assume

  - *The radix β is greater than 1, the precision is greater than 3 and the Underflow threshold β^{-E_i} is smaller than 1.*
  - *We either have $\beta = 2$ or t is even.*
  - *r_1 and r_2 are computed by Algorithm 2.*

  Then $-E_i \leq e_x + e_y$ implies that $x \times y = r_1 + r_2$.
  And anyway, $|x \times y - (r_1 + r_2)| \leq \frac{7}{2}\beta^{-E_i}$.

4.4   Conclusion on Exact Multiplication

We finally proved the correctness of the algorithm under mild assumptions. Even if the hypothesis "the radix is 2 or the precision is even" is far from elegant, it is very easy to check. More, it is indeed the case on the decimal basic formats of the revision of the IEEE-754 standard [18] on 64 bits ($t = 16$) or 128 bits ($t = 34$) but not on the decimal storage format on 32 bits ($t = 7$). In this last case, some extra-precision may be available, then the computation can be exact if the result of $x_2 \times y_2$ can be stored with at least one more digit.

In most real cases, the exact multiplication algorithm will work, but the other cases should not be ignored as they might make some higher-level algorithm fail. The study of Underflow is enlightening: it was clear from the start that the error in that case would not be zero, but a multiple of the Underflow threshold, but proving it was not that easy. We had to create some unintuitive property that carried all the information we need to be sure that "no Underflow" meant correct and "Underflow" meant a small error. Thanks to the tricky definition, we rather easily propagated this property till the end of the computation to give us an upper bound. This strategy was efficient but quite unusual. A more common solution would have been to split into many subcases:

  - if $x_1 \times y_1$ is subnormal, then...
  - if $x_1 \times y_1$ is normal, but if $x_1 \times y_2$ or $x_2 \times y_1$ is subnormal, then...
  - if $x_1 \times y_1$, $x_1 \times y_2$ and $x_2 \times y_1$ are normal, but $x_2 \times y_2$ is subnormal, then...

It would probably have worked and given a similar result (the author would not dare to guess which solution gives the better bound). The proof cost would have been much greater. We do not think this amount of work would have been worth it: the Underflow case must be studied, so that we can guarantee that the error cannot become huge without warning. As soon as the error is reasonably bounded, it does not always need to be sharpened.

As the previous algorithm, the main drawback of this exact multiplication is that it might Overflow either in the splitting of x or y or in the computation of $\circ(x \times y)$ or $\circ(x_1 \times y_1)$. In any case, either r_1 or r_2 or both will be exceptional values (infinities or NaNs) so this can be detected afterwards.

5 Perspectives

These algorithms are well-known, but the fact that the Veltkamp algorithm works in rounding to nearest, ties to even and that it does not work in rounding to nearest, ties away from zero are new. It was never proved before as only rounding to nearest (and an error bounded by half-an ulp) was ever considered before. Of course, it gives a rounding to nearest, but the tie-breaking case is not as it should be. The tie-breaking is not important for the Dekker algorithm but it may be decisive in other cases. The point is that it is difficult to guess the correctness of the tie-breaking: yes when to even and no when away from zero.

There are various striking things in this case study of floating-point algorithms. The first one is that a generic radix proof is tricky. Most existing proofs are radix-2 and are said to be "easily generalized". We are aware of the fact that tackling an odd radix seems excessive but many basic facts do not hold when the radix is 10. It might change the exponent of some variables. It changes the fact that the tail of the float may be on $s - 1$ or s digits. It might make the algorithm of exact multiplication fail. This can often be looked as patches for the proof as the differences may be small. In some cases unfortunately, it cannot: the basic path of the proof relies on some lemma that can be contradicted or some inequality that does not hold anymore. We were flabbergasted by the gap that sometimes exists between a radix-2 proof and its generic counterpart.

The second one is the overall complexity of the proofs. The algorithms are only a few lines long, but the formal proofs are above 6 600 lines. This is mostly real computations and inequalities. Justifying that a float is a/the rounding to nearest/ties to even is a painstaking work and computations on powers are entirely left to the user. Some tactics could be written to prove goals such as $\beta^{p-1} + \beta^{p-3} + 1 < \beta^p$ assuming $\beta > 1$.

Another perspective is the flexibility of the formal proof checker. When we apply a theorem on a goal that does not have the exact required shape, we would like it to be able to make it fit, even if it means an additional proof. For example, we would like the proof assistant to be able to unfold some definitions or to guess that, if the goal has the form $|a \times b - c| \leq d$ and the theorem has the form $|c - a \times b| \leq d$, then the theorem should be applied and an additional goal $|a \times b - c| = |c - a \times b|$ be added (or deduced). A real example is the following goal: let r be a real number and f a float. The theorem `ClosestUlp` states that $2*|r-f| \leq \mathrm{ulp}(f)$ with $\mathrm{ulp}(f) = \beta^{e_{\mathcal{N}(f)}}$ where $\mathcal{N}$ is a known function. To prove that $2*|f-r| \leq \beta^e$, we would like to apply this theorem and just prove that e is $e_{\mathcal{N}(f)}$ (it would be enough to prove that $e \leq e_{\mathcal{N}(f)}$ but this may be too much).

The third striking aspect is the unexpected difficulty of dealing with Underflows. Underflow creates unpredictable behaviors and these behaviors are difficult to detect as they give no warning at the end of the computation, contrary to Overflow here. Each theorem has a first proof "when no Underflow occur", usually it means that the inputs are normal floats. Then either the proof can be extended to subnormal floats. It usually means a unintuitive proof: here, we considered the same format with a smaller Underflow threshold. There is left to prove that the results of the roundings are similar whatever the format used. Or the proof fails. What can be guaranteed then is usually a bound on the error (a small multiple of the Underflow threshold is good). Some weaker property could also be guaranteed: a variable is non-zero, the final result is normal...

Dealing with Underflow is highly unintuitive as subnormal floats behave like fixed-point numbers with a constant maximal error on each operation (note that we have some interesting properties: for example, addition of subnormal numbers is always exact). The theorems and methods of floating-point studies are then highly non-adapted to these cases, especially when there might be a mix between normal and subnormal floats: it means a mix between a fixed error term and a proportional error term that usually do not mix well. New methods should be considered to treat more easily the Underflow problem. This is no simple task as the behavior of subnormal floats can go from a dream (addition is exact) to a hell (the error is 50 % of the value of the result) and there is no way to deduce the behavior of an algorithm when Underflow happens from its normal behavior.

References

1. Davis, P.J.: Fidelity in mathematical discourse: Is one and one really two? Amer. Math. Monthly **79** (1972) 252–263
2. Lamport, L., Melliar-Smith, P.M.: Synchronizing clocks in the presence of faults. Journal of the ACM **32**(1) (1985) 52–78
3. Rushby, J., von Henke, F.: Formal verification of algorithms for critical systems. In: Conference on Software for Critical Systems, New Orleans, Louisiana (1991)
4. Carreño, V.A., Miner, P.S.: Specification of the IEEE-854 floating-point standard in HOL and PVS. In: 1995 International Workshop on Higher Order Logic Theorem Proving and its Applications, Aspen Grove, Utah (1995) supplemental proceedings.
5. Russinoff, D.M.: A mechanically checked proof of correctness of the amd k5 floating point square root microcode. Formal Methods in System Design **14**(1) (1999) 75
6. Jacobi, C.: Formal Verification of a Fully IEEE Compliant Floating Point Unit. PhD thesis, Saarland University, Saarbrucken, Germany (2002)
7. Harrison, J.: A machine-checked theory of floating point arithmetic. In: 12th International Conference on Theorem Proving in Higher Order Logics, Nice (1999)
8. Harrison, J.: Formal verification of floating point trigonometric functions. In Hunt, W.A., Johnson, S.D., eds.: Proceedings of the Third International Conference on Formal Methods in Computer-Aided Design, Austin, Texas (2000) 217–233

9. The Coq Development Team, LogiCal Project, INRIA: The Coq Proof Assistant: Reference Manual, Version 8.0. (2004)
10. Daumas, M., Rideau, L., Théry, L.: A generic library of floating-point numbers and its application to exact computing. In: 14th International Conference on Theorem Proving in Higher Order Logics, Edinburgh, Scotland (2001) 169–184
11. Veltkamp, G.W.: Algolprocedures voor het berekenen van een inwendig product in dubbele precisie. RC-Informatie 22, Technische Hogeschool Eindhoven (1968)
12. Veltkamp, G.W.: ALGOL procedures voor het rekenen in dubbele lengte. RC-Informatie 21, Technische Hogeschool Eindhoven (1969)
13. Dekker, T.J.: A floating point technique for extending the available precision. Numerische Mathematik **18**(3) (1971) 224–242
14. Priest, D.M.: Algorithms for arbitrary precision floating point arithmetic. In: 10th Symposium on Computer Arithmetic, Grenoble, France (1991) 132–144
15. Shewchuk, J.R.: Adaptive precision floating-point arithmetic and fast robust geometric predicates. In: Discrete and Computational Geometry. Volume 18. (1997)
16. Stevenson, D., et al.: A proposed standard for binary floating point arithmetic. IEEE Computer **14**(3) (1981) 51–62
17. Stevenson, D., et al.: An American national standard: IEEE standard for binary floating point arithmetic. ACM SIGPLAN Notices **22**(2) (1987) 9–25
18. of the Microprocessor Standards Subcommittee of the Standards Committee of the IEEE Computer Society, F.P.W.G.: IEEE standard for floating-point arithmetic (2006) Work in progress.
19. Cody, W.J., Karpinski, R., et al.: A proposed radix and word-length independent standard for floating point arithmetic. IEEE Micro **4**(4) (1984) 86–100
20. Harrison, J.: Verifying the accuracy of polynomial approximations in HOL. In: Proceedings of the 10th International Conference on Theorem Proving in Higher Order Logics, Murray Hill, New Jersey (1997) 137–152
21. Muller, J.M.: On the definition of ulp(x). Technical Report LIP RR2005-09 INRIA RR-5504, Laboratoire de l'Informatique du Parallélisme (2005)
22. Sterbenz, P.H.: Floating point computation. Prentice Hall (1974)
23. Linnainmaa, S.: Software for doubled-precision floating-point computations. ACM Transactions on Mathematical Software **7**(3) (1981) 272–283
24. Boldo, S., Daumas, M.: Representable correcting terms for possibly underflowing floating point operations. In: Symposium on Computer Arithmetic, Spain (2003)
25. Ogita, T., Rump, S.M., Oishi, S.: Accurate sum and dot product. SIAM Journal on Scientific Computing **26**(6) (2005) 1955–1988

Using the TPTP Language for Writing Derivations and Finite Interpretations

Geoff Sutcliffe[1], Stephan Schulz[2], Koen Claessen[3], and Allen Van Gelder[4]

[1] University of Miami, USA
geoff@cs.miami.edu
[2] Technische Universität München, Germany
schulz@eprover.org
[3] Chalmers University of Technology, Sweden
koen@chalmers.se
[4] University of California at Santa Cruz, USA
avg@cs.ucsc.edu

Abstract. One of the keys to the success of the TPTP and related projects is their consistent use of the TPTP language. The ability of the TPTP language to express solutions as well as problems, in conjunction with the simplicity of the syntax, sets it apart from other languages used in ATP. This paper provides a complete definition of the TPTP language, and describes how the language should be used to write derivations and finite interpretations.

1 Introduction

The TPTP problem library [19] is a well known standard set of test problems for first order automated theorem proving (ATP) systems. The TSTP solution library [18], the "flip side" of the TPTP, is becoming known as a resource for contemporary ATP systems' solutions to TPTP problems. The SystemOnTPTP [16] and associated software have been employed in a range of application projects, e.g., [4,21,23]. One of the keys to the success of these projects is their consistent use of the TPTP language, which enables convenient communication between different systems and researchers.

TPTP v3.0.0 introduced a new version of the TPTP language [20]. The language was designed to be suitable for writing both ATP problems and ATP solutions, to be flexible and extensible, and easily processed by both humans and computers. The entry barrier for using the TPTP language is (and has always been) very low. The syntax shares many features with Prolog, a language that is widely known in the ATP community. Indeed, with a few operator definitions, units of TPTP data can be read in Prolog using a single `read/1` call, and written with a single `writeq/1` call. Development, or at least prototyping, of reasoning software in Prolog is common, and Prolog compatibility eliminates the mundane task of writing IO routines for the reasoning software.

The key development from the old (pre-v3.0.0) TPTP language to the new one was the addition of features for writing solutions to ATP problems. The features were designed for writing derivations, but their flexibility makes it possible to

U. Furbach and N. Shankar (Eds.): IJCAR 2006, LNAI 4130, pp. 67–81, 2006.

write a range of DAG structures. Additionally, there are features of the language that make it possible to conveniently specify finite interpretations. This paper provides a complete definition of the TPTP language, and describes how the language should be used to write derivations and finite interpretations.

The ability of the TPTP language to express solutions as well as problems, in conjunction with the simplicity of the syntax, sets it apart from other languages used in ATP. Some languages, e.g., the LOP format [13], were designed for writing problems, and do not support writing solutions. Some languages for writing solutions are limited in scope, e.g., the PCL language [5] is limited to solutions to to equational problems, and the OpenTheory language [8] is designed only to be a computer processible form for systems that implement the HOL logic [6]. There are some general purpose languages that have features for writing derivations, e.g., Otter's `proof_object` format [11,10] and the DFG syntax [7], but none of these (that we know of) also provide support for writing finite interpretations. Mark-up languages such as OmDoc [9], OpenMath [2], and MathML [2] are quite expressive (especially for mathematical content), but their XML based format is not suitable for human processing. Overall, the TPTP language is more expressive and usable than other languages. Interoperability with other languages is supported in some cases, through translation tools.

2   The TPTP Language

The new TPTP language was first used in TPTP v3.0.0, released in November 2004. It has been taken up by a number of developers and received valuable comments and feedback. As a consequence, since that first release there have been some small, but significant, changes and extensions. The BNF definition of the language has recently been thoroughly overhauled. A principal goal has been to make it easy to translate the BNF into `lex/yacc/flex/bison` input, so that construction of parsers (in languages other than Prolog) can be a reasonably easy task. The BNF definition is in the appendix of this paper.

The TPTP language definition uses a modified BNF meta-language that separates semantic, syntactic, lexical, and character-macro rules. Syntactic rules use the standard : : = separator, e.g.,

        <source>   : : = <general_term>

When only a subset of the syntactically acceptable values for a non-terminal make semantic sense, a second rule for the non-terminal is provided using a : == separator, e.g.,

        <source>   : == <dag_source> | <internal_source> | , etc.

Any further semantic rules that may be reached only from the right hand side of a semantic rule are also written using the : == separator, e.g.,

        <dag_source>   : == <name> | <inference_record>

This separation of syntax from semantics eases the task of building a syntactic analyzer, as only the : : = rules need be considered. At the same time, the semantic rules provide the detail necessary for semantic checking. The rules that produce tokens from the lexical level use a : : - separator, e.g.,

  `<lower_word>` : : - `<lower_alpha><alpha_numeric>*`

with the bottom level character-macros defined by regular expressions in rules using a : : : separator, e.g.,

  `<lower_alpha>` : : : `[a-z]`

The BNF is documented with comments.

The top level building blocks of TPTP files are *annotated formulae, include directives*, and *comments*. An annotated formula has the form:

  language(name, role, formula, source, [useful_info]) .

The *languages* currently supported are `fof` - formulae in full first order form, and `cnf` - formulae in clause normal form. The *role* gives the user semantics of the *formula*, e.g., axiom, lemma, `conjecture`, and hence defines its use in an ATP system - see the BNF for the list of recognized roles and their meaning. The logical *formula*, in either FOF or CNF, uses a consistent and easily understood notation [20] that can be seen in the BNF. The *source* describes where the formula came from, e.g., an input file or an inference. The *useful_info* is a list of arbitrary useful information, as required for user applications. The *useful_info* field is optional, and if it is not used then the *source* field becomes optional. An example of a FOF formula, supplied from a file, is:

```
fof(formula_27,axiom,
  ! [X,Y] :
   ( subclass(X,Y) <=>
    ! [U] :
      ( member(U,X) => member(U,Y) )),
  file('SET005+0.ax',subclass_defn),
  [description('Definition of subclass'), relevance(0.9)]).
```

An example of an inferred CNF formula is:

```
cnf(175,lemma,
   ( rsymProp(ib,sk_c3)
   | sk_c4 = sk_c3 ),
   inference(factor_simp,[status(thm)],[
      inference(para_into,[status(thm)],[96,78,theory(equality)])]),
   [iquote('para_into,96.2.1,78.1.1,factor_simp')]).
```

A novel feature of the TPTP language, which is employed in the representation of finite interpretations, is the recognition of interpreted predicates and functors. These come in two varieties: *defined* predicates and functors, whose interpretation is specified by the TPTP language, and *system* predicates and functors, whose interpretation is ATP system specific. Interpreted predicates and functors are syntactically different from uninterpreted predicates and functors. Defined predicates and functors either start with a $, or are composed of non-alphanumeric characters. System predicates and functors start with $$. Uninterpreted predicates and functors start with a lower case alphabetic. The defined predicates recognized so far are $true and $false, with the obvious interpretations, and = and != for equality and inequality. The defined functors recognized so far are "distinct object"s, written in double quotes, and numbers. A "distinct object" is interpreted as the domain element in the double quotes. Numbers are interpreted as themselves (as domain elements). A consequence of the predefined interpretations is that all different "distinct object"s and numbers are known to be unequal, e.g., "Apple" != "Microsoft" and 1 != 2 are implicit axioms. Such implicit axioms may be built into an ATP system, e.g., [14], or generated. System predicates and functors are used for interpreted predicates and functors that are available in particular ATP tools. The names are not controlled by the TPTP language, so they must be used with caution.

The source field of an annotated formula is most commonly a `file` record or an `inference` record. A `file` record stores the name of the file from which the annotated formula was read, and optionally the name of the annotated formula as it occurs in the file (this may be different from the name of the annotated formula itself, e.g., if the ATP system renames the annotated formulae that it reads in). An `inference` record stores three items of information about an inferred formula: the name of the inference rule provided by the ATP system, i.e., there are no standards; a list of useful information items, e.g., the semantic `status` of the formula and with respect to its parents as an SZS ontology value [20] (commonly inferred formulae are theorems of their parents, but in some cases the semantic relationship is weaker, as in Skolemization steps); and a list of the parents, which most commonly are parent annotated formula names, nested `inference` records, and `theory` records. A theory record is used when the axioms of some theory are built into the inference rule, e.g., equality axioms are built into paramodulation.

The `include` directives of the TPTP language are analogous to C's #include directives. An `include` directive may include an entire file, or may specify the names of the annotated formulae that are to be included from the file, thus providing a more finely grained include mechanism.

Regular comments in the TPTP language extend from a % character to the end of the line, or may be block comments within /* ...*/ bracketing. System comments in the TPTP language are used for system specific annotations. They extend from a %$$ sequence to the end of the line, or may be block comments within /*$$ ...*/ bracketing. System comments look like regular comments, so normally they would be discarded. However, a wily user of the language can store/extract information from the comment before discarding it. System comments should identify the ATP system, followed by a :, e.g., /*$$Otter 3.3: Demodulator */. Comments may occur between any two tokens.

Parsing tools written in C are available for the TPTP language, conversion of the BNF into `lex`/`yacc` input is available [22], and the `tptp2X` utility distributed with the TPTP is compatible with the language.

3   Derivations

A derivation is a directed acyclic graph (DAG) whose leaf nodes are formulae from the input, whose interior nodes are formulae inferred from parent formulae, and whose root nodes are the final derived formulae. For example, a proof of a FOF theorem from some axioms, by refutation of the CNF of the axioms and negated conjecture, is a derivation whose leaf nodes are the FOF axioms and conjecture, whose internal nodes are formed from the process of clausification and then from inferences performed on the clauses, and whose root node is the *false* formula.

The information required to record a derivation is, minimally, the leaf formulae, and each inferred formula with references to its parent formulae. More detailed information that may be recorded and useful includes: the role of each formula; the name of the inference rule used in each inference step; sufficient details of each inference step to deterministically reproduce the inference; and the semantic relationships of inferred formulae with respect to their parents. The TPTP language is sufficient for recording all this, and more. A comprehensively recorded derivation provides the information required for various forms of processing, such as proof verification [17], proof visualization [15], and lemma extraction [5].

A derivation written in the TPTP language is a list of annotated formulae. Each annotated formula has a name, a role, and the logical formula. Each inferred formula has an **inference** record with the inference rule name, the semantic relationship of the formula to its parents as an SZS ontology value in a **status** record, and a list of references to its parent formulae.

Example. Consider the following toy FOF problem, to prove the **conjecture** from the **axioms** (not all the axioms are needed for the proof - the extra axioms come into play when the example is used again in Section 4 to illustrate the finite interpretation format):

```
%--------------------------------------------------------------------
%----All (hu)men are created equal. John is a human. John got an F grade.
%----There is someone (a human) who got an A grade. An A grade is not
%----equal to an F grade. Grades are not human. Therefore there is a
%----human other than John.
fof(all_created_equal,axiom,(
    ! [H1,H2] : ( ( human(H1) & human(H2) ) => created_equal(H1,H2) ) )).
fof(john,axiom,(
    human(john) )).
fof(john_failed,axiom,(
    grade(john) = f )).
fof(someone_got_an_a,axiom,(
    ? [H] : ( human(H) & grade(H) = a ) )).
fof(distinct_grades,axiom,(
    a != f )).
fof(grades_not_human,axiom,(
    ! [G] : ~ human(grade(G)) )).
fof(someone_not_john,conjecture,(
    ? [H] : ( human(H) & H != john ) )).
%--------------------------------------------------------------------
```

Here is a derivation recording a proof by refutation of the CNF, adapted (removing inferences that simply copy the parent formula) from the one produced by the ATP system EP v0.91 [12]:

```
%------------------------------------------------------------------
fof(3,axiom,(
    grade(john) = f ),
    file('CreatedEqual.p',john_failed)).
fof(4,axiom,(
    ? [X3] : ( human(X3) & grade(X3) = a ) ),
    file('CreatedEqual.p',someone_got_an_a)).
fof(5,axiom,(
    a != f ),
    file('CreatedEqual.p',distinct_grades)).
fof(7,conjecture,(
    ? [X3] : ( human(X3) & X3 != john ) ),
    file('CreatedEqual.p',someone_not_john)).
fof(8,negated_conjecture,(
    ~ ? [X3] : ( human(X3) & X3 != john ) ),
    inference(assume_negation,[status(cth)],[7])).
cnf(14,plain,
    ( grade(john) = f ),
    inference(split_conjunct,[status(thm)],[3])).
fof(16,plain,
    ( human(esk1_0) & grade(esk1_0) = a ),
    inference(skolemize,[status(sab)],[4])).
cnf(17,plain,
    ( grade(esk1_0) = a ),
    inference(split_conjunct,[status(thm)],[16])).
cnf(18,plain,
    ( human(esk1_0) ),
    inference(split_conjunct,[status(thm)],[16])).
cnf(19,plain,
    ( a != f ),
    inference(split_conjunct,[status(thm)],[5])).
fof(22,negated_conjecture,(
    ! [X3] : ( ~ human(X3) | X3 = john ) ),
    inference(fof_nnf,[status(thm)],[8])).
cnf(24,negated_conjecture,
    ( X1 = john | ~ human(X1) ),
    inference(split_conjunct,[status(thm)],[22])).
cnf(25,negated_conjecture,
    ( john = esk1_0 ),
    inference(spm,[status(thm)],[24,18,theory(equality)])).
cnf(28,plain,
    ( f = a ),
    inference(rw,[status(thm)],[
        inference(rw,[status(thm)],[17,25,theory(equality)]),
        14,theory(equality)])).
cnf(29,plain,
    ( $false ),
    inference(sr,[status(thm)],[28,19,theory(equality)])).
%------------------------------------------------------------------
```

4 Finite Interpretations

A finite interpretation (or "finite model" of some identified formulae) consists of a finite *domain*, an *interpretation of functors* - a functor applied to domain elements is interpreted as a domain element, and an *interpretation of predicates* - a predicate applied to domain elements is interpreted as *true* or *false*. The elements of the domain are known to be distinct. The interpretation of functors and predicates is total, i.e., there is an interpretation for every functor and predicate for every pattern of domain element arguments.

The TPTP language is sufficient for recording a finite interpretation. The domain, interpretation of functors, and interpretation of predicates, are written as FOF annotated formulae. A recorded interpretation provides the information required for various forms of processing, such as model verification, interpretation of formulae, and identification of isomorphic interpretations.

The domain of a finite interpretation is written in the form:

> fof (fi_name, fi_domain,
> ! [X] : (X = e_1 | X = e_2 | ... | X = e_n)).

where the e_i are all "distinct object"s, or all distinct integers, or all distinct constant terms. If "distinct object" or integer terms appear in the interpreted signature, then all those terms must appear in the domain. If constant terms are used they are freely chosen constant terms that do not appear in the signature being interpreted. The e_i values then provide an exhaustive list of constant terms whose interpretation form the domain (there is a bijection from the constant terms to the domain, so one may think of the constant terms directly as the domain elements). The use of "distinct object"s or integer terms for a domain is preferred over constant terms, because that takes advantage of the predefined interpretation of such terms - all such terms and corresponding domain elements are known to be distinct (see Section 2). If the domain elements are constant terms then their inequality must be explicitly stated in annotated formulae of the form:

> fof (e_i_not_e_j, fi_domain,
> e_i != e_j).

The interpretation of functors is written in the form:

> fof (fi_name, fi_functors,
> (f(e_1, ..., e_m) = e_r
> & f(e_1, ..., e_p) = e_s
> ...)).

specifying that, e.g., f(e_1, ..., e_m) is interpreted as the domain element e_r. If "distinct object"s or integer terms appear in the interpreted signature, then those terms are necessarily interpreted as themselves and must not be interpreted in the fi_functors.

The interpretation of predicates is written in the form:

> fof (fi_name, fi_predicates,
> (p(e_1, ..., e_m)
> & ~ p(e_1, ..., e_p)
> ...)).

specifying that, e.g., $p(e_1, \ldots, e_m)$ is interpreted as *true* and $p(e_1, \ldots, e_p)$ is interpreted as *false*. Equality is interpreted naturally by the domain, with the understanding that identical elements are equal.

Example. Consider again the FOF problem from Section 3, but with the conjecture replaced by:

```
fof(equality_lost,conjecture,(
    ! [H1,H2] :
      ( created_equal(H1,H2)
    <=> H1 = H2 ) )).
```

The resultant problem is `CounterSatisfiable`, i.e., there is a model for the axioms and negated conjecture. Here is one such model, adapted (by converting constant term domain elements to "distinct object" domain elements) from the one found by the model finding system Paradox 1.3 [3]:

```
%-------------------------------------------------------------------
fof(equality_lost,fi_domain,
    ! [X] : ( X = "a" | X = "f" | X = "john" | X = "got_a") ).

fof(equality_lost,fi_functors,
    ( a = "a"  & f = "f"  & john = "john"
    & grade("a") = "f"    & grade("f") = "a"
    & grade("john") = "f" & grade("got_a") = "a" ) ).

fof(equality_lost,fi_predicates,
    ( human("john")                  & human("got_a")
    & ~ human("a")                   & ~ human("f")
    & ~ created_equal("a","a")       & ~ created_equal("a","f")
    & ~ created_equal("a","john")    & ~ created_equal("a","got_a")
    & ~ created_equal("f","a")       & ~ created_equal("f","f")
    & ~ created_equal("f","john")    & ~ created_equal("f","got_a")
    & ~ created_equal("john","a")    & ~ created_equal("john","f")
    & created_equal("john","john")   & created_equal("john","got_a")
    & ~ created_equal("got_a","a")   & ~ created_equal("got_a","f")
    & created_equal("got_a","john")  & created_equal("got_a","got_a") ) ).
%-------------------------------------------------------------------
```

Variations, Layout, and Verification

Normally every functor and predicate is interpreted once for every pattern of domain element arguments. No functor or predicate may be interpreted more than once for an argument pattern. If a functor or predicate is not interpreted for a given argument pattern then multiple interpretations are being represented, in which that functor or predicate applied to the argument pattern is interpreted as each of the possible values (each domain element for a functor, both *true* and *false* for a predicate).

It is recommended that interpretations follow a standard layout, as illustrated by the examples above. However, the conjuncts of functor and predicate interpretations may be separated into individual annotated formulae. Compact forms are possible using universally quantified formulae, e.g.,

```
fof(equality_lost,fi_predicates,
    ( human("john") & human("got_a")
    & ~ human("a")  & ~ human("f")
    & ! [X] : ~ created_equal("a",X)
    & ! [X] : ~ created_equal("f",X)
    & ! [X] : ~ created_equal(X,"a")
    & ! [X] : ~ created_equal(X,"f")
    & created_equal("john","john")  & created_equal("john","got_a")
    & created_equal("got_a","john") & created_equal("got_a","got_a") ) ).
```

An interpretation can be verified as a model of a set of formulae by directly evaluating each formula in the model. The TPTP format also provides an alternative approach - the interpretation is adjoined to the formulae, and a trusted model finder is then used to find a model of the combined formula set.

5 Conclusion

Standards for writing derivations and finite interpretations have been presented. These standards should be adopted by the ATP community, to increase the range of ATP tools that can be seamlessly integrated into more complex and effective reasoning systems. Increased interoperability will contribute to the usability and uptake of ATP technology in application domains.

Current work is extending the TPTP language for higher order logic [22]. When this is available, it will be used for extending the TPTP to higher order logic [1]. Future work will include the design of standards for representing infinite interpretations. As a first step, it is planned to represent Herbrand interpretations by term grammars, e.g., formulae of the form:

```
! [X,Y] : (p(X,Y) <=> ((X != a & Y != a) | (X = a & Y = a)))
```

There are decision procedures for the truth of ground atoms in the context of such formulae. Compaction of finite interpretations using normal-form theory from relational databases is also being considered.

References

1. C. Benzmüller and C. Brown. A Structured Set of Higher-Order Problems. In J. Hurd and T. Melham, editors, *Proceedings of the 18th International Conference on Theorem Proving in Higher Order Logics*, LNAI 3606, pages 66–81, 2005.
2. O. Caprotti and D. Carlisle. OpenMath and MathML: Semantic Mark Up for Mathematics. *ACM Crossroads*, 6(2), 1999.
3. K. Claessen and N. Sorensson. New Techniques that Improve MACE-style Finite Model Finding. In P. Baumgartner and C. Fermueller, editors, *Proceedings of the CADE-19 Workshop: Model Computation - Principles, Algorithms, Applications*, 2003.
4. E. Denney, B. Fischer, and J. Schumann. Using Automated Theorem Provers to Certify Auto-generated Aerospace Software. In M. Rusinowitch and D. Basin, editors, *Proceedings of the 2nd International Joint Conference on Automated Reasoning*, LNAI 3097, pages 198–212, 2004.

5. J. Denzinger and S. Schulz. Recording and Analysing Knowledge-Based Distributed Deduction Processes. *Journal of Symbolic Computation*, 21:523–541, 1996.
6. M. Gordon and T. Melham. *Introduction to HOL, a Theorem Proving Environment for Higher Order Logic*. Cambridge University Press, 1993.
7. R. Hähnle, M. Kerber, and C. Weidenbach. Common Syntax of the DFG-Schwerpunktprogramm Deduction. Technical Report TR 10/96, Fakultät für Informatik, Universät Karlsruhe, Karlsruhe, Germany, 1996.
8. J. Hurd and R. Arthan. OpenTheory. http://www.cl.cam.ac.uk/ jeh1004/research/opentheory, URL.
9. M. Kohlhase. OMDOC: Towards an Internet Standard for the Administration, Distribution, and Teaching of Mathematical Knowledge. In J.A. Campbell and E. Roanes-Lozano, editors, *Proceedings of the Artificial Intelligence and Symbolic Computation Conference, 2000*, LNCS 1930, pages 32–52, 2000.
10. W. McCune and O. Shumsky-Matlin. Ivy: A Preprocessor and Proof Checker for First-Order Logic. In M. Kaufmann, P. Manolios, and J. Strother Moore, editors, *Computer-Aided Reasoning: ACL2 Case Studies*, number 4 in Advances in Formal Methods, pages 265–282. Kluwer Academic Publishers, 2000.
11. W.W. McCune. Otter 3.3 Reference Manual. Technical Report ANL/MSC-TM-263, Argonne National Laboratory, Argonne, USA, 2003.
12. S. Schulz. E: A Brainiac Theorem Prover. *AI Communications*, 15(2-3):111–126, 2002.
13. S. Schulz. LOP-Syntax for Theorem Proving Applications. http://www4.informatik.tu-muenchen.de/~schulz/WORK/lop.syntax, URL.
14. S. Schulz and Maria Paola Bonacina. On Handling Distinct Objects in the Superposition Calculus. In B. Konev and S. Schulz, editors, *Proceedings of the 5th International Workshop on the Implementation of Logics*, pages 66–77, 2005.
15. G. Steel. Visualising First-Order Proof Search. In C. Aspinall, D. Lüth, editor, *Proceedings of User Interfaces for Theorem Provers 2005*, pages 179–189, 2005.
16. G. Sutcliffe. SystemOnTPTP. In D. McAllester, editor, *Proceedings of the 17th International Conference on Automated Deduction*, LNAI 1831, pages 406–410, 2000.
17. G. Sutcliffe. Semantic Derivation Verification. *International Journal on Artificial Intelligence Tools*, page To appear, 2006.
18. G. Sutcliffe. The TSTP Solution Library. http://www.TPTP.org/TSTP, URL.
19. G. Sutcliffe and C.B. Suttner. The TPTP Problem Library: CNF Release v1.2.1. *Journal of Automated Reasoning*, 21(2):177–203, 1998.
20. G. Sutcliffe, J. Zimmer, and S. Schulz. TSTP Data-Exchange Formats for Automated Theorem Proving Tools. In W. Zhang and V. Sorge, editors, *Distributed Constraint Problem Solving and Reasoning in Multi-Agent Systems*, number 112 in Frontiers in Artificial Intelligence and Applications, pages 201–215. IOS Press, 2004.
21. J. Urban. MPTP - Motivation, Implementation, First Experiments. *Journal of Automated Reasoning*, 33(3-4):319–339, 2004.
22. A. Van Gelder and G. Sutcliffe. Extending the TPTP Language to Higher-Order Logic with Automated Parser Generation. In U. Furbach and N. Shankar, editors, *Proceedings of the 3rd International Joint Conference on Automated Reasoning*, Lecture Notes in Artificial Intelligence, 2006.
23. J. Zimmer. A New Framework for Reasoning Agents. In V. Sorge, S. Colton, M. Fisher, and J. Gow, editors, *Proceedings of the Workshop on Agents and Automated Reasoning, 18th International Joint Conference on Artificial Intelligence*, pages 58–64, 2003.

Appendix

```
%------------------------------------------------------------------------------
%----README ... this header provides important meta- and usage information
%----
%----Intended uses of the various parts of the TPTP syntax are explained
%----in the TPTP technical manual, linked from www.tptp.org.
%----
%----Four kinds of separators are used, to indicate different types of rules:
%----  ::= is used for regular grammar rules, for syntactic parsing.
%----  :== is used for semantic grammar rules. These define specific values
%----      that make semantic sense when more general syntactic rules apply.
%----  ::- is used for rules that produce tokens.
%----  ::: is used for rules that define character classes used in the
%----      construction of tokens.
%----
%----White space may occur between any two tokens. White space is not specified
%----in the grammar, but the are some restrictions to ensure that the grammar
%----is campatible with standard Prolog: a <TPTP_file> should be readable with
%----read/1.
%----
%----The syntax of comments is defined by the <comment> rule. Comments may
%----occur between any two tokens, but do not act as white space. Comments
%----will normally be discarded at the lexical level, but may be processed
%----by systems that understand them e.g., if the system comment convention
%----is followed).
%------------------------------------------------------------------------------
%----Files. Empty file is OK.
<TPTP_file>            ::= <TPTP_input>*
<TPTP_input>           ::= <annotated_formula> | <include>

%----Formula records
<annotated_formula>  ::= <fof_annotated> | <cnf_annotated>
%----Future languages may include ...  english | efof | tfof | mathml | ...
<fof_annotated>        ::= fof(<name>,<formula_role>,<fof_formula><annotations>).
<cnf_annotated>        ::= cnf(<name>,<formula_role>,<cnf_formula><annotations>).
<annotations>          ::= <null> | ,<source><optional_info>
%----In derivations the annotated formulae names must be unique, so that
%----parent references (see <inference_record>) are unambiguous.

%----Types for problems.
%----Note: The previous <source_type> from ...
%----   <formula_role> ::= <user_role>-<source>
%----... is now gone. Parsers may choose to be tolerant of it for backwards
%----compatibility.
<formula_role>         ::= <lower_word>
<formula_role>         :== axiom | hypothesis | definition | lemma | theorem |
                           conjecture | lemma_conjecture | negated_conjecture |
                           plain | fi_domain | fi_functors | fi_predicates |
                           unknown
%----"axiom"s are accepted, without proof, as a basis for proving "conjecture"s
%----and "lemma_conjecture"s in FOF problems. In CNF problems "axiom"s are
%----accepted as part of the set whose satisfiability has to be established.
%----There is no guarantee that the axioms of a problem are consistent.
%----"hypothesis"s are assumed to be true for a particular problem, and are
%----used like "axiom"s.
%----"definition"s are used to define symbols, and are used like "axiom"s.
%----"lemma"s and "theorem"s have been proven from the "axiom"s, can be used
%----like "axiom"s, but are redundant wrt the "axiom"s. "lemma" is used as the
%----role of proven "lemma_conjecture"s, and "theorem" is used as the role of
%----proven "conjecture"s, in output. A problem containing a "lemma" or
%----"theorem" that is not redundant wrt the "axiom"s is ill-formed. "theorem"s
%----are more important than "lemma"s from the user perspective.
%----"conjecture"s occur in only FOF problems, and are to all be proven from
%----the "axiom"(-like) formulae. A problem is solved only when all
%----"conjecture"s are proven.
%----"lemma_conjecture"s are expected to be provable, and may be useful to
%----prove, while proving "conjecture"s.
```

```
%----"negated_conjecture"s occur in only CNF problems, and are formed from
%----negation of a "conjecture" in a FOF to CNF conversion.
%----"plain"s have no special user semantics, and can be used like "axiom"s.
%----"fi_domain", "fi_functors", and "fi_predicates" are used to record the
%----domain, interpretation of functors, and interpretation of predicates, for
%----a finite interpretation.
%----"unknown"s have unknown role, and this is an error situation.

%----FOF formulae. All formulae must be closed.
<fof_formula>        ::= <binary_formula> | <unitary_formula>
<binary_formula>     ::= <nonassoc_binary> | <assoc_binary>
%----Only some binary connectives are associative
%----There's no precedence among binary connectives
<nonassoc_binary>    ::= <unitary_formula> <binary_connective> <unitary_formula>
<binary_connective>  ::= <=> | => | <= | <~> | ~<vline> | ~&
%----Associative connectives & and | are in <assoc_binary>
<assoc_binary>       ::= <or_formula> | <and_formula>
<or_formula>         ::= <unitary_formula> <vline> <unitary_formula>
                         <more_or_formula>*
<more_or_formula>    ::= <vline> <unitary_formula>
<and_formula>        ::= <unitary_formula> & <unitary_formula>
                         <more_and_formula>*
<more_and_formula>   ::= & <unitary_formula>
%----<unitary_formula> are in ()s or do not have a <binary_connective> at the
%----top level.
<unitary_formula>    ::= <quantified_formula> | <unary_formula> |
                         (<fof_formula>) | <atomic_formula>
<quantified_formula> ::= <quantifier> [<variable_list>] : <unitary_formula>
<quantifier>         ::= ! | ?
%----! is universal quantification and ? is existential. Syntactically, the
%----quantification is the left operand of :, and the <unitary_formula> is
%----the right operand. Although : is a binary operator syntactically, it is
%----not a <binary_connective>, and thus a <quantified_formula> is a
%----<unitary_formula>.
%----Universal   example: ! [X,Y] : ((p(X) & p(Y)) => q(X,Y)).
%----Existential example: ? [X,Y] : (p(X) & p(Y)) & ~ q(X,Y).
%----Quantifiers have higher precedence than binary connectives, so in
%----the existential example the quantifier applies to only (p(X) & p(Y)).
<variable_list>      ::= <variable> | <variable>,<variable_list>
%----Future variables may have sorts and existential counting
%----Unary connectives bind more tightly than binary
<unary_formula>      ::= <unary_connective> <unitary_formula>
<unary_connective>   ::= ~

%----CNF formulae (variables implicitly universally quantified)
<cnf_formula>        ::= (<disjunction>) | <disjunction>
<disjunction>        ::= <literal> <more_disjunction>*
<more_disjunction>   ::= <vline> <literal>
<literal>            ::= <atomic_formula> | ~ <atomic_formula>

%----Atoms (<predicate> is not used currently)
<atomic_formula>     ::= <plain_atom> | <defined_atom> | <system_atom>
<plain_atom>         ::= <plain_term>
%----A <plain_atom> looks like a <plain_term>, but really we mean
%----  <plain_atom>       ::= <proposition> | <predicate>(<arguments>)
%----  <proposition>      ::= <atomic_word>
%----  <predicate>        ::= <atomic_word>
%----Using <plain_term> removes a reduce/reduce ambiguity in lex/yacc.
<arguments>          ::= <term> | <term>,<arguments>
<defined_atom>       ::= $true | $false |
                         <term> <defined_infix_pred> <term>
<defined_infix_pred> ::= = | !=
%----A more general formulation, which syntactically admits more defined atoms,
%----is as follows. Developers may prefer to adopt this.
%----  <defined_atom>     ::= <defined_prop> | <defined_pred>(<arguments>) |
%----                         <term> <defined_infix_pred> <term>
%----  <defined_prop>     ::= <atomic_defined_word>
%----  <defined_prop>     ::== $true | $false
```

```
%----   <defined_pred>        ::= <atomic_defined_word>
%----   <defined_pred>        :==
%----Some systems still interpret equal/2 as equality. The use of equal/2
%----for other purposes is therefore discouraged. Please refrain from either
%----use. Use infix '=' for equality. Note: <term> != <term> is equivalent
%----to ~ <term> = <term>
%----More defined atoms may be added in the future.
<system_atom>          ::= <system_term>
%----<system_atom>s are used for evaluable predicates that are available
%----in particular tools. The predicate names are not controlled by the
%----TPTP syntax, so use with due care. The same is true for <system_term>s.

%----Terms
<term>                 ::= <function_term> | <variable>
<function_term>        ::= <plain_term> | <defined_term> | <system_term>
<plain_term>           ::= <constant> | <functor>(<arguments>)
<constant>             ::= <atomic_word>
<functor>              ::= <atomic_word>
<defined_term>         ::= <number> | <distinct_object>
%----A more general formulation, which syntactically admits more defined terms,
%----is as follows. Developers may prefer to adopt this.
%----   <defined_term>        ::= <number> | <distinct_object> |
%----                             <defined_constant> |
%----                             <defined_functor>(<arguments>) |
%----                             <term> <defined_infix_func> <term>
%----   <defined_constant>    ::= <atomic_defined_word>
%----   <defined_constant>    :==
%----   <defined_functor>     ::= <atomic_defined_word>
%----   <defined_functor>     :==
%----   <defined_infix_func>  ::=
%----System terms have system specific interpretations
<system_term>          ::= <system_constant> | <system_functor>(<arguments>)
<system_functor>       ::= <atomic_system_word>
<system_constant>      ::= <atomic_system_word>
<variable>             ::= <upper_word>

%----Formula sources
<source>               ::= <general_term>
<source>               :== <dag_source> | <internal_source> | <external_source> |
                           unknown
%----Only a <dag_source> can be a <name>, i.e., derived formulae can be
%----identified by a <name> or an <inference_record>
<dag_source>           :== <name> | <inference_record>
<inference_record>     :== inference(<inference_rule>,<useful_info>,
                               [<parent_list>])
<inference_rule>       :== <atomic_word>
%----Examples are         deduction | modus_tollens | modus_ponens | rewrite |
%                         resolution | paramodulation | factorization |
%                         cnf_conversion | cnf_refutation | ...
<parent_list>          :== <parent_info> | <parent_info>,<parent_list>
<parent_info>          :== <source><parent_details>
<parent_details>       :== :<atomic_word> | <null>
<internal_source>      :== introduced(<intro_type><optional_info>)
<intro_type>           :== definition | axiom_of_choice | tautology
%----This should be used to record the symbol being defined, or the function
%----for the axiom of choice
<external_source>      :== <file_source> | <theory> | <creator_source>
<file_source>          :== file(<file_name><file_info>)
<file_info>            :== ,<name> | <null>
<theory>               :== theory(<theory_name><optional_info>)
<theory_name>          :== equality | ac
%----More theory names may be added in the future. The <optional_info> is
%----used to store, e.g., which axioms of equality have been implicitly used,
%----e.g., theory(equality,[rst]). Standard format still to be decided.
<creator_source>       :== creator(<creator_name><optional_info>)
<creator_name>         :== <atomic_word>

%----Useful info fields
```

```
<optional_info>        ::= ,<useful_info> | <null>
<useful_info>          ::= <general_term_list>
<useful_info>          :== [] | [<info_items>]
<info_items>           :== <info_item> | <info_item>,<info_items>
<info_item>            :== <formula_item> | <inference_item> | <general_function>
%----Useful info for formula records
<formula_item>         :== <description_item> | <iquote_item>
<description_item>     :== description(<atomic_word>)
<iquote_item>          :== iquote(<atomic_word>)
%----<iquote_item>s are used for recording exactly what the system output about
%----the inference step. In the future it is planned to encode this information
%----in standardized forms as <parent_details> in each <inference_record>.
%----Useful info for inference records
<inference_item>       :== <inference_status> | <refutation>
<inference_status>     :== status(<status_value>) | <inference_info>
%----These are the status values from the SZS ontology
<status_value>         :== tau | tac | eqv | thm | sat | cax | noc | csa | cth |
                           ceq | unc | uns | sab | sam | sar | sap | csp | csr |
                           csm | csb
%----The most commonly used status values are:
%----   thm - Every model (and there are some) of the parent formulae is a
%----         model of the inferred formula. Regular logical consequences.
%----   cth - Every model (and there are some) of the parent formulae is a
%----         model of the negation of the inferred formula. Used for negation
%----         of conjectures in FOF to CNF conversion.
%----   sab - There is a bijection between the models (and there are some) of
%----         the parent formulae and models of the inferred formula. Used for
%----         Skolemization steps.
%----For the full hierarchy see the SZSOntology file distributed with the TPTP.
<inference_info>       :== <inference_rule>(<atomic_word>,<general_list>)
<refutation>           :== refutation(<file_source>)
%----Useful info for creators is just <general_function>

%----Include directives
<include>              ::= include(<file_name><formula_selection>).
<formula_selection>    ::= ,[<name_list>] | <null>
<name_list>            ::= <name> | <name>,<name_list>

%----Non-logical data
<general_term>         ::= <general_data> | <general_data>:<general_term> |
                           <general_list>
<general_data>         ::= <atomic_word> | <atomic_word>(<general_arguments>) |
                           <number> | <distinct_object>
<general_arguments>    ::= <general_term> | <general_term>,<general_arguments>
<general_list>         ::= [] | [<general_term_list>]
<general_term_list>    ::= <general_term> | <general_term>,<general_term_list>

%----General purpose
<name>                 ::= <atomic_word> | <unsigned_integer>
<atomic_word>          ::= <lower_word> | <single_quoted>
%----This maybe useful in the future
%----    <atomic_defined_word> ::= <dollar_word>
<atomic_system_word> ::= <dollar_dollar_word>
<number>               ::= <real> | <signed_integer> | <unsigned_integer>
%----Numbers are always interpreted as themselves, and are thus implicitly
%----distinct if they have different values, e.g., 1 != 2 is an implicit axiom.
%----All numbers are base 10 at the moment.
<file_name>            ::= <atomic_word>
<null>                 ::=

%-------------------------------------------------------------------------------
%----Rules from here on down are for defining tokens (terminal symbols) of the
%----grammar, assuming they will be recognized by a lexical scanner.
%----A ::- rule defines a token, a ::: rule defines a macro that is not a
%----token. Usual regexp notation is used. Single characters are always placed
%----in []s to disable any special meanings (for uniformity this is done to
%----all characters, not only those with special meanings).
```

```
%----These are tokens that appear in the syntax rules above. No rules
%----defined here because they appear explicitly in the syntax rules.
%----Keywords:    fof cnf include
%----Punctuation: ( ) , . [ ] :
%----Operators:   ! ? ~ & | <=> => <= <~> ~| ~&
%----Predicates:  = != $true $false

<comment>              ::- <comment_line>|<comment_block>
<comment_line>        ::: [%]<printable_char>*
<comment_block>       ::: [/][*]<not_star_slash>[*][*]*[/]
<not_star_slash>      ::: ([^*][*][*][*]*[^/*])*[^*]*
%----System comments are a convention used for annotations that may used as
%----additional input to a specific system. They look like comments, but start
%----with %$$ or /*$$. A wily user of the syntax can notice the $$ and extract
%----information from the "comment" and pass that on as input to the system.
%----The specific system for which the information is intended should be
%----identified after the $$, e.g., /*$$Otter 3.3: Demodulator */
%----To extract these separately from regular comments, the rules are:
%----   <system_comment>        ::- <sys_comment_line>|<sys_comment_block>
%----   <sys_comment_line>      ::: [%]<dollar_dollar><printable_char>*
%----   <sys_comment_block>     ::: [/][*]<dollar_dollar><not_star_slash>[*][*]*[/]
%----A string that matches both <system_comment> and <comment> should be
%----recognized as <system_comment>, so put these before regular comments.

<single_quoted>       ::- [']([^\\']|[\\][']|[\\][\\])*[']
%----<single_quoted>         ::- '<printable_char>*', but ' and \ are escaped.
%----\ is used as the escape character for ' and \, i.e., if \' is  encountered
%----the ' is not the end of the <single_quoted>, and if \\ is encountered the
%----second \ is not an escape. Both characters (the escape \ and the following
%----' or \) are retained and printed on output. Behaviour is undefined if the
%----escape \ is followed by anything other than ' or \. Behaviour is undefined
%----if a non-<printable_char> is encountered. If the contents of a <single
%----quoted> constitute a <lower_word>, then the ''s should be stripped to
%----produce a <lower_word>.
<distinct_object>     ::- ["]([^\\"]|[\\]["]|[\\][\\])*["]
%----<distinct_object>   ::- "<printable_char>*", but " and \ are escaped. The
%----comments for <single_quoted> apply, with ' replaced by ".
%----Distinct objects are always interpreted as themselves, and are thus
%----implicitly distinct if they look different, e.g., "Apple" != "Microsoft"
%----is an implicit axiom.

<dollar_dollar_word> ::- <dollar_dollar><lower_word>
<upper_word>         ::- <upper_alpha><alpha_numeric>*
<lower_word>         ::- <lower_alpha><alpha_numeric>*

%----Numbers
<real>                ::- (<signed_decimal>|<unsigned_decimal>)<fraction_decimal>
<signed_integer>      ::- <sign><unsigned_integer>
<unsigned_integer>    ::- <unsigned_decimal>
<signed_decimal>      ::: <sign><unsigned_decimal>
<sign>                ::: [+-]
<unsigned_decimal>    ::: ([0]|<non_zero_numeric><numeric>*)
<fraction_decimal>    ::: [.]<numeric><numeric>*

%----Character classes
<numeric>             ::: [0-9]
<non_zero_numeric>    ::: [1-9]
<lower_alpha>         ::: [a-z]
<upper_alpha>         ::: [A-Z]
<alpha_numeric>       ::: (<lower_alpha>|<upper_alpha>|<numeric>|[_])
<dollar_dollar>       ::: [$][$]
<printable_char>      ::: .
%----<printable_char>      ::: any printable ASCII character, codes 32-126
%----<printable_char> thus includes spaces, but not tabs, newlines, bells, etc.
%----This definition does not capture that.
<vline>               ::: [|]
%------------------------------------------------------------------------
```

Stratified Context Unification Is NP-Complete[*]

Jordi Levy[1], Manfred Schmidt-Schauß[2], and Mateu Villaret[3]

[1] IIIA, CSIC, Campus de la UAB, Barcelona, Spain
http://www.iiia.csic.es/~levy
[2] Institut für Informatik, FB Informatik und Mathematik,
Johann Wolfgang Goethe-Universität,
Postfach 11 19 32, D-60054 Frankfurt, Germany
http://www.ki.informatik.uni-frankfurt.de/persons/schauss/schauss.html
[3] IMA, UdG, Campus de Montilivi, Girona, Spain
http://ima.udg.es/~villaret

Abstract. Context Unification is the problem to decide for a given set of second-order equations E where all second-order variables are unary, whether there exists a unifier, such that for every second-order variable X, the abstraction $\lambda x.r$ instantiated for X has exactly one occurrence of the bound variable x in r. Stratified Context Unification is a specialization where the nesting of second-order variables in E is restricted.

It is already known that Stratified Context Unification is decidable, NP-hard, and in PSPACE, whereas the decidability and the complexity of Context Unification is unknown. We prove that Stratified Context Unification is in NP by proving that a size-minimal solution can be represented in a singleton tree grammar of polynomial size, and then applying a generalization of Plandowski's polynomial algorithm that compares compacted terms in polynomial time. This also demonstrates the high potential of singleton tree grammars for optimizing programs maintaining large terms.

A corollary of our result is that solvability of rewrite constraints is NP-complete.

1 Introduction

Higher-order logic and higher-order deduction system (see e.g. [Dow01, PS99, Pau94, And86, Hue75]) provide very expressive frameworks and highly developed tools for deduction. One of the operations used in different variants is *higher-order unification* (see [Hue75, Dow01]). A specialization is *second-order unification*, which in turn is a generalization of *first-order unification*, where variables (i.e., second-order variables) at the position of function symbols are permitted in equations. In solving an equation, the second-order variables can stand for an arbitrary first-order term, with holes for plugging in the arguments, which must be terms. In lambda-notation, a second-order variable may be instantiated with a term $\lambda x_1, \ldots, x_n . t$, where t is a first-order term, and the variables

---

[*] First and third author's has been partially founded by the CICYT research projects iDEAS (TIN2004-04343) and Mulog (TIN2004-07933-C03-01/03).

U. Furbach and N. Shankar (Eds.): IJCAR 2006, LNAI 4130, pp. 82–96, 2006.

x_i also stand for first-order terms. It is known that second-order unification is undecidable, even under severe syntactic restrictions [Gol81, Far91, LV00, LV02].

A variant of second-order unification is *context unification*, which is also a generalization of *string unification*, which is decidable [Mak77] and known to be in PSPACE [Pla04]. Context unification is like second-order unification, where the arity of second-order variables is one, and the possible instantiations of second-order variables are restricted to abstractions where the number of occurrences of the bound variable is one. It is currently open, whether context unification is (un)decidable. A generalization is *linear second-order unification*, see [Lev96], where context variables may have arity more than one, and λ-bindings and bound variables may occur in the terms of the equations. It's decidability is also unknown. A decidable specialization of context unification is *stratified context unification* (SCU) [SS02], which allows only equations, where the nesting of variables obeys a stratification property: For every variable Z, every two positions p_1, p_2 of Z in terms in equations, the sequences of context variables on the paths p_1, p_2 must be the same. It is known that SCU is NP-hard [SSS98] and that the corresponding matching problem is NP-complete [SSS04]. There is a large gap in its precise complexity, since the algorithm for SCU described in [SS02] is non-elementary.

Context unification is also of practical use in computational linguistics [NPR97a, EN00], mainly in the field of compositional semantics of natural language. In fact, SCU subsumes *dominance constraints*, a first-order language that is used to represent scope underspecification [NPR97b, NK01], which has an NP-complete satisfiability problem [KNT98]. Another variant of context unification with interest in computational linguistics is *well-nested context-unification* [LNV05], which restricts the overlap of context variables in the solution; it was recently shown to be in NP.

Another, different, variant of second-order unification with a related algorithmic solution is *bounded second-order unification* (BSOU), with its specialization *monadic second-order unification*. Both problems were recently shown to be NP-complete [LSSV04, LSSV06], using similar methods as in this paper. The difference between BSOU and SCU are semantic: in BSOU the second-order variables may also be instantiated by abstractions without occurrences of the bound variable; and syntactic: the nesting of variables in BSOU may be arbitrary.

In this paper we prove that SCU is in NP, which means that it is NP-complete, closing this complexity gap. The proof-method is interesting in itself: it uses so-called *singleton tree grammars* (STG) [SS05, BLM05, Pla94, LSSV04] as a very general mechanism for compressing terms, i.e. solutions. The known decision algorithm for SCU is adapted and used for showing that the construction of a compressed representation of a size-minimal solution leads to a polynomial-sized STG. Using non-deterministic guessing and an algorithm that can compare compressed terms in polynomial time shows that SCU is in NP. One contribution of compression is to represent C^n with a number n bounded by the exponent of periodicity in polynomial space. The second contribution, together with the implicit representation of the equation during construction of the STG, is to show that the number of first-order variables remains polynomial. Then "in-NP"- result also implies that the complexity of *rewrite-constraints* is NP-complete (see [NTT00]). The result also demonstrates the high potential of singleton tree grammars for optimizing programs maintaining large terms. The upper complexity bound for SCU also shows the practical potential of SCU, since there is a community that has specialized on providing optimal programs that solve NP-complete problems (see [SAT06]). However, the available upper bound on the order of the involved polynomials is rather high: $O(size(E)^{16})$ for the size of a compressed size-minimal solution, and the upper bound for the time-complexity is further increased by the equality-check.

The paper is structured as follows: After an introduction and the preliminary definitions to explain the basic notions, in Section 3 the compression method using singleton tree grammars (STGs) is described, which permits to represent exponentially large and also exponentially deep terms in polynomial space allowing sharing of terms and contexts. We provide a road-map of the proof in Section 4. In Section 5 we introduce generalized stratified equations. In Sections 6 and 7 it is shown, how the non-elementary SCU decision algorithm can be adapted to the compression method. In Section 8 we summarize the estimations and obtain the result that SCU is in NP.

2   Preliminary Definitions

We consider one base (first-order) type o, and second-order types with the syntax $\tau ::= o \to o \mid o \to \tau$, with the usual convention that $\to$ is associative to the right. We use a *signature* $\Sigma = \bigcup_{i \geq 0} \Sigma_i$, where constants of Σ_i are i-ary, and a set of *variables* $\mathcal{X} = \bigcup_{i=0,1} \mathcal{X}_i$, where variables of $\mathcal{X}_i$ are also i-ary. Variables of $\mathcal{X}_0$ are therefore *first-order variables* and those of $\mathcal{X}_1$ are second-order typed and called *context variables*. We assume that the signature contains at least one 0-ary constant. We denote variables with capital letters Z if it may be first-order as well as context variables, and use the convention that X, Y mean context variables, and x, y, z mean first-order variables. Constants are denoted by lower-case letters $a, b, f, g \ldots$ respectively. *Second-order terms* are denoted as $s, t, u, v, \ldots$. The set of variables occurring in terms or other syntactic objects is denoted as $FV(\cdot)$. A term without occurrences of free variables is said to be *ground*. The *size* of a term t is denoted $|t|$ and defined as its number of symbols when written in $\beta\eta$-normal form. We use *positions* in terms, denoted p, q, as sequences of non-negative integers following Dewey notation. In $f(t_1, \ldots, t_n)$ or $X(r)$, respectively, the position of the function symbol and the context variable is 0 and the position of the ith argument is i. The symbol at position 0 is also called the *head* of the term. The empty word is notated ϵ, $p \prec q$ denotes the prefix relation, $p \cdot q$ the concatenation, and $t|_p$ the subterm at position p of t.

For ease of notation, we denote linear second-order terms $\lambda x.t$, where x has exactly one occurrence in t as $t[\cdot]$, where $[\cdot]$ indicates the position of the variable, also called *hole*. We call these terms also *contexts*. We denote contexts by upper case letters C, D. If the term s or context D, respectively, is plugged into the hole of $C[\cdot]$, we denote the result as the term $C[s]$ or the context $C[D]$, also denoted as $C \cdot D$. The position of the hole in a context D is called *main path*, denoted $mp(D)$, and the length of the main path is called the *main depth* of D. If $D_1 = D_2[D_3]$ for contexts D_i, then D_2 is called a *prefix* of D_1, and D_3 is called a *suffix* of D_1. Concatenation $C_1[\ldots[C_n]\ldots]$ is written $C_1 \cdot \ldots \cdot C_n$. The notation D^n for a context D and $n \in \mathbb{N}$ means concatenation of n copies of the context D. If $t = D[s]$, then D is a *prefix context* of the term t. A *subcontext* of a context or term is a prefix of some suffix or a prefix context of some subterm. *Second-order substitutions* denoted by greek letters $\sigma, \theta, \ldots$, are functions from terms to terms, defined as usual, where we in addition assume that context variables can only be instantiated with contexts. The application of a substitution σ to a term t is written $\sigma(t)$, where we always assume that the result is beta-reduced.

An instance of the *stratified context unification problem* (SCU) is a *set of equations* $E = \{t_1 \stackrel{?}{=} u_1, \ldots, t_n \stackrel{?}{=} u_n\}$ where t_i and u_i are second-order terms of type o, i.e. terms not containing λ-abstractions. In addition, for every variable $Z \in FV(E)$ and every two positions p_1, p_2 of Z in terms in equations, the sequence of context variables on the path p_1, p_2 is the same. Here we mean that X is *on the path* p in t, iff for some prefix p' of p, $t_{|p'}$ is of the form $X(r)$. The size of an equation E is denoted as $|E|$ and is its number of symbols. We assume that equations are symmetric. A substitution σ is said to be a *unifier* of E, iff for all $i : \sigma(t_i) = \sigma(u_i)$. A unifier σ is said to be a *solution* of E, iff for all $i :$ $\sigma(t_i)$ and $\sigma(u_i)$ are ground.   It is easy to see that the following holds:

Lemma 2.1. *Let σ be a solution of the SCU-problem E.*

- *If E contains a function symbol f with $ar(f) \geq 2$, then there is also a solution σ', such that every function symbol g with $ar(g) \geq 1$ occurring in $\sigma'(E)$, also occurs in E.*
- *If for all function symbols f occurring in E we have $ar(f) \leq 1$, if $\sigma(E)$ contains function symbols not in E and h is a function symbol with $ar(h) = 2$, then there is also a solution σ', such that for every function symbol g with $ar(g) \geq 1$ occurring in $\sigma'(E)$: either $g = h$ holds, or g occurs in E.*
- *E is unifiable iff E is solvable.*

It is reasonable to assume that the maximal arity of function symbols is not greater than $size(E)$. In this case the necessary transformations in the proof of Lemma 2.1 can be done in $O(size(E))$. Note that the second case occurs in the equation $X(a) \stackrel{?}{=} Y(b)$, with a solution $\{X \mapsto f(b, [\cdot]), Y \mapsto f([\cdot], a)\}$, but there is no solution using only the symbols occurring in the equation.

It is not a restriction to assume that E contains at least one binary function symbol by adding $f(x, y) = f(x, y)$ to E for a binary function symbol f if necessary. This also allows to restrict E to consist of just one equation.

A solution σ of E is said to be *size-minimal* if it minimizes $\sum_{Z \in FV(E)} |\sigma(Z)|$ among all solutions of E. Size-minimal solutions of a SCU-problem satisfy the exponent of periodicity lemma [Mak77, KP96, SSS98, SS02]:

Lemma 2.2 ([SS02]). *There exists a constant $\alpha \in \mathbb{R}$ such that, for every SCU-problem E, every size-minimal solution σ, every variable X (or x, respectively),* contexts u, v and term w, if $\sigma(X) = \lambda y \,.\, u\, v^n(w)$, or if $\sigma(x) = u\, v^n(w)$, and v is not empty, then $n \leq 2^{\alpha|E|}$.

In the following, we denote by $eop(\sigma)$ the maximal n such that for nontrivial D, $D^n([\cdot])$ is a subcontext of $\sigma(x)$ or $\sigma(X)(a)$ for variables x, X.

3   Singleton Tree Grammars

We define singleton tree grammars as a generalization of singleton context free grammars (SCFG) [LSSV04, Pla94], extending the expressivity of SCFGs by terms and contexts. This is consistent with [SS05] and [BLM05], and also with the context free tree grammars in [CDG+97], however, it is a special case.

Definition 3.1. A singleton tree grammar (STG) is a 4-tuple $G = (\mathcal{TN}, \mathcal{CN}, \Sigma, R)$, where $\mathcal{TN}$ are tree nonterminals, $\mathcal{CN}$ are context nonterminals, and Σ is a signature of function symbols and constants (the terminals), such that the sets $\mathcal{TN}$, $\mathcal{CN}$, Σ are pairwise disjoint. The set of nonterminals $\mathcal{N}$ is defined as $\mathcal{N} = \mathcal{TN} \cup \mathcal{CN}$. The rules in R may be of the form:

- $A ::= f(A_1, \ldots, A_n)$, where $A, A_i \in \mathcal{TN}$, and $f \in \Sigma_n$.
- $A_1 ::= C[A_2]$ where $A_1, A_2 \in \mathcal{TN}$, and $C \in \mathcal{CN}$.
- $C ::= [\cdot]$.
- $C_1 ::= C_2 C_3$, where $C_i \in \mathcal{CN}$.
- $C ::= f(A_1, \ldots, A_{i-1}, [\cdot], A_{i+1}, \ldots, A_n)$, where $A_i \in \mathcal{TN}$, $C \in \mathcal{CN}$, $[\cdot]$ is the hole, and $f \in \Sigma$ an n-ary function symbol.

Let $D' >_G D''$ for two nonterminals D', D'', iff $D' ::= t$, and D'' occurs in t. The STG must be non-recursive, i.e. the transitive closure $>_G^*$ must be terminating. Furthermore, for every non-terminal N there is exactly one rule having N as left hand side. Given a term t with occurrences of nonterminals, the derivation by G is an exhaustive iterated replacement of the nonterminals by the corresponding right hand sides, using the convention for second-order terms. The result is denoted as $w_{G,t}$. In this case we also say, that G defines $w_{G,t}$. Ê If the grammar G is clear, we omit the index in our notation. As a short hand for $mp(w_C)$ we use $mp(C)$ for context nonterminals C.

We will also allow variables Z from $\mathcal{X}_0$ and $\mathcal{X}_1$ in the grammar. The convention is that in case there is a rule with left hand side Z, then it is a nonterminal, otherwise we treat Z as terminal.

Definition 3.2. The size $|G|$ of a grammar (STG) G is the number of its rules. The depth of a nonterminal D is defined as the maximal number of $>_G$-steps from D. The depth of a grammar is the maximum of the depths of all nonterminals, denoted as $depth(G)$.

As a generalization of the theorem in Plandowski [Pla94, Pla95], in [SS05] and [BLM05], there are proofs of the following theorem, (where we have to simplify away the occurrences of holes):

Theorem 3.3. *Given an STG G, and two tree nonterminals A, B from G, it is decidable in polynomial time depending on $|G|$ whether $w_A = w_B$.*

The following lemmas state how the size and the depth of the grammar are increased by extending the grammar with concatenations, exponentiation, prefixes and suffixes of contexts. The depth/size bounds for these operations are related to balancing conditions for trees. When using log, we mean the binary logarithm. The proofs of the following three lemmas are easy and can be copied from the corresponding proofs for SCFGs in the forthcoming journal version of [LSSV04].

Lemma 3.4. *Let G be an STG defining the contexts $D_1, \ldots, D_n$ for $n \geq 1$. Then there exists a STG $G' \supseteq G$ that defines the context $D_1 \cdots \cdots D_n$ and satisfies $|G'| \leq |G| + n - 1$ and $depth(G') \leq depth(G) + \lceil \log n \rceil$.*

Lemma 3.5. *Let G be an STG defining the context D. For any $n \geq 1$, there exists an STG $G' \supseteq G$ that defines the context D^n and satisfies $|G'| \leq |G| + 2 \lfloor \log n \rfloor$ and $depth(G') \leq depth(G) + \lceil \log n \rceil$.*

Lemma 3.6. *Let G be an STG defining the context D or term t. For any nontrivial prefix, suffix or subterm D' of the context D, and for every subterm t' of the term t or context D, there exists an STG $G' \supseteq G$ that defines D' or t', respectively, and satisfies $|G'| \leq |G| + depth(G)$ and $depth(G') = depth(G)$.*

Lemma 3.7 covers the case that the main path of the desired prefix context of a term t deviates from the paths as given in the STG. The naïve construction may lead to an exponential blow-up. This case does not occur for words in SCFGs and requires an extra treatment. The prefix context of a context can be constructed as for words, whereas the same construction idea used for constructing a prefix context of a term t may lead to an exponential blow-up for several extensions, since too much rules are required. Hence this case requires an extra treatment.

Lemma 3.7. *Let G be an STG defining the term t. For any nontrivial prefix context D of the term t, there exists an STG $G' \supseteq G$ that defines D and satisfies $|G'| \leq |G| + 2\ depth(G)\ (\log(depth(G)) + 1)$ and $depth(G') \leq depth(G) + 2 + \log(depth(G))$,*

Proof. Let A be the non-terminal symbol defining the term $t = w_A$ and let p be a position in w_A that is the position of the hole of the desired context D. First we show by induction that we can generate a list of context nonterminals that can be concatenated to construct D. The induction is on $depth(A)$.

The base case is that $|p| = 0$ at some depth. In this case the empty context is the result, which is omitted in the list. For the induction step we consider the different possibilities for rules:

1. The rule is $A ::= f(A_1, \ldots, A_n)$ and $p = kp'$. Then we return the context defined by the rule $C_1 ::= f(A_1, \ldots, [\cdot]_k, \ldots, A_n)$, and the list for A_k, p'.

2. The rule is $A ::= C[A_2]$. There are some subcases:
If p is a prefix of $mp(C)$, then return C_1, constructed such that $p = mp(C_1)$ using Lemma 3.6.
If p is within A_2, and $p = p_1 p_2$, where $p_1 = mp(C)$, then we return C, and the list of contexts generated for A_2, p_2.
The position p is within C. Then let $p = p_1 p_2 p_3$, where p_1 is the maximal common prefix of p and $mp(C)$, and $|p_2| = 1$. Then construct C_1 for the prefix of w_C with $p_1 = mp(C_1)$ by Lemma 3.6. Let $p_1 k$ with $k \in \mathbb{N}$ be a prefix of $mp(C)$. Let C_3 be a new symbol defining the subcontext of w_C starting at position $p_1 k$ using Lemma 3.6. Moreover, there is a defined rule $C_2 ::= f(B_1, \ldots, [\cdot]_k, \ldots B_n)$, corresponding to the subcontext of w_C for position p_1, whose existence can be verified by induction. Since $p_2 \neq k$, we have to define the following new symbols and rules: $A_3 ::= C_3[A_2]$, $C_4 ::= f(B_1, \ldots, [\cdot]_{p_2}, \ldots, B_{k-1}, A_3, B_{k+1}, \ldots, B_n)$. Then return C_1, C_4 and the list generated for B_{p_2}, p_3.

Summarizing, we obtain a list of contexts of length at most $2\,depth(G)$, which can be concatenated defining a new symbol C_D. An upper bound on the total number of new rules is $(2 \log(depth(G)) + 2) * depth(G)$, since the induction hypothesis in case 2 is called for $depth(A) - 2$. Notice that the depth of all the contexts that we build up is bounded by $depth(G)+1$ because of the construction of C_4, hence the depth of C_D is at most $depth(G) + 2 + \log(depth(G))$, which is the depth contribution of the final concatenation. □

3.1 Estimations for Several Grammar Extensions

Definition 3.8. *Let G, G' be STGs, let $M \in \mathbb{R}$ with $M \geq 2$. Then we write $G \rightarrow_{sd(M)} G'$ for a grammar extension by size and depth, iff*

$$|G'| \quad \leq |G| + 3 \log(depth(G))\,depth(G) + 2M$$
$$depth(G') \leq depth(G) + \log(depth(G)) + M$$

As an abbreviation, we write $G \rightarrow^k_{sd(M)} G'$, iff $G \rightarrow_{sd(M)} G_1 \ldots G_{k-1} \rightarrow_{sd(M)} G'$ for appropriate STGs G_i and an integer $k \geq 2$.

Proposition 3.9. *Let G, G' be STGs, let $M \in \mathbb{R}$, such that $G \rightarrow^n_{sd(M)} G'$. Then with $M' = \max(M, depth(G))$ and $\beta(M, n) := (n + 2)M' + n\log(M') + n^2$:*

$$|G'| \quad \leq |G| + 3n\beta(M', n) \log(\beta(M', n)) + 2Mn$$
$$depth(G') \leq \beta(M', n)$$

Proof. Let $G = G_0, G_1, \ldots G_n = G'$ be a sequence of STGs, such that for every $i = 0, \ldots, n - 1$: $G_i \rightarrow_{sd} G_{i+1}$. To verify the bound for $depth(G_n)$, let $d_i := depth(G_i), i = 1, \ldots, n$. Then $d_{i+1} = d_i + \log(d_i) + M$, which implies $depth(G_n) \leq d_0 + nM + \sum(\log(d_i))$. Using $\log(d_i + a) \leq \log(d_i) + a/d_i$, it follows that $\log(d_{i+1}) - \log(d_i) \leq 1$ for $i \geq 2$. Then we obtain $depth(G_n) \leq d_0 + nM + n(2 + \log(M')) + n^2 \leq (n + 2)M' + n\log(M') + n^2$. The bound for $|G_n|$ can be derived from $|G_n| \leq |G_0| + 3 \sum_i \big(\log(\beta(M', n)) * \beta(M', n) \big) + 2Mn$. □

Corollary 3.10. *Let G be an STG, and G' be constructed from G by n grammar extensions according to Lemmas 3.4, 3.5, 3.6 and 3.7. Assume $M = max(\lceil \log(\text{eop}) \rceil, k)$, where k is the maximal number of concatenated nonterminals in Lemma 3.4, and the exponent in 3.5 is bounded by eop. For an initial system of equations E_0, let $M = O(|E_0|)$, $|G| = O(|E_0|)$, $depth(G) = O(|E_0|)$, and $n = O(|E_0|^h)$, where $h > 1$. Then*

4   Overview of the Proof Idea

Given a solvable stratified equation, we show that we can construct a polynomial sized solution and test it also in polynomial time. The second part, i.e. the test, is delegated to STGs. Showing the first part is the new contribution: Given a solvable stratified equation, the idea is to first fix a size-minimal solution σ, and then to compute a compressed representation. The algorithm in [SS02] is used, however, using a representation, where nonterminals from an STG and variables are also allowed in equations as abbreviations for larger terms. The solution σ will be used as a guide to perform a step-by-step computation of a representation of the solution σ together with an STG. We do not care about the efficiency of this algorithm, since only the size of the computed representation is of interest.

The computation will proceed as follows: After some initialization, the state consists of three components: an equation E, an STG G, and the solution σ. Variables from E may be terminals or non-terminals in the STG. As in [SS02], there will be a distinction between the cases:

1. there is no chain of equations that constitutes a cycle, or
2. there is at least one cycle of equations.

If $FV(E)$ is empty, the construction is finished. In the first case, we extend the partial solution by using a decomposition-like detection of decomposable subequations. In the second case, we use the algorithm in [SS02] and show that a cycle allows to compute a complete instantiation of at least one context variable. The algorithm will terminate and constructs an at most polynomial size representation of σ by an STG.

5   Generalized Stratified Equations

In the following we compact partial solutions as well as equations using STGs, where STG-symbols are permitted in equations. We also allow rules of the form $C ::= C'$, which does not extend the expressive power, since it can be easily removed later by the appropriate replacements in the STG.

5.1   Basic Definitions

Definition 5.1. *Let G be an STG, and E be a single stratified equation, where symbols from G are permitted in E. Then (E, G) is a generalized stratified equation (GSE). We denote the set of variables occurring in E after expansion of nonterminals using G by $FV_G(E)$, where the variables that are nonterminals in G are not considered.*

We fix a size-minimal solution σ_0 for the initial stratified equation $E_{initial} = \{u_1 \stackrel{?}{=} u_2\}$, and denote its size by M_0, and the exponent of periodicity bound of σ_0 according to Lemma 2.2 by eop. Let $W := FV(E_{initial})$. The partial solution, denoted by θ, is always given by the right hand sides in G of the variables in W, i.e. by $\theta(Z) := w_Z$ for all $Z \in W$. The corresponding initial GSE is (E_0, G_0), where G_0 encodes the terms u_1, u_2 as tree nonterminals U_1, U_2, and $E_0 := \{U_1 \stackrel{?}{=} U_2\}$. The initial state of the construction is $((E_0, G_0), \sigma_0)$. A solution σ of an intermediate GSE (E, G) is called *correct*, iff $\sigma\theta(Z) = \sigma_0(Z)$ for all variables $Z \in W$. The construction of the solution uses a state $((E, G), \sigma)$ where σ is a correct solution. For all correct solutions σ, we will have $eop(\sigma) \leq$ eop, since all concerned subcontexts are also subcontexts of $\sigma_0(Z)$ for $Z \in W$.

A *surface position* in a term t is a position p in t, such that for all prefixes p' of p: $t_{|p'}$ has a function symbol as head. We denote w_{U_i} as w_i for $i = 1, 2$ in the following. We repeat the definitions in [SS02] adapted to our representation.

Definition 5.2 (cycles). *Let (E, G) be a GSE. Let the surface equations of (E, G) be all equations $w_{1|p} \stackrel{?}{=} w_{2|p}$, that can be derived by decomposition from $w_1 \stackrel{?}{=} w_2$, where p is a surface position of w_1 and w_2. We denote the surface equations by surfE(E). Let $\approx$ be an equivalence relation on $FV_G(E)$ generated by all the relations $x \approx Y$ for surface equations $x \stackrel{?}{=} Y(s)$, $x \approx y$ for surface equations $x \stackrel{?}{=} y$, and $X \approx Y$ for surface equations $X(s) \stackrel{?}{=} Y(t)$. Let $\succ$ on $FV_G(E)$ be defined as follows: $x \succ Z$ if $x \stackrel{?}{=} s$ is in surfE(E), the head of w_s is a function symbol, and Z occurs in w_s at a surface position, i.e. there is some surface position p such that $w_{s|p} = Z(r)$ for some r; $X \succ Z$ if $X(r) \stackrel{?}{=} s$ is in surfE(E) and the head of w_s is a function symbol. Let $\succeq$ be the smallest preorder generated by $\approx$ and $\succ$. If for all $Z_1, Z_2 \in FV_G(E)$: $Z_1 \succ Z_2$ implies that $Z_1 \not\preceq Z_2$, then (E, G) is cycle-free, otherwise, (E, G) is cyclic.*

A cycle is a sequence of surface equations, which in expanded form is as follows: $Z_1(\ldots) \stackrel{?}{=} D_1(Z_2(\ldots)), Z_2(\ldots) \stackrel{?}{=} D_2(Z_3(\ldots)), \ldots, Z_h(\ldots) \stackrel{?}{=} D_h(Z_1(\ldots))$, where Z_i may be context-variables or first-order variables, D_i is a context for all i, and at least one D_i is a nontrivial context. The indicated occurrences directly correspond to the definition of $\approx$ and $\succ$. However, note that there may be different occurrences of the Z_i on the right hand side, and that D_i may not be unique. The length of the cycle is the number of the equations occurring in it.

Lemma 5.3 (Occurs-check). *In a solvable GSE (E, G), there is no cycle where all variables $Z_1, \ldots, Z_h$ are first-order variables.*

We define an ordering that will be reduced by mimicking the SCU-algorithm from [SS02] and use it for the construction of a representation of σ_0.

Definition 5.4. *Given a GSE (E, G), the measure $\mu(E)$ is the lexicographic combination $\langle \mu_1(E), \mu_2(E), \mu_3(E) \rangle$ of the following components:*

1. *$\mu_1(E) = |FV_G(E)|$.*
2. *$\mu_2(E) = 0$ if (E, G) is cyclic, and 1, otherwise.*

3. $\mu_3(E) = \mu_1(E) - |\{[Z]_\approx \mid Z \in FV_G(E)\}|$ if E is not cyclic, and 0 otherwise.
4. $\mu_4(E)$ is the number of variables in $FV_G(E)$ that are not $\succ$-maximal.

The transformations will never increase $|FV_G(E)|$ and they will transform a stratified equation into a stratified equation (see [SS02]).

6 GSE Without Cycles

The SCU-algorithm in [SS02] treats systems of equations without cycles by iteratedly guessing and instantiating parts of the solution σ. The potential number of these guessing, instantiating and decomposition steps in that paper may be exponential. We have to avoid steps that lead to unnecessary constructions of symbols and rules in G. Hence we have to adapt the algorithm given in [SS02] to our compressing method. Let a *var-term* be a term of the form x or $X(r)$.

Algorithm 6.1 (Rule: Transform-non-cyclic GSE). Let (E, G) be a non-cyclic GSE with $E = \{U_1 \stackrel{?}{=} U_2\}$, $w_i = w_{U_i}$, for $i = 1, 2$, and let σ be a correct solution. Depending on E, there are several possibilities:

1. w_1, w_2 are ground and $w_1 = w_2$. Then stop further instantiation.
2. There is a context variable $X \in FV_G(E)$ with $\sigma(X) = [\cdot]$. Then add $X ::= [\cdot]$ to G.
3. Assume cases (1) and (2) are not applicable.
   Let p be a surface position in w_1 and w_2 such that p is a position of a first-order variable in w_1 or w_2 which is also in $FV_G(E)$. Also assume that $w_{1|p} \neq w_{2|p}$. W.l.o.g. let $w_{1|p}$ be the first order variable, say x. Add a nonterminal A defining $w_{2|p}$, and add $x ::= A$ to the grammar.
4. Assume that the cases (1) – (3) are not applicable. Then let V be a $\succ$-maximal $\approx$-equivalence class in $FV_G(E)$, that is in addition not $\succ$-minimal. Note that V consists only of context variables. Let s be a term with a function symbol as head (such an s must exist), such that there is a surface position p and $w_{1|p} = s$, and $w_{2|p} = X(r)$ for some $X \in V$.
   Let q be the maximal position such that q is a prefix of all main paths of $\sigma(X)$ for all $X \in V$, and such that q is a surface position in s. There are some subcases:
   (a) q is the main path of some context $\sigma(X)$ where $X \in V$. Then construct A_s with $w_{A_s} = s$, and the symbol C for the prefix of A_s with main path q. For all $X \in V$, add $X ::= CX'$ or $X ::= C$ to G, where the X' are new context variables. The latter case is used iff $\sigma(X)$ has main path q.
   (b) If $s_{|q}$ is a var-term, then construct A_s with $w_{A_s} = s$, and the prefix symbol C of A_s with main path q. For all $X \in V$, add $X ::= CX'$ to G.
   (c) Case (4a) does not apply and $s_{|q}$ is not a var-term. This is the situation where the contexts go into different directions. Then let $V = \{X_1, \ldots, X_n\}$ and for all $i = 1, \ldots, n$ let q_i be a position of length 1, such that qq_i is a prefix of the main path of $\sigma(X_i)$. Construct A_s with $w_{A_s} = s$, and for every $i = 1, \ldots, n$ the prefix context C_i of A_s with main path qq_i. For all $X_i \in V$, add $X_i ::= C_iX_i'$ to G where X_i' are new context variables.

5. Assume that the cases (1) – (4) are not applicable. Let $V = \{X_1, \ldots, X_n\}$ be a $\succeq$-maximal $\approx$ −equivalence class in $FV_G(E)$, that is in addition $\succeq$-minimal. Note that V consists only of context variables. For $i = 1, \ldots, n$ let q_i be a position of length 1 that is a prefix of $\sigma(X_i)$. Minimality of σ_0 implies that $|\{q_i \mid i = 1, \ldots, n\}| \geq 2$. Since $\sigma(X_i) \neq [\cdot]$, there is a function symbol f, also occurring in E, which is the head of all $\sigma(X_i)$. Construct the context symbols C_i with rules $C_i ::= f(A_{i,1}, \ldots, [\cdot]_{q_i}, \ldots, A_{i,n})$, where q_i is the first integer on the main path of $\sigma(X_i)$. The symbol $A_{i,j}$ stands for a constant a_j, if for all i: $\sigma(X_i)_{|j} = a_j \in \mathcal{F}_0$. Let $J \subset \{1, \ldots, n\}$ be the indices, for which this is false. Note that $|J| \geq 2$. For indices $j \in J$, let $A_{i,j}$ be new first-order variables. Define the rules $X_i ::= C_i(X_i')$ for new context variables X_i'.

Since we have added first-order variables, we apply now the decomposition in (3) for all positions of $A_{i,j}$ for $j \in J$, successively, until for every first-order variable $A_{i,j}$, there is a rule in G. These rules are only of the form $A_{i,j} ::= A_{i',j}$ or $A_{i,j} ::= X_{i'}'(r)$.

In every case, we define the new solution $\sigma'(Z) := \sigma(r)$ for variables Z, if $Z ::= r$ is the new rule for Z, perhaps in several steps.

Case (5) is the key difference between SCU and context unification: in SCU the context variables X_i are only at the surface, and so an instantiation can be guessed, whereas in CU the occurrences of X_i may also be elsewhere, and guessing and instantiating these variables in general makes no progress in solving the equation.

Theorem 6.2. *If $((E, G), \sigma)$ is a GSE with a correct solution σ, then the transformations in (Transform-non-cyclic GSE) are correct. The order μ is strictly decreased. The number of grammar extensions of a single execution can be estimated for the different cases as follows:*

(2) requires 1 extension step, (3) requires 2 extension steps, (4) requires at most $2 + 2M_0$ extension steps, and (5) requires at most $2M_0 + M_0^2$ grammar extension steps.[1]

Proof. The standard cases for correctness follow from [SS02]. The only non-standard case is in case (5). If there is an equivalence class $V = \{X_1, \ldots, X_n\}$ that is $\succeq$-maximal and $\succeq$-minimal, consisting only of context variables, and $\sigma(X_i)$ is not trivial for all i, then the common prefix of the holes of all $\sigma(X_i)$ must have length 0, since σ_0 was chosen as size-minimal. Hence the algorithm part (5) covers all cases. Moreover, the class V will be replaced by at least two $\approx$-classes after the execution. Since also the number of variables is not increased, in this case, $\mu(\cdot)$ is strictly decreased. $\mu(\cdot)$ is also strictly decreased in all other cases: Either a cycle is introduced, or the number of variables is strictly decreased in cases (2), (3), and (4a). In case (4b), the number of non-maximal variables is strictly decreased, and in case (4c), the number of equivalence classes is increased, hence μ_3 is strictly decreased.

---

[1] $M_0 := |E_0|$ is defined in subsection 5.1.

The number of grammar extensions as given in the theorem can be checked by simply scanning the cases of the algorithm. □

7 GSE with Cycles

Given a cyclic GSE (E, G) and a solution σ, we mimic the algorithm in [SS02]. A cycle K in the expanded representation is of the form

$$X_1(s_1) \overset{?}{=} D_1(X_2(t_1)), \ldots, X_{h-1}(s_{h-1}) \overset{?}{=} D_{h-1}(X_h(t_{h-1})), X_h(s_h) \overset{?}{=} D_h(X_1(t_h))$$

provided there are no first-order variables in the cycle. Note that the contexts D_i are not necessarily unique, since there may be further occurrences of X_{i+1}, respectively X_1 in D_h.

We use the measure $\chi(K) = (\chi_1(K), \chi_2(K))$ for a cycle K as above, where $\chi_1(K)$ is the length of the cycle K, and $\chi_2(K)$ is h minus the maximal number i, such that $D_1, \ldots, D_i$ are trivial contexts, perhaps after a rotation of the cycle.

Algorithm 7.1 (Rulc: Solve-cycle). This step is applied to a cycle K that is minimal w.r.t. χ. There are four cases.

1. There is a first-order variable in the cycle. Then apply step (3) of rule 6.1.
2. There is a context-variable X with $\sigma(X) = [\cdot]$. Then apply step (2) of rule 6.1 to eliminate one context variable.
3. Some D_i for $i \neq h$ is nontrivial and (1) and (2) do not apply. Then let k be the minimal index such that D_k is nontrivial. Let q be the maximal common prefix of $mp(D_k)$ and of $mp(\sigma(X_i))$ for $i = 1, \ldots, k$. Construct C that represents the prefix context of D_k with hole at position q, and add $X_i ::= C X_i'$ for $i = 1, \ldots, k$.
4. The cases (1) – (2) do not apply, and only D_h is nontrivial. Then let q be the maximal common prefix of $mp(D_k^{\text{eop}+1})$ and $mp(\sigma(X_i))$ for $i = 1, \ldots, h$. Construct C_0 as the subcontext of $D_k^{\text{eop}+1}$ with hole at position q.
   (a) The position q is the main path of some $\sigma(X_i)$ where $i = 1, \ldots, h$. For all $i = 1, \ldots, h$ add $X_i ::= C_0 X_i'$ or $X_i ::= C_0$ to G; the latter if $\sigma(X_i) = C_0$.
   (b) Otherwise, for $i = 1, \ldots, h$ let $q q_i$ be the prefix of $mp(\sigma(X_i))$ with $|q_i| = 1$. Note that all contexts $\sigma(X_i)_{|q}$ have the same function symbol f as head, which also occurs in E. Construct the contexts symbols C_i with rules $C_i ::= f(x_{i,1}, \ldots, [\cdot]_{q_i}, \ldots, x_{i,n})$, and $C_i' ::= C_0 C_i$, where $x_{i,j}$ are fresh first-order variables. Define the rules $X_i ::= C_i'(X_i')$ for new context variables X_i'. Then apply the step (3) of rule 6.1 several times until all the variables $x_{i,j}$ are instantiated.

Theorem 7.2. *Given a GSE (E, G) with cycles and a solution σ with $\text{eop}(\sigma) \leq$ eop. Then it is possible to construct a GSE (E', G'), such that $\mu_1(E', G') < \mu_1(E, G)$, and there are at most $O(M_0^4)$ grammar extension steps necessary until this happens, and there is a correct solution σ' with $\text{eop}(\sigma') \leq$ eop.*

Proof. Since we have mimicked the algorithm in [SS02], we have only to check the number of grammar-extension steps. In every step, a cycle can be chosen that is χ-minimal. We estimate the number of applications until $\mu_1(\cdot)$ is strictly decreased. First, the number of applications of (Solve-cycle) is at most M_0^2, since in case $\mu_1(\cdot)$ is unchanged, χ of a minimal cycle is strictly decreased, which follows from [SS02]. The number of grammar-extension of one application can be estimated as follows: The construction of C_i requires $O(M_0)$ grammar extensions, the removal of the variables in case (4b) requires $O(M_0^2)$ extensions. Since we have at most M_0^2 executions and every execution requires $O(M_0^2)$ grammar extensions, we have $O(M_0^4)$ as an upper bound.   □

8 Upper Bound on the Complexity of Stratified Context Unification

Lemma 8.1. *There are at most $O(M_0^3)$ steps that strictly decrease the order μ.*

Proof. Three components in the lexicographic ordering are at most M_0, and the remaining one is bound by a constant.

Summarizing the estimations results in a NP upper bound:

Theorem 8.2. *Stratified context unification is in NP.*

Proof. Given a solvable stratified context unification problem E_{initial} of size M_0 and a size-minimal solution σ_0, we know that there is an upper bound on the exponent of periodicity, denoted as eop, which is of order $O(M_0)$. Theorem 7.2 shows that there are at most $O(M_0 * M_0^4)$ grammar extensions due to cyclic GSE. Theorem 6.2 and Lemma 8.1 show that there are at most $O(M_0^3 * M_0^2)$ grammar extensions due to non-cyclic GSE.

This means the number of grammar extensions is of order $O(M_0^5)$. Since the initial grammar has size and depth of order $O(M_0)$, Corollary 3.10 shows that the size of the final STG is of order $O(M_0^{3*5+1}) = O(M_0^{16})$.

Now the complexity estimation is as follows: Given E_{initial}, we compute E_0, G_0 as above. Then we guess a solution θ represented by an STG that is an extension of G_0 of size at most $O(M_0^{16})$. The variables can be used exactly as we had done it in the computation. The final equation is of the form $U_1 \stackrel{?}{=} U_2$ where U_1, U_2 are defined by the STG. Rules of the form $C ::= [\cdot]$, and $C ::= C'$, which may be generated by the guessing can easily be removed by performing the appropriate replacements in the STG. Now Theorem 3.3 (see [SS05, BLM05]) shows that we can decide equality of U_1, U_2 in polynomial time. This shows that stratified context unification is in NP.   □

Corollary 8.3. *Stratified context unification is NP-complete and solvability of rewrite constraints (as defined in [NTT00]) is NP-complete.*

Proof. The first claim follows from Theorem 8.2 and from NP-hardness shown in [SSS98]. The second claim follows from the equivalence proof in [NTT00].

It is not clear whether unifiability of generalized stratified context-unification problems (E, G) is in NP, since the usual encoding does not produce a stratified unification problem. However, the following is easy:

Corollary 8.4. *Unifiability of generalized SCU-problems is in NEXPTIME.*

Proof. We can first expand the equation to get rid of the STG, which results in an at most exponentially large SCU-problem, and then we apply Theorem 8.2.

9   Conclusion and Further Research

We have shown that stratified context unification is NP-complete by exploiting compaction of terms and polynomial comparison of the compactions using singleton tree grammars. This also determines the complexity of rewrite constraints to be NP-complete. The result in this paper is a hint that the complexity of distributive unification, which was shown to be decidable in [SS98], may also be in NP, since the algorithm can be seen as an extension of the algorithm for SCU. The compressing mechanism via STGs deserves further investigations to obtain better bounds for the operations on STGs.

References

[And86]   P. Andrews. *An introduction to mathematical logic and type theory: to truth through proof.* Academic Press, 1986.

[BLM05]   G. Busatto, M. Lohrey, and S. Maneth. Efficient memory representation of XML documents. In *Proc. DBPL 2005*, LNCS 3774, pages 199–216, 2005.

[CDG+97]   H. Comon, M. Dauchet, R. Gilleron, F. Jacquemard, D. Lugiez, S. Tison, and M. Tommasi. Tree automata techniques and applications. Available on: http://www.grappa.univ-lille3.fr/tata, 1997. release 1.10.2002.

[Dow01]   G. Dowek. Higher-order unification and matching. In A. Robinson and A. Voronkov, editors, *Handbook of Automated Reasoning*, volume II, chapter 16, pages 1009–1062. Elsevier Science, 2001.

[EN00]   K. Erk and J. Niehren. Parallelism constraints. In *RTA-11*, LNCS 1833, pages 110–126, 2000.

[Far91]   W. M. Farmer. Simple second-order languages for wich unification is undecidable. *Theoretical Computer Science*, 87:173–214, 1991.

[Gol81]   W. D. Goldfarb. The undecidability of the second-order unification problem. *Theoretical Computer Science*, 13:225–230, 1981.

[Hue75]   G. Huet. A unification algorithm for typed λ-calculus. *Theoretical Computer Science*, 1:27–57, 1975.

[KNT98]   A. Koller, J. Niehren, and R. Treinen. Dominance constraints: Algorithms and complexity. In *3rd LACL '98*, LNCS 2014, pages 106–125, 1998.

[KP96]   A. Kościelski and L. Pacholski. Complexity of Makanin's algorithm. *Journal of the ACM*, 43(4):670–684, 1996.

[Lev96]   J. Levy. Linear second order unification. In *RTA-7*, LNCS 1103, pages 332–346, 1996.

[LNV05]   J. Levy, J. Niehren, and M. Villaret. Well-nested context unification. In *CADE 2005*, LNCS 3632, pages 149–163, 2005.

[LSSV04]   J. Levy, M. Schmidt-Schauß, and M. Villaret. Monadic second-order unification is NP-complete. In *RTA-15*, LNCS 3091, pages 55–69, 2004.

[LSSV06]   J. Levy, M. Schmidt-Schauß, and M. Villaret. Bounded second-order unification is NP-complete. to appear in Proc. RTA' 06, 2006.

[LV00]   J. Levy and M. Veanes. On the undecidability of second-order unification. *Information and Computation*, 159:125–150, 2000.

[LV02]   J. Levy and M. Villaret. Currying second-order unification problems. In *RTA-13*, LNCS 2378, pages 326–339, 2002.

[Mak77]   G. S. Makanin. The problem of solvability of equations in a free semigroup. *Math. USSR Sbornik*, 32(2)·129–198, 1977.

[NK01]   J. Niehren and A. Koller. Dominance constraints in context unification. In *LACL'98*, LNAI 2014, pages 199–218, 2001.

[NPR97a]   J. Niehren, M. Pinkal, and P. Ruhrberg. On equality up-to constraints over finite trees, context unification, and one-step rewriting. In *CADE-14*, LNCS 1249, pages 34–48, 1997.

[NPR97b]   J. Niehren, M. Pinkal, and P. Ruhrberg. A uniform approach to underspecification and parallelism. In *35th ACL'97*, pages 410–417, Madrid, 1997.

[NTT00]   J. Niehren, S. Tison, and R. Treinen. On rewrite constraints and context unification. *Information Processing Letters*, 74:35–40, 2000.

[Pau94]   Lawrence C. Paulson. *Isabelle*. LNCS 828. Springer-Verlag, 1994.

[Pla94]   W. Plandowski. Testing equivalence of morphisms in context-free languages. In J. van Leeuwen, editor, *2nd ESA'94*, LNCS 855, pages 460–470, 1994.

[Pla95]   W. Plandowski. *The Complexity of the Morphism Equivalence Problem for Context-Free Languages*. PhD thesis, Dept. of Mathematics, Informatics and Mechanics, Warsaw University, 1995.

[Pla04]   W. Plandowski. Satisfiability of word equations with constants is in PSPACE. *Journal of the ACM*, 51(3):483–496, 2004.

[PS99]   F. Pfenning and C. Schürmann. System description: Twelf - a meta-logical framework for deductive systems. In H. Ganzinger, editor, *Proc. CADE-16*, LNAI 1632, pages 202–206. Springer-Verlag, 1999.

[SAT06]   2006. http://www.satlive.org/.

[SS98]   M. Schmidt-Schauß. A decision algorithm for distributive unification. *TCS*, 208:111–148, 1998.

[SS02]   M. Schmidt-Schauß. A decision algorithm for stratified context unification. *Journal of Logic and Computation*, 12(6):929–953, 2002.

[SS05]   M. Schmidt-Schauß. Polynomial equality testing for terms with shared substructures. Frank report 21, Institut für Informatik. FB Informatik und Mathematik. J. W. Goethe-Universität Frankfurt am Main, November 2005.

[SSS98]   M. Schmidt-Schauß and K. U. Schulz. On the exponent of periodicity of minimal solutions of context equations. In *9th RTA'98*, LNCS 1379, pages 61–75, Tsukuba, Japan, 1998.

[SSS04]   M. Schmidt-Schauß and J. Stuber. On the complexity of linear and stratified context matching problems. *Theory of Computing Systems*, 37:717–740, 2004.

A Logical Characterization of Forward and Backward Chaining in the Inverse Method

Kaustuv Chaudhuri, Frank Pfenning, and Greg Price*

Department of Computer Science
Carnegie Mellon University
{kaustuv, fp}@cs.cmu.edu, gprice@andrew.cmu.edu

Abstract. The inverse method is a generalization of resolution that can be applied to non-classical logics. We have recently shown how Andreoli's focusing strategy can be adapted for the inverse method in linear logic. In this paper we introduce the notion of focusing bias for atoms and show that it gives rise to forward and backward chaining, generalizing both hyperresolution (forward) and SLD resolution (backward) on the Horn fragment. A key feature of our characterization is the structural, rather than purely operational, explanation for forward and backward chaining. A search procedure like the inverse method is thus able to perform both operations as appropriate, even simultaneously. We also present experimental results and an evaluation of the practical benefits of biased atoms for a number of examples from different problem domains.

1 Introduction

Designing and implementing an efficient theorem prover for a non-classical logic requires deep knowledge about the structure and properties of proofs in this logic. Fortunately, proof theory provides a useful guide, since it has isolated a number of important concepts that are shared between many logics of interest. The most fundamental is Gentzen's cut-elimination property [7] which allows us to consider only subformulas of a goal during proof search. Cut elimination gives rise to the inverse method [6] for theorem proving which applies to many non-classical logics. A more recent development is Andreoli's focusing property [1,2] which allows us to translate formulas into derived rules of inference and then consider only the resulting big-step derived rules without losing completeness. Even though Andreoli's system was designed for classical linear logic, similar focusing systems for many other logics have been discovered [10,8].

In prior work we have constructed a focusing system for *intuitionistic* linear logic which is consonant with Andreoli's classical version [5], and shown that restricting the inverse method to work only with big-step rules derived from focusing dramatically improves its efficiency [4]. The key feature of focusing is that each logical connective carries an intrinsic attribute called polarity that determines its behavior under focusing. In the case of linear logic, polarities are uniquely determined for each connective. However, as Andreoli noted, polarities may be chosen freely for atomic formulas as long as duality is consistently maintained. In this paper we prove that, despite

---

* This work has been supported by the Office of Naval Research (ONR) under grant MURI N00014-04-1-0724 and by the National Science Foundation (NSF) under grant CCR-0306313.

U. Furbach and N. Shankar (Eds.): IJCAR 2006, LNAI 4130, pp. 97–111, 2006.
© Springer-Verlag Berlin Heidelberg 2006

the asymmetric nature of intuitionistic logic, a similar observation can be made here. Furthermore, we show that proof search on Horn formulas with the inverse method behaves either like hyperresolution or SLD resolution, depending on the chosen polarity for atoms. If different atoms are ascribed different polarities we can obtain combinations of these strategies that remain complete. The focused inverse method therefore directly generalizes these two classical proof search strategies. We also demonstrate through an implementation and experimental results that this choice can be important in practical proof search situations and that the standard polarity assumed for atoms in intuitionistic [9] or classical [14] logic programming is often the less efficient one.

Since focusing appears to be an almost universal phenomenon among non-classical logics, we believe these observations have wide applicability in constructing theorem provers. The fact that we obtain well-known standard strategies on the Horn fragment, where classical, intuitionistic, and even linear logic coincide, provides further evidence. We are particularly interested in intuitionistic linear logic and its extension by a monad, since it provides the foundation for the logical framework CLF [3] which we can use to specify stateful and concurrent systems. Theorem proving in CLF thereby provides a means for analyzing properties of such systems.

The remainder of the paper is organized as follows. In Section 2 we present the backward focusing calculus that incorporates focusing bias on atoms. In Section 2.1 we describe the derived rules that are generated with differently biased atoms. We then sketch the focused inverse method in Section 3, noting the key differences between sequents and rules in the forward direction from their analogues in the backward direction. In Section 4 we concentrate on the Horn fragment, where we show that the derived rules generalize hyperresolution (for right-biased atoms) and SLD resolution (for left-biased atoms). Finally, section 5 summarizes our experimental results on an implementation of the inverse method presented in Section 3.

2   Biased Focusing

We consider intuitionistic linear logic including the following connectives: linear implication ($\multimap$), multiplicative conjunction ($\otimes$, 1), additive conjunction ($\&$, $\top$), additive disjunction ($\oplus$, 0), the exponential ($!$), and the first-order quantifiers ($\forall$, $\exists$). Quantification is over a simple term language consisting of variables and uninterpreted function symbols applied to a number of term arguments. Propositions are written using capital letters ($A, B, \ldots$), and atomic propositions with lowercase letters ($p, q, \ldots$). We use a standard dyadic sequent calculus for this logic, having the usual nice properties: identity principle, cut-admissibility, structural weakening and contraction for unrestricted hypotheses. The rules of this calculus are standard and can be found in [4]. In this section we shall describe the focused version of this calculus.

In classical linear logic the synchronous or asynchronous nature of a given connective is identical to its polarity; the negative connectives ($\&$, $\top$, $\invamp$, $\bot$, $\forall$) are asynchronous, and the positive connectives ($\otimes$, 1, $\oplus$, 0, $\exists$) are synchronous. In intuitionistic logic, where the left- and right-hand side of a sequent are asymmetric and no convolutive negation exists, we derive the properties of the connectives via the rules and phases of search: an asynchronous connective is one for which decomposition is complete in the *active phase*; a synchronous connective is one for which decomposition is complete in the *focused phase*.

As our backward linear sequent calculus is two-sided, we have left- and right-
synchronous and asynchronous connectives.
For non-atomic propositions a left-synchronous connective is right-asynchronous, and
a left-asynchronous connective right-syn-

symbol	connectives
P	left-synchronous (&, ⊤, $-\!\circ$)
Q	right-synchronous ($\otimes$, $\mathbf{1}$, !)
L	left-asynchronous ($\otimes$, $\mathbf{1}$, !)
R	right-asynchronous (&, ⊤, $-\!\circ$)

chronous; this appears to be universal in well-behaved logics. We define the notations in the adjacent table for *non-atomic* propositions. The contexts in sequents contain linear and unrestricted zones as is usual in dyadic formulations of the sequent calculus. The *unrestricted* zone, written Γ, contains propositions that may be consumed arbitrarily often. The *passive linear* zone, written Δ, contains propositions that must be consumed exactly once. We further restrict this zone to contain only the left-synchronous proposi-tions. We also require a third kind of zone in active rules. This zone, written Ω, contains propositions that must be consumed exactly once, but unlike the passive linear zone, can contain arbitrary propositions. We treat this *active linear* zone as an ordered con-text and use a centered dot ($\cdot$) instead of commas to join active zones together. As we are in the intuitionistic setting, the right hand side must contain exactly one proposition. If the right proposition C is asynchronous, then we write the right hand side as C ; $\cdot$. If it is synchronous and not participating in any active rule, then we write it as $\cdot$; C. If the shape of the right hand side does not matter, we write it as γ. We have the follow-ing kinds of sequents: *right-focal* sequents Γ ; $\Delta \gg A$, *left-focal* sequents Γ ; Δ ; $A \ll Q$ (focus on A in both cases), and *active sequents* Γ ; Δ ; $\Omega \Longrightarrow \gamma$.

Active rules work on active sequents. In each case, a rule either decomposes an asyn-chronous connective (e.g. $\otimes L$) or transfers a synchronous proposition into one of the passive zones. The order in which propositions are examined is immaterial.

$$\frac{\Gamma;\Delta;\Omega\cdot A\cdot B\cdot\Omega'\Longrightarrow\gamma}{\Gamma;\Delta;\Omega\cdot A\otimes B\cdot\Omega'\Longrightarrow\gamma}\otimes L \qquad \frac{\Gamma;\Delta,P;\Omega\cdot\Omega'\Longrightarrow\gamma}{\Gamma;\Delta;\Omega\cdot P\cdot\Omega'\Longrightarrow\gamma}\text{ lact} \qquad \frac{\Gamma;\Delta;\Omega\Longrightarrow\cdot;Q}{\Gamma;\Delta;\Omega\Longrightarrow Q;\cdot}\text{ ract}$$

Because the ordering of propositions in Ω is immaterial, it is then sufficent to designate a particular ordering in which these rules will are applied. We omit the standard details here. Eventually the active sequent is reduced to the form Γ ; Δ ; $\cdot \Longrightarrow \cdot$; Q, which we call a neutral sequent. We will often write neutral sequents simply as Γ ; $\Delta \Longrightarrow Q$.

A *focusing phase* is launched from a neutral sequent by selecting a proposition from Γ, Δ, or the right hand side:

$$\frac{\Gamma;\Delta;P\ll Q}{\Gamma;\Delta,P\Longrightarrow Q}\text{ lf} \qquad \frac{\Gamma,A;\Delta;A\ll Q}{\Gamma,A;\Delta\Longrightarrow Q}\text{ copy} \qquad \frac{\Gamma;\Delta'\gg Q \quad Q\text{ non atomic}}{\Gamma;\Delta\Longrightarrow Q}\text{ rf}$$

This focused formula is decomposed under focus until the proposition becomes asyn-chronous. For example:

$$\frac{\Gamma;\Delta\gg A \quad \Gamma;\Delta'\gg B}{\Gamma;\Delta,\Delta'\gg A\otimes B}\otimes R \qquad \frac{\Gamma;\Delta;A\ll Q}{\Gamma;\Delta;A\,\&\,B\ll Q}\&L_1 \qquad \frac{\Gamma;\Delta;B\ll Q}{\Gamma;\Delta;A\,\&\,B\ll Q}\&L_2$$

As mentioned before, atomic propositions are somewhat special. Andreoli observed in [1] that it is sufficient to assign arbitrarily a synchronous or asynchronous nature to the atoms as long as duality is preserved; here, the asymmetric nature of the intuition-istic sequents suggests that they should be synchronous. However, we are still left with two possibilities for the initial sequents.

$$\overline{\Gamma ; \cdot ; p \ll p} \qquad \text{and} \qquad \overline{\Gamma ; q \gg q}$$

In previous work [4,5], we always selected the first of these two possibilities for the initial sequent. In this paper, we allow both kinds of initial sequents depending on the kind of *focusing bias* with regard to specific atoms. A *right-biased* atom has the Horn-like interpretation; here initial sequents have a *left* focus, and the right hand side is treated like the neutral "goal" in logic programming. A *left-biased* atom has the state-like interpretation; here initial sequents have a right focus, and the constitution of the linear context corresponds more directly to the evolution of the state.

The full set of rules is omitted; they can be reconstructed from [5,4]. We will briefly mention below the completeness theorem which proceeds via cut-elimination for the focusing calculus. This kind of theorem is not a contribution of this paper; we provided a similar proof for the right-focused system in [5]. The basic idea is to interpret every non-focusing sequent as an active sequent in the focusing calculus, then to show that the backward rules are admissible in the focusing calculus using cut. Because proposi-tions have dual synchronicities based on which side of the sequent arrow they appear in, a left-focal sequent matches only an active sequent in a cut; similarly for right-synchronous propositions. Cuts destroy focus as they generally require commutations spanning phase boundaries; this is not significant for our purposes as we interpret non-focusing sequents as active sequents.

Theorem 1 (cut). *If*

1. $\Gamma ; \Delta \gg A$ and:

    (a) $\Gamma ; \Delta' ; \Omega \cdot A \Longrightarrow \gamma$ then $\Gamma ; \Delta, \Delta' ; \Omega \Longrightarrow \gamma$.

    (b) $\Gamma ; \Delta', A ; \Omega \Longrightarrow \gamma$ then $\Gamma ; \Delta, \Delta' ; \Omega \Longrightarrow \gamma$.

2. $\Gamma ; \cdot \gg A$ and $\Gamma, A ; \Delta ; \Omega \Longrightarrow \gamma$ then $\Gamma ; \Delta ; \Omega \Longrightarrow \gamma$.

3. $\Gamma ; \Delta ; \Omega \Longrightarrow A ; \cdot$ or $\Gamma ; \Delta ; \Omega \Longrightarrow \cdot ; A$ and:

    (a) $\Gamma ; \Delta' ; A \ll Q$ then $\Gamma ; \Delta, \Delta' ; \Omega \Longrightarrow Q$.

    (b) $\Gamma ; \Delta' ; \Omega' \cdot A \Longrightarrow \gamma$ then $\Gamma ; \Delta, \Delta' ; \Omega \cdot \Omega' \Longrightarrow \gamma$.

    (c) $\Gamma ; \Delta', A ; \Omega' \Longrightarrow \gamma$ then $\Gamma ; \Delta, \Delta' ; \Omega \cdot \Omega' \Longrightarrow \gamma$.

4. $\Gamma ; \cdot ; \cdot \Longrightarrow A ; \cdot$ or $\Gamma ; \cdot ; \cdot \Longrightarrow \cdot ; A$ and $\Gamma, A ; \Delta ; \Omega \Longrightarrow \gamma$, then $\Gamma ; \Delta ; \Omega \Longrightarrow \gamma$.

The proof is by lexicographic induction over the structure of the two input derivations. It has one important difference from similar structural cut-admissibility proofs: when permuting a cut into an active derivation, we sometimes need to reorder the input deriva-tion in order to allow permuting the cut to the point where it becomes a principal cut. Thus, we have to generalize the induction hypothesis to be applicable not only to struc-turally smaller derivations, but also permutations of the smaller derivations that differ in the order of the active rules. For lack of space, we omit the details of this proof.

Theorem 2 (completeness). *If $\Gamma ; \Delta \Longrightarrow C$ in non-focused intuitionistic linear logic, then $\Gamma ; \cdot ; \Delta \Longrightarrow C ; \cdot$.*

The proof uses cut to show that the non-focusing rules are admissible in the focusing system.

2.1   Derived Inference Rules

The primary benefit of focusing is the ability to generate derived "big step" inference rules: the intermediate results of a focusing or active phase are not important. Andreoli called these rules "bipoles" because they combine two phases with principal formulas of opposite polarities. Each derived rule starts (at the bottom) with a neutral sequent from which a synchronous proposition is selected for focus. This is followed by a sequence of focusing steps until the proposition under focus becomes asynchronous. Then, the active rules are applied, and we eventually obtain a collection of neutral sequents as the leaves of this fragment of the focused derivation. These neutral sequents are then treated as the premisses of the derived rule that produces the neutral sequent with which we started.

For lack of space, we omit a formal presentation of the derived rule calculus; instead, we will motivate it with an example. Consider the negative proposition $q \otimes n \multimap d \otimes d \otimes d^1$ in the unrestricted context Γ. We start with focus on this proposition, and construct the following derivation tree.

$$
\dfrac{
\dfrac{
\dfrac{\dfrac{\Gamma ; \Delta_1 \Longrightarrow q}{\Gamma ; \Delta_1 ; \cdot \Longrightarrow q ; \cdot}\ \text{rb}}{\Gamma ; \Delta_1 \gg q}
\quad
\dfrac{\dfrac{\Gamma ; \Delta_2 \Longrightarrow n}{\Gamma ; \Delta_2 ; \cdot \Longrightarrow n ; \cdot}\ \text{rb}}{\Gamma ; \Delta_2 \gg n}
}{\Gamma ; \Delta_1, \Delta_2 \gg q \otimes n}\ \otimes R
\quad
\dfrac{\dfrac{\dfrac{\Gamma ; \Delta_3, d, d, d \Longrightarrow Q}{\Gamma ; \Delta_3 ; d \otimes d \otimes d \Longrightarrow \cdot ; Q}\ \otimes L; \otimes L; \text{lact} \times 3}{\Gamma ; \Delta_3 ; d \otimes d \otimes d \ll Q}\ \text{lb}}{\ }
}{
\dfrac{\Gamma ; \Delta_1, \Delta_2, \Delta_3 ; q \otimes n \multimap d \otimes d \otimes d \ll Q}{\Gamma ; \Delta_1, \Delta_2, \Delta_3 \Longrightarrow Q}\ \text{copy}
}\ \multimap L
$$

Here we assume that all atoms are right-biased, so none of the branches of the derivation can be closed off with an "init" rule. Thus, we obtain the derived rule:

$$
\dfrac{\Gamma ; \Delta_1 \Longrightarrow q \quad \Gamma ; \Delta_2 \Longrightarrow n \quad \Gamma ; \Delta_3, d, d, d \Longrightarrow Q}{\Gamma ; \Delta_1, \Delta_2, \Delta_3 \Longrightarrow Q}
\tag{D_1}
$$

The situation is considerably different if we assume that all atoms are left-biased. In this case, we get the following derivation:

$$
\dfrac{
\dfrac{\dfrac{\ }{\Gamma ; q \gg q}\ \text{linit} \quad \dfrac{\ }{\Gamma ; n \gg n}\ \text{linit}}{\Gamma ; q, n \gg q \otimes n}\ \otimes R
\quad
\dfrac{\dfrac{\dfrac{\Gamma ; \Delta, d, d, d \Longrightarrow \cdot ; Q}{\Gamma ; \Delta ; d \otimes d \otimes d \Longrightarrow \cdot ; Q}\ \otimes L; \otimes L; \text{lact} \times 3}{\Gamma ; \Delta ; d \otimes d \otimes d \ll Q}\ \text{lb}}{\ }
}{
\dfrac{\Gamma ; q, n, \Delta ; q \otimes n \multimap d \otimes d \otimes d \ll Q}{\Gamma ; q, n, \Delta \Longrightarrow Q}\ \text{copy}
}\ \multimap L
$$

In this left-biased case, we can terminate the left branch of the derivation with a pair of "init" rules. This rule forces the linear context in this branch of the proof to contain just the atoms q and n. The derived rule we obtain is, therefore,

$$
\dfrac{\Gamma ; \Delta, d, d, d \Longrightarrow Q}{\Gamma ; \Delta, q, n \Longrightarrow Q}
\tag{D_2}
$$

There are two key differences to observe between the derived rules (D_1) and (D_2). The first is that simply altering the bias of the atoms has a huge impact on the kinds of rules that are generated; even if we completely ignore the semantic aspect, the rule (D_2) is vastly preferable to (D_1) because it is much easier to use single premiss rules.

---

[1] Standing roughly for "quarter and nickel goes to three dimes".

The second — and more important — observation is that the rule that was generated for the left-biased atoms has a stronger and more obvious similarity to the proposition $q \otimes n \multimap d \otimes d \otimes d$ that was under focus. If we view the linear zone as the "state" of a system, then the rule (D_2) corresponds to transforming a portion of the state by replacing q and n by three ds (reading the rule from bottom to top). If, as is common for linear logic, the unrestricted context Γ contains state transition rules for some encoding of a stateful system, then the derived rules generated by left-biasing allows us to directly observe the evolution of the state of the system by looking at the composition of the linear zone.

3   The Focused Inverse Method

In this section we will briefly sketch the inverse method using the focusing calculus of the previous section. The construction of the inverse method for linear logic is described in more detail in [4]. To distinguish forward from backward sequents, we shall use a single arrow ($\longrightarrow$), but keep the names of the rules the same. In the forward direction, the primary context management issue concerns rules where the conclusion cannot be simply assembled from the premises. The backward $\top R$ rule has an arbitrary linear context Δ, and the unrestricted context Γ is also unknown in several rules such as init and $\top R$. For the unrestricted zone, this problem is solved in the usual (non-linear) inverse method by collecting only the needed unrestricted assumptions and remembering that they can be weakened if needed [6]. We adapt the solution to the linear zone, which may either be precisely determined (as in the case for initial sequents) or subject to weakening (as in the case for $\top R$). We therefore differentiate sequents whose linear context can be weakened and those whose can not.

Definition 3 (forward sequents). A forward sequent *is of the form* Γ ; $[\Delta]_w \longrightarrow \gamma$, *with w a Boolean (0 or 1) called the* weak-flag, *and* γ *being either empty* $(\cdot)$ *or a singleton. The sequent* Γ ; $[\Delta]_w \longrightarrow \gamma$ *corresponds to the backward sequent* Γ' ; $\Delta' \Longrightarrow C$ *if* $\Gamma \subseteq \Gamma'$, $\gamma \subseteq C$; *and* $\Delta = \Delta'$ *if* $w = 0$ *and* $\Delta \subseteq \Delta'$ *if* $w = 1$. *Sequents with* $w = 1$ *are called* weakly linear *or simply* weak, *and those with* $w = 0$ *are* strongly linear *or* strong.

Initial sequents are always strong, since their linear context cannot be weakened. On the other hand, $\top R$ always produces a weak sequent. For binary rules, the unrestricted zones are simply juxtaposed. We can achieve the effect of taking their union by applying the explicit contraction rule (which is absent, but admissible in the backward calculus). For the linear zone we have to distinguish cases based on whether the sequent is weak or not. We write the rules using two operators on the linear context – multiplicative composition ($\times$) and additive composition ($+$).

$$\frac{\Gamma \, ; [\Delta]_w \longrightarrow A \quad \Gamma' \, ; [\Delta']_{w'} \longrightarrow B}{\Gamma, \Gamma' \, ; [\Delta]_w \times [\Delta']_{w'} \longrightarrow A \otimes B} \ \otimes R \qquad \frac{\Gamma \, ; [\Delta]_w \longrightarrow^w A \quad \Gamma' \, ; [\Delta']_{w'} \longrightarrow B}{\Gamma, \Gamma' \, ; [\Delta]_w + [\Delta']_{w'} \longrightarrow A \,\&\, B} \ \&R$$

These compositions are defined as follows: For multiplicative rules, it is enough for one premiss to be weak for the conclusion to be weak; the weak flags are therefore joined with a disjunction ($\vee$). Dually, for additive rules, both premisses must be weak for the conclusion to be weak; in this case the weak flags are joined with a conjunction ($\wedge$).

Definition 4 (context composition). *The partial operators* $\times$ *and* $+$ *on forward linear contexts are defined as follows:* $[\Delta]_w \times [\Delta']_{w'} =_{def} [\Delta, \Delta']_{w \vee w'}$, *and*

$$[\Delta]_w + [\Delta']_{w'} =_{def} \begin{cases} [\Delta]_0 & \text{if } w = 0 \text{ and either } w' = 0 \text{ and } \Delta = \Delta', \text{ or } w' = 1 \text{ and } \Delta' \subseteq \Delta \\ [\Delta']_0 & \text{if } w' = 0, \ w = 1 \text{ and } \Delta \subseteq \Delta' \\ [\Delta \sqcup \Delta']_1 & \text{if } w = w' = 1 \end{cases}$$

Here $\Delta \sqcup \Delta'$ is the multiset union of Δ and Δ'.

In the lifted version of this calculus with free variables, there is no longer a single context represented by $\Delta \sqcup \Delta'$ because two propositions might be equalized by substitution. The approach taken in [4] was to define an additional "context simplification" procedure that iteratively calculates a set of candidates that includes every possible context represented by $\Delta \sqcup \Delta'$ by means of contraction. Many of these candidates are then immediately rejected by subsumption arguments. We refer to [4] for the full set of rules, the completeness theorem, and the lifted version of this forward calculus.

3.1 Focused Forward Search

The sketched calculus in the previous section mentioned only single-step rules. We are interested in doing forward search with derived inference rules generated by means of focusing. We therefore have to slightly generalize the context composition operators into a language of context expressions. In the simplest case, we merely have to add a given proposition to the linear context, irrespective of the weak flag. This happens, for instance, in the "lf" rule where the focused proposition is transferred to the linear context. We write this adjunction as usual using a comma. In the more general case, however, we have to combine two context expressions additively or multiplicatively depending on the kind of rule they were involved in; for these uses, we appropriate the same syntax we used for the single step compositions in the previous section.

$$\text{(context expressions)} \qquad \mathcal{D} \quad ::= \quad [\Delta]_w \mid \mathcal{D}, A \mid \mathcal{D}_1 + \mathcal{D}_2 \mid \mathcal{D}_1 \times \mathcal{D}_2$$

Context expressions can be *simplified* into forward contexts in a bottom-up procedure. We write $\mathcal{D} \hookrightarrow [\Delta]_w$ to denote that $\mathcal{D}$ simplifies into $[\Delta]_w$; it has the following rules.

$$\frac{}{[\Delta]_w \hookrightarrow [\Delta]_w} \qquad \frac{\mathcal{D} \hookrightarrow [\Delta]_w}{\mathcal{D}, A \hookrightarrow [\Delta, A]_w} \qquad \frac{\mathcal{D}_1 \hookrightarrow [\Delta_1]_{w_1} \quad \mathcal{D}_2 \hookrightarrow [\Delta_2]_{w_2}}{\mathcal{D}_1 + \mathcal{D}_2 \hookrightarrow [\Delta_1]_{w_1} + [\Delta_2]_{w_2}} \qquad \frac{\mathcal{D}_1 \hookrightarrow [\Delta_1]_{w_1} \quad \mathcal{D}_2 \hookrightarrow [\Delta_2]_{w_2}}{\mathcal{D}_1 \times \mathcal{D}_2 \hookrightarrow [\Delta_1]_{w_1} \times [\Delta_2]_{w_2}}$$

The forward version of backward derived rules can be written with these context expressions in a natural way by allowing unsimplified context expressions in the place of linear contexts in forward sequents. As an example, the negative unrestricted proposition $q \otimes n \multimap d \otimes d \otimes d$ has the following derived rule with right-biased atoms

$$\frac{\Gamma_1 ; [\Delta_1]_{w_1} \longrightarrow q \quad \Gamma_2 ; [\Delta_2]_{w_2} \longrightarrow n \quad \Gamma_3 ; [\Delta_3]_{w_3}, d, d, d \longrightarrow Q}{\Gamma_1, \Gamma_2, \Gamma_3 ; [\Delta_1]_{w_1} \times [\Delta_2]_{w_2} \times [\Delta_3]_{w_3} \longrightarrow Q}$$

After constructing the neutral sequent with a context expression we then simplify it. Note that context simplification is a partial operation, so we may not obtain any conclusions, for example, if the premises to an additive rule are strong sequents but the linear contexts do not match.

3.2 Focusing in the Inverse Method

The details of the focused inverse method have been sketched in detail in [5]; here we briefly summarize the major differences that arise as a result of focusing bias. The key calculation as laid out in [5] is of the *frontier literals* of the goal sequent, i.e., those sub-formulas that are available in neutral sequents to be focused on. For all but the atoms the calculation is the same as before, and for the atoms we make the following modifications.

1. A positive atom is in the frontier if it lies in the boundary of a phase transition from active to focus, and it is left-biased.
2. A negative atom is in the frontier if it lies in the boundary of a phase transition from active to focus, and it is right-biased.

We then specialize the inference rules to these frontier literals by computing the derived rules that correspond to giving focus to these literals.

Although the addition of bias gives us different rules for focusing, the use of the rules in the search engine is no different from before. The details of the implementation of the main loop can be found in [4]. The main innovation in our formulation of the inverse method in comparison with other descriptions in the literature is the use of a lazy variant of the OTTER loop that both simplifies the design of the rules and performs well in practice.

3.3 Globalization

The final unrestricted zone Γ_g is shared in all branches in a proof of $\Gamma_g ; \Delta_g \Longrightarrow \gamma_g$. One thus thinks of Γ_g as part of the ambient state of the prover, instead of representing it explicitly as part of the current goal. Hence, there is never any need to explicitly record Γ_g or portions of it in the sequents themselves. This gives us the following global and local versions of the copy rule in the forward direction.

$$\frac{\Gamma ; [\Delta]_w ; A \ll \gamma \quad A \in \Gamma_g}{\Gamma ; [\Delta]_w \longrightarrow \gamma} \; \text{delete} \qquad \frac{\Gamma ; [\Delta]_w ; A \ll \gamma \quad A \notin \Gamma_g}{\Gamma, A ; [\Delta]_w \longrightarrow \gamma} \; \text{copy}$$

Globalization thus corresponds to a choice of whether to add the constructed principal formula of a derived rule into the unrestricted zone or not, depending on whether or not it is part of the unrestricted zone in the goal sequent.

4 The Horn Fragment

In complex specifications that employ linearity, there are often significant sub-specifications that lie in the Horn fragment. Unfortunately, the straightforward inverse method is quite inefficient on Horn formulas, something already noticed by Tammet [16]. His prover switches between hyperresolution for Horn and near-Horn formulas and the inverse method for other propositions.

With focusing, this *ad hoc* strategy selection becomes entirely unnecessary. The focused inverse method for intuitionistic linear logic, when applied to a classical, non-linear Horn formula, will exactly behave as classical hyperresolution or SLD resolution depending on the focusing bias of the atomic propositions. This remarkable property gives further credence to the power of focusing as a technique for forward reasoning. In the next two sections we will describe this correspondence in slightly more detail.

A Horn clause has the form $\neg p_1, \ldots, \neg p_n, p$ where the p_i and p are atomic predicates over their free variables. This can easily be generalized to include conjunction and truth, but we restrict our attention to this simple clausal form, as theories with conjunction and truth can be simplified into this form. A Horn theory Ψ is just a set of Horn clauses, and a Horn query is of the form $\Psi \vdash g$ where g is a ground atomic "goal" formula[2]. In the following section we use a simple translation $(-)^o$ of these Horn clauses into linear logic where $\neg p_1, \ldots, \neg p_n, p$ containing the free variables $\vec{x}$ is translated into $\forall \vec{x}.\ p_1 \multimap \cdots \multimap p_n \multimap p$, and the query $\Psi \vdash g$ is translated as $(\Psi)^o ; [\cdot]_0 \longrightarrow g$. This is a special case of a general, focusing-preserving translation from intuitionistic to intuitionistic linear logic [5].

4.1 Hyperresolution

The hyperresolution strategy for the Horn query $\Psi \vdash g$ is just forward reasoning with the following rule (for $n > 1$):

$$\frac{p'_1 \quad \cdots \quad p'_n}{\theta p} \quad \left\{ \begin{array}{l} \text{where } \neg p_1, \ldots, \neg p_n, p \in \Psi; \rho_1, \ldots, \rho_n \text{ are renaming substs; and} \\ \theta = \mathrm{mgu}(\langle \rho_1 p'_1, \ldots, \rho_n p'_n \rangle, \langle p_1, \ldots, p_n \rangle) \end{array} \right.$$

The hyperresolution procedure begins with the collection of unit clauses in Ψ and $\neg g$ as the initial set of facts. The proof succeeds if the empty fact (contradiction) is generated. Because every clause in the theory has a positive literal, the only way an empty fact can be generated is if it proves the fact g itself (note that g is ground).

Consider the goal sequent in the translation $(\Psi)^o ; [\cdot]_0 \longrightarrow g$ where the atoms are all right-biased. The frontier is every clause $\forall \vec{x}.\ p_1 \multimap \cdots \multimap p_n \multimap p \in (\Psi)^o$. Focusing on one such clause gives the following abstract derivation in the forward direction (using lifted sequents):

$$\frac{\dfrac{\dfrac{\dfrac{\Gamma_1 ; [\Delta_1]_{w_1} \longrightarrow p_1}{\Gamma_1 ; [\Delta_1]_{w_1} ; \cdot \longrightarrow p_1 ; \cdot}}{\Gamma_1 ; [\Delta_1]_{w_1} \gg p_1} \quad \cdots \quad \dfrac{\dfrac{\Gamma_n ; [\Delta_n]_{w_n} \longrightarrow p_n}{\Gamma_n ; [\Delta_n]_{w_n} ; \cdot \longrightarrow p_n ; \cdot}}{\Gamma_n ; [\Delta_n]_{w_n} \gg p_n} \quad \dfrac{}{\Gamma ; [\cdot]_0 ; p \ll p} \text{ rinit}}{\dfrac{\dfrac{\Gamma_1, \ldots, \Gamma_n ; \Delta ; p_1 \multimap \cdots \multimap p_n \multimap p \ll p}{\Gamma_1, \ldots, \Gamma_n ; [\Delta_1]_{w_1}, \ldots, [\Delta_n]_{w_n} ; \forall \vec{x}.\ p_1 \multimap \cdots \multimap p_n \multimap p \ll p} \text{ } \forall L}{\Gamma_1, \ldots, \Gamma_n ; [\Delta_1]_{w_1} \times \cdots \times [\Delta_n]_{w_n} \longrightarrow p} \text{ delete}} \text{ } \multimap L}$$

In other words, the derived rule is

$$\frac{\Gamma_1 ; \Delta_1 \longrightarrow p_1 \quad \cdots \quad \Gamma_n ; [\Delta_n]_{w_n} \longrightarrow p_n}{\Gamma_1, \ldots, \Gamma_n ; [\Delta_1]_{w_1} \times \cdots \times [\Delta_n]_{w_n} \longrightarrow p}$$

In the case where $n = 0$, i.e., the clause in the Horn theory was a unit clause p, we obtain an initial sequent of the form $\cdot ; [\cdot]_0 \longrightarrow p$. As this clause has an empty left hand side, and none of the derived rules add elements to the left, we can make an immediate observation (lem.5) that gives us an isomorphism of rules (thm.6).

Lemma 5. *Every sequent generated in the proof of the goal $(\Psi)^o ; [\cdot]_0 \longrightarrow g$ has an empty left hand side.* □

---

[2] Queries with more general goals can be compiled to this form by adding an extra clause to the theory from the desired goal to a fresh ground goal literal.

Theorem 6 (isomorphism of rules). *Every hyperresolution rule for the query $\Psi \vdash g$ is isomorphic to an instance of a derived rule for the overall goal sequent $(\Psi)^0$; $[\cdot]_0 \longrightarrow g$ with empty left-hand sides.* □

These facts let us establish an isomorphism between hyperresolution and right-biased focused derivations.

Theorem 7. *Every hyperresolution derivation for the Horn query $\Psi \vdash g$ has an isomorphic focused derivation for the goal sequent $(\Psi)^o$; $[\cdot]_0 \longrightarrow g$ with right-biased atoms.*

Proof (Sketch). For every fact p' generated by the hyperresolution strategy, we have a corresponding fact $\cdot$; $[\cdot]_0 \longrightarrow p'$ in the focused derivation (up to a renaming of the free variables). When matching these sequents for consideration as input for a derived rule corresponding to the Horn clause $\neg p_1, \ldots, \neg p_n, p$, we calculate the simultaneous mgu of all the p_i and p'_i for a Horn clause, which is precisely the operation also performed in the hyperresolution rule. The required isomorphism then follows from thm. 6.   □

4.2 SLD Resolution

SLD Resolution [11] is a variant of linear resolution that is complete for Horn theories. For the Horn query $\Psi \vdash g$, we start with just the initial clause g, and then perform forward search using the following rule (using Ξ to stand for a clauses).

$$\frac{\Xi, q}{\theta(\Xi, p_1, p_2, \ldots, p_n)} \quad \begin{cases} \text{where } \neg p_1, \ldots, \neg p_n, p \in \Psi; \rho \text{ is a renaming subst; and} \\ \theta = \mathrm{mgu}(\rho p, q) \end{cases}$$

The composition of a clause is thus a contraction-free collection of atoms. When $n = 0$, i.e., for unit clauses in the Horn theory, this rule corresponds to simply deleting the member of the input clause that was unifiable with the unit clause. The search procedure succeeds when it is able to derive the empty clause.

To show how SLD resolution is modeled by our focusing system, we reuse the translation from before, but this time all atoms are given a left bias. The derivation that corresponds to focusing on the translation of the Horn clause $\neg p_1, \ldots, \neg p_n, p$ is:

$$\frac{\cfrac{}{\cdot; p_1 \gg p_1} \text{ linit} \quad \cdots \quad \cfrac{}{\cdot; p_n \gg p_n} \text{ linit} \quad \cfrac{\cfrac{\cfrac{\Gamma; [\Delta]_w, p \longrightarrow Q}{\Gamma; [\Delta]_w ; p \longrightarrow \cdot; Q}}{\Gamma; [\Delta]_w ; p \ll \cdot; Q}}{} \ {-\!\!\circ L}}{\cfrac{\Gamma; [\Delta]_w, p_1, \ldots, p_n ; p_1 -\!\!\circ \cdots p_n -\!\!\circ p \ll \cdot; Q}{\Gamma; [\Delta]_w, p_1, \ldots, p_n \Longrightarrow Q} \text{ delete}}$$

In other words, the derived rule is:

$$\frac{\Gamma; [\Delta, p]_w \longrightarrow Q}{\Gamma; [\Delta, p_1, \ldots, p_n]_w \longrightarrow Q}$$

The frontier of the goal $(\Psi)^0$; $[\cdot]_0 \longrightarrow g$ in the left-biased setting contains every member of $(\Psi)^0$, so we obtain one such derived rule for each clause in the Horn theory. The frontier contains, in addition, the positive atom g; assuming there is a negative instance of g somewhere in the theory, we will thus generate a single initial sequent, $\cdot$; $[g]_0 \longrightarrow g$. We immediately observe that:

Lemma 8. *Every sequent generated in the focused derivation of* $(\Psi)^0$ *;* $[\cdot]_0 \longrightarrow g$ *is of the form* $\cdot$ *;* $[\Delta]_0 \longrightarrow g$. $\qquad\square$

Theorem 9 (isomorphism of rules). *Every SLD resolution rule for the Horn query* $\Psi \vdash g$ *is isomorphic to an instance of a derived inference rule for the overall goal sequent* $(\Psi)^0$ *;* $[\cdot]_0 \longrightarrow g$ *with empty unrestricted zones and g on the right.* $\qquad\square$

As should be clear, the interpretation of a clause Ξ is the linear zone of the forward sequent, which also does not admit contraction.

Theorem 10. *Every SLD resolution derivation for the Horn query* $\Psi \vdash g$ *has an isomorphic focused derivation for the goal sequent* $(\Psi)^0$ *;* $[\cdot]_0 \longrightarrow g$ *with left-biased atoms.*

Proof (Sketch). Very similar argument as thm. 7, except we note that in the matching conditions in the derived rules we rename the input sequents, whereas in the SLD resolution case we rename the Horn clause itself. However, this renaming is merely an artifact of the procedure and does not itself alter the derivation. $\qquad\square$

Although the derivations are isomorphic, the focused derivations may not be as efficient as the SLD resolution in practice because of the need to rename (i.e., copy) the premises as part of the matching conditions of a derived rule– premises might contain many more components than the Horn clause itself.

5 Experiments

5.1 Propositional Linear Logic

The first class of experiments we performed were on propositional linear logic. We implemented several minor variants of an inverse method prover for propositional linear logic. The propositional fragment is the only fragment where we can compare with external provers, as we are not aware of any first order linear logic provers besides our own. The external prover we compared against is Tammet's Gandalf "nonclassical" distribution (version 0.2), compiled using a packaged version of the Hobbit Scheme compiler. This classical linear logic prover comes in two flavors: resolution (**Gr**) and tableau (**Gt**). Neither version incorporates focusing or globalization, and we did not attempt to bound the search for either prover. Other provers such as LinTAP [13] and llprover [17] fail to prove all but the simplest problems, so we did not do any serious comparisons against them. Our experiments were all run on a 3.4GHz Pentium 4 machine with 1MB L1 cache and 1GB main memory; our provers were compiled using MLTon version 20060213 using the default optimization flags; all times indicated are wall-clock times in seconds and includes the GC time; × denotes unprovability within a time limit of 1 hour. In the following tables, iters refers to number of iterations of the lazy OTTER loop, gen the number of generated sequents, and subs the number of subsumed sequents.

Stateful system encodings. In these examples, we encoded the state transition rules for stateful systems such as a change machine, a Blocks World problem with a fixed number of blocks, a few sample Petri nets. For the Blocks World example, we also compared a version that uses the CLF monad [3] and one without.

name	right-biased				left-biased				Gt time	Gr time
	iters	gen	subs	time	iters	gen	subs	time		
blocks	20	43	18	0.001	12	84	61	0.001	×	×
blocks-clf	27	65	26	0.002	5	24	7	<**0.001**	N/A	N/A
change	16	22	7	0.001	11	20	6	0.001	0.63	0.31
petri-1	23	38	23	**0.001**	284	1099	921	0.062	×	7.08
petri-2	57	133	105	**0.003**	393	1654	1433	0.068	×	7.13

Graph exploration algorithms. In these examples we encode the algorithm for exploring graph for calculating Euler or Hamiltonian tours. The problems have an equal balance of proofs (i.e., a tour exists) and refutations (i.e., no tour exists).

name	right-biased				left-biased			
	iters	gen	subs	time	iters	gen	subs	time
euler-1	6291	11853	5565	9.010	6291	11853	5565	**8.570**
euler-2	15640	34329	18689	152.12	15640	34329	18689	**145.9**
euler-3	64360	159194	94834	3043.35	64360	159194	94834	**2938.55**
hamilton	708	911	185	0.11	165	178	0	<**0.001**

The Euler tour computation uses a symmetric algorithm, so both backward and forward chaining generate the same facts, though, interestingly, a left-biased search performs slightly better than the right-biased system. For the Hamiltonian tour examples, the left-biased search is vastly superior.

Affine logic encoding. Linearity is often too stringent a requirement for situations where we simply need *affine* logic, i.e., where every hypothesis is consumed *at most* once. Affine logic can be embedded into linear logic by translating every affine arrow $A \to B$ as either $A \multimap B \otimes \top$ or $A \& 1 \multimap B$. Of course, one might select complex encodings; for example choosing $A \& !(0 \multimap X) \multimap B$ (for some arbitrary fresh proposition X) instead of $A \& 1 \multimap B$. Even though the two translations are equivalent, the prover performs poorly on the former. The Gandalf provers **Gt** and **Gr** fail on these examples.

encoding	right-biased				left-biased			
	iters	gen	subs	time	iters	gen	subs	time
$A \multimap B \otimes \top$	38	108	73	0.003	34	107	73	**0.002**
$A \& 1 \multimap B$	252	1103	828	0.098	62	229	126	**0.019**
$A \& !(0 \multimap X) \multimap B$	264	7099	6793	2.028	235	841	578	**0.042**

Quantified Boolean formulas. In these examples we used two variants of the algorithm from [12] for encoding QBFs in linear logic. The first variant uses exponentials to encode reusable "copy" rules; this variant performs very well in practice, so the table below collates the results of all the example QBFs in one entry. The second variant maps to the multiplicative-additive fragment of linear logic without exponentials. This variant produces problems that are considerably harder, so we have divided the problems in three sets in increasing order of complexity.

encodings	right-biased				left-biased			
	iters	gen	subs	time	iters	gen	subs	time
qbf-exp	1508	1722	140	**0.13**	7948	17610	9590	2.69
qbf-nonexp-1	1457	5590	4067	**0.54**	1581	4352	2612	0.58
qbf-nonexp-2	15267	517551	502174	368.92	9469	49777	37716	**29.55**
qbf-nonexp-3	28556	990196	961494	2807.64	21233	89542	115917	**308.24**

For these examples, when the number of iterations is low (i.e., the problems are simple), the right-biased search appears to perform better than the left-biased system. However, as the problems get harder, the left-biased system becomes dominant.

5.2   First-Order Linear Logic

We have also implemented a first-order prover for linear logic. Experiments with an early version of the first-order were documented in [4]. Since then we have made several improvements to the prover, including a complete reimplmentation of the focused rule generation engine, and also increased our collection of sample problems.

First-order stateful systems. The first experiments were with first-order encodings of various stateful systems. We selected a first-order Blocks World encoding (both with and without the CLF monad), Dijkstra's Urn Game, and an AI planning problem for a certain board game. The left-biased system performs consistently better than the right-biased system for these problems.

problem	right-biased				left-biased			
	iters	gen	subs	time	iters	gen	subs	time
blocks	45	424	317	0.12	26	387	337	**0.04**
blocks-clf	64	697	412	0.264	15	81	69	**0.006**
urn	29	72	27	0.24	13	58	55	**0.11**
board	349	7021	3138	3.26	166	5296	1752	**0.88**

Purely intuitionistic problems. Unfortunately, we are unable to compare our implementation with any other linear provers; to the best of our knowledge, our prover is the only first-order linear prover in existence. We therefore ran our prover on some problems drawn from the SICS benchmark [15]. These intuitionistic problems were translated into linear logic in two different ways– the first uses Girard's original encoding of classical logic in classical linear logic where every subformula is affixed with the exponential, and the second is a focus-preserving encoding as described in [5]. We also compared our prover with *Sandstorm*, a focusing inverse method theorem prover for intuitionistic logic implemented by students at CMU. The focus-preserving translation is always better than the Girard-translation; however, the complexity of linear logic, particularly the significant complexity of linear contraction, makes it uncompetitive with the intuitionistic prover.

problem	right-biased				left-biased				SS
	iters	gen	subs	time	iters	gen	subs	time	time
SICS1-gir	360	1948	1394	1.312	368	2897	2181	0.6	0.04
SICS1-foc	56	365	313	0.056	64	496	415	0.04	
SICS2-gir	3035	16391	11732	11.04	3460	27192	20389	5.856	0.06
SICS2-foc	489	3133	2688	0.472	616	4672	3902	0.376	
SICS3-gir	20958	1131823	810085	762.312	12924	1015552	761517	218.712	1.12
SICS3-foc	3377	21659	18646	33.096	2300	17464	14969	23.296	
SICS4 gir	×	×	×	×	×	×	×	×	3.89
SICS4-foc	8896	57056	49047	87.184	6144	46818	39993	62.24	

Horn examples from TPTP. For our last example, we selected 20 non-trivial Horn problems from the TPTP version 3.1.1. The selection of problems was not systematic, but we did not constrain our selection to any particular section of the TPTP. We used the translation described in sec. 4. For lack of space we omit the list of selected problems, which can be found from the first author's web-page.[3]

right-biased				left-biased			
iters	gen	subs	time	iters	gen	subs	time
4911	314640	287004	**462.859**	6289	704482	526207	638.818

For Horn problems, the right-biased system, which models hyperresolution, performs better than the left-biased system, which models SLD resolution. This observation is not unprecedented— the Gandalf system switches to a Hyperresolution strategy for Horn theories [16]. The likely reason is that in the left-biased system, unlike in SLD resolution system, the derived rule renames the input sequent rather than the rule itself.

6   Conclusion

We have presented an improvement of the focusing inverse method that exploits the flexibility in assigning polarity to atoms which we call bias. This strictly generalizes both hyperresolution and SLD resolution on (classical) Horn clauses to all of intuitionistic linear logic. This strategy shows significant improvement on a number of example problems. Among the future work will be to explore strategies for determining appropriate bias for atoms from the problem statement to optimize overall search behavior.

References

1. Jean-Marc Andreoli. Logic programming with focusing proofs in linear logic. *Journal of Logic and Computation*, 2(3):297–347, 1992.
2. Jean-Marc Andreoli. Focussing and proof construction. *Annals of Pure and Applied Logic*, 107:131–163, 2001.
3. Iliano Cervesato, Frank Pfenning, David Walker, and Kevin Watkins. A concurrent logical framework I & II. Technical Report CMU-CS-02-101 and 102, Department of Computer Science, Carnegie Mellon University, 2002. Revised May 2003.

---

[3] http://www.cs.cmu.edu/~kaustuv/papers/ijcar06

4. Kaustuv Chaudhuri and Frank Pfenning. A focusing inverse method theorem prover for first-order linear logic. In *Proceedings of CADE-20*, pages 69–83, Tallinn, Estonia, July 2005. Springer-Verlag LNAI-3632.
5. Kaustuv Chaudhuri and Frank Pfenning. Focusing the inverse method for linear logic. In Luke Ong, editor, *Proceedings of CSL 2005*, pages 200–215, Oxford, UK, August 2005. Springer-Verlag LNCS-3634.
6. Anatoli Degtyarev and Andrei Voronkov. The inverse method. In James Alan Robinson and Andrei Voronkov, editors, *Handbook of Automated Reasoning*, pages 179–272. MIT Press, September 2001.
7. Gerhard Gentzen. Untersuchungen über das logische Schließen. *Mathematische Zeitschrift*, 39:176–210, 405–431, 1935. English translation in M. E. Szabo, editor, *The Collected Papers of Gerhard Gentzen*, pages 68–131, North-Holland, 1969.
8. Jean-Yves Girard. Locus solum: from the rules of logic to the logic of rules. *Mathematical Structures in Computer Science*, 11:301–506, 2001.
9. Joshua S. Hodas and Dale Miller. Logic programming in a fragment of intuitionistic linear logic. *Information and Computation*, 110(2):327–365, 1994.
10. Jacob M. Howe. *Proof Search Issues in Some Non-Classical Logics*. PhD thesis, University of St. Andrews, September 1998.
11. R. Kowalski and D. Kuehner. Linear resolution with selection function. *Artificial Intelligence*, 2:227–260, 1971.
12. Patrick Lincoln, J. C. Mitchell, Andre Scedrov, and Natarajan Shankar. Decision problems for propositional linear logic. *Annals of Pure and Applied Logic*, 56:239–311, 1992.
13. Heiko Mantel and Jens Otten. LinTAP: A tableau prover for linear logic. In A. Murray, editor, *International Conference TABLEAUX'99*, pages 217–231, New York, June 1999. Springer-Verlag LNAI 1617.
14. D. Miller. A multiple-conclusion meta-logic. In S. Abramsky, editor, *Ninth Annual Symposium on Logic in Computer Science*, pages 272–281, Paris, France, July 1994. IEEE Computer Society Press.
15. Dan Sahlin, Torkel Franzén, and Seif Haridi. An intuitionistic predicate logic theorem prover. *Journal of Logic and Computation*, 2(5):619–656, 1992.
16. Tanel Tammet. Resolution, inverse method and the sequent calculus. In *Proceedings of KGC'97*, pages 65–83. Springer-Verlag LNCS 1289, 1997.
17. Naoyuki Tamura. Llprover. At: `http://bach.istc.kobe-u.ac.jp/llprover`.

Connection Tableaux with Lazy Paramodulation

Andrei Paskevich

Université Paris 12, Laboratoire d'Algorithmique,
Complexité et Logique, 94010 Créteil Cedex, France
andrei@capet.iut-fbleau.fr

Abstract. It is well-known that the connection refinement of clause tableaux with paramodulation is incomplete (even with weak connections). In this paper, we present a new connection tableau calculus for logic with equality. This calculus is based on a lazy form of paramodulation where parts of the unification step become auxiliary subgoals in a tableau and may be subjected to subsequent paramodulations. Our calculus uses ordering constraints and a certain form of the basicness restriction.

1 Introduction

The Model Elimination proof procedure was originally introduced by Loveland as a resolution-based calculus with clauses of a special form [1]. Later it was reconsidered as a clause tableau calculus, where proof search is guided by connections between clauses [2]. In this form, the method is also referred to as *connection tableaux*.

Connection tableaux are a powerful goal-directed refinement of general clause tableaux. Moreover, strong search pruning methods and efficient implementation techniques were developed for this calculus [3].

It is tempting to adapt connection tableaux for logic with equality by introducing paramodulation. That is, we could make a pair (equality to paramodulate by, literal to paramodulate in) constitute a connection, too, and add rules for paramodulation in a branch. Unfortunately, such a calculus turns out to be incomplete. Consider the following set of clauses: $\{a \approx b, \ c \approx d, \ \neg P(f(a), f(b)), \ \neg Q(g(c), g(d)), \ P(x,x) \vee Q(y,y)\}$. Let us try to build a refutation of S in that hypothetical calculus:

$$
\begin{array}{cc}
\dfrac{a \approx b}{\dfrac{\neg P(f(a), f(b))}{\neg P(f(b), f(b))}} &
\dfrac{\neg Q(g(c), g(d))}{\dfrac{c \approx d}{\neg Q(g(d), g(d))}}
\end{array}
$$

$$
\begin{array}{cccc}
P(x,x) & Q(y,y) & P(x,x) & Q(y,y) \\
\hline
\bot \cdot (x = f(b)) & ? & ? & \bot \cdot (y = g(d))
\end{array}
$$

We cannot continue the first inference because the literal $Q(y,y)$ does not match $Q(g(c), g(d))$ and the equality $c \approx d$ cannot be applied to $Q(y,y)$, either. The second inference will fail in a similar way.

U. Furbach and N. Shankar (Eds.): IJCAR 2006, LNAI 4130, pp. 112–124, 2006.

The fact that paramodulation works fine in resolution-style calculi [4] and general clause tableaux [5,6] is due to a flexible order of inferences which is impossible in a goal-directed calculus. The calculus could be made complete if we allow paramodulation into variables and add the axioms of *functional reflexivity* ($f(x) \approx f(x)$, $g(x) \approx g(x)$, etc) in order to construct new terms [7]. However, this approach is quite inefficient in practice, since functional reflexivity allows us to substitute an arbitrary term for any variable.

In order to solve problems with equality, existing competitive connection tableau provers [8] employ various forms of Brand's modification method [9,10,11]. This method transforms a clause set with equality into an equiconsistent set where the equality predicate does not occur. In addition, a complete procedure was developed upon a combination of goal-directed proof search in tableaux and a bottom-up equality saturation using basic ordered paramodulation [12].

In this paper we propose an alternative approach for equality handling in connection tableaux which is based on *lazy paramodulation*. This technique was originally introduced by J. Gallier and W. Snyder as a method for general E-unification [13] and used later to overcome incompleteness of the set-of-support strategy (another example of a goal-directed method) in the classical paramodulation calculus [14].

So, what is lazy paramodulation? Above, we noted that the literal $Q(y, y)$ cannot be unified with $Q(g(c), g(d))$. But let us postpone unification until the equality $c \approx d$ is applied to the second literal. Let us make the equality $Q(y, y) = Q(g(c), g(d))$ not a constraint to solve but an additional subgoal to prove. The clause set from the previous counter-example can be easily refuted in such a calculus:

$$
\begin{array}{cc}
\dfrac{P(x,x)}{\neg P(f(a), f(b))} & \dfrac{Q(y,y)}{\neg Q(g(c), g(d))}
\end{array}
$$

$$
\dfrac{f(a) \not\approx x \qquad f(b) \not\approx x}{\qquad} \qquad \dfrac{g(c) \not\approx y \qquad g(d) \not\approx y}{\qquad}
$$

$$
\dfrac{a \approx b}{f(b) \not\approx x} \quad \bot \cdot (f(b) = x) \qquad \dfrac{c \approx d}{g(d) \not\approx y} \quad \bot \cdot (g(d) = y)
$$

$$
\dfrac{}{\bot \cdot (f(b) = x)} \quad \dfrac{a \not\approx a}{\bot} \qquad \dfrac{}{\bot \cdot (g(d) = y)} \quad \dfrac{c \not\approx c}{\bot}
$$

Though the approach seems to work, an unrestricted procedure will be no better than the use of functional reflexivity. Indeed, if we postpone any unification, we can apply any equality to any non-variable term. Can we refine the method? Would it be complete? In what follows, we give positive answers to these questions.

The paper is organized as follows. The next section contains preliminary material. In Section 3 we explain the method of constrained equality elimination [11] in a form adapted for the completeness proof in the next section. A refined version of connection tableaux with lazy paramodulation is introduced and its completeness is proved in Section 4. We conclude with a brief summary and plans for future work.

2 Preliminaries

We work in first-order logic with equality in clausal form. A *clause* is a disjunction of literals; a *literal* is either an atomic formula or the negation of an atomic formula. We consider clauses as unordered multisets.

The equality predicate is denoted by the symbol $\approx$. We abbreviate the negation $\neg(s \approx t)$ as $s \not\approx t$. Negated equalities will be called *disequalities* to be distinguished from inequalities used in constraints (see below). We consider equalities as unordered pairs of terms, i.e. $a \approx b$ and $b \approx a$ stand for the same formula.

The symbol $\simeq$ will denote "pseudoequality", a binary predicate without any specific semantics. We use it to replace the symbol $\approx$ when we pass to logic without equality. The order of arguments becomes significant here: $a \simeq b$ and $b \simeq a$ denote different formulas. The expression $s \not\simeq t$ stands for $\neg(s \simeq t)$.

In what follows, we denote non-variable terms by the letters p and q, and arbitrary terms with the letters l, r, s, and t. Substitutions are denoted by the letters σ and τ. The result of applying a substitution σ to an expression (term, literal, or clause) E is denoted by $E\sigma$. We write $E[s]$ to indicate that s is a subterm of E and write $E[t]$ to denote the expression obtained from E by replacing one occurrence of s by t. Letters in bold ($\boldsymbol{s}$, $\boldsymbol{x}$, etc) stand for sequences of terms and variables.

We use *constraints* as defined in [11]. A *constraint* is a, possibly empty, conjunction of *atomic constraints* $s = t$ or $s \succ t$ or $s \succeq t$. The letters γ and δ are used to denote constraints; the symbol $\top$ denotes the empty conjunction. A compound constraint $(a = b \wedge b \succ c)$ can be written in an abbreviated form $(a = b \succ c)$. An equality constraint $(\boldsymbol{s} = \boldsymbol{t})$ stands for $(s_1 = t_1 \wedge \cdots \wedge s_n = t_n)$.

A substitution σ *solves* an atomic constraint $s = t$ if the terms $s\sigma$ and $t\sigma$ are syntactically identical. It is a solution of an atomic constraint $s \succ t$ ($s \succeq t$) if $s\sigma > t\sigma$ ($s\sigma \geqslant t\sigma$, respectively) with respect to some reduction ordering $>$ that is total on ground terms. We say that σ is a solution of a general constraint γ if it solves all atomic constraints in γ; γ is called *satisfiable* whenever it has a solution.

A *constrained clause tableau* is a finite tree $\mathbb{T}$. The root node of $\mathbb{T}$ contains the initial set of clauses to be refuted. The non-root nodes are pairs $L \cdot \gamma$ where L is a literal and γ is a constraint.

Any branch that contains the literal $\bot$ (denoting the propositional *falsum*) is considered as *closed*. A tableau is *closed*, whenever each branch in it is closed and the overall set of constraints in it is satisfiable.

An inference starts from the single root node (the initial clause set). Each inference step expands some branch in the tableau by adding new leaves under the leaf of the branch in question. Symbolically, we describe an inference rule as follows:

$$\frac{\mathcal{S} \parallel \Gamma}{L_1 \cdot \gamma_1 \quad \cdots \quad L_n \cdot \gamma_n}$$

where $\mathcal{S}$ is the initial set of clauses (the root node), Γ is the branch being expanded (with constraints not mentioned), and $(L_1 \cdot \gamma_1), \ldots, (L_n \cdot \gamma_n)$ are the added nodes (empty constraints will be omitted). Whenever we choose some

---

Start rule:

$$\mathcal{S}, (L_1 \vee \cdots \vee L_k) \parallel$$
$$\overline{\rule{0pt}{0pt}}$$
$$L_1 \quad \cdots \quad L_k$$

Expansion rules:

$$\frac{\mathcal{S}, (\neg P(s) \vee L_1 \vee \cdots \vee L_k) \parallel \Gamma, P(r)}{\bot \cdot (s = r) \quad L_1 \quad \cdots \quad L_k} \qquad \frac{\mathcal{S}, (P(s) \vee L_1 \vee \cdots \vee L_k) \parallel \Gamma, \neg P(r)}{\bot \cdot (s = r) \quad L_1 \quad \cdots \quad L_k}$$

Termination rules:

$$\frac{\mathcal{S} \parallel \Gamma, \neg P(s), \Delta, P(r)}{\bot \cdot (s - r)} \qquad \frac{\mathcal{S} \parallel \Gamma, P(s), \Delta, \neg P(r)}{\bot \cdot (s = r)}$$

Fig. 1. Connection tableaux **CT**

clause C in $\mathcal{S}$ to participate in the inference, we implicitly rename all variables in C to some fresh variables.

A closed tableau built from the initial set $\mathcal{S}$ will be called a *refutation* of $\mathcal{S}$.

In order to illustrate the proposed notation, we present the classical connection tableau calculus (denoted by **CT**) in Figure 1.

This calculus is sound and complete in first-order logic without equality [3]:

Proposition 1. *An equality-free set of clauses $\mathcal{S}$ is unsatisfiable if and only if $\mathcal{S}$ can be expanded to a closed **CT**-tableau. Moreover, if $\mathcal{S}$ is unsatisfiable but any proper subset of $\mathcal{S}$ is consistent, then for any $C \in \mathcal{S}$, there is a **CT**-refutation of $\mathcal{S}$ that starts with C.*

3 Constrained Equality Elimination

Constrained equality elimination (CEE) was proposed by L. Bachmair et al. in [11]. This is a variation of Brand's modification method improved by the use of ordering constraints. Here, we describe CEE-transformation in a slightly modified form as compared with the original explanation in [11]. First, we allow non-equality predicate symbols. Second, we require any two different occurrences of a non-variable subterm to be abstracted separately, introducing two different fresh variables during monotonicity elimination (*flattening*). Third, we apply the monotonicity elimination rules after symmetry elimination. Fourth, we work with traditional clauses and incorporate the ordering constraints into the inference rules. Fifth, we handle occurrences of negated variable equality $x \not\approx y$ in a different way. These modifications are minor and do not affect the main result (Proposition 2).

The four groups of rewriting rules in Figure 2 are applied in the order of their appearance to clauses from the initial set $\mathcal{S}$. Let us denote the intermediate result of transformation after the i-th group by $CEE^i(\mathcal{S})$. Variables with caret are considered to be new in the corresponding clause. Recall that p and q stand for non-variable terms, whereas l, r, s, and t denote arbitrary terms.

1. Elimination of symmetry:

$$\frac{s \approx t \lor C}{s \simeq t \lor C \qquad t \simeq s \lor C} \qquad \frac{p \not\approx s \lor C}{p \not\simeq s \lor C} \qquad \frac{x \not\approx q \lor C}{q \not\simeq x \lor C}$$

2. Elimination of monotonicity:

$$\frac{P(s_1, p, s_2) \lor C}{P(s_1, \hat{u}, s_2) \lor p \not\simeq \hat{u} \lor C} \qquad \frac{\neg P(s_1, p, s_2) \lor C}{\neg P(s_1, \hat{u}, s_2) \lor p \not\simeq \hat{u} \lor C}$$

$$\frac{f(s_1, p, s_2) \simeq t \lor C}{f(s_1, \hat{u}, s_2) \simeq t \lor p \not\simeq \hat{u} \lor C} \qquad \frac{f(s_1, p, s_2) \not\simeq t \lor C}{f(s_1, \hat{u}, s_2) \not\simeq t \lor p \not\simeq \hat{u} \lor C}$$

$$\frac{t \simeq f(s_1, p, s_2) \lor C}{t \simeq f(s_1, \hat{u}, s_2) \lor p \not\simeq \hat{u} \lor C} \qquad \frac{t \not\simeq f(s_1, p, s_2) \lor C}{t \not\simeq f(s_1, \hat{u}, s_2) \lor p \not\simeq \hat{u} \lor C}$$

3. Elimination of transitivity:

$$\frac{t \simeq q \lor C}{t \simeq \hat{u} \lor q \not\simeq \hat{u} \lor C} \qquad \frac{p \not\simeq q \lor C}{p \not\simeq \hat{u} \lor q \not\simeq \hat{u} \lor C}$$

4. Introduction of reflexivity:

$$\frac{}{z \simeq z}$$

Fig. 2. Constrained equality elimination

The first group replaces the equality symbol $\approx$ with the non-logical predicate symbol $\simeq$ and eliminates the need for explicit symmetry axioms for $\simeq$. The second group flattens the terms, thus eliminating the need for explicit monotonicity axioms for $\simeq$. The third group splits equality literals, thus eliminating the need for explicit transitivity axioms for $\simeq$. The last rule explicitly adds the reflexivity axiom to the clause set.

In the resulting set of clauses $\text{CEE}(\mathcal{S})$ $(= \text{CEE}^4(\mathcal{S}))$, resolutions correspond to paramodulations in the initial set. The introduced variables are, in some sense, "values" of the terms on the left hand side of new disequalities. By "value" we mean the result of all paramodulations into and under the term.

Now, we assign an atomic constraint $p \succeq s$ to each negative literal $p \not\simeq s$ that occurs in $\text{CEE}(\mathcal{S})$. We assign a constraint $x = y$ to each negative literal $x \not\simeq y$ in $\text{CEE}(\mathcal{S})$. We assign a constraint $s \succ t$ to each positive literal $s \simeq t$ in $\text{CEE}(\mathcal{S})$, except for the reflexivity axiom $z \simeq z$ which does not acquire any constraint. A *constrained ground instance* of a clause C from $\text{CEE}(\mathcal{S})$ is any ground clause $C\sigma$ such that the substitution σ is a solution of all atomic ordering constraints assigned for equalities and disequalities in C.

The following proposition is a counterpart of Theorem 4.1 from [11].

Proposition 2. *A clause set $\mathcal{S}$ is satisfiable if and only if the set of all constrained ground instances of clauses from $\text{CEE}(\mathcal{S})$ is satisfiable.*

In the Start and Expansion rules, the chosen clause is not $(z \simeq z)$

Start rule:	Reduction rule:
$$\frac{\mathcal{S}, (L_1 \vee \cdots \vee L_k) \parallel}{L_1 \quad \cdots \quad L_k}$$	$$\frac{\mathcal{S}, (z \simeq z) \parallel \Gamma, s \not\simeq t}{\bot \cdot (s = t)}$$

Expansion rules:

$$\frac{\mathcal{S}, (\neg P(s) \vee L_1 \vee \cdots \vee L_k) \parallel \Gamma, P(r)}{\bot \cdot (s = r) \quad L_1 \quad \cdots \quad L_k} \qquad \frac{\mathcal{S}, (P(s) \vee L_1 \vee \cdots \vee L_k) \parallel \Gamma, \neg P(r)}{\bot \cdot (s = r) \quad L_1 \quad \cdots \quad L_k}$$

$$\frac{\mathcal{S}, (p \not\simeq t \vee L_1 \vee \cdots \vee L_k) \parallel \Gamma, l \simeq r}{\bot \cdot (p = l \succ r = t) \quad L_1 \quad \cdots \quad L_k} \qquad \frac{\mathcal{S}, (l \simeq r \vee L_1 \vee \cdots \vee L_k) \parallel \Gamma, p \not\simeq t}{\bot \cdot (p = l \succ r = t) \quad L_1 \quad \cdots \quad L_k}$$

Termination rules:

$$\frac{\mathcal{S} \parallel \Gamma, \neg P(s), \Delta, P(r)}{\bot \cdot (s = r)} \qquad\qquad \frac{\mathcal{S} \parallel \Gamma, P(s), \Delta, \neg P(r)}{\bot \cdot (s = r)}$$

$$\frac{\mathcal{S} \parallel \Gamma, p \not\simeq t, \Delta, l \simeq r}{\bot \cdot (p = l \succ r = t)} \qquad\qquad \frac{\mathcal{S} \parallel \Gamma, l \simeq r, \Delta, p \not\simeq t}{\bot \cdot (p = l \succ r = t)}$$

Fig. 3. Connection tableaux for CEE-clauses ($\mathbf{CT}^{\simeq}$)

Consider the calculus $\mathbf{CT}^{\simeq}$ in Figure 3. In essence, it is just an extension of $\mathbf{CT}$ with ordering constraints for equality literals.

Proposition 3. *A clause set $\mathcal{S}$ is unsatisfiable if and only if the set* CEE($\mathcal{S}$) *can be refuted in the* $\mathbf{CT}^{\simeq}$ *calculus.*

Proof. We give just an outline of the proof, since the details are quite obvious. First, let us show the soundness of $\mathbf{CT}^{\simeq}$ with respect to CEE-transformed clause sets. Consider a closed $\mathbf{CT}^{\simeq}$-tableau $\mathbb{T}$ refuting the set CEE($\mathcal{S}$).

The substitution that solves the overall set of constraints from $\mathbb{T}$, can be completed to a ground substitution, giving us a set of ground instances of clauses from CEE($\mathcal{S}$). This set is unsatisfiable since we can transform $\mathbb{T}$ to a well-formed $\mathbf{CT}$-refutation by erasing ordering constraints.

It is easy to see that these ground instances are valid constrained ground instances mentioned in Proposition 2. Indeed, each positive equality literal $(l \simeq r)$ (except the reflexivity axiom) that takes part in the inference acquires the corresponding strict inequality constraint $(l \succ r)$ during an expansion or a termination step. Each disequality $(s \not\simeq t)$ is either reduced with the help of the reflexivity axiom or resolved with some positive equality literal. In both cases, the constraint $(s \succeq t)$ will be satisfied. A disequality $(x \not\simeq y)$ can only be reduced by reflexivity, so that the constraint $(x = y)$ will be satisfied, too.

Let us prove the completeness of $\mathbf{CT}^{\simeq}$ with respect to CEE-transformed clause sets. Consider the set S of all constrained ground instances of clauses from CEE(S). By Proposition 2, S is unsatisfiable, therefore we can build a **CT**-refutation of S that does not start with the reflexivity axiom ($z \simeq z$). Then we simply lift the inference to the first order and transform that **CT**-tableau into a **CT$^\simeq$**-refutation of CEE(S).   □

4   Connection Tableaux with Lazy Paramodulation

Now we present a refined version of the calculus sketched in the introduction. The inference rules of the calculus **LPCT** are given in Figure 1. The variables with bar are considered to be fresh in the tableau.

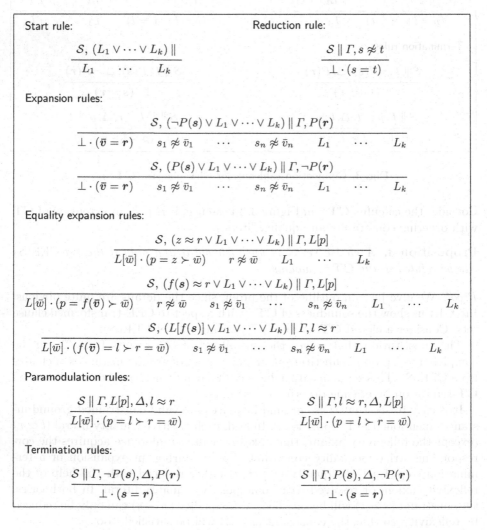

Fig. 4. Connection tableaux with lazy paramodulation **LPCT**

The proposed calculus contains several improvements in comparison with what was sketched at the beginning of the paper. First of all, we use lazy paramodulation only in expansion steps; paramodulation and termination steps do not postpone unification. Second, the "laziness" itself is more restricted now: any two non-variable terms whose unification is postponed should have the same functional symbol at the top. Third, we use ordering constraints. Fourth, we use basic paramodulation.

It should be noted that there are two different forms of the basicness restriction. The first one forbids paramodulation into terms introduced by instantiation. The corresponding refinement of lazy paramodulation was described by M. Moser [15]. This restriction is fully adopted in **LPCT**, since we work with constrained literals and do not apply substitutions in the course of inference.

The second, stronger form additionally prevents paramodulation into terms introduced by the earlier paramodulation steps [16]. In this form, basicness is used in **LPCT**, too (note the variables with bar), though not everywhere: two of the three equality expansion rules leave the inserted term "on the surface", allowed for subsequent paramodulations.

The soundness of **LPCT** can be shown directly, by checking that inference rules generate only what follows from the initial clause set and the current branch.

We prove completeness of **LPCT** by transforming a $\mathbf{CT}^{\simeq}$-refutation of the set of CEE-rewritten clauses into an **LPCT**-refutation of the initial clause set.

Proposition 4. *For any unsatisfiable clause set S there exists a refutation of S in* **LPCT**.

Proof. We begin by introducing an intermediate calculus $\mathbf{LPCT}^{\simeq}$, whose inference rules are those of **LPCT** with the equality symbol $\approx$ replaced with $\simeq$.

At the first stage we build a closed $\mathbf{CT}^{\simeq}$-tableau refuting the set $\mathrm{CEE}(S)$ (by Proposition 3) and transform it into an $\mathbf{LPCT}^{\simeq}$-refutation $\mathbb{T}$ of $\mathrm{CEE}^3(S)$. In Figure 5, we show how the termination and expansion rules of $\mathbf{CT}^{\simeq}$ can be simulated in $\mathbf{LPCT}^{\simeq}$, so that leaves in open branches and generated constraints stay the same. Recall that every equality or disequality in $\mathrm{CEE}(S)$ has a variable on the right hand side (by definition of CEE).

At the second stage we unflatten the clauses. We will call *suspicious* those variables with caret which were introduced by CEE-transformation. We will call a clause *suspicious* if a suspicious variable occurs in it. We will call an $\mathbf{LPCT}^{\simeq}$-inference step *suspicious* if it is a start step or expansion step or equality expansion step that involves a suspicious initial clause.

Let $S^{(0)}$ be $\mathrm{CEE}^3(S)$ and $\mathbb{T}^{(0)}$ be $\mathbb{T}$. We are going to construct a sequence of clause sets and $\mathbf{LPCT}^{\simeq}$-refutations such that the following statements will hold for every $i > 0$:

- $\mathbb{T}^{(i)}$ is a well-formed refutation of $S^{(i)}$ in $\mathbf{LPCT}^{\simeq}$;
- there are fewer different suspicious variables in $\mathbb{T}^{(i)}$ than in $\mathbb{T}^{(i-1)}$;
- any suspicious variable $\hat{u}$ occurs exactly twice in a clause from $S(i)$: once in a disequality of the form $(p \not\simeq \hat{u})$ and once in some other literal (but never as the left argument of a (dis)-equality);
- any non-suspicious clause in $S^{(i)}$ belongs to $\mathrm{CEE}^1(S)$.

$$\mathbf{CT}^{\simeq}\text{-Termination} \implies \mathbf{LPCT}\text{-Paramodulation:}$$

$$\frac{S \parallel \Gamma, f(\boldsymbol{x}) \not\simeq y, \Delta, l \simeq u}{\bot \cdot (f(\boldsymbol{x}) = l \succ u = y)} \implies \frac{S \parallel \Gamma, f(\boldsymbol{x}) \not\simeq y, \Delta, l \simeq u}{\dfrac{\bar{w} \not\simeq y \cdot (f(\boldsymbol{x}) = l \succ u = \bar{w})}{\bot \cdot (\bar{w} = y)}}$$

$$\mathbf{CT}^{\simeq}\text{-Expansion} \implies \mathbf{LPCT}\text{-Expansion:}$$

$$\frac{S, (\neg P(\boldsymbol{x}) \vee L_1 \vee \cdots \vee L_k) \parallel \Gamma, P(\boldsymbol{y})}{\bot \cdot (\boldsymbol{x} = \boldsymbol{y}) \qquad L_1 \qquad \cdots \qquad L_k} \implies$$

$$\frac{S, (\neg P(\boldsymbol{x}) \vee L_1 \vee \cdots \vee L_k) \parallel \Gamma, P(\boldsymbol{y})}{\dfrac{\bot \cdot (\bar{\boldsymbol{v}} = y)}{} \quad \dfrac{x_1 \not\simeq \bar{v}_1}{\bot \cdot (x_1 = \bar{v}_1)} \quad \cdots \quad \dfrac{x_n \not\simeq \bar{v}_n}{\bot \cdot (x_n = \bar{v}_n)} \quad L_1 \quad \cdots \quad L_k}$$

$$\mathbf{CT}^{\simeq}\text{-Expansion} \implies \mathbf{LPCT}\text{-EqualityExpansion:}$$

$$\frac{S, (f(\boldsymbol{x}) \not\simeq y \vee L_1 \vee \cdots \vee L_k) \parallel \Gamma, l \simeq u}{\bot \cdot (f(\boldsymbol{x}) = l \succ u = y) \qquad L_1 \qquad \cdots \qquad L_k} \implies$$

$$\frac{S, (f(\boldsymbol{x}) \not\simeq y \vee L_1 \vee \cdots \vee L_k) \parallel \Gamma, l \simeq u}{\dfrac{\bar{w} \not\simeq y \cdot (f(\bar{\boldsymbol{v}}) = l \succ u = \bar{w})}{\bot \cdot (\bar{w} = y)} \quad \dfrac{x_1 \not\simeq \bar{v}_1}{\bot \cdot (x_1 = \bar{v}_1)} \quad \cdots \quad \dfrac{x_n \not\simeq \bar{v}_n}{\bot \cdot (x_n = \bar{v}_n)} \quad L_1 \quad \cdots \quad L_k}$$

$$\frac{S, (z \simeq u \vee L_1 \vee \cdots \vee L_k) \parallel \Gamma, f(\boldsymbol{x}) \not\simeq y}{\bot \cdot (f(\boldsymbol{x}) = z \succ u = y) \qquad L_1 \qquad \cdots \qquad L_k} \implies$$

$$\frac{S, (z \simeq u \vee L_1 \vee \cdots \vee L_k) \parallel \Gamma, f(\boldsymbol{x}) \not\simeq y}{\dfrac{\bar{w} \not\simeq y \cdot (f(\boldsymbol{x}) = z \succ \bar{w})}{\bot \cdot (\bar{w} = y)} \quad \dfrac{u \not\simeq \bar{w}}{\bot \cdot (u = \bar{w})} \quad L_1 \quad \cdots \quad L_k}$$

$$\frac{S, (f(z) \simeq u \vee L_1 \vee \cdots \vee L_k) \parallel \Gamma, f(\boldsymbol{x}) \not\simeq y}{\bot \cdot (f(\boldsymbol{x}) = f(z) \succ u = y) \qquad L_1 \qquad \cdots \qquad L_k} \implies$$

$$\frac{S, (f(z) \simeq u \vee L_1 \vee \cdots \vee L_k) \parallel \Gamma, f(\boldsymbol{x}) \not\simeq y}{\dfrac{\bar{w} \not\simeq y \cdot (f(\boldsymbol{x}) = f(\bar{\boldsymbol{v}}) \succ \bar{w})}{\bot \cdot (\bar{w} = y)} \quad \dfrac{u \not\simeq \bar{w}}{\substack{\bot \cdot \\ (u = \bar{w})}} \quad \dfrac{z_1 \not\simeq \bar{v}_1}{\substack{\bot \cdot \\ (z_1 = \bar{v}_1)}} \quad \cdots \quad \dfrac{z_n \not\simeq \bar{v}_n}{\substack{\bot \cdot \\ (z_n = \bar{v}_n)}} \quad L_1 \quad \cdots \quad L_k}$$

Fig. 5. Transforming $\mathbf{CT}^{\simeq}$ to $\mathbf{LPCT}^{\simeq}$

Consider a lowermost suspicious inference I in $\mathbb{T}^{(i-1)}$ (i.e. there are no suspicious steps under that one). Let $\hat{u}$ be a suspicious variable that comes into the tableau with this step. The corresponding suspicious clause is of the form $(L[\hat{u}] \vee p \not\simeq \hat{u} \vee C)$. Let $\mathcal{S}^{(i)}$ be $\mathcal{S}^{(i-1)} \cup \{\, L[p] \vee C \,\}$.

Note that one of these two literals (containing an occurrence of $\hat{u}$) may be an "active literal" in I. This literal will not appear in $\mathbb{T}^{(i-1)}$ in its original form. Nevertheless, we can affirm that $\mathbb{T}^{(i-1)}$ contains two disjoint subtrees, $\mathbb{T}^{\circ}$ and $\mathbb{T}^{\bullet}$, such that the following holds:

- $\mathbb{T}^{\circ}$ and $\mathbb{T}^{\bullet}$ are introduced at the step I;
- $\hat{u}$ does not occur outside of $\mathbb{T}^{\circ}$ and $\mathbb{T}^{\bullet}$;
- the root literal of $\mathbb{T}^{\bullet}$ is of the form $s \not\simeq \hat{u}$ and $\hat{u}$ does not occur in s;
- moreover, $\hat{u}$ occurs in $\mathbb{T}^{\bullet}$ only in disequalities $(t \not\simeq \hat{u})$ and constraints $(t - \hat{u})$ introduced by a reduction step; $\hat{u}$ does not occur in these t (indeed, all we can do with $(t \not\simeq \hat{u})$ is to reduce it or to paramodulate in t);
- $\hat{u}$ occurs exactly once in the root literal of $\mathbb{T}^{\circ}$;
- $\hat{u}$ does not occur in the root node constraint of $\mathbb{T}^{\circ}$.

Let $\mathbb{T}^{\circ}$ have the form:

$$\frac{M[\hat{u}] \cdot \delta}{\mathbb{T}_1 \quad \cdots \quad \mathbb{T}_n}$$

Below, $\mathbb{T}_k[\hat{u} \leftarrow t]$ denotes the tree $\mathbb{T}_k$ where all occurrences of $\hat{u}$ (both in literals and constraints) are replaced with t. It is easy to see that this substitution does not make $\mathbb{T}_k$ ill-formed, provided that $\hat{u}$ and t are equal with respect to the constraints in $\mathbb{T}^{(i-1)}$. A tree transformation $[T]^{\mathbb{T}^{\circ}}$ is defined as follows:

$$\left[\frac{t \not\simeq \hat{u} \cdot \gamma}{\bot \cdot (t = \hat{u})}\right]^{\mathbb{T}^{\circ}} \implies \frac{M[t] \cdot \gamma}{\mathbb{T}_1[\hat{u} \leftarrow t] \quad \cdots \quad \mathbb{T}_n[\hat{u} \leftarrow t]}$$

$$\left[\frac{t \not\simeq \hat{u} \cdot \gamma}{T_1 \quad \cdots \quad T_n}\right]^{\mathbb{T}^{\circ}} \implies \frac{M[t] \cdot \gamma}{[T_1]^{\mathbb{T}^{\circ}} \quad \cdots \quad [T_n]^{\mathbb{T}^{\circ}}}$$

$$\left[\frac{L \cdot \gamma}{T_1 \quad \cdots \quad T_n}\right]^{\mathbb{T}^{\circ}} \implies \frac{L \cdot \gamma}{[T_1]^{\mathbb{T}^{\circ}} \quad \cdots \quad [T_n]^{\mathbb{T}^{\circ}}}$$

Consider the tableau $[\mathbb{T}^{\bullet}]^{\mathbb{T}^{\circ}}$. We can affirm the following:

- The suspicious variable $\hat{u}$ does not occur in $[\mathbb{T}^{\bullet}]^{\mathbb{T}^{\circ}}$.
- Given that $(s \not\simeq \hat{u})$ is the root literal of $\mathbb{T}^{\bullet}$, the literal $M[s]$ is the root literal of $[\mathbb{T}^{\bullet}]^{\mathbb{T}^{\circ}}$.
- Every paramodulation made in a literal of the form $(t \not\simeq \hat{u})$ in $\mathbb{T}^{\bullet}$ was made in the term t. Therefore it can also be made in the corresponding literal $M[t]$ in $[\mathbb{T}^{\bullet}]^{\mathbb{T}^{\circ}}$.
- Every literal $(t \not\simeq \hat{u})$ reduced in $\mathbb{T}^{\bullet}$ becomes the literal $M[t]$ in $[\mathbb{T}^{\bullet}]^{\mathbb{T}^{\circ}}$ and is extended further with the subtrees $\mathbb{T}_i[\hat{u} \leftarrow t]$. Since $\hat{u}$ and t are equal with respect to the constraints of $\mathbb{T}^{(i-1)}$, the tree $[\mathbb{T}^{\bullet}]^{\mathbb{T}^{\circ}}$ is closed.

Then we add the constraint δ to the root node constraint of $[\mathbb{T}^{\bullet}]^{\mathbb{T}^{\circ}}$ and replace $\mathbb{T}^{\circ}$ and $\mathbb{T}^{\bullet}$ in $\mathbb{T}^{(i-1)}$ with that tree. Also, we replace $\mathcal{S}^{(i-1)}$ with $\mathcal{S}^{(i)}$ in the root. The resulting well-formed closed **LPCT$^{\simeq}$**-tableau will be $\mathbb{T}^{(i)}$.

In $\mathbb{T}^{(i)}$, the step I is made with the clause $L[p] \vee C$. Then we make all paramodulations in p that were made in $\mathbb{T}^\bullet$ and proceed where needed with the inferences that were made in $\mathbb{T}^\circ$. The variable $\hat{u}$ disappeared from $\mathbb{T}^{(i)}$ and no other suspicious variables were introduced. It is not difficult to verify that other required conditions are satisfied, too.

By repeating this procedure, we will eventually get a closed tableau $\mathbb{T}^{(N)}$ where suspicious variables do not occur at all. This tableau is, essentially, an $\mathbf{LPCT}^\simeq$-refutation of the set $\mathrm{CEE}^1(\mathcal{S})$. It remains to undo the symmetry elimination step. We replace the symbol $\simeq$ with $\approx$ and reorient equalities to their initial form in $\mathcal{S}$.

Altogether, we obtain an $\mathbf{LPCT}$-refutation of $\mathcal{S}$.   □

Despite the way in which we prove completeness of the calculus, $\mathbf{LPCT}$ is not just a reformulation of the CEE method. In fact, there is an essential difference between flattening and lazy paramodulation. We said above that variables with caret introduced in CEE-clauses can be considered as "values" of the terms they replace. That is, the term that is finally substituted for a variable $\hat{u}$, in fact, is the result of all paramodulations made under and in the term t which was replaced with $\hat{u}$ by CEE. Therefore, in a given CEE-clause, each term has exactly one "value". It is not the case for $\mathbf{LPCT}$.

Let $\mathcal{S}$ be the set $\{\, x \approx c \vee x \approx g(h(x)),\ f(c) \approx d,\ f(g(z)) \approx d,\ f(a) \not\approx d\,\}$. The following tableau built in a simplified version of $\mathbf{LPCT}$ cannot be obtained from any $\mathbf{CT}^\simeq$-refutation of $\mathrm{CEE}(\mathcal{S})$.

$$
\begin{array}{c}
\mathcal{S} \\ \hline
f(a) \not\approx d
\end{array}
$$

$x \approx c$		$x \approx g(h(x))$	
$f(c) \not\approx d$	$x \not\approx a$	$f(g(h(x))) \not\approx d$	$x \not\approx a$
$f(c) \approx d$	$\bot \cdot (x = a)$	$f(g(z)) \approx d$	$\bot \cdot (x = a)$
$d \not\approx d$ $f(c) \not\approx f(c)$		$d \not\approx d$ $f(g(z)) \not\approx f(g(h(x)))$	
$\bot$ $\bot$		$\bot$ $\bot \cdot (z = h(x))$	

Here, we replace the constant a in the starting clause with two different terms, c and $g(h(x))$. If we make inferences with CEE-clauses, we should take two different instances of the starting clause. Based on this example, one can show that $\mathbf{LPCT}$ can give an exponential shortening of the minimal inference size as compared with $\mathbf{CT}^\simeq$ (but at the same time the number of possible inferences increases).

Another noteworthy point is the weakness of unification. The lazy unification procedure used in $\mathbf{LPCT}$ which matches top functional symbols immediately and postpones the rest is the one proposed for lazy paramodulation in [13]. This form of unification is much weaker than *top unification* (introduced in [17] and used in [14]) which descends down to variables. Top unification allows us to restrict drastically the weight of postponed "unification obligations". In particular, top unifiability of two ground terms is decided immediately.

Unfortunately, top unification and ordering constraints cannot be used together in the framework of connection tableaux. Consider the ordering $a > b > c$ and the set $\mathcal{S} = \{\, P(c) \vee Q(c), \neg P(a), \neg Q(b), b \approx c, a \approx c \,\}$. Ordering constraints prohibit paramodulations into c. The only way to refute $\mathcal{S}$ in **LPCT** is to resolve $P(c)$ with $\neg P(a)$ or $Q(c)$ with $\neg Q(b)$. However, these pairs are not top unifiable.

It is unclear whether ordered inferences for a stronger kind of lazy unification is a good trade-off. The author is not aware about any adaptation of connection tableaux for lazy paramodulation with top unification. One of the directions for further research is to develop and study one.

5   Conclusion

We have presented a new connection tableau calculus for first-order clausal logic with equality. This calculus employs lazy paramodulation with ordering constraints and a restricted form of basicness. The refutational completeness of the calculus is demonstrated by transforming proofs given by the (almost) traditional connection tableau calculus applied to a set of flattened clauses (in the spirit of Brand's modification method). Thus a connection is established between lazy paramodulation and equality elimination via problem transformation.

For the future, we plan to investigate the compatibility of the proposed calculus with various refinements of connection tableaux; first of all, with the regularity restriction. Unfortunately, the existing completeness proof is not well-suited for this task, some semantic argument would be useful here. It is also interesting to study more restricted forms of laziness, probably, giving up orderings and basicness.

Finally, we hope to implement the proposed calculus and compare it in practice with other methods of equality handling in tableau calculi.

Acknowledgment. The author is grateful to Alexander Lyaletski and Konstantin Verchinine for their guidance and expertise through the course of this work.

References

1. Loveland, D.W.: Mechanical theorem proving by model elimination. Journal of the ACM **16**(3) (1968) 349–363
2. Letz, R., Schumann, J., Bayerl, S., Bibel, W.: SETHEO: a high-performance theorem prover. Journal of Automated Reasoning **8**(2) (1992) 183–212
3. Letz, R., Stenz, G.: Model elimination and connection tableau procedures. In Robinson, A., Voronkov, A., eds.: Handbook for Automated Reasoning. Volume II. Elsevier Science (2001) 2017–2116
4. Nieuwenhuis, R., Rubio, A.: Paramodulation-based theorem proving. In Robinson, A., Voronkov, A., eds.: Handbook for Automated Reasoning. Volume I. Elsevier Science (2001) 371–443
5. Degtyarev, A., Voronkov, A.: What you always wanted to know about rigid E-unification. Journal of Automated Reasoning **20**(1) (1998) 47–80

6. Giese, M.: A model generation style completeness proof for constraint tableaux with superposition. In Egly, U., Fermüller, C.G., eds.: Automated Reasoning with Analytic Tableaux and Related Methods: International Conference, TABLEAUX 2002. Volume 2381 of Lecture Notes in Computer Science., Springer-Verlag (2002) 130–144

7. Loveland, D.W.: Automated Theorem Proving: A Logical Basis. Volume 6 of Fundamental studies in Computer Science. North-Holland (1978)

8. Moser, M., Ibens, O., Letz, R., Steinbach, J., Goller, C., Schumann, J., Mayr, K.: SETHEO and E-SETHEO — the CADE-13 systems. Journal of Automated Reasoning 18(2) (1997) 237–246

9. Brand, D.: Proving theorems with the modification method. SIAM Journal of Computing 4 (1975) 412–430

10. Moser, M., Steinbach, J.: STE-modification revisited. Technical Report AR-97-03, Fakultät für Informatik, Technische Universität München, München (1997)

11. Bachmair, L., Ganzinger, H., Voronkov, A.: Elimination of equality via transformation with ordering constraints. In Kirchner, C., Kirchner, H., eds.: Automated Deduction: 15th International Conference, CADE-15. Volume 1421 of Lecture Notes in Computer Science., Springer-Verlag (1998) 175–190

12. Moser, M., Lynch, C., Steinbach, J.: Model elimination with basic ordered paramodulation. Technical Report AR-95-11, Fakultät für Informatik, Technische Universität München, München (1995)

13. Gallier, J., Snyder, W.: Complete sets of transformations for general E-unification. Theoretical Computer Science 67 (1989) 203–260

14. Snyder, W., Lynch, C.: Goal directed strategies for paramodulation. In Book, R., ed.: Rewriting Techniques and Applications: 4th International Conference, RTA 1991. Volume 488 of Lecture Notes in Computer Science., Springer-Verlag (1991) 150–161

15. Moser, M.: Improving transformation systems for general E-unification. In Kirchner, C., ed.: Rewriting Techniques and Applications: 5th International Conference, RTA 1993. Volume 690 of Lecture Notes in Computer Science., Springer-Verlag (1993) 92–105

16. Bachmair, L., Ganzinger, H., Lynch, C., Snyder, W.: Basic paramodulation. Information and computation 121(2) (1995) 172–192

17. Dougherty, D.J., Johann, P.: An improved general E-unification method. In Stickel, M.E., ed.: Automated Deduction: 10th International Conference, CADE-10. Volume 449 of Lecture Notes in Computer Science., Springer-Verlag (1990) 261–275

Blocking and Other Enhancements for Bottom-Up Model Generation Methods

Peter Baumgartner[1] and Renate A. Schmidt[2]

[1] National ICT Australia (NICTA)
Peter.Baumgartner@nicta.com.au
[2] The University of Manchester
schmidt@cs.man.ac.uk

Abstract. In this paper we introduce several new improvements to the bottom-up model generation (BUMG) paradigm. Our techniques are based on non-trivial transformations of first-order problems into a certain implicational form, namely range-restricted clauses. These refine existing transformations to range-restricted form by extending the domain of interpretation with new Skolem terms in a more careful and deliberate way. Our transformations also extend BUMG with a blocking technique for detecting recurrence in models. Blocking is based on a conceptually rather simple encoding together with standard equality theorem proving and redundancy elimination techniques. This provides a general-purpose method for finding small models. The presented techniques are implemented and have been successfully tested with existing theorem provers on the satisfiable problems from the TPTP library.

1 Introduction

The bottom-up model generation (BUMG) paradigm encompasses a wide family of calculi and proof procedures that explicitly try to construct a model of a given (first-order) clause set by reading clauses as rules and applying them in a bottom-up way until completion. For instance, variants of hyperresolution and certain tableau calculi belong to this family. BUMG methods have been known for a long time to be refutationally complete. Comparably little effort has however been undertaken to exploit them for the dual task of refutational theorem proving, namely, computing models for satisfiable problems. This is somewhat surprising, as computing models is recognized as being important in software engineering, model checking, and other applications, and is becoming increasingly important for building and maintaining web ontologies. The BUMG methods we develop and study in this paper are intended to be used for consistency testing of ontologies and software specifications, and for aiding with the debugging through the generation of (counter-)models. Our techniques are partially inspired by techniques already successfully used in the area. For instance, we show how blocking techniques of description and modal logic tableau-based theorem provers can be generalized to full first-order logic. In our approach blocking is encoded on the clausal level and is combined with standard resolution techniques. In this way, suitable provers can be utilised to construct (small) models which can be easily read off from the derived clauses. Our other contributed techniques are significant improvements to the well-known "transformation to range-restricted form" as introduced in the context of the SATCHMO prover

U. Furbach and N. Shankar (Eds.): IJCAR 2006, LNAI 4130, pp. 125–139, 2006.
© Springer-Verlag Berlin Heidelberg 2006

in the eighties [15] and later improved in e.g. [4]. The existing transformations have the disadvantage that they force BUMG methods to enumerate the entire Herbrand universe and are therefore non-terminating except in the simplest cases. Our method extends and combines the transformation introduced in [21] for reducing first-order formulae and clauses into range-restricted clauses, which was used to develop general-purpose resolution decision procedures for the Bernays-Schönfinkel class. Our approach is similar in spirit to the methods in e.g. [10,13], by capitalizing on available *first-order* (equational) automated reasoning technology.

Other methods for model computation can be classified as methods that directly search for a finite model, like the extended PUHR tableau method [7], the method in [6] and the methods in the SEM-family [22,26,17]. In contrast, MACE-style model builders [9,16, e.g.] reduce model search to testing of propositional satisfiability. Being based on translation, the MACE-style approach is conceptually related, but different, to our approach. Both SEM- and MACE-style methods search for finite models, essentially, by searching the space of interpretations with domain sizes $1, 2, \ldots$, in increasing order, until a model is found. Our method operates significantly differently, as it is *not* parametrized by a domain size. Consequently, there is no iterative deepening over the domain size, and the search for finite models works differently. This way, we address a problem often found with models computed by these methods: from a pragmatic perspective, they tend to identify too many terms. For instance, for the two unit clauses $P(a)$ and $Q(b)$ there is a model that identifies a and b with the same object. Such models can be counterintuitive, for instance, in a description logic setting, where unique names are often assumed. Our transformations are careful at identifying objects than the methods mentioned and thus work closer to a Herbrand semantics. The difference in operation also shows up experimentally. Our methods can solve an overlapping, but disjoint set of the satisfiable TPTP problems solvable by the state-of-the-art MACE-style model builder Paradox.

The structure of the paper is as follows. Sections 1.1 and 2 give basic definitions and recall the characteristic properties of BUMG methods. Section 3 defines new techniques for generating small models and generating them more efficiently. The techniques are based on a series of transformations which include an improved range-restricting transformation (Section 3.1), instances of standard renaming and flattening (Section 3.2), and the introduction of blocking through an encoding and standard saturation-based equality reasoning (Section 3.3). In Section 4 we present and discuss results of experiments carried out with our methods on all satisfiable TPTP problems. Details and proofs, which are omitted due to lack of space, can be found in the long version [5].

1.1 Preliminaries

We use standard terminology from automated reasoning. We assume as given a signature $\Sigma = \Sigma_f \cup \Sigma_P$ of function symbols Σ_f (including constants) and predicate symbols Σ_P. As we are working (also) with equality, we assume Σ_P contains a distinguished binary predicate symbol $\approx$, which is used in infix form. Terms, atoms, literals and formulas over Σ and a given (denumerable) set of variables V are defined as usual.

A clause is a (finite) implicitly universally quantified disjunction of literals. We write clauses in a logic-programming style, i.e. we write $H_1 \vee \cdots \vee H_m \leftarrow B_1 \wedge \cdots \wedge B_k$ rather than $H_1 \vee \cdots \vee H_m \vee \neg B_1 \vee \cdots \vee \neg B_k$, where $m, k \geq 0$. Each H_i is called a *head atom*, and each B_j is called a *body atom*. When writing expressions like $H \vee \mathcal{H} \leftarrow B \wedge \mathcal{B}$ we mean any clause whose head literals are H and those in the disjunction of literals $\mathcal{H}$, and whose body literals are B and those in the conjunction of literals $\mathcal{B}$. A *clause set* is a finite set of clauses. A clause $\mathcal{H} \leftarrow \mathcal{B}$ is said to be *range-restricted* iff the body $\mathcal{B}$ contains all the variables in it. A clause set is range-restricted iff it contains only range-restricted clauses. For a given atom $P(t_1, \ldots, t_n)$ the terms $t_1, \ldots, t_n$ are also called the *top-level* terms of $P(t_1, \ldots, t_n)$ (P being $\approx$ is permitted). This notion generalizes to clause bodies, clause heads and clauses as expected. E.g., for a clause $\mathcal{H} \leftarrow \mathcal{B}$ the top-level terms of its body $\mathcal{B}$ are exactly the top-level terms of its body atoms. A *proper functional term* is a term which is neither a variable nor a constant.

With regards to semantics, we use the notions of (first-order) *satisfiability* and *E-satisfiability* in a completely standard way.

2   BUMG Methods

Proof procedures based on model generation approaches establish the satisfiability of a problem by trying to build a model for the problem. In this paper we are interested in bottom-up model generation approaches (BUMG). BUMG approaches use a forward reasoning approach where implications, or clauses, $\mathcal{H} \leftarrow \mathcal{B}$ are read as rules and are repeatedly used to derive (instances of) $\mathcal{H}$ from (instances of) $\mathcal{B}$ until a completion is found. The family of BUMG includes many familiar calculi and proof procedures, such as SATCHMO [15,12], PUHR [8,7], MGTP [11] and hyper tableaux [3]. The oldest and perhaps most widely known BUMG method is hyperresolution [19].

Hyperresolution consists of two inference rules, hyperresolution and factoring. The hyperresolution rule applies to a non-positive clause $H \leftarrow B_1 \wedge \ldots \wedge B_n$ and n positive clauses $C_1 \vee B'_1 \leftarrow \top, \ldots, C_n \vee B'_n \leftarrow \top$, and derives $(C_1 \vee \ldots \vee C_n \vee H)\sigma \leftarrow \top$, where σ is the most general unifier such that $B'_i\sigma = B_i\sigma$ for every $i \in \{1, \ldots, n\}$. The factoring rule derives the clause $(C \vee B)\sigma \leftarrow \top$ from a positive clause $C \vee B \vee B' \leftarrow \top$, where σ is the most general unifier of B and B'. A crucial requirement for the effective use of blocking (Section 3.3) is support of equality reasoning, for example, ordered paramodulation or superposition [18], in combination with simplification techniques based on orderings.

Our experiments show that a certain form of the splitting rule, or the β-rule, is quite useful for our approach. For the blocking transformation, splitting on the positive part of (ground) clauses is in fact mandatory to make it effective. This type of splitting will replace the branch of a derivation containing the positive clause $C \vee D \leftarrow \top$, say, by two copies of the branch in which the clause is replaced by $C \leftarrow \top$ and $D \leftarrow \top$, respectively, provided that C and D do not share any variables. Most BUMG procedures support this splitting technique, in particular the provers that we used do.

3   Transformations

3.1   Range-Restriction

Existing transformations to range-restricted form follow Manthey and Bry [15] (or are variations of it). The transformation can be defined by a procedure carrying out the following steps on a given set M of clauses.

(0) Initialization. Initially, let $\mathrm{crr}(M) := M$.

(1) Add a constant. Let dom be a "fresh" unary predicate symbol not in Σ_P, and let c be some constant. Extend $\mathrm{crr}(M)$ by the clause $\mathrm{dom}(c) \leftarrow$. (The constant c can be "fresh" or belong to Σ_f.)

(2) Range-restriction. For each clause $\mathcal{H} \leftarrow \mathcal{B}$ in $\mathrm{crr}(M)$, let $\{x_1, \ldots, x_k\}$ be the set of variables occurring in $\mathcal{H}$ but not in $\mathcal{B}$. Replace $\mathcal{H} \leftarrow \mathcal{B}$ by the clause

$$\mathcal{H} \leftarrow \mathcal{B} \wedge \mathrm{dom}(x_1) \wedge \cdots \wedge \mathrm{dom}(x_k).$$

(3) Enumerate the Herbrand universe. For each n-ary $f \in \Sigma_f$, add the clauses:

$$\mathrm{dom}(f(x_1, \ldots, x_n)) \leftarrow \mathrm{dom}(x_1) \wedge \cdots \wedge \mathrm{dom}(x_n).$$

We refer to the computed set $\mathrm{crr}(M)$ as the *classical range-restricting transformation* of M. It is not difficult to see that $\mathrm{crr}(M)$ is indeed range-restricted for any clause set M. The transformation is sound and complete, i.e. M is satisfiable iff $\mathrm{crr}(M)$ is satisfiable [15,8]. Clearly, the size of $\mathrm{crr}(M)$ is linear in the size of M and can be computed in linear time.

Perhaps the easiest way to understand the transformation is to imagine we use a BUMG method, e.g. hyperresolution. The idea is to build the model(s) during the derivation. The clause added in Step (1) ensures that the domain of interpretation given by the domain predicate dom is non-empty. Step (2) turns clauses into range-restricted clauses by shielding variables in the head that do not occur negatively within the added negative domain literals. Clauses that are already range-restricted are unaffected by this step. Step (3) ensures that all elements of the Herbrand universe of the (original) clause set are added to the domain via hyperresolution inference steps. As a consequence a clause set M with at least one non-nullary function symbols causes hyperresolution derivations to be unbounded for $\mathrm{crr}(M)$, unless M is unsatisfiable. This is a distinct drawback of the classical range-restricting transformation. However, the method has been shown to be useful for (domain-)minimal model generation when combined with other techniques [8,7].

In Section 4 we consider the combination of the classical range-restricting transformation crr with the blocking transformation which is introduced in Section 3.3.

Let us first turn to a new transformation to range-restricted form which aims to help avoid the brute-force enumeration of the entire Herbrand universe by BUMG approaches. The transformation involves extracting the non-variable top-level terms in an atom. Let $P(t_1, \ldots, t_n)$ be an atom and suppose $x_1, \ldots, x_n$ are fresh variables. For all $i \in \{1, \ldots, n\}$ let $s_i = t_i$, if t_i is a variable, and $s_i = x_i$, otherwise. The atom $P(s_1, \ldots, s_n)$ is called the *term abstraction* of $P(t_1, \ldots, t_n)$. Let the *abstraction substitution* α be defined by $\alpha = \{x_i \mapsto t_i \mid 1 \le i \le n \text{ and } t_i \text{ is not a variable}\}$. Hence, $P(s_1, \ldots, s_n)\alpha = P(t_1, \ldots, t_n)$, i.e. α reverts the term abstraction. Now, the new *range-restricting transformation*, denoted by rr, of a clause set M is the clause set obtained by carrying out the following steps (explanations and an example are given afterwards):

(0) Initialization. Initially, let $\mathrm{rr}(M) := M$.

(1) Add a constant. Same as Step (1) in the definition of crr.

(2) Domain elements from clause bodies. For each clause $\mathcal{H} \leftarrow \mathcal{B}$ in M and each atom $P(t_1, \ldots, t_n)$ from $\mathcal{B}$, let $P(s_1, \ldots, s_n)$ be the term abstraction of $P(t_1, \ldots, t_n)$ and let α be the corresponding abstraction substitution. Extend $rr(M)$ by the set

$$\{\mathsf{dom}(x_i)\alpha \leftarrow P(s_1, \ldots, s_n) \mid 1 \leq i \leq n \text{ and } x_i \mapsto t_i \in \alpha\}.$$

(3) Range-restriction. Same as Step (2) in the definition of crr.

(4) Domain elements from Σ_P. For each n-ary P in Σ_p, extend $rr(M)$ by the set

$$\{\mathsf{dom}(x_i) \leftarrow P(x_1, \ldots, x_n) \mid i \leq i \leq n\}.$$

(5) Domain elements from Σ_f. For each n-ary f in Σ_f, extend $rr(M)$ by the set

$$\{\mathsf{dom}(x_i) \leftarrow \mathsf{dom}(f(x_1, \ldots, x_n)) \mid i \leq i \leq n\}.$$

The intuition of the transformation reveals itself if we think of what happens when using hyperresolution. The idea is again to build the model(s) during the derivation, but this time terms are added to the domain only *as necessary*. Steps (1) and (3) are the same as Steps (1) and (2) in the definition of crr. The clauses added in Step (2) cause functional terms that occur negatively in the clauses to be inserted into the domain. Step (4) ensures that positively occurring functional terms are added to the domain, and Step (5) ensures that the domain is closed under subterms.

To illustrate the steps of the transformation consider the following clause.

$$q(x, g(x,y)) \vee r(y,z) \leftarrow p(a, f(x,y), x) \qquad (\dagger)$$

The term abstraction of the body literal is $p(x_1, x_2, x)$ and the abstraction substitution is $\alpha = \{x_1 \mapsto a, x_2 \mapsto f(x,y)\}$. The clauses added in Step (2) are thus:

$$\mathsf{dom}(a) \leftarrow p(x_1, x_2, x) \qquad\qquad \mathsf{dom}(f(x,y)) \leftarrow p(x_1, x_2, x) \qquad (\ddagger)$$

Notice that among the clauses so far the clauses ($\dagger$) and ($\ddagger$) are not range-restricted, but are turned into range-restricted clauses in Step (3), yielding the following.

$$q(x, g(x,y)) \vee r(y,z) \leftarrow p(a, f(x,y), x) \wedge \mathsf{dom}(z)$$
$$\mathsf{dom}(f(x,y)) \leftarrow p(x_1, x_2, x) \wedge \mathsf{dom}(y)$$

Step (4) generates clauses responsible for inserting the terms that occur in the heads of clauses into the domain. I.e. for each $i \in \{1, 2, 3\}$ and each $j \in \{1, 2\}$:

$$\mathsf{dom}(x_i) \leftarrow p(x_1, x_2, x_3) \qquad \mathsf{dom}(x_j) \leftarrow q(x_1, x_2) \qquad \mathsf{dom}(x_j) \leftarrow r(x_1, x_2)$$

For instance, when a model assigns true to the instance $q(a, g(a, f(a, a)))$ of one of the head atoms of the clause above, then $\mathsf{dom}(a)$ and $\mathsf{dom}(g(a, f(a, a)))$ will also be true. It is not necessary to insert the terms of the instance of the other head atom into the domain. The reason is that it does not matter how these (extra) terms are evaluated, or whether the atom is evaluated to true or false in order to satisfy the disjunction. The clauses added in Step (4) alone are not sufficient, however. For each term in the domain all its subterms have to be in the domain, too. This is achieved with the clauses obtained in Step (5). I.e. for each $j \in \{1, 2\}$:

$$\mathsf{dom}(x_j) \leftarrow \mathsf{dom}(f(x_1, x_2)) \qquad\qquad \mathsf{dom}(x_j) \leftarrow \mathsf{dom}(g(x_1, x_2))$$

Proposition 3.1 (Completeness of range-restriction (wrt. E-interpretations)). *Let M be a clause set. (i) If rr(M) is satisfiable then M is satisfiable. (ii) If $rr(M) \cup \{x \approx x \leftarrow dom(x)\}$ is E-satisfiable then M is E-satisfiable.*

Consider the clause $r(x) \leftarrow q(x) \wedge p(f(x))$ which might be part of the translation of a modal logic formula or a description logic knowledge base. Applying Steps (2) and (3) of our transformation give us a clause,

$$dom(f(x)) \leftarrow dom(x) \wedge p(y), \qquad\qquad (*)$$

which is splittable into $dom(f(x)) \leftarrow dom(x)$ and $\perp \leftarrow p(y)$. The first split component clause is unpleasant, because it is an example of an "enumerate the Herbrand universe" clause from existing standard transformations (Step (2) in the definition of crr). Such clauses cause the entire Herbrand universe to be enumerated with BUMG approaches. One solution is to switch off splitting when using a BUMG approach, but this is not necessarily the best or the only solution. (Indeed, our experiments below demonstrate that splitting is advisable.) Before describing a solution let us analyze the problem further.

The main rationale of our rr transformation is to constrain the generation of domain elements and limit the number of inference steps. The general form of clauses produced by Step (2), followed by Step (3), is the following, where $\bar{y} \subseteq \bar{x}$, $\bar{x} \subseteq \bar{y} \cup \bar{z}$ and $\bar{u} \subseteq \bar{z}$.

$$dom(f(\bar{x})) \leftarrow dom(y_1) \wedge \ldots \wedge dom(y_n) \wedge P(\bar{z}) \qquad dom(f(\bar{u})) \leftarrow P(\bar{z})$$

Clauses of the first form are often splittable (as in the example above), and can produce clauses of the unwanted form $dom(f(\bar{y})) \leftarrow dom(y_1) \wedge \ldots \wedge dom(y_n)$. Suppose therefore that splitting of any clause is forbidden when this splits the negative part of the clause (neither (M)SPASS nor hyper tableaux prover do this anyway). Although, compared to the classical range-restricting transformation methods, the two types of clauses above both *do* reduce the number of possible inferences, the constraining effect of the first type of clauses is a bit limited. Terms $f(\bar{s})$ are not generated, only when no fact $P(\bar{t})$ is present or has been derived. When a clause $P(\bar{t})$ is present, or as soon as such a clause is derived (for *any* (ground) terms $\bar{t}$), then terms are freely generated from terms already in the domain with f as the top symbol. Here is an example of a clause set for which the derivation is infinite on the transformation.

$$p(b) \leftarrow \top \qquad\qquad r(x) \leftarrow q(x) \wedge p(f(x))$$

Notice the derivation will be infinite on the classical range-restricting transformation as well, due to the generated clauses $dom(b) \leftarrow \top$ and $dom(f(x)) \leftarrow dom(x)$.

The second type of clauses, $dom(f(\bar{u})) \leftarrow P(\bar{z})$, are less problematic. Here is a concrete example. For $\perp \leftarrow r(x, f(x))$, Step (2) produces the clause $dom(f(x)) \leftarrow r(x, y)$. Although this clause, and the general form, still cause larger terms to be built with hyperresolution type inferences, the constraining effect is larger.

In the next two sections we discuss ways of improving the transformation further.

3.2 Shifting

The clauses introduced in Step (2) of the new transformation rr to range-restricted form insert instantiations of terms occurring in the clause bodies into the domain. This is sometimes unnecessary and can lead to non-termination of BUMG procedures. The *shifting* transformation addresses this problem. It consists of two sub-transformations, *basic shifting* and *partial flattening*.

If A is an atom $P(t_1, \ldots, t_n)$ then let not_A denote the atom not_$P(t_1, \ldots, t_n)$, where not_P is a fresh predicate symbol which is uniquely associated with the predicate symbol P. If P is the equality symbol $\approx$ we write not_P as $\not\approx$ and use infix notation. Now, the *basic shifting transformation* of a clause set M is the clause set $\mathrm{bs}(M)$ obtained from M by carrying out the following steps.

(0) Initialization. Initially, let $\mathrm{bs}(M) :- M$.

(1) Shifting deep atoms. Replace each clause in $\mathrm{bs}(M)$ of the form $\mathcal{H} \leftarrow B_1 \wedge \cdots \wedge B_m \wedge \mathcal{B}$, where each atom $B_1, \ldots, B_m$ contains at least one proper functional term and $\mathcal{B}$ contains no proper functional term, by the clause

$$\mathcal{H} \vee \mathrm{not\_}B_1 \vee \cdots \vee \mathrm{not\_}B_m \leftarrow \mathcal{B}.$$

Each of the atoms $B_1, \ldots, B_m$ is called a *shifted atom*.

(2) Shifted atoms consistency. Extend $\mathrm{bs}(M)$ by the clause set

$$\{\bot \leftarrow P(x_1, \ldots, x_n) \wedge \mathrm{not\_}P(x_1, \ldots, x_n) \mid$$
$$P \text{ is the } n\text{-ary predicate symbol of a shifted atom}\}.$$

Notice that we do *not* add clauses complementary to the "shifted atoms consistency" clauses, i.e., $P(x_1, \ldots, x_n) \vee \mathrm{not\_}P(x_1, \ldots, x_n) \leftarrow \top$. They could be included but are evidently superfluous.

Let us continue the example given at the end of the previous section. We can use basic shifting to move negative occurrences of functional terms into heads. In the example, instead of the clause ($*$) we get the following.

$$\begin{aligned} \mathrm{dom}(x) &\leftarrow \mathrm{not\_}p(x) & r(x) \vee \mathrm{not\_}p(\mathrm{f}(x)) &\leftarrow q(x) & (**)\\ \mathrm{dom}(x) &\leftarrow r(x) & \bot &\leftarrow \mathrm{not\_}p(x) \wedge p(x) \end{aligned}$$

This gets rid of the problematic clause ($*$). Even in the presence of an additional clause, say, $q(x) \leftarrow \top$, which leads to the clauses $\mathrm{dom}(\mathrm{a}) \leftarrow \top$ and $q(x) \leftarrow \mathrm{dom}(x)$, termination of BUMG can be achieved. For instance, in a hyperresolution-like setting and with splitting enabled the MSPASS prover [20] splits the derived clause $r(\mathrm{a}) \vee \mathrm{not\_}p(\mathrm{f}(\mathrm{a}))$, considers the case with the smaller literal $r(\mathrm{a})$ first *and terminates with a model*. This is because a finite completion is found without considering the case of the bigger literal $\mathrm{not\_}p(\mathrm{f}(\mathrm{a}))$, which would have added the deeper term $\mathrm{f}(\mathrm{a})$ to the domain. The same behaviour can be achieved for example with the KRHyper BUMG prover.

As can be seen in the example, the basic shifting transformation trades the generation of new domain elements for a smaller clause body (by removing literals from it). Of course, a smaller clause body is undesirable for BUMG methods, as then the clause can be used as a premise more often. To (partially) avoid this effect, we propose an additional transformation to be performed prior to the basic shifting transformation.

For a clause set M, the *partial flattening transformation* is the clause set $\mathrm{pf}(M)$ obtained by applying the following steps.

(0) Initialization. Initially, let $\mathrm{pf}(M) := M$.
(1) Reflexivity. Extend $\mathrm{pf}(M)$ by the unit clause $x \approx x \leftarrow \top$.
(2) Partial flattening. For each clause $\mathcal{H} \leftarrow \mathcal{B}$ in $\mathrm{pf}(M)$, let $t_1, \ldots, t_n$ be all top-level terms occurring in the non-equational literals in the body $\mathcal{B}$ that are proper functional terms, for some $n \geq 0$. Let $x_1, \ldots, x_n$ be fresh variables. Replace the clause $\mathcal{H} \leftarrow \mathcal{B}[t_1, \ldots, t_n]$ by the clause

$$\mathcal{H} \leftarrow \mathcal{B}[x_1, \ldots, x_n] \wedge t_1 \approx x_1 \wedge \cdots \wedge t_n \approx x_n.$$

It should be noted that the equality symbol $\approx$ need not be interpreted as equality, but could. (Un-)satisfiability (and logical equivalence) is preserved even when reading it just as "unifiability". This is achieved by the clause $x \approx x \leftarrow \top$.

In our running example, applying the transformations pf, bs and rr, in this order, yields the following clauses (among other clauses, which are omitted because they are not relevant to the current discussion).

$$\mathrm{r}(x) \vee \mathrm{f}(x) \not\approx u \leftarrow \mathrm{q}(x) \wedge \mathrm{p}(u) \qquad \mathrm{dom}(x) \leftarrow x \not\approx y \qquad \mathrm{dom}(x) \leftarrow \mathrm{r}(x)$$
$$\bot \leftarrow x \not\approx y \wedge x \approx y \qquad \mathrm{dom}(y) \leftarrow x \not\approx y$$

Observe that the first clause is more restricted than the clause $(\ast\ast)$ above because of the additional body literal $\mathrm{p}(u)$.

The reason for not extracting constants during partial flattening is that adding them to the domain will not cause non-termination of BUMG methods. It is preferable to leave them in place in the body literals because they have a stronger constraining effect than the variables introduced otherwise. Extracting top-level terms from equations has no effect at all. Consider the unit clause $\bot \leftarrow f(a) \approx b$, and its partial flattening $\bot \leftarrow x \approx b \wedge f(a) \approx x$. Applying basic shifting yields $f(a) \not\approx x \leftarrow x \approx b$, and, hyperresolution with $x \approx x \leftarrow \top$ gives $f(a) \not\approx b \leftarrow \top$. This is the same result as obtained by the transformations as defined. This explains why top-level terms of equational literals are excluded from the definition. (One could consider using "standard" flattening, i.e. recursively extracting terms, but this does not lead to any improvements over the defined transformations.)

Finally, combine basic shifting and partial flattening to give the *shifting transformation*, formally defined by $\mathrm{sh} := \mathrm{pf} \circ \mathrm{bs}$, i.e. $\mathrm{sh}(M) = \mathrm{bs}(\mathrm{pf}(M))$, for any clause set M.

Proposition 3.2 (Completeness of shifting (wrt. E-interpretations)). *Let M be a clause set. (i) If $\mathrm{sh}(M)$ is satisfiable then M is satisfiable. (ii) If $\mathrm{sh}(M)$ is E-satisfiable then M is E-satisfiable.*

3.3 Blocking

Our final transformation is intended to be a mechanism for detecting periodicity in the derived models. By definition, the *blocking transformation* of a clause set M is the clause set $\mathrm{bl}(M)$ obtained from M by carrying out the following steps.

(0) Initialization. Initially, let $\text{bl}(M) := M$.

(1) Axioms describing the subterm relationship. Let sub be a "fresh" binary predicate symbol not in Σ_P. Extend $\text{bl}(M)$ by $\text{sub}(x,x) \leftarrow \text{dom}(x)$ and, for every n-ary function symbol $f \in \Sigma_f$ and all $i \in \{1,\ldots,n\}$, add the clauses

$$\text{sub}(x, f(x_1,\ldots,x_n)) \leftarrow \text{sub}(x,x_i) \wedge \text{dom}(x) \wedge \text{dom}(f(x_1,\ldots,x_n)).$$

(2) Subterm equality case analysis. Extend $\text{bl}(M)$ by these clauses.

$$x \approx y \vee x \not\approx y \leftarrow \text{sub}(x,y) \qquad\qquad \leftarrow x \approx y \wedge x \not\approx y$$

The blocking transformation preserves range-restrictedness. In fact, because the dom predicate symbol is mentioned in the definition, the blocking transformation can be applied meaningfully only in combination with range-restricting transformations.

Reading $\text{sub}(s,t)$ as "s is a subterm of t", the Step (1) in the blocking transformation might seem overly involved, because an apparently simpler specification of the subterm relationship for the terms of the signature Σ_f can be given. Namely:

$$\text{sub}(x,x) \leftarrow \text{dom}(x) \qquad\qquad \text{sub}(x, f(x_1,x_2\ldots,x_n)) \leftarrow \text{sub}(x,x_i)$$

for every n-ary function symbol $f \in \Sigma_f$ and all $i \in \{1,\ldots,n\}$. This clause set is range-restricted. Yet, this specification is not suitable for our purposes. For example, for a given constant a and a unary function symbol f, when just $\text{dom}(\text{a})$ alone has been derived, a BUMG procedure derives an infinite sequence clauses: $\text{sub}(\text{a},\text{a})$, $\text{sub}(\text{a},\text{f}(\text{a}))$, $\text{sub}(\text{a},\text{f}(\text{f}(\text{a})))$, ... This does not happen with the specification in Step (1). It ensures that conclusions of BUMG inferences involving sub are about terms currently in the domain, and the domain is always finite.

To justify the clauses added in Step (2) we continue this example and suppose an interpretation that contains $\text{dom}(\text{a})$ and $\text{dom}(\text{f}(\text{a}))$. These might have been derived earlier in the run of a BUMG prover. Then, from the clauses added by blocking, the (necessarily ground) disjunction $\text{f}(\text{a}) \approx \text{a} \vee \text{f}(\text{a}) \not\approx \text{a} \leftarrow \top$ is derivable. Now, it is important to use a BUMG prover with support for splitting and to equip it with an appropriate search strategy. In particular, when deriving a disjunction like the one above, the $\approx$-literal should be split off and the clause set obtained in this case should be searched *first*. The reason is that the (ground) equation $\text{f}(\text{a}) \approx \text{a}$ thereby obtained can then be used for simplification and redundancy testing purposes. For example, should $\text{dom}(\text{f}(\text{f}(\text{a})))$ be derivable now (in the current branch), then any prover based a modern, saturation-based theory of equality reasoning will be able to prove it redundant from $\text{f}(\text{a}) \approx \text{a}$ and $\text{dom}(\text{a})$. Consequently, the domain will *not* be extended *explicitly*. The information that $\text{dom}(\text{f}(\text{f}(\text{a})))$ is in the domain is however implicit via the theory of equality.

The blocking transformation was designed to realize a "loop check" for the construction of a domain, by capitalizing on available, powerful equality reasoning technology and redundancy criteria from saturation-based theorem proving. To be suitable, a resolution-based prover, for instance, should support *hyperresolution-style inference, strong equality inference e.g. superposition, splitting, and the possibility to search for split-off equations first and standard redundancy elimination techniques.* Among the well-known, current resolution theorem provers splitting is not standard, but it is available in the saturation-based prover SPASS (and the extension MSPASS) and VAMPIRE.

Unfortunately, the hyper tableau prover KRHyper does not include suitable equality inference rules. Otherwise its splitting could easily be configured to meet our needs.

The blocking transformation is inspired by a technique with the same name (and same purpose) implemented in tableau provers for description and modal logics. Indeed, when comparing these techniques in detail it becomes clear that our transformation $rr \circ bl$, when applied to a knowledge base of a description logic with the finite model property, in conjunction with a suitable BUMG method (see above), is powerful enough to simulate various forms of blocking techniques, including (dynamic and static) subset blocking and equality blocking [1]. But notice that our transformation applies to any first-order clause set, not only to clauses from the translation of description logic problems. This makes our approach more widely applicable. For instance, our approach makes it possible to extend description logics with arbitrary (first-order expressible) "rule" languages. "Rules" provide a connection to (deductive) databases and are being used to represent information that is currently not expressible in the description logics associated with OWL DL.

Proposition 3.3 (Completeness of blocking wrt. E-interpretations). *Let M be any clause set. If $bl(M)$ is E-satisfiable then M is E-satisfiable.*

Our main theoretical result is the following.

Theorem 3.4 (Completeness of the combined transformations with respect to E-interpretations). *Let M be a clause set and suppose tr is any of the transformations in $\{rr, sh \circ rr, rr \circ bl, sh \circ rr \circ bl\}$. Then: (i) $tr(M)$ is range-restricted. (ii) $tr(M)$ can be computed in quadratic time. (iii) If $tr(M) \cup \{x \approx x \leftarrow dom(x)\}$ is E-satisfiable then M is E-satisfiable.*

By carefully modifying the definition of rr it is possible to compute the reductions in linear time. The reverse directions of (iii), i.e. soundness of the respective transformations, hold as well. The theorem is also true if rr is replaced by crr.

4 Experiments

We have implemented the transformations described in the previous section and carried out experiments on problems from the TPTP library, Version 3.1.1. (The implementation, in SWI-Prolog, is available from the first author's website.) Since the emphasis in this paper is on *disproving* theorems, i.e. on reporting whether a given clause set is satisfiable, we have selected for the experiments only satisfiable (clausal) problems from the TPTP suite, yet all 514 of them. The test were carried out with the BUMG systems MSPASS (Version 2.0g.1.4+) [20],[1] using ordered resolution with maximal selection of negative literals, and to a lesser extent the KRHyper theorem prover [25]. Both were run on a Linux PC with an Intel Pentium 4 3.80GHz processor and 1 GByte main memory.

Table 1 is a summary of the results of the MSPASS runs. The column with the heading "#" gives the number of problems in the listed TPTP categories. The subsequent

---

[1] MSPASS is an extension of the prover SPASS [24], but except for a small modification in the code we did not use any of the extra features of MSPASS. We used MSPASS because it satisfies the suitability criteria (see previous section), the source code is available, the options are documented and we are familiar with it.

Table 1. Result summary of MSPASS runs on the satisfiable clausal TPTP problems

Category	#	rr −sp	rr +sp	sh∘rr −sp	sh∘rr +sp	rr∘bl +sp	sh∘rr∘bl +sp	crr∘bl +sp
ALG	1	0	0	0	0	1	0	0
BOO	13	0	0	0	0	2	3	2
COL	5	0	0	0	0	0	0	0
GEO	1	0	0	0	0	0	0	0
GRP	25	7	7	7	8	15	14	12
KRS	8	1	1	4	8	4	6	4
LAT	1	0	0	0	0	1	1	0
LCL	4	0	1	1	1	1	1	1
MGT	10	1	1	3	4	4	5	0
MSC	1	1	1	1	1	1	1	1
NLP	236	49	79	68	96	87	160	68
NUM	1	1	1	1	1	1	1	1
PUZ	20	6	6	6	6	10	10	9
RNG	4	0	0	0	0	0	0	0
SWV	8	0	0	0	0	1	1	0
SYN	176	20	50	20	52	124	125	120
All	514	86	147	111	177	252	328	218

columns give the number of problems solved within the given time limit of five minutes (CPU time) and 300 MByte main memory consumption (which was not a bottleneck). Results are presented for the different transformations that were used. For example, sh∘rr∘bl means that shifting, the new range-restriction and blocking was used; +sp, respectively −sp, indicate whether splitting was enabled or disabled. The last column, crr∘bl, contains the results for the classical range-restricting transformation in combination with blocking. (For the reasons mentioned before, evaluating the classical range-restricting transformation without blocking is not of interest for satisfiable problems.) Testing the crr∘bl setting is interesting because it allows us to assess the significance of the shifting and our new range-restricting transformations in comparison with classical range-restriction. As can be seen from the number of problems solved, the sh, rr, and in particular, the sh∘rr transformations performed much better than crr in combination with bl. This demonstrates the need for *all* our new transformations. The runtimes for the problems solved spanned the whole range, from less than one second to almost all of the time allowed. It is not a mistake that no results are given for transformations with blocking but no splitting; this would not make sense.

Let us now compare the individual combinations and discuss our observations from the experiments conducted with MSPASS. Broadly, the results indicate that the performance for the combination (rr, −sp) was inferior to that for (rr, +sp) and for (sh∘rr, −sp), and each of these was inferior to the performance for (sh∘rr, +sp). There were only very few problems that were solved by an "inferior" combination alone. This suggests that switching splitting on is advisable, and that shifting is an effective improvement, in particular in combination with splitting. In that combination, splitting helps in particular to "forget" those atoms in the head of a clause that were introduced by shifting, which otherwise generates new domain elements.

The combination (sh ∘ rr, −sp) was inferior to (rr ∘ bl, +sp). Our explanation is that shifting without splitting often generates many deep and long clauses in the search space which are not redundant according to standard redundancy criteria. Nevertheless, these clauses are redundant in the sense that they are satisfied by a finite model.

The results obtained for the combinations (sh ∘ rr, +sp) and (rr ∘ bl, +sp) are incomparable. There were many problems over all categories that were solved by either approach. This confirms our expectation that the shifting and range-restriction techniques are orthogonal. Shifting tries to avoid the generation of domain elements, but it is sometimes not strong enough. Blocking, by contrast, is a strong technique, which helps to discover finite models more often, but creates a larger search space.

The combination (sh ∘ rr, +sp) was strictly inferior to (sh ∘ rr ∘ bl, +sp). It suggests that adding blocking to shifting is advisable. This result is somewhat surprising. We expected that the additional search space introduced by blocking renders some examples unsolvable that can be solved with shifting alone. Interestingly, not even time-wise did blocking cause a penalty when shifting alone was sufficient.

The combination (rr ∘ bl, +sp) was in most cases inferior to (sh ∘ rr ∘ bl, +sp). The result was not as uniform as in the previous case, though. There were some satisfiable problems that were solved with the (rr ∘ bl, +sp) combination *alone* (but no other combination). It is not entirely clear, why. On the other hand, there were also some problems that were not solved with rr ∘ bl, but were solved with most other transformations. For these problems the search overhead when using blocking seems too big.

We also used KRHyper [25], which is an efficient implementation of the hyper tableau calculus [3]. On range-restricted clause sets, the hyper tableau calculus is closely related to resolution with maximal selection and splitting, the instance of MSPASS that we used. KRHyper, as a tableau calculus, has splitting "built-in", but it does not include equality inference rules. It therefore lacks the refinements needed to support the blocking transformation effectively. We therefore selected all satisfiable TPTP problems without equality for the tests. There are 309 of these (out of a total of 514).

The results were as follows. The performance of KRHyper for the transformation rr was inferior to sh ∘ rr. The latter was better on almost all problems, over all categories. The results parallel those above obtained with MSPASS. This was expected.

Perhaps the most interesting comparison is between KRHyper equipped with the transformation sh ∘ rr and MSPASS equipped with the combination (sh ∘ rr, +sp). With these settings 134 problems were solved by KRHyper and 121 problems were solved by MSPASS. Specifically, there are 17 problems that were solved by KRHyper but not by MSPASS, in any combination. The rating of these problems is between 0.00 and 0.80. Most of them are from the NLP category. The reason why KRHyper performed better than MSPASS lies in its splitting strategy, which is more suitable for our purposes than the one utilized in MSPASS. (Due to lack of space we do not give details.) It would therefore be interesting to modify the way splitting is done in MSPASS so that it mimics KRHyper's splitting. Other (probably) significant differences are the non-chronological backtracking schemes employed in KRHyper and MSPASS.

Table 2 summarizes the results with respect to problem rating. The column with the heading "MSPASS" reflects how many problems were solved, among all the combinations mentioned in Table 1 except crr ∘ bl. The "KRHyper additional" column says how

Table 2. Result summary wrt. problem rating

Rating	#	MSPASS	KRHyper additional	Rating	#	MSPASS	KRHyper additional
1.00	4	0		0.40	47	26	1
0.80	57	24	4	0.33	8	4	1
0.67	26	5		0.20	70	50	
0.60	44	23	10	0.17	31	10	
0.50	5	0		0.00	223	198	1

many problems were solved by KRHyper (using the transformation sh ○ rr) that were not solvable in any combination with MSPASS. As far as we know, problems with rating 0.80 have so far been solved by one theorem prover only. It was notable that each problem with a rating 0.80 or 0.67 solvable by MSPASS required blocking. On the other hand, there were several unsolvable "easy" problems.

Together, this indicates that the approach presented here and the more established methods are orthogonal. This finding was confirmed by a comparison with MSPASS (in autonomous mode) and Paradox [9], a state-of-the-art MACE-style finite model builder. We ran Paradox on the same problem set, with the same time limit of five minutes (CPU time) and a limit on 400 MByte main memory consumption. There were several problems that were solved by Paradox but not with our methods. On the other side, there were 21 problems, all of the NLP category, that were be solved with our methods but not by Paradox. Each of these problems required shifting (and splitting) to be solvable by our methods. In about half of the cases blocking was essential, while the other half were solved by shifting alone. Without shifting (with or without splitting), none of these problems were solved. The runtimes varied between two and at most 15 seconds. Memory consumption was not an issue at all. By contrast, for 13 of these 21 problems Paradox was stopped prematurely because the memory limit was exceeded before the time limit was reached. We sampled some of these problems and re-ran Paradox without artificial limits. For the problem NLP049-1, for instance, about 10 million (ground) clauses were generated for a domain size of 8 elements, consuming about 1 GByte of main memory, and the underlying SAT solver did not complete its run within 15 minutes (we stopped it then). This picture seems typical for these problems. Regarding the comparison with MSPASS in autonomous mode, the differences in which problems were solvable were more pronounced.

5   Conclusions

We have presented and tested a number of enhancements for BUMG methods. An important aspect is that our enhancements exploit the strengths of readily available BUMG system without any, or only little modifications. Our techniques have the advantage over existing approaches based on transformations to range-restricted clauses that terms are added to the domain of interpretation on a "by need" basis. Moreover, we present methods that allow us to extend BUMG methods with a blocking technique, which has only been used in more the specialized setting for non-classical logics (with tree model properties). Related research in automated theorem proving has concentrated on developing refinements of resolution, mainly ordering refinements, for deciding numerous fragments of first-order logic. These fragments are complementary to the fragments that can be decided by refinements using the techniques presented in this paper. We thus extend the set of techniques available for resolution methods to turn them into more effective and efficient (terminating) automated reasoning methods. For example, based on the results of [21] we can use our transformations to decide the Bernays-Schönfinkel (BS) class. In particular, we can show that all procedures based on hyperresolution or BUMG can decide the class of BS formulae and the class of BS clauses (with equality).

Our approach is especially suitable for generating small models and we believe the approach allows us to compute finite models when they exist. The generated models do not need to be Herbrand models. It follows from how the transformations work that the generated models are quasi-Herbrand models, in the following sense. Whenever dom(s) and dom(t) hold in the (Herbrand) model constructed by the BUMG method, then (as in Herbrand interpretations) the terms s and t are mapped to themselves in the associated (possibly non-Herbrand) model. Reconsidering the example in the Introduction of the two unit clauses P(a) and Q(b), the associated model will map a and b to themselves, regardless as to which transformations are applied (as long as it includes rr). In this way, more informative models are produced than those computed by, e.g., MACE- and SEM-style finite model searchers.

We have implemented the approach and tested it with existing first-order logic theorem provers. The results demonstrate that our transformations are quite effective and many difficult TPTP problems can now be solved by BUMG methods, especially resolution with maximal selection or hyperresolution in MSPASS, and KRHyper. However, the results are far from conclusive, and we plan to develop and evaluate variants of our transformations, and experiment with alternative splitting strategies (particularly for MSPASS). Studying how well the ideas and techniques discussed in this paper can be exploited and behave in BUMG provers, and also tableau-based provers and other provers (including resolution-based provers) is very important but is beyond the scope of the present paper. We have started experimenting with another prover, Darwin [2], and first results are very encouraging. An in-depth comparison and analysis of BUMG approaches with our techniques and MACE-style or SEM-style model generation would also be of interest. Another source for future work is to combine our transformations with available BUMG techniques and improvements, such as magic sets transformations [14,23], a typed version of range-restriction [4], and minimal model computation. We speculate that our transformations carry over to the case with default negation, thus advancing, for example, answer-set programming beyond its current limitations.

Acknowledgement. Thanks to U. Furbach for comments on the paper and discussions.

References

1. F. Baader and U. Sattler. An overview of tableau algorithms for description logics. *Studia Logica*, 69:5–40, 2001.
2. P. Baumgartner, A. Fuchs, and C. Tinelli. DARWIN. http://goedel.cs.uiowa.edu/Darwin/.
3. P. Baumgartner, U. Furbach, and I. Niemelä. Hyper tableaux. In *Proc. JELIA 96*, vol. 1126 of *LNAI*. Springer, 1996.

4. P. Baumgartner, U. Furbach, and F. Stolzenburg. Computing answers with model elimination. *Artificial Intelligence*, 90(1–2):135–176, 1997.

5. P. Baumgartner and R. A. Schmidt. Blocking and other enhancements for bottom-up model generation methods. Technical report, National ICT Australia, http://www.nicta. com.au/director/research/publications/technical_reports.cfm, 2006.

6. M. Bezem. Disproving distributivity in lattices using geometry logic. In *Proc. CADE-20 Workshop on Disproving*, 2005.

7. F. Bry and S. Torge. A deduction method complete for refutation and finite satisfiability. In *Logics in Artificial Intelligence: JELIA'98*, vol. 1489 of *LNCS*, pp. 1–17. Springer, 1998.

8. F. Bry and A. Yahya. Positive unit hyperresolution tableaux for minimal model generation. *J. Automated Reasoning*, 25(1):35–82, 2000.

9. K. Claessen and N. Sörensson. New techniques that improve MACE-style finite model building. In *Proc. CADE-19 Workshop on Model Computation*, 2003.

10. C. Fermüller and A. Leitsch. Model building by resolution. In *Computer Science Logic: CSL'92*, vol. 702 of *LNCS*, pp. 134–148. Springer, 1993.

11. M. Fujita, J. Slaney, and F. Bennett. Automatic generation of some results in finite algebra. In *Proc. IJCAI'95*, pp. 52–57. Morgan Kaufmann, 1995.

12. T. Geisler, S. Panne, and H. Schütz. Satchmo: The compiling and functional variants. *J. Automated Reasoning*, 18(2):227–236, 1997.

13. L. Georgieva, U. Hustadt, and R. A. Schmidt. Computational space efficiency and minimal model generation for guarded formulae. In *Logic for Programming, Artificial Intelligence, and Reasoning: LPAR 2001*, vol. 2250 of *LNAI*, pp. 85–99. Springer, 2001.

14. R. Hasegawa, K. Inoue, Y. Ohta, and M. Koshimura. Non-horn magic sets to incorporate top-down inference into bottom-up theorem proving. In *Automated Deduction: CADE-14*, vol. 1249 of *LNCS*, pp. 176–190. Springer, 1997.

15. R. Manthey and F. Bry. SATCHMO: a theorem prover implemented in Prolog. In *Proc. CADE'88*, vol. 310 of *LNCS*, pp. 415–434. Springer, 1988.

16. W. McCune. A Davis-Putnam Program and its Application to Finite First-Order Model Search: Quasigroup Existence Problems. Technical Report MCS-TM-194, ANL, 1994.

17. W. McCune. Mace4 reference manual and guide. Technical Memorandum 264, Argonne National Laboratory, 2003.

18. R. Nieuwenhuis and A. Rubio. Paramodulation-based theorem proving. In J. Robinson and A. Voronkov, editors, *Handbook of Automated Reasoning*. Elsevier and MIT Press, 2001.

19. J. A. Robinson. Automatic deduction with hyper-resolution. *Internat. J. Computer Math.*, 1(3):227–234, 1965.

20. R. A. Schmidt. MSPASS. http://www.cs.man.ac.uk/~schmidt/mspass/.

21. R. A. Schmidt and U. Hustadt. Solvability with resolution of problems in the Bernays-Schönfinkel class. Presented at Dagstuhl Seminar 05431 and ARW 2006, Bristol, 2005.

22. J. Slaney. FINDER (finite domain enumerator): Notes and guide. Technical Report TR-ARP-1/92, Australian National University, 1992.

23. M. E. Stickel. Upside-down meta-interpretation of the model elimination theorem-proving procedure for deduction and abduction. *J. Automated Reasoning*, 13(2):189–210, 1994.

24. C. Weidenbach. SPASS. http://spass.mpi-sb.mpg.de.

25. C. Wernhard. System description: KRHyper. In *Proc. CADE-19 Workshop on Model Computation: Principles, Algorithms, Applications Systems*, 2003.

26. H. Zhang. Sem: a system for enumerating models. In *Proc. IJCAI'95*, pp. 298–303. Morgan Kaufmann, 1995.

The MathServe System
for Semantic Web Reasoning Services

Jürgen Zimmer[1] and Serge Autexier[1,2]

[1] FB Informatik, Universität des Saarlandes, D-66041 Saarbrücken, Germany
[2] DFKI, Stuhlsatzenhausweg 3, D-66123 Saarbrücken, Germany
{jzimmer, autexier}@ags.uni-sb.de

1 Introduction

In recent years, formal verification of hardware and software components has increasingly attracted interest from both academia and industry. The widespread use of automated reasoning techniques requires tools that are easy to use and support standardised protocols and data exchange formats. In [1] the first author presented the MathWeb Software Bus, a first step towards re-usable reasoning services. The MathWeb-SB had several drawbacks which limited its usability. For example, it had no service brokering capabilities and *the user* had to know exactly which reasoning system to use to solve a problem and how to access it.

Here we present the MathServe system that overcomes the limitations of the MathWeb-SB. MathServe offers reasoning systems as Semantic Web Services described in OWL-S [2]. MathServe's service broker can automatically find suitable services (and compositions of services) to solve a given reasoning problem. The use of Semantic Web technology allows applications and humans to automatically retrieve and access reasoning services via the Internet. MathServe complements similar projects, such as the *MathBroker* project [3], which describe computational services as Semantic Web Services. We provide and overview of the MathServe system in § 2 and describe the evaluation of the system at CASC-20 in § 3. We conclude and discuss future work in § 4.

2 The MathServe System

The MathServe system is based on state-of-the-art technologies for Semantic Web Services: It integrates reasoning systems as *Web Services*. The semantics of these Web Services is described in the OWL-S upper ontology for Web Services [2]. OWL-S *service profiles* define the inputs and outputs as well as the preconditions and effects of Web Services. MathServe services and the service broker are accessed by means of standard Web Service languages and protocols.

Client applications can interact with MathServe in two principal ways: All reasoning services can be invoked individually with reasoning problems. Complex queries can be sent to the MathServe broker which can perform service

U. Furbach and N. Shankar (Eds.): IJCAR 2006, LNAI 4130, pp. 140–144, 2006.
© Springer-Verlag Berlin Heidelberg 2006

matchmaking and automated service composition. Given a query containing a reasoning problem, service matchmaking returns a list of standalone services that can potentially answer that query. So far, service matchmaking simply performs class subsumption tests on the types of input and output parameters of available services and the query provided. If no single service can answer a query, MathServe's *service composer* can automatically combine services using classical AI planning and decision-theoretic reasoning.

Reasoning problems and their solutions are encoded in OWL/RDF format [4]. The primary interface to MathServe is the standard Web Service interface defined in the Web Service Description Language (WSDL). Services are invoked via the Simple Object Access Protocol (SOAP). Tools and libraries for WSDL and SOAP are available in many mainstream programming languages. Next to the SOAP interface, the MathServe broker offers an XML-RPC interface with convenient interface methods similar to the ones described in [1].

Reasoning Services in MathServe. MathServe provides several reasoning systems for classical first-order logic with equality as Semantic Web Services: 1) Services for clause normal form transformation of first-order problems are provided by the tptp2X utility and the FLOTTER system (available with SPASS [5]). 2) A problem analysing service can determine the *Specialist Problem Class* of a theorem proving problem (see below). 3) Deduction services are provided by state-of-the-art Automated Theorem Proving (ATP) systems. 4) Transformations of formal proofs are performed by the systems Otterfier [6] and TRAMP [7]. We cannot describe all these services in this paper. Detailed descriptions of the services provided by Otterfier and TRAMP can be found in [6]. In this paper, we focus on first-order ATP services. With respect to ATP services, MathServe is similar to the SSCPA system[1], which has been developed for human users, while MathServe's services can be consumed by software applications.

The latest version of MathServe offers the ATP systems DCTP 10.21p, EP 0.91, Otter 3.3, SPASS 2.2, Vampire 8.0 and Waldmeister 704 as Semantic Web Services (see [5] for ATP system descriptions). All theorem proving services support the same Web Service interface and can be invoked with a theorem proving problem, a CPU time limit, and (optionally) prover-specific options. The answers provided by ATP services specify unambiguously what has been established by the underlying system. For this, we developed an ontology of 18 well-defined ATP statuses [8]. Furthermore, results of ATP services contain the complete output of the prover, a reference to the problem submitted, the CPU and wall-clock time used, and, if available, resolution proofs in the new TPTP format.

OWL-S Descriptions of ATP Services. The performance of an ATP system depends on the computational resources given to the prover as well as the type of the problem to solve. *Sutcliffe* and *Suttner* [9] identified six "objective problem features" that have an impact on the performance of ATP systems. The

---
[1] Accessible via the TPTP web site (http://www.tptp.org).

```
profile VampireATP:
inputs:   tptp_problem :: mw#TptpProblem
          time_res :: mw#TimeResource
outputs:  atp_result :: mw#FoAtpResult
preconds:
effects:  resultFor(atp_result, tptp_problem)
categs:
params:   problemClass(tptp_problem, mw#FOF_NKC_EPR)
          ⇒ status(atp_result, stat#Theorem) (0.93) (4755ms)
          problemClass(tptp_problem, mw#CNF_NKS_RFO_SEQ_NHN)
          ⇒ status(atp_result, stat#Unsatisfiable) (0.52) (20984ms)
          ...
stat = http://www.mathweb.org/owl/status.owl
mw = http://www.mathweb.org/owl/mathserv.owl
```

Fig. 1. The OWL-S service profile of VampireATP

meaningful combinations of these features define 21 *Specialist Problem Classes* (SPCs) [9]. [2] All OWL-S service profiles for the above-mentioned ATP systems are annotated with data reflecting the performance of the system on the TPTP Library v3.1.1. For every SPC and every ATP system we have calculated the ratio of (TPTP Library) problems in that SPC solved by the system. We assume this ratio to be a good estimate for the system's probability of success on that SPC. The average CPU time for solved problems represents the average cost of the ATP service on that SPC. The performance data is modelled as conditional probabilistic effects of ATP service profiles and is used by the MathServe broker to choose the most suitable service for given proving problems.

Fig. 1 shows the OWL-S service profile of the service for Vampire 8.0.[3] Like all ATP services VampireATP takes a problem in the new TPTP format and a TimeResouce as inputs. It returns a first-order ATP result as described above. The *service parameters* contain the performance information, which indicates, for instance, that the service can prove the input problem with probability 93% if the problem is in the SPC FOF_NKC_EPR. The average time for proving conjectures in this SPC is 4.8 secs. For CNF_NKS_RFO_SEQ_NHN the probability of success is only 52% and the average CPU time for proving is 21 secs. The service profile contains similar statements for the remaining 19 SPCs.

Automated Reasoning Service Composition. Service composition in MathServe is a two-stage process. In the first stage the classical AI planning system PRODIGY [10] is used to find suitable sequences of reasoning services that can potentially answer a given query. In the second stage, the plans found by PRODIGY are combined and the probabilistic effects of a service (e.g., the

[2] For instance, CNF_NKS_RFO_SEQ_NHN is the SPC of problems in clause normal form that are potential "theorems" (not known to be satisfiable, NKS), are real first-order problems (RFO), contain some equality literals (SEQ) and non-Horn clauses (NHN).

[3] The XML namespaces stat and mw refer to MathServe's domain ontologies.

performance data in Fig. 1) are taken into account. A decision-theoretic reasoner computes an *optimal policy*, i.e. a program with conditional statements that maximises the probability of success by choosing different (parts of) plans in the context of a particular reasoning problem. In the case of ATP services, for instance, the optimal policy first analyses the problem at hand and then chooses the most promising ATP service depending on the SPC of the problem.

3 System Evaluation

MathServe participated in the demonstration division of the 20th CADE ATP System Competition (CASC-20) [5]. We evaluated MathServe's brokering capabilities for theorem proving services. Since MathServe does not constitute a new ATP system, but employs other ATP systems, it participated in the *demonstration division* in which systems are not formally ranked. As a preparation for the system competition we measured the performance of the ATP systems EP 0.82, Otter 3.3, SPASS 2.1 and Vampire 7.0 on the TPTP Library (v3.0.1) with a CPU time limit of 300 seconds per problem. The OWL-S profiles were annotated with the resulting performance information as described in the previous section. The MathServe broker computed an optimal policy from this data. The problem set of CASC-20 was composed of 660 randomly chosen problems from the TPTP Library (v3.1.0). 147 of these problems had not been seen by the competition participants before. A MathServe client was run sequentially on all 660 problems with a 600sec CPU time limit. The broker's optimal policy determined the SPC of each problem and chose the most promising ATP service according to the performance data recorded before. MathServe could solve 392 problems. Table 1 shows that MathServe could not solve as many problems as the leading ATP systems EP (409) and Vampire (430). This was due to the significant improvements made to the most recent versions of these ATP systems. These improved systems were not available to MathServe at the time of the competition. Furthermore, MathServe could not handle six problems of extraordinary size (> 2MB). If MathServe had used the competition versions of EP and Vampire (and the corresponding optimal policy) it would have solved 440 problems. After CASC-20 we improved MathServe by integrating the latest versions of the ATP systems EP and Vampire as well as the specialised provers DCTP and Waldmeister. We also changed the problem processing of MathServe such that it can now handle large problems.

Table 1. MathServe's performance at CASC-20 compared to EP and Vampire

System	Problems given	Problems solved	Percentage of given	Percentage complete
MathServe 0.62	660	392	59.4%	59.4%
Ep 0.9pre3	660	409	62.0%	62.0%
Vampire 8.0	540	430	79.6%	65.2%

4   Conclusions and Future Work

We described the MathServe system which offers several reasoning systems as Semantic Web Services. All services are accessible via standard Web Service protocols. MathServe's service broker can automatically find suitable services (and service compositions) for a given reasoning problem. The evaluation of MathServe in CASC-20 showed that the system performs well in a competition environment. In the future we will extend MathServe with services provided by finite model finding systems and decision procedures. Furthermore, we are planning to enhance the semantic descriptions of composite services by allowing parallel execution (as offered by the SCCPA system) and explicit time resource assignments.

The MathServe system is free software available under the GNU Public License. A binary distribution of the MathServe system is available from the system web page at http://www.ags.uni-sb.de/~jzimmer/mathserve.html. The system sources can be obtained via anonymous CVS.

References

1. Zimmer, J., Kohlhase, M.: System Description: The Mathweb Software Bus for Distributed Mathematical Reasoning. In Voronkov, A., ed.: Proc. of CADE-18. Number 2392 in LNAI, Springer Verlag, Berlin (2002) 139–143
2. Martin, D., et al.: OWL-S: Semantic Markup for Web Services. http://www.daml.org/services/owl-s/1.1/overview(2004)
3. Schreiner, W., Caprotti, O.: The MathBroker Project. http://poseidon.risc.uni-linz.ac.at:8080/mathbroker/ (2001)
4. Bechhofer, S., van Harmelen, F., Hendler, F.U.A.J., Horrocks, I., McGuinness, D.L., Patel-Schneider, P.F., Stein, L.A.: OWL Web Ontology Language Reference. http://www.w3.org/TR/owl-ref/ (2004)
5. Sutcliffe, G.: The CADE-20 Automated Theorem Proving Competition. AI Communications (2006)
6. Zimmer, J., Meier, A., Sutcliffe, G., Zhang, Y.: Integrated Proof Transformation Services. In Benzmüller, C., Windsteiger, W., eds.: Proc. of the Workshop on Computer-Supported Mathematical Theory Development, Cork, Ireland (2004)
7. Meier, A.: TRAMP: Transformation of Machine-Found Proofs into Natural Deduction Proofs at the Assertion Level. In McAllester, D., ed.: Proc. of CADE-17. Volume 1831 of LNAI., Springer Verlag (2000) 460–464
8. Sutcliffe, G., Zimmer, J., Schulz, S.: Communication Fomalisms for Automated Theorem Proving Tools. In Sorge, V., Colton, S., Fisher, M., Gow, J., eds.: Proc. of the IJCAI'03 Workshop on Agents and Automated Reasoning. (2003)
9. Sutcliffe, G., Suttner, C.: Evaluating General Purpose Automated Theorem Proving Systems. Artificial Intelligence 131(1-2) (2001) 39–54
10. Veloso, M., et al.: Integrating Planning and Learning: The PRODIGY Architecture. Journal of Experimental and Theoretical Artificial Intelligence 7(1) (1995)

System Description: GCLCprover + GeoThms

Predrag Janičić[1,*] and Pedro Quaresma[2,**]

[1] Faculty of Mathematics, University of Belgrade
Studentski trg 16, 11000 Belgrade, Serbia & Montenegro
janicic@matf.bg.ac.yu
[2] CISUC – Department of Mathematics, University of Coimbra
3001-454 Coimbra, Portugal
pedro@mat.uc.pt

1 Introduction

Dynamic geometry tools (e.g., *Cinderella, Geometer's Sketchpad, Cabri, Euklei-des*[1]) visualise geometric objects, allow interactive work, and link formal, axiomatic nature of geometry (most often — Euclidean) with its standard models (e.g., Cartesian model) and corresponding illustrations. These tools are used in teaching and studying geometry, some of them also for producing digital illustrations. The common experience is that dynamic geometry tools significantly help students to acquire knowledge about geometric objects. However, despite the fact that geometry is an axiomatic theory, most (if not all) of these tools concentrate only on concrete models of some geometric constructions and not on their abstract properties — their properties in deductive terms. The user can vary some initial objects and parameters and test if some property holds in all checked cases, but this still does not mean that the given property is valid.

We have extended GCLC, a widely used dynamic geometry package,[2] with a module that allows formal, deductive reasoning about constructions made in the main, drawing module. The built-in theorem prover (GCLCprover in the following text), is based on the area method [1,2,6]. It produces proofs that are human-readable (in LaTeX form), and with a justification for each proof step. It is also possible, via a conversion tool, to reason about constructions made with Eukleides [7,9]. Hence, the prover can be used in conjunction with other dynamic

---

* This work was partially supported by the programme POSC, by the Centro Internacional de Matemática (CIM), under the programme "Research in Pairs", while visiting Coimbra University under the Coimbra Group Hospitality Scheme. Also, partially supported by Serbian Ministry of Science and Technology grant 144030.
** This work was partially supported by programme POSC.
[1] See   http://www.cinderella.de,   http://www.keypress.com/sketchpad/, http://www.cabri.com, http://www.eukleides.org
[2] GCLC (originally a tool for producing geometrical illustrations for LaTeX, hence its name — *Geometrical Constructions → LaTeX Converter*) [3,4] provides support for a range of geometrical constructions, isometric transformations, parametric curves, but also for symbolic expressions, and program loops. The basic idea behind GCLC is that constructions are formal procedures, rather than drawings. Thus, producing illustrations is based on "describing figures" rather than of "drawing figures".

U. Furbach and N. Shankar (Eds.): IJCAR 2006, LNAI 4130, pp. 145–150, 2006.

geometry tools, which demonstrates the flexibility of the developed deduction module. Closely linked to the mentioned tools is GeoThms — a web tool that integrates dynamic geometry tools, geometry theorem provers, and a repository of geometry theorems and proofs. This integrated framework for constructive geometry, provides an environment suitable for new ways of studying and teaching geometry at different levels.

2   GCLCprover

Automated theorem proving in geometry has two major lines of research: synthetic proof style and algebraic proof style (see, for instance, [5] for a survey). Algebraic proof style methods are based on reducing geometric properties to algebraic properties expressed in terms of Cartesian coordinates. These methods are usually very efficient, but the proofs they produce do not reflect the geometric nature of the problem and they give only a yes/no conclusion. Synthetic methods attempt to automate traditional geometry proof methods.

The area method. This method (in the core of the prover built into GCLC) is a synthetic method providing traditional (not coordinate-based), human-readable proofs [1,2,6]. The proofs are expressed in terms of higher-level geometric lemmas and expression simplifications. The main idea of the method is to express hypotheses of a theorem using a set of constructive statements, each of them introducing a new point, and to express a conclusion by an equality of expressions in geometric quantities (e.g., signed area of a triangle), without referring to Cartesian coordinates. The proof is then based on eliminating (in reverse order) the points introduced before, using for that purpose a set of appropriate lemmas. After eliminating all introduced points, the current goal becomes an equality between two expressions in quantities over independent points. If it is trivially true, then the original conjecture was proved valid, if it is trivially false, then the conjecture was proved invalid, otherwise, the conjecture has been neither proved nor disproved. In all stages, different simplifications are applied to the current goal. Some steps require proving some lemmas (giving proofs on different levels).

Geometrical quantities. In our implementation of the area method, we deal with the following basic geometric quantities: *ratio of directed segments* ($\frac{\overline{AB}}{\overline{CD}}$), *signed area* ($S_{ABC}$ — signed area of a triangle ABC) and *Pythagoras difference* (P_{ABC} $= AB^2 + CB^2 - AC^2$) (for details see [8]). The conjecture is built from these geometric quantities (over points already introduced within the current construction), eventually combined together by standard arithmetic operators. A wide range of geometric conjectures can be simply stated in that way.

Properties of the area method. The procedure based on the area methods is terminating, sound, and complete: it can prove *any* geometry theorem expressed in terms of geometric quantities, and involving only points introduced by using a specific set of constructions (see below). Therefore, the procedure is a decision procedure for the described fragment of geometry. This fragment can be defined as axiomatic quantifier-free theory with the set of axioms equal to the set of all simplification and elimination rules (taken as not-oriented equalities). It can be easily shown that this theory is a sub-theory of Euclidean geometry augmented by the theory of real numbers. The method does not have any branching, which makes it very efficient for many non-trivial geometry theorems. The method can transform a conjecture given as a geometry quantity of a degree d, involving n constructed points, to a quantity not involving constructed points, and with a degree at most $5d3^{5n}$ [1], while this number is usually much less, and not reached, also thanks to the used simplification steps.

Primitive steps. Our theorem prover is a sort of rational reconstruction of the area method. The proofs are built from primitive steps: elimination steps and simplification steps. Simplifications are made explicit and based on rewrite rules. We divide simplification steps into two groups: *(i)* algebraic simplifications — apply simplification rewrite rules (not directly related to geometry, but to the properties of reals) such as: $x + 0 \to x$, $\frac{x}{y} + \frac{u}{v} \to \frac{x \cdot v + u \cdot y}{y \cdot v}$, etc; *(ii)* geometric simplifications — apply simplification rewrite rules, directly related to geometric quantities such as: $P_{AAB} \to 0$, $S_{ABC} \to S_{BCA}$. All simplifications and elimination lemmas are proved in full details in [8].

Integration. It is often the case that an application providing different functionalities is built around a theorem prover. In GCLC, we have faced the challenging problem of integrating a theorem prover into well-developed tool with well defined set of functionalities, and we have succeeded in building a system where the prover is tightly integrated. This means that one can use the prover to reason about a GCLC construction (i.e., about objects introduced in it), without adapting it for the deduction process — the user only needs to add the conclusion he/she wants to prove. GCLC and GCLCprover share (only) the parsing module, which is responsible for processing the input file and passing to GCLCprover the construction steps performed. These steps are internally transformed into primitive constructions of the area method, and in some cases, some auxiliary points are introduced. The constructions accepted by GCLCprover are: construction of a line given two points; an intersection of two lines; the midpoint of a segment; a segment bisector; a line passing through a given point, perpendicular to a given line; a foot from a point to a given line; a line passing through a given point, parallel to a given line; an image of a point in a given translation; an image of a point in a given scaling transformation; a random point on a given line.

3   GeoThms

GeoThms is a framework that links dynamic geometry tools (GCLC, Eukleides), geometry theorem provers (GCLCprover), and a repository of geometry problems (geoDB). GeoThms provides a Web workbench in the field of constructive problems in Euclidean geometry. Its tight integration with dynamic geometry software and automatic theorem provers (GCLC, Eukleides, and GCLCprover, for the moment) and its repository of theorems, figures and proofs, gives the user the possibility to easily browse through the list of geometric problems,

148   P. Janičić and P. Quaresma

their statements (both in natural-language form and as GCLC/Eukleies code),
illustrations and proofs, and also to interactively use the drawing and proving
programs.

4   Implementation and Experiences

The GCLCprover was implemented in C++ (having around 7000 lines of code)
and is very efficient. The theorem prover produces proofs in LaTeX form and a report about the proving process: whether the conjecture was proved or disproved,
data about CPU time spent, and the number of proof steps performed (in several
categories). At the beginning of the proof, auxiliary points are defined. For each
proof step, there is a justification, and (optionally) its semantics counterpart
(not used in the proof itself, but it can be used for testing conjectures). The
prover can prove many complex geometric problems in milliseconds, producing
short and readable proofs.[3] Results shown in Table 1 were obtained on a PC
Intel Pentium-IV, 3.2GHz, 1GB RAM. Let us consider, as a simple example, the
Midpoint's theorem, which can be expressed and proved within GCLC. The proof
produced in 0.002s is very small and readable (see Figure 1).

Table 1. Experimental results

Theorem	elimination steps	geometric steps	algebraic steps	time (sec)
Ceva	3	6	23	0.001
Gauss line	14	51	234	0.029
Midpoint	8	19	45	0.002
Thales	6	18	34	0.001
Menelaus	5	9	39	0.002
Pappus' Hexagon	24	65	269	0.040
Areas of Parallelograms	62	152	582	0.190

GeoThms is implemented in MySQL and PHP and uses LaTeX (and some
other auxiliary tools) to format the output and show data in a web-page.

GCLC is available from: http://www.matf.bg.ac.yu/~janicic/gclc/, and
GeoThms is accessible from: http://hilbert.mat.uc.pt/~geothms.

5   Future Work and Conclusion

The GCLCprover and GeoThms are parts of an integrated framework for constructive geometry, providing an environment suitable for studying and teaching
geometry. In this system, the axiomatic nature of geometric objects is tightly
linked to their standard representation (in Cartesian plane) and the formal reasoning is linked to human intuition. We believe that such a system brings new

---

[3] Some theorems need more then 10000 steps to be proved.

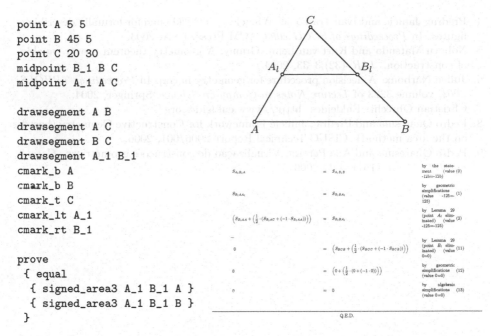

```
point A 5 5
point B 45 5
point C 20 30
midpoint B_1 B C
midpoint A_1 A C

drawsegment A B
drawsegment A C
drawsegment B C
drawsegment A_1 B_1
cmark_b A
cmark_b B
cmark_t C
cmark_lt A_1
cmark_rt B_1

prove
{ equal
  { signed_area3 A_1 B_1 A }
  { signed_area3 A_1 B_1 B }
}
```

Fig. 1. Midpoint's Theorem: the GCLC code with the conjecture ($AB \| A_1B_1$, expressed as $S_{A_1B_1A}=S_{A_1B_1B}$) (left), the corresponding illustration and a part of the proof (right)

dimension in teaching and studying geometry. This system, and the GEX tool[4] (new version is currently under development) are, to our knowledge, the only dynamic geometry tools with automated deduction modules (however, unlike GCLCprover, the GEX prover implements an algebraic proof method).

We are planning to extend the prover with support for additional sets of constructions and additional heuristics, and to use the prover for run-time control of correct geometric constructions. We are also considering implementing (and linking to dynamic geometry tools) other methods for automated proving of geometry theorems. Regarding GeoThms, we are planning to work on further integration of the visualisation tools and proving tools, and on further functionalities for interactive work.

References

1. Shang-Ching Chou, Xiao-Shan Gao, and Jing-Zhong Zhang. Automated production of traditional proofs for constructive geometry theorems. *Proceedings LICS*, pages 48–56. IEEE Computer Society Press, June 1993.
2. Shang-Ching Chou, Xiao-Shan Gao, and Jing-Zhong Zhang. Automated generation of readable proofs with geometric invariants, I. *JAR*, 17:325–347, 1996.
3. Mirjana Djorić and Predrag Janičić. Constructions, instructions, interactions. *Teaching Mathematics and its Applications*, 23(2):69–88, 2004.

---

[4] GEX tool: http://woody.cs.wichita.edu/gex/7-10/gex.html

4. Predrag Janičić and Ivan Trajković. Wingclc — a workbench for formally describing figures. In *Proceedings of SCCG 2003*, ACM Press, USA, 2003.
5. Noboru Matsuda and Kurt van Lehn. Gramy: A geometry theorem prover capable of construction. *JAR*, (32):3–33, 2004.
6. Julien Narboux. A decision procedure for geometry in coq. In *Proceedings TPHOLS 2004*, volume 3223 of *Lecture Notes in Computer Science*. Springer, 2004.
7. Christian Obrecht. Eukleides. http://www.eukleides.org/.
8. Pedro Quaresma and Predrag Janičić Framework for Constructive Geometry (based on the area method). CISUC Technical Report 2006/001, 2006.
9. Pedro Quaresma and Ana Pereira. Visualização de construções geométricas. *Gazeta de Matemática*, (151), July 2006.

A Sufficient Completeness Checker for Linear Order-Sorted Specifications Modulo Axioms*

Joe Hendrix[1], José Meseguer[1], and Hitoshi Ohsaki[2]

[1] University of Illinois at Urbana-Champaign
{jhendrix, meseguer}@uiuc.edu
[2] National Institute of Advanced Industrial Science and Technology
ohsaki@ni.aist.go.jp

Abstract. We present a tool for checking the sufficient completeness of left-linear, order-sorted equational specifications modulo associativity, commutativity, and identity. Our tool treats this problem as an equational tree automata decision problem using the tree automata library CETA, which we also introduce in this paper. CETA implements a semi-algorithm for checking the emptiness of a class of tree automata that are closed under Boolean operations and an equational theory containing associativity, commutativity and identity axioms. Though sufficient completeness for this class of specifications is undecidable in general, our tool is a decision procedure for subcases known to be decidable, and has specialized techniques that are effective in practice for the general case.

1   Introduction

An equational specification is sufficiently complete when enough equations have been specified so that the functions defined by the specification are fully defined on all relevant data elements. This is an important property to check, both to debug and formally reason about specifications and equational programs. For example, many inductive theorem proving techniques are based on the constructors building up the data and require that the specification is sufficiently complete.

Sufficient completeness was introduced in the Ph.D. thesis of Guttag. (see [4] for a more accessible treatment). For a good review of literature up to the late 80s, as well as some key decidability/undecidability results see [8, 9]. More recent developments show sufficient completeness as a tree automata decision problem (see [2] and references there). For unsorted, unconditional, weakly-normalizing, and confluent specifications, the problem is EXPTIME-complete [3].

Over the last 20 years, there have been numerous rewriting-based programming languages developed which support increasingly more expressive equational logics, including OBJ, Maude, ELAN, and CafeOBJ. These developments lead to a corresponding demand for reasoning tools that support these formalisms. In particular, there is a practical need for sufficient completeness checkers supporting: (1) conditional rewrite rules; (2) more expressive type formalisms such as order-sorted logic and membership equational logic; and (3) rewriting modulo

* Research supported by ONR Grant N00014-02-1-0715.

U. Furbach and N. Shankar (Eds.): IJCAR 2006, LNAI 4130, pp. 151–155, 2006.
© Springer-Verlag Berlin Heidelberg 2006

associativity, commutativity, and identity. Our earlier work in [5] addresses (1) and (2) through integration with an inductive theorem prover. Other recent work in [1] also addresses (1) using tree automata with constraints. The new tool we present in this paper addresses (2) and (3). Our checker is publicly available for download along with documentation and examples at the website: http://maude.cs.uiuc.edu/tools/scc/.

In an equational specification $\mathcal{E} = (\Sigma, E)$ with rewriting modulo axioms, the equations are partitioned into two disjoint sets A and R. The set A consists of any combination of associativity, commutativity, and identity axioms. The other equations $l = r \in R$ are treated as rewrite rules $l \rightarrow r$ modulo A. A term t rewrites to u modulo A, denoted $t \rightarrow_{R/A} u$ when there is a context C and substitution θ such that $t =_A C[l\theta]$ and $C[r\theta] =_A u$.

Our checker casts the left-linear, order-sorted sufficient completeness problem with rewriting modulo A as a decision problem for *equational tree automata* [10]. Equational tree automata over left-linear theories recognize precisely the equational closure of regular tree languages. However, since equational tree automata with associative symbols are not closed under Boolean operations [10], for checking properties such as inclusion, universality, and intersection-emptiness, we found it useful to introduce a new tree automata framework in [6], called *Propositional Tree Automata* (PTA), that is closed with respect both to Boolean operations and an equational theory.

2 Order-Sorted Sufficient Completeness

The motivation for sufficient completeness of a specification stems from the idea that introducing a new defined function should leave the underlying data elements unchanged. From a model-theoretic perspective, the initial model of the specification with the defined functions should be isomorphic to the initial model with only the constructor declarations. In the order-sorted context, we want to preserve this view of sufficient completeness, but the picture becomes more subtle due to the subsort relation and overloading — a symbol may be overloaded so that it is a constructor on one domain, and a defined symbol on another domain. As an example, we present a specification of lists of natural numbers with an associative append operator in Maude syntax.

```
fmod NATLIST is
  sorts Nat List NeList .     subsorts Nat < NeList < List .
  op 0 : -> Nat [ctor].   op s : Nat -> Nat [ctor].
  op nil : -> List [ctor].
  op __ : NeList NeList -> NeList [ctor assoc id: nil].
  op __ : List List -> List [assoc id: nil].
  op head : NeList -> Nat .   op tail : NeList -> List .
  op reverse : List -> List .
  var N : Nat .    var L : List .
  eq head(N L) = N .   eq tail(N L) = L .
  eq reverse(N L) = reverse(L) N .    eq reverse(nil) = nil .
endfm
```

In this specification, the signature Σ is defined by the sort, subsort, and operator declarations. The ctor attribute specifies an operator as a constructor. The operator attributes assoc and id: nil define the axioms in A. The equations declarations define the rules in R. The append operator $\_\_$ is overloaded: it is defined on all lists, but only a constructor on non-empty lists.

In the unsorted context, sufficient completeness for weakly-normalizing and confluent specifications is usually checked by showing that every term containing a defined symbol at the root is reducible. In an order-sorted context in which the same symbol can be both a constructor and defined symbol, this check is *too strong*. Instead, we need to check that that for each term $f(t_1, \ldots, t_n)$ where $f : s_1 \ldots s_n \rightarrow s$ is a defined symbol and every t_i is a constructor term of sort s_i, either $f(t_1, \ldots, t_n)$ is reducible, or $f(t_1, \ldots, t_n)$ is itself a constructor term of sort s. For details on why this property implies sufficient completeness, see [6] (which shows this in an even more general membership-equational context). It should be noted that there is an additional requirement for order-sorted specifications: the equations should be *sort-decreasing*. By this we mean that applying an equation $l = r$ to a term $l\theta$ of sort s should yield a term $r\theta$ whose sort is less than or equal to s.

Our paper [6] shows in detail how to convert the sufficient completeness property into a propositional tree automata emptiness problem. The key idea is that given an order-sorted specification $\mathcal{E} = (\Sigma, A \cup R)$ with sorts S, we can construct the following automata for each sort $s \in S$: (1) an automaton $\mathcal{A}_s^c$ accepting constructor terms of sort s; (2) an automaton $\mathcal{A}_s^d$ accepting terms whose root is a defined symbol of sort s and whose subterms are constructor terms; and (3) an automaton $\mathcal{A}^r$ accepting any term reducible by equations in R. If $\mathcal{E}$ is weakly-normalizing, ground confluent, and ground sort-decreasing modulo A, then $\mathcal{E}$ is sufficiently complete iff. $\mathcal{L}(\mathcal{A}_s^d) \subseteq \mathcal{L}(\mathcal{A}^r) \cup \mathcal{L}(\mathcal{A}_s^c)$ for each sort $s \in S$. Using our propositional tree automata framework, we in turn translate this problem into checking the emptiness of $\bigcup_{s \in S} \mathcal{L}(\mathcal{A}_s^d) - (\mathcal{L}(\mathcal{A}^r) \cup \mathcal{L}(\mathcal{A}_s^c))$.

This emptiness problem is decidable when the axioms in the specification are any combination of associativity, commutativity, and identity, except when a symbol is associative but not commutative. For the case of commutativity alone, this was shown in [10]. For symbols that are both associative and commutative, this was shown in [11]. Identity equations are transformed into identity rewrite rules using a specialized completion procedure along the lines of coherence completion in [13]. Our emptiness test identifies terms that are in normal form with respect to the identity rewrite rules. For symbols that are associative and not commutative, the emptiness problem is undecidable. For these symbols, our tool uses the semi-algorithm in [7], which we have found works well in practice. Collectively, these results allow our tool to handle specifications with any combination of associativity, commutativity, and identity axioms.

3   The Sufficient Completeness Checker (SCC)

The SCC has two major components: an analyzer written in Maude that generates the tree automaton emptiness problem from a Maude specification; and a C++ library called CETA that performs the emptiness check.

Analyzer: The analyzer accepts commands from the user, generates PTA from Maude specifications, forwards the PTA decision problems to CETA, and presents the user with the results. If the specification is not sufficiently complete, the tool shows the user a counterexample illustrating the error. The analyzer consists of approximately 900 lines of Maude code, and exploits Maude's support for reflection. The specifications it checks are also written in Maude.

If the user asks the tool to check the sufficient completeness of a specification that is not left-linear and unconditional, the tool transforms the specification by renaming variables and dropping conditions in to a checkable order-sorted left-linear specification. Even if the tool is able to verify the sufficient completeness of the transformed specification, it warns the user that it cannot show the sufficient completeness of the original specification. However, any counterexamples found in the transformed specification are also counterexamples in the original specification. We have found this feature quite useful to identify errors in Maude specifications falling outside the decidable class — including the sufficient completeness checker itself.

CETA: The propositional tree automaton generated by the analyzer is forwarded to the tree automata library CETA which we have developed. CETA is a complex C++ library with approximately 10 thousand lines of code. Emptiness checking is performed by a subset construction algorithm extended with support for associative and commutativity axioms as described in [7]. The reason that CETA is so large is that the subset construction algorithm relies on quite complex algorithms on context free grammars, semilinear sets, and finite automata. We have found that CETA performs quite well for our purposes. Most examples can be verified in seconds. The slowest specification that we have checked is the sufficient completeness analyzer itself — the library requires just under a minute on a Pentium 4 desktop to check the 900 lines of Maude code in the analyzer. As an example, we present a tool session in which we check two specifications: NATLIST from the previous section; and NATLIST-ERROR which updates NATLIST to change the operator declaration of head from op head : NeList -> Nat to op head : List -> Nat.

```
Maude> in natlist.maude
==========================================
fmod NATLIST
==========================================
fmod NATLIST-ERROR
Maude> load scc.maude
Maude> loop init-scc .
Starting the Maude Sufficient Completeness Checker.
Maude> (scc NATLIST .)
Checking sufficient completeness of NATLIST ...
Success: NATLIST is sufficiently complete under the assumption that it is
   weakly-normalizing, ground confluent, and sort-decreasing.
Maude> (scc NATLIST-ERROR .)
Checking sufficient completeness of NATLIST-ERROR ...
Failure: The term head(nil)is a counterexample as it is an irreducible
   term with sort Nat in NATLIST-ERROR that does not have sort Nat in
   the constructor subsignature.
```

4 Conclusions

Our work in developing sufficient completeness checkers for more complex equational specifications has already led to two complementary approaches, each able to handle specifications outside classes that could be handled by previous approaches. Although significant progress has been made, there is a great deal of opportunity both to develop new techniques and to improve the performance of existing techniques. Additionally, the tools and techniques we have developed are not restricted to sufficient completeness. Recently, the CETA library has been integrated into the reachability analysis tool ACTAS [12]. For more details on this, see CETA's website at: `http://formal.cs.uiuc.edu/ceta/`.

Bibliography

[1] A. Bouhoula and F. Jacquemard. Automatic verification of sufficient completeness for conditional constrained term rewriting systems. Technical Report LSC-05-17, ENS de Cachan, 2006. Available at: `http://www.lsv.ens-cachan.fr/Publis/`.

[2] H. Comon, M. Dauchet, R. Gilleron, F. Jacquemard, D. Lugiez, S. Tison, and M. Tommasi. Tree automata techniques and applications. Available at: `http://www.grappa.univ-lille3.fr/tata`, 1997. release October, 1st 2002.

[3] H. Comon and F. Jacquemard. Ground reducibility is EXPTIME-complete. *Information and Computation*, 187(1):123–153, 2003.

[4] J. V. Guttag and J. J. Horning. The algebraic specification of abstract data types. *Acta Informatica*, 10:27–52, 1978.

[5] J. Hendrix, M. Clavel, and J. Meseguer. A sufficient completeness reasoning tool for partial specifications. In J. Giesl, editor, *Proc. of RTA*, volume 3467 of *Lecture Notes in Computer Science*, pages 165–174. Springer, 2005.

[6] J. Hendrix, H. Ohsaki, and J. Meseguer. Sufficient completeness checking with propositional tree automata. Technical Report UIUCDCS-R-2005-2635, University of Illinois at Urbana-Champaign, 2005. Available at: `http://maude.cs.uiuc.edu/tools/scc/`.

[7] J. Hendrix, H. Ohsaki, and M. Viswanathan. Propositional tree automata. Technical Report UIUCDCS-R-2006-2695, University of Illinois at Urbana-Champaign, 2006. Available at: `http://maude.cs.uiuc.edu/tools/scc/`.

[8] D. Kapur, P. Narendran, D. J. Rosenkrantz, and H. Zhang. Sufficient-completeness, ground-reducibility and their complexity. *Acta Informatica*, 28(4):311–350, 1991.

[9] D. Kapur, P. Narendran, and H. Zhang. On sufficient-completeness and related properties of term rewriting systems. *Acta Informatica*, 24(4):395–415, 1987.

[10] H. Ohsaki. Beyond regularity: Equational tree automata for associative and commutative theories. In L. Fribourg, editor, *Proc. of CSL*, volume 2142 of *Lecture Notes in Computer Science*, pages 539–553. Springer, 2001.

[11] H. Ohsaki and T. Takai. Decidability and closure properties of equational tree languages. In S. Tison, editor, *Proc. of RTA*, volume 2378 of *Lecture Notes in Computer Science*, pages 114–128. Springer, 2002.

[12] H. Ohsaki and T. Takai. ACTAS : A system design for associative and commutative tree automata theory. In *Proc. of RULE*, volume 124 of *ENTCS*, pages 97–111. Elsevier, 2005.

[13] P. Viry. Equational rules for rewriting logic. *Theoretical Computer Science*, 285(2):487–517, 2002.

Extending the TPTP Language to Higher-Order Logic with Automated Parser Generation

Allen Van Gelder[1] and Geoff Sutcliffe[2]

[1] University of California at Santa Cruz, USA
http://www.cse.ucsc.edu/~avg
[2] University of Miami, USA
geoff@cs.miami.edu

Abstract. A stable proposal for extending the first-order TPTP (Thousands of Problems for Theorem Provers) language to higher-order logic, based primarily on lambda-calculus expressions, is presented. The purpose of the system is to facilitate sharing of theorem-proving problems in higher-order logic among many researchers. Design goals are discussed. BNF2, a new specification language, is presented. Unix/Linux scripts translate the specification document into a *lex* scanner and *yacc* parser.

1 Introduction

The goal of this work is to extend the current TPTP (Thousands of Problems for Theorem Provers) language [9] to include adequate support for higher-order logic, while continuing to recognize the existing first-order language. It was motivated by a panel discussion at the Workshop on Experimentally Successful Automated Reasoning in Higher-Order Logic held in conjunction with LPAR-12, December 2005. The panel discussion conveyed the desire to have a common language in which various researchers could express benchmark problems in higher-order logics that would be contributed to a common library along the lines of the TPTP problem library [8].

The new language developed in this project is tentatively named HOTPTP. Some of the design goals were

1. The rules of the language should be simple and regular, so that humans can understand them without too much trouble.
2. The rules of the language should be presented in a specification document that has sufficient formality and rigor to be unambiguous, yet is not so technical and complicated that its meaning is obscured.
3. The language should be amenable to *straightforward* automated parser generation, with established tools such as *lex* and *yacc*, or *flex* and *bison*. These tools accept LALR-1 languages. It would be undesirable to rely on tricks and extensions that might be supported in one tool and not another.
4. It should be straightforward to set up a Prolog parser for the language, using Prolog's `read()` procedure to accomplish most of the parsing drudgery.

U. Furbach and N. Shankar (Eds.): IJCAR 2006, LNAI 4130, pp. 156–161, 2006.
© Springer-Verlag Berlin Heidelberg 2006

The rules of the TPTP language, as released with TPTP v3.0.0, already achieved goals (1), (2), and (4) above quite well. The first step of the project was to achieve goal (3). During this initial phase, a few ambiguities were discovered in the existing language, and minor revisions of the rules were implemented to remove these ambiguities without changing the underlying language. Following that work, the task of extending the language to accommodate higher order constructs began.

Briefly, the contributions arising from this project are:

1. The development of BNF2, a new variant of Backus-Naur form. BNF2 is oriented toward the modern practice of two-level syntax for programming languages and is easy for humans to read.
2. Unix/Linux scripts to translate BNF2 into input readable by *lex* and *yacc*.
3. Stable BNF2 rules that extend the TPTP language and accept a variety of higher-order logic expressions in a human-readable language.

Software and documents are at http://www.cse.ucsc.edu/~avg/TPTPparser.

2   Specifications with BNF2

The TPTP language was specified in TPTP v3.0.0 using the original standard Backus-Naur form (BNF) [6], with informal explanations to get over some rough spots. In this simple and easy-to-read format, which is found in many programming-language texts, grammar symbols are enclosed in < >, and the only meta-symbols are the production symbol "::=", the alternative symbol "|", and the repetition symbol "*"; any other character sequence stands for itself, and is called a *self-declared token*. More sophisticated variants have been proposed over the years; see Section 5.

While trying to write scripts to translate BNF into inputs for *lex* and *yacc* it was realized that standard BNF is ill-suited for specifying *tokens*. That is, the modern two-level style of programming-language specification defines *tokens* using regular expressions, and defines *grammar symbols* using context-free production rules. A lexical analyzer parses the raw input into tokens, while the production rules treat tokens as terminal symbols. This distinction is blurred in standard BNF. Another aspect of the TPTP language that was observed was that some production rules went beyond specifying the *form* of the input, and specified a list of acceptable words. This presented a conflict in that such words became self-declared tokens. Without making a context-sensitive lexical analyzer, such words became unavailable for user identifiers.

To overcome these limitations of standard BNF we designed BNF2, a simple extension of BNF that preserves the easy-to-read format for production rules and adds different formats to specify semantic rules, tokens, and macros for tokens. *Semantic* production rules are ignored for purposes of syntactic parsing, but are available to specify more detail about the semantic content of certain sentential forms. All the extensions are implemented by using additional meta-symbols to specify various rule types, according to the following table. As the

Meta-Symbol	Rule Type	Examples (some are simplified from the TPTP language)		
::=	Grammar	`<TPTP input>`	`::=`	`<annotated formula>` | `<comment>`
		`<nonassoc op>`	`::=`	`<=>` | `=>` | `<=` | `<~>`
		`<formula role>`	`::=`	`<lower word>`
:==	Semantic	`<formula role>`	`:==`	`axiom` | `conjecture` | `lemma` |
				`theorem` | `negated_conjecture`
::-	Token	`<lower word>`	`::-`	`<lower><alphanum>*`
::=	Macro	`<lower>`	`:::`	`[a-z]`
		`<alphanum>`	`:::`	`[A-Za-z0-9_]`

table shows, a symbol that has a *semantic* rule must also have a normal grammar rule if it appears on the right side of any normal grammar rule. The string "`<=>`" and following strings are self-declared tokens: grammar symbols must consist of alphanumerics. The right sides of token and macro rules are *lex*-ready regular expressions, except that "`< >`" need to be converted to "`{ }`".

3   System Description

This section describes the system that evaluates a proposed HOTPTP language, based on a BNF2 specification document produced manually. The system includes both manual and automated elements. This is not a system to process an arbitrary BNF2 document; its main purpose is to support TPTP-related development. Figure 1 provides an overview.

The primary automated part of the system generates an executable parser from a BNF2 specification document for HOTPTP, following the right branch of the diagram. This parser is extremely simple, to ensure that the input being checked is really in the language of the specification document. The first step to generate a parser is to translate the (ASCII text) BNF2 specification document, say `hotptp-bnf2.txt`, into a pair of files, `hotptp-1.lex0` and `hotptp-1.y`, which are input files for *lex* (or *flex*) and *yacc* (or *bison*). Unix/Linux scripts accomplish this translation, invoking *sed*, *awk*, *grep*, *sort*, etc. No errors are detected during this step. There is a clear correspondence between grammar rules in `hotptp-bnf2.txt` and `hotptp-1.y`. Tokens have mnemonic names and are easy to locate in `hotptp-1.lex0`.

The analysis and compilation of `hotptp-1.y` by *yacc* or *bison* is a critical step. Grammar errors and ambiguities are often located here after the BNF2 document has passed human inspection. The default library routines are used for all procedures that are expected to be supplied by the programmer. A standard semantic action is attached to each grammar rule, which builds a naive parse tree for each sentence, which may be printed in verbose mode. A syntax error causes "syntax error" on the `stderr` stream and a nonzero exit code; the exit code is zero upon success.

Testing against the full TPTP Problem library requires several minutes. All files with extension ".p" should be accepted, whereas the TSTP library contains files that are known to have syntax errors. The most volatile files are the

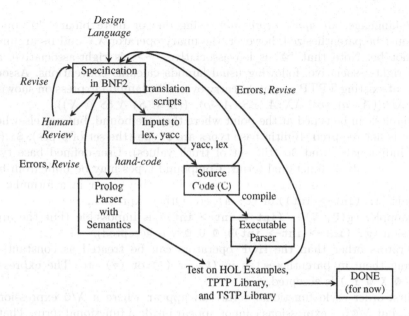

Fig. 1. Overview of the system evaluate a proposed HOTPTP language. Human activities are shown in *italics*.

HOL examples, which use the higher order extensions. When a syntax error or unexpected parse tree occurs, analysis is needed to determine if fault lies with the formula or the language specification. Based on available examples, the HOTPTP language has stabilized after about ten iterations of the left branch of the system diagram.

4   The HOTPTP Syntax Proposal

The complete BNF2 document for the proposed HOTPTP syntax is available as `hotptp-bnf2.txt` at the URL given at the end of Section 1. The following example illustrates many of the features added to express higher order constructs. TPTP follows the Prolog convention that variables begin with capital letters, and uses "?" for ∃ and "!" for ∀.

```
hof(1, definition,
    set_union := lambda [A: $type]: lambda [D: ((A-> $o)-> $o), X: A]:
                 ? [S: (A-> $o)]: ( (D @ S) & (S @ X) ) ).
```

The new operator "`:=`" permits a definition at the top level of a "formula" (Hudak uses "≡" [5]). Other new operators are: "`lambda`" for lambda abstraction, "`@`" for application, and "`->`" for type mappings. The colon "`:`" operator has several new meanings, for typing and lambda expressions. Also, "`^`" is a synonym for `lambda` and "`>`" is a synonym for "`->`". We call these new operators the HOF operators.

Logical operators and HOF operators can be mixed in λ/@ expressions,, subject to using parentheses as needed. Following the general principle in the

TPTP language, an *apply expression*, using one or more binary "@" operators, must be parenthesized; however, the unary operator λX and its argument need not be. Note that "@" is left-associative, "->" is right-associative, and ":" is right-associative, following usual lambda-calculus conventions. Associativities of existing TPTP operators carry over. The lambda expression shown is: $\lambda A{:}\tau.\ \lambda D{:}((A{\rightarrow}o){\rightarrow}o).\ \lambda X{:}A.\ \exists S{:}(A{\rightarrow}o).\ ((D\ @\ S)\ \wedge\ (S\ @\ X))$.

Variables can be typed at the point where they are bound, but not elsewhere. Typing is not required. Builtin base types are $type (the set of types), $i (the set of individuals), and $o (the set of truth values). User-defined base types can be constants or functional terms. Compound types may be built from base types with "->". Constants can be typed where they occur in a formula; the syntax is (c: (int-> int)) or (c: A), etc. Other expressions cannot be typed. For example, (g(U, V) : (int-> int-> int)) is impossible (but the apply expression (g: (int-> int-> int)) @ U @ V is accepted).

Operators other than the HOF operators can be treated as constants by enclosing them in parentheses, as in (&) or (~) or (=) etc. The expression ((&) @ X @ Y) is accepted.

A first-order style functional term can appear where a λ/@ expression is needed, but λ/@/$\rightarrow$ expressions cannot appear inside a functional term. That is, p((S @ X)) is impossible, but (S @ p(X)) is accepted.

5   Related Work and Acknowledgments

Other variants of BNF have been proposed before BNF2. Extended BNF (EBNF) was designed by a standards committee to have great generality but is quite complicated, with about a dozen meta-symbols, and does not distinguish tokens from grammar symbols. Labeled BNF (LBNF) is designed to generate parsers automatically [3], and distinguishes tokens from grammar symbols, but is even more complicated than EBNF.

HOTPTP requirements were culled from Hudak's exposition of lambda calculus [5], and descriptions of *Coq* [2], *LF* [4], and *ELF* [7]. We thank Chad Brown and Chris Benzmüller for contributing examples of formulas that should be expressible in HOTPTP syntax, based on their work [1].

References

1. Benzmüller, C., Brown, C.: A Structured Set of Higher-Order Problems. In: Proc. 18th Theorem Proving in Higher Order Logics. (2005) 66–81
2. Felty, D., et al.: The Coq Proof Assistant. http://pauillac.inria.fr/coq (URL)
3. Forsberg, M., Ranta, A.: The Labelled BNF Grammar Formalism. Technical report, Chalmers, Gothenburg, Sweden (2005)
   http://www.cs.chalmers.se/~markus/BNFC.
4. Harper, R., Honsell, F., Plotkin, G.: A Framework for Defining Logics. Journal of the ACM **40** (1993) 143–184
5. Hudak, P.: Conception, Evolution, and Application of Functional Programming Languages. ACM Computing Surveys **21** (1989) 359–411

6. Naur *et al.*, P.: Report on Algorithmic Language ALGOL 60. Communications of the ACM **3** (1960) 299–314
7. Pfenning, F.: ELF: A meta-language for deductive systems (system description). In: CADE. (1994)
8. Sutcliffe, G., Suttner, C.: The TPTP Problem Library: CNF Release v1.2.1. Journal of Automated Reasoning **21** (1998) 177–203
9. Sutcliffe, G., Zimmer, J., Schulz, S.: TSTP Data-Exchange Formats for Automated Theorem Proving Tools. In: Distributed Constraint Problem Solving and Reasoning in Multi-Agent Systems. IOS Press (2004) 201–215

Extracting Programs from Constructive HOL Proofs Via IZF Set-Theoretic Semantics

Robert Constable and Wojciech Moczydłowski*

Department of Computer Science, Cornell University,
Ithaca, NY 14853, USA
{rc, wojtek}@cs.cornell.edu

Abstract. Church's Higher Order Logic is a basis for proof assistants — HOL and PVS. Church's logic has a simple set-theoretic semantics, making it trustworthy and extensible. We factor HOL into a constructive core plus axioms of excluded middle and choice. We similarly factor standard set theory, ZFC, into a constructive core, IZF, and axioms of excluded middle and choice. Then we provide the standard set-theoretic semantics in such a way that the constructive core of HOL is mapped into IZF. We use the disjunction, numerical existence and term existence properties of IZF to provide a program extraction capability from proofs in the constructive core.

We can implement the disjunction and numerical existence properties in two different ways: one modifying Rathjen's realizability for CZF and the other using a new direct weak normalization result for intensional IZF by Moczydłowski. The latter can also be used for the term existence property.

1 Introduction

Church's Higher-Order logic [1] has been remarkably successful at capturing the intuitive reasoning of mathematicians. It was distilled from *Principia Mathematica*, and is sometimes called the Simple Theory of Types based on that legacy. It incorporates the λ calculus as its notation for functions, including propositional functions, thus interfacing well with computer science.

One of the reasons Higher-Order logic is successful is that its axiomatic basis is very small, and it has a clean set-theoretic semantics at a low level of the cummulative hierarchy of sets (up to $\omega + \omega$) and can thus be formalized in a small fragment of ZFC set theory . This means it interfaces well with standard mathematics and provides a strong basis for trust. Moreover, the set theory semantics is the basis for many extensions of the core logic; for example, it is straightforward to add arrays, recursive data types, and records to the logic.

Church's theory is the logical basis of two of the most successful interactive provers used in hardware and software verification, HOL and PVS. This is due in part to the two characteristics mentioned above in addition to its elegant automation based on Milner's tactic mechanism and its elegant formulation in the ML metalanguage.

---

* This research was supported by NSF grants DUE-0333526 and 0430161.

U. Furbach and N. Shankar (Eds.): IJCAR 2006, LNAI 4130, pp. 162–176, 2006.
© Springer-Verlag Berlin Heidelberg 2006

Until recently, one of the few drawbacks of HOL was that its logical base did not allow a way to express a constructive subset of the logic. This issue was considered by Harrison for HOL-light [2], and recently Berghofer implemented a constructive version of HOL in the Isabelle implementation [3,4] in large part to enable the extraction of programs from constructive proofs. This raises the question of finding a semantics for HOL that justifies this intuitively sound extraction.

The standard justification for program extraction is based on logics that embedded extraction deeply into their semantics; this is the case for the Calculus of Inductive Constructions (CIC) [5,6], Minlog [7], Computational Type Theory (CTT) [8,9] or the closely related Intuitionistic Type Theory (ITT) [10,11]. The mechanism of extraction is built deeply into logic and the provers based on it, e.g. Agda [12] on ITT, Coq [13] on CIC, MetaPRL [14] and Nuprl [15] on CTT.

In this paper we show that there is a way to provide a clean set-theoretic semantics for HOL and in the same stroke use it to semantically justify program extraction. The idea is to first factor HOL into its constructive core, say Constructive HOL, plus the axioms of excluded middle and choice. The semantics for this language can be given in ZFC set theory, and if that logic is factored into its constructive core, called IZF, plus excluded middle and choice (choice is sufficient to give excluded middle), then in the standard semantics, IZF provides the semantics for Constructive HOL. Moreover, we can base program extraction on the IZF semantics.

The constructive content of IZF is not as transparent as in the constructive set theories of Aczel, introduced in [16], however, in these set theories it is not possible to express the impredicative nature of Higher-Order Logic. Also, IZF is not as expressive as Howe's ZFC [17,18] with inaccessible cardinals and computational primitives, but this makes IZF a more standard theory.

Our semantics is appealing not only because it factors so elegantly, but also because the computational issues and program extraction can be reduced to the standard constructive properties of IZF — the disjunction, numerical existence and term existence properties.

We can implement the disjunction and numerical existence properties in two different ways: one modifying Rathjen's realizability for CZF [19] and the other using a new direct weak normalization result for intensional IZF by Moczydłowski [20]. The latter can also be used for the term existence property.

In this paper, we provide a set-theoretic semantics for HOL which has the following properties:

 - It is as simple as the standard semantics, presented in Gordon and Melham's [21].
 - It works in constructive set-theory.
 - It provides a semantical basis for program extraction.
 - It can be applied to the constructive version of HOL recently implemented in Isabelle-HOL as a means of using constructive HOL proofs as programs.

This paper is organized as follows. In section 2 we present a a version of HOL. In section 3 we define set-theoretic semantics. Section 4 defines constructive set theory IZF and states its main properties. We show how these properties can be used for program extraction in section 5.

2   Higher-Order Logic

In this section, we present in detail higher-order logic. There are two syntactic categories: *terms* and *types*. The types are generated by the following abstract grammar:

$$\tau ::= nat \mid bool \mid prop \mid \tau \to \tau \mid (\tau, \tau)$$

The distinction between *bool* and *prop* corresponds to the distinction between the two-element type and the type of propositions in type theory, or between the two-element object and the subobject classifier in category theory or, as we shall see, between 2 and the set of all subsets of 1 in constructive set theory.

The terms of HOL are generated by the following abstract grammar:

$$t ::= x_\tau \mid c_\tau \mid (t_{\tau \to \sigma}\, u_\tau)_\sigma \mid (\lambda x_\tau.\ t_\sigma)_{\tau \to \sigma} \mid (t_\tau, s_\sigma)_{(\tau, \sigma)}$$

Thus each term t_α in HOL is annotated with a type α, which we call *the type of t*. We will often skip annotating of terms with types, this practice should not lead to confusion, as the implicit type system is very simple. Terms of type *prop* are called *formulas*.

The free variables of a term t are denoted by $FV(t)$ and defined as usual. We consider α-equivalent terms equal. Our version of HOL has a set of builtin constants. To increase readability, we write $c : \tau$ instead of c_τ to provide the information about the type of c. If the type of a constant involves α, it is a constant *schema*, there is one constant for each type τ substituted for α. There are thus constants $=_{bool}$, $=_{nat}$ and so on.

$$\bot : prop \qquad \top : prop \qquad =_\alpha : (\alpha, \alpha) \to prop$$

$$\to : (prop, prop) \to prop \qquad \land : (prop, prop) \to prop \qquad \lor : (prop, prop) \to prop$$

$$\forall_\alpha : (\alpha \to prop) \to prop \qquad \exists_\alpha : (\alpha \to prop) \to prop \qquad \varepsilon_\alpha : (\alpha \to prop) \to \alpha$$

$$0 : nat \qquad S : nat \to nat \qquad false : bool \qquad true : bool$$

We present the proof rules for HOL in a sequent-based natural deduction style. A *sequent* is a pair (Γ, t), where Γ is a list of formulas and t is a formula. Free variables of a context are the free variables of all its formulas. A sequent (Γ, t) is written as $\Gamma \vdash t$. We write binary constants (equality, implication, etc.) using infix notation. We use standard abbreviations for quantifiers: $\forall a : \tau.\ \phi$ abbreviates $\forall_\tau(\lambda a_\tau.\ \phi)$, similarly with $\exists a : \tau.\ \phi$. The proof rules for HOL are:

$$\frac{}{\Gamma \vdash t}\, t \in \Gamma \qquad \frac{}{\Gamma \vdash t = t} \qquad \frac{\Gamma \vdash t = s}{\Gamma \vdash \lambda x_\tau.\ t = \lambda x_\tau.\ s}\, x_\tau \notin FV(\Gamma)$$

$$\frac{\Gamma \vdash t \quad \Gamma \vdash s}{\Gamma \vdash t \land s} \qquad \frac{\Gamma \vdash t \land s}{\Gamma \vdash t} \qquad \frac{\Gamma \vdash t \land s}{\Gamma \vdash s} \qquad \frac{}{\Gamma \vdash \top}$$

$$\frac{\Gamma \vdash t}{\Gamma \vdash t \vee s} \qquad \frac{\Gamma \vdash s}{\Gamma \vdash t \vee s} \qquad \frac{\Gamma \vdash t \vee s \quad \Gamma, t \vdash u \quad \Gamma, s \vdash u}{\Gamma \vdash u}$$

$$\frac{\Gamma, t \vdash s}{\Gamma \vdash t \to s} \qquad \frac{\Gamma \vdash s \to t \quad \Gamma \vdash s}{\Gamma \vdash t} \qquad \frac{\Gamma \vdash s = u \quad \Gamma \vdash t[u]}{\Gamma \vdash t[s]}$$

$$\frac{\Gamma \vdash f_{\alpha \to prop} \, t_\alpha}{\Gamma \vdash \exists_\alpha (f_{\alpha \to prop})} \qquad \frac{\Gamma \vdash \exists_\alpha (f_{\alpha \to prop}) \quad \Gamma, f_{\alpha \to prop} \, x_\alpha \vdash u}{\Gamma \vdash u} \; x_\alpha \text{ new}$$

Finally, we list HOL axioms.

1. (FALSE) $\bot = \forall b : prop. \; b$.
2. (FALSENOTTRUE) $false = true \to \bot$.
3. (BETA) $(\lambda x_\tau. \; t_\sigma) s_\tau = t_\sigma[x_\tau := s_\tau]$.
4. (ETA) $(\lambda x_\tau. \; f_{\tau \to \sigma} \; x_\tau) = f_{\tau \to \sigma}$.
5. (FORALL) $\forall_\alpha = \lambda P_{\alpha \to prop}. \; (P = \lambda x_\alpha. \; \top)$.
6. (P3) $\forall n : nat. \; (0 = S(n)) \to \bot$.
7. (P4) $\forall n, m : nat. \; S(n) = S(m) \to n = m$.
8. (P5) $\forall P : nat \to prop. \; P(0) \wedge (\forall n : nat. \; P(n) \to P(S(n))) \to \forall n : nat. \; P(n)$.
9. (BOOL) $\forall x : bool. \; (x = false) \vee (x = true)$.
10. (EM) $\forall x : prop. \; (x = \bot) \vee (x = \top)$.
11. (CHOICE) $\forall P : \alpha \to prop. \; \forall x : \alpha. \; P \; x \to P(\varepsilon_{(\alpha \to prop) \to \alpha}(P))$.

Our choice of rules and axioms is redundant. Propositional connectives, for example, could be defined in terms of quantifiers and *bool*. However, we believe that this makes the account of the semantics clearer and shows how easy it is to define a sound semantics for such system.

The theory CHOL (Constructive HOL) arises by taking away from HOL axioms (CHOICE) and (EM).

We write $\vdash_H \phi$ and $\vdash_C \phi$ to denote that HOL and CHOL, respectively, proves ϕ. We will generally use letters P, Q to denote proof trees. A notation $P \vdash_C \phi$ means that P is a proof tree in CHOL of ϕ.

3 Semantics

3.1 Set Theory

The set-theoretic semantics needs a small part of cumulative hierarchy — $R_{\omega+\omega}$ is sufficient to carry out all the constructions. The Axiom of Choice is necessary in order to define the meaning of the ε constant. For this purpose, C will denote a[1] blatantly non-constructive function such that for any $X, Y \in R_{\omega+\omega}$, if X is non-empty, then $C(X, Y) \in X$, and if X is empty then $C(X, Y) = Y$.

Recall that in the world of set theory, $0 = \emptyset$, $1 = \{0\}$ and $2 = \{0, 1\}$. Classically $P(1)$, the set of all subsets of 1, is equal to 2. This is not the case constructively; there is no uniform way of transforming an arbitrary subset A of 1 into an element of 2.

---

[1] Note that if we want to pinpoint C, we need to assume more than AC, as the existence of a definable choice function for $R_{\omega+\omega}$ is not provable in ZFC.

The following helpful lemma, however, does hold in a constructive world:

Lemma 1. *If $A \in P(1)$, then $A = 1$ iff $0 \in A$.*

We will use lambda notation in set theory to define functions: $\lambda x \in A.\ B(x)$ means $\{(x, B(x)) \mid x \in A\}$.

3.2 The Definition of the Semantics

We first define a meaning $[\![\tau]\!]$ of a type τ by structural induction on τ.

- $[\![nat]\!] = \mathbb{N}$.
- $[\![bool]\!] = 2$.
- $[\![prop]\!] = P(1)$.
- $[\![(\tau, \sigma)]\!] = [\![\tau]\!] \times [\![\sigma]\!]$, where $A \times B$ denotes the cartesian product of sets A and B.
- $[\![\tau_1 \to \tau_2]\!] = [\![\tau_1]\!] \to [\![\tau_2]\!]$, where $A \to B$ denotes the set of all functions from A to B.

The meaning of a constant c_α is denoted by $[\![c_\alpha]\!]$ and is defined as follows.

- $[\![=_\alpha]\!] = \lambda(x_1, x_2) \in ([\![\alpha]\!] \times [\![\alpha]\!]).\ \{x \in 1 \mid x_1 = x_2\}$.
- $[\![\to]\!] = \lambda(b_1, b_2) \in [\![prop]\!] \times [\![prop]\!].\ \{x \in 1 \mid x \in b_1 \to x \in b_2\}$.
- $[\![\vee]\!] = \lambda(b_1, b_2) \in [\![prop]\!] \times [\![prop]\!].\ b_1 \cup b_2$.
- $[\![\wedge]\!] = \lambda(b_1, b_2) \in [\![prop]\!] \times [\![prop]\!].\ b_1 \cap b_2$.
- $[\![false]\!] = [\![\bot]\!] = 0$.
- $[\![true]\!] = [\![\top]\!] = 1$.
- $[\![\forall_\alpha]\!] = \lambda f \in [\![\alpha]\!] \to [\![prop]\!].\ \bigcap_{a \in [\![\alpha]\!]} f(a)$.
- $[\![\exists_\alpha]\!] = \lambda f \in [\![\alpha]\!] \to [\![prop]\!].\ \bigcup_{a \in [\![\alpha]\!]} f(a)$.
- $[\![\varepsilon_\alpha]\!] = \lambda P \in [\![\alpha]\!] \to [\![prop]\!].\ C(P^{-1}(1), [\![\alpha]\!])$.
- $[\![0]\!] = 0$.
- $[\![S]\!] = \lambda n \in \mathbb{N}.\ n + 1$

Standard semantics, presented for example by Gordon and Melham in [21], uses a truth table approach — implication $\phi \to \psi$ is false iff ϕ is true and ψ is false etc. It is easy to see that with excluded middle, our semantics is equivalent to the standard one.[2]

To present the rest of the semantics, we need to introduce environments. An *environment* is a partial function from HOL variables to sets such that $\rho(x_\tau) \in [\![\tau]\!]$. We will use the symbol ρ exclusively for environments. The meaning $[\![t]\!]_\rho$ of a term t is parameterized by an environment ρ and defined by structural induction on t:

- $[\![c_\tau]\!]_\rho = [\![c_\tau]\!]$.
- $[\![x_\tau]\!]_\rho = \rho(x_\tau)$
- $[\![s\ u]\!]_\rho = App([\![s]\!]_\rho, [\![u]\!]_\rho)$.
- $[\![\lambda x_\tau.\ u]\!] = \{(a, [\![u]\!]_{\rho[x_\tau := a]}) \mid a \in [\![\tau]\!]\}$.
- $[\![(s, u)]\!]_\rho = ([\![s]\!]_\rho, [\![u]\!]_\rho)$.

---

[2] For the interested reader, our definition of the meaning of logical constants is essentially a combination of the fact that any complete lattice with pseudo-complements is a model for higher-order logic and that $P(1)$ is a complete lattice with pseudo-complement defined in the clause for $\to$.

3.3   Properties

There are several standard properties of the semantics we have defined. The following two lemmas are proved by induction on t:

Lemma 2 (Substitution lemma). *For any terms t, s and environments ρ,*
$[\![t]\!]_{\rho[x:=[\![s]\!]_\rho]} = [\![t[x := s]]\!]_\rho$.

Lemma 3. *For any ρ, $[\![t_\alpha]\!]_\rho \in [\![\alpha]\!]$.*

In particular, this implies that for any formula t, $[\![t]\!] \subseteq 1$. So if we want to prove that $[\![t]\!] = 1$, then by Lemma 1 it suffices to show that $0 \in [\![t]\!]$.

3.4   Soundness

The soundness theorem establishes validity of the proof rules and axioms with respect to the semantics.

Definition 1. $\rho \models \Gamma \vdash t$ *means that ρ is defined for $x_\tau \in FV(\Gamma) \cup FV(t)$.*

By the definition of environments, if $\rho \models \Gamma \vdash \bar{t}$, then for all $x_\tau \in FV(\Gamma) \cup FV(t)$, $\rho(x_\tau) \in [\![\tau]\!]$.

Definition 2. *We write $[\![\Gamma]\!]_\rho = 1$ if $[\![t_1]\!]_\rho = 1, \ldots, [\![t_n]\!]_\rho = 1$, where $\Gamma = t_1, t_2, \ldots, t_n$.*

Theorem 1 (Soundness). *If $\Gamma \vdash t$, then for all $\rho \models \Gamma \vdash t$, if $[\![\Gamma]\!]_\rho = 1$, then $[\![t]\!] = 1$.*

Proof. Straightforward induction on $\Gamma \vdash t$. We show some interesting cases. Case $\Gamma \vdash t$ of:

$$\frac{\Gamma \vdash t = s}{\Gamma \vdash \lambda x_\tau.\, t = \lambda x_\tau.\, s}$$

Take any $\rho \models \Gamma \vdash \lambda x_\tau.\, t = \lambda x_\tau.\, s$. We need to show that $\{(a, [\![t]\!]_{\rho[x_\tau:=a]}) \mid a \in [\![\tau]\!]\} = \{(a, [\![s]\!]_{\rho[x_\tau:=a]} \mid a \in [\![\tau]\!]\}$. That is, that for any $a \in [\![\tau]\!]$, $[\![t]\!]_{\rho[x_\tau:=a]} = [\![s]\!]_{\rho[x_\tau:=a]}$. Let $\rho' = \rho[x_\tau := a]$. Since $\rho' \models \Gamma \vdash t = s$, by the inductive hypothesis we get the claim.

$$\frac{\Gamma, t \vdash s}{\Gamma \vdash t \to s}$$

Suppose $[\![\Gamma]\!]_\rho = 1$. We need to show that $0 \in \{x \in 1 \mid x \in [\![t]\!]_\rho \to x \in [\![s]\!]_\rho\}$. Since $0 \in 1$, assume $0 \in [\![t]\!]_\rho$. Then $[\![\Gamma, t]\!]_\rho = 1$, so by the inductive hypothesis $[\![s]\!]_\rho = 1$ and $0 \in [\![s]\!]_\rho$.

$$\frac{\Gamma \vdash t \to s \quad \Gamma \vdash t}{\Gamma \vdash s}$$

Suppose $[\![\Gamma]\!]_\rho = 1$. By the inductive hypothesis, $0 \in \{x \in 1 \mid x \in [\![t]\!]_\rho \to x \in [\![s]\!]_\rho\}$ and $0 \in [\![t]\!]_\rho$, so easily $0 \in [\![s]\!]_\rho$.

$$\frac{\Gamma \vdash s = u \quad \Gamma \vdash t[x := u]}{\Gamma \vdash t[x := s]}$$

The proof is straightforward, using the Substitution Lemma.

$$\frac{\Gamma \vdash f\ t_\alpha}{\Gamma \vdash \exists_\alpha(f_{\alpha \to prop})}$$

Assume $[\![\Gamma]\!]_\rho = 1$. We have to show that $0 \in \bigcup_{a \in [\![\alpha]\!]}[\![f]\!]_\rho(a)$, so that there is $a \in [\![\alpha]\!]$ such that $0 \in f(a)$. By Lemma 3, $[\![t_\alpha]\!]_\rho \in [\![\alpha]\!]$, so taking $a = [\![t_\alpha]\!]_\rho$ we get the claim by the inductive hypothesis.

$$\frac{\Gamma \vdash \exists_\alpha(f_{\alpha \to prop}) \quad \Gamma, f\ x_\alpha \vdash u}{\Gamma \vdash u}\ x_\alpha\ \text{new}$$

Suppose $[\![\Gamma]\!]_\rho = 1$. By the inductive hypothesis, there is $a \in [\![\alpha]\!]$ such that $0 \in [\![f]\!]_\rho(a)$. Let $\rho' = \rho[x_\alpha := a]$. Then $\rho' \models \Gamma, f\ x_\alpha \vdash u$, so by the inductive hypothesis we get $0 \in [\![u]\!]_\rho$, which is what we want.

Having verified the soundness of the HOL proof rules, we proceed to verify the soundness of the axioms.

Theorem 2. *For any axiom t of HOL and any ρ, $0 \in [\![t]\!]_\rho$.*

Proof. We proceed axiom by axiom and sketch the respective proofs.

- (FALSE) $[\![\bot]\!]_\rho = \emptyset = \bigcap_{a \in P(1)} a = [\![\forall b : prop.\ b]\!]_\rho$. The second equality follows by $0 \in P(1)$.
- (BETA) Follows by the Substitution Lemma.
- (ETA) Follows by the fact that functions in set theory are represented by their graphs.
- (FORALL) We have:

$$[\![\forall_\alpha]\!]_\rho = \{(P, \bigcap_{a \in [\![\alpha]\!]} P(a)) \mid P \in [\![\alpha]\!] \to P(1)\}$$

Also:

$$[\![(\lambda P_{\alpha \to prop}.\ P = \lambda x_\alpha.\ \top)]\!]_\rho = \{(P, \{x \in 1 \mid P = \lambda x \in [\![\alpha]\!].\ 1\}) \mid P \in [\![\alpha]\!] \to P(1)\}$$

Take any $P \in [\![\alpha]\!] \to P(1)$. It suffices to show that $\bigcap_{a \in [\![\alpha]\!]} P(a) = \{x \in 1 \mid P = \lambda y \in [\![\alpha]\!].\ 1\}$. But $x \in \bigcap_{a \in [\![\alpha]\!]} P(a)$ iff for all $a \in [\![\alpha]\!]$, $x \in P(a)$ and $x = 0$. This happens if and only if $x = 0$ and for all $a \in [\![\alpha]\!]$, $P(a) = 1$ which is equivalent to $x \in \{x \in 1 \mid P = \lambda y \in [\![\alpha]\!].\ 1\}$. The sets in question are therefore equal.

- The axioms $P3, P4, P5$ follow by the fact that natural numbers satisfy the respective Peano axioms.

- (BOOL) We need to show that $[\![\forall_{bool}. \ (\lambda x_{bool}. \ x = false \lor x = true)]\!]_{\rho} = 1$. Unwinding the definition, this is equivalent to $\bigcap_{x \in 2}(\{z \in 1 \mid x = 0\} \cup \{z \in 1 \mid x = 1\}) = 1$. and furthermore to: for all $x \in 2$, $x \in \{z \in 1 \mid x = 0\} \cup \{z \in 1 \mid x = 1\}$. If $x \in 2$, then either $x = 0$ or $x = 1$. In the former case, $0 \in \{z \in 1 \mid x = 0\}$, in the latter $0 \in \{z \in 1 \mid x = 1\}$.

- (EM) We need to show that $[\![\forall_{prop}. \ (\lambda x_{prop}. \ x = \bot \lor x = \top)]\!]_{\rho} = 1$. Reasoning as in the case of (BOOL), we find that this is equivalent to: for all $x \in P(1)$, $x \in \{z \in 1 \mid x = 0\} \cup \{z \in 1 \mid x = 1\}$. Suppose $x \in P(1)$. At this point, it is impossible to proceed further constructively, all we know is that x is a subset of 1, which doesn't provide enough information to decide whether $x = 0$ or $x = 1$. However, classically, using the rule of excluded middle, $P(1) = 2$ and we proceed as in the previous case.

- (CHOICE) Straightforward.

Corollary 1. *HOL is consistent: it is not the case that* $\vdash_H \bot$.

Proof. Otherwise we would have $[\![\bot]\!] = [\![\top]\!]$, that is $0 = 1$.

4   IZF

The essential advantage of the semantics in the previous section over a standard one is that for the constructive part of HOL this semantics can be defined in constructive set theory IZF.

An obvious approach to creating a constructive version of ZFC set theory is to replace the underlying first-order logic with intuitionistic first-order logic. As many authors have explained [22,23,24], the ZF axioms need to be reformulated so that they don't imply the law of excluded middle.

In a nutshell, to get IZF from ZFC, the Axiom of Choice and Excluded Middle are taken away and Foundation is reformulated as $\in$-induction. The axioms of IZF are thus Extensionality, Union, Infinitiy, Power Set, Separation, Replacement or Collection[3] and $\in$-Induction. The detailed account of the theory can be found for example in Friedman's [25]. Besoon's book [23] contains a lot of information on metamathematical properties of IZF and related set theories. For convenience, we assume that the first-order logic has built-in terms and bounded quantifiers.

The properties of IZF important for us, proven for the first time by Myhill in [22], are:

- Disjunction Property (DP) : If IZF $\vdash \phi \lor \psi$, then IZF $\vdash \phi$ or IZF $\vdash \psi$.
- Numerical Existence Property (NEP) : If IZF $\vdash \exists x \in \mathbb{N}. \ \phi(x)$, then there is a natural number n such that IZF $\vdash \phi(\overline{n})$, where $\overline{n} = S(S(\ldots(0)))$ and $S(x) = x \cup \{x\}$.
- Term Existence Property (TEP) : If IZF $\vdash \exists x. \ \phi(x)$, then for some term t, IZF $\vdash \phi(t)$.

---

[3] There is a difference, in particular the version with Collection doesn't satisfy TEP. A concerned reader can replace IZFz with IZF$_R$ whenever TEP is used.

Moreover, the semantics and the soundness theorem for CHOL work in IZF, as neither Choice nor Excluded Middle were necessary to carry out these developments. Note that the existence of $P(1)$ is crucial for the semantics.

All the properties are constructive — there is a recursive procedure extracting a natural number, a disjunct or a term from a proof. A trivial one is to look through all the proofs for the correct one. For example, if IZF $\vdash \phi \lor \psi$, a procedure could enumerate all theorems of IZF looking for either ϕ or ψ; its termination would be ensured by DP. We discuss more efficient alternatives in section 5.3.

5   Extraction

We will show that the semantics we have defined can serve as a basis for program extraction for proofs. All that is necessary for program extraction from constructive HOL proofs is provided by the semantics and the soundness proof. Therefore, if one wants to provide an extraction mechanism for the constructive part of the logic, it may be sufficient to carefully define set-theoretic semantics, prove the soundness theorem and the extraction mechanism for IZF would take care of the rest. We speculate on practical uses of this approach in section 6.

5.1   IZF Extraction

We first describe extraction from IZF proofs. To facilitate the description, we will use a very simple fragment of type theory, which we call TT^0.

The *types* of TT^0 are generated by the following abstract grammar. They should not be confused with HOL types; the context will make it clear which types we refer to.

$$\tau ::= * \mid P_\phi \mid nat \mid bool \mid (\tau, \tau) \mid \tau + \tau \mid \tau \to \tau$$

We associate with each type τ of TT^0 a set of its elements, which are finitistic objects. The set of elements of τ is denoted by $El(\tau)$ and defined by structural induction on τ:

- $El(*) = \{*\}$.
- $El(P_\phi)$ is the set of all IZF proofs of formula ϕ.
- $El(nat) = \mathbb{N}$, the set of natural numbers.
- $El(bool) = \{true, false\}$.
- $M \in El((\tau_1, \tau_2)) = El(\tau_1) \times El(\tau_2)$.
- $M \in El(\tau_1 + \tau_2)$ iff either $M = inl(M_1)$ and $M_1 \in El(\tau_1)$ or $M = inr(M_1)$ and $M_1 \in El(\tau_2)$.
- $M \in El(\tau_1 \to \tau_2)$ iff M is a method which given any element of $El(\tau_1)$ returns an element of $El(\tau_2)$.

In the last clause, we use an abstract notion of "method". It will not be necessary to formalize this notion, but for the interested reader, all "methods" we use are functions provably recursive in $ZF + Con(ZF)$.

The notation $M : \tau$ means that $M \in El(\tau)$.

We call a TT^0 type *pure* if it doesn't contain $*$ and P_ϕ. There is a natural mapping of pure types TT^0 to sets. It is so similar to the meaning of the HOL types that we will use the same notation, $[\![\tau]\!]$:

- $[\![nat]\!] = \mathbb{N}$.
- $[\![bool]\!] = 2$.
- $[\![(\tau,\sigma)]\!] = [\![\tau]\!] \times [\![\sigma]\!]$.
- $[\![\tau + \sigma]\!] = [\![\tau]\!] + [\![\sigma]\!]$, the disjoint union of $[\![\tau]\!]$ and $[\![\sigma]\!]$.
- $[\![\tau \to \sigma]\!] = [\![\tau]\!] \to [\![\sigma]\!]$.

If a set (and a corresponding IZF term) is in a codomain of the map above, we call it *type-like*. If a set A is type-like, then there is a unique pure type τ such that $[\![\tau]\!] = A$. We denote this type $Type(A)$.

Before we proceed further, let us extend TT^0 with a new type Q_τ, where τ is any pure type of TT^0. The members of $El(Q_\tau)$ are pairs $(t, \mathcal{P})$ such that $\mathcal{P} \vdash_{IZF} t \in [\![\tau]\!]$ ($\mathcal{P}$ is an IZF proof of $t \in [\![\tau]\!]$). Note that there is a natural mapping from HOL terms M of type τ into Q_τ — it is easy to construct using Lemma 3 a proof $\mathcal{P}$ of the fact that $[\![M]\!]_\emptyset \in [\![\tau]\!]$, so the pair $([\![M]\!]_\emptyset, P) : Q_\tau$. In particular, any natural number n can be injected into Q_{nat}. The set of pure types stays unchanged.

We first define a helper function T, which takes a pure type τ and returns another type. Intuitively, $T(\tau)$ is the type of the extract from a statement $\exists x \in [\![\tau]\!]$. T is defined by induction on τ:

- $T(bool) = bool$.
- $T(nat) = nat$.
- $T((\tau,\sigma)) = (T(\tau), T(\sigma))$
- $T(\tau + \sigma) = T(\tau) + T(\sigma)$.
- $T(\tau \to \sigma) = Q_\tau \to T(\sigma)$ (in order to utilize an IZF function from $[\![\tau]\!]$ to $[\![\sigma]\!]$ we need to supply an element of a set $[\![\tau]\!]$, that is an element of Q_τ)

Now we assign to each formula ϕ of IZF a TT^0 type $\overline{\phi}$, which intuitively describes the *computational content* of an IZF proof of ϕ. We do it by induction on ϕ:

- $\overline{a \in b} = *$.
- $\overline{a = b} = *$ (atomic formulas carry no useful computational content).
- $\overline{\phi_1 \vee \phi_2} = \overline{\phi_1} + \overline{\phi_2}$.
- $\overline{\phi_1 \wedge \phi_2} = (\overline{\phi_1}, \overline{\phi_2})$.
- $\overline{\phi_1 \to \phi_2} = P_{\phi_1} \to \overline{\phi_2}$.
- $\overline{\exists a \in A.\ \phi_1} = (T(Type(A)), \overline{\phi_1})$, if A is type-like.
- $\overline{\exists a \in A.\ \phi_1} = *$, if A is not type-like.
- $\overline{\exists a.\ \phi_1} = *$.
- $\overline{\forall a \in A.\ \phi_1} = Q_{Type(A)} \to \overline{\phi_1}$, if A is type-like.
- $\overline{\forall a \in A.\ \phi_1} = *$, if A is not type-like.
- $\overline{\forall a.\ \phi_1} = *$.

The definition is tailored for HOL logic and could be extended to allow meaningful extraction from a larger class of formulas, i.e. we could extract a term from $\exists a.\ \phi_1$ using TEP. We present some natural examples of this translation in action:

1. $\overline{\exists x \in \mathbb{N}.\ x = x} = \langle nat, * \rangle$.
2. $\overline{\forall x \in \mathbb{N} \exists y \in \mathbb{N}.\ \phi} = Q_{nat} \to \langle nat, \overline{\phi} \rangle$.
3. $\overline{\forall f \in \mathbb{N} \to \mathbb{N} \exists x \in \mathbb{N}.\ f(x) = 0} = Q_{nat \to nat} \to \langle nat, * \rangle$.

These types are richer than what we intuitively would expect — nat in the first case, $nat \to nat$ in the second and $(nat \to nat) \to nat$ in the third, because any HOL term of type nat or $nat \to nat$ can be injected into Q_{nat} or $Q_{nat \to nat}$. The extra $*$ can be easily discarded from types (and extracts).

Lemma 4. *For any natural number n, $\overline{\phi[a := \overline{n}]} = \overline{\phi}$.*

Proof. Straightforward induction on ϕ.

Lemma 5 (IZF). $(\exists a \in 2.\ \phi(a))$ *iff* $\phi(0) \vee \phi(1)$.

We are now ready to describe the extraction function E, which takes an IZF proof $\mathcal{P}$ of a formula ϕ and returns an object of TT^0 type $\overline{\phi}$. We do it by induction on ϕ, checking on the way that the object returned is of type $\overline{\phi}$. Recall that DP, TEP and NEP denote Disjunction, Term and Numerical Existence Property, respectively. Case ϕ of:

- $a \in b$ — return $*$. We have $* : *$.
- $a = b$ — return $*$. We have $* : *$, too.
- $\phi_1 \vee \phi_2$. Apply DP to $\mathcal{P}$ to get a proof $\mathcal{P}_1$ of either ϕ_1 or ϕ_2. In the former case return $inl(E(\mathcal{P}_1))$, in the latter return $inr(E(\mathcal{P}_1))$. By the inductive hypothesis, $E(\mathcal{P}_1) : \overline{\phi_1}$ (or $E(\mathcal{P}_1) : \overline{\phi_2}$), so $E(\mathcal{P}) : \overline{\phi}$ follows.
- $\phi_1 \wedge \phi_2$. Then there are proofs $\mathcal{P}_1$ and $\mathcal{P}_2$ such that $\mathcal{P}_1 \vdash \phi_1$ and $\mathcal{P}_2 \vdash \phi_2$. Return a pair $(E(\mathcal{P}_1), E(\mathcal{P}_2))$. By the inductive hypothesis, $E(\mathcal{P}_1) : \overline{\phi_1}$ and $E(\mathcal{P}_2) : \overline{\phi_2}$, so $(E(\mathcal{P}_1), E(\mathcal{P}_2)) : \overline{\phi_1 \wedge \phi_2}$.
- $\phi_1 \to \phi_2$. Return a function G which takes an IZF proof $\mathcal{Q}$ of ϕ_1, applies $\mathcal{P}$ to $\mathcal{Q}$ (using the modus-ponens rule of the first-order logic) to get a proof $\mathcal{R}$ of ϕ_2 and returns $E(\mathcal{R})$. By the inductive hypothesis, any such $E(\mathcal{R})$ is in $El(\overline{\phi_2})$, so $G : P_{\phi_1} \to \overline{\phi_2}$.
- $\exists a \in A.\ \phi_1(a)$, where A is type-like. Let $T = Type(A)$. We proceed by induction on T, case T of:
  - *bool*. By Lemma 5, we have $\phi_1(0) \vee \phi_1(1)$. Apply DP to get a proof $\mathcal{Q}$ of either $\phi_1(0)$ or $\phi_1(1)$. Let b be *false* or *true*, respectively. Return a pair $(b, E(\mathcal{Q}))$. By the inductive hypothesis, $E(\mathcal{Q}) : \overline{\phi_1(\llbracket b \rrbracket)}$. By Lemma 4, $E(\mathcal{Q}) : \overline{\phi_1}$.
  - *nat*. Apply NEP to $\mathcal{P}$ to get a natural number n and a proof $\mathcal{Q}$ of $\phi_1(\overline{n})$. Return a pair $(n, E(\mathcal{Q}))$. By the inductive hypothesis, $E(\mathcal{Q}) : \overline{\phi_1(\overline{n})}$, by Lemma 4, $E(\mathcal{Q}) : \overline{\phi_1}$, so $(n, E(\mathcal{Q})) : (nat, \overline{\phi_1})$.

- (τ, σ). Construct a proof $\mathcal{Q}$ of $\exists a_1 \in [\![\tau]\!] \exists a_2 \in [\![\sigma]\!]. \, a = \langle a_1, a_2 \rangle \wedge \phi_1$. Let $M = E(\mathcal{Q})$. By the inductive hypothesis M is a pair $\langle M_1, M_2 \rangle$ such that $M_1 : T(\tau)$ and $M_2 : \overline{\exists a_2 \in [\![\sigma]\!]. \, a = \langle a_1, a_2 \rangle \wedge \phi_1}$. Therefore M_2 is a pair $\langle M_{21}, M_{22} \rangle$, $M_{21} : T(\sigma)$ and $M_{22} : \overline{a = \langle a_1, a_2 \rangle \wedge \phi_1}$. Therefore M_{22} is a pair $\langle N, O \rangle$, where $O : \overline{\phi_1}$. Therefore $\langle M_1, M_{21} \rangle : T((\tau, \sigma))$, so $\langle \langle M_1, M_{21} \rangle, O \rangle \; : \; (T((\tau, \sigma)), \overline{\phi_1})$ and we are justified to return $\langle \langle M_1, M_{21} \rangle, O \rangle$.

- $\tau + \sigma$. Construct a proof $\mathcal{Q}$ of $(\exists a_1 \in [\![\tau]\!]. \, \phi_1) \vee (\exists a_1 \in [\![\sigma]\!]. \, \phi_1)$. Apply DP to get the proof $\mathcal{Q}_1$ of (without loss of generality) $\exists a_1 \in [\![\tau]\!]. \, \phi_1$. Let $M = E(\mathcal{Q}_1)$. By the inductive hypothesis, $M = \langle M_1, M_2 \rangle$, where $M_1 : T(\tau)$ and $M_2 : \overline{\phi_1}$. Return $\langle inl(M_1), M_2 \rangle$, which is of type $(T(\tau + \sigma), \overline{\phi_1})$.

- $\tau \rightarrow \sigma$. Use TEP to get a term f such that $(f \in [\![\tau]\!] \rightarrow [\![\sigma]\!]) \wedge \phi_1(f)$. Construct proofs $\mathcal{Q}_1$ of $\forall x \in [\![\tau]\!] \exists y \in [\![\sigma]\!].f(x) = y$ and $\mathcal{Q}_2$ of $\phi_1(f)$. By the inductive hypothesis and Lemma 4, $E(\mathcal{Q}_2) : \overline{\phi}$. Let G be a function which works as follows: G takes a pair $t, \mathcal{R}$ such that $\mathcal{R} \vdash t \in [\![\tau]\!]$, applies $\mathcal{Q}_1$ to $t, \mathcal{R}$ to get a proof $\mathcal{R}_1$ of $\exists y \in [\![\sigma]\!]. \, f(t) = y \wedge \phi_1(f)$ and calls $E(\mathcal{R}_1)$ to get a term M. By inductive hypothesis, $M : \exists y \in [\![\sigma]\!]. \, f(t) = y$, so $M = \langle M_1, M_2 \rangle$, where $M_1 : T(\sigma)$. G returns M_1. Our extraction procedure $E(\mathcal{P})$ returns $\langle G, E(\mathcal{Q}_2) \rangle$. The type of $\langle G, E(\mathcal{Q}_2) \rangle$ is $\langle \mathcal{Q}_\tau \rightarrow T(\sigma), \overline{\phi_1} \rangle$ which is equal to $\langle T(\tau \rightarrow \sigma), \overline{\phi_1} \rangle$.

- $\exists a \in A. \; \phi_1(a)$, where A is not type-like. Return $*$.

- $\exists a. \; \phi_1(a)$, $\forall a. \; \phi_1(a)$. Return $*$.

- $\forall a \in A. \; \phi_1(a)$, where A is type-like. Return a function G which takes an element $(t, \mathcal{Q})$ of $Q_{Type(A)}$, applies $\mathcal{P}$ to t and $\mathcal{Q}$ to get a proof R of $\phi_1(t)$, and returns $E(\mathcal{R})$. By the inductive hypothesis and Lemma 4, $E(\mathcal{R}) : \overline{\phi_1}$, so $G : Q_{Type(A)} \rightarrow \overline{\phi_1}$.

- $\forall a \in A. \; \phi_1(a)$, where A is not type-like. Return $*$.

5.2 HOL Extraction

As in case of IZF, we will show how to do extraction from a subclass of CHOL proofs. The choice of the subclass is largely arbitrary, our choice illustrates the method and can be easily extended.

We say that a CHOL formula is *extractable* if it is generated by the following abstract grammar, where τ varies over pure TT^0 types and $\oplus \in \{\wedge, \vee, \rightarrow\}$.

$$\phi ::= \forall x : \tau. \, \phi \mid \exists x : \tau. \, \phi \mid \phi \oplus \phi \mid \bot \mid t = t,$$

We will define extraction for CHOL proofs of extractable formulas. By Theorem 2, if $CHOL \vdash \phi$, then $IZF \vdash 0 \in [\![\phi]\!]$. We need to slightly transform this IZF proof in order to come up with a valid input to E from the previous section. To this means, for any extractable ϕ (with possibly free variables) we define a formula ϕ' such that $IZF \vdash 0 \in [\![\phi]\!] \leftrightarrow \phi'$. The formula ϕ' is essentially ϕ with type membership information replaced by set membership information. We define ϕ' by induction on ϕ. The correctness follows trivially in each case. In all the cases we work in IZF. Case ϕ of:

- $\bot$. Then $\phi' = 0 \in [\![\bot]\!]$.
- $t = s$. Then $\phi' = 0 \in [\![t = s]\!]$.
- $\phi_1 \vee \phi_2$. $0 \in [\![\phi_1 \vee \phi_2]\!]$ iff $0 \in [\![\phi_1]\!]$ or $0 \in [\![\phi_2]\!]$. By the inductive hypothesis we get ϕ_1' and ϕ_2' such that $0 \in [\![\phi_1]\!] \leftrightarrow \phi_1'$ and $0 \in [\![\phi_2]\!] \leftrightarrow \phi_2'$. Take $\phi' = \phi_1' \vee \phi_2'$.
- $\phi_1 \wedge \phi_2$. Then $0 \in [\![\phi]\!]$ iff $0 \in [\![\phi_1]\!]$ and $0 \in [\![\phi_2]\!]$. Take ϕ_1' and ϕ_2' from the inductive hypothesis and set $\phi' = \phi_1' \wedge \phi_2'$.
- $\phi_1 \to \phi_2$. Then $0 \in [\![\phi_1 \to \phi_2]\!]$ iff $0 \in \{x \in 1 \mid x \in [\![\phi_1]\!] \to x \in [\![\phi_2]\!]\}$ iff $0 \in [\![\phi_2]\!] \to 0 \in [\![\phi_2]\!]$. By the inductive hypothesis get ϕ_1' such that $0 \in [\![\phi_1]\!] \leftrightarrow \phi_1'$ and ϕ_2' such that $0 \in [\![\phi_2]\!] \leftrightarrow \phi_2'$. Set $\phi' = \phi_1' \to \phi_2'$.
- $\forall a : \tau. \phi_1$. Then $0 \in [\![\phi]\!]$ iff for all $A \in [\![\tau]\!]$, $0 \in App([\![\lambda a : \tau. \phi_1]\!], A)$ iff for all $A \in [\![\tau]\!]$, $0 \in App(\{(x, [\![\phi_1]\!]_{\rho[a:=x]}) \mid x \in [\![\tau]\!]\}, A)$ iff for all $A \in [\![\tau]\!]$ $0 \in [\![\phi_1]\!]_{\rho[a:=A]}$ iff, by the Substitution Lemma, for all $A \in [\![\tau]\!]$, $0 \in [\![\phi_1[a := A]]\!]$ iff for all $A \in [\![\tau]\!]$, $0 \in [\![\phi_1]\!]$. Take ϕ_1' from the inductive hypothesis and set $\phi' = \forall a \in [\![\tau]\!]. 0 \in \phi_1'$.
- $\exists a : \tau. \phi_1$. Then $0 \in [\![\phi]\!]$ iff $A \in [\![\tau]\!]$ iff $0 \in [\![\phi_1[a := A]]\!]$. Just as in the previous case, get ϕ_1' from the inductive hypothesis and set $\phi' = \exists a \in [\![\tau]\!]. \phi_1'$.

Now we can finally define the extraction process. Suppose CHOL $\vdash \phi$, where ϕ is extractable. Using the soundness theorem, construct an IZF proof P that $0 \in [\![\phi]\!]$. Use the definition above to get ϕ' such that IZF $\vdash 0 \in [\![\phi]\!] \leftrightarrow \phi'$ and using P obtain a proof R of ϕ'. Finally, apply the extraction function E to R to get the computational extract.

5.3   Implementation Issues

The extraction process is parameterized by the implementation of NEP, DP and TEP for IZF. Obviously, searching through all IZF proofs to get a witnessing natural number, term or a disjunct would not be a very effective method. We discuss two alternative approaches.

The first approach is based on realizability. Rathjen defines a realizability relation in [19] for weaker, predicative constructive set theory CZF. For any CZF proof of a formula ϕ, there is a realizer e such that the realizability relation $e \Vdash \phi$ holds, moreover, this realizer can be found constructively from the proof. Realizers provide the information for DP and NEP — which of the disjuncts holds and the witnessing number. They could be implemented using lambda terms. Adapting these results to IZF should be a straightforward matter and according to [19] the proof will appear in the forecoming paper. This approach has the drawback of not providing the proof of TEP, which would restrict the extraction process from statements of the form $\exists x \in [\![\tau]\!]. \phi$ to atomic types τ. Moreover, the gap between the existing theoretical result and possible implementation is quite wide.

The second, more direct approach is based on Moczydłowski's proof in [20] of weak normalization of the lambda calculus λZ corresponding to proofs in IZF. The normalization is used to prove NEP, DP and TEP for the theory and the necessary information is extracted from the normal form of the lambda term corresponding to the IZF proof. Thus in order to provide the implementation of DP, NEP and TEP for IZF, it would suffice to implement λZ, which is specified completely in [20].

6   Conclusion

We have presented a computational semantics for HOL via standard interpretation in intuitionistic set theory. The semantics is clean, simple and agrees with the standard one.

The advantage of this approach is that the extraction mechanism is completely external to Constructive HOL. Using only the semantics, we can take any constructive HOL proof and extract from it computational information. No enrichment of the logic in the normalizing proof terms is necessary.

The separation of the extraction mechanism from the logic makes the logic very easily extendable. For example, inductive datatypes and subtyping have clean set-theoretic semantics, so can easily be added to HOL preserving consistency, as witnessed in PVS. As the semantics would work constructively, the extraction mechanisms from section 5 could be easily adapted to incorporate them. Similarly, one could define a set-theoretic semantics for the constructive version of HOL implemented in Isabelle ([3,4]) in the same spirit, with the same advantages.

The modularity of our approach and the fact that it is much easier to give set-theoretic semantics for the logic than to prove normalization, could make the development of new trustworthy provers with extraction capabilities much easier and faster.

We would like to thank anonymous reviewers for their helpful comments.

References

1. Church, A.: A formulation of the simple theory of types. The Journal of Symbolic Logic **5** (1940) 55–68
2. Harrison, J.: HOL Light: A tutorial introduction. In: Formal Methods in Computer-Aided Design (FMCAD'96). Volume 1166 of Lecture Notes in Computer Science., Springer (1996) 265–269
3. Berghofer, S.: Proofs, Programs and Executable Specifications in Higher Order Logic. PhD thesis, Technische Universität München (2004)
4. Berghofer, S., Nipkow, T.: Executing higher order logic. In Callaghan, P., Luo, Z., McKinna, J., Pollack, R., eds.: Types for Proofs and Programs: TYPES'2000. Volume 2277 of Lecture Notes in Computer Science., Springer-Verlag (2002)
5. Coquand, T., Paulin-Mohring, C.: Inductively defined types, preliminary version. In: COLOG '88, International Conference on Computer Logic. Volume 417 of Lecture Notes in Computer Science., Springer, Berlin (1990) 50–66
6. Bertot, Y., Castéran, P.: Interactive Theorem Proving and Program Development; Coq'Art: The Calculus of Inductive Constructions. Springer-Verlag (2004)
7. Benl, H., Berger, U., Schwichtenberg, H., et al.: Proof theory at work: Program development in the Minlog system. In Bibel, W., Schmitt, P.G., eds.: Automated Deduction. Volume II. Kluwer (1998)
8. Allen, S.F., et al.: Innovations in computational type theory using Nuprl. To appear in 2006 (2006)
9. Constable, R.L., et al.: Implementing Mathematics with the Nuprl Proof Development System. Prentice-Hall, NJ (1986)
10. Martin-Löf, P.: Constructive mathematics and computer programming. In: Proceedings of the Sixth International Congress for Logic, Methodology, and Philosophy of Science, Amsterdam, North Holland (1982) 153–175

11. Nordström, B., Petersson, K., Smith, J.M.: Programming in Martin-Löf's Type Theory. Oxford Sciences Publication, Oxford (1990)
12. Augustsson, L., Coquand, T., Nordström, B.: A short description of another logical framework. In: Proceedings of the First Annual Workshop on Logical Frameworks, Sophia-Antipolis, France (1990) 39–42
13. The Coq Development Team: The Coq Proof Assistant Reference Manual – Version V8.0. (2004) http://coq.inria.fr.
14. Hickey, J., et al.: MetaPRL — A modular logical environment. In Basin, D., Wolff, B., eds.: Proceedings of the TPHOLs 2003. Volume 2758 of Lecture Notes in Computer Science., Springer-Verlag (2003) 287–303
15. Allen, S., et al.: The Nuprl open logical environment. In McAllester, D., ed.: Proceedings of the 17th International Conference on Automated Deduction. Volume 1831 of Lecture Notes in Artificial Intelligence., Springer Verlag (2000) 170–176
16. Aczel, P.: The type theoretic interpretation of constructive set theory. In MacIntyre, A., Pacholski, L., Paris, J., eds.: Logic Colloquium '77, North Holland (1978)
17. Howe, D.J.: Semantic foundations for embedding HOL in Nuprl. In Wirsing, M., Nivat, M., eds.: Algebraic Methodology and Software Technology. Volume 1101 of Lecture Notes in Computer Science. Springer-Verlag, Berlin (1996) 85–101
18. Howe, D.J.: Toward sharing libraries of mathematics between theorem provers. In: Frontiers of Combining Systems, FroCoS'98, ILLC, Kluwer Academic Publishers (1998)
19. Rathjen, M.: The disjunction and related properties for constructive Zermelo-Fraenkel set theory. Journal of Symbolic Logic 70 (2005) 1233–1254
20. Moczydłowski, W.: Normalization of IZF with Replacement. Technical Report 2006-2024, Computer Science Department, Cornell University (2006)
21. Gordon, M., Melham, T.: Introduction to HOL: A Theorem Proving Environment for Higher-Order Logic. Cambridge University Press, Cambridge (1993)
22. Myhill, J.: Some properties of intuitionistic Zermelo-Fraenkel set theory. In: Cambridge Summer School in Mathematical Logic. Volume 29., Springer (1973) 206–231
23. Beeson, M.J.: Foundations of Constructive Mathematics. Springer-Verlag (1985)
24. McCarty, D.: Realizability and recursive set theory. Journal of Pure and Applied Logic 32 (1986) 153–183
25. Friedman, H.: The consistency of classical set theory relative to a set theory with intuitionistic logic. The Journal of Symbolic Logic (1973) 315–319

Towards Self-verification of HOL Light

John Harrison

Intel Corporation, JF1-13
2111 NE 25th Avenue
Hillsboro OR 97124
johnh@ichips.intel.com

Abstract. The HOL Light prover is based on a logical kernel consisting
of about 400 lines of mostly functional OCaml, whose complete formal
verification seems to be quite feasible. We would like to formally verify
(i) that the abstract HOL logic is indeed correct, and (ii) that the OCaml
code does correctly implement this logic. We have performed a full verification of an imperfect but quite detailed model of the basic HOL Light
core, without definitional mechanisms, and this verification is entirely
conducted with respect to a set-theoretic semantics within HOL Light
itself. We will duly explain why the obvious logical and pragmatic difficulties do not vitiate this approach, even though it looks impossible or
useless at first sight. Extension to include definitional mechanisms seems
straightforward enough, and the results so far allay most of our practical
worries.

1 Introduction: Quis Custodiet Ipsos Custodes?

Mathematical proofs are subjected to peer review before publication, but there
are plenty of cases where published results turned out to be faulty [13,4]. Such
errors seem more likely in mathematical correctness proofs of algorithms, protocols etc. These tend to be more messy and intricate than (most) proofs in pure
mathematics, and those performing the proofs are often not primarily trained
as mathematicians. So while there are still some voices of dissent [6], there is a
general consensus in the formal verification world that correctness proofs should
be at least checked, and perhaps partly or wholly generated, by computer. In
pure mathematics a similar opinion is still controversial, but we expect it to
slowly percolate into the mathematical mainstream over the coming decades.

One obvious and common objection to computer-checked proofs is: why should
we believe that they are any more reliable than human proofs? Well, for most
practical purposes, computers can be considered mechanically infallible. Though
'soft errors' resulting from particle bombardment are increasingly significant as
miniaturization advances, techniques for controlling these and other related effects are well-established and already in widespread use for high-integrity systems. The issue is not so much one of mechanical reliability, but rather the
correctness of the proof-checking program itself, as well as potentially the stack
of software it runs on. We may be willing to accept a machine-checked proof
that we couldn't conceivably 'survey' ourselves, provided we understand and

U. Furbach and N. Shankar (Eds.): IJCAR 2006, LNAI 4130, pp. 177–191, 2006.
© Springer-Verlag Berlin Heidelberg 2006

have confidence in the checking program — in this sense a proof checker provides intellectual leverage [16]. But how can we, or why should we? Who checks the checker?

2   LCF

Many practitioners consider worries about the fallibility of provers somewhat pointless. Experience shows unambiguously that typical mainstream proof checkers *are* far more reliable than human hand proofs, and abstract theorizing to the contrary is apt to look like empty chatter. Yet bugs in proof checkers are far from being unknown, and on at least one occasion, there was an announcement that an open problem had been solved by a theorem prover, later traced to a bug in the prover. For example, versions of HOL [9] have in the past had errors of two kinds:[1]

- Errors in the underlying logic, e.g. early versions allowed constant definitions with type variables occurring in the definiens but not the constant.
- Errors in the implementation, e.g. functions implementing logical operations were found not to rename variables to avoid free variable capture.

So what if we want to achieve the highest levels of confidence? We have no fully satisfactory answer to the thoroughgoing skeptic who doubts the integrity of the implementation language, compiler, operating system or hardware. But at least let us assume those are correct and consider how we might reassure ourselves about the proof checker itself, proving the absence of logical *or* implementation errors.

Since serious proof checkers are large and complex systems of software, their correctness is certainly open to doubt. However, there are established approaches to this problem. Some systems satisfy the *de Bruijn criterion* [2]: they can output a proof that is checkable by a much simpler program. Others based on the LCF approach [10] generate all theorems internally using a small logical kernel: only this is allowed to create objects of the special type 'theorem', just as only the kernel of an operating system is allowed to execute in privileged mode. From a certain point of view, one can say that an LCF prover satisfies the de Bruijn criterion, except that the proof exists only ephemerally and is checked by the kernel as it is created. And it is straightforward to instrument an LCF kernel so that it does actually output separately checkable proofs [22].

The original Edinburgh LCF system was designed to support proofs in a special 'Logic of Computable Functions' [19], hence the name LCF. But the key idea, as Gordon [8] emphasizes, is equally applicable to more orthodox logics supporting conventional mathematics, and subsequently many 'LCF-style' proof checkers have been designed using the same principles. In particular, the original HOL system [9] and its descendant HOL Light [11] are LCF-style provers. HOL Light is constructed on top of a logical kernel consisting of only around 400 lines of Objective CAML. Thus, if we accept that the interface to the trusted kernel is correct,

---

[1] In the absence of a highly rigorous abstract specification of the logic, it's not always easy to categorize errors in this way, but these examples seem clear.

we need only verify those 400 lines of code. In the present paper, we describe significant though imperfect progress towards this goal.

3   On Self-verification

Tarski's theorem on the undefinability of truth tells us that no logical system (capable of formalizing a certain amount of arithmetic) can formalize its own semantics, and Gödel's second incompleteness theorem tells us that it cannot prove its own consistency in any way at all — unless of course it *isn't* consistent, in which case it can prove anything [21]. So, regardless of implementation details, if we want to prove the consistency of a proof checker, we need to use a logic that in at least some respects goes beyond the logic the checker itself supports.

The most obvious approach, therefore, would be to verify HOL Light using a system whose logic is at least strong enough to formalize HOL Light's semantics, e.g. Mizar [18] based on Tarski-Grothendieck set theory. Instead, simply on the grounds of personal expertise with it, we have chosen to verify HOL Light *in itself*. Of course, in the light of the above observations, we cannot expect to prove consistency of HOL in itself, $\vdash_{HOL} Con(\text{HOL})$. Instead, we have proven two similar results: consistency of HOL within a stronger variant of HOL, and of a weaker variant of HOL within ordinary HOL:[2]

- $I \vdash_{HOL} Con(\text{HOL})$ for a new axiom I about sets.
- $\vdash_{HOL} Con(\text{HOL} - \{\infty\})$ where $\text{HOL} - \{\infty\}$ is HOL with no axiom of infinity.

One can still take the view that these results are pointless, but they cover most of the problems we worry about. Almost all implementation bugs in HOL Light and other versions of HOL have involved variable renaming, and manifest themselves in a contradiction regardless of whether we assume the axiom of infinity. So having a correctness proof of something close to the actual *implementation* of $\text{HOL} - \{\infty\}$, rather than merely the abstract logic, is a real reassurance.

Naturally, it is possible that a soundness bug in HOL Light could mean that these correctness statements themselves are not true, but have only been 'proved' by means of this bug! There are two counterarguments. Intuitively, it seems unlikely that some logical or implementation bug, never spotted in any other domain, should just happen to manifest itself in the proof of consistency. And HOL Light is able to generate proof logs that can be checked in Isabelle/HOL, thanks to work by Steven Obua. Thus, having a proof in HOL Light, we effectively have a proof in Isabelle/HOL too, which implements a similar logic but is quite different in terms of internal organization and so unlikely to feature the same implementation bugs.

4   HOL Light Foundations and Axioms

HOL Light's logic is simple type theory [3,1] with polymorphic type variables. The terms of the logic are those of simply typed lambda calculus, with formulas being

---

[2] Thanks to Rob Arthan for pointing out this kind of possibility.

terms of boolean type, rather than a separate category. Every term has a single
welldefined type, but each constant with polymorphic type gives rise to an infinite
family of constant terms. There are just two primitive types: bool (boolean) and
ind (individuals), and given any two types σ and τ one can form the function type
$\sigma \to \tau$.[3]

For the core HOL logic, there is essentially only one predefined logical constant,
equality ($=$) with polymorphic type $\alpha \to \alpha \to$ bool. However to state one of the
mathematical axioms we also include another constant $\varepsilon : (\alpha \to$ bool$) \to \alpha$,
explained further below. For equations, we use the conventional concrete syntax
$s = t$, but this is just surface syntax for the λ-calculus term $((-)s)t$, where juxtaposition represents function application. For equations between boolean terms
we often use $s \Leftrightarrow t$, but this again is just surface syntax.

The HOL Light deductive system governs the deducibility of one-sided sequents
$\Gamma \vdash p$ where p is a term of boolean type and Γ is a set (possibly empty) of terms
of boolean type. There are ten primitive rules of inference, rather similar to those
for the internal logic of a topos [12].

$$\frac{}{\vdash t = t} \text{ REFL}$$

$$\frac{\Gamma \vdash s = t \quad \Delta \vdash t = u}{\Gamma \cup \Delta \vdash s = u} \text{ TRANS}$$

$$\frac{\Gamma \vdash s = t \quad \Delta \vdash u = v}{\Gamma \cup \Delta \vdash s(u) = t(v)} \text{ MK\_COMB}$$

$$\frac{\Gamma \vdash s = t}{\Gamma \vdash (\lambda x.\ s) = (\lambda x.\ t)} \text{ ABS}$$

$$\frac{}{\vdash (\lambda x.\ t)x = t} \text{ BETA}$$

$$\frac{}{\{p\} \vdash p} \text{ ASSUME}$$

$$\frac{\Gamma \vdash p \Leftrightarrow q \quad \Delta \vdash p}{\Gamma \cup \Delta \vdash q} \text{ EQ\_MP}$$

$$\frac{\Gamma \vdash p \quad \Delta \vdash q}{(\Gamma - \{q\}) \cup (\Delta - \{p\}) \vdash p \Leftrightarrow q} \text{ DEDUCT\_ANTISYM\_RULE}$$

$$\frac{\Gamma[x_1, \ldots, x_n] \vdash p[x_1, \ldots, x_n]}{\Gamma[t_1, \ldots, t_n] \vdash p[t_1, \ldots, t_n]} \text{ INST}$$

$$\frac{\Gamma[\alpha_1, \ldots, \alpha_n] \vdash p[\alpha_1, \ldots, \alpha_n]}{\Gamma[\gamma_1, \ldots, \gamma_n] \vdash p[\gamma_1, \ldots, \gamma_n]} \text{ INST\_TYPE}$$

[3] In Church's original notation, also used by Andrews, these are written o, ι and $\tau\sigma$
respectively. Of course the particular concrete syntax has no logical significance.

In MK_COMB it is necessary for the types to agree so that the composite terms are well-typed, and in ABS it is required that the variable x not be free in any of the assumptions Γ. Our notation for term and type instantiation assumes capture-avoiding substitution, which we discuss in detail later.

All the usual logical constants are defined in terms of equality — see below for exactly what we mean by *defined*. The conventional syntax $\forall x.\, P[x]$ for quantifiers is surface syntax for $(\forall)(\lambda x.\, P[x])$, and we also use this 'binder' notation for the ε operator.

$$\top =_{def} (\lambda p.\, p) = (\lambda p.\, p)$$
$$\wedge =_{def} \lambda p.\, \lambda q.\, (\lambda f\ f\ p\ q) - (\lambda f.\, f \top \top)$$
$$\Longrightarrow =_{def} \lambda p.\, \lambda q.\, p \wedge q \Leftrightarrow p$$
$$\forall =_{def} \lambda P.\, P = \lambda x.\, \top$$
$$\exists =_{def} \lambda P.\, \forall q.\, (\forall x.\, P(x) \Longrightarrow q) \Longrightarrow q$$
$$\vee =_{def} \lambda p.\, \lambda q.\, \forall r.\, (p \Longrightarrow r) \Longrightarrow (q \Longrightarrow r) \Longrightarrow r$$
$$\bot =_{def} \forall p.\, p$$
$$\neg =_{def} \lambda p.\, p \Longrightarrow \bot$$
$$\exists! =_{def} \lambda P.\, \exists P \wedge \forall x.\, \forall y.\, P\, x \wedge P\, y \Longrightarrow x = y$$

These definitions allow us to derive all the usual (intuitionistic) natural deduction rules for the connectives in terms of the primitive rules above. All of the core 'logic' is derived in this way. But then we add three mathematical axioms:

- The axiom of extensionality, in the form of an eta-conversion axiom ETA_AX: $\vdash (\lambda x.\, t\ x) = t$. We could have considered this as part of the core logic rather than a mathematical axiom; this is largely a question of taste.
- The axiom of choice SELECT_AX, asserting that the Hilbert operator ε is a choice operator: $\vdash P\ x \Longrightarrow P((\varepsilon)P)$. It is only from this axiom that we can deduce that the HOL logic is classical [5].
- The axiom of infinity INFINITY_AX, discussed further below.

In addition, HOL Light includes two principles of definition, which allow one to extend the set of constants and the set of types in a way guaranteed to preserve consistency. The rule of constant definition allows one to introduce a new constant c and an axiom $\vdash c = t$, subject to some conditions on free variables and polymorphic types in t, and provided no previous definition for c has been introduced. All the definitions of the logical connectives above are introduced in this way. Note that this is 'object-level' definition: the constant and its defining axiom exist in the object logic. However, in our verification we don't formalize the rule of definition, instead regarding the definitions of the connectives as 'meta-level' definitions. When we write, say, $\bot$, it is merely an abbreviation for the term $\forall p.\, p$ and so on. We took this path to avoid technical complications over the changing signature of the logic, but eventually we want to generalize our proof to cover the actual HOL definitional principles. Neither do we presently formalize the rule of type definition, though we would eventually like to do so.

5   Added and Removed Axioms

Since in our self-verifications we either remove the axiom of infinity '∞' or add
a new axiom I, we will explain these carefully. The HOL Light axiom of infinity
asserts that the type ind of individuals is Dedekind-infinite, i.e. that there is a
function from ind to itself that is injective but not surjective:

```
|- ∃f:ind->ind. ONE_ONE f ∧ ¬ONTO f
```

where the subsidiary concepts are defined as follows:

```
|- ∀f. ONE_ONE f ⇔ (∀x1 x2. f x1 = f x2 ⟹ x1 = x2)
|- ∀f. ONTO f ⇔ (∀y. ∃x. y = f x)
```

This is the only rule or axiom that says anything specifically about ind. If we
exclude it, we can find a model for the HOL logic where ind is modelled by (say)
a 1-element set, and bool as usual by a 2-element set. Then any type we can construct from those using the function space constructor will also have an interpretation as a finite set. Thus we can find a model for the entire type hierarchy inside
any infinite set, which we have in the full HOL logic.

But to model all of HOL including its axiom of infinity, we must take an infinite
set, say $\mathbb{N}$, to model the type of individuals. We then need to be able to model at
least the infinite hierarchy of types ind, ind → bool, (ind → bool) → bool and so
on, so we need a set for the universe of types that can contain $\wp^n(\mathbb{N})$, the n-fold
application of the power set operation to $\mathbb{N}$, for all $n \in \mathbb{N}$. Since for successive n
these have cardinality $\aleph_0$, $2^{\aleph_0}$, $2^{2^{\aleph_0}}$ and so on, we cannot prove in HOL that there
is any set large enough. So we add a new axiom I that gives us a 'larger' universe
of sets. In the traditional terminology of cardinal arithmetic it asserts that there
is a cardinal ι with the property that it is strictly larger than the cardinality of $\mathbb{N}$
and is closed under exponentiation applied to smaller cardinals: $\aleph_0 < \iota \wedge (\forall \kappa. \kappa <
\iota \implies 2^\kappa < \iota)$. This is unproblematic in ZF set theory (e.g. take ι to be the cardinal
of $V_{\omega+\omega}$ in the hierarchy of sets) so there is nothing dubious or recherché about our
new axiom.

In order to deal with the two cases of removing and adding an axiom almost
entirely uniformly, we start each proof by defining a type ind_model to model the
type ind, as well as the type I that will model the whole type universe. In proving
$I \vdash Con(HOL)$, we introduce such types and assert our higher axiom of infinity
for them:

```
|- (:ind_model) <_c (:I) ∧
   (∀s:A->bool. s <_c (:I) ⟹ {t | t SUBSET s} <_c (:I)
```

Here '(:I)' is a HOL Light shorthand for the universal set on type I, and '$<_c$'
is strict cardinal comparison, defined as the irreflexive form of non-strict cardinal
comparison, itself defined in terms of the existence of an injective map from one
set to the other.[4]

---

[4] In simple type theory, it is problematic defining a general type of cardinals, but many
arguments can be rephrased in terms of cardinal comparison and set operations [7].

In the case of proving $\vdash_{\text{HOL}} Con(\text{HOL} - \{\infty\})$, we just *define* a type `ind_model` in bijection with a finite nonempty set and `I` in bijection with $\mathbb{N}$. In this case we can easily *prove* the statement about cardinal closure, instead of taking it as an axiom. The subsequent proofs are all completely identical based on this cardinality property, except that right at the end we need in one case to show how we can model the axiom of infinity.

6   Formalized Syntax

The various OCaml types representing logical entities of types and terms are formalized inside the HOL logic using analogous recursive type definitions. However, there is an important difference, which we will explain for types first. In the code, the type of HOL types is declared by the following OCaml recursive type definition:

```
type hol_type = Tyvar of string
              | Tyapp of string * hol_type list
```

The second clause allows a type constructor with any name and arity. However, the constructors themselves are hidden by an abstract type interface, which permits only types using type constructors that have been declared. In the initial state these amount to just the base types `bool`, `ind` and the binary function space constructor `fun`, but later type definitions can extend the list. In the HOL formalization, we do not consider the potentially extensible type signature, and just 'hardwire' the base types we will consider:

```
define_type "type = Tyvar string
                  | Bool
                  | Ind
                  | Fun type type";;
```

Similarly, the basic type of HOL terms is defined in OCaml without any well-typedness restriction, with any term as the "bound variable" of a lambda-abstraction, with these restrictions imposed by the abstract type interface.

```
type term = Var of string * hol_type
          | Const of string * hol_type
          | Comb of term * term
          | Abs of term * term
```

In the HOL formalization, we wire in the two primitive constants, where 'Equal α' represents $(=) : \alpha \to \alpha \to$ bool and 'Select α' represents $(\varepsilon) : (\alpha \to$ bool$) \to \alpha$, and we syntactically force the bound variable of a lambda-abstraction to be a (typed) variable and not any other kind of term:

```
define_type "term = Var string type
                  | Equal type | Select type
                  | Comb term term
                  | Abs string type term";;
```

This allows ill-typed terms that could not be constructed using the abstract type interface of HOL Light, so we often need to state side-conditions connected with well-typedness on our theorems. This notion is defined as

```
|- welltyped tm ⇔ ∃ty. tm has_type ty
```

where the typing judgement, written infix, is defined inductively as follows; every welltyped term then has a unique type, extracted by a function typeof.

```
|- (∀n ty. (Var n ty) has_type ty) ∧
   (∀ty. (Equal ty) has_type (Fun ty (Fun ty Bool))) ∧
   (∀ty. (Select ty) has_type (Fun (Fun ty Bool) ty)) ∧
   (∀s t dty rty. s has_type (Fun dty rty) ∧ t has_type dty
        ⟹ (Comb s t) has_type rty) ∧
   (∀n dty t rty. t has_type rty ⟹ (Abs n dty t) has_type (Fun dty rty))';;
```

Subject to these systematic differences, we model much of the OCaml code in the core faithfully. Most syntax functions are purely functional, and we "naively" transcribe them into corresponding definitional theorems in the logic, following [20]. In general, recursive functions in OCaml may fail to terminate, and this aspect is not adequately modelled by our encoding.[5] In practice all the functions we use do terminate, and without some inductive argument we would not be able to prove anything non-trivial about them. So this distinction is somewhat academic, and generally speaking the structural similarity is very clear. (It's particularly important to emphasize this point, since most of our discussion here is devoted to differences.) For example, the function that performs a union of term lists modulo alpha-equivalence in OCaml is:

```
let rec term_union l1 l2 =
  match l1 with
    [] -> l2
  | (h::t) -> let subun = term_union t l2 in
           if exists (aconv h) subun then subun else h::subun;;
```

and the HOL formalization is:

```
|- (TERM_UNION [] l2 = l2) ∧
   (TERM_UNION (CONS h t) l2 =
       let subun = TERM_UNION t l2 in
       if EX (ACONV h) subun then subun else CONS h subun)
```

At the other end of the spectrum, the worst case for the correspondence between code and HOL formalization is the type instantiation function, which replaces type variables $\alpha_1, \ldots, \alpha_n$ with other types $\sigma_1, \ldots, \sigma_n$ in some term. The OCaml code involves exceptions and pointer-equality tests:

---

[5] HOL Light's derived rules can prove consistency of various recursive definitions, in particular all tail-recursive ones (I owe the observation that these are always consistent to J Moore). This does *not* imply termination of the analogous functional program.

```
let rec inst env tyin tm =
  match tm with
    Var(n,ty)   -> let ty' = type_subst tyin ty in
                   let tm' = if ty' == ty then tm else Var(n,ty') in
                   if rev_assocd tm' env tm = tm then tm'
                   else raise (Clash tm')
  | Const(c,ty) -> let ty' = type_subst tyin ty in
                   if ty' == ty then tm else Const(c,ty')
  | Comb(f,x)   -> let f' = inst env tyin f and x' = inst env tyin x in
                   if f' == f & x' == x then tm else Comb(f',x')
  | Abs(y,t)    -> let y' = inst [] tyin y in
                   let env' = (y,y')::env in
                   try let t' = inst env' tyin t in
                       if y' == y & t' == t then tm else Abs(y',t')
                   with (Clash(w') as ex) ->
                   if w' <> y' then raise ex else
                   let ifrees = map (inst [] tyin) (frees t) in
                   let y'' = variant ifrees y' in
                   let z = Var(fst(dest_var y''),snd(dest_var y)) in
                   inst env tyin (Abs(z,vsubst[z,y] t))
```

The tyin argument is an association list $[\sigma_1, \alpha_1; \cdots; \sigma_n, \alpha_n]$ specifying the desired instantiation, tm is the term to instantiate, and env is used to keep track of correspondences between original and instantiated variables to detect name clash problems. Note first that the recursive cases are optimized to avoid rebuilding the same term. For example, the case for Comb(f,x) checks if the instantiated subterms f' and x' are pointer identical ('==') to the originals, and if so just returns the full original term. This optimization is not, and cannot be, reflected in our naive model.

The main complexity in this function is detecting and handling variable capture. For example, the instantiation of α to bool in the constant function λx : bool. $x : \alpha$ would, if done naively, result in the identity function λx : bool. x : bool. We want to ensure instead that we get something like $\lambda x'$: bool. x : bool. So each time a variable is type-instantiated (first clause) we check that it is consistent with the list env, which roughly means that if after instantiation it is bound by some abstraction, it was already bound by the same one before. If this property fails, an exception Clash is raised with the problem term. This exception is supposed to be caught by exactly the outer recursive call for that abstraction, which renames the variable appropriately and tries again (last line).

Exceptions also have no meaning in our naive model. Instead, we include the possibility of exceptions by extending the return type of the function in our HOL formalization to a disjoint sum type defined by:

```
define_type "result = Clash term | Result term";;
```

In all expressions we manually 'propagate' the Clash exception with the help of discriminator (IS_RESULT and IS_CLASH) and extractor (RESULT and CLASH) functions. These are also used at the end to take us back to a simple analog INST of the OCaml code's main inst function.[6] With all these caveats, the overall structure should faithfully model the OCaml code:

---

[6] The main recursion for inst shown above is used internally in the definition of the main inst, which simply provides the empty list as the initial env argument. The

```
|- (INST_CORE env tyin (Var x ty) =
     let tm = Var x ty
     and tm' = Var x (TYPE_SUBST tyin ty) in
   if REV_ASSOCD tm' env tm = tm then Result tm' else Clash tm') ∧
 (INST_CORE env tyin (Equal ty) = Result(Equal(TYPE_SUBST tyin ty))) ∧
 (INST_CORE env tyin (Select ty) = Result(Select(TYPE_SUBST tyin ty))) ∧
 (INST_CORE env tyin (Comb s t) =
     let sres = INST_CORE env tyin s in
     if IS_CLASH sres then sres else
     let tres = INST_CORE env tyin t in
     if IS_CLASH tres then tres else
     let s' = RESULT sres and t' = RESULT tres in
     Result (Comb s' t')) ∧
 (INST_CORE env tyin (Abs x ty t) =
     let ty' = TYPE_SUBST tyin ty in
     let env' = CONS (Var x ty,Var x ty') env in
     let tres = INST_CORE env' tyin t in
     if IS_RESULT tres then Result(Abs x ty' (RESULT tres)) else
     let w = CLASH tres in
     if ¬(w = Var x ty') then tres else
     let x' = VARIANT (RESULT(INST_CORE [] tyin t)) x ty' in
     INST_CORE env tyin (Abs x' ty (VSUBST [Var x' ty,Var x ty] t)))
```

The termination of this function needs a careful argument. The last line can result in a recursive call on a term of the same size, but the choice of new variable means that the subcall will then not raise the same exception that would lead to yet another subcall from this level.

We now introduce a handy abbreviation for equations (an exact counterpart to a function `mk_eq` in the OCaml code):

```
|- (s === t) = Comb (Comb (Equal(typeof s)) s) t
```

and are ready to model the HOL Light deductive system using an inductively defined 'is provable' predicate '|-'. For reasons of space, we only show clauses for rules REFL, TRANS and INST_TYPE, but none of them are complex or surprising:

```
|- (∀t. welltyped t ⟹ [] |- t === t) ∧
   (∀asl1 asl2 l m1 m2 r.
       asl1 |- l === m1 ∧ asl2 |- m2 === r ∧ ACONV m1 m2
       ⟹ TERM_UNION asl1 asl2 |- l === r) ∧
   ...
   (∀tyin asl p. asl |- p ⟹ MAP (INST tyin) asl |- INST tyin p) ∧
   ...
```

7   Set Theory

We next develop a HOL type V of 'sets' big enough to model all types. The sets are arranged in levels somewhat analogous to the Zermelo-Fraenkel hierarchy, each containing all subsets of the levels below it. The membership symbol in V is written as an infix <:, and has type $V \to V \to$ bool. (This is quite distinct from the usual HOL set/predicate membership operation IN with type $\alpha \to (\alpha \to$ bool) $\to \alpha$.) Many of the axioms and constructs familiar from ZF set theory appear, e.g 's suchthat p' is the subset of elements of s satisfying p, whose existence is assured by the ZF separation axiom:

choice of names is a bit confusing: this is used in the inference rule INST_TYPE; the rule INST is term instantiation and the corresponding term operation is called VSUBST.

```
|- (level(s suchthat p) = level s) ∧ ∀x. x <: s suchthat p ⇔ x <: s ∧ p x
```

Similarly we have a choice function `ch` satisfying:

```
|- ∀s. (∃x. x <: s) ⟹ ch(s) <: s
```

But we have no need of 'mixed level' sets like $\{\emptyset, \{\emptyset\}\}$, so we make the hierarchy non-cumulative, with the levels all distinct. This means that there are multiple empty sets at all levels of the hierarchy, so we don't have simple extensionality. We also have a primitive notion of pairing (it is not defined as is usually done in ZF set theory), and we start with two basic sets of 'ur-elements' `booloct` (with elements `true` and `false`) and `indset` to model the base HOL types. We will not show the technical details of the construction, since they are not particularly interesting or challenging. We just observe some notation for later use.

The set of functions from set `s` to set `t` (constructed much as in ZF set theory, as a certain set of ordered pairs) is denoted by `funspace s t`, and function application is `apply`. We also define a set-theoretic analog `abstract` of lambda-abstraction to allow us to construct certain functions explicitly. Here are a few relevant lemmas to help the reader to get a picture of the setup.

```
|- x <: s ∧ f(x) <: t ⟹ (apply(abstract s t f) x = f(x))

|- x <: s ∧ f <: funspace s t ⟹ apply f x <: t

|- (∀x. x <: s ⟹ f(x) <: t) ⟹ abstract s t f <: funspace s t
```

Note that everything in the construction of this set-theoretic hierarchy is based on the key cardinality property we noted earlier; no other axioms are used. Of course, this property was designed exactly to allow the construction of such a type.

8   Formalized Semantics

HOL is a fairly simple logic, and it isn't so difficult to give it a set-theoretic semantics. However, the presence of polymorphic type variables makes it a bit trickier than it first appears. Our approach is inspired by the semantics given by Andy Pitts [9], though we use more traditional valuation-based formulation rather than using contexts, since it seems (to us) technically simpler. The semantics is parameterized throughout by a valuation τ : `string` $\to$ V of the type variables. We require only that it always returns a nonempty set:

```
|- type_valuation tau ⇔ ∀x. (∃y. y <: tau x)
```

Given such a type valuation, each HOL type is allocated a corresponding set in V using the following straightforward definition:

```
|- (typeset tau (Tyvar s) = tau(s)) ∧
   (typeset tau Bool = boolset) ∧
   (typeset tau Ind = indset) ∧
   (typeset tau (Fun a b) = funspace (typeset tau a) (typeset tau b))
```

Now we come to the semantics of terms. As well as the valuation τ of type variables, this has as another parameter a valuation σ of term variables, or more precisely of name-type pairs. This should always be consistent with τ, i.e. should map each variable-type pair into the set corresponding to that type:

```
|- term_valuation tau sigma ⇔ ∀n ty. sigma(n,ty) <: typeset tau ty
```

The definition of the semantics is:

```
|- (semantics sigma tau (Var n ty) = sigma(n,ty)) ∧
   (semantics sigma tau (Equal ty) =
     abstract (typeset tau ty) (typeset tau (Fun ty Bool))
       ((λx. abstract (typeset tau ty) (typeset tau Bool)
                      (λy. boolean(x = y)))) ∧
   (semantics sigma tau (Select ty) =
     abstract (typeset tau (Fun ty Bool)) (typeset tau ty)
              (λs. if ∃x. x <: ((typeset tau ty) suchthat (holds s))
                   then ch ((typeset tau ty) suchthat (holds s))
                   else ch (typeset tau ty))) ∧
   (semantics sigma tau (Comb s t) =
      apply (semantics sigma tau s) (semantics sigma tau t)) ∧
   (semantics sigma tau (Abs n ty t) =
      abstract (typeset tau ty) (typeset tau (typeof t))
               (λx. semantics (((n,ty) |-> x) sigma) tau t))
```

The first clause is easy: just apply the valuation σ. The fourth and fifth clauses are also fairly natural: they just map application and abstraction into their set-theoretic counterparts. The semantics of a term $\lambda n : ty.\ t$ is a function taking an argument x that recursively evaluates the semantics of t in a modified valuation with $n : ty$ mapped to x but which is otherwise the same as σ. (The modification is done by an infix function update '|->'.) The second and third clauses look involved only because we actually need to interpret $=$ and ε as functions of the appropriate type, but they just give the right sets for the obvious equality and choice functions. (If it would otherwise be applied to an empty set, we force the choice operator to pick any element of the right type.) When the equality constant is actually used in an equation in the usual way, the semantics, with reasonable side-conditions, is about what we would expect. Note that here and above `boolean` just maps a HOL boolean into the corresponding member of `boolset` in V:[7]

```
|- (s === t) has_type Bool ∧ type_valuation tau ∧ term_valuation tau sigma
   ⟹ (semantics sigma tau (s === t) =
       boolean(semantics sigma tau s = semantics sigma tau t))
```

We proceed with various lemmas about how the semantics interacts with syntactic operations. The most complex governs the type instantiation operation whose definition we considered earlier:

```
|- ∀tyin tm sigma tau.
     welltyped tm ∧ type_valuation tau ∧ term_valuation tau sigma
     ⟹ (semantics sigma tau (INST tyin tm) =
         semantics
         (λ(x,ty). sigma(x,TYPE_SUBST tyin ty))
         (λs. typeset tau (TYPE_SUBST tyin (Tyvar s))) tm)
```

---

[7] The typing condition is a shorthand for saying that both subterms are welltyped; an equation always has boolean type if so.

where TYPE_SUBST is substitution of types for type variables within a *type*, defined by straightforward recursion. Finally, we define the semantic notion of entailment:

```
|- asms |= p ⇔ ALL (λa. a has_type Bool) (CONS p asms) ∧
              ∀sigma tau. type_valuation tau ∧ term_valuation tau sigma ∧
                ALL (λa. semantics sigma tau a = true) asms
                ⟹ (semantics sigma tau p = true)
```

and hence by induction, considering the various inference rules, we deduce that HOL is sound:

```
|- ∀asl p. asl |- p ⟹ asl |= p
```

and consistent in the sense that there is an unprovable formula:

```
|- ∃p. p has_type Bool ∧ ¬([] |- p)
```

9   Conclusions and Related Work

We believe that this is the first time anything close to the implementation of a 'real' theorem prover has been verified against a semantic model, though syntactic features of the HOL logic have been formalized before [23], and full correctness for a first-order proof checker [14] and a simple first-order tableau prover [17] have been verified. We believe that a proof based on a semantics is more valuable than one relative to an abstract description of the same deductive system: even the abstract definitions of notions like capture-avoiding substitution are somewhat involved, and it is much more satisfactory to characterize them by their (relatively) simple semantics — cf. the key theorem about the semantics of INST above. On the other hand, it might be a fruitful separation of concerns to use a more abstract description of the logic as an intermediate step between the implementation and the semantics.

As for practical consequences, we are genuinely pleased to have finally convinced ourselves that the variable renaming methods (notably the rather involved mechanism in type instantiation) are correct. This is where our practical worries lay. Still, we view the present work only as a proof of concept: we have shown that all the key things can be made to work as we would wish; there is not much intellectual work involved in taking it further. But there are many obvious shortcomings in the work so far that need to be addressed. First of all, we need to properly model the full extensible signatures and the definitional principles that extend them. It would also be desirable to use a more detailed model of the implementation language. Our present work certainly does little to guard against language issues. In fact there is one that we know about: OCaml's strings are mutable, and this leads to imperfect protection of the abstract types of types and terms.

Another avenue for future work would be to extend the semantics to cover extensions to the logic, such as the introduction of quantifiers over type variables suggested in [15]. Tom Ridge has already updated large parts of HOL Light to incorporate them, and we believe the extension of the semantics is straightforward.

Acknowledgements

I would like to thank Rob Arthan, who first pointed out the feasibility of this kind of self-verification, and John Matthews and Tom Ridge who suggested extending this work to cover quantified type variables. Members of WG 2.3 provided some valuable feedback on an earlier version of this work. The anonymous referees, who evidently read the submitted version with great care, provided helpful remarks and caught several errors.

References

1. P. B. Andrews. *An Introduction to Mathematical Logic and Type Theory: To Truth Through Proof.* Academic Press, 1986.
2. H. Barendregt. The impact of the lambda calculus on logic and computer science. *Bulletin of Symbolic Logic*, 3:181–215, 1997.
3. A. Church. A formulation of the Simple Theory of Types. *Journal of Symbolic Logic*, 5:56–68, 1940.
4. P. J. Davis. Fidelity in mathematical discourse: Is one and one really two? *The American Mathematical Monthly*, 79:252–263, 1972.
5. R. Diaconescu. Axiom of choice and complementation. *Proceedings of the American Mathematical Society*, 51:176–178, 1975.
6. E. W. Dijkstra. Formal techniques and sizeable programs (EWD563). In E. W. Dijkstra, editor, *Selected Writings on Computing: A Personal Perspective*, pages 205–214. Springer-Verlag, 1976. Paper prepared for Symposium on the Mathematical Foundations of Computing Science, Gdansk 1976.
7. T. Forster. *Reasoning about theoretical entities*, volume 3 of *Advances in Logic*. World Scientific, 2003.
8. M. J. C. Gordon. Representing a logic in the LCF metalanguage. In D. Néel, editor, *Tools and notions for program construction: an advanced course*, pages 163–185. Cambridge University Press, 1982.
9. M. J. C. Gordon and T. F. Melham. *Introduction to HOL: a theorem proving environment for higher order logic.* Cambridge University Press, 1993.
10. M. J. C. Gordon, R. Milner, and C. P. Wadsworth. *Edinburgh LCF: A Mechanised Logic of Computation*, volume 78 of *Lecture Notes in Computer Science*. Springer-Verlag, 1979.
11. J. Harrison. HOL Light: A tutorial introduction. In M. Srivas and A. Camilleri, editors, *Proceedings of the First International Conference on Formal Methods in Computer-Aided Design (FMCAD'96)*, volume 1166 of *Lecture Notes in Computer Science*, pages 265–269. Springer-Verlag, 1996.
12. J. Lambek and P. J. Scott. *Introduction to higher order categorical logic*, volume 7 of *Cambridge studies in advanced mathematics*. Cambridge University Press, 1986.
13. M. Lecat. *Erreurs de Mathématiciens.* Brussels, 1935.
14. W. McCune and O. Shumsky. Ivy: A preprocessor and proof checker for first-order logic. In M. Kaufmann, P. Manolios, and J. S. Moore, editors, *Computer-Aided Reasoning: ACL2 Case Studies*, pages 265–281. Kluwer, 2000.
15. T. F. Melham. The HOL logic extended with quantification over type variables. In L. J. M. Claesen and M. J. C. Gordon, editors, *Proceedings of the IFIP TC10/WG10.2 International Workshop on Higher Order Logic Theorem Proving and its Applications*, volume A-20 of *IFIP Transactions A: Computer Science and Technology*, pages 3–18, IMEC, Leuven, Belgium, 1992. North-Holland.

16. R. Pollack. How to believe a machine-checked proof. In G. Sambin and J. Smith, editors, *Twenty-Five Years of Constructive Type Theory*. Oxford University Press, 1998. Also available on the Web as http://www.brics.dk/~ pollack/export/believing.ps.gz.

17. T. Ridge. A mechanically verified, efficient, sound and complete theorem prover for first order logic. Available via http://homepages.inf.ed.ac.uk/s0128214/, 2005.

18. P. Rudnicki. An overview of the MIZAR project. Available on the Web as http://web.cs.ualberta.ca/~piotr/Mizar/MizarOverview.ps, 1992.

19. D. Scott. A type-theoretical alternative to ISWIM, CUCH, OWHY. *Theoretical Computer Science*, 121:411–440, 1993. Annotated version of a 1969 manuscript.

20. K. Slind. *Reasoning about terminating functional programs*. PhD thesis, Institut für Informatik, Technische Universität München, 1999. Available from http://tumb1.biblio.tu-muenchen.de/publ/diss/in/1999/slind.html.

21. R. M. Smullyan. *Gödel's Incompleteness Theorems*, volume 19 of *Oxford Logic Guides*. Oxford University Press, 1992.

22. W. Wong. Recording HOL proofs. Technical Report 306, University of Cambridge Computer Laboratory, New Museums Site, Pembroke Street, Cambridge, CB2 3QG, UK, 1993.

23. J. von Wright. Representing higher-order logic proofs in HOL. In T. F. Melham and J. Camilleri, editors, *Higher Order Logic Theorem Proving and Its Applications: Proceedings of the 7th International Workshop*, volume 859 of *Lecture Notes in Computer Science*, pages 456–470, Valletta, Malta, 1994. Springer-Verlag.

An Interpretation of Isabelle/HOL in HOL Light

Sean McLaughlin

Carnegie Mellon University

Abstract. We define an interpretation of the Isabelle/HOL logic in HOL Light and its metalanguage, OCaml. Some aspects of the Isabelle logic are not representable directly in the HOL Light object logic. The interpretation thus takes the form of a set of elaboration rules, where features of the Isabelle logic that cannot be represented directly are elaborated to functors in OCaml. We demonstrate the effectiveness of the interpretation via an implementation, translating a significant part of the Isabelle standard library into HOL Light.

1 Introduction

The vast advances in computer technology of the last century facilitated the construction of computer programs that could check logical proofs in full detail. These programs, called *proof assistants* or *interactive theorem provers*, were an extension of, and improvement upon, formal logical reasoning in the spirit of Russell and Whitehead [33] and Landau [17]. Such proof assistants, from the pioneer DeBruijn's Automath [5] to its modern counterparts (*e.g.*, Coq [4], HOL4 [10], HOL Light [16], Isabelle [25], Nuprl [6], PVS [24]), seek fully foundational proofs of deep mathematical and scientific problems. While the technical challenges of such developments can be significant, many important theorems have been fully checked in these systems. Some recent examples are the Four Color Theorem [9], the Prime Number Theorem [2], and the Jordan Curve Theorem [12].

Unfortunately, each system has its own library of theorems. The extensive effort involved in constructing a proof in one system must be duplicated to prove the theorem in another. For instance, the three examples cited above are all constructed in different proof assistants, and as of this writing, none have been ported to another system. Indeed, little infrastructure exists to support the sharing of proofs between proof assistants. This dissonance is a serious concern for large verification efforts. For example, the Flyspeck Project [11] seeks to formally prove the Kepler Conjecture [13] in HOL Light. Recently, Nipkow verified an important algorithm in the proof using Isabelle/HOL [22]. Researchers elsewhere are working on other parts of the project using the Coq proof assistant. For the Kepler Conjecture to exist as a single HOL Light theorem, there must be a way to import the Isabelle and Coq developments.

This paper describes a mechanism and provides an implementation for interpreting formulas and proofs of Isabelle/HOL in HOL Light. The interpretation is interesting because Isabelle/HOL supports features not found in ordinary higher order logic. These include *axiomatic type classes* and *constant overloading*. We therefore do not attempt a direct translation into HOL Light logic. Instead, we

U. Furbach and N. Shankar (Eds.): IJCAR 2006, LNAI 4130, pp. 192–204, 2006.
© Springer-Verlag Berlin Heidelberg 2006

elaborate Isabelle's types, terms, and proofs to functors in the HOL Light meta-language, Objective Caml (OCaml) [31]. We demonstrate the effectiveness of this interpretation via an implementation, translating a significant portion of the Isabelle/HOL standard library into HOL Light, including many proofs which rely on overloading and axiomatic type classes.

We use the term *interpretation* to mean a systematic translation from one logic to another. Because HOL Light is simply a set of OCaml types and functions, a proof in Isabelle corresponds to an OCaml value. More precisely, we show below how some proofs of Isabelle actually correspond to a family of OCaml values in HOL Light. This gives rise to our use of functors for representing these families.

A note on fonts: Isabelle text appears in sans serif font. OCaml keywords appear in **bold**. OCaml identifiers, which are also HOL Light inference rules and types, appear in SMALL CAPITAL LETTERS. Meta-functions, such as `tv` which returns the free type variables of a term, are in `typewriter face`.

2 Related Work

There are two different approaches to the sharing of formal theories. In one view, which we will call the *trusting* view, we interpret the logic of one proof assistant in another, prove (on paper) some semantic properties of the translation, verify that the axioms of the source system hold in the target interpretation, and finally accept the interpreted formulas that correspond to theorems in the source logic as theorems in the target logic. No translation of proof objects is attempted or, indeed, is necessary. The user of such a translation supposes the soundness of the source theorem prover.

In the other view, which we call the *skeptical* view, a given proof assistant is the final arbiter of correct reasoning. Relying on other systems, which are possibly unsound, is undesirable. Indeed, the very *raison d'être* of the given assistant is to distill the essential axioms and to build rich mathematical structures from these axioms alone. Trusting a large body of computer code would be anathema. To import theorems we check their proofs. There is no need to rely upon a model theory because the proof theory of the target system will guarantee the correctness of the translation.

Examples of the trusting view include work by Howe[7] and Naumov [20]. This work imports formulas of HOL and Isabelle/HOL, respectively, into Nuprl. Felty and Howe [8] show how the connection described in [7] can be used in a larger example. The skeptical outlook can be seen in the work of Naumov [21], Stehr [30] and the author [18]. Obua and Skalberg [23] describe an analogue to our work in the opposite direction, translating HOL Light proofs into Isabelle/HOL. There is also some related work involving general translation infrastructure, which we discuss in section 7.

3 Isabelle/HOL in HOL Light

HOL Light is an interactive prover in the LCF style based on Church's simple theory of types. Isabelle is a logical framework for defining logics [26]. The most

194   S. McLaughlin

well-developed instantiation is the interpretation of higher-order logic, Isabelle/HOL. In addition, Isabelle is extended with axiomatic type classes and constant overloading [32][1]. Though the logics are very similar, these additional features make the Isabelle logic more expressive, in the sense that a single theorem in Isabelle/HOL corresponds to a set of theorems in HOL Light. We thus appeal to the metalanguage to support type classes and overloading.

Note that in the following exposition we give a syntax for Isabelle that is convenient for our purposes. We do not present the actual concrete syntax of Isabelle. We take similar liberties with the OCaml syntax.

3.1 Type Class Example

Reasoning with type classes can be seen as a generalization of polymorphism. In a logic with polymorphism we avoid constructing similar theorems at different types and instead simply instantiate a polymorphic theorem at any type. In a logic with type classes we do the same, except that we also assert axiomatic properties of the type. An example is the class of partial orders.

$$\text{axclass order } [] =$$
$$[\leq: \alpha \to \alpha \to \text{bool}]$$
$$[\text{refl is } x : \alpha :: \text{order} \leq x,$$
$$\text{antisym is } x \leq y \wedge y \leq x \supset x = y,$$
$$\text{trans is } x \leq y \wedge y \leq z \supset x \leq z]$$

An axclass declaration consists of an Isabelle name (order), a list of ancestor classes, a list of constants that should be defined at that type, and a list of named axioms that hold on the universe of α and the constants. The syntax $x : \alpha :: \text{order}$ means x is a variable of type α where α is an *instance* of the class order. A type is an instance of a class if the constants of the class are defined on the type and satisfy the class axioms. More generally, $x : \alpha :: [c_1, \ldots, c_n]$ means that x is a variable of type α where α is an instance of all of $c_1, \ldots, c_n$. The collection $[c_1, \ldots, c_n]$ is called a *sort*. In this case the class has no ancestors.

We can now prove theorems with free type variables $\alpha :: \text{order}$. For instance, we can prove the theorem called order_eq_refl :

$$\forall x : \alpha :: \text{order. } x = y \supset x \leq y.$$

The proof term makes use of the class axioms.

To use theorems involving type classes, we must prove that concrete types are instances of the class. We prove that such a concrete type satisfies the class axioms, and then we instantiate the free type variables.

---

[1] Isabelle also includes a *locale* mechanism that extends the genericity of its reasoning capabilities [3]. Locales are eliminated in the construction of proof terms in Isabelle, however, and thus we needn't account for them in our interpretation, where we work directly with the proof terms.

instance real :: [order] ...

instance nat :: [order] ...

$\forall x : \text{real. } x = y \supset x \leq y$

$\forall x : \text{nat. } x = y \supset x \leq y$

where the ... stand for an Isabelle proof that the real, nat types satisfy the axioms. Then we may instantiate order_eq_refl twice to get the specific theorems Since HOL Light does not have such capabilities, we use the OCaml module system to emulate this behavior. The class order corresponds to an OCaml signature, while the Isabelle types real and nat correspond to modules *containing* the HOL Light types REAL and NAT.

signature ORDER =	module REAL =
sig	struct
val α : TYPE	let α = REAL
val $\leq$: TERM	let $\leq$ = REAL_LE
val REFL : THM	let REFL = REAL_LE_REFL
val ANTISYM : THM	let ANTISYM = REAL_LE_ANTISYM
val TRANS : THM	let TRANS = REAL_LE_TRANS
end	end

It is understood that REAL_LE is a predefined HOL Light constant, and that REAL_LE_REFL, *etc.* are predefined theorems. We can assume a similar definiton of a NAT module (though the HOL Light name of the type of natural numbers is NUM).

The Isabelle proof of order_eq_refl becomes a functor, encapsulating the reasoning involved.

functor ORDER_EQ_REFL(A : ORDER) =
struct
let THM = (proof involving A. $\leq$, A.REFL, *etc.*)
end

To instantiate the proof, we apply the functor to a module containing a type and the necessary constants and axioms on that type. Functor application "replays" the proof on the new type. The applications followed by projections evaluate to the HOL Light theorems

$$\text{ORDER\_EQ\_REFL}(\text{REAL}).\text{THM} = \forall x : \text{REAL. } x = y \supset x \leq y,$$

$$\text{ORDER\_EQ\_REFL}(\text{NAT}).\text{THM} = \forall x : \text{NUM. } x = y \supset x \leq y.$$

4 Elaboration

The translation from Isabelle/HOL to HOL Light is a set of syntax-directed elaboration rules. Many of the cases are routine. We give some illustrative cases here.

A complete list, along with a complete abstract syntax for Isabelle/HOL and HOL Light, can be found in an extended version of this paper at [1].

Our judgments have the form $Ctx \vdash X \leadsto Y$, understood to mean "X elaborates to Y in context Ctx," where it is understood that Ctx and X are input arguments and Y is an output argument. We define such a judgment for each syntactic class of Isabelle/HOL. In the following sections we explain the various contexts of the judgments and their elaboration rules.

Note that we introduce judgments in their order of importance, and thus some judgments of lesser interest will be used before they are defined. The curious reader may consult the extended paper for the full definitions of the judgments.

4.1   The Module System

While in fact Isabelle/HOL theorems are elaborated to OCaml functors, for clarity of presentation we are taking some liberties with the notation. In particular, we allow projections from functor applications. Such functors are called *applicative* in the literature. This is in contrast to the *generative* functors of OCaml [15]. Because our modules save no state, such projections are unproblematic and have the same semantics in both views. We can easily convert these functors to a generative form accepted by OCaml by inventing a new module identifier M (which does not bind anything seen so far in the OCamlenvironment), binding the functor application to that name, and projecting directly from M. *E.g.* ORDER_EQ_REFL(A).THM becomes

$$\textbf{module } \mathrm{X} = \mathrm{ORDER\_EQ\_REFL}(\mathrm{A})$$
$$\mathrm{X}.\textsc{thm}$$

For clarity, we also use the keyword **signature** instead of OCaml's **module type**.

We assume that before elaboration begins, the following signatures are defined. These represent HOL Light types, terms and theorems.

signature TYPE =	**signature** TERM =	**signature** THM =
sig	**sig**	**sig**
val TYPE : TYPE	**val** TERM : TERM	**val** THM : THM
end	**end**	**end**

Name Mapping. There is some amount of bookkeeping involved in mapping Isabelle identifiers to their OCaml counterparts. The details are not interesting. We assume the existence of a function $\ulcorner x \urcorner$ mapping the Isabelle identifier x to its counterpart. For example, $\ulcorner \mathsf{order\_eq\_refl} \urcorner = \mathrm{ORDER\_EQ\_REFL}$. In some cases $\ulcorner x \urcorner$ requires additional arguments. We note such places explicitly. An example is type constructors that are indexed in HOL Light by the sorts of their arguments.

An Isabelle theory is a sequence of declarations that introduce new names into a global environment. To ease the notational burden of frequently inventing new names, we extend the definition of $\ulcorner x \urcorner$ to generate a fresh name for the HOL Light counterpart of a declaration x, that will thereafter be returned by $\ulcorner x \urcorner$. For instance, when we elaborate $\mathsf{order\_eq\_refl}$, $\ulcorner \mathsf{order\_eq\_refl} \urcorner$ generates the name

ORDER_EQ_REFL and from the point of that declaration on, $\ulcorner$order_eq_refl$\urcorner$ = ORDER_EQ_REFL.

4.2   Contexts

The elaborator manages a number of distinct contexts during elaboration.

Δ is a map from Isabelle type variables to OCaml functor arguments. In the example above, Δ would consist of the single pair $\langle \alpha, A \rangle$, where α is the type variable from the Isabelle theorem order_eq_refl and A is the argument of the OCaml functor ORDER_EQ_REFL. The type variable α is elaborated to A.TYPE in the OR-DER_EQ_REFL functor. We often look up a block of type variables in Δ. Thus, $\Delta(\alpha_1, \ldots, \alpha_k) = (T_1, \ldots, T_k)$ means $\Delta(\alpha_1) = T_1, \ldots, \Delta(\alpha_k) = T_k$.

Γ maps Isabelle term variables to types, and Isabelle proof variables to Isabelle terms.

Σ As we wish to make no reference to a global data structure, Σ simply maintains the state of the elaboration process, mapping Isabelle declarations to their previously elaborated OCaml functors.

4.3   Functions

We assume the existence of a function tv which returns the free type variables in a term with their sorts, and a predicate $(A_1, \ldots, A_n)$ fresh indicating that the names $A_1, \ldots, A_n$ are new.

4.4   Classes

The elaboration of type classes is one of the the most interesting parts of the translator. The Isabelle abstract syntax for a class is

$$\text{axclass } c < [c_1, \ldots, c_k] = [con_1, \ldots, con_l],$$
$$[name_1 \text{ is } axm_1, \ldots, name_m \text{ is } axm_m]$$

where c is a new Isabelle class identifier, the c_i are previously defined type classes, the con_i are new constants of the class, and the axm_i are formulas representing type class axioms referred to by $name_i$. The evidence for a type τ being an instance of the class c is a proof that, for each i, τ has constants of the class c_i (in addition to $con_1, \ldots, con_l$) and that those constants satisfy the axioms of c_i (in addition to $axm_1, \ldots, axm_m$).

$$\Sigma \vdash \text{axclass } c < [c_1, \ldots, c_k] = [con_1, \ldots, con_l],$$
$$[name_1 \text{ is } axm_1, \ldots, name_m \text{ is } axm_m] \rightsquigarrow$$

> **signature** $\ulcorner c \urcorner$ =
> **sig**
>   **include** $\ulcorner c_1 \urcorner$ ... **include** $\ulcorner c_k \urcorner$
>   **val** $\ulcorner con_1 \urcorner$: TERM ... **val** $\ulcorner con_l \urcorner$: TERM
>   **val** $\ulcorner name_1 \urcorner$: THM ... **val** $\ulcorner name_m \urcorner$: THM
> **end**, Σ

The **include** statements textually replace the $\ulcorner c_i \urcorner$ with their definitions, thus capturing the semantics of the Isabelle class hierarchy. Note how the formulas axm_i are totally ignored. Here we make note of the phase distinction between *elaborating* the Isabelle theories and *using* the elaborated theorems. During the elaboration stage, the inability to specify the form of the axioms of a class is unproblematic. Both the signatures and the concrete types are created directly from Isabelle declarations, and, barring a bug in Isabelle, the concrete theorems match the declared class axioms. After the elaboration, however, when attempting to use these theorems with new types not defined by Isabelle, it is the HOL Light user's responsibility to ensure the well-formedness of the theorems she supplies. If the theorem supplied to a user-created module is not well-formed, a run-time error occurs during the functor application.

4.5   Instance

In Isabelle, instance declarations allow theorems with type variables of a class to be instantiated with concrete classes. The abstract syntax is

$$\text{instance } \tau :: (\langle \alpha_1, \sigma_1 \rangle, \ldots, \langle \alpha_n, \sigma_n \rangle)\, c = \langle [con_1, \ldots, con_k], p \rangle$$

which means that type constructor τ, when given arguments of sort σ_i is an instance of class c, where con_i are the constants required by c, and p is a proof that the axioms of c are satisfied by the type $\tau(\alpha_1, \ldots, \alpha_n)$, where α_i has sort σ_i.

$$\texttt{fresh}(A_1, \ldots, A_k) \quad \Delta = (\langle \alpha_1, A_1 \rangle, \ldots, \langle \alpha_k, A_k \rangle)$$
$$\Delta, \cdot \vdash con_1 \rightsquigarrow c_1 \quad \ldots \quad \Delta, \cdot \vdash con_n \rightsquigarrow c_n$$
$$\Delta, \cdot \vdash p \rightsquigarrow thm \quad thm = (thm_1 \wedge \ldots \wedge thm_m)$$

$$\left.
\begin{array}{l}
\textbf{signature } \ulcorner c \urcorner = \\
\textbf{sig} \\
\quad \textbf{val } \ulcorner con_1 \urcorner : \text{TERM} \ldots \textbf{val } \ulcorner con_l \urcorner : \text{TERM} \\
\quad \textbf{val } axm_1 : \text{THM} \ldots \textbf{val } axm_m : \text{THM} \\
\textbf{end}
\end{array}
\right\} \in \Sigma$$

$$A = \ulcorner \tau(\sigma_i, \ldots, \sigma_n) \urcorner$$

$\Sigma \vdash \texttt{instance } \tau :: (\langle \alpha_1, \sigma_1 \rangle, \ldots, \langle \alpha_n, \sigma_n \rangle)\, c = \langle [con_1, \ldots, con_k], p \rangle \rightsquigarrow$

$\quad \textbf{functor } A(A_1 : \ulcorner \sigma_1 \urcorner) \ldots (A_k : \ulcorner \sigma_n \urcorner) =$

$\textbf{struct}$

$\quad \textbf{let } \ulcorner con_1 \urcorner = c_1 \ldots \textbf{let } \ulcorner con_k \urcorner = c_k$

$\quad \textbf{let } axm_1 = thm_1 \ldots \textbf{let } axm_m = thm_m$

$\quad \textbf{end}, \Sigma$

To elaborate an instance, we begin by creating Δ from the free sorted type variables α. Then we translate the required constants and the proof of the axioms. Finally, we look up the definition of the class to get the signature identifiers for constants and axioms.

Note that the name of the generated functor depends on the sorts of the instance declaration. This is inevitable. Consider the Isabelle product type $\alpha \times \beta$. The generated functor for the type definition would be

$$\textbf{functor } \ulcorner \times \urcorner (A_1 : \text{Type})(A_2 : \text{Type}) : \text{Type} = \ldots$$

In Isabelle we can declare

$$\textsf{instance} \times :: (\langle \alpha_1, \textsf{order} \rangle, \langle \alpha_2, \textsf{order} \rangle) \textsf{ order} = \ldots$$

where we use the lexicographic ordering from α_1 and α_2. The elaboration of this instance declaration becomes

$$\textbf{functor } \ulcorner \times \urcorner (A_1 : \text{Order})(A_2 : \text{Order}) : \text{Order} = \ldots .$$

If $\ulcorner \times \urcorner$ were not indexed by sorts, the first functor would be shadowed by the second, and thus inaccessible. Since not all types are instances of ORDER, in such a situation it would be impossible to create product types of unordered types.

4.6 Theorems

Theorems in Isabelle are a name together with a formula and a proof. The abstract syntax is $\textsf{Thm}(id, t, p)$. Because in general the free type variables have nontrivial sorts, we abstract the type variables into functor arguments of the appropriate signature.

$$\frac{\textbf{tv}(t) = (\langle \alpha_1, \sigma_1 \rangle, \ldots, \langle \alpha_k, \sigma_k \rangle) \quad \textbf{fresh}(A_1, \ldots, A_k)}{\Delta = (\langle \alpha_1, A_1 \rangle, \ldots, \langle \alpha_k, A_k \rangle) \quad \Delta, \cdot \vdash p \rightsquigarrow thm}{\Sigma \vdash \textsf{Thm}(id, t, p) \rightsquigarrow}$$

$$\textbf{functor } \ulcorner id \urcorner (A_1 : \ulcorner \sigma_1 \urcorner) \ldots (A_k : \ulcorner \sigma_k \urcorner) : \text{THM} =$$
$$\textbf{struct}$$
$$\textbf{val } \text{THM} = thm$$
$$\textbf{end}, \Sigma$$

4.7 Types

As both Isabelle/HOL and HOL Light have their basis in classical higher order logic, translating terms and proofs is straightforward. We include the rules in the extended paper for completeness. Translating types has one complication, which is that a type variable corresponds to a functor argument instead of a specific HOL Light type. In order to make type translation syntax directed (in the sense that to translate a type constructor, it is enough to translate its arguments) we elaborate types to module variables. When the types themselves are needed, we simply project the TYPE component.

$$\frac{\Delta(\alpha) = A}{\Delta \vdash \alpha :: \sigma \rightsquigarrow A}$$

$$\frac{\Delta \vdash \tau_1 \rightsquigarrow A_1 \quad \ldots \quad \Delta \vdash \tau_k \rightsquigarrow A_k}{\Delta \vdash con(\tau_1, \ldots, \tau_k) \rightsquigarrow \ulcorner con \urcorner (A_1) \ldots (A_k)}$$

This completes our overview of the elaboration rules. A complete list can be found in the extended paper.

5 Name Mapping

The name map $\ulcorner x \urcorner$ from Isabelle identifiers to HOL Light identifiers plays an important role in many of the elaboration judgments. Some declarations, *e.g.*, axioms, refer to HOL Light identifiers that are assumed already to be mapped before the translation begins. In order for the user to extend the translator without modifying the source code, we include a simple specification language that allows a user to include these identifier maps in $\ulcorner x \urcorner$. In addition, the systems have a number of types and constants in common. The language allows a user to specify mappings between them. This avoids creating a second copy of the type or constant in HOL Light. For instance, both Isabelle/HOL and HOL Light have a type of natural numbers nat and NUM respectively. They are both similarly constructed from an axiom of infinity. Instead of having two separate developments of the natural numbers in HOL Light, we can map one to the other with the *typemap* declaration, followed by a number of *thmmap* declarations mapping the peano axioms.

$$\text{typemap} \ : \ \text{nat} \rightsquigarrow \text{NUM}$$
$$\text{thmmap} \ : \ \text{Suc\_not\_zero} \rightsquigarrow \text{NOT\_SUC} \dots$$

The complete language definition and description can be found at [1].

6 Implementation

While we believe that the elaboration makes novel use of the OCaml module system, the real contribution of this work is not theoretical, but practical. We have a working implementation of the elaboration rules written in Standard ML [19]. We have used the implementation to translate approximately 2000 theorems of the Isabelle/HOL standard library. While this is only about a third of more than 6000 theorems in the library, we foresee no difficulties in translating the rest. Already included in the first 2000 are all the difficulties of type classes, type definitions, and instances. Most of the effort of translation goes into carefully defining the theory in the given specification language and in proving the necessary HOL Light theorems corresponding to an Isabelle theory.

A typical example is mapping the definition of the propositional connective $\wedge$. In HOL Light, $P \wedge Q \overset{\text{def}}{=} \lambda f. \ f \ P \ Q = \lambda f. \ f \ True \ True$. In Isabelle, $P \wedge Q \overset{\text{def}}{=} \forall R. \ (P \supset Q \supset R) \supset R)$. We map the two notions of $\wedge$ by first proving their equivalence, eg,

```
let ISA_AND_DEF = prove
 ('(P /\ Q) <=> (!R. (P ==> Q ==> R) ==> R)',
  ASM_MESON_TAC[AND_DEF]);;
```

and declaring the mapping to the elaborator in a configuration file.

```
constmap : "op &" ~~> "(/\)" [And]
defmap : HOL.and_def ~~> ISA_AND_DEF
```

We expect the rest of the library to be completed in the near future. The translated libraries and the SML source code of the elaborator are available on the web at [1].

7   Future Work

7.1   More Libraries, More Logics

The most natural direction for this work is to translate more libraries. Indeed, we would like to import the rest of the standard library[2] and continue on to Avigad's prime number theorem. We also intend to use the implementation to translate the Isabelle portions of the Flyspeck project. Nipkow's algorithm verification relies on a reflection mechanism, whereby an algorithm is verified formally, code is extracted, and the code is run directly. There is no analogue to this mechanism in HOL Light, so this too presents a challenge for future work. We would also like to perform similar translations for more diverse deductive systems. An interpretation of Coq will be essential for Flyspeck, though the logics are so different that this will be a significant challenge.

7.2   Formalizing the Translation in LF

As effective as it is in practice, the interpretation given is unsatisfying in a number of ways. To begin, the elaboration of classes includes no information about what formula the declared axioms should prove. This is no oversight, as it would require OCaml to allow dependently typed terms. We therefore do not discover an error when using the functors until run-time. Given the length of time required to load a library into OCaml, this is a significant disadvantage. The problem occurs both in the elaboration phase when the HOL Light programmer must supply translations of the Isabelle axioms and in the usage phase when instantiating functors at concrete types. (*cf.* Section 4.4). HOL Light inference rule calls fail for many reasons, for instance, when the supplied theorem does not have exactly the right form. It would be much better to catch such errors at compile-time.

Moreover, the interpretation given has no obvious metatheoretic properties. For one, there is not an obvious relationship between the formula of an imported proof to the translation of the initial Isabelle/HOL formula. We would hope, for example, that if a proof p of t elaborates to p', then t elaborates to $\texttt{concl}(p')$. Another such property is completeness. We believe that the translation is total in the sense that every Isabelle/HOL theorem could be translated to an OCaml functor that, when run on any "correctly" implemented type modules, would yield the desired theorem instance. A formal proof of these facts, though, would involve reasoning about the operational semantics of the OCaml module system in addition to the logics involved. While we may convince ourselves on paper that our reasoning is correct, the full details of the proof would be overwhelming.

These concerns can be addressed by modeling the translation in LF [14], via the Twelf [27] implementation. Using the Twelf methodology, and that generally espoused by the Logosphere Project [28], we could formalize the Isabelle/HOL and HOL Light logics and give an operational semantics to a subset of the OCaml module language. We could then hope to prove theorems about the interpretation.

---

[2] What I call the standard library is the contents of the theories included in Main.

An example of this kind of formalization, from HOL to Nuprl, can be found in Schurmann [29].

8 Conclusion

The usefulness and importance of sharing libraries between proof assistants is abundantly clear. As a step in this direction, we presented an interpretation of the Isabelle/HOL logic in HOL Light and demonstrated its effectiveness through an implementation that produces executable OCaml functors. These functors construct HOL Light proofs. A significant part of the Isabelle/HOL standard library was translated in this way. In addition we provide a specification language that allows the translator to be extended easily to new theories. We hope that our work will be useful to the formal mathematics community.

Acknowledgments

We would like to thank Frank Pfenning for his advice and support throughout this work. John Reynolds, Tom Murphy, and William Lovas gave helpful suggestions. Thanks also to the members of the Isabelle mailing list who patiently answered many questions on the minutiae of Isabelle, and to John Harrison for reading a draft of the paper. This work was supported by NSF grant CCR-ITR-0325808.

References

1. http://www.cs.cmu.edu/~{}seanmcl/projects/logosphere/isabelle-holl.
2. J. Avigad, K. Donnelly, D. Gray, and P. Raff. A formally verified proof of the prime number theorem. To appear in the ACM Transactions on Computational Logic.
3. C. Ballarin. Locales and locale expressions in Isabelle/Isar. In S. B. *et al*, editor, *Types for Proofs and Programs: International Workshop*, 2003.
4. Y. Bertot and P. Castéran. *CoqArt: The Calculus of Inductive Constructions*. Texts in Theoretical Computer Science. Springer, 2004.
5. N. G. d. Bruijn. A survey of the project AUTOMATH. In J. P. Seldin and J. R. Hindley, editors, *To H. B. Curry: Essays in Combinatory Logic, Lambda Calculus, and Formalism*, pages 589–606. Academic Press, 1980.
6. R. Constable. *Implementing Mathematics with The Nuprl Proof Development System*. Prentice-Hall, 1986.
7. D. J. Howe. Importing mathematics from HOL into Nuprl. In J. Von Wright, J. Grundy, and J. Harrison, editors, *Ninth International Conference on Theorem Proving in Higher Order Logics TPHOL*, volume LNCS 1125, pages 267–282, Turku, Finland, 1996. Springer Verlag.
8. A. P. Felty and D. J. Howe. Hybrid interactive theorem proving using Nuprl and HOL. In *Fourteenth International Conference on Automated Deduction*, pages 351–365. Springer-Verlag Lecture Notes in Computer Science, 1997.
9. G. Gonthier. A computer-checked proof of the four colour theorem. Available on the Web via http://research.microsoft.com/~gonthier/, 2005.

10. M. J. C. Gordon and T. F. Melham. *Introduction to HOL: a theorem proving environment for higher order logic.* Cambridge University Press, 1993.
11. T. Hales. The Flyspeck Project fact sheet. Project description available at `http://www.math.pitt.edu/~thales/flyspeck/`, 2005.
12. T. Hales. The Jordan Curve Theorem in HOL Light. Source code available at `http://www.math.pitt.edu/~thales/`, 2005.
13. T. C. Hales. A proof of the the Kepler conjecture. *Annals of Mathematics*, 162:1065–1185, 2005.
14. R. Harper, F. Honsell, and G. Plotkin. A framework for defining logics. In *Proceedings of the Second Annual Symposium on Logic in Computer Science*, pages 194–204, Ithaca, NY, 1987. IEEE Computer Society Press.
15. R. Harper and B. C. Pierce. Design issues in advanced module systems. In B. C. Pierce, editor, *Advanced Topics in Types and Programming Languages.* MIT Press, 2005.
16. J. Harrison. HOL Light: A tutorial introduction. In M. Srivas and A. Camilleri, editors, *Proceedings of the First International Conference on Formal Methods in Computer-Aided Design (FMCAD'96)*, volume 1166 of *Lecture Notes in Computer Science*, pages 265–269. Springer-Verlag, 1996.
17. E. Landau. *Grundlagen der Analysis.* Leipzig, 1930. English translation by F. Steinhardt: 'Foundations of analysis: the arithmetic of whole, rational, irrational, and complex numbers. A supplement to textbooks on the differential and integral calculus', published by Chelsea; 3rd edition 1966.
18. S. McLaughlin, C. Barrett, and Y. Ge. Cooperating theorem provers: A case study combining CVC Lite and HOL Light. In A. Armando and A. Cimatti, editors, *Proceedings of the Third Workshop on Pragmatics of Decision Procedures in Automated Reasoning*, volume 144, pages 43–51, 2005.
19. R. Milner, M. Tofte, and R. Harper. *The Definition of Standard ML.* The MIT Press, 1990.
20. P. Naumov. Importing Isabelle formal mathematics into Nuprl. Technical Report TR99-1734, Cornell University, 26, 1999.
21. P. Naumov, M.-O. Stehr, and J. Meseguer. The HOL/NuPRL proof translator - a practical approach to formal interoperability. In *Theorem Proving in Higher Order Logics, 14th International Conference*, volume 2152 of *Lecture Notes in Computer Science*. Springer-Verlag, 2001.
22. T. Nipkow, G. Bauer, and P. Schultz. Flyspeck I: Tame Graphs. Technical report, Institut für Informatik, TU München, Jan. 2006.
23. S. Obua and S. Skalberg. Importing HOL into Isabelle/HOL. submitted, 2006.
24. S. Owre, J. M. Rushby, and N. Shankar. PVS: A prototype verification system. In D. Kapur, editor, *11th International Conference on Automated Deduction*, volume 607 of *Lecture Notes in Computer Science*, pages 748–752, Saratoga, NY, 1992. Springer-Verlag.
25. L. C. Paulson. *Isabelle: a generic theorem prover*, volume 828 of *Lecture Notes in Computer Science*. Springer-Verlag, 1994. With contributions by Tobias Nipkow.
26. F. Pfenning. Logical frameworks. In *Handbook of Automated Reasoning*, pages 1063–1147. MIT Press, 2001.
27. F. Pfenning and C. Schürmann. System description: Twelf - a meta-logical framework for deductive systems. In H. Ganzinger, editor, *Proceedings of the 16th International Conference on Automated Deduction*, pages 202–206, 1999.
28. F. Pfenning, C. Schürmann, M. Kohlhase, N. Shankar, and S. Owre. The Logosphere Project. Project description available at `http://www.logosphere.org`, 2005.

29. C. Schürmann and M.-O. Stehr. An Executable Formalization of the HOL/NuPRL Connection in Twelf. In *11th International Conference on Logic for Programming Artificial Intelligence and Reasoning*, 2005.
30. M.-O. Stehr, P. Naumov, and J. Meseguer. A proof-theoretic approach to the HOL-NuPRL connection with applications to proof-translation. In *WADT/CoFI'01*, 2001.
31. P. Weis and X. Leroy. *Le langage Caml*. InterEditions, 1993. See also the CAML Web page: http://pauillac.inria.fr/caml/.
32. M. Wenzel. Type Classes and Overloading in Higher-Order Logic. In E. Gunter and A. Felty, editors, *TPHOLs '97*, pages 307–322, Murray Hill, New Jersey, 1997.
33. A. N. Whitehead and B. Russell. *Principia Mathematica (3 vols)*. Cambridge University Press, 1910.

Combining Type Theory and Untyped Set Theory

Chad E. Brown

Universität des Saarlandes, Saarbrücken, Germany
cebrown@ags.uni-sb.de

Abstract. We describe a dependent type theory with proof irrelevance. Within this framework, we give a representation of a form of Mac Lane set theory and discuss automated support for constructing proofs within this set theory. One of the novel aspects of the representation is that one is allowed to use any class (in the set theory) as a type (in the type theory). Such class types allow a natural way of representing partial functions (e.g., the first and second operators on the class of Kuratowski ordered pairs). We also discuss how automated search can be used to construct proofs. In particular, the first-order prover Vampire can be called to solve a challenge problem (the injective Cantor Theorem) which is notoriously difficult for higher-order automated provers.

1 Introduction

In order to resolve mathematical conjectures, either a person or a system must know enough mathematics. Very few conjectures can be resolved by going back to first principles. One can imagine having a large library of mathematical definitions and theorems. An automated prover for mathematics should be able to make effective use of this library. First-order provers are designed to deal with large numbers of clauses. On the other hand, it is often difficult and unnatural to force higher-order or set-theoretic concepts into first-order logic.

What is the best language for automated reasoning in mathematics? We sketch two answers:

1. Experience shows first-order logic is the appropriate language for automated reasoning. Some forms of set theory such as von Neumann-Bernays-Gödel (NBG) are finitely axiomatizable in first-order logic and sufficient for representing much of mathematics. The best language is first-order logic with a finitely axiomatized set theory as in [6,18,5].
2. Higher-order logic (e.g., Church's type theory) allows more natural representations of mathematical propositions. In particular, λ-terms allow a more computational treatment of sets and functions than first-order set theory. Furthermore, higher-order logic supports type distinctions mathematicians make implicitly. While automated reasoning in higher-order logic is more complicated than in first-order logic, systems such as Tps can automatically prove some theorems which are difficult to even represent in first-order [2].

Of course, a third answer is simply that we do not yet know.

U. Furbach and N. Shankar (Eds.): IJCAR 2006, LNAI 4130, pp. 205–219, 2006.

We introduce a new alternative for automated reasoning in mathematics. Instead of trying to force mathematics into first-order logic, we use an LF-style dependent type theory (or, logical framework) with proof irrelevance. This type theory is implemented in a mathematical assistance system Scunak.

The Scunak type theory itself is too weak to represent interesting mathematics. We must "axiomatize" (give a signature for) a theory strong enough to represent mathematical propositions and proofs. The axiomatic theory presented here is a form of Mac Lane set theory (as advocated by Mac Lane in [13]). If we insisted on implementing this set theory in first-order logic, then we would need to use axiom schemes.

Another advantage of using a logical framework is that one can use proof terms to naturally represent partial functions by insisting that a proof of a certain condition is required for a term to be well-typed. One can further improve the treatment of partial functions by including certain (very restricted) product types and the notion of proof irrelevance in the logical framework. Essentially, one can make any predicate (or, in semantic terms, "class") into a type at the meta-level.

By noting certain properties of the language, we can argue that automated reasoning is possible in this setting. However, the implementation of Scunak does not currently include an automated theorem prover. Instead, we have written an interface between Scunak and the first-order prover Vampire [20] which has been able to find a proof of a challenge problem discussed in [3].

2   A Type Theory with Proof Irrelevance

The type theory of Scunak is a modified version of the type theory LF (also called λP) as implemented in Twelf [17]. A thorough development of the LF meta-theory can be found in [11] and of a similar version of Martin-Löf type theory can be found in [15]. We conjecture that the type theory we are presenting can be interpreted in the presumably more generally setting with proof irrelevance investigated in [19]. The Scunak type theory is not intended to be used as a logical framework, but as a type theory for encoding foundational systems for mathematics. A more thorough investigation of the Scunak type theory is planned for future work. Here, we define terms, types, and give algorithmic typing judgments. These correspond closely to the implementation. Afterwards, we consider a denotational semantics for terms and types.

Let $\mathcal{V}$ be an infinite set of variables and $\mathcal{C}$ be a set of constants. We use $x, y, z, x^1, \ldots$ to denote variables and $c, d, c^1, \ldots$ to denote constants. We define terms and types as follows:

Terms. $M, N, P, Q, R, \phi, \ldots := x|c|(\lambda x.M)|(M\ N)|\langle M, N\rangle|\pi_1(M)|\pi_2(M)$
Types. $A, B, C, \ldots \qquad := \mathtt{obj}|\mathtt{prop}|(\mathtt{pf}\ P)|(\mathtt{class}\ \phi)|(\Pi x : A.B)$

Intuitively, P should have type $\mathtt{prop}$ in the type ($\mathtt{pf}\ P$), and ϕ should have type ($\Pi x : \mathtt{obj.prop}$) in the type ($\mathtt{class}\ \phi$). These conditions are checked in the typing rules.

As usual we identify terms and types up to α-conversion. We assume all the usual notions of λ-calculus: substitution, β-reduction, η-reduction and the following pairing reductions:

$(\pi_1) : \pi_1(\langle M, N \rangle) \to_{\pi_1} M$ $\qquad$ $(\pi_2) : \pi_2(\langle M, N \rangle) \to_{\pi_2} N$
$(\pi) : \langle \pi_1(M), \pi_2(M) \rangle \to_\pi M$

We say a term or type is normal if it contains no redexes. We write $W^\downarrow$ for the normal form of W, if a unique normal form of W exists. In practice we will consider terms and types which are of a certain class (respecting simple types) which satisfy strong normalization and the Church-Rosser property. For such terms and types, $W^\downarrow$ exists (see, for example, [12]). For this purpose, we define the set of simple types as follows:

Simple Types. $\alpha, \beta, \gamma, \ldots := \texttt{obj}|\texttt{prop}|\texttt{pf}^-|(\texttt{obj} \times \texttt{pf}^-)|(\alpha \to \beta)$

Note that we allow one product type ($\texttt{obj} \times \texttt{pf}^-$).

For some rules in the typing judgment we will η- or π-expand on the fly. We introduce some notation to facilitate this.

If M is a term of the form $(\lambda x N)$, then let $\mathbf{x}_\lambda^M$ denote x and $\mathbf{B}_\lambda^M$ denote N. If M is any other term, then let $\mathbf{x}_\lambda^M$ be a variable not occurring in M and $\mathbf{B}_\lambda^M$ denote $(M\mathbf{x}_\lambda^M)$. Note that in the first case, $(\lambda \mathbf{x}_\lambda^M \mathbf{B}_\lambda^M)$ is identical to M. In the second case, $(\lambda \mathbf{x}_\lambda^M \mathbf{B}_\lambda^M)$ η-reduces to M.

If M is a term of the form $\langle N, P \rangle$, then let $\mathbf{fst}^M$ denote N and $\mathbf{snd}^M$ denote P. If M is any other term, then let $\mathbf{fst}^M$ denote $\pi_1(M)$ and $\mathbf{snd}^M$ denote $\pi_2(M)$. In the first case, $\langle \mathbf{fst}^M, \mathbf{snd}^M \rangle$ is identical to M. In the second case, $\langle \mathbf{fst}^M, \mathbf{snd}^M \rangle$ π-reduces to M.

A signature Σ is a list of distinct constants associated with types, and a type context Γ is a list of distinct variables associated with types. A simple type signature Ξ is a list of distinct constants associated with simple types, and a simple type context Δ is a list of distinct variables associated with simple types.

The dependencies of types on objects can be erased to obtain a simple type as follows: $\lceil \texttt{obj} \rceil := \texttt{obj}$, $\lceil \texttt{prop} \rceil := \texttt{prop}$, $\lceil \texttt{pf } M \rceil := \texttt{pf}^-$, $\lceil \texttt{class } M \rceil := (\texttt{obj} \times \texttt{pf}^-)$, and $\lceil (\Pi x : A.B) \rceil := (\lceil A \rceil \to \lceil B \rceil)$. We can use this operation to obtain a simple type signature Ξ (resp., simple type context Δ) from a signature Σ (resp., type context Γ).

In Scunak, terms and types are always given in $\beta\pi_1\pi_2$-normal form, so that the types of λ-abstractions and pairs can be inferred from the given intended type.

We assume two simple typing judgments are given:

- "$\Delta \vdash_\Xi M : \alpha$" In words, M has simple type α. The rules for this judgment are standard and omitted here. The main reason to consider this judgment is to guarantee strong normalization and Church-Rosser.
- "$\Delta \vdash_\Xi A$ sv" In words, A is *simply valid*. The rules are omitted. The idea is that if A is $\texttt{pf } P$ (resp., $\texttt{class } \phi$), then $\Delta \vdash_\Xi P : \texttt{prop}$ (resp., $\Delta \vdash_\Xi \phi : \texttt{obj} \to \texttt{prop}$) must hold.

$$\frac{x : A \in \Gamma}{\Gamma \vdash x \sim x \downarrow A} \; xv \qquad \frac{c : A \in \Sigma}{\Gamma \vdash c \sim c \downarrow A} \; xs \qquad \frac{\Gamma \vdash M \sim N \downarrow \text{class } \phi}{\Gamma \vdash \pi_2(M) \sim \pi_2(N) \downarrow \text{pf } (\phi \, \pi_1(M))} \; xpi2$$

$$\frac{\Gamma \vdash M \sim P \downarrow (\Pi x : A.B) \quad \Gamma \vdash N \sim Q \uparrow A}{\Gamma \vdash (MN) \sim (PQ) \downarrow ([N/x]B)} \; xa \qquad \frac{\Gamma \vdash M \sim N \downarrow \text{class } \phi}{\Gamma \vdash \pi_1(M) \sim \pi_1(N) \downarrow \text{obj}} \; xpi1$$

$$\frac{\Gamma, z : A \vdash [z/\mathbf{x}_\lambda^M]\mathbf{B}_\lambda^M \sim [z/\mathbf{x}_\lambda^N]\mathbf{B}_\lambda^N \uparrow [z/x]B \quad z \in \mathcal{V} \text{ fresh}}{\Gamma \vdash M \sim N \uparrow (\Pi x : A.B)} \; c\lambda^z$$

$$\frac{\Gamma \vdash_\Sigma \mathbf{fst}^M \sim \mathbf{fst}^N \uparrow \text{obj} \quad \Gamma \vdash_\Sigma \mathbf{snd}^M \sim \mathbf{snd}^N \uparrow \text{pf } (\phi \, \mathbf{fst}^M)}{\Gamma \vdash_\Sigma M \sim N \uparrow \text{class } \phi} \; cp$$

$$\frac{\Gamma \vdash M \sim N \downarrow B \quad B \in \{\text{obj}, \text{prop}\}}{\Gamma \vdash M \sim N \uparrow B} \; coerce$$

$$\frac{\begin{array}{l} \Gamma \vdash M \sim M \downarrow \text{pf } Q \quad [\Gamma] \vdash_{\lceil \Sigma \rceil} Q : \text{prop} \quad \Gamma \vdash Q^\downarrow \sim P \uparrow \text{prop} \\ \Gamma \vdash N \sim N \downarrow \text{pf } R \quad [\Gamma] \vdash_{\lceil \Sigma \rceil} R : \text{prop} \quad \Gamma \vdash R^\downarrow \sim P \uparrow \text{prop} \end{array}}{\Gamma \vdash_\Sigma M \sim N \uparrow \text{pf } P} \; coercepf$$

$$\frac{\Gamma \vdash A : Type \quad \Gamma, z : A \vdash [z/x]B : Type \quad z \in \mathcal{V} \text{ fresh}}{\Gamma \vdash (\Pi x : A.B) : Type} \; vt\Pi \qquad \frac{}{\Gamma \vdash \text{obj} : Type} \; vto$$

$$\frac{}{\Gamma \vdash \text{prop} : Type} \; vtp \qquad \frac{\Gamma \vdash M \sim M \uparrow \text{prop}}{\Gamma \vdash \text{pf } M : Type} \; vtpf \qquad \frac{\Gamma \vdash M \sim M \uparrow (\text{obj} \to \text{prop})}{\Gamma \vdash \text{class } M : Type} \; vtcl$$

Fig. 1. Rules for Algorithmic Typing Judgments

The main algorithmic typing judgments are as follows:

- "⊢ Σ sig" Intuitively, Σ is a valid signature. The idea is to ensure $\vdash_\Sigma A :$ $Type$ before adding $c : A$ to Σ. We omit the rules. Note, however, that unlike LF, new families are never added to the signature.
- "⊢$_\Sigma$ Γ ctx" Intuitively, Γ is a valid context. The idea is to ensure $\Gamma \vdash_\Sigma A :$ $Type$ holds before adding $x : A$ to Γ. We omit the rules.
- "$\Gamma \vdash_\Sigma M \sim N \uparrow A$" Intuitively, M can be checked to be A-related to N. The rules are given in Figure 1.
- "$\Gamma \vdash_\Sigma M \sim N \downarrow A$" Intuitively, the type A can be extracted as a type in which M is A-related to N. The rules are given in Figure 1.
- "$\Gamma \vdash_\Sigma A : Type$" In words, A is a valid type. The rules are given in Figure 1.

We usually omit the dependence on Σ in the judgments. Note that the rule *coercepf* which normalizes terms includes premises to ensure the terms are simply typable, hence that unique normal forms exist. Under certain conditions, one can eliminate these premises.

In order to clarify the type theory above and prepare for the set theory in the next section, we consider a particular model for terms and types. Since we only consider terms which can be given a simple type, we start by giving domains corresponding to the simple types. Intuitively, obj contains all the (untyped) mathematical objects of interest, prop contains propositions, and $\mathtt{pf}^-$ contains proofs. We take $\mathcal{D}_{\mathtt{obj}}$ to be V_{ω^2} in the usual von Neumann heirarchy of sets: $V_\emptyset = \emptyset$, $V_{\epsilon+1} = \mathcal{P}(V_\epsilon)$ and $V_\gamma = \bigcup_{\epsilon<\gamma} V_\epsilon$ for each limit ordinal γ. In set theory, the important properties of sets are given by the membership and equality relations. Fix four distinct values $\dot\in, \dot\notin, \dot=, \dot\neq$. We take $\mathcal{D}_{\mathtt{prop}}$ to be the set

$$\{(R,x,y) \mid R \in \{\dot\in, \dot\notin, \dot=, \dot\neq\}, x,y \in V_{\omega^2}\}$$

Intuitively, for any $x,y \in V_{\omega^2}$, $(\dot\notin, x, y)$ represents the proposition that $x \notin y$. Only some propositions should be "true" and true propositions should have "proofs". Since we wish to model proof irrelevance, a true proposition should have exactly *one* proof. An easy way to model this is to take the set of proofs to be a subset of the set of propositions. We take $\mathcal{D}_{\mathtt{pf}^-}$ to be the subset

$$\{(\dot\in, x, y) \mid x,y \in V_{\omega^2}, x \in y\} \cup \{(\dot\notin, x, y) \mid x,y \in V_{\omega^2}, x \notin y\}$$
$$\cup \{(\dot=, x, x) \mid x \in V_{\omega^2}\} \cup \{(\dot\neq, x, y) \mid x,y \in V_{\omega^2}, x \neq y\}.$$

of $\mathcal{D}_{\mathtt{prop}}$. The intention is that $p \in \mathcal{D}_{\mathtt{pf}^-}$ is a (the) proof of p. Taking $\mathcal{D}_{\mathtt{obj}\times\mathtt{pf}^-}$ to be $\mathcal{D}_{\mathtt{obj}} \times \mathcal{D}_{\mathtt{pf}^-}$ and $\mathcal{D}_{\alpha\to\beta}$ to be the set of all functions from $\mathcal{D}_\alpha$ to $\mathcal{D}_\beta$ for any α and β we obtain a standard frame for these simple types. The frame $\mathcal{D}$ is sufficient to evaluate simply typed λ-terms (with pairing between obj and $\mathtt{pf}^-$).

We can interpret any simply valid type as a binary relation over some $\mathcal{D}_\alpha$. The interpretation of valid types should be pers. For each α, let $\mathcal{R}_\alpha$ denote the set of all binary relations over $\mathcal{D}_\alpha$. For a relation R, let $|R|$ be $\{x \mid \langle x,x \rangle \in R\}$.

We will interpret $\mathtt{pf}\ P$ using a function $\overline{pf}$ from $\mathcal{D}_{\mathtt{prop}}$ to $\mathcal{R}_{\mathtt{pf}^-}$ taking a proposition p to the per $\{\langle p, p \rangle\}$ if $p \in \mathcal{D}_{\mathtt{pf}^-}$ and to the empty per otherwise. Hence $\overline{pf}(p)$ is a per with one equivalence class if p has a proof, and $\overline{pf}(p)$ is empty if p has no proof.

The type (class ϕ) depends on $\phi \in \mathcal{D}_{\mathtt{obj}\to\mathtt{prop}}$. Note that such a ϕ determines a subset $\{x \in \mathcal{D}_{\mathtt{obj}} \mid \phi(x) \in \mathcal{D}_{\mathtt{pf}^-}\}$ of $\mathcal{D}_{\mathtt{obj}}$. Intuitively, this is the "class" (relative to V_{ω^2}) of $x \in V_{\omega^2}$ such that $\phi(x)$ has a proof. This subset is isomorphic to the set $\{\langle x, p \rangle \in \mathcal{D}_{\mathtt{obj}} \times \mathcal{D}_{\mathtt{pf}^-} \mid p = \phi(x)\}$. This set is the domain of the per on $\mathcal{D}_{\mathtt{obj}} \times \mathcal{D}_{\mathtt{pf}^-}$ given by $\{\langle\langle x, \phi(x)\rangle, \langle x, \phi(x)\rangle\rangle \mid x \in \mathcal{D}_{\mathtt{obj}}, \phi(x) \in \mathcal{D}_{\mathtt{pf}^-}\}$. We take $\overline{class}(\phi)$ to be this per.

The remaining dependent types correspond to Π-types. Semantically, given $R \in \mathcal{R}_\alpha$ and $F : \mathcal{D}_\alpha \to \mathcal{R}_\beta$, we define $\overline{\Pi}(R,F) \in \mathcal{R}_{\alpha\to\beta}$ by $f(\overline{\Pi}(R,F))g$ iff $f(x)\,F(x)\,g(y)$ for all xRy.

We can interpret $c : \alpha \in \Xi$ by giving $[\![c]\!] \in \mathcal{D}_\alpha$. We can interpret $[\![\Delta]\!]$ as $\{0\} \times \mathcal{D}_{\alpha^1} \times \cdots \times \mathcal{D}_{\alpha^n}$. when Δ is $x^1 : \alpha^1, \ldots, x^n : \alpha^n$. (Special Case: $[\![\cdot]\!] := \{0\}$.)

Semantically, assume we have fixed $[\![c]\!] \in \mathcal{D}_\alpha$ for each $c : \alpha \in \Xi$. Then, when $\Delta \vdash_\Xi M : \alpha$ holds, we can define $[\![\Delta | M : \alpha]\!]$ to be a function from $[\![\Delta]\!]$ to $\mathcal{D}_\alpha$ (in the obvious way). For $d \in [\![\Delta]\!]$, we write $[\![\Delta | M : \alpha]\!]_d$ instead of $[\![\Delta | M : \alpha]\!](d)$.

When $\Delta \vdash_\Xi A$ sv holds, we can define $[\![\Delta|A]\!]$ to be a function from $[\![\Delta]\!]$ to $\mathcal{R}_{\lceil A \rceil}$. In particular, $[\![\Delta|\mathrm{obj}]\!]$ and $[\![\Delta|\mathrm{prop}]\!]$ are the identity relations on $\mathcal{D}_{\mathrm{obj}}$ and $\mathcal{D}_{\mathrm{prop}}$, $[\![\Delta|\mathrm{pf}\ P]\!](d)$ is $\overline{pf}([\![\Delta|P:\mathrm{prop}]\!]_d)$, class types are interpreted using $\overline{class}$, and function types are interpreted using $\overline{\Pi}$. For $d \in [\![\Delta]\!]$, we write $[\![\Delta|A]\!]_d$ instead of $[\![\Delta|A]\!](d)$.

We have described how to interpret simply typed terms and simply valid dependent types in the model. We can further interpret dependently typed contexts Γ by taking $[\![\Gamma]\!]$ to be a binary relation over $[\![\lceil\Gamma\rceil]\!]$. Let $[\![\cdot]\!]$ be the identity relation over $\{0\}$ and let $[\![\Gamma, x:A]\!]$ be $\{\langle\langle d,y\rangle,\langle e,z\rangle\rangle | d([\![\Gamma]\!])e$ and $y[\![\lceil\Gamma\rceil|A]\!]_d z\}$.

An interpretation of constants respects Σ if for all $c:A \in \Sigma$, $[\![c]\!] \in [\![[\cdot]|A]\!]_0$. Assume we have an interpretation which respects Σ. We conjecture the following soundness results:

1. If $\lceil\Gamma\rceil \vdash_{\lceil\Sigma\rceil} M : \lceil A \rceil$, $\lceil\Gamma\rceil \vdash_{\lceil\Sigma\rceil} N : \lceil A \rceil$, and $\lceil\Gamma\rceil \vdash_{\lceil\Sigma\rceil} A$ sv hold, and either $\Gamma \vdash_\Sigma M \sim N \uparrow A$ or $\Gamma \vdash_\Sigma M \sim N \downarrow A$ holds, then for all $d[\![\Gamma]\!]e$, we have $\langle[\![\lceil\Gamma\rceil|M:\lceil A\rceil]\!]_d, [\![\lceil\Gamma\rceil|N:\lceil A\rceil]\!]_e\rangle \in [\![\lceil\Gamma\rceil|A]\!]_d$.
2. If $\lceil\Gamma\rceil \vdash_{\lceil\Sigma\rceil} A$ sv and $\Gamma \vdash_\Sigma A : Type$ hold, then for all $d[\![\Gamma]\!]e$, $[\![\lceil\Gamma\rceil|A]\!]_d$ is a per on $\mathcal{D}_{\lceil A \rceil}$ and $[\![\lceil\Gamma\rceil|A]\!]_d = [\![\lceil\Gamma\rceil|A]\!]_e$.
3. If $\vdash_\Sigma \Gamma$ ctx holds, then $[\![\Gamma]\!]$ is a per over $[\![\lceil\Gamma\rceil]\!]$.

3 Mac Lane Set Theory with Universes

The axiomatic kernel of Mac Lane set theory with Universes (abbreviated **MU**) is implemented in Scunak using a signature of 29 constants. (In particular, the signature is finite.) There are three constants for constructing propositions.

- $\neg : \mathrm{prop} \to \mathrm{prop}$, i.e., $\neg M$ is a proposition whenever M is a proposition.
- $\in: \mathrm{obj} \to \mathrm{obj} \to \mathrm{prop}$, i.e., if x and y are objects (sets), then $(x \in y)$ (infix for $(\in y\,x)$) is a proposition.[1]
- $=: \mathrm{obj} \to \mathrm{obj} \to \mathrm{prop}$, i.e., if x and y are objects (sets), then $(x = y)$ (infix for $(= x\,y)$) is a proposition.

Note that we take negation as the *only* logical connective. The other connectives will be definable (making use of sets). Bounded quantifiers will also be definable.

There are six constants corresponding to basic set constructors.

- $\emptyset : \mathrm{obj}$, the empty set is a set.
- $\mathrm{dsetconstr} : \Pi A : \mathrm{obj}.(\mathrm{class}\ (\in A) \to \mathrm{prop}) \to \mathrm{obj}$, i.e., if A is a set and ϕ is a predicate on the set A, then $(\mathrm{dsetconstr}\ A\,\phi)$ (informally written $\{x \in A|\phi(x)\}$) is a set. In the future, we will often simply write A for the class type $\mathrm{class}\ (\in A)$ induced by the set A. The constant $\mathrm{dsetconstr}$ corresponds to the separation axiom.
- $\mathrm{setadjoin} : \mathrm{obj} \to \mathrm{obj} \to \mathrm{obj}$, i.e., if A and B are sets, then $\{A\} \cup B$ is a set. We take this operation of adjoining to sets as primitive instead of the more common primitive: unordered pair.

---

[1] The order of the arguments are reversed so that $(\in y)$, representing the predicate version of the set y, has a nice η-short form.

- $\mathcal{P}$: obj → obj, i.e., if A is a set, then the powerset $\mathcal{P}(A)$ of A is a set.
- $\bigcup$: obj → obj, i.e., if A is a set, then the union $\bigcup A$ of A is a set.
- univ : obj → obj, i.e., if A is a set then the "universe" of A is a set. A universe of a set A is a set containing A and closed under dsetconstr, setadjoin, $\mathcal{P}$ and $\bigcup$. We expect universes to be useful when one begins to represent so-called "large" categories.

Note that one can easily represent any finite enumeration $\{x_1, \dots, x_n\}$ using the empty set and the setadjoin operation: $(\{x_1\} \cup \cdots (\{x_n\} \cup \emptyset) \cdots)$.

While one could take more constructors for propositions and objects as primitive, there is a very important reason to prefer a minimal set: *primitive substitutions*. When forming a complete automated reasoning procedure, it seems inevitable that sometimes one will need to "guess" the use of one of the basic constants in an instantiation. In higher-order theorem proving, such guessing is performed by primitive substitutions (or, *primsubs*). In Church's type theory, the set of possible primsubs is infinite since there is a logical constant Π^α for each type α. In formulating **MU**, we have attempted to keep this set not only finite but also as small as possible.

We can easily interpret the constants above in our model. Briefly,

$$\llbracket \neg \rrbracket(\dot{\in}, x, y) := (\dot{\notin}, x, y) \quad \llbracket \neg \rrbracket(\dot{\notin}, x, y) := (\dot{\in}, x, y) \quad \llbracket \neg \rrbracket(\dot{=}, x, y) := (\dot{\neq}, x, y)$$
$$\llbracket \neg \rrbracket(\dot{\neq}, x, y) := (\dot{=}, x, y) \quad \llbracket \in \rrbracket(y)(x) := (\dot{\in}, x, y) \quad \llbracket = \rrbracket(x)(y) := (\dot{=}, x, y)$$
$$\llbracket \emptyset \rrbracket := \emptyset \qquad \llbracket \mathcal{P} \rrbracket(A) := \mathcal{P}(A) \qquad \llbracket \bigcup \rrbracket(A) := \bigcup(A).$$

Also, $\llbracket \text{setadjoin} \rrbracket(A)(B) := \{A\} \cup B$. Interpreting dsetconstr requires a bit more explanation. Let $A \in \mathcal{D}_{\text{obj}}$ and $\phi \in \mathcal{D}_{\text{obj} \times \text{pf}^- \to \text{prop}}$ be given. The intention is that ϕ is a property of the set A. As such, ϕ depends on an object $x \in \mathcal{D}_{\text{obj}}$ and a proof that x is in A. In our frame, $(\dot{\in}, x, A)$ is the only possible proof, and is only a proof if $(\dot{\in}, x, A) \in \mathcal{D}_{\text{pf}^-}$ (i.e., x is actually in A). We let $\llbracket \text{dsetconstr} \rrbracket(A)(\phi) := \{x \in A | \phi(\langle x, (\dot{\in}, x, A)\rangle) \in \mathcal{D}_{\text{pf}^-}\}$. Also, we interpret $\llbracket \text{univ} \rrbracket(A)$ to be $V_{\delta+\omega} \in V_{\omega^2}$ where $\delta < \omega^2$ is an ordinal such that $A \in V_\delta$.

Finally, there are 20 constants corresponding to natural deduction proof rules. These are shown in natural deduction style in Figure 2. To ease the presentation, some of the rules in Figure 2 are simplified. For example, the premiss $\Gamma \vdash P, Q$: prop of the rule xmcases stands for two premisses: $\Gamma \vdash P$: prop and $\Gamma \vdash Q$: prop. Variables named A, B, C and D are always of type obj and variables named P and Q are always of type prop. When we add these variables to the context Γ, we do not explicitly write the type. Also, we sometimes write $a : \phi$ for $a :$ class ϕ and we write $b : A$ for $b :$ class $(\in A)$. These rules are "sound" in our intended semantics. That is, there is an obvious interpretation (respecting the relevant pers). For example, we can interpret setunionI so that $\llbracket \text{setunionI} \rrbracket(A)(B)(C)(\dot{\in}, B, C)(\dot{\in}, C, A) := (\dot{\in}, B, \bigcup A)$ for $A, B, C \in V_{\omega^2}$ and $(\dot{\in}, B, C), (\dot{\in}, C, A) \in \mathcal{D}_{\text{pf}^-}$. Note that given these arguments, $(\dot{\in}, B, \bigcup A) \in \mathcal{D}_{\text{pf}^-}$ precisely because $B \in C$ and $C \in A$ and so $B \in \bigcup A$. Given arguments from $\mathcal{D}_{\text{pf}^-}$ which do not fall into the pattern above, setunionI can be arbitrary

$$\frac{\Gamma \vdash P, Q : \mathrm{prop} \quad \Gamma, P \vdash Q \quad \Gamma, \neg P \vdash Q}{\Gamma \vdash Q} \; \mathrm{xmcases} \qquad \frac{\Gamma \vdash P, Q : \mathrm{prop} \quad \Gamma \vdash P \quad \Gamma \vdash \neg P}{\Gamma \vdash Q} \; \mathrm{notE}$$

$$\frac{\Gamma, A \vdash (\phi A) : \mathrm{prop} \quad \Gamma \vdash a, b : \phi \quad \Gamma, c : \phi \vdash (\psi c) : \mathrm{prop} \quad \Gamma \vdash \pi_1(a) = \pi_1(b) \quad \Gamma \vdash \psi a}{\Gamma \vdash \psi b} \; \mathrm{eqCE}$$

$$\frac{\Gamma \vdash A, B : \mathrm{obj} \quad \Gamma, C, C \in A \vdash C \in B \quad \Gamma, D, D \in B \vdash D \in A}{\Gamma \vdash A = B} \; \mathrm{setext}$$

$$\frac{\Gamma \vdash A : \mathrm{obj} \quad \Gamma \vdash A \in \emptyset \quad \Gamma \vdash P : \mathrm{prop}}{\Gamma \vdash P} \; \mathrm{emptysetE}$$

$$\frac{\Gamma \vdash A : \mathrm{obj} \quad \Gamma, a : A \vdash (\phi a) : \mathrm{prop} \quad \Gamma \vdash b : A \quad \Gamma \vdash \phi b}{\Gamma \vdash \pi_1(b) \in \{x \in A | \phi x\}} \; \mathrm{dsetconstrI}$$

$$\frac{\Gamma \vdash A : \mathrm{obj} \quad \Gamma, a : A \vdash (\phi a) : \mathrm{prop} \quad \Gamma \vdash B : \mathrm{obj} \quad \Gamma \vdash B \in \{x \in A | \phi x\}}{\Gamma \vdash B \in A} \; \mathrm{dsetconstrEL}$$

$$\frac{\Gamma \vdash A : \mathrm{obj} \quad \Gamma, a : A \vdash (\phi a) : \mathrm{prop} \quad \Gamma \vdash B : \mathrm{obj} \quad \Gamma \vdash u : (B \in \{x \in A | \phi x\})}{\Gamma \vdash \phi \langle B, (\mathrm{dsetconstrEL}\, A\, \phi\, B\, u) \rangle} \; \mathrm{dsetconstrER}$$

$$\frac{\Gamma \vdash A, B : \mathrm{obj}}{\Gamma \vdash A \in \{A\} \cup B} \; \mathrm{setadjoinIL} \qquad \frac{\Gamma \vdash A, B : \mathrm{obj} \quad \Gamma \vdash C : \mathrm{obj} \quad \Gamma \vdash C \in B}{\Gamma \vdash C \in \{A\} \cup B} \; \mathrm{setadjoinIR}$$

$$\frac{\Gamma \vdash A, B, C : \mathrm{obj} \quad \Gamma \vdash C \in \{A\} \cup B \quad \Gamma \vdash P : \mathrm{prop} \quad \Gamma, C = A \vdash P \quad \Gamma, C \in B \vdash P}{\Gamma \vdash P} \; \mathrm{setadjoinE}$$

$$\frac{\Gamma \vdash A, B : \mathrm{obj} \quad \Gamma, C, C \in B \vdash C \in A}{\Gamma \vdash B \in \mathcal{P}(A)} \; \mathrm{powersetI}$$

$$\frac{\Gamma \vdash A, B, C : \mathrm{obj} \quad \Gamma \vdash B \in \mathcal{P}(A) \quad \Gamma \vdash C \in B}{\Gamma \vdash C \in A} \; \mathrm{powersetE}$$

$$\frac{\Gamma \vdash A, B, C : \mathrm{obj} \quad \Gamma \vdash B \in C \quad \Gamma \vdash C \in A}{\Gamma \vdash B \in \bigcup A} \; \mathrm{setunionI}$$

$$\frac{\Gamma \vdash A, B : \mathrm{obj} \quad \Gamma \vdash B \in \bigcup A \quad \Gamma \vdash P : \mathrm{prop} \quad \Gamma, C, B \in C, C \in A \vdash P}{\Gamma \vdash P} \; \mathrm{setunionE}$$

$$\frac{\Gamma \vdash A : \mathrm{obj}}{\Gamma \vdash A \in \mathrm{univ}(A)} \; \mathrm{univHas} \qquad \frac{\Gamma \vdash A : \mathrm{obj} \quad \Gamma \vdash a : \mathrm{univ}(A) \quad \Gamma, b : \pi_1(a) \vdash (\phi b) : \mathrm{prop}}{\Gamma \vdash \{x \in \pi_1(a) | \phi x\} \in \mathrm{univ}(A)} \; \mathrm{univSep}$$

$$\frac{\Gamma \vdash A : \mathrm{obj} \quad \Gamma \vdash a : \mathrm{univ}(A) \quad \Gamma \vdash b : \mathrm{univ}(A)}{\Gamma \vdash \{\pi_1(a)\} \cup \pi_1(b) \in \mathrm{univ}(A)} \; \mathrm{univAdj}$$

$$\frac{\Gamma \vdash A : \mathrm{obj} \quad \Gamma \vdash a : \mathrm{univ}(A)}{\Gamma \vdash \mathcal{P}(\pi_1(a)) \in \mathrm{univ}(A)} \; \mathrm{univPow} \qquad \frac{\Gamma \vdash A : \mathrm{obj} \quad \Gamma \vdash a : \mathrm{univ}(A)}{\Gamma \vdash \bigcup \pi_1(a) \in \mathrm{univ}(A)} \; \mathrm{univSU}$$

Fig. 2. Basic Set Theory Deduction Rules

in $\mathcal{D}_{\mathrm{pf}}-$. Only the pattern above is used to check $[\![\mathtt{setunionI}]\!]$ is in the domain of the per determined by the type

$$\Pi A : \mathtt{obj}.\Pi B : \mathtt{obj}.\Pi C : \mathtt{obj}.\mathtt{pf}\ (B \in C) \to \mathtt{pf}\ (C \in A) \to \mathtt{pf}\ (B \in \bigcup A)$$

so that the interpretation will respect the signature.

The rules $\mathtt{xmcases}$ and $\mathtt{notE}$ are natural deduction rules for classical negation. Consider the typed constants corresponding to these rules:

$\mathtt{xmcases}$: $\Pi P : \mathtt{prop}.\Pi Q : \mathtt{prop}.(\mathtt{pf}\ P \to \mathtt{pf}\ Q) \to (\mathtt{pf}\ (\neg P) \to \mathtt{pf}\ Q) \to \mathtt{pf}\ Q$
$\mathtt{notE}$: $\quad \Pi P : \mathtt{prop}.\Pi Q : \mathtt{prop}.\mathtt{pf}\ P \to \mathtt{pf}\ (\neg P) \to \mathtt{pf}\ Q$

One can use these two basic rules to derive a natural deduction rule for negation introduction $\mathtt{notIp}$ as well as the classical double negation rule $\mathtt{dnegE}$. That is, we can make two abbreviations using terms of the appropriate types:

$\mathtt{notIp}$: $(\Pi P : \mathtt{prop}.(\mathtt{pf}\ P \to \Pi Q : \mathtt{prop}.\mathtt{pf}\ Q) \to \mathtt{pf}\ (\neg P))$
$\quad = (\lambda P \lambda u(\mathtt{xmcases}\ P\ (\neg P)\ (\lambda v(u\ v\ (\neg P)))\ (\lambda ww)))$
$\mathtt{dnegE}$: $(\Pi P : \mathtt{prop}.\mathtt{pf}\ (\neg\neg P) \to \mathtt{pf}\ P)$
$\quad = (\lambda P \lambda u(\mathtt{xmcases}\ P\ P\ (\lambda vv)(\lambda w(\mathtt{notE}\ (\neg P)\ P\ w\ u))))$

This demonstrates how one represents **MU** theorems and proofs in Scunak. A "theorem" is a function type which returns a proof type and a "proof" is a term which can be judged to be a member of this type.

The rule $\mathtt{eqCE}$ allows one to replace equals by equals even when the objects are used in a "typed" way. Suppose ϕ is a predicate and a and b are in the class type of ϕ. Technically, a is a pair of an untyped set $\pi_1(a)$ and a proof $\pi_2(a)$ of $(\phi\,\pi_1(a))$. The "typed" object b is a similar pair. We cannot directly represent the proposition that a and b are equal, since we only have equality between objects (i.e., untyped sets). The proposition that a and b are equal as *untyped sets* is $\pi_1(a) = \pi_1(b)$ (one of the premises of $\mathtt{eqCE}$). Suppose ψ is a predicate that is only defined relative to the class ϕ. If we know ψ is true for the ϕ-object a, and we know a and b are equal as untyped sets, then $\mathtt{eqCE}$ allows us to conclude ψ is true for the ϕ-object b.

The only other rules which may require any explanation are $\mathtt{dsetconstrI}$, $\mathtt{dsetconstrEL}$ and $\mathtt{dsetconstrER}$ for introducing and eliminating the (dependent) set constructor. In each case we have premises indicating A is an object (i.e., untyped set) in context and ϕ is a predicate on A. Since ϕ can only be applied to members of the class type $\mathtt{class}\ (\in A)$, we must take care.

In the introduction rule $\mathtt{dsetconstrI}$, we assume we have b as a member of this class type and a proof that $(\phi\,b)$ holds. In such a case we wish to conclude that b is in the set $\{x \in A | (\phi\,x)\}$. This is not quite correct since $\in$ is a relation between objects, and b is a pair. Hence we recover the object using π_1 and conclude $\pi_1(b) \in \{x \in A | (\phi\,x)\}$.

The elimination rules $\mathtt{dsetconstrEL}$ and $\mathtt{dsetconstrER}$ form a kind of converse. Assume we have an untyped set B and a proof that B is in $\{x \in A | (\phi\,x)\}$. The first rule $\mathtt{dsetconstrEL}$ allows us to conclude $B \in A$. The second rule $\mathtt{dsetconstrER}$ intuitively allows us to conclude B satisfies ϕ. However, ϕ cannot be simply applied to B. Instead we *coerce* the untyped object B to be in the class determined by A *using* the previous rule dsetconstrEL. The term (dsetconstrEL $A \phi B$) takes a proof of $B \in \{x \in A | (\phi x)\}$ (the premiss named by u in dsetconstrER) to a proof of $B \in A$. Hence $\langle B, (\text{dsetconstrEL} A \phi B u) \rangle$ is in the class type (class ($\in A$)).

The basic set theoretic concepts and rules satisfy a kind of *logical purity*. Unlike most presentations of set theory, the basic rules only mention the basic concepts. In particular, all "axioms" are given before any definitions are made.

Although one starts with negation, one can define the other logical connectives and derive the appropriate rules. For example, for any propositions P and Q, one can define disjunction of P and Q using the term

$$\{\emptyset\} \in \{\{x \in \{\emptyset\} | P\}, \{x \in \{\emptyset\} | Q\}\}.$$

Once the appropriate rules for disjunction are proven, one need not unfold this definition of disjunction.

One can also define bounded quantifiers. For example, for a set A and predicate $\phi(x)$ depending on an element $x \in A$, $\forall x \in A.\phi(x)$ can be defined by $(\{x \in A.\phi(x)\} = A)$. Note that the predicate ϕ is relative to the set A. That is, $\phi(x)$ is only defined for x in the class type corresponding to A. Thus one could sensibly represent a proposition such as $\forall x \in Positive.\frac{1}{x} > 0$ where $Positive$ represents the set of positive real numbers. Forming the term $\frac{1}{x}$ would require a proof that x is nonzero and such a proof would depend on the assumption $x \in Positive$.

Note that two common set theory axioms, choice and foundation, are omitted from **MU**.

Starting from the basic concepts and rules defining the theory **MU**, we can make new definitions using terms of certain types. If the type returns a proof type, then we can interpret the type as a derived rule (or theorem) and we can interpret the term as a proof. We briefly outline some definitions which have been constructed interactively in Scunak. After getting starting, this follows the usual development of basic mathematics in an axiomatic set theory.

- Propositional connectives and bounded quantifiers are defined and corresponding rules are derived.
- The usual set theoretic notions are defined ($\subset$, binary union and intersection, etc.) are defined and relevant rules are derived.
- A description operator is defined on the class of singleton sets.
- Ordered pairs (as Kuratowski pairs) are defined, along with "first" and "second" operations which are only defined on the class of Kuratowski pairs. (To prevent confusion with pairing in the Scunak type theory, we write $\langle\langle x, y \rangle\rangle$ for the Kuratowski pair of x and y.)
- Using Kuratowski pairs, Cartesian products ($A \times B$) of sets A and B are defined.
- Given any sets A and B and (meta-level) relation $\phi : A \rightarrow B \rightarrow$ prop, we can define the subset of $A \times B$ of Kuratowski pairs $\langle\langle a, b \rangle\rangle$ such that $(\phi a b)$ holds. In Scunak, we include notation of the form {<<x,y>>:A \times B| ...} for

specifying such sets of pairs. This is especially useful when defining constructors for functions and relations.

- Using Cartesian products, binary relations are defined.
- For any two sets A and B, a function from A to B is defined as a functional (untyped) binary relation on A and B.
- For sets A and B, we define the *set* B^A of functions from A to B.
- Using the description operator, an application operator ap2 can be defined taking an element f of the set B^A and an element a of A to (intuitively) $f(a)$ in B.
- Given a "meta-level" function g from A to B (i.e., a term g of type $A \to B$), we can obtain an "object-level" function $(\text{lam2}\,A\,B\,g)$ from A to B (i.e., a member of B^A) by $\{\langle\langle x, y\rangle\rangle \in (A \times B)|(\pi_1(gx) = \pi_1(y))\}$. This is an internalized λ binder and (along with ap2) allows us to internalize standard models of Church's type theory.

Of particular note are the operations that are "partial" (i.e., only defined on subclasses of the untyped universe). Consider first the description operator. The predicate singleton is defined in the obvious way. One can easily prove if U is in the class of singletons, then $(\bigcup U) \in U$. Using the previous fact, we define a description operator the taking a singleton U : (class singleton) into (the class determined by) U. The important fact is that the description operator is defined *precisely* on the class of singleton sets. The type of the is ΠU : (class singleton).U. The definition of the is $(\lambda U\langle \bigcup U, (\text{theprop}\,U)\rangle)$ where theprop is an abbreviation for the proof, given a singleton U, that $(\bigcup U) \in U$.

Two other examples of such "partial" functions are given by the first and second operators for Kuratowski pairs. Both kfst and ksnd take an argument u of type (class iskpair) and return an object (i.e., an element of type obj).

4 Proving the Injective Cantor Theorem

A common example which has been considered many times is Cantor's Theorem. Intuitively, Cantor's Theorem states that $\mathcal{P}(A)$ is bigger than A. One way to formally state this property is that there is no surjection from A onto $\mathcal{P}(A)$. This is the *surjective Cantor Theorem* which was one of the earliest interesting theorems proven automatically by TPS [3]. The relevant diagonal set can be constructed by TPS using higher-order unification.

Otter was also able to prove the surjective Cantor theorem formalized in NBG. As discussed in [18], the diagonal set was defined by the user and certain lemmas about this diagonal set were explicitly given. For this reason, Quaife describes the proof as "semi-automatic."

An alternative formulation of Cantor's Theorem states that there is no injection from $\mathcal{P}(A)$ into A. This is the *injective Cantor Theorem*. As discussed in [3], this is a very challenging problem for higher-order theorem provers. The only known cut-free proofs of the injective Cantor Theorem are of quantificational depth at least 3. (Roughly speaking, one must do a primsub for a variable introduced by a quantifier which itself was introduced by a primsub.)

A different approach was suggested by Dana Scott: reduce the injective version to the surjective version by using the fact that an injection h from $\mathcal{P}(A)$ to A induces a surjection g from A to $\mathcal{P}(A)$. It is not reasonable to expect a theorem prover to "guess" such a lemma, but it may be reasonable for a theorem prover to find such a lemma in a library and use it, along with the surjective Cantor Theorem, to prove the injective Cantor Theorem. This is the "semi-automatic" approach we have taken here.

First we must represent the main lemma about one-sided inverse functions. A general version is not true: there can be an injection from A to B without there existing a surjection from B onto A. The counterexample is when A is empty and B is nonempty. We could formulate the lemma as follows: If A is nonempty and there is an injection from A to B, then there is a surjection from B onto A. Given a default value $a \in A$ and an injection h from A to B, we can actually *define* the relevant surjection g as follows:

$$\{\langle\langle y, x\rangle\rangle | \langle\langle x, y\rangle\rangle \in h\} \cup \{\langle\langle y, a\rangle\rangle | \neg\exists x \in A. \langle\langle x, y\rangle\rangle \in h\}. \tag{1}$$

That is, $g(y) = x$ if $h(x) = y$ and $g(y)$ is the default value a if no such x exists.

Let $iF(A, B)$ denote the set of injective functions from A to B and let $sF(A, B)$ denote the set of surjective functions from A to B. We can represent the construction above in Scunak by defining an abbreviation leftInvOfInj which takes two sets A and B, a member h of the set $iF(A, B)$ and a member a of the set A and returns a member of the set $sF(B, A)$. Since leftInvOfInj returns a member of a class type, it returns a pair. The object part of the pair is defined as indicated by (1) above. The proof part of the pair is a proof that (1) defines a member of $sF(B, A)$ (a surjective function from B to A). Instead of representing the main lemma as a proposition, we define an operation, which we can denote by $(h)_a^{-1}$, taking $h \in iF(A, B)$ and $a \in A$ to a member of $sF(B, A)$.

By the time we state the injective Cantor Theorem in Scunak, we have defined 57 concepts and proven 222 lemmas. Furthermore, 15 of the defined concepts are functions which return elements of class types and hence have proof content (namely, the proof that the resulting untyped object belongs to the class). For each definition (not counting lemmas), there are two rules for folding and unfolding abbreviations, giving 114 more facts. Combining this with the 20 basic proof rules from Figure 2, we have 371 facts which can be used to prove the injective Cantor Theorem.

Among these facts, we only send 114 to Vampire. We do not translate any fact which depends on variables of propositional type. This filters out, for example, the basic rules xmcases, notE and eqCE for negation and equality. However, since we translate negation and equality in Scunak to negation and equality in Vampire, these rules need not be translated. We also only translate types which are first-order (in the λ-calculus sense). This is more restrictive than necessary and filters out some important facts such as the basic set extensionality rule setext. Of course, the fewer clauses we send to Vampire, the less likely it becomes that there is a proof, but the more likely it becomes that Vampire will find a proof if one exists. Dependence of object terms on proof terms are deleted in the translation.

In addition to the 114 facts, two formulas corresponding to the injective Cantor theorem are sent to Vampire. Namely, the "axiom" that a constant h is in the set $A^{\mathcal{P}(A)}$ and the "conjecture" that h is not injective.

Vampire (version 8.0) was called with 116 first-order formulas and a five minute time limit. In less than 5 seconds, Vampire generated over $80,000$ clauses and found a refutation. Most of the given 116 clauses are not used in the refutation. We describe the relevant clauses used by Vampire:

1. $h \in A^{\mathcal{P}(A)}$.
2. h is injective (the negation of the conclusion).
3. (Surjective Cantor Theorem) If $g \in \mathcal{P}(X)^X$, then g is not surjective.
4. (Main Lemma) If $f \in iF(X,Y)$ and $a \in X$, then $(f)_a^{-1} \in sF(Y,X)$.
5. For any X, $\emptyset \in \mathcal{P}(X)$.
6. If $g \in sF(X,Y)$, then g is surjective.
7. If $g \in sF(X,Y)$, then $g \in Y^X$.
8. If an element f is in Y^X and is injective from X to Y, then $f \in iF(X,Y)$.
9. If $X \subseteq Y$ and $x \in X$, then $x \in Y$.
10. For any X, $\bigcup\{X\} \subseteq X$.
11. (Basic rule `setunionI`) If $x \in X$ and $X \in Y$, then $x \in \bigcup Y$.
12. (Basic rule `setadjoinIL`) For any x and Y, $x \in \{x\} \cup Y$.

The first facts (1-4) are at the heart of the refutation. Fact 5 is used so that the empty set can act as the necessary default value in $\mathcal{P}(A)$. Facts (6-8) must be used to pass from the sets $iF(X,Y)$ or $sF(X,Y)$ to the properties defining these sets. The remaining facts (9-12) are not strictly necessary for the proof, but are used by Vampire. If one modifies the input file for Vampire to include only facts (1-8), then Vampire finds a simpler refutation after generating only 16 clauses.

Upon inspection, the original refutation found by Vampire is a bit roundabout. Part of the refutation is clear: By the surjective Cantor theorem, nothing is in $sF(X, \mathcal{P}(X))$ for any X. Using this with main lemma, if something is in $\mathcal{P}(X)$, then nothing is in $iF(\mathcal{P}(X), X)$. At this point, we could finish the refutation using $\emptyset \in \mathcal{P}(A)$ (from 5) and $h \in iF(\mathcal{P}(A), A)$ (from 1, 2 and 8). However, the actual refutation found by Vampire proceeds as follows.

Using 8 and 11, if $f \in Y^X$ is injective and $iF(X,Y) \in Z$, then $f \in \bigcup Z$. Hence (using our assumptions 1 and 2), we conclude $h \in \bigcup Z$ whenever $iF(\mathcal{P}(A), A) \in Z$. Since $iF(\mathcal{P}(A), A) \in \{iF(\mathcal{P}(A), A)\} \cup Y$ by 12, we have $h \in \bigcup(\{iF(\mathcal{P}(A), A)\} \cup Y)$. In particular, $h \in \bigcup\{iF(\mathcal{P}(A), A)\}$. Using 9 and 10, $h \in iF(\mathcal{P}(A), A)$. Hence nothing is in $\mathcal{P}(A)$, contradicting $\emptyset \in \mathcal{P}(A)$.

5   Related Work

A similar idea of axiomatizing set theory in higher-order logic, as well as an internalization of higher-order logic within the set theory, was explored in [10]. The ZF-theory in Isabelle also encodes set theory within a form of simple type theory [16]. More recently, a variety of foundational systems including ZFC (Zermelo-Fraenkel set theory with the axiom of choice) were finitely represented and compared in Automath [22]. Decidable fragments of set theory have been studied extensively (see, e.g., [7]). Several different forms of mechanized set theory have been formulated and investigated in recent years, including [8], [9], [21], [4] and [22].

The idea of calling a first-order theorem prover to solve subgoals has been explored in several papers, including [14,1]. The work in [14] describes extensive experiments with a connection between Vampire and Isabelle-ZF. The work in [1] connects a first-order prover with a logical framework.

6 Conclusion

We have presented a type theory with proof irrelevance and class types implemented in the system Scunak. This type theory is designed with the intention of supporting both the construction of a large mathematical library and automated search using the library. Within this type theory, a form of Mac Lane set theory has been implemented. We argue this is a reasonably practical representation language for mathematics. Enough of a library has been interactively constructed to define function spaces as well as object-level versions of application and abstraction. In particular, we have represented the injective Cantor theorem and mapped this representation (along with much of the previously constructed theory) to the first-order prover Vampire. Vampire proves this challenge problem quickly. Hopefully, in the future we will have a larger library of mathematics in Scunak which can be used effectively during automated search.

References

1. Andreas Abel, Thierry Coquand, and Ulf Norell. Connecting a logical framework to a first-order logic prover. In Bernhard Gramlich, editor, *5th International Workshop on Frontiers of Combining Systems, FroCoS'05, Vienna, Austria, September 19-21, 2005*, Lecture Notes in Computer Science, 2005.
2. Peter B. Andrews and Matthew Bishop. On sets, types, fixed points, and checkerboards. In Pierangelo Miglioli, Ugo Moscato, Daniele Mundici, and Mario Ornaghi, editors, *Theorem Proving with Analytic Tableaux and Related Methods. 5th International Workshop. (TABLEAUX '96)*, volume 1071 of *Lecture Notes in Artificial Intelligence*, pages 1–15, Terrasini, Italy, May 1996. Springer-Verlag.
3. Peter B. Andrews, Matthew Bishop, and Chad E. Brown. System description: TPS: A theorem proving system for type theory. In David McAllester, editor, *Proceedings of the 17th International Conference on Automated Deduction*, volume 1831 of *Lecture Notes in Artificial Intelligence*, pages 164–169, Pittsburgh, PA, USA, 2000. Springer-Verlag.
4. Arnon Avron. Formalizing set theory as it is actually used. In Andrea Asperti, Grzegorz Bancerek, and Andrzej Trybulec, editors, *MKM*, volume 3119 of *Lecture Notes in Computer Science*, pages 32–43. Springer, 2004.
5. J.G.F. Belinfante. Computer Proofs in Gödel's class theory with equational definitions for composite and cross. *Journal of Automated Reasoning*, 22:311–339, 1999.

6. Robert Boyer, Ewing Lusk, William McCune, Ross Overbeek, Mark Stickel, and Lawrence Wos. Set theory in first-order logic: Clauses for Gödel's axioms. *Journal of Automated Reasoning*, 2:287–327, 1986.

7. Domenico Cantone, Calogero G. Zarba, and Rosa Ruggeri-Cannata. A tableau-based decision procedure for a fragment of set theory with iterated membership. *Journal of Automated Reasoning*, 34(1):49–72, 2005.

8. Gilles Dowek. Collections, sets and types. *Mathematical Structures in Computer Science*, 9(1):109–123, 1999.

9. William M. Farmer. Stmm: A set theory for mechanized mathematics. *J. Autom. Reasoning*, 26(3):269–289, 2001.

10. Michael J. C. Gordon. Set theory, higher order logic or both? In Joakim von Wright, Jim Grundy, and John Harrison, editors, *TPHOLs*, volume 1125 of *Lecture Notes in Computer Science*, pages 191–201. Springer, 1996.

11. Robert Harper, Furio Honsell, and Gordon Plotkin. A framework for defining logics. *Journal of the Association for Computing Machinery*, 40(1):143–184, January 1993.

12. J. Lambek and P. Scott. *Introduction to Higher Order Categorial Logic*. Cambridge University Press, Cambridge, UK, 1986.

13. Saunders Mac Lane. *Mathematics, Form and Function*. Springer-Verlag, 1986.

14. Jia Meng. Integration of interactive and automatic provers. In Manuel Carro and Jesus Correas, editors, *Second CologNet Workshop on Implementation Technology for Computational Logic Systems*, 2003. http://www.cl.cam.ac.uk/users/jm318/papers/integration.pdf.

15. Bengt Nordström, Kent Petersson, and Jan Smith. Martin-löf's type theory. In Samson Abramsky et al., editors, *Handbook of Logic in Computer Science*, volume 5. Oxford University Press, 2000.

16. Lawrence C. Paulson. Set Theory for Verification: II. Induction and Recursion. *Journal of Automated Reasoning*, 15(2):167–215, 1995.

17. Frank Pfenning and Carsten Schürmann. System Description: Twelf-A Meta-Logical Framework for Deductive Systems. In Harald Ganzinger, editor, *Proceedings of the 16th International Conference on Automated Deduction*, volume 1632 of *Lecture Notes in Artificial Intelligence*, pages 202–206, Trento, Italy, 1999. Springer-Verlag.

18. Art Quaife. *Automated Development of Fundamental Mathematical Theories*. Kluwer Academic Publishers, Norwell, MA, USA, 1992.

19. Jason Reed. Proof irrelevance and strict definitions in a logical framework. Technical Report 02-153, School of Computer Science, Carnegie Mellon University, 2002.

20. A. Riazanov and A. Voronkov. Vampire 1.1. (system description). In Rajeev Goré, Alexander Leitsch, and Tobias Nipkow, editors, *Automated Reasoning, First International Joint Conference, IJCAR*, volume LNAI 2083 of *Lecture Notes in Artificial Intelligence*, pages 376–380, Siena, Italy, January 2001. Springer Verlag.

21. Raymond Turner. Type inference for set theory. *Theor. Comput. Sci.*, 266(1-2):951–974, 2001.

22. Freek Wiedijk. Is ZF a hack? Comparing the complexity of some (formalist interpretations of) foundational systems for mathematics. *Journal of Applied Logic*, 4, 2006. to appear.

Cut-Simulation in Impredicative Logics

Christoph E. Benzmüller[1], Chad E. Brown[1], and Michael Kohlhase[2]

[1] Saarland University, Saarbrücken, Germany
{chris, cebrown}@ags.uni-sb.de
[2] International University Bremen, Bremen, Germany
m.kohlhase@iu-bremen.de

Abstract. We investigate cut-elimination and cut-simulation in impredicative (higher-order) logics. We illustrate that adding simple axioms such as Leibniz equations to a calculus for an impredicative logic — in our case a sequent calculus for classical type theory — is like adding cut. The phenomenon equally applies to prominent axioms like Boolean- and functional extensionality, induction, choice, and description. This calls for the development of calculi where these principles are built-in instead of being treated axiomatically.

1   Introduction

One of the key questions of automated reasoning is the following: "When does a set Φ of sentences have a model?" In fact, given reasonable assumptions about calculi, most inference problems can be reduced to determining (un)-satisfiability of a set Φ of sentences. Since building models for Φ is hard in practice, much research in computational logic has concentrated on finding sufficient conditions for satisfiability, e.g. whether there is a Hintikka set $\mathcal{H}$ extending Φ.

Of course in general the answer to the satisfiability question depends on the class of models at hand. In classical first-order logic, model classes are well-understood. In impredicative higher-order logic, there is a whole landscape of plausible model classes differing in their treatment of functional and Boolean extensionality. Satisfiability then strongly depends on these classes, for instance, the set $\Phi := \{a, b, qa, \neg qb\}$ is unsatisfiable in a model class where the universes of Booleans are required to have at most two members (see property $\mathfrak{b}$ below), but satisfiable in the class without this restriction.

In [5] we have shown that certain (i.e. *saturated*) Hintikka sets always have models and have derived syntactical conditions (so-called *saturated* abstract consistency properties) for satisfiability from this fact. The importance of abstract consistency properties is that one can check completeness for a calculus $\mathcal{C}$ by verifying proof-theoretic conditions (checking that $\mathcal{C}$-irrefutable sets of formulae have the saturated abstract consistency property) instead of performing model-theoretic analysis (for historical background of the method in first-order logic, cf. [10,13,14]). Unfortunately, the saturation condition (if Φ is abstractly consistent, then one of $\Phi \cup \{\mathbf{A}\}$ or $\Phi \cup \{\neg\mathbf{A}\}$ is as well for all sentences $\mathbf{A}$) is very difficult to prove for machine-oriented calculi (indeed as hard as cut elimination).

U. Furbach and N. Shankar (Eds.): IJCAR 2006, LNAI 4130, pp. 220–234, 2006.
© Springer-Verlag Berlin Heidelberg 2006

In this paper we investigate further the relation between the lack of the sub-formula property in the saturation condition (we need to "guess" whether to extend Φ by $\mathbf{A}$ or $\neg\mathbf{A}$ on our way to a Hintikka set for all sentences $\mathbf{A}$) and the cut rule (where we have to "guess", i.e. search for in an automated reasoning setting" the cut formula $\mathbf{A}$). A side result is the insight that there exist "cut-strong" formulae which support the effective simulation of cut in calculi for impredicative logics.

In Section 2, we will fix notation and review the relevant results from [5]. We define in Section 3 a basic sequent calculus and study the correspondence between saturation in abstract consistency classes and cut-elimination. In Section 4 we introduce the notion of "cut-strong" formulae and sequents and show that they support the effective simulation of cut. In Section 5 we demonstrate that the pertinent extensionality axioms are cut-strong. We develop alternative extensionality rules which do not suffer from this problem. Further rules are needed to ensure Henkin completeness for this calculus with extensionality. These new rules correspond to the acceptability conditions we propose in Section 6 to ensure the existence of models and the existence of saturated extensions of abstract consistence classes.

2 Higher-Order Logic

In [5] we have re-examined the semantics of classical higher-order logic with the purpose of clarifying the role of extensionality. For this we have defined eight classes of higher-order models with respect to various combinations of Boolean extensionality and three forms of functional extensionality. We have also developed a methodology of abstract consistency (by providing the necessary model existence theorems) needed for instance, to analyze completeness of higher-order calculi with respect to these model classes. We now briefly summarize the main notions and results of [5] as required for this paper. Our impredicative logic of choice is Church's classical type theory.

Syntax: Church's Simply Typed λ-Calculus. As in [9], we formulate higher-order logic ($\mathcal{HOL}$) based on the simply typed λ-calculus. The set of simple types $\mathcal{T}$ is freely generated from basic types o and ι using the function type constructor $\rightarrow$.

For formulae we start with a set $\mathcal{V}$ of (typed) variables (denoted by $X_\alpha, Y, Z,$ $X_\beta^1, X_\gamma^2 \ldots$) and a signature Σ of (typed) constants (denoted by $c_\alpha, f_{\alpha\rightarrow\beta}, \ldots$). We let $\mathcal{V}_\alpha$ (Σ_α) denote the set of variables (constants) of type α. The signature Σ of constants includes the logical constants $\neg_{o\rightarrow o}$, $\vee_{o\rightarrow o\rightarrow o}$ and $\Pi_{(\alpha\rightarrow o)\rightarrow o}^\alpha$ for each type α; all other constants in Σ are called parameters. As in [5], we assume there is an infinite cardinal $\aleph_s$ such that the cardinality of Σ_α is $\aleph_s$ for each type α (cf. [5](3.16)). The set of $\mathcal{HOL}$-formulae (or terms) are constructed from typed variables and constants using application and λ-abstraction. We let $wf\!f_\alpha(\Sigma)$ be the set of all terms of type α and $wf\!f(\Sigma)$ be the set of all terms.

We use vector notation to abbreviate k-fold applications and abstractions as $\mathbf{A}\overline{\mathbf{U}^k}$ and $\lambda\overline{X^k}.\mathbf{A}$, respectively. We also use Church's dot notation so that . stands for a (missing) left bracket whose mate is as far to the right as possible (consistent with given brackets). We use infix notation $\mathbf{A} \vee \mathbf{B}$ for $((\vee\mathbf{A})\mathbf{B})$ and binder notation $\forall X_\alpha.\mathbf{A}$ for $(\Pi^\alpha(\lambda X_\alpha.\mathbf{A}_o))$. We further use $\mathbf{A} \wedge \mathbf{B}$, $\mathbf{A} \Rightarrow \mathbf{B}$, $\mathbf{A} \Leftrightarrow \mathbf{B}$ and $\exists X_\alpha.\mathbf{A}$ as shorthand for formulae defined in terms of $\neg$, $\vee$ and Π^α (cf. [5]). Finally, we let $(\mathbf{A}_\alpha \doteq^\alpha \mathbf{B}_\alpha)$ denote the Leibniz equation $\forall P_{\alpha\to o}.(P\mathbf{A}) \Rightarrow .P\mathbf{B}$.

Each occurrence of a variable in a term is either bound by a λ or free. We use $free(\mathbf{A})$ to denote the set of free variables of $\mathbf{A}$ (i.e., variables with a free occurrence in $\mathbf{A}$). We consider two terms to be equal if the terms are the same up to the names of bound variables (i.e., we consider α-conversion implicitly). A term $\mathbf{A}$ is closed if $free(\mathbf{A})$ is empty. We let $cwff_\alpha(\Sigma)$ denote the set of closed terms of type α and $cwff(\Sigma)$ denote the set of all closed terms. Each term $\mathbf{A} \in wff_o(\Sigma)$ is called a proposition and each term $\mathbf{A} \in cwff_o(\Sigma)$ is called a sentence.

We denote substitution of a term $\mathbf{A}_\alpha$ for a variable X_α in a term $\mathbf{B}_\beta$ by $[\mathbf{A}/X]\mathbf{B}$. Since we consider α-conversion implicitly, we assume the bound variables of $\mathbf{B}$ avoid variable capture.

Two common relations on terms are given by β-reduction and η-reduction. A β-redex $(\lambda X.\mathbf{A})\mathbf{B}$ β-reduces to $[\mathbf{B}/X]\mathbf{A}$. An η-redex $(\lambda X.\mathbf{C}X)$ (where $X \notin free(\mathbf{C})$) η-reduces to $\mathbf{C}$. For $\mathbf{A}, \mathbf{B} \in wff_\alpha(\Sigma)$, we write $\mathbf{A}\equiv_\beta\mathbf{B}$ to mean $\mathbf{A}$ can be converted to $\mathbf{B}$ by a series of β-reductions and expansions. Similarly, $\mathbf{A}\equiv_{\beta\eta}\mathbf{B}$ means $\mathbf{A}$ can be converted to $\mathbf{B}$ using both β and η. For each $\mathbf{A} \in wff(\Sigma)$ there is a unique β-normal form (denoted $\mathbf{A}{\downarrow}_\beta$) and a unique $\beta\eta$-normal form (denoted $\mathbf{A}{\downarrow}_{\beta\eta}$). From this fact we know $\mathbf{A}\equiv_\beta\mathbf{B}$ ($\mathbf{A}\equiv_{\beta\eta}\mathbf{B}$) iff $\mathbf{A}{\downarrow}_\beta \equiv \mathbf{B}{\downarrow}_\beta$ ($\mathbf{A}{\downarrow}_{\beta\eta} \equiv \mathbf{B}{\downarrow}_{\beta\eta}$).

A non-atomic formula in $wff_o(\Sigma)$ is any formula whose β-normal form is of the form $[c\overline{\mathbf{A}^n}]$ where c is a logical constant. An atomic formula is any other formula in $wff_o(\Sigma)$.

Semantics: Eight Model Classes. For each $* \in \{\beta, \beta\eta, \beta\xi, \beta f, \beta b, \beta\eta b, \beta\xi b, \beta f b\}$ (the latter set will be abbreviated by ⊕ in the remainder) we define $\mathfrak{M}_*$ to be the class of all Σ-models $\mathcal{M}$ such that $\mathcal{M}$ satisfies property $\mathfrak{q}$ and each of the additional properties $\{\eta, \xi, f, b\}$ indicated in the subscript $*$ (cf. [5](3.49)). Special cases of Σ-models are Henkin models and standard models (cf. [5](3.50 and 3.51)). Every model in $\mathfrak{M}_{\beta f b}$ is isomorphic to a Henkin model (see the discussion following [5](3.68)).

Saturated Abstract Consistency Classes and Model Existence. Finally, we review the model existence theorems proved in [5]. There are three stages to obtaining a model in our framework. First, we obtain an abstract consistency class Γ_Σ (usually defined as the class of irrefutable sets of sentences with respect to some calculus). Second, given a (sufficiently pure) set of sentences Φ in the abstract consistency class Γ_Σ we construct a Hintikka set $\mathcal{H}$ extending Φ. Third, we construct a model of this Hintikka set (and hence a model of Φ).

A Σ-abstract consistency class Γ_Σ is a class of sets of Σ-sentences. An abstract consistency class is always required to be closed under subsets (cf. [5](6.1)). Sometimes we require the stronger property that Γ_Σ is compact, i.e., a set Φ is in Γ_Σ iff every finite subset of Φ is in Γ_Σ (cf. [5](6.1,6.2)).

To describe further properties of abstract consistency classes, we use the notation $S * a$ for $S \cup \{a\}$ as in [5]. The following is a list of properties a class Γ_Σ of sets of sentences can satisfy with respect to arbitrary $\Phi \in \Gamma_\Sigma$ (cf. [5](6.5)):

∇_c If **A** is atomic, then **A** $\notin \Phi$ or $\neg$**A** $\notin \Phi$.

$\nabla_\neg$ If $\neg\neg$**A** $\in \Phi$, then $\Phi * $**A** $\in \Gamma_\Sigma$.

∇_β If **A**$\equiv_\beta$**B** and **A** $\in \Phi$, then $\Phi * $**B** $\in \Gamma_\Sigma$.

∇_η If **A**$\equiv_{\beta\eta}$**B** and **A** $\in \Phi$, then $\Phi * $**B** $\in \Gamma_\Sigma$.

$\nabla_\vee$ If **A** $\vee$ **B** $\in \Phi$, then $\Phi * $**A** $\in \Gamma_\Sigma$ or $\Phi * $**B** $\in \Gamma_\Sigma$.

$\nabla_\wedge$ If $\neg($**A** $\vee$ **B**$) \in \Phi$, then $\Phi * \neg$**A** $* \neg$**B** $\in \Gamma_\Sigma$.

$\nabla_\forall$ If Π^α**F** $\in \Phi$, then $\Phi * $**FW** $\in \Gamma_\Sigma$ for each **W** $\in cwff_\alpha(\Sigma)$.

$\nabla_\exists$ If $\neg\Pi^\alpha$**F** $\in \Phi$, then $\Phi * \neg($**F**$w) \in \Gamma_\Sigma$ for any parameter $w_\alpha \in \Sigma_\alpha$ which does not occur in any sentence of Φ.

∇_b If $\neg($**A** $\doteq^o$ **B**$) \in \Phi$, then $\Phi * $**A** $* \neg$**B** $\in \Gamma_\Sigma$ or $\Phi * \neg$**A** $* $**B** $\in \Gamma_\Sigma$.

∇_ξ If $\neg(\lambda X_\alpha.$**M** $\doteq^{\alpha\to\beta} \lambda X_\alpha.$**N**$) \in \Phi$, then $\Phi * \neg([w/X]$**M** $\doteq^\beta [w/X]$**N**$) \in \Gamma_\Sigma$ for any parameter $w_\alpha \in \Sigma_\alpha$ which does not occur in any sentence of Φ.

∇_f If $\neg($**G** $\doteq^{\alpha\to\beta}$ **H**$) \in \Phi$, then $\Phi * \neg($**G**$w \doteq^\beta$ **H**$w) \in \Gamma_\Sigma$ for any parameter $w_\alpha \in \Sigma_\alpha$ which does not occur in any sentence of Φ.

∇_{sat} Either $\Phi * $**A** $\in \Gamma_\Sigma$ or $\Phi * \neg$**A** $\in \Gamma_\Sigma$.

We say Γ_Σ is an abstract consistency class if it is closed under subsets and satisfies $\nabla_c, \nabla_\neg, \nabla_\beta, \nabla_\vee, \nabla_\wedge, \nabla_\forall$ and $\nabla_\exists$. We let $\mathfrak{Acc}_\beta$ denote the collection of all abstract consistency classes. For each $* \in \boxtimes$ we refine $\mathfrak{Acc}_\beta$ to a collection $\mathfrak{Acc}_*$ where the additional properties $\{\nabla_\eta, \nabla_\xi, \nabla_f, \nabla_b\}$ indicated by $*$ are required (cf. [5](6.7)). We say an abstract consistency class Γ_Σ is saturated if ∇_{sat} holds.

Using ∇_c (atomic consistency) and the fact that there are infinitely many parameters at each type, we can show every abstract consistency class satisfies non-atomic consistency. That is, for every abstract consistency class Γ_Σ, **A** $\in cwff_o(\Sigma)$ and $\Phi \in \Gamma_\Sigma$, we have either **A** $\notin \Phi$ or $\neg$**A** $\notin \Phi$ (cf. [5](6.10)).

In [5](6.32) we show that sufficiently Σ-pure sets in saturated abstract consistency classes extend to saturated Hintikka sets. (A set of sentences Φ is sufficiently Σ-pure if for each type α there is a set $\mathcal{P}_\alpha$ of parameters of type α with cardinality $\aleph_s$ and such that no parameter in $\mathcal{P}$ occurs in a sentence in Φ.)

In the Model Existence Theorem for Saturated Sets [5](6.33) we show that these saturated Hintikka sets can be used to construct models $\mathcal{M}$ which are members of the corresponding model classes $\mathfrak{M}_*$. Then we conclude (cf. [5](6.34)):

Model Existence Theorem for Saturated Abstract Consistency Classes: *For all* $* \in \boxtimes$, *if* Γ_Σ *is a saturated abstract consistency class in* $\mathfrak{Acc}_*$ *and* $\Phi \in \Gamma_\Sigma$ *is a sufficiently* Σ*-pure set of sentences, then there exists a model* $\mathcal{M} \in \mathfrak{M}_*$ *that satisfies* Φ. *Furthermore, each domain of* $\mathcal{M}$ *has cardinality at most* $\aleph_s$.

In [5] we apply the abstract consistency method to analyze completeness for different natural deduction calculi. Unfortunately, the saturation condition is very difficult to prove for machine-oriented calculi (indeed as we will see in Section 3 it is equivalent to cut elimination), so Theorem [5](6.34) cannot be easily used for this purpose directly.

In Section 6 we therefore motivate and present a set of extra conditions for $\mathfrak{Acc}_{\beta f b}$ we call **acceptability** conditions. The new conditions are sufficient to prove model existence.

Basic Rules
$$\frac{\mathbf{A} \text{ atomic (and } \beta\text{-normal)}}{\Delta * \mathbf{A} * \neg \mathbf{A}} \mathcal{G}(\mathit{init}) \qquad \frac{\Delta * \mathbf{A}}{\Delta * \neg\neg \mathbf{A}} \mathcal{G}(\neg)$$

$$\frac{\Delta * \neg \mathbf{A} \quad \Delta * \neg \mathbf{B}}{\Delta * \neg(\mathbf{A} \vee \mathbf{B})} \mathcal{G}(\vee_-) \qquad \frac{\Delta * \mathbf{A} * \mathbf{B}}{\Delta * (\mathbf{A} \vee \mathbf{B})} \mathcal{G}(\vee_+)$$

$$\frac{\Delta * \neg (\mathbf{AC}){\downarrow}_\beta \quad \mathbf{C} \in \mathit{cwff}_\alpha(\Sigma)}{\Delta * \neg \Pi^\alpha \mathbf{A}} \mathcal{G}(\Pi^{\mathcal{C}}_-) \qquad \frac{\Delta * (\mathbf{Ac}){\downarrow}_\beta \quad c_\alpha \in \Sigma \text{ new}}{\Delta * \Pi^\alpha \mathbf{A}} \mathcal{G}(\Pi^c_+)$$

Inversion Rule
$$\frac{\Delta * \neg\neg \mathbf{A}}{\Delta * \mathbf{A}} \mathcal{G}(\mathit{Inv}^\neg)$$

Weakening and Cut Rules
$$\frac{\Delta}{\Delta \cup \Delta'} \mathcal{G}(\mathit{weak}) \qquad \frac{\Delta * \mathbf{C} \quad \Delta * \neg \mathbf{C}}{\Delta} \mathcal{G}(\mathit{cut})$$

Fig. 1. Sequent Calculus Rules

3   Sequent Calculi, Cut and Saturation

We will now study cut-elimination and cut-simulation with respect to (one-sided) sequent calculi.

Sequent Calculi $\mathcal{G}$. We consider a sequent to be a finite set Δ of β-normal sentences from $\mathit{cwff}_o(\Sigma)$. A sequent calculus $\mathcal{G}$ provides an inductive definition for when $\Vdash_\mathcal{G} \Delta$ holds. We say a sequent calculus rule

$$\frac{\Delta_1 \quad \cdots \quad \Delta_n}{\Delta} r$$

is **admissible** in $\mathcal{G}$ if $\Vdash_\mathcal{G} \Delta$ holds whenever $\Vdash_\mathcal{G} \Delta_i$ for all $1 \leq i \leq n$. For any natural number $k \geq 0$, we call an admissible rule r k-**admissible** if any instance of r can be replaced by a derivation with at most k additional proof steps. Given a sequent Δ, a model $\mathcal{M}$, and a class $\mathfrak{M}$ of models, we say Δ is *valid for $\mathcal{M}$* (or *valid for $\mathfrak{M}$*), if $\mathcal{M} \models \mathbf{D}$ for some $\mathbf{D} \in \Delta$ (or Δ is valid for every $\mathcal{M} \in \mathfrak{M}$). As for sets in abstract consistency classes, we use the notation $\Delta * \mathbf{A}$ to denote the set $\Delta \cup \{\mathbf{A}\}$ (which is simply Δ if $\mathbf{A} \in \Delta$). Figure 1 introduces several sequent calculus rules. Some of these rules will be used to define sequent calculi, while others will be shown admissible (or even k-admissible).

Abstract Consistency Classes for Sequent Calculi. For any sequent calculus $\mathcal{G}$ we can define a class $\Gamma^\mathcal{G}_\Sigma$ of sets of sentences. Under certain assumptions, $\Gamma^\mathcal{G}_\Sigma$ is an abstract consistency class. First we adopt the notation $\neg\Phi$ and $\Phi{\downarrow}_\beta$ for the sets $\{\neg\mathbf{A}|\mathbf{A} \in \Phi\}$ and $\{\mathbf{A}{\downarrow}_\beta |\mathbf{A} \in \Phi\}$, resp., where $\Phi \subseteq \mathit{cwff}_o(\Sigma)$. Furthermore, we assume this use of $\neg$ binds more strongly than $\cup$ or $*$, so that $\neg\Phi \cup \Delta$ means $(\neg\Phi) \cup \Delta$ and $\neg\Phi * \mathbf{A}$ means $(\neg\Phi) * \mathbf{A}$.

Definition 1. *Let $\mathcal{G}$ be a sequent calculus. We define $\Gamma_\Sigma^{\mathcal{G}}$ to be the class of all finite $\Phi \subset cwff_o(\Sigma)$ such that $\Vdash_{\mathcal{G}} \neg \Phi\!\downarrow_\beta$ does not hold.*

In a straightforward manner, one can prove the following results (see [7]).

Lemma 2. *Let $\mathcal{G}$ be a sequent calculus such that $\mathcal{G}(Inv^\neg)$ is admissible. For any finite sets Φ and Δ of sentences, if $\Phi \cup \neg\Delta \notin \Gamma_\Sigma^{\mathcal{G}}$, then $\Vdash_{\mathcal{G}} \neg \Phi\!\downarrow_\beta \cup \Delta\!\downarrow_\beta$ holds.*

Theorem 3. *Let $\mathcal{G}$ be a sequent calculus. If the rules $\mathcal{G}(Inv^\neg)$, $\mathcal{G}(\neg)$, $\mathcal{G}(weak)$, $\mathcal{G}(init)$, $\mathcal{G}(\vee_-)$, $\mathcal{G}(\vee_+)$, $\mathcal{G}(\Pi_-^C)$ and $\mathcal{G}(\Pi_+^c)$ are admissible in $\mathcal{G}$, then $\Gamma_\Sigma^{\mathcal{G}} \in \mathfrak{Acc}_\beta$.*

We can furthermore show the following relationship between saturation and cut (see [7]).

Theorem 4. *Let $\mathcal{G}$ be a sequent calculus.*

1. *If $\mathcal{G}(cut)$ is admissible in $\mathcal{G}$, then $\Gamma_\Sigma^{\mathcal{G}}$ is saturated.*
2. *If $\mathcal{G}(\neg)$ and $\mathcal{G}(Inv^\neg)$ are admissible in $\mathcal{G}$ and $\Gamma_\Sigma^{\mathcal{G}}$ is saturated, then $\mathcal{G}(cut)$ is admissible in $\mathcal{G}$.*

Since saturation is equivalent to admissibility of cut, we need weaker conditions than saturation. A natural condition to consider is the existence of saturated extensions.

Definition 5 (Saturated Extension). *Let $* \in \boxed{\boldsymbol{\beta}}$ and $\Gamma_\Sigma, \Gamma_\Sigma' \in \mathfrak{Acc}_*$ be abstract consistency classes. We say Γ_Σ' is an **extension** of Γ_Σ if $\Phi \in \Gamma_\Sigma'$ for every sufficiently Σ-pure $\Phi \in \Gamma_\Sigma$. We say Γ_Σ' is a **saturated extension** of Γ_Σ if Γ_Σ' is saturated and an extension of Γ_Σ.*

There exist abstract consistency classes Γ in $\mathfrak{Acc}_{\beta\mathfrak{fb}}$ which have no saturated extension.

Example 6. *Let $a_o, b_o, q_{o \to o} \in \Sigma$ and $\Phi := \{a, b, (qa), \neg(qb)\}$. We construct an abstract consistency class Γ_Σ from Φ by first building the closure Φ' of Φ under relation $\equiv_\beta$ and then taking the power set of Φ'. It is easy to check that this Γ_Σ is in $\mathfrak{Acc}_{\beta\mathfrak{fb}}$. Suppose we have a saturated extension Γ_Σ' of Γ_Σ in $\mathfrak{Acc}_{\beta\mathfrak{fb}}$. Then $\Phi \in \Gamma_\Sigma'$ since Φ is finite (hence sufficiently pure). By saturation, $\Phi * (a \doteq^o b) \in \Gamma_\Sigma'$ or $\Phi * \neg(a \doteq^o b) \in \Gamma_\Sigma'$. In the first case, applying $\nabla_\forall$ with the constant q, $\nabla_\vee$ and ∇_c contradicts $(qa), \neg(qb) \in \Phi$. In the second case, ∇_b and ∇_c contradict $a, b \in \Phi$.*

Existence of any saturated extension of a sound sequent calculus $\mathcal{G}$ implies admissibility of cut. The proof uses the model existence theorem for saturated abstract consistency classes (cf. [5](6.34)). The full proof is in [7].

Theorem 7. *Let $\mathcal{G}$ be a sequent calculus which is sound for $\mathfrak{M}_*$. If $\Gamma_\Sigma^{\mathcal{G}}$ has a saturated extension $\Gamma_\Sigma' \in \mathfrak{Acc}_*$, then $\mathcal{G}(cut)$ is admissible in $\mathcal{G}$.*

Sequent Calculus $\mathcal{G}_\beta$. We now study a particular sequent calculus $\mathcal{G}_\beta$ defined by the rules $\mathcal{G}(init)$, $\mathcal{G}(\neg)$, $\mathcal{G}(\vee_-)$, $\mathcal{G}(\vee_+)$, $\mathcal{G}(\Pi_-^C)$ and $\mathcal{G}(\Pi_+^c)$ (cf. Figure 1). It is easy to show that $\mathcal{G}_\beta$ is sound for the eight model classes and in particular for class $\mathfrak{M}_\beta$.

The reader may easily prove the following Lemma.

Lemma 8. *Let* $\mathbf{A} \in cwff_o(\Sigma)$ *be an atom,* $\mathbf{B} \in cwff_\alpha(\Sigma)$*, and* Δ *be a sequent. In* $\mathcal{G}_\beta$

1. $\Delta * \mathbf{A} \Leftrightarrow \mathbf{A} := \Delta * \neg(\neg(\neg\mathbf{A} \vee \mathbf{A}) \vee \neg(\neg\mathbf{A} \vee \mathbf{A}))$ *is derivable in 7 steps and*
2. $\Delta * \mathbf{B} \doteq^\alpha \mathbf{B} := \Delta * \Pi^\alpha(\lambda P_{\alpha\to o}.\neg(P\mathbf{B}) \vee (P\mathbf{B})$ *is derivable in 3 steps.*

The proof of the next Lemma is by induction on derivations and is given in [7].

Lemma 9. *The rules* $\mathcal{G}(Inv^-)$ *and* $\mathcal{G}(weak)$ *are* 0*-admissible in* $\mathcal{G}_\beta$*.*

Theorem 10. *The sequent calculus* $\mathcal{G}_\beta$ *is complete for the model class* $\mathfrak{M}_\beta$ *and the rule* $\mathcal{G}(cut)$ *is admissible.*

Proof. By Theorem 3 and Lemma 9, $\Gamma_\Sigma^{\mathcal{G}_\beta} \in \mathfrak{Acc}_\beta$. Suppose $\nvdash_{\mathcal{G}_\beta} \Delta$ does not hold. Then $\neg\Delta \in \mathfrak{Acc}_\beta$ by Lemma 2. By the model existence theorem for $\mathfrak{Acc}_\beta$ (cf. [6](8.1)) there exists a model for $\neg\Delta$ in $\mathfrak{M}_\beta$. This gives completeness of $\mathcal{G}_\beta$. We can use completeness to conclude cut is admissible in $\mathcal{G}_\beta$. □

Andrews proves admissibility of cut for a sequent calculus similar to $\mathcal{G}_\beta$ in [1]. The proof in [1] contains the essential ingredients for showing completeness.

We will now show that $\mathcal{G}(cut)$ actually becomes k-admissible in $\mathcal{G}_\beta$ if certain formulae are available in the sequent Δ we wish to prove.

4   Cut-Simulation

Cut-Strong Formulae and Sequents. k-cut-strong formulae can be used to effectively simulate cut. Effectively means that the elimination of each application of a cut-rule introduces maximally k additional proof steps, where k is constant.

Definition 11. *Given a formula* $\mathbf{A} \in cwff_o(\Sigma)$*, and an arbitrary but fixed number* $k > 0$*. We call formula* $\mathbf{A}$ k**-cut-strong** *for* $\mathcal{G}$ *(or simply* **cut-strong***) if the cut rule variant*

$$\frac{\Delta * \mathbf{C} \quad \Delta * \neg\mathbf{C}}{\Delta * \neg\mathbf{A}} \; \mathcal{G}(cut^\mathbf{A})$$

is k*-admissible in* $\mathcal{G}$*.*

Our examples below illustrate that cut-strength of a formula usually only weakly depends on calculus $\mathcal{G}$: it only presumes standard ingredients such as β-normalization, weakening, and rules for the logical connectives.

We present some simple examples of cut-strong formulae for our sequent calculus $\mathcal{G}_\beta$. A corresponding phenomenon is observable in other higher-order calculi, for instance, for the calculi presented in [1,4,8,11].

Example 12. *Formula* $\forall P_o.P := \Pi^o(\lambda P_o.P)$ *is 3-cut-strong in* $\mathcal{G}_\beta$*. This is justified by the following derivation which actually shows that rule* $\mathcal{G}(cut^\mathbf{A})$ *for this specific choice of* $\mathbf{A}$ *is derivable in* $\mathcal{G}_\beta$ *by maximally 3 additional proof steps. The* *only interesting proof step is the instantiation of P with formula* $\mathbf{D} := \neg\mathbf{C}\vee\mathbf{C}$ *in rule* $\mathcal{G}(\Pi_-^{\mathbf{D}})$. *(Note that* $\mathbf{C}$ *must be* β-*normal; sequents such as* $\Delta * \mathbf{C}$ *by definition contain only* β-*normal formulae.)*

$$\cfrac{\cfrac{\Delta * \mathbf{C}}{\Delta * \neg\neg\mathbf{C}}\ \mathcal{G}(\neg) \qquad \Delta * \neg\mathbf{C}}{\cfrac{\Delta * \neg(\neg\mathbf{C}\vee\mathbf{C})}{\Delta * \neg\Pi^o(\lambda P_o.P)}\ \mathcal{G}(\Pi_-^{\mathbf{D}})}\ \mathcal{G}(\vee_-)$$

Clearly, $\forall P_o.P$ *is not a very interesting cut-strong formula since it implies false-hood, i.e. inconsistency.*

Example 13. *The formula* $\forall P_o.P \Rightarrow P := \Pi^o(\lambda P_o.\neg P \vee P)$ *is 3-cut-strong in* $\mathcal{G}_\beta$. *This is an example of a tautologous cut-strong formula. Now* P *is simply instantiated with* $\mathbf{D} := \mathbf{C}$ *in rule* $\mathcal{G}(\Pi_-^{\mathbf{D}})$. *Except for this first step the derivation is identical to the one for Example 12.*

Example 14. *Leibniz equations* $\mathbf{M} \doteq^\alpha \mathbf{N} := \Pi^\alpha(\lambda P.\neg P\mathbf{M} \vee P\mathbf{N})$ *(for arbitrary formulae* $\mathbf{M}, \mathbf{N} \in cwff_\alpha(\Sigma)$ *and types* $\alpha \in \mathcal{T}$ *) are 3-cut-strong in* $\mathcal{G}_\beta$. *This includes the special cases* $\mathbf{M} \doteq^\alpha \mathbf{M}$. *Now* P *is instantiated with* $\mathbf{D} := \lambda X_\alpha.\mathbf{C}$ *in rule* $\mathcal{G}(\Pi_-^{\mathbf{D}})$. *Except for this first step the derivation is identical to the one for Example 12.*

Example 15. *The original formulation of higher-order logic (cf. [12]) contained comprehension axioms of the form* $\mathcal{C} := \exists P_{\alpha^1 \to \cdots \to \alpha^n \to o}\forall \overline{X^n}.P\overline{X^n} \Leftrightarrow \mathbf{B}_o.$ *where* $\mathbf{B}_o \in wff_o(\Sigma)$ *is arbitrary with* $P \notin free(\mathbf{B})$. *Church eliminated the need for such axioms by formulating higher-order logic using typed* λ-*calculus. We will now show that the instance* $\mathcal{C}^I := \exists P_{\iota \to o}.\forall X_\iota.PX \Leftrightarrow X \doteq^\iota X$ *is 16-cut-strong in* $\mathcal{G}_\beta$ *(note that* $\mathcal{G}(weak)$ *is 0-admissible). This motivates building-in comprehension principles instead of treating comprehension axiomatically.*

$$\cfrac{\cfrac{\cfrac{\cfrac{\cfrac{\cfrac{\cfrac{\begin{array}{c}3\ steps;\ see\ Lemma\ 8\\ \vdots\\ \Delta * \neg(pa \Rightarrow a \doteq^\iota a) * a \doteq^\iota a\end{array}}{\Delta * \neg(pa \Rightarrow a \doteq^\iota a) * \neg\neg(a \doteq^\iota a)}\ \mathcal{G}(\neg) \qquad \mathcal{D}}{\Delta * \neg(pa \Rightarrow a \doteq^\iota a) * \neg(\neg(a \doteq^\iota a) \vee pa)}\ \mathcal{G}(\vee_-)}{\Delta * \neg(pa \Rightarrow a \doteq^\iota a) \vee \neg(a \doteq^\iota a \Rightarrow pa)}\ \mathcal{G}(\vee_+)}{\Delta * \neg\neg(\neg(pa \Rightarrow a \doteq^\iota a) \vee \neg(a \doteq^\iota a \Rightarrow pa))}\ \mathcal{G}(\neg)}{\Delta * \neg\Pi^\iota(\lambda X_\iota.pX \Leftrightarrow X \doteq^\iota X)}\ \mathcal{G}(\Pi_-^{a_\iota})}{\Delta * \Pi^{\iota \to o}(\lambda P^{\iota \to o}.\neg\Pi^\iota(\lambda X_\iota.pX \Leftrightarrow X \doteq^\iota X))}\ \mathcal{G}(\Pi_+^{p_{\iota \to o}})}{\Delta * \mathcal{C}^I}\ \mathcal{G}(\neg)$$

Derivation $\mathcal{D}$ *is:*

$$\cfrac{\cfrac{\overline{\Delta * pa * \neg pa}\ \mathcal{G}(init)}{\Delta * \neg\neg pa * \neg pa}\ \mathcal{G}(\neg) \qquad \cfrac{\begin{array}{c}\Delta * \mathbf{C}\quad \Delta * \neg\mathbf{C}\\ \vdots\ 3\ steps;\ see\ Example\ 14\\ \Delta * \neg(a \doteq^o a)\end{array}}{\Delta * \neg(a \doteq^\iota a) * \neg pa}\ \mathcal{G}(weak)}{\Delta * \neg(\neg pa \vee a \doteq^\iota a) * \neg pa}\ \mathcal{G}(\vee_-)$$

As we will show later, many prominent axioms for higher-order logic also belong to the class of cut-strong formulae.

Next we define cut-strong sequents.

Definition 16. *A sequent Δ is called k-cut-strong (or simply **cut-strong**) if there exists a a k-cut-strong formula $\mathbf{A} \in cwff_o(\Sigma)$ such that $\neg\mathbf{A} \in \Delta$.*

Cut-Simulation. The cut-simulation theorem is a main result of this paper. It says that cut-strong sequents support an effective simulation (and thus elimination) of cut in $\mathcal{G}_\beta$. Effective means that the size of cut-free derivation grows only linearly for the number of cut rule applications to be eliminated.

We first fix the following calculi: Calculus $\mathcal{G}_\beta^{cut}$ extends $\mathcal{G}_\beta$ by the rule $\mathcal{G}(cut)$ and calculus $\mathcal{G}_\beta^{cut^{\mathbf{A}}}$ extends $\mathcal{G}_\beta$ by the rule $\mathcal{G}(cut^{\mathbf{A}})$ for some arbitrary but fixed cut-strong formula $\mathbf{A}$.

Theorem 17. *Let Δ be a k-cut-strong sequent such that $\neg\mathbf{A} \in \Delta$ for some k-cut-strong formula $\mathbf{A}$. For each derivation $\mathcal{D}$: $\vdash_{\mathcal{G}_\beta^{cut}} \Delta$ with d proof steps there exists an alternative derivation $\mathcal{D}'$: $\vdash_{\mathcal{G}_\beta^{cut^{\mathbf{A}}}} \Delta$ with d proof steps.*

Proof. Note that the rules $\mathcal{G}(cut)$ and $\mathcal{G}(cut^{\mathbf{A}})$ coincide whenever $\neg\mathbf{A} \in \Delta$. Intuitively, we can replace each occurrence of $\mathcal{G}(cut)$ in $\mathcal{D}$ by $\mathcal{G}(cut^{\mathbf{A}})$ in order to obtain a $\mathcal{D}'$ of same size. Technically, in the induction proof one must weaken to ensure $\neg\mathbf{A}$ stays in the sequent and carry out a parameter renaming to make sure the eigenvariable condition is satisfied. □

Theorem 18. *Let Δ be a k-cut-strong sequent such that $\neg\mathbf{A} \in \Delta$ for some k-cut-strong formula $\mathbf{A}$. For each derivation $\mathcal{D}$: $\vdash_{\mathcal{G}_\beta^{cut^{\mathbf{A}}}} \Delta$ with d proof steps and with n applications of rule $\mathcal{G}(cut)$ there exists an alternative derivation $\mathcal{D}'$: $\vdash_{\mathcal{G}_\beta} \Delta$ with maximally $d + nk$ proof steps.*

Proof. $\mathbf{A}$ is k-cut-strong so by definition $\mathcal{G}(cut^{\mathbf{A}})$ is k-admissible in $\mathcal{G}_\beta$. This means that $\mathcal{G}(cut^{\mathbf{A}})$ can be eliminated in $\mathcal{D}$ and each single elimination of $\mathcal{G}(cut^{\mathbf{A}})$ introduces maximally k new proof steps. Now the assertion can be easily obtained by a simple induction over n. □

Corollary 19. *Let Δ be a k-cut-strong sequent. For each derivation $\mathcal{D}$: $\vdash_{\mathcal{G}_\beta^{cut}} \Delta$ with d proof steps and n applications of rule $\mathcal{G}(cut)$ there exists an alternative cut-free derivation $\mathcal{D}'$: $\vdash_{\mathcal{G}_\beta} \Delta$ with maximally $d + nk$ proof steps.*

5   The Extensionality Axioms Are Cut-Strong

We have shown comprehension axioms can be cut-strong (cf. Example 15). Further prominent examples of cut-strong formulae are the Boolean and functional extensionality axioms. The Boolean extensionality axiom (abbreviated $\mathcal{B}_o$ in the remainder) is

$$\forall A_o.\forall B_o.(A \Leftrightarrow B) \Rightarrow A \doteq^o B$$

The infinitely many functional extensionality axioms (abbreviated $\mathcal{F}_{\alpha\beta}$) are parameterized over $\alpha, \beta \in \mathcal{T}$.

$$\forall F_{\alpha \to \beta}.\forall G_{\alpha \to \beta}.(\forall X_\alpha.FX \doteq^\beta GX) \Rightarrow F \doteq^{\alpha \to \beta} G$$

These axioms usually have to be added to higher-order calculi to reach Henkin completeness, i.e. completeness with respect to model class $\mathfrak{M}_{\beta\mathfrak{fb}}$. For example, Huet's constrained resolution approach as presented in [11] is not Henkin complete without adding extensionality axioms. For instance, the need for adding Boolean extensionality is actually illustrated by the set of unit literals $\Phi := \{a, b, (qa), \neg(qb)\}$ from Example 6. As the reader may easily check, this clause set Φ, which is inconsistent for Henkin semantics, cannot be proven by Huet's system without, e.g, adding the Boolean extensionality axiom. By relying on results in [1], Huet essentially shows completeness with respect to model class $\mathfrak{M}_\beta$ as opposed to Henkin semantics.

We will now investigate whether adding the extensionality axioms to a machine-oriented calculus in order to obtain Henkin completeness is a suitable option.

Theorem 20. *The Boolean extensionality axiom $\mathcal{B}_o$ is a 14-cut-strong formula in $\mathcal{G}_\beta$.*

Proof. The following derivation justifies this theorem (a_o is a parameter).

$$
\frac{\dfrac{\begin{array}{c} \vdots \; \text{7 steps; see Lemma 8} \\ \Delta * a \Leftrightarrow a \end{array}}{\Delta * \neg\neg(a \Leftrightarrow a)}\; \mathcal{G}(\neg) \qquad \dfrac{\Delta * \mathbf{C} \quad \Delta * \neg\mathbf{C} \;\; \vdots \; \text{3 steps; see Example 14}}{\Delta * \neg(a \doteq^o a)}\; \mathcal{G}(\vee_-)}{\dfrac{\Delta * \neg(\neg(a \Leftrightarrow a) \vee a \doteq^o a)}{\Delta * \neg\mathcal{B}_o}\; 2 \times \mathcal{G}(\Pi_-^a)} \qquad \square
$$

Theorem 21. *The functional extensionality axioms $\mathcal{F}_{\alpha\beta}$ are 11-cut-strong formulae in $\mathcal{G}_\beta$.*

Proof. The following derivation justifies this theorem ($f_{\alpha \to \beta}$ is a parameter).

$$
\frac{\dfrac{\dfrac{\begin{array}{c} \vdots \; \text{3 steps; see Lemma 8} \\ \Delta * fa \doteq^\beta fa \end{array}}{\Delta * (\forall X_\alpha.fX \doteq^\beta fX)}\; \mathcal{G}(\Pi_+^{a_\alpha})}{\Delta * \neg\neg\forall X_\alpha.fX \doteq^\beta fX}\; \mathcal{G}(\neg) \qquad \dfrac{\Delta * \mathbf{C} \quad \Delta * \neg\mathbf{C} \;\; \vdots \; \text{3 steps; see Example 14}}{\Delta * \neg(f \doteq^{\alpha \to \beta} f)}\; \mathcal{G}(\vee_-)}{\dfrac{\Delta * \neg(\neg(\forall X_\alpha.fX \doteq^\beta fX) \vee f \doteq^{\alpha \to \beta} f)}{\Delta * \neg\mathcal{F}_{\alpha\beta}}\; 2 \times \mathcal{G}(\Pi_-^f)} \qquad \square
$$

In [4] and [8] we have already argued that the extensionality principles should not be treated axiomatically in machine-oriented higher-order calculi and there

$$\frac{\Delta * \neg \mathcal{F}_{\alpha\beta} \quad \alpha \to \beta \in \mathcal{T}}{\Delta} \, \mathcal{G}(\mathcal{F}_{\alpha\beta}) \qquad \frac{\Delta * \neg \mathcal{B}_o}{\Delta} \, \mathcal{G}(\mathcal{B})$$

Fig. 2. Axiomatic Extensionality Rules

we have developed resolution and sequent calculi in which these principles are built-in. Here we have now developed a strong theoretical justification for this work: Theorems 20, 21 and 19 tell us that adding the extensionality principles $\mathcal{B}_o$ and $\mathcal{F}_{\alpha\beta}$ as axioms to a calculus is like adding a cut rule.

In Figure 2 we show rules that add Boolean and functional extensionality in an axiomatic manner to $\mathcal{G}_\beta$. More precisely we add rules $\mathcal{G}(\mathcal{F}_{\alpha\beta})$ and $\mathcal{G}(\mathcal{B})$ allowing to introduce the axioms for any sequent Δ; this way we address the problem of the infinitely many possible instantiations of the type-schematic functional extensional axiom $\mathcal{F}_{\alpha\beta}$. Calculus $\mathcal{G}_\beta$ enriched by the new rules $\mathcal{G}(\mathcal{F}_{\alpha\beta})$ and $\mathcal{G}(\mathcal{B})$ is called $\mathcal{G}_\beta^E$. Soundness of the the new rules is easy to verify: In [5](4.3) we show that $\mathcal{G}(\mathcal{F}_{\alpha\beta})$ and $\mathcal{G}(\mathcal{B})$ are valid for Henkin models.

Replacing the Extensionality Axioms. In Figure 3 we define alternative extensionality rules which correspond to those developed for resolution and sequent calculi in [4] and [8]. Calculus $\mathcal{G}_\beta$ enriched by $\mathcal{G}(\mathfrak{f})$ and $\mathcal{G}(\mathfrak{b})$ is called $\mathcal{G}_{\beta\mathfrak{f}\mathfrak{b}}^-$. Soundness of $\mathcal{G}(\mathfrak{f})$ and $\mathcal{G}(\mathfrak{b})$ for Henkin semantics is again easy to show.

Our aim is to develop a machine-oriented sequent calculus for automating Henkin complete proof search. We argue that for this purpose $\mathcal{G}(\mathfrak{f})$ and $\mathcal{G}(\mathfrak{b})$ are more suitable rules than $\mathcal{G}(\mathcal{F}_{\alpha\beta})$ and $\mathcal{G}(\mathcal{B})$.

Our next step now is to show Henkin completeness for $\mathcal{G}_\beta^E$. This will be relatively easy since we can employ cut-simulation. Then we analyze whether calculus $\mathcal{G}_{\beta\mathfrak{f}\mathfrak{b}}^-$ has the same deductive power as $\mathcal{G}_\beta^E$.

First we extend Theorem 3. The proof is given in [7].

Theorem 22. *Let $\mathcal{G}$ be a sequent calculus such that $\mathcal{G}(Inv^\neg)$ and $\mathcal{G}(\neg)$ are admissible.*

1. *If $\mathcal{G}(\mathfrak{f})$ and $\mathcal{G}(\Pi_+^c)$ are admissible, then $\Gamma_\Sigma^\mathcal{G}$ satisfies $\nabla_\mathfrak{f}$.*
2. *If $\mathcal{G}(\mathfrak{b})$ is admissible, then $\Gamma_\Sigma^\mathcal{G}$ satisfies $\nabla_\mathfrak{b}$.*

Theorem 23. *The sequent calculus $\mathcal{G}_\beta^E$ is Henkin complete and the rule $\mathcal{G}(cut)$ is 12-admissible.*

Proof. $\mathcal{G}(cut)$ can be effectively simulated and hence eliminated in $\mathcal{G}_\beta^E$ by combining rule $\mathcal{G}(\mathcal{F}_{\alpha\beta})$ with the 11-step derivation presented in the proof of Theorem 21.

Let $\Gamma_\Sigma^{\mathcal{G}_\beta^E}$ be defined as in Definition 1. We prove Henkin completeness of $\mathcal{G}_\beta^E$ by showing that the class $\Gamma_\Sigma^{\mathcal{G}_\beta^E}$ is a saturated abstract consistency class in $\mathfrak{Acc}_{\beta\mathfrak{f}\mathfrak{b}}$. We here only analyze the crucial conditions $\nabla_\mathfrak{b}$, $\nabla_\mathfrak{f}$ and ∇_{sat}. For the other conditions we refer to Theorem 3. Note that 0-admissibility of $\mathcal{G}(Inv^\neg)$ and $\mathcal{G}(weak)$ can be shown for $\mathcal{G}_\beta^E$ by a suitable induction on derivations as in Lemma 9.

$$\frac{\Delta * (\forall X_\alpha.AX \doteq^\beta BX)\big\downarrow_\beta}{\Delta * (A \doteq^{\alpha\to\beta} B)}\; \mathcal{G}(\mathfrak{f}) \qquad\qquad \frac{\Delta * \neg A * B \quad \Delta * \neg B * A}{\Delta * (A \doteq^o B)}\; \mathcal{G}(\mathfrak{b})$$

Fig. 3. Proper Extensionality Rules

$\nabla_{\mathfrak{f}}$ $\mathcal{G}(\Pi_+^c)$ is a rule of $\mathcal{G}_\beta^E$ and thus admissible. According to Theorem 22 it is thus sufficient to ensure admissibility of rule $\mathcal{G}(\mathfrak{f})$ to show $\nabla_{\mathfrak{f}}$. This is justified by the following derivation where $\mathbf{N} := \mathbf{A} \doteq^{\alpha\to\beta} \mathbf{B}$ and $\mathbf{M} := (\forall X_\alpha.\mathbf{A}X \doteq^\beta \mathbf{B}X)\big\downarrow_\beta$ (for β-normal $\mathbf{A}, \mathbf{B}$).

$$\cfrac{\cfrac{\cfrac{\cfrac{\cfrac{\cfrac{\Delta * (\forall X_\alpha.\mathbf{A}X \doteq^\beta \mathbf{B}X)\big\downarrow_\beta}{\Delta * \mathbf{N} * \mathbf{M}}\; \mathcal{G}(weak) \quad \begin{array}{c}\text{derivable}\\ \vdots\end{array}}{\Delta * \mathbf{N} * \neg\neg\mathbf{M}}\; \mathcal{G}(\neg) \qquad \cfrac{}{\Delta * \mathbf{N} * \neg\mathbf{N}}\; \mathcal{G}(\vee_-)}{\Delta * \mathbf{N} * \neg(\neg\mathbf{M} \vee \mathbf{N})}}{\Delta * \mathbf{N} * \neg\mathcal{F}_{\alpha\beta}}\; \mathcal{G}(\Pi_-^A), \mathcal{G}(\Pi_-^B)}{\Delta * \mathbf{A} \doteq^{\alpha\to\beta} \mathbf{B}}\; \mathcal{G}(\mathcal{F}_{\alpha\beta})}$$

$\nabla_{\mathfrak{b}}$ With a similar derivation using $\mathcal{G}(\mathcal{B})$ we can show that $\mathcal{G}(\mathfrak{b})$ is admissible. We conclude $\nabla_{\mathfrak{b}}$ by Theorem 22.

∇_{sat} Since $\mathcal{G}(cut)$ is admissible we get saturation by Theorem 4. □

Does $\mathcal{G}_{\beta\mathfrak{fb}}^-$ have the same deductive strength as $\mathcal{G}_\beta^E$? I.e., is $\mathcal{G}_{\beta\mathfrak{fb}}^-$ Henkin complete? We show this is not yet the case.

Theorem 24. *The sequent calculus $\mathcal{G}_{\beta\mathfrak{fb}}^-$ is not complete for Henkin semantics.*

We illustrate the problem by a counterexample.

Example 25. *Consider the sequent $\Delta := \{\neg a, \neg b, \neg(qa), (qb)\}$ where $a_o, b_o,$ $q_{o\to o} \in \Sigma$ are parameters. For any $\mathcal{M} \equiv (\mathcal{D}, @, \mathcal{E}, v) \in \mathfrak{M}_{\beta\mathfrak{fb}}$, either $v(\mathcal{E}(a)) \equiv F$, $v(\mathcal{E}(b)) \equiv F$ or $\mathcal{E}(a) \equiv \mathcal{E}(b)$ by property $\mathfrak{b}$. Hence sequent Δ is valid for every $\mathcal{M} \in \mathfrak{M}_{\beta\mathfrak{fb}}$. However, $\Vdash_{\mathcal{G}_{\beta\mathfrak{fb}}^-} \Delta$ does not hold. By inspection, Δ cannot be the conclusion of any rule.*

In order to reach Henkin completeness and to show cut-elimination we thus need to add further rules. Our example motivates the two rules presented in Figure 4. $\mathcal{G}(Init^{\doteq})$ introduces Leibniz equations such as $qa \doteq^o qb$ as is needed in our example and $\mathcal{G}(d)$ realizes the required decomposition into $a \doteq^o b$.

We thus extend sequent calculus $\mathcal{G}_{\beta\mathfrak{fb}}^-$ to $\mathcal{G}_{\beta\mathfrak{fb}}$ by adding the decomposition rule $\mathcal{G}(d)$ and the rule $\mathcal{G}(Init^{\doteq})$ which generally checks if two atomic sentences of opposite polarity are provably equal (as opposed to syntactically equal).

Is $\mathcal{G}_{\beta\mathfrak{fb}}$ complete for Henkin semantics? We will show in the next Section that this indeed holds (cf. Theorem 28).

With $\mathcal{G}^E$ and $\mathcal{G}_{\beta\mathfrak{fb}}$ we have thus developed two Henkin complete calculi and both calculi are cut-free. However, as our exploration shows "cut-freeness" is

$$\frac{\Delta * (\mathbf{A} \doteq^o \mathbf{B}) \quad (\dagger)}{\Delta * \neg \mathbf{A} * \mathbf{B}} \; \mathcal{G}(\mathit{Init}^{\doteq}) \qquad\qquad \frac{\Delta * (\mathbf{A}^1 \doteq^{\alpha_1} \mathbf{B}^1) \; \cdots \; \Delta * (\mathbf{A}^n \doteq^{\alpha_n} \mathbf{B}^n) \quad (\ddagger)}{\Delta * (h\overline{\mathbf{A}^n} \doteq^\beta h\overline{\mathbf{B}^n})} \; \mathcal{G}(d)$$

(†) $\mathbf{A},\mathbf{B}$ atomic $\qquad\qquad\qquad$ (‡) $n \geq 1, \beta \in \{o, \iota\}, h_{\overline{\alpha^n} \to \beta} \in \Sigma$ parameter

Fig. 4. Additional Rules $\mathcal{G}(\mathit{Init}^{\doteq})$ and $\mathcal{G}(d)$

not a well-chosen criterion to differentiate between their suitability for proof search automation: $\mathcal{G}^E$ inherently supports effective cut-simulation and thus cut-freeness is meaningless.

The criterion we propose for the analysis of calculi in impredicative logics is "freeness of effective cut-simulation".

Other Rules for Other Model Classes. In [6] we developed respective complete and cut-free sequent calculi not only for Henkin semantics but for five of the eight model classes. In particular, no additional rules are required for the β, $\beta\eta$ and $\beta\xi$ case. Meanwhile, the $\beta\mathfrak{f}$ case requires additional rules allowing η-conversion. The limited space does not allow us to present and analyze these cases here.

6   Acceptability Conditions

We now turn our attention again to the existence of saturated extension of abstract consistency classes.

As illustrated by the Example 6, we need some extra abstract consistency properties to ensure the existence of saturated extensions. We call these extra properties **acceptability conditions**. They actually closely correspond to additional rules $\mathcal{G}(\mathit{Init}^{\doteq})$ and $\mathcal{G}(d)$.

Definition 26 (Acceptability Conditions). *Let Γ_Σ be an abstract consistency class in $\mathfrak{Acc}_{\beta\mathfrak{f}\mathfrak{b}}$. We define the following properties:*

∇_m *If $\mathbf{A}, \mathbf{B} \in \mathit{cwff}_o(\Sigma)$ are atomic and $\mathbf{A}, \neg\mathbf{B} \in \Phi$, then $\Phi * \neg(\mathbf{A} \doteq^o \mathbf{B}) \in \Gamma_\Sigma$.*

∇_d *If $\neg(h\overline{\mathbf{A}^n} \doteq^\beta h\overline{\mathbf{B}^n}) \in \Phi$ for some types α_i where $\beta \in \{o, \iota\}$ and $h_{\overline{\alpha^n} \to \beta} \in \Sigma$ is*

   a parameter, then there is an i ($1 \leq i \leq n$) such that $\Phi * \neg(\mathbf{A}^i \doteq^{\alpha^i} \mathbf{B}^i) \in \Gamma_\Sigma$.

We now replace the strong saturation condition used in [5] by these acceptability conditions.

Definition 27 (Acceptable Classes). *An abstract consistency class $\Gamma_\Sigma \in \mathfrak{Acc}_{\beta\mathfrak{f}\mathfrak{b}}$ is called **acceptable** in $\mathfrak{Acc}_{\beta\mathfrak{f}\mathfrak{b}}$ if it satisfies the conditions ∇_m and ∇_d.*

One can show a model existence theorem for acceptable abstract consistency classes in $\mathfrak{Acc}_{\beta\mathfrak{f}\mathfrak{b}}$ (cf. [6](8.1)). From this model existence theorem, one can conclude $\mathcal{G}_{\beta\mathfrak{f}\mathfrak{b}}$ is complete for $\mathfrak{M}_{\beta\mathfrak{f}\mathfrak{b}}$ (hence for Henkin models) and that cut is admissible in $\mathcal{G}_{\beta\mathfrak{f}\mathfrak{b}}$.

Theorem 28. *The sequent calculus $\mathcal{G}_{\beta\mathfrak{f}\mathfrak{b}}$ is complete for Henkin semantics and the rule $\mathcal{G}(\mathit{cut})$ is admissible.*

Proof: The argumentation is similar to Theorem 10 but here we employ the acceptability conditions ∇_m and ∇_d.   □

One can further show the **Saturated Extension Theorem** (cf. [6](9.3)):

Theorem 29. *There is a saturated abstract consistency class in $\mathfrak{Acc}_{\beta\mathfrak{fb}}$ that is an extension of all acceptable Γ_Σ in $\mathfrak{Acc}_{\beta\mathfrak{fb}}$.*

Given Theorem 7, one can view the Saturated Extension Theorem as an abstract cut-elimination result.

The proof of a model existence theorem employs Hintikka sets and in the context of studying Hintikka sets we have identified a phenomenon related to cut-strength which we call the **Impredicativity Gap**. That is, a Hintikka set $\mathcal{H}$ is saturated if any cut-strong formula $\mathbf{A}$ (e.g. a Leibniz equation $\mathbf{C} \doteq \mathbf{D}$) is in $\mathcal{H}$. Hence we can reasonably say there is a "gap" between saturated and unsaturated Hintikka sets. Every Hintikka set is either saturated or contains no cut-strong formulae.

7 Conclusion

We have shown that adding cut-strong formulae to a calculus for an impredicative logic is like adding cut. For machine-oriented automated theorem proving in impredicative logics — such as classical type theory — it is therefore not recommendable to naively add cut-strong axioms to the search space. In addition to the comprehension principle and the functional and Boolean extensionality axioms as elaborated in this paper the list of cut-strong axioms includes:

Other Forms of Defined Equality. Formulas $\mathbf{A} \doteq^\alpha \mathbf{B}$ are 4-cut-strong in $\mathcal{G}_\beta$ where $\doteq^\alpha$ is $\lambda X_\alpha.\lambda Y_\alpha.\forall Q_{\alpha\to\alpha\to o}.(\forall Z_\alpha.(Q\ Z\ Z)) \Rightarrow (Q\ X\ Y)$ (cf. [3]).
    Proof. Instantiate Q with $\lambda X_\alpha.\lambda Y_\alpha.\mathbf{C}$.   □

Axiom of Induction. The axiom of induction for the naturals $\forall P_{\iota\to o}.P0 \wedge (\forall X_\iota.PX \Rightarrow P(sX)) \Rightarrow \forall X_\iota.PX$ is 18-cut-strong in $\mathcal{G}_\beta$. (Other well-founded ordering axioms are analogous.)
    Proof. Instantiate P with $\lambda X_\iota.a \doteq^o a$ for some parameter a_o.   □

Axiom of Choice. $\exists I_{(\alpha\to o)\to o}.\forall Q_{\alpha\to o}.\exists X_\alpha.QX \Rightarrow Q(IQ)$ is 7-cut-strong in $\mathcal{G}_\beta$.
    Proof. Instantiate Q with $\lambda X_\alpha.\mathbf{C}$.   □

Axiom of Description. The description axiom $\exists I_{(\alpha\to o)\to o}.\forall Q_{\alpha\to o}.(\exists_1 Y_\alpha.QY) \Rightarrow Q(IQ)$ (see [2]), where $\exists_1 Y_\alpha.QY$ stands for $\exists Y_\alpha.QY \wedge (\forall Z_\alpha.QZ \Rightarrow Y \doteq Z)$ is 25-cut-strong in $\mathcal{G}_\beta$.
    Proof. Instantiate Q with $\lambda X_\alpha.a \doteq^\alpha X$ for some parameter a_α.   □

As Example 15 shows, comprehension axioms can be cut-strong. Church's formulation of type theory (cf. [9]) used typed λ-calculus to build comprehension principles into the language. One can view Church's formulation as a first step in the program to eliminate the need for cut-strong axioms. For the extensionality axioms a start has been made by the sequent calculi in this paper (and [6]), for resolution in [4] and for sequent calculi and extensional expansion proofs in [8]. The extensional systems in [8] also provide a complete method for using primitive equality instead of Leibniz equality. For improving the automation of higher-order logic our exploration thus motivates the development of higher-order calculi which directly include reasoning principles for equality, extensionality, induction, choice, description, etc., without using cut-strong axioms.

References

1. P. B. Andrews. Resolution in type theory. *Journal of Symbolic Logic*, 36(3):414–432, 1971.
2. P. B. Andrews. General models and extensionality. *Journal of Symbolic Logic*, 37(2):395–397, 1972.
3. P. B. Andrews. *An Introduction to Mathematical Logic and Type Theory: To Truth Through Proof*. Kluwer Academic Publishers, second edition, 2002.
4. C. E. Benzmüller. *Equality and Extensionality in Automated Higher-Order Theorem Proving*. PhD thesis, Saarland University, 1999.
5. C. E. Benzmüller, C. E. Brown, and M. Kohlhase. Higher-order semantics and extensionality. *Journal of Symbolic Logic*, 69(4):1027–1088, 2004.
6. C. E. Benzmüller, C. E. Brown, and M. Kohlhase. Semantic techniques for higher-order cut-elimination. Seki Report SR-2004-07, Saarland University, 2004.
7. C. E. Benzmüller, C. E. Brown, and M. Kohlhase. Cut-simulation in impredicative logics (extended version). Seki Report SR-2006-01, Saarland University, 2006.
8. C. E. Brown. *Set Comprehension in Church's Type Theory*. PhD thesis, Department of Mathematical Sciences, Carnegie Mellon University, 2004.
9. A. Church. A formulation of the simple theory of types. *Journal of Symbolic Logic*, 5:56–68, 1940.
10. K. J. J. Hintikka. Form and content in quantification theory. *Acta Philosophica Fennica*, 8:7–55, 1955.
11. G. P. Huet. A mechanization of type theory. In *Proceedings of the 3rd International Joint Conference on Artificial Intelligence*, pages 139–146, 1973.
12. B. Russell. Mathematical logic as based on the theory of types. *American Journal of Mathematics*, 30:222–262, 1908.
13. R. M. Smullyan. A unifying principle for quantification theory. *Proc. Nat. Acad Sciences*, 49:828–832, 1963.
14. R. M. Smullyan. *First-Order Logic*. Springer, 1968.

Interpolation in Local Theory Extensions

Viorica Sofronie-Stokkermans

Max-Planck-Institut für Informatik,
Stuhlsatzenhausweg 85, Saarbrücken, Germany
sofronie@mpi-inf.mpg.de

Abstract. In this paper we study interpolation in local extensions of
a base theory. We identify situations in which it is possible to obtain
interpolants in a hierarchical manner, by using a prover and a procedure for generating interpolants in the base theory as black-boxes. We
present several examples of theory extensions in which interpolants can
be computed this way, and discuss applications in verification, knowledge representation, and modular reasoning in combinations of local
theories.

1 Introduction

Many problems in mathematics and computer science can be reduced to proving
satisfiability of conjunctions of (ground) literals modulo a background theory.
This theory can be a standard theory, the extension of a base theory with additional functions, or a combination of theories. It is therefore very important
to find efficient methods for reasoning in standard as well as complex theories.
However, it is often equally important to find local causes for inconsistency.
In distributed databases, for instance, finding local causes of inconsistency can
help in locating errors. Similarly, in abstraction-based verification, finding the
cause of inconsistency in a counterexample helps to rule out spurious counterexamples.

The problem can be formally described as follows: Let A and B be sets of
ground clauses in a theory $\mathcal{T}$. Assume that $A \wedge B$ is inconsistent with respect
to $\mathcal{T}$. Can we find a ground formula I, containing only constants and function
symbols common to A and B, such that I is a consequence of A w.r.t. $\mathcal{T}$, and
$B \wedge I$ is inconsistent modulo $\mathcal{T}$? If so, I is an *interpolant* of A and B, and can
be regarded as a "local" explanation for the inconsistency of $A \wedge B$.

In this paper we study possibilities of obtaining ground interpolants in theory
extensions. We identify situations in which it is possible to do this in a hierarchical manner, by using a prover and a procedure for generating interpolants in
the base theory as "black-boxes".

The main contributions of the paper are summarized below:

- First, we identify new examples of local theory extensions. In these, hierarchical reasoning is possible.
- Second, we present a method for generating interpolants in extensions of a
  base theory by means of sets of clauses. The method is general, in the sense
  that it can be applied to an extension $\mathcal{T}_1$ of a theory $\mathcal{T}_0$ provided that:

U. Furbach and N. Shankar (Eds.): IJCAR 2006, LNAI 4130, pp. 235–250, 2006.

(a) (i) T_0 is convex; (ii) T_0 is P-interpolating for a specified set P of predicates (cf. the definition in Section 4.2); (iii) in T_0 every inconsistent conjunction of ground clauses $A \wedge B$ allows a ground interpolant.

(b) the extension clauses have a special form (i.e. type (3) in Section 4.2). The method is *hierarchical*: the problem of finding interpolants in T_1 is reduced to that of finding interpolants in the base theory T_0. We can use the properties of T_0 to control the form of interpolants in the extension T_1.

- Third, we identify examples of theory extensions with properties (a) and (b).
- Fourth, we discuss application domains such as: modular reasoning in combinations of local theories (characterization of the type of information which needs to be exchanged), reasoning in distributed databases, and verification.

The existence of ground interpolants has been studied in several recent papers, mainly motivated by abstraction-refinement based verification [3,4,5,10]. In [4] McMillan presents a method for generating ground interpolants from proofs in an extension of linear rational arithmetic with uninterpreted function symbols. The use of free function symbols is sometimes too coarse (cf. the example in Section 1.1). Here, we show that similar results also hold for other types of extensions of a base theory, provided that the base theory has some of the properties of linear rational arithmetic. Another method for generating interpolants for combinations of theories over disjoint signatures from Nelson-Oppen-style unsatisfiability proofs was proposed by Yorsh and Musuvathi in [10]. Although we impose similar conditions on T_0, our method is orthogonal to theirs, as it also allows to consider combinations of theories over non-disjoint signatures.

Structure of the paper: In Section 1.1 we provide motivation for the study. In Section 2 the basic notions needed in the paper are introduced. Section 3 contains results on local theory extensions. In Section 4 local extensions allowing hierarchical interpolation are identified and some applications (modular reasoning in combinations of theories, reasoning in complex databases, and verification) are presented. We end with conclusions and plans for future work.

1.1 Motivation

We present two fields of applications: knowledge representation and verification.

Knowledge representation. Consider a simple (and faulty) terminological database for chemistry, consisting of two extensions of a common kernel Chem (basic chemistry): AChem (anorganic chemistry) and BioChem (biochemistry). Assume that Chem contains a set $C_0 = \{\text{process, reaction, substance, organic, anorganic}\}$ of concepts and a set Γ_0 of constraints:

$$\Gamma_0 = \{\text{organic} \wedge \text{anorganic} = \emptyset, \quad \text{organic} \subseteq \text{substance}, \quad \text{anorganic} \subseteq \text{substance}\}$$

Let AChem be an extension of Chem with concepts $C_1 = \{\text{cat-oxydation, oxydation}\}$, a rôle $R_1 = \{\text{catalyzes}\}$, terminology T_1 and constraints Γ_1:

$$T_1 = \{\text{cat-oxydation} = \text{substance} \wedge \exists\text{catalyzes(oxydation)}\}$$
$$\Gamma_1 = \{\text{reaction} \subseteq \text{oxydation}, \quad \text{cat-oxydation} \subseteq \text{anorganic}, \quad \text{cat-oxydation} \neq \emptyset\}.$$

Let BioChem be an extension of Chem with a concept $C_2 = \{enzyme\}$, rôles $R_2 = \{produces, catalyzes\}$, terminology T_2 and constraints Γ_2:

$T_2 = \{reaction=process \wedge \exists produces(substance), enzyme = organic \wedge \exists catalyzes(reaction)\}$
$\Gamma_2 = \{enzyme \neq \emptyset\}$

The combination of Chem, AChem and BioChem is inconsistent (we wrongly added to Γ_1 the constraint reaction $\subseteq$ oxydation instead of oxydation $\subseteq$ reaction). This can be proved as follows: By results in ([7], p.156 and p.166) the combination of Chem, AChem and BioChem is inconsistent iff

$$\Gamma_0 \wedge (T_1 \wedge \Gamma_1) \wedge (T_2 \wedge \Gamma_2) \models_{\mathcal{T}} \bot \qquad (1)$$

where $\mathcal{T}$ is the extension $\mathsf{SLat} \wedge \bigcup_{f \in R_1 \cup R_2} \mathsf{Mon}_f$ of the theory of semilattices with first element 0 and monotone function symbols corresponding to $\exists r$ for each rôle $r \in R_1 \cup R_2$. Using, for instance, the hierarchical calculus presented in [8] (see also Section 3), the contradiction can be found in polynomial time. In order to find the mistake we look for an explanation for the inconsistency in the common language of AChem and BioChem. (Common to AChem and BioChem are the concepts substance, organic, anorganic, reaction and of rôle catalyzes.) This can be found by computing an interpolant for the conjunction in (1) in the theory of semilattices with monotone operators. In this paper we show how such interpolants can be found in an efficient way.

Verification. Consider a water level controller modeled as follows: Changes in the water level by inflow/outflow are represented as functions in, out, depending on time t and water level L. Alarm and overflow levels $L_{alarm} < L_{overflow}$ are known.

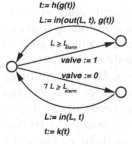

$t := h(g(t))$
$L := in(out(L, t), g(t))$

$L \geq L_{alarm}$
valve := 1
valve := 0
$\neg L \geq L_{alarm}$

$L := in(L, t)$
$t := k(t)$

- If $L \geq L_{alarm}$ then a valve is opened until time $g(t)$, the water level changes by $L' := in(out(L, t), g(t))$ and time by $t' := h(g(t))$.

- If $L < L_{alarm}$ then the valve is closed; the water level changes by $L' := in(L, t)$ and time by $t' := k(t)$.

We want to show that if initially $L < L_{alarm}$ then the water level always remains below $L_{overflow}$.

In [4], McMillan proposed a method in which interpolation (e.g. for linear arithmetic + free functions) is used for abstraction refinement. If in, out are free functions then $L < L_{alarm} \wedge L' \approx in(L, t) \wedge t' \approx k(L) \wedge \neg L' \leq L_{overflow}$ is satisfiable, so there exists a path from an initial state to an error state. To prove safety, we need to impose restrictions on in and out, e.g.:

$$\forall L, t \ (L < L_{alarm} \rightarrow in(L, t) < L_{overflow}), \qquad \forall L, t \ (L < L_{overflow} \rightarrow out(L, t) < L_{alarm}) \qquad (2)$$

The method we present here allows us to efficiently generate ground interpolants for extensions with functions satisfying condition (2), and also for a whole class of more general axioms. An immediate application is to verification by abstraction-refinement; there are other potential applications (e.g. goal-directed overapproximation for achieving faster termination, or automatic invariant generation).

2 Preliminaries

Theories and models. Theories can be regarded as sets of formulae or as sets of models. In this paper, whenever we speak about a theory T – if not otherwise specified – we implicitly refer to the set $\mathsf{Mod}(T)$ of all models of T. Let T be a theory in a given signature $\Pi = (\Sigma, \mathsf{Pred})$, where Σ is a set of function symbols and Pred a set of predicate symbols. Let ϕ and ψ be formulae over the signature Π with variables in a set X. The notion of truth of formulae and of entailment is the usual one in logic. We say that ϕ is true w.r.t. T (denoted $\models_T \phi$) if ϕ is true in each model $\mathcal{M}$ of T. ϕ is satisfiable w.r.t. T if there exists at least one model $\mathcal{M}$ of T and an assignment $\beta : X \to \mathcal{M}$ such that $(\mathcal{M}, \beta) \models \phi$. Otherwise we say that ϕ is unsatisfiable. We say that ϕ entails ψ w.r.t. T (denoted $\phi \models_T \psi$) if for every model $\mathcal{M}$ of T and every valuation β, if $(\mathcal{M}, \beta) \models \phi$ then $(\mathcal{M}, \beta) \models \psi$. Note that ϕ is unsatisfiable w.r.t. T iff $\phi \models_T \bot$.

Interpolation. A theory T has interpolation if, for all formulae ϕ and ψ in the signature of T, if $\phi \models_T \psi$ then there exists a formula I containing only symbols which occur in both ϕ and ψ such that $\phi \models_T I$ and $I \models_T \psi$. First order logic has interpolation but even if ϕ and ψ are e.g. conjunctions of ground literals I may still be an arbitrary formula. It is often important to identify situations in which ground clauses have ground interpolants.

We say that a theory T has the *ground interpolation property* (or, shorter, that T has *ground interpolation*) if for all ground clauses $A(\bar{c}, \bar{d})$ and $B(\bar{c}, \bar{e})$, if $A(\bar{c}, \bar{d}) \wedge B(\bar{c}, \bar{e}) \models_T \bot$ then there exists a ground formula $I(\bar{c})$, containing only the constants $\bar{c}$ occurring both in A and B, such that $A(\bar{c}, \bar{d}) \models_T I(\bar{c})$ and $B(\bar{c}, \bar{e}) \wedge I(\bar{c}) \models_T \bot$.

There exist results which relate ground interpolation to amalgamation or the injection transfer property [2,1,9] and thus allow us to recognize many theories with ground interpolation. Thus it can be proved that the following equational classes have ground interpolation: (abelian) groups, partially-ordered sets, lattices, semilattices, distributive lattices and Boolean algebras. However, in many applications one needs to consider extensions or combinations of theories, and proving amalgamation properties can be complicated. On the other hand, just knowing that ground interpolants exist is not sufficient: we would like to construct the interpolants fast, and to use the advantages of modular or hierarchical reasoning for constructing them. This is why in this paper we aim at giving methods for *constructing* interpolants in a hierarchical way.

3 Local Theory Extensions

Let T_0 be a theory with signature $\Pi_0 = (\Sigma_0, \mathsf{Pred})$. We consider extensions T_1 of T_0 with signature $\Pi = (\Sigma, \mathsf{Pred})$, where $\Sigma = \Sigma_0 \cup \Sigma_1$ (i.e. the signature is extended by new *function symbols*) and T_1 is obtained from T_0 by adding a set $\mathcal{K}$ of (universally quantified) clauses. Thus, $\mathsf{Mod}(T_1)$ consists of all Π-structures which are models of $\mathcal{K}$ and whose reduct to Π_0 is a model of T_0.

A *partial Π-structure* is a structure $\mathcal{M} = (M, \{f_M\}_{f \in \Sigma}, \{P_M\}_{P \in \mathsf{Pred}})$, where $M \neq \emptyset$ and for every $f \in \Sigma$ with arity n, f_M is a partial function from M^n to M. The notion of evaluating a term t with respect to a variable assignment $\beta : X \to M$ for its variables in a partial structure $\mathcal{M}$ is the same as for total algebras, except that this evaluation is undefined if $t = f(t_1, \ldots, t_n)$ and at least one of $\beta(t_i)$ is undefined, or else $(\beta(t_1), \ldots, \beta(t_n))$ is not in the domain of f_M. Let $\mathcal{M}$ be a partial Π-structure, C a clause and $\beta : X \to M$. Then $(\mathcal{M}, \beta) \models_w C$ iff either (i) for some term t in C, $\beta(t)$ is undefined, or else (ii) $\beta(t)$ is defined for all terms t of C, and there exists a literal L in C s.t. $\beta(L)$ is true in $\mathcal{M}$. $\mathcal{M}$ *weakly satisfies* C (notation: $\mathcal{M} \models_w C$) if $(\mathcal{M}, \beta) \models_w C$ for all assignments β. $\mathcal{M}$ *weakly satisfies a set of clauses* $\mathcal{K}$ ($\mathcal{M} \models_w \mathcal{K}$) if $\mathcal{M} \models_w C$ for all $C \in \mathcal{K}$.

3.1 Definition and Examples

Let $\mathcal{K}$ be a set of (universally quantified) clauses in the signature $\Pi = (\Sigma, \mathsf{Pred})$, where $\Sigma = \Sigma_0 \cup \Sigma_1$. In what follows, when referring to sets G of ground clauses we assume they are in the signature $\Pi^c = (\Sigma \cup \Sigma_c, \mathsf{Pred})$ where Σ_c is a set of new constants. An extension $\mathcal{T}_0 \subseteq \mathcal{T}_0 \cup \mathcal{K}$ is *local* if, in order to prove unsatisfiability of a set G of clauses with respect to $\mathcal{T}_0 \cup \mathcal{K}$, it is sufficient to use only those instances $\mathcal{K}[G]$ of $\mathcal{K}$ in which the terms starting with extension functions are in the set $\mathsf{st}(G, \mathcal{K})$ of ground terms which already occur in G or $\mathcal{K}$. Formally, $\mathcal{T}_0 \subseteq \mathcal{T}_1 = \mathcal{T}_0 \cup \mathcal{K}$ is a local extension if it satisfies condition (Loc):

(Loc)   For every set G of ground clauses, $G \models_{\mathcal{T}_1} \bot$ iff there is no partial Π^c-structure P such that $P_{|\Pi_0}$ is a total model of $\mathcal{T}_0$, all terms in $\mathsf{st}(\mathcal{K}, G)$ are defined in P, and P weakly satisfies $\mathcal{K}[G] \wedge G$.

In [8] we gave several examples of local theory extensions: any extension of a theory with free functions; extensions with selector functions for a constructor which is injective in the base theory; extensions of $\mathbb{R}$ with a Lipschitz function in a point x_0; extensions of partially ordered theories – in a class Ord consisting of the theories of posets, (dense) totally-ordered sets, semilattices, (distributive) lattices, Boolean algebras, or $\mathbb{R}^\infty$ – with a monotone function f, i.e. satisfying:

$$(\mathsf{Mon}_f) \quad \bigwedge_{i=1}^{n} x_i \leq y_i \to f(x_1, \ldots, x_n) \leq f(y_1, \ldots, y_n),$$

Below, we give some additional examples with particular relevance in verification.

Theorem 1. *The following theory extensions are local:*

(1) Extensions of any theory $\mathcal{T}_0$ for which $\leq$ is reflexive with functions satisfying boundedness (Bound_f^t) or guarded boundedness (GBound_f^t) conditions

$(\mathsf{Bound}_f^t) \qquad \forall x_1, \ldots, x_n (f(x_1, \ldots, x_n) \leq t(x_1, \ldots, x_n))$

$(\mathsf{GBound}_f^t) \quad \forall x_1, \ldots, x_n (\phi(x_1, \ldots, x_n) \to f(x_1, \ldots, x_n) \leq t(x_1, \ldots, x_n)),$

where $t(x_1, \ldots, x_n)$ is a term in the base signature Π_0 and $\phi(x_1, \ldots, x_n)$ a conjunction of literals in the signature Π_0, whose variables are in $\{x_1, \ldots, x_n\}$.

(2) *Extensions of any theory in* Ord *with* $\mathsf{Mon}_f \wedge \mathsf{Bound}_f^t$, *if* $t(x_1,\ldots,x_n)$ *is monotone in the variables* $x_1,\ldots,x_n$.

(3) *Extensions of any theory in* Ord *with functions satisfying* $\mathsf{Leq}(f,g) \wedge \mathsf{Mon}_f$.

$(\mathsf{Leq}(f,g))$ $\forall x_1,\ldots,x_n(\bigwedge_{i=1}^n x_i \leq y_i \rightarrow f(x_1,\ldots,x_n) \leq g(y_1,\ldots,y_n))$

(4) *Extensions of any totally-ordered theory in* Ord *with functions satisfying* $\mathsf{SGc}(f,g_1,\ldots,g_n) \wedge \mathsf{Mon}(f,g_1,\ldots,g_n)$.

$(\mathsf{SGc}(f,g_1,\ldots,g_n))$ $\forall x_1,\ldots,x_n, x(\bigwedge_{i=1}^n x_i \leq g_i(x) \rightarrow f(x_1,\ldots,x_n) \leq x)$

(5) *Extensions of theories in* Ord *with functions satisfying* $\mathsf{SGc}(f,g_1) \wedge \mathsf{Mon}(f,g_1)$.

3.2   Hierarchic Reasoning in Local Theory Extensions

Let $\mathcal{T}_0 \subseteq \mathcal{T}_1 = \mathcal{T}_0 \cup \mathcal{K}$ be a local theory extension. To check the satisfiability of a set G of ground clauses w.r.t. $\mathcal{T}_1$ we can proceed as follows (for details cf. [8]):

Step 1: Use locality. By the locality condition, we know that G is unsatisfiable w.r.t. $\mathcal{T}_1$ iff $\mathcal{K}[G] \wedge G$ has no weak partial model in which all the subterms of $\mathcal{K}[G] \wedge G$ are defined, and whose restriction to Π_0 is a total model of $\mathcal{T}_0$.

Step 2: Flattening and purification. As in $\mathcal{K}[G]$ and G the functions in Σ_1 have as arguments only ground terms, $\mathcal{K}[G] \wedge G$ can be purified and flattened by introducing new constants for the arguments of the extension functions as well as for the (sub)terms $t = f(g_1,\ldots,g_n)$ starting with extension functions $f \in \Sigma_1$, together with new corresponding definitions $c_t \approx t$. The set of clauses thus obtained has the form $\mathcal{K}_0 \wedge G_0 \wedge D$, where D is a set of ground unit clauses of the form $f(c_1,\ldots,c_n) \approx c$, where $f \in \Sigma_1$ and $c_1,\ldots,c_n,c$ are constants, and $\mathcal{K}_0, G_0$ are clauses without function symbols in Σ_1.

Step 3: Relational translation. We represent the function symbols in Σ_1 as partial, but functional relations. We thus obtain a relational translation D^* of D, in which each literal $f(c_1,\ldots,c_n) \approx c$ is replaced by $r_f(c_1,\ldots,c_n,c)$, and corresponding functionality axioms $\mathsf{Fun}(D^*)$ are added.

Step 4: Reduction to testing satisfiability in $\mathcal{T}_0$. We reduce the problem of testing satisfiability of G w.r.t. $\mathcal{T}_1$ to a satisfiability test in $\mathcal{T}_0$ as shown in Theorem 2.

Theorem 2 ([8]). *With the notation above, the following are equivalent:*

(1) $\mathcal{T}_0 \wedge \mathcal{K} \wedge G$ *has a model.*

(2) $\mathcal{T}_0 \wedge \mathcal{K}[G] \wedge G$ *has a weak partial model where all terms in* $\mathrm{st}(\mathcal{K},G)$ *are defined.*

(3) $\mathcal{T}_0 \wedge \mathcal{K}_0 \wedge G_0 \wedge D$ *has a weak partial model with all terms in* $\mathrm{st}(\mathcal{K},G)$ *defined.*

(4) $\mathcal{T}_0 \wedge \mathcal{K}_0 \wedge G_0 \wedge \mathsf{Fun}(D^*) \wedge D^*$ *has a relational model, where*

$$\mathsf{Fun}(D^*) = \{\bigwedge_{i=1}^n c_i \approx d_i \wedge r_f(c_1,\ldots,c_n,c) \wedge r_f(d_1,\ldots,d_n,d) \rightarrow c \approx d \mid$$
$$f \in \Sigma_1, r_f(c_1,\ldots,c_n,c), r_f(d_1,\ldots,d_n,d) \in D^*\}.$$

(5) $\mathcal{T}_0 \wedge \mathcal{K}_0 \wedge G_0 \wedge N_0$ *has a (total)* Σ_0-*model, where*

$$N_0 = \bigwedge\{\bigwedge_{i=1}^n c_i \approx d_i \rightarrow c \approx d \mid f(c_1,\ldots,c_n) \approx c, f(d_1,\ldots,d_n) \approx d \in D\}.$$

Example 1. Let $T_1 = \mathsf{SLat} \cup \mathsf{SGc}(f,g) \cup \mathsf{Mon}(f,g)$ be the extension of the theory of semilattices with two monotone functions f, g satisfying the semi-Galois condition $\mathsf{SGc}(f,g)$. Consider the ground formulae A, B in the signature of T_1:

$$A: \quad d \leq g(a) \ \wedge \ a \leq c \qquad B: \quad b \leq d \ \wedge \ f(b) \not\leq c.$$

where c and d are shared constants. By Theorem 1(5), T_1 is a local extension of the theory of semilattices. To prove that $A \wedge B \models_{T_1} \bot$ we proceed as follows:

We purify and flatten the formula $A \wedge B$ by replacing the ground terms starting with f and g with new constants. The clauses are separated into a part containing definitions for terms starting with extension functions, $D_A \wedge D_B$, and a conjunction of formulae in the base signature, $A_0 \wedge B_0$. As the extension $\mathsf{SLat} \subseteq T_1$ is local, $A \wedge B \models_{T_1} \bot$ iff $A_0 \wedge B_0 \wedge N_0 \wedge \mathsf{Mon}_0 \wedge \mathsf{SGc}_0$ is unsatisfiable w.r.t. SLat, where N_0 consists of the flattened form of those instances of the congruence axioms containing only f- and g-terms which occur in D_A or D_B, and $\mathsf{Mon}_0 \wedge \mathsf{SGc}_0$ consists of those instances of axioms in $\mathsf{Mon}(f,g) \wedge \mathsf{SGc}(f,g)$ containing only f- and g-terms which occur in D_A or D_B.

Extension	Base		
$D_A \wedge D_B$	$A_0 \wedge B_0 \wedge N_0 \wedge \mathsf{Mon}_0 \wedge \mathsf{SGc}_0$		
$a_1 \approx g(a)$	$A_0 = d \leq a_1 \wedge a \leq c$	$N_A \wedge \mathsf{Mon}_A = a \vartriangleleft a \to a_1 \vartriangleleft a_1, \vartriangleleft \in \{\approx, \leq\}$	
$b_1 \approx f(b)$	$B_0 = b \leq d \wedge b_1 \not\leq c$	$N_B \wedge \mathsf{Mon}_B = b \vartriangleleft b \to b_1 \vartriangleleft b_1, \ \vartriangleleft \in \{\approx, \leq\}$	
		$\mathsf{SGc}_0 = b \leq a_1 \to b_1 \leq a$	

It is easy to see that $A_0 \wedge B_0 \wedge N_0 \wedge \mathsf{Mon}_0 \wedge \mathsf{SGc}_0$ is unsatisfiable w.r.t. T_0: $A_0 \wedge B_0$ entails $b \leq a_1$, together with SGc_0 this yields $b_1 \leq a$, which together with $a \leq c$ and $b_1 \not\leq c$ leads to a contradiction.

4   A Hierarchical Interpolation Procedure

Let $T_0 \subseteq T_1 = T_0 \cup \mathcal{K}$ be a theory extension by means of a set of clauses $\mathcal{K}$. Assume that $A \wedge B \models_{T_1} \bot$, where A and B are two sets of ground clauses. Our goal is to find a ground *interpolant*, that is a ground formula I containing only constants and extension functions which are common to A and B such that

$$A \models_{T_1} I \quad \text{and} \quad I \wedge B \models_{T_1} \bot.$$

Flattening and purification do not influence the existence of ground interpolants:

Lemma 3. *Let A and B be two sets of ground clauses in the signature Π^c. Let $A_0 \wedge D_A$ and $B_0 \wedge D_B$ be obtained from A resp. B by purification and flattening. If I is an interpolant of $(A_0 \wedge D_A) \wedge (B_0 \wedge D_B)$ then the formula $\overline{I}$, obtained from I by replacing, recursively, all newly introduced constants with the terms in the original signature which they represent, is an interpolant for $A \wedge B$.*

Therefore we can restrict without loss of generality to finding interpolants for the *purified and flattened* conjunction of formulae $(A_0 \wedge D_A) \wedge (B_0 \wedge D_B)$.

We focus on interpolation in *local theory extensions*. Let $\mathcal{T}_0 \subseteq \mathcal{T}_1 = \mathcal{T}_0 \cup \mathcal{K}$ be a local theory extension. From Theorem 2 we know that in such extensions hierarchical reasoning is possible [8]: if A and B are sets of ground clauses in a signature Π^c, and $A_0 \wedge D_A$ (resp. $B_0 \wedge D_B$) are obtained from A (resp. B) by purification and flattening then:

$$(A_0 \wedge D_A) \wedge (B_0 \wedge D_B) \models_{\mathcal{T}_1} \bot \qquad \text{iff} \qquad \mathcal{K}_0 \wedge A_0 \wedge B_0 \wedge N_0 \models_{\mathcal{T}_0} \bot,$$

where $\mathcal{K}_0$ is obtained from $\mathcal{K}[D_A \wedge D_B]$ by replacing the Σ_1-terms with the corresponding constants contained in the definitions D_A and D_B and

$$N_0 = \bigwedge_{i=1}^{n} \{ \bigwedge c_i \approx d_i \rightarrow c \approx d \mid f(c_1, \dots, c_n) \approx c, f(d_1, \dots, d_n) \approx d \in D_A \cup D_B \}.$$

In general we cannot use Theorem 2 for generating a ground interpolant because:

(i) $\mathcal{K}[D_A \wedge D_B]$ (hence also $\mathcal{K}_0$) may contain free variables.
(ii) The clauses in $\mathcal{K}[D_A \wedge D_B]$ and the instances of congruence axioms (and therefore the clauses in $\mathcal{K}_0 \wedge N_0$) may contain combinations of constants and extension functions from A and B.
(iii) If some clause in $\mathcal{K}$ contains two or more different extension functions, it is unlikely that these extension functions can be separated in the interpolants.

To solve (iii), we define a relation $\sim$ between extension functions, where $f \sim g$ if f and g occur in the same clause in $\mathcal{K}$. This defines an equivalence relation $\sim$ on Σ_1. We henceforth consider that a function $f \in \Sigma_1$ is common to A and B if there exist $g, h \in \Sigma_1$ such that $f \sim g$, $f \sim h$, g occurs in A and h occurs in B.

Example 2. Consider the reduction to the base theory in Example 1. *Ad* (ii): The clause $b \leq a_1 \rightarrow b_1 \leq a$ of SGc_0 is mixed, i.e. contains combinations of constants from A and B. *Ad* (iii): As $\mathsf{SGc}(f, g)$ contains occurrences of both f and g, it is not likely to find an interpolant with no occurrence of f and g, even if g only occurs in A and f only occurs in B. We assume that both f and g are shared.

4.1 Main Idea

The idea of our approach is to separate mixed instances of axioms in $\mathcal{K}_0$, or of congruence axioms in N_0, into an A-part and a B-part. This is, if $A \wedge B \models_{\mathcal{T}_1} \bot$ we find a set T of $\Sigma_0 \cup \Sigma_1$-terms containing only constants and extension functions common to A and B, such that $\mathcal{K}[A \wedge B]$ can be separated into a part $\mathcal{K}[A, T]$ consisting of instances with extension terms occurring in A and T, and a part $\mathcal{K}[B, T]$ containing only instances with extension terms in B and T, such that:

$$\mathcal{K}[A, T] \wedge A_0 \wedge \mathsf{Fun}((D_A \wedge D_T)^*) \wedge \mathcal{K}[B, T] \wedge B_0 \wedge \mathsf{Fun}((D_B \wedge D_T)^*)$$

has no weak partial model where all ground terms in $\mathcal{K}, D_A, D_B, T$ are defined.

Example 3. Consider the conjunction $A_0 \wedge D_A \wedge B_0 \wedge D_B \wedge N_0 \wedge \mathsf{Mon}_0 \wedge \mathsf{SGc}_0$ in Example 1. We obtain a separation for the clause $b \leq a_1 \rightarrow b_1 \leq a$ of SGc_0 as follows: Note that $A_0 \wedge B_0 \models b \leq a_1$. We can find an SLat-term t containing only shared constants of A_0 and B_0 such that $A_0 \wedge B_0 \models b \leq t \wedge t \leq a_1$. (Indeed, such a term is $t = d$.) We show that, instead of the axiom $a \leq g(b) \rightarrow f(a) \leq b$, whose flattened form is in SGc_0, we can use, without loss of unsatisfiability:

(1) an instance of the monotonicity axiom for f: $b \leq d \rightarrow f(b) \leq f(d)$, and
(2) another instance of SGc, namely: $d \leq g(a) \rightarrow f(d) \leq a$.

We introduce a new constant $c_{f(d)}$ for $f(d)$ (its definition, $c_{f(d)} \approx f(d)$, is stored in a set D_T), and the corresponding instances $\mathcal{H}_{\mathsf{sep}} = \mathcal{H}_{\mathsf{sep}}^A \wedge \mathcal{H}_{\mathsf{sep}}^B$ of the congruence, monotonicity and $\mathsf{SGc}(f, g)$-axioms, which are now separated into an A-part ($d \leq a_1 \rightarrow c_{f(d)} \leq a$) and a B-part ($b \leq d \rightarrow b_1 \leq c_{f(d)}$). We thus obtain a separated conjunction $\overline{A}_0 \wedge \overline{B}_0$ (where $\overline{A}_0 = \mathcal{H}_{\mathsf{sep}}^A \wedge A_0$ and $\overline{B}_0 = \mathcal{H}_{\mathsf{sep}}^B \wedge B_0$), which can be proved to be unsatisfiable in $\mathcal{T}_0 = \mathsf{SLat}$. To compute an interpolant in SLat for $\overline{A}_0 \wedge \overline{B}_0$ note that $\overline{A}_0$ is logically equivalent to the conjunction of unit literals $d \leq a_1 \wedge a \leq c \wedge c_{f(d)} \leq a$ and $\overline{B}_0$ is logically equivalent to $b \leq d \wedge b_1 \not\leq c \wedge b_1 \leq c_{f(d)}$. An interpolant is $I_0 = c_{f(d)} \leq c$. By replacing the new constants with the terms they denote we obtain the interpolant $I = f(d) \leq c$ for $A \wedge B$.

4.2 Examples of Theory Extensions with Hierarchic Interpolation

We identify a class of theory extensions for which interpolants can be computed hierarchically (and efficiently) using a procedure for generating interpolants in the base theory $\mathcal{T}_0$. This allows us to exploit specific properties of $\mathcal{T}_0$ for obtaining simple interpolants in $\mathcal{T}_1$. We make the following assumptions about $\mathcal{T}_0$:

Assumption 1: $\mathcal{T}_0$ is *convex* with respect to the set Pred of all predicates (including equality $\approx$), i.e., for all conjunctions Γ of ground atoms, relations $R_1, \ldots, R_m \in$ Pred and ground tuples of corresponding arity $\bar{t}_1, \ldots, \bar{t}_n$, if $\Gamma \models_{\mathcal{T}_0} \bigvee_{i=1}^{m} R_i(\bar{t}_i)$ then there exists $j \in \{1, \ldots, m\}$ such that $\Gamma \models_{\mathcal{T}_0} R_j(\bar{t}_j)$.
Assumption 2: $\mathcal{T}_0$ is *P-interpolating*, i.e. for all conjunctions A and B of ground literals, all binary predicates $R \in P$ and all constants a and b such that a occurs in A and b occurs in B (or vice versa), if $A \wedge B \models_{\mathcal{T}_0} aRb$ then there exists a term t containing only constants common to A and B with $A \wedge B \models_{\mathcal{T}_0} aRt \wedge tRb$. (If we can always guarantee that $A \models_{\mathcal{T}_0} aRt$ and $B \models_{\mathcal{T}_0} tRb$ we say that $\mathcal{T}_0$ is *strongly P-interpolating*.)
Assumption 3: $\mathcal{T}_0$ has ground interpolation.

Some examples of theories satisfying these properties are given below.

Theorem 4. *The following theories have ground interpolation and are convex and P-interpolating w.r.t. the indicated set P of predicate symbols:*

(1) The theory of $\mathcal{EQ}$ of pure equality without function symbols (for $P = \{\approx\}$).
(2) The theory PoSet of posets (for $P = \{\approx, \leq\}$).

(3) *Linear rational arithmetic* LI($\mathbb{Q}$) *and linear real arithmetic* LI($\mathbb{R}$) *(convex w.r.t.* $P = \{\approx\}$, *strongly P-interpolating for* $P = \{\approx, \leq\}$).

(4) *The theories* Bool *of Boolean algebras,* SLat *of semilattices and* DLat *of distributive lattices (strongly P-interpolating for* $P = \{\approx, \leq\}$).

For the sake of simplicity we only consider sets A, B of unit clauses, i.e. conjunctions of ground literals. This is not a restriction, since if we can obtain interpolants for conjunctions of ground literals then we also can construct interpolants for conjunctions of arbitrary clauses by using standard methods[1] discussed e.g. in [4] or [10]. By Lemma 3, we can restrict w.l.o.g. to finding an interpolant for the purified and flattened conjunction of unit clauses $A_0 \wedge B_0 \wedge D_A \wedge D_B$.

By Theorem 2, $A_0 \wedge D_A \wedge B_0 \wedge D_B \models_{\mathcal{T}_1} \bot$ iff $\mathcal{K}_0 \wedge A_0 \wedge B_0 \wedge N_0 \models_{\mathcal{T}_0} \bot$, where $\mathcal{K}_0$ is obtained from $\mathcal{K}[D_A \wedge D_B]$ by replacing the Σ_1-terms with the corresponding constants contained in the definitions $D_A \wedge D_B$ and

$$N_0 = \bigwedge_{i=1}^{n} \{\bigwedge c_i \approx d_i \rightarrow c \approx d \mid f(c_1, \ldots, c_n) \approx c, f(d_1, \ldots, d_n) \approx d \in D_A \cup D_B\}.$$

In general, $N_0 = N_0^A \wedge N_0^B \wedge N_{\text{mix}}$ and $\mathcal{K}_0 = \mathcal{K}_0^A \wedge \mathcal{K}_0^B \wedge \mathcal{K}_{\text{mix}}$, where $N_0^A, \mathcal{K}_0^A$ only contain extension functions and constants which occur in A, $N_0^B, \mathcal{K}_0^B$ only contain extension functions and constants which occur in B, and $N_{\text{mix}}, \mathcal{K}_{\text{mix}}$ contain mixed clauses with constants occurring in both A and B. Our goal is to separate N_{mix} and $\mathcal{K}_{\text{mix}}$ into an A-local and a B-local part. We show that, under Assumptions 1 and 2, N_{mix} can always be separated, and $\mathcal{K}_{\text{mix}}$ can be separated if $\mathcal{K}$ contains the following type of combinations of clauses:

$$\begin{cases} x_1 \, R_1 \, s_1 \wedge \cdots \wedge x_n \, R_n \, s_n \rightarrow f(x_1, \ldots, x_n) \, R \, g(y_1, \ldots, y_n) \\ x_1 \, R_1 \, y_1 \wedge \cdots \wedge x_n \, R_n \, y_n \rightarrow f(x_1, \ldots, x_n) \, R \, f(y_1, \ldots, y_n) \end{cases} \tag{3}$$

where $n \geq 1$, $x_1, \ldots, x_n$ are variables, $R_1, \ldots, R_n, R$ are binary relations with $R_1, \ldots, R_n \in P$ and R transitive, and each s_i is either a variable among the arguments of g, or a term of the form $f_i(z_1, \ldots, z_k)$, where $f_i \in \Sigma_1$ and all the arguments of f_i are variables occurring among the arguments of g. [2]

Example 4. The following local extensions are in the class above:

(a) Any extension with free functions ($\mathcal{K} = \emptyset$).
(b) Extensions of any theory in Ord (cf. Section 3.1) with monotone functions.
(c) Extensions of any totally-ordered theory in Ord with functions satisfying $\mathsf{SGc}(f, g_1, \ldots, g_n) \wedge \mathsf{Mon}(f, g_1, \ldots, g_n)$.
(d) Extensions of theories in Ord with functions satisfying $\mathsf{SGc}(f, g_1) \wedge \mathsf{Mon}(f, g_1)$.
(e) Extensions of theories in Ord with functions satisfying $\mathsf{Leq}(f, g) \wedge \mathsf{Mon}_f$.

---

[1] E.g. in a DPLL-style procedure partial interpolants are generated for the unsatisfiable branches and then recombined using ideas of Pudlák.
[2] More general types of clauses, in which instead of variables we can consider arbitrary base terms, can be handled if $\mathcal{T}_0$ has a P-interpolation property for terms instead of constants. Due to space limitations, such extensions are not discussed here.

Note: If the clauses in $\mathcal{K}$ are of type (3), then (i) the cardinality of $\mathcal{K}_0 \cup N_0$ is quadratic in the size of $A \wedge B$, (ii) all clauses in $\mathcal{K}_0$ are of the form $C = \bigwedge_{i=1}^{n} c_i\,R_i\,d_i \rightarrow c\,R\,d$, where $R_i \in P$, R is transitive, and c_i, d_i, c, d are constants.

Proposition 5. *Assume that $\mathcal{T}_0$ satisfies Assumptions 1 and 2. Let $\mathcal{H}$ be a set of Horn clauses $\bigwedge_{i=1}^{n} c_i R_i d_i \rightarrow c R d$ in the signature Π_0^c (with R transitive and $R_i \in P$) which are instances of flattened and purified clauses of type (3) and of congruence axioms. Let A_0 and B_0 be conjunctions of ground literals in the signature Π_0^c such that $A_0 \wedge B_0 \wedge \mathcal{H} \models_{\mathcal{T}_0} \bot$. Then there exists a set T of $\Sigma_0 \cup \Sigma_c$-terms containing only constants common to A_0 and B_0 such that $A_0 \wedge B_0 \wedge (\mathcal{H} \backslash \mathcal{H}_{\mathsf{mix}}) \wedge \mathcal{H}_{\mathsf{sep}} \models_{\mathcal{T}_0} \bot$, where*

$$\mathcal{H}_{\mathsf{mix}} = \{\bigwedge_{i=1}^{n} c_i R_i d_i \rightarrow c R d \in \mathcal{H} \mid c_i, c \text{ constants in } A, d_i, d \text{ constants in } B\} \cup$$
$$\{\bigwedge_{i=1}^{n} c_i R_i d_i \rightarrow c R d \in \mathcal{H} \mid c_i, c \text{ constants in } B, d_i, d \text{ constants in } A\}$$
$$\mathcal{H}_{\mathsf{sep}} = \{(\bigwedge_{i=1}^{n} c_i R_i t_i \rightarrow c R c_{f(t_1,\dots,t_n)}) \wedge (\bigwedge_{i=1}^{n} t_i R_i d_i \rightarrow c_{f(t_1,\dots,t_n)} R d) \mid$$
$$\bigwedge_{i=1}^{n} c_i R_i d_i \rightarrow c R d \in \mathcal{H}_{\mathsf{mix}}, d_i \approx s_i(e_1,\dots,e_n), d \approx g(e_1,\dots,e_n) \in D_B,$$
$$c \approx f(c_1,\dots,c_n) \in D_A \text{ or vice versa } \} = \mathcal{H}_{\mathsf{sep}}^A \wedge \mathcal{H}_{\mathsf{sep}}^B$$

and $c_{f(t_1,\dots,t_n)}$ are new constants in Σ_c (considered common to A_0, B_0) introduced for the terms $f(t_1,\dots,t_n)$.

Proof (Sketch). Proof by induction on the number of clauses in $\mathcal{H}$. Convexity and P-interpolation ensure that for each clause $C = \bigwedge c_i R_i d_i \rightarrow c R d \in \mathcal{H}_{\mathsf{mix}}$, e.g. obtained from the following instance of a clause of type (3):

$$c_1 R_1 s_1(e_1,\dots,e_m) \wedge \dots \wedge c_n R_n s_n(e_1,\dots,e_m) \rightarrow f(c_1,\dots,c_n) R g(e_1,\dots,e_m)$$

there exist terms $t_1,\dots,t_n$ containing only constants common to A_0 and B_0 such that $A_0 \wedge B_0 \wedge (\mathcal{H} \backslash \{C\}) \models_{\mathcal{T}_0} c_i R_i t_i \wedge t_i R_i d_i$. We thus can replace C with the conjunction of an instance of the monotonicity axiom, $C_A : \bigwedge_{i=1}^{n} c_i R_i t_i \rightarrow c R c_{f(t_1,\dots,t_n)}$ and an instance of the clause of type (3), $C_B : \bigwedge_{i=1}^{n} t_i R_i d_i \rightarrow c_{f(t_1,\dots,t_n)} R d$. $\square$

In what follows we assume that $\mathcal{K}$ only contains combinations of clauses of type (3). An immediate consequence of Proposition 5 is Theorem 6.

Theorem 6. *Assume $\mathcal{T}_0$ satisfies Assumptions 1, 2 and $\mathcal{K}_0 \wedge A_0 \wedge B_0 \wedge N_0 \models_{\mathcal{T}_0} \bot$. Then there exists a set T of $\Sigma_0 \cup \Sigma_c$-terms containing only constants common to A_0 and B_0 such that (if $N_0^D = N_0^{DA} \wedge N_0^{DB} = N_{0\mathsf{sep}}$ and $\mathcal{K}_0^D = \mathcal{K}_0^{DA} \wedge \mathcal{K}_0^{DB} = \mathcal{K}_{0\mathsf{sep}}$):*

$$\mathcal{K}_0^A \wedge \mathcal{K}_0^B \wedge \mathcal{K}_0^D \wedge A_0 \wedge B_0 \wedge N_0^A \wedge N_0^B \wedge N_0^D \models_{\mathcal{T}_0} \bot. \tag{4}$$

(As before, Σ_c contains the new constants $c_{f(t_1,\dots,t_n)}$, considered to be common to A_0 and B_0, introduced for terms $f(t_1,\dots,t_n)$, with $t_1,\dots,t_n \in T$.)

Corollary 7. *Assume $\mathcal{T}_0$ satisfies Assumptions 1–3 and $\mathcal{K}_0 \wedge A_0 \wedge B_0 \wedge N_0 \models_{\mathcal{T}_0} \bot$.*

(1) There exists a Π_0^c-formula I_0 containing only constants common to A_0, B_0 with $\mathcal{K}_0^A \wedge \mathcal{K}_0^{DA} \wedge A_0 \wedge N_0^A \wedge N_0^{DA} \models_{\mathcal{T}_0} I_0$ and $\mathcal{K}_0^B \wedge \mathcal{K}_0^{DB} \wedge B_0 \wedge N_0^B \wedge N_0^{DB} \wedge I_0 \models_{\mathcal{T}_0} \bot$.
(2) There exists a ground Π^c-formula I containing only constants and function symbols which occur both in A and B such that $A \models_{\mathcal{T}_1} I$ and $B \wedge I \models_{\mathcal{T}_1} \bot$.

Proof. If T_0 has ground interpolation, (1) is a direct consequence of Theorem 6, since $\mathcal{K}_0^A, \mathcal{K}_0^{AD}, \mathcal{K}_0^B, \mathcal{K}_0^{BD}$ are ground. (2) Let I be obtained from I_0 by recursively replacing each constant c_t introduced in the separation process with the term t. Then I is an interpolant of $(A_0 \wedge D_A) \wedge (B_0 \wedge D_B)$.   □

We obtain the following procedure for computing interpolants for $A \wedge B$:

Preprocess: Using locality, flattening and purification we obtain a set $\mathcal{H} \wedge A_0 \wedge B_0$ of formulae in the base theory, where $\mathcal{H}$ is as in Prop. 5. Let $\Delta := \mathsf{T}$.

Repeat as long as possible: Let $C \in \mathcal{H}$ whose premise is entailed by $A_0 \wedge B_0 \wedge \Delta$. If C is mixed, compute terms t_i which separate the premises in C, and separate the clause into an instance C_1 of monotonicity and an instance C_2 of a clause in $\mathcal{K}$ as in Prop. 5. Remove C from $\mathcal{H}$, and add C_1, C_2 to $\mathcal{H}_{\mathsf{sep}}$ and their conclusions to Δ. Otherwise move C to $\mathcal{H}_{\mathsf{sep}}$ and add its conclusion to Δ.

Compute interpolant: in T_0 for the separated formula obtained this way, and construct an interpolant for the extension as explained in Corollary 7(2).

Theorem 8. *Assume that the cycle of the procedure above stops after moving the processed clauses $\mathcal{H}_{\mathsf{proc}}$ into the set $\mathcal{H}_{\mathsf{sep}}$. The following are equivalent:*

(1) $A_0 \wedge D_A \wedge B_0 \wedge D_B \models_{T_1} \bot$.   *(2) $A_0 \wedge B_0 \wedge (\mathcal{H} \backslash \mathcal{H}_{\mathsf{proc}}) \wedge \mathcal{H}_{\mathsf{sep}} \models_{T_0} \bot$.*

Proof. (1)⇒(2) is a consequence of Theorems 2 and 6. As the conjunction in (2) corresponds to a subset of instances of $\mathcal{K} \wedge A_0 \wedge D_A \wedge B_0 \wedge D_B$, (2) imples (1).   □

Note. If $\mathcal{K}_0 \wedge A_0 \wedge B_0 \wedge N_0 \models_{T_0} \bot$ then no matter which terms are chosen for separating mixed clauses in $N_0 \wedge \mathcal{K}_0$, we obtain a separated conjunction of clauses unsatisfiable w.r.t. T_0. Theorem 8 shows that if the set of clauses obtained when the procedure stops is satisfiable then $A \wedge B$ was satisfiable, and conversely, so the procedure can be used to test satisfiability and to compute interpolants at the same time. (However, it is more efficient to first test $A \wedge B \models_{T_1} \bot$.)

Complexity. Assume that in T_0 for a formula of length n (a) interpolants can be computed in time $g(n)$, (b) P-interpolating terms can be computed in time $h(n)$, (c) entailment can be checked in time $k(n)$. The size n of the set of clauses obtained after the preprocessing phase is quadratic in the size of the input. The procedure above computes an interpolant in time of order $n \cdot (k(n) + h(n)) + g(n)$.

Remark 9. *If T_0 satisfies Assumptions 1,3 and is strongly P-interpolating, the procedure above can be changed to separate all clauses in $\mathcal{H}$ and store the conclusions of the separated clauses in $\Delta = \Delta_A \cup \Delta_B$. If $\mathcal{K}_0 \wedge A_0 \wedge B_0 \wedge N_0 \models_{T_0} \bot$ then there exists a set T of $\Sigma_0 \cup \Sigma_c$-terms containing only constants common to A_0 and B_0, and common new constants in a set Σ_c such that the terms in T can be used to separate $N_0 \cup \mathcal{K}_0$ into $\mathcal{H}_{\mathsf{sep}} = (\mathcal{K}_0^{DA} \wedge N_0^{DA}) \wedge (\mathcal{K}_0^{DB} \wedge N_0^{DB})$, where:*

$$\mathcal{H}_{\mathsf{sep}} = \{ (\bigwedge_{i=1}^n c_i R_i t_i \rightarrow cRc_{f(t_1,\dots,t_n)}) \wedge (\bigwedge_{i=1}^n t_i R_i d_i \rightarrow c_{f(t_1,\dots,t_n)} Rd) \mid$$
$$\bigwedge_{i=1}^n c_i R_i d_i \rightarrow cRd \in N_0 \cup \mathcal{K}_0 \} = (\mathcal{K}_0^{DA} \wedge N_0^{DA}) \wedge (\mathcal{K}_0^{DB} \wedge N_0^{DB})$$

such that for each premise $c_i R_i d_i$ of a rule in $N_0 \cup K_0$, at some step in the procedure $A_0 \wedge B_0 \wedge \Delta_A \wedge \Delta_B \models c_i R_i d_i$ and there exists $t_i \in T$ such that $A_0 \wedge \Delta_A \models c_i R_i t_i$ and $B_0 \wedge \Delta_B \models t_i R_i d_i$. In this case $A_0 \wedge K_0^{DA} \wedge N_0^{DA}$ is logically equivalent to $\overline{A}_0$, and $B_0 \wedge K_0^{DB} \wedge N_0^{DB}$ is logically equivalent to $\overline{B}_0$, where $\overline{A}_0, \overline{B}_0$ are the following conjunctions of literals:

$$\overline{A}_0 = A_0 \wedge \bigwedge \{ cRc_{f(\overline{t})} \mid \text{conclusion of some clause } (\Gamma \to cRc_{f(\overline{t})}) \in K_0^{DA} \cup N_0^{DA} \}$$
$$\overline{B}_0 = B_0 \wedge \bigwedge \{ c_{f(\overline{t})} Rd \mid \text{conclusion of some clause } (\Gamma \to c_{f(\overline{t})} Rd) \in K_0^{DB} \cup N_0^{DB} \}.$$

Thus, if for instance in T_0 interpolants for conjunctions of ground literals are again conjunctions of ground literals, the same is also true in the extension.

Example 6. The following theory extensions have ground interpolation:

(a) Extensions of any theory in Theorem 4(1)–(4) with free function symbols.
(b) Extensions of the theories in Theorem 4(2),(4) with monotone functions.
(c) Extensions of the theories in Theorem 4(2),(4) with $\mathsf{Leq}(f,g) \wedge \mathsf{Mon}_f$.
(d) Extensions of the theories in Theorem 4(2),(4) with $\mathsf{SGc}(\mathsf{f}, \mathsf{g_1}) \wedge \mathsf{Mon}(f, g_1)$.
(e) Extensions of any theory in Theorem 4(1)–(4) with Bound_f^t or GBound_f^t (where t is a term and ϕ a set of literals in the base theory).
(f) Extensions of the theories in Theorem 4(2),(4) with $\mathsf{Mon}_f \wedge \mathsf{Bound}_f^t$, if t is monotone in its variables.
(g) $\mathbb{R} \cup (\mathsf{L}_f^\lambda)$, the extension of the theory of reals with a unary function which is λ-Lipschitz in a point x_0, where (L_f^λ) is $\forall x \, |f(x) - f(x_0)| \le \lambda \cdot |x - x_0|$.

Proof. (a)–(d) are direct consequences of Corollary 7, since all sets of extension clauses are of type (3). For extensions of linear arithmetic note that due to the totality of $\le$ we can always assume that A and B are positive, so convexity w.r.t. $\approx$ is sufficient (cf. proof of Proposition 5). (e)–(g) follow from Corollary 7 and the fact that if each clause in K contains only one occurrence of an extension function, no mixed instances can be generated when computing $K[A \wedge B]$. $\square$

4.3 Applications

Modular Reasoning in Local Combinations of Theories. Let $T_i = T_0 \cup K_i$, $i = 1, 2$ be local extensions of a theory T_0 with signature $\Pi_0 = (\Sigma_0, \mathsf{Pred})$, where $\Sigma_0 = \Sigma_1 \cap \Sigma_2$. Assume that (a) all variables in K_i occur below some extension function, (b) the extension $T_0 \subseteq T_0 \cup K_1 \cup K_2$ is local[3], and (c) T_0 has ground interpolation.

Let G be a ground clause in the signature $\Pi^c = (\Sigma_0 \cup \Sigma_1 \cup \Sigma_2 \cup \Sigma_c, \mathsf{Pred})$. G can be flattened and purified, so we assume w.l.o.g. that $G = G_1 \wedge G_2$, where G_1, G_2 are flat and linear sets of clauses in the signatures Π_1, Π_2 respectively, i.e. for $i = 1, 2$, $G_i = G_i^0 \wedge G_0 \wedge D_i$, where G_i^0 and G_0 are clauses in the base theory and D_i conjunctions of unit clauses of the form $f(c_1, \dots, c_n) = c, f \in \Sigma_i$.

Theorem 10. *With the notations above, assume that $G_1 \wedge G_2 \models_{T_1 \cup T_2} \bot$. Then there exists a ground formula I, containing only constants shared by G_1 and G_2, with $G_1 \models_{T_1 \cup T_2} I$ and $I \wedge G_2 \models_{T_1 \cup T_2} \bot$.*

---

[3] If T_0 is a $\forall\exists$ theory then (b) is implied by (a) and the locality of T_1, T_2 [6].

Proof. By Theorem 2, the following are equivalent:

(1) $\mathcal{T}_0 \cup \mathcal{K}_1 \cup \mathcal{K}_2 \cup (G_1^0 \wedge G_0 \wedge D_1) \wedge (G_2^0 \wedge G_0 \wedge D_2) \models \perp$,

(2) $\mathcal{T}_0 \cup \mathcal{K}_1[G_1] \wedge \mathcal{K}_2[G_2] \wedge (G_1^0 \wedge G_0 \wedge D_1) \wedge (G_2^0 \wedge G_0 \wedge D_2) \models \perp$,

(3) $\mathcal{K}_1^0 \wedge \mathcal{K}_2^0 \wedge (G_1^0 \wedge G_0) \wedge (G_2^0 \wedge G_0) \wedge N_1 \wedge N_2 \models_{\mathcal{T}_0} \perp$, where, for $j = 1, 2$,

$$N_j = \bigwedge_{i=1}^{n} \{ \bigwedge c_i \approx d_i \rightarrow c = d \mid f(c_1, \ldots, c_n) \approx c, f(d_1, \ldots, d_n) \approx d \in D_j \},$$

and $\mathcal{K}_i^0$ is the formula obtained from $\mathcal{K}_i[G_i]$ after purification and flattening, taking into account the definitions from D_i. Let $A = \mathcal{K}_1^0 \wedge (G_1^0 \wedge G_0) \wedge N_1$ and $B = \mathcal{K}_2^0 \wedge (G_2^0 \wedge G_0) \wedge N_2$. By assumption (a), A and B are both ground. As A and B have no function symbols in common and only share the constants which G_1 and G_2 share, there exists an interpolant I_0 in the signature Π_0, containing only Σ_0-function symbols and only constants shared by G_1, G_2, such that $A \models_{\mathcal{T}_0} I_0$ and $B \wedge I_0 \models_{\mathcal{T}_0} \perp$. An interpolant for $G_1 \wedge G_2$ w.r.t. $\mathcal{T}_1$ can now be obtained by replacing the newly introduced constants by the terms they replaced.   □

By Remark 9, if $\mathcal{T}_0$ is strongly P-interpolating and has equational interpolation then I is a conjunction of literals, so for modularily proving $G_1 \wedge G_2 \models_{\mathcal{T}_1} \perp$ only conjunctions of ground literals containing constants shared by G_1, G_2 need to be exchanged between specialized provers for $\mathcal{T}_1$ and $\mathcal{T}_2$.

Verification. Consider the example presented in the verification example in Section 1.1. We illustrate our method for generating interpolants for a formula corresponding to a path of length 2 from an initial state to an unsafe state:

$$G = l{<}L_{\mathsf{alarm}} \wedge l'{\approx}\mathsf{in}(l, t) \wedge t'{\approx}k(l) \wedge$$
$$l'{\geq}L_{\mathsf{alarm}} \wedge l''{\approx}\mathsf{in}(\mathsf{out}(l', t'), g(t')) \wedge t''{\approx}h(g(t')) \wedge \neg l''{\leq}L_{\mathsf{overflow}}$$

Hierarchic reasoning. The extension $\mathcal{T}_1$ of linear arithmetic with the clauses (2) in Section 1.1 is local, so to prove $G \models_{\mathcal{T}_1} \perp$ it is sufficient to consider ground instances $\mathcal{K}[G]$ of (2) in which all extension terms already occur in G: After flattening and purifying $\mathcal{K}[G] \wedge G$, we separate the problem into an extension part Ext and a base part Base. By Theorem 2 [8], the problem can be reduced to testing the satisfiability in the base theory of the conjunction Base $\wedge N_0$. As this conjunction is unsatisfiable w.r.t. $\mathcal{T}_0$, G is unsatisfiable.

Ext		Base $\wedge N_0$		
$c \approx \mathsf{in}(l, t)$	$d \approx k(t)$	$l < L_{\mathsf{alarm}}$	$l' \approx c$	$\mathcal{K}_0 : l < L_{\mathsf{alarm}} \rightarrow c < L_{\mathsf{overflow}}$
$l_o \approx \mathsf{out}(l', t')$	$t_o \approx g(t')$	$l' \geq L_{\mathsf{alarm}}$	$t' \approx d$	$l_o < L_{\mathsf{alarm}} \rightarrow c' < L_{\mathsf{overflow}}$
$c' \approx \mathsf{in}(l_o, t_o)$	$d' \approx h(t_o)$	$\neg l'' \leq L_{\mathsf{overflow}}$	$l'' \approx c'$	$l' < L_{\mathsf{overflow}} \rightarrow l_o < L_{\mathsf{alarm}}$
			$t'' \approx d'$	$N_0 : l \approx l_o \wedge t \approx t_o \rightarrow c \approx c'$

Interpolation. Let $A = l{<}L_{\mathsf{alarm}} \wedge l'{\approx}\mathsf{in}(l, t) \wedge t'{\approx}k(l)$ and $B = l'{\geq}L_{\mathsf{alarm}} \wedge l''{\approx}\mathsf{in}(\mathsf{out}(l', t'), g(t')) \wedge t''{\approx}h(g(t')) \wedge \neg l''{\leq}L_{\mathsf{overflow}}$. To generate an interpolant for $A \wedge B$, we partition the clauses in Base as $A_0 \wedge B_0$, where $A_0 = l{<}L_{\mathsf{alarm}} \wedge l'{\approx}c \wedge t'{\approx}d \wedge \mathcal{K}_0^A$ and $B_0 = l'{\geq}L_{\mathsf{alarm}} \wedge l''{\approx}c' \wedge t''{\approx}d' \wedge \neg l''{\leq}L_{\mathsf{overflow}} \wedge \mathcal{K}_0^B$. The clause in

N_0 is mixed. Since already the conjunction of the formulae in Base is unsatisfiable, N_0 is not needed to prove unsatisfiability. The conjunction of the formulae in Base is equivalent to $A_0' \wedge B_0'$, where $A_0' = l < L_{\mathsf{alarm}} \wedge l' \approx c \wedge t' \approx d \wedge c < L_{\mathsf{overflow}}$ and $B_0' = l' > L_{\mathsf{alarm}} \wedge l'' \approx c' \wedge t'' \approx d' \wedge \neg l'' \leq L_{\mathsf{overflow}} \wedge c' < L_{\mathsf{overflow}} \wedge l_o < L_{\mathsf{alarm}}$. The interpolant for $A_0' \wedge B_0'$ is $L' < L_{\mathsf{overflow}}$, which is also an interpolant for $A \wedge B$.

For the database example in Section 1.1 the interpolant is computed similarily.

5   Conclusions

We presented a method for obtaining simple interpolants in theory extensions. We identified situations in which it is possible to do this in a hierarchical manner, by using a prover and a procedure for generating interpolants in the base theory as "black-boxes". This allows us to use the properties of T_0 (e.g. the form of interpolants) to control the form of interpolants in the extension T_1. We discussed applications of interpolation in verification and knowledge representation.

The method we presented is more general than the results of McMillan [4] on interpolation in extension of linear rational arithmetic with uninterpreted function symbols. Our method is orthogonal to the method for generating interpolants for combinations of theories over disjoint signatures from Nelson-Oppen-style unsatisfiability proofs proposed by Yorsh and Musuvathi in [10], as it allows us to consider combinations of theories over non-disjoint signatures.

The hierarchical interpolation method presented here (for the special case of the extension of linear arithmetic with free function symbols) was implemented by Andrey Rybalchenko in Prolog. First tests suggest that our method is considerably faster than other existing methods. Details about the implementation and benchmarks for the special case of linear arithmetic + free function symbols are the subject of a separate joint paper.

Acknowledgements. I thank Andrey Rybalchenko for interesting discussions. This work was partly supported by the German Research Council (DFG) as part of the Transregional Collaborative Research Center "Automatic Verification and Analysis of Complex Systems" (SFB/TR 14 AVACS). See www.avacs.org for more information.

References

1. P.D. Bacsich. Amalgamation properties and interpolation theorem for equational theories. *Algebra Universalis*, 5:45–55, 1975.
2. B Jónsson. Extensions of relational structures. In J.W. Addison, L. Henkin, and A. Tarski, editors, *The Theory of Models, Proc. of the 1963 Symposium at Berkeley*, pages 146–157, Amsterdam, 1965. North-Holland.
3. K.L. McMillan. Interpolation and SAT-based model checking. In *CAV'2003: Computer Aided Verification, LNCS 2725*, pages 1–13. Springer, 2003.
4. K.L. McMillan. An interpolating theorem prover. In *TACAS'2004: Tools and Algorithms for the Construction and Analysis of Systems, LNCS 2988*, pages 16–30. Springer, 2004.

5. K.L. McMillan. Applications of Craig interpolants in model checking. In *TACAS'2005: Tools and Algorithms for the Construction and Analysis of Systems, LNCS 3440*, pages 1–12. Springer, 2005.
6. V. Sofronie-Stokkermans. On combinations of local theory extensions. Submitted.
7. V. Sofronie-Stokkermans. Automated theorem proving by resolution in non-classical logics. In *4th Int. Conf. Journees de l'Informatique Messine: Knowledge Discovery and Discrete Mathematics (JIM-03)*, pages 151–167, 2003.
8. V. Sofronie-Stokkermans. Hierarchic reasoning in local theory extensions. In R. Nieuwenhuis, editor, *20th International Conference on Automated Deduction (CADE-20), LNAI 3632*, pages 219–234. Springer, 2005.
9. A. Wroński. On a form of equational interpolation property. In *Foundations of logic and linguistics (Salzburg, 1983)*, pages 23–29, New York, 1985. Plenum.
10. G. Yorsh and M. Musuvathi. A combination method for generating interpolants. In R. Nieuwenhuis, editor, *20th International Conference on Automated Deduction (CADE-20), LNAI 3632*, pages 353–368. Springer, 2005.

Canonical Gentzen-Type Calculi with (n,k)-ary Quantifiers

Anna Zamansky and Arnon Avron

Tel Aviv University, Ramat Aviv, Israel
{annaz, aa}@post.tau.ac.il

Abstract. Propositional canonical Gentzen-type systems, introduced in [1], are systems which in addition to the standard axioms and structural rules have only logical rules in which exactly one occurrence of a connective is introduced and no other connective is mentioned. [1] provides a constructive coherence criterion for the non-triviality of such systems and shows that a system of this kind admits cut-elimination iff it is coherent. The semantics of such systems is provided using two-valued nondeterministic matrices (2Nmatrices). [14] extends these results to systems with unary quantifiers of a very restricted form. In this paper we substantially extend the characterization of canonical systems to (n, k)-ary quantifiers, which bind k distinct variables and connect n formulas. We show that the coherence criterion remains constructive for such systems, and that for the case of $k \in \{0, 1\}$: (i) a canonical system is coherent iff it has a strongly characteristic 2Nmatrix, and (ii) if a canonical system is coherent, then it admits cut-elimination.

1 Introduction

An (n, k)-*ary quantifier* (for $n > 0$, $k \geq 0$) is a generalized logical connective, which binds k variables and connects n formulas. Any n-ary propositional connective can be thought of as an $(n, 0)$-ary quantifier. For instance, the standard $\wedge$ connective binds no variables and connects two formulas: $\wedge(\psi_1, \psi_2)$. The standard first-order quantifiers $\exists$ and $\forall$ are $(1, 1)$-quantifiers, as they bind one variable and connect one formula: $\forall x \psi, \exists x \psi$. Bounded universal and existential quantification used in syllogistic reasoning $(\forall x(p(x) \rightarrow q(x))$ and $\exists x(p(x) \wedge q(x)))$ can be represented as $(2,1)$-ary quantifiers $\overline{\forall}$ and $\overline{\exists}$, binding one variable and connecting two formulas: $\overline{\forall} x(p(x), q(x))$ and $\overline{\exists} x(p(x), q(x))$. An example of (n, k)-ary quantifiers for $k > 1$ are Henkin quantifiers[1] ([9,10]). The simplest Henkin quantifier Q_H binds 4 variables and connects one formula:

$$Q_H \begin{matrix} \forall x_1 & \exists y_1 \\ \forall x_2 & \exists y_2 \end{matrix} \psi(x_1, x_2, y_1, y_2)$$

According to a long tradition in the philosophy of logic, established by Gentzen in his classical paper *Investigations Into Logical Deduction* ([7]), an "ideal" introduction rule for a logical connective is a rule which determines the *meaning*

---

[1] Although the semantic interpretation of quantifiers used in this paper is not sufficient for treating such quantifiers.

U. Furbach and N. Shankar (Eds.): IJCAR 2006, LNAI 4130, pp. 251–265, 2006.

of the connective. In [1,2] the notion of a "canonical propositional Gentzen-type rule" was first defined in precise terms. A constructive *coherence* criterion for the non-triviality of such systems was then provided, and it was shown that a system of this kind admits cut-elimination iff it is coherent. It was further proved that the semantics of such systems is provided by two-valued non-deterministic matrices (2Nmatrices), which form a natural generalization of the classical matrix. In fact, a characteristic 2Nmatrix was constructed for every coherent canonical propositional system.

In [14] the results were extended to systems with unary quantifiers. A characterization of a "canonical unary quantificational rule" in such calculi was proposed (the standard Gentzen-type rules for $\forall$ and $\exists$ are canonical according to it), and a constructive extension of the coherence criterion of [1,2] for canonical systems of this type was given. 2Nmatrices were extended to languages with unary quantifiers, using a *distribution* interpretation of quantifiers ([12]). Then it was proved that again a canonical Gentzen-type system of this type admits cut-elimination iff it is coherent, and that it is coherent iff it has a characteristic 2Nmatrix. However, the canonical systems in [14] are of a very restricted form: they use unary quantifiers and only one atomic (monadic) formula is allowed in each clause.

In this paper we make the intuitive notion of a "well-behaved" introduction rule for (n, k)-ary quantifiers formally precise. We considerably extend the scope of the characterizations of [1,2,14] to "canonical (n, k)-ary quantificational rules", so that both the propositional systems of [1,2] and the restricted quantificational systems of [14] are specific instances of the proposed definition. However, in contrast to the systems in [14], there are no limitations on the size of the clauses in our formulation. It is then shown that the coherence criterion for the defined systems remains constructive. Then we turn to the class of canonical systems with (n, k)-ary quantifiers for $k \in \{0, 1\}$ and show that every coherent canonical calculus G has a characteristic 2Nmatrix and admits cut-elimination. The other direction, however, does not hold: we shall see that in contrast to the canonical systems of [1,14], the ability to eliminate cuts in a canonical calculus G does *not* necessarily imply its coherence.

2   Preliminaries

For any $n > 0$ and $k \geq 0$, if a quantifier $\mathcal{Q}$ is of arity (n, k), then $\mathcal{Q}x_1...x_k$ $(\psi_1, ..., \psi_n)$ is a formula whenever $x_1, ..., x_k$ are distinct variables and $\psi_1, ..., \psi_n$ are formulas of L.

For interpretation of quantifiers, we use a generalized notion of *distribution functions* ([12]). Given a set S, $P^+(S)$ is the set of all the nonempty subsets of S.

Definition 1. *Given a set of truth value $\mathcal{V}$, a distribution of a (1,1)-ary quantifier $\mathcal{Q}$ is a function $\lambda_\mathcal{Q} : P^+(\mathcal{V}) \to \mathcal{V}$.*

(1,1)-ary distribution quantifiers have been extensively studied and axiomatized in many-valued logic. See, for instance, [5,13,8].

In what follows, L is a language with (n, k)-ary quantifiers, that is with quantifiers $\mathcal{Q}_1, ..., \mathcal{Q}_m$ with arities (n_1, k_1), ..., (n_m, k_m) respectively. Denote by Frm_L^{cl} the set of closed L-formulas and by Trm_L^{cl} the set of closed L-terms.

$\equiv_\alpha$ is the α-equivalence relation between formulas, i.e identity up to the renaming of bound variables. We use [ ] for application of functions in the metalanguage, leaving the use of ( ) to the object language. $A\{t/x\}$ denotes the formula obtained from A by substituting t for x. Given an L-formula A, $Fv[A]$ is the set of variables occurring free in A. We denote $\mathcal{Q}x_1...x_kA$ by $\mathcal{Q}\overrightarrow{x}A$, and $A(x_1, ..., x_k)$ by $A(\overrightarrow{x})$.

3   Canonical Systems with (n,k)-ary Quantifiers

In this section we formulate a precise definition of a "canonical (n, k)-ary quantificational Gentzen-type rule".

Using an introduction rule for an (n, k)-ary quantifier $\mathcal{Q}$, we should be able to derive a sequent of the form $\Gamma \Rightarrow \mathcal{Q}x_1...x_k(\psi_1, ..., \psi_n), \Delta$ or of the form $\Gamma, \mathcal{Q}x_1...x_k(\psi_1, ..., \psi_n) \Rightarrow \Delta$, based on some information about the subformulas of $\mathcal{Q}x_1...x_k(\psi_1, ..., \psi_n)$ contained in the premises of the rule. For instance, consider the following standard rules for the $(1,1)$-ary quantifier $\forall$:

$$\frac{\Gamma, A\{t/w\} \Rightarrow \Delta}{\Gamma, \forall w\, A \Rightarrow \Delta} \; (\forall \Rightarrow) \qquad \frac{\Gamma \Rightarrow A\{z/w\}, \Delta}{\Gamma \Rightarrow \forall w\, A, \Delta} \; (\Rightarrow \forall)$$

where t, z are free for w in A and z does not occur free in the conclusion. Our key observation is that the internal structure of A, as well as the exact term t or variable w used, are immaterial for the meaning of $\forall$. What is important here is the side of the sequent, on which A appears, as well as whether a term variable t or an eigenvariable z is used.

Hence, the internal structure of the formulas of L can be abstracted by using a simplified first-order language, i.e. the formulas of L in an introduction rule of a (n, k)-ary quantifier, will be represented by *atomic* formulas with predicate symbols of arity k. The case when the substituted term is any L-term, will be signified by a constant, and the case when it is a variable satisfying the above conditions - by a variable. In other words, constants serve as term variables, while variables are eigenvariables.

Hence, in addition to our original language L with (n, k)-ary quantifiers we define another, simplified language.

Definition 2. *For $k \geq 0$, $n \geq 1$ and a set of constants Con, $L_k^n(Con)$ is the language with n k-ary predicate symbols $p_1, ..., p_n$ and the set of constants Con (and no quantifiers or connectives).*

Definition 3 (Canonical Rules)

1. *Let Con be some set of constants. A canonical quantificational rule of arity (n, k) is an expression of the form $\{\Pi_i \Rightarrow \Sigma_i\}_{1 \leq i \leq m}/C$, where $m \geq 0$, C is*

either $\Rightarrow Qx_1...x_k(p_1(x_1,...,x_k),...,p_n(x_1,...,x_k))$ *or* $Qx_1...x_k(p_1(x_1,...,x_k),$
$...,p_n(x_1,...,x_k)) \Rightarrow$ *for some* (n,k)-*ary quantifier* Q *of* L *and for every*
$1 \le i \le m$: $\Pi_i \Rightarrow \Sigma_i$ *is a clause*[2] *over* $L_k^n(Con)$.

2. *Let* $R = \Theta/C$ *be an* (n,k)-*ary canonical rule, where* C *is of one of the forms*
$(Q\vec{x}(p_1(\vec{x}),...,p_n(\vec{x})) \Rightarrow)$ *or* $(\Rightarrow Q\vec{x}(p_1(\vec{x}),...,p_n(\vec{x})))$.
Let Con_Θ *be the set of constants occurring in* Θ. *Let* Γ *be a set of* L-*formulas*
and $z_1,...,z_k$ - *distinct variables.*
An $\langle R, \Gamma, z_1,...,z_k\rangle$-*mapping is any function* χ *from the predicate symbols*
and terms of $L_k^n(Con_\Theta)$ *to formulas and terms of* L, *satisfying the following*
conditions:
 - *For every* $1 \le i \le n$, $\chi[p_i]$ *is an* L-*formula.*
 - $\chi[y]$ *is a variable of* L.
 - $\chi[x] \ne \chi[y]$ *for every two variables* $x \ne y$.
 - $\chi[c]$ *is an* L-*term.*
 - *For every* $1 \le i \le n$, *every* $p_i(t_1,...,t_k)$ *occurring in* Θ *and every* $1 \le$
   $j \le k$: $\chi[t_j]$ *is a term free for* z_j *in* $\chi[p_i]$, *and if* t_j *is a variable, then*
   $\chi[t_j]$ *does not occur free in* $\Gamma \cup \{Qz_1...z_k(\chi[p_1],...,\chi[p_n])\}$.

We extend χ *to* $L_k^n(Con_\Theta)$-*formulas and sets of* $L_k^n(Con)$-*formulas as fol-*
lows:

$$\chi[p_i(t_1,...,t_k)] = \chi[p_i]\{\chi[t_1]/z_1,...,\chi[t_k]/z_k\}$$

$$\chi[\Gamma] = \{\chi[\psi] \mid \psi \in \Gamma\}$$

An application *of a canonical quantificational rule of arity* (n,k)
$R = \{\Pi_i \Rightarrow \Sigma_i\}_{1 \le i \le m}/Qx_1...x_k(p_1(x_1,...,x_k),...,p_n(x_1,...,x_k)) \Rightarrow$ *is any*
inference step of the form:

$$\frac{\{\Gamma, \chi[\Pi_i] \Rightarrow \Delta, \chi[\Sigma_i]\}_{1 \le i \le m}}{\Gamma, Qz_1...z_k\ (\chi[p_1],...,\chi[p_n]) \Rightarrow \Delta}$$

where $z_1,...,z_k$ *are variables,* Γ, Δ *are any sets of* L-*formulas and* χ *is some*
$\langle R, \Gamma \cup \Delta, z_1,...,z_k\rangle$-*mapping.*
An application of a canonical quantificational rule of the form
$\{\Pi_i \Rightarrow \Sigma_i\}_{1 \le i \le m}/ \Rightarrow Qx_1...x_k(p_1(x_1,...,x_k),...,p_n(x_1,...,x_k))$ *is defined*
similarly.

In other words, an application of an (n,k)-ary canonical rule $\Theta/ \Rightarrow Q\vec{z}$
$(p_1(\vec{z}),...,p_n(\vec{z}))$ is obtained by "instantiating" the rule, i.e. by replacing every $L_k^n(Con_\Theta)$-formula $p_i(c)$ in Θ by some L-formula $\psi_i\{\mathbf{t}_c/z\}$, every $p_j(x)$ - by
some L-formula $\psi_j\{y_x/z\}$, and $Q\vec{z}(p_1(\vec{z}),...,p_n(\vec{z}))$ - by $Qz(\psi_1,...,\psi_n)$, with
the restrictions on $\mathbf{t}_c$ and y_x which are specified above.

Below we demonstrate the above definition by a number of examples.

Example 1. The standard right introduction rule for $\wedge$, which can be thought of as
an $(2,0)$-ary quantifier is $\{\Rightarrow p_1, \Rightarrow p_2\}/ \Rightarrow p_1 \wedge p_2$. Its application is of the form:

$$\frac{\Gamma \Rightarrow \psi_1, \Delta \quad \Gamma \Rightarrow \psi_2, \Delta}{\Gamma \Rightarrow \psi_1 \wedge \psi_2, \Delta}$$

---

[2] By a clause we mean a sequent containing only atomic formulas.

Example 2. The two standard introduction rules for the $(1,1)$-ary quantifier $\forall$ can be formulated as follows:

$$\{p(c) \Rightarrow\}/\forall x\, p(x) \Rightarrow \quad \{\Rightarrow p(y)\}/ \Rightarrow \forall x\, p(x)$$

Applications of these rules have the forms:

$$\frac{\Gamma, A\{t/w\} \Rightarrow \Delta}{\Gamma, \forall w\, A \Rightarrow \Delta} \ (\forall \Rightarrow) \qquad \frac{\Gamma \Rightarrow A\{z/w\}, \Delta}{\Gamma \Rightarrow \forall w\, A, \Delta} \ (\Rightarrow \forall)$$

where z is free for w in A, z is not free in $\Gamma \cup \Delta \cup \{\forall w A\}$, and $\mathbf{t}$ is any term free for w in A.

Example 3. Consider the bounded existential and universal $(2,1)$-ary quantifiers $\overline{\forall}$ and $\overline{\exists}$ (corresponding to $\forall x.p_1(x) \rightarrow p_2(x)$ and $\exists x.p_1(x) \wedge p_2(x)$ used in syllogistic reasoning). Their corresponding rules can be formulated as follows:

$$\{p_2(c) \Rightarrow , \ \Rightarrow p_1(c)\}/\overline{\forall}x \ (p_1(x), p_2(x)) \Rightarrow \quad \{p_1(y) \Rightarrow p_2(y)\}/ \Rightarrow \overline{\forall}x \ (p_1(x), p_2(x))$$

$$\{p_1(y), p_2(y) \Rightarrow\}/\overline{\exists} \ x(p_1(x), p_2(x)) \Rightarrow \quad \{\Rightarrow p_1(c) , \ \Rightarrow p_2(c)\}/ \Rightarrow \overline{\exists}x(p_1(x), p_2(x))$$

Applications of these rules are of the form:

$$\frac{\Gamma, \psi_2\{t/z\} \Rightarrow \Delta \quad \Gamma \Rightarrow \psi_1\{t/z\}, \Delta}{\Gamma, \overline{\forall}z \ (\psi_1, \psi_2) \Rightarrow \Delta} \qquad \frac{\Gamma, \psi_1\{y/z\} \Rightarrow \psi_2\{y/z\}, \Delta}{\Gamma \Rightarrow \overline{\forall}z \ (\psi_1, \psi_2), \Delta}$$

$$\frac{\Gamma, \psi_1\{y/z\}, \psi_2\{y/z\} \Rightarrow \Delta}{\Gamma, \overline{\exists}z \ (\psi_1, \psi_2) \Rightarrow \Delta} \qquad \frac{\Gamma, \psi_1\{t/x\} \Rightarrow \Delta \quad \Gamma \Rightarrow \psi_2\{t/x\}, \Delta}{\Gamma \Rightarrow \overline{\exists}z \ (\psi_1, \psi_2), \Delta}$$

where $\mathbf{t}$ and y are free for z in ψ_1 and ψ_2, y does not occur free in $\Gamma \cup \Delta \cup \{\overline{\exists}z(\psi_1, \psi_2)\}$.

Example 4. Consider the $(2,2)$-ary rule

$$\{p_1(x, z) \Rightarrow , \ p_1(y, d) \Rightarrow p_2(c, d)\}/ \Rightarrow Qz_1z_2(p_1(z_1, z_2), p_2(z_1, z_2))$$

Its application is of the form:

$$\frac{\Gamma, \psi_1\{w_1/z_1, w_2/z_2\} \Rightarrow \Delta \quad \Gamma, \psi_1\{w_3/z_1, t_1/z_2\} \Rightarrow \Delta, \psi_2\{t_2/z_1, t_1/z_2\}}{\Gamma \Rightarrow \Delta, Qz_1z_2(\psi_1, \psi_2)}$$

where w_1, w_2, w_3, t_1, t_2 satisfy the appropriate conditions.

Henceforth, in cases where the set of constants Con_Θ is clear from the context (it is the set of all constants occurring in a canonical rule), we will write L_k^n instead of $L_k^n(Con_\Theta)$.

Definition 4. *A Gentzen-type calculus G is canonical if in addition to the α-axiom $A \Rightarrow A'$ for $A \equiv_\alpha A'$ and the standard structural rules, G has only canonical quantificational rules, such that the sets of constants and variables of every two rules are disjoint.*

Although we can define arbitrary canonical systems using our simplified language L_k^n, our quest is for systems, the syntactic rules of which define the semantic meaning of logical connectives. Thus we are interested in calculi with a "reasonable" or "non-contradictory" set of rules, which allows for defining a sound and complete semantics for the system. This can be captured syntactically by the *coherence* criterion of [1,14]:

Definition 5 (Coherence). [3] *A canonical calculus G is coherent if for every two canonical rules of G of the form $\Theta_1/ \Rightarrow A$ and $\Theta_2/A \Rightarrow$, the set of clauses $\Theta_1 \cup \Theta_2$ is classically inconsistent.*

Proposition 1 (Decidability of coherence). *The coherence of a canonical calculus G is decidable.*

Proof. The question of classical consistency of a finite set of clauses without quantifiers can be easily shown to be equivalent to satisfiability of a finite set of universal formulas in a language with no function symbols, which is decidable.

Notation. (Following [1], notations 3-5.) Let $-t = f$, $-f = t$ and $ite(t, A, B) = A$, $ite(f, A, B) = B$. Let Φ, A^s (where Φ may be empty) denote $ite(s, \Phi \cup \{A\}, \Phi)$. For instance, the sequents $A \Rightarrow$ and $\Rightarrow A$ are denoted by $A^a \Rightarrow A^{-a}$ for $a = t$ and $a = f$ respectively.

According to this notation, a (n, k)-ary canonical rule is of the form

$$\{\Sigma_j \Rightarrow \Pi_j\}_{1 \leq j \leq m}/$$

$$\mathcal{Q}\overrightarrow{z}(p_1(\overrightarrow{z}), ..., p_n(\overrightarrow{z}))^s \Rightarrow \mathcal{Q}\overrightarrow{z}(p_1(\overrightarrow{z}), ..., p_n(\overrightarrow{z}))^{-s}$$

for $s \in \{t, f\}$. For further abbreviation, we denote such rule by $\{\Sigma_j \Rightarrow \Pi_j\}_{1 \leq j \leq m}/\mathcal{Q}(s)$.

4   The Semantic Framework

4.1   Non-deterministic Matrices

Our main semantic tool are non-deterministic matrices (Nmatrices), first introduced in [1] and used in [2,14]. These structures are a generalization of the standard concept of a many-valued matrix, in which the truth-value of a formula is chosen non-deterministically from a given non-empty set of truth-values. Thus, given a set of truth-values $\mathcal{V}$, we can generalize the notion of a distribution function of an (n, k)-ary quantifier $\mathcal{Q}$ (from Definition. 1) to a function $\lambda_{\mathcal{Q}} : P^+(\mathcal{V}^n) \rightarrow P^+(\mathcal{V})$. In other words, given some distribution Y of n-ary vectors of truth values, the interpretation function non-deterministically chooses the truth value assigned to $\mathcal{Q}\overrightarrow{z}(\psi_1, ..., \psi_n)$ out from $\lambda_{\mathcal{Q}}[Y]$.

---

[3] Strongly related coherence criterions are defined in [11], where linear logic is used to reason about various sequent systems, and in [6], where a characterization of cut-elimination is given for a general class of propositional single-conclusion sequent calculi.

Definition 6 (Non-deterministic matrix). *A non-deterministic matrix (henceforth Nmatrix) for L is a tuple $\mathcal{M} = <\mathcal{V}, \mathcal{G}, \mathcal{O}>$, where:*

- $\mathcal{V}$ *is a non-empty set of truth values.*
- $\mathcal{G}$ *(designated truth values) is a non-empty proper subset of $\mathcal{V}$.*
- $\mathcal{O}$ *is a set of interpretation functions: for every (n, k)-ary quantifier Q of L, $\mathcal{O}$ includes the corresponding distribution function $\tilde{Q}_{\mathcal{M}} : P^+(\mathcal{V}^n) \to P^+(\mathcal{V})$.*

At this point a remark on our treatment of propositional connectives is in order. In [1,14], an Nmatrix includes an interpretation function $\tilde{\diamond} : \mathcal{V}^n \to P^+(\mathcal{V})$ for every n-ary connective of the language; given a valuation v, the truth value $v[\diamond(\psi_1, ..., \psi_n)]$ is chosen non-deterministically from $\tilde{\diamond}[\langle v[\psi_1], ..., v[\psi_n]\rangle]$. In the definition above, the interpretation of a propositional connective $\diamond$ is a function of another type: $\tilde{\diamond} : P^+(\mathcal{V}^n) \to P^+(\mathcal{V})$. This can be thought as a generalization of the previous definition, identifying the tuple $\langle v[\psi_1], ..., v[\psi_n]\rangle$ with the singleton $\{\langle v[\psi_1], ..., v[\psi_n]\rangle\}$. The advantage of this generalization is that it allows for a uniform treatment of both quantifiers and propositional connectives.

Definition 7 (L-structure). *Let $\mathcal{M}$ be an Nmatrix for L. An L-structure for $\mathcal{M}$ is a pair $S = \langle D, I \rangle$ where D is a (non-empty) domain and I is a function interpreting constants, predicate symbols and function symbols of L, satisfying the following conditions: $I[c] \in D$, $I[p^n] : D^n \to \mathcal{V}$ is an n-ary predicate, and $I[f^n] : D^n \to D$ is an n-ary function.*
I is extended to interpret closed terms of L as follows:

$$I[f(t_1, ..., t_n)] = I[f][I[t_1], ..., I[t_n]]$$

Definition 8 (L(D)). *Let $S = \langle D, I \rangle$ be an L-structure for an Nmatrix $\mathcal{M}$. $L(D)$ is the language obtained from L by adding to it the set of individual constants $\{\bar{a} \mid a \in D\}$. $S' = \langle D, I' \rangle$ is the $L(D)$-structure, such that I' is an extension of I satisfying: $I'[\bar{a}] = a$.*

Given an L-structure $S = \langle D, I \rangle$, we shall refer to the extended $L(D)$-structure $\langle D, I' \rangle$ as S and to I' as I when the meaning is clear from the context.

Definition 9 (Congruence of terms and formulas). *Let S be an L-structure for an Nmatrix $\mathcal{M}$. The relation $\sim^S$ between terms of $L(D)$ is defined inductively as follows:*

- $x \sim^S x$
- *For closed terms t, t' of $L(D)$: $t \sim^S t'$ when $I[t] = I[t']$.*
- *If $t_1 \sim^S t'_1, ..., t_n \sim^S t'_n$, then $f(t_1, ..., t_n) \sim^S f(t'_1, ..., t'_n)$.*

The relation $\sim^S$ between formulas of $L(D)$ is defined as follows:

- *If $t_1 \sim^S t'_1, t_2 \sim^S t'_2, ..., t_n \sim^S t'_n$, then $p(t_1, ..., t_n) \sim^S p(t'_1, ..., t'_n)$.*
- *If $\psi_1\{\overrightarrow{z}/\overrightarrow{x}\} \sim^S \varphi_1\{\overrightarrow{z}/\overrightarrow{y}\}, ..., \psi_n\{\overrightarrow{z}/\overrightarrow{x}\} \sim^S \varphi_n\{\overrightarrow{z}/\overrightarrow{y}\}$, where $\overrightarrow{x} = x_1...x_k$ and $\overrightarrow{y} = y_1...y_k$ are distinct variables and $\overrightarrow{z} = z_1...z_k$ are new distinct variables, then $Q\overrightarrow{x}(\psi_1, ..., \psi_n) \sim^S Q\overrightarrow{y}(\varphi_1, ..., \varphi_n)$ for any (n, k)-ary quantifier Q of L.*

Lemma 1. *Let S be an L-structure for an Nmatrix $\mathcal{M}$. Let ψ, ψ' be formulas of $L(D)$. Let t, t' be closed terms of $L(D)$, such that $t \sim^S t'$.*

1. *If $\psi \equiv_\alpha \psi'$, then $\psi \sim^S \psi'$.*
2. *If $\psi \sim^S \psi'$, then $\psi\{t/x\} \sim^S \psi'\{t'/x\}$.*

Definition 10 (Legal valuation). *Let $S = \langle D, I \rangle$ be an L-structure for an Nmatrix $\mathcal{M}$. An S-valuation $v : Frm_L^{cl} \to \mathcal{V}$ is legal in $\mathcal{M}$ if it satisfies the following conditions: $v[\psi] = v[\psi']$ for every two sentences ψ, ψ' of $L(D)$, such that $\psi \sim^S \psi'$, $v[p(t_1, ..., t_n)] = I[p][I[t_1], ..., I[t_n]]$, and:*

$$v[Qx_1, ..., x_k(\psi_1, ..., \psi_n)] \in$$

$$\tilde{Q}_{\mathcal{M}}[\{\langle v[\psi_1\{\bar{a}_1/x_1, ..., \bar{a}_k/x_k\}], ..., v[\psi_n\{\bar{a}_1/x_1, ..., \bar{a}_k/x_k\}]\rangle \mid a_1, ..., a_k \in D\}]$$

for every (n, k)-ary quantifier Q of L.

Note that in case Q is a propositional connective (for $k = 0$), the function $\tilde{Q}$ is applied to a singleton, as was explained above.

Definition 11 (Model, $\mathcal{M}$-validity, $\vdash_{\mathcal{M}}$). *Let $S = \langle D, I \rangle$ be an L-structure for an Nmatrix $\mathcal{M}$.*

1. *An $\mathcal{M}$-legal S-valuation v is a model of a sentence ψ in $\mathcal{M}$, denoted by $S, v \models_{\mathcal{M}} \psi$, if $v[\psi] \in \mathcal{G}$.*
2. *A formula ψ is $\mathcal{M}$-valid in S if for every S-substitution σ and every $\mathcal{M}$-legal S-valuation v, $S, v \models_{\mathcal{M}} \sigma[\psi]$. A formula ψ (a set of formulas Γ) is $\mathcal{M}$-valid if ψ (every $\psi \in \Gamma$) is $\mathcal{M}$-valid in every L-structure for $\mathcal{M}$.*
3. *A sequent $\Gamma \Rightarrow \Delta$ is $\mathcal{M}$-valid in S if for every $\mathcal{M}$-legal S-valuation v and every S-substitution σ: $S, v \models_{\mathcal{M}} \sigma[\Gamma]$ implies that there exists some $\psi \in \Delta$, such that $S, v \models_{\mathcal{M}} \sigma[\psi]$. A sequent is $\mathcal{M}$-valid if it is $\mathcal{M}$-valid in every structure.*
4. *The consequence relation $\vdash_{\mathcal{M}}$ induced by $\mathcal{M}$ is defined as follows: $\Gamma \vdash_{\mathcal{M}} \Delta$ if $\Gamma \Rightarrow \Delta$ is $\mathcal{M}$-valid.*
5. *An Nmatrix $\mathcal{M}$ is sound for a system G if $\vdash_G \subseteq \vdash_{\mathcal{M}}$. An Nmatrix $\mathcal{M}$ is complete for a system G if $\vdash_{\mathcal{M}} \subseteq \vdash_G$.*

Definition 12 (Strong soundness). *An Nmatrix $\mathcal{M}$ is strongly sound for a system G if: (i) $\mathcal{M}$ is sound for G, and (ii) for every inference rule R of G and every L-structure S: if the premises of R are $\mathcal{M}$-valid in S, the conclusion of R is $\mathcal{M}$-valid in S.*

Definition 13. *An Nmatrix $\mathcal{M}$ is a characteristic Nmatrix for a canonical system G if $\vdash_{\mathcal{M}} = \vdash_G$.*

A characteristic Nmatrix $\mathcal{M}$ for G is strongly characteristic if it is strongly sound for G.

4.2 Semantics for Simplified Languages L_k^n

In addition to L-structures for languages with (n, k)-ary quantifiers, we also use L_k^n-structures for the simplified languages L_k^n, using which the canonical rules are formulated. To make the distinction clearer, we shall use the metavariable S for the former and $\mathcal{N}$ for the latter. Since the formulas of L_k^n are always atomic, the specific 2Nmatrix for which $\mathcal{N}$ is defined is immaterial, and can be omitted. We may even speak of classical validity of sequents over L_k^n. Furthermore, instead of speaking of $\mathcal{M}$-validity of a set of clauses Θ over L_k^n, we may speak simply of validity.

Next we define the notion of a *distribution* of L_k^n-structures.

Definition 14. *Let $\mathcal{N}$ be a structure for L_k^n. $Dist_{\mathcal{N}}$, the distribution of $\mathcal{N}$ is defined as follows:*

$$Dist_{\mathcal{N}} = \{\langle I[p_1][a_1, ..., a_k], ..., I[p_n][a_1, ..., a_k]\rangle \mid a_1, ..., a_k \in D\}$$

We say that an L_k^n-structure is $\mathcal{E}$-characteristic if $Dist_{\mathcal{N}} = \mathcal{E}$.

Note that the distribution of an $\mathcal{L}_0^n$-structure $\mathcal{N}$ is $Dist_{\mathcal{N}} = \{\langle I[p_1], ..., I[p_n]\rangle\}$ and so it is always singleton. Furthermore, the validity of a set of clauses over $\mathcal{L}_0^n$ can be reduced to propositional satisfiability as stated in the following lemma.

Lemma 2. *For every $\mathcal{L}_0^n$-structure $\mathcal{N}$, such that $Dist_{\mathcal{N}} = \{\langle a_1, ..., a_n\rangle\}$, let $v_{Dist_{\mathcal{N}}}$ be any propositional valuation satisfying $v[p_i] = a_i$. A set of clauses Θ is valid in a $Dist_{\mathcal{N}}$-characteristic $\mathcal{L}_0^n$-structure $\mathcal{N}$ iff $v_{Dist_{\mathcal{N}}}$ propositionally satisfies Θ.*

Now we turn to the case $k = 1$. In this case it is convenient to define a special kind of $\mathcal{L}_1^n$-structures which we call *canonical* structures, which will be sufficient to reflect the behavior of all possible $\mathcal{L}_1^n$-structures.

Definition 15. *Let $\mathcal{E} \in P^+(\{t, f\}^n)$. A $\mathcal{L}_1^n$-structure $\mathcal{N} = \langle D, I \rangle$ is $\mathcal{E}$-canonical if $D = \mathcal{E}$ and for every $b = \langle a_1, ..., a_n \rangle \in D$ and every $1 \leq i \leq n$: $I[p_i][b] = a_i$.*

Clearly, every $\mathcal{E}$-canonical $\mathcal{L}_1^n$-structure is $\mathcal{E}$-characteristic.

Lemma 3. *Let Θ be a set of clauses over $\mathcal{L}_1^n$, which is valid in a structure $\mathcal{N} = \langle D, I \rangle$. Then there exists a $Dist_{\mathcal{N}}$-canonical structure $\mathcal{N}'$ in which Θ is valid.*

Proposition 2. *Let $\mathcal{E} \in P^+(\{t, f\}^n)$. For a finite set of clauses Θ over L_k^n, the question whether Θ is valid in a $\mathcal{E}$-characteristic structure is decidable.*

5 Canonical Systems with (n,k)-ary Quantifiers for $k \in \{0, 1\}$

Now we turn to the class of systems with (n, k)-ary quantifiers for $k \in \{0, 1\}$ and $n \geq 1$. Henceforth, unless stated otherwise, assume that $k \in \{0, 1\}$. For a uniform treatment of both $k = 0$ and $k = 1$, we use the following notation. For any variable x and any constant c, let x^0 and c^0 denote the empty string, and x^1, c^1 denote the strings 'x' and 'c' respectively. When we write $\mathcal{Q}x^k(\psi_1, ..., \psi_n)$, we mean $\mathcal{Q}x(\psi_1, ..., \psi_n)$ if $k = 1$ and $\mathcal{Q}(\psi_1, ..., \psi_n)$ if $k = 0$; when we write $\psi\{\mathbf{t}/x^k\}$, we mean $\psi\{\mathbf{t}/x\}$ for $k = 1$, and ψ for $k = 0$.

In this section we show that any coherent canonical calculus G has a characteristic 2Nmatrix and admits cut-elimination. We start by defining the notion of *suitability* for G.

Definition 16 (Suitability for G). *Let G be a canonical calculus over L. A 2Nmatrix $\mathcal{M}$ is* suitable *for G if for every (n, k)-ary canonical rule $\Theta/A^{-s} \Rightarrow A^s$ of G, where $s \in \{t, f\}$ and $A = \mathcal{Q}x^k(p_1(x^k), ..., p_n(x^k))$ it holds that for every L_k^n-structure $\mathcal{N}$ in which Θ is valid: $\tilde{\mathcal{Q}}_\mathcal{M}[Dist_\mathcal{N}] = \{s\}$.*

Next we prove that any 2Nmatrix $\mathcal{M}$ suitable for G is strongly sound for G. But first we transform G into a canonical calculus G', satisfying a certain property defined below.

Lemma 4 (Elimination of constants). *Let G be a canonical calculus with a canonical $(1,n)$-ary rule $R = \Theta/\mathcal{Q}(s)$ for some $s \in \{t, f\}$, where there are two clauses of the form $\Sigma_1, p_i(c) \Rightarrow \Pi_1$ and $\Sigma_2 \Rightarrow p_i(c), \Pi_2$ in Θ. Let $R' = \Theta'/\mathcal{Q}(s)$, where Θ' is obtained from Θ by replacing these two clauses for the clause $\Sigma_1, \Sigma_2 \Rightarrow \Pi_1, \Pi_2$. Let G' be the calculus obtained from G by replacing R for R'. Then any 2Nmatrix strongly sound for G', is also strongly sound for G.*

Corollary 1. *Let G be a canonical calculus. Then there exists a calculus G', such that (i) any 2Nmatrix strongly sound for G', is also strongly sound for G, and (ii) for every $(n,1)$-ary rule $\Theta/\mathcal{Q}(s)$ of G' and every clause $\Sigma_1, p_i(c)^r \Rightarrow \Pi_1, p_i(c)^{-r} \in \Theta$: there is no clause of the form $\Sigma_2, p_i(c)^{-r} \Rightarrow \Pi_2, p_i(c)^r$ in Θ.*

Proof. Easily follows by repeatedly applying lemma 4.

Theorem 1. *Let G be a canonical calculus over L and $\mathcal{M}$ - a 2Nmatrix suitable for G. Then $\mathcal{M}$ is strongly sound for G.*

Proof. Clearly, we may assume that G satisfies condition (ii) from corollary 1. Let S be an L-structure. Let R be an (n, k)-ary rule $R = \{\Sigma_j \Rightarrow \Pi_j\}_{1 \le j \le m}/ \Rightarrow \mathcal{Q}x^k(p_1(x^k), ..., p_n(x^k))$ of G'. Consider an application of R:

$$\frac{\{\Gamma, \chi[\Sigma_j] \Rightarrow \chi[\Pi_j], \Delta\}_{1 \le j \le m}}{\Gamma \Rightarrow \Delta, \mathcal{Q}z^k(\chi[p_1], ..., \chi[p_n])}$$

where χ is some $\langle R, \Gamma \cup \Delta, z^k \rangle$-mapping. It suffices to show that if the premises are $\mathcal{M}$-valid in S, then the conclusion is $\mathcal{M}$-valid in S. Let σ be an S-substitution and v an $\mathcal{M}$-legal valuation, such that $S, v \models_\mathcal{M} \sigma[\Gamma]$ and for every $\psi \in \Delta$: $S, v \not\models_\mathcal{M} \sigma[\psi]$. Denote by $\overrightarrow{\psi}$ the L-formula obtained from a formula ψ by substituting every free occurrence of $w \in Fv[\psi] - \{z^k\}$ for $\sigma[w]$. Let

$$\mathcal{E} = \{\langle v[\overrightarrow{\chi[p_1]}\{\overline{a}/z^k\}], ..., v[\overrightarrow{\chi[p_n]}\{\overline{a}/z^k\}]\rangle \mid a \in D\}$$

Define the L_k^n-structure $\mathcal{N} = \langle D', I' \rangle$: $D = D'$ and I' is defined as follows:

- For every $p_i(c) \in ite(s, \Sigma_j, \Pi_j)$ for some $1 \leq j \leq m$ and $s \in \{t, f\}$: if there is some $a \in D$, such that $v[\overrightarrow{\chi[p_i]}\{\overline{a}/z\}] = -s$, choose $I'[c]$ to be any such a (note that in this case $\Pi_j \Rightarrow \Sigma_j$ becomes valid); otherwise, choose $I'[c]$ to be any $a \in D$. It is important to stress that this is well-defined due to the special property of G', namely that $p_i(c)$ cannot occur on two different sides of a clause.
- For every $a \in D$: $I'[p_i][a^k] = v[\overrightarrow{\chi[p_i]}\{\overline{a}/z^k\}]$

It is easy to show that $\{\Sigma_j \Rightarrow \Pi_j\}_{1 \leq j \leq m}$ is valid in $\mathcal{N}$. Obviously, $Dist_{\mathcal{N}} = \mathcal{E}$ and since $\mathcal{M}$ is suitable for G: $\tilde{Q}_{\mathcal{M}}[\mathcal{E}] = \{t\}$ and so $v[\sigma[Qz(\chi[p_1], ..., \chi[p_n])]] = t$ and the conclusion of the application is $\mathcal{M}$-valid in S. $\qquad \square$

Now we come to the construction of a characteristic 2Nmatrix for a coherent canonical calculus.

Definition 17. *Let G be a coherent canonical calculus. The Nmatrix $\mathcal{M}_G$ for L is defined as follows. For every (n, k)-ary quantifier Q of L, every $s \in \{t, f\}$ and every $\mathcal{E} \in P^+(\{t, f\}^n)$:*

$$\tilde{Q}_{\mathcal{M}_G}[\mathcal{E}] = \begin{cases} \{s\} & \text{if } \Theta/Q(s) \in G \text{ and} \\ & \Theta \text{ is valid in some } \mathcal{E} - \text{characteristic structure} \\ \{t, f\} & \text{otherwise} \end{cases}$$

First let us show that $\mathcal{M}_G$ is well-defined. Assume by contradiction that there are two rules $\Theta_1/ \Rightarrow A$ and $\Theta_2/A \Rightarrow$, such that both Θ_1 and Θ_2 are valid in some $\mathcal{E}$-characteristic structures $\mathcal{N}_1 = \langle D_1, I_1 \rangle, \mathcal{N}_2 = \langle D_2, I_2 \rangle$ respectively. If $k = 0$, by lemma 2, the set of clauses $\Theta_1 \cup \Theta_2$ is propositionally satisfiable by $v_{\mathcal{E}}$ and is thus classically consistent, in contradiction to the coherence of G.

If $k = 1$, by lemma 3 there are $\mathcal{E}$-canonical structures $\mathcal{N}_1', \mathcal{N}_2'$ in which Θ_1, Θ_2 are valid. Recall that the only difference between different $\mathcal{E}$-canonical structures is in the interpretation of constants, and since the sets of constants occurring in Θ_1 and Θ_2 are disjoint, an $\mathcal{E}$-canonical structure $\mathcal{N}' = \langle D', I' \rangle$ (for the extended language containing the constants of both Θ_1 and Θ_2) can be constructed, in which $\Theta_1 \cup \Theta_2$ are valid. Thus the set $\Theta_1 \cup \Theta_2$ is classically consistent, in contradiction to the coherence of G.

Let us demonstrate the construction of a characteristic 2Nmatrix for some simple coherent canonical calculi.

Example 5. It is easy to see that for any canonical coherent calculus G including the standard $(1,1)$-ary rules for $\forall$ and $\exists$ from Example 2:

$$\tilde{\forall}_{\mathcal{M}_G}[\{t, f\}] = \tilde{\forall}_{\mathcal{M}_G}[\{f\}] = \tilde{\exists}_{\mathcal{M}_G}[\{f\}] = \{f\}$$

$$\tilde{\forall}_{\mathcal{M}_G}[\{t\}] = \tilde{\exists}_{\mathcal{M}_G}[\{t, f\}] = \tilde{\exists}_{\mathcal{M}_G}[\{t\}] = \{t\}$$

Example 6. Consider the canonical calculus G' consisting of the following two $(1,2)$-ary rules from Example 3:

$$\{p_1(y) \Rightarrow p_2(y)\}/ \Rightarrow \bar{\forall} x\ (p_1(x), p_2(x))$$

and

$$\{\Rightarrow p_1(c)\ ,\ \Rightarrow p_2(c)\}/ \Rightarrow \bar{\exists} x (p_1(x), p_2(x))$$

It is easy to see that G' is coherent. The 2Nmatrix $\mathcal{M}_{G'}$ is defined as follows for every $H \in \Gamma^+(\{t,f\}^2)$:

$$\tilde{\bar{\forall}}[H] = \begin{cases} \{t\} & \text{if } \langle t,f \rangle \notin H \\ \{t,f\} & \text{otherwise} \end{cases} \qquad \tilde{\bar{\exists}}[H] = \begin{cases} \{t\} & \text{if } \langle t,t \rangle \in H \\ \{t,f\} & \text{otherwise} \end{cases}$$

Remark. The construction of $\mathcal{M}_G$ above is much simpler than the constructions carried out in [1,14]: a canonical calculus there is first transformed into an equivalent normal form calculus, which is then used to construct the characteristic Nmatrix. The idea is to transform the calculus so that each rule dictates the interpretation for only one $\mathcal{E}$. However, the above definitions show that the transformation into normal form is actually not necessary and we can construct $\mathcal{M}_G$ directly from G.

Now we come to the main theorem, establishing that $\mathcal{M}_G$ is sound and complete for any coherent calculus G.

Theorem 2 (Soundness and cut-free completeness). *Let G be a coherent canonical calculus. Then a sequent $\Gamma \Rightarrow \Delta$ satisfying the free-variable condition[4] has a cut-free proof in G iff $\Gamma \vdash_{\mathcal{M}_G} \Delta$.*

Proof. *Soundness*: It is easy to see that $\mathcal{M}_G$ is suitable for G. By theorem 1, $\mathcal{M}_G$ is strongly sound for G, and thus $\vdash_G \subseteq \vdash_{\mathcal{M}_G}$.

Cut-free completeness: Let $\Gamma \Rightarrow \Delta$ be a sequent satisfying the free-variable condition. Suppose that $\Gamma \Rightarrow \Delta$ has no cut-free proof in G. We will show that it is not $\mathcal{M}_G$-valid.

It is easy to see that we can limit ourselves to the language L^*, which is a subset of L, consisting of all the constants and predicate and function symbols, occurring in $\Gamma \Rightarrow \Delta$. Let $\mathbf{T}$ be the set of all the terms in L^* which do not contain variables occurring bound in $\Gamma \Rightarrow \Delta$. It is a standard matter to show that Γ, Δ can be extended to two (possibly infinite) sets Γ', Δ' (where $\Gamma \subseteq \Gamma'$ and $\Delta \subseteq \Delta'$), satisfying the following properties:

1. For every $\Gamma_1 \subseteq \Gamma'$ and $\Delta_1 \subseteq \Delta'$, $\Gamma_1 \Rightarrow \Delta_1$ does not have a cut-free proof in G.
2. There are no $A \in \Gamma'$ and $B \in \Delta'$, such that $A \equiv_\alpha B$.
3. If $\{\Pi_j \Rightarrow \Sigma_j\}_{1 \le j \le m}/\mathcal{Q}(r)$ is an (n,k)-ary rule of G and $\mathcal{Q}z^k\ (A_1, ..., A_n) \in ite(r, \Delta', \Gamma')$, then there is some $1 \le j \le m$, such that:

---

[4] By the free-variable condition we mean that the set of bound variables of $\Gamma \cup \Delta$ is disjoint from its set of free variables.

- If $p_i(c^k) \in ite(r, \Pi_j, \Sigma_j)$ for some $1 \leq i \leq n$, then $A_i\{\mathbf{t}/z^k\} \in ite(r, \Gamma', \Delta')$ for every $\mathbf{t} \in \mathbf{T}$.
- If $p_i(y^k) \in ite(r, \Pi_j, \Sigma_j)$ for some $1 \leq i \leq n$, then there exists some $\mathbf{t} \in \mathbf{T}$, such that $A_i\{\mathbf{t}/z^k\} \in ite(r, \Gamma', \Delta')$.

Note that for the case of $k = 1$, $\mathbf{t}$ is free for z in A_i by the free-variable condition.

Let $S = \langle \mathbf{T}, I \rangle$ be the L^*-structure defined as follows:

- $I[c] = c$ for every constant c of L^*.
- $I[p][\mathbf{t}_1, ..., \mathbf{t}_n] = t$ iff $p(\mathbf{t}_1, ..., \mathbf{t}_n) \in \Gamma'$ for every n-ary predicate symbol p.
- $I[f][\mathbf{t}_1, ..., \mathbf{t}_n] = f(\mathbf{t}_1, ..., \mathbf{t}_n)$ for every n-ary function symbol f.

Let σ^* be any S-substitution satisfying $\sigma^*[x] = \overline{x}$ for every $x \in \mathbf{T}$. (Note that every $x \in \mathbf{T}$ is also a member of the domain and thus has an individual name referring to it in $L^*(D)$.)

It is easy to show that (i) $I^*[\sigma^*[\mathbf{t}]] = \mathbf{t}$ for every $\mathbf{t} \in \mathbf{T}$, and (ii) for every $A, B \in \Gamma' \cup \Delta'$: if $\sigma^*[A] \sim^S \sigma^*[B]$, then $A \equiv_\alpha B$.

Define the S-valuation v as follows:

- $v[p(\mathbf{t}_1, ..., \mathbf{t}_n)] = I[p][I[\mathbf{t}_1], ..., I[\mathbf{t}_n]]$.
- For every (n, k)-ary quantifier Q, if there is some $C \in \Gamma' \cup \Delta'$, such that $\sigma^*[C] \equiv_\alpha Qx^k(\psi_1, ..., \psi_n)$, then $v[Qx^k(\psi_1, ..., \psi_n)] = t$ iff $C \in \Gamma'$. Otherwise $v[Qx^k(\psi_1, ..., \psi_n)] = t$ iff $\tilde{Q}[\{\langle v[\psi_1\{\overline{a}/x^k\}], ..., v[\psi_n\{\overline{a}/x^k\}]\rangle \mid a \in D\}] = \{t\}$.

Lemma 5. *1. v is legal in $\mathcal{M}_G$.*
2. For every $\psi \in \Gamma' \cup \Delta'$: $v(\sigma^*[\psi]) = t$ iff $\psi \in \Gamma'$.

Since v is legal in $\mathcal{M}_G$, $\Gamma \subseteq \Gamma'$ and $\Delta \subseteq \Delta'$, by the above lemma v refutes $\Gamma \Rightarrow \Delta$. $\square$

Corollary 2. *If G is coherent, then $\mathcal{M}_G$ is strongly characteristic for G.*

Corollary 3. *For any canonical calculus G, the following two statements are equivalent:*

1. *G has a strongly characteristic 2Nmatrix.*
2. *G is coherent.*

Proof. The proof of $(1 \Rightarrow 2)$ is easy and is left to the reader. $(2 \Rightarrow 1)$ follows from corollary 2.

Corollary 4. *The existence of a strongly characteristic 2Nmatrix for a canonical calculus G is decidable.*

Remark. It is important to note that the coherence of G is *not* a necessary condition for the existence of a characteristic 2Nmatrix for G and, consequently, for cut-elimination. Consider, for instance the canonical calculus G_1 consisting of the following two inference rules:

$$(1) \ \{p_1(y) \Rightarrow p_2(y) \ , \ p_1(c_1) \Rightarrow \ , \ p_2(c_1) \Rightarrow \ ,$$

$$p_1(c_2) \Rightarrow \ , \ \Rightarrow p_2(c_2) \ , \ \Rightarrow p_1(c_3) \ , \ \Rightarrow p_2(c_3)\}/ \Rightarrow \mathcal{Q}z(p_1(z), p_2(z))$$

$$(2) \ \{p_1(y) \Rightarrow p_2(y) \ , \ p_1(c_4) \Rightarrow \ , \ p_2(c_4) \Rightarrow \ ,$$

$$p_1(c_5) \Rightarrow \ , \ \Rightarrow p_2(c_5) \ , \ \Rightarrow p_1(c_6) \ , \ \Rightarrow p_2(c_6)\}/\mathcal{Q}z(p_1(z), p_2(z)) \Rightarrow$$

It is easy to see that G_1 is not coherent, but the only sequents provable in it are logical axioms, and so G_1 has a characteristic 2Nmatrix and admits cut-elimination. This is in contrast to the systems in [1,14], where the fact that a canonical calculus admits cut-elimination implies that G is coherent.

6   Summary and Further Research

In this paper we have considerably extended the characterization of canonical calculi of [1,14] to (n, k)-ary quantifiers. For the case of $k \in \{0, 1\}$, we have shown that any coherent calculus admits cut-elimination and has a characteristic 2Nmatrix, but the converse does not necessary hold (unlike in [1,14]). In fact, a calculus is coherent iff it has a strongly characteristic 2Nmatrix. In addition to some proof-theoretical results for a natural type of multiple conclusion Gentzen-type systems with $(n, 1)$-ary quantifiers, our work also provides further evidence for the thesis that the meaning of a logical constant is given by its introduction (and "elimination") rules . We have shown that at least in the framework of multiple-conclusion consequence relations, any "reasonable" set of canonical quantificational rules completely determines the semantics of the quantifier.

Some of the most immediate research directions are:

1. Defining an exact criterion for the ability to eliminate cuts in canonical systems and developing a syntactic method for cut-elimination for the case of $k \in \{0, 1\}$, i.e. a stepwise transformation of any derivation of a canonical calculus into a cut-free derivation, possibly along the lines of [3].
2. Developing a general theory, extending the results of the previous section to the case of $k > 1$. This might lead to new insights on Henkin quantifiers and other important extensions, such as Transitive Closure operations. However, already for the simplest quantifiers this is not straightforward. First of all, the coherence of a canonical calculus G with general quantifiers *does not* imply that a 2Nmatrix suitable for G exists. For instance, consider the calculus G, consisting of the following two (1,2)-ary rules:

$$\{p(c, x) \Rightarrow\}/ \Rightarrow \mathcal{Q}z_1 z_2 p(z_1, z_2) \quad \{\Rightarrow p(y, d)\}/\mathcal{Q}z_1 z_2 p(z_1, z_2) \Rightarrow$$

G is coherent, but it is easy to see that $\mathcal{M}_G$ is not well-defined in this case. Secondly, even if a 2Nmatrix $\mathcal{M}$ suitable for G does exist, it is not necessarily sound for G. Therefore, a more complex interpretation of quantifiers is needed, which in its turn will lead to various extensions of the simplified language L_k^n (e.g. adding function symbols), and the cost of losing the decidability of the coherence criterion in this case seems inevitable.

Aknowledgement

This research was supported by the *Israel Science Foundation* founded by the Israel Academy of Sciences and Humanities.

References

1. Avron, A. and I. Lev, 'Canonical Propositional Gentzen-type Systems', *Proceedings of the 1st International Joint Conference on Automated Reasoning (IJCAR 2001)*, R. Gore, A. Leitsch, T. Nipkow, eds., Springer Verlag, LNAI 2083, 529–544, Springer Verlag, 2001.
2. Avron, A. and I. Lev, 'Non-deterministic Multi-valued Structures', *Journal of Logic and Computation*, vol. 15, 241–261, 2005.
3. Baaz M., C.G. Fermüller and R.Zach, 'Elimination of Cuts in First-order Finite-valued Logics', *Information Processing Cybernetics*, vol. 29, no. 6, 333–355, 1994.
4. Baaz M., C.G. Fermüller, G. Salzer and R.Zach, 'Labeled Calculi and Finite-valued Logics', *Studia Logica*, vol. 61, 7–33, 1998.
5. Carnielli W., 'Systematization of Finite Many-valued Logics through the method of Tableaux', *Journal of Symbolic Logic*, vol. 52 (2), 473–493, 1987.
6. Ciabattoni A. and Terui K., 'Towards a semantic characterization of cut elimination', *Studia Logica*, vol. 82(1), 95–119, 2006.
7. Gentzen, G., 'Investigations into Logical Deduction', in *The collected works of Gerhard Gentzen* (M.E. Szabo, ed.), 68–131, North Holland, Amsterdam , 1969.
8. Hähnle, R., 'Commodious Axiomatization of Quantifiers in Many-valued Logic', *Studia Logica*, vol. 61, 101–121, 1998.
9. Henkin, L., 'Some remarks on infinitely long formulas', *Infinistic Methods*, 167–183. Pergamon Press, Oxford, 1961.
10. Krynicki, M. and M.Mostowski, 'Henkin Quantifiers', *Quantifiers: logics, models and computation, M. Krynicki, M. Mostowski and L. Szcerba eds.*, vol. 1, 193–263, Kluwer Academic Publishers, 1995.
11. Miller, D. and E. Pimentel, 'Using Linear logic to reason about sequent systems', *Tableaux'02, LNAI*, 2–23, 2002.
12. Mostowski, A., 'Axiomatizability of some Many-valued Predicate Calculi', *Fundamenta Mathematicae*, , vol. 15, 165–190, North Holland, Amsterdam , 1961.
13. Salzer, G., 'Optimal axiomatizations for multiple-valued operators and quantifiers based on semilattices', *Proceedings of 13-th CADE, Springer, M. McRobbie and J. Slaney eds.*, vol. 1104, 688–702, 1996.
14. Zamansky, A. and A. Avron, 'Cut Elimination and Quantification in Canonical Systems', *Studia Logica (special issue on Cut Elimination)*, vol. 82(1), 157–176, 2006.

Dynamic Logic with Non-rigid Functions
A Basis for Object-Oriented Program Verification

Bernhard Beckert[1] and André Platzer[2]

[1] University of Koblenz-Landau, Department of Computer Science
beckert@uni-koblenz.de
[2] University of Oldenburg, Department of Computing Science
platzer@informatik.uni-oldenburg.de

Abstract. We introduce a dynamic logic that is enriched by non-rigid functions, i.e., functions that may change their value from state to state (during program execution), and we present a (relatively) complete sequent calculus for this logic. In conjunction with dynamically typed object enumerators, non-rigid functions allow to embed notions of object-orientation in dynamic logic, thereby forming a basis for verification of object-oriented programs. A semantical generalisation of substitutions, called state update, which we add to the logic, constitutes the central technical device for dealing with object aliasing during function modification. With these few extensions, our dynamic logic captures the essential aspects of the complex verification system KeY and, hence, constitutes a foundation for object-oriented verification with the principles of reasoning that underlie the successful KeY case studies.

Keywords: Dynamic logic, sequent calculus, program logic, software verification, logical foundations of programming languages, object-orientation.

1 Introduction

Overview. Dynamic logic serves two purposes: (*a*) theoretical investigations of programs, programming languages, and verification calculi; and (*b*) formal verification of particular programs. Deductive verification of real-world object-oriented programs requires the use of a program logic that is suitable for object-orientation instead of a logic for a simple WHILE language (e.g. [11]). In this paper, we add a succinct set of features to a dynamic logic for WHILE, which forms a basis for handling object-oriented programming languages; and we present a sound and (relatively) complete sequent calculus for the extended logic. The logic that we introduce, called ODL, is a minimal extension of dynamic logic [11], i.e., only very few essential notions of object-orientation are directly included.

For inclusion in ODL, we have identified the following essentials: (1) an object type system; (2) object creation; and, most importantly, (3) non-rigid functions that can be used to represent object attributes. Using such a minimal extension that is not cluttered with too many constructs is necessary for theoretical investigations (*a*). A case in point are the soundness and completeness proofs

U. Furbach and N. Shankar (Eds.): IJCAR 2006, LNAI 4130, pp. 266–280, 2006.

for the ODL calculus, which are—though not trivial—still readable, understandable and, hence, accessible to investigation. Furthermore, ODL is sufficient for
verifying programs written in real-world programming languages (b), because
they can be transformed into ODL programs uniformly (as practical experience
with the KeY prover implementation shows, see below). ODL thus serves both
purposes of a dynamic logic. In this paper, JAVA-like languages are considered
for transformation into ODL programs.

In addition to providing a sound and complete calculus for ODL, a prime
contribution of this paper is the logic ODL itself, which forms a coherent basis
for object-oriented verification.

The KeY Project and ODL. The work reported in this paper has been carried out
as part of the KeY project [2], the goal of which is to develop a comprehensive
tool supporting formal specification and verification of JAVA CARD programs
within a commercial platform for UML/JML-based software development. This
approach is based on the design-by-contract paradigm. In KeY, contracts are
verified statically using a semi-automatic, interactive theorem prover on the
basis of a dynamic logic for 100% JAVA CARD [5].

ODL captures the essence of reasoning underlying the KeY approach. Here,
we consolidate the foundational principles of KeY into this concise logic, which
is not only (relatively) complete in theory but also provides sufficient means for
practical object-oriented verification. Practical applicability has been demonstrated in successful case studies (e.g. [15]) with the KeY prover. Now, using
ODL, we focus on more theoretical aspects in this paper.

Dynamic Logic. The principle of dynamic logic (DL) is to facilitate the formulation of statements about program behaviour by integrating programs and
formulas within a single specification language (see e.g. [11] for a general exposition of DL). By permitting arbitrary programs α as actions of a labelled
multi-modal logic, dynamic logic provides formulas of the form $[\alpha]\phi$ and $\langle\alpha\rangle\phi$,
where $[\alpha]\phi$ expresses that all (terminating) executions of program α lead to states
in which ϕ holds, whereas $\langle\alpha\rangle\phi$ expresses that there is at least one terminating
execution of α after which ϕ holds. A Hoare-style specification $\{\phi\}\alpha\{\psi\}$ can be
expressed as $\phi \rightarrow [\alpha]\psi$. In contrast to Hoare logic and temporal logic approaches,
dynamic logic further permits to express structural relationships between differ-
ent programs, for example, $\langle\alpha\rangle\phi \rightarrow \langle\alpha'\rangle\phi$ and $[\alpha](c \geq 0 \rightarrow \langle\alpha\rangle'c \leq d \cdot d)$.

Object-orientation. Typical features of object-oriented programming languages
include structured object data types with inheritance and subtyping, resolving
method invocation by dynamic dispatch, overloading, hiding of fields, object
creation, exception handling (as well as other means of abrupt completion) and
side-effects during expression evaluation. There is no general consensus on the
question which of these features constitute the heart of object-orientation and
which are just contingent features of object-oriented languages (see, e.g., [14] for
a discussion why exception handling is orthogonal to object-orientation). We
are *not* trying to answer this question by including some features into ODL and

others not. Instead, our choice was to include those features that are (*a*) frequently used in object-oriented languages and (*b*) cannot be removed easily by program transformation. We put more emphasis on the latter criterion (*b*) than on a general philosophy of what should be considered object-oriented.

Related Work. Stärk and Nanchen [20] define a dynamic logic for single steps of abstract state machines and develop a calculus. Their dynamic logic has some features in common with ODL; it uses a related but distinct notion of parallel updates. Their calculus, however, is unwieldy as it uses a multitude of axioms and necessitates several successive translations with complicated reasoning on termination conditions and the absence of clashes. Due to the limitation to single steps, their logic is not suitable for verification of proper algorithms.

Von Oheimb and Nipkow [22] describe a Hoare calculus for NANOJAVA, which has many more native language features than ODL. Their calculus, that is accordingly more complicated and harder to use than ours, has been formulated in Isabelle/HOL and proven sound and complete relative to a semantics of NANO-JAVA specified in Isabelle. In [16], Nipkow defines a programming language to capture the essentials of object-orientation (without giving a calculus). Yet, this language keeps more built-in features than ODL, like exceptions and casts.

Pierik and de Boer [17] present a wp-calculus for a moderate abstraction of an object-oriented programming language with a fairly rich set of features (without exceptions) and a focus on method invocation, using an assertion language with quantification over sequences of objects. Their calculus uses a complicated treatment of object creation and is proven complete only relative to the strongest postconditions of programs, which is a comparably weak notion of completeness.

Abadi and Leino [1] present a logic for reasoning about a programming language with prototype-based object inheritance. Their logic resembles a formal type system enriched with pre- and postconditions.

Igarashi *et al.* [12] define a λ-calculus for functional JAVA (without assignments) and use it to investigate type-safety as well as parametric type genericity.

Other approaches [2,9,13,19,3], which aim to define and use calculi for verifying full (or large fragments of) JAVA or C# are too complex for our second goal (besides verification) of a small and easy to understand basis that allows theoretical investigations of programs, program languages, and calculi.

The strength of the ODL approach compared to others lies primarily in an (even) smaller amount of language features and a simple language semantics building on classical first-order dynamic logic. With this basis, the ODL calculus is straightforward and behaves reasonably in practical application scenarios. On a proof-theoretical level, a noteworthy difference is that ODL completeness is even proven relative to first-order arithmetic.

Structure of this Paper. After introducing syntax and semantics of the logic ODL in Section 2, the transformation from existing object-oriented languages into ODL is surveyed in Section 3. As the central contribution of this paper, Section 4 introduces a sound and relatively complete calculus for ODL. Finally, in Section 5 we draw conclusions and discuss future work.

2 Syntax and Semantics of ODL

Overview. In addition to dynamic logic for a standard WHILE programming language [11], we use three important concepts.

Type System. The ODL type system needs to represent types of existing object-oriented programming languages. Since classes are a central concept of object-orientation, ODL uses a proper type system rather than an indirect encoding of types as formulas or numbers. Program constructs whose behaviour depends on dynamic typing (like method invocation) can be translated into ODL code with instanceof formulas (see Section 4) to access the dynamic type of expressions.

Dynamic Object Creation. ODL needs to have a way to represent object creation and dynamic types. We introduce object enumerators: for each natural number n there is one distinct object, denoted by the term $\text{obj}_C(n)$, of each object-type C. Then, dynamic type-checks simply amount to checking from which of these free type generators an object originates. As opposed to memory models [21], each type has a disjoint set of created objects. Hence, objects of different types are never aliased. The prover can profit from this higher level of abstraction and the resulting simplicity. This design prohibits arbitrary pointer arithmetic, though.

State Updates. Object-oriented programming languages allow to modify object attributes. ODL represents attributes as *non-rigid* function symbols, i.e., functions that may change their value during program execution. Changes to such non-rigid functions are promoted throughout a formula by means of *state updates*, which can be seen as a "semantical" generalisation of syntactic substitutions. The update mechanism of ODL provides a means for handling symbol aliasing and for applying state updates to modalities. Moreover, bundling changes of multiple locations to one *parallel* update of simultaneous effect, accelerates the prover considerably.

Modelling object attributes as non-rigid function symbols emphasises the logical properties of object states. This avoids encoding objects states in memory structures and improves readability (as compared to memory-model-based approaches). For ODL, the usual object access $o.x$ is a notational variant of $x(o)$.

Syntax of ODL. A (nearly) arbitrary type system can be plugged into ODL. For simplicity, it is assumed to form a lattice (which is no real restriction as any type structure can be embedded into a lattice) satisfying additional conditions.

Definition 1. *The type system* TYP *is a (decidable) lattice with sub-type relation* $\leq$. *Within* TYP, *there is a designated subset of* object-types *(which are subject to object creation). The type lattice conforms to the following restrictions: (a) the type* nat *of natural numbers is an element of* TYP; *(b) object-types have only finitely many subtypes; (c) the bottom type* $\perp$ *is not an object-type; (d) all subtypes of an object type (except* $\perp$) *are object-types; (e) there is an object-type* Null, *which is a subtype of all object-types.*

Note that function and tuple types are *not* part of the object-level type system TYP. Instead, the typing of a function symbol with n parameters of types $\sigma_1, \ldots, \sigma_n \in$ TYP and result type $\tau \in$ TYP is $\sigma_1 \times \cdots \times \sigma_n \to \tau$. Despite (b), TYP may contain infinitely many object-types (that are not subtypes of each other). Assumptions $(c-e)$ are not essential but simplify notation in the sequel.

Figure 1 shows part of an ODL type system embedding JAVA types. Of the types shown, Object, Date, and String, are object-types. Unlike the JAVA-type int, they permit object creation during program execution. The special object-type Null represents the type of the single JAVA null-pointer, which is a possible value for expressions of any object-type but not for those of integer types. In the case of JAVA, nat will not occur in the original programs but emerge during the transformation in Section 3.

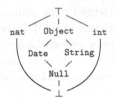

Fig. 1. Lattice for part of JAVA

Terms and Formulas. The formulas of ODL are built over a set V of variables and a signature Σ of function and predicate symbols, which have a fixed static type. Function symbols are either *rigid* or *non-rigid*, with only non-rigid symbols being subject to assignment during program execution (program variables are represented by non-rigid constants, object attributes by non-rigid functions). Our calculus assumes the presence of sufficiently many symbols of each kind.

The signature Σ is assumed to contain the traditional rigid function and predicate symbols for type nat, such as $0, 1, +, \cdot, \leq, \geq$, as well as the rigid symbol null of type Null. For object-types $C \in$ TYP, in addition to a non-rigid symbol next_C of type nat (the number of the next object to be created), Σ contains a rigid function symbol obj_C of the typing nat $\to$ C. The intended semantics of such an *object enumerator* obj_C is to enumerate all objects of type C.

The set $\text{Trm}(\Sigma \cup V)_\tau$ of *terms* of type τ (or subtypes thereof) is defined as in classical many-sorted first-order logic. Additionally, we use *conditional terms* of the form $(if\, \phi\, then\, t\, else\, t'\, fi)$. They evaluate to the value of t if ϕ is true and to the value of t' otherwise (conditional terms are no essential ingredient of ODL, primarily used to simplify concepts and notation).

The *formulas* of ODL are defined as common in first-order dynamic logic. That is, they are built using the connectives $\wedge, \vee, \to, \neg$, equality $\doteq$ and the quantifiers $\forall, \exists$ (first-order part). In addition, if ϕ is a formula and α a program, then $[\alpha]\phi, \langle\alpha\rangle\phi$ are formulas (dynamic part). Refer to [18] for a detailed definition of the syntax and semantics of ODL. For enhanced readability, we sometimes use the notation $\forall x : \tau\ \phi$ for quantification when x is of type τ.

Programs. The control structures of ODL are those commonly found in a WHILE programming language: ODL *programs* are constructed using (a) sequential composition $\alpha; \gamma$, (b) conditional execution $if(\phi)\, \alpha\, else\, \gamma$, and (c) loops $while(\phi)\, \alpha$, with quantifier-free first-order formulas ϕ as conditions. The *atomic* programs of ODL are *state updates*:

Definition 2 (State updates). *Let $n \in \mathbb{N}$ and, for $1 \leq i \leq n$, let f_i a non-rigid function symbol of type $\sigma_i^1 \times \cdots \times \sigma_i^{k_i} \to \tau_i$, $f_i(t_i^1, \ldots, t_i^{k_i}) \in \text{Trm}(\Sigma \cup V)_{\tau_i}$,*

and $t_i \in \mathrm{Trm}(\Sigma \cup V)_{\tau_i}$ with types σ_i^j, τ_i. Then, a (state) update has the form
$$f_1(t_1^1, \ldots, t_1^{k_1}) := t_1, \ldots, f_n(t_n^1, \ldots, t_n^{k_n}) := t_n.$$

The intended effect of $f(t) := t'$ is to change the interpretation of f at location t to t', with multiple modifications $(n > 1)$ working in parallel, i.e., the t_i^j and t_i are all evaluated prior to the (parallel) modifications.

Method calls can be added to ODL by permitting $c := m(t_0, \ldots, t_n)$ as an atomic program that represents an invocation of the method m on parameters $t_i \in \mathrm{Trm}(\Sigma \cup V)$ and assignment of the result (if any) to c. For most programming languages, t_0 is the object on which m is invoked. Fixed-point semantics then defines the effect of a method invocation. For simplicity, the particularities of method calls are not formally investigated further here.

Semantics. The interpretations of ODL consist of worlds (states) that are first-order structures, associating total functions and relations of appropriate type with function and predicate symbols.

Definition 3 (Interpretation). *An interpretation I is a non-empty set of (typed) first-order structures, called* states, *over a signature Σ such that: (1) all states have the same interpretation of rigid symbols; (2) the set of states of I is closed under the modification (see below) of finitely many non-rigid symbols at finitely many locations; (3) for each type τ, all states share the same set $I(\tau)$ as the set of objects of type τ; the universe of all states is the union of the $I(\tau)$; (4) for all types σ, τ: if $\sigma \leq \tau$ then $I(\sigma) \subseteq I(\tau)$; (5) obj_C is interpreted as a bijection from $\mathbb{N}$ into the set of objects having C as their most-specific type, i.e., that are of type C but not of any subtype of C; (6) the interpretations of the obj_C symbols have disjoint ranges; (7) nat is interpreted as the set of natural numbers, with operators as usual; (8) the interpretation of the Null type is a singleton; that of $\perp$ is empty.*

In the following, s denotes a state of I and β an assignment of variables, i.e., a mapping from V to the universe of I that respects types. Non-rigid symbols, like program variables or attributes, are allowed to assume different interpretations in different states. Logical variable symbols, however, are rigid in the sense that their value is determined by β alone and does not depend on the state. We use $s[f(e) \mapsto d]$ to denote the *semantic modification* of state s that is identical to s except for the interpretation of the non-rigid symbol f at position e, which is d.

Definition 4 (Valuation of terms and formulas). *For terms and formulas, the valuation $val_{I,\beta}(s, \cdot)$ with respect to I, β, s is defined as usual for first-order modal logic [10], i.e., using the following definitions for the modal operators:*
$val_{I,\beta}(s, [\alpha]\phi) = $ *true iff* $val_{I,\beta}(s', \phi) = $ *true for all s' with $(s, s') \in \rho_{I,\beta}(\alpha)$ and*
$val_{I,\beta}(s, \langle \alpha \rangle \phi) = $ *true iff* $val_{I,\beta}(s', \phi) = $ *true for some s' s.t. $(s, s') \in \rho_{I,\beta}(\alpha)$.*

With the exception of state updates, the semantics—$\rho_{I,\beta}(\alpha)$—of programs is as customary. In order to demonstrate how concise and simple the ODL language semantics is devised, the full formal definition is provided.

Definition 5 (Semantics of programs). *The* valuation $\rho_{I,\beta}(\alpha)$ *of a program* α *is a relation on the states of* I. *It specifies which state* s' *(if any) is reachable from a state* s *by executing program* α *and is defined as follows:*

1. $(s,s') \in \rho_{I,\beta}(f_1(t_1^1,\ldots,t_1^{k_1}) := t_1,\ldots,f_n(t_n^1,\ldots,t_n^{k_n}) := t_n)$ *iff* $s = s_0, s' = s_n$, *and* $s_i = s_{i-1}[f_i(val_{I,\beta}(s,t_i^1),\ldots,val_{I,\beta}(s,t_i^{k_i})) \mapsto val_{I,\beta}(s,t_i)]$ *($1 \le i \le n$).*

2. $(s,s') \in \rho_{I,\beta}(\alpha;\gamma)$ *iff* $(s,u) \in \rho_{I,\beta}(\alpha)$ *and* $(u,s') \in \rho_{I,\beta}(\gamma)$ *for some state* u.

3. $(s,s') \in \rho_{I,\beta}(\mathtt{if}(\phi)\,\alpha\,\mathtt{else}\,\gamma)$ *iff (1)* $val_{I,\beta}(s,\phi) = true$ *and* $(s,s') \in \rho_{I,\beta}(\alpha)$, *or (2)* $val_{I,\beta}(s,\phi) - false$ *and* $(s,s') \in \rho_{I,\beta}(\gamma)$.

4. $(s,s') \in \rho_{I,\beta}(\mathtt{while}(\phi)\,\alpha)$ *iff there are* $n \in \mathbb{N}$ *and* $s=s_0,\ldots,s_n=s'$ *such that (1) for* $0 \le i < n$, $val_{I,\beta}(s_i,\phi) = true$ *and* $(s_i,s_{i+1}) \in \rho_{I,\beta}(\alpha)$, *and (2)* $val_{I,\beta}(s_n,\phi) = false$.

Note that according to this definition, the modifications of a state update are executed simultaneously in the sense that the terms t_i^j, t_i are evaluated in the initial state $s = s_0$. However, if there is a clash, i.e., if two modifications assign different values to the same location, then the rightmost modification wins, which turns out to be more natural for sequential programs than alternative approaches to clash semantics [18]. Like classical dynamic logic, ODL focuses on the input/output behaviour of programs and program parts. Hence it cannot be used to express properties of programs during an infinite run, which would require an extension of ODL to trace semantics (versions of DL with trace semantics are described in [7] for classical DL and in [6] for JAVA CARD).

3   ODL as a Basis for Handling Real-World Languages

In this section, we survey the transformation from real-world object-oriented programs into ODL as a basis for their verification. The particular transformation that we consider here is implemented by schematic inference rules in the KeY deduction engine. It transforms JAVA CARD programs into a sublanguage of JAVA that corresponds to ODL, except for notation. Experience with KeY in practice shows that the transformation leads to a linear increase in the size of the program and that the time complexity of the transformation is linear in the size of the program. The resulting program retains the structure of the original, as the transformation only locally replaces language features that are not part of ODL. Hence, the relation between JAVA and ODL programs is easy to grasp for users. Due to space limitations, we have to restrict this presentation to the key ideas enriched with illustrative examples; see [5,18] for more details.

Type Transformations. As the subtype relation of the class hierarchy is integrated directly, fields and methods undergo a simple translation. An attribute $f : \sigma_1 \times \ldots \times \sigma_n \rightarrow \tau$ of class ζ is represented as a non-rigid function symbol $f : \zeta \times \sigma_1 \times \ldots \times \sigma_n \rightarrow \tau$, which stores at position $(o, a_1, \ldots, a_n)$ the value that field f of object o has at position $(a_1, \ldots, a_n)$ (for array types $n > 0$).

Code Transformations. Most features of current programming languages have a simple uniform transformation into ODL, which accomplishes their effects with more elementary means and without introducing memory or machine models.

Object Creation. Object creation has to support dynamic type-checks, establish object identity and maintain the current type extension. Because of the properties of ODL object enumerators, these demands are fulfilled by translating occurrences of $c := \mathtt{new\,C}()$ into the state update $c := \mathtt{obj}_C(\mathtt{next}_C)$, $\mathtt{next}_C := \mathtt{next}_C + 1$.

Two objects created by distinct invocations of **new** are always different, which is achieved by means of the disjoint bijection constraints on $\mathtt{obj}_C$ and the increment of $\mathtt{next}_C$. Maintaining the extension, i.e., a set of all objects created by program execution so far, is needed in order to express properties ϕ of all objects that have already been created with an invocation of **new**. As $\mathtt{next}_C$ counts the number of objects created of type C, this corresponds to: $\forall n\,(n < \mathtt{next}_C \rightarrow \phi(\mathtt{obj}_C(n)))$. Using object enumerators, it is further possible to express dynamic type-checks. For a term t and object-type C, we define the type-check formula t **instanceof** C to be an abbreviation of $\exists n : \mathtt{nat}\ \bigvee_{\mathtt{Null} < \tau \leq C} t \doteq \mathtt{obj}_\tau(n)$.

Despite the static typing of symbols in Σ, ODL needs dynamic type-checks because the *interpretation* of a constant symbol c of (static) type τ in Σ can have any subtype $\sigma \leq \tau$ depending on the current state.

The ODL treatment of object creation is still safe in the presence of garbage collection due to the absence of pointer arithmetics and resource limitations [18]. A further advantage of object enumerators is the simplicity of the contribution of natural numbers—which are already part of ODL for completeness reasons—to object identity without the need to use Skolem symbols for object creation.

Side-effects. Expressions with side-effects can be replaced by a sequence of state updates to temporary program variables, each of which encapsulates one effect of the original expression. Therefore, the order of assignments has to respect the evaluation order constraints of the investigated real-world language. For example, the JAVA fragment a[i++] = b−− + b can be *schematically* translated into an ODL program $vi := i;\ i := i + 1;\ vb := b;\ b := b - 1;\ a(vi) := vb + b$ that does not have side-effects. This ODL program can be condensed to a single parallel update using our simplification rules (see Section 4), which results in $i := i + 1, b := b - 1, a(i) := b + (b - 1)$. ODL updates can be more verbose than side-effecting JAVA expressions, but they are also more explicit. For the purpose of verification, it is beneficial to have the actual effects readily identifiable.

Exception Handling. Exceptions are not built into ODL, but have to be emulated by preprocessing program transformations. Exception raising can be simulated by introducing appropriate conditions on a (local) program variable that stores the raised exception (which is passed up the call trace when it is not caught). Consider the following example with exception raising and handling:

```
try { while (d != 0)
        {if (d < 0) {throw new RangeEx(d);} else {d=d-1;}}
      /* do something */
    } catch (RangeEx r) {/* handle range */}
```

It can be transformed into a program that uses exception polling instead:

```
Exception r = null;
while (r == null && d != 0)
   {if (d < 0) {r = new RangeEx(d);} else {d=d−1;}}
if (r == null) {/* do something */}
else if (r instanceof RangeEx) {/* handle range */}
else {return r; /* pass up the call trace */}
```

In favour of a simple logic and calculus, ODL compromises on readability when handling exceptions by program transformation. This is non-crucial in the sense that exceptions are not an inherently object-oriented feature.

The main advantage of banning exceptions and undefinedness from ODL is that no special features like, e.g., a third truth value, have to be introduced to handle partiality. For example, with built-in exception handling, a logic would have to promote the exceptional case of values being null throughout the inductive valuation, which clutters both semantics and inference rules. In contrast, ODL just considers null as an ordinary—though designated—object. Further, the truth-value of an expression like $c.a \doteq c.a + 2$ is always consistently false, even in the case of $c \doteq \text{null}$, whereas $c.a \doteq c.a$ is consistently true.

Dynamic Dispatch. Dynamic dispatch of method calls can be reduced to static method calls by dynamic type-check cascades with **instanceof** along the *reverse* topological order of the type lattice (which also works for multiple inheritance). An important advantage of the ODL way of dynamic dispatch is its simplicity: the basic idea is to implement dispatch "tables" from classical compiler construction technology with ODL primitives. Dynamic dispatch occurs in situations like the one sketched in the following JAVA fragment:

```
class Car { int follow (Car d) {...} }
class Van extends Car { int follow (Car d) {...} }
... return b. follow (d);
```

Having renamed the methods follow that are subject to overriding to Car_follow or Van_follow, respectively, this code snippet is transformed as follows (type casts are expressible in ODL using existential quantification: $\exists v : \text{Van } v \doteq b$):

```
class Car { int Car_follow (Car d) {...} }
class Van extends Car { int Van_follow (Car d) {...} }
...    if (b instanceof Van) {return ((Van)b). Van_follow (d);}
else if (b instanceof Car) {return ((Car)b). Car_follow (d);}
else {/* cannot happen when all types are known */}
```

Built-in Operators. From a theoretical perspective, extending ODL by built-in operators is straightforward when assuming a suitable axiomatisation of the operator semantics. For example, modular arithmetic can be axiomatised as [8]:
$r \doteq a \bmod n \quad \leftrightarrow \quad \exists z : \text{nat } a \doteq z \cdot n + r \wedge r < n.$

Running Example. Consider the following JAVA fragment that illustrates sequence number generation in object database applications and also is a typical part of the implementation of enumeration types in JAVA (sequence numbers are assumed to be multiples of 5, for example):

```
class E { static int g; int id;
          E create() {E r=new E(); r.id=g;g=g+5; return r;}}
```

With return-value r, the method body of create() has the ODL representation $\alpha = r := \mathrm{obj}_E(\mathrm{next}_E), \mathrm{next}_E := \mathrm{next}_E+1;\ r.\mathrm{id} := g;\ g := g + 5$ (using JAVA notation for field access). An important property of class E is that sequence numbers in the field id are unique Identifiers for E-objects, which is expressed by the global state invariant $\forall x : \mathrm{E}\ \forall y : \mathrm{E}\ (x.\mathrm{id} \doteq y.\mathrm{id} \to x \doteq y)$. In this context, a typical conjecture is that two objects generated with successive invocations of α have distinct identifiers, which is represented by the ODL formula: $\forall x\,[\alpha](x \doteq r \to [\alpha]\,(x.\mathrm{id} < r.\mathrm{id}))$.

Discussion. Assignment to non-rigid function symbols cannot be removed from ODL without losing the operational basis for object-oriented programming that permits the change of structured and dynamically typed data or terms.

Likewise, object creation constitutes an essential ingredient to the dynamics of object-oriented systems. Allocating objects at run-time is characteristic of object-oriented programming. With the presence of object enumerator symbols, ODL does not need a native allocation operator. Both the axiomatisation and the translation are convincing and the practical performance achieved with object enumerators is appropriate [18] (similar reasons apply for dynamic dispatch).

4 A Sequent Calculus for ODL

Overview. In this section, we present a sound and (relatively) complete sequent calculus for ODL. The basic idea of the ODL calculus is to perform a symbolic program execution, thereby successively analysing programs and transforming them into logical formulas describing their effects. Yet, rule applications for first-order reasoning and program reasoning are not separated but intertwined.

For first-order and propositional logic standard rule schemata are listed in Table 1, including an integer induction scheme. Within the rules for the program logic part (Table 2), state update rules R29–R30 constitute a peculiarity of ODL and will be discussed after defining rule applications. Essentially, the ODL inference rules have the effect of reducing more complex formulas to simpler ones. Prior to handling loops by R27 or R22, they transform formulas to the normal form $\langle \mathcal{U} \rangle \langle \mathtt{while}(e)\, \alpha \rangle \phi$ or $[\mathcal{U}][\mathtt{while}(e)\, \alpha]\phi$ with some update $\mathcal{U}$. The rules for treating control structures work similar to the case of the WHILE programming language.

Rules of the Calculus. A *sequent* is of the form $\Gamma \vdash \Delta$, where Γ and Δ are sets of formulas. Its informal semantics is the same as that of $\bigwedge_{\phi \in \Gamma} \phi \ \to \ \bigvee_{\psi \in \Delta} \psi$.

Table 1. First-order logic part of the ODL calculus

(R1) $\dfrac{\vdash A}{\neg A \vdash}$	(R4) $\dfrac{A, B \vdash}{A \wedge B \vdash}$	(R7) $\dfrac{A \vdash \quad B \vdash}{A \vee B \vdash}$	(R10) $\dfrac{\vdash A \quad B \vdash}{A \to B \vdash}$
(R2) $\dfrac{A \vdash}{\vdash \neg A}$	(R5) $\dfrac{\vdash A \quad \vdash B}{\vdash A \wedge B}$	(R8) $\dfrac{\vdash A, B}{\vdash A \vee B}$	(R11) $\dfrac{A \vdash B}{\vdash A \to B}$
(R3) $\dfrac{\vdash A_x^X}{\vdash \forall x\, A}$	(R6) $\dfrac{A_x^t, \forall x\, A \vdash}{\forall x\, A \vdash}$	(R9) $\dfrac{A_x^X \vdash}{\exists x\, A \vdash}$	(R12) $\dfrac{\vdash A_x^t, \exists x\, A}{\vdash \exists x\, A}$
(R13) $\dfrac{}{A \vdash A}$	(R15) $\dfrac{\Gamma_t^{t'}, t \doteq t' \vdash \Delta_t^{t'}}{\Gamma, t \doteq t' \vdash \Delta}$	(R17) $\dfrac{}{\vdash t \doteq t}$	
(R14) $\dfrac{A \vdash \quad \vdash A}{\vdash}$	(R16) $\dfrac{\Gamma_t^{t'}, t' \doteq t \vdash \Delta_t^{t'}}{\Gamma, t' \doteq t \vdash \Delta}$	(R18) $\dfrac{\vdash \phi(0) \quad \phi(X) \vdash \phi(X+1)}{\vdash \forall n\, \phi(n)}$	

ODL inference rules use substitutions that replace terms (not only variables) by terms and take effect within formulas *and* programs. The result of applying to ϕ the substitution that replaces s by t is defined as usual; it is denoted by ϕ_s^t. Yet, only admissible substitutions are applicable, which is crucial for soundness:

Definition 6 (Admissible substitution). *An application of a substitution θ is admissible if no replaced term s occurs (a) in the scope of a quantifier binding a variable of $\theta(s)$ or s, nor (b) in the scope of a modality in which an update to a non-rigid function symbol of $\theta(s)$ or s occurs.*

As common in sequent calculus, although the direction of entailment is from premisses (sequents above bar) to conclusion (sequent below), the order of reasoning is converse in practice. Rules are applied analytically, starting with the proof obligation at the bottom. To highlight the logical essence of inference rules, the ODL calculus provides the rule *schemata* R1–R30 to which the following definition associates the inference rules that are applicable during an ODL proof.

Definition 7 (Rules). *The rule schemata in Tables 1 and 2 induce rules by:*

1. *If $\Phi_1 \vdash \Psi_1 \ldots \Phi_n \vdash \Psi_n \,/\, \Phi \vdash \Psi$ is an instance of one of the rule schemata R1–R26, then*

$$\frac{\Gamma, \langle \mathcal{U} \rangle \Phi_1 \vdash \langle \mathcal{U} \rangle \Psi_1, \Delta \quad \ldots \quad \Gamma, \langle \mathcal{U} \rangle \Phi_n \vdash \langle \mathcal{U} \rangle \Psi_n, \Delta}{\Gamma, \langle \mathcal{U} \rangle \Phi \vdash \langle \mathcal{U} \rangle \Psi, \Delta}$$

is an inference rule of the ODL calculus, where $\mathcal{U}$ is an arbitrary (or empty) state update, and Γ, Δ are finite sets of context formulas. The formulas within the schemata R19–R22 can occur on either side of the sequent.
2. *Instances of the rule schemata R27 and R28 can be applied as an inference rule of the ODL calculus.*
3. *If (a) $s \rightsquigarrow t$ is an instance of term rewrite rule R29 or R30, (b) $\Phi' \vdash \Psi'$ results from a sequent $\Phi \vdash \Psi$ by substituting t for s, and (c) that substitution is admissible, then the ODL calculus contains the rule $\Phi' \vdash \Psi' \,/\, \Phi \vdash \Psi$.*

Table 2. Program logic part of the ODL sequent calculus

(R19) $\dfrac{\langle\!\langle\alpha\rangle\!\rangle\,\langle\!\langle\gamma\rangle\!\rangle\,\phi}{\langle\!\langle\alpha;\gamma\rangle\!\rangle\,\phi}$

(R24) $\dfrac{}{\vdash\ \mathsf{obj}_\mathsf{C}(i)\doteq\mathsf{obj}_\mathsf{C}(j)\to i\doteq j}$

(R20) $\dfrac{(e\to\langle\!\langle\alpha\rangle\!\rangle\,\phi)\wedge(\neg e\to\langle\!\langle\gamma\rangle\!\rangle\,\phi)}{\langle\!\langle\texttt{if}(e)\,\alpha\,\texttt{else}\,\gamma\rangle\!\rangle\,\phi}$

(R25) $\dfrac{}{\vdash\ \neg(\mathsf{obj}_\mathsf{C}(i)\doteq\mathsf{obj}_\mathsf{D}(j))}$

(R21) $\dfrac{(e\to\phi(t))\wedge(\neg e\to\phi(t'))}{\phi(\textit{if}\,e\,\textit{then}\,t\,\textit{else}\,t'\,\textit{fi})}$

(R26) $\dfrac{}{\vdash\ \forall o:\mathsf{C}\ (o\,\texttt{instanceof}\,\mathsf{C}\vee o\doteq\texttt{null})}$

(R22) $\dfrac{\langle\!\langle\texttt{it}(e)\,\{\alpha;\texttt{while}(e)\,\alpha\}\rangle\!\rangle\,\phi}{\langle\!\langle\texttt{while}(e)\,\alpha\rangle\!\rangle\,\phi}$

(R27) $\dfrac{\Gamma\vdash\langle\mathcal{U}\rangle p,\Delta\quad p,e\vdash[\alpha]p\quad p,\neg e\vdash\phi}{\Gamma\vdash\langle\mathcal{U}\rangle[\texttt{while}(e)\,\alpha]\phi,\Delta}$

(R23) $\dfrac{A\vdash B}{\exists x\,A\vdash\exists x\,B}$

(R28) $\dfrac{A\vdash B}{\langle\!\langle\alpha\rangle\!\rangle A\vdash\langle\!\langle\alpha\rangle\!\rangle B}$

(R29) $\langle\mathcal{U}\rangle f(u)\ \rightsquigarrow$
  $\textit{if}\,s_{i_r}\doteq\langle\mathcal{U}\rangle u\,\textit{then}\,t_{i_r}\,\textit{else}\,\ldots\,\textit{if}\,s_{i_1}\doteq\langle\mathcal{U}\rangle u\,\textit{then}\,t_{i_1}\,\textit{else}\,f(\langle\mathcal{U}\rangle u)\,\textit{fi}\ldots\textit{fi}$
  where $i_1<\cdots<i_r$ are all those indices with $f_{i_j}=f$, for some $r\geq0$

(R30) $\langle\tilde{\mathcal{U}}\rangle\langle\mathcal{U}\rangle\phi\ \rightsquigarrow\ \langle\tilde{\mathcal{U}},f_1(\langle\tilde{\mathcal{U}}\rangle s_1):=\langle\tilde{\mathcal{U}}\rangle t_1,\ldots,f_n(\langle\tilde{\mathcal{U}}\rangle s_n):=\langle\tilde{\mathcal{U}}\rangle t_n\rangle\phi$

In the rule schemata, t,t' are terms, X is a new logical variable, $\mathsf{C}\neq\mathsf{D}$ are object-types and $\langle\mathcal{U}\rangle,\langle\tilde{\mathcal{U}}\rangle$ are updates. All substitutions are admissible, in particular the (implicit) substitution that inserts t into $\phi(t)$ must be admissible. In R29 and R30, $\langle\mathcal{U}\rangle$ is of the form $\langle f_1(s_1):=t_1,\ldots,f_n(s_n):=t_n\rangle$, working accordingly for other arities of f. Moreover, in all rule schemata, the schematic modality $\langle\!\langle\cdot\rangle\!\rangle$ can be instantiated with both $[\cdot]$ and $\langle\cdot\rangle$. The same modality instance has to be chosen within a single schema instantiation, though.

It is of utmost importance for soundness that only the rule schemata R1–R26 allow to add an update prefix $\mathcal{U}$ and a sequent context Γ,Δ (case 1 in the above definition), while that is not possible for rule schemata R27 and R28 (case 2) because of their global form of reasoning.

Rule R26 expresses that all objects, except **null**, that will ever exist are generated by object creation expressions. In addition to the standard treatment of equalities, it can be used to discharge proof obligations depending on dynamic types, which typically occur during object-oriented verification. Similarly, R24 and R25 directly express the disjoint bijection restrictions on object enumerators (see Subsection 3) that are needed to reflect the impact of the type system.

The rewrite schema R29 symbolically executes a state update. Besides promoting the effect of updates to the arguments inductively, R29 basically unfolds changes to the top-level symbol in the order appearing within update $\mathcal{U}$. Thereby, it respects the last-win semantics that ODL uses for clashing updates. In case of a singleton state update $\mathcal{U}$ of the form $f(s):=t$, the rewrite simplifies to $\langle\mathcal{U}\rangle f(u)\ \rightsquigarrow\ \textit{if}\,s\doteq\langle\mathcal{U}\rangle u\,\textit{then}\,t\,\textit{else}\,f(\langle\mathcal{U}\rangle u)\,\textit{fi}$. The conditional terms introduced

Table 3. Proof of sequence number generation (with $o \equiv \mathrm{obj}_E$ and $n \equiv \mathrm{next}_E$)

$$
\begin{array}{cl}
& \qquad\qquad\qquad\qquad * \qquad\qquad\qquad\qquad\qquad\qquad\qquad\qquad \ldots \\
\mathrm{R17} & \overline{X.\mathrm{id} < g, \neg o(n) \doteq X \vdash X.\mathrm{id} < g} \qquad \overline{X.\mathrm{id} < g, o(n) \doteq X \vdash g < g} \\
\mathrm{R5} & \overline{X.\mathrm{id} < g \vdash (\neg o(n) \doteq X \,\to\, X.\mathrm{id} < g) \,\wedge\, (o(n) \doteq X \,\to\, g < g)} \\
\mathrm{R21} & \overline{X.\mathrm{id} < g \vdash (\mathrm{if}\, o(n) \doteq X \,\mathrm{then}\, g\, \mathrm{else}\, X.\mathrm{id}\, \mathrm{fi}) < g} \\
\mathrm{R29} & \overline{X.\mathrm{id} < g \vdash [r := o(n), n := n{+}1, o(n).\mathrm{id} := g, g := g + 5]\,(X.\mathrm{id} < r.\mathrm{id})} \\
\mathrm{R30} & \overline{X.\mathrm{id} < g \vdash [r := o(n), n := n{+}1, o(n).\mathrm{id} := g][g := g + 5]\,(X.\mathrm{id} < r.\mathrm{id})} \\
\mathrm{R30} & \overline{X.\mathrm{id} < g \vdash [r := o(n), n := n{+}1][r.\mathrm{id} := g][g := g + 5]\,(X.\mathrm{id} < r.\mathrm{id})} \\
\mathrm{R19} & \overline{X.\mathrm{id} < g \vdash [r := o(n), n := n{+}1][r.\mathrm{id} := g; g := g + 5]\,(X.\mathrm{id} < r.\mathrm{id})} \\
\mathrm{R19} & \overline{X.\mathrm{id} < g \vdash [\alpha]\,(X.\mathrm{id} < r.\mathrm{id})} \\
\mathrm{R11} & \overline{\vdash X.\mathrm{id} < g \to [\alpha]\,(X.\mathrm{id} < r.\mathrm{id})} \\
\mathrm{R3} & \overline{\vdash \forall x : E\,(x.\mathrm{id} < g \to [\alpha]\,(x.\mathrm{id} < r.\mathrm{id}))}
\end{array}
$$

herewith can, in turn, vanish according to schema R21 once the substitution is admissible. Deferring R21 avoids branching until necessary for progress.

The rules R23 and R28, which are required for completeness but are rarely used in practice, characterise a global consequence relation.

Definition 8 (Provability, derivability). *A formula ψ is* provable *from a set Φ of formulas, denoted by $\Phi \vdash_{ODL} \psi$ iff there is a finite subset $\Phi_0 \subseteq \Phi$ for which the sequent $\Phi_0 \vdash \psi$ is derivable. In turn, a sequent $\Phi \vdash \Psi$ is* derivable *iff there is an inference rule of the* ODL *calculus (Definition 7) with conclusion $\Phi \vdash \Psi$ such that all premises of the rule are derivable.*

Verification Example. Continuing the example of Subsection 3, we consider a specification of the body α (with return value r) of the create() method: $\forall x : E\,(x.\mathrm{id} < g \to [\alpha]\,(x.\mathrm{id} < r.\mathrm{id}))$. On this basis, uniqueness of E-identifiers is due to the fact that create() is the only source for E-objects and that identifiers do not change after object creation (which needs to be proven separately).

Table 3 shows (part of) the proof for the above formula (the right branch remains open). Apart from reducing object creation to object enumerators, the proof essentially consists in update merging and applying the final update $\mathcal{U} = [r := o(n), n := n{+}1, o(n).\mathrm{id} := g, g := g + 5]$, which involves rewriting: $[\mathcal{U}]X.\mathrm{id} \rightsquigarrow \mathrm{if}\, o(n) \doteq [\mathcal{U}]X\, \mathrm{then}\, g\, \mathrm{else}\, ([\mathcal{U}]X).\mathrm{id}\, \mathrm{fi} \rightsquigarrow \mathrm{if}\, o(n) \doteq X\, \mathrm{then}\, g\, \mathrm{else}\, X.\mathrm{id}\, \mathrm{fi}$.

With results about reasoning with created objects [18], the proof can be extended such that the right branch closes as well. That makes use of the fact that X—when it is restricted to objects that have already been created—must differ from the newly created $r = o(n)$. This manifests as an additional antecedent $\exists k\,(X \doteq o(k) \wedge k < n)$, which contradicts $o(n) \doteq X$ in the right branch using R24.

Soundness and Completeness. With the usual notions of soundness and relative completeness, the ODL calculus is proven sound and a complete extension of first-order arithmetic [18]. Using the proof technique from [11], a central lemma is that all ODL formulas have an equivalent first-order arithmetic formula. This requires Gödelisation of sequences, which is more complicated in the presence of non-rigid functions of finite but unbounded change.

Theorem 1 (Soundness and relative completeness). *(1) The ODL calculus (Definition 8) is sound, i.e., derivable formulas are valid (true in all states of all interpretations).*

(2) The ODL calculus is complete with respect to first-order arithmetic, i.e., if an ODL formula is valid, then it can be derived from a set of tautologies of first-order arithmetic.

Moreover, we have shown that relative completeness is preserved for conservative extensions of ODL with language features that so-called locally equivalent inference rules can reduce to original ODL [18].

Example 1 (Relatively complete coverage of for *loops).* Adding to ODL the rule " $\vdash \langle \mathcal{U}; \mathtt{while}(\chi) \{\alpha; \gamma\}\rangle\phi$ / $\vdash \langle \mathtt{for}(\mathcal{U}; \chi; \gamma)\alpha\rangle\phi$" yields a calculus for ODL extended with for loops that is complete w.r.t. first-order arithmetic. Similarly, constructor calls and side-effecting expression evaluation can be added to ODL without loss of relative completeness.

5   Conclusions and Future Work

We have introduced a dynamic logic, ODL, with non-rigid functions, and presented a sound and relatively complete calculus. The conceptual design of the logic ODL is guided by the ambition to capture the essence of reasoning for a coherent basis of object-oriented verification at an adequate level of abstraction.

ODL provides dynamically typed object enumerators and state updates, i.e., operations to change the interpretation of non-rigid function symbols. State updates work in parallel for multiple pointwise changes at once. With these extensions, notions of object-orientation can be embedded in ODL.

The ODL calculus is based on a classical sequent calculus for the WHILE programming language [11]. In order to deal with function modification, rewrite rules have been introduced that promote the effect of a state update throughout the affected formula, with case distinctions to resolve potential aliasing. State update applications can be delayed to defer branching of the proof.

The completeness proof for our ODL calculus in [18] has revealed and fixed a flaw in the classical completeness proofs for dynamic logic (for WHILE) [11,7] concerning the treatment of multiple variables.

Future work includes a closer investigation of the pragmatic effects of the ODL approach to software verification. It is useful to build a modular set of verification components for object-oriented calculi by providing add-on inference rules for additional language features on the basis of the extension theorem in [18]. An investigation of the impact of parametric genericity for the type system seems worthwhile to a similar degree.

To sum up, the feasibility of defining an insightful essentials-only verification calculus for object-oriented programming, which is sound and complete relative to classical first-order arithmetic, has been demonstrated.

References

1. M. Abadi and K. R. M. Leino. A logic of object-oriented programs. In M. Bidoit and M. Dauchet, editors, *TAPSOFT '97*, volume 1214. Springer-Verlag, 1997.
2. W. Ahrendt, T. Baar, B. Beckert, R. Bubel, M. Giese, R. Hähnle, W. Menzel, W. Mostowski, A. Roth, S. Schlager, and P. H. Schmitt. The KeY tool. *Software and System Modeling*, 4:32–54, 2005.
3. M. Barnett, K. R. M. Leino, and W. Schulte. The Spec# programming system: An overview. In Barthe et al. [4].
4. G. Barthe, L. Burdy, M. Huisman, J.-L. Lanet, and T. Muntean, editors. *CASSIS 2004, Revised Selected Papers*, volume 3362 of *LNCS*. Springer, 2005.
5. B. Beckert. A dynamic logic for the formal verification of Java Card programs. In I. Attali and T. Jensen, editors, *Java on Smart Cards: Programming and Security*, volume 2041 of *LNCS*, pages 6–24, 2001.
6. B. Beckert and W. Mostowski. A program logic for handling Java Card's transaction mechanism. In *FASE'03*, LNCS. Springer, 2003.
7. B. Beckert and S. Schlager. A sequent calculus for first-order dynamic logic with trace modalities. In R. Goré, A. Leitsch, and T. Nipkow, editors, *IJCAR*, volume 2083 of *LNCS*, pages 626–641. Springer, 2001.
8. B. Beckert and S. Schlager. Software verification with integrated data type refinement for integer arithmetic. In E. A. Boiten, J. Derrick, and G. Smith, editors, *IFM*, volume 2999 of *LNCS*, pages 207–226. Springer, 2004.
9. D. R. Cok and J. Kiniry. ESC/Java2: Uniting ESC/Java and JML. In Barthe et al. [4], pages 108–128.
10. M. Fitting and R. L. Mendelsohn. *First-Order Modal Logic*. Kluwer Academic Publishers, Norwell, MA, USA, 1999.
11. D. Harel. *First-Order Dynamic Logic*. Springer-Verlag, New York, 1979.
12. A. Igarashi, B. C. Pierce, and P. Wadler. Featherweight Java: A minimal core calculus for Java and GJ. *ACM Trans. Program. Lang. Syst.*, 23(3):396–450, 2001.
13. B. Jacobs and E. Poll. A logic for the Java modeling language JML. In *FASE '01*, pages 284–299, London, UK, 2001. Springer-Verlag.
14. R. Miller and A. Tripathi. Issues with exception handling in object-oriented systems. In *ECOOP*, pages 85–103, 1997.
15. W. Mostowski. *Formal Development of Safe and Secure Java Card Applets*. PhD thesis, Chalmers University of Technology, Göteborg, Sweden, February 2005.
16. T. Nipkow. Jinja: Towards a comprehensive formal semantics for a Java-like language. In *Proc. Marktoberdorf Summer School*, 2003.
17. C. Pierik and F. S. de Boer. A syntax-directed Hoare logic for object-oriented programming concepts. In E. Najm, U. Nestmann, and P. Stevens, editors, *FMOODS*, volume 2884 of *LNCS*, pages 64–78. Springer, 2003.
18. A. Platzer. An object-oriented dynamic logic with updates. Master's thesis, University of Karlsruhe, September 2004. Available at www.key-project.org.
19. A. Poetzsch-Heffter and P. Müller. A programming logic for sequential Java. In D. Swierstra, editor, *ESOP '99*, volume 1576 of *LNCS*. Springer, 1999.
20. R. Stärk and S. Nanchen. A logic for abstract state machines. *J. UCS*, 7(11), 2001.
21. J. van den Berg, M. Huisman, B. Jacobs, and E. Poll. A type-theoretic memory model for verification of sequential Java programs. In D. Bert, C. Choppy, and P. D. Mosses, editors, *WADT*, volume 1827 of *LNCS*, pages 1–21. Springer, 1999.
22. D. von Oheimb and T. Nipkow. Hoare logic for NanoJava: Auxiliary variables, side effects, and virtual methods revisited. In L.-H. Eriksson and P. A. Lindsay, editors, *FME*, volume 2391 of *LNCS*, pages 89–105. Springer, 2002.

AProVE 1.2: Automatic Termination Proofs in the Dependency Pair Framework*

Jürgen Giesl, Peter Schneider-Kamp, and René Thiemann

LuFG Informatik II, RWTH Aachen, Ahornstr. 55, 52074 Aachen, Germany
{giesl, thiemann, psk}@informatik.rwth-aachen.de

Abstract. AProVE 1.2 is one of the most powerful systems for auto-mated termination proofs of term rewrite systems (TRSs). It is the first tool which automates the new *dependency pair framework* [8] and there-fore permits a completely flexible combination of different termination proof techniques. Due to this framework, AProVE 1.2 is also the first termination prover which can be fully configured by the user.

1 Introduction

AProVE 1.2 (<u>A</u>utomated <u>P</u>rogram <u>V</u>erification <u>E</u>nvironment) is a system for automated termination and innermost termination proofs of TRSs. Its prede-cessor AProVE 1.0 [7] already offered a variety of termination proof techniques. However, there the techniques were applied in a fixed order which could not be influenced by the user. AProVE 1.2 has been totally re-structured (and partly re-implemented) to permit a completely modular combination of the available termination techniques. This increase in modularity of the termination tech-niques also increases the power of AProVE substantially. The theoretical basis for this re-design is the new *dependency pair (DP) framework* which is briefly recapitulated in Sect. 2. Sect. 3 explains AProVE's structure and shows how the user can configure the tool in order to experiment with self-defined strategies. We conclude in Sect. 4 and describe how to use AProVE in a fully automatic way.

2 The Dependency Pair Framework

The DP framework [8] (which was inspired by the cycle analysis algorithm of [12] and which is related to the constraint-based approach of [2, Chapter 7]) is a modular reformulation and improvement of Arts and Giesl's dependency pair approach [1,5]. Here, root symbols of left-hand sides of rules are called *defined* and all other symbols are *constructors*. For each defined symbol f we introduce a fresh *tuple symbol* F. Then for each rule $f(s_1, \ldots, s_n) \to r$ and each subterm $g(t_1, \ldots, t_m)$ of r with defined root g, we build a dependency pair $F(s_1, \ldots, s_n) \to G(t_1, \ldots, t_m)$. $DP(\mathcal{R})$ denotes the set of dependency pairs of a TRS $\mathcal{R}$.

In the following screenshot, the Source window **(A)** contains the TRS $\mathcal{R}$ under consideration. Here, minus and quot are defined symbols and s and 0 are

---

* Supported by the Deutsche Forschungsgemeinschaft DFG under grant GI 274/5-1.

U. Furbach and N. Shankar (Eds.): IJCAR 2006, LNAI 4130, pp. 281–286, 2006.

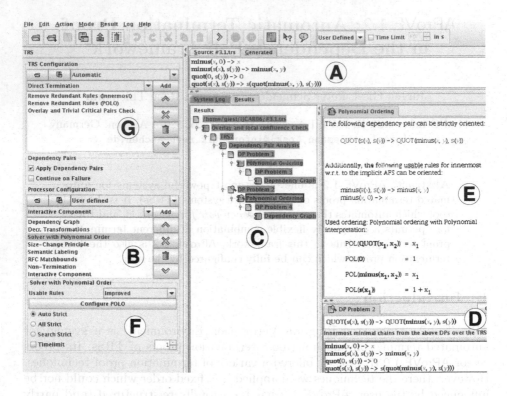

constructors. Therefore, we have $DP(\mathcal{R}) = \{\mathsf{MINUS}(\mathsf{s}(x), \mathsf{s}(y)) \to \mathsf{MINUS}(x, y),$ $\mathsf{QUOT}(\mathsf{s}(x), \mathsf{s}(y)) \to \mathsf{MINUS}(x, y), \mathsf{QUOT}(\mathsf{s}(x), \mathsf{s}(y)) \to \mathsf{QUOT}(\mathsf{minus}(x, y), \mathsf{s}(y))\}$.

The DP framework operates on *DP problems* $(\mathcal{P}, \mathcal{R})$ where initially, $\mathcal{P} = DP(\mathcal{R})$.[1] A DP problem $(\mathcal{P}, \mathcal{R})$ is called *finite* if there is no infinite $(\mathcal{P}, \mathcal{R})$-chain, i.e., no infinite sequence of pairs $s_1 \to t_1, s_2 \to t_2, \ldots$ from $\mathcal{P}$ with substitutions σ_i such that $t_i\sigma_i$ is terminating w.r.t. $\mathcal{R}$ and such that $t_i\sigma_i \to_{\mathcal{R}}^* s_{i+1}\sigma_{i+1}$ for all i. As shown in [1], a TRS $\mathcal{R}$ is terminating iff there is no infinite *chain* of its dependency pairs. So our goal is to prove that the problem $(DP(\mathcal{R}), \mathcal{R})$ is finite.

Termination techniques now operate on DP problems instead of TRSs and are called *DP processors*. Formally, a DP processor *Proc* takes a DP problem as input and returns a new set of DP problems which then have to be solved instead. Alternatively, it can also return "no". A processor *Proc* is *sound* if for all DP problems d, d is finite whenever $Proc(d)$ is not "no" and all DP problems in $Proc(d)$ are finite. *Proc* is *complete* if for all DP problems d, d is infinite whenever $Proc(d)$ is "no" or when $Proc(d)$ contains an infinite DP problem.

Soundness of a DP processor *Proc* is required to prove termination (in particular, to conclude that d is finite if $Proc(d) = \varnothing$). Completeness is needed to prove non-termination (in particular, to conclude that d is infinite if $Proc(d) = $ no).

So termination proofs in the DP framework start with the initial DP problem $(DP(\mathcal{R}), \mathcal{R})$. Then this problem is transformed repeatedly by sound DP proces-

---

[1] For efficiency, AProVE uses a slightly simpler notion of DP problems than [8].

sors. If the final processors return empty sets of DP problems, then termination is proved. If one of the processors returns "no" and all processors used before were complete, then one has disproved termination of the TRS $\mathcal{R}$. So in contrast to AProVE 1.0, AProVE 1.2 can also prove *non-termination*, cf. [9].

3   Structure of AProVE 1.2

Our description of AProVE's structure is based on the windows **(A)** – **(G)** in the screenshot. AProVE 1.2 offers 22 different DP processors. These include virtually all recent techniques and improvements for termination analysis with dependency pairs [6,8,9,10,12,17] (whereas no other tool implements all of these refinements) as well as processors based on other termination techniques like the *size-change principle* [15,16], *semantic labeling* [20], and *match-bounds* [4].

In the **Processor Configuration** window **(B)**, the user can select which processors should be used in which order. Whenever AProVE has to solve a DP problem, it first tries the first processor from the list in this window. So in the screenshot, one first applies the **Dependency Graph** processor. Only if a processor does not modify the current problem (i.e., if $Proc(\mathcal{P}, \mathcal{R}) = \{(\mathcal{P}, \mathcal{R})\}$), then AProVE tries the next processor in the list.

In our example, the dependency graph processor determines that any potentially infinite chain either contains infinitely many occurrences of the MINUS- or of the QUOT-dependency pair. Therefore, it transforms the initial DP problem $(DP(\mathcal{R}), \mathcal{R})$ into two new problems (1) $(\{\mathsf{MINUS}(\mathsf{s}(x), \mathsf{s}(y)) \to \mathsf{MINUS}(x, y)\}, \mathcal{R})$ and (2) $(\{\mathsf{QUOT}(\mathsf{s}(x), \mathsf{s}(y)) \to \mathsf{QUOT}(\mathsf{minus}(x, y), \mathsf{s}(y))\}, \mathcal{R})$. Now finiteness of the problems (1) and (2) can be proved separately.

This is reflected in the **Results** window **(C)** which depicts the corresponding proof tree. Nodes in the tree (marked with ▣) represent proof obligations. Edges (marked with ▤) represent proof techniques that transform a proof obligation into new proof obligations. In the screenshot, the node "TRS2" is the proof obligation which corresponds to the TRS $\mathcal{R}$ and the edge "**Dependency Pair Analysis**" is the proof technique which transforms $\mathcal{R}$ into the initial DP problem $(DP(\mathcal{R}), \mathcal{R})$ and immediately applies the dependency graph processor. All further nodes in the resulting subtrees are DP problems and all further edges are applications of DP processors. So "**DP Problem 1**" and "**DP Problem 2**" are the MINUS- and QUOT-problems (1) and (2) above.

If one clicks on a node or on an edge of the proof tree, then more information on the respective proof obligation or proof technique is displayed in the windows on the right. In the screenshot, the **Proof Obligation** window **(D)** depicts **DP Problem 2** and the **Proof Technique** window **(E)** provides details on the DP processor which was used to transform **DP Problem 2** further. Here, a *reduction pair processor based on polynomial orders* was applied (called "**Solver with Polynomial Order**").[2] For a DP problem $(\mathcal{P}, \mathcal{R})$, this processor tries to find a polynomial order such that all rules in $\mathcal{P}$ and $\mathcal{R}$ are at least weakly decreasing (i.e., $l \succsim r$ for all $l \to r \in \mathcal{P} \cup \mathcal{R}$) and it removes all pairs from $\mathcal{P}$ which are strictly

---

[2] AProVE also offers RPOS, KBO, or polynomial orders with negative coefficients [11].

decreasing (i.e., all $l \rightarrow r \in \mathcal{P}$ with $l \succ r$). Moreover, under some conditions, it is sufficient if just certain "usable" rules in $\mathcal{R}$ are weakly decreasing. In the screenshot, AProVE found a polynomial order where the only dependency pair of DP Problem 2 is strictly decreasing. Hence, applying this processor results in DP Problem 4, which is $(\varnothing, \mathcal{R})$. Finally, another application of the dependency graph processor to DP Problem 4 results in no remaining proof obligations. DP Problem 1 can be solved in a similar way. Therefore, termination of this example is proved. The generated proof can then be exported as an html- or LaTeX-file.

AProVE 1.2 is indeed fully configurable by the user, since the user can compose the list of processors in the Processor Configuration window (**B**). Moreover, for each processor, the user can determine its parameters in window (**F**). So for the Solver with Polynomial Order, the user can impose a timeout, choose the method to compute the usable rules and the algorithm for finding strictly decreasing dependency pairs, and determine the degree of the polynomials and the range for their coefficients (by clicking on "Configure POLO").

For particularly challenging examples and to develop new heuristics, one can include an "Interactive Component" processor in the Processor Configuration window (**B**). The interactive component displays the current DP problem together with all available DP processors. Then the user can select a processor manually and apply it. Afterwards, the list of processors in the Processor Configuration window is applied again on the resulting DP problems. Thus, to use the interactive component only if all other DP processors fail, this component should be at the end of the list in the Processor Configuration window.

For efficiency, it is often recommendable to simplify the initial TRS before transforming it into a DP problem. Suitable simplification techniques can be chosen in the TRS Configuration window (**G**). Here, the user can select which simplifications should be applied in which order. AProVE starts with applying the first technique in the list to the given TRS. In contrast to the application of DP processors, AProVE does not start with the first technique in the list again when the TRS has been modified by one of the simplifications. Instead, then the second technique is applied to the modified TRS, etc.

One of the most important simplifications is the Overlay and Trivial Critical Pairs Check. Under certain conditions, the obligation to prove termination of a TRS can be relaxed to prove only *innermost* termination. The advantage is that innermost termination is often easier to show than termination. Therefore, DP problems also have a flag which indicates whether one wants to prove full or just innermost termination. Depending on this flag, the DP processors behave differently and they are often more powerful for innermost termination.

Finally, AProVE has an extensive online Help (by clicking on ⬚) and a context-dependent help (by clicking on ⬚? and selecting any item in the GUI).

4   Using AProVE 1.2

For users who do not want to configure AProVE themselves, the "User Defined Mode" in the top right corner can be changed into a fully "Automatic Mode", where AProVE runs with a fixed list of DP processors. In this setting, processors are even applied in parallel. This mode of AProVE 1.2 corresponds to the one used in the *International Competition of Termination Tools* 2005. In this competition, AProVE 1.2 was the most powerful system for termination analysis of TRSs.[3] The reason is that AProVE is the only tool which features most modern termination techniques for TRSs and which permits to combine them in a completely flexible way. This combination can even be determined and configured by the user. In addition to ordinary TRSs, AProVE 1.2 also analyzes the termination of several other formalisms, e.g., of conditional TRSs and logic programs. In contrast to AProVE 1.0 it also handles TRSs modulo AC and context-sensitive TRSs. Its power in these areas is again demonstrated by the respective competitions. AProVE 1.2 is written in Java and can be downloaded from http://aprove.informatik.rwth-aachen.de/. At this URL one can also run AProVE in fully "Automatic Mode" directly via the web on a parallel computer.

References

1. T. Arts and J. Giesl. Termination of term rewriting using dependency pairs. *Theoretical Computer Science*, 236:133–178, 2000.
2. C. Borralleras. *Ordering-based methods for proving termination automatically*. PhD thesis, Universitat Politècnica de Catalunya, 2003.
3. E. Contejean, C. Marché, B. Monate, and X. Urbain. CiME. http://cime.lri.fr.
4. A. Geser, D. Hofbauer, and J. Waldmann. Match-bounded string rewriting systems. *Applicable Algebra in Eng., Comm. and Computing*, 15(3,4):149–171, 2004.
5. J. Giesl, T. Arts, and E. Ohlebusch. Modular termination proofs for rewriting using dependency pairs. *Journal of Symbolic Computation*, 34(1):21–58, 2002.
6. J. Giesl, R. Thiemann, P. Schneider-Kamp, and S. Falke. Improving dependency pairs. In *Proc. 10th LPAR*, LNAI 2850, pages 165–179, 2003.
7. J. Giesl, R. Thiemann, P. Schneider-Kamp, and S. Falke. Automated termination proofs with AProVE. In *Proc. 15th RTA*, LNCS 3091, pages 210–220, 2004.
8. J. Giesl, R. Thiemann, and P. Schneider-Kamp. The DP framework: Combining techn. for aut. termination proofs. *Proc. 11th LPAR*, LNAI 3452, p. 301-331, 2005.
9. J. Giesl, R. Thiemann, and P. Schneider-Kamp. Proving and disproving termination of higher-order functions. *Proc. 5th FroCoS*, LNAI 3717, pp. 216–231, 2005.
10. N. Hirokawa and A. Middeldorp. Dependency pairs revisited. In *Proc. 15th RTA*, LNCS 3091, pages 249–268, 2004.
11. N. Hirokawa and A. Middeldorp. Polynomial interpretations with negative coefficients. In *Proc. 7th AISC*, LNAI 3249, pages 185–198, 2004.
12. N. Hirokawa and A. Middeldorp. Automating the dependency pair method. *Information and Computation*, 199(1,2):172–199, 2005.
13. N. Hirokawa and A. Middeldorp. Tyrolean Termination Tool. In *Proc. RTA '05*, LNCS 3467, pages 175–184, 2005.
14. A. Koprowski. TPA: Termination proved automatically. In *Proc. 17th RTA*, LNCS, 2006. To appear.

---

[3] The other termination provers for TRSs were CiME [3], Matchbox [19], Teparla [18], TPA [14], TTT [13], cf. http://www.lri.fr/~marche/termination-competition/.

15. C. S. Lee, N. D. Jones, and A. M. Ben-Amram. The size-change principle for program termination. In *Proc. 28th POPL*, pages 81–92, 2001.
16. R. Thiemann and J. Giesl. The size-change principle and dependency pairs for termination of term rewriting. *AAECC*, 16(4):229–270, 2005.
17. R. Thiemann, J. Giesl, and P. Schneider-Kamp. Improved modular termination proofs using dependency pairs. *Proc. 2nd IJCAR*, LNAI 3097, pp. 75–90, 2004.
18. J. v. d. Wulp. Teparla. http://www.win.tue.nl/~hzantema/torpa.html
19. J. Waldmann. Matchbox: A tool for match-bounded string rewriting. In *Proc. 15th RTA*, LNCS 3091, pages 85–94, 2004.
20. H. Zantema. Termination of term rewriting by semantic labelling. *Fundamenta Informaticae*, 24:89–105, 1995.

CEL— A Polynomial-Time Reasoner
for Life Science Ontologies

Franz Baader, Carsten Lutz, and Boontawee Suntisrivaraporn

Theoretical Computer Science, TU Dresden, Germany
{baader, lutz, meng}@tcs.inf.tu-dresden.de

Abstract. CEL (Classifier for $\mathcal{EL}$) is a reasoner for the small description logic $\mathcal{EL}^+$ which can be used to compute the subsumption hierarchy induced by $\mathcal{EL}^+$ ontologies. The most distinguishing feature of CEL is that, unlike all other modern DL reasoners, it is based on a polynomial-time subsumption algorithm, which allows it to process very large ontologies in reasonable time. In spite of its restricted expressive power, $\mathcal{EL}^+$ is well-suited for formulating life science ontologies.

1 The Description Logic Underlying CEL

The system CEL[1] is a first step towards realizing the dream of a description logic system that offers both sound and complete polynomial-time algorithms and expressive means that allow its use in real-world applications. It is based on recent theoretical advances that have shown that the description logic (DL) $\mathcal{EL}$, which allows for conjunction and existential restrictions, and some of its extensions have a polynomial-time subsumption problem even in the presence of concept definitions and so-called general concept inclusions (GCI) [1]. The DL $\mathcal{EL}^+$ handled by CEL extends $\mathcal{EL}$ by so-called role inclusions (RI). On the practical side, it has turned out that the expressive power of $\mathcal{EL}^+$ is sufficient to express several large life science ontologies. In particular, the Systematized Nomenclature of Medicine (SNOMED) [4] employs $\mathcal{EL}$ with RIs and acyclic concept definitions. The Gene Ontology (GO) [3] can also be expressed in $\mathcal{EL}$ with acyclic concept definitions and one transitive role (which is a special case of an RI). Finally, large parts of the Galen Medical Knowledge Base (GALEN) [5] can be expressed in $\mathcal{EL}$ with GCIs and RIs.

Because of the space limitations, we cannot introduce the syntax and semantics of $\mathcal{EL}^+$ in detail. We just mention the syntax elements, and illustrate their use by a small example. Full definitions can be found in [1,2]. Like in other DLs, $\mathcal{EL}^+$ *concepts* are inductively defined starting with the sets of *concept names* N_C and *role names* N_R. Each concept name A is a concept, and so are the *top concept* $\top$, *conjunction* $C \sqcap D$, and *existential restriction* $\exists r.C$. An $\mathcal{EL}^+$ *ontology* is a finite set of *general concept inclusions (GCI)* of the form $C \sqsubseteq D$ for concepts C, D, and *complex role inclusions (RI)* of the form $r_1 \circ \cdots \circ r_n \sqsubseteq s$ for roles $r_1, \ldots, r_n, s$. A *primitive concept definition* (PCDef) $A \sqsubseteq D$ is a GCI with the

---

[1] CEL can be downloaded from http://lat.inf.tu-dresden.de/systems/cel/

U. Furbach and N. Shankar (Eds.): IJCAR 2006, LNAI 4130, pp. 287–291, 2006.
© Springer-Verlag Berlin Heidelberg 2006

$$\text{Endocardium} \sqsubseteq \text{Tissue} \sqcap \exists\text{cont-in.HeartWall} \sqcap$$
$$\exists\text{cont-in.HeartValve}$$
$$\text{HeartWall} \sqsubseteq \text{BodyWall} \sqcap \exists\text{part-of.Heart}$$
$$\text{HeartValve} \sqsubseteq \text{BodyValve} \sqcap \exists\text{part-of.Heart}$$
$$\text{Endocarditis} \sqsubseteq \text{Inflammation} \sqcap \exists\text{has-loc.Endocardium}$$
$$\text{Inflammation} \sqsubseteq \text{Disease} \sqcap \exists\text{acts-on.Tissue}$$
$$\text{HeartDisease} \equiv \text{Disease} \sqcap \exists\text{has-loc.Heart}$$
$$\text{part-of} \sqsubseteq \text{cont-in}$$
$$\text{has-loc} \circ \text{cont-in} \sqsubseteq \text{has-loc}$$

Fig. 1. An example $\mathcal{EL}^+$ ontology (motivated by GALEN)

left-hand side a concept name, while a (non-primitive) *concept definition* (CDef) $A \equiv D$ can be expressed using two GCIs. It is worthwhile to note that RIs generalize at least three expressive means important in bio-medical applications: role hierarchy, transitive role, and so-called right-identity axioms [4]. One of the most prominent inference problems for DL ontologies is *classification*: compute the subsumption hierarchy of all concept names occurring in the ontology.

As an example, we consider the $\mathcal{EL}^+$ ontology in Fig. 1, where all capitalized words are concept names and all lowercase words are role names. This small ontology contains 5 GCIs (which are indeed PCDefs), a CDef, and 2 RIs (more precisely a role hierarchy and a right-identity axiom) expressing a piece of clinical knowledge about *endocarditis* and related concepts and roles. It is not hard to infer from this ontology that endocarditis is classified as heart disease, i.e., Endocarditis $\sqsubseteq_{\mathcal{O}}$ HeartDisease. In fact, (*i*) Endocarditis implies Inflammation and thus Disease, which yields the first conjunct in the definition of HeartDisease. Moreover, (*ii*) $\exists$has-loc.Endocardium implies $\exists$has-loc.$\exists$cont-in.HeartWall and thus $\exists$has-loc.$\exists$cont-in.$\exists$part-of.Heart, which, in the presence of both RIs, implies $\exists$has-loc.Heart, satisfying the second conjunct in the definition of HeartDisease.

2   The CEL System

The algorithm implemented in CEL is based on the restriction to $\mathcal{EL}^+$ of the polytime classification algorithm for the more expressive DL $\mathcal{EL}^{++}$ introduced in [1]. To classify an ontology, the algorithm first transforms it into *normal form*, which requires all GCIs and RIs to be in one of the forms shown in the left part of Fig. 2. By introducing new concept and role names and applying a number of straightforward rewriting rules, any $\mathcal{EL}^+$ ontology $\mathcal{O}$ can be transformed into a normalized one such that subsumption between the concept names occurring in $\mathcal{O}$ is preserved. The normalization can be carried out in linear time, yielding an ontology whose size is linear in the size of the original one [1]. After normalization, the algorithm computes two mappings: $S : \mathsf{N_C^\top} \longrightarrow 2^{\mathsf{N_C^\top}}$ and $R : \mathsf{N_R} \longrightarrow 2^{(\mathsf{N_C^\top} \times \mathsf{N_C^\top})}$ where $\mathsf{N_C^\top}$ is $\mathsf{N_C}$ augmented by $\top$. The intuition is that these mappings make implicit subsumption relationships explicit in the sense that $B \in S(A)$ implies $A \sqsubseteq_{\mathcal{O}} B$, and $(A, B) \in R(r)$ implies $A \sqsubseteq_{\mathcal{O}} \exists r.B$. The mappings are initialized by setting $S(A) := \{A, \top\}$ and $R(r) := \emptyset$. Then the sets

$$A_1 \sqcap \cdots \sqcap A_n \sqsubseteq B$$

CR1 If $\{A_1, \ldots, A_n\} \subseteq S(X)$, $A_1 \sqcap \cdots \sqcap A_n \sqsubseteq B \in \mathcal{O}$,
and $B \notin S(X)$
then $S(X) := S(X) \cup \{B\}$

$$A \sqsubseteq \exists r.B$$

CR2 If $A \in S(X)$, $A \sqsubseteq \exists r.B \in \mathcal{O}$, and $(X, B) \notin R(r)$
then $R(r) := R(r) \cup \{(X, B)\}$

$$\exists r.A \sqsubseteq B$$

CR3 If $(X, Y) \in R(r)$, $A \in S(Y)$, $\exists r.A \sqsubseteq B \in \mathcal{O}$,
and $B \notin S(X)$
then $S(X) := S(X) \cup \{B\}$

$$r \sqsubseteq s$$

CR4 If $(X, Y) \in R(r)$, $r \sqsubseteq s \in \mathcal{O}$, and $(X, Y) \notin R(s)$
then $R(s) := R(s) \cup \{(X, Y)\}$

$$r \circ o \sqsubseteq t$$

CR5 If $(X, Z) \in R(r)$, $(Z, Y) \in R(s)$, $r \circ s \sqsubseteq t \in \mathcal{O}$,
and $(X, Y) \notin R(t)$
then $R(t) := R(t) \cup \{(X, Y)\}$

Fig. 2. Normal Form and Completion Rules

$S(A)$ and $R(r)$ are extended by applying the completion rules shown in the right part of Fig. 2 until no more rule applies. As a result, the mapping S computed this way satisfies $B \in S(A)$ iff $A \sqsubseteq_{\mathcal{O}} B$, i.e., $S(A)$ contains all subsumers of A. Note that this algorithm computes the subsumption relationships between *all* pairs of concept names.

It is obvious that, when implementing this algorithm, an efficient approach for finding an applicable rule must be developed. To avoid searching for such rules, we use a set of queues, one for each concept name appearing in the input ontology, to guide the application of completion rules. Intuitively, the queues list modifications to $S(A)$ and $R(A)$ that still have to be carried out. The fact that such an addition triggers other rules is taken into account by appropriately extending the queues when the addition is performed (see [2] for a detailed description). With a relatively straightforward implementation (in Common LISP) of this idea, we were able to classify the large SNOMED ontology (see below) in less than 4 hours (see [2] for this and other experimental results). Since then, however, we have further improved the implementation by changing the strategy of rule applications, changing the encoding of concept and role names, and low-level optimizations on the data structures. These optimizations have enhanced the performance of CEL on large real-world ontologies. In particular, CEL can now classify SNOMED in less than half an hour (see below).

The CEL Interface. CEL currently accepts input based on a small extension of the KRSS syntax.[2] It is currently equipped with a very simple shell-like interface that provides users with all essential functionalities, including a simple interactive help command. The user can either load an $\mathcal{EL}^+$ ontology formulated in KRSS syntax into the system from a file by calling (`load-ontology filename`) or enter interactively at the prompt each axiom of the ontology. The normalization is carried out while the ontology is being loaded, and once normalization is finished, (`classify-ontology`) can be invoked to classify all concept names occur-

---

[2] See `http://dl.kr.org/krss-spec.ps`

ring in the ontology (eager subsumption approach). We have modified the algorithm described above to a goal-directed variant such that a single subsumption query between 2 concept names (subsumes? B A) can be answered without needing to classify the whole ontology first (lazy subsumption approach). After having classified the whole ontology, CEL allows the user to output the classification results in different formats: (output-supers) to output the sets $S(A)$ for all concept names A occurring in $\mathcal{O}$; (output-taxonomy) to output the Hasse diagram of the subsumption hierarchy, i.e., just the *direct* parent-child relationships; and (output-hierarchy) to output the hierarchy as a graphical indented tree.

Through its command-line options, CEL can also work as a stand-alone reasoner without interaction from users. For instance, the command line:

$$\$cel\ -l\ \textit{filename}\ -c\ -outputHierarchy\ -q$$

can be entered to load and classify an ontology from *filename*, and then output the hierarchy. For a more detailed description of the CEL interface, we refer to the CEL user manual (available on the CEL homepage).

Performance Evaluation. The empirical results for the performance of CEL described below show that it can compete with, and often outperforms, the fastest tableau-based DL systems. We have compared the performance of CEL with three of the most advanced DL systems: FaCT^{++} (v1.1.0), RacerMaster (v1.9.0), and Pellet (v1.3b). These systems implement tableau-based decision procedures for expressive DLs in which subsumption is EXPTIME-complete. All experiments have been performed on a PC with 2.8GHz Intel Pentium 4 processor and 512MB memory running Linux v2.6.14. For Pellet, we used JVM v1.5 and set the Java heap space to 256MB (as recommended by the implementers).

Our experiments are based on three important bio-medical ontologies: GO, GALEN, and SNOMED. Since GALEN uses some expressivity that CEL cannot handle, we have simplified it by removing inverse role axioms and treating functional roles as ordinary ones, and obtained an $\mathcal{EL}^+$ ontology $\mathcal{O}^{\text{GALEN}}$. (Of course, also the other reasoners, which could have handled inverse and functional roles, were applied to $\mathcal{O}^{\text{GALEN}}$ rather than full GALEN.) We have obtained two other benchmarks, $\mathcal{O}^{\text{GO}}$ and $\mathcal{O}^{\text{SNOMED}}$, from the other two ontologies. However, SNOMED has one right-identity rule similar to the last axiom in our example (see Fig. 1). This axiom is passed to CEL, but not to the other reasoners, as the latter do not support right identities. Additionally, to get a smaller version of SNOMED that can be dealt with by standard DL reasoners, we also consider a fragment obtained by keeping only CDefs, and call it $\mathcal{O}^{\text{SNOMED}}_{\text{core}}$. Some information on the size and structure of these benchmarks is given in the upper part of Table 1, where the first row shows the numbers of PCDef, CDef, and GCI axioms, respectively. The results of our experiments are summarized in the lower part of Table 1, where all classification times are shown in seconds and *unattainable* means that the reasoner failed due to memory exhaustion. Notable, CEL outperforms all the reasoners in all benchmarks except $\mathcal{O}^{\text{GALEN}}$, where RacerMaster is as fast. CEL and FaCT^{++} are the only reasoners that can classify $\mathcal{O}^{\text{SNOMED}}$, whereas RacerMaster and Pellet fail. Pellet and the original version of FaCT (not

Table 1. Benchmarks and Evaluation Results

	$\mathcal{O}^{\text{Go}}$	$\mathcal{O}^{\text{GALEN}}$	$\mathcal{O}^{\text{SNOMED}}_{\text{core}}$	$\mathcal{O}^{\text{SNOMED}}$
concept axioms	20,465/0/0	2,041/699/1,214	0/38,719/0	340,972/38,719/0
role axioms	1	438	0	11 + 1
$|N_C|$	20,465	2,740	53,234	379,691
$|N_R|$	1	413	52	52
CEL	5.8	14	95	1,782
FaCT^{++}	6.9	50	740	3,859
RacerMaster	19	14	34,709	*unattainable*
Pellet	1,357	75	*unattainable*	*unattainable*

shown in the table) even fail to classify $\mathcal{O}^{\text{SNOMED}}_{\text{core}}$. It seems worth noting that the performance of FaCT^{++} degrades dramatically if $\mathcal{O}^{\text{SNOMED}}$ is extended with real GCIs. For instance, FaCT^{++} needs about 3,000 more seconds to classify $\mathcal{O}^{\text{SNOMED}}$ for each additional GCI of the form $\exists r.C \sqsubseteq D$, whereas the performance of CEL does not change noticeably if we add such GCIs.

3   Conclusion

We view these results as a strong argument for the use of tractable DLs based on extensions of $\mathcal{EL}$. As illustrated by the above performance evaluation, CEL is suitable for practical reasoning on very large life science ontologies. Developing CEL is ongoing work. We plan to extend its capabilities to the DL $\mathcal{EL}^{++}$ [1], with which one can express, among other things, *nominals* and *disjoint concepts*. We also plan to implement the DIG and OWL interface, so that CEL can be used as a backend reasoner for ontology editors such as OilEd and Protégé, which would also make their sophisticated user-interfaces available to users of CEL.

References

1. F. Baader, S. Brandt, and C. Lutz. Pushing the $\mathcal{EL}$ envelope. In *IJCAI-05*, Edinburgh, UK, 2005. Morgan-Kaufmann Publishers.
2. F. Baader, C. Lutz, and B. Suntisrivaraporn. Is tractable reasoning in extensions of the description logic $\mathcal{EL}$ useful in practice? In *Proceedings of the 2005 International Workshop on Methods for Modalities (M4M-05)*, 2005.
3. The Gene Ontology Consortium. Gene Ontology: Tool for the unification of biology. *Nature Genetics*, 25:25–29, 2000.
4. R. Cote, D. Rothwell, J Palotay, R. Beckett, and L. Brochu. The systematized nomenclature of human and veterinary medicine. Technical report, SNOMED International, Northfield, IL: College of American Pathologists, 1993.
5. A. Rector and I. Horrocks. Experience building a large, re-usable medical ontology using a description logic with transitivity and concept inclusions. In *Proceedings of the Workshop on Ontological Engineering, AAAI Spring Symposium (AAAI'97)*, Stanford, CA, 1997. AAAI Press.

FaCT++ Description Logic Reasoner: System Description

Dmitry Tsarkov and Ian Horrocks

School of Computer Science
The University of Manchester
Manchester, UK
{tsarkov, horrocks}@cs.man.ac.uk

Abstract. This is a system description of the Description Logic reasoner
FaCT++. The reasoner implements a tableaux decision procedure for the well
known $\mathcal{SHOIQ}$ description logic, with additional support for datatypes, including strings and integers. The system employs a wide range of performance en-
hancing optimisations, including both standard techniques (such as absorption
and model merging) and newly developed ones (such as ordering heuristics and
taxonomic classification). FaCT++ can, via the standard DIG interface, be used
to provide reasoning services for ontology engineering tools supporting the OWL
DL ontology language.

1 Introduction

Description Logics (DLs) are a family of logic based knowledge representation formalisms [1]. Although they have a range of applications, they are perhaps best known as
the basis for widely used ontology languages such as OIL, DAML+OIL and OWL [5].

A key motivation for basing ontology languages on DLs is that DL systems can then
be used to provide computational services for ontology tools and applications [8,9].
The increasing use of ontologies, along with increases in their size and complexity,
brings with it a need for efficient DL reasoners. Given the high worst case complexity
of the satisfiability/subsumption problem for the DLs in question (at least ExpTime-
complete), optimisations that exploit the structure of typical ontologies are crucial to
the viability of such reasoners.

FaCT++ is a new sound and complete DL reasoner designed as a platform for experimenting with new tableaux algorithms and optimisation techniques.[1] It incorporates
most of the standard optimisation techniques, including those introduced in the FaCT
system [3], but also employs many novel ones. This includes a new "ToDo list" architecture that is better suited to more complex tableaux algorithms (such as those used to
reason with OWL ontologies), and allows for a wider range of heuristic optimisations.

2 Tableaux Reasoning and Architecture

DL systems take as input a knowledge base (equivalently an ontology) consisting of a
set of axioms describing constraints on the conceptual schema (often called the TBox)

---

[1] FaCT++ is available at http://owl.man.ac.uk/factplusplus.

U. Furbach and N. Shankar (Eds.): IJCAR 2006, LNAI 4130, pp. 292–297, 2006.

and a set of axioms describing some particular situation (often called the ABox). They are then able to answer both "intensional" queries (e.g., regarding concept satisfiability and subsumption) and "extensional" queries (e.g., retrieving the instances of a given concept) w.r.t. the input knowledge base (KB). For the expressive DLs implemented in modern systems, these reasoning tasks can all be reduced to checking KB satisfiability.

Most modern DL systems are based on tableaux decision procedures, as first introduced by Schmidt-Schauß and Smolka [10], and subsequently extended to deal with ever more expressive logics [1]. Many systems now implement the $\mathcal{SHIQ}$ or $\mathcal{SHOIQ}$ DLs, tableaux algorithms for which were presented in [7,6]; these logics are very expressive, and correspond closely to the OWL ontology language. In spite of the high worst case complexity of the KB satisfiability problem for these logics (ExpTime-complete and NExpTime-complete respectively), highly optimised implementations have been shown to work well in many realistic (ontology) applications [3].

When reasoning with a KB, FaCT++ proceeds as follows. A first *preprocessing* stage is applied to the KB when it is loaded into reasoner; it is normalised and transformed into an internal representation. During this process several optimisations (that can be viewed as a syntactic re-writings) are applied.

The reasoner then performs *classification*, i.e., computes and caches the subsumption partial ordering (taxonomy) of named concepts. Several optimisations are applied here, mainly involving choosing the order in which concepts are processed so as to reduce the number of subsumption tests performed.

The classifier uses a KB *satisfiability* checker in order to decide subsumption problems for given pairs of concepts. This is the core component of the system, and the most highly optimised one.

3   FaCT++ Optimisations

3.1   Preprocessing Optimisations

Lexical normalisation and *simplification* is a standard rewriting optimisation primarily designed to promote early clash (inconsistency) detection, although it can also simplify concepts and even detect relatively trivial inconsistencies [4]. The basic idea is that all concepts are transformed into a *simplified normal form* (SNF), where the only operators allowed in SNF are negation ($\neg$), conjunction ($\sqcap$), universal restriction ($\forall$) and (qualified) at-most restriction ($\leq$). In FaCT++, the translation into SNF is performed on the fly, during the parsing process. At the same time, some simplifications are applied to concept expressions, including constant elimination (e.g., $C \sqcap \bot \rightarrow \bot$), expression elimination (e.g., $\neg\neg C \rightarrow C$), and subsumer elimination (e.g., $C \sqcap D \rightarrow C$ for D a known subsumer of C).

Absorption is a widely used rewriting optimisation that tries to eliminate General Concept Inclusion axioms (GCIs, axioms in the form $C \sqsubseteq D$, where both C and D are complex concept expressions), as GCIs left in the TBox invariably lead to a significant decrease in the performance of tableaux based satisfiability/subsumption testing procedures [3]. In FaCT++, GCIs are eliminated by absorbing them into either concept definition axioms (*concept absorption*) or role domain axioms (*role absorption*). Role absorption is particularly beneficial from the point of view of the CD-classification optimisation (see Section 3.3), as it eliminates GCIs without reducing the number of concepts to which CD-classification can be applied.

Told Cycle Elimination is a technique that we assume is used in most modern reasoners, although we know of no reference to it in the literature. Definitional cycles in the TBox can lead to several problems, and in particular cause problems for algorithms that exploit the told subsumer hierarchy (see Section 3.3). These cycles are, however, often quite easy to eliminate. Assume, for example, that $A_1 \ldots A_n$ are concept names, $C_1 \ldots C_n$ are arbitrary concept expressions, and $\bowtie$ is either $\sqsubseteq$ or $=$. The axioms $A_1 \bowtie A_2 \sqcap C_2, A_2 \bowtie A_3 \sqcap C_3, \ldots, A_n \bowtie A_1 \sqcap C_1$ include a definitional cycle, because the r.h.s. of the first axiom (indirectly) refers to the name on its l.h.s. The cycle can, however, be eliminated by transforming the axioms into $A_2 \equiv A_1, \ldots, A_n \equiv A_1, A_1 \sqsubseteq C_1 \sqcap C_2 \ldots \sqcap C_n$.

Synonym Replacement is used to extend simplification possibilities and improve early clash detection. If the only axiom with C on the left hand side is $C \equiv D$, then C is called a *synonym* of D. For a set of concept names, all of which are synonymous, FaCT++ uses a single "canonical" name in all concept expressions in the KB.

FaCT++ first translates all input concepts into SNF, with subsequent transformations being designed to preserve this form. After simplification and absorption, FaCT++ repeatedly performs cycle and synonym elimination steps until there are no further changes to the KB.

3.2 Satisfiability Checking Optimisations

The FaCT++ system was designed with the intention of implementing DLs that include inverse roles, and of investigating new optimisation techniques, including new ordering heuristics. In order to deal more easily with inverse roles, and to allow for more flexible ordering of the tableaux expansion, FaCT++ uses a *ToDo list*, instead of the usual top-down approach, to control the application of the expansion rules [13]. The basic idea behind this approach is that rules may become applicable whenever a concept is added to a node label. When this happens, the relevant node/concept pair is added to the ToDo list. The ToDo list sorts entries according to some order, and gives access to the "first" element in the list. The tableaux algorithm repeatedly removes and processes list entries until either a clash occurs or the list becomes empty.

Dependency-directed backtracking (Backjumping) is a crucial and widely used optimisation. Each concept in a completion tree label is labelled with a *dependency set* containing information about the branching decisions on which it depends. In case of a clash, the system backtracks to the most recent branching point where an alternative choice might eliminate the cause of the clash.

Boolean constant propagation (BCP) is another widely used optimisation. As well as the standard tableau expansion rules, additional inference rules can be applied to the formulae occurring in a node label, usually with the objective of simplifying them and reducing the number of nondeterministic rule applications. BCP is probably the most commonly used simplification, the basic idea being to apply the inference rule

$$\frac{\neg C_1, \ldots, \neg C_n, C_1 \sqcup \ldots \sqcup C_n \sqcup C}{C}$$

to concepts in a node labels.

Semantic Branching is another rewriting optimisation, the idea being to rewrite disjunctions of the form $C \sqcup D$ as $C \sqcup (\neg C \sqcap D)$. If choosing C leads to clash, then the $\neg C$ in the second disjunct (along with BCP) ensures that C will not be added to the node label again by some other nondeterministic expansion.

Ordering Heuristics can be very effective, and have been extensively investigated in FaCT++ [13]. Changing the order in which nondeterministic expansions are explored can result in huge (up to several orders of magnitude) differences in reasoning perfor mance. Heuristics can be used to choose a "good" order in which to try the different possible expansions. In practise, this usually means using heuristics to select the way in which expansion rules are applied to the disjunctive concepts in a node label, with a heuristic function being used to compute the relative "goodness" of each candidate expansion.

Heuristics may select an expansion-ordering based on, e.g., (ascending or descending order of) concept size, maximum quantifier depth, or frequency of usage. In order to reduce the cost of computing the heuristic function, FaCT++ computes and caches relevant values for each concept as the KB is loaded. As no one heuristic performs well in all cases, FaCT++ also selects the heuristics to be used based on an analysis of the structure of the input KB.

3.3 Classification Optimisations

As mentioned above, the focus here is on reducing the number of subsumption tests performed during classification. In FaCT++, this is achieved by both reducing the number of comparisons and by substituting cheaper (but incomplete) comparisons where possible.

Definitional Ordering is a well known technique that uses the syntactic structure of TBox axioms to optimise the order in which the taxonomy is computed. E.g., given an axiom $C \sqsubseteq D$, with C a concept name, FaCT++ will delay adding C to the taxonomy until all of the concepts occurring in D have been classified. In some cases this technique allows the taxonomy to be computed "top down", thereby avoiding the need to check for subsumees of newly added concepts.

Similarly, the structure of TBox axioms can be used to avoid (potentially) expensive subsumption tests by computing a set of (trivially obvious) *told subsumers* and *told disjoints* of a concept C. E.g., if the TBox contains an axiom $C \sqsubseteq D_1 \sqcap D_2$, then FaCT++ treats both D_1 and D_2, as well as all *their* told subsumers, as told subsumers of C, and if the TBox contains an axiom $C \sqsubseteq \neg D \sqcap \ldots$, then D is treated as a told disjoint of C. The classification algorithm can then exploit obvious (non-) subsumptions between concepts an their told subsumers (disjoints).

Model Merging is a widely used technique that exploits cached partial models in order to perform a relatively cheap but incomplete non-subsumption test. If the cached models for D and $\neg C$ can be merged to give a model of $D \sqcap \neg C$, then the subsumption $C \sqsubseteq D$ clearly does not hold.

Completely Defined Concepts is a novel technique used in FaCT++ to deal more effectively with wide (and shallow) taxonomies [12]. In this case, some concepts in the taxonomy may have very many direct subsumees, rendering classification ordering optimisations ineffective. It is often possible, however, to identify a significant subset of concepts whose subsumption relationships are completely defined by told subsumptions. FaCT++ computes a taxonomy for these concepts without performing any subsumption tests.

Clustering is another technique that addresses the same problem [2]. The idea here is to introduce new "virtual concepts" into the taxonomy in order to produce a deeper and more uniform structure. These concepts are asserted to be equivalent to the union of a number of sibling concepts and are inserted in the taxonomy in between these concepts and their common parent.

4   Discussion and Future Directions

We have presented FaCT++, a sound and complete reasoner for $\mathcal{SHOIQ}$ (and so OWL DL) which uses a new ToDo list architecture and incorporates a wide range of optimisations, including several novel ones.

Future directions for FaCT++ include both algorithmic and technological improvements. The next version of FaCT++ will support the more expressive $\mathcal{SROIQ}$ DL needed by the OWL 1.1 ontology language (see http://owl-workshop.man. ac.uk/OWL1_1.html). Some new optimisations, including optimised reasoning with nominals [11] and more elaborate heuristics are also planned. Regarding technological improvements, we plan to add direct support for OWL's XML syntax, and to parallelise the reasoning process.

References

1. F. Baader, D. Calvanese, D. McGuinness, D. Nardi, and P. F. Patel-Schneider, editors. *The Description Logic Handbook: Theory, Implementation and Applications*. CUP, 2003.
2. V. Haarslev and R. Möller. High performance reasoning with very large knowledge bases: A practical case study. In *Proc. of IJCAI 2001*, pages 161–168, 2001.
3. I. Horrocks. Using an expressive description logic: FaCT or fiction? In *Proc. of KR'98*, pages 636–647, 1998.
4. I. Horrocks. Implementation and optimisation techniques. In F. Baader, D. Calvanese, D. McGuinness, D. Nardi, and P. F. Patel-Schneider, editors, *The Description Logic Handbook: Theory, Implementation, and Applications*, pages 306–346. CUP, 2003.
5. I. Horrocks, P. F. Patel-Schneider, and F. van Harmelen. From $\mathcal{SHIQ}$ and RDF to OWL: The making of a web ontology language. *J. of Web Semantics*, 1(1):7–26, 2003.
6. I. Horrocks and U. Sattler. A tableaux decision procedure for $\mathcal{SHOIQ}$. In *Proc. of IJCAI 2005*, 2005.
7. I. Horrocks, U. Sattler, and S. Tobies. Practical reasoning for expressive description logics. In *Proc. of LPAR'99*, number 1705 in LNAI, pages 161–180, 1999.
8. H. Knublauch, R. Fergerson, N. Noy, and M. Musen. The protégé OWL plugin: An open development environment for semantic web applications. In *Proc. of ISWC 2004*, number 3298 in LNCS, pages 229–243, 2004.

9. A. Rector. Medical informatics. In F. Baader, D. Calvanese, D. McGuinness, D. Nardi, and P. F. Patel-Schneider, editors, *The Description Logic Handbook: Theory, Implementation, and Applications*, pages 415–435. CUP, 2003.
10. M. Schmidt-Schauß and G. Smolka. Attributive concept descriptions with complements. *Artificial Intelligence*, 48(1):1–26, 1991.
11. E. Sirin, B. C. Grau, and B. Parsia. From wine to water: Optimizing description logic reasoning for nominals. In *Proc. of KR 2006*, 2006. To Appear.
12. D. Tsarkov and I. Horrocks. Optimised classification for taxonomic knowledge bases. In *Proc. of the 2005 Description Logic Workshop (DL 2005)*, 2005.
13. D. Tsarkov and I. Horrocks. Ordering heuristics for description logic reasoning. In *Proc. of IJCAI 2005*, 2005.

Importing HOL into Isabelle/HOL

Steven Obua* and Sebastian Skalberg

Technische Universität München
D-85748 Garching, Boltzmannstr. 3, Germany

Abstract. We developed an importer from both HOL 4 and HOL-light into Isabelle/HOL. The importer works by replaying proofs within Isabelle/HOL that have been recorded in HOL 4 or HOL-light and is therefore completely safe. Concepts in the source HOL system, that is types and constants, can be mapped to concepts in Isabelle/HOL; this facilitates a true integration of imported theorems and theorems that are already available in Isabelle/HOL. The importer is part of the standard Isabelle distribution.

1 Introduction

The idea of sharing theorems between different proof-assistants is not new; there has been previous work on translating from HOL to NuPRL [1,2,3], from Isabelle to NuPRL [4] and from HOL to Coq [5,6]. Only [1,3,4,5] provide implementations; of these implementations only [3,5] translate *proofs* instead of just theorems. Both implementations can deal only with a subset of the HOL inference rules and have not been used for large developments.

Our translator from HOL 4 [10] and HOL-light [11] to Isabelle/HOL [9] is therefore the first one that fulfills both of the following two criteria:

- The translation process is safe relative to the correctness of the destination system, in this case Isabelle/HOL. This is achieved by replaying *proofs* that have been recorded in the source system (HOL 4 or HOL-light) in the destination system (Isabelle/HOL).
- Large developments have been translated with our translator, in fact almost all of the entire HOL 4 distribution and all of base HOL-light.

In contrast to previous work is also that our translation is basically *between systems, not between logics*. Although some complications result from the fact that Isabelle/HOL is an object logic instance of the Isabelle framework, and HOL 4 and HOL-light directly implement higher-order logic, all these systems still share the same logic: classical simply-typed polymorphic higher-order logic (HOL). The HOL community has always profited from the fact that while the implementations of their systems has been relatively stable, a large database of proven theorems has been developed in each of the systems. Now the time has come to go a step further and to make theorems in one HOL system available in

---

* Supported by the Ph.D. program "Logik in der Informatik" of the "Deutsche Forschungsgemeinschaft".

U. Furbach and N. Shankar (Eds.): IJCAR 2006, LNAI 4130, pp. 298–302, 2006.

the other systems, thus unifying these large databases. Other work sharing this vision is that of McLaughlin who translates Isabelle/HOL to HOL-light [7].

Our translator consists of two components. First there is the proof-recording component which resides in HOL 4 and HOL-light and which records the theorems together with their proofs so that they can be saved as a collection of XML files. Second there is the importer component which takes this collection as input and uses it to re-prove the exported theorems in Isabelle/HOL. The importer component can be configured to map imported concepts to concepts that are already available in Isabelle/HOL. This makes it for example possible to map the type of real numbers of HOL 4 or HOL-light to the type of real numbers of Isabelle, because they represent the same abstract concept independent of their specific construction. Another example of this versatility is that the importer can also be configured to map HOL 4's LET constant to Isabelle's Let constant although the constants differ in their names (different capitalization) and the order in which they take their arguments.

The importer component is part of the standard Isabelle distribution since 2004; the proof-recording component for HOL-light is part of the HOL-light distribution since release 2.0; the proof-recording component for HOL 4 can currently only be obtained by contacting the authors of this paper. There is also a simple importer implementation available which has been written in Java; although this implementation misses some features it can be used to check all of HOL-light; it can be downloaded [12].

2   The Proof-Recording Component

Each HOL system is based on the central idea of an abstract datatype thm. Instances of thm can be created and manipulated only according to the rules of the logic. The part of the HOL system that implements this abstract datatype, together with theory extension mechanisms like constant and type definition, is called the *kernel* of the system. The rest of the system is built on top of it.

Thanks to the concept of a kernel, adding proof-recording to an HOL system is relatively easy: first one adds a new component proof to the internal representation of thm, then one modifies the functions that manipulate thm to record these manipulations in the new component. Basically, each constructor of the proof component corresponds to an inference rule of the kernel. In HOL 4, which is implemented in Standard ML, these changes were transparent to the rest of the system; in HOL-light, whose implementation language is OCaml, unexpected problems arose from the fact that the built-in equality on theorems leaked through the abstractness of the datatype; this equality had changed, of course, because now for two theorems to be equal they have to have the same proof, too! Therefore all places in the HOL-light system had to be found and modified that made use of equality on theorems.

A proof can be considered a tree consisting of other proofs, terms and types. Saving this tree to disk naively is not feasible in practice; it is simply just to big. This might come as a surprise: after all, the proof has to fit into the main memory of the computer! The solution to this puzzle is that a proof in main memory is not a tree, but a DAG; unfolding this DAG into a tree when saving can lead to exponential blow-up. Therefore we go through the following steps during saving a collection of proofs:

- Apply $\alpha\beta\eta$-normalization to all terms; therefore we need no proof constructors for the β and η inference rules, which degenerate to reflexivity.
- Simplify proofs that involve reflexivity; the proof TRANS (REFL t) p for example can be simplified to just p.
- Identify all proofs that are shared in main memory; each shared proof is saved into a separate XML file. When saving a proof A that has a shared proof B as its child, instead of B only a link to the XML file of B is saved in the XML file of A.
- For each proof that is saved into a separate XML file, share all the terms and types within that proof, using a DAG representation.

These simple measures yield manageable proof-on-disk sizes: The base HOL 4 distribution results in 80,000 files, taking up 350MB disk space (13MB when gzipped). The base HOL-light system results in 130,000 files, taking up 229MB disk space (21MB when gzipped).

One extreme case is the proof of the Jordan Curve theorem in HOL-light by Thomas Hales. It produces about 1,000,000 files; unix commands like ls broke down when used naively. Therefore it would be better not to shift the proof sharing to the file system, but design an own file format for this purpose. This format could also deal with gzip-like compression issues.

Note that we use a first-order representation of proofs with sharing as our compression technique; Berghofer [8] uses another approach where proofs are represented as higher-order terms. It is not clear which approach is superior, or whether a combination of both approaches would be beneficial.

Adding proof-recording to the kernel of an HOL system does not change the runtime of this HOL system significantly. Saving the recorded proofs to disk is a time-consuming task, though: the base HOL 4 system needs 50 minutes, the base HOL-light system about 30 minutes. Saving the Jordan Curve theorem took a couple of hours.

The semantics of the proof constructors establishes an abstract HOL kernel [1] which is the union of the HOL 4 and HOL-light kernel, but operates not only modulo α-, but also modulo β- and η-equivalence. One inefficiency of this kernel is its current storage format, as mentioned before. Another improvement of it would be to incorporate higher inference rules such as rewriting which would certainly reduce the size of proofs considerably. Taking this one step further, a "golden" kernel should also provide the possibility of *coding higher rules and storing this code along with the proof objects*. Such a kernel could then serve as a standard kernel for exchanging theorems between HOL systems, and find also its applications in areas such as proof-carrying code, where the size of proof objects is regarded an important factor.

---

[1] For a description of this kernel, see [12].

3   The Importer Component

The import of the recorded proofs is done in two phases:

1. A *configuration Isabelle theory* transforms a set of XML proof files into a set of Isabelle/HOL theories.
2. The generated Isabelle/HOL theories can now be used just as other Isabelle theories; because the statements in these theories are proven with the help of the recorded proofs, the XML proof files must still be present when using these generated theories.

The critical phase is the first one; here it is decided via the configuration file how the imported concepts are mapped onto already existing ones. The importer does not accept axioms; this means that all constants that are specified via axioms in the source HOL system must be mapped onto existing Isabelle constants, and statements must be proven in Isabelle about these existing constants that correspond to the imported axioms. Further mappings are desirable for a better integration of the imported theories with already existing theories, but these additional mappings are not required.

There are mainly three mapping constructs: the command *const-maps* which maps constants, the command *type-maps* which maps types, and the attribute *hol4rew* which can be attached to Isabelle theorems. Furthermore there is the additional command *ignore-thms* which is currently also essential for the mapping process; its purpose is to ignore certain theorems and to not import them. Unfortunately one currently has to make explicit use of *ignore-thms* when mapping constants or types: the defining theorems/proofs for these constants and types have to be ignored. This is bound to confuse particularly the novice user, and is still annoying also the experienced one.

The importing process can be described as follows:

- A list is fetched from the collection of XML proof files that describes all *named* theorems in that collection; theorems that are not named occur also among the proof files, they have been created because of proof sharing.
- All entries of the list are imported one after another. If the entry corresponds to a theorem flagged by *ignore-thms*, it is skipped. Otherwise first the statement S of the theorem is fetched from the file. Then the types and constants of that statement are mapped according to *const-maps* and *type-maps*, yielding a statement $S' = \text{map}\,(S)$.
- After this, the *shuffler* is applied to S', yielding a statement $S'' = \text{shuffle}\,(S')$. The shuffler makes a statement more "Isabelle-like", converting for example quantified variables into unquantified schematic variables. The shuffler also applies all rewriting rules to the statement that have been defined via the *hol4rew* attribute.
- If S'' can be looked up in the Isabelle theorem database, then the import of the theorem has been successful. For mapped constants, this is very often the case. Otherwise the proof P is fetched from the XML proof file; mapping yields $P' = \text{map}\,(P)$. Then P' is replayed in Isabelle, mimicking the inference rules of the abstract HOL kernel, yielding a theorem T. The theorem T is

stored so that other proofs referencing this proof can access it. Furthermore $T' = \text{shuffle}\,(T)$ is stored and dumped to the generated theories.

- Thus, all shared proofs are replayed at most once. While this is desirable for obvious performance reasons, there is also a functional aspect to it. Certain proofs do have *side-effects*, because definition of constants and types are also encoded as proofs. The side-effect of replaying a constant definition is that this constant is now defined in the generated Isabelle theory; the same holds for type definitions. Replaying a proof at most once ensures that a side-effect is executed at most once.

4 Conclusion

We have described an importer/translator from HOL 4 and HOL-light to Isabelle/HOL; other source systems can be supported given that they adhere to the contract of the abstract kernel. The translator has been used to import large developments like the real analysis libraries of HOL 4 and base HOL-light and facilitates an integration of imported and already existing theories; thus it sets new standards for safe interoperability between HOL systems, though its user-friendliness could be improved.

Acknowledgments. Thanks to John Harrison for including the proof-recorder in his HOL-light distribution and for putting time and effort into making that inclusion as smooth as possible; also thanks to Virgile Prevosto for OCaml-related help.

References

1. D. J. Howe. Importing Mathematics from HOL into Nuprl. *TPHOLs'96*, LNCS 1125, Springer 1996.
2. C. Schürmann, M. Stehr. An Executable Formalization of the HOL/Nuprl Connection in the Metalogical Framework Twelf. *LPAR 2004*, to appear.
3. P. Naumov, M. Stehr, J. Meseguer. The HOL/NuPRL Proof Translator: A Practical Approach to Formal Interoperability. *TPHOLs'01*, LNCS 2152, Springer 2001.
4. P. Naumov. Importing Isabelle Formal Mathematics into NuPRL. *TPHOLs'99*, LNCS 1690, Springer 1999.
5. E. Denney. A Prototype Proof Translator from HOL to Coq. *TPHOLs'00*, LNCS 1869, Springer 2000.
6. F. Wiedijk. Encoding the HOL Light logic in Coq. Unpublished notes.
7. S. McLaughlin. An interpretation of Isabelle/HOL in HOL Light, submitted.
8. S. Berghofer, T. Nipkow. Proof terms for simply typed higher order logic. *TPHOLs'00*, LNCS 1869, Springer 2000.
9. T. Nipkow, L. C. Paulson, M. Wenzel. *Isabelle/HOL: A Proof Assistant for Higher-Order Logic*, Springer 2002
10. The HOL System Description. http://hol.sourceforge.net
11. J. Harrison. The HOL Light manual.
    http://www.cl.cam.ac.uk/users/jrh/hol-light/manual-1.1.pdf
12. S. Obua. http://www4.in.tum.de/~obua/importer

Geometric Resolution:
A Proof Procedure Based on Finite
Model Search

Hans de Nivelle and Jia Meng

Max-Planck Institut für Informatik, Germany
nivelle@mpi-inf.mpg.de
National ICT Australia, Australia
Jia.Meng@nicta.com.au

Abstract. We present a proof procedure that is complete for first-order logic, but which can also be used when searching for finite models. The procedure uses a normal form which is based on geometric formulas. For this reason we call the procedure *geometric resolution*. We expect that the procedure can be used as an efficient proof search procedure for first-order logic. In addition, the procedure can be implemented in such a way that it is complete for finding finite models.

1   Introduction

For many applications of automated theorem proving, knowing a counter model to a wrong conjecture is as useful as knowing that a conjecture is true. When a theorem prover fails to find a proof, the user might try to give more resources to the prover, tune the settings of the prover, or try to get another theorem prover. When the prover returns a model, the user will concentrate on trying to correct the conjecture.

Variants of resolution [11,1] are quite succesful in finding proofs. Although resolution can be modified into decision procedures for many decidable fragments [6,7,8], there is no general way of extracting models from these procedures. Also there exists no known general method for making resolution complete in finding finite models.

The model evolution calculus of [2] is complete and is guaranteed to terminate on clause sets without function symbols. However, because the model evolution calculus operates on Skolemized formulas, this not include formulas with existential quantifiers in the scope of universal quantifiers. In contrast, our proof procedure can be implemented in such a way that it terminates on all formulas that have a finite model.

There exist various approaches to searching for finite models: One approach is based on guessing a possible size of the domain, instantiating the clauses within the domain, and applying propositional reasoning on the result. If the result is satisfiable, then a model has been found. Otherwise, the size of the domain has to be increased. Approaches among this line are the systems MACE [10] and

U. Furbach and N. Shankar (Eds.): IJCAR 2006, LNAI 4130, pp. 303–317, 2006.

ModGen [9]. Alternatively, one can search for a model by direct search. This approach is followed for example in [12], [13] and [14].

Our algorithm is somewhat related to this last approach but it has also elements from other approaches. It consists of a search algorithm which is almost identical to the algorithm in [5], but enhanced with lemma generation. In [5], the algorithm searches for a model by exhaustive search. When a disjunction is encountered, all members of the disjunction are tried. When an existential quantifier is encountered, first all existing elements in the interpretation are tried. If this fails, a new element is tried.

This naive model search algorithm is refutationally complete, and also guaranteed to find finite models when breadth-first search is used, but very inefficient. The major source of inefficiency are the existential quantifiers. Every time, when a subformula of form $\exists y \; P(\overline{d}, y)$ needs to be made true, all elements in the interpretation have to be tried as candidates for y.

In order to reduce the search complexity, we add lemma learning to the procedure. We introduce a calculus with which it is always possible, at each choice point, after all subbranches have been refuted, to derive a new formula which closes the search attempt before the choice point. Because the derived lemmas contain variables, the lemmas give a most general reason why the branch has been closed. In this way, repetition of identical work can be largely reduced. In particular, we will show that in many cases enumeration of domain elements can be avoided.

The way we use lemma generation is related to lemma generation in DPLL [15]. The main difference with lemma generation in DPLL is that our calculus operates on formulas with variables. In fact, one could say that our calculus for lemma generation relates to the naive model search algorithm in the same way as resolution with superposition relates to the model construction procedure of [1]. The essential difference is that we actually run the naive search algorithm and use the lemma calculus to improve its efficiency. For superposition, the model construction procedure is used only as a tool for proving completeness. Our lemma calculus could also be used in this way (i.e. as a saturation-based proof search method), but one would loose the ability to find finite models.

2   Geometric Formulas

The model search algorithm and the lemma calculus operate on what we call *geometric formulas*. The formulas are related to the formulas used in [4], but not exactly the same. In [4], the right hand side of a formula is a disjunction of existentially quantified conjunctions. Here we simplified the right hand sides by allowing only one operator at the same time.

Geometric formulas play a role similar to clauses in saturation-based theorem proving. The main difference is that geometric formulas do not contain constant and function symbols. Instead they may contain existential quantifiers. We show in Section 3 that every first-order formula (possibly containing equality) can be transformed to a set of geometric formulas, so that no generality is lost.

Definition 1. *We assume an infinite set of* variables $\mathcal{V}$. *A variable atom is defined by one of the following two forms:*

- $x_1 \not\approx x_2$, *with* $x_1, x_2 \in \mathcal{V}$ *and* $x_1 \neq x_2$.
- $p(x_1, \ldots, x_n)$ *with* $n \geq 0$ *and the* $x_i \in \mathcal{V}$.

There are no constants and no function symbols in variable atoms. There are no positive equalities. In principle, one could allow disequalities of form $v \not\approx v$, but since these are known to be false, there is no need to keep such equalities. Geometric formulas are built from variable atoms. We give the definition:

Definition 2. *A* geometric formula *has form*

$$\forall \overline{x} \; A_1(\overline{x}) \wedge \cdots \wedge A_p(\overline{x}) \wedge x_1 \not\approx x_1' \wedge \cdots \wedge x_q \not\approx x_q' \rightarrow Z(\overline{x}),$$

in which $p \geq 0$, $q \geq 0$, *and the* $x_1, x_1', \ldots, x_q, x_q' \in \overline{x} \subseteq \mathcal{V}$.
The right hand side $Z(\overline{x})$ *must have one of the following three forms:*

1. *The false constant* $\bot$.
2. *A non-empty disjunction of atoms* $B_1(\overline{x}) \vee \cdots \vee B_r(\overline{x})$ *with* $r > 0$.
3. *An existential formula of form* $\exists y \; B(\overline{x}, y)$ *with* $y \in \mathcal{V}$ *but* $y \notin \overline{x}$. *The variable* y *must occur in* $B(\overline{x}, y)$.

A formula of the first type is called lemma. *A formula of the second type is called* disjunctive. *A formula of the third type is called* existential.

Our notations can be clarified as follows:

- In $\forall \overline{x}$, $\overline{x}$ denotes an enumeration of $\overline{x}$, in arbitrary order, mentioning each variable of $\overline{x}$ exactly once. The scope of $\forall \overline{x}$ is the complete geometric formula.
- In $A(\overline{x})$, $\overline{x}$ denotes a sequence of variables from $\overline{x}$. Variables may be repeated, and variables may be omitted.
- Latin letters A, B denote variables atoms that are not disequalities.
- In later sections, we will use expressions of form $\Phi(\overline{x})$ or $\phi_1(\overline{x}) \wedge \cdots \wedge \phi_p(\overline{x})$ for conjunctions of variable atoms of both types with variables in $\overline{x}$.

Note that in each of the three cases, the free variables of $Z(\overline{x})$ are within $\overline{x}$. However, since $A_1(\overline{x}) \wedge \cdots \wedge A_p(\overline{x})$ need not contain all variables of $\overline{x}$, this does not imply that geometric formulas are range restricted. (An implication is range restricted if each variable occurring in the right hand side also occurs in the left hand side) Types 1 and 2 could be merged if we would allow $r = 0$ in type 2. We prefer to keep the types distinct, because the roles of the formulas will be different in the calculus.

Example 1. Propositional clauses can be replaced by geometric formulas of type 1 or type 2 with empty $\overline{x}$. For example, $A \vee B \vee \neg C$ can be replaced by $C \rightarrow A \vee B$. The clause $A \vee B$ is already a geometric formula. The clause $\neg A \vee \neg B$ can be replaced by $A \wedge B \rightarrow \bot$.

Example 2. Equalities can be translated into geometric formulas. Consider the positive equality $f(a) \approx f(b)$. First one introduces relations A, B, F and geometric formulas: $\exists y\, A(y)$, $\exists y\, B(y)$, $\forall x\, \exists y\, F(x,y)$. Using those, the equality can be expressed by $\forall x_1, x_2, x_3, x_4\, A(x_1) \wedge F(x_1, x_2) \wedge B(x_3) \wedge F(x_3, x_4) \wedge x_2 \not\approx x_4 \rightarrow \bot$.

The negative equality $f(a) \not\approx f(b)$ can be expressed by the geometric formula $\forall x_1, x_2, x_3\, A(x_1) \wedge S(x_1, x_2) \wedge B(x_3) \wedge S(x_3, x_2) \rightarrow \bot$.

3 Conversion from FOL to Geometric Logic

The conversion from first-order logic to geometric logic is analogous to the clause transformation that is used for resolution. The main difference is that functions are replaced by existential quantifiers, instead of replacing existential quantifiers by functions.

Theorem 1. *There exists a transformation from first-order formulas to finite sets of geometric formulas, which can be efficiently computed. For each non-empty set D holds: The formula F has a model D as domain iff the translation $G_1, \ldots, G_m$ (read as conjunction) has a model with D as domain.*

It is possible to obtain a polynomial transformation, but we prefer not to stress this, because a polynomial transformation need not be the best in practical cases. We stress the domain of the interpretations (instead of simply stating equisatisfiability) because we are interested both in models and in proofs.

As a starting point of the transformation, we assume that F is a formula in negation normal form. Because geometric formulas do not allow function symbols, we will replace functions by serial relations, somewhat similar to the transformation in [9]. The difference is that here we use only seriality axioms, while there also functionality axioms are needed.

When removing functions, constants are treated as 0-arity functions, these will be also deleted. We call the removal operation *anti Skolemization*. In the transformation, we assume that F is standardized apart. (A formula is standardized apart if there are no two quantifiers that quantify the same variable)

Definition 3. *Let F be a formula in negation normal form. We assume that for each function symbol f occurring in F with arity a, there exists a unique predicate symbol P_f with arity $(a+1)$. We define S_f as the seriality axiom for P_f,*

$$\forall x_1, \ldots, x_a\, \exists y\, P_f(x_1, \ldots, x_a, y).$$

We define a replacement sequence $F_1, F_2, \ldots, F_n$ which starts with $F_1 = F$, and which eliminates occurrences of function symbols one-by-one.

Let $f(x_1, \ldots, x_a)$ be a term which occurs in F_i, and in which the $x_1, \ldots, x_a$ are variables. (not necessarily distinct)

Let A be the smallest subformula of F_i containing all occurrences of $f(x_1, \ldots, x_a)$. Write F_i in the form $F_i[\, A[\, f(x_1, \ldots, x_a)\,]\,]$.

Let P_f be the predicate symbol assigned to f. Let α be a variable that does not occur in F_i. Then F_{i+1} is defined as

$$F_i[\ \forall \alpha\ (\neg P_f(x_1,\ldots,x_a,\alpha) \vee A[\alpha]\ )\ ].$$

At some point, the sequence will reach a formula F_n which has no remaining function symbols. Then the anti-Skolemization *of F equals*

$$S_{f_1} \wedge \cdots \wedge S_{f_q} \wedge F_n.$$

Theorem 2. *We use the term D-model for a model with D as domain.*

Let F be a formula. Let F_n be its anti-Skolemization. Let D be a non-empty set. Then F has a D-model iff F_n has a D-model.

Proof. Let the seriality axioms S_f and the sequence $F_1, F_1, \ldots, F_n$ with $F = F_1$ be defined as in Definition 3.

First assume that F_1 has a D-model. We need to show that $S_{f_1} \wedge \cdots \wedge S_{f_q} \wedge F_n$ has a D-model. In order to do this, one can interpret each predicate $P_f(x_1,\ldots,x_a,y)$ as $f(x_1,\ldots,x_a) \approx y$. Then the seriality axioms $S_{f_1},\ldots,S_{f_q}$ are provable. For each i with $1 \leq i < n$, we have $F_i \leftrightarrow F_{i+1}$, because $A[\ f(x_1,\ldots,x_n)\ ]$ is equivalent to $(\ \forall \alpha\ f(x_1,\ldots,x_n) \approx \alpha \rightarrow A[\alpha]\ )$. Iterating $n-1$ times, it follows that $S_{f_1} \wedge \cdots \wedge S_{f_q} \wedge F_n$ has a D-model.

Now assume that $S_{f_1} \wedge \cdots \wedge S_{f_q} \wedge F_n$ has a D-model. We first Skolemize the formulas of S_f. Because F_n contains no function symbols, we may assume without losing generality, that the Skolem function for S_f is f. Write Sk_f for the formula $\forall x_1,\ldots,x_a\ P_f(x_1,\ldots,x_a,f(x_1,\ldots,x_a))$.

From the soundness of Skolemization, it follows that $Sk_{f_1} \wedge \cdots \wedge Sk_{f_q} \wedge F_n$ has a D-model. Assume that the term being replaced at stage i is $f(x_1,\ldots,x_a)$. It is easily seen (using resolution) that

$$Sk_f, \forall \alpha\ (\neg P_f(x_1,\ldots,x_a,\alpha) \vee A[\alpha]\ ) \vdash A[\ [f(x_1,\ldots,x_a)]\ ].$$

Iterating $n-1$ times, it follows that $Sk_{f_1} \wedge \cdots \wedge Sk_{f_q} \wedge F_0$ has a D-model.

Definition 4. *A formula is in CUDEN normal form if the operator path to each atom has form $\wedge^* \forall^* \vee^* \exists^? \neg^?$. (CUDEN stands for Conjunction, Universal quantifier, Disjunction, Existential quantifier, Negation.)*

Theorem 3. *The following replacements transform a formula from NNF to CUDEN normal form:*

1. $\forall x(A \wedge B) \Rightarrow (\forall x\ A) \wedge (\forall x\ B),$
    $(A \wedge B) \vee C \Rightarrow (A \vee C) \wedge (B \vee C),$
    $A \vee (B \wedge C) \Rightarrow (A \vee B) \wedge (A \vee C),$

    $(\forall x\ A) \vee B \Rightarrow \forall x\ (A \vee B),$
    $A \vee (\forall x\ B) \Rightarrow \forall x\ (A \vee B).$

2. *If F contains a subformula $\exists y\ A(x_1,\ldots,x_a,y)$ in which $A(x_1,\ldots,x_a,y)$ is either an equality, a disequality, or not an atom, then let p be a new predicate symbol with arity $a+1$ Replace $F[\ \exists y\ A(x_1,\ldots,x_a,y)\ ]$ by*

$$F[\ \exists y\ p(x_1,\ldots,x_a,y)\ ] \wedge \forall x_1,\ldots,x_a,y\ (\ \neg p(x_1,\ldots,x_a,y) \vee A(x_1,\ldots,x_a,y)\ ).$$

Finally, a function-free formula in CUDEN normal form can be transformed into a set of geometric formulas by the following replacements:

1. Delete negative equalities from disjunctions as follows: Replace
   $$\forall x_1, \ldots, x_p \ (\ \neg(x \approx x') \vee A_1 \vee \cdots \vee A_q \ ) \text{ by}$$
   $$\forall x_1, \ldots, x_p \ (\ A_1[x := x'] \vee \cdots \vee A_q[x := x'] \ ).$$
2. Replace positive equalities $x \approx x'$ by negative disequalities $\neg(x \not\approx x')$.
3. If there is a disjunction of form $\forall x_1, \ldots, x_p \ A_1 \vee \cdots \vee A_q$ in which one of the A_i has form $\exists y \ B(x_1', \ldots, x_r', y)$, and another A_j is a positive non-equality atom, then replace $\exists y \ B(x_1', \ldots, x_r', y)$ by $q(x_1', \ldots, x_r')$ and add a new disjunction

$$\forall x_1', \ldots, x_r' \ \neg q(x_1', \ldots, x_r') \vee \exists y \ B(x_1', \ldots, x_r', y).$$

4   Model Search Without Lemma Generation

We present the model search algorithm without lemma generation. It is closely related to the methods in [4] and [5]. The main difference is that our method is able to handle equality. The algorithm with lemma generation will be presented in Section 5.

Definition 5. *We assume an infinite set of elements $\mathcal{E}$. A ground atom is an object of form $p(e_1, \ldots, e_a)$, with $a \geq 0$ and $e_1, \ldots, e_a \in \mathcal{E}$.*

If for some $E \subseteq \mathcal{E}$, all $e_1, \ldots, e_n$ are in E, then we call $p(e_1, \ldots, e_n)$ a ground atom over E.

In contrast to variable atoms, ground atoms have no disequalities. Ground disequalities $e \not\approx e'$ can always be evaluated.

Definition 6. *An interpretation is a pair (E, M) in which $E \subseteq \mathcal{E}$ is a set of elements, and M is a set of ground atoms over E.*

We will $+$ both for insertion of elements to E, and for insertion of atoms to M. If we want to add an element e to a set of elements E, we can write $E + e$. If $E = \{e_1, e_2, e_3\}$ we can write $E = e_1 + e_2 + e_3$. Similarly, if we add an atom $p(e_1, e_2)$ to M, we can write $M + p(e_1, e_2)$. A complete interpretation can be written as $(\ 0 + 1, \ \ p(0) + q(1) + p(0, 1) \ )$.

Definition 7. *A ground substitution Θ is a substitution from $\mathcal{V}$ to $\mathcal{E}$. We write $A(\overline{x})\Theta$ or $A(\overline{x}\Theta)$ for the application of Θ on $A(\overline{x})$. Let (E, M) be an interpretation, let Θ be a ground substitution:*

1. *If Θ is defined for $x_1, \ldots, x_a$, then Θ makes a variable atom of form $p(x_1, \ldots, x_a)$ true in (E, M) if $p(x_1, \ldots, x_a)\Theta \in M$.*
2. *If Θ is defined for x, x', then Θ makes the disequality $(x \not\approx x')$ true if $x\Theta \neq x'\Theta$.*

If Θ is defined for all variables in $\overline{x}$, then Θ makes a conjunction $\phi_1(\overline{x}) \wedge \cdots \wedge \phi_p(\overline{x})$ of variable atoms true in (E, M) if Θ makes all $\phi_i(\overline{x})$ true in (E, M).

Definition 8. *Let* $r = \forall \overline{x}\ \Phi(\overline{x}) \rightarrow Z(\overline{x})$ *be a geometric formula. Let* (E, M) *be an intepretation. We say that* (E, M) *makes* r *true if every ground substitution* Θ *that is defined for* $\overline{x}$, *either does not make* $\Phi(\overline{x})$ *true in* (E, M), *or*

1. $Z(\overline{x})$ *has form* $B_1(\overline{x}) \vee \cdots \vee B_q(\overline{x})$ *and* Θ *makes one of the* $B_j(\overline{x})$ *true in* (E, M).
2. $Z(\overline{x})$ *has form* $\exists y\ B(\overline{x}, y)$ *and there exists an element* $e \in E$ *such that the ground substitution* $\Theta + (y := e)$ *makes* $B(\overline{x}, y)$ *true in* (E, M).

Definition 9. *Let* $r = \forall \overline{x}\ \phi_1(\overline{x}) \wedge \cdots \wedge \phi_p(\overline{x}) \rightarrow Z(\overline{x})$ *be a geometric rule. Let* (E, M) *be an interpretation, and let* Θ *be a substitution which is defined on* $\overline{x}$. *If* Θ *makes* $\phi_1(\overline{x}) \wedge \cdots \wedge \phi_p(\overline{x})$ *true in* (E, M), *then we call the rule* r *applicable on* (E, M) *with substitution* Θ, *if one the following conditions is met, depending on the type of* r :

1. $Z(\overline{x}) = \perp$. *In this case we call* r *a closing lemma of* (E, M).
2. $Z(\overline{x})$ *has form* $B_1(\overline{x}) \vee \cdots \vee B_q(\overline{x})$ *and* Θ *makes none of the* $B_j(\overline{x})$ *true in* (E, M).
3. $Z(\overline{x})$ *has form* $\exists y\ B(\overline{x}, y)$ *and there exists no* $e \in E$, *for which* $\Theta + (y := e)$ *makes* $B(\overline{x}, y)$ *true in* (E, M).

Lemma 1. *An interpretation* (E, M) *makes a set of rules* G *true if and only if there there is no applicable rule in* G.

We present the model search algorithm. It starts with an empty model. At each stage it looks for a rule r that is applicable with some substitution Θ. If there is no applicable rule, then the interpretation makes all rules true. Otherwise, the interpretation is extended in such a way that r is not applicable anymore with Θ. In case the interpretation can be extended in more than one possible way, the algorithm has to attempt all possibilities. When applicable rules are explored in a fair fashion, the search algorithm is refutationally complete.

Definition 10. *Let* G *be a set of geometric formulas.* $S_t(G)$ *is initially defined as* $S_t(G, \emptyset, \emptyset)$.

$S_t(G, E, M)$ *returns either* $\perp$ *or an interpretation* (E', M'), *s.t.* $E \subseteq E'$, $M \subseteq M'$, *and* (E', M') *makes all rules in* G *true.* $S_t(G, E, M)$ *is defined by the following cases:*

1. *If* G *contains a lemma* $\forall \overline{x}\ \phi_1(\overline{x}) \wedge \cdots \wedge \phi_p(\overline{x}) \rightarrow \perp$, *which is applicable on* (E, M) *with ground substitution* Θ, *then* $S_t(G, E, M)$ *returns* $\perp$.
2. *If* G *contains a disjunctive rule* $\forall \overline{x}\ \phi_1(\overline{x}) \wedge \cdots \wedge \phi_p(\overline{x}) \rightarrow B_1(\overline{x}) \vee \cdots \vee B_q(\overline{x})$ *which is applicable on* (E, M) *with ground substitution* Θ, *then compute, for each* j *with* $1 \leq j \leq q$, $\lambda_j := S_t(G, E, M + B_j(\overline{x})\Theta)$. *If* $\lambda_1 = \cdots = \lambda_q = \perp$, *then* $S_t(G, E, M)$ *returns* $\perp$. *Otherwise* $S_t(G, E, M)$ *returns one of the* λ_j *which is different from* $\perp$.
3. *If* G *contains an existential rule* $\forall \overline{x}\ \phi_1(\overline{x}) \wedge \cdots \wedge \phi_p(\overline{x}) \rightarrow \exists y\ B(\overline{x}, y)$, *which is applicable in* (E, M) *with ground substitution* Θ, *then define, for each* $e \in E$, $\Theta_e = \Theta + (y := e)$, *and recursively compute* $\lambda_e := S_t(G, E, M + B(\overline{x}, y)\Theta_e)$.

In addition, define $\Theta_{\hat{e}} = \Theta + (y := \hat{e})$ for some $\hat{e} \notin E$, and compute $\lambda_{\hat{e}} := S_t(G, E + \hat{e}, M + B(\overline{x}, y)\Theta_{\hat{e}})$.
If, for each $e \in E$, $\lambda_e = \perp$, and also $\lambda_{\hat{e}} = \perp$, then $S_t(G, E, M)$ returns $\perp$. Otherwise, $S_t(G, E, M)$ returns one of the λ_e or $\lambda_{\hat{e}}$ which is different from $\perp$.

4. *If there exists no applicable rule, then $S_t(G, E, M)$ returns (E, M).*

It is easily seen that the algorithm $S_t(G)$ is complete, as long as applicable rules are expanded in a fair way. Due to the way existential quantifiers are treated, $S_t(G)$ also has a reasonable chance of finding finite models, but it is not guaranteed to find a finite model in case there exists one. As an example consider the set of formulas $A \vee B$, $\forall x \; A \rightarrow \exists y \; P(x, y)$, $\forall xyz \; P(x, y) \wedge P(y, z) \rightarrow P(x, z)$, $\forall x \; P(x, x) \rightarrow \perp$. The interpretation $(\emptyset, B)$ makes all rules true. However, $S_t(G)$ will probably first attempt A in the first disjunction, after which it has to construct an infinite P-chain. Completeness for finite models can be obtained by using breadth-first search, but this would make search for refutations less efficient. Although complete in theory, $S_t(G)$ is of course inefficient.

5   The Algorithm with Lemma Generation

We modify the algorithm of the previous section in such a way that it is able to learn in the following way: Whenever it cannot extend (E, M) to a model of G, the improved algorithm will not simply return $\perp$, but a lemma that closes (E, M). The lemma ensures that, whenever the algorithm enters a similar situation again, it will not search another time for a refutation, but instead reuse the lemma. It will be also possible to avoid enumerating the complete domain for an existential quantifier, in case the lemma does not depend on the actual witness chosen. Another advantage of learning is that the algorithm will be able to output proofs which can be verified in a formal calculus.

Definition 11. *A* variable substitution *Σ is a substitution from $\mathcal{V}$ to $\mathcal{V}$. Most general unifiers* between non-disequality variable atoms *are defined as usual.*

Note that, because we consider only variable atoms, atoms with the same predicate symbol are always unifiable. We define the rules with which lemmas are derived. Variable merging and disjunction resolution are standard. The existential resolution rules are different from the standard paramodulation/superposition rules.

We assume that premises in geometric formulas can be freely permuted. As a consequence, in disjunction resolution, the resolved atoms are not necessarily the first atoms in the lemmas. We always assume that lemmas are normalized in the following ways:

1. Quantified variables that do not occur in the body are removed.
2. Repeated quantifications over the same variable are removed.
3. Identical copies of atoms are removed. This includes the case where the formula contains two orientations $v \not\approx w$ and $w \not\approx v$ of a disequality.

Definition 12. *We the rules of the lemma calculus. When a rule has more than one premise, we implictly assume that variables in the premises are renamed, s.t. no two premises have a variable in common.*

Variable merging: *Let* $\lambda = \forall \overline{x} \quad A_1(\overline{x}) \wedge \cdots \wedge A_p(\overline{x}) \wedge x_1 \not\approx x_1' \wedge \cdots \wedge x_q \not\approx x_q' \to \bot$. *Let* Σ *be a substitution of form* $x := x'$, *for two distinct* $x, x' \in \overline{x}$. *Then the following lemma is a* variable merging *of* λ :

$$\forall \overline{x}\Sigma \quad A_1(\overline{x})\Sigma \wedge \cdots \wedge A_p(\overline{x})\Sigma \wedge x_1\Sigma \not\approx x_1'\Sigma \wedge \cdots \wedge x_q\Sigma \not\approx x_q'\Sigma \to \bot.$$

Disjunction resolution: *Let* $\rho = \forall \overline{x} \ \Phi(\overline{x}) \to B_1(\overline{x}) \vee B_2(\overline{x}) \vee \cdots \vee B_q(\overline{x})$ *be a disjunctive formula. Let*

$$\lambda = \forall \overline{y} \ D_1(\overline{y}) \wedge D_2(\overline{y}) \wedge \cdots \wedge D_r(\overline{y}) \wedge y_1 \not\approx y_1' \wedge \cdots \wedge y_s \not\approx y_s' \to \bot$$

be a lemma. Assume that $B_1(\overline{x})$ *and* $D_1(\overline{y})$ *are unifiable with mgu* Σ. *Then*

$$\forall \overline{x}\Sigma \ \overline{y}\Sigma \quad \Phi(\overline{x})\Sigma \wedge D_2(\overline{y})\Sigma \wedge \cdots \wedge D_r(\overline{y})\Sigma \wedge$$

$$y_1\Sigma \not\approx y_1'\Sigma \wedge \cdots \wedge y_s\Sigma \not\approx y_s'\Sigma \to B_2(\overline{x})\Sigma \vee \cdots \vee B_q(\overline{x})\Sigma$$

is a disjunction resolvent *of* ρ *with* λ.

Existential resolution: *Let* $\rho = \forall \overline{x} \ \Phi(\overline{x}) \to \exists y \ B(\overline{x}, y)$ *be an existential formula. Let*

$$\lambda = \forall \overline{z} \ \forall v \ \Psi(\overline{z}) \wedge B(\overline{z}, v) \wedge v \not\approx z_1 \wedge \cdots \wedge v \not\approx z_s \to \bot$$

be a lemma, such that $z_1, \ldots, z_s \in \overline{z}$, *and* $v \notin \overline{z}$. *Assume that* $B(\overline{x}, y)$ *and* $B(\overline{z}, v)$ *have most general unifier* Σ. *Furthermore, assume that* $y\Sigma = v\Sigma$, $y\Sigma \notin \overline{x}\Sigma$, $v\Sigma \notin \overline{z}\Sigma$. *Then*

$$\forall \overline{x}\Sigma \ \overline{z}\Sigma \quad \Phi(\overline{x})\Sigma \wedge \Psi(\overline{z})\Sigma \to B(\overline{z}, z_1)\Sigma \vee \cdots \vee B(\overline{z}, z_s)\Sigma$$

is an existential resolvent *of* ρ *with* λ. *Note that in case* $s = 0$, *the existential resolvent is a lemma. Otherwise it is a disjunctive rule.*

Existential resolution (degenerated): *Let* $\rho = \forall \overline{x} \ \Phi(\overline{x}) \to \exists y \ B(\overline{x}, y)$ *be an existential formula. Let*

$$\lambda = \forall \overline{z} \ \forall v \ \Psi(\overline{z}) \wedge v \not\approx z_1 \wedge \cdots \wedge v \not\approx z_s \to \bot$$

be a lemma, such that $z_1, \ldots, z_s \in \overline{z}$, *and* $v \notin \overline{z}$. *Then*

$$\forall \overline{x} \ \overline{z} \ \Phi(\overline{x}) \wedge \Psi(\overline{z}) \to B(\overline{x}, z_1) \vee \cdots \vee B(\overline{x}, z_s)$$

is a (degenerated) existential resolvent *of* ρ *with* λ. *In case* $s = 0$, *the degenerated existential resolvent is a lemma. Otherwise, it is a disjunctive rule.*

Disjunction resolution will be used only as hyperresolution rule. For a given rule ρ, the algorithm will find q lemmas, and resolve all the conclusions away at once. Note that it is not possible to resolve upon a disequality. Variable merging will be used only in combination with the other rules. In existential resolution, the conjunction $\Phi(\overline{z})$ may contain disequalities. However, these disequalities are not allowed to contain v, because v cannot occur in $\Phi(\overline{z})$ at all. We give examples of disjunction resolution:

Example 3. $\forall x\ A(x) \to \exists y\ P(x,y),\quad \forall z \forall t\ B(z) \land P(z,t) \to \perp \Rightarrow$
$\quad \forall z\ A(x) \land B(x) \to \perp.$
$\forall x\ A(x) \to \exists y\ P(x,y),\quad \forall z \forall t\ B(z) \land P(z,t) \land z \not\approx t \to \perp \Rightarrow$
$\quad \forall z\ A(x) \land B(x) \to P(x,x).$
$\forall x_1 x_2\ \exists y\ F(x_1,y,x_2,y),$
$\quad \forall z_1 z_2 \forall t\ G(z_1,z_2) \land F(z_1,t,z_2,t) \land z_1 \not\approx t \land z_2 \not\approx t \to \perp \Rightarrow$
$\quad \forall x_1 x_2\ G(x_1,x_2) \to F(x_1,x_1,x_2,x_1) \lor F(x_1,x_2,x_2,x_2).$

Theorem 4. *The rules of Definition 12 are sound.*

Proof. Lemma factoring and disjunction resolution are standard rules. The correctness of existential resolution can be seen as follows: The lemma λ is equivalent to $\lambda' = \forall \overline{z}\ \Psi(\overline{z}) \to \forall v[\ B(\overline{z},v) \to v \approx z_1 \lor \cdots \lor v \approx z_s]$. This implies $\lambda'' = \forall \overline{z}\ \Psi(\overline{z}) \to [\exists v\ B(\overline{z},v)] \to B(\overline{z},z_1) \lor \cdots \lor B(\overline{z},z_s)$. Now $\exists v\ B(\overline{z},v)$ can resolve with $\exists y\ B(\overline{x},y)$ in ρ.

In the case of degenerated existential resolution, λ is equivalent to $\lambda' = \forall \overline{z}\ \Psi(\overline{z}) \to \forall v[v \approx z_1 \lor \cdots \lor v \approx z_s]$. From this, the conclusion can be derived by case analysis.

We call the improved algorithm S_m. It uses the rules of Definition 12 in order to compute closing lemmas. Whenever an interpretation (E, M) cannot be extended to an interpretation that makes G true, $S_m(G, E, M)$ returns a closing lemma of (E, M).

We explain how the algorithm of Definition 10 is modified: In case 1, $S_m(G, E, M)$ can simply return the lemma $\forall \overline{x}\ \phi_1(\overline{x}) \land \cdots \land \phi_p(\overline{x}) \to \perp$. In case 4, nothing needs to be changed. For cases 2 and 3, we will show that when the recursive calls have returned closing lemmas, $S_m(G, E, M)$ is able to construct a closing lemma for (E, M). In case 2, it uses disjunction resolution. In case 3, it uses one step of (possibly degenerated) existential resolution and several steps of disjunction resolution. Before we can prove this, we need to establish two properties of variable merging.

Lemma 2. *Let $\forall \overline{x}\ \Phi(\overline{x}) \to \perp$ be a lemma. Let Θ be a ground substitution, for which there exist distinct variables $x_1, \ldots, x_m \in \overline{x}$, such that $x_1 \Theta = \cdots = x_m \Theta$. Then one can obtain in $m - 1$ variable merging steps, a lemma of form $\forall\ (\overline{x}\Sigma)\ \Phi(\overline{x})\Sigma \to \perp$, for which there exists a ground substitution Θ', such that $\Theta = \Sigma \cdot \Theta'$ and the new lemma contains exactly one variable x' for which $x'\Theta' = x_1\Theta = \cdots x_m\Theta$.*

Proof. It follows from the definition of most general unifier, because Σ is the mgu of x and x'.

Lemma 3. *Let $\forall \overline{x}\ \Phi(\overline{x}) \to \perp$ be a lemma. Let Θ be a ground substitution, for which there exist some non-disequality atoms $A_1(\overline{x}), \ldots, A_m(\overline{x}) \in \Phi(\overline{x})$, s.t. $A_1(\overline{x})\Theta = \cdots = A_m(\overline{x})\Theta$. Then one can obtain, by iterated variable mergings, a lemma $\forall\ (\overline{x}\Sigma)\ \Phi(\overline{x})\Sigma \to \perp$, for which there exists a ground substitution Θ', s.t. $\Theta = \Sigma \cdot \Theta'$, and $\Phi(\overline{x})\Sigma$ contains exactly one atom B, s.t. $B\Theta' = A_1(\overline{x})\Theta = \cdots = A_m(\overline{x})\Theta.$*

Proof. The proof is by induction on the number of distinct variables in $A_1(\overline{x}), \ldots, A_m(\overline{x})$. If $m = 1$, then there is nothing to prove. Otherwise, we have $m > 1$, and there exists a position on which $A_1(\overline{x})$ and $A_2(\overline{x})$ contain a different variable. Call the variables x_1 and x_2 (So one can write $A_1(\overline{x}) = A_1(\ldots, x_1, \ldots)$) and $A_2(\overline{x}) = A_2(\ldots, x_2, \ldots)$. Apply Lemma 2 with x_1 and x_2. In the resulting variable merging, the number of variables has decreased by one.

The following theorem guarantees that S_t can be modified to return a closing lemma in case 2.

Theorem 5. *Suppose that we have:*

1. *An interpretation (E, M).*
2. *A disjunctive formula $r = \forall \overline{x} \; \Phi(\overline{x}) \to B_1(\overline{x}) \vee \cdots \vee B_q(\overline{x})$, which is applicable to (E, M) with ground substitution Θ.*
3. *For each j, $1 \le j \le q$,   a closing lemma λ_j of $(\; E, \; M + B_j(\overline{x})\Theta \;)$.*

Then one can construct a closing lemma for (E, M) using at most q applications of disjunction resolution. (and possibly several variable mergings)

Proof. If we are lucky, one of the closing lemmas λ_j also closes (E, M). Otherwise, we show by induction on q that a closing lemma of (E, M) can be constructed in at most q disjunction resolution steps.

First consider λ_1. Write λ_1 in the form $\forall \overline{y} \; \Psi(\overline{y}) \to \bot$. Let Θ_1 be the ground substitution with which λ_1 closes $(\; E, M + B_1(\overline{x})\Theta \;)$. Because λ_1 does not close (E, M), there must be some atoms $A_1(\overline{y}), \ldots, A_m(\overline{y})$ in $\Psi(\overline{y})$, such that $A_j(\overline{y})\Theta_1 = B_1(\overline{x})\Theta$. According to Lemma 3, one can obtain by repeated variable merging a lemma λ_1' of form $\forall \overline{y}' \; A(\overline{y}') \wedge \Psi'(\overline{y}) \to \bot$, for which there exists a ground substitution Θ_1', s.t.

$$A(\overline{y}')\Theta_1' = B_1(\overline{x})\Theta \text{ and } \Psi'(\overline{y}')\Theta_1' \subseteq M.$$

Because $A(\overline{y}')$ and $B_1(\overline{x})$ are unifiable with mgu Σ, one can construct the following disjunction resolvent from r and λ_1' :

$$\rho = \forall \; \overline{x}\Sigma \; \overline{y}'\Sigma \; \Phi(\overline{x})\Sigma \wedge \Psi'(\overline{y}')\Sigma \to B_2(\overline{x})\Sigma \vee \cdots \vee B_q(\overline{x})\Sigma.$$

Because Σ is the mgu of $A(\overline{y}')$ and $B_1(\overline{x})$, there is a ground substitution Θ_1', s.t. $\Theta_1 = \Sigma \cdot \Theta_1'$. As a consequence ρ is applicable to (E, M). If $q = 1$, then ρ is a closing lemma. Otherwise, it can be checked that ρ and $\lambda_2, \ldots, \lambda_q$ satisfy the conditions $(1) \cdots (3)$ with $q - 1$, so that it is possible to apply induction.

The following guarantees that S_t can be modified to return a closing lemma in case 3.

Theorem 6. *Suppose that we have:*

1. *An interpretation (E, M).*
2. *An existential formula $r = \forall \overline{x} \; \Phi(\overline{x}) \to \exists y \; B(\overline{x}, y)$, which is applicable to (E, M) with ground substitution Θ.*

3. *For each $e \in E$, a closing lemma λ_e of $(E, M + B(\overline{x}, y)\Theta_e)$, with $\Theta_e = \Theta + (y := e)$.*
4. *For some $\hat{e} \notin E$, a closing lemma $\lambda_{\hat{e}}$ of $(E + \hat{e}, M + B(\overline{x}, y)\Theta_{\hat{e}})$, with $\Theta_{\hat{e}} = \Theta + (y := \hat{e})$.*

Then it is possible to construct a closing lemma for (E, M) using at most one application of existential resolution (possibly degenerated) and at most $|E|$ applications of disjunction resolution.

Proof. Again, if we are lucky, one of the closing lemmas λ_e with $e \in E$, or $\lambda_{\hat{e}}$ with $\hat{e} \notin E$ already closes (E, M).

Otherwise consider $\lambda_{\hat{e}}$. Let Θ_λ be the substitution with which $\lambda_{\hat{e}}$ closes $(E + \hat{e}, B(\overline{x}, y)\Theta_{\hat{e}})$. Write $\lambda_{\hat{e}}$ in the form $\lambda_{\hat{e}} = \forall \overline{z} \; \overline{v} \; \Psi(\overline{z}, \overline{v}) \rightarrow \bot$, where $\overline{v}$ are the variables v for which $v\Theta_\lambda = \hat{e}$ and $\overline{z}$ are the remaining variables.

Because $\lambda_{\hat{e}}$ closes $(E + \hat{e}, M + B(\overline{x}, y)\Theta_{\hat{e}})$ but not (E, M), the sequence of variables $\overline{v}$ is not empty.

In case $\overline{v}$ contains more than one variable, one can apply Lemma 2 and obtain a new closing lemma $\lambda_{\hat{e}} = \forall \overline{z} v \; \Psi(\overline{z}, v) \rightarrow \bot$, which closes $(E + \hat{e}, M + B(\overline{x}, y)\Theta_{\hat{e}})$ with a ground substitution Θ_λ for which v is the only variable with $v\Theta_\lambda' = \hat{e}$.

The sequence of atoms $\Psi(\overline{z}, v)$ contains at least one atom containing v. We show that atoms containing v are either disequalities, or atoms of form $B(\overline{z}, v)$ with $B(\overline{z}, v)\Theta_\lambda = B(\overline{x}, y)\Theta_{\hat{e}}$. Let $A(\overline{z}, v)$ be a non-disequality atom that contains v. Then the instance $A(\overline{z}, v)\Theta_\lambda$ contains $\hat{e}$. Since M does not contain $\hat{e}$, and $A(\overline{z}, v)\Theta_\lambda \in M + B(\overline{x}, y)\Theta_{\hat{e}}$, it must be the case that $B(\overline{z}, v)\Theta_\lambda = B(\overline{x}, y)\Theta_{\hat{e}}$.

In case there is more than one atom $A(\overline{z}, v)$ containing v, for all of them holds that $A(\overline{z}, v)\Theta_\lambda = B(\overline{x}, y)\Theta_{\hat{e}}$. Therefore, we can apply Lemma 3 and obtain a new lemma $\lambda_{\hat{e}}$ which contains only one non-disequality atom which contains v. We distinguish two cases, dependent on whether $\Psi(\overline{z}, v)$ contains a non-disequality atom $B(\overline{z}, v)$ which is matched into $B(\overline{x}, y)\Theta_{\hat{e}}$.

1. $\lambda_{\hat{e}}$ can be written in the form $\forall \overline{z} \; v \; \Psi(\overline{z}) \wedge B(\overline{z}, v) \wedge v \not\approx z_1 \wedge \cdots \wedge v \not\approx z_s \rightarrow \bot$. We have assumed that the existential rule r and the lemma $\lambda_{\hat{e}}$ have no variables in common. Hence we can define $\Theta_{\lambda, r} = \Theta_\lambda + \Theta_{\hat{e}}$. We have

$$\Phi(\overline{x})\Theta_{\lambda, r} \subseteq M, \quad \Psi(\overline{z})\Theta_{\lambda, r} \subseteq M,$$

$$B(\overline{x}, y)\Theta_{\lambda, r} = B(\overline{x}, y)\Theta_{\hat{e}}, \quad B(\overline{z}, v)\Theta_{\lambda, r} = B(\overline{x}, y)\Theta_{\hat{e}}.$$

Let Σ be the mgu of $B(\overline{x}, y)$ and $B(\overline{z}, v)$. There exists a ground substitution Θ_{rest}, s.t. $\Theta_{\lambda, r} = \Sigma \cdot \Theta_{rest}$.

We know that $B(\overline{x}, y)$ contains y, and that $y\Theta_{\lambda, r} = \hat{e}$. Because v is the only variable in $B(\overline{z}, v)$ with $v\Theta_{\lambda, r} = \hat{e}$, it must the case that $B(\overline{z}, v)$ contains v at every position where $B(\overline{x}, y)$ contains y. From this it follows that $v\Sigma = y\Sigma$. In order to show that $y\Sigma \notin \overline{x}\Sigma$ and $v\Sigma \notin \overline{z}\Sigma$, it is sufficient to observe that $y\Theta_{\lambda, r} \notin \overline{x}\Theta_{\lambda, r}$ and $v\Theta_{\lambda, r} \notin \overline{z}\Theta_{\lambda, r}$.

We can apply existential resolution, and obtain the rule

$$\forall \overline{x}\Sigma \; \overline{z}\Sigma \; \Phi(\overline{x})\Sigma \wedge \Psi(\overline{z})\Sigma \rightarrow B(\overline{z}, z_1)\Sigma \vee \cdots \vee B(\overline{z}, z_s)\Sigma.$$

Because of the fact that $\Theta_{\lambda,r} = \Sigma \cdot \Theta_{rest}$, we have

$$(\Phi(\overline{x})\Sigma)\Theta_{rest} \subseteq M, \quad (\Psi(\overline{z})\Sigma)\Theta_{rest} \subseteq M.$$

In case that $s = 0$, we already have a closing lemma. Otherwise, we will show that it is possible to apply Theorem 5.

First we show that for each j, $1 \leq j \leq s$, there is an $e \in E$, such that $B(\overline{z}, z_j)\Theta_\lambda = B(\overline{x}, y)\Theta_e$.

The left hand side $B(\overline{z}, z_j)\Theta_\lambda$ equals $B(\overline{z}\Theta_\lambda, z_j\Theta_\lambda)$. This in turn is equal to $B(\overline{x}\Theta, z_j\Theta_\lambda)$. If we define $e = z_j\Theta_\lambda$, (which is in E), then $B(\overline{x}\Theta, z_j\Theta_\lambda)$ is equal to $B(\overline{x}\Theta, y[y := e])$. Because $y \notin \overline{x}$, this equals $B(\overline{x}, y)(\Theta + (y := e))$, which in tuern equals $B(\overline{x}, y)\Theta_e$.

As a consequence each $B(\overline{z}, z_j)\Theta_{\lambda,r}$ is not true in (E, M). Hence the existential resolvent is applicable in (E, M). Because for each z_j, there is an $e \in E$, such that $B(\overline{z}, z_j)\Theta_{\lambda,r} = B(\overline{x}, y)\Theta_e$, and we have a closing lemma λ_e of $(E, M + B(\overline{z}, z_j)\Theta_{\lambda,r})$. This ensures that we can apply Theorem 5 and obtain a closing lemma for (E, M).

2. $\lambda_{\hat{e}}$ can be written in the form $\forall \overline{z} \; v \; \Psi(\overline{z}) \wedge v \not\approx z_1 \wedge \cdots \wedge v \not\approx z_s \rightarrow \bot$. We have assumed that the existential rule r and the lemma $\lambda_{\hat{e}}$ have no variables in common. We can construct the degenerated existential resolvent

$$\forall \overline{x} \; \overline{z} \; \Phi(\overline{x}) \wedge \Psi(\overline{z}) \rightarrow B(\overline{x}, z_1) \vee \cdots \vee B(\overline{x}, z_s).$$

It is easily checked that this rule is applicable on (E, M) with ground substitution $\Theta_\lambda + \Theta_{\hat{e}}$.

By similar reasoning as in the the previous case, we can see that Theorem 5 can be applied.

Note that the fact that $S_m(G, E, M)$ can always return a closing lemma, as a side effect implies that the calculus of Definition 12 is complete when used as a saturation calculus. The algorithm $S_m(G, E, M)$ can be made complete for finite-models by applying depth-first search. Because the learnt lemmas are kept, the loss in efficiency can be expected to be much less than the loss of efficiency that $S_t(G, E, M)$ would have. We give an example that shows that $S_m(G)$ improves over $S_t(G)$.

Example 4. Consider the set of rules $G = \exists x \; P_0(x), \quad \exists x \; P_1(x), \quad \exists x \; P_2(x), \quad \exists x \; P_3(x), \quad \forall x_0 x_1 x_2 x_3 \; P_0(x_0) \wedge P_1(x_1) \wedge P_2(x_2) \wedge P_3(x_3) \rightarrow \bot$. $S_t(G)$ will consider a large sequence of interpretations of form:

$$(e_0, \; P_0(e_0) + P_1(e_0) + P_2(e_0) + P_3(e_0)),$$
$$(e_0 + e_1, \; P_0(e_0) + P_1(e_0) + P_2(e_0) + P_3(e_1)),$$
$$(e_0 + e_1, \; P_0(e_0) + P_1(e_0) + P_2(e_1) + P_3(e_0)),$$
$$(e_0 + e_1, \; P_0(e_0) + P_1(e_0) + P_2(e_1) + P_3(e_1)),$$
$$\cdots$$
$$(e_0 + e_1 + e_2, \; P_0(e_0) + P_1(e_1) + P_2(e_2) + P_3(e_0)),$$
$$(e_0 + e_1 + e_2, \; P_0(e_0) + P_1(e_1) + P_2(e_2) + P_3(e_1)),$$
$$(e_0 + e_1 + e_3, \; P_0(e_0) + P_1(e_1) + P_2(e_2) + P_3(e_2)),$$
$$\cdots$$
$$(e_0 + e_1 + e_2 + e_3, \; P_0(e_0) + P_1(e_1) + P_2(e_2) + P_2(e_3)).$$

The algorithm $S_m(G)$ will close the first interpretation $(e_0, P_0(e_0) + P_1(e_0) + P_2(e_0) + P_3(e_0))$ with rule $\forall x_0 x_1 x_2 x_3 \ P_0(x_0) \wedge P_1(x_1) \wedge P_2(x_2) \wedge P_3(x_3) \to \bot$. Using existential resolution with $\exists x \ P_3(x)$ it will derive the lemma $\eta_1 = \forall x_0 x_1 x_2 \ P_0(x_0) \wedge P_1(x_1) \wedge P_2(x_2) \to \bot$. Since η_1 closes $(e_0, P_0(e_0) + P_1(e_1) + P_2(e_2))$, it will apply one more time existential resolution, and derive $\eta_2 = \forall x_0 x_1 \ P_0(x_0) \wedge P_1(x_1) \to \bot$. Continuing, it will derive $\eta_4 = \top \to \bot$ which closes $(\emptyset, \emptyset)$.

How many elements actually need to be tried, in addition to the first one, depends on the number s of disequalities in the first closing lemma $\forall \overline{x} y \ \Psi(\overline{x}) \wedge B(\overline{x}, y) \to y \not\approx x_1 \wedge \cdots \wedge y \not\approx x_s \to \bot$. Only those elements for which one of the disequalities is false, need to be tried. In the example, we always had $s = 0$.

6 Conclusions and Future Work

We have introduced a calculus, which is refutationally complete for first-order logic with equality. It can be implemented in such a way (using breadth-first search) that it is complete for finding finite models. In addition, it can be expected that our calculus will be good at handling problems containing *partial functions*.

We are in the process of implementing the calculus and studying refinements. The most successful refinement is *functional reduction*. It is best explained from an example. If one has a rule r of form $r = \forall \overline{x} \ \Phi(\overline{x}) \to \exists y \ P(\overline{x}, y)$, and there are no other positive occurrences of P in the set of formulas G, then P will be always functional in all attempted interpretations, because $\exists y \ P(\overline{x}, y)$ is extended only when it is false. As a consequence, whenever some lemma contains among its premises two occurrences of P of form $P(\overline{x}, y_1)$ and $P(\overline{x}, y_2)$, one can unify y_1 and y_2 without losing possible applications. This has turned out a good refinement, which improves performance by a factor of one hundred, especially on harder problems.

Another refinement that we tried is *lemma subsumption*. In analogy to resolution, one can define that λ_1 *subsumes* λ_2 if there exists a variable substitution Σ, s.t. $\lambda_1 \Sigma \subseteq \lambda_2$. Due to the way $S_m(G)$ operates, only backward subsumption needs to be considered. Our experiments show that approximately one fourth of the lemmas can be deleted with backward subsumption.

In future work, we intend to study other refinements, prove that they do not increase proof length whenever this is possible, and extend our experiments. We intend to take part in CASC with our implementation.

In addition, we would also like to obtain theoretical results that compare our calculus to superposition.

Acknowledgements

We thank Peter Baumgartner for reading a draft version of this report, and for discussions in the early stages of this work. Thanks also to Marc Bezem because the idea for this research came after attending a talk about [3]. We thank him also for useful discussions on the topic of geometric logic.

References

1. Leo Bachmair and Harald Ganzinger. Rewrite-based equational theorem proving with selection and simplification. *Journal of Logic and Computation*, 4(3):217–247, 1994.
2. Peter Baumgartner and Cesare Tinelli. The model evolution calculus. In Franz Baader, editor, *CADE-19 - 19th International Conference on Automated Deduction*, volume 2741 of *LNAI*, pages 350–364. Springer, 2003.
3. Marc Bezem. Disproving distributivity in lattices using geometric logic. In *Workshop on Disproving, Non-Theorems, Non-Validity, Non-Provability*, pages 24–31. informal proceedings, July 2005.
4. Marc Bezem and Thierry Coquand. Automating coherent logic. In Geoff Sutcliffe and Andrei Voronkov, editors, *LPAR*, volume 3835 of *LNCS*, pages 246–260. Springer, 2005.
5. François Bry and Sunna Torge. A deduction method complete for refutation and finite satisfiability. In Jürgen Dix, Luis Fariñas del Cerro, and Ulrich Furbach, editors, *JELIA*, volume 1489 of *LNCS*, pages 122–138. Springer Verlag, 1998.
6. Hans de Nivelle and Maarten de Rijke. Deciding the guarded fragments by resolution. *Journal of Symbolic Computation*, 35(1):21–58, January 2003.
7. H. Ganzinger and H. de Nivelle. A superposition decision procedure for the guarded fragment with equality. In *LICS'99*, pages 295–303, 1999.
8. Yevgeny Kazakov and Hans de Nivelle. A resolution decision procedure for the guarded fragment with transitive guards. In Michaël Rusinowitch and David Basin, editors, *Second International Joint Conference on Automated Reasoning (IJCAR 2004)*, volume 3097 of *Lecture Notes in Artificial Intelligence*, pages 122–136, Cork, Ireland, July 2004. Springer Verlag.
9. Sun Kim and Hantao Zhang. ModGen: Theorem proving by model generation. In Barbara Hayes-Roth and Richard Korf, editors, *Proceedings of AAAI-94*, pages 162–167, 1994.
10. William McCune. Models and counter examples MACE2 (system). http://www-unix.mcs.anl.gov/AR/mace2/ .
11. J. A. Robinson. A machine oriented logic based on the resolution principle. *Journal of the ACM*, 12:23–41, 1965.
12. John Slaney. Scott: A model-guided theorem prover. In *IJCAI-93*, pages 109–114, 1993.
13. Jian Zhang. Constructing finite algebras with FALCON. *Journal of Automated Reasoning*, 17:1–22, 1996.
14. Jian Zhang and Hantao Zhang. SEM: a system for enumerating models. In *IJCAI*, pages 298–303, 1995.
15. Lintao Zhang and Sharad Malik. The quest for efficient boolean satisfiability solvers. In Andrei Voronkov, editor, *CADE-18*, volume 2392 of *LNAI*, pages 295–313. Springer, 1992.

A Powerful Technique to Eliminate Isomorphism in Finite Model Search

Xiangxue Jia[1,2] and Jian Zhang[1]

[1] Laboratory of Computer Science
Institute of Software, Chinese Academy of Sciences
[2] Graduate University, Chinese Academy of Sciences

Abstract. We propose a general-purpose technique, called DASH (De-cision Assignment Scheme Heuristic), to eliminate isomorphic subspaces when generating finite models. Like LNH, DASH is based on inherent iso-morphism in first order clauses on finite domains. Unlike other methods, DASH can completely eliminate isomorphism during the search. There-fore, DASH can generate all the models none of which are isomorphic. And DASH is an efficient technique for finite model enumeration. The main idea is to cut the branch of the search tree which is isomorphic to a branch that has been searched. We present a new method to describe the class of isomorphic branches. We implemented this technique by modify-ing SEM1.7B, and the new tool is called SEMD. This technique proves to be very efficient on typical problems like the generation of finite groups, rings and quasigroups. The experiments show that SEMD is much faster than SEM on many problems, especially when generating all the models and when there is no model. SEMD can generate all the non-isomorphic models with little extra cost, while other tools like MACE4 will spend more time.

Keywords: Isomorphism; scheme; symmetry breaking; LNH; DASH.

1 Introduction

Many problems from various application domains can be regarded as deciding the satisfiability of certain logical formulas. In fact, the satisfiability problem in the propositional logic, known as SAT, is a fundamental problem in computer science and artificial intelligence. Many researchers have been working on SAT, and many algorithms have been proposed to solve the problem. In the 1980's, the algorithms are typically analyzed theoretically. Recently, tool development and empirical evaluation received more attention. Several efficient SAT solvers have been implemented, such as SATO [6], MiniSat [17] and zchaff [3].

However, practical problems are often more naturally described by a set of first-order formulas. In the problem library TPTP [5], fewer than 1% of the prob-lems are described in pure propositional logic. The satisfiability problem in the first-order logic is undecidable in general. But we can try to satisfy first-order formulas in finite domains. This problem is known as finite model generation or finite model searching. Of course, it can be transformed into SAT. But it can

U. Furbach and N. Shankar (Eds.): IJCAR 2006, LNAI 4130, pp. 318–331, 2006.

also be solved directly, through exhaustive search. During the past 15 years, several efficient finite model searchers have been developed, such as FINDER [11], FALCON [12], SEM [14], Mace4 [22], MACE [21] and Paradox [15]. Although these tools are quite successful in solving some open problems in mathematics, we can still do something to improve their performances. In particular, we can eliminate more symmetric subspaces in the search space. This paper describes such an attempt.

2 Preliminaries and Notations

2.1 Finite Models

A **model** of a set of first-order formulas is an interpretation that gives a value to constant and every entry of function or predicate. A finite model of size n is often defined on the domain $D_n = \{0, 1, \ldots, n-1\}$.

When the arity of a function (predicate) is no more than 2, the function (predicate) can be described by a table. We call an entry of the table a **cell**. Syntactically a cell is given by a term whose arguments are elements of the domain. For example, both $f(0, 2)$ and $P(1)$ denote cells, if P is a unary predicate and f is a binary function. A model gives a value to all the cells.

A **partial model** gives values to some cells. We use $Pmod$ to denote a partial model.

2.2 Basic Search Procedure

Finite model searchers often work on a set of ground formulas, which are obtained by instantiating the input formulas over the domain D_n. For example, suppose $n = 2$ and the input contains the formula $f(x, y) = x$. We get the following set of ground formulas:

$$f(0, 0) = 0; \qquad f(0, 1) = 0; \qquad f(1, 0) = 1; \qquad f(1, 1) = 1.$$

To search for a model, we can use the following backtrack search procedure:

Algorithm 1. The standard search function

```
Srh(S: set of assignments, G: set of ground formulas): Boolean;
{
  for each assignment a in S, Propagate(a,G,S);
  if S contains incompatible assignments then return(FALSE);
  if G has been satisfied then return(TRUE);
  select one unassigned cell c;
  forall v in Dn
    if Srh(S and (c=v), G) then return(TRUE);
  return FALSE;
}
```

We can regard the execution of the search procedure as a search tree. In each node of the tree, we try to choose a value for a cell. Every choice correspomds to a **decision**, and every branch of the search tree correspomds to a **decision sequence**. Each decision sequence leads to a partial model, which also includes the cell assignments derived from the sequence by constraint propagation.

The **depth** of a cell assignment is the depth of the search tree at which the cell is assigned its value.

3   Isomorphism Elimination

Two models can be isomorphic to each other. This is due to symmetries on the domain elements.

Definition 1. *A **permutation** of D_n is a one to one mapping (bijection) from D_n onto itself. Such a permutation is called a **symmetry** if it maps models to models.*

Definition 2. *A set G of ground clauses is **symmetric** with respect to a subset of D_n, if G remains the same under any permutation of that subset.*

Because symmetry leads to isomorphism, we use symmetry breaking and isomorphism elimination for the same meaning.

There are two ways of eliminating isomorphism. The first is adding constraints of isomorphism elimination, and the second is eliminating isomorphism during search.

Adding constraints of isomorphism elimination is a kind of preprocessing. It changes the original problem to a new problem by constraining the search path. Paradox [15] uses this static way. Usually it does not get the minimal search space because adding full constraints to eliminate isomorphism will cost too much time to check those constraints.

For the second way, the disadvantage is that if we do not implement a quick symmetry detection method, the time cost by eliminating isomorphism may be more than the time we save. In [9], the authors point out that the computational complexity of the symmetry detection problem is equivalent (within a polynomial factor) to that of the graph isomorphism problem.

When generating finite models of first order logic, some isomorphic branches in the search tree can be cut based on the following observation: all individual values in D_n that are not used as a cell index or as a cell value in previous decisions are interchangeable. This intuition led to the idea of the Least Number Heuristic (LNH) [12]. When implementing this technique, we can use a special variable mdn to denote the maximal designated number. All elements in the subset $\{mdn + 1, \ldots, n - 1\}$ should be interchangeable.

Definition 3. *Let $imdn$ denote the **initial maximal designated number** in the input file. If the input problem does not contain constants, $imdn = -1$.*

However, the LNH alone may not cut all unwanted search branches. And it has been extended in various ways, such as [4]. The current paper also focuses on this issue. We examine each new branch to find out whether it is isomorphic to a branch searched before, and cut all such branches.

4 Decision Assignment Scheme Heuristic

Now we describe a new isomorphism elimination technique: DASH (which stands for Decision Assignment Scheme Heuristic). All that DASH does is to eliminate branches which are isomorphic to some searched branches.

Definition 4. *There are two meanings of* **branch** *in the paper. One is the original meaning for the search tree, and the other is the partial model which is derived from the decision sequence on the branch.*

Let $Pmod_1$ stand for a branch that has been searched, and $Pmod_2$ stand for the current branch which is isomorphic to a sub-branch $Pmod_1'$ of $Pmod_1$. In this situation, we call $Pmod_1$ as **scheme branch**, and $Pmod_2$ as **iso-branch**.

Given a decision sequence, for each domain element in the sequence which is larger than $imdn$, we introduce a distinct auxiliary variable. We call these variables **scheme variables**. Usually we name a scheme variable by one letter, which stands for the sort, and use the integer corresponding to the domain element as its index.

Then we substitute each domain element by the auxiliary variable. The decision (cell assignment) after the substitution is called a **decision scheme**, and the conjunction of all such schemes is called a **scheme**. The number of decision schemes in a scheme is called the **length** of the scheme.

For example, suppose $imdn = 0$, and there is a branch of the search tree which corresponds to the decision sequence: $g(1) = 1, g(2) = 4, f(1,2) = 3, f(2,2) = 4$. We can introduce 4 scheme variables: x_1, x_2, x_3, x_4, and get the scheme $g(x_1) = x_1 \land g(x_2) = x_4 \land f(x_1, x_2) = x_3 \land f(x_2, x_2) = x_4$. The length of this scheme is 4.

Definition 5. *For every decision sequence α, there is a scheme denoted by $\hat{\alpha}$ and a partial model denoted by $\bar{\alpha}$ which is derived from α by through constraint propagation.*

Remarks
We should remember that distinct scheme variables can't have the same value and they can't have values smaller than or equal to $imdn$.

In this paper, we assume there is only one sort to simplify the presentation. If there are more than one sorts, we can name the scheme variables as x_1, y_2 and so on. Every different sort has a different letter.

Example 1
Consider the following axioms for the Abelian Group:

$$g(0) = 0$$
$$g(x) \neq y \lor g(y) = x$$
$$f(x, 0) = x$$
$$f(0, x) = x$$
$$f(x, g(x)) = 0$$
$$f(g(x), x) = 0$$
$$f(f(x, y), z) = f(x, f(y, z))$$
$$f(x, y) = f(y, x)$$

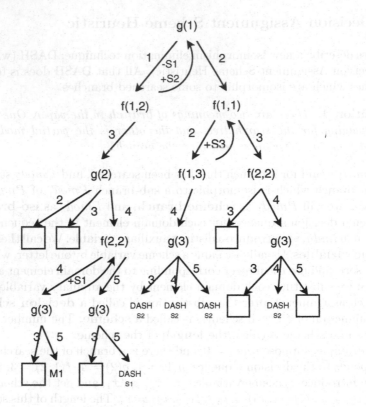

Fig. 1. The search tree for AG6

We can see that $imdn = 0$. Set the order to 6 (i.e., let $n = 6$). If a decision sequence is $g(1) = 1, g(2) = 4, f(1,2) = 3, f(2,2) = 4$, then after the substitution, we get four decision schemes, namely $g(x_1) = x_1, g(x_2) = x_4, f(x_1, x_2) = x_3, f(x_2, x_2) = x_4$. The scheme constructed from them is $g(x_1) = x_1 \land g(x_2) = x_4 \land f(x_1, x_2) = x_3 \land f(x_2, x_2) = x_4$.

The whole search tree using DASH is shown in Fig.1. It is found that there is only one non-isomorphic model of Abelian group of order 6.

In Fig.1, there are three schemes used in the search, namely $S1$, $S2$, $S3$:

$S1 : g(x_1) = x_1 \land g(x_2) = x_4 \land f(x_1, x_2) = x_3 \land f(x_2, x_2) = x_4$
$S2 : g(x_1) = x_1$
$S3 : g(x_1) = x_2 \land f(x_1, x_1) = x_2$

Though there are many other schemes that can be added, they are redundant for our method.

The search tree is a depth-first search tree, from left to right. In the figure, the $\square$ means that there exists a contradiction when doing constraint propagation. And the arrows point out the trace of search. M1 means we got a model at that node. DASH S1 means we will backtrack at this node because of the current partial model satisfies S1.

In the rest of this section, we shall discuss how to use the above concepts to describe the branches in the search tree and how to use them to eliminate isomorphism.

First, we realize that we can use some schemes to describe all the branches we have searched. Then when we are exploring a new branch, we would like to know whether it is isomorphic to some previous branch. This can be done by checking whether the partial model derived from the new decision sequence satisfies some existing scheme.

Definition 6. *If there is a series of assignments to all the scheme variables in a scheme such that the scheme becomes a series of assignments in the partial model, we say that "the partial model which is derived from the new decision sequence satisfies the scheme", or in short, "a decision sequence satisfies the scheme".*

Please see Example 2 below.

Proposition 4.1. Consider a decision sequence α , the scheme $\hat{\alpha}$ which is derived from α and the partial model $\bar{\alpha}$ which is extended from α by constraint propagation. If we don't consider the symmetry between the values not bigger than $imdn$, the scheme represents all the branches which are isomorphic to some branch $\bar{\alpha}'$ extended from $\bar{\alpha}$.

That is, for any branch $\bar{\beta}$ which is isomorphic to $\bar{\alpha}'$ and the isomorphism preserves the values which are not bigger than $imdn$, the isomorphism mapping θ leads to one assignment σ to all the scheme variables in the scheme $\hat{\alpha}$ such that $\sigma(\hat{\alpha})$ is consistent with $\bar{\beta}$.

For any assignment σ to the scheme variables in $\hat{\alpha}$ which gives distinct values to distinct scheme variables, the scheme becomes a decision sequence which is isomorphic to α.

Proof. By the definition of scheme, obviously the original decision sequence satisfies the scheme. The assignment σ just gives every variable's index as the variable's value.

For any branch $\bar{\beta}$ which is isomorphic to $\bar{\alpha}'$ and the isomorphism preserves the values which are not bigger than $imdn$, denote the isomorphism mapping as θ. Here θ is a mapping: $D_n \to D_n$, such that $\theta(\bar{\alpha}')$ equals to $\bar{\beta}$.

Then θ can derive an assignment σ such that $\sigma(\hat{\alpha})$ is consistent with $\bar{\beta}$. Here for any scheme variable x_i in $\hat{\alpha}$, $\sigma(x_i) = \theta(i)$.

And for any assignment σ to the scheme variables in $\hat{\alpha}$ which gives distinct values to distinct scheme variables, the scheme becomes a decision sequence β which is isomorphic to α.

The isomorphism mapping $\theta : D_n \to D_n$ is defined as follows:

- for any scheme variable x_i in $\hat{\alpha}$, $\theta(i) = \sigma(x_i)$.
- for other undefined j in D_n, $\theta(j) = j$.

It is easy to check that $\theta(\alpha) = \beta$.

Proposition 4.2. If the partial model which is derived from the current decision sequence satisfies some scheme, then we can cut the current branch to eliminate isomorphism.

Proof. By Proposition 4.1 and Definition 6, the partial model (also called a branch) is isomorphic to some sub-branch of the branch which the scheme is derived from. Therefore, cutting the current branch can eliminate isomorphism.

Example 2

Consider the Abelian Group of order 6 in Example 1. We have the scheme $g(x_1) = x_1 \wedge g(x_2) = x_4 \wedge f(x_1, x_2) = x_3 \wedge f(x_2, x_2) = x_4$. When we come to a decision sequence which is $g(1) = 1, g(2) = 4, f(1, 2) = 3, f(2, 2) = 5, g(3) = 5$, we will find that the partial model which is derived from this sequence satisfies the scheme by assignments $x_1 = 1, x_2 = 3, x_3 = 2, x_4 = 5, x_5 = 4$, so we get the isomorphic bijection $(23)(45)$ which maps the partial model to some sub-branch of $g(1) = 1, g(2) = 4, f(1, 2) = 3, f(2, 2) = 4$.

After the assignments $x_1 = 1, x_2 = 3, x_3 = 2, x_4 = 5, x_5 = 4$, the scheme becomes a series of assignments, namely, $g(1) = 1, g(3) = 5, f(1, 3) = 2, f(3, 3) = 5$. Here, $f(1, 3) = 2$ and $f(3, 3) = 5$ don't occur in the current decision sequence $g(1) = 1, g(2) = 4, f(1, 2) = 3, f(2, 2) = 5, g(3) = 5$, but these two assignments are obtained by constraint propagation.

Thus the partial model which is derived by $g(1) = 1, g(2) = 4, f(1, 2) = 3, f(2, 2) = 5, g(3) = 5$ satisfies the scheme $g(x_1) = x_1 \wedge g(x_2) = x_4 \wedge f(x_1, x_2) = x_3 \wedge f(x_2, x_2) = x_4$.

So the current branch which is derived from $g(1) = 1, g(2) = 4, f(1, 2) = 3, f(2, 2) = 5, g(3) = 5$ can be eliminated.

4.1   When to Add and Delete Schemes

In this subsection, we discuss how to use schemes to detect and eliminate isomorphism. In particular, we will show how to use as few schemes as possible to describe the searched branches and when to add or delete schemes.

If we add all the schemes, the number of schemes is too large. But if we only add the necessary ones, the experiments show that the number is much smaller.

Generally speaking, the number of schemes increases during the search. But in fact, if the original problem has many isomorphic subspaces, the number is small. Because many schemes can be simplified and the branches which satisfy some scheme do not lead to any new scheme.

In many experiments, the maximum number of schemes is not bigger than several hundred. If there is not plenty of isomorphism, using isomorphism elimination techniques is not a good choice.

First of all, every searched branch can lead to a scheme. We should eliminate the redundant ones. Because the schemes are used to eliminate isomorphism, we need not add the scheme derived from the current branch. When we will choose a value for a new cell, we add a scheme derived from the past branch unless that branch is backtracked due to the conflict obtained from constraint propagation.

For instance, consider Example 1. After we have searched the branch derived from the sequence $g(1) = 1, g(2) = 4, f(1, 2) = 3, f(2, 2) = 4$, before we try the case $f(2, 2) = 5$, we add the scheme $g(x_1) = x_1 \wedge g(x_2) = x_4 \wedge f(x_1, x_2) = x_3 \wedge f(x_2, x_2) = x_4$.

Obviously if the past branch already satisfies some scheme, we need not add a new scheme.

When we get a model, we must add a scheme to describe the model.

After all possible values of a cell have been tried, we must backtrack. Before backtracking we will delete all the schemes which are derived from trying values of the current cell.

Consider the above example, after we tried the case $f(2,2) = 5$, we must backtrack. Then we delete the scheme $g(x_1) = x_1 \wedge g(x_2) = x_4 \wedge f(x_1, x_2) = x_3 \wedge f(x_2, x_2) = x_4$. Because after backtracking, we will add a new scheme $g(x_1) = x_1$, and this scheme includes the above one.

Proposition 4.3. Using DASH will not lose any non-isomorphic model, and the generated models are all non-isomorphic ones.

Proof. By using DASH, we only cut the branches which are isomorphic to some searched branches. The models in those branches must be isomorphic to some model which we obtained. So we do not lose any non-isomorphic model.

If there are two generated models which are isomorphic to each other, then the second one must satisfy the scheme derived from the first one. This contradicts with the DASH process.

Therefore, the proposition holds.   □

So by the above propositions, we can cut all the iso-branches, and at the same time, without losing any isomorphic class of models.

4.2 The Scheme Checking Process

The time used for adding and deleting schemes is so small that it can be ignored. Almost all the time of the DASH process is spent on checking whether a branch satisfies some scheme. In our implementation, we just use a simple backtracking process for scheme checking. When we check an iso-branch, the depth of the checked branch is not smaller than the length of any scheme. And we check from the earliest scheme to the latest one.

After we select one scheme, we use backtracking search on the scheme variables, trying to find whether there is a set of assignments of the scheme variables such that the scheme becomes a set of assignments which is a subset of the current partial model. Please also see Example 2.

4.3 Adjustable Parameters

Eliminating all the isomorphism during search is not the most efficient way, since as the depth of search becomes bigger, the cost of eliminating isomorphism increases significantly and the benefit of doing so decreases. Thus, we can improve the efficiency by avoiding some improper checking of isomorphism.

We can adjust some parameters to achieve this goal. The most important parameter is the checking depth (i.e., using DASH up to a certain depth). This is easy to understand, since as the checking depth increases, the cost of checking increases greatly.

So in our implementation, we use a variable $maxD$ to record the current maximum depth of the search tree. And we can adjust three parameters, denoted by $factor1, factor2, factor3$. When the current depth is not larger than $factor1 * maxD$, we check all the schemes to find out whether the current branch satisfies some scheme.

When the current depth is larger than $factor1 * maxD$ and smaller than $factor2 * maxD$, we check all the schemes whose lengths are not bigger than $factor3 * maxD$.

Through our experiments, we found that it is often good to set the parameters $factor1, factor2, factor3$ to the values $0.6, 0.9, 0.3$, respectively.

Because the cost of adding and deleting schemes is very small, we still do these things. If we only want to get the non-isomorphic models, we can use DASH to check whether the new model is isomorphic to some existing model which has already been generated.

4.4   The New Algorithm

In this subsection, we describe an abstract procedure about DASH. We shall use the notations introduced earlier. The new search procedure is shown in Fig 2. It is extended from the basic search procedure of SEM [14]. We use upper-case letters to denote the new statements.

```
Void srh() {
    forward = TRUE;
    while (TRUE)  {
        if (forward)     {
           choose one cell whose value has not been fixed;
           if (all cells are assigned values)  {
               Number_Mod++;
               if (Number_Mod == Max_N_Mod) return;
               else forward = FALSE;
           }
        }
        if (forward) push stack;
        else {
           if (stack is empty)  return;
           ADD a scheme for the current decision sequence;
           restore stack;
        }
        forward = FALSE;
        for each of current cell's possible values do  {
           assign the value to the cell;
           propagate the effect of this assignment;
           if (contradiction does not occur )   {
               CHECK all schemes;
               if (the current partial model satisfies some scheme)
                   { restore stack; continue; }
```

```
            else {
                forward = TRUE;
                break;
            }
        }
        else  restore stack;
    }
    if (forward == FALSE) {
        DELETE schemes of current depth;
        pop stack;
    }
  }
}
```

Fig. 2. The Search Procedure with DASH

5   Experimental Results

Using the above ideas, we have implemented an automatic tool, called SEMD, based on SEM [14]. We have tested the tool on a number of well-known problems and compared it with SEM, newSEM [4], Mace4 [22] and Paradox [15]. The problems include:

- Logic and abstract algebra: the problems "Finite Abelian Groups". We try to find all the finite Abelian Groups of every order. In Table 1, we set $factor1 = factor2 = factor3 = 1$. Table 2 shows that adjusting factors can improve the efficiency. We denote $factor1, factor2, factor3$ by $t1, t2, t3$ respectively, in Table 2. From the fundamental theorem on finite Abelian groups, we

Table 1. Abelian Groups

	SEM + LNH			SEM + DASH				newSEM + XLNH			Mace 4	
n	m	t	r	m	t	r	Cuts	m	t	r	m	t
6	6	0	30	1	0	23	5	2	0	40	6	0
16	135	0.68	2347	5	0.21	479	71	44	0.41	696	135	1.79
26	16	8.90	10480	1	2.25	1291	178	2	7.87	3308	16	98.28
32	2295	133.72	76483	7	12.55	2623	404	529	63.92	11313	2295	802.24
33	15	71.85	48659	1	8.95	2527	351	15	11.57	3347	+	+
34	20	78.96	51306	1	9.76	2611	356	2	66.75	12786	+	+
35	13	185.86	95009	1	16.81	3097	457	13	14.55	3711	+	+
36	2142	309.79	146386	4	22.26	3524	553	321	145.07	21601	+	+
37	1	239.30	112003	1	20.01	3407	478	1	23.35	4779	+	+
38	22	240.40	115528	1	22.51	3533	511	2	175.14	23366	+	+
39	17	397.98	174819	1	29.20	4017	600	17	34.82	5811	+	+
40	2220	589.14	233198	3	35.61	4407	671	282	303.37	39124	+	+
49	+	+	+	2	78.77	6420	874	8	188.26	12858	+	+
50	+	+	+	2	87.58	6570	934	+	+	+	+	+

Table 2. Abelian Groups with Different DASH Factors

		$t1 = t2 = t3 = 1$			$t1 = 0.6, t2 = 0.9, t3 = 0.3$				newSEM + XLNH		
n	m	t	r	Cuts	m	t	r	Cuts	m	t	r
43	1	43.62	4929	708	1	40.01	7443	669	1	61.35	7781
44	2	50.83	5188	750	2	45.98	7858	699	31	662.61	66025
45	2	56.34	5494	801	2	52.78	8930	749	180	93.24	9024
46	1	57.41	5498	786	1	53.31	8602	733	+	+	+
47	1	61.88	5795	803	1	58.49	8103	784	1	86.70	9329
48	5	106.08	6913	1058	5	91.05	14082	912	+	+	+
49	2	78.77	6420	874	2	73.29	9673	829	8	188.26	12858
50	2	87.58	6570	934	2	83.30	10547	867	+	+	+

know that the number of nonisomorphic Abelian groups of order n, where $n = p_1^{e_1} \ldots p_n^{e_n}$, is $f(e_1) \ldots f(e_n)$, where $f(x)$ denotes the number of out-of-order partitions of x. Thus we can verify that the number of models obtained by SEMD is just the number of nonisomorphic Abelian groups.

- Combinatorics: Quasigroup existence problems described in [16]. For this problem, we only compare SEMD with SEM. Since there is no unary function in this problem and newSEM is based on unary functions, newSEM can not

Table 3. Quasigroup Existence Problem

	SEM +LNH		SEM + DASH		
Order	Time	Rounds	Time	Rounds	Cuts
10	62.44	18423609	33.02	6717481	35
11	190.46	69742027	113.97	25427909	33

speed up in this problem. In Table 3, we only search for one quasigroup for each different order. For an order which is less than 10, DASH can not cut any branch for the first model. In Table 4, we search for one quasigroup which satisfies the QG5 identity. Though we can cut some branches, the scheme checking process costs too much time and the total time used by SEMD is a little longer than that for SEM.

Table 4. QG5 Existence Problem

	SEM +LNH			SEM + DASH			
Order	Models	Time	Rounds	Models	Time	Rounds	Cuts
9	0	0	66	0	0	52	1
10	0	0	166	0	0	134	2
11	1	0.01	421	1	0.01	297	4
12	0	0.05	2878	0	0.05	1770	79
13	0	0.51	27764	0	0.68	14894	834
14	0	8.66	430040	0	11.91	182304	10060

Table 5. HSI Problem

	SEM +LNH			SEM + DASH			
Order	Models	Time	Rounds	Models	Time	Rounds	Cuts
2	5	0	15	5	0	15	0
3	68	0	228	44	0	182	15
4	2199	0.05	7867	657	0.23	3259	375

- HSI problem [13]: This problem also comes from Algebra, and there are some results about order 2 and order 3 in [19].

In these tables, all running times ("t") are given in seconds. We use "+" to indicate that the running time is more than 600 seconds. "Rounds" ("r") means the number of rounds of the search loop, and "Cuts" means the number of branches which are cut by DASH, while "n" means the size of the model, "m" means the number of models. The experimental results are obtained on a personal computer with Pentium 4 2.6G, 512M memory.

We can see that, when using SEMD (SEM+DASH), the numbers of models are quite small, and the running times are acceptable. It should be noted that SEMD gets all the non-isormorphic models, while the other tools just find out all models without eliminating the redundant ones.

Paradox is quite slow on this type of problems, because it is weak in symmetry breaking and when the order increases, the SAT instance generated by Paradox becomes too large. So we do not give the experimental data for Paradox.

6   Related Works and Conclusions

During the past several years, symmetry breaking and isomorphism elimination have attracted much attention from researchers. It was shown that they can play a key role in the solution of many problems. Sophisticated symmetry breaking methods have been developed, such as the addition of symmetry breaking constraints (see for example [10]), symmetry breaking during search (SBDS) [7], or symmetry breaking by dominance detection (SBDD) [20]. Especially the latter is quite interesting.

SBDD works by checking whether the current choice point under investigation represents a symmetric variant of a part of the search space that has been investigated completely before. The core of an SBDD symmetry breaking code is dominance detection which was automated in [8] by using the generic computational group theory tool, yielding a method named GAP-SBDD.

The basic idea of this paper is similar to that of SBDS and SBDD. But the latter deals with constraint satisfaction problems (CSPs) and they mainly consider the symmetries among variables in a CSP. We try to solve the finite model generation problem, in which the symmetries are different.

For finite model enumeration, there are some isomorphism elimination methods which are similar to the Least Number Heuristic (LNH) or are extensions to the LNH, see for example, [1,18,4]. It is worth mentioning that the tool newSEM

[4] is quite close to ours. But it requires that the problem has a unary function, so it is useless for some problems. For instance, in QG problems, SEMD can work well, but newSEM does not work. From Table 1, we can see that SEMD is almost always better than newSEM on the Abelian group problem. More recently, Boy de la Tour and Countcham [2] investigated the integration of SEM-style search procedure and McKay's general method of isomorph-free exhaustive enumeration. But their tool SEMK is not available yet.

One of the advantages of DASH is that we can get all the nonisomorphic models with just a little overhead. We can tell the program to find all the models and use DASH to eliminate all the models which are isomorphic to some nonisomorphic model. We have tried to do this by using other tools such as Mace4. They check isomorphism after all the models are generated. And much more time is needed. Therefore, DASH becomes an efficient technique for finite model enumeration.

The most important contribution of our work is presenting a new method of describing the isomorphism class. The experiments show that it is efficient. But we still have something to do in the future. Most importantly, we need to find a more efficient scheme checking method.

Acknowledgements

We are grateful to the anonymous reviewers for their comments and suggestions. This work was partially supported by NSFC grant No. 60125207.

References

1. Jackson D., Jha S., and Damon C.A. Isomorph-free model enumeration: A new method for checking relational specifications. *ACM Transactions on Programming Languages and Systems*, 20(2):302–343, 1998.
2. Boy de la Tour T. and Countcham P. An isomorph-free SEM-like enumeration of models. *Electr. Notes Theor. Comput. Sci.*, 125(2):91–113, 2005.
3. Moskewicz M et al. Chaff: Engineering an efficient SAT solver. In *Proc. 39th Design Automation Conference*, pages 530–535, 2001.
4. Audemard G. and Henocque L. The extended least number heuristic. In *Proc. of the 1st Int'l Joint Conference on Automated Reasoning*, pages 427–442, 2001.
5. Sutcliffe G. and Suttner C.B. The TPTP problem library – CNF release v1.2.1. *Journal of Automated Reasoning*, 21(2):177–203, 1998.
6. Zhang H. An efficient propositional prover. In *Proc. 14th Int'l Conf. on Automated Deduction (CADE-14)*, pages 272–275, 1997.
7. Gent I. and Smith B. Symmetry breaking in constraint programming. In *Proc. ECAI'00*, pages 599–603, 2000.
8. Gent I., Harvey W., Kelsey T., and Linton S. Generic SBDD using computational group theory. In *Proc. CP'03*, pages 333–347, 2003.
9. Crawford J. A theoretical analysis of reasoning by symmetry in first order logic. Technical report, AT&T Bell Laboratories, 1996.
10. Crawford J., Ginsberg M., Luks E., and Roy A. Symmetry-breaking predicates for search problems. In *Proc. KR'96*, pages 149–159, 1996.

11. Slaney J. Finite domain enumerator. system description. In *Proc. 12th Int'l Conf. on Automated Deduction (CADE-12)*, pages 798–801, 1994.
12. Zhang J. Constructing finite algebras with FALCON. *Journal of Automated Reasoning*, 17(1):1–22, 1996.
13. Zhang J. Computer search for counterexamples to Wilkie's identity. In *Proc. 20th International Conference on Automated Deduction (CADE-20)*, pages 441–451, 2005.
14. Zhang J. and Zhang H. SEM: a system for enumerating models. In *Proc. 14th Int'l Joint Conf. on Artificial Intelligence (IJCAI)*, pages 298–303, 1995.
15. Claessen K. and Sörensson N. New techniques that improve mace-style finite model finding. In *Proceedings of the CADE-19 Workshop: Model Computation - Principles, Algorithms, Applications (Miami, USA)*, 2003.
16. Fujita M., Slaney J., and Bennett F. Automatic generation of some results in finite algebra. In *Proc. 13th Int'l Joint Conf. on Artificial Intelligence (IJCAI)*, pages 52–57, 1993.
17. Eén N. and Sörensson N. The MiniSat page. Webpage, Chalmers University, http://www.cs.chalmers.se/Cs/Research/FormalMethods/MiniSat/, 2005.
18. Peltier N. A new method for automated finite model building exploiting failures and symmetries. *J. of Logic and Computation*, 8(4):511–543, 1998.
19. Burris S. and Lee S. Small models of the high school identities. *Intl J. of Algebra and Computatio*, 2:139–178, 1992.
20. Fahle T., Schamberger S., and Sellmann M. Symmetry breaking. In *Proc. CP'01*, pages 93–107, 2001.
21. McCune W. MACE 2.0 reference manual and guide. Technical Report No. 249, Argonne National Laboratory, Argonne, IL, USA, 2001.
22. McCune W. Mace4 reference manual and guide. Technical Report No. 264, Argonne National Laboratory, Argonne, IL, USA, 2003.

Automation of Recursive Path Ordering
for Infinite Labelled Rewrite Systems

Adam Koprowski and Hans Zantema

Eindhoven University of Technology
Department of Computer Science
P.O. Box 513, 5600 MB, Eindhoven, The Netherlands
{A.Koprowski, H.Zantema}@tue.nl

Abstract. Semantic labelling is a transformational technique for proving termination of Term Rewriting Systems (TRSs). Only its variant with finite sets of labels was used so far in tools for automatic termination proving and variants with infinite sets of labels were considered not to be suitable for automation. We show that such automation can be achieved for semantic labelling with natural numbers, in combination with recursive path ordering (RPO). In order to do so we developed algorithms to deal with recursive path ordering for these infinite labelled systems. Using these techniques TPA, a tool developed by the first author, is the only current tool that can prove termination of the SUBST system automatically.

1 Introduction

Semantic labelling ([12]) is a well-known transformational termination technique for TRSs. The core of the idea is to interpret the function symbols in some model and use this interpretation to label the system. After this labelling all function symbols are equipped with a label and the resulting TRS is terminating if and only if the original one is terminating. This approach is often successful in the sense that proving termination for the labelled system is easier than for the original one. Typically, non simply terminating systems are often transformed to systems for which termination is easily proved by polynomials or recursive path ordering (RPO).

In recent years research in this area has focussed towards the automation of the termination proving process. Any termination technique, to be regarded successful, apart from being widely applicable needs to be suitable for automation. The best evidence of that is the annual termination competition ([1]) where termination tools written by different authors compete on a set of termination problems.

Automation of semantic labelling can be done straightforwardly if the models contain only finitely many elements, or in particular only 2 elements. For instance, this technique is used by the tools AProVE [6], TORPA [14] and TeParLa. However if we consider labelling with infinite sets of labels, like natural numbers, some complications show up as then the labelled system has an infinite

U. Furbach and N. Shankar (Eds.): IJCAR 2006, LNAI 4130, pp. 332–346, 2006.

signature and contains infinitely many rules. For that reason such variants of semantic labelling were regarded as not feasible for automation and were not used in termination tools before 2005.

The main claim of this paper is that semantic labelling with a model consisting of the infinite set of natural numbers can be automated in combination with extending RPO implementation to the corresponding infinite signatures. By doing so, in the setting we are about to describe, one gets a widely applicable new termination technique. We give examples where this technique easily yields a termination proof whereas all other known techniques fail.

Apart from developing the theory we also implemented this technique in TPA[1] (Termination Proved Automatically), a termination tool developed by the first author, for which semantic labelling with natural numbers in combination with RPO is one of the main techniques.

Before presenting the details of this technique, we give a motivating example.

Example 1. Consider the following TRS:

$$
\begin{aligned}
&(1) \quad \lambda(x) \circ y \to \lambda(x \circ (1 \star (y \circ \uparrow))) \\
&(2) \quad (x \star y) \circ z \to (x \circ z) \star (y \circ z) \\
&(3) \quad (x \circ y) \circ z \to x \circ (y \circ z) \\
&(4) \quad \mathsf{id} \circ x \to x \\
&(5) \quad 1 \circ \mathsf{id} \to 1 \\
&(6) \quad \uparrow \circ \mathsf{id} \to \uparrow \\
&(7) \quad 1 \circ (x \star y) \to x \\
&(8) \quad \uparrow \circ (x \star y) \to y
\end{aligned}
$$

This system, named σ_0 in [4] and essentially equivalent to system SUBST in [7] describes the process of substitution in combinatory categorical logic with 'λ' corresponding to currying, '$\circ$' to composition, 'id' to identity, '$\star$' to pairing and '1' and '$\uparrow$' to projections.

Termination of this system (implying termination of the process of explicit substitution in un-typed λ-calculus) is non-trivial and was the main result of [4] and [7]. However in [12,13] a very simple proof was given using only semantic labelling with natural numbers followed by an application of RPO on the transformed system. Ability to reproduce this proof completely automatically was a first goal of this work, while a next goal was to make this approach fruitful in general. Both goals have been achieved.

This TRS will be a running example in this paper.

The outline of this paper is as follows. In Section 2 we present the required preliminaries on RPO. We continue in Section 3 by briefly introducing the technique of semantic labelling with natural numbers. Section 4 concentrates on adopting the recursive path ordering (RPO) to deal with infinite labelled systems. In section 5 we present practical evaluation of this technique along with two examples for which it is particularly suitable. We conclude in Section 6.

---

[1] For more information about TPA see http://www.win.tue.nl/tpa.

2   Recursive Path Ordering

Recursive path ordering (RPO) is an ordering introduced by Dershowitz [5] for proving termination of TRSs. We will briefly present it here. For a general introduction to term rewriting we refer to [2].

Let Σ be any signature, possibly infinite. Let $\succ$ be a well-founded order on Σ, called a precedence. Let τ be a status function on Σ, i.e., for every $f \in \Sigma$ the status $\tau(f)$ describes how to compare sequences of arguments of f: by multiset ordering or by lexicographic comparison in some direction. Then the corresponding recursive path ordering $\succ_{RPO}$ is defined as:

$$s \succ_{RPO} t \iff s = f(s_1, \ldots, s_n) \text{ and}$$

  (1) $s_i = t$ or $s_i \succ_{RPO} t$ for some $1 \leq i \leq n$, or
  (2) $t = g(t_1, \ldots, t_m)$, $s \succ_{RPO} t_i$ for all $1 \leq i \leq m$, and either
    (a) $f \succ g$, or
    (b) $f = g$ and $\langle s_1, \ldots, s_n \rangle \succ_{RPO}^{\tau(f)} \langle t_1, \ldots, t_m \rangle$.

The main property of this ordering is the following:

  If $\ell \succ_{RPO} r$ for every rule $\ell \to r$ of a TRS R, then R is terminating.

So for proving termination by RPO one has to find a well-founded precedence $\succ$ and a status function τ such that $\ell \succ_{RPO} r$ for every rule $\ell \to r$. In tools this is typically done by collecting constraints on $\succ$ and checking whether these constraints give rise to a well-founded precedence $\succ$. In searching for these collections of constraints often choices are possible, also choices on τ, giving rise to back-tracking. The crucial algorithm required in this back-tracking procedure is to check whether a set of constraints on $\succ$ gives rise to a well-founded precedence $\succ$. For finite signatures this coincides with checking whether the corresponding graph is acyclic. For the infinite signatures, as we consider in this paper, it is more involved, but the basic frame of the algorithm remains the same. We will concentrate on the question of how to construct a well-founded precedence out of a collection of constraints on such a precedence.

3   Semantic Labelling with Natural Numbers

First we recall the main theory of semantic labelling.

A Σ-algebra (A, Σ_A) is defined to be a non-empty set A together with a map $[f] : A^n \to A$ for every $f \in \Sigma$, where n is the arity of f. Let $\mathcal{V}$ be a set of variables. For $\alpha : \mathcal{V} \to A$ we inductively define $[x, \alpha] = \alpha(x)$ for $x \in \mathcal{V}$, and $[f(t_1, \ldots, t_n), \alpha] = [f]([t_1, \alpha], \ldots, [t_n, \alpha])$.

A Σ-algebra (A, Σ_A) equipped with a partial order $\geq$ is called a *quasi-model* for a TRS R if $[\ell, \alpha] \geq [r, \alpha]$ for all rules $\ell \to r$ in R and all $\alpha : \mathcal{V} \to A$, and $[f]$ is weakly monotone in all arguments for all $f \in \Sigma$.

In case the partial order $\geq$ coincides with equality then weak monotonicity holds for every operation, and the only requirement is $[\ell, \alpha] = [r, \alpha]$ for all rules $\ell \to r$ in R and all $\alpha : \mathcal{V} \to A$. In this case the quasi-model is called a *model*.

For labelling here we do not introduce an arbitrary labelling function as in [12,13], but choose the particular case where this labelling function is the identity. This means that given a quasi-model $(A, \Sigma_A, \geq)$ for a TRS R over Σ, the labelled TRS $\overline{R}$ is defined as follows. The signature $\overline{\Sigma}$ consists of n-ary symbols $f_{a_1,\ldots,a_n}$, where f is an n-ary symbol from Σ and $a_1,\ldots,a_n \in A$. Given $\alpha : \mathcal{V} \to A$, the labelling function lab is defined inductively by

$$\mathsf{lab}(x, \alpha) = x,$$

$$\mathsf{lab}(f(t_1,\ldots,t_n), \alpha) = f_{[t_1,\alpha],\ldots,[t_n,\alpha]}(\mathsf{lab}(t_1, \alpha),\ldots,\mathsf{lab}(t_n, \alpha))$$

for $x \in \mathcal{V}$ and $f \in \Sigma$. Now $\overline{R}$ is defined to consist of the rules

$$\mathsf{lab}(\ell, \alpha) \to \mathsf{lab}(r, \alpha)$$

for all $\alpha : \mathcal{V} \to A$ and all rules $\ell \to r$ of R. The TRS Decr is defined to consist of the rules

$$f_{a_1,\ldots,a_n}(x_1,\ldots,x_n) \to f_{b_1,\ldots,b_n}(x_1,\ldots,x_n)$$

for all $f \in \Sigma$ and $a_1,\ldots,a_n,b_1,\ldots,b_n$ satisfying $a_i > b_i$ for some i and $a_j = b_j$ for all $j \neq i$. Here $>$ denotes the strict part of $\geq$. Note that Decr is empty in the model case, i.e., if $\geq$ coincides with equality.

The main property of semantic labelling is the following:

R is terminating if and only if $\overline{R} \cup$ Decr is terminating.

In this paper we focus on the case where $A = \mathbb{N}$, the natural numbers. The approach is as follows: for a TRS R for which we want to prove termination, search for interpretations in A such that $(A, \Sigma_A, \geq)$ is a quasi-model, and next try to prove termination of the infinite TRS $\overline{R} \cup$ Decr by means of RPO. If this succeeds, then according to the main property of semantic labelling we have proved termination of R. In case $(A, \Sigma_A, \geq)$ happens to be a model, i.e., for all rules we have equality, then we choose $\geq$ on $A = \mathbb{N}$ to be equality, by which Decr is empty. In the other case we choose $\geq$ to be the usual order on $\mathbb{N}$. In this case Decr is not empty, but we may and shall restrict Decr to all rules of the shape

$$f_{a_1,\ldots,a_n}(x_1,\ldots,x_n) \to f_{b_1,\ldots,b_n}(x_1,\ldots,x_n)$$

for $f \in \Sigma$ and $a_1,\ldots,a_n,b_1,\ldots,b_n$ satisfying $a_i = b_i + 1$ for some i and $a_j = b_j$ for all $j \neq i$. This is valid since if $a_i > b_i$ then a_i can be obtained from b_i by taking the successor a number of times, so the rewrite relation $\to_{\mathsf{Decr}}^+$ is not changed by this modification of Decr. In the sequel we refer to $\overline{R} \cup$ Decr as the *labelled system*.

Example 2. As an example, we apply this approach to the TRS R from Example 1 and the following interpretation in $\mathbb{N}$:

$$[\lambda](x) = x + 1 \qquad\qquad [1] = 0$$
$$[\star](x, y) = \mathsf{max}(x, y) \qquad\qquad [\uparrow] = 0$$
$$[\circ](x, y) = x + y \qquad\qquad [\mathsf{id}] = 0$$

This interpretation is a quasi-model and after application of semantic labelling we obtain $\overline{R}$ consisting of the rules

$$
\begin{array}{lll}
(1) & \lambda_i(x) \circ_{i+1,j} y \to \lambda_{i+j}(x \circ_{i,j} (1 \star_{0,j} (y \circ_{j,0} \uparrow))) & \\
(2a) & (x \star_{i,j} y) \circ_{i,k} z \to (x \circ_{i,k} z) \star_{i+k,j+k} (y \circ_{j,k} z) & \text{for } i \geq j \\
(2b) & (x \star_{i,j} y) \circ_{j,k} z \to (x \circ_{i,k} z) \star_{i+k,j+k} (y \circ_{j,k} z) & \text{for } i < j \\
(3) & (x \circ_{i,j} y) \circ_{i+j,k} z \to x \circ_{i,j+k} (y \circ_{j,k} z) & \\
(4) & \text{id} \circ_{0,i} x \to x & \\
(5) & 1 \circ_{0,0} \text{id} \to 1 & \\
(6) & \uparrow \circ_{0,0} \text{id} \to \uparrow & \\
(7a) & 1 \circ_{0,i} (x \star_{i,j} y) \to x & \text{for } i \geq j \\
(7b) & 1 \circ_{0,j} (x \star_{i,j} y) \to x & \text{for } i < j \\
(8a) & \uparrow \circ_{0,i} (x \star_{i,j} y) \to y & \text{for } i \geq j \\
(8b) & \uparrow \circ_{0,j} (x \star_{i,j} y) \to y & \text{for } i < j
\end{array}
$$

and Decr consisting of the rules

$$
\begin{array}{ll}
(D_1) & \lambda_{i+1}(x) \to \lambda_i(x) \\
(D_{2a}) & x \circ_{i+1,j} y \to x \circ_{i,j} y \\
(D_{2b}) & x \circ_{i,j+1} y \to x \circ_{i,j} y \\
(D_{3a}) & x \star_{i+1,j} y \to x \star_{i,j} y \\
(D_{3b}) & x \star_{i,j+1} y \to x \star_{i,j} y.
\end{array}
$$

Here variables i, j, k run over $\mathbb{N}$.

The goal now is to represent such an infinite labelled system $\overline{R} \cup$ Decr in such a way that we can search systematically for a suitable RPO proving its termination. Before doing so first we say something about the search for (quasi-)models.

As long as all basic interpretations are polynomials, checking whether this interpretation is a model coincides with checking whether $[\ell, \alpha] = [r, \alpha]$ for all rules $\ell \to r$ and all α. This is simply checking whether polynomials are equal. Checking whether an interpretation is a quasi-model coincides with checking whether $[\ell, \alpha] \geq [r, \alpha]$; this can be done along the lines of the standard way of checking for polynomial interpretations as described in [3,9].

In TPA as an initial step symbols of arity > 2 are transformed to a number of binary symbols, so no symbols of arity > 2 occur anymore. Then in the basic setting the functions used as interpretations for constant, unary and binary symbols, respectively, are as follows[2]:

$$\{0, 1\}$$

$$\{\lambda x.0, \ \lambda x.1, \ \lambda x.x, \ \lambda x.x + 1, \ \lambda x. \max(0, x - 1), \ \lambda x.2x, \ \lambda x.7x\}$$

$$\{\lambda x\, y.0, \ \lambda x\, y.1, \ \lambda x\, y.x + y, \ \lambda x\, y.x + y + 3, \ \lambda x\, y.xy,$$

$$\lambda x\, y.x, \ \lambda x\, y.y, \ \lambda x\, y. \max(0, x - y), \ \lambda x\, y. \max(x, y), \ \lambda x\, y. \min(x, y)\}$$

---

[2] Note that, for technical reasons, TPA actually uses $A = \mathbb{N} \setminus \{0, 1\}$ not $A = \mathbb{N}$ hence the actual functions being used are slight variants of those presented here.

So we may also want to use non-polynomial functions like min or max. Checking whether the required (in-)equalities hold is accomplished by first removing min and max functions by simple case analysis and then using the standard approach for polynomials.

Note however that while doing this case analysis we introduce side conditions, just like in Example 2. For F being a polynomial over $\mathbb{N}$ in n variables $a_1, \ldots, a_n$ let us abbreviate $\forall a_1, \ldots, a_n \in \mathbb{N}.F(a_1, \ldots, a_n) > 0$ by $F > 0$. So now the problem of comparing polynomials is not to check whether $F > 0$, as in the standard setting, but to check whether $\{F_i \geq 0\}_i \implies F > 0$ where the premise is a set of side conditions introduced by case analysis. This problem is undecidable as it is a generalization of polynomial comparison which is already undecidable. TPA uses a very simple and naive approximation of this problem and concludes $\{F_i \geq 0\}_i \implies F > 0$ only if $F > 0 \vee \exists i \in \{1, \ldots, n\}.F - F_i > 0$. For instance comparison of function symbols $\circ_{i,k}$ and $\circ_{j,k}$ in rule (2a) may require comparing polynomials $i + k$ and $j + k$ if the two indices of $\circ$ are added. For that we have to use the side condition of this rule, $i \geq j$. We cannot conclude $i + k \geq j + k$ in general but by using the side condition and subtracting i from the left hand side of this inequality and j from the right hand side we get $i + k - i \geq j + k - j$ which is trivially satisfied.

4   RPO for Infinite Labelled Systems

In this section we describe how RPO can be adapted to deal with labelled systems, more precisely, for infinite systems over infinite signatures obtained by labelling with natural numbers. In fact we do not change the definition of RPO, but we restrict the search space for possible precedences on the labelled symbols in such a way that this search can be automated and we have algorithms checking whether constraints on the precedence give rise to a well-founded precedence or not.

First in 4.1 we present theoretical foundations of those results and then in 4.2 we discuss the algorithmic approach for searching for a precedence satisfying given set of constraints.

4.1   Well-Foundedness of a Precedence

The final precedence $\succ$ we search for will be of the following shape:

Definition 1 (Precedence description). *A precedence description* consists *of:*

- *for every $f \in \Sigma$ of arity n, $\phi_f : \mathbb{N}^n \to \mathbb{N}$ (we will call those functions* label synthesis functions*) and*
- $\mathsf{pd} : \Sigma \times \Sigma \to \{\perp, >, \geq, \top\}$.

These ingredients give rise to the following relation $\succ$:

$$f_{k_1, \ldots, k_n} \succ g_{l_1, \ldots, l_m} \iff \mathsf{pd}(f, g) = \top \vee$$
$$(\mathsf{pd}(f, g) = \geq \wedge \phi_f(k_1, \ldots, k_n) \geq \phi_g(l_1, \ldots, l_m)) \vee$$
$$(\mathsf{pd}(f, g) = > \wedge \phi_f(k_1, \ldots, k_n) > \phi_g(l_1, \ldots, l_m)).$$

So $\mathsf{pd}(f, g)$ indicates when we can conclude $f_{k_1,\ldots,k_n} \succ g_{l_1,\ldots,l_m}$ with: $\bot$ indicating that this can never be the case; $\top$ that it is always the case regardless of the labels of f and g; and $\geq$ and $>$ let us conclude $f_{k_1,\ldots,k_n} \succ g_{l_1,\ldots,l_m}$ if $\phi_f(k_1,\ldots,k_n)$ is, respectively, greater equal/strictly greater than $\phi_g(l_1,\ldots,l_m)$.

Typically this relation $\succ$ will not be an ordering as it may not be transitive but then it may be replaced by its transitive closure so by abuse of terminology we will call it a precedence.

We need criteria under which in the above setting we can conclude well-foundedness of $\succ$. If these criteria hold then termination of the labelled system, and hence of the original TRS, can be concluded if $\ell \succ_{RPO} r$ for all rules $\ell \to r$ in the labelled system. So our approach can be summarized as follows: collect constraints on pd and the label synthesis functions ϕ_f from the requirement that $\ell \succ_{RPO} r$ for all rules $\ell \to r$, and then check whether this gives rise to a well-founded precedence $\succ$.

This well-foundedness criterion is captured by the following theorem. A function $\mathsf{pd} : \Sigma \times \Sigma \to \{\bot, >, \geq, \top\}$ gives rise to a *precedence graph* having Σ as its node set, and having three kinds of directed edges:

- an *unconditional* edge from f to g if $\mathsf{pd}(f, g) = \top$, denoted by a double arrow $\Longrightarrow$;
- a *strict* edge from f to g if $\mathsf{pd}(f, g) = >$, denoted by a single arrow $\longrightarrow$;
- a *non-strict* edge from f to g if $\mathsf{pd}(f, g) = \geq$, denoted by a dotted arrow $\cdots\cdots\!\!\!>$;

Theorem 1 (Well-foundedness of a precedence). *In the above setting a precedence description* pd *gives rise to a well-founded precedence* $\succ$ *if every cycle in the corresponding precedence graph*

(1) contains no unconditional edge, and
(2) contains at least one strict edge.

Proof. Suppose that the precedence is not well-founded. This means that there is an infinite sequence $f_{k_1,\ldots,k_n} \succ g_{l_1,\ldots,l_m} \succ \ldots$. Every step in this reduction corresponds to an edge in the precedence graph. Since this sequence is infinite it must traverse some cycle in the precedence graph (which is finite) infinitely often. Every cycle contains only strict and non-strict edges due to (1), which gives rise to the inequalities on ϕ functions as depicted below.

$$\cdots \longrightarrow f \longrightarrow g \longrightarrow \cdots$$

$$\cdots \geq \phi_f(k_1,\ldots,k_n) \geq \phi_g(l_1,\ldots,l_m) \geq \cdots$$

Due to (2) at least one of those inequalities is strict which gives rise to a decreasing weight along a cycle. Hence no cycle can be traversed infinitely often. Contradiction, we conclude well-foundedness of $\succ$.   □

To make the approach feasible, but still applicable to interesting examples, it is natural to restrict the choice for the label synthesis functions. In TPA the choice has been made to choose ϕ to always be identity for unary symbols. For binary symbols ϕ is chosen to be one of the three functions: summation $+$, left projection π_1 and right projection π_2. This set of synthesis functions may seem quite restricted but it works reasonably well in practice whereas a bigger set would lead to a bigger search space.

One of the constraints implied by the rule

$$\lambda_i(x) \circ_{i+1,j} y \ \rightarrow \ \lambda_{i+j}(x \circ_{i,j} (1 \star_{0,j} (y \circ_{j,0} \uparrow)))$$

where i, j runs over the naturals, will be $\circ_{i+1,j} \succ \lambda_{i+j}$, for all i, j. Since ϕ_λ is fixed to be the identity, according to the definition of $\succ$ this gives three possibilities.

1. $\mathsf{pd}(\circ, \lambda) = \top$,
2. $\mathsf{pd}(\circ, \lambda) = \geq \ \wedge \ \phi_\circ(i+1, j) \geq i + j$ for all i, j,
3. $\mathsf{pd}(\circ, \lambda) = > \ \wedge \ \phi_\circ(i+1, j) > i + j$ for all i, j.

By re-using the algorithm for comparing polynomials it can be determined that among the three possibilities for $\phi_\circ$ cases 2 and 3 only hold if $\phi_\circ = +$, from which case 3 is preferred since by Theorem 1 strict edges are preferred over non-strict edges.

4.2   Algorithm for Computing a Well-Founded Precedence

In general for every pair (f, g) the RPO constraints will give rise to a list of cases. Each case consists of a choice for $\mathsf{pd}(f, g)$ being $\top$, $\geq$ or $>$, and in case this is not $\top$, also a choice for ϕ_f and ϕ_g. Now the question is whether for every pair (f, g) a choice can be made in such a way that conditions of Theorem 1 are satisfied so that this choice gives rise to a well-founded precedence. Note that for every $f \in \Sigma$ in a precedence there is a single, global function ϕ_f corresponding to it. However in the search procedure we do not know what this ϕ_f should be and hence during the search we allow using different functions for comparison with different symbols and only at the end we conclude which one should be chosen for every function symbol. We will express all those choices for ϕ and pd, in, what we call, a precedence description scheme.

Definition 2 (Precedence description scheme). *We define a precedence description scheme as a function* pds *from pairs of function symbols to the set of precedence description possibilities, more precisely,*

$$\mathsf{pds}(f, g) \subseteq \{\bot\} \cup (\{>, \geq\} \times \mathbb{N}^{\mathbb{N}^n} \times \mathbb{N}^{\mathbb{N}^m}) \cup \{\top\}$$

where n is the arity of f and m arity of g.

We say that a precedence description $(\{\phi_f\}_{f \in \Sigma}, \mathsf{pd})$ *is compatible with a precedence description scheme* pds *if:*

$$\forall f, g \in \Sigma \ . \ \begin{cases} \mathsf{pd}(f, g) = \top \implies \top \in \mathsf{pds}(f, g) \\ \mathsf{pd}(f, g) = \geq \implies (\geq, \phi_f, \phi_g) \in \mathsf{pds}(f, g) \\ \mathsf{pd}(f, g) = > \implies (>, \phi_f, \phi_g) \in \mathsf{pds}(f, g) \end{cases}$$

Let us illustrate the notion of precedence description scheme on an example.

Example 3. Consider the labelled system from Example 2. A possible branching of an application of RPO to that system gives the following sets of constraints for respective rules; note that for $\circ$ a lexicographic left-to-right status is essential.

$$(1) \quad \{\circ_{i+1,j} > \lambda_{i+j}, \ \circ_{i+1,j} > \circ_{i,j}, \ \circ_{i+1,j} > \star_{0,j},$$
$$\circ_{i+1,j} > 1, \ \circ_{i+1,j} > \circ_{j,0}, \ \circ_{i+1,j} > \uparrow\}$$
$$(2a) \quad \{\circ_{i,k} > \star_{i+k,j+k}, \ \circ_{i,k} \geq \circ_{j,k}\} \text{ with } i \geq j$$
$$(2b) \quad \{\circ_{j,k} > \star_{i+k,j+k}, \ \circ_{j,k} \geq \circ_{i,k}\} \text{ with } i < j$$
$$(3) \quad \{\circ_{i+j,k} = \circ_{i,j+k}, \ \circ_{i+j,k} > \circ_{j,k}\}$$
$$(D_1) \quad \{\lambda_{i+1} > \lambda_i\}$$
$$(D_{2a}) \quad \{\circ_{i+1,j} > \circ_{i,j}\}$$
$$(D_{2b}) \quad \{\circ_{i,j+1} > \circ_{i,j}\}$$
$$(D_{3a}) \quad \{\star_{i+1,j} > \star_{i,j}\}$$
$$(D_{3b}) \quad \{\star_{i,j+1} > \star_{i,j}\}$$

Now with a finite set of label synthesis function, transformation of those constrains to a precedence description scheme can be easily accomplished. For instance for $\mathsf{pds}(\circ, \star)$ we need to consider the following three constraints:

$$\circ_{i+1,j} > \star_{0,j} \qquad \circ_{i,k} > \star_{i+k,j+k} \text{ with } i \geq j \qquad \circ_{j,k} > \star_{i+k,j+k} \text{ with } i < j$$

Given a finite set of label synthesis functions we can consider all possible combinations of synthesis functions for $\circ$ and $\star$ and analyze the resulting polynomial constraints. In TPA the set of label synthesis functions for binary symbols consists of π_1, π_2 and $+$. If $\circ$ always bigger than $\star$ then we trivially have those inequalities, so $\top \in \mathsf{pds}(\circ, \star)$. For remaining conditional cases we easily observe that only $+$ is possible as a label synthesis function for $\circ$ whereas only projections are allowed for $\star$. We get $(\geq, +, \pi_1) \in \mathsf{pds}(\circ, \star)$ because $(i+1) + j \geq \pi_1(0, j)$, $i + k \geq \pi_1(i + k, j + k)$ and $i < j \implies j + k \geq \pi_1(i + k, j + k)$. Similarly $(\geq, +, \pi_2) \in \mathsf{pds}(\circ, \star)$. Continuing such analysis we end up with the following precedence description scheme. For all f and g for which $\mathsf{pds}(f, g)$ is not listed in the table below we have $\mathsf{pds}(f, g) = \{\bot\}$.

$$\mathsf{pds}(\circ, 1) = \{\top\} \qquad\qquad \mathsf{pds}(\circ, \lambda) = \{(>, +, \mathsf{id}), \top\}$$
$$\mathsf{pds}(\circ, \uparrow) = \{\top\} \qquad\qquad \mathsf{pds}(\circ, \star) = \{(\geq, +, \pi_1), (\geq, +, \pi_2), \top\}$$
$$\mathsf{pds}(\circ, \circ) = \{(>, +, +)\} \qquad \mathsf{pds}(\lambda, \lambda) = \{(>, \mathsf{id}, \mathsf{id})\}$$
$$\mathsf{pds}(\star, \star) = \{(>, +, +)\}$$

To summarize our approach: given TRS find an interpretation that is a (quasi-)model and label the system. Now find a RPO termination proof for that system. This proof gives rise to a number of constraints on precedence that can be transformed to a precedence description scheme pds as in Example 3. Now our task is to find a precedence that satisfies those constraints and is well-founded. That is we are looking for a precedence description pd which is: (a) compatible with pds and (b) satisfies conditions of Theorem 1.

Before presenting an appropriate algorithm we first observe that a simpler problem of finding any precedence description compatible with a given precedence description scheme is NP-complete.

Theorem 2. *Suppose at least three different φ functions are allowed. Then given a precedence description scheme* pds, *the problem of finding a precedence description compatible with it is NP-complete.*

Proof. Reduction to the 3-coloring problem of graphs; for details see [11].   □

Before we present the algorithm let us put the problem in a more practical light by discussing it in the context in which it occurs in TPA. As mentioned before TPA uses precisely three different φ functions for binary symbols meaning that we are on the border of conditions posted in Theorem 2. If it had two the problem would correspond to 2-coloring which can be solved in polynomial time. But we believe that all three functions are important and we do not want to get rid of any of them. Moreover we are about to describe an algorithm that in practice performs very well and takes negligible time in the whole search procedure.

First let us observe that from the precedence description scheme pds we can already determine the structure of the precedence graph for a precedence description pd compatible with pds. Let us note that due to the construction of the precedence description scheme for any f and g we either have $pds(f, g) = \{\bot\}$ or $\top \in pds(f, g) \wedge \bot \notin pds(f, g)$. Now if $pds(f, g) = \{\bot\}$ then we can simply choose $pd(f, g) = \bot$ and hence there is no edge from f to g in the precedence graph. Otherwise f and g are connected with an edge although at this point we do not know yet what is the type of this edge.

The key to get an efficient algorithm is the observation that we can detect strongly connected components (SCCs) in the precedence graph and treat them separately. Since precedence graphs are typically spare, meaning that SCCs are small, by doing so we increase the efficiency greatly. Note that all the edges between f and g belonging to different SCCs do not lie on any cycle and hence cannot violate conditions of the Theorem 1. Thus they can safely be changed to unconditional edges (as then $\top \in pds(f, g)$). On the other hand there cannot be an unconditional edge connecting two nodes from the same SCC since all the edges within SCC belong to some cycle, so all such options can be dropped from the precedence description scheme.

So now we can localize further reasoning to a single SCC and we can limit to strict and non-strict edges only. We still need to find φ functions for all function symbols and the appropriate ordering of those symbols.

Firstly for all function symbols we compute their predecessors and successors in the precedence graph:

$$\mathsf{IN}_f = \{g \mid pds(g, f) \neq \{\bot\},\ g\ \text{in the same SCC as f}\}$$
$$\mathsf{OUT}_f = \{g \mid pds(f, g) \neq \{\bot\},\ g\ \text{in the same SCC as f}\}$$

Now we can compute possible label synthesis functions for every function symbol:

$$PSF_f = \bigcap_{g \in OUT_f} \{\phi_f \mid (\geq / >, \phi_f, \phi_g) \in pds(f, g)\} \cap$$

$$\bigcap_{g \in IN_f} \{\phi_f \mid (\geq / >, \phi_g, \phi_f) \in pds(g, f)\}$$

If for any f, $PSF_f = \emptyset$ then we can finish with a negative answer. Otherwise we refine ps in the following way:

$$pds'(f, g) := \{(\geq / >, \phi_f, \phi_g) \in pds(f, g) \mid \phi_f \in PSF_f, \ \phi_g \in PSF_g\}$$

We continue this procedure as long as there are some changes in the refinement of pds. If at any point for any f and g, $pds(f, g) = \emptyset$ we finish with negative answer. Hopefully we arrive at pds with all entries being singletons in which case we have only one potential solution; otherwise we need to consider all the possible choices. At the end we check whether condition (2) of Theorem 1 is satisfied that is whether there are no cycles containing non-strict edges only.

For a more detailed summary of the whole procedure we refer the reader to [11].

5   Practical Evaluation

The technique of semantic labelling with natural numbers has been implemented in TPA. In Section 5.1 we discuss the role of this technique in TPA and in Section 5.2 we discuss two examples.

5.1   TPA - Termination Proved Automatically

The results presented below come from the evaluation of TPA on the database of 773 TRSs, which is used for the Termination Competition and is available at the following address: http://www.lri.fr/~marche/tpdb.

Semantic labelling with natural numbers is one of the techniques implemented in TPA. For a recent version of the tool out of 432 successful proofs in 85 this techniques has been applied. Moreover after semantic labelling with natural numbers has been switched off 32 of those systems could not be proven terminating anymore.

Another interesting experiment is the evaluation of the claim we made in Section 4.2, namely that typically SCCs in the precedence graph are small and hence the algorithm is efficient. For 115 systems for which semantic labelling with natural numbers was applicable we calculated the size of the biggest SCC occurring in the analysis of that system (note that often many different labellings are tried resulting in many applications of the algorithm from Section 4.2). The average of those values was less than 5 confirming the claim that in practice SCCs are very small. Also the time spent on the execution of the algorithm in question on average summed up to less than 1% of the total running time of TPA.

5.2   Examples

In this section we would like to finish our analysis of the SUBST system introduced in Example 1 and also present one new example. We will show that using our approach both those systems can be easily proved terminating. Indeed TPA produces termination proof for them whereas, at the time being, no other termination tool can deal with those systems.

Example 4. Let us continue with Example 3, where we presented a precedence description scheme for this system. Below we depict the precedence graph corresponding to this scheme.

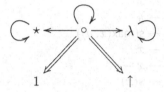

Using algorithm from Section 4.2 we first observe that all nodes are in separate SCCs. So first we replace all edges between different nodes by unconditional edges. Then we are left with no choice and we end up with the following precedence:

$$\mathsf{pd}(\circ, \lambda) = \top$$
$$\mathsf{pd}(\circ, \star) = \top$$
$$\mathsf{pd}(\circ, 1) = \top \qquad \phi_\circ = +$$
$$\mathsf{pd}(\circ, \uparrow) = \top \qquad \phi_\lambda = \mathsf{id}$$
$$\mathsf{pd}(\circ, \circ) = > \qquad \phi_\star = +$$
$$\mathsf{pd}(\lambda, \lambda) = >$$
$$\mathsf{pd}(\star, \star) = >$$

which can be written down as:

$$\circ_{i,j} > \lambda_k \qquad \text{for all } i, j, k$$
$$\circ_{i,j} > \star_{k,l} \qquad \text{for all } i, j, k, l$$
$$\circ_{i,j} > 1 \qquad \text{for all } i, j$$
$$\circ_{i,j} > \uparrow \qquad \text{for all } i, j$$
$$\circ_{i,j} > \circ_{k,l} \qquad \text{if } i + j > k + l$$
$$\lambda_i > \lambda_k \qquad \text{if } i > k$$
$$\star_{i,j} > \star_{k,l} \qquad \text{if } i + j > k + l$$

One can easily check that all the rules of the SUBST TRS can be oriented using RPO with this precedence. This is also essentially the same solution as presented in [13].

In the termination competition it is allowed that tool authors submit up to 5 TRS, the so-called secret problems. Those problems are then merged into the main database and all the tools compete on them trying to prove their termination. All 5 systems submitted by TPA in the 2005 competition could be proven terminating using semantic labelling with natural numbers and RPO and for 4 of those systems TPA was the only tool that could prove their termination. Below we present one of those systems. Please note that this is a very natural TRS and not some artificial, cooked-up system.

Example 5. Consider the following TRS describing a GCD (*Greatest common divisor*) computation in a straightforward way.

$$\min(x, 0) \to 0$$
$$\min(0, y) \to 0$$
$$\min(\mathsf{s}(x), \mathsf{s}(y)) \to \mathsf{s}(\min(x, y))$$
$$\max(x, 0) \to x$$
$$\max(0, y) \to y$$
$$\max(\mathsf{s}(x), \mathsf{s}(y)) \to \mathsf{s}(\max(x, y))$$
$$x - 0 \to x$$
$$\mathsf{s}(x) - \mathsf{s}(y) \to x - y$$
$$\gcd(\mathsf{s}(x), 0) \to \mathsf{s}(x)$$
$$\gcd(0, \mathsf{s}(y)) \to \mathsf{s}(y)$$
$$\gcd(\mathsf{s}(x), \mathsf{s}(y)) \to \gcd(\max(x, y) - \min(x, y), \mathsf{s}(\min(x, y)))$$

Consider the following interpretation of function symbols in $\mathbb{N}$:

$$[\mathsf{s}](x) = x + 1 \qquad\qquad [0] = 0$$
$$[\min](x, y) = \min(x, y) \qquad\qquad [\max](x, y) = \max(x, y)$$
$$[-](x, y) = x \qquad\qquad [\gcd](x, y) = x + y$$

This interpretation is a quasi-model and after application of semantic labelling it gives the following TRS:

$$\min_{i,0}(x, 0) \to 0$$
$$\min_{0,j}(0, y) \to 0$$
$$\min_{i+1,j+1}(\mathsf{s}_i(x), \mathsf{s}_j(y)) \to \mathsf{s}_j(\min_{i,j}(x, y)) \qquad\qquad \text{for } i \geq j$$
$$\min_{i+1,j+1}(\mathsf{s}_i(x), \mathsf{s}_j(y)) \to \mathsf{s}_i(\min_{i,j}(x, y)) \qquad\qquad \text{for } i < j$$
$$\max_{i,0}(x, 0) \to x$$
$$\max_{0,j}(0, y) \to y$$
$$\max_{i+1,j+1}(\mathsf{s}_i(x), \mathsf{s}_j(y)) \to \mathsf{s}_i(\max_{i,j}(x, y)) \qquad\qquad \text{for } i \geq j$$
$$\max_{i+1,j+1}(\mathsf{s}_i(x), \mathsf{s}_j(y)) \to \mathsf{s}_j(\max_{i,j}(x, y)) \qquad\qquad \text{for } i < j$$
$$x -_{i,0} 0 \to x$$
$$\mathsf{s}_i(x) -_{i+1,j+1} \mathsf{s}_j(y) \to x -_{i,j} y$$
$$\gcd_{i+1,j+1}(\mathsf{s}_i(x), \mathsf{s}_j(y)) \to \gcd_{i-j,j}(\max_{i,j}(x, y) -_{i,j} \min_{i,j}(x, y), \qquad \text{for } i \geq j$$
$$\mathsf{s}_j(\min_{i,j}(x, y)))$$
$$\gcd_{i+1,j+1}(\mathsf{s}_i(x), \mathsf{s}_j(y)) \to \gcd_{j-i,i}(\max_{i,j}(x, y) -_{j,i} \min_{i,j}(x, y), \qquad \text{for } i < j$$
$$\mathsf{s}_j(\min_{i,j}(x, y)))$$

Termination of the union of the above rules and decreasing rules can be proved with RPO. This time the description scheme leaves more choice for the label synthesis functions for different symbols but again all nodes are in separate

SCCs and our algorithm easily yields the following precedence description:

$$\phi_{min} = \pi_1$$
$$\phi_{max} = \pi_1$$
$$\phi_s = \mathsf{id}$$
$$\phi_- = \mathsf{id}$$
$$\phi_{gcd} = +$$

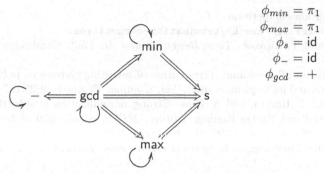

which corresponds to the following well-founded precedence:

$\mathsf{min}_{i,j} > \mathsf{min}_{k,l}$ if $i > k$ $\mathsf{gcd}_{i,j} > \mathsf{gcd}_{k,l}$ if $i + j > k + l$

$\mathsf{min}_{i,j} > \mathsf{s}_k$ for all i, j, k $\mathsf{gcd}_{i,j} > \mathsf{min}_{k,l}$ for all i, j, k, l

$\mathsf{max}_{i,j} > \mathsf{max}_{k,l}$ if $i > k$ $\mathsf{gcd}_{i,j} > \mathsf{s}_k$ for all i, j, k

$\mathsf{max}_{i,j} > \mathsf{s}_k$ for all i, j, k $\mathsf{gcd}_{i,j} > \mathsf{max}_{k,l}$ for all i, j, k, l

$-_{i,j} > -_{k,l}$ if $i > k$ $\mathsf{gcd}_{i,j} > -_{k,l}$ for all i, j, k, l

Another option to tackle this system would be to use predictive labelling [8]. Roughly speaking that would allow us not to give an interpretation for gcd symbol and ignore the rules defining gcd while checking the quasi-model conditions.

6 Conclusions and Further Research

In this paper we presented a way of automating RPO extended to infinite systems. This allows its use for systems that were transformed using semantic labelling with natural numbers. We explained how the combination of those two techniques can be employed for proving termination of rewriting and presented examples where it is successful whereas all other techniques seem to fail. Our description of automation makes it possible to use this technique in termination tools. Finally we briefly described the way in which it has been implemented and its evaluation in a termination tool TPA, developed by the first author.

Several extensions are possible. There is quite a lot of choice and questions that arise while employing this technique: what functions to use for interpretations? And for label synthesis functions? How to deal with case analysis and corresponding extended problem of comparing polynomials? Those questions can be studied further in order to make the most out of this technique. Another interesting issue is investigation of combination of other standard techniques, like for instance Knuth-Bendix order (KBO, [10]), with semantic labelling with natural numbers.

Acknowledgments

Authors would like to thank Gerhard Woeginger for his valuable ideas and remarks that contributed to the material presented in Section 4.2.

References

1. The termination competition.
   http://www.lri.fr/~marche/termination-competition.
2. F. Baader and T. Nipkow. *Term Rewriting and All That.* Cambridge University Press, 1998.
3. A. B. Cherifa and P. Lescanne. Termination of rewriting systems by polynomial interpretations and its implementation. *Sci. Comput. Program.*, 9(2):137–159, 1987.
4. P.-L. Curien, T .Hardin, and A. Ríos. Strong normalization of substitutions. In Ivan M. Havel and Václav Koubek, editors, *MFCS*, volume 629 of *Lecture Notes in Computer Science*, pages 209–217. Springer, 1992.
5. N. Dershowitz. Orderings for term-rewriting systems. *Theor. Comput. Sci.*, 17:279–301, 1982.
6. J. Giesl, R. Thiemann, P. Schneider-Kamp, and S. Falke. Automated termination proofs with AProVE. In Vincent van Oostrom, editor, *RTA*, volume 3091 of *Lecture Notes in Computer Science*, pages 210–220. Springer, 2004.
7. T. Hardin and A. Laville. Proof of termination of the rewriting system SUBST on CCL. *Theor. Comput. Sci.*, 46(2-3):305–312, 1986.
8. N. Hirokawa and A. Middeldorp. Predictive labeling. In F. Pfenning, editor, *Proceedings of the 17th Conference on Rewriting Techniques and Applications (RTA)*, Lecture Notes in Computer Science. Springer, 2006.
9. H. Hong and D. Jakus. Testing Positiveness of Polynomials. *J. Autom. Reasoning*, 21(1): 23–38, 1998
10. D. Knuth and P. Bendix. Simple word problems in universal algebras. *Computational Problems in Abstract Algebra*, pages 263–297, 1970.
11. A. Koprowski and H. Zantema. Recursive Path Ordering for Infinite Labelled Rewrite Systems. Technical Report CS-Report 06-17, Eindhoven Univ. of Tech., April 2006.
12. H. Zantema. Termination of term rewriting by semantic labelling. *Fundamenta Informaticae*, 24(1/2):89–105, 1995.
13. H. Zantema. Term Rewriting Systems. Volume 55 of *Cambridge Tracts in TCS*, chapter 6, pages 181–259. Cambridge University Press, 2003.
14. H. Zantema. TORPA: Termination of rewriting proved automatically. In Vincent van Oostrom, editor, *RTA*, volume 3091 of *Lecture Notes in Computer Science*, pages 95–104, 2004.

Strong Cut-Elimination Systems for Hudelmaier's Depth-Bounded Sequent Calculus for Implicational Logic

Roy Dyckhoff[1], Delia Kesner[2], and Stéphane Lengrand[1,2]

[1] School of Computer Science, University of St Andrews, Scotland
[2] PPS, CNRS and Université Paris 7, France

Abstract. Inspired by the Curry-Howard correspondence, we study *normalisation* procedures in the depth-bounded intuitionistic sequent calculus of Hudelmaier (1988) for the implicational case, thus strengthening existing approaches to *Cut*-admissibility. We decorate proofs with terms and introduce various term-reduction systems representing proof transformations. In contrast to previous papers which gave different arguments for *Cut*-admissibility suggesting *weakly normalising* procedures for *Cut*-elimination, our main reduction system and all its variations are *strongly normalising*, with the variations corresponding to different optimisations, some of them with good properties such as confluence.

1 Introduction

The sequent calculus **G4ip** (as it is called in [TS00]) for intuitionistic propositional logic was independently developed in [Hud89, Hud92] and [Dyc92]; see also [LSS91]; it has the strong property of being *depth-bounded*, in that proofs are of bounded depth and thus (for root-first proof search) no loop-checking is required. This contrasts with other calculi for this logic such as Kleene's **G3ip**, where proofs can be of unbounded depth. Its essential ingredients appeared already in 1952 work of Vorob'ev, published in detail in [Vor70].

Its completeness can be shown by various means, either indirectly, using the completeness of another calculus and a permutation argument [Dyc92], or directly, such as in [DN00] where cut-admissibility is proved without reference to the completeness of any other sequent calculus. This admissibility proof could be seen, via the Curry-Howard correspondence, as a *weakly normalising* proof-reduction system. Developing this idea, this paper presents a formulation of implicational **G4ip** with derivations represented by terms; strong (instead of weak) normalisation is proved by the use of a multi-set path ordering. Several variations, *all of them being strongly normalising*, are considered.

The merits of **G4ip** for proof-search and automated reasoning have been discussed in many papers (see [ORK05] for some recent pointers; note its use of an old name **LJT** for **G4ip**). However, a question that has been less investigated is the following: what are the proofs expressed in **G4ip** and what is their semantics ? Here we investigate operational, rather than denotational, semantics

U. Furbach and N. Shankar (Eds.): IJCAR 2006, LNAI 4130, pp. 347–361, 2006.

because it is more directly related to inductive proofs of cut-admissibility (such as in [DN00]). Further work will investigate denotational semantics, by relating these proofs and their reductions to the simply-typed λ-calculus.

This paper presents **G4ip** with a term syntax, so sequents are of the form $\Gamma \Rightarrow M : A$ where A is a type, M is a term and Γ is a consistent finite set of "declarations" of the form $x : B$, where x is a variable and B a type. Results about such sequents translate directly to results about traditional "logical sequents".

Our approach to cut-elimination using terms differs from that in [DN00], which showed (using logical sequents) first the admissibility of *Contraction* and then the admissibility of "context-splitting" (or "multiplicative") *Cut*. Given our interest in term calculi, it is appropriate to use rather a "context-sharing" (or "additive") *Cut*; admissibility of *Contraction* then follows as a special case of that of *Cut*.

To some extent, Matthes [Mat02] also investigated terms and reductions corresponding to cut-elimination in **G4ip**, with a variety of motivations, such as that of understanding better Pitts' algorithm [Pit92] for uniform interpolation. His work is similar to ours in using terms to represent derivations; but it differs conceptually from ours by considering not the use of explicit operators for the *Cut*-rule but the closure of the syntax under (implicit) substitution, as in pure λ-calculus, where the general syntax of λ-terms may be regarded as the extension of the normal λ-terms by such a closure. His reduction rules are global (using implicit substitutions) rather than local (using explicit operators); strong normalisation is shown for a subset of the reductions, but unfortunately not for all that are required.

Structure of the Paper. The paper is organised as follows. Section 2 presents the term syntax and typing rules of our calculus for **G4ip** and its auxiliary (admissible) rules. Section 3 studies proof transformations and reduction rules of the calculus. Section 4 shows a translation from the calculus to a first-order syntax and Section 5 shows that every reduction step satisfies subject reduction and decreases first-order terms associated to derivations with respect to a multi-set path ordering, thus proving strong normalisation. In Section 6 we give different variants for the reduction system introduced in Section 3, some of them being confluent. Finally we conclude and give some ideas for further work. We refer the reader to the full version [DKL06] of this paper for further details such as complete proofs.

2 Syntax

2.1 Grammar

We assume we are given an infinite set of *base types* P (known as *proposition variables* or *atomic formulae* in the logical interpretation) and an infinite set of *variables* x. We consider the following grammars for *types* (also known as *formulae*) and *terms*:

Definition 1 (Grammar of Types and Terms)

$$A, B ::= P \mid A{\supset}B$$
$$M, N ::= x \mid \lambda x.M \mid x(y, z.M) \mid x(u.v.M, z.N) \mid$$
$$\texttt{inv}(x, y.M) \mid \texttt{of}(M, x) \mid \texttt{dec}(x, y, z.M) \mid \texttt{cut}(M, x.N)$$

In this definition, the first line defines the syntax for types, the second gives the syntax for *normal* or *constructor* terms (corresponding to primitive derivations) and the third gives the extra syntax for *auxiliary* terms, which may be built up using also the "auxiliary constructors" that appear in bold teletype font, such as cut. Six of the eight term constructors use variable binding: in $\lambda x.M$, x binds in M; in $x(y, z.M)$, z binds in M; in $x(u.v.M, z.N)$, u and v bind in M and z binds in N; in $\texttt{inv}(x, y.M)$, y binds in M; in $\texttt{dec}(x, y, z.M)$, z binds in M; and in $\texttt{cut}(M, x.N)$, x binds in N. Lack of space here does not allow a formal treatment of variable binding using e.g. De Bruijn indices or nominal logic [Pit03].

Barendregt's convention is used to avoid confusion of free and bound variables, and α-convertible terms are, as usual, regarded as identical.

Certain constraints on the use of the term syntax will be evident once we present the typing rules; these constraints are captured by the following notion of *well-formed term*:

Definition 2. *A term L is* well-formed *if in any sub-term of the form*

- $x(y, z.M)$, *we have $x \neq y$, with x not free in M;*
- $x(u.v.M, z.N)$, *we have $u \neq v$, with x not free in M and not free in N;*
- $\texttt{inv}(x, y.M)$, *we have x not free in M;*
- $\texttt{of}(M, x)$, *we have x not free in M;*
- $\texttt{dec}(x, y, z.M)$, *we have $x \neq y$, with both of them not free in M.*

Definition 3 (Ordering on (multi-sets of) types). *The weight $w(A)$ of a type A is defined by: $w(P) = 1$ for any base type P and $w(A{\supset}B) = 1 + w(A) + w(B)$. Types are compared by their weight, i.e. we say that A is* smaller *than B iff $w(A) < w(B)$.*

We shall then compare multi-sets of types, equipped with the traditional multi-set ordering *[DM79, BN98], denoted $<_{mul}$, generated by the order relation on types.*

The weight is chosen to ensure that, for every rule of the logical sequent calculus **G4ip**, the multi-set of types appearing in the conclusion is greater than that of each premiss. Hence, we say that **G4ip** is *depth-bounded*. See [Dyc92] or [TS00] for details, and see the next section for the corresponding property in our version of **G4ip** with terms.

2.2 Typing

A *context* Γ is a finite mapping from variables to types. The variable x is *declared* in Γ when $\Gamma(x)$ is defined. When we write a context in the form $\Gamma, x\!:\!A$ (i.e. the extension of Γ with $x \mapsto A$), it is always implicit that x is not declared in Γ. We denote by $m(\Gamma)$ the range (considered as a multi-set) of a context Γ.

A *sequent* consists of a context Γ, a term M and a type A; it is written $\Gamma \Rightarrow M : A$.

The next definition adds term notation to the rules for implication of **G4ip**; another view is that it shows how the untyped normal terms of the above grammar may be typed.

Definition 4 (Typing Rules for Normal Terms)

$$\frac{}{\Gamma, x:A \Rightarrow x:A} Ax \qquad \frac{\Gamma, x:A \Rightarrow M:B}{\Gamma \Rightarrow \lambda x.M : A{\supset}B} R{\supset}$$

$$\frac{\Gamma, y:A, z:B \Rightarrow M:E}{\Gamma, x:A{\supset}B, y:A \Rightarrow x(y, z.M):E} L0{\supset}$$

$$\frac{\Gamma, u:C, v:D{\supset}B \Rightarrow M:D \qquad \Gamma, z:B \Rightarrow N:E}{\Gamma, x:(C{\supset}D){\supset}B \Rightarrow x(u.v.M, z.N):E} L{\supset}{\supset}$$

These rules only construct well-formed terms; e.g. the notation $\Gamma, x:A{\supset}B, y:A$ in the conclusion of $L0{\supset}$ forces $x \neq y$ and x to be not already declared in Γ (hence not free in M).

These rules are the extensions with terms of the logical rules of **G4ip** in [TS00] (note a slight difference of the $L{\supset}{\supset}$ rule from that of [Dyc92]), with the variation that both in Ax and in $L0{\supset}$ the type A need not be atomic. In the rules $R{\supset}$, $L0{\supset}$ and $L{\supset}{\supset}$ the types $A{\supset}B$, $A{\supset}B$ and $(C{\supset}D){\supset}B$ respectively are *principal*; in $L0{\supset}$ the type A is *auxiliary*. (This use of "auxiliary" is not to be confused with its use in Definition 1 to describe certain kinds of term.)

Note that in every instance of a rule in Definition 4 with conclusion $\Gamma \Rightarrow M:A$, each premiss $\Gamma' \Rightarrow N:B$ is such that $m(\Gamma) \cup A >_{\mathsf{mul}} m(\Gamma') \cup B$, where $\cup$ denotes the union of multi-sets. As a consequence, given Γ and A, there are finitely many derivations concluding, for some (normal) term M, the sequent $\Gamma \Rightarrow M:A$.

Definition 5 (Typing Rules for Auxiliary Terms)

$$\frac{\Gamma, y:C{\supset}D \Rightarrow M:E}{\Gamma, x:D \Rightarrow \mathsf{inv}(x, y.M):E} Inv \qquad \frac{\Gamma \Rightarrow M:A{\supset}B}{\Gamma, x:A \Rightarrow \mathsf{of}(M, x):B} Of$$

$$\frac{\Gamma, z:(C{\supset}D){\supset}B \Rightarrow M:A}{\Gamma, x:C, y:D{\supset}B \Rightarrow \mathsf{dec}(x, y, z.M):A} Dec \qquad \frac{\Gamma \Rightarrow M:A \quad x:A, \Gamma \Rightarrow N:B}{\Gamma \Rightarrow \mathsf{cut}(M, x.N):B} Cut$$

These rules only construct well-formed terms; e.g. the notation $\Gamma, x:A$ in the conclusion of Inv forces x to be not declared in Γ and hence not free in M.

In the *Cut*-rule, we say that A is the *cut-type*. *Derivations* are built as usual from the rules (Definitions 4 and 5). A derivation is *normal* if it uses only the primitive rules, i.e. those of Definition 4. The *height* of a derivation is just its height as a tree; so a tree with one node has height 0.

We will occasionally find it necessary to rename free variables. The *renaming* by the variable y of all the free occurrences of x in M, written $\{y/x\}M$, is defined whenever y and x are distinct variables, M is a well-formed term and y is not free in M. This is an implicit substitution rather than explicit (i.e. a meta-notation rather than a term constructor). Renaming is sound with respect to typing, as shown by the first of the two following results of admissibility, in the standard sense [TS00].

Lemma 1. *The following rules are admissible both in the system of normal derivations and in the full system with auxiliary terms, with the proviso that $y \neq x$ in the* (Ren) *rule. (We use dashed lines and parenthesize the names of the rules to emphasise their admissibility in these systems.)*

$$\frac{\Gamma, x\!:\!B \Rightarrow M\!:\!A}{\Gamma, y\!:\!B \Rightarrow \{y/x\}M\!:\!A} \ (Ren) \qquad \frac{\Gamma \Rightarrow M\!:\!A}{\Gamma, y\!:\!B \Rightarrow M\!:\!A} \ (W)$$

Proof. Routine induction on the height of the derivation of the premiss. Some swapping of bound variable names may be necessary. Note that the notation $\Gamma, y\!:\!B$ forces y to be not declared in Γ and hence not free in M.   □

Remark 1. Note that for each proved sequent $\Gamma \Rightarrow M\!:\!A$ there is a unique derivation tree (up to renaming, in sub-derivations, of the variables bound in M), which can be reconstructed using the structure of the term M that *represents* the proof (hence the notion of *proof-term*).

3   Proof Transformations and Reduction Rules

The starting point of this section is the admissibility in the   logical sequent calculus **G4ip** of the following inference rules (i.e. the logical counter-part of the typing rules for auxiliary terms given in Definition 5):

$$\frac{\Gamma, C \supset D \Rightarrow E}{\Gamma, D \Rightarrow E} \ Inv \qquad\qquad \frac{\Gamma \Rightarrow A \supset B}{\Gamma, A \Rightarrow B} \ Of$$

$$\frac{\Gamma, (C \supset D) \supset B \Rightarrow A}{\Gamma, C, D \supset B \Rightarrow A} \ Dec \qquad \frac{\Gamma \Rightarrow A \qquad A, \Gamma \Rightarrow B}{\Gamma \Rightarrow B} \ Cut$$

The admissibility of *Inv* and *Of* in **G4ip** can be proved, independently, by induction on the heights of the derivations of the premisses. For the admissibility of *Dec* and *Cut* we can use a simultaneous induction, the admissibility of one rule being recursively used for the admissibility of the other. The measure now uses the multi-set of types appearing in the unique premiss for *Dec* and in the second premiss for *Cut*. In other words, the induction can be done on $\{\!\{\Gamma, (C \supset D) \supset B, A\}\!\}$ for *Dec* and on $\{\!\{\Gamma, A, B\}\!\}$ for *Cut*.

We do not include here the detail of these proofs of admissibility, because the property turns out to be a consequence (Corollary 2) of our strong normalisation result for our calculus with terms.

Indeed, the admissibility property means, in our framework with terms, that a term M with auxiliary constructors inv, of, dec or cut can be transformed into another term M' with the same type in the same context that does not use these constructors.

This motivates the notion of *term-irrelevant admissibility* in a system with terms:

Definition 6. *A rule R is* term-irrelevantly admissible *in system S if, given an instance with conclusion $\Gamma \Rightarrow M:A$ and derivations in system S of its premiss(es), there exists a derivation in S of $\Gamma \Rightarrow M':A$ for some term M'.*

Remark that this notion corresponds to the standard notion of admissibility when term annotations are erased.

Moreover, the inductive arguments of admissibility above can be seen as *weakly normalising* term reduction systems that specify how to eliminate the auxiliary constructors inv, of, dec and cut.

The reduction systems, given hereafter, must satisfy the following properties:

1. A term containing an auxiliary constructor is reducible by these systems.
2. They satisfy the Subject Reduction property, i.e. preservation of typing.
3. They satisfy some termination property.

Concerning point 3, the weak normalisation property of these systems suffices to prove the results of admissibility, and the proofs suggested above can be expressed as a terminating innermost strategy for these reduction systems. Nevertheless, we give in this paper reduction systems that are in fact *strongly normalising*. While this might be inferred for the orthogonal systems that we present in Section 6 (since weak innermost normalisation is equivalent to strong normalisation for orthogonal first-order systems [O'D77]), the result is certainly not so straightforward for the non-orthogonal ones. However, the measures for induction mentioned above can be taken as part of a *Multi-Set Path Ordering* [KL80, BN98] in order to conclude strong normalisation as well (see Section 4).

We give in Tables 1, 2 and 3 the reduction systems that eliminate the auxiliary constructors of, inv and dec. All these rules that we call system oid will be part of the different variants that we are going to introduce.

In order to reduce the cuts we now suggest a general system called cegs for cut-elimination in Tables 4 and 5 (variants are presented in Section 6). The whole system is called gs and contains the reduction rules in cegs (Tables 4 and 5) plus the ones in oid (Tables 1, 2 and 3).

Summing up :

Name of the System	Reduction Rules
oid	Tables 1, 2 and 3
cegs	Tables 4, 5
gs	oid $\cup$ cegs

Table 1. Reduction Rules for of-terms

$\mathbf{of}(y,x)$	$\longrightarrow_{o1}$	$y(x,z.z)$
$\mathbf{of}(\lambda y.M,x)$	$\longrightarrow_{o2}$	$\{x/y\}M$
$\mathbf{of}(y(z,w.N),x)$	$\longrightarrow_{o3}$	$y(z,w.\mathbf{of}(N,x))$
$\mathbf{of}(y(u.v.M,w.N),x)$	$\longrightarrow_{o4}$	$y(u.v.M,w.\mathbf{of}(N,x))$

Table 2. Reduction Rules for inv-terms

$\mathbf{inv}(x,y.z)$	$\longrightarrow_{i_1}$	z
$\mathbf{inv}(x,y.y)$	$\longrightarrow_{i_2}$	$\lambda z.x$
$\mathbf{inv}(x,y.\lambda z.M)$	$\longrightarrow_{i_3}$	$\lambda z.\mathbf{inv}(x,y.M)$
$\mathbf{inv}(x,y.y(w,z.N))$	$\longrightarrow_{i_4}$	$\{x/z\}N$
$\mathbf{inv}(x,y.y(u.v.M,z.N))$	$\longrightarrow_{i_5}$	$\{x/z\}N$
$\mathbf{inv}(x,y.w(y,z.N))$	$\longrightarrow_{i_6}$	$w(u.v.x,z.\mathbf{inv}(x,y.N))$
$\mathbf{inv}(x,y.y'(w,z.N))$	$\longrightarrow_{i_7}$	$y'(w,z.\mathbf{inv}(x,y.N))$
$\mathbf{inv}(x,y.y'(u.v.M,z.N))$	$\longrightarrow_{i_8}$	$y'(u.v.\mathbf{inv}(x,y.M),z.\mathbf{inv}(x,y.N))$

Table 3. Reduction Rules for dec-terms

$\mathbf{dec}(x,y,z.w)$	$\longrightarrow_{d_1}$	w
$\mathbf{dec}(x,y,z.z)$	$\longrightarrow_{d_2}$	$\lambda v.v(x,w.y(w,u.u))$
$\mathbf{dec}(x,y,z.\lambda w.M)$	$\longrightarrow_{d_3}$	$\lambda w.\mathbf{dec}(x,y,z.M)$
$\mathbf{dec}(x,y,z.w(u.v.M,w'.N))$	$\longrightarrow_{d_4}$	$w(u.v.\mathbf{dec}(x,y,z.M),w'.\mathbf{dec}(x,y,z.N))$
$\mathbf{dec}(x,y,z.w(y',z'.M))$	$\longrightarrow_{d_5}$	$w(y',z'.\mathbf{dec}(x,y,z.M))$
$\mathbf{dec}(x,y,z.z(y',z'.M))$	$\longrightarrow_{d_6}$	$y'(x,z''.y(z'',z'.\mathbf{inv}(z'',y'.M)))$
$\mathbf{dec}(x,y,z.x'(z,z'.M))$	$\longrightarrow_{d_7}$	$x(u.v.v(x,z''.y(z'',w.w)),z'.\mathbf{dec}(x,y,z.M))$
$\mathbf{dec}(x,y,z.z(u.v.M,z'.N))$	$\longrightarrow_{d_8}$	$\mathbf{cut}(\{x/u\}\{y/v\}M,y'.y(y',z'.N))$

Table 4. Cut Elimination Rules cegs (Kind_1 and Kind_2)

Kind_1		
$\mathbf{cut}(M,x.x)$	$\longrightarrow_{c1}$	M
$\mathbf{cut}(M,x.y)$	$\longrightarrow_{c2}$	y
$\mathbf{cut}(M,x.\lambda y.N)$	$\longrightarrow_{c3}$	$\lambda y.\mathbf{cut}(M,x.N)$
$\mathbf{cut}(M,x.y(z,w.N))$	$\longrightarrow_{c4}$	$y(z,w.\mathbf{cut}(\mathbf{inv}(w,y.M),x.N))$
$\mathbf{cut}(M,x.y(u.v.N',w.N))$	$\longrightarrow_{c5}$	$y(u.v.P,w.\mathbf{cut}(\mathbf{inv}(w,y.M),x.N))$
		where $P=\mathbf{cut}(\mathbf{dec}(u,v,y.M),x.N')$
$\mathbf{cut}(\lambda z.M,x.y(x,w.N))$	$\longrightarrow_{c6}$	$y(u.v.P,w.\mathbf{cut}(\mathbf{inv}(w,y.\lambda z.M),x.N))$
		where $P=\mathbf{cut}(u,z.\mathbf{dec}(u,v,y.M))$
$\mathbf{cut}(z,x.y(x,w.N))$	$\longrightarrow_{c7}$	$y(z,w.\mathbf{cut}(z,x.N))$
Kind_2		
$\mathbf{cut}(y(z,w.M),x.N)$	$\longrightarrow_{c8}$	$y(z,w.\mathbf{cut}(M,x.\mathbf{inv}(w,y.N)))$
$\mathbf{cut}(y(u.v.M',w.M),x.N)$	$\longrightarrow_{c9}$	$y(u.v.M',w.\mathbf{cut}(M,x.\mathbf{inv}(w,y.N)))$

As in most cut-elimination systems, the cut-reduction rules can be split into three kinds ($\text{Kind}_1, \text{Kind}_2, \text{Kind}_3$), according to whether they push cuts to the right, to the left, or they break a cut into cuts on smaller types.

Table 5. Cut Elimination Rules cegs (Kind$_3$)

Kind$_3$
$\text{cut}(M, x.x(z, w.N))$ $\longrightarrow_A$ $\text{cut}(\text{cut}(z, y.\text{of}(M, y)), w.N)$
$\text{cut}(M, x.x(u.v.N', w.N))$ $\longrightarrow_B$ $\text{cut}(P, w.N)$
where $P = \text{cut}(\lambda u.\text{cut}(\lambda z.\text{inv}(z, y.\text{of}(M, y)), v.N'), y.\text{of}(M, y))$

Here, owing to the particular inference rules of **G4ip** and the well-formedness constraints they impose on terms, the first two kinds must use the auxiliary constructs `inv` and `dec`, rather than just propagate the cuts.

For the third kind of cut-reduction rules, we usually expect both sub-proofs of the cut to introduce the cut-type (on the right and on the left, respectively). In particular, this requires the first argument of the cut-constructor to be a *value*, i.e. a variable or an abstraction, with a functional type, i.e. an implication $A \supset B$. However, just as *any* λ-term can be turned into a value by an η-expansion, here *any* term can be turned into a value by the use of the `of` constructor, with the following rule, which we also call η:

$$M \longrightarrow_\eta \lambda x.\text{of}(M, x) \qquad \text{if } x \notin FV(M)$$

Note that in both cases this is only sound with respect to typing if the type of the original term is an implication.

Lemma 2. *All rules of system* gs *are such that well-formed terms reduce to well-formed terms.*

Proof. Routine.

4   A First-Order Syntax for Typed G4ip-Terms

Termination of the above rewrite systems on typed terms will be proved by the decrease of a measure associated to typing derivations. The latter are mapped to a first-order syntax with the following infinite signature:

$$\Sigma = \{\star/0, \mathsf{I}/1, \mathsf{K}/2, \mathsf{J}/1\} \cup \{\mathsf{D}^m/1, \mathsf{C}^m/2 \mid m \text{ is a multiset of types}\}$$

where the notation f/n is used to say that the symbol f has arity n, and the symbols have the following precedence relation:

$$\mathsf{C}^n \succ \mathsf{D}^n \succ \cdots \succ \cdots \succ \mathsf{C}^m \succ \mathsf{D}^m \succ \mathsf{J} \succ \mathsf{K} \succ \mathsf{I} \succ \star \qquad \text{if } n >_{\mathsf{mul}} m$$

The precedence relation on symbols provides a *Multi-set Path Ordering* $\gg_{mpo}$ (mpo) on first-order terms [KL80, BN98].

Remark 2.

1. The order on types (Def. 3) is well-founded, so $>_{\mathsf{mul}}$ is well-founded [DM79].
2. The order $>_{\mathsf{mul}}$ is well-founded, so $\succ$ is also well-founded.
3. The order $\succ$ is well-founded, so the Multi-Set Path Ordering $\gg_{mpo}$ is also well-founded.

Derivations are mapped to this first-order syntax. In particular, since each sequent $\Gamma \Rightarrow M:A$ has at most one derivation, we write $\overline{\Gamma \Rightarrow M:A}$ for such a translation, and even $\overline{M}$ when the context and type are clear from the text, as in the right-hand sides of the following definition.

$$
\begin{array}{ll}
\overline{\Gamma, x:A \Rightarrow x:A} & = \star \\
\overline{\Gamma \Rightarrow \lambda x.M:A{\supset}B} & = \mathsf{I}(\overline{M}) \\
\overline{\Gamma, x:A{\supset}B, y:A \Rightarrow x(y,z.M):E} & = \mathsf{I}(\overline{M}) \\
\overline{\Gamma, x:(C{\supset}D){\supset}B \Rightarrow x(u.v.M, z.N):E} & = \mathsf{K}(\overline{M}, \overline{N}) \\
\overline{\Gamma, x:D \Rightarrow \mathtt{inv}(x, y.M):E} & - \mathsf{J}(\overline{M}) \\
\overline{\Gamma, x:A \Rightarrow \mathtt{of}(M,x):B} & = \mathsf{J}(\overline{M}) \\
\overline{\Gamma, x:C, y:D{\supset}B \Rightarrow \mathtt{dec}(x,y,z.M):A} & = \mathsf{D}^k(\overline{\Gamma, z:(C{\supset}D){\supset}B \Rightarrow M:A}) \\
& \qquad \text{where } k = \{\!\!\{\Gamma, (C{\supset}D){\supset}B, A\}\!\!\} \\
\overline{\Gamma \Rightarrow \mathtt{cut}(M, x.N):B} & = \mathsf{C}^k(\overline{\Gamma \Rightarrow M:A}, x:A, \overline{\Gamma \Rightarrow N:B}) \\
& \qquad \text{where } k = \{\!\!\{\Gamma, A, B\}\!\!\}
\end{array}
$$

Observe that $\overline{M} = \overline{\{x/y\}M}$ for any renaming of M.

5 Subject Reduction and Strong Normalisation

In this section we show two fundamental properties of system **gs**. The first one is subject reduction and it guarantees that types are preserved by the reduction system. The second one is strong normalisation and it guarantees that there is no infinite reduction sequence starting from a typed term. Strong normalisation is shown by a decreasing measure given by the Multi-Set Path Ordering of Section 4.

Theorem 1. *If* $\Gamma \Rightarrow L:E$ *and* $L \longrightarrow_{\mathsf{gs}} L'$, *then* $\Gamma \Rightarrow L':E$ *and* $\overline{L} \gg_{mpo} \overline{L'}$.

Proof. By induction on the derivation of $\Gamma \Rightarrow L:E$. For brevity we show only the most important case of rule B, which reduces $\mathtt{cut}(M, x.x(u.v.N, z.N'))$ to $\mathtt{cut}(\mathtt{cut}(\lambda u.\mathtt{cut}(\lambda y'.\mathtt{inv}(y', y.\mathtt{of}(M,y)), v.N), y.\mathtt{of}(M,y)), z.N')$.

The derivation

$$
\cfrac{
\cfrac{\cdots}{\Gamma \Rightarrow M:(C{\supset}D){\supset}B}
\quad
\cfrac{
\cfrac{\cdots}{u:C, v:D{\supset}B, \Gamma \Rightarrow N:D}
\quad
\cfrac{\cdots}{z:B, \Gamma \Rightarrow N':E}
}{x:(C{\supset}D){\supset}B, \Gamma \Rightarrow x(u.v.N, z.N'):E} \; L{\supset}
}{\Gamma \Rightarrow \mathtt{cut}(M, x.x(u.v.N, z.N')):E} \; Cut
$$

rewrites to

$$
\cfrac{
\cfrac{
\cfrac{\mathcal{D}}{\Gamma \Rightarrow M':C{\supset}D}
\quad
\cfrac{
\cfrac{\cdots}{\Gamma \Rightarrow M:(C{\supset}D){\supset}B}
}{\Gamma, y:C{\supset}D \Rightarrow \mathtt{of}(M,y):B} \; Of
}{\Gamma \Rightarrow \mathtt{cut}(M', y.\mathtt{of}(M,y)):B} \; Cut
\quad
\cfrac{\cdots}{z:B, \Gamma \Rightarrow N':E}
}{\Gamma \Rightarrow \mathtt{cut}(\mathtt{cut}(M', y.\mathtt{of}(M,y)), z.N'):E} \; Cut
$$

where $M' = \lambda u.\mathsf{cut}(\lambda y'.\mathsf{inv}(y', y.\mathsf{of}(M,y)), v.N)$ and $\mathcal{D}$ is the following derivation:

$$
\cfrac{
  \cfrac{
    \cfrac{
      \cfrac{
        \cfrac{
          \cfrac{
            \cdots
          }{\Gamma \Rightarrow M:(C{\supset}D){\supset}B}
        }{\Gamma, y:C{\supset}D \Rightarrow \mathsf{of}(M,y):B} \; Of
      }{\Gamma, u:C, y:C{\supset}D \Rightarrow \mathsf{of}(M,y):B} \; (W)
    }{\Gamma, u:C, y':D \Rightarrow \mathsf{inv}(y', y.\mathsf{of}(M,y)):B} \; Inv
  }{\Gamma, u:C \Rightarrow \lambda y'.\mathsf{inv}(y', y.\mathsf{of}(M,y)):D{\supset}B} \; R{\supset}
  \qquad
  \cfrac{\cdots}{u:C, v:D{\supset}B, \Gamma \Rightarrow N:D}
}{
  \cfrac{
    \Gamma, u:C \Rightarrow \mathsf{cut}(\lambda y'.\mathsf{inv}(y', y.\mathsf{of}(M,y)), v.N):D
  }{\Gamma \Rightarrow \lambda u.\mathsf{cut}(\lambda y'.\mathsf{inv}(y', y.\mathsf{of}(M,y)), v.N):C{\supset}D} \; R{\supset}
} \; Cut
$$

Let $k = \{(C{\supset}D){\supset}B, \Gamma, E\}$ and $j = \{B, \Gamma, E\}$ and $i = \{\Gamma, C{\supset}D, B\}$ and $h = \{C, D{\supset}B, \Gamma, D\}$. Since $k >_{\mathsf{mul}} j, i, h$, we have $\mathsf{C}^k \succ \mathsf{I}, \mathsf{J}, \mathsf{C}^j, \mathsf{C}^i, \mathsf{C}^h$ and

$$
\overline{L} = \mathsf{C}^k(\overline{M}, \mathsf{K}(\overline{N}, \overline{N'})) \gg_{mpo} \mathsf{C}^j(\mathsf{C}^i(\mathsf{I}(\mathsf{C}^h(\mathsf{I}(\mathsf{J}(\mathsf{J}(\overline{M})))), \overline{N})), \mathsf{J}(\overline{M})), \overline{N'}) = \overline{L'}
$$

Full details can be found in [DKL06]. $\qquad\qquad\qquad\qquad\qquad\qquad\qquad\qquad$ $\square$

Corollary 1 (Strong Normalisation). *System* gs *is strongly normalising on typed terms.*

Proof. This is a consequence of Theorem 1 and Remark 2. $\qquad\qquad\qquad$ $\square$

Corollary 2. *Rules* Inv, Of, Dec, *and* Cut *are term-irrelevantly admissible in the system of Definition 4.*

Proof. Every term with an auxiliary constructor is reducible by system gs. $\square$

6   Variants of Reduction Systems

We investigate in this section some variants of the cut-elimination system of Section 3.

We discuss in Section 6.1 the rules of Kind$_3$, noticing that the of-constructor is only introduced by the reductions of gs in order to include η-conversion in the system. We present two variations without η-conversion, called system rs and system ars, that no longer use the of-constructor.

Without η-conversion, the only critical pairs of those variations are between the rules of Kind$_1$ and those of Kind$_2$, so in Section 6.2, which only concerns rules of Kind$_1$ and Kind$_2$, we present two ways of removing those critical pairs, i.e. of making systems rs and ars orthogonal.

6.1   Avoiding the of-Constructor

In this section we remove η-expansion from the reduction system so that the of-constructor is no more used by the cut elimination rules. We obtain two variants, depending on whether we want variables to behave like their η-expansions or we want the elimination of a cut with a variable to be simpler and closer to renaming.

The rules A and B of system gs (Table 5) introduce the of-constructor to model η-expansion, turning the first argument of the cut into an abstraction.

Theorem 2. *Rule A (resp. B) can be factorised into an η-expansion followed by rule C (resp. D) below:*

$$\mathsf{cut}(\lambda y.M, x.x(z, w.N)) \longrightarrow_C \mathsf{cut}(\mathsf{cut}(z, y.M), w.N)$$
$$\mathsf{cut}(\lambda y.M, x.x(u.v.N', w.N))$$
$$\longrightarrow_D \mathsf{cut}(\mathsf{cut}(\lambda u.\mathsf{cut}(\lambda z.\mathsf{inv}(z, y.M), v.N'), y.M), w.N)$$

Proof.

Rule A:	$\mathsf{cut}(M, x.x(z, w.N))$
	$\longrightarrow_\eta \mathsf{cut}(\lambda y.\mathsf{of}(M, y), x.x(z, w.N))$
	$\longrightarrow_C \mathsf{cut}(\mathsf{cut}(z, y.\mathsf{of}(M, y)), w.N)$
Rule B:	$\mathsf{cut}(M, x.x(u.v.N', w.N))$
	$\longrightarrow_\eta \mathsf{cut}(\lambda y.\mathsf{of}(M, y), x.x(u.v.N', w.N))$
	$\longrightarrow_D \mathsf{cut}(\mathsf{cut}(\lambda u.\mathsf{cut}(\lambda z.\mathsf{inv}(z, y.\mathsf{of}(M, y)), v.N'), y.\mathsf{of}(M, y)), w.N)$

$\square$

Note that the η-expansion of an abstraction reduces, by direct elimination of the of, to the abstraction itself:

$$\lambda y.M \longrightarrow_\eta \lambda x.\mathsf{of}(\lambda y.M, x) \longrightarrow_{\mathsf{o2}} \lambda x.\{x/y\}M =_\alpha \lambda y.M \text{ with } x \notin FV(M)$$

This justifies the following theorem:

Theorem 3. *Rules C and D can be respectively derived from rules A and B using system* oid.

Proof. Similar to Theorem 2. $\square$

Similarly, direct elimination of the of-constructor is allowed by rule o1 in the case of a variable ($y \longrightarrow_\eta \lambda x.\mathsf{of}(y, x) \longrightarrow_{\mathsf{o1}} \lambda x.y(x, z.z)$ with $x \notin FV(M)$), so this suggests that two rules E and F, treating the case of a variable, can also be derived from rules A and B:

Theorem 4. *The following rules E and F can be respectively derived from A and B using system* gs:

$$\mathsf{cut}(y, x.x(z, w.N)) \longrightarrow_E y(z, w'.\mathsf{cut}(w', w.\mathsf{inv}(w', y.N)))$$
$$\mathsf{cut}(y, x.x(u.v.N', w.N)) \longrightarrow_F y(u'.v'.\mathsf{cut}(u', u.P), w'.\mathsf{cut}(w', w.\mathsf{inv}(w', y.N)))$$
$$\text{where } P = \mathsf{dec}(u', v', y.\mathsf{cut}(\lambda y''.y(u.v.y'', z.z), v.N'))$$

Proof. Similar to Theorem 2. $\square$

Now, *by construction*, rules E and F make variables have the same functional behaviour as their η-expansion.

Note also that the new rules C, D, E and F (together with rules c8 and c9) can now replace any use of rules A and B, thus forming a system, called cers, that is still complete for cut-elimination and makes no use of the of-constructor. We show in Table 6 only the cut reduction rules of $Kind_3$, in which cegs and cers differ, the rules of $Kind_1$ and $Kind_2$ being the same. System cegs can thus be seen as system cers to which η-expansion has been integrated by the use of the auxiliary constructor of.

Table 6. Cut Elimination Rules in System cers ($Kind_3$)

$Kind_3$
$\mathsf{cut}(\lambda y.M, x.x(z, w.N)) \quad\longrightarrow_C \mathsf{cut}(\mathsf{cut}(z, y.M), w.N)$
$\mathsf{cut}(\lambda y.M, x.x(u.v.N', w.N)) \!\longrightarrow_D \mathsf{cut}(\mathsf{cut}(\lambda u.\mathsf{cut}(\lambda z.\mathsf{inv}(z, y.M), v.N'), y.M), w.N)$
$\mathsf{cut}(y, x.x(z, w.N)) \quad\longrightarrow_E y(z, w'.\mathsf{cut}(w', w.\mathsf{inv}(w', y.N)))$
$\mathsf{cut}(y, x.x(u.v.N', w.N)) \quad\longrightarrow_F y(u'.v'.\mathsf{cut}(u', u.P), w'.\mathsf{cut}(w', w.\mathsf{inv}(w', y.N)))$
$\qquad\qquad\text{where } P = \mathsf{dec}(u', v', y.\mathsf{cut}(\lambda y''.y(u.v.y'', z.z), v.N'))$

The behaviour of functionals is interesting in **G4ip**, because it is a depth-bounded calculus: for instance, among all Church's numerals only 0 and 1 can be represented in **G4ip**. So when reducing the term that represents (using cuts) "$1+1$", we should expect some semantical anomaly in the reductions (which is quite similar to the one reported by Vestergaard in [Ves99]). Such an anomaly is to be found in rules B and D, and for abstractions we have no alternative choice. However in system rs we have made the choice of making variables have the same functional behaviour as their η-expansions, hence rule F inherits the anomaly. But instead we might rather follow the intuition that cutting a variable with a another variable is almost renaming, and replace rule F with a new rule G, thus forming system cears presented in Table 7 (again we only show rules of $Kind_3$, but rules of $Kind_1$ and $Kind_2$ are the same as in cegs or cers). This new rule is simpler and more natural than rule F; however the reducts are semantically different and thus the choice of rule G breaks the property that a variable and its η-expansion have the same behaviour.

Table 7. Cut Elimination Rules in System cears ($Kind_3$)

$Kind_3$
$\mathsf{cut}(\lambda y.M, x.x(z, w.N)) \quad\longrightarrow_C \mathsf{cut}(\mathsf{cut}(z, y.M), w.N)$
$\mathsf{cut}(\lambda y.M, x.x(u.v.N', w.N)) \!\longrightarrow_D \mathsf{cut}(\mathsf{cut}(\lambda u.\mathsf{cut}(\lambda z.\mathsf{inv}(z, y.M), v.N'), y.M), w.N)$
$\mathsf{cut}(y, x.x(z, w.N)) \quad\longrightarrow_E y(z, w'.\mathsf{cut}(w', w.\mathsf{inv}(w', y.N)))$
$\mathsf{cut}(y, x.x(u.v.N', w.N)) \quad\longrightarrow_G y(u'.v'.\mathsf{cut}(u', u.P'), w'.\mathsf{cut}(w', w.\mathsf{inv}(w', y.N)))$
$\qquad\qquad\qquad\text{where } P' = \mathsf{cut}(v', v.\mathsf{dec}(u', v', y.N'))$

Since all the rules of system rs are derived from system gs, it is clear that the former inherits from the latter the Subject Reduction property as well as the Strong Normalisation of typed terms. However, for system ars, those properties are not inherited, even if it is easy to check that rule G satisfies the Subject

Reduction property and decreases with respect to the multi-set path ordering in Section 4.

The systems presented so far in this paper can be summarised in the following table:

of, inv and dec	cut =	(Kind$_1$ + Kind$_2$) +	Kind$_3$	Whole system
oid	cegs =	Table 4	+ Table 5	gs
oid	cers =	Table 4	+ Table 6	rs
oid	cears =	Table 4	+ Table 7	ars

6.2   Orthogonal Systems

In this section we suggest two ways of restricting the rules of Kind$_1$ and Kind$_2$ to make systems rs and ars orthogonal, and hence confluent.

In the restricted systems gs and ars there are overlaps between the right and left propagation sub-systems, i.e. there is a critical pair between any rule in $\{c1, c2, c3, c4, c5\}$ and any rule in $\{c8, c9\}$. This is shown in Table 8, where column headers represent the different cases concerning the first premiss of the cut, while row headers represent the different cases for the second one (marking inside parentheses the status of the cut-type).

Table 8. Overlaps of reduction rules

	Axiom	$R\supset$	$L0\supset$	$L\supset\supset$
Axiom (Principal)	c1	c1	c1, c8	c1, c9
Axiom (Non-Principal)	c2	c2	c2, c8	c2, c9
$R\supset$	c3	c3	c3, c8	c3, c9
$L0\supset$ (Non-Principal, Non-Auxiliary)	c4	c4	c4, c8	c4, c9
$L\supset\supset$ (Non-Principal)	c5	c5	c5, c8	c5, c9
$L0\supset$ (Non-Principal, Auxiliary)	c7	c6	c8	c9
$L0\supset$ (Principal)	E	C	c8	c9
$L\supset\supset$ (Principal)	F (rs) or G (ars)	D	c8	c9

The overlaps pointed out in Table 8 are well-known in sequent calculus, and correspond to the choice of whether to push a cut into the proof of its left premiss or into the proof of its right premiss. The former corresponds to a *call-by-value* strategy and the latter corresponds to a *call-by-name* strategy.

Since the overlaps only concerns cut-reduction rules of Kind$_1$ and Kind$_2$, we discuss in the following possible ways to make them non-overlapping.

Call-By-Name. One way to make the system orthogonal is to give preference to rules c1-c2-c3-c4-c5 over rules c8-c9, thus restricted to the case when N is an x-covalue Q, i.e. is of the form $x(y, w.N)$ or $x(u.v.M, w.N)$.

Note that in order to reduce a term like $\mathbf{cut}(M, x.y(x, w.N))$, there is no choice other than left-propagation (rules c8 and c9) until a similar redex is found in which M is a value, and then only rules c6 or c7 can be applied.

Call-By-Value. Alternatively, preference might be given to rules c8 and c9, which we can formalise as restricting rules c1-c2-c3-c4-c5 to the case when M is a value V (variable or abstraction).

The choice of call-by-value is more natural than that of call-by-name because the two rules of right-propagation c6 and c7 only apply to cuts whose first argument is a value. This suggests that **G4ip** has an inherent *call-by-value* flavour, echoing the idea that it is somehow based on the call-by-value sequent calculus **LJQ**. Indeed, completeness of **LJQ** gives a short proof of the completeness of **G4ip** [DL06].

We finish this section by stating the following property of cbn and cbv.

Theorem 5. *Reduction systems* cbn *and* cbv *are confluent.*

Proof. Systems cbn and cbv can be seen as particular *orthogonal CRS*, so they enjoy confluence (see [vOvR94] for details). □

7   Conclusion

This paper defines various term calculi for the depth-bounded intuitionistic sequent calculus of Hudelmaier. Using standard techniques of rewriting, we prove subject-reduction and strong normalisation for all of them, so *Cut*-admissibility turns out to be a corollary. The cbn and cbv systems presented in this paper are also orthogonal, which guarantees confluence (and uniqueness of normal forms).

Some relations between **G4ip** and other calculi for intuitionistic logic are studied in [DL06]. Also, from our term calculi for **G4ip**, which use explicit operators, we could extract term calculi with *implicit* operators (as in λ-calculus). This would bring our calculus closer to that of Matthes [Mat02], and with a strong normalising cut-elimination procedure. As mentioned in the introduction, defining a denotational semantics for our calculi as well as investigating the connexions with the simply-typed λ-calculus would reveal more properties of the proofs in **G4ip**.

References

[BN98]   F. Baader and T. Nipkow. *Term Rewriting and All That.* Cambridge University Press, 1998.

[DKL06]   R. Dyckhoff, D. Kesner, and S. Lengrand. Strong cut-elimination systems for Hudelmaier's depth-bounded sequent calculus for implicational logic, 2006. Full version. Available at http://www.pps.jussieu.fr/~lengrand/Work/Papers.html.

[DL06]   R. Dyckhoff and S. Lengrand. **LJQ**, a strongly focused calculus for intuitionistic logic. In A. Beckmann, U. Berger, B. Loewe, and J. V. Tucker, editors, *Proc. of the 2nd Conf. on Computability in Europe (CiE'06)*, volume 3988 of *LNCS*. Springer-Verlag, July 2006.

[DM79]   N. Dershowitz and Z. Manna. Proving termination with multiset orderings. *Communications of the ACM*, 22(8):465–476, 1979.

[DN00]   R. Dyckhoff and S. Negri. Admissibility of structural rules for contraction-free systems of intuitionistic logic. *The Journal of Symbolic Logic*, 65(4):1499–1518, 2000.

[Dyc92]   R. Dyckhoff. Contraction-free sequent calculi for intuitionistic logic. *The Journal of Symbolic Logic*, 57(3):795–807, 1992.

[Hud89]   J. Hudelmaier. *Bounds for Cut Elimination in Intuitionistic Logic*. PhD thesis, Universität Tübingen, 1989.

[Hud92]   J. Hudelmaier. Bounds on cut-elimination in intuitionistic propositional logic. *Archive for Mathematical Logic*, 31:331–354, 1992.

[KL80]   S. Kamin and J.-J. Lévy. Attempts for generalizing the recursive path orderings. Handwritten paper, University of Illinois, 1980.

[LSS91]   P. Lincoln, A. Scedrov, and N. Shankar. Linearizing intuitionistic implication. In *Proc. of the Sixth Annual IEEE Symposium on Logic in Computer Science*, pages 51–62, Amsterdam, The Netherlands, 1991.

[Mat02]   R. Matthes. Contraction-aware λ-calculus, 2002. Seminar at Oberwolfach.

[O'D77]   M. J. O'Donnell. *Computing in Systems Described by Equations*, volume 58 of *LNCS*. Springer-Verlag, 1977.

[ORK05]   J. Otten, T. Raths, and C. Kreitz. The ILTP Library: Benchmarking automated theorem provers for intuitionistic logic. In B. Beckert, editor, *International Conference TABLEAUX-2005*, volume 3702 of *LNAI*, pages 333–337. Springer Verlag, 2005.

[Pit92]   A. M. Pitts. On an interpretation of second order quantification in first-order intuitionistic propositional logic. *Journal of Symbolic Logic*, 57:33–52, 1992.

[Pit03]   A. M. Pitts. Nominal logic, a first order theory of names and binding. *Information and Computation*, 186:165–193, 2003.

[TS00]   A. S. Troelstra and H. Schwichtenberg. *Basic Proof Theory*. Cambridge University Press, 2000.

[Ves99]   R. Vestergaard. Revisiting Kreisel: A computational anomaly in the Troelstra-Schwichtenberg **g3i** system, March 1999. Available at http://www.cee.hw.ac.uk/~jrvest/.

[Vor70]   N. N. Vorob'ev. A new algorithm for derivability in the constructive propositional calculus. *American Mathematical Society Translations*, 94(2):37–71, 1970.

[vOvR94]   V. van Oostrom and F. van Raamsdonk. Weak orthogonality implies confluence: the higher-order case. In A. Nerode and Y. Matiyasevich, editors, *Proc. of the 3rd Int. Symp. on Logical Foundations of Computer Science*, volume 813 of *LNCS*, pages 379–392. Springer-Verlag, July 1994.

Eliminating Redundancy in Higher-Order Unification: A Lightweight Approach

Brigitte Pientka

School of Computer Science,
McGill University
Montreal, Canada

Abstract. In this paper, we discuss a lightweight approach to eliminate the overhead due to implicit type arguments during higher-order unification of dependently-typed terms. First, we show that some implicit type information is uniquely determined, and can therefore be safely skipped during higher-order unification. Second, we discuss its impact in practice during type reconstruction and during proof search within the logical framework Twelf. Our experimental results show that implicit type arguments are numerous and large in size, but their impact on run-time is between 10% and 20%. On the other hand optimizations such as eliminating the occurs check are shown to be crucial to achieve significant performance improvements.

1 Introduction

In recent years, logical frameworks which support formalizing language specifications together with their meta-theory have been pervasively used in small and large-scale applications, from certifying code [1] to advocating a general infrastructure for formalizing language meta-theory and semantics [2]. In particular, the logical framework LF [6], based on the dependently typed lambda-calculus, and light-weight variants of it like LF_i [11] have played a major role in these applications. While the acceptance of logical framework technology has grown and they have matured, one of the most criticized points is concerned with the run-time performance. To address this problem, we concentrate in this paper on one of the most common operations in type reconstruction and proof search: higher-order unification. In prior work, we have proposed to optimize higher-order pattern unification by eliminating unnecessary occurs checks during proof search [16]. This optimization leads to significant performance improvements in many example applications. In this work, we consider a different optimization where we skip some redundant implicit type arguments during unification. Unlike our prior optimization which is restricted to proof search, skipping some redundant type arguments during unification is a general optimization and hence impacts not only the proof search performance, but also any other algorithm relying on unification such as type-reconstruction, coverage checking, termination checking etc. Our approach is light-weight in the sense that we do not translate or change our internal representation of terms and types. This has the advantage that it can be seamlessly incorporated into the current implementation of the

U. Furbach and N. Shankar (Eds.): IJCAR 2006, LNAI 4130, pp. 362–376, 2006.

Twelf system [14] and it can be easily compared to other existing optimizations. Adapting this lightweight approach is not just a matter of practical engineering convenience. A change to a different internal representation of terms impacts the foundation of LF itself and it remains unclear whether other algorithms such as mode, termination, and coverage checking would still remain correct.

Our work is motivated by Necula and Lee's [11] observation that the amount of implicit type arguments can be substantial when representing terms with a deep dependent type structure. Their main concern [11] however was in compactly representing terms in a fragment of LF called LF_i by allowing some implicit type arguments to be omitted. Reed [17] has proposed an extension of their idea to full LF. In contrast, we are interested in investigating the run-time overhead due to implicit type arguments during higher-order unification and its impact on type reconstruction and proof search in logical frameworks. In an early empirical study, Michaylov and Pfenning [7] have conjectured that the impact of redundant types during run-time may be significant. This paper investigates this question in theory and practice. The contributions of this paper are two-fold: 1) We identify arguments which can be safely omitted during higher-order unification based on a static analysis of the declared type of constants. This information is then taken into account during run-time by looking up the relevant information for each constant and exploiting it when unifying its arguments. We justify this optimization theoretically using a contextual modal type theory. 2) We have implemented this optimization as part of the Twelf system [14], and discuss its impact in practice. Our experimental results show that although the size of redundant arguments is large and there is a substantial number of them, their impact on run-time performance is surprisingly limited (roughly 20% improvement). Our experimental results also demonstrate that optimizations such as eliminating the occurs checks are more important than previously thought. These results provide interesting insights into efficient implementations of dependently typed systems in general, and can provide guidance for future implementations.

The paper is organized as follows: First, we give an example to illustrate the idea, and present some background on dependent type theory and type checking algorithm. Our presentation follows ideas discussed in [10], where meta-variables are first-class objects. Next, we present a formal algorithm which identifies redundant type arguments and show the correctness of optimized higher-order pattern unification where redundant type arguments are skipped. Finally, we present experimental results and discuss related work.

2   Example: Translating Natural Deduction Proofs

To illustrate the problem of redundant arguments in dependently typed systems, let us consider the following example, where we translate natural deduction proofs into Hilbert-style proofs. We only consider a subset containing rules for implication and universal quantification and provide an implementation within the logical framework Twelf. Assuming o and i represent the type family for propositions and individuals respectively, we declare implication and universal quantification as imp:o->o->o. and all:(i->o)->o. using higher-order abstract syntax. The judgment for natural deduction is then implemented via a type family nd which is indexed by propositions. Following the judgements-as-types principle, we define constants impi, impe, alli, and alle whose types correspond to introduction and elimination rules for implication and universal quantifiers.

```
nd: o -> type.
impi:(nd A -> nd B) -> nd (A imp B). alli:({a}nd A a) -> nd (all [x] A x).
impe:nd (A imp B) -> nd A -> nd B.    alle:nd (all [x] A x) -> nd (A T).
```

The lambda-abstraction $\lambda x.M$ is denoted by [x] M and the dependent function type $\Pi x{:}A_1.A_2$ is represented as {x:A₁}A₂. Using higher-order abstract syntax we have define the type of all:(i->o)->o. As a consequence, the constant all takes a function as an argument. We typically use capital letters to denote meta-variables (or schematic variables), while small letters denote ordinary bound variables and meta-variables are assumed to be implicitly quantified at the outside. For example, the type of impi is in fact {A:o}{B:o}(nd A -> nd B) -> nd (A imp B). Following similar ideas, we define constants k, s, mp, f1, and f2 for the Hilbert-style formulation.

```
hil: o -> type.
k : hil (A imp B imp A).
s : hil ((A imp B imp C) imp (A imp B) imp A imp C).
mp: hil (A imp B) -> hil A -> hil B.
f1: hil ((all [x] A x) imp (A T)).
f2: hil ((all [x] (B imp A x)) imp (B imp all [x] A x)).
```

Note that in the axiom f2 bound variable dependencies are crucial, since we are only allowed to move the universal quantifier inside an implication iff the formula B does not depend on the bound variable x. Next, we define the translation of natural deduction proofs into Hilbert-style proofs using the type family hildn. We refer the reader not familiar with representing derivations in the logical framework LF to [13].

```
hilnd :hil A -> nd A -> type.
hnd_k :hilnd k (impi [u] impi [v] u).
hnd_s :hilnd s (impi [u] impi [v] impi [w] impe (impe u w) (impe v w)).
hnd_mp:hilnd H2 D2 -> hilnd H1 D1 -> hilnd (mp H1 H2) (impe D1 D2).
```

The code only reflects the explicit arguments describing the natural deduction and Hilbert-style derivations respectively. To illustrate, consider the second clause where we translate the Hilbert axiom s to a natural deduction derivation. The correctness of this translation hinges on the underlying dependent type structure and the translation hilnd takes in fact three arguments: the actual proposition being considered, a constant k representing the Hilbert-style proof and the natural deduction proof. Similarly, when we build the natural deduction derivation, we record how we instantiate the implication introduction and elimination rules. This leads to the following explicit representation of the clause hnd_s, where we marked implicit type arguments X with brackets ⌊X⌋.

```
hilnd ⌊((A imp (B imp C)) imp ((A imp B) imp (A imp C)))⌋ (s ⌊A⌋ ⌊B⌋ ⌊C⌋)
  (impi ⌊(A imp (B imp C))⌋ ⌊((A imp B) imp (A imp C))⌋
    ([u] impi ⌊(A imp B)⌋ ⌊(A imp C)⌋
      ([v] impi ⌊A⌋ ⌊C⌋
        ([w] impe ⌊B⌋ ⌊C⌋ (impe ⌊A⌋ ⌊(B imp C)⌋ u w) (impe ⌊A⌋ ⌊B⌋ v w))))).
```

When we execute this translation via a proof search interpretation, we must unify a goal with a given clause head. This will involve unifying not only its explicit arguments, but also all its implicit type arguments. In this paper, we investigate how much type computation can be eliminated during unification, and what its effect and impact is on run-time performance. We exploit and make precise a simple idea that some of the implicit type arguments in a term M are uniquely determined by the type of the object M and therefore may be skipped during unification.

3   Contextual Modal Type Theory

In this section we present the foundation for logical frameworks. We will follow our development in [10] where we present a contextual modal dependent type theory with first-class meta-variables. The presentation exploits a recent presentation technique for logical frameworks due to Watkins et al. [18] in which only canonical forms are well-typed. The key idea underlying is to introduce hereditary substitutions which always yields terms in canonical form after the substitution has been applied. In the object calculus, we distinguish between *atomic objects* R and *normal objects* M. Meta-variables together with a mediating substitution σ are in this presentation first-class and denoted by $u[\sigma]$. They are declared in the modal context Δ and carry their own context of bound variables Ψ and type A. Note that the substitution σ is part of the syntax of meta-variables. This eliminates the need of pre-cooking [4] which raises existential variables to the correct context. This is a conservative extension of LF [6] so we suppress some routine details such as signatures. For a full extension of this fragment as a contextual dependent type theory we refer the reader to [10].

Normal Kinds	$K ::= \text{type} \mid \Pi x{:}A.K$	Contexts	$\Gamma, \Psi ::= \cdot \mid \Gamma, x{:}A$
Atomic Types	$P, Q ::= a \cdot S$	Modal Context	$\Delta ::= \cdot \mid \Delta, u{::}A[\Psi]$
Normal Types	$A, B ::= P \mid \Pi x{:}A.B$	Substitution	$\sigma ::= \cdot \mid \sigma, M/x$
Atomic Objects	$R ::= x \cdot S \mid c \cdot S \mid u[\sigma] \cdot S$	Modal subst.	$\theta ::= \cdot \mid \theta, M/u$
Normal Objects	$M, N ::= \lambda x.\, M \mid R$		
Spines	$S ::= \text{nil} \mid M; S$		

Typing at the level of objects is divided into the following three judgments:

$\Delta; \Gamma \vdash M \Leftarrow A$ Check object M against canonical A

$\Delta; \Gamma \vdash R \Rightarrow A$ Synthesize canonical A for atomic object R

$\Delta; \Gamma \vdash S : A \Rightarrow P$ Synthesize a canonical P by checking a spine S against type A

$\Delta; \Gamma \vdash \sigma \Leftarrow \Psi$ Check substitution σ against context Ψ

The central idea is based on two observations: First, we can characterize canonical forms via bi-directional type-checking. Second, we can formalize normalization as a primitive recursive functional exploiting the structure of types and objects. The key idea is to replace ordinary substitution operation with one which will always yield a canonical term, i.e. in places where the ordinary substitution operation would create a redex, we must make sure to normalize during substitutions. In particular, when applying the substitution $[M/x]$ to a term $x \cdot S$, we must apply the substitution $[M/x]$ to the spine S, but we also must reduce the redex $(M \cdot [M/x]S)$ which would be created, since it is not meaningful in the defined setting. Since when applying $[M/x]$ to the spine S, we again may encounter situations which require us to contract a redex, the substitution $[M/x]$ must be hereditary. We therefore call this operation *hereditary substitution*. Before we discuss this substitution operation further, let us first present the bi-directional type checking rules.

Check normal object M against type

$$\frac{\Delta; \Gamma, x{:}A \vdash M \Leftarrow B}{\Delta; \Gamma \vdash \lambda x.\, M \Leftarrow \Pi x{:}A.B} \qquad\qquad \frac{\Delta; \Gamma \vdash R \Rightarrow P' \quad P = P'}{\Delta; \Gamma \vdash R \Leftarrow P}$$

Synthesize atomic type P for atomic object R

$$\frac{\Delta; \Gamma \vdash S : A \Rightarrow P \quad \Sigma(c) = A}{\Delta; \Gamma \vdash c \cdot S \Rightarrow P} \qquad\qquad \frac{\Delta; \Gamma \vdash S : A \Rightarrow P \quad \Gamma(x) = A}{\Delta; \Gamma \vdash x \cdot S \Rightarrow P}$$

$$\frac{(\Delta_1, u{::}A[\Psi], \Delta_2); \Gamma \vdash \sigma \Leftarrow \Psi \quad (\Delta_1, u{::}A[\Psi], \Delta_2); \Gamma \vdash S : [\sigma]^a_\Psi(A) \Rightarrow P}{(\Delta_1, u{::}A[\Psi], \Delta_2); \Gamma \vdash u[\sigma] \cdot S \Rightarrow P}$$

Synthesize atomic type P from spine S and type A

$$\frac{}{\Delta; \Gamma \vdash \mathsf{nil} : P \Rightarrow P} \qquad\qquad \frac{\Delta; \Gamma \vdash M \Leftarrow A \quad \Delta; \Gamma \vdash S : [M/x]^a_A(B) \Rightarrow P}{\Delta; \Gamma \vdash (M; S) : \Pi x{:}A.B \Rightarrow P}$$

Next we will describe the hereditary substitution operation. As we mentioned above, we must carefully design it such that it also ensures that the result of applying a substitution σ to a canonical object M yields again a canonical object. We define hereditary substitutions as a primitive recursive functional where we pass in the type of the variable we substitute for. This will be crucial in determining termination of the overall substitution operation. If we hereditarily substitute $[\lambda y.M/x](x \cdot S)$, then if everything is well-typed, $x{:}A_1 \to A_2$ for some A_1 and A_2 and we will write $[\lambda y.M/x]_{A_1 \to A_2}(x \cdot S)$ indexing the substitution with the type of x. These will all be total operations since any side condition can be satisfied by α-conversion. It is worth pointing out that it suffices for the type annotation A of the substitution $[M/x]_A$ to be "approximately" correct[1].

---

[1] In [10] we define approximate types as dependent types where dependencies have been erased. This is not necessary for the correctness of substitution, but it clarifies the role of the type annotation of substitutions.

The definition for $[R/x]^n_P(M)$ is straightforward, and we omit it here, since no redices will be produced. Instead we concentrate on the ordinary substitution $[M/x]^n_A(N)$ where potentially redices are created. We define substitution as a primitive recursive functional $[M/x]^n_A(N)$, and $[M/x]^r_A(R)$. Similar operations can be defined for $[M/x]^l_A(S)$, $[M/x]^s_A(\sigma)$, $[M/x]^g_A(\Gamma)$ and $[M/x]^a_A(B)$.

$$[M/x]^n_A(\lambda y.\,N) \quad = \lambda y.\,N' \quad \text{where } N' = [M/x]^n_A N,\ y \notin \mathsf{FV}(M) \text{ and } y \neq x$$
$$[M/x]^n_A(R) \quad\quad = R' \quad\quad\ \text{where } R' = [M/a]^r_A R$$

$$[M/x]^r_A(c \cdot S) \quad = c \cdot S' \quad\ \text{where } S' = [M/x]^l_A S$$
$$[M/x]^r_A(x \cdot S) \quad = R \quad\quad\ \text{where } S' = [M/x]^l_A S \text{ and } R = \text{reduce}(M : A, S')$$
$$[M/x]^r_A(y \cdot S) \quad = y \cdot S' \quad\ \text{if } y \neq x \text{ and } S' = [M/x]^l_A S$$
$$[M/x]^r_A(u[\sigma] \cdot S) = u[\sigma'] \cdot S' \text{ where } \sigma' = [M/x]^s_A \sigma \text{ and } S' = [M/x]^l_A$$

The interesting case is when we substitute a term M for a variable x in the term $x \cdot S$. As we outlined above, we need to possibly reduce the resulting redex to maintain canonical forms. Hence we define the $\text{reduce}(M : A, S) = R$ next.

$$\text{reduce}(\lambda y.M : \Pi x{:}A_1.A_2, (N; S)) = M'' \quad \text{where } [N/y]^n_{A_1} M = M'$$
$$\text{and } \text{reduce}(M' : A_2, S) = M''$$
$$\text{reduce}(R : P, \mathsf{nil}) \quad\quad\quad\quad\quad = R$$
$$\text{reduce}(M : A, S) \quad\quad\quad\quad\quad\quad \text{fails otherwise}$$

Substitution may fail to be defined only if substitutions into the subterms are undefined. The side conditions $y \notin \mathsf{FV}(M)$ and $y \neq x$ do not cause failure, because they can always be satisfied by appropriately renaming y. However, substitution may be undefined if we try for example to substitute an atomic term R for x in the term $x \cdot S$ where the spine S is non-empty. Similarly, the reduce operation is undefined. The substitution operation is well-founded since recursive appeals to the substitution operation take place on smaller terms with equal type A, or the substitution operates on smaller types (see the case for $\text{reduce}(\lambda y.M : A_1 \to A_2, (N; S)))$.

Hereditary substitution operations terminate, independently of whether the terms involved are well-typed or not. The operation may fail, in particular if we have ill-typed terms, or yield a canonical term as a result.

Theorem 1 (Substitution on Terms)

1. If $\Delta; \Gamma \vdash M \Leftarrow A$ and $\Delta; \Gamma, x{:}A, \Gamma' \vdash N \Leftarrow B$ and
   $[M/x]^n_A N = N'$, $[M/x]^a_A B = B'$ and $[M/x]^g_A(\Gamma') = \Gamma''$
   then $\Delta; \Gamma, \Gamma'' \vdash N' \Leftarrow B'$.
2. If $\Delta; \Gamma \vdash M \Leftarrow A$ and $\Delta; \Gamma, x{:}A, \Gamma' \vdash R \Rightarrow P$ and
   $R' = [M/x]^r_A R$, $[M/x]^a_A P = P'$ and $[M/x]^g_A(\Gamma') = \Gamma''$
   then $\Delta; \Gamma, \Gamma' \vdash R' \Rightarrow P'$.

Substitutions for meta-variables u are a little more difficult. Recall that meta-variables u are always associated with a postponed substitution and $u[\sigma]$ forms a closure. As soon as we know which term u stands for we can apply σ to it.

Moreover, because of α-conversion, the ordinary variables occurring in the term M being substituted and the domain of σ may be different. As a result, substitution for a meta-variable must carry a context, written as $[\Psi.M/u]N$ and $[\Psi.M/u]\sigma$ where Ψ binds all free variables in M. This complication can be eliminated in an implementation of our calculus based on de Bruijn indexes.

Finally, just as with ordinary substitutions we must be careful to only construct canonical terms. In particular, when we substitute M into the term $u[\sigma] \cdot S$ the resulting term $[\sigma]M \cdot S$ is not in canonical form. Hence similar to ordinary hereditary substitutions we will define a primitive recursive functional for contextual substitutions which is indexed by the type of the contextual variable and ensure that the result is always in normal form.

$$
\begin{aligned}
&[\Psi.M/u]^n_{A[\Psi]}(\lambda y.\, N) = \lambda y.\, N' && \text{where } N' = [\Psi.M/u]^n_{A[\Psi]}N \\
&[\Psi.M/u]^n_{A[\Psi]}(R) = R' && \text{where } R' = [\Psi.M/u]^r_{A[\Psi]}(R) \\
&[\Psi.M/u]^r_{A[\Psi]}(c \cdot S) = c \cdot S' && \text{where } S' = [\Psi.M/u]^r_{A[\Psi]}S \\
&[\Psi.M/u]^r_{A[\Psi]}(x \cdot S) = x \cdot S' && \text{where } S' = [\Psi.M/u]^r_{A[\Psi]}S \\
&[\Psi.M/u]^r_{A[\Psi]}(u[\tau] \cdot S) = R && \text{where } \tau' = [\Psi.M/u]^s_{A[\Psi]}(\tau), \; M' = [\tau'/\Psi]^n_\Psi(M) \\
& && \quad S' = [\Psi.M/u]^l_{A[\Psi]}(S) \text{ and } \mathsf{reduce}(M' : A, S') = R \\
&[\Psi.M/u]^r_{A[\Psi]}(v[\tau] \cdot S) = v[\tau'] \cdot S' \text{ where } v \neq u, \; \tau' = [\Psi.M/u]^s_{A[\Psi]}\tau \\
& \qquad\qquad\qquad\qquad\qquad \text{and } S' = [\Psi.M/u]^l_{A[\Psi]}S
\end{aligned}
$$

Applying $[\Psi.M/u]$ to the term $u[\tau] \cdot S$ will first apply $[\Psi.M/u]$ to the closure $u[\tau]$. This will yield the simultaneous substitution $\tau' = [\Psi.M/u]\tau$, but instead of returning $M[\tau']$, it proceeds to eagerly apply τ' to M. Before τ' can be carried out, however, it's domain must be renamed to match the variables in Ψ, denoted by τ'/Ψ. In addition, the substitution $[\Psi.M/u]$ must be applied to the spine S yielding S'. Since the result $M' \cdot S'$ may not be canonical, we again must call the reduce operation. Contextual substitutions are compositional, and contextual substitution properties hold. We only show the one for normal terms but the other can be stated similarly.

Theorem 2 (Contextual Substitution on Terms)
If $\Delta; \Psi \vdash M : A$ and $(\Delta, u::A[\Psi], \Delta'); \Gamma \vdash N : B$ and $[\Psi.M/u]^n_{A[\Psi]}N = N'$, $[\Psi.M/u]^a_{A[\Psi]}B = B'$, and $[\Psi.M/u]^g_{A[\Psi]}\Gamma = \Gamma'$ then $(\Delta, \Delta'); \Gamma' \vdash N' : B'$.

Remark 1. Although our theory allows for meta-variables $u[\sigma] \cdot S$, it is often convenient to require that meta-variables are lowered and their spine S is therefore empty. This optimization is based on the observation that meta-variables $u::(\Pi x{:}A_1.A_2)[\Psi]$ must always be instantiated with λ-abstractions, because λ-abstractions are the only canonical objects of function type. We can therefore anticipate part of the structure of the instantiation of u and create a new variable $u'::A_2[\Psi, x{:}A_1]$. Note that u' has a simpler type, although a longer context. In this way we can always lower existential variables until they have atomic type, $v::P[\Psi]$. As a consequence, the only occurrences of meta-variables are as $u[\sigma] \cdot \mathsf{nil}$ and we often abbreviate this term simply by writing $u[\sigma]$. Finally it is worth pointing out that any instantiation of u must be an atomic object R, and applying a substitution $[\![\Psi.R/u]\!]$ to a term M will always directly yield a canonical object.

Remark 2. Often it is convenient to refer to the pattern fragment [8,12]. We call a normal term M an *atomic pattern*, if all the subterms of the form $u[\sigma] \cdot$ nil are such that $u::Q[\Psi]$ and $\sigma = y_1/x_1, \ldots y_k/x_k$ where $y_1, \ldots, y_k$ are distinct bound variables. This is already implicitly assumed for $x_1, \ldots, x_k$ because all variables defined by a substitution must be distinct. Such a substitution is called a *pattern substitution*. In addition, the type of any occurrence of $u[\sigma]$ is atomic and we will write Q for atomic types. Finally, we can show that pattern substitutions and contextual substitutions commute [15].

To illustrate the use of meta-variables and ordinary variables, let us briefly reconsider the previous example of translating natural deduction proofs to proofs in Hilbert-style. Recall that bound variable dependencies are crucial when defining in f2:hil ((all [x:i] (B imp A x)) imp (B imp all [x:i] A x)), since we are only allowed to move the universal quantifier inside an implication if the formula B does not depend on the bound variable x. Our contextual modal type theory, will give us an elegant way of distinguishing between meta-variables and ordinary variables, and describing possible dependencies between them. We can represent these clauses as follows: A, B, and T are meta-variables and will be represented by contextual variables u, v, t.

```
f1: hil ((all λx.u[x/x']) imp (u[t[·]/x'])).
f2: hil ((all λx.(v[·] imp u[x/x'])) imp (v[·] imp (all λx.u[x/x']))).
```

Note that meta-variables u and v are associated with a substitution which precisely characterizes their dependencies. Since v cannot depend on the bound variable x, it is associated with the empty substitution. The instantiation for meta-variable u on the other hand may refer to the bound variable x, which is characterized by the associated substitution [x/x']. In this example the type of the constant f1 is not a higher-order pattern since it contains a subterm u[t[·]/x'] where the substitution associated with the modal variable u is not a pattern substitution. On the other hand the type of the constants f2 is a higher-order pattern, since both meta-variable occurrences are patterns.

4   Synthesizing Spine Arguments from Types

As we saw in the previous section, typing proceeds in a bi-directional way where the type of atomic objects is synthesized. The central idea behind bi-directional type-checking is to distinguish between objects whose type is uniquely determined and hence can be synthesized and objects whose type we already know and we may not be able to uniquely determine from the surrounding information and hence need to be checked against a given type. In this section, we will take a slightly different view. In particular, we ask what information in the object is uniquely determined, if we know its type. For example in the rule for the object

$c \cdot S$ we always synthesize the type P, by first looking up the type A of the constant c and then inferring P from the spine S and the type A. Switching perspectives we ask what information in the spine S can be synthesized if we know the type A and its final target type P. In other words, we will think of the object $c \cdot S$ as a normal object and we can check it against a given type P. Intuitively, we can always recover argument M_i occurring in a spine S if $[M_i/x_i]P$ is injective in the argument M_i. Therefore some information already present in P is duplicated in S. Hence we will target the rule for checking a term $c \cdot S$ and the rules for type checking spines. In particular, we will introduce a new judgment which says that we can synthesize a substitution θ by checking a canonical P against the type A and a spine S:

$$\Delta; \Theta; \Gamma \vdash S : A \Leftarrow P/\theta$$

The context Θ characterizes the holes in the type A which can be uniquely inferred from target type P. θ is a contextual substitution with domain Θ. Holes are described by meta-variables and we will ensure that only A can refer to these meta-variables characterized by Θ. Hence we will replace the rule for synthesizing an atomic type P for $c \cdot S$ with the following rule which checks $c \cdot S$ against an atomic type P.

$$\frac{\Delta; \cdot; \Gamma \vdash S : A \Leftarrow P/\cdot \quad \Sigma(c) = A}{\Delta; \Gamma \vdash c \cdot S \Leftarrow P}$$

Next, we show the rules for synthesizing a substitution θ by checking the spine S and the type A against the atomic type P.

$$\frac{\Delta; \Theta; \Gamma \vdash P \doteq P'/\theta}{\Delta; \Theta; \Gamma \vdash \mathsf{nil} : P' \Leftarrow P/\theta}$$

$$\frac{\Delta; \Theta; \Gamma \vdash \mathsf{strict}\ (x, B) \quad \Delta; \Theta, u{::}A[\Gamma]; \Gamma \vdash S : [u[\mathsf{id}_\Gamma]/x]_A^a(B) \Leftarrow P/(\theta, \Gamma.M/u)}{\Delta; \Theta; \Gamma \vdash (M; S) : \Pi x{:}A.B \Leftarrow P/\theta}$$

$$\frac{\Delta; \Theta; \Gamma \nvdash (\mathsf{strict}\ (x, B) \quad \Delta; \Gamma \vdash M \Leftarrow [\![\theta]\!]_\Theta^a(A) \quad \Delta; \Theta; \Gamma \vdash S : [M/x]_A^a(B) \Leftarrow P/\theta}{\Delta; \Theta; \Gamma \vdash (M; S) : \Pi x{:}A.B \Leftarrow P/\theta}$$

Assume $S = M_1; \ldots; M_n; \mathsf{nil}$, $A = \Pi x_1{:}A_1. \ldots. \Pi x_n{:}A_n.P'$, and atomic type P. Then for every x_i where x_i occurs strict in P', we can retrieve M_i from P. θ will exactly keep track of those M_i which we can synthesize from P. When we encounter $\Pi x_i{:}A_i.B$ where x_i is strict in the target type of B, we will introduce a fresh meta-variable u which will later be instantiated by higher-order pattern matching Note that the criteria of x_i being strict in P is crucial because only for those x_i can we ensure that higher-order pattern matching will find a unique instantiation.

If u occurs strict in the target type of $[u[\mathsf{id}_\Gamma]/x]_A^a(B)$ and u occurs as a higher-order pattern, then we can always reconstruct M, the information which is present in the spine $(M; S)$. Otherwise, we will continue to type check the spine S and infer an instantiation for all the meta-variables occurring in Θ. Next, we can show that the new type-checking algorithm which skips over some elements is correct. The crucial lemma needed is the following:

Lemma 1

1. If $\Delta; \Theta; \Gamma \vdash S : B \Leftarrow P/\theta$ then $\Delta; \Gamma \vdash S : [\![\theta]\!]^a_\Theta B \Rightarrow P$
2. If $\Delta; \Gamma \vdash S : [\![\theta]\!]^a_\Theta B \Rightarrow P$ then $\Delta; \Theta; \Gamma \vdash S : B \Leftarrow P/\theta$.

The type A of a constant c determines therefore which arguments in the spine of the term $c \cdot S$ can be omitted. Therefore, we generate a simple binary recipe from the type A which is associated with the constant c. Let $A = \Pi x_1{:}A_1 \ldots x_n{:}A_n.P$. If x_i occurs strict as a higher-order pattern in P, then we record 0 at the i-th position in the recipe b. If x_i does not occur strict as a higher-order pattern in P, then we record 1 at the i-th position in the recipe b. Consider the constant f1:hil ((all λx.u[x/x']) imp (u[t[·]/x'])). The type has one occurrence of the meta-variable u which is not a pattern, namely u[t[·]/x']. As a consequence, every time we encounter a term of type P with head f1, we must also consider the instantiations for u and t, because their instantiation cannot be uniquely determined from the type P. The recipe associated with f1 is therefore 11. On the other hand the type of constant f2 only contains occurrences of the meta-variable u which are higher-order patterns. If we encounter a term of type P with head f2, we can uniquely recover the instantiations for u and v. The recipe associated with f2 will be 00.

We will then modify higher-order unification as follows: when we are unifying two terms $c \cdot S$ and $c \cdot S'$, we will first lookup the recipe b associated with c, and then unify the spines S and S' taking into account the recipe b. If the i-th position in the recipe lists 0 then the i-th position in the spine S and S' will be skipped. If the i-th position in the recipe lists 1 then the i-th position in the spine S and S' must be unified. Crucial to the correctness of this optimization is the fact that the synthesized modal substitution θ is uniquely determined by the target type P and the type of the spine A.

Lemma 2. If $\Delta; \Theta; \Gamma \vdash S : A \Leftarrow P/\theta$ and $\Delta; \Theta; \Gamma \vdash S' : A \Leftarrow P/\theta'$ then $\theta = \theta'$.

Therefore, we already know that the spine S and S' agree on some of its arguments, and those arguments must not be unified..

5   Experimental Evaluation

The optimization of skipping some redundant type arguments during higher-order unification is a general optimization which can affect any algorithm relying on it. In this section, we discuss the impact of unifying redundant type arguments during proof search and report on our experience in type reconstruction. All experiments are done on a machine with the following specifications: 3.40GHz Intel Pentium Processor, 1024 MB RAM. We are using SML of New Jersey 110.55 under the Linux distribution Gentoo 16.14. Times are measured in seconds. For the timing analysis, we have done five runs, and we report on the average over these runs as well as the standard deviation observed.

5.1 Proof Search

Unification is a central operation during proof search and its performance directly impacts the overall run-time performance. In previous work [16], we investigated optimizing higher-order pattern unification by linearizing terms and delaying the occurs check together with other expensive checks concerning bound variable occurrences. This optimization is called linear head compilation, since the head of a logic programming clause is translated into a linear term and constraints during compilation. This optimization can only be exploited during proof search since it relies on the fact that the meta-variables in the head of a clause and the meta-variables in the query are distinct. Here, we will first compare the impact of eliminating the need to unify redundant type arguments when no optimization of unification is done. Next, we will compare it to linear head compilation, and finally we will report results of combining linear head compilation with eliminating the need to unify redundant type arguments.

Labeling of table: The first column NO describes the runtime in seconds when no optimization is done to unification. The second column TE describes the runtime when we skip redundant type arguments. LH describes the time using linear head compilation, and TELH gives the time when we combine linear head compilation with skipping redundant type arguments. The column #op refers to the number of skipped arguments during unification, and the column Av(size) refers to the average size of the omitted arguments.

Compiler translations for MiniML. We consider some examples from compiler verification [5]. When given an evaluation of some programs using a big-step semantics, we translate this evaluation to a sequence of transitions on an abstract machine and vice versa. The implicit type arguments denote the actual program being evaluated, and hence depending on the size of the program, this may be large. The standard deviation on the reported examples was less than 1%.

The first set of examples uses a continuation based machine, and the example programs being translated are simple programs involving multiplication, addition, square, and minus.

CPM – Proof search

	NO	TE	LH	TELH	no-te	no-lh	lh-telh	#op	Av(size)
addMin1	134.61	133.32	12.26	12.21	1%	91%	0%	829	31.02
square4b	779.55	766.23	153.62	121.73	2%	80%	21%	488	28.20
squmin3a	435.52	423.91	69.92	62.10	3%	84%	11%	1128	33.74
squmin4a	743.83	622.08	140.03	130.21	16%	81%	7%	1496	30.75

Unifying redundant type arguments has limited impact on the overall performance compared to no optimization. The last example shows an improvement by 16%. This can be substantial if we consider the absolute runtime. However, in many cases, the improvement is almost negligible given the standard deviation of 1%. The results clearly demonstrate that linear head optimization is crucial to achieve good performance. Redundant type elimination combined with linear head compilation, can give an additional improvement between 0% and 21%.

In our examples many redundant type arguments were skipped (up to 1496), the average size of the skipped argument was around 30 constructors, and the maximum size of argument skipped was 185. Given this set-up, we expected a much stronger impact on run-time performance. We believe that the reason for the limited impact is that at the time when we need to unify redundant type arguments they are syntactically equal. This means it is very cheap to unify two arguments which are already syntactically equal.

The second set of examples uses a CLS abstract machine. Examples are similar to the CPM machine involving programs with addition, multiplication, square and minus. We are interested in translating evaluations of terms to reductions of their de Bruijn representation. Since de Bruijn representations can be very large in size, our examples exhibit very large redundant arguments. On average the size of omitted arguments was up to 549.38, and the maximum size of omitted argument was 75218. In the examples considered there was also a substantial number of omitted terms (up to 6219). If the time limit of 3h had been exceeded and no solution was found, this is indicated by – in the table below.

CLS – Proof search

	NO	TE	LH	TELH	no-te	no-lh	lh-telh	#op	Av(size)	max
cls01	4044.18	3821.47	1.94	1.72	5.51%	99.95%	11.48%	1875	121.90	240
cls02	–	–	30.29	23.67	–	–	21.87%	1852	214.30	596
cls03	4450.01	4417.17	1.35	1.20	0.74%	99.97%	11.19%	1741	121.90	240
cls04	–	–	482.61	413.28	–	–	14.36%	6219	549.38	75218

Again there is almost no impact of skipping redundant arguments when we compare it to no optimization at all. Linear head optimization is however crucial to execute some examples. If we combine skipping over redundant type arguments with linear head optimization, we can see an additional improvement between 8% and 22%.

Translating classical proofs into cut-free proofs. The next few examples exploit a translation of proofs in classical logic into cut-free sequent calculi proofs. Relative standard deviation was up to 2.7%.

Cut-elimination – Proof search producing cut-free proofs

	NO	TE	LH	TELH	no-te	no-lh	lh-telh	#op	Av(size)
ndcf01	13.26	13.16	6.39	6.22	1%	52%	3%	97687	1.305
ndcf02	30.24	29.65	17.16	15.45	2%	43%	10%	264387	7.15

Due to space constraints, we only show here two significant examples. Although there may be many redundant type arguments (up to 264,387) their size may not be very large, and their impact on runtime behavior is limited.

Summary of results. Redundant type arguments occur often as we can see by the large number of arguments skipped and they are substantial in size. Their impact on runtime in the current Twelf implementation ranges up to 20% especially if we combine it with linear head compilation. Surprisingly optimizations such as linear head compilation are crucial to overcome some performance barriers, even in examples with a deeply nested dependent type structures.

5.2   Type Reconstruction

Higher-order unification does not only play an important role during proof search, but is used in many algorithms, such as type reconstruction, termination, and totality checking. Skipping redundant type arguments during unification therefore impacts these algorithms.

We have experimented with a wide variety of type reconstruction examples, from Kolmogoroff proof translation, Hilbert-style proof translations, typed assembly language [3]. Similar to proof search, we observe that although there is quite a large number of redundant implicit type arguments (< 1488) in some of these test-suites), the impact on the performance during type reconstruction is up to 13% on our examples. In the CPM compilation examples for example, we observe between 2% and 13% runtime improvement, The maximum size of omitted argument was 159, and the average size was between 13.37 and 32.33.

6   Related Work

J. Reed [17] investigates a bi-directional type checking algorithm for the logical framework LF where some implicit type arguments can be omitted. The motivation for his work is to compactly represent proofs and check them. However the price is a complicated meta-theory, and a different dependently typed lambda calculus where some terms are explicitly annotated with types. The motivation of his work lies in generalizing Necula and Lee's work on compact proof representations to the full power of dependent types. If we would want to adopt his approach as a foundation for optimizing unification, proof search and type-reconstruction, we would need to abandon our current representation of terms. This could be not only a bothersome and daunting engineering task, but it is also not clear whether other algorithms such as mode, termination, and coverage checking would still continue to work on this variant of LF. In contrast, we propose a lightweight approach which does not impact our foundations itself, but can be employed locally to optimize unification.

Although the problem of index arguments is due to the dependent type structure of LF, a similar problem arises in λProlog due to polymorphism [9]. A similar criteria as the one described in this paper, has been exploited by Nadathur and Qi [9] in recent work on optimizing λProlog. They explore optimizations such as eliminating typing annotations at lambda-labels and some implicit type arguments due to polymorphism within the WAM for λProlog. However, their proposal does not provide a high-level justification for this optimization and no experimental comparison or discussion is given how much impact these optimizations have in practice.

7 Conclusion

We have presented a lightweight approach to eliminate overhead of redundant type information during unification. We have presented a clean theoretical foundation for it based on contextual modal types, and evaluated the impact of redundant type arguments in practice. Although redundant arguments arise frequently and they are large in size, their impact on run-time is in the current Twelf implementation between 10% and 20%. This may seem surprising at first, since it is commonly believed that redundant type arguments can yield up to a factor of two improvement. Our experimental results however seem to indicate that unifying two arguments which are syntactically the same is very cheap. A few interesting lessons we have learned from this work is that we have underestimated the impact of linearization and delaying the occurs check during unification and proof search. Linearization allows for quick failure, and more importantly reduces the overhead of trailing during runtime, which can substantially improve the performance. As our results indicate, the size of omitted arguments is in fact substantial, and reducing the overall size of terms may yield better run-time performance, since most computation seems to be memory bound. This seems to suggest that generating compact representations of terms for proof search may be desirable in order to improve performance. On the other hand, choosing a different more compact representation of terms as a basis of the implementation could be a bothersome and daunting engineering task. In addition, it is also not clear whether other algorithms such as mode, termination, and coverage checking would still continue to work on this dependently typed variant of LF. Nevertheless, it may be worthwhile to consider a compact term representation if a system is newly designed and is specialized towards proof search.

References

1. Andrew Appel. Foundational proof-carrying code. In J. Halpern, editor, *Proceedings of the 16th Annual Symposium on Logic in Computer Science (LICS'01)*, pages 247–256. IEEE Computer Society Press, June 2001.
2. B. Aydemir *et. al.* Mechanized metatheory for the masses: The poplmark challenge. In J. Hurd and T. F. Melham, editors, *Eighteenth International Conference on Theorem Proving in Higher Order Logics (TPHOLs), Oxford, UK, August*, volume 3603 of *Lecture Notes in Computer Science(LNCS)*, pages 50–65. Springer, 2005.
3. Karl Crary and Susmit Sarkar. Foundational certified code in a metalogical framework. In F. Baader, editor, *19th International Conference on Automated Deduction*, Lecture Notes in Artificial Intelligence (LNAI) 2741, pages 106–120. Springer-Verlag, July 2003.
4. Gilles Dowek, Thérèse Hardin, Claude Kirchner, and Frank Pfenning. Unification via explicit substitutions: The case of higher-order patterns. In M. Maher, editor, *Proceedings of the Joint International Conference and Symposium on Logic Programming*, pages 259–273, Bonn, Germany, September 1996. MIT Press.
5. John Hannan and Frank Pfenning. Compiler verification in LF. In Andre Scedrov, editor, *Seventh Annual IEEE Symposium on Logic in Computer Science*, pages 407–418, Santa Cruz, California, June 1992.

6. Robert Harper, Furio Honsell, and Gordon Plotkin. A framework for defining logics. *Journal of the Association for Computing Machinery*, 40(1):143–184, January 1993.
7. Spiro Michaylov and Frank Pfenning. An empirical study of the runtime behavior of higher-order logic programs. In D. Miller, editor, *Proceedings of the Workshop on the λProlog Programming Language*, pages 257–271, Philadelphia, Pennsylvania, July 1992. University of Pennsylvania.
8. Dale Miller. Unification of simply typed lambda-terms as logic programming. In *Eighth International Logic Programming Conference*, pages 255–269, Paris, France, June 1991. MIT Press.
9. Gopalan Nadathur and Xiaochu Qi. Optimizing the runtime processing of types in polymorphic logic programming languages. In G. Sutcliffe and A. Voronkov, editors, *12th International Conference on Logic for Programming, Artificial Intelligence, and Reasoning (LPAR), Montego Bay, Jamaica, December, 2005*, volume 3835 of *Lecture Notes in Computer Science*, pages 110–124. Springer, 2005.
10. Aleksandar Nanevski, Frank Pfenning, and Brigitte Pientka. A contextual modal type theory. 2005.
11. George C. Necula and Peter Lee. Efficient representation and validation of logical proofs. In Vaughan Pratt, editor, *Proceedings of the 13th Annual Symposium on Logic in Computer Science (LICS'98)*, pages 93–104, Indianapolis, Indiana, June 1998. IEEE Computer Society Press.
12. Frank Pfenning. Unification and anti-unification in the Calculus of Constructions. In *Sixth Annual IEEE Symposium on Logic in Computer Science*, pages 74–85, Amsterdam, The Netherlands, July 1991.
13. Frank Pfenning. Logical frameworks. In A. Robinson and A. Voronkov, editors, *Handbook of automated reasoning*, pages 1063–1147, Amsterdam, The Netherlands, The Netherlands, 2001. Elsevier Science Publishers B. V.
14. Frank Pfenning and Carsten Schürmann. System description: Twelf — a metalogical framework for deductive systems. In H. Ganzinger, editor, *Proceedings of the 16th International Conference on Automated Deduction (CADE-16)*, pages 202–206, Trento, Italy, July 1999. Springer-Verlag Lecture Notes in Artificial Intelligence (LNAI) 1632.
15. Brigitte Pientka. *Tabled higher-order logic programming*. PhD thesis, Department of Computer Sciences, Carnegie Mellon University, Dec 2003. CMU-CS-03-185.
16. Brigitte Pientka and Frank Pfennning. Optimizing higher-order pattern unification. In F. Baader, editor, *19th International Conference on Automated Deduction, Miami, USA*, Lecture Notes in Artificial Intelligence (LNAI) 2741, pages 473–487. Springer-Verlag, July 2003.
17. Jason Reed. Redundancy Elimination for LF. In Carsten Schuermann, editor, *Fourth Workshop on Logical Frameworks and Meta-languages(LFM'04)*, Cork, Ireland, July 2004.
18. Kevin Watkins, Iliano Cervesato, Frank Pfenning, and David Walker. A concurrent logical framework I: Judgments and properties. Technical Report CMU-CS-02-101, Department of Computer Science, Carnegie Mellon University, 2002.

First-Order Logic with Dependent Types

Florian Rabe*

Carnegie Mellon University and International University Bremen
florian@cs.cmu.edu

Abstract. We present DFOL, an extension of classical first-order logic with dependent types, i.e., as in Martın-Lof type theory, signatures may contain type-valued function symbols. A model theory for the logic is given that stays close to the established first-order model theory. The logic is presented as an institution, and the logical framework LF is used to define signatures, terms and formulas. We show that free models over Horn theories exist, which facilitates its use as an algebraic specification language, and show that the classical first-order axiomatization is complete for DFOL, too, which implies that existing first-order theorem provers can be extended. In particular, the axiomatization can be encoded in LF.

1 Introduction and Related Work

Classical first-order logic (FOL) and its variations are folklore knowledge. Lots of variations classify the elements of a model into different sorts, e.g., many-sorted or order-sorted FOL. Type theory may also be viewed as an extension of FOL, introducing function sorts. Further extensions of type theory include type operators, type polymorphism and dependent types. All these extensions have varying advantages and disadvantages and various implementations exist. Surprisingly, not much work has been undertaken to extend FOL with just dependent types.

PVS ([ORS92]) is a classical verification system that extends simply-typed higher order logic with dependent function, record and product types and other concepts. Its type system is undecidable, and a set theoretic semantics for an idealized language exists ([OS97]). Coq ([BC04]), Nuprl ([CAB+86]) and LF ([Pfe01]) implement Martin-Löf's intuitionistic type theory with dependent types ([ML74]); while the first two add further concepts and are directed at general mathematics, the main purpose of LF is the specification of logics. A semantics for Martin-Löf type theory was introduced in [Car86], where also algebraic theories are treated. It was linked with locally cartesian closed categories as analogues of FOL structures in [See84] (see also [Hof94] and [Dyb95] for related approaches). However, these concepts are mathematically very complex and not tightly connected to research on theorem proving. Neither are they easy to specialize to FOL, even if intuitionistic FOL is used.

---

* The author was supported by a fellowship for Ph.D. research of the German Academic Exchange Service.

U. Furbach and N. Shankar (Eds.): IJCAR 2006, LNAI 4130, pp. 377–391, 2006.

We could only locate one attempt at combining FOL with just dependent types ([Mak], never published), which is mainly directed at studying equivalence of categories. It adds connectives and quantifiers to the treatment in [Car86] and gives an axiomatization, but does not allow general equality and function symbols (without which dependent types are significantly less interesting). Their type hierarchy is similar to ours, but the chosen notation is completely different from the usual one.

Our motivation in defining DFOL is to add as little as possible to FOL, keeping not only notation and intuition but also the results and applications. Thus, both researchers and implementations can use DFOL more easily. Therefore, we deliberately dispense with one feature of dependent types, namely circular dependencies, which greatly simplifies the model theory while hardly excluding interesting applications.

DFOL is presented as an institution. Institutions were introduced in [GB92] as a unifying concept for model theory. Examples for institutional definitions of logics are OBJ ([GWM+93]) and Maude ([CELM96]). The syntax of DFOL is presented directly in LF (see [HST94] for other logic specifications in LF) because even in our special case the inherent complexity of dependent types makes any independent introduction inconvenient. We introduce DFOL in section 2, sections 3 to 5 treat free models, axiomatization and examples.

2   Syntax and Semantics

2.1   Preliminary Definitions

Institutions. An institution is a tuple $(Sig, Sen, Mod, \models)$ where Sig is a category of signatures; signature morphisms are notation changes, usually mappings between the symbols of the signatures; $Sen : Sig \to Set$ is a functor that assigns to each signature its set of formulas and with each signature morphism the induced formula translation; $Mod : Sig \to Cat^{op}$ is a functor that assigns to every signature its category of models, and with every signature morphism the induced model reduction; and for every signature Σ, the satisfaction relation $\models_\Sigma \subseteq |Mod(\Sigma)| \times Sen(\Sigma)$ between models and sentences determines truth. Institutions must satisfy the satisfaction condition which can be paraphrased as "Truth is invariant under change of notation.". We refer to [GB92] for a thorough introduction.

LF. The logical framework LF and its implementation Twelf ([Pfe01], [PS99]) implement Martin-Löf type theory ([ML74]). LF will be used as a meta-language to define the syntax of DFOL. An LF signature[1] consists of a sequence $c : T$ of declarations, where c is a new symbol, and T is its type, which may depend on the previously declared symbols. T is of the form $\Pi x_1 : T_1. \ldots . \Pi x_n : T_n. T_{n+1}$, which means that c is a function symbol taking arguments of the types $T_1, \ldots, T_n$, called $x_1, \ldots, x_n$, and returning an argument of the type T_{n+1}; dependent types means that x_i may occur in $T_{i+1}, \ldots, T_{n+1}$. If $T_{n+1} = type$, c is not a function

---

[1] Readers familiar with LF will notice that our introduction is highly simplified.

symbol but returns a new dependent type for every argument tuple. If x does not occur in B, $\Pi x\!:\!A.\,B$ is abbreviated by $A \to B$.

To illustrate this, look at the signature Σ_B which represents our meta-language:

$\textbf{S}:\textit{type}.$ $\quad$ $\textit{Univ}:\textbf{S} \to \textit{type}.$ $\quad$ $o:\textit{type}.$

$\textit{true},\textit{false}:o.$ $\quad\quad$ $\wedge,\vee,\Rightarrow:o \to o \to o.$ $\quad$ $\neg:o \to o.$

$\forall,\exists:\Pi S\!:\!\textbf{S}.\,(\textit{Univ } S \to o) \to o.$ $\quad$ $\doteq:\Pi S\!:\!\textbf{S}.\,\textit{Univ } S \to \textit{Univ } S \to o.$

In this signature, $\textbf{S}$ is a type, the type of sorts declared in a DFOL signature. $\textit{Univ}$ is a dependent type family that returns a new type for each sort S, namely the type of terms of sort S; models will interpret the type $\textit{Univ } S$ as the universe for the sort S. o is the type of formulas. The remainder of the signature encodes the usual grammar for FOL formulas. Higher-order abstract syntax is used, i.e., λ is used to bind the free variables in a formula, and quantifiers are operators taking a λ expression as an argument.[2] Quantifiers and the equality symbol take the sort they operate on as their first argument; we will omit this argument if no ambiguities arise. When we refer to sorts, terms or formulas, we always mean objects with the respective type that do not contain any lambda abstractions except for those preceded by quantifiers.

A context for a signature Σ is a sequence of typed variables $x : \textit{Univ } S$, where previously declared variables and symbols declared in Σ may occur in S. Sorts, terms and formulas in context C may contain the variables declared in C.

We introduce abbreviations to make the LF syntax more familiar: The usual infix notation and bracket conventions of FOL are used, and conjunction binds stronger than implication; $\forall \lambda x : \textit{Univ } S.\,F$ is abbreviated as $\forall x : S.\,F$, and we write $\forall x, y : S,\, z : S'$ instead of $\forall x : S.\,\forall y : S.\,\forall z : S'$, and similarly for $\exists$. Note that application is written as $f\,t_1\,\dots\,t_n$ instead of the familiar $f(t_1,\dots t_n)$ and that substitution is written as β-reduction.

We allow a harmless[3] extension of LF: Contexts and signatures need not be finite but may contain infinitely many declarations of the form $c : \textit{Univ } S$. The reason for this is purely technical: It allows to have an infinite reservoir of names c for elements that occur in the universe of S, which facilitates some proofs.

2.2 Signatures

We are now ready to introduce DFOL signatures as certain LF signatures. A DFOL signature will consist of Σ_B followed by declarations of the form

$$c:\Pi x_1\!:\!\textit{Univ } S_1.\,\dots.\Pi x_m\!:\!\textit{Univ } S_m.\,T$$

where $m \in \mathbb{N}$, $T = \textbf{S}$, $T = \textit{Univ } S$ or $T = o$, and $S_1,\dots,S_m,S$ are sorts. c is called a sort symbol if $T = \textbf{S}$, a function symbol with target S if $T = \textit{Univ } S$,

---

[2] The reflexivity of LF is used to encode the sort dependencies. Alternatively, $\textbf{S}$ could be replaced with $\textit{type}$ and $\textit{Univ}$ omitted everywhere. But then sorts could not be used as arguments since LF does not support polymorphism.

[3] It is not harmless in general, only in our setting as explained below.

and a predicate symbol if $T = o$. The sorts S_i are called arguments of c. If we only allow sort symbols without arguments, we obtain the usual many-sorted FOL. Sort symbols with arguments construct dependent sorts.

Definition 1 (Signatures). *Let Σ_i be partial LF signatures such that $\Sigma = \Sigma_B \, \Sigma_0 \, \ldots \, \Sigma_d$ is an LF signature, and let Σ^n abbreviate $\Sigma_B \, \Sigma_0 \, \ldots \, \Sigma_n$ for $n \leq d$. Σ is called a DFOL signature if*

1. *only sort, function or predicate symbols are declared in $\Sigma_0 \, \ldots \, \Sigma_d$,*
2. *all sort symbol declarations in Σ_n have only arguments from Σ^{n-1},*
3. *the target of a function symbol declaration in Σ_n is not an LF term over Σ^{n-1} (i.e., only over Σ_n).*

Condition 1 prevents the use of more expressive LF declarations[4]. Condition 2 establishes an acyclic sort dependency: Every sort declared in Σ_n may only depend on sorts that have been declared in Σ^{n-1}. d is called the depth of Σ. A sort, term or formula has depth n if it is defined over Σ^n (for some context) but not over Σ^{n-1}. Condition 3 is the most important one: It requires that a function symbol that takes a sort of depth n as an argument may not return an element of a smaller depth.[5]

Condition 3 is rather restrictive to ensure the existence of free models. It excludes, e.g., projection functions π from a sort $T\ n$ of n-tuples (at depth 1) over B to B (at depth 0). A weaker restriction that is still sufficient for free models could allow π if there are equality axioms that identify every term $\pi\ x$ with a term of depth 0, i.e., if π does not generate new objects.

We have the following property.

Lemma 1. *Let Σ be a DFOL signature of depth d. Then Σ^n, for $0 \leq n \leq d$, is a DFOL signature such that the sorts of Σ^n are precisely the sorts of Σ that have depth at most n; and such that the terms of a sort S of Σ^n are precisely the terms of sort S over Σ.*

Proof. Trivial but note how condition 3 is needed.   □

This ensures that infinitely many declarations of the form $c : Univ\ S$ are indeed harmless: S may depend on the previously declared symbols but these must have strictly smaller depth than S and so on; therefore, S can only depend on finitely many symbols. From now on let the word signature only refer to DFOL signatures.

In general every sort symbol in Σ_n has a type of the form

$$\Pi\, x_1 : Univ\ S_1. \ \ldots\ .\Pi\, x_m : Univ\ S_m.\ \mathbf{S} \tag{F 1}$$

where $S_1, \ldots, S_m$ have depth smaller than n. Without loss of generality, we can assume that every function symbol in Σ_n has a type of the form

$$\Pi\, x_1 : Univ\ S_1. \ \ldots\ .\Pi\, x_r : Univ\ S_r.\ Univ\ S_{r+1} \to \ldots \to Univ\ S_m \to Univ\ S \tag{F 2}$$

---

[4] In particular, function types may not occur as arguments.
[5] In the terminology of [Vir96], this corresponds to dependence relations between sort symbols given by $s \prec t$ iff s has at most the depth of t.

where $S_1, \ldots, S_r$ have depth smaller than n and $S_{r+1}, \ldots, S_m$ have depth n. Similarly, we can assume that every predicate symbol in Σ_n has a type of the form

$$\Pi\, x_1 : Univ\ S_1.\ \ldots\ .\Pi\, x_r : Univ\ S_r.\ Univ\ S_{r+1} \to \ldots \to Univ\ S_m \to o. \quad \text{(F 3)}$$

A signature morphism $\sigma : \Sigma \to \Sigma'$ is a mapping of Σ symbols to Σ' symbols such that (i) σ is the identity for symbols declared in Σ_B; (ii) σ respects types and depths of all mapped symbols. We omit the formal definition. For example, the identity mapping is a signature morphism from $\Sigma_B\, \Sigma_0\ \ldots\ \Sigma_c$ to $\Sigma = \Sigma_B\, \Sigma_0\ \ldots\ \Sigma_d$ for $c \leq d$. These morphisms are called extensions.

Running Example. We will use a running example. Consider the signature Σ

$t :$ **S**. $i : Univ\ t$. $j : Univ\ t$. $d : Univ\ t \to$ **S**.
$f : \Pi\, x : Univ\ t.\ Univ\ d\, x$. $c : Univ\ d\, i$. $p : \Pi\, x : Univ\ t.\ Univ\ d\, x \to o$

Σ has depth 1 (Σ_0 consists of the declarations for t, i and j.) and declares three sorts, t, $d\, i$ and $d\, j$, and five terms, i and j with sort t, $f\, i$ and c with sort $d\, i$, and $f\, j$ with sort $d\, j$, and one predicate.

2.3 Sentences and Models

Definition 2 (Sentences). *$Sen(\Sigma)$, the set of formulas over Σ, is the set of LF objects $F = \lambda x_1 : Univ\ S_1. \ldots .\lambda x_n : Univ\ S_n.\ G$ where G is of type o and all λ's in G are preceded by $\forall$ or $\exists$. For a signature morphism σ, $Sen(\sigma)$ is the mapping between formulas induced by σ.*

Taking the above lambda closure over the free variables in G is not needed in FOL. In DFOL, however, it is helpful to keep track of the sorts of the free variables in G because x_i may occur in $S_{i+1}, \ldots, S_n$. For simplicity, we identify G and F if it does not cause confusion. We do not distinguish between, e.g., F and $\lambda x : Univ\ S.\ F$ if x does not occur in F. Closed and atomic formulas are defined in the obvious way.

Running Example. Examples for closed formulas are $E_1 = \forall x : t.\ (i \doteq x \Rightarrow p\, x\, f\, x)$ and $E_2 = \forall x : t.\ \exists y : d\, x.\ (p\, x\, y)$.

Definition 3 (Models, Assignments). *Let Σ have depth d. We define Σ-models and assignments by induction on d. If $d = 0$, $Mod(\Sigma)$ is the category of many-sorted FOL models of Σ, i.e., interpretation functions M given by*

- *a universe s^M for every sort symbol $s :$ **S** $\in \Sigma$,*
- *a function $f^M : s_1^M \times \ldots \times s_m^M \to s^M$ for every function symbol f with m arguments,*
- *a mapping $p^M : s_1^M \times \ldots \times s_m^M \to \{0, 1\}$ for every predicate symbol p with m arguments.*

If $d > 0$ and Mod is defined for signatures of depth $d - 1$, the objects $M \in Mod(\Sigma)$ are interpretation functions $\cdot^M$ that interpret the sort, function and predicate symbols of Σ in the following way.

1. $\cdot^M$ restricted to Σ^{d-1} (which has depth $d-1$) is a Σ^{d-1}-model. We denote this restriction by N.
2. Let $C = (x_i : \text{Univ } S_i)_{i=1,\dots,n}$ be a context over Σ^{d-1}. We define assignments and model extensions through two entwined recursions:
   - An assignment from C into N is a mapping u that assigns to every $x_i :$ Univ S_i in C an element $u(x_i) \in S_i^N(u)$. Here, $S_i^N(u)$ is the extension of $\cdot^N$ to sorts induced by the assignment u.
   - The extension of $\cdot^N$ to sorts and terms for an assignment u from the respective free variables into N, is defined recursively by $x_i^N(u) = u(x_i)$ and
   $$(c\, t_1\, \dots\, t_m)^N(u) = c^N(t_1^N(u), \dots, t_m^N(u))$$
   for a sort or function symbol c and terms t_i.
3. For every sort symbol of the form (F 1) declared in Σ_d and every assignment u from $(x_i : \text{Univ } S_i)_{i=1,\dots,m}$ into N,
   $$s^M(u(x_1), \dots, u(x_m)) \text{ is a set.}$$
4. Note that at this point, $\cdot^M$ is defined for all sort symbols in Σ_d and all terms of depth at most $d-1$. As in step 2, we define assignments into M and the extension $\cdot^M$ to sorts of depth d.
5. For every function symbol f of the form (F 2) declared in Σ_d and every assignment u from $(x_i : \text{Univ } S_i)_{i=1,\dots,m}$ into M,
   $$f^M(u(x_1), \dots, u(x_m)) \in S^M.$$
6. As in step 2, we define $\cdot^M$ for all terms of depth n.
7. For every predicate symbol p of the form (F 3) declared in Σ_d and every assignment u from $(x_i : \text{Univ } S_i)_{i=1,\dots,m}$ into M,
   $$p^M(u(x_1), \dots, u(x_m)) \in \{0,1\}.$$

For a sort S, S^M is called the universe of M. A model morphism $\phi : M \to N$ for Σ-models M and N maps from each universe of M to some universe of N as follows.[6] For every assignment u from $(x_i : \text{Univ } S_i)_{i=1,\dots,m}$ into M, we put $\boldsymbol{u} = (u(x_1), \dots, u(x_m))$; then $\phi(\boldsymbol{u}) = (\phi(u(x_1)), \dots, \phi(u(x_m)))$ is an assignment into N. We require that for every d and every appropriate assignment u into M

1. for every sort symbol s declared in Σ_d, ϕ is a mapping from $s^M(\boldsymbol{u})$ to $s^N(\phi(\boldsymbol{u}))$,
2. for every function symbol f declared in Σ_d, $\phi(f^M(\boldsymbol{u})) = f^N(\phi(\boldsymbol{u}))$,
3. for every predicate symbol p declared in Σ_d, $p^M(\boldsymbol{u}) \leq p^N(\phi(\boldsymbol{u}))$. [7]

Note that for $d = 0$, this reduces to the usual first-order definition of homomorphisms.

---

[6] Since the universes of M are not required to be pairwise disjoint, ϕ should be indexed with the universes to distinguish these mappings. We omit these indexes and rely on the context.

[7] Using $\leq$ means that truth of atomic formulas is preserved along homomorphisms.

For a signature morphism $\sigma : \Sigma \to \Sigma'$, $Mod(\sigma)$ is the usual model reduction functor from $Mod(\Sigma')$ to $Mod(\Sigma)$, i.e., $Mod(\sigma)$ maps a Σ'-model N to a Σ-model M defined by $c^M = \sigma(c)^N$ for every symbol c of Σ (Thus every universe of M is also a universe of N.); and $Mod(\sigma)$ maps a Σ'-model morphism from N to N' to its restriction to the universes of $Mod(\sigma)(N)$. We omit the formal proof that Mod is indeed a functor.

In particular for an extension $\phi : \Sigma^n \to \Sigma^d$ for $n \leq d$, $Mod(\phi)$ maps every Σ^d-model M to its restriction M^n over Σ^n.

Running Example. A model M for the example signature is given by $t^M = \mathbb{N} \setminus \{0\}$, $i^M = 2$, $j^M = 3$, $d^M(n) = \mathbb{N}^n$, $f(n) = (1, \dots, n)$, and $p(n, (m_1, \dots, m_n)) = 1 \Leftrightarrow m_1 = n$. Note how all interpretations must be defined for all elements regardless of whether they can be named by terms.

2.4 Satisfaction

Satisfaction $M \models_\Sigma F$ is defined in the usual way: $M \models_\Sigma F \Leftrightarrow F^M(u) = 1$ for all assignments u from the free variables in F into M, where $\cdot^M$ is extended to all formulas by

- if $F = p\, t_1 \dots t_m$ for a predicate symbol p, then
  $F^M(u) = p^M(t_1^M(u), \dots, t_m^M(u))$,
- if $F = t_1 \doteq t_2$, then $F^M(u) = 1 \Leftrightarrow t_1^M(u) = t_2^M(u)$,
- the usual definition for propositional connectives,
- if $F = \forall x : S.\ G$, then $F^M(u) = \inf\{G^M(u\{x \mapsto v\}) \mid v \in S^M(u)\}$,
- if $F = \exists x : S.\ G$, then $F^M(u) = \sup\{G^M(u\{x \mapsto v\}) \mid v \in S^M(u)\}$,

where $u\{x \mapsto v\}$ is as u but with $u(x) = v$. We omit the formal proof of the satisfaction condition.

Running Example. We have $M \not\models_\Sigma E_1$ since for $u(x) = 2$, we have $(i \doteq x)^M(u) = 1$ but $(f\ x)^M(u) = (1, 2)$ and therefore, $(p\ x\ f\ x)^M(u) = 0$. And we have $M \models_\Sigma E_2$ since for every $n \in t^M$ there is an $m \in d^M(n)$ such that $p^M(n, m) = 1$, for example $m = (n, 1, \dots, 1)$.

3   Free Models

A theory $K = (\Sigma, T)$ consists of a signature Σ and a set T of closed Σ-formulas. *Sen* and *Mod* are extended to theories by putting $Sen(\Sigma, T) = Sen(\Sigma)$ and $Mod(\Sigma, T) = \{M \in Mod(\Sigma) \mid M \models F \text{ for all } F \in T\}$.

For many-sorted first-order logic there is the standard result (see for example [Tar85]) that for a Horn theory (Σ, T) and sets A_s of generators for all sort symbols s, there is a Σ-model $Free_\Sigma(A)/T$ of T such that for every $M \in Mod(\Sigma, T)$ and every family of mappings $\phi_s : A_s \to s^M$ there is a unique Σ-morphism $\overline{\phi} : Free_\Sigma(A)/T \to M$ that extends ϕ.

The purpose of this section is to establish the corresponding result for DFOL. Horn formulas over a DFOL signature Σ are defined in the usual way (i.e., a universally closed implication $T \Rightarrow H$ in which the tail T is a conjunction of atomic formulas and the head H is an atomic formula except for $false$). A Horn formula is hierarchic if the depth of its head is at least as big as the depth of its tail. We can allow only hierarchic Horn formulas because, informally, otherwise axioms of a greater depth could influence the interpretation of symbols of a lower depth. As generators, we might use a family A_S where S runs over all sorts, but a stronger result is possible that also allows generators for sorts that depend on other generators. The most elegant way to describe such generators is by using signatures that contain arbitrarily many constant declarations of the form $a : Univ\ S$.[8] Then DFOL has free models over hierarchic Horn theories in the following sense.

Lemma 2. *For a hierarchic Horn theory $K = (\Sigma, T)$, there is a K-model $Free_\Sigma / T$ such that for every K-model M there is a unique Σ-morphism from $Free_\Sigma / T$ to M.*

Proof. Let Σ and T be as stated. Let T^n be the restriction of T to depth at most n. We define $Free_\Sigma / T$ by induction on the depth of Σ, say d. If $d = 0$, $F^0 = Free_{\Sigma^0} / T^0$ is the classical result; note that the universes of F^0 arise by taking equivalence classes of terms.

By the induction hypothesis, we assume

$$F^{d-1} = Free_{\Sigma^{d-1}} / T^{d-1} \in Mod(\Sigma^{d-1}, T^{d-1})$$

all universes of which consist of equivalence classes of terms, let $[\cdot]$ denote these equivalence classes. We define Herbrand models to be (Σ^d, T^d)-models M that satisfy the following conditions:

- M agrees with F^{d-1} for all symbols in Σ^{d-1},
- for all sort symbols s of the form (F 1) in Σ_d: $s^M([t_1], \ldots, [t_m]) = U/\equiv$ where U contains those terms that have any of the sorts $s\ b_1\ \ldots\ b_m$ for $b_i \in [t_i]$, and $\equiv$ is some equivalence relation[9]; let $\langle \cdot \rangle$ denote the equivalence classes of $\equiv$; clearly, all universes are disjoint, so that we can use the symbols $\equiv$ and $\langle \cdot \rangle$ for all universes,
- for a function symbol f of the form (F 2) in Σ_d:

$$f^M([t_1], \ldots, [t_r], \langle t_{r+1} \rangle, \ldots, \langle t_m \rangle) = \langle f\ t_1\ \ldots\ t_m \rangle,$$

- for a predicate symbol p of the form (F 3) in Σ_d:

$$p^M([t_1], \ldots, [t_r], \langle t_{r+1} \rangle, \ldots, \langle t_m \rangle) = 1 \Leftrightarrow M \models_{\Sigma^d} p\ t_1\ \ldots\ t_m.$$

We put F^d to be the Herbrand model that satisfies the least atomic formulas. By definition, it is a (Σ^d, T^d)-model in which all universes arise by taking equivalence classes of terms.

---

[8] This is why we allow infinite signatures.

[9] Note that $\equiv$ identifies more terms than the relation $(t \doteq t')^M = 1$: Term identification in F^{d-1} may lead to sort identification at depth d, thus causing terms of different sorts to become equal.

We have to prove that the above F^d exists. This is done in essentially the same way as for the FOL case. Informally, a Herbrand model is uniquely determined by the equivalence $\equiv$ and the set P of atomic formulas of depth d that it satisfies. Let $(\equiv_i, P_i)_{i \in I}$ be all Herbrand models. This family is not empty: It contains the model in which all atomic formulas of depth d are true. Then it is easy to show that this family also contains the model determined by $\bigcap_{i \in I} \equiv_i$ and $\bigcap_{i \in I} P_i$, which we can put to be F^d. This completes the induction.

The unique morphism into M simply maps the equivalence class of a term t to t^M. This is well-defined because M satisfies T and by the definition of F^d.

Running Example. The free model F for the example signature with the axioms $\forall x : t. (p\, x\, f\, x)$ and $c \doteq f\, i$ is given by $t^F = \{\{i\}, \{j\}\}$, $d^F(\{i\}) = \{\{c, f\, i\}\}$, $d^F(\{j\}) = \{\{f\, j\}\}$ and $(p\, x\, y)^F(u) = 1$ for both possible assignments u.

Generators. Since we allow infinite signatures, Lem. 2 contains the result where there are arbitrarily many generators. We make this more precise: Let $\Sigma(A)$ be the signature Σ enriched with the declarations from a context A over Σ. Then every Σ-model M and every assignment u from A into M induce a $\Sigma(A)$-model, which we call (M, u).

Theorem 1. *For a signature Σ, a context A over Σ, and a set T of hierarchic Horn formulas over $\Sigma(A)$, there is a $\Sigma(A)$-model $Free_\Sigma(A)/T$ of T such that for every Σ-model M and every assignment u from A into M such that (M, u) models T, there is a unique $\Sigma(A)$-morphism $\overline{u} : Free_\Sigma(A)/T \to (M, u)$ that extends u.*

Proof. Simply put $Free_\Sigma(A)/T$ to be $Free_{\Sigma(A)}/T$. □

Of particular interest is the case where T does not depend on A. Then $Free_\Sigma(A)/T$ is a (Σ, T)-model and every assignment u from A into a (Σ, T)-model M has a unique extension to a Σ-morphism, namely the extension of the interpretation function M under the assignment u.

We abstain from a categorical interpretation in terms of adjoint functors and simply remark that $Free_\Sigma(\emptyset)/T$ is initial in the category $Mod(\Sigma, T)$.

Running Example. The free model F for the example signature with the generators $A = a_1 : t$, $a_2 : f\, a_1$ with the axioms E_1 (from the running example above) and $i \doteq a_1$ is given by: $t^F = \{\{i, a_1\}, \{j\}\}$, $d^F(\{i, a_1\}) = \{\{f\, i, f\, a_1, \{c\}, \{a_2\}\}$, $d^F(\{j\}) = \{\{f\, j\}\}$ and $(p\, x\, y)^F(u) = 1$ precisely for $u(x) = \{i, a_1\}$, $u(y) = \{f\, i, f\, a_1\}$.

4 Axiomatization

Completeness. To enhance readability, we omit the operator *Univ* completely from now on. We show that the classical axiomatizations are sufficient for DFOL. We use the common Gentzen style notation for sequents and rules. For simplicity, we only give the completeness result for the case that empty universes are forbidden. The general case is similar.

$$\frac{}{\vdash A} \text{ for every } A \in T \qquad \frac{\Gamma \vdash A, \Delta}{\Gamma, \neg A \vdash \Delta} \qquad \frac{\Gamma, A \vdash \Delta}{\Gamma \vdash \neg A, \Delta}$$

$$\frac{}{\Gamma \vdash true, \Delta} \qquad \frac{\Gamma, A, B \vdash \Delta}{\Gamma, A \wedge B \vdash \Delta} \qquad \frac{\Gamma \vdash A, \Delta \quad \Gamma \vdash B, \Delta}{\Gamma \vdash A \wedge B, \Delta}$$

$$\frac{\Gamma, A \vdash \Delta}{\Gamma, \exists x : S. A \vdash \Delta} \qquad \frac{\Gamma \vdash (\lambda x : S. A) t, \Delta}{\Gamma \vdash \exists x : S. A, \Delta}$$

$$\vdash \forall x_1 : S_1, \ldots x_r : S_r, x_{r+1}, x'_{r+1} : S_{r+1}, \ldots, x_m, x'_m : S_m.$$
$$x_{r+1} \doteq x'_{r+1} \wedge \ldots \wedge x_m \doteq x'_m \Rightarrow$$
$$f\, x_1 \ldots x_r\, x_{r+1} \ldots x_m \doteq f\, x_1 \ldots x_r\, x'_{r+1} \ldots x'_m$$
$$\text{for all } f \text{ of the form (F 2)}$$

In the ∃left rule, we assume that x does not occur free in Γ or Δ. In the ∃right rule, t is a term of sort S in which the free variables from Γ, S, A and Δ may occur. We omit the structural rules (axioms, cut, weakening, contraction and exchange), the remaining equality rules (reflexivity, symmetry and transitivity) and the rules for definable connectives and quantifiers.

Fig. 1. Axiomatization for $SC(\Sigma, T)$

Theorem 2. *Let $K = (\Sigma, T)$ be a finite theory (i.e., Σ and T are finite), and let the rules of $SC(K)$ be as in classical sequent style axiomatizations for FOL with equality (see [Gal86]) with slight modifications as given in Fig. 1. Then $SC(K)$ is sound and complete for $Mod(K)$.*

The modifications mainly serve to account for free variables. Only the congruence axiom has an unfamiliar form and may even look incomplete, but note that the putatively underivable formulas are not well-typed in the first place.

Proof. We only sketch the completeness proof since it is almost the same as the classical Henkin style proof (see [Hen49]). There are only a few minor technical differences in the notation of free variables and quantifiers. Firstly, a set of formulas Γ such that $\Gamma \cup T$ is consistent is extended to a maximal consistent set $\overline{\Gamma}$ with witnesses. To do that, we use a context A containing infinitely many declarations for each sort over Σ and A.

Then $M = Free_\Sigma(A)/T$, where T is the set of atomic formulas in $\overline{\Gamma}$, is a $(\Sigma(A), T)$-model of $\overline{\Gamma}$. The proof proceeds by induction on the number of occurrences of logical symbols in $F \in \overline{\Gamma}$.

Then the $\Sigma(A)$-model M yields a Σ-model M' by forgetting the interpretations of the symbols from A (formally $M' = Mod(\sigma)(M)$ where $\sigma : \Sigma \to \Sigma(A)$ is the injection). M' is a model of $\Gamma \cup T$ because no symbols from A occur in $\Gamma \cup T$. From this model existence result, the theorem follows as in the classical case. $\qquad \square$

As in the classical case, Thm. 2 yields the compactness theorem and the Löwenheim-Skolem result that any consistent set of sentences has a countable model.

Running Example. Let an axiom for Σ be given by $i \doteq j$. This implies that the sorts $d\,i$ and $d\,j$ are equal, it also implies $(f\,i)^M = (f\,j)^M$ in every model M. Note, however, that $f\,i \doteq f\,j$ cannot be derived because it is not a well-formed formula. It cannot be well-formed because it only makes sense in the presence of the axiom $i \doteq j$. If equations between terms of the same depth but different sorts were allowed, and if equations in this broader sense were forbidden to occur in the axioms of a theory, the completeness result would still hold.

Implementation. It follows that a Gentzen style theorem prover of FOL can be turned into one for DFOL, if its syntax is extended to support DFOL signatures. In the case of the existing implementation of FOL in LF, which is part of the Twelf distribution, only rules for equality need to be added.

Completeness results for resolution based proving as in Vampire ([RV02]) require additional work. The transformation into conjunctive normal form is as for FOL with the exception of skolemization, which transforms

$$\lambda\,x_1 : S_1. \ \ldots . \lambda\,x_n : S_n.\ \exists x : S.\ G \text{ to } \lambda\,x_1 : S_1. \ \ldots . \lambda\,x_n : S_n.\ (\lambda\,x : S.\ G)(f x_1 \ldots x_n).$$

Here $x_1, \ldots, x_n$ also contain the free variables of S, and the substitution must also operate on S. If paramodulation (see for example [NR01]) is used to replace a subterm s of F with t, both the sorts of s and t as well as s and t themselves must be unified (see [PP03] for unification with dependent types in LF).

5 Examples

In the examples, we use infix notation for some symbols without giving the corresponding Twelf declarations. And we use the implicit arguments notation of Twelf, i.e., if a free variable X which, due to the context, must have type T occurs in a declaration, it is assumed that the type is prefixed with $\Pi\,X : T$. If such a free variable occurs in an axiom, we assume an implicit universal quantification.

Categories. Let *Cat* be the following theory of depth 1 (where we leave a blank line between signature and axioms)

$Ob :$ **S**.
$Mor :\ \Pi\,A, B : Ob.$ **S**.
$id :\ \Pi\,A : Ob.\ Mor\,A\,A.$
$\circ :\ Mor\,A\,B\ \rightarrow\ Mor\,B\,C\ \rightarrow\ Mor\,A\,C.$

$\forall f : Mor\,A\,B.\ f \doteq f \circ id\,B$
$\forall f : Mor\,A\,B.\ f \doteq id\,A \circ f$
$\forall f : Mor\,A\,B,\ g : Mor\,B\,C,\ h : Mor\,C\,D.\ (f \circ g) \circ h \doteq f \circ (g \circ h)$

Then $Mod(Cat)$ is the category of small categories. For example the formula $\lambda\,X : Ob.\ \forall A : Ob.\ \exists f : Mor\,A\,X.\ \forall g : Mor\,A\,X.\ f \doteq g$ expresses the property that $X : Ob$ is a terminal element.

The free category over a generating graph G can be obtained by applying
Thm. 1 to Cat where A contains declarations $N : Ob$ for every node N and
$E : Mor\ N\ N'$ for every edge $E = (N, N')$ of G. Note that the theorem also
allows to impose specific equalities, e.g., an axiom $E = E_1 \circ E_2$ if the composition
of E_1 and E_2 is already part of G.

A theory extension consists of additional declarations and additional axioms;
it is simple, if it does not add sort declarations. Let $2Cat$ be the following
extension of Cat

$2cell :\ \Pi\ f, g\!:\!Mor\ A\ B.\ \mathbf{S}.$
$Id_2 :\ \Pi\ f\!:\!Mor\ A\ B.\ 2cell\ f\ f.$
$\circ_{vert} :\ \Pi\ f, g, h\!:\!Mor\ A\ B.\ 2cell\ f\ g\ \rightarrow\ 2cell\ g\ h\ \rightarrow\ 2cell\ f\ h.$
$\circ_{hor} :\ \Pi\ f, g\!:\!Mor\ A\ B.\ \Pi\ f', g'\!:\!Mor\ B\ C.$
$\quad 2cell\ f\ g\ \rightarrow\ 2cell\ f'\ g'\ \rightarrow\ 2cell\ f \circ f'\ g \circ g'.$

If we also add appropriate axioms, $Mod(2Cat)$ becomes the category of small
2-categories. Bi-categories can be specified similarly, e.g., using the axiom

$\forall f : Mor\ A\ B,\ g : Mor\ B\ C,\ h : Mor\ C\ D,\ k, l : Mor\ A\ D.$
$\quad k \doteq (f \circ g) \circ h\ \wedge\ l \doteq f \circ (g \circ h)\ \Rightarrow\ \exists \alpha : 2cell\ k\ l.\ \exists \beta : 2cell\ l\ k.$
$\quad\quad \alpha \circ_{vert} \beta \doteq Id_2\ k\ \wedge\ \beta \circ_{vert} \alpha \doteq Id_2\ l.$

Under the Curry-Howard-Tait correspondence, a 2-category corresponds to a
logic with formulas, proofs and rewrites. If a simple extension of $2Cat$ declares
function symbols for connectives, proof rules and conditional rewrite rules of a
logic, Thm. 1 yields its free 2-category of proofs.

Let $OCat$ be the extension of Cat with

$\leadsto:\ Mor\ A\ B\ \rightarrow\ Mor\ A\ B\ \rightarrow\ o.$

$\forall f : Mor\ A\ B.\ f \leadsto f$
$\forall f, g, h : Mor\ A\ B.\ (f \leadsto g\ \wedge\ g \leadsto h\ \Rightarrow\ f \leadsto h)$

where we interpret $\leadsto$ as rewritability between morphisms. Let K be a simple
extension of $OCat$, and let K' be as K but with the additional axioms

$\forall X_1 : S_1 \ldots X'_m : S_m.$
$\quad X_1 \leadsto X'_1\ \wedge\ \ldots\ \wedge\ X_m \leadsto X'_m\ \Rightarrow\ f\ X_1\ \ldots\ X_m \leadsto f\ X'_1\ \ldots\ X'_m$

for every function symbol f of depth 1. We call $Mod(K')$ the category of small
order-enriched K-categories. The added axioms in K' are simply the congruence
conditions for all function symbols with respect to rewriting. The arising axiomatization of rewriting is the same as in rewriting logic (see [BM03], which also
allows frozen arguments).

In particular, this yields free order-enriched K-categories over Horn theories,
and a complete axiomatization of this category. This allows a succinct view of
logics under the Curry-Howard-Tait correspondence.[10]

---

[10] Having a simple meta-language that supports dependent types while allowing axiomatization and free models was the original motivation to introduce DFOL. The idea
for these specifications and the introduction of DFOL is due to Till Mossakowski
and discussions with him and others.

Linear Algebra. Let Σ be the following signature of depth 1

N : **S**.
one : N
succ : $N \to N$.
Mat : $N \to N \to$ **S**.
0 : R.
1 : R.
RowAppend : $Mat\ m\ one \to R \to Mat\ succ\ m\ one$.
ColAppend : $Mat\ m\ n \to Mat\ m\ one \to Mat\ m\ succ\ n$.
E : $Mat\ m\ m$.
$+$: $Mat\ m\ n \to Mat\ m\ n \to Mat\ m\ n$.
$-$: $Mat\ m\ n \to Mat\ m\ n \to Mat\ m\ n$.
$\cdot$: $Mat\ l\ m \to Mat\ m\ n \to Mat\ l\ n$.
det : $Mat\ m\ m \to R$.
inv : $Mat\ m\ m \to o$.
eigenvalue : $Mat\ m\ n \to R \to o$.

(where we use R to abbreviate $Mat\ one\ one$). Clearly, Σ can be used to axiomatize linear algebra over any ring that can be axiomatized in first-order logic. Examples for axioms are

$\forall M : Mat\ m\ m.\ (inv\ M \Leftrightarrow \neg\ det\ M \doteq 0)$ and
$\forall M : Mat\ m\ n,\ r : R.\ (eigenvalue\ M\ r \Leftrightarrow \exists v : Mat\ n\ one.\ M \cdot v \doteq v \cdot r)$
(with the usual abbreviation $\Leftrightarrow$).

6 Conclusion

We have introduced an extension of FOL with dependent types such that the generalization of definitions, results and implementations is very natural. The formulation of DFOL as an institution allows to apply the established institution-independent results (see the book [Dia05]). The formulation of the syntax in LF immediately yields implementations of type checking, proof checking and simple theorem proving.

Of course, DFOL does not permit anything that has not been possible before. For example, category theory has been specified in Coq ([HS98]) or simply using FOL.[11] However, the simple model theory and the performance of automated theorem provers provide good arguments to stick to FOL if possible. The research presented here is targeted at those situations where specifications in (partial) FOL are desirable but awkward. In the examples, we demonstrated that only one or two dependent sort constructors can allow an elegant specification of a mathematical theory that would be awkward in FOL, but for which tools like Coq are far more powerful than necessary.

---

[11] DFOL cannot in general be encoded in partial many-sorted FOL since there may be more universes in a DFOL model then there are closed sort terms in the language. An encoding in FOL is straightforward and can provide an alternative completeness result but is very awkward.

It can be argued that signatures of depth greater than 1 or 2 are not interesting. And in fact, the general case was not our original goal. But it turned out that the step from depth 0 to depth 1 is already almost as complex as the induction step for the general case so that no simplifications are to be expected from restricting the depth.

Although further work is needed (e.g., on resolution or Craig interpolation), it turned out that crucial classical results can be extended to DFOL. Free models make DFOL valuable as an algebraic specification language, and we plan to integrate it into CASL ([BM04]). And the axiomatization indicates that existing provers can be extended for DFOL. The FOL encoding in Twelf can be adapted easily so that both pure LF and the Twelf meta-theorem prover ([SP96]) can be applied.

References

[BC04]   Y. Bertot and P. Castéran. *Coq'Art: The Calculus of Inductive Constructions.* Springer, 2004.

[BM03]   R. Bruni and J. Meseguer. Generalized rewrite theories. In *Proceedings of ICALP '03.* Springer, 2003.

[BM04]   Michel Bidoit and Peter D. Mosses. *Casl User Manual.* LNCS 2900 (IFIP Series). Springer, 2004.

[CAB+86] R. Constable, S. Allen, H. Bromley, W. Cleaveland, J. Cremer, R. Harper, D. Howe, T. Knoblock, N. Mendler, P. Panangaden, J. Sasaki, and S. Smith. *Implementing Mathematics with the Nuprl Development System.* Prentice-Hall, 1986.

[Car86]   J. Cartmell. Generalized algebraic theories and contextual category. *Annals of Pure and Applied Logic*, 32, 1986.

[CELM96] M. Clavel, S. Eker, P. Lincoln, and J. Meseguer. Principles of Maude. In J. Meseguer, editor, *Proceedings of the First International Workshop on Rewriting Logic*, volume 4, pages 65–89, 1996.

[Dia05]   R. Diaconescu. *Institution-independent Model Theory.* 2005.

[Dyb95]   P. Dybjer. Internal type theory. In *TYPES*, pages 120–134, 1995.

[Gal86]   J. Gallier. *Foundations of Automatic Theorem Proving.* Wiley, 1986.

[GB92]   J. A. Goguen and R. M. Burstall. Institutions: Abstract model theory for specification and programming. *Journal of the Association for Computing Machinery*, 39(1):95–146, 1992.

[GWM+93] J. Goguen, Timothy Winkler, J. Meseguer, K. Futatsugi, and J. Jouannaud. Introducing OBJ. In Joseph Goguen, editor, *Applications of Algebraic Specification using OBJ.* Cambridge, 1993.

[Hen49]   L. Henkin. The completeness of the first-order functional calculus. *Journal of Symbolic Logic*, 14:159–166, 1949.

[Hof94]   M. Hofmann. On the interpretation of type theory in locally cartesian closed categories. In *CSL*, pages 427–441, 1994.

[HS98]   G. Huet and A. Saïbi. Constructive category theory. In G. Plotkin, C. Stirling, and M. Tofte, editors, *Proof, Language and Interaction: Essays in Honour of Robin Milner.* MIT Press, 1998.

[HST94]   R. Harper, D. Sannella, and A. Tarlecki. Structured presentations and logic representations. *Annals of Pure and Applied Logic*, 67:113–160, 1994.

[Mak]   M. Makkai. First order logic with dependent sorts (FOLDS). Unpublished.

[ML74]   P. Martin-Löf. An intuitionistic theory of types: Predicative part. In *Proceedings of the '73 Logic Colloquium*. North-Holland, 1974.

[NR01]   R. Nieuwenhuis and A. Rubio. Paramodulation-Based theorem proving. In *Handbook of Automated Reasoning*, pages 371–443. Elsevier Science Publishers, 2001.

[ORS92]   S. Owre, J. M. Rushby, and N. Shankar. PVS: A prototype verification system. In Deepak Kapur, editor, *11th International Conference on Automated Deduction (CADE)*, volume 607 of *Lecture Notes in Artificial Intelligence*, pages 748–752, Saratoga, NY, 1992. Springer.

[OS97]   S. Owre and N. Shankar. The formal semantics of PVS. Technical Report SRI-CSL-97-2, SRI International, 1997.

[Pfe01]   F. Pfenning. Logical frameworks. In *Handbook of automated reasoning*, pages 1063–1147. Elsevier, 2001.

[PP03]   B. Pientka and F. Pfenning. Optimizing higher-order pattern unification. In *19th International Conference on Automated Deduction*, pages 473–487. Springer, 2003.

[PS99]   F. Pfenning and C. Schürmann. System description: Twelf - a metalogical framework for deductive systems. *Lecture Notes in Computer Science*, 1632:202–206, 1999.

[RV02]   A. Riazanov and A. Voronkov. The design and implementation of Vampire. *AI Communications*, 15:91–110, 2002.

[See84]   R. Seely. Locally cartesian closed categories and type theory. *Math. Proc. Cambridge Philos. Soc.*, 95:33–48, 1984.

[SP96]   C. Schürmann and F. Pfenning. Automated theorem proving in a simple meta-logic for LF. In C. Kirchner and H. Kirchner, editors, *Proceedings of the 15th International Conference on Automated Deduction*, pages 286–300. Springer, 1996.

[Tar85]   A. Tarlecki. On the existence of free models in abstract algebraic institutions. *Theoretical Computer Science*, 37:269–301, 1985.

[Vir96]   R. Virga. Higher-order superposition for dependent types. In H. Ganzinger, editor, *Proceedings of the 7th International Conference on Rewriting Techniques and Applications*, pages 123–137. Springer, 1996.

Automating Proofs in Category Theory

Dexter Kozen[1], Christoph Kreitz[1,2], and Eva Richter[2]

[1] Computer Science Department,
Cornell University, Ithaca, NY 14853-7501, USA
[2] Institut für Informatik,
Universität Potsdam, 14482 Potsdam, Germany

Abstract. We introduce a semi-automated proof system for basic category-theoretic reasoning. It is based on a first-order sequent calculus that captures the basic properties of categories, functors and natural transformations as well as a small set of proof tactics that automate proof search in this calculus. We demonstrate our approach by automating the proof that the functor categories Fun[C × D, E] and Fun[C, Fun[D, E]] are naturally isomorphic.

1 Introduction

Category theory is a popular framework for expressing abstract properties of mathematical structures. Since its invention in 1945 by Samuel Eilenberg and Saunders Mac Lane [12], it has had a wide impact in many areas of mathematics and computer science. The beauty of category theory is that it allows one to be completely precise about general mathematical concepts. Abstract algebraic notions such as free constructions, universality, naturality, adjointness, and duality have precise formulations in the theory. Many algebraic constructions become exceedingly elegant at this level of abstraction.

However, there are some disadvantages too. Many basic facts, although easy to state, can be quite tedious to verify formally. Diagrams can be used to illustrate essential insights, but complete proofs based on precise definitions often involve an enormous number of low-level details that must be checked. In many cases, it is not considered worth the effort to carry out such a detailed verification, and readers are frequently asked to accept "obvious" assertions on faith.

Another issue is that category theory is considerably more abstract than many other branches of mathematics. Because of this abstraction, it is easy to lose sight of the connection with concrete motivating examples. One works in a rarified atmosphere in which much of the intuition has been stripped away, so the verification at the lowest level becomes a matter of pure symbol manipulation, devoid of motivating intuition.

On the other hand, precise proofs in category theory often rely on standard patterns of reasoning that may lend themselves well to automation. Providing such an automation serves two purposes. It enables users to generate completely formal proofs of elementary category-theoretic facts without having to go through all the details themselves, thus providing assurance that the statement is in fact true and allowing them to inspect details if desired. It also demonstrates that the proofs that many authors do not bother to provide, which may

U. Furbach and N. Shankar (Eds.): IJCAR 2006, LNAI 4130, pp. 392–407, 2006.
© Springer-Verlag Berlin Heidelberg 2006

be considered trivial from an intellectual point of view, actually may contain a tremendous amount of hidden detail, and may identify conditions that formally should be checked, but that the author might have taken for granted or overlooked entirely.

In this paper we introduce a proof system for automating basic category-theoretic reasoning. We first give a formal first-order axiomatization of elementary category theory that is amenable to automation in Section 2. This axiomatization is a slight modification of a system presented in [18]. We then describe an implementation of this calculus within the proof environment of the Nuprl system [9,1] in Section 3 and strategies for automated proof search in Section 4. These strategies attempt to capture the general patterns of formal reasoning that we have observed in hand-constructed proofs using this calculus. These patterns were alluded to in [18], but the description there was quite vague and there was no attempt at implementation.

We demonstrate the feasibility of our approach by giving a completely automated proof of the statement that the functor categories Fun[C × D, E] and Fun[C, Fun[D, E]] are naturally isomorphic. The process of automating this proof has given us significant insights into the formal structure of category-theoretic proofs and has taught us much about how to streamline the automation. We describe these technical insights below in the context of the proof itself.

1.1 Related Work

The published approaches to a formalization of category theory essentially aim at three different purposes. The first is a formal reconstruction of mathematical knowledge in a computer-oriented environment. This is done in the Mizar project of Bialystok University [29]. Mizar statements are formulated in first order logic and proved using a declarative proof language. Mizar's library contains a comprehensive collection of theorems mostly proved already in 1990-1996, but is still under active research. The last entries concerning special functor behavior and duality of categories were done in 2001 [3,4,5]. One disadvantage of the Mizar approach is that it has only little automation: although Mizar's basic inference steps are quite expressive, it does not provide a mechanism for automating domain-specific reasoning tasks.

A second purpose is to provide calculi for category theory to use its machinery in several domains of computer science (for example denotational semantics). One of these approaches is Caccamo's and Winskel's *Higher order calculus for categories* [10]. The authors present a second order calculus for a fragment of category theory. Their approach is at a level higher than ours. Their basic types are (small) categories and the syntactic judgments describe functorial behavior of expressions. The rules allow the construction of new functors. A consequence of this approach is that for example Yoneda's lemma occurs as a rule rather than a theorem. Another approach to be mentioned here is Rydeheard's and Burstall's *Computational Category Theory* [24]. This work is a programming language representation of the subject, i.e., a collection of structures and functions that represent the main concepts of category theory. One of the merits of the book is that it emphasizes the constructive flavor of categorial concepts. The representation is mainly regarded a basis for the use of category theory in program design.

A third group consists of formalizations of category theory in interactive proof systems. In these formalizations, practical issues like feasibility, automation and elegance of the design (in the sense of [15]) play an important role. There are at least two formalizations of category theory in Isabelle/HOL that should be mentioned here. Glimming's 2001 master thesis [13] describes a development of basic category theory and a couple of concrete categories. As HOL does not admit the definition of partial functions, Glimming had to address the problem of the composition of uncomposable arrows. This problem is solved by the introduction of an error object, which is never a member of any set of arrows. Since his interests lie in a formalization of the Bird-Meertens formalism [7], there are no attempts to improve automation beyond Isabelle's generic prover.

Another formalization of category theory in Isabelle is O'Keefe's work described in [22]. His main focus is on the readability of the proofs, aiming at a representation close to one in a mathematical textbook. Therefore he uses a sectioning concept provided by Isabelle. This saves a lot of repetition and is an elegant way to emulate informal mathematical reasoning. Although this formalization contains definitions of functors and natural transformations, it does not include functor categories. O'Keefe mentions another formalization of category theory in HOL by Lockwood Morris whose focus is on automation, but unfortunately neither a description nor the sources have been published.

In the Coq library there are two contributions concerning category theory. The development of Saïbi and Huet [16,26] contains definitions and constructions up to cartesian closed categories, which are then applied to the category of sets. The authors formulate the theory of functors including Freyd's adjoint functor theorem, i.e., their work covers nearly all of chapters I–V of [20]. The formalization of Saïbi and Huet is directly based on the constructive type theory of Coq. Simpson [27], on the other hand, makes only indirect use of it. Instead, his formalization is set up in a ZFC-like environment. In addition to some basic set theory and algebra, he develops category theory including functors, natural transformations, limits and colimits, functor categories, and a theorem about the existence of (co)limits in functor categories. Simpson has written some tactics to improve the automation, but, as for the work of Saïbi and Huet, there are no official papers available.

A key difference between these works and our approach is that we have identified an independent calculus for reasoning about category theory and given a full implementation in Nuprl. In addition, we have provided a family of tactics that allow many proofs to be automated. None of the other extant implementations we have encountered make any attempt to isolate an independent formal axiomatization of the elementary theory. Instead, they embed category theory into some other logic, and reasoning relies mostly on the underlying logic.

2   An Axiomatization of Elementary Category Theory

2.1   Notational Conventions

We assume familiarity with the basic definitions and notation of category theory [6,20]. To simplify notation, we will adhere to the following conventions.

- Symbols in sans serif, such as C, always denote categories. The categories Set and Cat are the categories of sets and set functions and of (small) categories and functors, respectively.
- If C is a category, we use the symbol C to denote both the category C and the set of objects of C.
- We write $A : C$ to indicate that A is an object of C. Composition is denoted by the symbol $\circ$ and the identity on object $A : C$ is denoted 1_A. The use of a symbol in sans serif, such as C, implicitly carries the type assertion C : Cat.
- We write $h : C(A, B)$ to indicate that h is an arrow of the category C with domain A and codomain B.
- Fun[C, D] denotes the functor category whose objects are functors from C to D and whose arrows are natural transformations on such functors. This is the same as the category denoted D^C in [20]. Thus $F : $ Fun[C, D] indicates that F is a functor from C to D and $\varphi : $ Fun[C, D](F, G) indicates that φ is a natural transformation with domain F and codomain G.
- C^{op} denotes the opposite category of C.
- $f : X \Rightarrow Y$ indicates that $f : $ Set(X, Y), that is, f is a set function from set X to set Y. We use the symbol $\Rightarrow$ only in this context. Function application is written as juxtaposition and associates to the left.
- F^1 and F^2 denote the object and arrow components, respectively, of a functor F. Thus if $F : $ Fun[C, D], $A, B : $ C, and $h : $ C(A, B), then $F^1A, F^1B : $ D and $F^2h : $ D(F^1A, F^1B).
- Function application binds tighter than the operators ^{1} and ^{2}. Thus the expression F^1A^2 should be parsed $(F^1A)^2$.
- $C \times D$ denotes the product of categories C and D. Its objects are pairs $(A, X) : C \times D$, where $A : $ C and $X : $ D, and its arrows are pairs $(f, h) : (C \times D)((A, X), (B, Y))$, where $f : $ C(A, B) and $h : $ D(X, Y). Composition and identities are defined componentwise; that is,

$$(g, k) \circ (f, h) \overset{\text{def}}{=} (g \circ f, k \circ h) \tag{1}$$

$$1_{(A,X)} \overset{\text{def}}{=} (1_A, 1_X). \tag{2}$$

2.2   Rules

The rules involve sequents $\Gamma \vdash \alpha$, where Γ is a type environment (set of type judgments on atomic symbols) and α is either a type judgment or an equation. There is a set of rules for functors and a set for natural transformations, as well as some rules covering the basic properties of categories and equational reasoning.

The rules for functors and natural transformations are the most interesting. They are divided into symmetric sets of rules for analysis (elimination) and synthesis (introduction).

Categories. There is a collection of rules covering the basic properties of categories, which are essentially the rules of typed monoids. These rules include typing rules for composition and identities

$$\frac{\Gamma \vdash A, B, C : \mathsf{C}, \quad \Gamma \vdash f : \mathsf{C}(A,B), \quad \Gamma \vdash g : \mathsf{C}(B,C)}{\Gamma \vdash g \circ f : \mathsf{C}(A,C)} \tag{3}$$

$$\frac{\Gamma \vdash A : \mathsf{C}}{\Gamma \vdash 1_A : \mathsf{C}(A,A)}, \tag{4}$$

as well as equational rules for associativity and two-sided identity.

Functors. A functor F from C to D is determined by its object and arrow components F^1 and F^2. The components must be of the correct type and must preserve composition and identities. These properties are captured in the following rules.

Analysis

$$\frac{\Gamma \vdash F : \mathsf{Fun}[\mathsf{C},\mathsf{D}], \quad \Gamma \vdash A : \mathsf{C}}{\Gamma \vdash F^1 A : \mathsf{D}} \tag{5}$$

$$\frac{\Gamma \vdash F : \mathsf{Fun}[\mathsf{C},\mathsf{D}], \quad \Gamma \vdash A, B : \mathsf{C}, \quad \Gamma \vdash f : \mathsf{C}(A,B)}{\Gamma \vdash F^2 f : \mathsf{D}(F^1 A, F^1 B)} \tag{6}$$

$$\frac{\Gamma \vdash F : \mathsf{Fun}[\mathsf{C},\mathsf{D}], \quad \Gamma \vdash A, B, C : \mathsf{C}, \quad \Gamma \vdash f : \mathsf{C}(A,B), \quad \Gamma \vdash g : \mathsf{C}(B,C)}{\Gamma \vdash F^2(g \circ f) = F^2 g \circ F^2 f} \tag{7}$$

$$\frac{\Gamma \vdash F : \mathsf{Fun}[\mathsf{C},\mathsf{D}], \quad \Gamma \vdash A : \mathsf{C}}{\Gamma \vdash F^2 1_A = 1_{F^1 A}} \tag{8}$$

Synthesis

$$\frac{\begin{array}{l}\Gamma, A : \mathsf{C} \vdash F^1 A : \mathsf{D} \\ \Gamma, A, B : \mathsf{C}, \ g : \mathsf{C}(A,B) \vdash F^2 g : \mathsf{D}(F^1 A, F^1 B) \\ \Gamma, A, B, C : \mathsf{C}, \ f : \mathsf{C}(A,B), \ g : \mathsf{C}(B,C) \vdash F^2(g \circ f) = F^2 g \circ F^2 f \\ \Gamma, A : \mathsf{C} \vdash F^2 1_A = 1_{F^1 A}\end{array}}{\Gamma \vdash F : \mathsf{Fun}[\mathsf{C},\mathsf{D}]} \tag{9}$$

Natural Transformations. A natural transformation $\varphi : \mathsf{Fun}[\mathsf{C},\mathsf{D}](F,G)$ is a function that for each object $A : \mathsf{C}$ gives an arrow $\varphi A : \mathsf{D}(F^1 A, G^1 A)$, called the *component* of φ at A, such that for all arrows $g : \mathsf{C}(A,B)$, the following diagram commutes:

$$
\begin{array}{ccc}
F^1 A & \xrightarrow{F^2 g} & F^1 B \\
\varphi A \downarrow & & \downarrow \varphi B \\
G^1 A & \xrightarrow{G^2 g} & G^1 B
\end{array} \tag{10}
$$

Composition and identities are defined by

$$(\varphi \circ \psi)A \stackrel{\mathrm{def}}{=} \varphi A \circ \psi A \tag{11}$$

$$1_F A \stackrel{\mathrm{def}}{=} 1_{F^1 A}. \tag{12}$$

The property (10), along with the typing of φ, are captured in the following rules.

Analysis

$$\frac{\Gamma \vdash \varphi : \mathsf{Fun}\,[\mathsf{C},\mathsf{D}]\,(F,G)}{\Gamma \vdash F,G : \mathsf{Fun}\,[\mathsf{C},\mathsf{D}]} \tag{13}$$

$$\frac{\Gamma \vdash \varphi : \mathsf{Fun}\,[\mathsf{C},\mathsf{D}]\,(F,G), \quad \Gamma \vdash A : \mathsf{C}}{\Gamma \vdash \varphi A : \mathsf{D}(F^1 A, G^1 A)} \tag{14}$$

$$\frac{\Gamma \vdash \varphi : \mathsf{Fun}\,[\mathsf{C},\mathsf{D}]\,(F,G), \quad \Gamma \vdash A,B : \mathsf{C}, \quad \Gamma \vdash g : \mathsf{C}(A,B)}{\Gamma \vdash \varphi B \circ F^{1?}g - G^2 y \cup \varphi A} \tag{15}$$

Synthesis

$$\frac{\begin{array}{l} \Gamma \vdash F,G : \mathsf{Fun}\,[\mathsf{C},\mathsf{D}] \\ \Gamma,\ A : \mathsf{C} \vdash \varphi A : \mathsf{D}(F^1 A, G^1 A) \\ \Gamma,\ A,B : \mathsf{C},\ g : \mathsf{C}(A,B) \vdash \varphi B \circ F^2 g = G^2 g \circ \varphi A \end{array}}{\Gamma \vdash \varphi : \mathsf{Fun}\,[\mathsf{C},\mathsf{D}]\,(F,G)} \tag{16}$$

Equational Reasoning. Besides the usual domain-independent axioms of typed equational logic (reflexivity, symmetry, transitivity, and congruence), certain domain-dependent equations on objects and arrows are assumed as axioms, including the associativity of composition and two-sided identity rules for arrows, the equations (1) and (2) for products, and the equations (11) and (12) for natural transformations.

We also provide extensionality rules for objects of functional type:

$$\frac{\Gamma \vdash F,G : \mathsf{Fun}\,[\mathsf{C},\mathsf{D}], \quad \Gamma, A : \mathsf{C} \vdash F^1 A = G^1 A}{\Gamma \vdash F^1 = G^1} \tag{17}$$

$$\frac{\Gamma \vdash F,G : \mathsf{Fun}\,[\mathsf{C},\mathsf{D}], \quad \Gamma,\ A,B : \mathsf{C},\ g : \mathsf{C}(A,B) \vdash F^2 g = G^2 g}{\Gamma \vdash F^2 = G^2} \tag{18}$$

$$\frac{\Gamma \vdash F,G : \mathsf{Fun}\,[\mathsf{C},\mathsf{D}], \quad \Gamma \vdash F^1 = G^1, \quad \Gamma \vdash F^2 = G^2}{\Gamma \vdash F = G} \tag{19}$$

$$\frac{\Gamma \vdash F,G : \mathsf{Fun}\,[\mathsf{C},\mathsf{D}], \quad \Gamma \vdash \varphi,\psi : \mathsf{Fun}\,[\mathsf{C},\mathsf{D}]\,(F,G), \quad \Gamma,\ A : \mathsf{C} \vdash \varphi A = \psi A}{\Gamma \vdash \varphi = \psi} \tag{20}$$

Finally, we also allow equations on types and substitution of equals for equals in type expressions. Any such equation $\alpha = \beta$ takes the form of a rule

$$\frac{\Gamma \vdash A : \alpha}{\Gamma \vdash A : \beta}. \tag{21}$$

Other Rules. There are also various rules for products, weakening, and other structural rules for manipulation of sequents. These are all quite standard and do not bear explicit mention.

3 Implementation of the Formal Theory

As a platform for the implementation of our proof calculus we have selected
the Nuprl proof development system [9,2,19,1]. Nuprl is an environment for the
development of formalized mathematical knowledge that supports interactive
and tactic-based reasoning, decision procedures, language extensions through
user-defined concepts, and an extendable library of verified formal knowledge.
Most of the formal theories in this library are based on Nuprl's Computational
Type Theory, but the system can accommodate other logics as well.

One of the key aspects of the implementation of a formal theory is faithfulness
with respect to the version on paper. Although Nuprl supports a much more
expressive formalism, reasoning mechanisms should be restricted to first-order
logic and the axiomatization of category theory given in the previous section.
To accomplish this we proceeded as follows.

Encoding Semantics and Syntax. We have used Nuprl's definition mechanism to
implement the vocabulary of basic category theory. For each concept we have
added an abstraction object to the library that defines the semantics of a new
abstract term in terms of Nuprl's Computational Type Theory. For instance,
the product of two categories C and D, each consisting of a set of objects, a
set of arrows, a domain and a codomain function, and composition and identity operations, is defined by an abstraction which states that objects and arrows are the cartesian products of the respective sets for C and D, domain
and codomain functions are paired, and composition and identity are computed
pointwise.

```
CatProd(C,D) == < C×D,  ArrC×ArrD,  λ(f,h).<dom(f),dom(h)>,
          λ(f,h).<cod(f),cod(h)>,  λ((f,h),(g,k)).<f∘g,h∘k>,  λ(A,X).<1A,1X> >
```

The outer appearance of abstract terms (display syntax) is defined separately
through *display forms*, which enable us to adjust the print and display representations of abstract terms to conform to a specific style without modifying the
term itself. Following [20], for instance, we denote the set of objects of a category
by the name of the category. For the product category, we use the same notation
as for the cartesian product.

```
C×D == CatProd(C,D)
```

Since the abstract terms are different, the proof system can easily distinguish
terms that look alike but have a different meaning. Display forms can also be
used to suppress information that is to be considered implicit. The composition
of two arrows f and g, for instance, depends on the category C to which f and
g belong, but it would be awkward to write down this information every time
the composition operator is used.

Currently, Nuprl's display is restricted to a single 8-bit font. This limits the
use of symbols, subscripts and superscripts to the characters defined in this
font. Identities, usually written as 1_A or $1_{(A,X)}$, have to be presented as 1A and
1<A,X>. Apart from these restrictions, all the basic category-theoretic vocabulary
appears in the system as described in Section 2.

Inference rules. Given the formal representation of basic category theory, there are several ways to implement the rules.

The standard approach would be to encode rules as tactics based on elementary inference rules. However, it is difficult to prove that these tactics actually represent a specific category-theoretic rule. Furthermore, the tactics may require executing hundreds of basic inferences for each category-theoretic inference step. A more efficient way is to write tactics based on formal theorems that establish properties of the fundamental concepts. For instance, rule (14) corresponds to the theorem

$$\forall C,D:\text{Categories}. \ \forall F,G:\text{Fun}[C,D]. \ \forall \varphi:\text{Fun}[C,D](F,G). \ \forall X:C. \ \varphi X \in D(F^1 X, G^1 X)$$

To apply the rule, one would instantiate the theorem accordingly. But this would lead to proof obligations that do not occur in the original rule, such as showing that C and D are categories and F and G are functors in $\text{Fun}[C,D]$.

The Nuprl system supports a more direct approach to encoding formal theories. Experienced users can add rule objects to the system's library that directly represent the inference rules of the theory, then prove formal theorems like the one above to justify the rules. Apart from the fact that rules have to be formulated as top-down sequent rules to accommodate Nuprl's goal-oriented reasoning style, the representation of the rules in the system is identical to the version on paper, which makes it easy to check its faithfulness. Rule (14), for instance, is represented by a rule object `NatTransApply` with the following contents.

```
+- RULE: NatTransApply @edd.standardplus @sara
H ⊢ φ X ∈ D(F¹X,G¹X)

  BY NatTransApply C

H ⊢ φ ∈ Fun[C,D](F,G)
H ⊢ X ∈ C
```

Nuprl's rule compiler converts rule objects into rules that match the first line of the object against the actual goal sequent and create the subgoal sequents by instantiating the two lower lines. Note that the rule requires the category C to be given as parameter, since it occurs in a subgoal but not in the main goal.

Since equalities in Nuprl are typed, we added types to all the inference rules that deal with equalities. For example, rule (15) is represented as follows:

```
+- RULE: NatTransCompEqual @edd.standardplus @sarah
H ⊢ ((φ Y)∘F²g) = (G²g∘(φ X)) ∈ D(F¹X,G¹Y)

  BY NatTransCompEqual C

H ⊢ φ ∈ Fun[C,D](F,G)
H ⊢ X ∈ C
H ⊢ Y ∈ C
H ⊢ g ∈ C(X,Y)
```

We have generated rule objects for all the rules described in Section 2, as well as rules for dealing with products. Logical rules and rules dealing with extensional equality and substitution are already provided by Nuprl.

For each inference rule, we have also proved formally that it is correct with respect to our formalization of basic category theory. Although this is not strictly necessary if one is mainly interested in automating proofs, it validates the consistency of the implemented inference system relative to the consistency of Nuprl.

4 Proof Automation

The implementation of the proof calculus described above enables us to create formal proofs for many theorems of basic category theory. But even the simplest such theorems lead to proofs with hundreds or even thousands of inference steps, as illustrated in [18]. Since most of these statements are considered mathematically trivial, it should be possible to find their proofs completely automatically.

We have developed strategies for automated proof search in basic category theory that attempt to capture the general patterns of reasoning that we have observed in hand-constructed proofs. In this section we discuss the key components of these strategies and some of the issues that had to be reckoned with.

Automated Rule Application. Most of the inference rules are simple refinements that describe how to decompose a proof obligation into simpler components. Given a specific proof goal, there are only few rules that can be applied at all. Thus to a large extent, proof search consists of determining applicable rules and their parameters from the context, applying the rule, and then continuing the search on all the subgoals.

To make this possible, all the basic inference rules had to be converted into simple tactics that automatically determine their parameters. Generating names for new variables in the subgoals, as in the case of the extensionality rules (17)–(20), is straightforward. All other parameters occur as types in one of the subgoals of a rule and are determined through an extended type inference algorithm.

An important issue is loop control. Since the synthesis rules for functors and natural transformations are the inverse of the corresponding analysis rules, we have to avoid applying analysis rules if they create a subgoal that has already been decomposed by a synthesis rule. Synthesis rules decrease the depth of functor types in a proof goal. It is therefore sufficient to keep track of proof goals to which a synthesis rule had been applied and block the application of analysis rules that would generate one of these as a subgoal.

Performance Issues. One of the disadvantages of refinement style reasoning is that proof trees may contain identical proof goals in different branches. This is especially true after the application of synthesis and extensionality rules, which must be used quite often in complex proofs. The first subgoal of rule (9) eventually reappears in the proof of the second, since F^1A occurs within the type of that goal and both subgoals reappear in the proofs of the third and fourth subgoals. In a bottom-up proof, one would prove these goals only once and reuse them whenever they are needed to complete the proof of another goal, while a standard refinement proof forces us to prove the same goal over and over again.

Obviously we could optimize the corresponding rules for top-down reasoning and drop the redundant subgoals. To retain faithfulness of the implemented inference system, however, we decided to leave the rules unchanged. Instead, we have wrapped the corresponding tactic with a controlled application of the cut rule: we assert the first two subgoals of rule (9) before applying the rule. As a result they appear as hypotheses of all subgoals and have to be proved only once.

Although this method is a simple trick, it leads to a significant reduction in the size of automatically generated proofs. A complete proof of the isomorphism between Fun[C × D, E] and Fun[C, Fun[D, E]] without cuts consists of almost 30,000 inference steps. Using the wrapper reduces this number to 3,000.

Equality Reasoning. Equality reasoning is a key component in formal category-theoretic proofs. Ten of the inference rules deal with equalities and can be used to replace a term by one that is semantically equal.

Since equalities can be used both ways, they can easily lead to infinite loops in an automated search for a proof. Our automated reasoning strategy therefore has to assign a direction to each of the equalities and attempt to rewrite terms into some normal form. Furthermore, it has to keep track of the types involved in these equalities, which are sometimes crucial for finding a proper match and, as in the case of rule (15), for determining the right-hand side of an equality from the left-hand side. The inference rules described in Section 2, including those dealing with associativity and identity, lead to the following typed rewrites.

Rewrite		Type	Rule
$\langle g, k \rangle \circ \langle f, h \rangle$	$\mapsto \langle g \circ f, k \circ h \rangle$	$C \times D(\langle A_1, X_1 \rangle, \langle A_3, X_3 \rangle)$	(01)
$1_{\langle A, X \rangle}$	$\mapsto \langle 1_A, 1_X \rangle$	$C \times D(\langle A, X \rangle, \langle A, X \rangle)$	(02)
$1_Y \circ f$	$\mapsto f$	$C(X, Y)$	(2a)
$f \circ 1_X$	$\mapsto f$	$C(X, Y)$	(2b)
$h \circ (g \circ f)$	$\mapsto (h \circ g) \circ f$	$C(X, T)$	(2c)
$F^2(g \circ f)$	$\mapsto F^2 g \circ F^2 f$	$D(F^1 X, F^1 Z)$	(07)
$F^2 1_X$	$\mapsto 1_{F^1 X}$	$D(F^1 X, F^1 X)$	(08)
$(\psi \circ \varphi) A$	$\mapsto \psi A \circ \varphi A$	$D(F^1 X, H^1 X)$	(11)
$1_F X$	$\mapsto 1_{F^1 X}$	$D(F^1 X, F^1 X)$	(12)
$\varphi Y \circ F^2 g$	$\mapsto G^2 g \circ \varphi X$	$D(F^1 X, G^1 Y)$	(15)

Each rewrite is executed by applying a substitution, which is validated by applying the corresponding equality rule mentioned in the table above.

The above rewrite system is incomplete, as it cannot prove the equality of some terms that can be shown equal with the inference rules. We have used the superposition-based Knuth-Bendix completion procedure [17] to generate the following additional typed rewrites.

Rewrite		Type	Rules
$F^2 \langle 1_A, 1_X \rangle$	$\mapsto 1_{F^1 \langle A, X \rangle}$	$E(F^1 \langle A, X \rangle, F^1 \langle A, X \rangle)$	(02),(08)
$F^2 \langle g, k \rangle \circ F^2 \langle f, h \rangle$	$\mapsto F^2 \langle g \circ f, k \circ h \rangle$	$E(F^1 \langle A, X \rangle, F^1 \langle C, X \rangle)$	(01),(07)
$(\varphi Y A) \circ (F^2 g A)$	$\mapsto (G^2 g A) \circ (\varphi X A)$	$E(F^1 X^1 A, G^1 Y^1 A)$	(15),(11)
$(\varphi Y \circ \psi Y) \circ F^2 g$	$\mapsto (G^2 g \circ \varphi X) \circ \psi X$	$E(F^1 X, G^1 Y)$	(11),(15)
$H^2(\varphi Y) \circ H^2(F^2 g)$	$\mapsto H^2(G^2 g) \circ H^2(\varphi X)$	$E(H^1 F^1 X, H^1 G^1 Y)$	(2c),(15)
$(h \circ \varphi Y) \circ F^2 g$	$\mapsto (h \circ G^2 g) \circ \varphi X$	$D(F^1 X, Z)$	(07),(15)
$((h \circ G^2 g) \circ \varphi X) \circ \psi X$	$\mapsto ((h \circ \varphi Y) \circ \psi Y) \circ F^2 g$	$E(F^1 X, Z)$	(2c),(11),(15)
$(h \circ H^2(\varphi Y)) \circ H^2(F^2 g)$	$\mapsto (h \circ H^2(G^2 g)) \circ H^2(\varphi X)$	$E(H^1 F^1 X, Z)$	(07),(07),(15)

402   D. Kozen, C. Kreitz, and E. Richter

First-Order Reasoning. One important aspect of our approach is demonstrating that reasoning in basic category theory is essentially first-order although some of its concepts are not. This means that functors and natural transformations can only be treated as abstract objects whose properties can only be described in terms of their first-order components.

For example, proving two categories C and D isomorphic (formally denoted by $C \hat{=} D$) requires showing the existence of two functors θ : Fun[C,D] and η : Fun[D,C] that are inverses of each other. In the formal proof, we cannot simply introduce θ as closed object, because this would be a pair of λ-terms mapping C-objects onto D-objects and C-arrows onto D-arrows. Instead we have to specify its object and arrow components $\theta^1 A$ and $\theta^2 f$ for A an object of C and f an arrow of C through first-order equations. If these components are again functors or natural transformations, we have to specify subcomponents until we have reached a first-order level. In our proof of the isomorphism between Fun[C × D, E] and Fun[C, Fun[D, E]], we need four equations to specify θ:

$$\theta^1 G^1 X^1 X1 \equiv G^1 <X, X1> \qquad \theta^1 G^2 f \ X \equiv G^2 <f, 1X>$$
$$\theta^1 G^1 X^2 h \equiv G^2 <1X, h> \qquad \theta^2 \varphi \ X \ X1 \equiv \varphi <X, X1>$$

Mathematically speaking, these four equations are sufficient for the proof, since any functor satisfying these equations can be used to complete the proof. However, the embedding of basic category theory into Nuprl's formal logic requires the existence of a functor satisfying these equations to be verified (this requirement could, of course, be turned off by providing a special rule). Constructing the functor from the equations is straightforward if it is uniquely specified by them. Since this part of the proof is higher-order and has nothing to do with basic category theory, it is generated automatically in the background.

Guessing Witnesses for Existential Quantifiers. The mechanisms described so far are sufficient to verify properties of given functors and natural transformations. But many proofs in basic category theory require proving the existence of functors or transformations with certain properties. For a trained mathematician this is a trivial task if there are only few "obvious" choices. Since the purpose of proof automation is automating what is considered obvious, we have developed a heuristic that attempts to determine specifications for functors or natural transformations that are most likely to make a proof succeed.

The most obvious approach is to start developing a proof where the functor or natural transformation has been replaced by a free variable and proceed until the decomposition cannot continue anymore. At this point we have generated typing subgoals for all first-order components of the functor. For the functor θ in our isomorphism proof we get (up to α-equality) four different typing conditions

$$\theta^1 G^1 X^1 X1 \in E \qquad\qquad \theta^1 G^2 f \ X \ \in E(\theta^1 G^1 A^1 X, \theta^1 G^1 B^1 X)$$
$$\theta^1 G^1 X^2 h \ \in E(\theta^1 G^1 X^1 X1, \theta^1 G^1 X^1 Y) \quad \theta^2 \varphi \ X \ X1 \in E(\theta^1 F^1 X^1 X1, \theta^1 G^1 X^1 X \ X1)$$

The heuristic then tries to determine the simplest term that is built from the component's parameters (whose types are known) and satisfies the given typing requirements. For this purpose it tries to identify parameters that are declared to be functors or natural transformations and to find a match between some part of their range type and the typing requirement for the component. Once the match has been found, the remaining parameters will be used to determine the arguments needed by the functor or natural transformation.

To solve the first of the above typing conditions, the heuristic finds the declarations $G : \mathsf{Fun}[\mathsf{C} \times \mathsf{D}, \mathsf{E}]$, $X : \mathsf{C}$, and $X_1 : \mathsf{D}$. The simplest term that has type E and is built from these parameters is the term $G^1{<}X, X_1{>}$.

Determining the arguments of a functor or natural transformation is not always straightforward. In some cases like the above, the remaining parameters are of the right type and can be used as arguments. In other cases we have an object where an arrow is needed or vice versa. The most obvious choice is turning an object into an identity arrow and an arrow into its domain or codomain, depending on the typing requirements.

To solve the second of the above conditions, the heuristic has to use the declarations $G : \mathsf{Fun}[\mathsf{C} \times \mathsf{D}, \mathsf{E}]$, $X : \mathsf{C}$, $h : \mathsf{D}(X_1, Y)$, and $X_1, Y : \mathsf{D}$. To create a term of type $\mathsf{E}(\theta^1 G^1 X^1 X_1, \theta^1 G^1 X^1 Y)$, one has to use G^2 and arrows from $\mathsf{C}(X, X)$ and $\mathsf{D}(X_1, Y)$. For the latter, we can pick h, while the only arrow in $\mathsf{C}(X, X)$ that can be built from the object X is the identity 1_X.

In some cases, none of the above choices satisfy the typing conditions, but a composition of natural transformation and functor as in rule (15) would do so. In this case, the heuristic will use the functor and its arguments twice in different ways. This choice is less obvious, but still considered standard.

5 An Application

To demonstrate the feasibility of our approach, we have generated a completely formal proof that the functor categories $\mathsf{Fun}[\mathsf{C} \times \mathsf{D}, \mathsf{E}]$ and $\mathsf{Fun}[\mathsf{C}, \mathsf{Fun}[\mathsf{D}, \mathsf{E}]]$

```
⌐                "- PRF : Currying Tactic Test @edd.standardplus @sarah           ⌐│▫│
* top
∀C,D,E:Categories.  Fun[C×D,E] ≙ Fun[C,Fun[D,E]]

BY Unfold `CatIso` 0 THEN prover·

* 1

1. C : Categories
2. D : Categories
3. E : Categories
⊢ ∃θ:Fun[Fun[C×D,E],Fun[C,Fun[D,E]]].
  ∃η:Fun[Fun[C,Fun[D,E]],Fun[C×D,E]]. θ and η are inverse

BY GUESS ⌐θ⌐ · THEN GUESS ⌐η⌐ ·

* 1 1

4. theta : Top
5. ∀phi,k,X1,X,f,G:Top.
      (θ¹G²f X ≡ G²<f, 1X>
    ∧ θ¹G¹X¹X1 ≡ G¹<X, X1>
    ∧ θ¹G¹X²k ≡ G²<1X, k>
    ∧ θ²φ X X1 ≡ φ <X, X1>)
6. eta : Top
7. ∀X1,phi,g,f,X,A,G:Top.
      (η¹G¹<A, X> ≡ G¹A¹X
    ∧ η¹G²<f, g> ≡ ((G²f cod(g))∘G¹dom(f)²g)
    ∧ η²φ <A, X1> ≡ φ A X1)
⊢ θ and η are inverse

BY Unfold `FunInverse` 0 THEN AutoCAT2
```

are naturally isomorphic. The structure of the proof is similar to the hand-constructed proof described in [18], which required several hours to complete and more than 10 pages to write down. Using our strategies, the creation of the proof was fully automated and took only a few seconds.

The screenshot above shows that the proof consists of only six proof steps. First we unfold the definition of isomorphisms and decompose the proof goal. We then ask the tactic to guess values for the functors θ and η. Finally, we unfold the definition of inverse functors and use the automated proof search procedure to validate that θ and η are indeed functors of the appropriate types and that they are inverse to each other.

This top-level version of the proof reveals the key idea that was necessary to solve the problem, but hides the tedious details involved in validating the solution. Users interested in proof details can inspect the complete proof tree that Nuprl will display on demand. However, one should be aware that the complete proof is huge. It takes 1046 and 875 basic inferences to prove that θ and η are indeed functors of the appropriate types and another 1141 inferences to prove that they are inverse to each other.

It should be noted that all six steps are straightforward when it comes to dealing with isomorphism problems. One could combine them into a single tactic IsoCAT, which would then give us the following proof.

```
* ∀C,D,E:Categories.  Fun[C×D,E] ≐ Fun[C,Fun[D,E]]
  BY IsoCAT
```

However, little insight is gained from such a proof, except that it has in fact been completed automatically.

Proving the naturality of the isomorphism is more demanding, since we have to show θ and η to be elements of $\mathsf{Fun}[\mathsf{Cat}^{\mathrm{op}} \times \mathsf{Cat}^{\mathrm{op}} \times \mathsf{Cat}, \mathsf{Cat}](U, V)$ for suitable functors U, V, that are inverse for every choice of categories C, D, and E. Guessing specifications for U, V, θ, and η automatically is now less trivial. Currently, our automated strategy (extended for dealing with categories of categories) can only validate U, V, θ, and η after they have been specified by hand.

6 Conclusion

We have presented a Gentzen-style deductive system for elementary category theory involving a mixture of typing and equational judgments. We have implemented this logic in Nuprl along with relevant proof tactics that go a long way toward full automation of elementary proofs. We have demonstrated the effectiveness of this approach by automatically deriving proofs of several nontrivial results in the theory, one example of which is presented in detail above. The system works very well on the examples we have tried.

We have found that careful planning in the order of application of tactics makes the proof search mostly deterministic. However, the proofs that are generated tend to be quite large because of the overwhelming amount of detail. Many of the necessary steps, especially those that involve basic typing judgments, are quite tedious and do not lend much insight from a human perspective. For this reason, they are typically omitted in the literature. Such arguments are nevertheless essential for automation, because they drive the application of tactics.

There are a number of technical insights that we have observed in the course of this work.

- Most of the ideas that we have applied in this work are in fact fairly standard and not too sophisticated. This shows that our calculus is well designed and integrates well with existing theorem proving technology.
- Formal proofs, even of quite elementary facts, have thousands of inferences. As mentioned, many of these steps are quite tedious and do not lend much insight. This indicates that the theory is a good candidate for automation.
- Almost all proof steps can be automated. Forward steps such as decomposition using the analysis rules and directed rewriting for equations tend to be quite successful. Since the proof system is normalizing and confluent (we did not show this), the time is mostly spent building the proof. Apart from guessing witnesses, there is virtually no backtracking involved and the bulk of the development is completely deterministic, being driven by typing considerations.
- Lookahead improves the performance of our strategy. Since inference rules may generate redundant subgoals, lemma generation can allow proof reuse.
- Display forms are crucial for comprehensibility. It is often very difficult to keep track of typing judgments currently in force. Judicious choice of the display form can make a great difference in human readability.

For the future, we plan to gain more experience by attempting to automate more of the basic theory. We need more experience with the different types of arguments that arise in category theory so that we will be better able to design those parts of the mechanism involved with the guessing of witnesses. Preliminary investigations show that automating the application of the Yoneda lemma will be key to many of the more advanced proofs.

Since our proof strategies can be viewed as encodings of proof plans for category theory, our approach may benefit from using generic proof planning techniques [8] to make these proof plans explicit.

Finally, we would like to mention an intriguing theoretical open problem. The proof of the result that we have described, namely that Fun[C × D, E] and Fun[C, Fun[D, E]] are naturally isomorphic, breaks down into two parts. The first part argues that the functor categories Fun[C × D, E] and Fun[C, Fun[D, E]] are isomorphic, and the second part argues that the isomorphism is natural. As Mac Lane describes it [20, p. 2], *naturality*, applied to a parameterized construction, says that the construction is carried out "in the same way" for all instantiations of the parameters. Of course, there is a formal definition of the concept of naturality in category theory itself, and it involves reparameterizing the result in terms of functors in place of objects, natural transformations in place of arrows. But any constructions in the formal proof π of the first part of the theorem, just the isomorphism of the two parameterized functor categories, would work "in the same way" for all instantiations of the parameters, by virtue of the fact that the formal proof π is similarly parameterized. This leads us to ask: Under what conditions can one extract a proof of naturality *automatically* from π? That is, under what conditions can a proof in our formal system be automatically retooled to additionally establish the naturality of the constructions involved? Extracting naturality in this way would be analogous to the extraction of programs from proofs according to the Curry–Howard isomorphism.

References

1. S. Allen et. al. Innovations in computational type theory using Nuprl. *Journal of Applied Logic*, 2006. (to appear).
2. S. Allen, R. Constable, R. Eaton, C. Kreitz, L. Lorigo The Nuprl open logical environment. *CADE-17*, LNCS 1831, pages 170–176. Springer, 2000.
3. G. Bancerek. Concrete categories. *J. formalized mathematics*, 13, 2001.
4. G. Bancerek. Miscellaneous facts about functors. *J. form. math.*, 13, 2001.
5. G. Bancerek. Categorial background for duality theory. *J. form. math.*, 13, 2001.
6. M. Barr, C. Wells. *Category Theory for Computing Science*. Prentice Hall, 1990.
7. R. Bird. *A Calculus of Functions for Program Derivation*, Research Topics in Functional Programming, pages 287–307, Addison-Wesley, 1990.
8. A. Bundy *The Use of Explicit Plans to Guide Inductive Proofs*. *CADE-9*, pages 111–120. Springer, 1988.
9. R. Constable et. al. *Implementing Mathematics with the Nuprl proof development system*. Prentice Hall, 1986.
10. M. J. Cáccamo, G. Winskel. A higher-order calculus for categories. Technical Report RS-01-27, BRICS, University of Aarhus, 2001.
11. P. Eklund et. al. A graphical approach to monad compositions. *Electronic Notes in Theoretical Computer Science*, 40, 2002.
12. S. Eilenberg, S. MacLane. General theory of natural equivalences. *Trans. Amer. Math. Soc.*, 58:231–244, 1945.
13. J. Glimming. Logic and automation for algebra of programming. Master thesis, University of Oxford, 2001.
14. J. Goguen. A categorical manifesto. *Mathematical Structures in Computer Science*, 1(1):49–67, 1991.
15. J. Harrison. Formalized mathematics. *Technical report of Turku Centre for Computer Science*, 36, 1996.
16. G. Huet, A. Saïbi. Constructive category theory. *Joint CLICS-TYPES Workshop on Categories and Type Theory*, 1995. MIT Press.
17. D. Knuth, P. Bendix. Simple word problems in universal algebra. *Computational Problems in Abstract Algebra*, pages 263–297. Pergamon Press, 1970.
18. D. Kozen. Toward the automation of category theory. Technical Report 2004-1964, Computer Science Department, Cornell University, 2004.
19. C. Kreitz. *The Nuprl Proof Development System, V5: Reference Manual and User's Guide*. Computer Science Department, Cornell University, 2002.
20. S. MacLane. *Categories for the Working Mathematician*. Springer, 1971.
21. E. Moggi. Notions of computation and monads. *Inf. and Comp.*, 93, 1991.
22. Greg O'Keefe. Towards a readable formalisation of category theory. *Electronic Notes in Theoretical Computer Science* 91:212–228. Elsevier, 2004.
23. L. Paulson. *Isabelle: A Generic Theorem Prover*, LNCS 828. Springer, 1994.

24. D. Rydeheard, R. Burstall. *Computational Category Theory*. Prentice Hall, 1988.
25. G. M. Reed, A. W. Roscoe, R. F. Wachter. *Topology and Category Theory in Computer Science*. Oxford University Press, 1991.
26. A. Saïbi. Constructive category theory, coq.inria.fr/contribs/category.tar.gz, 1995.
27. C. Simpson. Category theory in ZFC, coq.inria.fr/contribs/CatsInZFC.tar.gz, 2004.
28. M. Takeyama. *Universal Structure and a Categorical Framework for Type Theory*. PhD thesis, University of Edinburgh, 1995.
29. A. Trybulec. Some isomorphisms between functor categories. *J. formalized mathematics*, 4, 1992.
30. P. Wadler. Monads for functional programming. *Advanced Functional Programming*, LNCS 925, pp. 24–52, Springer, 1995.

Formal Global Optimisation with Taylor Models

Roland Zumkeller

École Polytechnique, 91128 Palaiseau Cedex, France

Abstract. Formal proofs and global optimisation are two research areas that have been heavily influenced by the arrival of computers. This article aims to bring both further together by formalising a global optimisation method based on Taylor models: a set of functions is represented by a polynomial together with an error bound. The algorithms are implemented in the proof assistant Coq's term language, with the ultimate goal to obtain formally proven bounds for any multi-variate smooth function in an efficient way. To this end we make use of constructive real numbers, interval arithmetic, and polynomial bounding techniques.

1 Introduction

Global optimisation, as it shall be understood in this article, is concerned with finding the minimum and maximum value of a given objective function $f : \mathbb{R}^n \to \mathbb{R}$ on a certain domain $[a_1; b_1] \times \ldots \times [a_n; b_n]$. Since this is generally difficult, we will in practice content ourselves with a bounding interval [c;d] such that $\forall x \in [a_1; b_1] \times \ldots \times [a_n; b_n]. \ f \, x \in [c; d]$, of course desiring $[c; d]$ as narrow as possible.

Problems of this kind arise in a wide spectrum of science, ranging from engineering (aeronautics [4], robotics [16]), over experimental physics (particle motion in accelerators [12]) to geometry. A prominent instance of the last class is the proof of the Kepler conjecture given by Thomas Hales [10], in which some thousand lemmata asserting bounds on geometric functions occur.

1.1 From Extremum Criteria to Global Optimisation Algorithms

In 1755 Euler gave (based on previous work by Fermat) the well-known necessary condition $\nabla f x = 0$ for f to assume an extremum at x [5]. However, in most interesting cases effectively solving this equation is an equally difficult problem. During the following centuries a lot of more sophisticated criteria have been developed, but like Euler's most of them reduced the original problem to another difficult one.

The arrival of computers changed this situation: Previously intractable optimisation problems entered the scope of what could be solved. Moreover, this led mathematicians to develop new methods to treat this kind of problems. In 1962 Ramon E. Moore described the use of interval arithmetic on a computer, refined by a branch-and-bound algorithm to optimise a function over an interval [18]. This work has been the basis for many sophisticated refinements, making up the core of numerous current global optimisation algorithms [11].

U. Furbach and N. Shankar (Eds.): IJCAR 2006, LNAI 4130, pp. 408–422, 2006.

1.2   From Formal Proof in Principle to Formal Proof in Fact

In 1879 Frege was first to introduce the notion of formal proof. With his *Begriffs-schrift* he gave a language to express propositions and rules to reason on them in a purely syntactical manner. While this work showed how formal proofs can *in principle* be constructed, its usefulness remained limited by practical con-straints: The amount of detail required to formally prove even relatively simple statements was unacceptably large for a human equipped only with pencil and paper.

Again, the arrival of computers changed this situation: In 1967, after mathe-matical logic had become a more thoroughly studied topic, Nicolaas G. de Bruijn developed the Automath system [3], which could syntactically verify that a given proof indeed demonstrates a given theorem. The fact that formal proofs could now be constructed and checked on a machine made their development more practical, and a certain amount of mathematics has been formalised in different systems since.

1.3   Formal Global Optimisation

The aim of the work described in this article is to apply formal proof techniques to global optimisation. More precisely, we are going to formalise an algorithm based on Taylor models [12] in the Coq system. Taylor models are the basis of one of the more recent global optimisation methods in the tradition of interval arithmetic, while Coq is a state-of-the-art proof assistant in the tradition of de Bruijn's system.

Solutions to other computationally difficult problems have already been for-malised: a formal proof of the Four Colour Theorem has been given by Georges Gonthier and Benjamin Werner [6]. Also, a verification algorithm for Pocklington certificates of prime numbers has been proven correct [7]. In a slightly different setting, other computational parts of the Kepler conjecture proof have been formalised, namely a large graph enumeration problem [20] and linear prog-rams [22].

Computational proofs are supported by an important characteristic of type theory: The so-called *conversion rule* identifies terms modulo β-conversion (com-putation). In fact, functional programs written in type theory can be referred to in proofs. For example assume that test : term $\rightarrow$ intvl $\rightarrow$ bool implements a global optimisation method which attempts to prove that a certain function (described by its term) is positive on a given interval. Its correctness lemma states:

$$\forall f : \text{term}, X : \text{intvl. test } f\, X = \text{true} \rightarrow \forall x : \mathbb{R}.\ x \in X \rightarrow [\![f]\!]\, x > 0$$

If the method used is reasonably good test $(\frac{1}{2} + \mathcal{X} + \mathcal{X}^2) [-1; 1]$ will evaluate to true. Then we can prove $\forall x : \mathbb{R}.\ x \in [-1; 1] \rightarrow \frac{1}{2} + x + x^2 > 0$ simply by applying the correctness lemma. The attractive feature of this technique, called *proof by reflection*, is that the computation steps do not have to be made explicit. It suffices in fact to refer to the decision procedure test, whose computational trace can be reproduced if the proof needs to be re-checked. Therefore the trace does not need to be stored, which can dramatically reduce the size of certain proofs.

The rest of this article presents an implementation of Taylor models in Coq. Its description has to remain on a rather abstract level, due to the number of different concepts involved. However, the implementation follows quite closely the theoretical presentation given here. Our ultimate goal is to entirely prove correct the Taylor model algorithm and to refine our implementation sufficiently, so that it can treat all of the above-mentioned lemmata appearing in the proof of the Kepler conjecture.

1.4   Outline

Section 2 presents interval arithmetic and its traditional use for global optimisation. The dependency problem and the loss of sharpness of the united extension are discussed. A solution to the latter is suggested in section 3 where we explain how constructive reals can be used as interval bounds. In particular, a generalisation of Moore's sign-based interval multiplication is given. In section 4 Taylor models are presented according to [12]. We simplify it by giving a new technique for composing smooth functions with Taylor models, not requiring the manual insertion of an addition theorem (4.2). Besides, it is shown that the choice of reference points for the development of smooth functions can be improved (4.3). Finally, we give some examples of our implementation's performance (section 5) before reaching the conclusions (section 6).

2   Interval Arithmetic

As mentioned, interval arithmetic on computers has been developed by Moore in the early 1960s. We will briefly describe its traditional use for global optimisation, thereby summarising its elementary notions. While we are not going to follow this approach here, Taylor models themselves make careful use of interval arithmetic.

Definition 1. *Given a set of bounds $B \subseteq \mathbb{R}$ the set of associated intervals is defined as $\mathbb{I}_B := \{[a; b] \mid a, b \in B\}$ where $[a; b] := \{x \in R \mid a \leq x \leq b\}$. We also note the set of n-dimensional boxes as $\mathbb{I}_{\mathbb{R}}^n := \{X_1 \times \ldots \times X_n \mid X_1, \ldots, X_n \in \mathbb{I}\}$, and $[x_1, \ldots, x_k]$ the smallest interval containing all of $x_1, \ldots, x_k$, each one of which is either a bound or an interval.*

Definition 2. *For any $B \subseteq \mathbb{R}$ the function $\hat{f} : \mathbb{I}_B^n \to \mathbb{I}_B$ is a B-interval extension of $f : \mathbb{R}^n \to \mathbb{R}$ iff:*

$$\forall X \in \mathbb{I}_B^n. \ \hat{f} X \supseteq \{f x \mid x \in X\}$$

If $\supseteq$ can be replaced by $=$ in the preceding line, $\hat{f}$ is called B-sharp.

We will first develop interval arithmetic on $\mathbb{I}_{\mathbb{R}}$. The problems to which other choices for the bounds lead will be discussed in section 2.3. However, in section 3 we will show that, in spite of tradition, a choice different from $\mathbb{R}$ is not mandatory for an implementation.

2.1 Operations

Interval extensions of some basic real functions are given in table 1. They are all sharp, as can be easily verified. Extensions of more complicated functions can be obtained by structural recursion on the term describing them. The result is referred to as the *natural interval extension*. Note that it is in general not sharp.

Table 1. Interval extensions of some real functions

$$[a; b] \mathbin{\hat{+}} [c; d] :- [a \mid c; b \mid d]$$
$$\mathbin{\hat{-}} [a; b] := [-b; -a]$$
$$[a; b] \mathbin{\hat{\cdot}} [c; d] := [\min\{ac, ad, bc, cd\}; \max\{ac, ad, bc, cd\}]$$
$$1 \mathbin{\hat{/}} [a; b] := [1/b; 1/a] \quad \text{if } 0 \notin [a; b]$$
$$\operatorname{arc\hat{t}an}[a; b] = [\arctan a; \arctan b]$$
$$\sqrt{\hat{[a; b]}} = [\sqrt{a}; \sqrt{b}] \quad \text{if } 0 \le a$$

The extension of multiplication is inefficient if implemented as suggested by the formula given in table 1, because all of ac, ad, bc, and bd are computed before determining their minimum and maximum. In fact this can be accelerated [17] by looking at the signs of a, b, c, and d, using the fact that $a \le b$ and $c \le d$.

Definition 3. *An interval* $[a; b]$ *has* sign + *if* $a > 0$, sign − *if* $b < 0$ *and sign* ± *if* $a \le 0 \le b$.

Given the signs of the two intervals $[a; b]$ and $[c; d]$ we can compute the extension of multiplication as described in the following table:

$[a; b]$	$[c; d]$	$\min\{ac, ad, bc, bd\}$	$\max\{ac, ad, bc, bd\}$
+	+	ac	bd
+	±	bc	bd
±	±	$\min\{ad, bc\}$	$\max\{ac, bd\}$

The other six cases can be reduced to these by the two equations:

$$[a; b] \mathbin{\hat{\cdot}} [c; d] = [c; d] \mathbin{\hat{\cdot}} [a; b] = -([-b; -a] \mathbin{\hat{\cdot}} [c; d])$$

2.2 Global Optimisation with Interval Arithmetic

In order to obtain bounds for a given function f on a domain X, it is now sufficient to construct an interval extension $\hat{f}$ of f (e.g. the natural one). Then, by the extension property, computing the interval $\hat{f} X$ provides bounds for f on X.

However, and this is why the story does not end here, these bounds are in general quite crude. Optimising $x \mapsto x - x$ on $[a; b]$ by this method yields

$[a-b; b-a]$, although it is easy to see that $[0;0]$ is a bound here. One might object that $x - x$ could easily be recognised and rewritten to 0. This is correct (and even helpful), but there are many other similar cases, e.g. $(\sin x)^2 + (\cos x)^2$. No general procedure is known to cover all of them.

It might seem surprising that the interval extension of the subtraction given in table 1 is sharp, while the result that it yields on the above example is not optimal. This point merits some study. To begin with, the extension property for $\hat{-}$ states that for any $X, Y \in \mathbb{I}$:

$$\forall x \in X, y \in Y.\ x - y \in X \mathbin{\hat{-}} Y$$

Furthermore, sharpness asserts that for any X, Y the interval $X \hat{-} Y$ is the narrowest one satisfying this statement. By setting Y to X we obtain:

$$\forall x, y \in X.\ x - y \in X \mathbin{\hat{-}} X$$

This shows the problem clearly: An argument to an interval extension does not contain any reference to the variable it represents. The term $X \mathbin{\hat{-}} X$ represents not only $x - y$, but of course also the less general $x - x$. It cannot be evaluated to $[0;0]$ because the information that both its arguments are the same has been lost. This phenomenon is often referred to as the *dependency problem*.

A simple strategy to improve the quality of the bounds is based on interval-splitting. In one dimension the *united extension* $\hat{f}_n$ of f is given by:

$$\hat{f}_n\,[a;b] = \bigcup_{i=1}^{n} \hat{f}\left[a + (i-1)\frac{b-a}{n}; a + i\frac{b-a}{n}\right]$$

Moore showed in his thesis [18] that $[a;b] \mapsto \lim_{n \to \infty} \hat{f}_n[a;b]$ is a sharp extension of f. This can – with exponential complexity – easily be generalised to the multi-dimensional case. Although important, this technique is not yet sufficient for most applications, which is why numerous other refinements [11,19] have been developed. In section 4 we are going to see how Taylor models address the dependency problem more directly and are able to overcome it in part.

2.3   The Set of Interval Bounds

Traditionally some set of "machine-representable" numbers $B \subset \mathbb{R}$ has been used to implement interval bounds. However, note that even when we are able to obtain a basic set of B-sharp functions (such as in table 1), the B-sharpness of the united extension can be lost, as shows the following example:

Example 1. Let $B = \{\frac{k}{1000} \mid k \in \mathbb{N}\}$. Denote $\lfloor x \rfloor = \max\{b \in B \mid b \le x\}$ and $\lceil x \rceil = \min\{b \in B \mid x \le b\}$. We then have the B-sharp extensions:

$$[a;b] \mathbin{\hat{-}_B} [c;d] = [a - d; b - c]$$
$$\sqrt{[a;b]}_B = \left[\lfloor \sqrt{a} \rfloor\,;\,\lceil \sqrt{b} \rceil\right]$$

Now consider the function $f = x \mapsto \sqrt{x} - \sqrt{x}$. Its natural B-interval extension is $\hat{f} = [a; b] \mapsto \left[\lfloor\sqrt{a}\rfloor - \lceil\sqrt{b}\rceil ; \lceil\sqrt{b}\rceil - \lfloor\sqrt{a}\rfloor \right]$. For its united extension we have

$$\hat{f}_n [0; 1] = \bigcup_{i=1}^{n} [-\delta_{i,n}; \delta_{i,n}] = [-\delta_{1,n}; \delta_{1,n}] \text{ where } \delta_{i,n} = \left[\sqrt{\frac{i}{n}} \right] - \left\lfloor \sqrt{\frac{i-1}{n}} \right\rfloor$$

Note that $\delta_{1,n} = \left\lceil \sqrt{\frac{1}{n}} \right\rceil \geq \frac{1}{1000}$ for any n. Thus $\lim_{n\to\infty} \hat{f}_n [0;1] = [0; \frac{1}{1000}] \neq [0;0]$, which means that $\hat{f}_n$ is not B-sharp. $\square$

The same phenomenon occurs with floating-point numbers. As an alternative, taking rational numbers allows us to have sharp interval extensions of basic arithmetic to $\mathbb{I}_{\mathbb{Q}}$. However, for the irrational functions (e.g. square root) there are no sharp extensions. In order to refine bounds for f obtained by computing $\hat{f}_n$ for some n we thus have two options:

- Recompute $\hat{f}_n$ for a larger n.
- Use a more precise set of bounds $B \subset \mathbb{R}$. In practice this can mean to increase some precision parameter.

The first option would be a good choice for $f\,x = x - x$, the second one for $f\,x = \sqrt{x}$ on $[0; 2]$. However, it is not easy to say which choice is better in general. Making the wrong one will lead to unnecessary computations.

3   Constructive Real Numbers

No solution has been given to the loss of sharpness for the united extension occurring when using numbers that are "machine-representable" in the traditional sense. We will explain how constructive analysis can be used to represent the whole of (constructively defined) $\mathbb{R}$ on a machine. This approach allows us to regain sharpness of the united extension.

Real numbers can be seen as equivalence classes of Cauchy sequences. $x : \mathbb{N} \to \mathbb{Q}$ is a Cauchy sequence if:

$$\forall \varepsilon > 0. \ \exists n. \ \forall k_1, k_2 \geq n. \ \left| x\,k_1 - x\,k_2 \right| < \varepsilon$$

By the Curry-Howard-isomorphism constructively proving this property for a given x amounts to providing a function $m : \mathbb{Q} \to \mathbb{N}$ (referred to as the *modulus*) such that

$$\forall \varepsilon > 0. \ \forall k_1, k_2 \geq m\,\varepsilon. \ \left| x\,k_1 - x\,k_2 \right| < \varepsilon$$

A real number can thus be defined as a pair $(x, m) \in (\mathbb{N} \to \mathbb{Q}) \times (\mathbb{Q} \to \mathbb{N})$ verifying this property. They are equipped with two families of ε-indexed relations:

$$(x_1, m_1) =_\varepsilon (x_2, m_2) :\Leftrightarrow \left| (x_1 \circ m_1)\,\varepsilon - (x_2 \circ m_2)\,\varepsilon \right| \leq 2\varepsilon$$
$$(x_1, m_1) <_\varepsilon (x_2, m_2) :\Leftrightarrow (x_1 \circ m_1)\,\varepsilon + 2\varepsilon \leq (x_2 \circ m_2)\,\varepsilon$$

We also note:

$$a < b :\Leftrightarrow \exists \varepsilon.\ a <_\varepsilon b \qquad \text{and} \qquad a = b :\Leftrightarrow \forall \varepsilon.\ a =_\varepsilon b$$

Note that $=_\varepsilon$ and $<_\varepsilon$ are decidable for a given ε, whereas $=$ and $<$ are not. We give here only a few examples of functions on constructive reals:

$$(x_1, m_1) + (x_2, m_2) := \left(k \mapsto x_1\,k + x_2\,k, \varepsilon \mapsto \max\left\{m_1\left(\frac{\varepsilon}{2}\right), m_2\left(\frac{\varepsilon}{2}\right)\right\}\right)$$

$$\min(x_1, m_1)(x_2, m_2) := (k \mapsto \min(x_1\,k)(x_2\,k), \varepsilon \mapsto \max(m_1\,\varepsilon)(m_2\,\varepsilon))$$

$$\mathrm{sgn}_\varepsilon(x, m) := \begin{cases} 1 & \text{if } x\varepsilon < -\varepsilon \\ -1 & \text{if } \varepsilon < x\varepsilon \\ 0 & \text{otherwise} \end{cases}$$

More details on constructive real numbers and their implementations can be found in [25,21,23,2,15]. Irrational functions (square root, trigonometry etc.) can be computed without rounding. This means that in order to obtain an approximation for a larger formula we have to provide only one precision argument.

Real numbers defined in this way are termed "constructive" because they serve as the basis of constructive analysis, in which every proof induces an algorithm. However, when one does not care for algorithms, it is of course acceptable to use the excluded middle to reason about them.

3.1   Interval Multiplication

When using constructive real numbers as interval bounds, the undecidability of their sign is not entirely harmless. For the multiplication of two intervals Moore's procedure (section 2.1) cannot be applied since it requires sign information for all four bounds involved. If sgn_ε yields 0 for one of the two intervals, we would have to fall back to the more inefficient version of table 1.

In order to avoid this, we propose a generalisation of Moore's efficient interval multiplication to intervals with constructive real numbers as bounds. It performs a finer case analysis, able to eliminate candidates among $\{ac, ad, bc, cd\}$ based on only partial sign information.

We note $(x_{-1}, x_1, y_{-1}, y_1) := (a, b, c, d)$. Under the assumptions $x_{-1} < x_1$ and $y_{-1} < y_1$ (which happens to be an invariant of all interval operations) we have for any ε:

$$\min\{x_i y_j \mid i, j \in \{-1, 1\}\} = \min\{x_i y_j \mid i, j \in \{-1, 1\} \wedge \neg(0 <_\varepsilon j x_i \vee 0 <_\varepsilon i y_j)\}$$

Proof. We have to show that for the smallest element $x_i y_j$ the property $\neg(0 <_\varepsilon j x_i \vee 0 <_\varepsilon i y_j)$ holds. If $0 <_\varepsilon j x_i$ then $x_i y_{-j} < x_i y_j$. Symmetrically, if $0 <_\varepsilon i y_i$ then $x_{-i} y_j < x_i y_j$. Both conclusions contradict the assumption that $x_i y_j$ is minimal. □

What ε should be chosen? Note that this choice does not affect the result of the given procedure but only its performance. If ε is chosen too small, the cost of determining $0 <_\varepsilon j x_i$ and $0 <_\varepsilon i y_j$ becomes high, if chosen too large the set which the min function is applied to is more likely to contain more than one element. Experiments show that this choice is in most cases not critical.

3.2 Partial Functions

Looking at table 1 we notice that the extension of the multiplicative inverse has $0 \notin [a; b]$ as a side condition. If it is not satisfied then the inverse function in our implementation returns the special interval $[-\infty; \infty]$, conveying the information that nothing can be pe proved about the result.

Because the condition is undecidable on constructive reals we can only give an ε-indexed family of interval extensions:

$$\hat{1/}_\varepsilon[a; b] := \begin{cases} [1/b; 1/a] & \text{if } 0 <_\varepsilon a \vee b <_\varepsilon 0 \\ [-\infty; \infty] & \text{otherwise} \end{cases}$$

Once a function has returned the interval $[-\infty; \infty]$ this result is propagated (e.g. $[-\infty; \infty] + [a; b] = [-\infty; \infty]$) and the computation thus aborted. Except for this error case the sharpness of the united extension remains ensured.

4 Taylor Models

The dependency problem described in section 2.2 gave rise to many refinements of interval arithmetic, such as variable centring, domain-splitting, domain projections, or gradient checks [11,19]. All of these provide a certain remedy, but they do not actually solve the problem. It has often been observed that Taylor expansions of the function to optimise can be used to obtain better results with interval arithmetic. Taylor *models* [12] exploit this fact systematically and combine it with methods for the efficient computation of derivatives.

As we have seen, the dependency problem stems from the fact that the information that $x - x$ is different from $x - y$ is lost on the interval level. This is because interval arithmetic is a *calculus of number sets*, unable to represent this kind of information. In contrast to this, Taylor models provide a *calculus of function sets*.

We note $\mathbb{R}[\mathcal{X}_1, \ldots, \mathcal{X}_k]$ the set of k-variate polynomials with real coefficients in the variables $\mathcal{X}_1, \ldots, \mathcal{X}_k$. Their addition and multiplication are assumed.

Definition 4. *The set of k-variate* Taylor models *is defined as* $\mathbb{T} := \mathbb{I}^k \times \mathbb{R}[\mathcal{X}_1, \ldots, \mathcal{X}_k] \times \mathbb{I}$. *For a Taylor model* $(X, P, \Delta) \in \mathbb{T}$ *the box X is called its domain, P its polynomial, and Δ its error bound. The set of all Taylor models over some given domain X is denoted by* $\mathbb{T}_X$.

A Taylor model represents a set of functions:

$$[\![(X, P, \Delta)]\!] = \{ f : X \to \mathbb{R} \mid \forall x.\ f\,x - P\,x \in \Delta \}$$

4.1 Arithmetic on Taylor Models

A polynomial bounder $B : \mathbb{R}[\mathcal{X}_1, \ldots, \mathcal{X}_k] \to \mathbb{I}^k \to \mathbb{I}$ is assumed to be available, e.g. by a Horner evaluation in interval arithmetic. $(P)_{\leq n}$ denotes the polynomial P up to the nth coefficient, and $(P)_{>n}$ the remaining part.

A binary operation on Taylor models $\odot_T$ correctly reflects $\odot_R$ on reals iff:

$$[\![T_1 \odot_T T_2]\!] \supseteq \{x \mapsto f\,x \odot_R g\,x \mid f \in [\![T_1]\!], g \in [\![T_2]\!]\}$$

This condition is satisfied by the following definitions, valid for two Taylor models with identical domain [12]:

$$(X, P_1, \Delta_1) \,\tilde{+}\, (X, P_2, \Delta_2) = (X, P_1 + P_2, \Delta_1 \hat{+} \Delta_2)$$
$$(X, P_1, \Delta_1) \,\tilde{\cdot}\, (X, P_2, \Delta_2) = (X, (P_1 \cdot P_2)_{\leq n}, B\,X\,(P_1 \cdot P_2)_{>n} \,\hat{+}$$
$$B\,P_1\,X \,\hat{\cdot}\, \Delta_2 \,\hat{+}\, \Delta_1 \,\hat{\cdot}\, B\,P_2\,X \,\hat{+}\, \Delta_1 \,\hat{\cdot}\, \Delta_2)$$

For multiplication the degree n can be arbitrarily chosen. Higher values will lead to better accuracy, but also to a higher computational cost.

4.2   Composing Smooth Functions with Taylor Models

After having defined addition and multiplication in the previous section we are able to evaluate any polynomial in $\mathbb{T}_X$. The natural next step is to construct Taylor model versions for the square root or trigonometric functions (the multiplicative inverse will be treated along with them).

We show how, given any smooth function $g : Y \to R$ (where $Y \subseteq \mathbb{R}$) and a Taylor model $F \in \mathbb{T}_X$ (where $X \in \mathbb{I}^k$) we can construct a new Taylor model $H \in \mathbb{T}_X$ such that:

$$\{g \circ f \mid f \in [\![F]\!]\} =: g \circ [\![F]\!] \subseteq H$$

The proposed solution of this problem is not going to use the fact that F is represented by a Taylor model. It would work as well for any other representation of function sets.

The idea is to apply Taylor's theorem to develop g around a freely chosen reference point $y_0 \in Y$. We thus have for any $f \in F$:

$$\forall x \in X.\; g\,(f\,x) \in \sum_{k=0}^{n} \frac{g^{(k)}\,y_0}{k!}(f\,x - y_0)^k + \frac{g^{(n+1)}[y_0, f\,x]}{(n+1)!}(f\,x - y_0)^{(n+1)} \quad (1)$$

The left summand can be written in notation of functions arithmetic, while we make the right summand an interval independent of x (by taking the union of all possibles values of f on X). (1) thus implies:

$$g \circ f \in \sum_{k=0}^{n} \frac{g^{(k)}\,y_0}{k!}(f - y_0)^k + \frac{g^{(n+1)}[y_0, f\,X]}{(n+1)!}(f\,X - y_0)^{(n+1)}$$

The last step is to include all possible choices within F and to bound it on X:

$$g \circ F \subseteq \sum_{k=0}^{n} \frac{g^{(k)}\,y_0}{k!}(F - y_0)^k + \frac{g^{(n+1)}[y_0, B\,F\,X]}{(n+1)!}(B\,F\,X - y_0)^{(n+1)} =: H \quad (2)$$

We're now done with the construction of H. It can actually be implemented: The left summand is a polynomial of Taylor models (or any other structure representing function sets), for which we have already defined the arithmetic operations. The right summand relies on the bounding of F and interval arithmetic. It contributes to the resulting Taylor model's error interval.

This construction is inspired by the strategy for composing smooth functions with Taylor models given in [12]: Note c the constant part of F (i.e. the first coefficient of its polynomial) and $\bar{F} := F - c$. Use an addition theorem for g to split $g \circ F = g \circ (c \tilde{+} \bar{F})$ into two parts. Then apply Taylor's theorem with reference point 0 to the part including $\bar{F}$. For the logarithm this strategy gives us:

$$\log \circ F = \log \circ (c + \bar{F}) = \log \circ \left\{ c \cdot \left(1 + \frac{\bar{F}}{c} \right) \right\} = \log c + \log \circ \left(1 + \frac{\bar{F}}{c} \right) \quad (3)$$

$$\in \log c + \sum_{k=1}^{n} \frac{(-1)^{k-1}}{k} \left(\frac{\bar{F}}{c} \right)^k + \frac{(-1)^n \left(\frac{B \bar{F} X}{c} \right)^{n+1}}{(n+1) \left(1 + \left[0, \frac{B \bar{F} X}{c} \right] \right)^{n+1}} \quad (4)$$

This kind of reasoning does of course not represent any difficulty for the working mathematician. However, finding an appropriate addition theorem for a given g requires a certain amount of creativity, which can only be provided by a human. This is why in [14] this strategy has been applied to many different functions manually: $x \mapsto \frac{1}{x}$, sin, cos, arctan, log etc., so that they could be implemented. In contrast, our construction (2) can entirely be carried out by a machine and is still general enough to cover all these functions. The idea was to apply Taylor's theorem immediately (i.e. without invocation of an addition theorem) with some carefully chosen y_0 (instead of 0) as reference point. For the logarithm (2) yields:

$$\log \circ F \subseteq \log y_0 + \sum_{k=1}^{n} \frac{(-1)^{k-1}}{k y_0^k} (F - y_0)^k + \frac{(-1)^n (B F X - y_0)^{n+1}}{(n+1)[y_0, B F X]^{n+1}}$$

Choosing $y_0 = c$ makes this equivalent to (4). The "creative part" of applying a function-dependent addition theorem, done in step (3), has been made superfluous, so a machine can entirely perform the task. Our Coq implementation actually contains a generic function that provides a Taylor model extension given only a function's Taylor coefficients as arguments.

4.3 What Reference Point to Choose?

With this procedure established, a point that merits some more study is the choice to be made for the reference point y_0. As mentioned, the strategy described in [13] is equivalent to setting $y_0 = c$. However Taylor's theorem can be applied with any $y_0 \in Y$ as reference point. A good choice is one that minimises the width of the resulting Taylor model's error interval. In fact, there are cases where a better choices for y_0 than the Taylor model's constant part can be made. We illustrate this by the following example:

Example 2

$$\frac{1}{(1 + X^2, [0; 0])} \subseteq \sum_{k=0}^{n} \frac{(-1)^k}{y_0^{k+1}} (1 + X^2, [0; 0])^k + \frac{(-1)^{n+1}}{[y_0, 1 + X^2]^{n+2}} (1 + X^2 - y_0)^{n+1}$$

At order $n = 2$ we obtain (assuming $y_0 \in 1 + X^2$):

$$\left(\frac{1 - 3y_0 + 3y_0^2}{y_0^3} + \frac{2 - 3y_0}{y_0^3} X^2, \frac{X^4}{y_0^3} - \frac{(1 + X^2 - y_0)^3}{(1 + X^2)^4} \right)$$

Let us further fix $X := [-\frac{1}{2}; \frac{1}{2}]$. For this example the optimal (i.e. minimising the width of the error interval) choice for the reference point is not $y_0 = c = 1$. For $y_0 = 1$ the error interval has the width 0.078125, and for $y_0 = \frac{5}{4}$ the width is 0.047625. Careful study shows that the latter is optimal. □

This example is limited to the multiplicative inverse and also to the case where the error part of the Taylor model given as an argument is zero. It is not obvious how to obtain an optimal value for y_0 in general. However, there are cases where better choices than c can be made. It would be interesting to see if a general procedure can be derived.

4.4 Implementation of Taylor Models

In Coq we represent a Taylor model as a record of two fields:

```
Record TaylorModel (degree : nat) (X : list intvl) : Type := TM {
  approx : Poly R (length X);
  error : intvl
}
```

This type is parameterised by the **degree** at which Taylor operations will be carried out (section 4.1) and the domain X. The field **approx** contains a polynomial with real coefficients in **length** X (the dimension of the domain) variables. The field **error** is the Taylor model's error interval.

Polynomials. An $(n+1)$-variate polynomial can be represented as a polynomial with n-variate polynomials as coefficients. This is justified by the canonical polynomial isomorphism:

$$\mathbb{R}[\mathcal{X}_1, \ldots, \mathcal{X}_{n+1}] \simeq \mathbb{R}[\mathcal{X}_1, \ldots, \mathcal{X}_n][\mathcal{X}_{n+1}]$$

This can be translated to Coq as follows [9]:

```
Fixpoint PolyN (n:nat) struct n : Type :=
match n with
| 0 => C
| S m => list (PolyN m)
end.
```

The coefficients of the Taylor models' polynomials are represented by constructive real numbers because they can become irrational. Other choices have different consequences:

- Floating-point numbers: Their usage as coefficients will only yield approximations without error bounds, which is unacceptable for formal proof. An explicit treatment of rounding errors is possible, as has been shown for addition and multiplication [24]. However this approach can be expected to be much more difficult for the Taylor development of general smooth functions.

– Intervals: Using intervals with rational or floating-point number bounds as coefficients is feasible, but they add to the complexity of proofs. Furthermore, they force the user to give a precision for the enclosure of irrational values, thereby affecting sharpness in a way difficult to control.

Bounding. Taylor models make use of polynomial bounding for multiplication (section 4.1) and composition with smooth functions (section 4.2). A simple way to bound polynomials is to evaluate their interval extension. However there are much better strategies yielding narrower bounds. For example it is well-known that a univariate quadratic function can be rewritten by:

$$c_2 x^2 + c_1 x + c_0 = c_2 \left(x + \frac{c_1}{2c_2} \right)^2 - \frac{c_1^2}{4c_2} + c_0$$

The natural interval extension of the right hand side will then yield sharp bounds. There are much more sophisticated techniques for multi-variate polynomials of several degrees, as described in section 5.4.3 of [12]. Our implementation does not include them yet.

Computing Taylor Coefficients. As we have seen, in order to apply a smooth function to a Taylor model it is necessary to compute the coefficients of its Taylor series. Doing this by symbolic derivation is prohibitively expensive, so we use combinatoric formulas to obtain the derivatives. For example:

$$\operatorname{inv}^{(k)} y = (-1)^k \frac{k!}{y^{k+1}} \qquad \log^{(k)} y = \operatorname{inv}^{(k-1)} y = (-1)^{(k-1)} \frac{(k-1)!}{y^k}$$

A perhaps less well-known formula is [1]:

$$\arctan^{(k)} y = \frac{n!}{(1+y^2)^n} \sum_{k=0,\, n+k\,\mathrm{odd}}^{n} (-1)^{\frac{n+k+1}{2}} \binom{n}{k} y^k$$

These formulas are evaluated both in real numbers and in the interval arithmetic, as required by equation 2.

5   Examples

Example 3. As a first example [13] we study the function $f\,x = \frac{1}{x} + x$ on the domain $[1.9; 2.1]$. Our implementation yields the following results (the last line of the table shows the actual bound):

order of Δ	width of Δ	bound interval
0	$5.0125313 \cdot 10^{-2}$	$[2.3761905; 2.6263158]$
1	$5.5401662 \cdot 10^{-2}$	$[2.3722992; 2.6277008]$
2	$1.4579385 \cdot 10^{-3}$	$[2.4250000; 2.5764579]$
3	$1.5346721 \cdot 10^{-4}$	$[2.4236733; 2.5763267]$
4	$4.0386107 \cdot 10^{-6}$	$[2.4236875; 2.5763165]$
∞	0	$[2.4263158; 2.5761905]$

All these results have been obtained in less than a second using Coq's compiler [8]. □

Example 4. Lemma I_751442360 in Thomas Hales' proof of the Kepler conjecture [10] states that

$$\frac{\begin{array}{c}-x_1x_3 - x_2x_4 + x_1x_5 + x_3x_6 - x_5x_6 + \\ x_2(-x_2 + x_1 + x_3 - x_4 + x_5 + x_6)\end{array}}{\sqrt{4x_2\left(\begin{array}{c}x_2x_4(-x_2 + x_1 + x_3 - x_4 + x_5 + x_6) + \\ x_1x_5(x_2 - x_1 + x_3 + x_4 - x_5 + x_6) + \\ x_3x_6(x_2 + x_1 - x_3 + x_4 + x_5 - x_6) \\ - x_1x_3x_4 - x_2x_3x_5 - x_2x_1x_6 - x_4x_5x_6\end{array}\right)}} < \tan\left(\frac{\pi}{2} - 0.74\right) \approx 1.09518$$

for all $x \in X_{751442360}$, which is a 6-dimensional box given in the proof. We bound the left-hand side on a sub-domain of $X_{751442360}$ which is smaller (of width $\approx \frac{1}{10}$ in every dimension), but still contains the global maximum. The results are:

order of Δ	width of Δ	bound interval
0	∞	$[-\infty; \infty]$
1	1.3025929	$[0.36246433; 1.6650572]$
2	$1.6105738 \cdot 10^{-2}$	$[0.94291234; 1.0905563]$
∞	0	$[0.95253193; 1.0849205]$

The result for order 3 has been obtained in about ten minutes[1]. Further work needs to be done in order to improve this performance. However, it is already sufficiently tight for proving the required statement on the given small sub-domain. □

6   Conclusion

The global optimisation problems included in Thomas Hales' proof of the Kepler are the most complex to have been included in a mathematical proof so far. Having shown that they are not entirely out of reach for current proof assistants encourages us to further pursue our direction of work. Many paths can be followed to improve our implementation, two of which we find worth mentioning:

- In order to bound the multi-variate polynomials appearing in the Taylor models our current implementation evaluates them in interval arithmetic using the Horner-scheme induced by the canonical polynomial isomorphism. However, many better methods are available, which should considerably tighten the resulting bounds.
- Implementations of constructive real numbers in a style of pure functional programming suffer from an important performance problem: the cost of evaluating $x + x$ to precision ϵ is twice that of evaluating x to precision $\frac{\epsilon}{2}$. The same computation is actually carried out twice. This problem could be avoided by stocking previously computed results in a global cache.

---

[1] On an Intel Pentium 4 running at 2.80GHz.

It should be kept in mind that we have to pay a certain performance penalty for the maximal security achieved by implementing algorithms inside a proof assistant. However, the speed of machines has been increasing at an exponential rate for a long time. Besides, algorithms become more and more efficient. As a consequence, today we are able to treat problems in a formal setting that twenty years ago were only in reach for implementations on machine level.

In order to diminish this gap, work on proof assistants itself is necessary: a more efficient mechanism for computation has recently been added to Coq [8]. A second step in this direction would be the usage of machine numbers for computations inside proofs. With such tools at hand, our implementation could become a powerful system performing verified optimisation for a large class of functions.

Acknowledgements

I would like to thank Bas Spitters, Milad Niqui, and Russell O'Connor for many instructive discussions on constructive real numbers. I'm grateful to my supervisor, Benjamin Werner, for advice he gave to me at various stages of this work. Furthermore I would like to thank the anonymous referees as well as Nathalie Revol for their valuable comments on earlier versions of this article.

References

1. Mohammad K. Azarian. A076741. In N. J. A. Sloane, editor, *The On-Line Encyclopedia of Integer Sequences*. www.research.att.com/~njas/sequences/, 2002.
2. Yves Bertot. Calcul de formules affines et de séries entières en arithmétique exacte avec types co-inductifs. Technical report, 2005.
3. Nicolaas G. de Bruijn. The mathematical language AUTOMATH, its usage, and some of its extensions. In M. Laudet, editor, *Proceedings of the Symposium on Automatic Demonstration*, pages 29–61, Versailles, France, December 1968. Springer-Verlag LNM 125.
4. G. Dowek, A. Geser, and C. Muñoz. Tactical conflict detection and resolution in a 3-D airspace. In *Proceedings of the 4th USA/Europe Air Traffic Management R&DSeminar, ATM 2001*, Santa Fe, New Mexico, 2001.
5. Leonhard Euler. Institutiones calculi differentialis, 1755.
6. Georges Gonthier. A computer-checked proof of the Four Colour Theorem. Preprint, 2005.
7. B. Grégoire, L. Thery, and B. Werner. A computational approach to pocklington certificates in type theory. FLOP 2006, to appear in LNCS.
8. Benjamin Grégoire and Xavier Leroy. A compiled implementation of strong reduction. In Proceedings ICFP'02.
9. Benjamin Grégoire and Assia Mahboubi. Proving equalities in a commutative ring done right in coq. In Joe Hurd and Tom Melham, editors, *Proceedings of TPHOLs'05*, volume 3603 of *Lecture Notes in Computer Science*, pages 98–113, Oxford, UK, August 2005. Springer-Verlag.
10. Thomas C. Hales. A proof of the Kepler Conjecture. Manuscript, 2004.
11. E. Hansen. *Global Optimization Using Interval Analysis*. M. Dekker, 1992.

12. Kyoko Makino. *Rigorous Analysis of Nonlinear Motion in Particle Accelerators.* PhD thesis, Michigan State University, East Lansing, MI, USA, 1998. Also MSUCL-1093.
13. Kyoko Makino and Martin Berz. Remainder differential algebras and their applications. In Martin Berz, Christian Bischof, George Corliss, and Andreas Griewank, editors, *Computational Differentiation: Techniques, Applications, and Tools*, pages 63–74. SIAM, Philadelphia, Penn., 1996.
14. Kyoko Makino and Martin Berz. Taylor models and other validated functional inclusion methods. *International Journal of Pure and Applied Mathematics*, 4(4):379–456, 2003.
15. Valérie Ménissier-Morain. *Arithmétique exacte: conception, algorithmique et performances d'une implémentation informatique en précision arbitraire.* Phd thesis, Université Paris 7, 1994.
16. Jean-Pierre Merlet. Solving the forward kinematics of a gough-type parallel manipulator with interval analysis. *International Journal of Robotics Research*, 23(3):221–236, 2004.
17. Ramon E. Moore. Automatic error analysis in digital computation. Technical Report LMSD-48421 Lockheed Missiles and Space Co, Palo Alto, CA, 1959.
18. Ramon E. Moore. *Interval Arithmetic and Automatic Error Analysis in Digital Computing.* PhD thesis, Department of Computer Science, Stanford University, 1962.
19. Ramon E. Moore. *Interval Analysis.* Prentice-Hall, Englewood Cliffs N. J., 1966.
20. Tobias Nipkow, Gertrud Bauer, and Paula Schultz. Flyspeck i: Tame graphs. In U. Furbach and N. Shankar, editors, *Int. Joint Conf. Automated Reasoning — IJCAR 2006*, volume 4130, pages 21–35.
21. Milad Niqui. *Formalising Exact Arithmetic: Representations, Algorithms and Proofs, Radboud University Nijmegen.* PhD thesis, Radboud University Nijmegen, September 2004.
22. Steven Obua. Proving bounds for real linear programs in isabelle/hol. In *TPHOLs*, pages 227–244, 2005.
23. Russell O'Connor. A monadic, functional implementation of real numbers. Preprint, 2005.
24. N. Revol, K. Makino, and M. Berz. Taylor models and floating-point arithmetic: proof that arithmetic operations are validated in COSY.
25. Helmut Schwichtenberg. Constructive analysis with witnesses, 2005. Manuscript.

A Purely Functional Library for Modular Arithmetic and Its Application to Certifying Large Prime Numbers

Benjamin Grégoire and Laurent Théry

INRIA Sophia-Antipolis, France
{Benjamin.Gregoire, Laurent.Thery}@sophia.inria.fr

Abstract. Computing efficiently with numbers can be crucial for some theorem proving applications. In this paper, we present a library of modular arithmetic that has been developed within the CoQ proof assistant. The library proposes the usual operations that have all been proved correct. The library is purely functional but can also be used on top of some native modular arithmetic. With this library, we have been capable of certifying the primality of numbers with more than 13000 digits.

1 Safe Computation and Theorem Proving

Recent formalisations such as the four colour theorem [9] and the Flyspeck project [17] have shown all the benefits one can get from having a formal system where both proving and computing are possible. In the CoQ proof assistant [18], computation is provided by the logic. A direct application of having computation inside the logic is the so-called two-level approach [4]. To illustrate it, let us consider the problem of proving the primality of some natural numbers. Suppose that we have defined a predicate *prime*: a number is prime if it has exactly two divisors, 1 and itself. How do we now prove that 17 is prime? The usual approach is to interactively build a proof object using tactics. Of course, this task can be automated by writing an ad-hoc tactic. Still, behind the scene, the system will have to build a proof object and the larger the number to be proved prime is, the larger the proof term will be. The two-level approach proposes an alternative strategy in two steps. In the first step, one writes a semi-decision procedure for the problem in the programming language of CoQ. In our case, it amounts to writing a function *test* from natural numbers to booleans such that if the function returns *true* then the number is prime. For example, if the natural number is n, the function can check that there is no divisor between 2 and $\sqrt{n}$ by a simple iteration. In the second step, one proves that the function meets its specification. This means proving for our function *test* that

$$\forall n, test\ n = \text{true} \rightarrow prime\ n$$

Note that implication is sufficient for the two-level approach to work. Proving equivalence would not be of much interest here. A better way of proving that

U. Furbach and N. Shankar (Eds.): IJCAR 2006, LNAI 4130, pp. 423–437, 2006.

a number n is not prime is to find externally a factor p of n and only check internally that p divides n.

Once the second step has been completed, for 17 to be certified as prime, it is sufficient to prove that the function *test* applied to 17 returns `true`. As the function *test* directly evaluates inside COQ, this last proof is simply the reflexivity of equality. Using the two-level approach, we have just transformed the problem of building a large proof object into a conversion problem: showing that *test* 17 is convertible to `true`. The size of the proof object is then independent of the number to be proved prime.

A recent improvement of the evaluation mechanism [10] has made the two-level approach much more attractive. The evaluation inside COQ is now as fast as the bytecode evaluation of the OCAML language [15]. The only restriction when writing programs inside COQ is that programs must be purely functional, i.e. side effects are not allowed, and must always terminate. This is the price to pay to safely combine proofs and computations. Obviously, for this approach to be used, the COQ system should provide efficient functional implementations for the usual data structures: numbers, strings, vectors, hash tables, . . .

The contribution of this paper is to propose a purely functional library to compute efficiently with large numbers inside COQ. The key idea of the library is to implement a representation of numbers that accommodates the divide and conquer strategy to speed up computation. The paper is organised as follows. In Section 2, we present the current arithmetic of COQ and explain why a new representation of numbers is needed in order to compute efficiently with large numbers. In Section 3, we give an overview of our new library based on this new representation. In Section 4, we detail two possible instantiations of the library. Finally, Section 5 presents an application of the library to the particular problem of certifying large prime numbers.

2   Linear Versus Tree Representation of Numbers

In the standard library of COQ, strictly positive numbers are represented as linear structures, low bits first.

```
Inductive positive : Set :=
  | xI : positive -> positive
  | xO : positive -> positive
  | xH : positive.
```

xH is 1, (xO p) is two times the value of p and (xI p) is two times plus one the value of p. For example, 17 and 18 are represented as xI (xO (xO (xO (xH)))) and xO (xI (xO (xO (xH)))) respectively. The choice of the representation has some direct impact on the way operations are implemented. To illustrate this on an example, let us consider the comparison function Pcmp. It takes two positive numbers and returns a comparison value

```
Inductive comparison: Set := Eq | Lt | Gt.
```

As numbers are represented low bits first, to compare two numbers one needs to walk down both numbers keeping track of what the current status of the comparison is. This is what the auxiliary function Pcompare does. The main function Pcomp starts the computation with the initial status being equality.

```
Fixpoint Pcompare (x y: positive) (r: comparison): comparison :=
  match x, y with
  |    xH,    xH => r
  |    xH,    _  => Lt
  |    _ ,    xH => Gt
  | xI x', xI y' => Pcompare x' y' r
  | x0 x', x0 y' => Pcompare x' y' r
  | xI x', x0 y' => Pcompare x' y' Gt
  | x0 x', xI y' => Pcompare x' y' Lt
  end.
```

```
Definition Pcmp x y := Pcompare x y Eq.
```

This is clearly not optimal but is the best one can do with this representation: recursive calls only skip a single bit. Efficient algorithms for large numbers, like Karatsuba multiplication [14], use a divide and conquer strategy. They require to be able to split numbers in parts efficiently. This motivates our representation based on a tree-like structure. Given an arbitrary one-word set w, we define the two-word set w2 w as follows

```
Inductive w2 (w: Set): Set :=   WW : w -> w -> w2 w.
```

For example, (WW true false) is of type (w2 bool). We choose in an arbitrary way that high bits are the first argument of WW, low bits the second one. Now we use a recursive type definition and define the type of numbers of height n as

```
Fixpoint word (w: Set) (n:nat): Set :=
  match n with
  | O => w
  | S n => w2 (word w n)
  end.
```

An object of type (word w n) is a complete binary tree that contains 2^n objects of type w. Given a number, one has to choose an appropriate height to represent it exactly. For example, taking the usual booleans for base words, a minimum height of 2 is necessary to represent the number 13. With this height, numbers have type (word bool 2) and (WW (WW true true) (WW false true)) denotes the number 13.

Arithmetic operations are not going to be defined on the type word directly. We use a technique similar to the one in [11]. A functor is first defined that allows to build a two-word modular arithmetic on top of a single-word one. The functor is then applied iteratively to get the final implementation. In the following, x, y are used to denote one-word variables and xx, yy to denote two-word variables.

When defining a new function f, we just need to explain how to compute the result on two-word values knowing how to compute it on one-word values. We use the notation w_f for the single-word version of f and ww_f for the two-word version. For example, let us go back to our comparison function Pcompare and try to define it on our trees. We first suppose the existence of the comparison on single words

```
Variable w_compare: w -> w -> comparison -> comparison.
```

and then define the function for two-word values

```
Definition ww_compare (xx yy: w2 w) (r: comparison) :=
  match xx, yy with
    WW xH xL, WW yH yL => w_compare xH yH (w_compare xL yL r)
  end.
```

This is not the function that is in our library. Instead, we can take advantage of the tree-like structure and compare high bits first.

```
Variable w_cmp: w -> w -> comparison.
```

```
Definition ww_cmp (xx yy: w2 w) :=
  match xx, yy with
    WW xH xL, WW yH yL =>
      match w_cmp xH yH with Eq => w_cmp xL yL | cmp => cmp end
  end.
```

The key property of our representation is that splitting number in two is for free. The next section details why this property is crucial to implement efficient algorithms for functions like multiplication, division and square root. Note that, in term of memory allocation, having a tree structure does not produce any overhead. In a functional setting, building a binary tree structure or building the equivalent linear list of words requires the same number of cells.

One main drawback of our representation is that we manipulate only complete binary trees. So, even if we choose carefully the appropriate height, half of the words could be unnecessary to compute the final result. To soften this problem, we have extended the definition of w2 to include an empty word W0.

```
Inductive w2 (w: Set): Set :=
| W0: w2
| WW: w -> w -> w2.
```

For example, the number 13 can be represented at height 3 as

```
WW W0 (WW (WW true true) (WW false true))
```

With this extension, we lose uniqueness of representation. Still, there is a notion of canonicity, W0 should always be preferred to a sub-tree full of zeros. Note that, in our development, all functions have been carefully written in order to preserve canonicity, but canonicity is not part of their specification since it is not necessary to ensure safe computations. Using w_0 to represent the one-word zero, the final version of the comparison function is then

```
Definition ww_cmp (xx yy: w2 w) :=
  match xx, yy with
  | W0, W0 => Eq
  | W0, WW yH yL =>
      match w_cmp w_0 yH  with Eq => w_cmp w_0 yL  | _   => Lt   end
  | WW xh xl, W0 =>
      match w_cmp xH  w_0 with Eq => w_cmp xL  w_0 | _   => Gt   end
  | WW xH xL, WW yH yL =>
      match w_cmp xH  yH  with Eq => w_cmp xL  yL  | cmp => cmp end
  end.
```

3   The Certified Library

Our library includes the usual functions: comparison, successor, predecessor, opposite, addition, subtraction, multiplication, square, Euclidean division, modulo, integer square root, gcd, and power. It is a modular library: we manipulate trees (or words) of the same height (resp. of the same size). For addition and subtraction, we also provide an exact version that returns a word and a carry. For multiplication, we also provide an exact version returning two words.

Since we want to use our library in the context of the two-level approach, we must carefully choose the algorithms we implement. Furthermore, semi-decision procedures must also be certified, so every function of our library must come along with its proof of correctness.

Specifications are expressed using predicates over integers. For this, we use two interpretation functions $[|\ |]$ and $[[\ ]]$. Given a one-word element x, its corresponding integer value is $[|x|]$. Given a two-word element xx, its corresponding integer value is $[[xx]]$. The base of the arithmetic, i.e. one plus the maximum value that fits in a single-word, is wB. We write w_0 (resp. w_1) for the word with corresponding integer value 0 (resp. 1). From these definitions, the following statement holds

$$\forall x\, y,\ [[\text{WW}\ x\ y]] = [|x|] * \text{wB} + [|y|]$$

Once a function is defined, its correctness has to be proved. For example, for the comparison defined in the previous section, one needs to prove that if the function w_cmp meets its specification

$$\forall x\, y,\ match\ \text{w\_cmp}\ x\ y\ with$$
$$|\ \text{Eq}\ \to\ [|x|] = [|y|]\ |\ \text{Lt}\ \to\ [|x|] < [|y|]\ |\ \text{Gt}\ \to\ [|x|] > [|y|]$$
$$end$$

so does the function ww_cmp

$$\forall xx\, yy,\ match\ \text{ww\_cmp}\ xx\ yy\ with$$
$$|\ \text{Eq}\ \to\ [[xx]] = [[yy]]\ |\ \text{Lt}\ \to\ [[xx]] < [[yy]]\ |\ \text{Gt}\ \to\ [[xx]] > [[yy]]$$
$$end$$

3.1 Words and Carries

Carries are important for operations like addition and subtraction. In our functional setting, carries encapsulate words

```
Inductive carry (w: Set): Set :=
 | C0: w -> carry
 | C1: w -> carry.
```

Two interpretation functions $[+|~|]$ and $[-|~|]$ are associated with carries. One interprets the carry positively: $[+|\text{C1 } x|] = \text{wB} + [|x|]$ and $[+|\text{C0 } x|] = [|x|]$. The other interprets it negatively (i.e. a borrow): $[-|\text{C1 } x|] = [|x|] - \text{wB}$ and $[-|\text{C0 } x|] = [|x|]$. To illustrate how carries are manipulated, let us consider the successor function. In our library, it is represented by two functions

```
w_succ: w -> w
w_succ_c: w -> carry w
```

The first function represents the modular version, the second the exact version. With these two functions, it is possible to define the version for two-word elements. For example, the definition for the modular version is

```
Definition ww_succ xx :=
  match xx with
  | W0 => WW w_0 w_1
  | WW xH xL =>
    match w_succ_c xL with
    | C0 l => WW xH l
    | C1 l => WW (w_succ xH) w_0
    end
  end.
```

Note that, unlike what happens in imperative languages, returning a carry allocates a memory cell. So in our implementation we avoid as much as possible to create them. When we know in advance that the result always returns (resp. does not return) a carry, we can call the modular function instead. An example of such a situation is a naive implementation of the exact function that adds 2 to a one-word element by calling twice the successor function:

```
Definition w_add2 x :=
  match w_succ_c x with
  | C0 y => w_succ_c y
  | C1 y => C1 (w_succ y)
  end.
```

In the case when the first increment has created a carry, we are sure that the second increment cannot raise any carry, so we can directly call the function w_succ. Also, we use a combination of partial evaluation and continuation passing style to get shorter definitions. This has proved to ease considerably the proving phase without changing the efficiency of functions.

3.2 Shifting Bits

If most of the operations work at word level, some functions (like the shifting operation) require to work at a lower level, i.e. the bit level. Surprisingly, all the operations we had to perform at bit level can be built using a single function

```
w_add_mul_div : positive -> w -> w -> w
```

Evaluating (w_add_mul_div p x y) returns a new word that is composed for its last p bits by the first bits of y and for the remaining bits by the last bits of x. Its specification is

$$\forall p\, x\, y,\ 2^p < \text{wB} \Rightarrow$$
$$[|\text{w\_add\_mul\_div}\, p\, x\, y|] = ([|x|] * 2^p + ([|y|] * 2^p)/\text{wB}) \bmod \text{wB}$$

Two degenerated versions of this function are of direct interest. Calling it with w_0 as second argument implements the shift left. Calling it with w_0 as first argument implements the shift right.

3.3 Divide and Conquer Algorithms

Karatsuba Multiplication. Speeding up the multiplication was the main motivation of our tree representation for numbers. The multiplication is represented in our library by the function

```
w_mul_c: w -> w -> w2 w
```

and its specification is

$$\forall x\, y,\ [|\text{w\_mul\_c}\, x\, y|] = [|x|] * [|y|]$$

The naive implementation on two-word elements follows the simple equation

$$[[\text{WW}\ x_h\ x_l]] * [[\text{WW}\ y_h\ y_l]] =$$
$$[|x_h|] * [|y_h|] * \text{wB}^2 + ([|x_h|] * [|y_l|] + [|x_l|] * [|y_h|]) * \text{wB} + [|x_l|] * [|y_l|]$$

Thus, performing a multiplication requires four submultiplications. Karatsuba multiplication [14] saves one of these submultiplications

$$[[\text{WW}\ x_h\ x_l]] * [[\text{WW}\ y_h\ y_l]] =$$
$$\text{let } h = [|x_h|] * [|y_h|] \text{ in}$$
$$\text{let } l = [|x_l|] * [|y_l|] \text{ in}$$
$$h * \text{wB}^2 + ((h + l) - ([|x_h|] - [|x_l|]) * ([|y_h|] - [|y_l|])) * \text{wB} + l$$

Karatsuba multiplication is more efficient than the naive one only when numbers are large enough. So our library includes both implementations for multiplication. They are used separately to define two different functors. The functor with the naive multiplication is only used for trees of "small" height.

Recursive Division. The general Euclidean division algorithm that we have used is the usual schoolboy method that iterates the division of two words by one word. It is then crucial to perform this two-by-one division efficiently. The algorithm we have implemented is the one presented in [6]. The idea is to use the recursive call on high bits to guess an approximation of the quotient and then to perform an appropriate adjustment to get the exact quotient.

In our development, the two-by-one division takes three words and returns a pair composed of the quotient and the remainder

```
Variable w_div21: w -> w -> w -> w * w
```

and its specification is

$$\forall x_1 \ x_2 \ y, \ let \ q, r = \texttt{w\_div21}\, x_1 \ x_2 \ y \ in$$
$$[[x_1]] < [[y]] \Rightarrow \texttt{wB}/2 \leq [[y]] \Rightarrow [[\texttt{WW}\ x_1\ x_2\,]] = [[q]] * [[y]] + [[r]] \wedge 0 \leq [[r]] < [[y]]$$

The two conditions deserve some explanation. The first one ensures that the quotient fits in one word. The second one ensures that the recursive call computes an approximation of the quotient that is not too far from the correct value.

Before defining the function `ww_div21` for two-word elements, we need to define the intermediate function `w_div32` that divides three one-word elements by two one-word elements. Its specification is

$$\forall x_1 \ x_2 \ x_3 \ y_1 \ y_2, \ let \ q, rr = \texttt{w\_div32}\ x_1 \ x_2 \ x_3 \ y_1 \ y_2 \ in$$
$$[[\texttt{WW}\ x_1\ x_2\,]] < [[\texttt{WW}\ y_1\ y_2\,]] \Rightarrow \texttt{wB}/2 \leq [[y_1]] \Rightarrow$$
$$[[x_1]] * \texttt{wB}^2 + [[x_2]] * \texttt{wB} + [[x_3]] = [[q]] * [[\texttt{WW}\ y_1\ y_2\,]] + [[rr]]\ \wedge$$
$$0 \leq [[rr]] < [[\texttt{WW}\ y_1\ y_2\,]]$$

The two conditions play the same roles as the ones in the specification of `w_div21`. As the code is a bit intricate, here we just explain how the function proceeds. It first calls `w_div21` to divide x_1 and x_2 by y_1. This gives a pair (q, r) such that

$$[[x_1]] * \texttt{wB} + [[x_2]] = [[q]] * [[y_1]] + [[r]]$$

q is considered as the approximation of the final quotient. The condition $\texttt{wB}/2 \leq [[y_1]]$ ensures that if this approximation is not exact, then it exceeds the real value of at most two units. So the quotient can only be q, $q - 1$ or $q - 2$. As we have

$$[[x_1]] * \texttt{wB}^2 + [[x_2]] * \texttt{wB} + [[x_3]] = [[q]] * [[\texttt{WW}\ y_1\ y_2\,]] + ([[\texttt{WW}\ r\ x_3\,]] - [[q]] * [[y_2]])$$

we know in which situation we are by testing the sign of the candidate remainder. In our modular arithmetic, it amounts to checking whether or not the subtraction of (`w_mul_c` q y_2) from (`WW` r x_3) produces a borrow. If it is positive or zero (no borrow), the quotient is q. If it is negative (a borrow), we have to consider $q - 1$ and add in consequence (`WW` y_1 y_2) to the candidate remainder. We test again the sign of this new candidate. If it is positive, the quotient is $q - 1$, otherwise is $q - 2$. The definition of `ww_div21` is now straightforward. Forgetting the `W0` constructor, we have

```
Definition ww_div21 xx1 xx2 yy :=
  match xx1, xx2, yy with
  ....
  | WW x1H x1L, WW x2H x2L, WW yH yL =>
      let (qH, rr) := w_div32 x1H x1L x2H yH yL in
      match rr with
      | W0 => (WW qH w_0, WW w_0 x2L)
      | WW rH rL =>
          let (qL, s) := w_div32 rH rL x2L yH yL in
          (WW qH qL, s)
      end
end.
```

These two divisions can only be used if the divisor y is greater than equal to $wB/2$. This is not restrictive because, if y is too small, we can always find an n such that $y * 2^n \geq wB/2$. If we have $x * 2^n = q * (y * 2^n) + r$ for some x and r, then r can be written as $r = 2^n * r'$, so $x = q * y + r'$. Hence, to perform the division of two numbers of the same size, we first shift divisor and dividend by n. The shifted dividend fits in two words and its high part is smaller than the shifted divisor. Then, we use the two-by-one division. The resulting quotient is correct and we just have to unshift the remainder.

Recursive Square Root. The algorithm for computing the integer square root is similar to the one for division. It was first described in [19] and has already been formalised in a theorem prover [3]. It requires the number to be split in four. For this reason it is represented by the following function in our library

```
w_sqrt2: w -> w -> w * carry w;
```

The function returns the integer square root and the rest. Its specification is

$$\forall x\, y,\ let\ s, r = \text{w\_sqrt2}\ x\ y\ in$$
$$wB/4 \leq [|x|] \Rightarrow [[WW\ x\ y]] = [|s|]^2 + [+|r|] \wedge [+|r|] \leq 2 * [|s|]$$

As for division, the input must be large enough so that the recursive call that computes the approximation is not too far from the exact value.

The definition of the square root needs a support function that implements a division by twice a number

```
w_div2s: carry w -> w -> w -> carry w * carry w
```

with its specification

$$\forall x_1\, x_2\, y,\ let\ q, r = \text{w\_div2s}\ x_1\ x_2\ y\ in$$
$$wB/2 \leq [|y|] \Rightarrow [+|x_1|] \leq 2 * [|y|] \Rightarrow$$
$$[+|x_1|] * wB + [|x_2|] = [+|q|] * (2 * [|y|]) + [+|r|] \wedge 0 \leq [+|r|] < 2 * [|y|]$$

The idea of the algorithm is summarised by the following equation

$$let\ q_h, r = \text{w\_sqrt2}\ x_h\ x_l\ \ in$$
$$let\ q_l, r_1 = \text{w\_div2s}\ r\ y_h\ q_h\ in$$
$$[[WW\ x_h\ x_l]] * wB^2 + [[WW\ y_h\ y_l]] = [[WW\ q_h\ q_l]]^2 + ([+|r_1|] * wB + [|y_l|] - [|q_l|]^2)$$

(WW q_h q_l) is a candidate for the square root of (WW (WW x_h x_l) (WW y_h y_l)).
Because of the condition on the input, we are sure that the integer square root
is either (WW q_h q_l) or (WW q_h q_l) − 1. It is the sign of $[+|r_1|] * \mathtt{wB} + [|y_l|] − [|q_l|]^2$
that indicates which one to choose.

4   Implementing Base Word Arithmetic

The final step to complete our library is to define the arithmetic for the base
words. Once defined, we get the modular arithmetic for the desired size by applying an appropriate number of times our functors on top of this base arithmetic.
In a classical implementation, these base words would be machine words. Unfortunately, machine words are not yet accessible from the COQ language.

4.1   Defined Modular Arithmetic

For the moment, the only way to have a modular arithmetic for base words
inside COQ is to define base words as a datatype. For example, we have for
two-bit words

```
Inductive word2 : Set := OO | OI | IO  | II.
```

The functions are then defined by simple case analysis. For example, the exact
successor function is defined as

```
Definition word2_succ_c x :=
 match x with
 | OO => CO OI
 | OI => CO IO
 | IO => CO II
 | II => C1 OO
 end.
```

We also need to give the proofs that every function meets its specification. These
proofs are also done by case analysis.

Rather than writing by hand functions and proofs, we have written an OCAML
program instead. This program takes the word size as argument and generates
the desired base arithmetic with all its proofs. It is a nice application of meta-
proving. Unfortunately, functions and their corresponding proofs grow quickly
with the word size. For example, the addition for word8 is a pattern matching
of 65536 cases. word8 is actually the largest size COQ can handle.

The main benefit of this approach is to get an arithmetic library that is entirely
expressed in the logic of COQ. The library is portable: no extension of the COQ
kernel is needed.

4.2   Native Modular Arithmetic

To test our library with some machine word arithmetic, we use the extraction
mechanism that converts automatically COQ functions into OCAML functions.

It is then possible to run the resulting program with the 31-bit native OCAML arithmetic or a simulated 64-bit arithmetic. Not all the functions that we have implemented have their corresponding functions in the native modular arithmetic, so some native code had to be developed for these functions. The formal verification of this code is also possible and we did it for some of these functions. Running the extracted library with machine word arithmetic gives an idea of the speed-up we could get if we had a native arithmetic in COQ.

5   Evaluating the Library

A way of applying the two-level approach for proving primality has been presented in [12]. It is based on the notion of prime certificate and more precisely of *Pocklington certificate*. A prime certificate is an object that witnesses the primality of a number. The Pocklington certificates we have been using are justified by the following theorem given in [5]:

Theorem 1. *Given a number n, a witness a and some pairs of natural numbers $(p_1, \alpha_1), \ldots, (p_k, \alpha_k)$ where all the p_i are prime numbers, let*

$$F_1 = p_1^{\alpha_1} \ldots p_k^{\alpha_k}$$
$$R_1 = (n-1)/F_1$$
$$s = R_1/(2F_1)$$
$$r = R_1 \bmod (2F_1)$$

it is sufficient for n to be prime that the following conditions hold:

$$F_1 \text{ is even, } R_1 \text{ is odd, and } F_1 R_1 = n - 1 \tag{1}$$
$$(F_1 + 1)(2F_1^2 + (r-1)F_1 + 1) > n \tag{2}$$
$$a^{n-1} = 1 (\bmod\ n) \tag{3}$$
$$\forall i \in \{1, \ldots, k\}\ \gcd(a^{\frac{n-1}{p_i}} - 1, n) = 1 \tag{4}$$
$$r^2 - 8s \text{ is not a square or } s = 0 \tag{5}$$

For a prime number n, the list $[a, p_1, \alpha_1, p_2, \alpha_2, \ldots, p_k, \alpha_k]$ represents its Pocklington certificate. Even if generating a certificate for a given n can be cpu-intensive, verifying conditions (1)-(5) is an order of magnitude simpler than evaluating (*test n*) (computing $a^{n-1}(\bmod\ n)$ requires a maximum of $2 log_2 n$ modular multiplications). In fact, only the verification of conditions (1)-(5) is crucial for asserting primality. This requires safe computation and is done inside COQ. The generation of the certificate is delegated to an external tool. This is a direct application of the skeptic approach described in [2,13]. Note that this method of certifying prime numbers is effective only if the prime number n is such that $n - 1$ can be easily partially factorised.

With respect to the usual approach for the same problem [7], the two-level approach gives a significant improvement in terms of size of the proof object and in terms of time. Figure 1 illustrates this on some examples (P_{150} is a random prime number with 150 digits and the millennium prime is a prime

prime	digits	size		time	
		standard	two-level	standard	two-level
1234567891	10	94K	0.453K	3.98s	0.50s
74747474747474747	17	145K	0.502K	9.87s	0.56s
1111111111111111111	19	223K	0.664K	17.41s	0.66s
$(2^{148}+1)/17$	44	1.2M	0.798K	350.63s	2.77s
P_{150}	150	–	1.902K	–	75.62s
millennium prime	2000	–	–	–	–

Fig. 1. Some verifications of certificates with the standard and two-level approaches

	digits	positive	word8
1234567891	10	0.50s	0.10s
74747474747474747	17	0.56s	0.12s
1111111111111111111	19	0.66s	0.20s
$(2^{148}+1)/17$	44	2.77s	0.36s
P_{150}	150	75.62s	8.44s
millennium prime	2000	–	5320.05s

Fig. 2. Some verifications of certificates with the standard and our CoQ arithmetics

number with 2000 digits discovered by John B. Cosgrave). However, due to the limitations of the linear representation of numbers in CoQ, even with the two-level approach, we were not capable of certifying large prime numbers (> 1000 digits) as illustrated by the millennium prime. The same occurred when applying the Lucas-Lehmer test for proving the primality of Mersenne numbers, i.e. numbers that can be written as $2^p - 1$.

Theorem 2. *Let (S_n) be recursively defined by $S_0 = 4$ and $S_{n+1} = S_n^2 - 2$. For $p > 2$, $2^p - 1$ is prime if and only if $(2^p - 1)|S_{p-2}$.*

The largest Mersenne number we could certify was $2^{4423} - 1$ that has 1332 digits.

The idea is then to use our new library based on a tree-like representation of numbers. The complete library with the corresponding contribution for prime numbers is available at http://gforge.inria.fr/projects/coqprime/. It consists of 9000 lines of hand-written definitions and proofs. The automatically generated word8 arithmetic is much bigger, 95 Mb: 41 Mb are used to define functions and 54 Mb for the proofs. This is the largest ever contribution that has been verified by CoQ. With this new library, we have been capable of proving that the Mersenne number $2^{44497} - 1$ was prime using CoQ with the Lucas-Lehmer test. As far as we know, it is the largest prime number that has been certified by a theorem prover.

The certification with our library is faster even for small numbers. This is illustrated in Figure 2 and the fifth and sixth columns of Figure 3. There is a maximum speed-up of 70. These benchmarks have been run on a Pentium 4 with 1 Gigabyte of RAM.

#	n	digits	year	positive	word8	w31	w64	Big_int
12	127	39	1876	0.73s	0.04s	0.01s	0.s	0.s
13	521	157	1952	53.00s	1.85s	0.02s	0.02s	0.s
14	607	183	1952	84.00s	2.78s	0.03s	0.03s	0.s
15	1279	386	1952	827.00s	20.21s	0.25s	0.16s	0.02s
16	2203	664	1952	4421.00s	89.1s	1.1s	0.8s	0.08s
17	2281	687	1952	4964.00s	97.59s	1.21s	0.82s	0.09s
18	3217	969	1957	14680.00s	237.65s	2.85s	2.14s	0.22s
19	4253	1281	1961	35198.00s	494.09s	6.4s	4.58s	0.6s
20	4423	1332	1961	39766.00s	563.27s	6.99s	4.99s	0.67s
21	9689	2917	1963		5304.08s	56.1s	39.98s	5.89s
22	9941	2993	1963		5650.63s	60.5s	42.53s	6.32s
23	11213	3376	1963		7607.00s	80.56s	57.47s	11.25s
24	19937	6002	1971		34653.12s	377.24s	268.09s	45.75s
25	21701	6533	1978		43746.21s	463.02s	338.04s	58.56s
26	23209	6987	1979		51210.56s	538.33s	403.48s	88.43s
27	44497	13395	1979		282784.09s	3282.23s	2208.45s	476.75s

Fig. 3. Times to verify Mersenne numbers

Comparing word8 with the 31-bit OCAML integer w31 shows all the benefit we could get from having machine words in COQ. There is a maximum speed-up of 95 with respect to word8. This means a speed-up of 6650 with respect to the standard COQ library.

The 64-bit OCAML integer w64 is a simulated arithmetic (our processor has only 32 bits). This is why there is not such a gap between w31 and w64. BIG_INT [16] is the standard exact library for OCAML. It has a purely functional interface but is written in C. The comparison is not bad. For the last Mersenne, w64 is only 4.6 times slower than BIG_INT. It is also very interesting that this gap is getting smaller as numbers get larger. On individual functions, random tests on addition give a ratio of 4 and on multiplication a ratio of 10.

We are still far away from getting the performance of the GMP [1] library. This library is written in C and uses in-place computation instead. This minimises considerably the number of memory allocations. Unfortunately, in-place computation is not compatible with the logic of COQ.

6   Conclusions

The main contribution of our work is to present a certified library for performing modular arithmetic. Individual arithmetic functions have already been proved correct, see for example [3]. To our knowledge, it is the first time verification has been applied successfully to a complete library with non-trivial algorithms. Our motivation was to improve integer arithmetic inside COQ. The figures given in Section 5 show that this goal has been reached: we are now capable of manipulating numbers with more than 13000 digits. These tests also show all the benefit we could get from a native base arithmetic. We hope this will motivate researchers to integrate machine word arithmetic inside COQ.

Expressing the arithmetic in the logic has a price: no side effect is possible, also numbers are allocated progressively, not in one block. A natural continuation of our work would be to prove the correctness of a library with side effects. This would require a much more intensive verification work since in-place computing is known to be much harder to verify. Note that directly integrating an existing library inside the prover with no verification would go against the philosophy of CoQ to keep its trusted computing base as small as possible.

From the methodological point of view, the most interesting aspect of this work has been the use of the meta-proving technique to generate our base arithmetic. This has proved to be a very powerful technique. Files for the base arithmetic are generated in an ad-hoc manner by concatenating strings. Developing a more adequate support for meta-proving inside the prover seems a very promising future work. Note that meta-proving could also be a solution to get more flexibility in the proof system. Slightly changing our representation, for example adding not only WO but also W1 and W-1 to the w2 type, would break most of our definitions and proofs. Meta-proving could be a solution for having a formal development for a family of data structures rather than just a single one.

Finally, on December 2005, a new prime Mersenne number has been discovered: $2^{30402457} - 1$. It took five days to perform its Lucas-Lehmer test on a super computer. The program uses a very intriguing algorithm for multiplication [8]. Proving the correctness of such an algorithm seems a very challenging task.

Acknowledgments

We would like to thank the anonymous referees for their careful reading of the paper and specially the referee who suggested a simplification to our implementation of Karatsuba multiplication.

References

1. *GNU Multiple Precision Arithmetic Library.* http://www.swox.com/gmp/.
2. Henk Barendregt and Erik Barendsen. Autarkic computations in formal proofs. *J. Autom. Reasoning*, 28(3):321–336, 2002.
3. Yves Bertot, Nicolas Magaud, and Paul Zimmermann. A proof of GMP square root. *Journal of Automated Reasoning*, 29(3-4):225–252, 2002.
4. Samuel Boutin. Using Reflection to Build Efficient and Certified Decision Procedures. In *TACS'97*, volume 1281 of *LNCS*, pages 515–529, Sendai, Japan, 1997.
5. John Brillhart, Derrick H. Lehmer, and John L. Selfridge. New primality criteria and factorizations of $2^m \pm 1$. *Mathematics of Computation*, 29:620–647, 1975.
6. Christoph Burnikel and Joachim Ziegler. Fast recursive division. Technical Report MPI-I-98-1-022, Max-Planck-Institut, 1998.
7. Olga Caprotti and Martijn Oostdijk. Formal and efficient primality proofs by use of computer algebra oracles. *Journal of Symbolic Computation*, 32(1/2):55–70, 2001.
8. Richard Crandall and Barry Fagin. Discrete weighted transforms and large-integer arithmetic. 62(205):305–324, 1994.
9. Georges Gonthier. A computer-checked proof of the Four Colour Theorem. Technical report. Available at http://research.microsoft.com/~gonthier/4colproof.pdf.

10. Benjamin Grégoire and Xavier Leroy. A compiled implementation of strong reduction. In *International Conference on Functional Programming 2002*, pages 235–246. ACM Press, 2002.
11. Benjamin Grégoire and Assia Mahboubi. Proving ring equalities done right in Coq. In *TPHOLS'05*, volume 3603 of *LNCS*, pages 98–113.
12. Benjamin Grégoire, Laurent Théry, and Benjamin Werner. A computational approach to Pocklington certificates in type theory. In *FLOPS'06*, volume 3945 of *LNCS*, pages 97–113.
13. John Harrison and Laurent Théry. A skeptic's approach to combining HOL and Maple. *J. Autom. Reasoning*, 21(3):279–294, 1998.
14. Anatolii A. Karatsuba and Yu Ofman. Multiplication of Many-Digital Numbers by Automatic Computers. *Soviet Physics-Doklad*, 7:595–596, 1963.
15. Xavier Leroy. Objective Caml. Available at http://pauillac.inria.fr/ocaml/, 1997.
16. Valérie Ménissier-Morain. The CAML Numbers Reference Manual. Technical Report 141, INRIA, 1992.
17. Tobias Nipkow, Gertrud Bauer, and Paula Schultz. Flyspeck I: Tame Graphs. Technical report. Available at http://www.in.tum.de/~nipkow/pubs/Flyspeck/.
18. The Coq development team. The Coq Proof Assistant Reference Manual v7.2. Technical Report 255, INRIA, 2002. Available at http://coq.inria.fr/doc.
19. Paul Zimmermann. Karatsuba square root. Research Report 3805, INRIA, 1999.

Proving Formally the Implementation of an Efficient gcd Algorithm for Polynomials

Assia Mahboubi

INRIA Sophia-Antipolis
2204, routes des Lucioles - B.P. 93
06902 Sophia Antipolis Cedex, France
Assia.Mahboubi@sophia.inria.fr

Abstract. We describe here a formal proof in the Coq system of the structure theorem for subresultants, which allows to prove formally the correctness of our implementation of the subresultants algorithm. Up to our knowledge it is the first mechanized proof of this result.

1 Introduction

Automation in formal proofs can greatly benefit from the marriage of proof assistants and computer algebra tools. Unfortunately these two kinds of tools, both intending to do mathematics on a computer, were not designed to talk to each other and importing the art of computer algebra inside a proof assistant can become a challenging problem. There are at least two different approaches to bridge this gap. One is to use (but not to trust!) skillful oracles like Maple and to prove correct the result of each computation [13,6]. An orthogonal solution is to integrate computer algebra algorithms inside the proof assistant and to provide a machine-checked correctness proof of the procedures [21]. The work we present here goes in this last direction.

We are using the Coq system [20,2], which is a proof assistant based on type theory : it contains a strongly typed programming language which we will use for computations. In fact, we first implement computer algebra algorithms using this language, and these programs will be executed inside Coq by the reduction mechanism of the system. Later we will state correctness theorems about these objects and build formal proofs of these statements. This approach, called *computational reflection*, contrasts with the one adopted for example by Théry in [21], where algorithms are *formalized* in the proof assistant and then *extracted* to a functional programming language like Ocaml, before being executed.

The recent introduction of a compiler [9] to the Coq system allows to expect a reasonable efficiency from these programs executed by Coq, taking into account that the average user of a proof assistant does not seek for the same level of performance as the one of a computer algebra system. The latter will expect from the system fast computations that are beyond human reach because they involve large entries, while the former will need a proof producing automated tool for small, but very tedious goals.

U. Furbach and N. Shankar (Eds.): IJCAR 2006, LNAI 4130, pp. 438–452, 2006.
© Springer-Verlag Berlin Heidelberg 2006

We present here an algorithm for computing efficiently greatest common divisors (gcd) for polynomials with coefficients in a unique factorization domain (UFD) (see for example Geddes et al. [7]). A UFD is a ring where it makes sense to define gcd but may be less than a field, like it is the case for integers or polynomial rings on a UFD. Computing polynomial gcds is a fundamental concern of algebraic manipulations: simplification of polynomial expressions, computation of partial fraction expansions, mechanization of proofs in geometry...

The algorithms for polynomial gcd computations implemented in computer algebra systems merely fall into three main classes. First come pseudo-remainder sequences based algorithms whose most efficient variant is called the subresultant algorithm, introduced by Collins [5]. Sparse modular algorithms are based on Hensel lemma (see Geddes et al. [7]), including probabilistic versions like in the work of Zippel [24]. Many heuristics are also used, taking benefit from trivial factorizations, using tricks based again on finite field decompositions or on reduction to integer gcds.

Choosing which algorithm will be the most efficient, even on a given entry, is quite tricky and there is no decision procedure for that problem. Most systems implement several methods, and define a default behavior with customization possibilities. According to Liao and Fateman [16], Maple will apply sparse modular methods when its heuristic fails, and Macsyma as well as Mathematica attempt a Zippel's approach [24] before calling a subresultant algorithm. This paper also points out that the subresultant algorithm turns out to be the fastest in half of the benchmarking problems. Moreover, a subresultant algorithm can be defined and used on arbitrary UFDs, whereas the two other kinds of procedures apply for polynomials with integer base constants.

The algorithm we have chosen to implement is a subresultant algorithm, as described by Basu et al. [1].

Up to our knowledge the only directly related work has been the preliminary study of Boulmé [3], which did not lead to a formalization, and it seems that there is no available mechanized proof of this result. Our feeling is that this well-known computer algebra algorithm had not been formalized before because, despite an abundant computer algebra literature on this topic (see for example the survey of von zur Gathen and Lücking [22]), pen and paper proofs are technical and seemed to require a large amount of preliminary formalizations. Our first contribution is to provide a guideline, which is certainly not a new proof from a computer algebra point of view since it essentially combines the two approaches of Brown and Traub [4] and Basu et al. [1]. Describing how to make the formal proofs tractable is on the other hand an original work.

Our second contribution is an implementation in Coq of this algorithm, on top of a certified library for polynomial arithmetic. Our last contribution is a formal proof in Coq of the fundamental theorem of subresultant, leading to the correctness of the algorithm implemented.

The paper is organized as follows : in section 2 we introduce our representation of polynomials and defined *pseudo-remainder sequences* (PRS). Then section 3, after pointing out the complexity trade-off in polynomial gcd computations, defines *polynomial determinants*, studies their links with PRS and describes the corresponding formalization. Finally, in section 4 we define *subresultant polynomials* and state the fundamental theorem. We will finally discuss complexity and formalization issues, before concluding with section 5.

For the sake of readability we try to avoid Coq syntax as much as possible. Coq files can however be retrieved from:

http://www-sop.inria.fr/marelle/Assia.Mahboubi/rech-eng.html

2   Preliminary Definitions and Formalizations

2.1   Formalization of Polynomials

In the sequel, we will work with polynomials in $D[X]$, where D is a UFD with characteristic 0. In fact, our motivation is to implement these algorithms for polynomials in $\mathbb{Q}[X_1, \ldots, X_n]$, which are represented as univariate polynomials in X_n with coefficients in $\mathbb{Q}[X_1] \ldots [X_{n-1}]$. In this latter case, $\mathbb{Q}$ being a field, the polynomial ring $D = \mathbb{Q}[X_1] \ldots [X_{n-1}]$ is be a unique factorization domain.

Polynomials of $D[X]$ are implemented in the *sparse Horner* representation. Given the set D of coefficients, elements of $D[X]$ are inductively defined as being either constants, built from an element of D, or of the form $P \times X^n + p$ where P is an element of $D[X]$, n is a positive integer and p is an element of D. Here is the Coq syntax for this definition:

Inductive $Pol(D : Set) : Set :=$
$| Pc : D \to Pol\ D$
$| PX : Pol\ D \to \mathbb{N}^+ \to D \to Pol\ D.$

The positive integer n in the non constant case allows more compact representations for sparse polynomials, but at the same time enables even more terms to represent the same mathematical object. For example, X^2 can be represented as $((1) \times X) \times X + 0$ or as $(1) \times X^2 + 0$. It is however possible to choose as a normal form the most compact of these representations, which has no head zeros and is factorized as much as possible.

Now we assume that D is equipped with a ring structure, and a decidable equivalence relation which is taken as an equality relation over D. Moreover all the operations on D are compatible with it. It is possible to endow $(Pol\ D)$ with a decidable equality, equating all the representations of a polynomial, and with a ring structure. We also implement usual operations on polynomials like degree, leading coefficient.

We suppose now that a partial operation of division is available on D. Given two elements x and y of D we suppose that if there exist $a \in D$ such that $y = ax$ then $div(y, x) = a$. Partiality is a sensitive issue in type theory : we choose here to make div total, and $div(y, x)$ will be 0 if the division fails. Therefore $div(y, x)$ fails iff $div(y, x) = 0$ and $y \neq 0$. From now on it is possible to program a (partial) *euclidean division* over $D[X]$, in the usual way, but again returning zero for the quotient and the remainder as soon as one of the divisions performed on coefficients fails. This choice is the one made for the integer division in the proof assistants HOL-Light [12] and Isabelle [18].

Remark 1. A nice property of our representation is that it allows the definition of euclidean division by structural induction over the divisor. We would otherwise have provided a termination proof for the definition of the division. In fact, the representation chosen is very close to the representation of numbers in a formal basis X.

2.2   Pseudo-remainder and Pseudo-remainder Sequences

In the sequel, given $P \in D[X]$, its degree is denoted by $deg(P)$ and its leading coefficient by $lcoef(P)$. In the process of the euclidean division of P by Q, the only "denominators" we may introduce are powers of the leading coefficient of Q and in fact the process of euclidean division of $lcoef(Q)^{deg(P)-deg(Q)+1}P$ by Q, performed in $D[X]$, will never fail. This was already observed and used by Jacobi in 1836 [14] and we call $lcoef(Q)^{deg(P)-deg(Q)+1}$ the Jacobi factor.

Definition 1 (Pseudo-division). *Let* $P = p_0 + \cdots + p_n X^n$ *and* $Q = q_0 + \ldots q_m X^m$, *with* $p_n, q_m \neq 0$ *and* $n \geq m$, *be two elements of* $D[X]$.

The unique remainder (resp. the quotient) of the euclidean division of $q_m^{n-m+1}P$ *by* Q *is called the* pseudo-remainder *(resp. pseudo-quotient) of* P *by* Q *and denoted by* $prem(P,Q)$ *(resp.* $pquo(P,Q)$*). This operation is called* pseudo-division *of* P *by* Q, *and* $prem(P,Q), pquo(P,Q) \in D[X]$.

Example 1. $P = X^2$, $Q = 2X + 1$: $pquo(P,Q) = 2X - 1$, $prem(P,Q) = 1$.
$P = 2X^2 + 2X$, $Q = 2X + 2$: $pquo(P,Q) = 4X$, $prem(P,Q) = 0$.

Definition 2 (Similar elements). *Let* $P, Q \in D[X]$. P *and* Q *are similar* $(P \sim Q)$ *if there exists* $a, b \in D$ *such that* $aP = bQ$.

The Euclidean algorithm computes the gcd of two polynomials with coefficients in a field by a sequence of euclidean divisions. We can now generalize this algorithm to the case of a ring. Each step of euclidean division is replaced by a step of *pseudo*-euclidean division, but since the correcting factors we have introduced to be able to perform the division may not be the smallest possible, we introduce the possibility of scalar factorizations in the polynomials by requiring only similarity to the pseudo-remainders:

Definition 3 (Pseudo-remainder sequences (PRS)). *Let* $F_1, F_2 \in D[X]$, *with* $deg(F_1) > deg(F_2)$. *Let* $F_1, \ldots, F_k \in D[X]$ *be a sequence of non-zero polynomials such that:*

$$F_i \sim prem(F_{i-2}, F_{i-1}) \text{ for } i = 3 \ldots k \quad and \quad prem(F_{k-1}, F_k) = 0$$

This sequence is called a pseudo-remainder sequence. *From the definitions above,*

$$\forall i = 3 \ldots k, \quad \exists \alpha_i, \beta_i \in D \text{ and } \exists Q_i \sim pquo(F_{i-2}, F_{i-1}) \text{ such that}$$

$$\beta_i F_i = \alpha_i F_{i-2} - Q_i F_{i-1} \quad deg(F_i) < deg(F_{i-1})$$

Informally, α ensures that we can perform a euclidean division inside $D[X]$, and β is a scalar factor we can remove from the remainder. Again to circumvent the problem of partiality, such sequences of polynomials are encoded in Coq as infinite sequences in $(D[X])_{n \in \mathbb{N}}$, whose elements are zero after some index k. We even know thanks to the decreasing of the degree that $k \leq deg(Q) + 2$.

2.3   Reduction to Primitive Polynomials

Finally, given $P \in D[X]$, its *content* ($cont(P)$) is defined as a gcd of its coefficients. It is unique up the multiplication by units of D. If the coefficients of P are relatively prime, P is said to be *primitive*. If not, the *primitive part* $pp(P)$ of P is defined by $P = cont(P)pp(P)$.

The gcd of two elements of $D[X]$ is the product of their contents by the gcd of their primitive parts. Moreover, if two polynomials F_1 and F_2 in $D[X]$ are primitive, so is their gcd, hence with the notations of the definition 3, $gcd(F_1, F_2) = pp(F_k)$. We suppose that we are able to compute gcd on D (we are interested in the case where D is a polynomial ring $\mathbb{Q}[X_1, \ldots X_n]$).Subsequently from now on we study the problem of computing the gcd and subresultants of two primitive polynomials, with distinct degrees.

3   Polynomial Determinants and PRS

In this section, we consider $F_1 = p_0 + \cdots + p_n X^n$ and $F_2 = q_0 + \ldots q_m X^m$ with $p_n, q_m > 0$ and $n > m$, two polynomials in $D[X]$ and $(F_i)_{i=1\ldots k}$ a PRS, such that for $i = 3\ldots k$:

$$\beta_i F_i = \alpha_i F_{i-2} - Q_i F_{i-1} \quad deg(F_i) < deg(F_{i-1}) \quad (1)$$

We denote $n_i = deg(F_i)$ and $c_i = lcoef(F_i)$ for $i = 1\ldots k$ and call (1) a *pseudo-euclidean relation*.

3.1   Control over the Growth of Coefficients

Computing efficiently the gcd of two polynomials is computing efficiently the last non zero element of a PRS. The naivest way of computing a PRS is to choose $F_i = prem(F_{i-2}, F_{i-1})$. This PRS is called the *Euclidean PRS* after Collins [5]. Unfortunately this may lead to a dramatical increase in the size of the coefficients of the polynomials in the PRS. In fact, the bit-size of the coefficients grows exponentially: an exponential lower bound is given by Yap [23] and Knuth describes this phenomenon [15]:"Thus the upper bound [...] would be approximately $N^{0.5(2.414)^n}$ and experiments show that the simple algorithm does in fact have this behavior, the number of digits in the coefficients grows exponentially at each step!". However according to von zur Gathen and Lücking [22] : "In a single division, say with random inputs, one cannot do much better than Jacobi's pseudo-division in trying to keep the remainder integral. But the results in Euclid's algorithm are so highly dependent that there are always large factors that can be extracted".

On the other hand, choosing $F_i = pp(prem(F_{i-2}, F_{i-1}))$ minimizes the growth of theses coefficients. This PRS is called the *primitive PRS*, again after Collins [5]. But recursive computations of gcds for each division step is in the general case too expensive.

The *Subresultant PRS algorithm* we are going to present is a compromise between the two preceding solutions, removing at each pseudo-division step a significant factor which is easier to compute than the content. This means it *predicts* suitable values for the α_i's and β_i's (using notations of definition 3), which ensure a reasonable (bit-size linear) growth for the coefficients of the polynomials (see section 4.3).

3.2 An Example of Computations

We reprint here the example of von zur Gathen and Lücking [22] to compare these three approaches. The α_i's are always the Jacobi factor of the pseudo-division, and the β_i's are factors we can extract from the pseudo-remainder.

i	α_i	β_i	F_i
1			$9X^6 - 27X^4 - 27X^3 + 72X + 18X - 45$
2			$3X^4 - 4X^2 - 9X + 21$
3	$3^3 = 27$	1	$-297x^2 - 729X + 1620$
4	-26198073	1	$3245333040X - 4899708873$
5	10532186540515641600	1	-16599458653306233453993

Euclidean PRS : no factorization ($\beta_i = 1$), exponential growth.

i	α_i	β_i	F_i
1			$9X^6 - 27X^4 - 27X^3 + 72X + 18X - 45$
2			$3X^4 - 4X^2 - 9X + 21$
3	$3^3 = 27$	3	$-11X - 27X + 60$
4	-1331	9	$18320X - 27659$
5	335622400	1959126851	-1

Primitive PRS : optimal factorization, expensive recursive computations.

i	α_i	β_i	F_i
1			$9X - 27X^4 - 27X^3 + 72X + 18X - 45$
2			$3X - 4X^2 - 9X + 21$
3	27	3	$297X^2 + 729X - 1620$
4	26198073	-243	$13355280X - 20163411$
5	178363503878400	2910897	9657273681

Subresultant PRS : a compromise, we remove smaller factors than in the Primitive case but computations are much cheaper.

3.3 Polynomial Determinants

We now roughly follow the presentation of Basu et al. [1] to introduce *polynomial determinants*. Let $\mathcal{F}_n$ be the set of polynomials in $D[X]$ whose degrees are less than n. It is a finitely generated free module, equipped with the usual monomial basis $\mathcal{B} = X^{n-1} \dots X, 1$.

Proposition 1 (Polynomial determinant definition). *Let $m \leq n$, two integers. There exists a unique multi-linear antisymmetric mapping, denoted* pdet, *from $(\mathcal{F}_n)^m$ to $\mathcal{F}_{n-m+1}$ such that for every $n > i_1 > \dots i_{m-1} > i$:*

$$
\begin{cases}
pdet_{n,m}(X^{i_1}, \dots, X^{i_{m-1}}, X^i) = X^i & \text{if for every } j < m \; i_j = n - j \\
pdet_{n,m}(X^{i_1}, \dots, X^{i_{m-1}}, X^i) = 0 & \text{otherwise}
\end{cases}
$$

Proof. Uniqueness comes from antisymmetry and multilinearity, after decomposing the arguments on the basis $\mathcal{B}$.

Let $Mat'(\mathcal{P})$ be the square matrix whose $m - 1$ first lines are the $m - 1$ first lines of $Mat(\mathcal{P})$, and the last line is built with the polynomials $P_1, \dots, P_m$:

$$
Mat'(\mathcal{P}) = \begin{bmatrix}
p_{n-1}^1 & \cdots & p_{n-1}^m \\
\vdots & & \vdots \\
p_{n-m+1}^1 & \cdots & p_{n-m+1}^m \\
P_1 & \cdots & P_m
\end{bmatrix}
$$

Now $pdet_{n,m} = det(Mat'(\mathcal{P}))$, where det is the usual determinant of matrices, here with polynomial coefficients. □

3.4 Formalization of Multilinear Applications in Coq

To date there exists no distributed contribution for multilinear algebra in the Coq system. Building such a formal theory of multilinear algebra on top of the existing Coq contributions on linear algebra finally appeared as a very costly solution for our purpose. One of the difficulties was to handle the hierarchy of coercions between the fields of dependent records, which underly these previous contributions. This piled and intricate structure representing inheritance in mathematical structures is tricky to handle and type-checking can become quite inefficient. Since we did not need the whole theory leading to the construction of determinants over rings, we have chosen to define determinants as (computable) functions and to prove on demand their required properties.

To fit the usual definition of multilinear applications, like determinants, let us consider temporarily a field K and E_K a vector space over K. Let l be the list of elements of E_K, we will compute the multilinear application by recursion over the length of l. We need to specify how to extract coordinates on the basis we have chosen, and therefore assume an extra parameter $coord : \text{nat} \to E_K \to K$, which is global and depends on n, the dimension of the vector space considered. The recursion will transform the problem into the same but with determinants of size one less. Now if n is the length of l, under the assumption that we know how to compute det for arguments of size $n-1$, we can compute $(det\ l)$ recursively and this job will be performed by the rec_det function (whose description we postpone).

Definition. det l := det_aux (length l) l.

```
let rec det_aux(n:nat)(l:list E_K):K :=
    match n with
    |O ⇒ 1_K
    |n_1 + 1 ⇒ rec_det (coord n) (det_aux n_1) l nil
    end.
```

To compute the determinant, we will develop along, say one line, recursively compute the cofactors, and finally build the appropriate linear combination of the cofactors, with alternate signs. Cofactors are determinants of the sublists of length $n-1$ of l. The line along which the development is performed is chosen by the values of $coord$. Now rec_det is defined by induction on the structure of l.

```
let rec rec_det(f:E_K → K)(rec : list E_K → K)(l_1 l_2:list E_K):K:=
    match l_1 with
    |nil ⇒ 0_K
    |a :: l_3 ⇒ f(a)*[rec (app l_2 l_3)] - [rec_det f rec l3 (app l2 (a::nil))]
    end.
```

The assumptions we have made on K and E_K were only for the sake of clarity : in fact the only requirements of our formalization are that:

- K is a commutative integral ring
- E_K is a set equipped with an internal additive law, an external linear product $E_K \to K \to E_K$ and linear $coord$ operator.

Proving that we can develop a determinant along the line determined by $coord$ is granted from the definition of det. We also prove formally that det is multilinear, antisymmetric, and alternate, by proving it successively for det_rec and det_aux, of course under the assumption that $coord$ is linear. We also formalize the notion of triangular system, and obtain the value of such a determinant as a product of diagonal values.

Taking $K = \mathbb{Z}$ and $E_K = list\ \mathbb{Z}$, we encode the usual determinant of a square matrix of integers, just by taking:

Definition. coord n l := nth (n - 1) l 0.

where $(nth\ k\ l\ a)$ computes the k-th element of the list l and returns a if n is out of bounds.

We would like to define the polynomial determinant as an application of type $(list\ D[X]) \to D[X]$, and this definition of det makes it possible. Here are the signatures of the auxiliary functions:

$$coord\ :\ nat \to D[X] \to D[X]$$
$$det\_aux\ :\ nat \to (list\ D[X]) \to D[X]$$
$$rec\_det\ :\ (D[X] \to D[X]) \to ((list\ D[X]) \to D[X]) \to (list\ D[X]) \to D[X]$$

We need to clarify the definition of $coord$. It corresponds to the development of the matrix $Mat'(\mathcal{P})$ along the penultimate line, because this is the way to get a definition of *pdet* by induction on the number of polynomials. We also need to give as a parameter *max_degree* (it was $n - 1$ in definition 1), the maximal degree of the polynomials involved, which determines the number of possible zero lines on top of $Mat'(\mathcal{P})$. This leads to the following definition:

Definition. coord max_degree j : $\rightarrow D[X] \rightarrow D[X]$:=
  if max_degree $+ 2 \leq$ j
    then (fun $P : Pol \Rightarrow P0$)
    else
      match j with
      $|O \Rightarrow$ (fun $P : Pol \Rightarrow P0$)
      $|1 \Rightarrow$ (fun $P : Pol \Rightarrow P$)
      $|_- \Rightarrow$ (fun $P : Pol \Rightarrow (-1)^{j+1} p_{\text{max\_degree}-j+2})$)
  end.
where p_k is the coefficient of P on X^k, here viewed as a constant polynomial. Now we are ready to define *subresultant polynomials*.

4   Structure of Subresultant Polynomials

4.1   Definition and First Properties

Definition 4 (Subresultant polynomials). *Let* $P, Q \in D[X]$ *be two polynomials with* $deg(P) = n$, $deg(Q) = m$ *and* $n > m$. *Then for* $i = 0 \ldots n$, *the* i-*th subresultant polynomial* $S_i(P, Q)$ *is defined by:*

- $S_n(P, Q) = P$
- $S_i(P, Q) = 0$ *for* $m < i < n$
- $S_i(P, Q) = pdet_{n+m-i,n+m-2i}(X^{m-i-1}, \ldots, XP, P, Q, XQ, \ldots, X^{n-i-1}Q)$ *otherwise*

Going back to the interpretation of *pdet* as a determinant of a matrix of polynomials (section 3.3), we can observe that:

$$S_i(P, Q) = det\,\mathbf{M}_{n_i} \text{ where } \mathbf{M}_{n_i} = \begin{bmatrix} p_n & & 0 & & q_m & & 0 \\ \vdots & \ddots & & & \vdots & & \ddots \\ p_{n-m+i+1} & \cdots & p_n & & & & \\ & & & & q_{m-n+i+1} & \cdots & q_m \\ \vdots & & \vdots & & \vdots & & \vdots \\ p_{2i+2-m} & \cdots & p_{i+1} & & q_{2i+2-n} & \cdots & q_{i+1} \\ X^{m-i-1}P & \cdots & & P & X^{n-i-1}Q & \cdots & Q \end{bmatrix}$$

Using the notations of section 3 and considering a PRS $F_1, \ldots, F_k$, from the relation (1) we can obtain Bezout-like relations by induction on i. Indeed for all $i = 3 \ldots k$, there exists $\gamma_i \in D$ and U_i, V_i in $D[X]$ such that :

$$U_i \times F_1 + V_i \times F_2 = \gamma_i F_i \quad deg(U_i) < m - n_{i-1}, \quad deg(V_i) < n - n_{i-1}$$

Reversing the problem, this relation can be seen as a system of linear equations in the coefficients of U_i and V_i, considering the relations equating coefficients of like powers on both sides. Gathering the last $n_i + 1$, inhomogeneous, equations in a single linear polynomial equation, this system can be described by

$$\mathbf{M}_{n_i} \times V = \begin{bmatrix} 0 \\ \vdots \\ 0 \\ \gamma_i F_i \end{bmatrix}$$

where V is the column vector of the coefficients of U_i and V_i, in decreasing order of subscript. There are in fact relations between the subresultant polynomials of two polynomials P and Q and the polynomials of a PRS starting with P and Q. From now on, we drop both subscripts of $pdet$; unless otherwise specified, $n + 1$ will always be the maximal degree of the polynomials given in arguments.

The following lemma (see [4]) shows that $S_j(P,Q)$ is a multiple of $S_j(Q, prem(P,Q))$, and this shift will be the elementary step of our main proof.

Lemma 1. *Let F, G, H, B be non zero polynomials in $D[X]$, of degree $\phi, \gamma, \eta, \beta$, respectively, such that :*

$$F + BG = H \quad with \quad \phi \geq \gamma > \eta \quad and \quad \beta = \phi - \gamma$$

Then,

$$
\begin{array}{lll}
(i) & S_j(F,G) = (-1)^{(\phi-j)(\gamma-j)} g_\gamma^{\phi-\eta} S_j(G,H) & 0 \leq j < \eta \\
(ii) & S_\eta(F,G) = (-1)^{(\phi-\eta)(\gamma-\eta)} g_\gamma^{\phi-\eta} h_\eta^{\gamma-\eta-1} H & \\
(iii) & S_j(F,G) = 0 & \eta < j < \gamma - 1 \\
(iv) & S_{\gamma-1}(F,G) = (-1)^{\phi-\gamma+1} g_{\phi-\gamma+1} H &
\end{array}
$$

Proof. Recall that for $j < \gamma$:

$$S_j(F,G) = pdet(X^{\gamma-j-1}F, \ldots, XF, F, G, XG, \ldots, X^{\phi-j-1}G)$$

In the right hand side, replacing each F by H is adding to each one of the $\gamma - i$ first arguments a linear combination of the $\phi - i$ last ones. Indeed $X^k F + X^k BG = X^k H$ with $\beta + k \leq \phi - j - 1$. The polynomial determinant being multilinear and alternate, this replacement does not alter the value of the $pdet$. Notice that these operations mimic the euclidean division of F by G. We have then:

$$S_j(F,G) = pdet(X^{\gamma-j-1}H, \ldots, XH, H, G, XG, \ldots, X^{\phi-j-1}G)$$

We now come back to the matrix representation of this $pdet$. We denote g_k (resp. h_k) the coefficient of G (resp. H) on the monomial X^k and swap the two blocks of columns:

$$S_j(F,G) = (-1)^{(\phi-j)(\gamma-j)} \det \begin{bmatrix} g_\gamma & 0 & h_\phi & 0 \\ \vdots & & \vdots & \ddots \\ \vdots & \ddots & \vdots & h_\phi \\ \vdots & & \vdots & \vdots \\ g_{\gamma-\phi+j+1} & \cdots & g_\gamma & h_{j+1} & \cdots & h_\gamma \\ \vdots & & \vdots & \vdots & & \vdots \\ g_{2i+2-\phi} & \cdots & g_{j+1} & h_{2j+2-\gamma} & \cdots & h_{j+1} \\ X^{\phi-i-1}G & \cdots & G & X^{\gamma-j-1}H & \cdots & H \end{bmatrix}$$

If $j \geq \eta$, then the matrix is triangular, and
$$S_\eta(F, G) = (-1)^{(\phi-\eta)(\gamma-\eta)} g_\gamma^{\phi-\eta} h_\eta^{\gamma-\eta-1} H \text{ for } \eta \leq j \leq \gamma - 1$$
This proves $(ii) - (iv)$. Now if $j < \eta$, the determinant has the block form:

$$S_j(F, G) = (-1)^{(\phi-j)(\gamma-j)} det \begin{bmatrix} A & 0 \\ B & S_j(G, H) \end{bmatrix}$$

where A is a triangular square block of size $\phi - \eta$, with all elements on its main diagonal equal to g_ϕ, which proves (i). □

Remark 2. The formal proof of this lemma relies on the fact that every polynomial in $D[X]$ of degree less than d is equal to a linear combination of monomials of degree less than d. Due to the choice of our representation (see section 2), we provide a theorem of equivalence of representations. Hereafter we can switch at any moment to the most convenient representation for the current goal to be proved.

4.2   Subresultants and PRS

The lemma 1 was describing the behavior of subresultant polynomials under with euclidean division. This result can be iterated to establish the link between subresultants and PRS. The multilinearity of *pdet* will lead to similarity relations between polynomials in the PRS and subresultant polynomials.

The fundamental theorem describes the structure of the sequence of subresultant polynomials : once the possible zero polynomials occurring in the subresultant polynomials sequence have been removed, polynomials in the sequence obtained are *pairwise similar* to the ones of the PRS.

Theorem 1 (Fundamental theorem). *Let $F_1, F_2, \ldots, F_k$ be a PRS in $D[X]$ and $n_i = deg(F_i)$. Using the notations of section 4.1:*

(i) $S_j(F_1, F_1) = 0$, *for* $0 \leq j < n_k$
(ii) $S_{n_i}(F_1, F_2)$ *and* F_i *are similar.*
(iii) $S_j(F_1, F_1) = 0$ *for* $n_i < j < n_{i-1} - 1$
(iv) $S_{n_{i-1}-1}(F_1, F_2)$ *and* F_i *are similar, for* $i = 3, \ldots k$.

Proof. The proof we have formalized is exactly the one published by Brown and Traub [4]. □

The similarity coefficients only depend on the values chosen for the α_i's and β_i's. The idea of a subresultants algorithm is to choose these values such that the non zeros subresultant polynomials are exactly the F_i of a PRS, which will be called the subresultant PRS. Fine customizations are possible in the choice of these α_i's and β_i's and this leads to several algorithms, which are all called subresultant algorithms. Here we have followed the presentation of Basu at al., [1] (see pp. 279 and 281) and we have implemented the corresponding algorithm, which computes successive subresultant polynomials by euclidean divisions using recursively defined appropriate α_i and β_i.

4.3   Complexity Issues

The unique factorization domain can in particular be instantiated by integers. Going back to our example in the section 3.2, we define $P := 9X^6 - 27X^4 - 27X^3 + 72X + 18X - 45$ and $Q := 3X^4 - 4X^2 - 9X + 21$, here is the output (instantly) computed by our Coq implementation:

```
Eval compute in (Pol_subres_list P Q).
   = PX (PX (PX (PX (PX (Pc 9) 2 -27) 1 -27) 1 72) 1 18) 1 -45
    :: PX (PX (PX (Pc 3) 2 -4) 1 -9) 1 21
     :: PX (PX (Pc -33) 1 -81) 1 180
      :: PX (Pc 18320) 1 -27659
       :: Pc -1471921 :: nil          : list Pol
```

Note that this result is slightly better than the one given in the former example, we are indeed here not very far from the primitive PRS, thanks to a more accurate choice of α_i's.

Basu et al. also give in [1] a detailed complexity analysis of their algorithm (see p. 298,Prop. 8.43).

Roughly speaking, the bit-size of the coefficients involved in the computation is linear in the sum of the degrees of the entries and in the bit-size of their coefficients. The theoretical (word operations) runtime complexity is quadratic in the degree of the entries.

Benchmarking Coq's output to get runtime results is not easy, because Coq's time measurement tool is not precise enough. Anyway, our implementation running in Coq is never slower that 20 times the implementation in Maple described by Liao and Fateman [16] on the 4 case problems where the subresultant algorithm wins the competition. This means for example that gcds of relatively prime polynomials of degree 10 with 5 variables are computed in Coq in less than one second.

4.4   Implementation and Formal Proofs

This formalization can be considered as a test case for the integration of a non-trivial computer algebra algorithm inside a proof assistant using computational reflection. Here is a review of the steps of such a development.

Implementation of the computational part. Working by computational reflection means here that we are using the proof assistant as a programming language to implement and execute programs, and not as a formal mirror of extracted programs. This can only be legitimated by a satisfactory efficiency in the reduction mechanism of the proof assistant. In this setting, formalizations have to be designed as efficient functional programs. For our purpose, one of the main gaps between the computer algebra on one hand and the context of a proof assistant on the other hand was the status of primitive computations on *numbers*. The integers we are computing with are Coq objects as well and not the machine integers a CAS has at its disposal. Fortunately, it is possible to work in Coq with a library for large numbers arithmetics [11], and this leads to the nice performances described above.

Ring structure for the polynomials. Dealing with *real* functional programs may lead to more intricate proofs than reasoning on an ad-hoc representation of mathematical objects like polynomials. Here the choice of the equality relation over polynomials is one of the most influential on the style of the formal proofs. We have chosen an inductive predicate describing all the possible degeneracies of the normal form of a given polynomial, which constitute its class. This equality is parametrized by the equality relation defined on coefficients. Such a non-syntactic equality is represented in Coq thanks to *setoid* structures [8].

Remark 2 shows that the computational representation we have chosen may not be the most appropriate for the proofs. One could have adopted this point of view from scratch, defining a second representation for polynomials, dedicated to the proofs (like streams of coefficients), together with an embedding of the Horner form in this non optimized representation. The Coq proofs of the ring structure for Horner polynomials is completed, but we are currently investigating this direction, since it could solve remaining problems due to setoid rewritings and provide and abstract formalization for further implementations of polynomials in the system.

Polynomial determinants, algebraic identities, automation. This part of the formalization was the most tedious of the development. The proofs of the fundamental properties of the determinant, like the development of a trigonal determinant along its diagonal, chain setoid rewritings at several levels and ring identities in quite large terms. We make here a heavy use of the re-shaped tactic for automating normalization and proofs of ring identities [10], which enhances the previously available tactic, specially by providing an efficient and convenient tool on abstract (axiomatically defined) structures. The proof of the fundamental theorem 1 involves a bunch of identities of the form:

$$S_{n_{i-1}-1}(F_1, F_2) \prod_{l=3}^i \alpha_l^{n_{l-1}-n_{i-1}+1} =$$
$$F_i c_{i-1}^{1-n_{i-1}+n_i} \prod_{l=3}^i [\beta_l^{n_{l-1}-n_{i-1}+1} c_{l-1}^{n_{l-2}-n_l} (-1)^{(n_{l-2}-n_{i-1}+1)(n_{l-1}-n_{i-1}+1)}]$$

The work of Sacerdoti [19], which has considerably enhanced setoid rewriting, has been a prerequisite for our formalization. For example, Coq now allows, after having defined the above $\prod$: $nat \to nat \to (nat \to Coef) \to Coef$, to fix an equality relation for each argument, and once the compatibility lemma automatically generated is proved, to rewrite any of the arguments in a transparent way. Unfortunately setoid rewriting becomes even so a limiting factor: automatic search of rewritable occurrences is very slow, and may even fail unexpectedly, demanding the user to program small ad-hoc tactics using the toplevel metalanguage Ltac [2] of Coq. Efficient equational reasoning may be one of the next challenge to handle the quotient structures (inducing setoid rewriting) which are pervasive in formalization of mathematics.

5   Conclusion

It is a common situation is formalizations of mathematics that no pen and paper proof available in the literature is literally adapted to a formal treatment. The case of the correction of the subresultant algorithm is yet another example of this gap. The historical paper [4] does not use the convenient definition of polynomial determinants and Basu et al. [1] use the fraction field of a UFD, which requires further non trivial developments in Coq.

This work is still in progress: the correctness proof of the implemented algorithm is not finished and we rely on axiomatic specifications of our euclidean division. Yet majors steps of the formalization are completed since we have formally proved Theorem 1. The code also needs to be cleaned up in order to be reusable as a stand-alone library for polynomial arithmetic and a reusable definition of determinants.

The approach we have chosen here is self-contained: programs are implemented, executed and checked by the same system. Thanks to the performances we obtain with such computations, we hope will be able to transpose the experiments described by Delahaye and Mayero [6], who were making the most of Maple's expertise in computation (of polynomial gcds), but spent time to the the answers of the CAS. We could compute less efficiently but the correctness proof of the gcd ensures once and for ever the correctness of all the outputs : time of computing is time of proving.

Computing polynomial gcds is at heart of several procedures which can automatize formal proofs. The most immediate byproduct we would like to get is a tactic for the simplification of field expressions, using factorizations of rational fractions.

This algorithm is a small piece of a decision procedure we have implemented in the Coq system, for the theory of real numbers [17]. This algorithm is a cylindrical algebraic decomposition [5,1], which uses extensively subresultant computations. Today, this procedure is completely programmed and our long-term goal is to provide a correctness proof for this program, which would then constitute a powerful tactic for real number arithmetic.

Acknowledgments. I would like to thank Laurent Théry for very fruitful discussions and in particular for his suggestions in the formalization of determinants, Laurence Rideau for her significant help in the pedestrian proofs of the ring axioms for polynomials and Marie-Françoise Roy for her detailed explanations on subresultants and elimination theory.

References

1. S. Basu, R. Pollack, and M.-F. Roy. *Algorithms in Real Algebraic Geometry*, volume 10 of *Algorithms and Computation in Mathematics*. Springer Verlag, 2003. draft for snd edition available at http://name.math.univ-rennes1.fr/marie-francoise.roy/bpr-posted1.html.
2. Y. Bertot and P.Casteran. *Interactive Theorem Proving and Program Development. Coq'Art : the Calculus of Inductive Constructions*. Texts in Theoretical Computer Science. Springer Verlag, 2004.
3. S. Boulmé. Vers la spécification formelle d'un algorithme non trivial de calcul formel : le calcul de pgcd de deux polynômes par la chaîne de pseudo-restes de sous-résultants. Master's thesis, SPI team, Paris VI University, September 1997.
4. W. S. Brown and J. F. Traub. On Euclid's Algorithm and the The Theory of Subresultants. *Journal of the ACM*, 18(4):505–514, 1971.

5. G. E. Collins. Subresultant and Reduced Polynomial Remainder Sequences. *Journal of the ACM*, 14:128–142, 1967.
6. D. Delahaye and M. Mayero. Quantifier Elimination over Algebraically Closed Fields in a Proof Assistant using a Computer Algebra System. In *Proceedings of Calculemus 2005*, 2005.
7. K. Geddes, S. R. Czapor, and G. Labahn. *Algorithms for Computer Algebra*. Kluwer Academic Publishers, 1992.
8. V. C. Gilles Barthe and O. Pons. Setoids in type theory. *Journal of Functional Programming*, 13(2):261–293, March 2003.
9. B. Grégoire and X. Leroy. A Compiled Implementation of Strong Reduction. In *International Conference on Functional Programming 2002*, pages 235–246. ACM Press, 2002.
10. B. Grégoire and A. Mahboubi. Proving Ring Equalities Done Right in Coq. In *TPHOLs'05*, LNCS. Springer Verlag, 2005.
11. B. Grégoire and L. Théry. A Purely Functional Library for Modular Arithmetic and its Application for Certifying Large Prime Numbers. In *IJCAR'06: Third International Joint Conference on Automated Reasoning*, 2006. to appear.
12. J. Harrison. *The HOL-Light System 2.20*. University of Cambrige, DSTO, SRI International, May 2006. http://www.cl.cam.ac.uk/~jrh/hol-light/.
13. J. Harrison and L. Théry. A Skeptic's Approach to Combining HOL and Maple. *Journal of Automated Reasoning*, 21:279–294, 1998.
14. C. Jacobi. De Eliminatione Variablilis e Duabus Aequationibus. *J. Reine Angew. Math*, 15:101–124, 1836.
15. D. Knuth. *The Art of Computer Programming, Semi-numerical Algorithms*, volume 2. Addison-Wesley, 1998.
16. H.-C. Liao and R. J. Fateman. Evaluation of the Heuristic Polynomial gcd. In *ISSAC '95: Proceedings of the 1995 international symposium on Symbolic and algebraic computation*, pages 240–247. ACM Press, 1995.
17. A. Mahboubi. Programming and Certifying a CAD Algorithm in the Coq system. In *Mathematics, Algorithms, Proofs*, number 05021 in Dagstuhl Seminar Proceedings. IBFI, Schloss Dagstuhl, Germany, 2006.
18. T. Nipkow, L. C. Paulson, and M. Wenzel. *Isabelle/HOL A Proof Assistant for Higher-Order Logic*, volume 2283 of *LNCS*. Springer, 2002.
19. C. Sacerdoti. A Semi-reflexive Tactic for (Sub-)Equational Reasoning. In *TYPES 2004*, volume 3839 of *Lecture Notes in Computer Sciences*, pages 98–114. Springer Verlag, 2006.
20. The Coq Development Team. *The Coq Proof Assistant Reference Manual – Version V8.0*, Apr. 2004. http://coq.inria.fr.
21. L. Théry. A Machine-Checked Implementation of Buchberger's Algorithm. *Journal of Automated Reasoning*, 26:107–137, 2001.
22. J. von zur Gathen and T. Lücking. Subresultants Revisited. *Theoretical Computer Science*, 297(1-3):199–239, 2003.
23. C. K. Yap. *Fundamental Problems of Algorithmic Algebra*. Oxford University Press, 2000.
24. R. Zippel. *Effective Polynomial Computation*. Kluwer Academic Publishers, 1993.

A SAT-Based Decision Procedure for the Subclass of Unrollable List Formulas in ACL2 (SULFA)

Erik Reeber and Warren A. Hunt Jr.

Department of Computer Sciences, 1 University Station, M/S C0500
The University of Texas, Austin, TX 78712-0233, USA
{hunt, reeber}@cs.utexas.edu

Abstract. We define the Subclass of Unrollable List Formulas in ACL2 (SULFA). SULFA is a subclass of ACL2 formulas based on list structures that is sufficiently expressive to include invariants of finite state machines (FSMs). We have extended the ACL2 theorem prover to include a new proof mechanism, which can recognize SULFA formulas and automatically verify them with a SAT-based decision procedure. When this decision procedure is successful, a theorem is added to the ACL2 system database as a lemma for use in future proof attempts. When unsuccessful, a counter-example to the SULFA property is presented.

We are using SULFA and its SAT-based decision procedure as part of a larger system to verify components of the TRIPS processor. Our verification system translates Verilog designs automatically into ACL2 models. These models are written such that their invariants are SULFA properties, which can be verified by our SAT-based decision procedure, traditional theorem proving, or a mixture of the two.

1 Introduction

Formal methods can be divided into several important areas, including theorem proving and model checking. Theorem proving scales to large systems, but requires human guidance. Model checking is more automatic, but the state explosion problem prevents it from verifying large systems. The integration of these two complementary techniques is an area of active research.

The ACL2 theorem prover has been used to formally verify large hardware designs, including the elementary floating-point operations on AMD's Athlon™processor [1]. It has the advantage of having a fast execution engine and a relative high degree of automation. The integration of model checking techniques within ACL2, however, has proven challenging. Due to ACL2's expressiveness, model checking techniques cannot apply to all ACL2 properties and since ACL2 is typeless, one cannot narrow its expressiveness through type restrictions.

In this paper, we present a new approach to integrating fully automatic techniques within ACL2. Our main contribution is the definition of the Subclass of

U. Furbach and N. Shankar (Eds.): IJCAR 2006, LNAI 4130, pp. 453–467, 2006.

Unrollable List Formulas in ACL2 (SULFA). SULFA is decidable, making it an ideal application for fully automatic techniques. Furthermore, SULFA is extendable, allowing restricted calls to user-defined recursive functions. This extensibility allows hardware models and their invariants to be succinctly described. Furthermore, SULFA is typeless and defined over an infinite domain—variables in a SULFA property can be instantiated with any ACL2 constant.

We added a recognizer for SULFA to the ACL2 theorem prover, which we describe in Sect. 3. We also extended the theorem prover to include the SAT-based decision procedure for SULFA described in Sect. 4. In Sect. 5 we apply this decision procedure to the verification of components of the TRIPS processor.

2   Background

2.1   Satisfiability Solving

Satisfiability (SAT) solving is the problem of determining whether there exists an instantiation of Boolean variables that satisfies a formula, typically in Conjunctive Normal Form (CNF). The following is an example of a CNF formula:

$$(x_0 \lor x_1 \lor x_2) \land (\neg x_0 \lor \neg x_1) \land (x_0 \lor \neg x_2)$$

SAT solving is known to be NP-Complete. Nevertheless, there are SAT-based tools that can solve a wide array of practical problems [2].

2.2   ACL2

ACL2, A Computation Logic for Applicative Common Lisp, is a functional subset of Common Lisp. For a thorough description of it, see the book by Kaufmann et al. [3]. In this paper, some understanding of Common Lisp is assumed.

ACL2 includes a large array of constants, including numbers, characters, strings, symbols, and ordered pairs (also referred to as list structures). In this paper, we focus mostly on the symbol nil, which represents both *false* and the empty list; the symbol t, which represents *true*; and ordered pairs, which are recognized by consp and created by cons. A fundamental axiom of ACL2 is that the different types of constants are disjoint. Therefore (cons x y)≠nil is

[1] (consp (cons x y))≠nil	[6]	(car (cons x y))=x
[2] (consp x)=nil → (car x)=nil	[7]	(cdr (cons x y))=y
[3] (consp x)=nil → (cdr x)=nil	[8]	t≠nil
[4] ((consp x)=t) ∨ ((consp x)=nil)	[9]	x=nil → (if x y z)=z
[5] (consp x)≠nil → (cons (car x) (cdr x))=x	[10]	x≠nil → (if x y z)=y

Fig. 1. Some relevant ACL2 axioms. Note that the axioms [1], [5], [6], and [7] also form the axioms of Nelson and Oppen's Theory of List Structure [4]. The axioms [2], [3], and [4] make car, cdr, and consp total functions.

an ACL2 theorem, where the unbound variables x and y are implicitly universally quantified. Other axioms regarding ACL2's ordered pair functions and if functions are shown in Fig. 1.

Fig. 2 illustrates a few example ACL2 definitions. Here concat concatenates two bit vectors and uand returns the conjunction of the bits in a bit vector. We also make use of the built in ACL2 function (zp N), which returns nil if N is a positive integer and t otherwise.

The functions uand and concat are defined recursively. ACL2 requires that these functions terminate on all inputs. This obligation is relieved by finding a *measure* that maps the function's inputs to an ordinal (up to ϵ_0), and proving that this measure decreases on each recursive call. In this case, a measure is found and proven to decrease without user guidance. A reasonable measure for both these functions is (nfix n), which returns n if n is a natural number, and zero otherwise. A function defined in this manner is total and ACL2 can execute the function to determine its value given any constant inputs.

```
(defun concat (n a b)
  (if (zp n)
      b
    (cons (car a) (concat (1- n) (cdr a) b))))

(defun uand (n a)
  (if (zp n)
      t
    (if (car a)
        (uand (1- n) (cdr a))
      nil)))

(defthm uand-concat
  (iff (uand (+ x y) (concat x a b)) (and (uand x a) (uand y b))))
```

Fig. 2. Some example ACL2 definitions and an example ACL2 theorem

Fig. 2 also illustrates an ACL2 theorem. This theorem states that the unary-and of the concatenation of two bit vectors is equivalent to the conjunction of the unary-and of each individual bit vector. Note that in ACL2 terms are used in place of formulas, where the implied formula is that the term is not equal to nil.

3   The Definition of SULFA

SULFA has the same syntax as ACL2, but places two semantic restrictions on function applications. First, all functions in a SULFA property must be executable. Second, all the non-list arguments to a function must be constant. A function is executable if it is a primitive or it is introduced using the lisp defun construct, rather than as an uninterpreted constrained function. The non-list arguments of a function are defined by considering the function's body, as follows:

- The *non-list arguments* of a function, intuitively, is the subset of formal arguments that must be constant in order for a function application to be unrolled into the primitives car, cdr, cons, consp, and if. For these primitives, the non-list arguments is their entire set of formals. For other primitives, the non-list arguments is the empty set. For non-primitives, the non-list arguments is defined as the minimal fix point that includes all unbound variables in the function's measure and all unbound non-list variables occurring in the function's body.
- An unbound variable in an expression is an *unbound non-list variable* if it occurs in any expression used to calculate the non-list argument of a function application.

Consider the example design of the 3-digit decimal counter shown in Fig. 3 and its corresponding ACL2 model in Fig. 4. The n argument of step-n-counter is

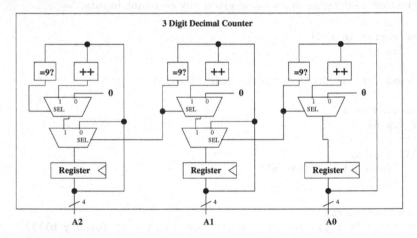

Fig. 3. A schematic for a 3-Digit Decimal Counter. Each individual digit is represented as a four bit, bit vector.

```
(defun step-n-counter (n count-state)
  (let ((digit (car count-state)))
    (if (zp n)
        nil
      (if (bv-eq 4 digit (bv-const 4 9))
          (cons (bv-const 4 0) (step-n-counter (1- n) (cdr count-state)))
        (cons (bv++ 4 digit) (cdr count-state))))))

(defun step-3-counter (count-state)
  (step-n-counter 3 count-state))
```

Fig. 4. An ACL2 model of the 3-Digit counter in Fig. 3. The function bv-eq determines if two n-bit, bit vectors are equal; the function bv-const returns the n-bit, bit vector representing a natural number; and the function bv++ increments an n-bit, bit vector.

a non-list argument, because of its use within the termination justifying measure of `step-n-counter` and its use in the applications of `zp`, `1-`, and the recursive call. The other formal arguments in Fig. 4 are list arguments.

The digits of `step-3-counter` always are intended to represent numbers between zero and nine. This invariant can be written as the ACL2 property:

```
(defthm counter-invariant-3
  (implies (all-3-below-tenp init-state)
           (all-3-below-tenp (Tth-3-count-state tao init-state))))
```

Here the function `Tth-3-count-state` produces the state of the counter after `tao` time steps and the function `all-below-ten-p` has the following definition, where `bv<` determines whether one n-bit, bit vector is less than another.

```
(defun all-below-ten-p (n count-state)
  (if (zp n)
      t
    (if (bv< 4 (car count-state) (bv-const 4 10))
        (all-below-ten-p (1- n) (cdr count-state))
      nil)))
```

This property follows by induction from the following ACL2 property:

```
(defthm counter-step-3
  (implies (all-below-ten-p 3 count-state)
           (all-below-ten-p 3 (step-3-counter count-state)))
  :hints (("Goal" :sat default)))
```

Note that the above property is proven with the `:sat` hint. ACL2 contains many hints to guide the theorem prover. Our SAT-based decision procedure is implemented as a new hint, `:sat`, which verifies valid SULFA properties automatically. If a SULFA property is invalid, our procedure gives a counter example.

4   A SAT-Based Decision Procedure

In this section we present a SAT-Based decision procedure for SULFA. We then discuss the optimizations needed to make this procedure practical, before showing how our procedure performs on some examples.

4.1   Conversion Algorithm

Our goal is to translate a SULFA formula into the negation of a formula in Boolean Conjunctive Normal Form (CNF). Therefore the CNF formula is unsatisfiable if and only if the SULFA formula is valid.

The first step is to create a negated-conjunction, by performing double-negation on the SULFA formula. Throughout the rest of the algorithm the formula is maintained as a negated conjunction. We refer to arguments of the conjunction as *clauses* and arguments to each clause's disjunction as *literals*.

Each literal is a *leaf expression* or its negation, where a leaf expression is a
SULFA expression. Note that the validity of any such negated conjunction is
not changed if every leaf expression X is mapped to the Boolean expression
$X \neq$ **nil**.

Our procedure starts with a single leaf expression, which is the negation of the
original formula. For an example, we illustrate how our procedure finds a counterexample to the invalid SULFA formula (implies (car a) (uand 2 a)),
where uand has the definition given in Fig. 2. The initial negated-conjunction is
(nand (not (implies (car a) (uand 2 a)))). Our decision procedure continues by executing the following phases:

Function Expansion. If a function application has constant arguments, it
is evaluated. Otherwise, unless it is an application of if, cons, car, cdr, or
consp, it is expanded according to its definition. If the function is recursive,
ACL2 contains an associated ordinal measure. Since the function application is
in SULFA, the measure is constant. If the measure fails to decrease on a recursive
call, then it follows from the proof of termination that the value returned by the
recursive call is irrelevant. To prevent further expansion, irrelevant recursive calls
are replaced with arbitrary constants. In our example, let the measure of (uand n
x) be equal to n when n is a natural number, and zero otherwise. Therefore when
expanding (uand 0 x), the recursive call is replace with an arbitrary constant.
This process leads to the following formula:

```
(nand
 (not
  (if (car a) (if nil t
      (if (car a) (if nil t
          (if (car (cdr a))
              (if t t (if (car (cdr (cdr a))) 'arbitrary-constant nil))
              nil))
          nil))
      t)))
```

IF Removal. Any if with a constant condition is simplified to either its true
or false branch. Any other clause of the form (or (f (if a b c)) x), where f
is car, cdr, or consp is replaced with two clauses: (or (f b) (not a) x) and
(or (f c) a x). For our example, this process leads to the following formula:

```
(nand (or (not t) (not (car (cdr a))) (not (car a)) (not (car a)))
      (or (not nil) (car (cdr a)) (not (car a)) (not (car a)))
      (or (not t) (not (car (cdr a))) (car a) (not (car a)))
      (or (not nil) (car (cdr a)) (car a) (not (car a)))
      (or (not t) (not (car (cdr a))) (not (car a)) (car a))
      (or (not t) (car (cdr a)) (not (car a)) (car a))
      (or (not t) (not (car (cdr a))) (car a) (car a))
      (or (not t) (car (cdr a)) (car a) (car a)))
```

Cons Simplification. Occurrences of (car (cons a b)) are replaced with a,
(cdr (cons a b)) with b, and (consp (cons a b)) with *true*. Any remaining

cons must appear at the top-level of a leaf expression. Such expressions are reduced to *true* by the theorem (not (equal (cons x y) nil)), since any leaf expression X can be substituted with $X \neq$ nil without affecting the validity of the negated-CNF formula. Our example formula does not contain cons, so this phase has no effect on it.

Local Simplification. Simplifications local to a clause are now performed. Occurrences of (car (consp X)) and (cdr (consp X)) are reduced to nil, constants are evaluated, *false* literals are removed, and redundant literals are removed. Also a clause is removed if it contains a *true* literal or a literal and its negation. In our example, most of the clauses are now removed, leading to the following:

```
(nand (or (not (car (cdr a))) (not (car a)))
      (or (not (car (cdr a))) (car a))
      (or (car (cdr a)) (car a)))
```

List Accessor Removal. At this point, every leaf expression contains only applications of car and cdr, with a possible top-level application of consp. Let Γ be the set of unique leaf expressions occurring in the formula. Next for each ACL2 expression X such that (car X) is in Γ, the clause (or (not (car X)) (consp X)) is added to the formula, and (consp X) is added to Γ if it is not already present. Similarly for each (cdr X) in Γ the clause (or (not (cdr X)) (consp X)) is added, and for each (consp X) in Γ the clause (or (not (consp X)) X) is added. In our example, the following new clauses are created:

```
(or (not (car (cdr a))) (consp (cdr a)))
(or (not (car a)) (consp a))
(or (not (consp (cdr a))) (cdr a))
(or (not (consp a)) a)
(or (not (cdr a)) (consp a))
```

Since these clauses are instantiations of ACL2 theorems, they are always satisfied. Their addition though allows the removal of the functions car, cdr, and consp. A new formula is created by substituting new Boolean variables for each each element of Γ. In our example, we create the variable y0 for (car a), y1 for (car (cdr a)), y2 for a, y3 for (cdr a), y4 for (consp (cdr a)), and y5 for (consp a). This leads to the following formula:

```
(nand (or (not y1) (not y0))   (or (not y1) y0)
      (or y1 y0)               (or (not y1) y4)
      (or (not y0) y5)         (or (not y4) y3)
      (or (not y5) y2)         (or (not y3) y5))
```

Note that the five new clauses ensure that a satisfying instance of the new variables does not correspond to an invalid ACL2 list structures in the original formula. For example, y0 = t and y5 = **nil** is not allowed because there is no ACL2 list structure that satisfies both (car a) $\neq$ **nil** and (consp a) = **nil**.

Counter Example Generation. We now use a SAT solver to find a satisfying instance of the conjunction. If there is no such instance, then the original SULFA formula is valid; otherwise, we construct a counterexample. For our example, the SAT solver finds the following instance:

```
y0 = (car a)          : true,    y3 = (cdr a)           : true,
y1 = (car (cdr a))    : false,   y4 = (consp (cdr a))   : true,
y2 = a                : true,    y5 = (consp a)         : true
```

Each of these variables represents a leaf expression X that is equivalent to $X \neq$ nil; therefore any variable that is *true* may be a cons structure.

To choose a counterexample, we define the function $\mathrm{CE}(expr, \Gamma, \mu)$, where $expr$ is an ACL2 expression, and μ is the mapping of expressions in Γ to values in the SAT instance. If $expr$ is not in Γ or if $expr$ is $false$ in μ, then $\mathrm{CE}(expr, \Gamma, \mu) =$ nil. Otherwise if (consp $expr$) is $false$ in μ, then $\mathrm{CE}(expr, \Gamma, \mu) = $ t. Otherwise, $\mathrm{CE}(expr, \Gamma, \mu)$ is a cons structure whose car is $\mathrm{CE}((\mathrm{car}\ expr), \Gamma, \mu)$ and whose cdr is $\mathrm{CE}((\mathrm{cdr}\ expr), \Gamma, \mu)$. CE terminates since $expr$ cannot expand indefinitely while staying in Γ.

We construct a counterexample by using CE to find a value for each variable in our original formula. For our example $\mathrm{CE}(\mathrm{a}, \Gamma, \mu)$ returns the counterexample (cons (cons nil nil) (cons nil nil)).

4.2   Correctness

The conversion algorithm cannot be verified by the ACL2 theorem prover, since it depends on meta-theoretical arguments, such as any function's body is equal to its definition and the measure of any recursive function decreases on each relevant recursive call. We could verify the algorithm on a case-by-case basis, but in practice these formulas are too large for the ACL2 theorem prover to handle. We therefore sketch a proof of the correctness of our algorithm by hand. In the interest of brevity, some details are skipped.

First we prove the equivalence of the original formula and the negated conjunction output by the Local Simplification Phase. For the most part, this equivalence follows from the definitional axioms and the axioms of Fig. 1. The only exception is the replacement of certain recursive function calls with arbitrary constants, which we already justified. Note that this fact is enough to prove the decidability of SULFA, since the formula output by the Local Simplification Phase is in the Theory of List Structure, shown decidable by Nelson and Oppen [4] (their theory usually does not include axioms [2] and [3] in Fig. 1, but their paper shows that the addition of these axioms does not affect decidability).

Next we prove that if the formula F output by the Local Simplification Phase is invalid, then there exists a satisfying instance to the final Boolean CNF formula. This represents the most important component of correctness, since it means that unsatisfiable CNF formulas correspond to valid ACL2 properties. Given that F is invalid, it must have a counterexample that satisfies all its clauses. This example also satisfies the clauses added during the Boolean Variable Creation Phase, since these are instantiations of valid ACL2 theorems, following from the axioms in Fig. 1. A counterexample to the formula output by the List Accessor Removal Phase can thus be created by mapping each variable in the output formula to the value of the expression it represents in the input formula under its counterexample. Replacing **nil** with *false* and any other value with *true*, then creates a satisfying instance to the Boolean CNF formula.

All that remains to be proven is that, given a satisfying instance to the Boolean CNF formula, the output of CE is a counterexample to the original formula. It is sufficient to show that each leaf expression in Γ is **nil** under the output of CE if and only if its corresponding Boolean CNF variable in μ is *false*. By the definition of CE, the value of any expression explicitly evaluated during counterexample generation has this characteristic. Furthermore CE is defined so that any expression not explicitly evaluated by it evaluates to **nil**. The corresponding values of these expressions in μ are *false* since the clauses added by the List Accessor Removal Phase force a variable representing (car x), (cdr x), and (consp x) to *false* if the variable representing x is *false*.

4.3 Optimization

The above procedure is too inefficient to be used directly, since the formula size quickly explodes. To a certain extent this explosion is unavoidable. Unrolling recursion creates a worst case explosion corresponding to the worst case complexity of any function one can prove terminates in ACL2, since any such function can be used to calculate the non-list argument on which a function recurs.

In practice, however, formula explosion can be greatly reduced by creating new variables, in a manner similar to that used by Tseitin [5]. Our optimized procedure creates new variables to avoid copying arguments during the Function Expansion Step and to avoid copying **if** conditions in the If Removal Step. New variables are initially constrained by clauses containing a positive literal of the form (equal x y), where x is a new variable. Then, through a mechanism similar to an outside-in cone-of-influence reduction, a finite number of relevant Boolean components of each variable is discovered. Then, without loss of generality, each clause containing (equal x y) is replaced with multiple clauses relating Boolean components of x with corresponding Boolean components of y.

Another optimization avoids adding new leaf expressions to Γ in the List Accessor Removal Phase by anticipating the application of the new clauses. For example, if a and (car (cdr a)) are in Γ, but not (cdr a), we create the clause (or (not (car (cdr a))) a), rather than adding clauses containing (cdr a).

Table 1 shows the performance of our optimized procedure on eight examples. First the associativity of 4 bit, 32 bit, and 200 bit ripple carry adders is verified. Next the commutativity of a 4 by 4 and a 8 by 8 multiplier is proven. Finally the invariant of the 10 and 100 digit instantiation of the decimal counter described in Sect. 3 is verified. For each example we show the number of lines of code required to write the model and specification, the time spent on the conversion to CNF, the number of variables and clauses in the CNF formula, the time spent SAT solving, and the total time required for the process (including I/O and other overhead). For this analysis the SAT solver zChaff, version 2004.11.15, was used

Table 1. The performance of the decision procedure on eight examples

N	Example	lines	Conv(s)	vars	clauses	SAT(s)	Total(s)
1	4-bit Adder Assoc	25	0.01	81	254	0.01	0.05
2	32-bit Adder Assoc	25	0.15	641	2298	2.08	2.29
3	200-bit Adder Assoc	25	2.82	4001	14562	144.62	147.80
4	4x4 Mult Commute	32	0.02	233	970	0.03	0.05
5	8x8 Mult Commute	32	0.09	913	4050	89.40	89.49
6	10 Digit Decimal Inv	44	0.04	300	1494	0.01	0.10
7	100 Digit Decimal Inv	44	6.70	2820	50454	3.69	13.13

on a 1.8GHz Intel $XEON^{TM}$ processor with 512 MB of RAM running ACL2 v2.9.1 on Allegro Common Lisp 6.2.

Table 1 shows that many interesting properties can be verified fully automatically through our approach. Note that it is common, but not universally true, that the conversion of a valid formula to CNF requires less time than the corresponding proof of unsatisfiability. This was also usually the case when verifying the TRIPS components described in Sect. 5. However, when an invalid property is converted to CNF, the SAT solver usually requires little time to find a satisfying instance to the corresponding CNF formula.

We have tried three other approaches within ACL2 to verify these examples: induction, clausification, and BDD comparison.

- The induction approach generalizes the problem and uses ACL2's induction proof engine. This approach scales well to large problems, but requires a significant amount of human guidance.
- The clausification approach expands the property into calls of `if` and relies on ACL2's internal clausification system to simplify `if`. This approach is nearly automatic, but has poor performance. The only example in Table 1 that can be verified by this approach is the associativity of a 4 bit adder.
- The BDD comparison approach reduces the problem to a finite domain and uses ACL2's built-in BDD system. The performance of the BDD system is similar to the performance of our SAT-based system, but is much less automatic. The BDD system often requires user guidance to expand recursive functions, detect relevant Boolean list structures, and provide a variable ordering for creating compact BDDs. For example, this approach requires 202 lines to model and specify the associativity of the 200 bit adder and 404 seconds to verify it. The BDD system also required 280 lines to model and specify the 100 digit decimal invariant, and 2.5 seconds to verify it.

5   Verifying TRIPS Processor Components

We are applying our SAT-based decision procedure to the verification of the TRIPS processor, which is a prototype of a next-generation processor that has been designed at the University of Texas [6] and is being built by IBM. One novel

LSQ Protocol Design

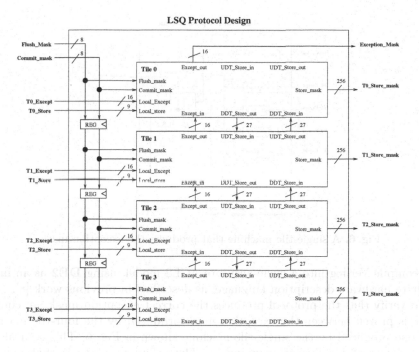

Fig. 5. An overview of the four tile exception protocol design

aspect of the TRIPS processor is that its memory is divided into four pieces; each piece has its own memory control tile, with its own cache and Load Store Queue (LSQ), as described by Sethumadhavan et al. [7]. We verified the protocol, implemented in Verilog, that manages communication between the four LSQs.

The LSQ protocol is illustrated in Fig. 5. The LSQs are arranged in a column, with each communicating with the one above it and below it. A tile communicates at the beginning of each cycle, sending information calculated in the previous cycle. Therefore, information input to tile 3 reaches tile 0 after a minimum of three cycles. The protocol is implemented in Verilog and uses the same design for each tile. Two tasks are accomplished:

1. **Generation of Exception Mask.** There are eight instruction blocks, each of which may generate an exception. A local exception is input to each tile as a three bit block address with an extra enable bit. Each tile sends all known exceptions to the tile above it and the top tile reports its exception mask to the rest of the processor. Eventually an exception should lead to a flush of the corresponding instruction block.
2. **Generation of Global Store Masks.** The protocol generates a global 256 bit mask of arrived stores, which is needed for the waking of deferred loads and completion detection. At most one new store is input to each LSQ each cycle, which is denoted by an eight bit address plus an enable bit. To generate the global store mask, each tile reports up to three recently-arrived stores to its neighbors.

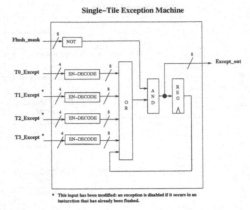

Fig. 6. A single-tile machine that produces the exception mask

We compile Verilog into a cycle-accurate ACL2 model, using **DE2** as an intermediate hardware description language, as described in previous work [8].

To verify that the protocol produces the correct exception mask, an equivalence is proven between the exception mask produced by the four-tile machine and one produced by the single-tile machine shown in Fig. 6. This equivalence has a safety and a liveness component. The safety property is that any exception reported by the four-tile machine is also reported by the single-tile machine. The liveness property is that eventually any exception reported by the single-tile machine will either be reported by the four-tile machine or be flushed.

We prove the safety property by proving three SULFA properties:

```
(defthm initial-except-inv
  (except-inv (initial-ext-state) (initial-4T-state) (initial-1T-state)))

(defthm implies-except-inv
  (and (inputs-good-p ext-state 4T-state 1T-state in)
       (except-inv ext-state 4T-state 1T-state))
  (submask-p 8
             (4T-except_out *tile-0* 4T-state in)
             (1T-except_out 1T-state in)))

(defthm step-except-inv
  (implies
   (and (inputs-good-p ext-state 4T-state 1T-state in)
        (except-inv ext-state 4T-state 1T-state))
   (except-inv (ext-step ext-state in)
               (4T-step 4T-state in)
               (1T-step 1T-state in)))))
```

Note that a third machine, with the state `ext-state`, stores information needed to constrain the inputs and define the invariant `except-inv`. The first theorem `initial-except-inv` states the invariant is true of the initial state. This theorem is proven by evaluation. The second theorem `implies-except-inv` states that the invariant implies that the exceptions produced by tile 0 in the four-tile machine are a subset of the exceptions produced by the single-tile machine. This theorem is proven directly with our SAT-based decision procedure. The final theorem `step-except-inv` states that the invariant implies itself in the next time step, given valid inputs `in`. This theorem is in SULFA, but requires too much time and memory to be proven directly with our SAT-based decision procedure. Instead the theorem prover is used to break it up into a number of lemmas, each of which is proven with our decision procedure.

To verify the liveness property we prove that after three cycles the top tile's exception mask includes all exceptions in the single-tile machine, which reduces to three SULFA properties, just as its safety counterpart did.

The verification of the global store mask is more difficult, but follows the same basic approach. We defined a single-tile machine and verified safety and liveness equivalence properties, similar to those used in the exception mask verification. The safety property reduced to three SULFA properties, which were proven using a mixture of theorem proving and the SAT-based decision procedure. To verify the liveness property, we used a different approach. We defined an ordinal measure that decreases whenever a store produced by the single-tile machine is not in a mask produced by the four-tile machine. Using this theorem we are able to prove the liveness property that a store output by the single-tile machine is eventually output by the four-tile machine. Although the ordinal property is not in SULFA, many of the lemmas used to complete its proof are in SULFA.

The use of SULFA properties significantly reduces the necessary human guidance in a proof effort, because once a property can be proven by the decision procedure no more guidance is needed. Furthermore, errors are immediately found and reported as counter-examples. Also note that many implementation details are only viewed by the decision procedure. If these details change, the design can be recompiled and the proof can be rerun without modification.

6   Related Work

The complementary techniques of theorem proving and model checking have been combined previously on many occasions. Issabelle, for example, incorporates a number of decision procedures inspired by model checking, including a SAT-based decision procedure for propositional logic. The general-purpose theorem prover PVS was designed with the combination of model-checking and theorem proving in mind [9]. Intel's FORTE system uses a HOL-based theorem prover built on top of an efficient procedure for symbolic trajectory evaluation [10]. The most general combination of theorem proving and model-checking of which we know is implemented by the SyMP model prover [11].

Fewer attempts have been made to integrate model checking with ACL2. A BDD-based engine has been built into the theorem prover for some time [12], but uses a significantly different approach. The BDD-based engine is not fully automatic over any clearly defined subclass of ACL2 formulas, but instead, with some human guidance, attempts to operate on a wider set of ACL2 formulas.

Other work incorporating fully automatic tools with ACL2 includes the definition in ACL2 of a simple model checker for the Mu-Calculus [13] and the partial integration of ACL2 with UCLID [14]. The main difference between our work and this work is the relative simplicity of the logic used by SAT solvers, which allows us to create a more natural embedding into the ACL2 logic. We also have used UCLID [15] to verify some of our examples from Sect. 4.3, but found that it was not designed with low-level hardware models in mind. When used with the zChaff SAT solver, UCLID required 6.33 seconds to verify the invariant of the ten digit decimal counter and after ten minutes was unable to verify the invariant of the hundred digit decimal counter. It may be possible to improve on these results, however, with the help of an experienced UCLID user.

7   Conclusion

We have defined a subclass of ACL2 formulas, SULFA, and shown that it is decidable. SULFA includes a variant of Nelson and Oppen's Theory of List Structure [4]. Unlike the Theory of List Structure, however, SULFA can be extended with user-defined functions, which allows hardware models and their invariants to be written succinctly. We implemented a SULFA recognizer and a SAT-based decision procedure for SULFA as an extension to the ACL2 theorem prover, which is publicly available [16].

Our work makes a number of contributions. We are the first to define a decidable subclass of ACL2 formulas that can succinctly express hardware invariants. To our knowledge, we are also the first to expand the hint mechanism of the ACL2 theorem prover to use an external tool. SAT solvers make an ideal external tool since the logic of SAT solvers embeds easily into ACL2. We are also the first to apply theorem proving techniques to the TRIPS processor. The TRIPS processor is unique in that it is not only a pipelined, out-of-order processor, but also has multiple memory and execution tiles.

Our approach represents a solid improvement over the verification of hardware with pure ACL2 theorem proving and has potential for greater improvement. We plan to apply our approach to a larger portion of the TRIPS processor and to explore the application of our approach to the verification of hardware generators. We are working with the authors of the ACL2 theorem prover to develop a more general mechanism for extending it. Once this mechanism is in place we will be able to include our SAT-based decision procedure as a dynamically-loaded book available with the standard ACL2 system. We also plan to further optimize our SAT-based decision procedure and explore the use of techniques other than SAT solving, such as BDD-based techniques.

References

1. Russinoff, D.: A Mechanically Checked Proof of IEEE Compliance of a Register-Transfer-Level Specification of the AMD K7 Floating Point Multiplication, Division and Square Root Instructions. London Mathematical Society Journal of Computation and Mathematics **1** (1998) 148–200
2. Moskewicz, M., Madigan, C., Zhao, Y., Zhang, L., Malik, S.: Chaff: Engineering an Efficient SAT Solver. In: Proceedings of the 38th Design Automation Conference (DAC 2001), ACM (2001) 530–535
3. Kaufmann, M., Manolios, P., Moore, J.S.: Computer Aided Reasoning: An Approach. Kluwer Academic (2000)
4. Nelson, G., Oppen, D.C.: Fast Decision Procedures Based on Congruence Closure. Journal of the ACM **27**(2) (1980) 356–364
5. Tseitin, G.: On the complexity of derivation in propositional calculus. Seminars in Mathematics **8** (1968)
6. Sankaralingam, K., Nagarajan, R., Liu, H., Kim, C., Huh, J., Burger, D., Keckler, S., Moore, C.: "exploiting ilp, tlp, and dlp with the polymorphous trips architecture". In: International Symposium on Computer Architecture, 2003. (2003) 422–433
7. Sethumadhavan, S., Desikan, R., Burger, D., Moore, C.R., Keckler, S.W.: Scalable Hardware Memory Disambiguation for High ILP Processors. In: Proceedings of the 36th Annual International Symposium on Microarchitecture (MICRO 36), ACM/IEEE (2003) 399–410
8. Hunt, Jr., W. A., Reeber, E.: Formalization of the DE2 Language. In: Correct Hardware Design and Verification Methods (CHARME 2005), Springer (2005) 20–34
9. Owre, S., Rajan, S., Rushby, J.M., Shankar, N., Srivas, M.K.: PVS: Combining Specification, Proof Checking, and Model Checking. In: CAV. (1996) 411–414
10. Jones, R.B., O'Leary, J.W., Seger, C.J.H., Aagaard, M., Melham, T.F.: Practical Formal Verification in Microprocessor Design. IEEE Design & Test of Computers **18**(4) (2001) 16–25
11. Berezin, S.: Model Checking and Theorem Proving: A Unified Framework. PhD thesis, Carnegie Mellon University (2002)
12. Moore, J.: Introduction to the OBDD Algorithm for the ATP Community. Journal of Automated Reasoning **12**(1) (1994) 33–45
13. Manolios, P.: Mechanical Verification of Reactive Systems. PhD thesis, The University of Texas at Austin (2001)
14. Manolios, P., Srinivasan, S.K.: Automatic Verification of Safety and Liveness for XScale-Like Processor Models Using WEB Refinements. In: DATE. (2004) 168–175
15. Lahiri, S.K., Bryant, R.E.: Deductive Verification of Advanced Out-of-Order Microprocessors. In: Computer Aided Verification, 15th International Conference (CAV 2003), Springer (2003) 341–353
16. The SAT-extended ACL2 Theorem Prover: www.cs.utexas.edu/users/reeber/sat-extended-acl2.html (2006)

Solving Sparse Linear Constraints

Shuvendu K. Lahiri and Madanlal Musuvathi

Microsoft Research
{shuvendu, madanm}@microsoft.com

Abstract. Linear arithmetic decision procedures form an important part of theorem provers for program verification. In most verification benchmarks, the linear arithmetic constraints are dominated by simple difference constraints of the form $x \leq y + c$. *Sparse linear arithmetic* (SLA) denotes a set of linear arithmetic constraints with a very few non-difference constraints. In this paper, we propose an efficient decision procedure for SLA constraints, by combining a solver for difference constraints with a solver for general linear constraints. For SLA constraints, the space and time complexity of the resulting algorithm is dominated solely by the complexity for solving the difference constraints. The decision procedure generates models for satisfiable formulas. We show how this combination can be extended to generate implied equalities. We instantiate this framework with an equality generating Simplex as the linear arithmetic solver, and present preliminary experimental evaluation of our implementation on a set of linear arithmetic benchmarks.

1 Introduction

Many program analysis and verification techniques involve checking the satisfiability of formulas containing linear arithmetic constraints. These constraints appear naturally when reasoning about integer variables and array operations in programs. As such, there is a practical need to develop solvers that effectively check the satisfiability of linear arithmetic constraints.

It has been observed [21] that many of the arithmetic constraints that arise in verification or program analysis comprise mostly of *difference* constraints. These constraints are of the form $x \leq y + c$, where x and y are variables and c is a constant. Although efficient polynomial algorithms exist for checking the satisfiability of such constraints, these algorithms cannot be directly used if non-difference constraints, albeit few, are present in the input. In practice, this makes it hard to exploit the efficiency of difference constraints in arithmetic solvers.

Motivated by this problem, we propose a mechanism for solving general linear arithmetic constraints that exploits the presence of difference constraints in the input. We define a set of linear arithmetic constraints as *sparse linear arithmetic(SLA)* constraints, when the fraction of non-difference constraints is very small compared to the fraction of difference constraints.

The main contribution of this paper is a framework for solving linear arithmetic constraints that combines a solver for difference constraints with a general

U. Furbach and N. Shankar (Eds.): IJCAR 2006, LNAI 4130, pp. 468–482, 2006.

linear arithmetic constraint solver. The former analyzes the difference constraints in the input while the latter processes only the non-difference constraints. These solvers then share relevant facts to check the satisfiability of the input constraints. When used to solve SLA constraints, the time and space complexity of our combination solver is determined solely by the complexity of the difference constraint solver. As a result, our algorithm retains the efficiency of the difference constraint solvers with the completeness of a linear arithmetic solver. Additionally, the combined solver can also generate models (satisfying assignments) for satisfiable formulas.

The second key contribution of this paper is an efficient algorithm for generating the set of implied variable equalities from the combined solver. Generating such equalities is essential when our solver is used in the Nelson-Oppen combination framework [19]. We show that for rationals, the difference and the non-difference solvers only need to exchange equalities with offsets (of the form $x = y + c$) over the shared variables to generate all the implied equalities.

We provide an instantiation of the framework by combining a solver for difference constraints based on *negative cycle detection* algorithms, and a solver for general linear arithmetic constraints based on Simplex [6]. We show that we can modify the Simplex implementation in Simplify [7] (that already generates all implied equalities of the form $x = y$) to generate implied equalities of the form $x = y + c$ without incurring any more overhead. Finally, we provide preliminary experimental results on a set of linear arithmetic benchmarks of varying complexity.

The rest of the paper is organized as follows: In Section 2, we describe the background work including solvers for difference logic. In Section 3, we formally describe the SLA constraints and provide a decision procedure. We extend the decision procedure to generate implied equalities in Section 4.1, and provide a concrete implementation with Simplex in Section 4.2. We present the results in Section 5. In Section 6, we present the related work. Details of the proofs can be found in an extended technical report [16].

2   Background

For a given theory T, a decision procedure for T checks if a formula ϕ in the theory is *satisfiable*, i.e. it is possible to assign values to the symbols in ϕ that are consistent with T, such that ϕ evaluates to **true**.

Decision procedures, nowadays, do not operate in isolation, but form a part of a more complex system that can decide formulas involving symbols shared across multiple theories. In such a setting, a decision procedure has to support the following operations efficiently: (i) *Satisfiability Checking*: Checking if a formula ϕ is satisfiable in the theory. (ii) *Model Generation*: If a formula in the theory is satisfiable, find values for the symbols that appear in the theory that makes it satisfiable. This is crucial for applications that use theorem provers for test-case generation. (iii) *Equality Generation*: The Nelson-Oppen framework for combining decision procedures [19] requires that each theory (at least) produces the set of equalities over variables that are implied by the constraints. (iv) *Proof Generation*: Proof generation can be used to certify the output of a theorem prover [18]. Proofs are also used to construct conflict clauses efficiently in a lazy SAT-based theorem proving architecture [8].

2.1 Linear Arithmetic

Linear arithmetic is the first-order theory where atomic formulas (also called linear constraints) are of the form $\sum_i a_i . x_i \bowtie c$, where x_i is a variable from the set X, each of a_i and c is a constant and $\bowtie \in \{\leq, <, =\}$. When the variables in X range over integers $\mathbb{Z}$, and each of the constants a_i and c is a integer constant, we refer to the theory as integer linear arithmetic. Otherwise, if the variables and the constants range over rationals $\mathbb{Q}$, we refer to it as simply linear arithmetic.

An assignment ρ maps each variable in X to either an integer or a rational value, depending on the underlying theory. A set of linear constraints $\{l_i | l_i \doteq \sum_j a_{i,j} . x_j \bowtie c_i\}$ is *satisfiable*, if there is an assignment ρ such that each l_i evaluates to **true**. Otherwise, the set of linear constraints is said to be *unsatisfiable*.

Given two assignments ρ_A and ρ_B over set of variables A and B respectively (A and B need not be disjoint), we define the resulting assignment $\rho \doteq \rho_A \circ \rho_B$ obtained by composing ρ_A and ρ_B as follows for any $x \in A \cup B$:

$$\rho_A \circ \rho_B(x) = \begin{cases} \rho_A(x) & \text{if } x \in A \\ \rho_B(x) & \text{otherwise} \end{cases}$$

Deciding the satisfiability of a set of integer linear arithmetic constraints is NP-complete [20]. For the rational counterpart, there exists polynomial algorithms for deciding satisfiability [13]. However, in spite of the polynomial complexity, these algorithms have large overhead that make them infeasible on large problems. Instead, Simplex [6] algorithm (that has worst-case exponential complexity) has been found to be efficient for most practical problems. We will describe more about the workings of Simplex in Section 4.2.

2.2 Difference Constraints and Negative Cycle Detection

A particularly useful fragment of linear arithmetic is the theory of *difference constraints*, where the atomic formulas are of the form $x_1 - x_2 \bowtie c$. Constraints of the forms $x \bowtie c$ are converted to the above form by introducing a special vertex x_{orig} to denote the origin, and expressing the constraint as $x - x_{orig} \bowtie c$. The resultant system of difference constraints is equisatisfiable with the original set of constraints. Moreover, if ρ satisfies the resultant set of difference constraints, then a satisfying assignment ρ' to the original set of constraints (that include $x \bowtie c$ constraints) can be obtained by simply assigning $\rho'(x) \doteq \rho(x) - \rho(x_{orig})$, for each variable. A set of difference constraints (both over integers and rationals) can be decided in polynomial time using *negative cycle detection* algorithms.

Given a weighted graph $G(V, E)$, the problem of determining if G has a cycle C, such that sum of the (weight on the) edges along the cycle is negative, is called the negative cycle detection problem. Various algorithms can be used to determine the existence of negative cycles in a graph [4]. Negative cycle detection (NCD) algorithms have two properties:

1. The algorithm determines if there is a negative cycle in the graph. In this case, the algorithm produces a particular negative cycle as a witness.
2. If there are no negative cycles, then the algorithm generates a *feasible* solution $\delta : V \to \mathbb{Q}$, such that for every $(u, v) \in E$, $\delta(v) \leq \delta(u) + w(u, v)$. Moreover, if all the weights $w(u, v) \in \mathbb{Z}$ for any $(u, v) \in E$, then δ assigns integral values to all vertices.

For example, the Bellman-Ford [3,9] algorithm for single-source shortest path in a graph can be used to detect negative cycles in a graph. If the graph contains n vertices and m edges, the Bellman-Ford algorithm can determine in $O(n.m)$ time and $O(n+m)$ space, if there is a negative cycle in G, and a feasible solution otherwise.

In this paper, we assume that we use one such NCD algorithm. We will define the complexity $O(\mathcal{NCD})$ as the complexity of the NCD algorithm under consideration. This allows us to leverage all the advances in NCD algorithms in recent years [4], which have complexity better than the Bellman-Ford algorithm.

Given a set of difference constraints, we can construct a weighted directed graph by creating a vertex for each variable in the set of constraints, and creating an edge from a vertex x to vertex y with a weight c for each constraint $y - x \leq c$. We will refer to the set of difference constraints and the underlying graph interchangeably in the rest of the paper.

3   Sparse Linear Arithmetic (SLA) Constraints

Pratt [21] observed that most queries that arise in software verification are dominated by difference constraints. Recently, more evidence has been presented strengthening the hypothesis [24], where the authors found more than 95% of the linear arithmetic constraints were restricted to difference constraints for a set of program verification benchmarks. Hence, it is crucial to construct decision procedures for linear arithmetic that can exploit the *sparse* nature of general linear constraints.

Let $\phi \doteq \bigwedge_i \left(\sum_j a_{i,j}.x_j \leq c_i \right)$ be the conjunction of a set of (integer or rational) linear arithmetic constraints over a set of variables X. Let us partition the set of constraints in ϕ into the set of difference constraints ϕ_D and the non-difference constraints ϕ_L, such that $\phi = \phi_D \wedge \phi_L$. Let D be the set of variables that appear in ϕ_D, L be the set of variables that appear in ϕ_L, and let Q be the set of variables in $D \cap L$. We assume that the variable x_{orig} to denote the origin, always belong to D, and any $x \bowtie c$ constraint has been converted to $x \bowtie x_{orig} + c$.

We define a set of constraints ϕ to be *sparse linear arithmetic* (SLA) constraints, if the fraction $|L|/|D| \ll 1$. Observe this also implies that $|Q|/|D| \ll 1$. Our goal is to devise an efficient decision procedure for SLA constraints, such that the complexity is polynomial in D but (possibly) exponential only over L. This would be particularly appealing for solving integer linear constraints, where the complexity of the decision problem is NP-complete. For rational linear arithmetic, the procedure will still retain its polynomial complexity, but will improve the robustness on practical benchmarks by mitigating the effect of the general linear arithmetic solver.

In this section, we describe one such decision procedure for SLA constraints. In Section 4, we show how to generate implied equalities between variable pairs from such a decision procedure and describe its integration with Simplex, for rational linear arithmetic.

3.1   Checking Satisfiability of SLA

We provide an algorithm for checking the satisfiability of a set of SLA constraints that has polynomial complexity in the size of the difference constraints. Moreover, the space complexity of the algorithm is *almost* linear in the size of the difference constraints. Finally, assuming we have a decision procedure for integer linear arithmetic that generates satisfying assignments, the algorithm can generate an integer solution when the input SLA formula is satisfiable over integers.

Let ϕ be a set of linear arithmetic constraints as before, and let Q be the set of variables common to the difference constraints ϕ_D and non-difference constraints ϕ_L. The algorithm (SLA-SAT) is simple, and operates in four steps:

1. Check the satisfiability of ϕ_D using a negative cycle detection algorithm.
2. If ϕ_D is unsatisfiable, return unsatisfiable. Else, let $SP(x, y)$ be the weight of the shortest path from the (vertices corresponding to) variable x to y in the graph induced by ϕ_D. Generate the set of difference constraints

$$\phi_Q \doteq \bigwedge \{y - x \le d \mid x \in Q, y \in Q, SP(x, y) = d\}, \tag{1}$$

   over Q.
3. Check the satisfiability of $\phi_L \wedge \phi_Q$ using a linear arithmetic decision procedure. If $\phi_L \wedge \phi_Q$ is unsatisfiable, then return unsatisfiable. Else, let ρ_L be a satisfying assignment for $\phi_L \wedge \phi_Q$ over L.
4. Generate a satisfying assignment ρ_D to the formula $\phi_D \wedge \bigwedge_{x \in Q} (x = \rho_L(x))$, using a negative cycle detection algorithm. Return $\rho_X \doteq \rho_D \circ \rho_L$ as a satisfying assignment for ϕ.

It is easy to see that the algorithm is sound. This is because we report unsatisfiable only when a set of constraints implied by ϕ is detected to be unsatisfiable. To show that the algorithm is complete (for both integer and rational arithmetic), we show that if ϕ_D and $\phi_Q \wedge \phi_L$ are each satisfiable, then ϕ is satisfiable. This is achieved by showing that a satisfying assignment ρ_L for $\phi_L \wedge \phi_Q$ can be extended to an assignment ρ_X for ϕ, such that ϕ is satisfiable.

Lemma 1. *If the assignment ρ_L over L satisfies $\phi_L \wedge \phi_Q$, then the assignment ρ_X over X satisfies ϕ.*

Since a model for ϕ_Q can be extended to be a model for ϕ_D, Lemma 1 also shows another useful fact, which we will utilize later:

Corollary 1. *Let $P \doteq D \setminus Q$ be the set of variables local to ϕ_D. Then ϕ_Q is equivalent to $(\exists P : \phi_D)$, denoted as $\phi_Q \Leftrightarrow (\exists P : \phi_D)$.*

The corollary says that ϕ_Q is the result of quantifier elimination of the variables $D \setminus Q$ local to ϕ_D. Hence, for any constraint ψ over Q, ϕ_D implies ψ (denoted as $\phi_D \Rightarrow \psi$) if and only if $\phi_Q \Rightarrow \psi$. We will make use of this fact throughout the paper.

Theorem 1. *The algorithm SLA SAT is a decision procedure for (integer and rational) linear arithmetic. Moreover, it also generates a satisfying assignment when the constraints are satisfiable.*

Complexity of *SLA-SAT*: Given m difference constraints over n variables, we denote $\mathcal{NCD}(n, m)$ as the complexity of the negative cycle detection algorithm. The space complexity for $\mathcal{NCD}(n, m)$ is $O(n + m)$, and the upper bound of the time complexity is $O(n.m)$, although many algorithms have a much better complexity [4]. Similarly, with m constraints over n variables, we denote $\mathcal{LAP}(n, m)$ as the complexity of the linear arithmetic procedure under consideration. For example, if we use Simplex as the (rational) linear arithmetic decision procedure, then the space complexity for $\mathcal{LAP}(n, m)$ is $O(n.m)$ and the time complexity is polynomial in n and m in practice. Finally, for a set of constraints ψ, let $|\psi|$ denote the the number of constraints in ψ.

Let us try to analyze the complexity of the procedure *SLA-SAT* described in the previous section. Step 1 takes $\mathcal{NCD}(|D|, |\phi_D|)$ time and space complexity. Step 2 requires generating shortest paths between every pair of variables $x \in Q$ and $y \in Q$. This can be obtained by using a variant of Johnson's algorithm for generating all-pair-shortest-paths [5] for a graph. For a graph with n nodes and m vertices, this algorithm has linear space complexity of $O(n+m)$. Assuming we have already performed a negative cycle detection algorithm, the time complexity of the algorithm is only $O(n^2. \log(n))$.

Instead of generating all-pair-shortest-paths for every pair of vertices using Johnson's algorithm, we adapt the algorithm to compute the shortest paths only for vertices in Q, the set of shared variables. This makes the time complexity of Step 2 of the algorithm $O(|Q|.|D|. \log(|D|))$. The space complexity of this step is $O(|\phi_Q|)$ which is bounded by $O(|Q|^2)$.

The complexity of Step 3 is $\mathcal{LAP}(|L|, |\phi_Q| + |\phi_L|)$. Finally, Step 4 incurs another $\mathcal{NCD}(|D|, |\phi_D|)$ complexity, since at most $|Q|$ constraints are added as $x = \rho_L(x)$ constraints to ϕ_D.

4   Equality Generation for SLA

In this section, we consider the problem of generating equalities between variables implied by the constraint ϕ. Equality generation is useful for combining the linear arithmetic decision procedure with other decision procedures in the

Nelson-Oppen combination framework. In Section 4.1, we describe the requirements from the difference and the non-difference decision procedures in SLA-SAT to generate all equalities implied by ϕ. In Section 4.2, we describe how to instantiate the framework when combining a negative cycle detection algorithm (as the decision procedure for difference constraints) with Simplex (as the decision procedure for non-difference constraints).

4.1   Equality Generation from SLA-SAT

In this section, we extend the basic SLA-SAT algorithm to generate all the equalities between pairs of variables, implied by the input formula ϕ. We will describe the procedure in an abstract fashion, without providing an implementation of the individual steps. The algorithm described in this section has only been proved complete for the case when the variables are interpreted over $\mathbb{Q}$; we are currently working on the case of $\mathbb{Z}$.

Throughout this section, we assume that ϕ is satisfiable. We carry the notations (e.g. ϕ_D, ϕ_L etc.) from Section 3. The key steps of the procedure are:

1. Assuming ϕ_D is satisfiable, generate ϕ_Q and solve $\phi_Q \wedge \phi_L$ using linear arithmetic decision procedure.
2. Generate the set of equalities (with offsets) implied by $\phi_Q \wedge \phi_L$

$$\mathcal{E}_1 \doteq \{x = y + c \mid x \in L, y \in L, \text{and } (\phi_Q \wedge \phi_L) \Rightarrow x = y + c\}, \quad (2)$$

   from the linear arithmetic decision procedure.
3. Let $\mathcal{E}_2 \subseteq \mathcal{E}_1$ be the set of equalities over the variables in Q:

$$\mathcal{E}_2 \doteq \{x = y + c \mid x \in Q, y \in Q, x = y + c \in \mathcal{E}_1 \}, \quad (3)$$

4. Generate all the implied equalities (with offset) from $\mathcal{E}_2$ (interpreted as a formula by conjoining all the equalities in $\mathcal{E}_2$) and ϕ_D:

$$\mathcal{E}_3 \doteq \{x = y + c \mid x \in D, y \in D, (\phi_D \wedge \mathcal{E}_2) \Rightarrow x = y + c\}, \quad (4)$$

5. Finally, the set of equalities implied by $\mathcal{E}_1$ and $\mathcal{E}_3$ is the set of equalities implied by ϕ:

$$\mathcal{E} \doteq \{x = y \mid x \in X, y \in X, (\mathcal{E}_1 \wedge \mathcal{E}_3) \Rightarrow x = y\} \quad (5)$$

Before proving the correctness of the equality generating algorithm (Theorem 2), we first state and prove a few intermediate lemmas.

For a set of linear arithmetic constraints $A \doteq \{e_1, \ldots, e_n\}$, we define a *linear combination* of A to be a summation $\sum_{e_j \in A} c_j.e_j$, such that each $c_j \in \mathbb{Q}$ and non-negative.

Lemma 2. *Let ϕ_A and ϕ_B be two sets of linear arithmetic constraints over variables in A and B respectively. If u is a linear arithmetic term over $A \setminus B$ and v is a linear arithmetic term over B such that $\phi_A \wedge \phi_B \Rightarrow u \bowtie v$, then there exists a term t over $A \cap B$ such that*

1. $\phi_A \Rightarrow u \bowtie t$, and
2. $\phi_B \Rightarrow t \bowtie v$,

where $\bowtie$ is either $\leq$ or $\geq$.

For the set of satisfiable difference constraints $\phi_D \doteq \{e_1, \ldots, e_n\}$, we say a linear combination $\sum_{e_j \in \phi_D} c_j.e_j$ contains a *cycle* (respectively, a *path from x to y), if there exists a subset of constraints in ϕ_D with positive coefficients (i.e. $c_j > 0$), such that they form a cycle (respectively, a path from x to y) in the graph induced by ϕ_D.

Lemma 3. *For any term t over D, if $\phi_D \Rightarrow t \leq 0$, then there exists a linear derivation of $t \leq 0$ that does not contain any cycles.*

Lemma 4 (Difference-Bounds Lemma). *Let $x, y \in D \setminus Q$, t be a term over Q, and ϕ_D a set of difference constraints.*

1. *If $\phi_D \Rightarrow x \bowtie t$, then there exists terms $u_1, u_2, \ldots, u_n$ such that all of the following are true*
   (a) *Each u_i is of the form $x_i + c_i$ for a variable $x_i \in Q$ and a constant c_i,*
   (b) *$\phi_D \Rightarrow \bigwedge_i x \bowtie u_i$, and*
   (c) *$\phi_D \Rightarrow 1/n . \sum_i u_i \bowtie t$*
2. *If $\phi_D \Rightarrow x - y \bowtie t$, then there exists terms $u_1, u_2, \ldots, u_n$ such that all of the following are true*
   (a) *Each u_i is either of the form c_i or $x_i - y_i + c_i$ for variables $x_i, y_i \in Q$ and a constant c_i,*
   (b) *$\phi_D \Rightarrow \bigwedge_i x - y \bowtie u_i$, and*
   (c) *$\phi_D \Rightarrow 1/n . \sum_i u_i \bowtie t$*

where $\bowtie$ is one of $\leq$ or $\geq$.

The proof makes use of a novel trick to split a linear combination of difference constraints to yield the desired results.

Lemma 5 (Sandwich Lemma). *Let $l_1, l_2, \ldots l_m$ and $u_1, u_2, \ldots u_n$ be terms such that $\bigwedge_{i,j} l_i \leq u_j$. Let $l_{avg} = 1/m . \sum_i l_i$ and $u_{avg} = 1/n . \sum_j u_j$ be the respective average of these terms. If l and u are terms such that $l \leq l_{avg}$ and $u_{avg} \leq u$, then*

$$l = u \Rightarrow \bigwedge_{i,j} l_i = u_j = l$$

Now, we can prove the correctness of the equality propagation algorithm.

Theorem 2. *For two variables $x \in X$ and $y \in X$, $\phi \Rightarrow x = y$ if and only if $x = y \in \mathcal{E}$.*

Proof. Case 1: The easiest case to handle is the case when both $x, y \in L$. Thus, $(\exists D \setminus L : \phi) = \phi_Q \wedge \phi_L \Rightarrow x = y$. Therefore, the equality $x = y$ is present in $\mathcal{E}_1$ and thus in $\mathcal{E}$.

Case 2: Consider the case when one of the variables, say, $x \in D \setminus L$ while $y \in L$. We have $\phi \Rightarrow x \leq y \wedge x \geq y$. Applying Lemma 2 twice, there exist terms $t, t' \in Q$ such

$$\phi_D \Rightarrow x \leq t \wedge x \geq t' \tag{6}$$
$$\phi_L \Rightarrow t \leq y \wedge t' \geq y \tag{7}$$

However, $\phi_D \wedge \phi_L \Rightarrow x = y = t = t'$. As $t, t' \in Q$, we have

$$\phi_Q \wedge \phi_L \Rightarrow t = t' = y \tag{8}$$

Using Lemma 4.1 twice on Equation 6, there exist terms $u_1, \ldots, u_m$ and terms $l_1, \ldots, l_n$ all of the form $v + c$ for a variable $v \in Q$ and a constant c such that

$$\phi_D \Rightarrow \left(\bigwedge_i x \leq u_i \wedge 1/m. \sum_i u_i \leq t \right) \wedge \left(\bigwedge_j x \geq l_j \wedge 1/n. \sum_j l_j \geq t' \right)$$

As the terms u_i and l_j are terms over Q, we have

$$\phi_Q \Rightarrow \left(\bigwedge_{i,j} l_j \leq u_i \right) \wedge \left(1/m. \sum_i u_i \leq t \right) \wedge \left(1/n. \sum_j l_j \geq t' \right)$$

Using Lemma 5 and Equation 8, we have

$$\phi_Q \wedge \phi_L \Rightarrow \bigwedge_{i,j} l_j = u_i = t = t' = y$$

All of the above equalities belong to $\mathcal{E}_1$. Moreover, the equalities between l_j and u_i are present in $\mathcal{E}_2$. Thus, the equality $x = l_j = u_i$ is present in $\mathcal{E}_3$. Thus $x = y$ is in $\mathcal{E}$.

Case 3: The final case involves the case when x, y are both in $D \setminus L$. The proof is similar to Case 2. We have $\phi \Rightarrow x - y \leq 0 \wedge x - y \geq 0$. Applying Lemma 2 twice, there exists terms $t, t' \in Q$ such

$$\phi_D \Rightarrow x - y \leq t \wedge x - y \geq t' \tag{9}$$
$$\phi_L \Rightarrow t \leq 0 \wedge t' \geq 0 \tag{10}$$

However, $\phi_D \wedge \phi_L \Rightarrow x - y = 0 = t = t'$. As $t, t' \in Q$, we have

$$\phi_Q \wedge \phi_L \Rightarrow t = t' = 0 \tag{11}$$

Using Lemma 4.2 twice on Equation 9, there exists terms $u_1, \ldots, u_m$ and terms $l_1, \ldots, l_n$ all of the form $u - v + c$ for variables $u, v \in Q$ and a constant c such that

$$\phi_D \Rightarrow \left(\bigwedge_i x - y \leq u_i \wedge 1/m. \sum_i u_i \leq t \right) \wedge \left(\bigwedge_j x - y \geq l_j \wedge 1/n. \sum_j l_j \geq t' \right)$$

As the terms u_i and l_j are terms over Q, we have

$$\phi_Q \Rightarrow \left(\bigwedge_{i,j} l_j \le u_i \right) \wedge \left(1/m. \sum_i u_i \le t \right) \wedge \left(1/n. \sum_j l_j \ge t' \right)$$

Using Lemma 5 and Equation 11, we have

$$\phi_Q \wedge \phi_L \Rightarrow \bigwedge_{i,j} l_j = u_i = t = t' = 0$$

All of the above equalities belong to $\mathcal{E}_1$. Moreover, the equalities between l_j and u_i are present in $\mathcal{E}_2$. Thus, the equality $x = l_j = u_i$ is present in $\mathcal{E}_3$. Thus $x = y$ is in $\mathcal{E}$.

4.2   Equality Generation with NCD and Simplex

In this section, we describe an instantiation of the SLA framework, where we use the Simplex algorithm for solving general linear arithmetic constraints. The Simplex algorithm [6] (although has a worst case exponential complexity) remains one of the most practical methods for solving linear arithmetic constraints, when the variables are interpreted over rationals. Although Simplex is incomplete for integers, various heuristics have been devised to solve most integer queries in practice [7].

The main contribution of this section is to show how to generate all equalities with offsets between a pair of variables, i.e. all the $x = y + c$ equalities implied by a set of linear constraints. The implementation of Simplex in Simplify [7] can generate all possible $x = y$ equalities implied by a set of constraints. We show that the same Simplex implementation also allows generating all $x = y + c$, without any additional overhead.[1] Due to space constraints, we only provide an informal high-level description of the algorithm. Details and proofs can be found in an extended technical report [16]. Finally, we also mention how to derive $x = y + c$ equalities from a set of difference constraints using NCD algorithms. Proof generation (for contradictions and the implied equalities with offsets) in Simplex is an easy adaptation of existing proof-generating Simplex [18].

Simplex Tableau. A *Simplex tableau* is used to represent a set of linear arithmetic constraints. Each linear inequality is first converted to linear equality by the introduction of a *slack variable*, which is restricted to be non-negative. The Simplex tableau is a two-dimensional matrix that consists of the following:

- Natural numbers n and m for the number of rows and columns for tableau respectively,
- The identifiers for the rows $y[0], \ldots, y[n]$ and the columns $x[1], \ldots, x[m]$. The column 0 corresponds to the constant column. We use u, u_1 etc. to range over the row and column identifiers.
- A two dimensional array of rational numbers $a[0,0], \ldots, a[n,m]$.

---

[1] In fact, readers familiar with the Simplify work [7] can see that Lemma 4 in Section 8 of [7], almost immediately generalizes to give us the desired result.

- A subset of identifiers (representing the slack variables) in $y[0], \ldots, y[n]$, $x[1], \ldots, x[m]$ have a *sign* $\in \{\geq, *\}$, and are called *restricted*. A variable u with *sign* of $*$ is called **-restricted*, and denotes that $u = 0$; otherwise a restricted variable u with sign $\geq$ denotes $u \geq 0$.
- The $y[0]$ of the Simplex tableau is a special row *Zero* to denote the value 0, and has 0 in all columns.

Each row in the tableau represents a *row constraint* of the form:

$$y[i] = a[i,0] + \Sigma_{1 \leq j \leq m} a[i,j].x[j] \tag{12}$$

A *feasible* tableau is one where the solution obtained by setting each of the column variables $x[j]$ to 0 and setting each of the $y[i]$ to $a[i,0]$, satisfies all the constraints (row constraints and sign constraints). A set of constraints is satisfiable iff such a feasible tableau exists. We will not go into the details of finding the feasible tableau, as it is a well-known method [6,7].

Equality Generation from Simplex Tableau. To generate equalities implied by the set of constraints, the tableau has to be constrained further in addition to being feasible. The tableau has to be constrained such that for any restricted variable u, the set of constraints imply $u = 0$, if and only if u is **-restricted* in the tableau. Such a tableau is called a *minimal* tableau. The Simplex implementation in Simplify [7] provides a procedure for obtaining a minimal tableau for a set of constraints. The set of all implied variable equalities (of the form $u_1 = u_2$) can be simply read off the minimal tableau. We show that, in fact, the set of all implied offset equalities (of the form $u_1 = u_2 + c$) can also be read off such a minimal tableau. The basic idea is that in a minimal tableau, the implied equalities do not depend on the $\geq$ sign constraints.

We now state the generalization of Lemma 2 (Section 8.2 [7]) to include offset equalities:

Lemma 6 (Generalization of Lemma 2 in Section 8.2 [7]). *For any two variables u_1 and u_2 in a feasible and minimal tableau, the set of constraints imply $u_1 = u_2 + c$, where c is a rational constant, if and only if at least one of the following conditions hold:*

1. *u_1 and u_2 are both *-restricted columns (here c is 0), or*
2. *both u_1 and u_2 are row variables $y[i]$ and $y[j]$ respectively, and apart from the *-restricted columns only (possibly) differ in the constant column, such that $a[i,0] = a[j,0] + c$, or*
3. *u_1 is a row variable $y[i]$, u_2 is a column variable $x[j]$, and the only non-zero entries in the row i outside the *-restricted columns are $a[i,0] = c$ and $a[i,j] = 1$.*
4. *u_2 is a *-restricted column, and u_1 is a row variable $y[i]$, such that $a[i,0] = c$ is the only non-zero entry outside *-restricted columns in row i.*

Therefore, obtaining the minimal tableau is sufficient to derive even $x = y + c$ facts from Simplex. This is noteworthy because the Simplex implementation does not incur any more overhead in generating these more general equalities than simple $x = y$ equalities.

Inferring Equalities from NCD. The algorithm for SLA equality generation described in Section 4.1 requires generating equalities of the form $x = y + c$ from the NCD component of SLA. Lemma 2 in [15] provides such an algorithm. The lemma is provided here.

Lemma 7 (Lemma 2 in [15]). *For an edge e in G_ϕ representing $y \leq x + c$, e can be strengthened to represent $y = x + c$ (called an equality-edge), if and only if e lies in a cycle of weight zero.*

Hence, using Lemma 6, Theorem 2 and Lemma 7, we obtain a complete equality generating decision procedure over rationals.

Theorem 3. *The SLA implementation by combining NCD and Simplex is an equality generating decision procedure for linear arithmetic over rationals.*

5   Implementation and Results

In this section, we describe our implementation of the SLA algorithm in the Zap [1] theorem prover and report preliminary results from our experiments. The implementation uses the Bellman-Ford algorithm as the NCD algorithm and the Simplex implementation (described in Section 4.2) for the non-difference constraints. We are currently working on the implementation of the proof generation from the SLA algorithm (namely, the proof of implied equalities from NCD [15]) , to integrate it into the lazy proof-generating theorem prover framework [2,8]. Hence, we are currently unable to evaluate our algorithm on more realistic benchmarks (such as the SMT-LIB benchmarks [26]), where we need the proofs to generate conflict clauses to reason about the Boolean structure in the formula. Instead, we evaluate on a set of randomly generated linear arithmetic benchmarks.

We report preliminary results comparing our algorithm with two different implementations for solving linear arithmetic constraints: (i) *Simplify-Simplex*: the linear arithmetic solver in the Simplify [7] theorem prover, and (ii) *Zap-UTVPI*: an implementation of Unit Two Variable Per Inequality (UTVPI) decision procedure [10,12] in Zap.[2] Even though *Zap-UTVPI* is not complete for general linear arithmetic, we chose this implementation to compare a transitive closure based decision procedure (as used by Sheini and Sakallah [25]) to a one based on NCD algorithms.

We generated the random benchmarks as follows. For different values for the total number of variables lying between 100 and 1000, we generated benchmarks with the number of constraints varying from half to five times the number of variables. To measure the effect of the sparseness of the constraints, we varied the ratio of non-difference constraints to difference constraints from 2% to 50%. For each difference constraint we picked the two variables at random. For each non-difference constraint we randomly picked 2 to 5 variables and chose a random

---

[2] UTVPI constraints are of the form $a.x + b.y \leq c$, where a and $b \in \{-1, 0, 1\}$ and c is an integer constant.

480   S.K. Lahiri and M. Musuvathi

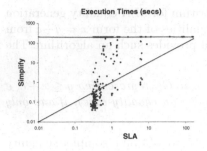 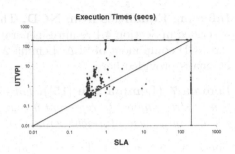

Fig. 1. Comparison of SLA with (a) *Simplify-Simplex* and (b) *Zap-UTVPI* on a set of randomly generated benchmarks

coefficient between -2 and 2. We ensured that the set of benchmarks when run on the SLA implementation involved all of the following: instances where the difference constraints alone were unsatisfiable, instances where the non-difference constraints alone were unsatisfiable, instances that required *both* difference and non-difference reasoning, and finally instances that were satisfiable.

Figure 1 (a) shows the comparison of the execution times of the SLA algorithm against *Simplify-Simplex*. In the graph, we indicate both the runs that took greater than 200 seconds and runs that incurred a crash due to an integer-overflow exception, as timeouts with 200 seconds. The overflow exception happens in Simplex (both in Simplify and Zap) due to the use of machine integers to represent large coefficients in the tableau. The following observations are evident from this graph. On those instances for which Simplify finished within a second, the SLA algorithm also finished within a second, but performed worse than Simplify. This is a result of the constant overhead Zap (implemented in C#) incurs loading the virtual machine of the C# language on every run. On the other hand, SLA solved instances within seconds for which Simplify required orders of magnitude longer time or timed out at 200 seconds. To our surprise, Simplify incurred an integer-overflow exception on many benchmarks for which pure difference reasoning was sufficient to prove the unsatisfiability of the query. The SLA implementation did incur an integer-overflow on certain instances for which Simplify completed successfully. This could be due to the fact that our Simplex implementation is not as optimized as the one in Simplify as we have not implemented the many pivot heuristics of Simplify.

Figure 1 (b) shows the execution time of the UTVPI decision procedure on these benchmarks. SLA performs better than the UTVPI decision procedure on a greater proportion of the instances. The transitive-closure based algorithm for the UTVPI decision procedure has a quadratic space complexity, resulting in orders of magnitude slowdown. There are instances, however, where the SLA algorithm results in an integer-overflow for which the UTVPI algorithm terminates. (Note, the UTVPI algorithm is incomplete for general linear arithmetic.) This suggests a possibility of combining the linear-space UTVPI algorithm [14] with a general linear arithmetic solver, along the lines of SLA. While this is an interesting problem for future work, we are unsure about its value in practice.

6   Related Work

Checking the satisfiability of a set of linear arithmetic constraints over integers is NP-complete [20]. Various algorithms based on branch-and-bound heuristics are implemented in various integer linear programming (ILP) solvers like LP_SOLVE [17] and commercial tools like CPLEX [11] to solve this fragment. These algorithms have a worst-case exponential time complexity. Even for the relaxation of the linear arithmetic problem over rationals (where polynomial time decision procedures exists [13]), most practical solvers use Simplex [6] algorithm that has a worst-case exponential complexity. Gomory cuts [23] can be used to extend Simplex over integers although the algorithm might require exponential space in the worst case. Ruess and Shankar [22] provide one such implementation. Their algorithm also generates equalities over variables. However, unlike our approach, their algorithm does not try to exploit the sparsity in linear arithmetic constraints, and the asymptotic complexity for solving sparse linear arithmetic constraints is still exponential.

Recently attempts have been made to exploit the sparsity in linear arithmetic constraints mostly dominated by difference logic queries. Seshia and Bryant [24] demonstrate that although one might incur a linear blowup for translating a Boolean formula over linear arithmetic constraints (over integers) to an equisatisfiable propositional formula, formulas with only a small number of non-difference constraints can be converted using a logarithmic blowup. This approach however does not help towards improving the complexity of solving a set of linear arithmetic constraints.

The closest approach to ours is the approach of Sheini and Sakallah [25], where they provide a decision procedure for integer linear arithmetic by combining a decision procedure for UTVPI constraints and a general linear arithmetic solver (CPLEX [11] in their case). Their algorithm relies on computing a transitive closure for the UTVPI constraints that incurs cubic time and quadratic space complexity, independent of the sparsity of the constraints. In contrast, our decision procedure retains the efficiency of the NCD algorithms thereby making our procedure robust even for non sparse linear arithmetic benchmarks. This is well demonstrated by our experimental results (Figure 1 (b)). Moreover, their combination does not generate models for satisfiable formulas. Finally, their algorithm does not provide a way to generate implied equalities that are crucial for a Nelson-Oppen framework.

References

1. T. Ball, S. K. Lahiri, and M. Musuvathi. Zap: Automated theorem proving for software analysis. In *Logic for Programming, Artificial Intelligence, and Reasoning (LPAR 2005)*, LNCS 3835, pages 2–22, 2005.
2. C. W. Barrett, D. L. Dill, and A. Stump. Checking satisfiability of first-order formulas by incremental translation to SAT. In *CAV 02: Computer-Aided Verification*, LNCS 2404, pages 236–249, 2002.
3. R. Bellman. On a routing problem. *Quarterly of Applied Mathematics*, 16(1):87–90, 1958.

4. B. V. Cherkassky and A. V. Goldberg. Negative-cycle detection algorithms. In *European Symposium on Algorithms*, pages 349–363, 1996.
5. T. H. Cormen, C. E. Leiserson, and R. L. Rivest. *Introduction to Algorithms*. MIT Press, 1990.
6. G. Dantzig. *Linear programming and extensions*. Princeton University Press, Princeton NJ, 1963.
7. D. L. Detlefs, G. Nelson, and J. B. Saxe. Simplify: A theorem prover for program checking. Technical report, HPL-2003-148, 2003.
8. C. Flanagan, R. Joshi, X. Ou, and J. Saxe. Theorem proving using lazy proof explication. In *CAV 03: Computer-Aided Verification*, LNCS 2725, pages 355–367, 2003.
9. L. R. Ford, Jr., and D. R. Fulkerson. *Flows in Networks*. 1962.
10. W. Harvey and P. J. Stuckey. A unit two variable per inequality integer constraint solver for constraint logic programming. In *Proceedings of the 20th Australasian Computer Science Conference (ACSC '97)*, pages 102–111, 1997.
11. ILOG CPLEX. Available at http://ilog.com/products/cplex.
12. J. Jaffar, M. J. Maher, P. J. Stuckey, and H. C. Yap. Beyond finite domains. In *PPCP 94: Principles and Practice of Constraint Programming*, LNCS 874, pages 86–94, 1994.
13. Narendra Karmarkar. A new polynomial-time algorithm for linear programming. *Combinatorica*, 4(4):373–396, 1984.
14. S. K. Lahiri and M. Musuvathi. An efficient decision procedure for UTVPI constraints. In *FroCos 05: Frontiers of Combining Systems*, LNCS 3717, pages 168–183, 2005.
15. S. K. Lahiri and M. Musuvathi. An Efficient Nelson-Oppen Decision Procedure for Difference Constraints over Rationals. Number 2 in ENTCS 144, pages 27—41, 2005.
16. S. K. Lahiri and M. Musuvathi. Solving sparse linear constraints. Technical Report MSR-TR-2006-47, Microsoft Research, 2006.
17. LP_SOLVE. Available at http://groups.yahoo.com/group/lp_solve/.
18. G. C. Necula and P. Lee. Proof generation in the touchstone theorem prover. In *Conference on Automated Deduction*, LNCS 1831, pages 25–44, 2000.
19. G. Nelson and D. C. Oppen. Simplification by cooperating decision procedures. *ACM Transactions on Programming Languages and Systems (TOPLAS)*, 2(1):245–257, 1979.
20. C. H. Papadimitriou. On the complexity of integer programming. *J. ACM*, 28(4):765–768, 1981.
21. V. Pratt. Two easy theories whose combination is hard. Technical report, Massachusetts Institute of Technology, Cambridge, Mass., September 1977.
22. H. Rueß and N. Shankar. Solving linear arithmetic constraints. Technical Report CSL-SRI-04-01, SRI International, January 2004.
23. A. Schrijver. *Theory of Linear and Integer Programming*. Wiley, 1986.
24. S. A. Seshia and R. E. Bryant. Deciding quantifier-free Presburger formulas using parameterized solution bounds. In *LICS 04: Logic in Computer Science*, pages 100–109, July 2004.
25. H. M. Sheini and K. A. Sakallah. A scalable method for solving satisfiability of integer linear arithmetic logic. In *Theory and Applications of Satisfiability Testing (SAT 2005)*, LNCS 3569, pages 241–256, 2005.
26. SMT-LIB: The Satisfiability Modulo Theories Library. Available at http://combination.cs.uiowa.edu/smtlib/.

Inferring Network Invariants Automatically

Olga Grinchtein[1,*], Martin Leucker[2], and Nir Piterman[3]

[1] Department of Computer Systems, Uppsala University, Sweden
[2] IT Department, TU Munich, Germany
[3] EPFL, Lausanne, Switzerland

Abstract. Verification by network invariants is a heuristic to solve uniform verification of parameterized systems. Given a system P, a network invariant for P is a system that abstracts the composition of every number of copies of P running in parallel. If there is such a network invariant, by reasoning about it, uniform verification with respect to the family $P[1] \parallel \cdots \parallel P[n]$ can be carried out. In this paper, we propose a procedure that searches systematically for a network invariant satisfying a given safety property. The search is based on algorithms for learning finite automata due to Angluin and Biermann. We optimize the search by combining both algorithms for improving successive possible invariants. We also show how to reduce the learning problem to SAT, allowing efficient SAT solvers to be used, which turns out to yield a very competitive learning algorithm. The overall search procedure finds a minimal such invariant, if it exists.

1 Introduction

One of the most challenging problems in verification is the *uniform verification of parameterized systems*. Given a parameterized system $S(n) = P[1] \parallel \cdots \parallel P[n]$ and a property φ, uniform verification attempts to verify that $S(n)$ satisfies φ for every $n > 1$. The problem is in general undecidable [AK86]. One possible approach is to look for restricted families of systems for which the problem is decidable (cf. [EK00, CTTV04]). Another approach is to look for sound but incomplete methods (e.g., explicit induction [EN95], regular model checking [JN00, PS00], or environment abstraction [CTV06]).

Here, we attack uniform verification of parameterized systems using the heuristic of network invariants [WL89, KM95]. In simple words[1], a *network invariant* for a given finite system P is a finite system I that abstracts the composition of every number of copies of P running in parallel. Thus, the network invariant contains all possible computations of every number of copies of P. If we find such a network invariant I, we can solve uniform verification with respect to the family $S(n) = P[1] \parallel \cdots \parallel P[n]$ by reasoning about I.

The general idea proposed in [WL89] and turned into a working method in [KM95], is to show by induction that I is a network invariant for P. The induction base is to prove that $P \sqsubseteq I$, for a suitable abstraction relation $\sqsubseteq$. The induction step is to show that $P \parallel I \sqsubseteq I$. After establishing that I is a network invariant we can prove $I \models \varphi$, turning

---

* Part of this work has been done during the author's stays in EPFL and TU München, funded by the Swedish Foundation for Strategic Research via the ARTES++ graduate school.

[1] We give a precise definition of the network invariants approach in Section 2.

U. Furbach and N. Shankar (Eds.): IJCAR 2006, LNAI 4130, pp. 483–497, 2006.
© Springer-Verlag Berlin Heidelberg 2006

I into a *proper* network invariant with respect to φ. Then we conclude that $S(n) \models \varphi$ for every value of n.

Coming up with a proper network invariant is usually an iterative process. We start with divining a candidate for a network invariant. Then, we try to prove by induction that it is a network invariant. When the candidate system is nondeterministic this usually involves deductive proofs [KPSZ02][2]. During this stage we usually need to refine the candidate until getting a network invariant. The final step is checking that this invariant is proper (by automatically model checking the system versus φ). If it is not, we have to continue refining our candidate until a proper network invariant is found. Coming up with the candidate network invariant requires great knowledge of the parameterized system in question and proving abstraction using deductive methods requires great expertise in deductive proofs and tools. Whether a network invariant exists is undecidable [WL89], hence all this effort can be done in vain.

In this paper, we propose a procedure searching systematically for a network invariant satisfying a given safety property. If one exists, the procedure finds a proper invariant with a minimal number of states. If no proper invariant exists, our procedure in general diverges (though in some cases it may terminate and report that no proper invariant exists). In the light of the undecidability result for the problem, this seems reasonable.

Network invariants are usually explained in the setting of *transition structures*[KP00]. Here, we use learning algorithms that are best explained in terms of deterministic finite state machines (DFAs). Operations like parallel composition are not very natural in the context of DFAs (while standard in the context of transition structures). Porting the learning algorithms to the context of transition structures is not complicated, however, explaining the learning algorithms in the context of transition structures is unnatural and renders the exposition hard to follow. Thus, we explain our work in the setting of checking safety properties of networks that are described in terms of (the parallel product of) DFAs.

As mentioned, this paper is about searching for network invariants. As the class of DFAs is enumerable, a naïve algorithm would be to enumerate all possible DFAs and check one after the other whether it is a proper invariant. Clearly, this algorithm is not feasible in practice. We improve the naïve search for a minimal proper invariant by employing *learning algorithms*. The learning algorithm queries for additional information like which strings should be accepted by the network invariant and which rejected. This information is gathered by checking the system P and the property φ. When the learning algorithm proposes an automaton that is not an invariant, we identify some string that should be accepted or rejected by a real invariant. This information can be fed back to the learning algorithm to improve the candidate for invariant.

Two types of inference (or learning) algorithms for DFAs can be distinguished, so-called *online* and *offline* algorithms. Online algorithms, such as Angluin's L^* algorithm [Ang87], query whether strings are in the language, before coming up with an automaton. Offline algorithms get a fixed set of examples and no further queries are allowed before computing a minimal DFA conforming to the examples. Typical algorithms of this type are based on a characterization in terms of a constraint satisfaction problem (CSP) over the natural numbers due to Biermann [BF72].

---

[2] For a recent attempt at mechanizing this step see [KPP05].

Clearly, an online algorithm like Angluin's should perform better than offline algorithms like Biermann's. Indeed, Angluin's algorithm is polynomial while without the ability to ask further queries the problem is known to be NP-complete [Gol78]. In our setting, however, we cannot rely completely on Angluin's algorithm. The definition of a network invariant does not identify an automaton completely. In consequence, in some cases we identify behaviors that can either be added to or equally well be removed from the candidate invariant. Thus, queries may be answered by *maybe*.

We therefore define an algorithm that is a combination of an online algorithm and an offline algorithm and is inspired by [PO98]. Similar to Angluin's algorithm, we round off the information on the automaton in question by asking queries. As queries can be answered by *maybe*, we may not be able to complete the information as in Angluin's setting to compute a DFA directly. For this, we use Biermann's approach for obtaining a DFA based on the enriched information. Our combination is conservative in the sense that in case all queries are answered by either *yes* or *no*, we obtain the same efficiency as for Angluin's algorithm. Furthermore, the encoding in terms of CSP is optimized based on the information collected in Angluin's algorithm. Both advantages are in contrast to the combination proposed in [PO98].

While in [OS01] an efficient implementation for solving the resulting CSP problem is explained, we give an encoding as a SAT problem featuring a simple yet—as the examples show—very efficient inference algorithm by employing powerful SAT solvers.

We note that there are efficient algorithms inferring a DFA that is not necessarily of minimal size, like [Lan92], [OG92] (known as RPNI). However, getting a minimum size automaton is essential to obtain our semi-computability result, which is why we cannot use these algorithms.

To validate our approach in practice, we have implemented it and tailored it to the intensively studied setting of *transition structures* [KP00]. Our implementation is based on the verification tool TLV [PS96] and on the SAT solver ZCHAFF [MMZ$^+$01]. We have tested our implementation on a well-studied example of mutual-exclusion protocol. We establish that the protocol is safe (i.e., no two processes are in the critical section simultaneously). The proper network invariant for this example is obtained in about 2 seconds.

Automatic inference of network invariants has been studied in [LHR97]. Their solution is based on *heuristically* solving a recursive equation for I. For some examples, a proper invariant has been found within seconds, while for others, no proper invariant was obtained automatically, though one exists. In contrast, in the case that a proper invariant exists, our algorithm would find one. Furthermore, the optimized yet systematic search for a proper invariant allows to inform the user of our tool about the current progress by saying up-to which size all possible invariants have been rejected. Such a requirement is extremely important especially for semi-terminating algorithms. In other words, while the general problem studied in this paper is undecidable, our algorithm decides the restricted problem of whether, for a given natural number n, a proper network invariant with at most n states exists.

Recently, several applications of learning techniques for verification problems have been proposed. In [HV05, VSVA04b], learning was used in the setting of regular model checking to verify safety properties. The approach was extended in [VSVA05] to checking ω-regular properties. An application to verify FIFO automata is given in [VSVA04a]. None of the approaches deals with queries that are possibly answered by *maybe*. Therefore, these papers do not address the combination of learning algorithms. Less related combinations of verification and learning are reported for example in [AMN05, CCST05].

Contribution. To the best of our knowledge, this is the first time learning techniques are applied to the problem of finding network invariants and the first efficient realization of a learning problem in terms of SAT solving. Furthermore, our combination of Angluin's L^* and Biermann's approach is more efficient than that of [PO98] due to additional optimizations.

Outline. We recall the framework of verification by network invariants tailored to the setting of DFAs in the next section. Section 3 recalls Angluin's and Biermann's inference algorithms, presents a simple combination of both of them, reduces it to SAT, and discusses some optimizations. The search procedure finding proper network invariants is described in Section 4. We examine the case study in Section 5, before we draw final conclusions.

2   Verification by Network Invariants

We recall the notion and notation of verification by network invariants, tailored to the setting of checking safety properties of system families built-up by DFAs.

For $n \in \mathbb{N}$, let $[n] := \{1, \ldots, n\}$. For the rest of this section, we fix an alphabet Σ. A *deterministic finite automaton* (DFA) $\mathcal{A} = (Q, q_0, \delta, Q^+)$ over Σ consists of a finite set of *states* Q, an *initial state* $q_0 \in Q$, a *transition function* $\delta : Q \times \Sigma \to Q$, and a set $Q^+ \subseteq Q$ of *accepting states*. A *run* of $\mathcal{A}$ is a sequence $r = q_0 \xrightarrow{a_1} q_1 \xrightarrow{a_2} \ldots \xrightarrow{a_n} q_n$ such that $a_i \in \Sigma$, $q_i \in Q$ and $\delta(q_{i-1}, a_i) = q_i$ for all $i \in [n]$. It is called *accepting* iff $q_n \in Q^+$. We say that r is a run *over* $w = a_1 a_2 \ldots a_n$ and say that w is *accepted* if r is accepting. The *language* accepted by $\mathcal{A}$, denoted by $\mathcal{L}(\mathcal{A})$, is the set of accepted strings. We extend δ to strings as usual by $\delta(q, \lambda) = q$ and $\delta(q, ua) = \delta(\delta(q, u), a)$, where λ denotes the empty string. Let $\mathfrak{D}$ denote the class of DFAs (over Σ).

In order to reason about network invariants we have to consider *abstraction relations*, *safety properties*, and *parallel composition*. These notions are well established in the context of transition structures [KP00], however, in the context of DFAs may seem out of place. In what follows, we should have in mind the properties of these notions. These are the properties that are required to make the algorithm work. In the context of transition structures, these notions are well known, can be checked (where appropriate), and have the required properties.

An *abstraction relation* on $\mathfrak{D}$ is a reflexive and transitive relation $\sqsubseteq \subseteq \mathfrak{D} \times \mathfrak{D}$. Here, let $\sqsubseteq \subseteq \mathfrak{D} \times \mathfrak{D}$ be defined by $\mathcal{A} \sqsubseteq \mathcal{B}$ iff $\mathcal{L}(\mathcal{A}) \subseteq \mathcal{L}(\mathcal{B})$. A *safety property* is a DFA φ that has a *prefix-closed* language, i.e., $ua \in \mathcal{L}(\varphi)$ implies $u \in \mathcal{L}(\varphi)$, defining the intended correct behavior. Thus, a system $\mathcal{A} \in \mathfrak{D}$ satisfies φ, denoted by $\mathcal{A} \models \varphi$, iff $\mathcal{L}(\mathcal{A}) \subseteq \mathcal{L}(\varphi)$. Clearly, in our setting, the abstraction relation is *sound* with respect to safety properties: For $\mathcal{A}, \mathcal{B} \in \mathfrak{D}$, $\varphi \in \mathfrak{D}$, $\mathcal{A} \sqsubseteq \mathcal{B}$ and $\mathcal{B} \models \varphi$ implies $\mathcal{A} \models \varphi$, as $\mathcal{L}(\mathcal{A}) \subseteq \mathcal{L}(\mathcal{B}) \subseteq \mathcal{L}(\varphi)$ implies $\mathcal{L}(\mathcal{A}) \subseteq \mathcal{L}(\varphi)$.

A *parallel operator* on $\mathfrak{D}$ is a mapping $\| : \mathfrak{D} \times \mathfrak{D} \to \mathfrak{D}$. For notational simplicity, we assume $\|$ to be *associative* and *commutative*, although this is not essential. We call $\|$ *compatible* with respect to $\sqsubseteq$ if, for all $C \in \mathfrak{D}$, $A \sqsubseteq B \implies A \| C \sqsubseteq B \| C$. Let us fix a parallel operator that is compatible with $\sqsubseteq$ for the rest of this paper.

A *projection operator* for $A \| B$ onto B is a mapping $pr^{B}_{A\|B} : \mathcal{L}(A \| B) \to \mathcal{L}(B)$ such that whenever $w \in \mathcal{L}(A \| B)$ then for all B' with $pr^{B}_{A\|B}(w) \in \mathcal{L}(B')$ also $w \in \mathcal{L}(A \| B')$. In other words, (at least) the projection of w has to be removed from B to (eventually) remove w from the parallel product.

Definition 1. *For $P \in \mathfrak{D}$, we call $I \in \mathfrak{D}$ a network invariant, iff* **(I1)** $P \sqsubseteq I$ *and* **(I2)** $P \| I \sqsubseteq I$. *If furthermore for $S \in \mathfrak{D}$ and a safety property $\varphi \in \mathfrak{D}$ we have* **(P)** $S \| I \models \varphi$ *we call I a proper network invariant for (S, P, φ).*

Often, we just say (proper) invariant instead of (proper) network invariant.

Theorem 1. [WL89] *Let S, P, I and φ in $\mathfrak{D}$ such that I is a proper network invariant for (S, P, φ). Then $S \| P[1] \| \cdots \| P[n] \models \varphi$, for all $n \in \mathbb{N}$ where, for every i, $P[i]$ is a copy of P.*

The problem studied in this paper can be phrased as follows:

Definition 2 (Proper Network Invariant Problem). *For systems S, P and a safety property φ in $\mathfrak{D}$, the* proper network invariant problem *is to compute a proper network invariant for (S, P, φ) (if it exists).*

Proposition 1. *The proper network invariant problem is semi-computable.*

Let us give a simple (but non-satisfactory) solution to the problem, based on the observation that the class of DFAs over a fixed alphabet is enumerable. Thus, let $I_1, I_2, \ldots$ be an enumeration of DFAs.

 – Check whether (I1) and (I2) hold for P and I_i. If yes, I_i is a network invariant.
 – If so, check whether $S \| I_i \models \varphi$. If yes, a proper invariant has been found and the procedure stops. If not, continue with $i + 1$.

It other words, the procedure finds a proper invariant, if one exists. Additionally, in case that DFAs are enumerated according to number of states, the resulting proper invariant is minimal with respect to its number of states.

   Of course, the algorithm outlined above is, in a way, naïve, and clearly inefficient in practice. We use learning techniques to accelerate the search for the proper invariants in question. Our procedure still produces a minimal proper invariant, if one exists. Conditions (I1), (I2), and (P) are used for inferring properties of the proper invariant we are looking for.

3   Inference of Deterministic Finite Automata

3.1   Angluin's Algorithm

Angluin's learning algorithm [Ang87] is designed for learning a regular language, $\mathcal{L} \subseteq \Sigma^*$, by constructing a minimal DFA A such that $\mathcal{L}(A) = \mathcal{L}$. In this algorithm a

Learner, who initially knows nothing about $\mathcal{L}$, is trying to learn $\mathcal{L}$ by asking a *Teacher*, who knows $\mathcal{L}$, two kinds of queries:

- A *membership query* consists of asking whether a string $w \in \Sigma^*$ is in $\mathcal{L}$.
- An *equivalence query* consists of asking whether a hypothesized DFA $\mathcal{H}$ is correct, i.e., whether $\mathcal{L}(\mathcal{H}) = \mathcal{L}$. The *Teacher* answers *yes* if $\mathcal{H}$ is correct, or else supplies a counterexample w, either in $\mathcal{L} \setminus \mathcal{L}(\mathcal{H})$ or in $\mathcal{L}(\mathcal{H}) \setminus \mathcal{L}$.

The *Learner* maintains a prefix-closed set $U \subseteq \Sigma^*$ of prefixes, which are candidates for identifying states, and a suffix-closed set $V \subseteq \Sigma^*$ of suffixes, which are used to distinguish such states. The sets U and V are increased when needed during the algorithm. The *Learner* makes membership queries for all words in $(U \cup U\Sigma)V$, and organizes the results into a *table* T that maps each $u \in (U \cup U\Sigma)$ to a mapping $T(u) : V \mapsto \{+, -\}$ where $+$ represents accepted and $-$ not accepted. In [Ang87], each function $T(u)$ is called a *row*. When T is

- *closed*, meaning that for each $u \in U$, $a \in \Sigma$ there is a $u' \in U$ such that $T(ua) = T(u')$, and
- *consistent*, meaning that $T(u) = T(u')$ implies $T(ua) = T(u'a)$,

the *Learner* constructs a hypothesized DFA $\mathcal{H} = (Q, q_0, \delta, Q^+)$, where (a) $Q = \{T(u) \mid u \in U\}$ is the set of distinct rows, (b) q_0 is the row $T(\lambda)$, (c) δ is defined by $\delta(T(u), a) = T(ua)$, and (d) $Q^+ = \{T(u) \mid u \in U, T(u)(\lambda) = +\}$ and submits $\mathcal{H}$ as an equivalence query. If the answer is *yes*, the learning procedure is completed, otherwise the returned counterexample is used to extend U and V, and subsequent membership queries are performed in order to make the new table closed and consistent producing a new hypothesized DFA, etc.

In our setting, queries are no longer answered by either *yes* or *no*, but also by *maybe*, denoted by ?. We therefore list the necessary changes to Angluin's algorithm. We keep the idea of a table but now, for every $u \in (U \cup U\Sigma)$, we get a mapping $T(u) : V \to \{+, -, ?\}$. For $u, u' \in (U \cup U\Sigma)$, we say that rows $T(u)$ and $T(v)$ *look similar*, denoted by $T(u) \equiv T(u')$, iff, for all $v \in V$, $T(u)(v) \neq?$ and $T(u')(v) \neq?$ implies $T(u)(v) = T(u')(v)$. Otherwise, we say that $T(u)$ and $T(v)$ are *obviously different*. We call T

- *weakly closed* if for each $u \in U$, $a \in \Sigma$ there is a $u' \in U$ such that $T(ua) \equiv T(u')$, and
- *weakly consistent* if $T(u) \equiv T(u')$ implies $T(ua) \equiv T(u'a)$.

Angluin's algorithm works as before, but using the weak versions of closed and consistent. However, extracting a DFA from a weakly closed and weakly consistent table is no longer straightforward. For this, we rely on Biermann's approach, described next.

3.2   Biermann's Algorithm

Biermann's learning algorithm [BF72] is also designed for learning a DFA $\mathcal{A}$. This time we are given a set of strings that are to be accepted by $\mathcal{A}$ and a set of strings that are to be rejected by $\mathcal{A}$. There is no possibility of asking queries and we have to supply a minimal possible DFA that accepts / rejects these strings. The set of positive and negative strings are called *sample*. We now formally describe samples and Biermann's algorithm.

A *sample* is a set of strings that, by the language in question, should either be accepted, denoted by $+$, or rejected, denoted by $-$. For technical reasons, it is convenient to work with prefix-closed samples. As the samples given to us are not necessarily prefix closed we introduce the value *maybe*, denoted by ?. Formally, a *sample* is a partial function $O : \Sigma^* \rightarrow \{+, -, ?\}$ that is defined for u whenever it is defined for some ua. For a string u the sample O yields whether u should be *accepted*, *rejected*, or we do not know. For strings u and u', we say that O *disagrees* on u and u' if $O(u) \neq ?$, $O(u') \neq ?$, and $O(u) \neq O(u')$. Clearly, Angluin's table (including entries with ?) can easily be translated to a sample, possibly by adding prefixes to $(U \cup U\Sigma)V$ with value ? to obtain a prefix-closed domain. An automaton $\mathcal{A}$ is said to *conform* with a sample O, if whenever O is defined for u we have $O(u) = +$ implies $u \in \mathcal{L}(\mathcal{A})$ and $O(u) = -$ implies $u \notin \mathcal{L}(\mathcal{A})$.

Given a sample O and a DFA $\mathcal{A}$ that is conform to O, let S_u denote the state reached in $\mathcal{A}$ when reading u. As long as we do not have $\mathcal{A}$, we can treat S_u as a variable ranging over states and derive constraints for the assignments of such a variable. More precisely, let $\mathrm{CSP}(O)$ denote the set of equations

$$\{S_u \neq S_{u'} \qquad\qquad | \; O \text{ disagrees on } u \text{ and } u'\} \quad (C1)$$
$$\cup \; \{S_u = S_{u'} \Rightarrow S_{ua} = S_{u'a} \mid a \in \Sigma, ua, u'a \in \mathcal{D}(O)\} \quad (C2)$$

Let the domain of $\mathcal{D}(\mathrm{CSP}(O))$ comprise the set of variables S_u used in the constraints. A *solution* of $\mathrm{CSP}(O)$ is mapping $\Gamma : \mathcal{D}(\mathrm{CSP}(O)) \rightarrow \mathbb{N}$ fulfilling the equations over the naturals, defined in the usual manner. The set $\mathrm{CSP}(O)$ is *solvable* over $[N]$ iff there is a solution with range $[N]$. It is easy to see that every solution of the CSP problem over the natural numbers can be turned into an automaton conforming with O.

Lemma 1 (Learning as CSP, [BF72]). *For a sample O, a DFA with N states conforming to O exists iff $\mathrm{CSP}(O)$ is solvable over $[N]$.*

We note that taking a different value for every S_u, trivially solves the CSP problem. Thus, a solution with minimum range exists and yields a DFA with a minimal number of states.

3.3 Pruning the Search Space of the CSP Problem

In general, one finds a minimum DFA by trying to solve the corresponding CSP problem with subsequently larger integer ranges. However, before doing so, let us make a simple yet important observation to simplify the CSP problem. We call a bijection $\iota : [N] \rightarrow [N]$ a *renaming* and say that Γ and Γ' are *equivalent modulo* renaming iff there is a renaming ι such that $\Gamma = \iota \circ \Gamma'$.

Since names or numbers of states have no influence on the accepted language of an automaton, we get

Lemma 2 (Name irrelevance). *For a sample O, $\Gamma : \mathcal{D}(\mathrm{CSP}(O)) \rightarrow [N]$ is a solution for $\mathrm{CSP}(O)$ iff for every renaming $\iota : [N] \rightarrow [N]$, $\iota \circ \Gamma$ is a solution of $\mathrm{CSP}(O)$.*

The previous lemma can be used to prune the search space for a solution: We can assign numbers to state variables, provided different numbers are used for different states.

Definition 3 (Obviously different). *S_u and $S_{u'}$ are said to be* obviously different *iff there is some $v \in \Sigma^*$ such that O disagrees on uv and $u'v$. Otherwise, we say that S_u and $S_{u'}$ look similar.*

A CSP problem with M obviously different variables needs at least M different states, which gives us together with Lemma 1:

Lemma 3 (Lower bound). *Let M be the number of obviously different variables. Then $\mathrm{CSP}(O)$ is not solvable over all $[N]$ with $N < M$.*

Note that solvability over $[M]$ is not guaranteed, as can easily be seen.

As a solution to the constraints system produces an automaton and in view of Lemma 2, we can fix the values of obviously different variables.

Lemma 4 (Fix different values). *Let $S_{u_1}, \ldots, S_{u_M}$ be M obviously different variables. Then $\mathrm{CSP}(O)$ is solvable iff $\mathrm{CSP}(O) \cup \{S_{u_i} = i \mid i \in [M]\}$ is solvable.*

The simple observation stated in the previous lemma improves the solution of a corresponding SAT problem defined below significantly, as described in Section 5.

Given a table $T : (U \cup U\Sigma) \times V \rightarrow \{+, -, ?\}$, we can easily approximate obviously different states: For $u, u' \in (U \cup U\Sigma)$. States S_u and $S_{u'}$ are obviously different, if the rows $T(u)$ and $T(u')$ are obviously different.

3.4   Translation of CSP to SAT

We would like to efficiently solve the CSP problem presented above. Such a solution is proposed in [OS01]. We follow, for reasons of simplicity, a different yet efficient approach. In order to solve the CSP problem, we translate it to an equivalent propositional-logic satisfiability problem in conjunctive normal form (CNF). Therefore, we need to represent the constraints formulated above in terms of equalities and inequalities as well as the possible assignments to values from $[N]$ in CNF form. More specifically, we have to encode in CNF constraints of the following form.

1. $S_u \in [N]$
2. $S_u \neq S_{u'}$
3. $S_u = S_{u'} \implies S_{ua} = S_{u'a}$
4. $S_u = i$ for some $i \in [N]$.

Namely, every constraint should be a conjunction of disjunctions of literals, where every literal is either a proposition or its negation. We propose two different encodings: *binary* and *unary*. While the first is more compact for representing large numbers, it turns out that the unary encoding speeds-up solving the resulting SAT problem.

Binary Encoding. We show how to encode the constraints by using binary encoding for numbers. In order to encode the restriction that a variable S_u takes a value in $[N]$ (case 1), we encode the value of S_u by m propositional variables $S_u^1 \ldots S_u^m$, where $m := \lceil \log_2 N \rceil$. Intuitively, the assignment to $S_u^1 \ldots S_u^m$ is the binary encoding of $S_u - 1$. Thus, we allocate m propositional variables for every string in the domain of O. Furthermore, we limit the range to exactly N, involving up-to $(\log N)^2$ clauses, unless the value of S_u is fixed (case 4).

In order to encode the restriction that $S_u \neq S_{u'}$ (case 2) we do the following. We have $S_u \neq S_{u'}$ iff there is a distinguishing bit in their binary representation. Thus, $S_u \neq S_{u'}$ iff $\bigvee_{k \in \{1,\dots,m\}} S_u^k \neq S_{u'}^k$ is satisfiable, which reads in CNF as

$$
\begin{aligned}
\varphi = (\ & S_u^1 \vee S_{u'}^1 \vee & \dots & & \vee S_u^m \vee S_{u'}^m \ ) \wedge \\
(\ & S_u^1 \vee S_{u'}^1 \vee & \dots & & \vee \neg S_u^m \vee \neg S_{u'}^m \ ) \wedge \\
(\ & S_u^1 \vee S_{u'}^1 \vee \dots \vee \neg S_u^{m-1} \vee \neg S_{u'}^{m-1} \vee S_u^m \vee S_{u'}^m \ ) \wedge \\
(\ & S_u^1 \vee S_{u'}^1 \vee \dots \vee \neg S_u^{m-1} \vee \neg S_{u'}^{m-1} \vee \neg S_u^m \vee \neg S_{u'}^m \ ) \wedge \\
& \vdots \\
(\ & \neg S_u^1 \vee \neg S_{u'}^1 \vee & \dots & & \vee \neg S_u^m \vee \neg S_{u'}^m \ )
\end{aligned}
$$

Thus, each inequality is encoded by 2^m clauses. Recall that m is logarithmic in the number of states of the prospective automaton. It follows that the number of clauses is linear with respect to the number of states of the target automaton.

In order to encode the restriction that $S_u = S_{u'} \rightarrow S_{ua} = S_{u'a}$ (case 3) we do the following. Clearly, $S_u = S_{u'} \rightarrow S_{ua} = S_{u'a}$ is equivalent to $(S_u \neq S_{u'} \vee S_{ua} = S_{u'a})$. We encode this restriction in CNF using the same scheme as for cases 1 and 2, except that we add clauses for $S_u = S_{u'}$. We obtain clauses of the form

$$
\begin{aligned}
(\ \varphi \vee\ & S_{ua}^1 \vee \neg S_{u'a}^1 \ ) \wedge \\
(\ \varphi \vee\ & \neg S_{ua}^1 \vee S_{u'a}^1 \ ) \wedge \\
& \vdots \\
(\ \varphi \vee\ & S_{ua}^m \vee \neg S_{u'a}^m \ ) \wedge \\
(\ \varphi \vee\ & \neg S_{ua}^m \vee S_{u'a}^m \ )
\end{aligned}
$$

where φ is as defined above. This can be easily translated to CNF. Thus, every such constraint yields $2^{m+1}m$ CNF clauses.

The restriction that $S_u = i$ (case 4) is encoded by requiring that the corresponding bits of the binary representation of i are set or unset. Thus, we get m clauses for every such constraint.

Let n be the number of strings in $\mathcal{D}(O)$ and N be the size of the automaton in question. Then $\mathrm{CSP}(O)$ has $\mathcal{O}(n^2)$ constraints. Thus, the binary SAT encoding yields $\mathcal{O}(n^2 N \log N)$ clauses over $\mathcal{O}(n \log N)$ variables.

Unary Encoding. Surely, we can translate the CSP problem to an equivalent SAT problem using a unary encoding for values. While in general, a unary encoding uses exponentially more propositional variables, we obtain a similar number of clauses, since the constraints can be encoded using less clauses. Furthermore, for the problem sizes in question this exponential blow-up seems to be admissible. In fact, it turns out, that the employed SAT solver performs much better with the unary encoding than with the binary encoding.

In order to encode the restriction that a variable S_u takes a value in $[N]$ (case 1), we allocate N propositional variables $S_u^1, \dots, S_u^N$ and require that $S_u^j = 1$ implies $\bigwedge_{k \neq j} S_u^k = 0$. Hence, N^2 clauses are used for all these constraints.

In order to encode the restriction that $S_u \neq S_{u'}$ (case 2) we do the following. We have $S_u \neq S_{u'}$ iff $(\neg S_u^1 \vee \neg S_{u'}^1) \wedge (\neg S_u^2 \vee \neg S_{u'}^2) \wedge \cdots \wedge (\neg S_u^N \vee \neg S_{u'}^N)$. Thus, we need N clauses for each inequality.

The restriction $S_u = S_{u'} \rightarrow S_{ua} = S_{u'a}$ (case 3) is encoded by clauses of the following form.

$$(\neg S_u^1 \vee \neg S_{u'}^1 \vee S_{ua}^1 \vee \neg S_{u'a}^1) \wedge$$
$$\vdots$$
$$(\neg S_u^1 \vee \neg S_{u'}^1 \vee S_{ua}^N \vee \neg S_{u'a}^N) \wedge$$
$$(\neg S_u^2 \vee \neg S_{u'}^2 \vee S_{ua}^1 \vee \neg S_{u'a}^1) \wedge$$
$$\vdots$$
$$(\neg S_u^2 \vee \neg S_{u'}^2 \vee S_{ua}^N \vee \neg S_{u'a}^N) \wedge$$
$$\vdots$$
$$(\neg S_u^N \vee \neg S_{u'}^N \vee S_{ua}^N \vee \neg S_{u'a}^N)$$

Thus, we require N^2 CNF clauses for each equation. Finally, the restriction $S_u = i$ (case 4) is trivial to represent.

Let n be the number of strings in $\mathcal{D}(O)$ and N the size of the target automaton. Totally, the unary encoding has $\mathcal{O}(n^2 N^2)$ clauses with $\mathcal{O}(nN)$ variables.

4   Inference of Network Invariants

We now describe how to compute a proper network invariant in the case that one exists. For the rest of this section, we fix systems S, P, and a property automaton φ.

We start with an informal explanation. We are using an unbounded number of *students* whose job it is to suggest possible invariants, one *teaching assistant* (TA) whose job it is to answer queries by the students, and one *supervisor* whose job it is to control the search process for a proper invariant. The search starts by the supervisor instructing one student to look for a proper invariant.

Like in Angluin's algorithm, every active student maintains a table (using $+$, $-$, and ?) and makes it weakly closed and weakly consistent by asking the TA membership queries. The TA answers with either $+$, $-$, or ?, as described below. When the table is weakly closed and consistent, the student translates the table to a sample O and this to a CSP problem. He solves the CSP problem using the SAT encoding. The solution with minimum range is used to form an automaton I that is proposed to the supervisor. The supervisor now checks whether I is indeed a proper invariant by checking (P), (I1), and (I2). If yes, the supervisor has found a proper invariant. If not, one of the following holds.

1. There is a string w such that $w \in \mathcal{L}(S \parallel I)$ but $w \notin \mathcal{L}(\varphi)$,
2. There is a string w such that $w \in \mathcal{L}(P)$ but $w \notin \mathcal{L}(I)$,
3. There a string w such that $w \in \mathcal{L}(P \parallel I)$ but $w \notin \mathcal{L}(I)$.

In the first case, the projection $pr^I_{S \parallel I}(w)$ should be removed from I. In the second case, the string w should be added to I. In these cases, the supervisor returns the appropriate string with the appropriate acceptance information to the student, who continues in the same manner as before.

In the last case, it is not clear, whether w should be added to I or removed from $P \parallel I$. For the latter, we have to remove the projection $pr^{I}_{P\parallel I}(w)$ from I. Unless w is listed negatively or $pr^{I}_{P\parallel I}(w)$ is listed positively in the table, both possibilities are meaningful. Therefore, the supervisor has to follow both tracks. She copies the table of the current student, acquires another student, and asks the current student to continue with w in I and the new student to continue with $pr^{I}_{P\parallel I}(w)$ not in I.

In order to give answers, the teaching assistant uses the same methods as the supervisor, however, whenever a choice is possible she just says ?.

Choices can sometimes yield conflicts that are observed later in the procedure. For example, w might be added to I and the new automaton I' proposed by the student together with S does not satisfy φ with w' as counter example. It is then possible that $pr^{I'}_{S\parallel I'}(w') = w$ requesting to set w's entry to $-$. Such a case reveals a conflicting assumption and requires the student to retire. If no working student is left, no proper invariant exists.

Clearly, the procedure sketched above finds a proper invariant if one exists. However, it consumes a lot of resources and may yield a proper invariant that is not minimal. We show how to adapt the supervisor so that it uses only one student at a given time and it stops with a minimal proper invariant. Intuitively, the supervisor keeps track of the active students as well as the sizes of recently suggested automata. Whenever a student proposes a new automaton of size N, the supervisor computes the appropriate answer, which is either a change of the student's table or the answer *proper invariant found*. However, she postpones answering the student (or stopping the algorithm), gives the student priority N, and puts the student on hold. Then the supervisor takes a student that is on hold with minimal priority and sends the pre-computed instrumentation to the corresponding student. In case the student's instrumentation was tagged *proper invariant found* the procedure stops by printing the final proper invariant. Note that students always propose automata of at least the same size as before since the learning algorithm returns a *minimal* automaton conforming to the sample. Thus, whenever a proper invariant is found, it is guaranteed that the proper invariant is eventually reported by the algorithm, unless a smaller proper invariant is found before.

To be a little more precise, consider the pseudo code for the supervisor given in Algorithm 1. The supervisor maintains a working set (set of students on hold) that contains triplets of the form $(n, table, automaton)$. Such a triplet consists of a table, a lower bound on the minimal-size of an automaton consistent with the table, and if the table yields a proper invariant a pointer to an automaton.

In line 2, the working set is initialized with the following triplet: size 1, empty table, no invariant. Then, we enter a loop in which a triplet with minimal number of states n is taken out of the working set. If the pointer to the automaton exists, then we have a proper invariant. Since the number of states is minimal, it is indeed a minimal proper invariant—and the algorithm terminates. If not, we ask the student to make the table closed and consistent and to propose a new automaton (based on SAT solving) and also list its number of states (line 8). The supervisor continuous by checking whether the proposed automaton is indeed an invariant. If a counter example is obtained by checking (P) or (I1), this counter example is added to the table, the automaton pointer is set to NULL (proposed automaton is not proper invariant), and the triplet is added

---

Algorithm 1. Pseudo code for the supervisor

```
1  Function supervisor ()
2    wset = { (1, getEmptyTable(),NULL) };
3    do
4      (wset,  (n,  table ,  automaton)) = takeOutWithMin_n(wset);
5      if (automaton ≠ NULL) then
6        print (automaton);  stop ();   // a previously found invariant is proved minimal
7        print ("Considered  all  automata up–to size  ", n−1);
8        (n,  table ,  automaton) = student ( table );
9        cex = checkP(automaton);
10       if cex ≠ NULL then
11         wset = wset ∪ addition( (n,  table ,  NULL), (pr(cex ),  −));
12         continue_while;
13       cex  = checkI1 (automaton);
14       if cex ≠ NULL then
15         wset = wset ∪ addition( (n,  table ,  NULL), (cex, +));
16         continue_while;
17       cex = checkI2 (automaton);
18       if cex = NULL then // we have an invariant, store it
19         wset = wset ∪ (n, table ,  automaton);
20       else
21         wset = wset ∪ addition( (n,  table ,  NULL), (pr(cex ),  −));
22                     ∪ addition( (n,  table ,  NULL), (cex, +));
23   while wset ≠ ∅;
24   print ("No invariant  exists ");
```

---

to the working set (lines 11,15). If the information that should be added to the table conflicts with the information already stored there, the addition function just returns the empty set, stopping further treatment of this triplet. If a counter example is found for case (I2), the supervisor tries to add both possibilities, possibly enlarging the working set (lines 21–22). If no counter example is obtained, we have a proper invariant and store it in the working set (line 19). Unless no smaller invariant is found, it is printed later in line 6. If we reach line 24, all possible invariants have been ruled out and no proper invariant exists. Overall, the procedure guarantees that at most one student is working and that the final proper invariant is indeed minimal.

Theorem 2. *For systems S, P and a safety property φ in $\mathfrak{D}$, the procedure outlined above computes minimal proper network invariant for (S, P, φ), if one exists.*

Proof (sketch). Clearly, whenever an automaton is printed, it is a proper invariant. Minimality follows from the way the supervisor searches for invariants as well as from the property that invariants proposed by the student are minimal. It remains to show that indeed one proper invariant is found, if it exists. The only way to fail this property would be to stay forever in the while loop, without examining new possible proper invariants. This is only possible if the triplets in the working set do not increase in the number of states n. However, the combined learning algorithm proposes always a new automaton

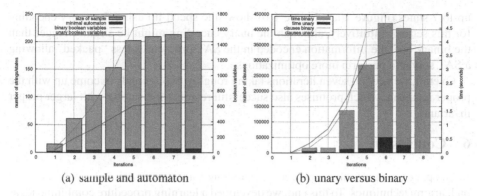

(a) sample and automaton   (b) unary versus binary

Fig. 1. Finding a proper invariant based on SAT solving

whenever a new string based on a counter example is added to the table. As there are
only finitely many automata of a fixed size, we obtain the desired contradiction.

5   Experimental Results

To validate our approach in practice, we have engineered the approach described in the
previous sections for the setting of *transition structures*, which have been used extensively in the context of network invariants [KP00].

We have implemented the procedure of finding a proper invariant, if one exists,
based on the verification tool TLV [PS96], which we employ for checking the abstraction relation and checking the safety property ((P), (I1), (I2)) and on the SAT solver
ZCHAFF [MMZ+01] used for computing prospective proper invariants. Using TLV and
ZCHAFF, the remaining effort was to come-up with code implementing the completion
of tables, and gluing the three tools together.

We used the well-studied example of a simple mutual exclusion protocol taken from
[KP00]. We were interested in a proper invariant showing that the safety property *no two
processes are in the critical section simultaneously* holds.

In first experiments we skipped the step of making the table complete and consistent,
thus using only Biermann's algorithm. In total, we examined 78 possible invariants
before finding the minimal one with 7 states after approximately 20 minutes, solving
78 SAT problems using the binary encoding.

To reduce the number of SAT instances, we have experimented with rounding off
the information in the table before applying Biermann's algorithm. Interestingly, this
idea alone fails. Extending the table yields less but larger SAT problems. With the binary encoding, one of the SAT problems alone took about 30 minutes. Using the unary
encoding, solving the SAT instances turns out to be much faster though the overall approach is still not satisfactory. Only by combining the optimization of fixing values for
obviously different variables we convert the approach to a working method.

In conclusion, it is the combination of Angluin's and Biermann's algorithms, reduced
to SAT solving based on unary encoding and fixing the variables of obviously different
variables that yields best results. Figure 1 reports the values of this combination for
our example. We needed up-to 217 entries in a sample yielding minimal automata of

up-to 7 states (Figure 1(a)). Figure 1(b) shows the speed-up using the unary encoding for this setting. Intuitively, although the unary encoding might be slightly bigger than the binary one, the information encoded in the SAT problem is less "packed" allowing a SAT solver to perform more optimizations.

Overall, we needed seven iterations taking roughly two seconds to come up with the proper invariant, which promises also successful results for a setting with larger proper invariants.

6 Conclusion

In this paper, we presented a procedure searching for a proper network invariant based on learning techniques. To this end, we developed a learning procedure combining ideas of Angluin's L^* and Biermann's inference algorithm. Moreover, we have shown that the resulting learning algorithm allows an efficient implementation via a reduction to SAT and using existing SAT solvers. The search for a proper invariant terminates with an invariant with a minimal number of states, provided one exists, and might otherwise not terminate. Since the studied problem is undecidable, this cannot be avoided.

While we have experienced that learning techniques do not scale easily to large systems [BJLS03], our approach should be understood as an alternative to finding invariants manually. For this, it has to be competitive for systems of sizes that could alternatively be handled by hand.

On the same line, it is important to note that our search procedure iteratively considers larger and larger prospective proper invariants. This implies that it can be used to decide the question whether a proper network invariant with up-to n states exists, for every fixed natural number n. Practically, it means that the algorithm is able to continuously report on its progress, i.e., the size of the current prospective invariant. Thus, even if no proper invariant is found after a while, a user can learn that no invariant with size up-to the one currently studied exists.

It would be interesting to combine learning methods for ω-automata in the search for network invariants. This would allow us to handle also more complex properties of the parameterized system in question.

Acknowledgment. We thank Bengt Jonsson and Christian Schallhart for valuable comments and discussions.

References

[AK86]   Krzysztof R. Apt and Dexter Kozen. Limits for automatic verification of finite-state concurrent systems. *IPL*, 22(6):307–309, 1986.

[AMN05]   R. Alur, P. Madhusudan, and W. Nam. Symbolic compositional verification by learning assumptions. In *17th CAV*, LNCS 3576, pages 548–562. 2005.

[Ang87]   Dana Angluin. Learning regaular sets from queries and counterexamples. *IC*, 75:87–106, 1987.

[BF72]   A. W. Biermann and J. A. Feldman. On the synthesis of finite-state machines from samples of their behaviour. *IEEE TOC*, 21:592–597, 1972.

[BJLS03]   Therese Berg, Bengt Jonsson, Martin Leucker, and Mayank Saksena. Insights to Angluin's learning. TR 2003-039, Uppsala University, 2003.

[CCST05]   S. Chaki, E. M. Clarke, N. Sinha, and P. Thati. Automated assume-guarrantee reasoning for simulation conformance. In 17th CAV, LNCS 3576, pages 534–547. 2005.

[CTTV04]   E. M. Clarke, M. Talupur, T. Touili, and H. Veith. Verification by network decomposition. In 15th Concur, LNCS 3170, pages 276–291. 2004.

[CTV06]   E. M. Clarke, M. Talupur, and H. Veith. Environment abstraction for parameterized verification. In 7th VMCAI, LNCS 3855, 126–141. 2006.

[EK00]   E.A. Emerson and V. Kahlon. Reducing model checking of the many to the few. In 17th CADE, LNCS 1831, pages 236–254, 2000.

[EN95]   E.A. Emerson and K.S. Namjoshi. Reasoning about rings. In POPL, 1995.

[Gol78]   E. M. Gold. Complexity of automaton identification from given data. IC, 37(3):302–320, 1978.

[HV05]   Peter Habermehl and Tomás Vojnar. Regular model checking using inference of regular languages. ENTCS, 138(3):21–36, 2005.

[JN00]   Bengt Jonsson and Marcus Nilsson. Transitive closures of regular relations for verifying infinite-state systems. In 6th TACAS, LNCS 1785, 2000.

[KM95]   R. P. Kurshan and K. L. McMillan. A structural induction theorem for processes. IC, 117(1):1–11, 1995.

[KP00]   Y. Kesten and A. Pnueli. Control and data abstraction: The cornerstones of practical formal verification. STTT, 2(4):328–342, 2000.

[KPP05]   Y. Kesten, N. Piterman, and A. Pnueli. Bridging the gap between fair simulation and trace inclusion. IC, 200(1):35–61, 2005.

[KPSZ02]   Y. Kesten, A. Pnueli, E. Shahar, and L. Zuck. Network invariants in action. In 13th Concur, LNCS 2421, 2002.

[Lan92]   Kevin J. Lang. Random dfa's can be approximately learned from sparse uniform examples. In COLT, pages 45–52, 1992.

[LHR97]   D. Lesens, N. Halbwachs, and P. Raymond. Automatic verification of parameterized linear networks of processes. In 24th POPL, 1997.

[MMZ$^+$01]   Matthew W. Moskewicz, Conor F. Madigan, Ying Zhao, Lintao Zhang, and Sharad Malik. Chaff: Engineering an efficient sat solver. In DAC, 530–535. ACM, 2001.

[OG92]   J. Oncina and P. Garcia. Inferring regular languages in polynomial update time. In Pattern Recognition and Image Analysis, Series in Machine Perception and AI 1, pages 49–61. World Scientific, 1992.

[OS01]   Arlindo L. Oliveira and João P. Marques Silva. Efficient algorithms for the inference of minimum size dfas. Machine Learning, 44(1/2):93–119, 2001.

[PO98]   Jorge M. Pena and Arlindo L. Oliveira. A new algorithm for the reduction of incompletely specified finite state machines. In ICCAD, 482–489, 1998.

[PS96]   A. Pnueli and E. Shahar. A platform for combining deductive with algorithmic verification. In 8th CAV, pages 184–195, 1996.

[PS00]   A. Pnueli and E. Shahar. Liveness and acceleration in parameterized verification. In 12th CAV, LNCS 1855, pages 328–343. Springer Verlag, 2000.

[VSVA04a]   A. Vardhan, K. Sen, M. Viswanathan, and G. Agha. Actively learning to verify safety for fifo automata. In FSTTCS, LNCS 3328, 494–505. 2004.

[VSVA04b]   A. Vardhan, K. Sen, M. Viswanathan, and G. Agha. Learning to verify safety properties. In ICFEM, LNCS 3308, 274–289. 2004.

[VSVA05]   A. Vardhan, K. Sen, M. Viswanathan, and G. Agha. Using language inference to verify omega-regular properties. In TACAS, LNCS 3440, 2005.

[WL89]   P. Wolper and V. Lovinfosse. Verifying properties of large sets of processes with network invariants. In Proceedings of the International Workshop on Automatic Verification Methods for Finite State Systems, LNCS 407, 1989.

A Recursion Combinator for Nominal Datatypes Implemented in Isabelle/HOL

Christian Urban and Stefan Berghofer

Technische Universität München
{urbanc, berghofe}@in.tum.de

Abstract. The nominal datatype package implements an infrastructure in Isabelle/HOL for defining languages involving binders and for reasoning conveniently about alpha-equivalence classes. Pitts stated some general conditions under which functions over alpha-equivalence classes can be defined by a form of structural recursion and gave a clever proof for the existence of a primitive-recursion combinator. We give a version of this proof that works directly over nominal datatypes and does not rely upon auxiliary constructions. We further introduce proving tools and a heuristic that made the automation of our proof tractable. This automation is an essential prerequisite for the nominal datatype package to become useful.

Keywords: Lambda-calculus, proof assistants, nominal logic, primitive recursion.

1 Introduction

The infrastructure provided by various datatype packages [2,6] dramatically simplifies the embedding of languages *without* binders inside HOL-based proof assistants [4]. Because such proof assistants emphasise the development of theories by definition rather than axiom postulation, simple tasks like reasoning about lists would be fiendishly complicated without such an infrastructure.

The purpose of the nominal datatype package[1] is to provide an infrastructure in Isabelle/HOL for embedding languages *with* binders and for reasoning conveniently about them. Many ideas for this package originate from the nominal logic work by Pitts ([7], see also [11]). Using this package, the user can define the terms of, for example, the lambda-calculus as follows:

$$
\begin{aligned}
&\textbf{atom\_decl name}\\
&\textbf{nominal\_datatype lam} = \text{Var "name"}\\
&\qquad\qquad\qquad\qquad\quad | \text{ App "lam" "lam"}\\
&\qquad\qquad\qquad\qquad\quad | \text{ Lam "«name»lam"}
\end{aligned}
\tag{1}
$$

where **name** is declared to be the type for variables and where «...» indicates that a name is bound in a lambda-term. Despite similarities with the usual datatype declaration of Isabelle/HOL and despite the fact that after this declaration one

---

[1] Available from http://isabelle.in.tum.de/nominal/

U. Furbach and N. Shankar (Eds.): IJCAR 2006, LNAI 4130, pp. 498–512, 2006.

can, as usual, write $(\text{Var }a)$, $(\text{App }t_1 \, t_2)$ and $(\text{Lam }a \, t)$ for the lambda-terms, the code above does *not* define a datatype in the usual sense, but rather defines *alpha-equivalence* classes. Indeed we can show that the *equation*

$$(\text{Lam }a \, (\text{Var }a)) = (\text{Lam }b \, (\text{Var }b)) \qquad (2)$$

holds for the nominal datatype lam.

By using alpha-equivalence classes and strong induction principles, that is induction principles which have the usual variable convention already built-in [10,11], one can often formalise with great ease informal proofs about languages involving binders. One example[2] is Barendregt's informal proof of the substitution lemma shown in Fig. 1. This lemma establishes a "commutation-property" for the function of capture-avoiding substitution. This substitution function is usually defined by the three clauses:

$$
\begin{aligned}
(\text{Var }a)[b := t'] &= \text{ if } a = b \text{ then } t' \text{ else } (\text{Var }a)\\
(\text{App }t_1 \, t_2)[b := t'] &= \text{ App }(t_1[b := t'])\,(t_2[b := t'])\\
(\text{Lam }a \, t)[b := t'] &= \text{ Lam }a\,(t[b := t'])
\end{aligned}
\qquad (3)
$$

where the last clause has the side-constraint that $a \neq b$ and $a \mathbin{\#} t'$ (the latter is the nominal logic terminology for a not being free in t'). While it is trivial to define functions by primitive recursion over datatypes, this is not so for nominal datatypes, because there functions need to respect equations such as (2); if *not*, then one can easily prove false in Isabelle/HOL. Consider for example the following two definitions that are intended, respectively, to calculate the set of bound names and to return the set of immediate subterms of a lambda-term:

$$
\begin{aligned}
bn\,(\text{Var }a) &= \varnothing & ist\,(\text{Var }a) &= \varnothing\\
bn\,(\text{App }t_1 \, t_2) &= (bn\,t_1) \cup (bn\,t_2) & ist\,(\text{App }t_1 \, t_2) &= \{t_1, t_2\}\\
bn\,(\text{Lam }a \, t) &= \{a\} \cup (bn\,t) & ist\,(\text{Lam }a \, t) &= \{t\}
\end{aligned}
$$

If bn and ist were functions, then they must return the same result for the two terms in (2)—that means $\{a\} = \{b\}$ in case of bn and $\{\text{Var }a\} = \{\text{Var }b\}$ in case of ist; however, if we assume $a \neq b$, then both equations lead to contradictions. Pitts gave in [8,9] some general conditions that allow to define the substitution function by the clauses in (3), but exclude definitions such as bn and ist.

In earlier versions of the nominal datatype package one could define functions on a case-by-case basis, but this involved some rather non-trivial reasoning—there was no uniform method for defining functions over the structure of nominal datatypes. Pitts gave in [9] two proofs for the existence of a primitive recursion operator that allows one to define functions by stating a clause for each term-constructor. His first proof is fairly complicated and involves auxiliary constructions: for example he does not show the existence directly for alpha-equivalence classes, but indirectly via the existence of primitive recursion for the corresponding "un-quotient" type (in case of the lambda-calculus "un-quotient" means

---

[2] Other examples such as Church-Rosser and strong normalisation can be found in the distribution of the nominal datatype package.

SUBSTITUTION LEMMA.

If $x \not\equiv y$ and $x \notin FV(L)$, then
$$M[x := N][y := L] \equiv M[y := L][x := N[y := L]].$$

PROOF. By induction on the structure of M.

Case 1: M is a variable.

Case 1.1. $M \equiv x$. Then both sides equal $N[y := L]$ since $x \not\equiv y$.

Case 1.2. $M \equiv y$. Then both sides equal L, for $x \notin FV(L)$ implies
$L[x := \ldots] \equiv L$.

Case 1.3. $M \equiv z \not\equiv x, y$. Then both sides equal z.

Case 2: $M \equiv \lambda z.M_1$. By the variable convention we may assume that $z \not\equiv x, y$ and z is not free in N, L. Then by induction hypothesis

$$\begin{aligned}
(\lambda z.M_1)[x := N][y := L] &\equiv \lambda z.(M_1[x := N][y := L]) \\
&\equiv \lambda z.(M_1[y := L][x := N[y := L]]) \\
&\equiv (\lambda z.M_1)[y := L][x := N[y := L]].
\end{aligned}$$

Case 3: $M \equiv M_1 M_2$. The statement follows again from the induction hypothesis. $\square$

```
lemma forget:
  assumes asm: "x#L"
  shows "L[x:=P] = L"
using asm by (nominal_induct L avoiding: x P rule: lam.induct)
              (auto simp add: abs_fresh fresh_atm)

lemma fresh_fact:
  fixes z::"name"
  assumes asm: "z#N" "z#L"
  shows "z#(N[y:=L])"
using asm by (nominal_induct N avoiding: z y L rule: lam.induct)
              (auto simp add: abs_fresh fresh_atm)

lemma substitution_lemma:
  assumes asm: "x≠y" "x#L"
  shows "M[x:=N][y:=L] = M[y:=L][x:=N[y:=L]]"
using asm by (nominal_induct M avoiding: x y N L rule: lam.induct)
              (auto simp add: fresh_fact forget)
```

Fig. 1. The informal proof shown at the top is taken from Barendregt [1]. In the lambda-case, the variable convention allows him to move the substitutions under the binder, to apply the induction hypothesis and finally to pull the substitutions back out from under the binder. Using the nominal datatype package one can formalise this proof in Isabelle/HOL by establishing first the lemmas forget and fresh_fact. Although hidden by the auto-tactic, the formal proof follows quite closely Barendregt's reasoning, including his use of the variable convention. One important part of this formalisation is the definition of the function for capture-avoiding substitution.

lambdas are defined having the type name×lam). Norrish formalised this proof quite faithfully, but needed, despite using the quotient package by Homeier [5] that automated some parts of the proof, approximately 600 lines of extremely dense HOL4-code. It is a fair comment[3] to say that this formalisation and the one included in early versions of the nominal datatype package are far too difficult for an automation.

We present in this paper a formalisation of Pitts second proof whose length is in case of the lambda-calculus only 150 lines of readable Isar-code. In contrast to [9], our proof is a direct proof not relying on any auxiliary constructions; also we prove directly the existence of a recursion combinator and do not make a detour via an iteration combinator. The automation of this proof will be part of the forthcoming release of the nominal datatype package. To ease the automation, we introduce here a heuristic that allowed us to write a tactic for solving some re-occurring proof obligations to do with finite support.

The paper introduces in Sec. 2 the central notions from the nominal logic work and some brief comments on the implementation of the nominal datatype package. Sec. 3 gives the proof of the *structural recursion combinator* for the type lam. Some examples are given in Sec. 4. The general case for all nominal datatypes is mentioned very briefly in Sec. 5; Sec. 6 draws conclusions and mentions related work.

2   Preliminaries

As can be seen from the declaration of lam shown in (1), there is a single type of variables in the lambda-calculus. We denote this type here by name and in the tradition of the nominal logic work call its elements *atoms*. While the structure of atoms is immaterial, two properties need to hold for the type name: one has to be able to distinguishing different atoms and one needs to know that there are countably infinitely many of them.

Permutations are finite bijective mappings from atoms to atoms; as in [11] permutations are implemented as finite lists whose elements are swappings (that is pairs of atoms). We write such permutations as $(a_1 b_1)(a_2 b_2) \cdots (a_n b_n)$; the empty list [] stands for the identity permutation. A permutation π *acting* on an atom a is defined as:

$$[] \cdot a \stackrel{\text{def}}{=} a$$

$$((a_1 a_2) :: \pi) \cdot a \stackrel{\text{def}}{=} \begin{cases} a_2 & \text{if } \pi \cdot a = a_1 \\ a_1 & \text{if } \pi \cdot a = a_2 \\ \pi \cdot a & \text{otherwise} \end{cases} \tag{4}$$

where $(a\,b) :: \pi$ is the composition of a permutation followed by the swapping $(a\,b)$. The composition of π followed by another permutation π' is given by list-concatenation, written as $\pi' @ \pi$, and the inverse of a permutation is given by list reversal, written as π^{-1}. Our representation of permutations as lists does

---

[3] Personal communication with Norrish.

not give unique representatives: for example, the permutation $(a\,a)$ is "equal" to the identity permutation. We equate the representations of permutations with a relation $\sim$:

Definition 1 (Permutation Equality). *Two permutations are* equal, *written* $\pi_1 \sim \pi_2$, *provided* $\pi_1 \cdot a = \pi_2 \cdot a$ *for all atoms* a.

To generalise the notion given in (4) of a permutation acting on an atom, the nominal datatype package takes advantage of the overloading mechanism in Isabelle by declaring a constant, written infix as $(-)\cdot(-)$, with the polymorphic type $(\texttt{name} \times \texttt{name})\,\texttt{list} \Rightarrow \alpha \Rightarrow \alpha$. A definition of the permutation action can then be given separately for each type-constructor; for lists, products, unit, sets and functions the definitions are as follows:

$$
\begin{aligned}
\alpha \text{ list}: \qquad & \pi \cdot [] \stackrel{\text{def}}{=} [] \\
& \pi \cdot (x :: t) \stackrel{\text{def}}{=} (\pi \cdot x) :: (\pi \cdot t) \\
\alpha_1 \times \alpha_2: \quad & \pi \cdot (x_1, x_2) \stackrel{\text{def}}{=} (\pi \cdot x_1, \pi \cdot x_2) \\
\text{unit}: \qquad & \pi \cdot () \stackrel{\text{def}}{=} () \\
\alpha \text{ set}: \qquad & \pi \cdot X \stackrel{\text{def}}{=} \{\pi \cdot x \mid x \in X\} \\
\alpha_1 \Rightarrow \alpha_2: \quad & \pi \cdot \mathit{fn} \stackrel{\text{def}}{=} \lambda x.\pi \cdot (\mathit{fn}\,(\pi^{-1} \cdot x))
\end{aligned}
\tag{5}
$$

The nominal datatype package also defines a permutation action for the type `lam`, which behaves as follows:

$$
\begin{aligned}
\pi \cdot (\mathsf{Var}\,a) &= \mathsf{Var}\,(\pi \cdot a) \\
\pi \cdot (\mathsf{App}\,t_1\,t_2) &= \mathsf{App}\,(\pi \cdot t_1)\,(\pi \cdot t_2) \\
\pi \cdot (\mathsf{Lam}\,a\,t) &= \mathsf{Lam}\,(\pi \cdot a)\,(\pi \cdot t)
\end{aligned}
\tag{6}
$$

(Since we have not yet derived a mechanism for defining functions by structural recursion over nominal datatypes, this permutation action cannot yet be defined directly, but needs to be lifted from the representing type for `lam`.)

The nominal datatype package assumes that every permutation action defined for a type satisfies three basic properties. For this we use the terminology from [11] of a *permutation type*:

Definition 2 (Permutation Type). *A type* α *will be referred to as* permutation type, *written* pt_α, *provided the permutation action satisfies the following three properties:*

$$
\begin{aligned}
(i) \quad & [] \cdot x = x \\
(ii) \quad & (\pi_1 @ \pi_2) \cdot x = \pi_1 \cdot (\pi_2 \cdot x) \\
(iii) \quad & \text{if } \pi_1 \sim \pi_2 \text{ then } \pi_1 \cdot x = \pi_2 \cdot x
\end{aligned}
$$

These properties entail that the permutations action behaves on elements of permutation types as one expects, for example we have $\pi^{-1} \cdot (\pi \cdot x) = x$. We note that:

Lemma 1. *Given pt_α, pt_{α_1} and pt_{α_2}, the types* name, unit, α list, α set, $\alpha_1 \times \alpha_2$, $\alpha_1 \Rightarrow \alpha_2$ *and* lam *are also permutation types.*

Proof. All properties follow by unwinding the definition of the corresponding permutation action and routine inductions. The property $pt_{\alpha_1 \Rightarrow \alpha_2}$ uses the fact that $\pi_1 \sim \pi_2$ implies $\pi_1^{-1} \sim \pi_2^{-1}$. $\qquad\qquad\square$

The permutation action on a function-type, say $\alpha_1 \Rightarrow \alpha_2$ with α_1 being a permutation type, is defined so that for every function *fn* we have the equation

$$\pi \bullet (fn\ x) = (\pi \bullet fn)(\pi \bullet x) \tag{7}$$

in Isabelle/HOL; this is because we have $\pi^{-1} \bullet (\pi \bullet x) = x$ for x of type α_1.

The most interesting feature of the nominal logic work is that as soon as one fixes a permutation action for a type, then the *support* for the elements of this type, very roughly speaking their set of free atoms, is fixed as well [3]. The definition of support and the derived notion of freshness is:

Definition 3 (Support and Freshness)

- *The* support *of x, written $supp(x)$, is the set of atoms defined as*

$$supp(x) \stackrel{def}{=} \{a \mid infinite\{b \mid (a\ b) \bullet x \neq x\}\}$$

- *An atom a is said to be* fresh *for an x, written $a \mathbin{\#} x$, provided $a \notin supp(x)$.*

The advantage of the quite unusual definition of support is that it generalises the notion of a free variable to functions (a fact that will play an important rôle later on). Unwinding this definition and the permutation action given in (5) and (6), one can calculate the support for the types:

$$
\begin{array}{lll}
\text{name:} & supp(a) = \{a\} & \\
\alpha_1 \times \alpha_2\text{:} & supp(x_1, x_2) = supp(x_1) \cup supp(x_2) & \\
\text{unit:} & supp(()) = \varnothing & \\
\alpha\,\text{list:} & supp([]) = \varnothing & \\
& supp(x :: xs) = supp(x) \cup supp(xs) & \\
\text{lam:} & supp(\text{Var}\ a) = \{a\} & \\
& supp(\text{App}\ t_1\ t_2) = supp(t_1) \cup supp(t_2) & \\
& supp(\text{Lam}\ a\ t) = supp(t) - \{a\} &
\end{array}
\tag{8}
$$

where the last clause uses the fact that alpha-equivalence for the type lam is given by:

$$\text{Lam}\ a\ t = \text{Lam}\ b\ t' \;\Leftrightarrow\; (a = b \wedge t = t') \vee (a \neq b \wedge t = (a\ b) \bullet t' \wedge a \mathbin{\#} t') \tag{9}$$

For permutation types the notion of support and freshness have very good properties as mentioned next (proofs are in [11]):

$$\pi \bullet a \mathbin{\#} \pi \bullet x \text{ if and only if } a \mathbin{\#} x \tag{10}$$

$$\text{if } a \mathbin{\#} x \text{ and } b \mathbin{\#} x \text{ then } (a\ b) \bullet x = x \tag{11}$$

A further restriction on permutation types filters out all those that contain elements with infinite support:

Definition 4 (Finitely Supported Permutation Types). *A permutation type α is said to be* finitely supported, *written fs_α, if every element of α has finite support.*

We shall write *finite(supp(x))/infinite(supp(x))* to indicate that an element x from a permutation type has finite/infinite support. The following holds:

Lemma 2. *Given fs_α, fs_{α_1} and fs_{α_2}, the types* name, unit, α list, $\alpha_1 \times \alpha_2$ *and* lam *are also finitely supported permutation types.*

Proof. Routine proofs using the calculations given in (8).

The crucial property entailed by Def. 4 is that if an element, say x, of a permutation type has finite support, then there must be a fresh atom for x, since there are infinitely many atoms. Therefore we have:

Proposition 1. *If x of permutation type has finite support, then there exists an atom a with $a \# x$.*

As a result, whenever we need to choose a fresh atom for an x of permutation type, we have to make sure that x has finite support. This task can be automatically performed by Isabelle's axiomatic type-classes [12] for most constructions occurring in informal proofs: Isabelle has to just examine the types of the construction using Lem. 2. Unfortunately, this is more difficult in case of functions, because not all functions have finite support, even if their domain and codomain are finitely supported permutation types (see [9, Example 9]). Therefore we have to establish whether a function has finite support on a case-by-case basis. In order to automate the corresponding proof obligations, we use the auxiliary notion of *supports* [3].

Definition 5. *A set S of atoms* supports *an x, written S supports x, provided:*

$$\forall a\,b.\ a \notin S \wedge b \notin S \;\Rightarrow\; (a\,b)\bullet x = x\,.$$

This notion allows us to approximate the support of an x from "above", because we can show that:

Lemma 3. *If a set S is finite and S supports x, then $supp(x) \subseteq S$.*

Proof. By contradiction we assume $supp(x) \not\subseteq S$, then there exists an atom $a \in supp(x)$ and $a \notin S$. From S supports x follows that for all $b \notin S$ we have $(a\,b)\bullet x = x$. Hence the set $\{b \mid (a\,b)\bullet x \neq x\}$ is a subset of S, and since S is finite by assumption, also $\{b \mid (a\,b)\bullet x \neq x\}$ must be finite. But this implies that $a \notin supp(x)$ which gives the contradiction.   □

Lem. 3 gives us in many cases some effective means to decide relatively easily whether a function has finite support: one only needs to find a finite set of atoms and then verify whether this set supports the function. For this we use the following heuristic:

Heuristic 1. *Assume an HOL-function, say fn, is given as a lambda-term. The support of the tuple consisting of the free variables of fn supports this function, more formally we have supp(FV(fn)) supports fn, where we assume FV is defined as usual, except that we group the free variables in tuples, instead of finite sets.*

This is a heuristic, because it can very likely not be established as a lemma inside Isabelle/HOL, since it is a property about HOL-functions. Nevertheless the heuristic is extremely helpful for deciding whether a function has finite support. Consider the following two examples:

Example 1. Given a function $fn \stackrel{\text{def}}{=} f_1 c$ where f_1 is a function of type name $\Rightarrow \alpha$. We also assume that f_1 has finite support. The question is whether fn has finite support? The free variables of fn are f_1 and c, that means $FV(fn) = (f_1, c)$. According to our heuristic we have to verify whether $supp(f_1, c)$ *supports* fn, which amounts to showing that

$$\forall a\, b.\ a \notin supp(f_1, c) \wedge b \notin supp(f_1, c) \Rightarrow (a\, b) \cdot fn = fn$$

To do so we can assume by the definition of freshness (Def. 3) that $a \mathbin{\#} (f_1, c)$ and $b \mathbin{\#} (f_1, c)$ and show that $(a\, b) \cdot fn = fn$. This equation follows from the calculation that pushes the swapping $(a\, b)$ inside fn:

$$(a\, b) \cdot fn \stackrel{\text{def}}{=} (a\, b) \cdot (f_1\, c) \stackrel{\text{by (7)}}{=} ((a\, b) \cdot f_1)\, ((a\, b) \cdot c) \stackrel{(*)}{=} f_1\, c \stackrel{\text{def}}{=} fn$$

where $(*)$ follows because we know that $a \mathbin{\#} f_1$ and $b \mathbin{\#} f_1$ and therefore by (11) that $(a\, b) \cdot f_1 = f_1$ (similarly for c).

We can conclude that $supp(fn)$ is a subset of $supp(f_1, c)$, because the latter is finite (since f_1 has finite support by assumption and c is finitely supported because the type name is a finitely supported permutation type). So fn must have finite support. $\square$

Example 2. Given the function $fn' \stackrel{\text{def}}{=} \lambda\pi.\ f_2\, (r_1\, \pi)\, (r_2\, \pi)$ where we assume that the free variables of fn', namely f_2, r_1 and r_2, are functions with finite support. In order to verify that fn' has finite support we need to verify (f_1, r_1, r_2) *supports* fn', that is decide the following equation

$$(a\, b) \cdot (\lambda\pi.\ f_2\, (r_1\, \pi)\, (r_2\, \pi)) = \lambda\pi.\ f_2\, (r_1\, \pi)\, (r_2\, \pi)$$

under the assumptions that $a \mathbin{\#} (f_2, r_1, r_2)$ and $b \mathbin{\#} (f_2, r_1, r_2)$. Pushing the swapping $(a\, b)$ under the λ and inside the applications using (5) and (7), the swapping will by (11) "vanish" in front of f_1, r_1 and r_2, and we have two identical terms. So fn' has finite support under the given assumptions. $\square$

As the examples indicate, by using the heuristic one can infer from a decision problem involving permutations whether or not a function has finite support. The main point is that the decision procedure involving permutations can be relatively easily automated in a special purpose tactic analysing permutations. This seems much more convenient than analysing the support of a function directly.

3 Recursion for the Lambda-Calculus

In this section we derive from an inductively defined relation the existence of
a recursion combinator that allows us to define functions over the structure of
the type lam. This way of introducing a recursion combinator is standard in
HOL-based theorem provers.

In contrast with the usual datatypes, such as lists and products, where the
term-constructors are always injective, the term-constructors of nominal
datatypes are because of the binders in general *not* injective, see equation (2).
That means when stating a function definition by characteristic equations like
the ones given for capture-avoiding substitution in (3), it is not obvious whether
the intended function, roughly speaking, preserves alpha-equivalence—we have
seen the counter-examples *bn* and *ist* in the Introduction. Pitts [8,9] stated some
general conditions for when functions do preserve alpha-equivalence.

A definition by structural recursion involves in case of the lambda-calculus
three functions (one for each term-constructor) that specify the behaviour of the
function to be defined—let us call these functions f_1, f_2, f_3 for the variable-,
application- and lambda-case respectively and let us assume they have the types:

$$f_1 : \text{name} \Rightarrow \alpha$$
$$f_2 : \text{lam} \Rightarrow \text{lam} \Rightarrow \alpha \Rightarrow \alpha \Rightarrow \alpha$$
$$f_3 : \text{name} \Rightarrow \text{lam} \Rightarrow \alpha \Rightarrow \alpha$$

with α being a permutation type. Then the first condition by Pitts states that
f_3—the function for the lambda case—needs to satisfy the following property:[4]

Definition 6 (Freshness Condition for Binders (FCB)). *A function f
with type* name $\Rightarrow$ lam $\Rightarrow \alpha \Rightarrow \alpha$ *satisfies the* FCB *provided* $\exists a.\ a \# f \wedge \forall t\, r.\, a \#
f\, a\, t\, r.$

As we shall see later on, this condition ensures that the result of f_3 is independent
of which particular fresh name one chooses for the binder a. The second condition
states that the functions f_1, f_2 and f_3 have finite support. This condition ensures
that we can use Prop. 1 to chose a fresh name.

With these two conditions we can define a recursion combinator, we call it
$rfun_{f_1 f_2 f_3}$, with the following properties:

Theorem 1 (Characteristic Equations for Recursion). *If f_1, f_2 and f_3
have finite support and f_3 satisfies the FCB, then:*

$$rfun_{f_1 f_2 f_3}\,(\text{Var}\, a) \quad = f_1\, a$$
$$rfun_{f_1 f_2 f_3}\,(\text{App}\, t_1\, t_2) = f_2\, t_1\, t_2\,(rfun_{f_1 f_2 f_3}\, t_1)\,(rfun_{f_1 f_2 f_3}\, t_2)$$
$$rfun_{f_1 f_2 f_3}\,(\text{Lam}\, a\, t) \quad = f_3\, a\, t\,(rfun_{f_1 f_2 f_3}\, t) \qquad\qquad \text{provided } a \# (f_1, f_2, f_3)$$

To give a proof of this theorem we start with the following inductive relation,
called $rec_{f_1 f_2 f_3}$ and of type $(\text{lam} \times \alpha)\,\text{set}$ where, like above, α is assumed to be
a permutation type:

---

[4] We slightly adapted the definition of Pitts to apply to our recursion combinator.

$$\overline{(\text{Var}\,a, f_1\,a) \in rec_{f_1 f_2 f_3}}$$

$$\frac{(t_1, r_1) \in rec_{f_1 f_2 f_3} \quad (t_2, r_2) \in rec_{f_1 f_2 f_3}}{(\text{App}\,t_1\,t_2, f_2\,t_1\,t_2\,r_1\,r_2) \in rec_{f_1 f_2 f_3}} \tag{12}$$

$$\frac{a\,\#\,(f_1, f_2, f_3) \quad (t, r) \in rec_{f_1 f_2 f_3}}{(\text{Lam}\,a\,t, f_3\,a\,t\,r) \in rec_{f_1 f_2 f_3}}$$

With this inductive definition comes the following induction principle:

$$\frac{\begin{array}{l} \forall a.\, P\,(\text{Var}\,a)\,(f_1\,a) \\ \forall t_1\,t_2\,r_1\,r_2.\, P\,t_1\,r_1 \wedge P\,t_2\,r_2 \Rightarrow P\,(\text{App}\,t_1\,t_2)\,(f_2\,t_1\,t_2\,r_1\,r_2) \\ \forall a\,t\,r.\,a\,\#\,(f_1, f_2, f_3) \wedge P\,t\,r \Rightarrow P\,(\text{Lam}\,a\,t) \end{array}}{(t, r) \in rec_{f_1 f_2 f_3} \Rightarrow P\,t\,r} \tag{13}$$

We shall show next that the relation $rec_{f_1 f_2 f_3}$ defines a function in the sense that for all lambda-terms t there exists a unique r so that $(t, r) \in rec_{f_1 f_2 f_3}$. From this we obtain a function from lam to α.

We first show that there exists an r for every t. For this we use the following strong structural induction principle [9,10,11] that the nominal datatype package generates for the type lam:

$$\frac{\begin{array}{l} \textit{finite}(S) \\ \forall a.\, P\,(\text{Var}\,a) \\ \forall t_1 t_2.\, P\,t_1 \wedge P\,t_2 \Rightarrow P\,(\text{App}\,t_1\,t_2) \\ \forall a\,t.\,a \notin S \Rightarrow P\,t \Rightarrow P\,(\text{Lam}\,a\,t) \end{array}}{P\,t} \tag{14}$$

This induction principle is called *strong*, because in the lambda-case one does not need to establish the property P for all binders a, but only for binders that are not in the finite set S. With this structural induction principle the proof of the next lemma is routine.

Lemma 4 (Totality). *Provided f_1, f_2 and f_3 have finite support, then for all t there exists an r such that $(t, r) \in rec_{f_1 f_2 f_3}$.*

Proof. By the strong induction principle, where we take S to be $supp(f_1, f_2, f_3)$, which we know by assumption is finite. Then in the lambda-case we can assume that $a \notin supp(f_1, f_2, f_3)$ holds, which is defined to be $a\,\#\,(f_1, f_2, f_3)$. All cases are then routine applying the rules in (12).

Next we establish that all r in the relation $rec_{f_1 f_2 f_3}$ have finite support.

Lemma 5 (Finite Support). *If f_1, f_2 and f_3 have finite support, then $(t, r) \in rec_{f_1 f_2 f_3}$ implies that r has finite support.*

Proof. By the induction principle give in (13). In the variable-case we have to show that $f_1\,a$ has finite support, which we inferred in Example 1 using our heuristic. The application- and lambda-case are similar.   □

In order to establish the "uniqueness" part of Theorem 1, we need the following two lemmas establishing that $rec_{f_1 f_2 f_3}$ is *equivariant* (see [7]) and that it preserves freshness.

Lemma 6 (Equivariance). *If* $(t, r) \in rec_{f_1 f_2 f_3}$ *then for all* π *also* $(\pi {\cdot} t, \pi {\cdot} r) \in$ $rec_{(\pi \bullet f_1)(\pi \bullet f_2)(\pi \bullet f_3)}$.

Proof. By the induction principle given in (13). All cases are routine by pushing the permutation π into t and r, except in the lambda-case where we have to apply (10) in order to infer $(\pi {\cdot} a) \# (\pi {\cdot} (f_1, f_2, f_3))$ from $u \# (f_1, f_2, f_3)$. □

Lemma 7 (Freshness). *If* f_1, f_2 *and* f_3 *have finite support and* f_3 *satisfies the FCB, then assuming* $(t, r) \in rec_{f_1 f_2 f_3}$ *and* $a \# (f_1, f_2, f_3, t)$ *implies* $a \# r$.

Proof. By the induction principle given in (13); non-routine is the lambda-case. In this case, say with the instantiations $(\mathrm{Lam}\, a'\, t)$, we have that $a' \# (f_1, f_2, f_3)$. We further have that $a \# (f_1, f_2, f_3, \mathrm{Lam}\, a'\, t)$ and have to show that $a \# f_3\, a'\, t\, r$. In case that $a = a'$, we know from the FCB, there exists an a'' such that $a'' \# f_3$ and $\forall t\, r.\, a'' \# f_3\, a''\, t\, r$. Using (10) we apply the swapping $(a\, a'')$ to both sides of our goal which gives $a'' \# ((a\, a'') {\bullet} f_3)\, a''\, ((a\, a'') {\bullet} t)\, ((a\, a'') {\bullet} r)$. Since $a \# f_3$ and $a'' \# f_3$ we have by (11) that $(a\, a'') {\bullet} f_3 = f_3$ and hence we are done. In case $a \neq a'$ we can infer from $a \# (f_1, f_2, f_3, \mathrm{Lam}\, a'\, t)$ that $a \# (f_1, f_2, f_3, t)$ holds and thus apply the induction hypothesis. □

Now we can show the crucial lemma about $rec_{f_1 f_2 f_3}$ being a "function".

Lemma 8 (Uniqueness). *If* f_1, f_2 *and* f_3 *have finite support and* f_3 *satisfies the FCB, then* $(t, r) \in rec_{f_1 f_2 f_3}$ *and* $(t, r') \in rec_{f_1 f_2 f_3}$ *implies that* $r = r'$.

Proof. By the induction principle given in (13); again the only non-routine case is the lambda-case. By assumption we know that $(\mathrm{Lam}\, a\, t, f_3\, a\, t\, r) \in rec_{f_1 f_2 f_3}$ from which we can infer that $a \# (f_1, f_2, f_3)$ and $(t, r) \in rec_{f_1 f_2 f_3}$; the induction hypothesis states that for all r', $(t, r') \in rec_{f_1 f_2 f_3}$ implies $r = r'$. Using the second assumption $(\mathrm{Lam}\, b\, t', r') \in rec_{f_1 f_2 f_3}$ we need to show that $f_3\, a\, t\, r = f_3\, b\, t'\, r'$ holds for all $\mathrm{Lam}\, b\, t'$ such that $b \# (f_1, f_2, f_3)$ and $\mathrm{Lam}\, a\, t = \mathrm{Lam}\, b\, t'$. The latter implies by (9) that either

$$(a = b \wedge t = t') \ \text{ or } \ (a \neq b \wedge t = (a\, b) {\bullet} t' \wedge a \# t')\,.$$

The first case is routine because by the induction hypothesis we can infer that $r = r'$. In the second case we have $((a\, b) {\bullet} t, r') \in rec_{f_1 f_2 f_3}$ and by Lem. 6 also that $(t, (a\, b) {\bullet} r') \in rec_{f_1 f_2 f_3}$ (where we also use (11) and the facts $a \# (f_1, f_2, f_3)$ and $b \# (f_1, f_2, f_3)$). By induction hypothesis we can therefore infer that $r = (a\, b) {\bullet} r'$. Hence we have to show that $f_3\, a\, ((a\, b) {\bullet} t')\, ((a\, b) {\bullet} r') = f_3\, b\, t'\, r'$ holds.

Since we know that $a \# t'$ and $a \# (f_1, f_2, f_3)$, we can use $(t', r') \in rec_{f_1 f_2 f_3}$ and Lem. 7 to show that $a \# r'$ holds. With this and the facts that $a \neq b$, $a \# t'$ and $a \# f_3$, we can infer that $a \# (f_3\, b\, t'\, r')$ (the latter is because (f_3, b, t', r') supports $(f_3\, b\, t'\, r')$ and therefore $supp(f_3\, b\, t'\, r') \subseteq (f_3, b, t', r')$).

We now show that also $b \mathrel{\#} (f_3 \, b \, t' \, r')$. From the FCB we know that there exists a b' such that $b' \mathrel{\#} f_3$ and $\forall t \, r. \, b' \mathrel{\#} f_3 \, b' \, t \, r$ holds. If $b = b'$ we are done; otherwise we use (10) and apply the swapping $(b \, b')$ to both sides of $b \mathrel{\#} (f_3 \, b \, t' \, r')$ which gives $b' \mathrel{\#} ((b \, b') \bullet f_3) \, b' \, ((b \, b') \bullet t') \, ((b \, b') \bullet r')$. Since $b \mathrel{\#} f_3$ and $b' \mathrel{\#} f_3$ we have by (11) that $(b \, b') \bullet f_3 = f_3$ and hence we are done.

Knowing that $a \mathrel{\#} (f_3 \, b \, t' \, r')$ and $b \mathrel{\#} (f_3 \, b \, t' \, r')$ hold, we can infer by (11) that $(a \, b) \bullet f_3 \, b \, t' \, r' = f_3 \, b \, t' \, r'$. The left-hand side of this equation is equal to $f_3 \, a \, ((a \, b) \bullet t') \, ((a \, b) \bullet r')$ which is what we had to show. $\qquad\square$

To prove our theorem about structural recursion we define $rfun_{f_1 f_2 f_3} \, t$ to be the unique r so that $(t, r) \in rec_{f_1 f_2 f_3}$. This is a standard construction in HOL-based theorem provers. The characteristic equations for $rfun_{f_1 f_2 f_3}$ are given by how the relation $rec_{f_1 f_2 f_3}$ is defined.

4 Examples

We are now going to give examples defining three functions by recursion over the structure of the nominal datatype lam. We use the functions:

$$sz_1 = \lambda a. \, 1$$
$$sz_2 = \lambda r_1 \, r_2. \, 1 + (\mathbf{max} \, r_1 \, r_2)$$
$$sz_3 = \lambda a \, r. \, 1 + r$$

$$frees_1 = \lambda a. \, \{a\}$$
$$frees_2 = \lambda \_ \_ r_1 \, r_2. \, r_1 \cup r_2$$
$$frees_3 = \lambda a \_ r. \, r - \{a\}$$

$$subst_1 \, b \, t' = \lambda a. \, \mathbf{if} \, a = b \, \mathbf{then} \, t' \, \mathbf{else} \, (\mathrm{Var} \, a)$$
$$subst_2 \, b \, t' = \lambda \_ \_ r_1 \, r_2. \, \mathrm{App} \, r_1 \, r_2$$
$$subst_3 \, b \, t' = \lambda a \_ r. \, \mathrm{Lam} \, a \, r$$

To verify the precondition for the function sz we need to define $\pi \bullet n = n$ as the permutation action over natural numbers. This definition implies that nat is a permutation type; this also implies that the support of sz_1, sz_2 and sz_3 is the empty set. Next we need to show that the FCB-condition, namely $\exists a. \, a \mathrel{\#} sz_3 \wedge \forall t' \, r. \, a \mathrel{\#} sz_3 \, a \, r$, holds. For this we can chose any atom a, because sz_3 has empty support and $sz_3 \, a \, r$ is a natural number and so has also empty support.

In order to define the function for the set of free names of a lambda-term in the nominal datatype package, we need to restrict the co-domain of frees to finite sets. This is because finite sets, as opposed to arbitrary sets, have much better properties w.r.t. the notion of support. In addition finite sets of names are permutation types. We can verify that $frees_n$ for $n = 1, 2, 3$ has empty support using our heuristic and the fact that the HOL-functions $\lambda x \, y. \, x \cup y$ and $\lambda x \, y. \, x - y$ have empty support. To verify the FCB-condition, namely $\exists a. \, a \mathrel{\#} frees_3 \wedge \forall t' \, r. \, a \mathrel{\#} frees_3 \, a \, r$, holds. For this we can chose any atom a, because $frees_3$ has empty support; next we have to verify that $\forall r. \, a \mathrel{\#} r - \{a\}$ holds, or equivalently $\forall r.\ a \notin supp(r-\{a\})$. Since we restricted the co-domain of **frees** to finite sets, we know that $r-\{a\}$ is finite for all r and further that $supp(r-\{a\}) = r-\{a\}$. Thus we are done.

For the substitution function we find that $supp(b,t')$ *supports* $\mathtt{subst}_n\,b\,t'$ for $n = 1,2,3$. The set $supp(b,t')$ is finite, because **name** and **lam** are finitely supported permutation types. The FCB-condition of $\mathtt{subst}_3$ holds for all atoms c with $c\ \#\ (b,t')$. Because $supp(b,t')$ *supports* $\mathtt{subst}_n\,b\,t'$, the preconditions of the recursion-combinator in the lambda-case simplify to $a\ \#\ (b,t')$ and thus we obtain the characteristic equation

$$\mathtt{subst}\,b\,t'\,(\mathtt{Lam}\,a\,t) = \mathtt{Lam}\,a\,(\mathtt{subst}\,b\,t'\,t)$$

with the side-conditions $a \neq b$ and $a\ \#\ t'$, as expected.

The "functions" bn and ist from the Introduction do not satisfy the FCB. In case of bn it is never true that $a\ \#\ r \cup \{a\}$, and in case of ist there does not exists an a such that for all t we have that $a\ \#\ \{t\}$ holds—it will fail for example for $t = \mathtt{Var}\,a$.

5   General Case

The nominal datatype package supports the declaration of more than one atom type and allows term-constructors to have more than one binder. The notions of support and freshness (see Def. 3) have in the implementation already polymorphic type to take several atom types into account. For the recursion combinator we have to make sure that the function f_i of the characteristic equations have finite support with respect to every atom type that occurs in binding position. By binding position we mean the types occurring inside the «...» that are used in a nominal datatype declaration. For example, given the term-constructor C with the type declaration

$$C \text{ "«atm}_1\text{» ... «atm}_n\text{» } \alpha\text{"}$$

then we have to consider all atom types $\mathtt{atm}_1 \ldots \mathtt{atm}_n$.

Similarly the FCB needs to be generalised for all atom types that occur in binding position. To explain the generalisations let us consider first the term-constructor **Let** "«name» lam" "lam". The type indicates that if we write, say **Let** $a\,t_1\,t_2$, then the scope of the binder a is t_1. Hence the characteristic equation for **Let** is

$$rfun_{f_1\,f_2\,f_3\,f_4}\,(\mathtt{Let}\,a\,t_1\,t_2) = f_4\,a\,t_1\,t_2\,(rfun_{f_1\,f_2\,f_3\,f_4}\,t_1)\,(rfun_{f_1\,f_2\,f_3\,f_4}\,t_2)$$
$$provided\ a\ \#\ (f_1, f_2, f_3, f_4, t_2)$$

As can be seen, the binder a needs to be fresh for f_1, f_2, f_3 and f_4 (like in the lambda-case), but also for t_2. The general rule is that a needs to be fresh for all terms that are *not* in its scope—in this example, this applies only to t_2. The FCB for **Let** is

$$\exists a. \, a \; \# \; f_4 \; \wedge \; \forall t_1 \, t_2 \, r_1 \, r_2. \, a \; \# \; t_2 \Rightarrow a \; \# \; f_4 \, a \, t_1 \, t_2 \, r_1 \, r_2$$

where in the second conjunct we may assume that a is fresh for all terms not in its scope.

Albeit not yet supported by the current version of the nominal datatype package, even more interesting is the term-constructor Letrec "«name»(lam × «name»lam)" where we have two binders. The characteristic equation for Letrec is

$$rfun_{f_1 \, f_2 \, f_3 \, f_4 \, f_5} \, (\mathtt{Letrec} \, a \, t_1 \, b \, t_2) = f_5 \, a \, t_1 \, b \, t_2 \, (rfun_{f_1 \, .. \, f_5} \, t_1) \, (rfun_{f_1 \, .. \, f_5} \, t_2)$$

$$provided \; a \; \# \; (f_1, f_2, f_3, f_4, f_5)$$

$$and \; b \; \# \; (f_1, f_2, f_3, f_4, f_5, t_1)$$

$$and \; a \neq b$$

where we need to have $b \; \# \; t_1$ since t_1 is not in the scope of the binder b. However, in case we have more than one binder in a term-constructor then we further need to add constraints that make sure every binder is distinct. With these generalisations the proofs we have given in Sec. 3 scale to all nominal datatypes.

6   Conclusion

We presented a structural recursion combinator for nominal datatypes. The details were given for the nominal datatype lam; we mentioned briefly the general case—further details are given in [9]. For the presentation we adapted the clever proof given also in [9]. The main difference is that we gave a direct proof for nominal datatypes and did not use auxiliary constructions. There are also a number of other differences: for example Pitts does not need to prove Lem. 5, which is however necessary in Isabelle/HOL, because one cannot conveniently introduce the type of finitely supported functions. In comparison with the formalisation by Norrish, our proof is much shorter—only about 150 lines of readable Isar-code compared to approximately 600 dense lines of HOL4-code. Our use of the heuristic that solves proof obligations to do with finite support made it tractable to automate our proof. The earlier formalisation were far too difficult for such an automation. This work removes the painful obstacle when defining functions over the structure of nominal datatypes using earlier versions of the nominal datatype package. In the future we are aiming at automating the process of verifying the FCB and finite support-conditions required in the recursion combinator.

Acknowledgements. We are very grateful to Andrew Pitts and Michael Norrish for the many discussions with them on the subject of the paper. The first author is supported by a fellowship from the Alexander-von-Humboldt foundation and by a Emmy-Noether fellowship from the German Research Council. The second author received funding via the BMBF project Verisoft.

512   C. Urban and S. Berghofer

References

1. H. Barendregt. *The Lambda Calculus: Its Syntax and Semantics*, volume 103 of *Studies in Logic and the Foundations of Mathematics*. North-Holland, 1981.
2. S. Berghofer and M. Wenzel. Inductive Datatypes in HOL - Lessons Learned in Formal-Logic Engineering. In *Proc. of the 12th International Conference Theorem Proving in Higher Order Logics (TPHOLs)*, number 1690 in LNCS, pages 19–36, 1999.
3. M. J. Gabbay and A. M. Pitts. A New Approach to Abstract Syntax Involving Binders. In *Logic in Computer Science*, pages 214–224. IEEE Computer Society Press, 1999.
4. M. Gordon. From LCF to HOL: a short history. In G. Plotkin, C. P. Stirling, and M. Tofte, editors, *Proof, Language, and Interaction*, pages 169–186. MIT Press, 2000.
5. P. Homeier. A Design Structure for Higher Order Quotients. In *Proc. of the 18th International Conference on Theorem Proving in Higher Order Logics (TPHOLs)*, volume 3603 of *LNCS*, pages 130–146, 2005.
6. T. Melham. Automating Recursive Type Definitions in Higher Order Logic. In G. Birtwistle and P. A. Subrahmanyam, editors, *Current Trends in Hardware Verification and Automated Theorem Proving*, pages 341–386. Springer-Verlag, 1989.
7. A. M. Pitts. Nominal Logic, A First Order Theory of Names and Binding. *Information and Computation*, 186:165–193, 2003.
8. A. M. Pitts. Alpha-Structural Recursion and Induction (Extended Abstract). In *Proc. of the 18th International Conference on Theorem Proving in Higher Order Logics (TPHOLs)*, volume 3603 of *LNCS*, pages 17–34, 2005.
9. A. M. Pitts. Alpha-Structural Recursion and Induction. *Journal of the ACM*, 200X. to appear.
10. C. Urban and M. Norrish. A Formal Treatment of the Barendregt Variable Convention in Rule Inductions. In *Proc. of the 3rd International ACM Workshop on Mechanized Reasoning about Languages with Variable Binding and Names*, pages 25–32, 2005.
11. C. Urban and C. Tasson. Nominal Techniques in Isabelle/HOL. In *Proc. of the 20th International Conference on Automated Deduction (CADE)*, volume 3632 of *LNCS*, pages 38–53, 2005.
12. M. Wenzel. *Using Axiomatic Type Classes in Isabelle*. Manual in the Isabelle distribution.

Decidability and Undecidability Results for Nelson-Oppen and Rewrite-Based Decision Procedures*

Maria Paola Bonacina[1], Silvio Ghilardi[2], Enrica Nicolini[3], Silvio Ranise[2,4],
and Daniele Zucchelli[2,4]

[1] Dipartimento di Informatica, Università degli Studi di Verona, Italia
[2] Dipartimento di Informatica, Università degli Studi di Milano, Italia
[3] Dipartimento di Matematica, Università degli Studi di Milano, Italia
[4] LORIA & INRIA-Lorraine, Nancy, France

Abstract. In the context of combinations of theories with disjoint signatures, we classify the component theories according to the decidability of constraint satisfiability problems in arbitrary and in infinite models, respectively. We exhibit a theory T_1 such that satisfiability is decidable, but satisfiability in infinite models is undecidable. It follows that satisfiability in $T_1 \cup T_2$ is undecidable, whenever T_2 has only infinite models, even if signatures are disjoint and satisfiability in T_2 is decidable.

In the second part of the paper we strengthen the Nelson-Oppen decidability transfer result, by showing that it applies to theories over disjoint signatures, whose satisfiability problem, in either arbitrary or infinite models, is decidable. We show that this result covers decision procedures based on rewriting, complementing recent work on combination of theories in the rewrite-based approach to satisfiability.

1   Introduction

In many applications of automated reasoning (for instance to software verification), it is important to decide the satisfiability of conjunctions of literals modulo a given background theory; quite often, it is also necessary to combine modularly such decision procedures to unions of background theories. If such theories have disjoint signatures and are stably infinite (which means that we can safely restrict to infinite models to decide satisfiability of literals), then the well-known Nelson-Oppen combination schema provides a combination transfer result. Recently, relaxing the stably infiniteness requirement has received a lot of attention in order to design combination schemas handling theories that are not stably-infinite. For instance,[1] Tinelli and Zarba [22] have shown how to combine an arbitrary theory with one satisfying requirements which are stronger than

---

* The full version of this paper is available as a Technical Report RI DSI 308-06, Università degli Studi di Milano, at http://homes.dsi.unimi.it/~zucchell/publications/techreport/BoGhiNiRaZu-RI308-06.pdf

[1] For lack of space, we only discuss results that are closely related to ours (see, e.g., [19] for an overview on combination of decision procedures and references).

U. Furbach and N. Shankar (Eds.): IJCAR 2006, LNAI 4130, pp. 513–527, 2006.

stable-infiniteness. Thus, contrary to the combination schema by Nelson-Oppen [14], such a schema is asymmetric in the sense that the requirements on the component theories are not the same.

In this paper, we consider combinations of theories whose signatures are disjoint and classify the component theories according to the decidability of their satisfiability problems in arbitrary and in infinite models. Assume that the satisfiability problem in a theory T_1 is decidable in arbitrary models but not in infinite models. Then, any combination of such a T_1 with a theory T_2 that does not have finite models yields an undecidable satisfiability problem. This holds even if T_1 and T_2 have disjoint signatures and even if satisfiability in T_2 is decidable in arbitrary models. As a consequence of this observation, we obtain the first (undecidability) result of the paper, by exhibiting a theory such that the satisfiability problem is decidable, whereas the satisfiability problem in infinite models is undecidable.

The second result of the paper is related to decision procedures based on rewriting. Armando et al [1] recently showed how to use a rewrite-based inference system to obtain decision procedures for (disjoint) unions of *variable-inactive* theories, when there exist rewrite-based decision procedures for the component theories. Here, we explain the relationship between variable-inactivity and stable-infiniteness. We show that if a theory is not stably infinite, then the inference system is guaranteed to generate clauses that constrain the cardinality of its models, so that the theory is not variable-inactive. This result has two applications: first, it complements the combination schema of [1] for (disjoint) unions of theories that have a rewrite-based satisfiability procedures. Second, it suggests a simple way to combine the rewrite-based approach with constraint-solving techniques that check satisfiability in finite models.

2   Preliminaries

A *signature* Σ is an (at most countable) set of functions and predicate symbols, each of them endowed with the corresponding arity. We assume the binary equality predicate symbol '=' to be always present in any signature Σ. The signature obtained from Σ by the addition of a set of new constants (that is, 0-ary function symbols) $\mathcal{K}$ is denoted by $\Sigma \cup \mathcal{K}$ or by $\Sigma^{\mathcal{K}}$; when the set of constants is finite, we use letters $\underline{a}, \underline{b}, \underline{c}$, etc. in place of $\mathcal{K}$. We have the usual notions of Σ-*term*, (full first order) -*formula*, -*atom*, -*literal*, -*clause*, -*positive clause*, etc.: e.g., an atom is an atomic formula, a literal is an atom or the negation of an atom, a clause is a multiset of literals, a positive clause is a multiset of atoms, etc. Abusing notation, we write a clause C either as the disjunction of its literals or as a sequent $\Delta_1 \Rightarrow \Delta_2$, meaning that Δ_1 (resp. Δ_2) contains the negative (resp. positive) literals of C. Terms, literals, clauses and formulæ are called *ground* whenever variables do not appear. Formulæ without free variables are called *sentences*. The universal (resp. existential) closure of a formula ϕ is the sentence obtained from ϕ by adding a prefix of universal (resp. existential) quantifiers binding all variables occurring free in ϕ. A Σ-*theory* T is a set of sentences (called the axioms of T) in the signature Σ. If T is finite, the theory is said to be finitely axiomatized. A *universal* theory is a theory whose axioms are universal closures of quantifier-free formulae.

From the semantic side, we have the standard notion of a Σ-*structure* $\mathcal{A}$: this is a support set endowed with an arity-matching interpretation of the function and predicate symbols from Σ. We use $f^{\mathcal{A}}$ (resp. $P^{\mathcal{A}}$) to denote the interpretation of the function symbol f (resp. predicate symbol P) in the structure $\mathcal{A}$. The support set of a structure $\mathcal{A}$ is indicated by the notation $|\mathcal{A}|$. We say that $\mathcal{A}$ is *finite* when there exists an integer $N > 0$ such that the cardinality of $|\mathcal{A}|$ is less than N; if such an integer does not exist, we say that $\mathcal{A}$ is *infinite*. The *truth* of a Σ-formula in $\mathcal{A}$ is defined in the standard way (so that truth of a formula is equivalent to truth of its *universal* closure). A formula ϕ is *satisfiable* in $\mathcal{A}$ iff its *existential* closure is true in $\mathcal{A}$.

A Σ-structure $\mathcal{A}$ is a *model* of a Σ-theory T (in symbols $\mathcal{A} \models T$) iff all axioms of T are true in $\mathcal{A}$. For models of a Σ-theory T we shall use the letters $\mathcal{M}, \mathcal{N}, \ldots$ to distinguish them from arbitrary Σ-structures. If ϕ is a formula, $T \models \phi$ ('ϕ *is a logical consequence of* T') means that ϕ is true in any model of T. A Σ-theory T is *complete* iff for every Σ-sentence ϕ, either ϕ or $\neg\phi$ is a logical consequence of T; T is *consistent* iff it has a model.

A Σ-*constraint* in a signature Σ is a finite set of ground $\Sigma^{\underline{a}}$-literals (where $\underline{a}$ is a finite set of new free constants). The *constraint satisfiability problem* for a Σ-theory T is the problem of deciding whether a Σ-constraint is satisfiable in a model of T: if this problem is decidable, we say that the theory T is $\exists$-*decidable*. Notice that, equivalently, T is $\exists$-decidable iff it is decidable whether a universal Σ-formula is entailed by the axioms of T.

3 Satisfiability in Infinite Models

Let T_1 and T_2 be theories such that the signature Σ_1 of T_1 is disjoint from the signature Σ_2 of T_2, i.e., $\Sigma_1 \cap \Sigma_2$ contains only the equality symbol. We consider the decidability of the constraint satisfiability problem of the theory $T_1 \cup T_2$. We are especially interested in establishing the relationships between the decidability of the constraint satisfiability problems in the component theories T_1 and T_2, and the decidability of the constraint satisfiability problem in $T_1 \cup T_2$.

3.1 Undecidability Result

Let us recall two simple facts. First, combined word problems are decidable whenever the word problems for the component theories are decidable [18]. Second, it is commonly believed that combining word problems is more difficult than combining constraint satisfiability problems - the reason is that the algorithms to be combined are less powerful, as they can handle only constraints formed by a single negative literal. From these two observations, one may conjecture that the decidability of the constraint satisfiability problem in $T_1 \cup T_2$ always follows from the decidability of the constraint satisfiability problem in T_1 and T_2. Contrary to expectation, all known combination results for the decidability of the constraint satisfiability problems in unions of theories (such as [14,22]) assume that the component theories satisfy certain requirements. The key observation is that such requirements are related to the satisfiability of constraints in infinite models of a component theory. For example, the Nelson-Oppen combination schema [14] requires the component theories to be stably-infinite. A Σ-theory T is *stably infinite* iff every Σ-constraint satisfiable in a model of T is satisfiable in an infinite model of T. Motivated by this observation, we introduce the following definition.

Definition 3.1. *Let T be a Σ-theory; we say that T is $\exists_\infty$-decidable iff it is $\exists$-decidable and moreover it is decidable whether any Σ-constraint Γ is satisfiable in some* infinite *model of T.*

From the definition, it is trivially seen that $\exists$-decidability is equivalent to $\exists_\infty$-decidability in the case of stably infinite theories. To illustrate the interest of studying the decidability of satisfiability in the infinite models of a theory, we state the following

Theorem 3.1. *Let T_i be a Σ_i-theory (for $i = 1, 2$) and let the signatures Σ_1, Σ_2 be disjoint. If T_1 is $\exists$-decidable but it is not $\exists_\infty$-decidable and if T_2 is consistent, $\exists$-decidable but does not admit finite models, then the constraint satisfiability for $T_1 \cup T_2$ is undecidable.*

Proof. We simply show that a Σ_1-constraint Γ is $T_1 \cup T_2$-satisfiable iff it is satisfiable in an infinite model of T_1. One side is obvious; for the other side, pick infinite models $\mathcal{M}_1$ of $T_1 \cup \Gamma$ and $\mathcal{M}_2$ of T_2 (the latter exists by consistency of T_2). By Löwhenheim-Skolem theorem, we can assume that both models are countable, i.e. that they have the same support (up to isomorphism). But then, we can simply put together the interpretations of functions and predicate symbols and get a model of $T_1 \cup T_2 \cup \Gamma$.   □

We notice that there are many theories which are $\exists$-decidable and have only infinite models. One such theory is Presburger Arithmetic, another one is the theory of acyclic lists [17]. More interestingly, one could ask the following

   QUESTION 1: *Are there $\exists$-decidable theories that are not $\exists_\infty$-decidable?*

If the answer is positive, then Theorem 3.1 implies that *there exist theories which are $\exists$-decidable and whose union is not $\exists$-decidable*. In Section 4, we exhibit some theories that are $\exists$-decidable but not $\exists_\infty$-decidable, thereby answering QUESTION 1 positively.

3.2 Decidability Result

Notwithstanding the negative result implied by Theorem 3.1, we observe that when both T_1 and T_2 are $\exists_\infty$-decidable, we are close to get the decidability of constraint satisfiability in $T_1 \cup T_2$. To understand why, recall the following well-known fact.

Lemma 3.1. *Let Λ be a set of first-order sentences. If Λ does not admit infinite models, then there must exist an integer $N > 0$ such that, for each model $\mathcal{M}$ of Λ, the cardinality of the support set of $\mathcal{M}$ is bounded by N.*

For a proof, the interested reader is referred to any introductory textbook about model theory (see, e.g., [23]). The key idea is to apply compactness to infinitely many 'at-least-n-elements' constraints (these are the constraints expressed by the formulæ $\exists x_1, \ldots, x_n \bigwedge_{i \neq j} x_i \neq x_j$). It is interesting to notice that the above bound on the cardinality of finite models can be effectively computed for $\exists$-decidable theories:

Lemma 3.2. *Let T be an $\exists$-decidable Σ-theory; whenever it happens[2] that a given Σ-constraint Γ is not satisfiable in an infinite model, one can compute a natural number N such that all models of $T \cup \Gamma$ have cardinality at most N.*

Proof. For $h = 2, 3, \ldots$, add the following set $\delta_h := \{c_i \neq c_j \mid 1 \leq i < j \leq h\}$ of literals to $T \cup \Gamma$, where the constants $c_1, \ldots, c_h$ are fresh.[3] Clearly, if $T \cup \Gamma \cup \delta_h$ is unsatisfiable, then we get a bound for the cardinality of the models of $T \cup \Gamma$. Since, by Lemma 3.1, such a bound exists, the process eventually terminates.   □

Definition 3.2. *An $\exists_\infty$-decidable Σ-theory T is said to be strongly $\exists_\infty$-decidable iff for any finite Σ-structure $\mathcal{A}$, it is decidable whether $\mathcal{A}$ is a model of T.*

It is not difficult to find strongly $\exists_\infty$-decidable theories. For example, any finitely axiomatizable $\exists_\infty$-decidable Σ-theory with a finite Σ is strongly $\exists_\infty$-decidable, since it is sufficient to check the truth of the axioms for finitely many valuations. Now, we are in the position to state and prove the following modularity property for $\exists_\infty$-decidable theories.

Theorem 3.2. *Let T_i be a strongly $\exists_\infty$-decidable Σ_i-theory (for $i = 1, 2$) such that Σ_1, Σ_2 are finite and disjoint. Then the combined theory $T_1 \cup T_2$ is $\exists$-decidable.[4]*

Proof. Let Γ be a finite set of ground $\Sigma_1 \cup \Sigma_2$-literals containing free constants. By well-known means (see, e.g., [5]), we can obtain an equisatisfiable set $\Gamma_1 \cup \Gamma_2$ such that Γ_i contains only $\Sigma_i^{\underline{a}}$-symbols, for $i = 1, 2$ and for some free constants $\underline{a}$. Let Γ_0 be an *arrangement* of the constants $\underline{a}$, i.e. a finite set of literals such that either $a_i = a_j \in \Gamma_0$ or $a_i \neq a_j \in \Gamma_0$, for $i \neq j$ and $a_i, a_j \in \underline{a}$. Clearly, $\Gamma_1 \cup \Gamma_2$ is satisfiable iff $\Gamma_1 \cup \Gamma_0 \cup \Gamma_2$ is satisfiable for some arrangement Γ_0 of the constants $\underline{a}$. From the fact that theories T_1, T_2 are both $\exists_\infty$-decidable, the following case analysis can be *effectively* performed:

- If $\Gamma_0 \cup \Gamma_i$ is satisfiable in an infinite model of T_i (for both $i = 1, 2$), then $\Gamma_0 \cup \Gamma_1 \cup \Gamma_2$ is satisfiable in an infinite model of $T_1 \cup T_2$ by the standard argument underlying the correctness of the Nelson-Oppen combination schema (see, e.g., [21,12]).

---

[2] There is a subtle point here: Lemma 3.2 applies to all $\exists$-decidable theories, but it is really useful only for $\exists_\infty$-decidable theories, because only for these theories the hypothesis 'Γ in not satisfiable in an infinite model of T' can be effectively checked.

[3] Notice that the literals in δ_h are simply the Skolemization of the 'at-least-h-elements' constraint.

[4] This result can be easily generalized to the combination of $n > 2$ theories.

– If $\Gamma_0 \cup \Gamma_i$ is unsatisfiable in any infinite model of T_i (for either $i = 1$ or $i = 2$), then (by Lemma 3.2) we can effectively compute an integer $N > 0$ such that each model $\mathcal{M}$ of $T \cup \Gamma_i \cup \Gamma_0$ has cardinality less than N. Hence, it is sufficient to exhaustively search through $\Sigma_1 \cup \Sigma_2 \cup \underline{a}$-structures up to cardinality N. The number of these structures is finite because Σ_1 and Σ_2 are finite and, by Definition 3.2, it is possible to effectively check whether each such a structure is a model of T_1 and T_2, and hence also of $T_1 \cup T_2 \cup \Gamma_0 \cup \Gamma_1 \cup \Gamma_2$. If a model is found, the procedure returns 'satisfiable', otherwise another arrangement Γ_0 (if any) is tried.   □

Since a stably infinite theory is $\exists$-decidable if and only if it is $\exists_\infty$-decidable, it is clear that Theorem 3.2 substantially generalizes Nelson-Oppen result (the further requirement of Definition 3.2 being only a technical condition which is usually fulfilled). Theorem 3.2 raises the following

> QUESTION 2: Is there a practical sufficient condition for a theory to be strongly $\exists_\infty$-decidable?

Clearly, stably infinite $\exists$-decidable theories are $\exists_\infty$-decidable. More interesting examples are given in Section 5, where we will show that, whenever a finitely axiomatized theory T admits a rewrite-based decision procedure for its constraint satisfiability problem [2,1], T is not only $\exists$-decidable but also strongly $\exists_\infty$-decidable.

4 Undecidability

In this section, we give an affirmative answer to QUESTION 1 by defining some $\exists$-decidable theories that are not $\exists_\infty$-decidable. Let Σ_{TM_∞} be the signature containing (in addition to the equality predicate) the following (infinite) set of propositional letters $\{P_{(e,n)} \mid e, n \in \mathbb{N}\}$. Consider the propositional letter $P_{(e,n)}$: we regard e as the index (i.e. the code) of a Turing Machine and n as the input to the Turing machine identified by e (this coding is possible because of basic results about Turing machines, see, e.g., [16]). We indicate by $k : \mathbb{N} \times \mathbb{N} \to \mathbb{N} \cup \{\infty\}$ the (non-computable) function associating to each pair (e, n) the number $k(e, n)$ of computation steps of the Turing Machine e on the input n. We write $k(e, n) = \infty$ when the computation does not halt. The axioms of the theory TM_∞ are the universal closures of the following formulæ:

$$P_{(e,n)} \to \bigvee_{i<j\leq m} x_i = x_j, \qquad \text{if } k(e,n) < m. \tag{1}$$

Two observations are in order. First, the property "being an axiom of TM_∞" is decidable, because the ternary predicate $k(e, n) < m$ is recursive. Indeed, it is sufficient to run the Turing Machine e on input n and wait at most m computation steps to verify whether e halts. Second, the consequent of implication (1) is an *at-most cardinality constraint*, i.e. it is a formula of the form

$$\bigvee_{i\neq j} x_i = x_j \tag{2}$$

where x_i, x_j are (implicitly universally quantified) distinct variables for $i, j = 1, \ldots, n$, which constrain the domain of any model to contain at most n elements. Thus, axioms of the form (1) tells us that if $P_{(e,n)}$ holds and the Turing Machine e halts in at most m steps, then the cardinality of the domains of a model is bounded by m. These properties allow us to state and prove the following key result:

Proposition 4.1. *The theory* TM_∞ *is* $\exists$-*decidable but it is not* $\exists_\infty$-*decidable.*

Proof. To show that the theory is $\exists$-decidable, consider a constraint Γ over the signature $\Sigma^a_{TM_\infty}$. First, guess an arrangement Γ_0 for the constants $\underline{a}$ and check the set of equations and inequations from $\Gamma \cup \Gamma_0$ for consistency in the pure theory of equality. Then, if the satisfiability check succeeds, Γ_0 explicitly gives the minimum cardinality m for $\Gamma \cup \Gamma_0$ to be satisfied. Clearly, $\Gamma \cup \Gamma_0$ is unsatisfiable if it contains both $P_{(e,n)}$ and $\neg P_{(e,n)}$. If this is not the case, we still have to consider the constraints represented by axiom (1), which states that if a literal of the kind $P_{(e,n)}$ is in a Σ_{TM_∞}-constraint, such a constraint can be only satisfied in a model whose cardinality is at most $k(e, n)$. Thus, if $P_{(e,n)} \in \Gamma \cup \Gamma_0$, we only need to check that $m \leq k(e, n)$, which can be effectively done since the ternary predicate $k(e, n) < m$ is recursive.

To see that TM_∞ is not $\exists_\infty$-decidable, notice that the constraint $\{P_{(e,n)}\}$ is TM_∞-satisfiable in an infinite structure iff $k(e, n) = \infty$. In turn, this is equivalent to check whether the computation of the Turing Machine e on the input n does not terminate, which is obviously undecidable, being the complement of the Halting problem. $\qquad\qquad\square$

The theory TM_∞ is defined on an infinite signature. However, it is possible to introduce a universal theory $TM_{\forall\omega}$ over a finite signature, with the same characteristics as TM_∞ as far as decidability in finite and infinite models is concerned. Since the proof that such theory is $\exists$-decidable but not $\exists_\infty$-decidable is similar to that of Proposition 4.1, modulo some technical details, we report it in the full TR version of the present paper. Thus, we are ready to state our first main result:

Theorem 4.1. *There exist* $\exists$-*decidable universal theories over finite and disjoint signatures, whose union is not* $\exists$-*decidable.*

5   Decidability

The answer to *QUESTION 2* rests on showing that (under suitable assumptions) rewrite-based methods give practical sufficient conditions for a theory to be strongly $\exists_\infty$-decidable. First, we need to introduce some technical definitions. In Section 5.1, we recall some basic notions underlying the superposition calculus [15] and we introduce superposition modules as suitable abstractions for the subsequent technical development. Then, in Section 5.2, we introduce the notion of invariant superposition modules and, in Section 5.3, we show that they can generate an "at most" cardinality constraint (cf. (2) in Section 4) whenever a theory does not admit infinite models. Last, in Section 5.4, we describe how to combine rewrite-based procedures [1,2] with Satisfiability Modulo Theory (SMT) tools, such as [9,3,10,11], in order to obtain automatic methods to solve constraint satisfiability problems involving theories admitting only finite models (e.g., enumerated data-types).

5.1   Superposition Calculi and Superposition Modules

From now on, we consider only universal, finitely axiomatized theories, whose signatures are finite. Without loss of generality, we may assume that signatures contain only function symbols (see, e.g., [15]). A fundamental assumption of superposition-based inference systems [15] is that the universe of terms is ordered by a *reduction ordering*. A reduction ordering on terms can be extended to literals and clauses by using standard techniques. The most commonly used orderings are the *Knuth-Bendix ordering (KBO)* and the *lexicographic path ordering (LPO)*. Definitions, results, and references on orderings can be found in, e.g., [4]. Since we have to deal with constraints involving finitely (but arbitrarily) many new constants, we consider a countable set[5] $\mathcal{K}$ disjoint from Σ to form the expanded signature $\Sigma^{\mathcal{K}}$. We collect all needed data in the following:

Definition 5.1 (Suitable Ordering Triple). *A* suitable ordering triple *is a triple* $(\Sigma, \mathcal{K}, \succ)$ *where: (a)* Σ *is a finite signature; (b)* $\mathcal{K} := \{c_1, c_2, c_3, \ldots\}$ *is a countably infinite set of constant symbols such that* Σ *and* $\mathcal{K}$ *are disjoint; (c)* $\succ$ *is a reduction ordering over* $\Sigma^{\mathcal{K}}$*-terms satisfying the following conditions:*

(i) $\succ$ *is total on ground* $\Sigma^{\mathcal{K}}$*-terms;*
(ii)   *for every ground* $\Sigma^{\mathcal{K}}$*-term* t *with root symbol* $f \in \Sigma$ *and for every* $c_i \in \mathcal{K}$, *we have* $t \succ c_i$;
(iii)   *for* $c_i, c_j \in \mathcal{K}$, *we have* $c_i \succ c_j$ *iff* $i > j$.

The above conditions on the reduction ordering are similar to those adopted in [2,1] to build rewrite-based decision procedures for the constraint satisfiability problem in theories of data structures, fragments of integer arithmetic, and their combinations. It is indeed very easy and natural to produce suitable ordering triples: for instance, if an LPO is adopted, it is sufficient to take a total precedence $>_p$ satisfying the condition $f >_p c_i >_p c_j$, for $f \in \Sigma$, $c_i \in \mathcal{K}$, $c_j \in \mathcal{K}$ and $i > j$.

Another key characteristic of a rewrite-based inference system is the possibility of associating a model to the set of derived clauses, defined by building incrementally a convergent term rewriting system.

Let $(\Sigma, \mathcal{K}, \succ)$ be a suitable ordering triple and let S be a set of $\Sigma^{\mathcal{K}}$-clauses not containing the empty clause. The set $gr(S)$ contains all ground $\Sigma^{\mathcal{K}}$-clauses that are instances of clauses in S. By transfinite induction on $C \in gr(S)$, we simultaneously define $Gen(C)$ and the ground rewrite system R_C as follows:

---

[5] Usual results on orderings can be extended to infinite signatures, see [13]; notice however that one can keep the signature $\Sigma^{\mathcal{K}}$ finite, by coding c_i as $s^i(0)$ (for new symbols $s, 0$), like e.g. in [8].

(a) $R_C := \bigcup_{D \in gr(S), C \succ D} Gen(D)$;

(b) $Gen(C) := \{l \to r\}$ in case C is of the kind $\Delta_1 \Rightarrow l = r, \Delta_2$ and the following conditions are satisfied:

1. $R_C \not\models \Delta_1 \Rightarrow \Delta_2$, i.e. (i) for each $l = r \in \Delta_1$, l and r have the same normal form with respect to R_C (in symbols, $l \downarrow_{R_C} r$) and (ii) for each $s = t \in \Delta_2$, $s \not\downarrow_{R_C} t$;

2. $l \succ r$, $l \succ u$ (for all u occurring in Δ_1), $\{l, r\} \succ^{ms} \{u, v\}$, for every equation $u = v$ occurring in Δ_2, where $\succ^{ms}$ is the multi-set extension [4] of $\succ$;

3. l is not reducible by $R_{C'}$, and

4. $R_C \not\models r = t'$, for every equation of the kind $l = t'$ occurring in Δ_2;

(c) $Gen(C) := \emptyset$, otherwise.

We say that C is *productive* if $Gen(C) \neq \emptyset$. Finally, let $R_S := \bigcup_{C \in gr(S)} Gen(C)$. Note that R_S is a convergent rewrite system, by conditions 2 and 3 above.

A set of clauses is *saturated* with respect to an inference system, if any clause that can be inferred from S is redundant in S (see, e.g., [7]). In a more abstract treatment, that makes saturation independent of the inference system and only requires a well-founded ordering on proofs, a set of formulæ is *saturated* if it contains all the premises of all normal-form proofs in the theory [6]. For the purposes of this paper, we are interested in a semantic notion of saturation based on model generation.

Definition 5.2. *A set S of $\Sigma^{\mathcal{K}}$-clauses is* model-saturated *iff the rewrite system R_S is a model of S (i.e. the quotient of the Herbrand universe of $\Sigma^{\mathcal{K}}$ modulo R_S-convergence is a model of the universal closures of the clauses in S).*

The following definition of reasoning module is precisely what we need to prove the main technical Lemma 5.2 below.

Definition 5.3 (Superposition Module). *Let $(\Sigma, \mathcal{K}, \succ)$ be a suitable ordering triple. A superposition module $\mathcal{SP}(\Sigma, \mathcal{K}, \succ)$ is a computable function which takes a finite set S_0 of $\Sigma^{\mathcal{K}}$-clauses as input and returns a (possibly infinite) sequence*

$$S_0, S_1, \ldots, S_n, \ldots \tag{3}$$

of finite sets of $\Sigma^{\mathcal{K}}$-clauses, called an S_0-derivation, such that (i) if S_0 is unsatisfiable, then there exists $k \geq 0$ such that the empty clause is in S_k; (ii) if S_0 is satisfiable, then the set

$$S_\infty := \bigcup_{j \geq 0} \bigcap_{i \geq j} S_i$$

of persistent clauses *is model-saturated, and (iii) the sets S_i and S_j are logically equivalent for $(0 \leq i, j \leq \infty)$. We say that $\mathcal{SP}(\Sigma, \mathcal{K}, \succ)$ terminates on the set of $\Sigma^{\mathcal{K}}$-clauses S_0 iff the S_0-derivation (3) is finite.*

Superposition modules are *deterministic*, i.e. there exists just one S_0-derivation starting with a given finite set S_0 of clauses. Any implementation of the superposition calculus [15] together with a fair strategy satisfies Definition 5.3.

5.2   Superposition Modules and Rewrite-Based Decision Procedures

For the proofs below, we need a class of superposition modules which are invariant (in a sense to be made precise) under certain renamings of finitely many constants. Formally, an *n-shifting* (where n is an integer such that $n > 0$) is the operation that applied to a $\Sigma^{\mathcal{K}}$-expression E returns the $\Sigma^{\mathcal{K}}$-expression E^{+n} obtained from E by simultaneously replacing each occurrence of the free constant $c_i \in \mathcal{K}$ by the free constant c_{i+n}, for $i > 0$ (where the word 'expression' may denote a term, a literal, a clause, or a set of clauses). In practice, an n-shifting rearranges the set of free constants occurring in the set of clauses by eliminating the constants $c_1, \ldots, c_n$ that are not in the range of the function $(\cdot)^{+n}$.

Example 5.1. Let us consider the set $S := \{f(c_1, c_4) = c_1, f(f(c_1, c_4), c_4) = c_2\}$ of ground $\Sigma^{\mathcal{K}}$-literals where $\Sigma := \{f\}$ and $\mathcal{K} := \{c_1, c_2, \ldots\}$. Then, we have that $S^{+5} := \{f(c_6, c_9) = c_6, f(f(c_6, c_9), c_9) = c_7\}$.

Definition 5.4 (Invariant Superposition Module). *Let $(\Sigma, \mathcal{K}, \succ)$ be a suitable ordering triple. A superposition module $SP(\Sigma, \mathcal{K}, \succ)$ is invariant iff for every S_0-derivation $S_0, S_1, \ldots, S_j, \ldots$ (with S_0 being a set of $\Sigma^{\mathcal{K}}$-clauses), we have that $(S_0)^{+n}, (S_1)^{+n}, \ldots, (S_j)^{+n}, \ldots$ is an $(S_0)^{+n}$-derivation, for all $n \geq 0$.*

Most of the actual implementations of superposition are *stable under signature extensions* (this is so because they need to handle Skolem symbols) and hence, the behavior of a superposition prover is not affected by any proper extension of the signature and the ordering. The property of producing derivations being invariant under shifting is weaker than stability under signature extensions. As a consequence, any superposition prover can be turned into an invariant superposition module. However, not all possible implementations of the superposition calculus are invariant superposition modules, as we point out in the full TR version of the paper.

Example 5.2. Suppose that in the suitable ordering triple $(\Sigma, \mathcal{K}, \succ)$, the term ordering $\succ$ is an LPO whose precedence satisfies $f >_p c_i >_p c_j$ (for $f \in \Sigma, c_i \in \mathcal{K}, c_j \in \mathcal{K}, i > j$). Let us consider the superposition module given by the standard superposition calculus and let us take again the situation in Example 5.1. The (model-)saturated set output by $SP(\Sigma, \mathcal{K}, \succ)$ when taking S as input is $S_s := \{f(c_1, c_4) = c_1, c_2 = c_1\}$. It is not difficult to see that the set $(S_s)^{+5} := \{f(c_6, c_9) = c_6, c_7 = c_6\}$ is exactly the set that we would obtain as output by the superposition module $SP(\Sigma, \mathcal{K}, \succ)$ when taking as input the set $(S)^{+5}$ (see Example 5.1).

Definition 5.5. *Let $(\Sigma, \mathcal{K}, \succ)$ be a suitable ordering triple. A universal and finitely axiomatized Σ-theory T is $\exists$-superposition-decidable iff there exists an invariant superposition module $SP(\Sigma, \mathcal{K}, \succ)$ that is guaranteed to terminate when taking as input $T \cup \Gamma$, where Γ is a $\Sigma^{\mathcal{K}}$-constraint.*

From the termination results for superposition given in [2,1], it follows that theories such as equality, (possibly cyclic) lists, arrays, and so on are $\exists$-decidable by superposition. According to Definition 5.5, any theory T which is $\exists$-superposition-decidable is $\exists$-decidable. In the following, we show that T is also $\exists_\infty$-decidable, which is the second main result of the paper.

5.3 Invariant Superposition Modules and Cardinality Constraints

A *variable clause* is a clause containing only equations between variables or their negations. The *antecedent-mgu* (a-mgu, for short) of a variable clause $\Delta_1 \Rightarrow \Delta_2$ is the most general unifier of the unification problem $\{x \stackrel{?}{=} y \mid x = y \in \Delta_1\}$. A *cardinality constraint clause* is a variable clause $\Delta_1 \Rightarrow \Delta_2$ such that $\Rightarrow \Delta_2\mu$ does not contain any trivial equation like $x = x$, where μ is the a-mgu of $\Delta_1 \Rightarrow \Delta_2$; the number of free variables of $\Delta_2\mu$ is called the *cardinal* of the cardinality constraint clause $\Delta_1 \Rightarrow \Delta_2$. For example, the clause $x = y \Rightarrow y = z_1, x = z_2$ is a cardinality constraint clause whose cardinal is 3 (notice that this clause is true only in the one-element model).

Lemma 5.1. *If a satisfiable set S of clauses contains a cardinality constraint clause $\Delta_1 \Rightarrow \Delta_2$, then S cannot have a model whose domain is larger than the cardinal of $\Delta_1 \Rightarrow \Delta_2$.*

Proof. Let μ be the a-mgu of $\Delta_1 \Rightarrow \Delta_2$. By definition of a cardinality constraint clause, the clause $\Rightarrow \Delta_2\mu$ does not contain trivial equations; if n is the number of distinct variables in $\Rightarrow \Delta_2\mu$, then there cannot be more than $n - 1$ distinct elements in any model of S. □

The next crucial lemma expresses the property that an invariant superposition module discovers a cardinality constraint clause whenever the input set of clauses does not admit infinite models.

Lemma 5.2. *Let $(\Sigma, \mathcal{K}, \succ)$ be a suitable ordering triple. Let $\mathcal{SP}(\Sigma, \mathcal{K}, \succ)$ be an invariant superposition module. If S_0 is a satisfiable finite set of clauses, then the following conditions are equivalent:*

  (i) *the set S_∞ of persistent clauses in an S_0-derivation of $\mathcal{SP}(\Sigma, \mathcal{K}, \succ)$ contains a cardinality constraint clause;*
  (ii) *S_0 does not admit infinite models.*

Proof. The implication (i) $\Rightarrow$ (ii) is proved by Lemma 5.1. To show (ii) $\Rightarrow$ (i), assume that the set S_0 does not have a model whose domain is infinite. By Lemma 3.1, there must exist a natural number N such that every model $\mathcal{M}$ of S_0 has a domain with at most N elements. Since a cardinality constraint clause does not contain constants, it is in S_∞ iff it is in $(S_\infty)^{+N}$. Hence, by Definition 5.4 of an invariant superposition module (considering $(S_0)^{+N}$ rather than S_0, if needed) we are free to assume that the constants $\{c_1, \ldots, c_N\}$ do not occur in S_∞. Recall also that, according to the definition of a suitable ordering triple, the constants $\{c_1, \ldots, c_N\}$ are the smallest ground $\Sigma^\mathcal{K}$-terms.

According to the definition of superposition module (cf. Definition 5.3), since S_0 is assumed to be satisfiable, S_∞ is model-saturated, which means that the convergent rewrite system R_{S_∞} is a model of S_∞ (hence also of S_0, which is logically equivalent to S_∞). Now, since S_0 does not have a model whose domain is of cardinality N or greater, there is at least one constant among $c_1, \ldots, c_N$ which is not in normal form (with respect to R_{S_∞}). Assume that c_i is not in normal form (with respect to R_{S_∞}) and that each c_j (for $j < i$) is. By model generation (see section 5.1), to reduce c_i we need a rule $l \to r$ from a productive clause C of the kind $\Delta_1 \Rightarrow l = r, \Delta_2 \in gr(S_\infty)$; furthermore, c_i can be reduced only to c_j for $j < i$. The maximality condition 2 of model generation in Section 5.1 on l implies that l is c_i and that the remaining terms in C are of the kind c_j for $j \leq i$.[6] By condition 1 of model generation in Section 5.1, the fact that all terms c_j ($j < i$) are in R_{S_∞}-normal form, and the fact that R_{S_∞} is a convergent rewrite system extending R_C, it follows that each equation in Δ_1 is of the form $c_j = c_j$. Furthermore, again by condition 1 of model generation in Section 5.1, there is no (trivial) equality of the form $c_j = c_j$ in Δ_2. Since the constants $\{c_1, \ldots, c_N\}$ do not occur in S_∞, we are entitled to conclude that the productive clause $\Delta_1 \Rightarrow l = r, \Delta_2$ is the ground instance of a variable clause, i.e. there must exist a variable clause $\tilde{C}$ of the form $\tilde{\Delta}_1 \Rightarrow \tilde{l} = \tilde{r}, \tilde{\Delta}_2$ in S_∞ such that $\tilde{C}\theta \equiv C$ for some ground substitution θ. Since the antecedent of C consists of trivial equalities, θ is less general than μ, where μ is the a-mgu of $\tilde{C}$, i.e. we have that $\theta = \mu\theta'$ for some substitution θ'. Furthermore, since there are no positive trivial equalities in $C \equiv \tilde{C}\mu\theta'$, there are no positive trivial equalities in $\tilde{C}\mu$ either, which implies that $\tilde{C}$ is a cardinality constraint clause belonging to S_∞. $\square$

The following result immediately follows from Lemma 5.2 above, because unsatisfiability in infinite models can be detected by looking for a cardinality constraint clause among the finitely many final clauses of a terminating derivation:

Theorem 5.1. *Let T be a finitely axiomatized universal Σ-theory where Σ is finite. If T is $\exists$-superposition-decidable, then T is strongly $\exists_\infty$-decidable.*

5.4   Combining Superposition Modules and SMT Procedures

Invariant superposition modules provide us with means to check whether a theory is strongly $\exists_\infty$-decidable (and this answers *QUESTION 2* in Section 3.2). However, the situation is not really clear in practice. By using available state-of-the-art implementations of the superposition calculus, such as SPASS [24] or E [20], with suitable ordering, we have run concrete invariant superposition modules for a theory $T^{\leq k}$, admitting only finite models with at most $k - 1$ elements, axiomatized by an appropriate "at most" cardinality constraint, see (2). Indeed, according to Definition 5.4, the hard part is to prove termination for arbitrary input clauses of the form $T^{\leq k} \cup \Gamma$, where Γ is a set of ground literals. Our preliminary experiments were quite discouraging. In fact, both SPASS and E were able to handle only the trivial theory $T^{\leq 1}$ (axiomatized by $\Rightarrow x = y$). Already for $T^{\leq 2}$ (axiomatized by $\Rightarrow x = y, x = z, y = z$), the provers do not

---

[6] More precisely (this is important for the proof): terms occurring positively can only be c_j for $j \leq i$ and terms occurring negatively can only be c_j for $j < i$.

function *Grounding* (N : *integer*, T: *axioms*, Γ: *Ground literals*)
1   introduce fresh constants $c_1, \ldots, c_N$;
2   for every k-ary function symbol f in $\Gamma \cup T$ (with $k \geq 0$), generate the positive
     clauses

$$\bigvee_{i=1}^{N} f(a_1, \ldots, a_k) = c_i$$

     for every $a_1, \ldots, a_k \in \{c_1, \ldots, c_N\}$ and let E be the resulting set of clauses;
3   for every clause $C \in T$, instantiate C in all possible ways by ground substitutions
     whose range is the set $\{c_1, \ldots, c_N\}$ and let T_g be the resulting set of clauses;
4   return the set $T_g \cup E \cup \Gamma$.
end

Fig. 1. Computing equisatisfiable sets of ground clauses for instances of the constraint
satisfiability problem of theories with no infinite models

terminate in a reasonable amount of time although we experimented with various settings. For example, while SPASS is capable of finding a saturation for $T^{\leq 2} \cup \Gamma$ when $\Gamma := \emptyset$, it seems to diverge when $\Gamma := \{a \neq b\}$. This seems to dramatically reduce the scope of applicability of Theorem 5.1 and hence of Theorem 3.2.

Fortunately, this problem can be solved by the following two observations. First, although a superposition module may not terminate on instances of the constraint satisfiability problem of the form $T \cup \Gamma$, where Γ is a constraint and T does not admit infinite models (such as $T^{\leq k}$, above), Lemma 5.2 ensures that a cardinality constraint clause will eventually be derived in a finite amount of time: if a clause C is in the set S_∞ of persistent clauses of a derivation $S_0, S_1, \ldots$, then there must exists an integer $k \geq 0$ such that $C \in S_k$ (recall Definition 5.3). Second, when a cardinality constraint clause C is derived from $T \cup \Gamma$, a bound on the cardinality of the domains of any model can be immediately obtained by the cardinal associated to C. It is possible to use such a bound to build an equisatisfiable set of clauses (see Figure 1) and pass it to an SMT procedure for the pure theory of equality (e.g., those in [9,3,10,11]) or to a model builder. The observations above motivate the following relaxation of the notion of an $\exists$-superposition-decidable theory.

Definition 5.6. *Let* $(\Sigma, \mathcal{K}, \succ)$ *be a suitable ordering triple. A universal and finitely axiomatized* Σ*-theory* T *is* weakly-$\exists$-superposition-decidable *iff there exists an invariant superposition module* $\mathcal{SP}(\Sigma, \mathcal{K}, \succ)$ *such that for every* $\Sigma^{\mathcal{K}}$*-constraint* Γ, *any* $T \cup \Gamma$*-derivation either* (i) *terminates or* (ii) *generates a cardinality constraint clause.*

We can easily adapt Theorem 5.1 to this new definition.

Theorem 5.2. *Let* T *be a universal and finitely axiomatized* Σ*-theory, where* Σ *is finite. If* T *is weakly-$\exists$-superposition-decidable, then* T *is strongly* $\exists_\infty$*-decidable.*

Proof. Decidability of Σ-constraints in T-models can be obtained by halting the invariant superposition module, as soon as a cardinality constraint clause is generated at some stage i, and applying an SMT procedure for the theory of equality or a model builder to the set of clauses produced by applying the function $Grounding$ of Figure 1 to S_i. Satisfiability in infinite models is answered negatively if a cardinality constraint clause is generated; otherwise, we have termination of the invariant superposition module and if the empty clause is not produced, satisfiability is reported by Lemma 5.2.   □

6 Conclusion and Future Work

By classifying the component theories according to the decidability of constraint satisfiability problems in arbitrary and in infinite models, respectively, we exhibited a theory T_1 such that T_1-satisfiability is decidable, but T_1-satisfiability in infinite models is undecidable. It follows that satisfiability in $T_1 \cup T_2$ is undecidable, whenever T_2 has only infinite models, even if signatures are disjoint and satisfiability in T_2 is decidable. In the second part of the paper we strengthened the Nelson-Oppen combination result, by showing that it applies to theories over disjoint signatures, whose satisfiability problem, in either arbitrary or infinite models, is decidable. We showed that this result covers decision procedures based on superposition, offering an alternative to the results in [1].

An interesting line of future work consists of finding $ad\ hoc$ contraction rules which allow the superposition calculus to terminate on theories that do not admit infinite models such as the $T^{\leq k}$'s considered in Section 5.4.

References

1. A. Armando, M. P. Bonacina, S. Ranise, and S. Schulz. On a rewriting approach to satisfiability procedures: extension, combination of theories and an experimental appraisal. In *Proc. of FroCoS'05*, volume 3717 of *LNCS*, pages 65–80. Springer, 2005. Full version available as DI RR 36/2005, Università degli Studi di Verona, http://www.sci.univr.it/~bonacina/verify.html.
2. A. Armando, S. Ranise, and M. Rusinowitch. A rewriting approach to satisfiability procedures. *Information and Computation*, 183(2):140–164, 2003.
3. G. Audemard, P. Bertoli, A. Cimatti, A. Korniłowicz, and R. Sebastiani. A SAT based approach for solving formulas over boolean and linear mathematical propositions. In *Proc. of CADE-18*, volume 2392 of *LNCS*, pages 195–210. Springer, 2002.
4. F. Baader and T. Nipkow. *Term Rewriting and All That*. Cambridge University Press, United Kingdom, 1998.
5. F. Baader and C. Tinelli. Deciding the word problem in the union of equational theories. *Information and Computation*, 178(2):346–390, 2002.
6. M. P. Bonacina and N. Dershowitz. Abstract canonical inference. *ACM Transactions on Computational Logic*, (to appear), 2006.
7. M. P. Bonacina and J. Hsiang. Towards a foundation of completion procedures as semidecision procedures. *Theoretical Computer Science*, 146:199–242, July 1995.
8. H. Comon, P. Narendran, R. Nieuwenhuis, and M. Rusinowitch. Decision problems in ordered rewriting. In *Proc. of LICS'98*, pages 276–286. IEEE Computer Society Press, 1998.

9. D. Déharbe and S. Ranise. Light-weight theorem proving for debugging and verifying units of code. In *Proc. of SEFM'03*. IEEE Computer Society Press, 2003.
10. J.-C. Filliâtre, S. Owre, H. Rueß, and N. Shankar. ICS: Integrated canonizer and solver. In *Proc. of CAV'01*, LNCS, pages 246–249. Springer, 2001.
11. H. Ganzinger, G. Hagen, R. Nieuwenhuis, A. Oliveras, and C. Tinelli. DPLL(T): Fast decision procedures. In *Proc. of CAV'04*, volume 3114 of *LNCS*, pages 175–188. Springer, 2004.
12. S. Ghilardi. Model theoretic methods in combined constraint satisfiability. *Journal of Automated Reasoning*, 33(3-3):221–249, 2005.
13. A. Middeldorp and H. Zantema. Simple termination revisited. In *Proc. of CADE'94*, LNCS, pages 451–465. Springer, 1994.
14. G. Nelson and D. C. Oppen. Simplification by cooperating decision procedures. *ACM Trans. on Programming Languages and Systems*, 1(2):245–257, 1979.
15. R. Nieuwenhuis and A. Rubio. Paramodulation-based theorem proving. In A. Robinson and A. Voronkov, editors, *Handbook of Automated Reasoning*. Elsevier and MIT Press, 2001.
16. P. Odifreddi. *Classical recursion theory*, volume 125 of *Studies in Logic and the Foundations of Mathematics*. North-Holland, 1989.
17. D. C. Oppen. Complexity, convexity and combinations of theories. *Theoretical Computer Science*, 12:291–302, 1980.
18. D. Pigozzi. The join of equational theories. *Colloquium Mathematicum*, 30(1):15–25, 1974.
19. S. Ranise, C. Ringeissen, and D.-K. Tran. Nelson-Oppen, Shostak and the extended canonizer: A family picture with a newborn. In *Proc. of ICTAC 2004*, LNCS. Springer, 2004.
20. S. Schulz. E - a brainiac theorem prover. *AI Communications*, 15(2/3):111–126, 2002.
21. C. Tinelli and M. T. Harandi. A new correctness proof of the Nelson-Oppen combination procedure. In *Proc. of FroCoS'96*, pages 103–120. Kluwer Academic Publishers, 1996.
22. C. Tinelli and C. G. Zarba. Combining non-stably infinite theories. *Journal of Automated Reasoning*, 2006. (to appear).
23. D. van Dalen. *Logic and Structure*. Springer-Verlag, 1989. Second edition.
24. C. Weidenbach. Combining superposition, sorts and splitting. In A. Robinson and A. Voronkov, editors, *Handbook of Automated Reasoning*. Elsevier and MIT Press, 2001.

Verifying Mixed Real-Integer Quantifier Elimination

Amine Chaieb

Institut für Informatik
Technische Universität München

Abstract. We present a formally verified quantifier elimination procedure for the first order theory over linear mixed real-integer arithmetics
in higher-order logic based on a work by Weispfenning. To this end we
provide two verified quantifier elimination procedures: for Presburger
arithmitics and for linear real arithmetics.

1   Introduction

The interest of theorem provers in decision procedures (dps.) for arithmetics is
inveterate. Noteworthily, the apparently first theorem prover [14] implements
a quantifier elimination procedure (qep.) for Presburger arithmetic ($\mathcal{Z}$). This
paper presents a formally verified qep. for $\mathcal{R}_{\lfloor . \rfloor} = \mathrm{Th}(\mathbb{R}, <, +, \lfloor . \rfloor, 0, 1)$ in higher-
order logic based on [38]. For a real number x, $\lfloor x \rfloor$ is the greatest integer
less than or equal to x. Our development environment is Isabelle/HOL [27].
Weispfenning presented in [38] a qep. for $\mathcal{R}_{\lfloor . \rfloor}$, which reduces the qe. problem to qe. in $\mathcal{Z}$ and $\mathcal{R} = \mathrm{Th}(\mathbb{R}, <, +, 0, 1)$. In this paper, we formalize not
only this reduction, but also a qep. for $\mathcal{Z}$ and a qep. for $\mathcal{R}$, which yields a
complete qep. for $\mathcal{R}_{\lfloor . \rfloor}$. In fact, our formalization is carried out in an executable fragment of HOL, for which code generation [7] is possible. The in-
terest in $\mathcal{R}_{\lfloor . \rfloor}$ is not only of theoretical nature (almost any non trivial extension of $\mathcal{R}_{\lfloor . \rfloor}$ is undecidable, see [38] for several impossibility results), but also
practically motivated, since mixed real-integer constraints naturally rise in
verification.

Generated ML code from HOL functions [7] yields smoothly integratable oracles returning sound answers, provided the code generator is correct. Accepting
these answers as equality proofs is often referred to by *reflection*. Many type
theory based theorem provers accept such proofs as part of their underlying
logic [21,8]. Reflection has been used and studied by many researchers and the
opinions range from enthusiasm [2,3] to scepticism concerning its utility in LCF
frameworks[19].

Regardless of reflection, implementations of dps. proved correct in the logic
are worthy for several reasons: (a) while even new considerations using dependent types [1,23] fail to guarantee completeness of (complex enough) dps., the
approach we adopt does; (b) sharing theorems between HOL theorem provers
[29,26] provides a mechanism of sharing dps., which is an important issue to
achieve faster progress in theorem proving; (c) an LCF-conservative integration

U. Furbach and N. Shankar (Eds.): IJCAR 2006, LNAI 4130, pp. 528–540, 2006.
© Springer-Verlag Berlin Heidelberg 2006

is *still* possible, e.g. by specializing the simplifier to the involved defining equations (fast rewriting techniques [4] play an important role) or by instrumenting code generators to produce LCF-proofs (Isabelle provides a prototypical implementation [6]); (d) no intimate knowledge of the internals of the underlying theorem prover is needed. This makes the dps. easily portable and enables other developers (and even normal users) insight into dps.-implementations, which are the till now arcane.

The main contributions of our work are: (a) the first-time verified formalization of a qep. for $\mathcal{R}_{\lfloor . \rfloor}$ and $\mathcal{R}$ (à la [15]) in a theorem prover; (b) a perspicuous and concise formalization (1000 lines including several optimizations) of a uniform treatment for linear arithmetics that is easily portable to other theorem provers; (c) the most substantial application of reflection in a theorem prover (as far as we are aware of); (d) a motivation to proof-producing code generators as an alternative of reflection in LCF-based theorem provers.

Related Work. In [38] $\mathcal{R}_{\lfloor . \rfloor}$ has been proved to admit quantifier elimination. The overall procedure reduces the problem to qe. in $\mathcal{R}$ and $\mathcal{Z}$. The decidability of $\mathcal{R}$ is arguably due to Fourier [18]. The decidability of $\mathcal{Z}$ has been shown independently by Presburger [31] and Skolem [34]. Several other qep. have been proposed for $\mathcal{R}$ [35,15,24] and for $\mathcal{Z}$ [12,33,32] and incited excellent complexity studies [30,17,16,36,37]. Alternative dps. use automata [39,22]. Many theorem provers include implementations of qep. for $\mathcal{Z}$ and $\mathcal{R}$ [28,10,25] or for some subsets [13]. A formalization of Cooper's qep. for $\mathcal{Z}$ has been presented in [11]. An automata based dp. for *closed* $\mathcal{R}_{\lfloor . \rfloor}$-formulae has been recently proposed [9]. Since this procedure is based on sorts distinction for variables, it does *not* provide a qep., see [38] for an excellent proof. An extension of [32] to deal with real and integer variables is presented in [5]. The said extension is noteworthily online and proof producing and hence useful for combination frameworks based on the Nelson and Oppen method. The considered formulae are *quantifier free*.

Notation. Datatypes are declared using datatype. Lists are built up from the empty list [] and consing ·; the infix @ appends two lists. For a list l, $\{\!\{l\}\!\}$ denotes the set of elements of l, and $l!n$ denotes its nth element. Functions are defined by pattern matching. We use the letters u, x, y, z for reals and c, d, i, j for integers and denote by $\underline{i}$ the injection of i into the reals. We call $\underline{i}$ a real integer. For i and j we write $i \mid j$ if i divides j. For x and y we define $x \mid y \leftrightarrow \exists i.y = x \cdot \underline{i}$. We use $i \nmid j$ (resp. $x \nmid y$) as a shorthand for $\neg i \mid j$ (resp. $\neg x \mid y$). For x we denote by $\lfloor x \rfloor$ the greatest integer i such that $\underline{i} \leq x$. Note that $\lfloor x \rfloor$ is an integer, not a real integer. We use $\lceil x \rceil$ as a shorthand for $-\lfloor -x \rfloor$.

The rest of this paper is structured as follows. In § 2 we set up the basis for our formalization and then present the qep. for $\mathcal{R}_{\lfloor . \rfloor}$ in a top-down fashion. In § 3 we formalize the overall procedure in terms of two qe. procedures: for $\mathcal{R}$, subject of § 4, and for $\mathcal{Z}$, subject of § 5. In § 6 we describe some formalization and integration issues.

2 Preliminaries

2.1 Syntax and Semantics

We define the syntax of terms and formulae as follows:

$$\text{datatype } \rho = \widehat{int} \mid v_{nat} \mid - \rho \mid \rho + \rho \mid \rho - \rho \mid int * \rho \mid \lfloor \rho \rfloor$$

$$\text{datatype } \phi = \rho < 0 \mid \rho > 0 \mid \rho \leq 0 \mid \rho \geq 0 \mid \rho = 0 \mid \rho \neq 0 \mid int \mid \rho \mid int \dagger \rho$$

$$\boldsymbol{T} \mid \boldsymbol{F} \mid \neg \phi \mid \phi \wedge \phi \mid \phi \vee \phi \mid \phi \rightarrow \phi \mid \phi \leftrightarrow \phi \mid \exists \phi \mid \forall \phi$$

The real integer constant i in the logic is represented by the term $\widehat{i}$. Bound variables are represented by de Bruijn indices: v_n represents the bound variable with index n (a natural number). Hence quantifiers need not carry variable names. The bold symbols $+$, ≤ 0, $\wedge$ etc are constructors and reflect their counterparts $+$, $\lambda x.x \leq 0$, $\wedge$ etc in the logic. We use $\bowtie 0$ as a place-holder for $=0, \neq 0, <0, \leq 0, >0$ or ≥ 0, all of them notably constructors with *only one* argument. We use $\lceil t \rceil$ to denote $- \lfloor - t \rfloor$.

Throughout the paper p and q (resp. s and t) are of type ϕ (resp. ρ).

$$
\begin{array}{lll}
[\widehat{i}]^{vs}_\rho = \widehat{i} & [\boldsymbol{T}]^{vs} = True & [\widehat{i} \mid t]^{vs} = (\widehat{i} \mid [t]^{vs}_\rho) \\
[v_n]^{vs}_\rho = vs!n & [\boldsymbol{F}]^{vs} = False & [\widehat{i} \dagger t]^{vs} = (\widehat{i} \dagger [t]^{vs}_\rho) \\
[-t]^{vs}_\rho = -[t]^{vs}_\rho & [t<0]^{vs} = ([t]^{vs}_\rho < 0) & [\neg p]^{vs} = (\neg [p]^{vs}) \\
[t+s]^{vs}_\rho = [t]^{vs}_\rho + [s]^{vs}_\rho & [t>0]^{vs} = ([t]^{vs}_\rho > 0) & [p \wedge q]^{vs} = ([p]^{vs} \wedge [q]^{vs}) \\
[t-s]^{vs}_\rho = [t]^{vs}_\rho - [s]^{vs}_\rho & [t \leq 0]^{vs} = ([t]^{vs}_\rho \leq 0) & [p \vee q]^{vs} = ([p]^{vs} \vee [q]^{vs}) \\
[\widehat{i} * t]^{vs}_\rho = \widehat{i} \cdot [t]^{vs}_\rho & [t \geq 0]^{vs} = ([t]^{vs}_\rho \geq 0) & [p \rightarrow q]^{vs} = ([p]^{vs} \rightarrow [q]^{vs}) \\
[\lfloor t \rfloor]^{vs}_\rho = \lfloor [t]^{vs}_\rho \rfloor & [t = 0]^{vs} = ([t]^{vs}_\rho = 0) & [p \leftrightarrow q]^{vs} = ([p]^{vs} \leftrightarrow [q]^{vs}) \\
& [t \neq 0]^{vs} = ([t]^{vs}_\rho \neq 0) & [\exists p]^{vs} = (\exists x.[p]^{x \cdot vs}) \\
& & [\forall p]^{vs} = (\forall x.[p]^{x \cdot vs})
\end{array}
$$

Fig. 1. Semantics of the shadow syntax

The interpretation functions ($[.]^{\cdot}_\rho$ and $[.]^{\cdot}$) in Fig. 1 map the representations back into logic. They are parameterized by an environment vs which is a list of real expressions. The de Bruijn index v_n picks out the nth element from that list. We say that x is a witness for p if $[p]^{x \cdot vs}$ holds. It will alway be clear from the context which vs is meant.

2.2 Generic Quantifier Elimination

Assume we have a function qe, that eliminates one $\exists$ in front of quantifier-free formulae. The function qelim_ϕ applies qe to all quantified subformulae in a bottom-up fashion. Let $\text{qfree } p$ formalize that p is quantifier-free (qf.). We prove by structural induction that if qe takes a qf. formula q and returns a qf. formula q' equivalent to $\exists q$, then $\text{qelim}_\phi qe$ is a qep.:

$$(\forall vs, q. \text{ qfree } q \rightarrow \text{qfree } (qe\ q) \wedge ([qe\ q]^{vs} \leftrightarrow [\exists q]^{vs}))$$
$$\rightarrow \text{qfree } (\text{qelim}_\phi\ qe\ p) \wedge ([\text{qelim}_\phi\ qe\ p]^{vs} \leftrightarrow [p]^{vs}). \tag{1}$$

In § 3 we present mir, an instance of qe satisfying the premise of (1).

2.3 Linearity

When defining a function (over ρ or ϕ) we assume the input to have a precise syntactical shape. This not only simplifies the function definition but is also crucial for its correctness proof. The fact that v_0 does not occur in a ρ-term t (resp. in a ϕ-formula p) is formalized by $\mathsf{unbound}_\rho\ t$ (resp. $\mathsf{unbound}_\phi\ p$). Substituting t for v_0 in p is defined by $p[t]$. Decreasing all variable indexes in p is defined by $\mathsf{decr}\ p$. These functions have such simple recursive definitions that the properties (2) are proved automatically.

$$\mathsf{unbound}_\phi\ p \to \forall x, y. [\![p]\!]^{x \cdot vs} \leftrightarrow [\![p]\!]^{y \cdot vs}$$

$$\mathsf{qfree}\ p \to ([\![p[t]]\!]^{x \cdot vs} \leftrightarrow [\![p]\!]^{([\![t]\!]^{x \cdot vs}_\rho) \cdot vs}) \tag{2}$$

$$\mathsf{unbound}_\phi\ p \to \forall x. [\![\mathsf{decr}\ p]\!]^{vs} \leftrightarrow [\![p]\!]^{x \cdot vs}$$

We define p to be $\mathcal{R}$-linear ($\mathsf{islin}_\mathcal{R}\ p$) if it is built up from $\wedge, \vee$ and atoms θ, either of the form $c * v_0 + t \bowtie 0$, such that $\mathsf{unbound}_\rho\ t \wedge c > 0$, or satisfying $\mathsf{unbound}_\phi\ \theta$. We define p to be $\mathcal{Z}$-linear in a context vs ($\mathsf{islin}_\mathcal{Z}\ p\ vs$) if in addition to the previous requirements every t represents an integer, i.e. $[\![\lfloor t \rfloor]\!]^{vs}_\rho = [\![t]\!]^{vs}_\rho$. Moreover $i \mid c * v_0 + t$ and $i \nmid c * v_0 + t$ such that $i > 0 \wedge c > 0 \wedge$ $\mathsf{unbound}_\rho\ t \wedge [\![t]\!]^{vs}_\rho = [\![\lfloor t \rfloor]\!]^{vs}_\rho$, are $\mathcal{Z}$-linear atoms. A $\mathcal{R}$- (resp. $\mathcal{Z}$-) linear formula can be regarded as a formula in $\mathcal{R}$ (resp. $\mathcal{Z}$), assuming v_0 will be interpreted by some $x \in \mathbb{R}$ (resp. by some $\underline{i}, i \in \mathbb{Z}$).

3 Quantifier Elimination for $\mathcal{R}_{\lfloor \cdot \rfloor}$

The main idea is: "$\lfloor \cdot \rfloor$ is burdensome, get rid of it". Notice that $\forall x. \underline{0} \le x - \lfloor x \rfloor <$ $\underline{1}$ and hence $\exists x. [\![p]\!]^{x \cdot vs} \leftrightarrow \exists i, u. \underline{0} \le u < \underline{1} \wedge [\![p]\!]^{(i+u) \cdot vs}$. Let $\widehat{0} \le v_0 < \widehat{1}$ be a shorthand for $1 * v_0 + \widehat{0} \ge 0 \wedge 1 * v_0 + \widehat{-1} < 0$. Let $\mathsf{split}_0\ p = \widehat{0} \le v_0 < \widehat{1} \wedge p'$, where p' results from p by replacing every occurrence of v_0 by $v_0 + v_1$ and v_i by v_{i+1} for $i > 0$. We easily prove

$$\mathsf{qfree}\ p \to ([\![\exists p]\!]^{vs} \leftrightarrow \exists i, u. [\![\mathsf{split}_0\ p]\!]^{i \cdot u \cdot vs}) \tag{3}$$

One main contribution of [38] is to supply two functions $\mathsf{lin}_\mathcal{R}$ and $\mathsf{lin}_\mathcal{Z}$, which, assuming that v_0 is interpreted by $u \in [\underline{0}, \underline{1})$ (resp. by $\underline{i}$), transform any qf. p into a $\mathcal{R}$- (resp. $\mathcal{Z}$-) linear formula, cf. (5) and (4).

$$\mathsf{qfree}\ p \to ([\![\mathsf{lin}_\mathcal{Z}\ p]\!]^{\underline{i} \cdot vs} \leftrightarrow [\![p]\!]^{\underline{i} \cdot vs}) \wedge \mathsf{islin}_\mathcal{Z}\ (\mathsf{lin}_\mathcal{Z}\ p)\ (\underline{i} \cdot vs) \tag{4}$$

$$\mathsf{qfree}\ p \wedge \underline{0} \le x < \underline{1} \to ([\![\mathsf{lin}_\mathcal{R}\ p]\!]^{x \cdot vs} \leftrightarrow [\![p]\!]^{x \cdot vs}) \wedge \mathsf{islin}_\mathcal{R}\ (\mathsf{lin}_\mathcal{R}\ p) \tag{5}$$

The next subsections exhibit $\mathsf{lin}_\mathcal{Z}$ and $\mathsf{lin}_\mathcal{R}$, which mainly "get rid of $\lfloor \cdot \rfloor$". Now given two qe. procedures $qe_{\mathcal{R}_l}$ for $\mathcal{R}$ and $qe_{\mathcal{Z}_l}$ for $\mathcal{Z}$ satisfying:

$$\mathsf{islin}_\mathcal{R}\ p \to ([\![qe_{\mathcal{R}_l}\ \widehat{0} \le v_0 < \widehat{1} \wedge p]\!]^{vs} \leftrightarrow [\![\exists \widehat{0} \le v_0 < \widehat{1} \wedge p]\!]^{vs}) \wedge \mathsf{qfree}(qe_{\mathcal{R}_l}\ p)$$

$$\mathsf{islin}_\mathcal{Z}\ p \to ([\![qe_{\mathcal{Z}_l}\ p]\!]^{vs} \leftrightarrow \exists i. [\![p]\!]^{i \cdot vs}) \wedge \mathsf{qfree}(qe_{\mathcal{Z}_l}\ p)$$

then it is simple to prove that $\mathsf{mir} = qe_{\mathcal{Z}_l} \circ \mathsf{lin}_\mathcal{Z} \circ qe_{\mathcal{R}_l} \circ \mathsf{lin}_\mathcal{R} \circ \mathsf{split}_0$ satisfies the premise of (1) and hence $\mathsf{qelim}_\phi\ \mathsf{mir}$ is a qep. for ϕ-formulae. In § 4 and § 5 we present instances of $qe_\mathcal{R}$ and $qe_\mathcal{Z}$.

3.1 lin$_{\mathbb{Z}}$

In order to define lin$_{\mathbb{Z}}$ and prove (4), we first introduce a function split$_{\mathbb{Z}}$ that, given a ρ-term t, returns an integer c and a ρ-term s (not involving v_0), such that (6) (Lemma 3.2 in [38]) holds. Note that v_0 is interpreted by a real integer i.

$$(\text{split}_{\mathbb{Z}}\ t = (c, s)) \rightarrow (\llbracket c * v_0 + s \rrbracket_\rho^{i \cdot vs} = \llbracket t \rrbracket_\rho^{i \cdot vs}) \wedge \text{unbound}_\rho s \qquad (6)$$

The definition of split$_{\mathbb{Z}}$ and the proof of (6) proceed by induction on t. If $t = \lfloor t' \rfloor$ then return $(c, \lfloor s \rfloor)$, where split$_{\mathbb{Z}}\ t' = (c, s)$. Remember that $\lfloor x + j \rfloor = \lfloor x \rfloor + j$ holds for any $j \in \mathbb{Z}$. The other cases are trivial.

Now lin$_{\mathbb{Z}}$ is simple: push negations inwards and transform atoms according to the result of split$_{\mathbb{Z}}$ and the properties (7), cf. example 1 for the $= 0$ case, where the first property in (7) is used . By induction on p, we easily prove (4) using the properties (6) and (7).

$$(\underline{c \cdot i} = y) \leftrightarrow (c \cdot i = \lfloor y \rfloor \wedge y = \lfloor y \rfloor)$$
$$(\underline{c \cdot i} < y) \leftrightarrow (c \cdot i < \lfloor y \rfloor \vee (c \cdot i = \lfloor y \rfloor \wedge \lfloor y \rfloor < y))$$
$$(\underline{d} \mid \underline{c \cdot i} + y) \leftrightarrow (\lfloor y \rfloor = y \wedge d \mid c \cdot i + \lfloor y \rfloor) \qquad (7)$$
$$\underline{0} \mid x \leftrightarrow (x = \underline{0})$$

Example 1

> lin$_{\mathbb{Z}}$ $(t = 0) =$ **let** $(c, s) =$ *split*$_{\mathbb{Z}}$ t *in*
>   **if** $c = 0$ **then** $s = 0$
>   **else if** $c > 0$ **then** $c * v_0 + \lceil s \rceil = 0 \wedge \lfloor s \rfloor - s = 0$
>   **else** $-c * v_0 + \lfloor -s \rfloor = 0 \wedge \lfloor s \rfloor - s = 0$

3.2 lin$_{\mathcal{R}}$

In order to define lin$_{\mathcal{R}}$ and prove (5), we first introduce a function split$_{\mathcal{R}} : \rho \rightarrow (\phi \times int \times \rho)list$ that, given a ρ-term t, yields a *complete* finite case distinction given by $\mathcal{R}$-linear formulae ϕ_i and corresponding ρ-terms s_i (not involving v_0) and integers c_i such that $\llbracket t \rrbracket_\rho^{u \cdot vs} = \llbracket c_i * v_0 + s_i \rrbracket_\rho^{u \cdot vs}$ whenever $\llbracket \phi_i \rrbracket^{u \cdot vs}$ holds (Lemma 3.3 in [38]), i.e.

$$\forall (\phi_i, c_i, s_i) \in \{\!\!\{\text{split}_{\mathcal{R}}\ t\}\!\!\}.(\llbracket \phi_i \rrbracket^{u \cdot vs} \rightarrow (\llbracket t \rrbracket_\rho^{u \cdot vs} = \llbracket c_i * v_0 + s_i \rrbracket_\rho^{u \cdot vs}))$$
$$\wedge \text{unbound}_\rho\ s_i \wedge \text{islin}_{\mathcal{R}}\ \phi_i \qquad (8)$$
$$\underline{0} \leq u < \underline{1} \rightarrow \exists (\phi_i, c_i, s_i) \in \{\!\!\{\text{split}_{\mathcal{R}}\ t\}\!\!\}.\llbracket \phi_i \rrbracket^{u \cdot vs} \qquad (9)$$

The definition of split$_{\mathcal{R}}$ and the proof of (8) and (9) proceed by induction on t. Assume $t = \lfloor t' \rfloor$, let $(\phi_i', c_i', s_i') \in \{\!\!\{\text{split}_{\mathcal{R}}\ t'\}\!\!\}$ and assume $\llbracket \phi_i' \rrbracket^{u \cdot vs}$ and $c_i' > 0$. From the induction hypothesis we have $\llbracket t' \rrbracket_\rho^{u \cdot vs} = \llbracket c_i' * v_0 + s_i' \rrbracket_\rho^{u \cdot vs}$ and since $\underline{0} \leq u < \underline{1}$ and $c_i' > 0$ we have $j \leq c_i' \cdot u < j + 1$ for some $j \in \{0 \ldots c_i'\}$, i.e.

$$\underline{j + \lfloor \llbracket s_i' \rrbracket_\rho^{u \cdot vs} \rfloor} \leq \llbracket c_i' * v_0 + s_i' \rrbracket_\rho^{u \cdot vs} < \underline{j + 1 + \lfloor \llbracket s_i' \rrbracket_\rho^{u \cdot vs} \rfloor}$$

and hence $\lfloor \llbracket c'_i * v_0 + s'_i \rrbracket_\rho^{u \cdot vs} \rfloor = j$. For $(\phi'_i, c'_i, s'_i) \in \{\mathsf{split}_\mathcal{R}\ t'\}$ $\mathsf{split}_\mathcal{R}$ returns the list of $(\phi'_i \wedge A_j, 0, \lfloor s \rfloor + \widehat{j})$, where $j \in \{0 \dots c'_i\}$, where $A_j = r - \widehat{j} \geq 0 \wedge r - \widehat{j+1} < 0$ and $r = c'_i * v_0 + s'_i - \lfloor s'_i \rfloor$. The cases $c'_i < 0$ and $c'_i = 0$, ignored in [38], are analogous. The other cases for t are simple.

The definition of $\mathsf{lin}_\mathcal{R}$ for atoms is involved, but very simple for the rest: it just pushes negations inwards. Due to the result of $\mathsf{split}_\mathcal{R}$, assume that atoms have the form $f(c * v_0 + s)$, where s does not involve v_0 and $f \in \{\bowtie 0, \lambda t.i \mid t, \lambda t.i \nmid t$ for some $i\}$. For every f, we define its corresponding $\mathcal{R}$-linear version $f_l : int \to \rho \to \phi$, and prove (10). Example 2 shows the case for $= 0$ and the corresponding definition of $\mathsf{lin}_\mathcal{R}$.

$$\underline{0} \leq u < \underline{1} \wedge \mathsf{unbound}_\rho\ s \wedge (\llbracket t \rrbracket_\rho^{u \cdot vs} = \llbracket c * v_0 + s \rrbracket_\rho^{u \cdot vs})$$
$$\to (\llbracket f_l\ c\ s \rrbracket^{u \cdot vs} \leftrightarrow \llbracket f\ t \rrbracket^{u \cdot vs}) \wedge \mathsf{islin}_\mathcal{R}\ (f_l\ c\ s) \tag{10}$$

Example 2

$$c * v_0 + s =_l 0 = \textbf{if } c = 0 \textbf{ then } s = 0 \textbf{ else}$$
$$\textbf{if } c > 0 \textbf{ then } c * v_0 + s = 0 \textbf{ else } -c * v_0 +- s = 0$$

$$\mathsf{lin}_\mathcal{R}(t = 0) = \textbf{let } [(p_0, c_0, s_0), ..., (p_n, c_n, s_n)] = \mathsf{split}_\mathcal{R}\ t$$
$$\textbf{in } (p_0 \wedge (c_0 * v_0 + s_0 =_l 0)) \vee ... \vee (p_n \wedge (c_n * v_0 + s_n =_l 0))$$

Since $\cdot \mid \cdot$ and $\cdot \nmid \cdot$ are not $\mathcal{R}$-linear, their corresponding linear versions eliminate them at the cost of a case distinction according to (11).

$$\underline{0} \leq u < \underline{1} \wedge c > 0 \to$$
$$(\underline{d} \mid \underline{c} \cdot u + s \leftrightarrow \exists j \in \{0..c-1\}.(\underline{c} \cdot u = \underline{j} + \lceil s \rceil - s) \wedge d \mid j + \lceil s \rceil) \tag{11}$$

We implement this case distinction by dvd and $\cdot \mid_l \cdot$ follows naturally, ie.

$$d \textbf{ dvd } c * v_0 + s = (c * v_0 + s - \lceil s \rceil - \widehat{0} = 0 \wedge d \mid \lceil s \rceil + \widehat{c-1}) \vee ...$$
$$\vee (c * v_0 + s - \lceil s \rceil - \widehat{c-1} = 0 \wedge d \mid \lceil s \rceil + \widehat{c-1})$$
$$d \mid_l c * v_0 + s = \quad \textbf{if } d = 0 \textbf{ then } c * v_0 + s =_l 0 \textbf{ else}$$
$$\textbf{if } c = 0 \textbf{ then } d \mid s \textbf{ else}$$
$$\textbf{if } c > 0 \textbf{ then } |d| \textbf{ dvd } c * v_0 + s$$
$$\textbf{else then } |d| \textbf{ dvd } -c * v_0 +- s$$

Now we define $\mathsf{lin}_\mathcal{R}(d \mid t)$ analogously to the $= 0$-case.

$$\mathsf{lin}_\mathcal{R}(d \mid t) = \textbf{let } [(p_0, c_0, s_0), ..., (p_n, c_n, s_n)] = \mathsf{split}_\mathcal{R}\ t$$
$$g = \lambda c, s.d \mid_l c * v_0 + s$$
$$\textbf{in } (p_0 \wedge (g\ c_0\ s_0)) \vee ... \vee (p_n \wedge (g\ c_n\ s_n))$$

Note that $\mathsf{lin}_\mathcal{R}$ has akin definitions for the atoms. In fact for an atom $f(t)$, the real definition is $\mathsf{lin}_\mathcal{R}(f(t)) = \mathsf{split}_l\ f_l\ t$, where

$$\mathsf{split}_l\ f_l\ t \equiv \textbf{let } [(p_0, c_0, s_0), ..., (p_n, c_n, s_n)] = \mathsf{split}_\mathcal{R}\ t$$
$$\textbf{in } (p_0 \wedge (f_l\ c_0\ s_0)) \vee ... \vee (p_n \wedge (f_l\ c_n\ s_n)) \tag{12}$$

We prove the following simple, yet generic property for split_l

$$\underline{0} \leq u < \underline{1} \wedge (\forall t, c, s.\mathsf{unbound}_\rho \ s \wedge (\llbracket t \rrbracket_\rho^{u \cdot vs} = \llbracket c * v_0 + s \rrbracket_\rho^{u \cdot vs})$$

$$\rightarrow (\llbracket f_l \ c \ s \rrbracket^{u \cdot vs} \leftrightarrow \llbracket f \ t \rrbracket^{u \cdot vs} \wedge \mathsf{islin}_\mathcal{R} \ (f_l \ c \ s))) \quad (13)$$

$$\rightarrow \mathsf{islin}_\mathcal{R} \ (\mathsf{split}_l \ f_l \ t) \wedge (\llbracket \mathsf{split}_l \ f_l \ t \rrbracket^{u \cdot vs} \leftrightarrow \llbracket f \ t \rrbracket^{u \cdot vs})$$

Note that the premise of (13), which expresses that f_l is a $\mathcal{R}$-linear version of f, will be discharged by the instances of (10) for the different f's. After all these preparations, it is not surprising that (5) is proved automatically.

4   Quantifier Elimination for $\mathcal{R}$

We present $\mathsf{ferrack}$, a verified qep. for $\mathcal{R}$ based on [15], and prove (14). To our knowledge, this is the first-time verified formalization of this qep.

$$\mathsf{islin}_\mathcal{R} \ p \rightarrow \llbracket \mathsf{ferrack}(\widehat{0} \leq v_0 < \widehat{1} \wedge p) \rrbracket^{vs} \leftrightarrow \llbracket \exists \widehat{0} \leq v_0 < \widehat{1} \wedge p \rrbracket^{vs} \quad (14)$$

The implementation of $\mathsf{ferrack}$ is based on (15) (Lemma 1.1 in [15]), a consequence of the nature of $\mathcal{R}$-expressible sets: for a $\mathcal{R}$-linear formula p, the set $\{x | \llbracket p \rrbracket^{x \cdot vs}\}$ is a finite union of *intervals*, whose endpoints are either $\frac{\llbracket t \rrbracket_\rho^{x \cdot vs}}{c}$ for some $(t, c) \in \{\mathcal{U} \ p\}$ (cf. Fig. 2), $-\infty$ or $+\infty$. In Fig. 2, p_- and p_+ are defined as

p	$\mathcal{U} \ p$	$\mathcal{B} \ p$	p_-	p_+
$p \wedge q$	$(\mathcal{U} \ p)@(\mathcal{U} \ q)$	$(\mathcal{B} \ p)@(\mathcal{B} \ q)$	$p_- \wedge q_-$	$p_+ \wedge q_+$
$p \vee q$	$(\mathcal{U} \ p)@(\mathcal{U} \ q)$	$(\mathcal{B} \ p)@(\mathcal{B} \ q)$	$p_- \vee q_-$	$p_+ \vee q_+$
$c * v_0 + t = 0$	$[(-t, c)]$	$[\widehat{-1} - t]$	F	F
$c * v_0 + t \neq 0$	$[(-t, c)]$	$[-t]$	T	T
$c * v_0 + t < 0$	$[(-t, c)]$	$[]$	T	F
$c * v_0 + t \leq 0$	$[(-t, c)]$	$[]$	T	F
$c * v_0 + t > 0$	$[(-t, c)]$	$[-t]$	F	T
$c * v_0 + t \geq 0$	$[(-t, c)]$	$[\widehat{-1} - t]$	F	T
$-$	$[]$	$[]$	p	p

Fig. 2. $\mathcal{U} \ p, \mathcal{B} \ p, p_-, p_+$

to simulate the behavior of p, where v_0 is interpreted by arbitrarily small (resp. big) real numbers.

$$\mathsf{islin}_\mathcal{R} \ p \rightarrow (\exists x. \llbracket p \rrbracket^{x \cdot vs} \leftrightarrow \llbracket p_- \rrbracket^{x \cdot vs} \vee \llbracket p_+ \rrbracket^{x \cdot vs}$$

$$\vee \exists ((t, i), (s, j)) \in \{\mathcal{U} \ p\}^2. \llbracket p \rrbracket^{((\llbracket t \rrbracket_\rho^{x \cdot vs}/\underline{i} + \llbracket s \rrbracket_\rho^{x \cdot vs}/\underline{j})/\underline{2}) \cdot vs}) \quad (15)$$

For the proof of (15), assume $\mathsf{islin}_\mathcal{R} \ p$. The conclusion of (15) has the form $A \leftrightarrow B \vee C \vee D$. Obviously $D \rightarrow A$ holds. We first prove $B \rightarrow A$ and $C \rightarrow A$. For this we prove the following properties for p_- and p_+ by induction on p. The proof is simple: we provide y.

$$\mathsf{islin}_\mathcal{R} \ p \rightarrow \mathsf{unbound}_\phi \ (p_-) \wedge \exists y. \forall x < y. \llbracket p_- \rrbracket^{x \cdot vs} \leftrightarrow \llbracket p \rrbracket^{x \cdot vs} \quad (16)$$

$$\mathsf{islin}_\mathcal{R} \ p \rightarrow \mathsf{unbound}_\phi \ (p_+) \wedge \exists y. \forall x > y. \llbracket p_+ \rrbracket^{x \cdot vs} \leftrightarrow \llbracket p \rrbracket^{x \cdot vs} \quad (17)$$

Now assume that $[\![p_-]\!]^{x \cdot vs}$ holds for some x. Since $\mathsf{unbound}_\phi \ p_-$ holds, we have by (2) that $[\![p_-]\!]^{z \cdot vs}$ holds for any z, e.g. for $z < y$, where y is obtained from (16). Consequently z is a witness for p. Analogously we prove $\exists x.[\![p_+]\!]^{x \cdot vs} \to \exists x.[\![p]\!]^{x \cdot vs}$. This finishes the proof of $B \vee C \vee D \to A$. Now we only have to prove $A \wedge \neg B \wedge \neg C \to D$. For this assume $[\![p]\!]^{x \cdot vs}$ for some x and $\neg [\![p_-]\!]^{x \cdot vs}$ and $\neg [\![p_+]\!]^{x \cdot vs}$. This means that x is a withness for p that is neither too large nor too small. Hence x must lie in an interval with endpoints in $M_p = \{ \frac{[\![t]\!]_\rho^{x \cdot vs}}{i} | (t, i) \in \{\mathcal{U} \ p\} \}$. This is expressed by (18).

$$\mathsf{islin}_{\mathcal{R}} \ p \wedge \neg [\![p_-]\!]^{x \cdot vs} \wedge \neg [\![p_+]\!]^{x \cdot vs} \wedge [\![p]\!]^{x \cdot vs}$$
$$\to \exists ((t, i), (s, j)) \in \{\mathcal{U} \ p\}^2 . \frac{[\![t]\!]_\rho^{x \cdot vs}}{i} \leq x \leq \frac{[\![s]\!]_\rho^{x \cdot vs}}{j} \tag{18}$$

The proof of (18) is easy. In fact its main part is done automatically. Now we conclude that either $x \in M_p$, in which case we are done (remember that $\frac{x+x}{2} = x$), or we can find the *smallest* interval with endpoints in M_p containing x, i.e. $l_x < x < u_x \wedge \forall y.l_x < y < u_x \to y \notin M_p$ for some $(l_x, u_x) \in M_p^2$. The construction of this *smallest* interval is simple.

Now we prove a main property of $\mathcal{R}$-formulae (19), which shows the the expressibility limitations of $\mathcal{R}$. A $\mathcal{R}$-formula p does *not* change its truth value over smallest intervals with endpoints in M_p, i.e.

$$\mathsf{islin}_{\mathcal{R}} \ p \wedge l < x < u \wedge (\forall y.l < y < u \to y \notin M_p)$$
$$\wedge [\![p]\!]^{x \cdot vs} \to \forall y.l < y < u \to [\![p]\!]^{y \cdot vs} \tag{19}$$

The proof of (19) is by induction on p. The cases $\neq 0$ and $= 0$ are trivial. Assume p is $c * v_0 + t < 0$ and let $z = -\frac{[\![t]\!]^{x \cdot vs}}{c}$. From $[\![p]\!]^{x \cdot vs}$ we have $x < z$. Since $l < y < u$ and $z \in M_p$ we have $y \neq z$. Hence $y < z$ (which is $[\![p]\!]^{y \cdot vs}$), for if $y > z$ then $l < z < u$, which contradicts the premises since $z \in M_p$. The other interesting cases are proved analogously.

Since $[\![p]\!]^{x \cdot vs}$ and $l_x < x < u_x \wedge \forall y.l_x < y < u_x \to y \notin M_p$ for some $(l_x, u_x) \in M_p^2$, we conclude that $[\![p]\!]^{z \cdot vs}$ for any z such that $l_x < z < u_x$. Taking $z = \frac{l_x + u_x}{2}$ finishes the proof of (15).

In order to provide an implementation of ferrack, we define in Fig. 3 a function to simulate the substitution of $(\frac{[\![t]\!]_\rho^{x \cdot vs}}{i} + \frac{[\![s]\!]_\rho^{x \cdot vs}}{j})/2$ for v_0 in p, since division is not included in our language. We use the notation $p[(\frac{t}{i} + \frac{s}{j})/2]$ for this substitution. The main property is expressed by

$$\mathsf{islin}_{\mathcal{R}} \ p \wedge i > 0 \wedge j > 0 \wedge \mathsf{unbound}_\rho \ t \wedge \mathsf{unbound}_\rho \ s$$
$$\to \mathsf{unbound}_\phi (p[(\frac{t}{i} + \frac{s}{j})/2]) \tag{20}$$
$$\wedge ([\![p[(\frac{t}{i} + \frac{s}{j})/2]]\!]^{x \cdot vs} \leftrightarrow [\![p]\!]^{(([\![t]\!]_\rho^{x \cdot vs}/i + [\![s]\!]_\rho^{x \cdot vs}/j)/2) \cdot vs})$$

For the implementation of the bounded existential quantifier in (15) we use a function $\mathsf{eval}_\vee$, which basically evaluates a function f lazily over a list $[a_0, \ldots, a_n]$. The result represents $f\, a_0 \vee \ldots \vee f\, a_n$, i.e.

$$\forall vs, ps. [\![\mathsf{eval}_\vee\, f\, ps]\!]^{vs} \leftrightarrow \exists p \in \{\!\{ps\}\!\}. [\![f\, p]\!]^{vs} \tag{21}$$

$$
\begin{aligned}
(p \wedge q)[(\tfrac{t}{i} + \tfrac{s}{j})/2] &= p[(\tfrac{t}{i} + \tfrac{s}{j})/2] \wedge q[(\tfrac{t}{i} + \tfrac{s}{j})/2] \\
(p \vee q)[(\tfrac{t}{i} + \tfrac{s}{j})/2] &= p[(\tfrac{t}{i} + \tfrac{s}{j})/2] \vee q[(\tfrac{t}{i} + \tfrac{s}{j})/2] \\
(c * v_0 + t' \bowtie 0)[(\tfrac{t}{i} + \tfrac{s}{j})/2] &= 2{\cdot}j * t + 2{\cdot}i * s + 2{\cdot}i{\cdot}j * t' \bowtie 0 \\
p[(\tfrac{t}{i} + \tfrac{s}{j})/2] &= p
\end{aligned}
$$

$$\mathsf{ferrack}\, p = \mathsf{let}\ \sigma = \lambda((t,i),(s,j)). p[(\tfrac{t}{i} + \tfrac{s}{j})/2];\ U = \mathcal{U}\, p$$
$$\mathsf{in}\ \mathsf{decr}(\mathsf{eval}_\vee\, \sigma\, (\mathsf{allpairs}\, U\, U))$$

Fig. 3. Substitution, $\mathsf{eval}_\vee$ and ferrack

The implementation of ferrack is given in Fig. 3. The function allpairs satisfies $\{\!\{\mathsf{allpairs}\, xs\, ys\}\!\} = \{\!\{xs\}\!\} \times \{\!\{ys\}\!\}$. For a $\mathcal{R}$-linear formula p, $[\![\mathsf{ferrack}\, p]\!]^{vs}$ is hence equivalent to

$$\exists ((t,i),(s,j)) \in \{\!\{\mathcal{U}\, p\}\!\}^2. [\![p]\!]^{(([\![t]\!]_\rho^{x \cdot vs}/i + [\![s]\!]_\rho^{x \cdot vs}/j)/2) \cdot vs}.$$

The proof of (14) needs the following observation. Recall that the input to $qe_{\mathcal{R}_l}$ in mir (cf. § 3) is $p = \widehat{0} \leq v_0 < \widehat{1} \wedge p'$, for some linear formula p' and hence $[\![p_-]\!]^{x \cdot vs} \leftrightarrow [\![p_+]\!]^{x \cdot vs} \leftrightarrow False$ and consequently ferrack correctly ignores p_- and p_+ (recall (15)). An implementation that covers all $\mathcal{R}$-linear formulae should simply include p_- and p_+.

5   Quantifier Elimination for $\mathcal{Z}$

We present cooper, a verified qep. for $\mathcal{Z}$ based on [12], and prove (22).

$$\mathsf{islin}_{\mathcal{Z}}\, p\, (\underline{i} \cdot vs) \rightarrow [\![\mathsf{cooper}\, p]\!]^{vs} \leftrightarrow \exists i. [\![p]\!]^{i \cdot vs} \tag{22}$$

The input to Cooper's algorithm is a $\mathcal{Z}$-linear formula p. We only consider linear formulae where the coefficients of v_0 are $\widehat{1}$, since $\exists i. Q(d{\cdot}i) \leftrightarrow \exists i.d \mid i \wedge Q(i)$ holds. It is straightforward to convert p into $p' = \mathsf{adjust}\, p\, d$, and prove (23), cf. [11].

$$\mathsf{islin}_{\mathcal{Z}}\, p\, (\underline{i} \cdot vs) \wedge \mathsf{dvd}_{\widehat{c}}\, p\, d \wedge d > 0 \rightarrow \mathsf{islin}_{\mathcal{Z}}\, (\mathsf{adjust}\, p\, d)\, (\underline{i} \cdot vs)$$
$$\wedge \mathsf{dvd}_{\widehat{c}}\, (\mathsf{adjust}\, p\, d)\, 1 \wedge [\![\mathsf{adjust}\, p\, d]\!]^{(d \cdot i) \cdot vs} \leftrightarrow [\![p]\!]^{i \cdot vs} \tag{23}$$
$$\mathsf{islin}_{\mathcal{Z}}\, p\, (\underline{i} \cdot vs) \rightarrow \mathsf{dvd}_{\widehat{c}}\, p\, (\mathsf{lcm}_{\widehat{c}}\, p) \wedge \mathsf{lcm}_{\widehat{c}}\, p > 0 \tag{24}$$

The predicate $\mathsf{dvd}_{\widehat{c}}\, p\, d$ is true exactly when all the coefficients $\widehat{c}$ of v_0 in p satisfy $c \mid d$. A candidate for d is $lcm\{c \mid c * v_0 \text{ occurs in } p\}$, which is computed recursively by $\mathsf{lcm}_{\widehat{c}}$, cf. (24).

$$\text{cooper } p = \textsf{let } d = \textsf{lcm}_{\hat{c}} \ p; q = d \mid 1 * v_0 + \widehat{0} \wedge (\textsf{adjust } p \ d); \delta = \delta_q;$$
$$M = \textsf{eval}_\vee \ (\lambda j.q_-[\widehat{j}])[1..\delta];$$
$$B = \textsf{eval}_\vee \ (\lambda(b,j).q[b+\widehat{j}]) \ (\textsf{allpairs } (\mathcal{B} \ q) \ [1..\delta]) \ \textsf{in}$$
$$\textsf{decr}(M \vee B)$$

Fig. 4. cooper

A fundamental property is that, for any $\mathbb{Z}$-linear p, the set $\{i | [\![p]\!]^{i \cdot vs}\}$ differs from a periodic subset of $\mathbb{Z}$ *only* by a finite set (involving $\mathcal{B} \ p$, cf. Fig. 2). Let δ_p be $lcm\{d | d \mid 1 * v_0 + t$ occurs in $p\}$, then (25) (Cooper's theorem [12]) expresses this fundamental property.

$$\textsf{islin}_\mathbb{Z} \ p \ (\underline{i} \cdot vs) \wedge \textsf{dvd}_{\hat{c}} \ p \ 1 \rightarrow$$
$$\exists i. [\![p]\!]^{i \cdot vs} \leftrightarrow \exists j \in \{1..\delta_p\}. [\![p_-]\!]^{j \cdot vs} \vee \exists b \in \{\!\{\mathcal{B} \ p\}\!\}. [\![p]\!]^{(j + [\![b]\!]_\rho^{i \cdot vs}) \cdot vs} \tag{25}$$

The proof is simple and we refer the reader to [12,28,10,20] for the mathematical details and to [11] for a verified formalization.

The implementation of cooper is shown in Fig. 4. First the coefficients of v_0 are normalized to one. This step is correct by (23) and (24). After computing $\delta \ p$ and $\mathcal{B} \ p$, the appropriate disjunction is generated using $\textsf{eval}_\vee$. The properties (21),(25) and (2) finish the proof of (22).

6 Formalization and Integration Issues

6.1 Normal Forms

When defining a function (over ρ or ϕ) we assume the input to have a precise syntactical shape, i.e. satisfy a given predicate. This not only simplifies the function definition but is also crucial for its correctness proofs. In [11], such functions used deeply nested pattern matching, which gives rise to a considerable number of equations, for the recursive definitions package avoids overlapping equations by performing completion. To avoid this problem, the ρ-datatype contains additional constructor CX int ρ, not shown so far. Its intended meaning is $[\![CX \ c \ t]\!]_\rho^{vs} = [\![c * v_0 + t]\!]_\rho^{vs}$. In fact all the previous occurrences of $c * v_0 + t$ can be understood as a syntactic sugar for CX c t. Both proofs and implementation are simpler. In the ρ-datatype definition we also included only multiplication by a constant and it was maladroit not to do so in [11].

6.2 Optimizations

Our implementation includes not only the optimization presented in § 4, i.e. omitting the generation of p_- and p_+ in ferrack, but also several others, left out for space limitations. For instance several procedures scrutinize and simplify ρ-terms and ϕ-formulae. These are also used to keep the $\mathcal{U}$, cf. § 4, and $\mathcal{B}$, cf. § 5, small, which considerably affects the output size of ferrack and cooper. The evaluation of large disjunctions is done lazily. In [12], Cooper proved a dual lemma to (25) that uses substitution of arbitrary large numbers, cf. p_+ in Fig. 2 and a set $\mathcal{A}$, dual to $\mathcal{B}$. We formalized this duality principle, cf. [11] for more details, and choose the smaller set in the implementation. The generic qep. qelim_ϕ, cf. § 2.2, pushes ∃ inwards before every elimination. *All these optimizations are formally proved correct.*

6.3 Integration

We integrate the formalized qep. by providing an ML-function *reif*. Given a HOL subgoal P, it constructs a ϕ-formula p and a HOL-list vs such that the theorem $[\![p]\!]^{vs} = P$ can be proved in HOL. Obviously we can replace $[\![p]\!]^{vs}$ by $[\![\mathsf{qelim}_\phi \; \mathsf{mir} \; p]\!]^{vs}$ and then we either use rewriting or run the generated code, depending on our trust in the code generator. Of course *reif* can not succeed on every subgoal, since ϕ-formulae represent only a (small) subset of HOL-formulae. Note that the completeness of the integrated qep. relies *entirely* on the completeness of *reif*.

6.4 Performance

Since our development is novice, we have only tested the qep.for small reasonable looking examples. The generated code proves e.g. $\forall x.2 \cdot \lfloor x \rfloor \leq \lfloor 2 \cdot x \rfloor \leq 2 \cdot \lfloor x + 1 \rfloor$ within 0.06 sec. but needs more than 10 sec. to prove $\forall x, y. \lfloor x \rfloor = \lfloor y \rfloor \rightarrow 0 \leq |y - x| \leq 1$. The main causes are as follows:

- mir reduces the problem blindly to $\mathcal{R}$ and $\mathcal{Z}$, while often only $qe_\mathcal{R}$ or $qe_\mathcal{Z}$ is sufficient to eliminate ∃.
- The substitution in Fig. 3 gratuitously introduces big coefficients, which *heavily* influences the output size of cooper.
- cooper introduces big coefficients (which appear in $\cdot \mid \cdot$ atoms!), due to the global nature of the method (see [33]), which *heavily* influences the output size of $\mathsf{lin}_\mathcal{R}$.

Solving these problems is part of our future work.

7 Conclusion

We presented a formally verified and executable qep. for $\mathcal{R}_{\lfloor \cdot \rfloor}$, based on [38], and corroborate the maturity of modern theorem provers to assist formalizing state of the art qep. within acceptable time (1 month) and space (4000 lines). Our formalization includes a qep. for $\mathcal{R}$ à la [15] and Copper's qep. for $\mathcal{Z}$, that could be replaced by more efficient yet verified ones, e.g. [24,33]. Our work represents a new substantial application of reflection as well as a challenge for code generators, e.g. [7], to generate proof-producing code. Decision procedures developed this way are easier to maintain and to share with other theorem provers. This is one key issue to deal with the growing challenges, such as Flyspeck[1], modern theorem provers have to face.

Acknowledgment. I am thankful to Tobias Nipkow for suggesting the topic and for advice. I am also thankful to Clemens Ballarin, Michael Norrish and Norbert Schirmer for useful comments on a draft.

---

[1] http://www.math.pitt.edu/~thales/flyspeck/

References

1. Andrew W. Appel and Amy P. Felty. Dependent types ensure partial correctness of theorem provers. *J. Funct. Program.*, 14(1):3–19, 2004.
2. Henk Barendregt. Reflection and its use: from science to meditation, 2002.
3. Henk Barendregt and Erik Barendsen. Autarkic computations in formal proofs. *J. Autom. Reasoning*, 28(3):321–336, 2002.
4. Bruno Barras. Programming and computing in HOL. In *Proceedings of the 13th International Conference on Theorem Proving in Higher Order Logics*, pages 17–37. Springer-Verlag, 2000.
5. Sergey Berezin, Vijay Ganesh, and David L. Dill. An online proof-producing decision procedure for mixed-integer linear arithmetic. In Hubert Garavel and John Hatcliff, editors, *TACAS*, volume 2619 of *LNCS*, pages 521–536. Springer, 2003.
6. Stefan Berghofer. Towards generating proof producing code from HOL definitions. Private communication.
7. Stefan Berghofer and Tobias Nipkow. Executing higher order logic. In *In Types for Proofs and Programs (TYPES 2000)*, volume 2277 of *LNCS*, pages 24–40. Springer-Verlag, 2002.
8. Y. Bertot and P. Castéran. *Coq'Art: The Calculus of Inductive Constructions*, volume XXV of *Text in theor. comp. science: an EATCS series*. Springer, 2004.
9. Bernard Boigelot, Sébastien Jodogne, and Pierre Wolper. An effective decision procedure for linear arithmetic over the integers and reals. *ACM Trans. Comput. Log.*, 6(3):614–633, 2005.
10. A. Chaieb and T. Nipkow. Generic proof synthesis for presburger arithmetic. Technical report, Technische Universität München, 2003.
11. A. Chaieb and T. Nipkow. Verifying and reflecting quantifier elimination for Presburger arithmetic. In G. Stutcliffe and A. Voronkov, editors, *Logic for Programming, Artificial Intelligence, and Reasoning*, volume 3835. Springer-Verlag, 2005.
12. D.C. Cooper. Theorem proving in arithmetic without multiplication. In B. Meltzer and D. Michie, editors, *Machine Intelligence*, volume 7, pages 91–100. Edinburgh University Press, 1972.
13. Pierre Crégut. Une procédure de décision réflexive pour un fragment de l'arithmétique de Presburger. In *Informal proceedings of the 15th journées francophones des langages applicatifs*, 2004. In French.
14. M. Davis. A computer program for presburger's algorithm. In *Summaries of talks presented at the Summer Inst. for Symbolic Logic, Cornell University*, pages 215–233. Inst. for Defense Analyses, Princeton, NJ, 1957.
15. Jeanne Ferrante and Charles Rackoff. A decision procedure for the first order theory of real addition with order. *SIAM J. Comput.*, 4(1):69–76, 1975.
16. Jeanne Ferrante and Charles Rackoff. *The Computational Complexity of Logical Theories*, volume 718 of *Lecture Notes in Mathematics*. Springer Verlag, NY, 1979.
17. Fischer and Rabin. Super-exponential complexity of presburger arithmetic. In *SIAMAMS: Complexity of Computation: Proc. of a Symp. in Appl. Math. of the AMS and the Society for Industrial and Applied Mathematics*, 1974.
18. J. Fourier. Solution d'une question particulière du calcul des inegalités. *Nouveau Bulletin des Sciences par la Scociété Philomatique de Paris*, pages 99–100, 1823.
19. John Harrison. Metatheory and reflection in theorem proving: A survey and critique. Technical Report CRC-053, SRI Cambridge, Millers Yard, Cambridge, UK, 1995. http://www.cl.cam.ac.uk/users/jrh/papers/reflect.dvi.gz.
20. John. R. Harrison. Introduction to logic and theorem proving. To appear.

21. Douglas J. Howe. Computational Metatheory in Nuprl. In Ewing L. Lusk and Ross A. Overbeek, editors, *CADE*, volume 310 of *LNCS*, pages 238–257, 1988.
22. Felix Klaedtke. On the automata size for Presburger arithmetic. In *Proceedings of the 19th Annual IEEE Symposium on Logic in Computer Science (LICS 2004)*, pages 110–119. IEEE Computer Society Press, 2004.
23. Robert Klapper and Aaron Stump. Validated Proof-Producing Decision Procedures. In C. Tinelli and S. Ranise, editors, *2nd Int. Workshop Pragmatics of Decision Procedures in Automated Reasoning*, 2004.
24. Rüdiger Loos and Volker Weispfenning. Applying linear quantifier elimination. *Comput. J.*, 36(5):450–462, 1993.
25. Sean McLaughlin and John Harrison. A proof-producing decision procedure for real arithmetic. volume 3632 of *LNCS*, pages 295–314. Springer-Verlag, 2005.
26. Sean McLauglin. An Interpretation of Isabelle/HOL in HOL Light. In U. Furbach and N. Shankar, editors, *Automated Reasoning — IJCAR 2006*, 2006. To appear.
27. Tobias Nipkow, Lawrence Paulson, and Markus Wenzel. *Isabelle/HOL — A Proof Assistant for Higher-Order Logic*, volume 2283 of *LNCS*. Springer-Verlag, 2002. http://www.in.tum.de/~nipkow/LNCS2283/.
28. Michael Norrish. Complete integer decision procedures as derived rules in HOL. In D.A. Basin and B. Wolff, editors, *Theorem Proving in Higher Order Logics, TPHOLs 2003*, volume 2758 of *LNCS*, pages 71–86. Springer-Verlag, 2003.
29. S. Obua and S. Skalberg. Importing HOL into Isabelle/HOL. In U. Furbach and N. Shankar, editors, *Automated Reasoning — IJCAR 2006*, 2006. To appear.
30. Derek C. Oppen. Elementary bounds for presburger arithmetic. In *STOC '73: Proceedings of the fifth annual ACM symposium on Theory of computing*, pages 34–37, New York, NY, USA, 1973. ACM Press.
31. Mojzesz Presburger. Über die Vollständigkeit eines gewissen Systems der Arithmetik ganzer Zahlen, in welchem die Addition als einzige Operation hervortritt. In *Comptes Rendus du I Congrès des Math. des Pays Slaves*, pages 92–101, 1929.
32. William Pugh. The Omega test: a fast and practical integer programming algorithm for dependence analysis. In *Proceedings of the 1991 ACM/IEEE conference on Supercomputing*, pages 4–13. ACM Press, 1991.
33. C. R. Reddy and D. W. Loveland. Presburger arithmetic with bounded quantifier alternation. In *STOC '78: Proceedings of the tenth annual ACM symposium on Theory of computing*, pages 320–325, New York, NY, USA, 1978. ACM Press.
34. T. Skolem. Über einige Satzfunktionen in der Arithmetik. In *Skrifter utgitt av Det Norske Videnskaps-Akademi i Oslo, I. Matematisk naturvidenskapelig klasse*, volume 7, pages 1–28. Oslo, 1931.
35. A. Tarski. *A Decision Method for Elementary Algebra and Geometry*. University of California Press, 2d edition, 1951.
36. Volker Weispfenning. The complexity of linear problems in fields. *J. Symb. Comput.*, 5(1/2):3–27, 1988.
37. Volker Weispfenning. The complexity of almost linear diophantine problems. *J. Symb. Comput.*, 10(5):395–404, 1990.
38. Volker Weispfenning. Mixed real-integer linear quantifier elimination. In *ISSAC '99: Proceedings of the 1999 international symposium on Symbolic and algebraic computation*, pages 129–136, New York, NY, USA, 1999. ACM Press.
39. Pierre Wolper and Bernard Boigelot. An automata-theoretic approach to presburger arithmetic constraints (extended abstract). In *SAS '95: Proc. of the Second Int. Symp. on Static Analysis*, pages 21–32, London, UK, 1995. Springer-Verlag.

Presburger Modal Logic Is PSPACE-Complete*

Stéphane Demri[1] and Denis Lugiez[2]

[1] Laboratoire Spécification et Vérification
CNRS & INRIA Futurs projet SECSI & ENS Cachan
demri@lsv.ens-cachan.fr
[2] Laboratoire d'Informatique Fondamentale, Marseille
UMR 6166 CNRS-Université de Provence
lugiez@lif.univ-mrs.fr

Abstract. We introduce a Presburger modal logic PML with regularity constraints and full Presburger constraints on the number of children that generalize graded modalities, also known as number restrictions in description logics. We show that PML satisfiability is only PSPACE-complete by designing a Ladner-like algorithm. This extends a well-known and non-trivial PSPACE upper bound for graded modal logic. Furthermore, we provide a detailed comparison with logics that contain Presburger constraints and that are dedicated to query XML documents. As an application, we show that satisfiability for Sheaves Logic SL is PSPACE-complete, improving significantly its best known upper bound.

1 Introduction

Logics for XML Documents. In order to query XML documents with Presburger and/or regular constraints, logical and automata-based formalisms have been recently introduced [ZL06, SSMH04, BT05] leading to various expressiveness and complexity results about logics and specialized tree automata. As usual, XML documents are viewed as labeled, unranked ordered trees. For instance, a logic with fixed-point operators, Presburger and regularity constraints is shown EXPTIME-complete in [SSMH04], improving results for description logics with qualified number restrictions [CG05]. At the same period, the sister logic SL ("Sheaves Logic") is shown decidable in [ZL03]. The more expressive logic GDL is however shown undecidable in [ZL06] since GDL can express properties about disjoint sequences of children. More generally, designing modal logics for semistructured data, either for tree-like models [Mar03, ABD+05] or for graph-like models [ADdR03, BCT04] has been a fruitful approach since it allows to reuse known technical machineries adapted to special purpose formalisms.

Our Motivation. The main goal of this work is to introduce a modal logic allowing Presburger constraints (more general than those in graded modal logics [BC85, Tob00] or description logics [HST00, CG05]) and with regularity constraints as in the logical formalisms from [Wol83, ZL03, SSMH04] but with a

---

* The second author has been supported by the research program ACI "Masse de données".

U. Furbach and N. Shankar (Eds.): IJCAR 2006, LNAI 4130, pp. 541–556, 2006.

satisfiability problem in polynomial space which would refine decidability and complexity results from [Tob00, SSMH04, ZL06]. Such an hypothetical logic would be much more helpful than the minimal modal logic K that is also known to be PSPACE-complete [Lad77] but K has not the ability to express such complex Presburger and regularity constraints. With such requirements, fixed-point operators are out of the game since modal μ-calculus is already EXPTIME-complete. Similarly, Presburger constraints should be in a normal form since full Presburger logic has already a complexity higher than 2EXPTIME. It is worth observing that as far as memory ressources are concerned, no EXPTIME-complete problem is known to be solved in polynomial space. Hence, the potential difference between EXPTIME-completeness and PSPACE-completeness remains, so far, a significant gap in practice for running algorithms.

Our Contribution. We consider a Presburger modal logic PML with full Presburger constraints on the number of children and with regularity constraints. It is a minor variant of either the fixed-point free fragment of [SSMH04] or the Sheaves Logic SL [ZL06]. The exact relationships between PML, SL and the logic from [SSMH04] are provided in the paper. We show that the satisfiability problem is PSPACE-complete (only the binary representation for integers is used). The complexity upper bound is proved with a Ladner-like algorithm, see the original one in [Lad77] and strongly related tableaux methods in [Gor99]. This result generalizes what is known about graded modal logic [Fin72, BC85, Tob00] and apart from its larger scope, we believe our proof is also much more transparent. Even though some of the bounds used in our algorithm are obtained by a careful analysis of proofs from [SSMH04], our algorithm can be viewed as the optimal composition between an algorithm that transforms a PML formula into a Presburger tree automata and an algorithm that tests emptiness for these peculiar Presburger tree automata. This provides a new and non-trivial PSPACE complexity upper bound that is not a direct consequence of [SSMH04] since composing a polynomial space reduction with a polynomial space test does not imply the existence of a direct polynomial space test for the composition. For example, runs of linearly-bounded alternating Turing machines can be computed in polynomial space and testing if a run is accepting can be done in polynomial space in the size of the run. However, since APSPACE = EXPTIME, it is unlikely that the composition can be done in PSPACE. Additionally, our algorithm substantially refines results from [ZL03, SSMH04]. Indeed, as by-products of the PSPACE-completeness of PML, we show that SL satisfiability [ZL06] is PSPACE-complete, the fixed-point free fragment of the main logic from [SSMH04] is also PSPACE-complete and the logic PDL$_{tree}$ from [ABD+05] is undecidable when extended with Presburger constraints. The complexity upper bounds are established via a logspace reduction whereas the PSPACE lower bound is proved by reducing satisfiability for the modal logic K restricted to the only truth constants as atomic formulae and characterized by the class of all the Kripke structures or equivalently by the class of all finite trees. Indeed, PSPACE-hardness of this very K fragment is already known [Hem01].

Omitted proofs can be found in the report [DL06].

2   Presburger Modal Logic

Given countably infinite sets $AP = \{p_1, p_2, \ldots\}$ of propositional variables and $\Sigma = \{R_1, R_2, \ldots\}$ of symbol relations, we define the set of formulae and terms inductively as follows: $\phi ::= p \mid \neg\phi \mid \phi \wedge \phi \mid t \sim b \mid t \equiv_k c \mid \mathcal{A}(R, \phi_1, \ldots, \phi_n)$ and $l ::= u \times \sharp^R \psi \mid l + a \times \sharp^R \phi$, where $p \in AP$, $R \in \Sigma$, $b, k, c \in \mathbb{N}$, $a \in \mathbb{Z}$, $\sim \in \{<, >, =\}$ and $\mathcal{A}$ is a nondeterministic finite-state automaton over an n-letter alphabet $\Sigma_\mathcal{A}$ in which the letters are linearly ordered $\Sigma_\mathcal{A} = a_1, \ldots, a_n$. The language accepted by $\mathcal{A}$ is denoted by $L(\mathcal{A})$. We write $|\phi|$ to denote the size of the formula ϕ with some reasonably succinct encoding and $md(\phi)$ to denote the "modal degree" of ϕ defined as the maximal number of imbrications of the symbol $\sharp$ in ϕ.

A term of the form $a_1 \times \sharp^{R_1}\phi_1 + \ldots + a_m \times \sharp^{R_m}\phi_m$ is abbreviated by $\Sigma_i a_i \sharp^{R_i}\phi_i$. Because of the presence of Boolean operators and quantifier-elimination for Presburger arithmetic, any kind of Presburger constraints can be expressed in this formalism, maybe less concisely with respect to an analogous language with quantifiers. We assume in the following that the automata are encoded reasonably succinctly and the elements in $\mathbb{Z}$ are represented with a binary encoding.

A model $\mathcal{M}$ for PML is a structure $\mathcal{M} = \langle T, (R_R)_{R \in \Sigma}, (<_{nd}^R)_{nd \in T}, l \rangle$ where

- T is the set of nodes (possibly infinite),
- $(R_R)_{R \in \Sigma}$ is a family of binary relations in $T \times T$ such that for all $R \in \Sigma$ and $nd \in T$, the set $\{nd' \in T : \langle nd, nd' \rangle \in T\}$ is finite (finite-branching),
- each relation $<_{nd}^R$ is a total ordering on the R_R-successors of nd,
- $l : T \to 2^{AP}$ is the valuation function.

In the rest of the paper, we write $R_R(nd) = nd_1 < \ldots < nd_\alpha$ to mean that $R_R(nd) \stackrel{\text{def}}{=} \{nd' \in T : \langle nd, nd' \rangle \in R_R\} = \{nd_1, \ldots, nd_\alpha\}$, and $nd_1 <_{nd}^R \ldots <_{nd}^R nd_\alpha$. Given a finite-branching binary relation $R \subseteq T \times T$, we write $R^\sharp(q)$ to denote the cardinal of the set $\{q' \in T : \langle q, q' \rangle \in R\}$. The satisfaction relation is inductively defined below where $\mathcal{M}$ is a model for PML and $nd \in T$:

- $\mathcal{M}, nd \models p$ iff $p \in l(nd)$; $\mathcal{M}, nd \models \neg\phi$ iff not $\mathcal{M}, nd \models \phi$,
- $\mathcal{M}, nd \models \phi_1 \wedge \phi_2$ iff $\mathcal{M}, nd \models \phi_1$ and $\mathcal{M}, nd \models \phi_2$,
- $\mathcal{M}, nd \models \Sigma_i a_i \sharp^{R_i}\phi_i \sim b$ iff $\Sigma_i a_i R_{R_i, \phi_i}^\sharp(nd) \sim b$ with $R_{R_i, \phi_i} = \{\langle nd', nd'' \rangle \in T \times T : \langle nd', nd'' \rangle \in R_{R_i}$, and $\mathcal{M}, nd'' \models \phi_i\}$,
- $\mathcal{M}, nd \models \Sigma_i a_i \sharp^{R_i}\phi_i \equiv_k c$ iff there is $n \in \mathbb{N}$ such that $\Sigma_i a_i R_{R_i, \phi_i}^\sharp(nd) = nk + c$,
- $\mathcal{M}, nd \models \mathcal{A}(R, \phi_1, \ldots, \phi_n)$ iff there is $a_{i_1} \cdots a_{i_\alpha} \in L(\mathcal{A})$ such that $R_R(nd) = nd_1 < \ldots < nd_\alpha$ and for every $j \in \{1, \ldots, \alpha\}$, $\mathcal{M}, nd_j \models \phi_{i_j}$.

The automata in PML are used exactly as those defining temporal operators in extended temporal logic [Wol83]. The modal operator $\Diamond$ (see e.g. [BdRV01]) is defined by $\Diamond\phi \approx \sharp^R\phi \geqslant 1$ (and dually $\Box\phi \approx \sharp^R\neg\phi = 0$) whereas formula $\Diamond_{\geqslant n}\phi$ from graded modal logic is defined by $\Diamond_{\geqslant n}\phi \approx \sharp^R\phi \geqslant n$. A basic example of what PML can express and graded modal logic cannot is that "there are twice more children satisfying p than children satisfying q" which can be stated by $\sharp^R p - 2\sharp^R q = 0$.

A formula ϕ of PML is satisfiable whenever there exist a model $\mathcal{M} = \langle T, (R_R)_{R\in\Sigma}, (<_{nd}^R)_{nd\in T}, l\rangle$ and $nd \in T$ such that $\mathcal{M}, nd \models \phi$. Even though PML models are defined from general Kripke structures (apart from the fact that they are finite-branching), we show below that we can restrict ourselves to finite unranked ordered trees.

Lemma 1. *For every PML formula ϕ, ϕ is satisfiable iff ϕ is satisfiable in a model $\mathcal{M}$ such that for all relation symbols R occurring in ϕ and $nd \in T$, the restriction of $\langle T, R_R\rangle$ to $R_R^*(nd)$ is a tree.*

Proof. Suppose that ϕ has a PML model $\mathcal{M} = \langle T, (R_R)_{R\in\Sigma}, (<_{nd}^R)_{nd\in T}, l\rangle$ and state $nd \in T$ such that $\mathcal{M}, nd \models \phi$. We build a model $\mathcal{M}'$ satisfying the tree condition by unfolding $\mathcal{M}$ in the standard way. However, it remains to define the corresponding linear ordering. The model $\mathcal{M}' = \langle T', (S_R)_{R\in\Sigma}, (<_{nd}^{'R})_{nd\in T'}, l'\rangle$ is defined as follows:

- T' is the set of finite non-empty sequences of the form $nd\,R_1\,nd_1\ldots R_k\,nd_k$,
- $(nd\,R_1\,nd_1\ldots R_n nd_n)\,S_R\,(nd\,R_1\,nd_1\ldots R_n\,nd_n\,R_{n+1}\,nd_{n+1})$ iff $\langle nd_n, nd_{n+1}\rangle \in R_R$ and $R = R_{n+1}$,
- $l'(nd\,R_1\,nd_1\ldots R_n\,nd_n) = l(nd_n)$ for every $nd\,R_1\,nd_1\ldots R_n\,nd_n \in T'$,
- each ordering $<_{nd'}^{'R}$ is the one induced by $<_{nd}^R$ by considering the last element nd of the sequence nd'.

One can show that for every $nd\,R_1\,nd_1\ldots R_n\,nd_n \in T'$ and PML formula ψ, $\mathcal{M}', nd\,R_1\,nd_1\ldots R_n\,nd_n \models \psi$ iff $\mathcal{M}, nd_n \models \psi$. In particular $\mathcal{M}, \langle nd\rangle \models \phi$.

Since the formula tree of every formula is finite and Presburger or regular constraints only speak about direct successors, we can establish the result below.

Lemma 2. *For every PML formula ϕ, ϕ is satisfiable iff ϕ is satisfiable in a model $\mathcal{M}$ such that T is finite and for all relation symbols R occurring in ϕ and $nd \in T$, the restriction of $\langle T, R_R\rangle$ to $R_R^*(nd)$ is a tree.*

Additionally, one relation symbol suffices as a consequent of the result below.

Lemma 3. *For every PML formula ϕ, one can compute in logspace a PML formula ϕ' with a unique relation symbol R such that ϕ is satisfiable on finite trees iff ϕ' is satisfiable on finite trees.*

In the rest of the paper, we assume that Σ is a singleton set $\{R\}$, we write $\mathcal{A}(\phi_1, \ldots, \phi_n)$ instead of $\mathcal{A}(R, \phi_1, \ldots, \phi_n)$ and $\sharp\phi_i$ instead of $\sharp^R\phi_i$. Models are written as tuples $\langle T, R, (<_{nd})_{nd\in T}, l\rangle$.

3   An Optimal Algorithm for PML Satisfiability

In this section, we show that PML satisfiability can be solved in polynomial space by using a Ladner-like algorithm [Lad77]. The original algorithm [Lad77] is designed for the modal logics K and S4, see a tense extension in [Spa93].

3.1   Consistent Sets of Formulae

We define below a notion of closure à la Fisher-Ladner [FL79] for finite sets of formulae. Intuitively, the closure $\mathrm{cl}(X)$ of X contains all the formulae useful to evaluate the truth of formulae in X.

Definition 1. *Let X be a finite set of formulae. $\mathrm{cl}(X)$ is the smallest set of formulae such that*

- *$X \subseteq \mathrm{cl}(X)$, $\mathrm{cl}(X)$ is closed under subformulae,*
- *if $\psi \in \mathrm{cl}(X)$, then $\neg\psi \in \mathrm{cl}(X)$ (we identify $\neg\neg\psi$ with ψ),*
- *if $t \sim b \in \mathrm{cl}(X)$, then $t \sim' b \in \mathrm{cl}(X)$ for every $\sim' \in \{<, >, =\}$,*
- *let K be the lcm of all the constants k occurring in subformulae of the form $t \equiv_k c$. Without any loss of generality, we can assume that $\equiv_K$ does not occur in ϕ. If $t \equiv_k c \in \mathrm{cl}(X)$, then $t \equiv_K c' \in \mathrm{cl}(X)$ for every $c' \in \{0, \ldots, K-1\}$.*

A set X of formulae is said to be closed iff $\mathrm{cl}(X) = X$. Observe that $\mathrm{card}(\mathrm{cl}(X))$ is exponential in $\mathrm{card}(X)$, which is usually not a good start to establish a polynomial space upper bound. Nevertheless, consistent sets of formulae, the ones that may be satisfiable, contain exactly one formula from $\{t \equiv_K c : c \in \{0, \ldots, K-1\}\}$ for each constraint $t \equiv_k c'$ in X. Hence, as shown below, encoding consistent sets will require only linear space.

We refine the notion of closure by introducing a new parameter n: the distance from the root node to the current node where the formulae are evaluated. Each set $\mathrm{cl}(n, \phi)$ is therefore a subset of $\mathrm{cl}(\phi)$.

Definition 2. *Let ϕ be a PML formula. For $n \in \mathbb{N}$, $\mathrm{cl}(n, \phi)$ is the smallest set such that:*

- *$\mathrm{cl}(0, \phi) = \mathrm{cl}(\{\phi\})$, for every $n \in \mathbb{N}$, $\mathrm{cl}(n, \phi)$ is closed,*
- *for all $n \in \mathbb{N}$ and $\sharp\psi$ occurring in some formula of $\mathrm{cl}(n, \phi)$, $\psi \in \mathrm{cl}(n+1, \phi)$,*
- *for all $n \in \mathbb{N}$ and $\mathcal{A}(\phi_1, \ldots, \phi_m) \in \mathrm{cl}(n, \phi)$, $\{\phi_1, \ldots, \phi_m\} \subseteq \mathrm{cl}(n+1, \phi)$.*

We are only interested in subsets of $\mathrm{cl}(n, \phi)$ whose conjunction of its elements is PML satisfiable. A necessary condition to be satisfiable is to be consistent locally, i.e. at the propositional level and at the level of Presburger constraints. As far as these latter constraints are concerned, we are more interested to introduce a notion of consistency that allows a polynomial space encoding of consistent sets than to guarantee that the Presburger constraints in a given set are indeed satisfiable. This latter property is checked with constraint systems (see below) in the main algorithm. This is analogous to the requirement to check maximal consistency at the propositional level but not PML satisfiability at once.

Definition 3. *A set $X \subseteq \mathrm{cl}(n, \phi)$ is said to be n-locally consistent iff the conditions below hold:*

- *if $\neg\psi \in \mathrm{cl}(n, \phi)$, then $\neg\psi \in X$ iff $\psi \notin X$,*
- *if $\psi_1 \wedge \psi_2 \in \mathrm{cl}(n, \phi)$, then $\psi_1 \wedge \psi_2 \in X$ iff $\psi_1, \psi_2 \in X$,*
- *if $t \sim b \in \mathrm{cl}(n, X)$ then there is a unique $\sim' \in \{<, >, =\}$ s.t. $t \sim' b \in X$,*
- *if $t \equiv_k c \in \mathrm{cl}(n, X)$, then there is a unique $c' \in \{0, \ldots, K - 1\}$ such that $t \equiv_K c' \in X$,*
- *if $t \equiv_k c \in \mathrm{cl}(n, X)$, then $\neg t \equiv_k c \in X$ iff there is $c' \in \{0, \ldots, K - 1\}$ such that $t \equiv_K c' \in X$ and not $c' \equiv_k c$,*
- *if $t \sim b \in \mathrm{cl}(n, X)$ then $\neg t \sim b \in X$ iff there is $\sim' \in \{<, >, =\} \setminus \{\sim\}$ such that $t \sim' b \in X$.*

Lemma 4. *Let ϕ be a PML formula and $n \in \mathbb{N}$. (I) Every n-locally consistent set has cardinal at most $2 \times |\phi|$ and can be encoded with a polynomial amount of bits with respect to $|\phi|$. (II) $\mathrm{cl}(|\phi|, \phi) = \emptyset$.*

Let X be an n-consistent subset of $\mathrm{cl}(n, \phi)$. The set X is encoded as follows. To each subformula ψ in $\mathrm{cl}(n, \phi)$ that is neither a periodicity constraint of the form $t \equiv_K c$, nor a constraint of the form $t \sim b$, we associate a bit encoding whether ψ belongs to X. To each formula of the form $t \sim b$ in $\mathrm{cl}(n, \phi)$, we associate a value $\sim'$ in $\{<, >, =\}$ encoding the fact that $t \sim' b$ belongs to X. Analogously, to each formula of the form $t \equiv_k c$ in $\mathrm{cl}(n, \phi)$, we associate a value c' in $\{0, \ldots, K - 1\}$ encoding the fact that $t \equiv_K c'$ belongs to X. This unique c' requires $\mathcal{O}(|\phi|)$ bits to be encoded. Hence, each n-consistent subset of $\mathrm{cl}(n, \phi)$ can be encoded with $\mathcal{O}(|\phi|^2)$ bits.

3.2   Constraint Systems

In this section, we explain how a consistent set induces solutions from numerical constraint systems based on the Presburger and regularity constraints. A constraint system $\mathcal{S}$ over the set of variables $\{x_1, \ldots, x_n\}$ is a Presburger formula built over $\{x_1, \ldots, x_n\}$ that is a Boolean combination of atomic constraints of the form $\Sigma_j a_j \times x_{i_j} = b$ with each $a_j \in \mathbb{Z}$ and $b \in \mathbb{N}$. A positive solution for $\mathcal{S}$ is an element $\overline{x} \in \mathbb{N}^n$ such that $\overline{x} \models \mathcal{S}$ in Presburger arithmetic. We base our analysis on the following lemma, which follows from a result of Papadimitriou [Pap81].

Lemma 5. *Let $\mathcal{S}$ be a constraint system over $\{x_1, \ldots, x_n\}$. $\mathcal{S}$ has a positive solution iff there is a positive solution s.t. all the coefficients are bounded by $(n + 2 \times m) \times (2 \times m + (a + 1))^{4m+1}$ where a is the maximal absolute value among the constants occurring in $\mathcal{S}$ and m is the number of atomic constraints in $\mathcal{S}$.*

Given a PML formula ϕ and an n-locally consistent set X, we associate a constraint system $\mathcal{S}_X$ as follows. The number of $(n + 1)$-locally consistent sets is bounded by $nb(n + 1) \stackrel{\mathrm{def}}{=} 2^{p_1(|\phi|)}$ for some polynomial $p_1(\cdot)$ and we denote below such sets by $Y_1, \ldots, Y_{nb(n+1)}$. The system $\mathcal{S}_X$ contains the variables $x_1, \ldots, x_{nb(n+1)}$. To each formula $\psi \in \mathrm{cl}(n + 1, \phi)$ that is not a periodicity constraint of the form $t \equiv_K c$, we associate the term $t_\psi = \Sigma_{i,\psi \in Y_i} x_i$. Remember that we have assumed wlog that formulae of the form $t \equiv_K c$ belongs to the closure sets but are not atomic formulae occurring in ϕ. We shall define $\mathcal{S}_X$ as a conjunction of the constraints below:

- Σ_{Y_i} is not satisfiable $x_i = 0$,
- if $\Sigma_i a_i \sharp \phi_i = b \in X$, then we add $\Sigma_i a_i t_{\phi_i} = b$,
- if $\Sigma_i a_i \sharp \phi_i < b \in X$, then we add $\Sigma_i a_i t_{\phi_i} + y = b - 1$ where y is new,
- if $\Sigma_i a_i \sharp \phi_i > b \in X$, then we add $\Sigma_i a_i t_{\phi_i} - y = b + 1$ where y is new,
- if $\Sigma_i a_i \sharp \phi_i \equiv_K c \in X$, then we add $\Sigma_i a_i t_{\phi_i} - Ky = c$ where y is new,
- if $\mathcal{A}_1(\phi_1^1, \ldots, \phi_{n_1}^1), \ldots, \mathcal{A}_l(\phi_1^l, \ldots, \phi_{n_l}^l)$ and $\neg \mathcal{A}_1'(\psi_1^1, \ldots, \psi_{m_1}^1), \ldots,$
  $\neg \mathcal{A}_{l'}'(\psi_1^{l'}, \ldots, \psi_{m_{l'}}^{l'})$ are all the automaton-based formulae in X, then we add
  the Presburger formula of the form

$$\bigvee \exists \ldots y_k^{i,j} \ldots z_k^{i,j} \ldots (\bigwedge_{i,j}(t_{\phi^j} = a_0^{i,j} + \Sigma_k y_k^{i,j} a_k^{i,j}) \wedge (\bigwedge_{i,j} t_{\psi^j} = b_0^{i,j} + \Sigma_k z_k^{i,j} b_k^{i,j}))$$

such that each disjunct has at most $2^{p_1(|\phi|)} + 2^{2 \times |\phi|^2}$ variables and the absolute values of the coefficients $a_k^{i,j}$ and $b_k^{i,j}$ are bounded by $2^{2 \times |\phi|}$.

The positive solutions form the Parikh image of the language $L(\mathcal{A}_1) \cap \cdots \cap L(\mathcal{A}_{n_1}) \cap -L(\mathcal{A}_1') \cap \cdots \cap -L(\mathcal{A}_{m_1}')$ over the alphabet $Y_1, \ldots, Y_{nb(n+1)}$. A transition $q \xrightarrow{a_i} q'$ in $\mathcal{A}_1(\phi_1^1, \ldots, \phi_{n_1}^1)$ is read as a concise representation for the transitions of the form $q \xrightarrow{Y} q'$ with $\phi_i^1 \in Y$. The existence of such a formula is a consequence of the proof of [SSMH04, Theorem 3] and the proof of [SSMH04, Theorem 6]. Indeed, computing the minimal and deterministic automaton for the product of $\mathcal{A}_1, \ldots, \mathcal{A}_l, \mathcal{A}_1', \ldots, \mathcal{A}_{l'}'$ over the alphabet $\{Y_1, \ldots, Y_{nb(n+1)}\}$ produces a constraint system of dimension $nb(n+1)$ with doubly exponential number of variables and coefficients bounded by an exponential value in $|\phi|$ [VSS05]. However, the constraints induced by the automaton-based formulae involve subformulae of ϕ and the latter system can be reduced to a system with only an exponential amount of variables using some combinatorial argument from [SSMH04, Theorem 6].

If we restrict ourselves to the fragment of PML with at most k regularity constraints per formulae and *deterministic* automata, say $\text{PML}_k^{\text{det}}$, then an automaton $\mathcal{A}$ accepting $L(\mathcal{A}_1) \cap \cdots \cap L(\mathcal{A}_{n_1}) \cap -L(\mathcal{A}_1') \cap \cdots \cap -L(\mathcal{A}_{m_1}')$ $(n_1 + m_1 \leqslant k)$ can be built in polynomial-time in $|\phi|$ and then a Presburger formula for the Parikh image of $L(\mathcal{A})$ in linear-time in $\mathcal{A}$ using [VSS05, Theorem 4]. In the case PML is studied in full generality instead of a specific $\text{PML}_k^{\text{det}}$, one needs to take advantage of this huge disjunction. The number of disjuncts may be (double) exponential but each disjunct will satisfy the good size properties to get PSPACE. The construction of $\mathcal{S}_X$ is done in the way that allows to state the result below:

Lemma 6. *Let ϕ be a PML formula, $d \in \{0, \ldots, |\phi|\}$ and X be a d-locally consistent of formulae. Then, X is PML satisfiable iff $\mathcal{S}_X$ has a positive solution.*

Because of the Presburger formula introduced by the regular constraints, the system $\mathcal{S}_X$ can be viewed as a disjunction of constraint systems $\mathcal{S}'$ such that the number of variables in $\mathcal{S}'$ is at most exponential in $|\phi|$, the number of atomic constraint in $\mathcal{S}'$ is polynomial in $|\phi|$ and the maximal absolute value among the constants occurring in $\mathcal{S}'$ is at most exponential in $|\phi|$. By Lemma 5, if $\mathcal{S}'$ has a solution, then each value can be encoded in polynomial space in $|\phi|$. Consequently, if $\mathcal{S}_X$ has a solution, then each value can be encoded in polynomial space in $|\phi|$. We write M to denote the maximal value for all the systems $\mathcal{S}_X$ from the d-locally consistent set of ϕ with $d \leqslant |\phi|$. M is actually in $\mathcal{O}(2^{p_2(|\phi|)})$.

3.3   The Algorithm

We define the function SAT such that ϕ is PML satisfiable iff there is $X \subseteq \mathrm{cl}(0, \phi)$ such that X is 0-locally consistent and $\mathrm{SAT}(\phi, X, 0)$ has a computation that returns true. The function $\mathrm{SAT}(X, \phi, d)$ is defined in Fig. 1. The first argument X is intended to be a subset of $\mathrm{cl}(d, \phi)$. SAT is a non-deterministic algorithm but it can be defined as a deterministic one by enumerating possibilities instead of guessing, in the standard way.

Observe that we do not need to guess values for the auxiliary variables (y, $y_k^{i,j}, z_k^{i,j}$) but their existence is taken into account in the bound M and in the (final-checking) step. Similarly, if we guess a set Y_x that contains some unsatisfiable formula then $\mathrm{SAT}(Y_x, \phi, d+1)$ has no accepting computation which also induces a non accepting computation for $\mathrm{SAT}(X, \phi, d)$. However, the bound M takes into account this type of constraints of unsatisfiable formulae. Moreover, we check on the fly that the regularity constraints hold true. In particular, we visit on the fly the automata obtained by the subset construction in order to check negative regularity constraints.

The algorithm described in SAT is a typical example of Ladner-like algorithm, see e.g. similar algorithms in [Lad77, Spa93, Dem03]. Indeed, it does not rely on any machinery such as automata or tableaux/sequent proof systems for checking satisfiability (but its correctness proof is indeed a kind of completeness proof). Moreover, the graph of recursive calls (here for SAT) induces a tree model for the argument formula. Since PML models are precisely trees, we get the PML model for free.

Observe also that comparing our algorithm from the one in [Tob00] for the poorer graded modal logic, our PSPACE upper bound is not based on any specific technique such as the trace technique and Presburger constraints are checked after guessing all the children.

3.4   Complexity Analysis and Correctness

Firstly, we prove that SAT requires only polynomial space.

Lemma 7. *For each 0-locally consistent set X, any computation of* $\mathrm{SAT}(\phi, X, 0)$ *requires polynomial space in* $|\phi|$.

Then we prove the correctness of the algorithm.

`function SAT(X, φ, d)`

(consistency) if X is not d-locally consistent then **abort**;
(base case) if X contains only propositional formulae then return **true**;
(witnesses)

> **(initialization-counters)** for every $\psi \in \mathrm{cl}(d+1, \phi)$ that is not a periodicity constraint of the form $t \equiv_K c$, $C_\psi := 0$;
> **(initialization-states)** for every $\mathcal{A}(\psi_1, \ldots, \psi_\alpha) \in X$, $q_{\mathcal{A}(\psi_1, \ldots, \psi_\alpha)} := q_0$ for some initial state q_0 of $\mathcal{A}$;
> **(initialization-states-complement)** for every $\neg\mathcal{A}(\psi_1, \ldots, \psi_\alpha) \in X$, $q_{\neg\mathcal{A}(\psi_1, \ldots, \psi_\alpha)} := I$ where I is the set of initial states of $\mathcal{A}$;
> **(guess-number-children)** guess nb in $\{0, \ldots, nb(d+1) \times M\}$;
> **(guess-children-from-left-to-right)** for $i = 1$ to nb do
>> 1. guess $x \in \{1, \ldots, nb(n+1)\}$;
>> 2. if not $\mathrm{SAT}(Y_x, \phi, d+1)$ then **abort**;
>> 3. for every $\psi \in \mathrm{cl}(d+1, \phi)$ that is not a periodicity constraint, if $\psi \in Y_x$, then $C_\psi := C_\psi + 1$;
>> 4. for every $\mathcal{A}(\psi_1, \ldots, \psi_\alpha) \in X$,
>>> (a) guess a transition $q_{\mathcal{A}(\psi_1, \ldots, \psi_\alpha)} \xrightarrow{a_i} q'$ in $\mathcal{A}$ with $\Sigma_\mathcal{A} = a_1, \ldots, a_\alpha$;
>>> (b) if $\psi_i \in Y_x$, then $q_{\mathcal{A}(\psi_1, \ldots, \psi_\alpha)} := q'$, otherwise **abort**;
>> 5. for every $\neg\mathcal{A}(\psi_1, \ldots, \psi_\alpha) \in X$,
>>> (a) guess a letter a_i in $\Sigma_\mathcal{A} = a_1, \ldots, a_\alpha$;
>>> (b) if $\psi_i \in Y_x$, then $q_{\neg\mathcal{A}(\psi_1, \ldots, \psi_\alpha)} := \{q : \exists q' \in q_{\neg\mathcal{A}(\psi_1, \ldots, \psi_\alpha)}, q' \xrightarrow{a_i} q\}$, otherwise **abort**;

(final-checking)
> 1. for every $\Sigma_i a_i \sharp \psi_i \sim b \in X$, if $\Sigma_i a_i \times C_{\psi_i} \sim b$ does not hold, then **abort**,
> 2. for every $\Sigma_i a_i \sharp \psi_i \equiv_k c \in X$, if $\Sigma_i a_i \times C_{\psi_i} \equiv_k c$ does not hold, then **abort**,
> 3. for every $\mathcal{A}(\psi_1, \ldots, \psi_\alpha) \in X$, if $q_{\mathcal{A}(\psi_1, \ldots, \psi_\alpha)}$ is not a final state of $\mathcal{A}$, then **abort**;
> 4. for every $\neg\mathcal{A}(\psi_1, \ldots, \psi_\alpha) \in X$, if $q_{\neg\mathcal{A}(\psi_1, \ldots, \psi_\alpha)}$ contains a final state of $\mathcal{A}$, then **abort**;

(return-true) return **true**.

Fig. 1. Satisfiability algorithm

Lemma 8. *A formula ϕ is PML satisfiable iff for some $X \subseteq \mathrm{cl}(0, \phi)$, SAT $(X, \phi, 0)$ has a computation that returns* **true**.

By Lemmas 7, 8, Savitch's Theorem and PSPACE-hardness of K, we establish our main result.

Theorem 1. *PML satisfiability is* PSPACE-*complete.*

Obviously, PML without regularity constraints is also in PSPACE.

4   Complexity Results for Similar Logics

In this section, we compare PML with other logics with Presburger constraints. This is the opportunity to clarify the relationships between PML and logics from [SSMH04, ZL06, ABD$^+$05] and to state some new PSPACE-completeness and undecidability results.

4.1 Graded Modal Logics

Graded modal logics are obviously the modal ancestors of PML where the formulae with Presburger constraints are of the form $\Diamond_{\geq n}\phi$ and the like, are considered, see e.g. the early [Fin72, BC85, vdH92, vdHdR95]. Such logics have been extended to fit more specific motivations, giving epistemic logics [vdHM91] and description logics (see e.g. [CG05]) with graded modalities. It is only in [Tob00] that minimal graded modal logic, counterpart of the modal logic K, is shown decidable in PSPACE, various decidability results being earlier established in a systematic way in [Cer94]. Our result about PML extends the main result from [Tob00]. Various extensions of known logics by adding graded modalities has been considered and undecidability is often obtained because the ability to count is often central to encode a grid, see e.g. [BP04]. However, the EXPTIME-completeness of graded μ-calculus [KSV02] remains a tour de force. Furthermore, there exist various attempts to encode concisely logics with counting into logics with no explicit counting mechanism, see e.g. [OSH96, MP97], but none of them implies a PSPACE upper bound. Modal-like logics with more expressive Presburger constraints on the number of children can be found in [SSMH04, ZL06] and this is the subject of the two next sections.

4.2 Sheaves Logic

Definition. In this section, we recall the syntax and semantics of the Sheaves Logic SL that is shown decidable in [ZL03, ZL06] with a non-elementary algorithm. For the sake of uniformity, we adopt a presentation of SL models similar to the one for PML models whereas the mode of representation for regular languages and semilinear sets is the same as for PML. Indeed, the choice of representations for such objects may induce sometimes complexity gaps because of the different conciseness of the formalisms. Similarly, we allow Boolean operators at the level of element formulae (denoted by E) as done for document formulae (denoted by D). The element formulae are inductively defined as follows:

- $E := \alpha[D] \mid \delta \mid \neg E \mid E \wedge E \mid \textbf{true}$,
- $D := \mathcal{A}(E_1, \ldots, E_p) \mid \exists x_1, \ldots, x_p : \phi(x_1, \ldots, x_p) : x_1 E_1 \& \cdots \& x_p E_p \mid$ $\textbf{true} \mid \neg D \mid D \wedge D'$,

where

- α belongs to a countably infinite set TAGS of tags,
- δ belongs to a countably infinite set DATATYPES of datatypes disjoint from TAGS,
- $\mathcal{A}$ is a nondeterministic finite-state automaton over an p-letter alphabet $\Sigma_{\mathcal{A}}$ in which the letters are linearly ordered $\Sigma_{\mathcal{A}} = \mathsf{a}_1, \ldots, \mathsf{a}_p$.

- $\phi(x_1, \ldots, x_p)$ is a Boolean combination of Presburger formulae built over the variables $x_1, \ldots, x_p$ of the form either $t \sim b$ or $t \equiv_k c$ with $t = \Sigma a_i x_i$.

A model $\mathcal{M}$ for SL is a structure $\mathcal{M} = \langle T, R, (<_{nd})_{nd \in T}, l \rangle$ where T is a finite set of states, $\langle T, R \rangle$ is a tree and each $<_{nd}$ is a total ordering on $R(nd)$ and $l : T \to \text{TAGS} \cup \text{DATATYPES}$ is a labeling function such that for every $nd \in T$, if nd is a leaf of $\langle T, R \rangle$ then $l(nd) \in \text{DATATYPES}$ and for every $nd \in T$, if nd is not a leaf of $\langle T, R \rangle$ then $l(nd) \in \text{TAGS}$. The satisfaction relation is inductively defined below where $\mathcal{M}$ is a model for SL and $nd \in T$ (we omit the clauses for Boolean operators):

- $\mathcal{M}, nd \models \delta$ iff $\delta = l(nd)$,
- $\mathcal{M}, nd \models \alpha[D_1 \wedge D_2]$ iff $\mathcal{M}, nd \models \alpha[D_1]$ and $\mathcal{M}, nd \models \alpha[D_2]$,
- $\mathcal{M}, nd \models \alpha[\neg D]$ iff $\alpha = l(nd)$ and not $\mathcal{M}, nd \models \alpha[D]$,
- $\mathcal{M}, nd \models \alpha[\textbf{true}]$ iff $\alpha = l(nd)$,
- $\mathcal{M}, nd \models \alpha[\exists x_1, \ldots, x_p : \phi(x_1, \ldots, x_p) : x_1 E_1 \& \cdots \& x_p E_p]$ iff $\alpha = l(nd)$, $R(nd) = nd_1 < \cdots < nd_k$, and there exist $i_1, \ldots, i_k$ such that for every $j \in \{1, \ldots, k\}$, $\mathcal{M}, nd_j \models E_{i_j}$ and $[x_1 \leftarrow n_1, \ldots, x_p \leftarrow n_p] \models \phi(x_1, \ldots, x_p)$ with $n_i = \text{card}(\{l \in \{1, \ldots, k\} : i_l = i\})$,
- $\mathcal{M}, nd \models \alpha[\mathcal{A}(E_1, \ldots, E_p)]$ iff $\alpha = l(nd)$, $R(nd) = nd_1 < \cdots < nd_k$, and there is $i_1, \ldots, i_k$ such that for every $j \in \{1, \ldots, k\}$, $\mathcal{M}, nd_j \models E_{i_j}$ and $\mathbf{a}_{i_1} \cdots \mathbf{a}_{i_k} \in L(\mathcal{A})$ with $\Sigma_{\mathcal{A}} = \{\mathbf{a}_1, \ldots, \mathbf{a}_p\}$.

A major difference with the semantics of PML (see also [SSMH04]) is that for SL in Presburger constraints each child counts only once.

PSPACE-Completeness. Let ϕ be an SL formula with tags $\{\alpha_1, \ldots, \alpha_n\}$ and datatypes $\{\delta_1, \ldots, \delta_{n'}\}$. We define a formula ϕ' built over the propositional variables (plus others, see below) $VP = \{p_{\alpha_1}, \ldots, p_{\alpha_n}, p_{\alpha_{new}}\} \cup \{p_{\delta_1}, \ldots, p_{\delta_{n'}}, p_{\delta_{new}}\}$.

Given a PML φ, we write $\forall^n \varphi$ as an abbreviation for $\bigwedge_{i=0}^{n} \overbrace{\Box \ldots \Box}^{i \text{ times}} \varphi$. The formula ϕ' is defined as the conjunction $\phi'_{val} \wedge t(\phi)$ where $t(\phi)$ is defined recursively on the structure of ϕ and ϕ'_{val} states constraints about the valuation of datatypes and tags in SL models. For each document formula of the form $D = \exists x_1 \cdots x_p : \phi(x_1, \ldots, x_p) : x_1 E_1 \& \cdots \& x_p E_p$ in ϕ, we introduce new propositional variables $p_D^1, \ldots, p_D^p$.

The formula ϕ'_{val} is defined as the conjunction below

$$\forall^{|\phi|} \bigvee_{p \in VP} (p \wedge \bigwedge_{q \in VP \setminus \{p\}} \neg q) \wedge \forall^{|\phi|} (\Diamond \textbf{true} \Rightarrow \overbrace{\bigvee_{\alpha \in \{\alpha_1, \ldots, \alpha_n, \alpha_{new}\}} p_\alpha}^{\text{internal nodes labeled by tags}}) \wedge$$

$$\forall^{|\phi|} (\Box \textbf{false} \Rightarrow \underbrace{\bigvee_{\delta \in \{\delta_1, \ldots, \delta_{n'}, \delta_{new}\}} p_\delta}_{\text{leaves labeled by constants of datatypes}}) \wedge$$

$$\forall^{|\phi|} \bigwedge_{D \text{ is of the form } \exists \ldots E_p} \bigvee_{i \in \{1, \ldots, p\}} (p_D^i \wedge \bigwedge_{j \in \{1, \ldots, p\} \setminus \{i\}} \neg p_D^j)$$

where $|\phi|$ is the size of ϕ. Actually, an optimal construction would consider $md(\phi)$. Let t be reduction from SL formulae to PML formulae:

- t is homomorphic for Boolean operators and $t(\text{true}) = \text{true}$,
- $t(\alpha_i[D]) = p_{\alpha_i} \wedge t(D)$, $t(\delta_i) = p_{\delta_i}$,
- $t(\mathcal{A}(E_1, \ldots, E_p)) = \mathcal{A}(t(E_1), \ldots, t(E_p))$,
- $t(\exists x_1 \cdots x_p : \phi(x_1, \ldots, x_p) : x_1 E_1 \& \cdots \& x_p E_p)$ equals the formula below:

$$\phi(x_1, \ldots, x_p)[x_1 \leftarrow \sharp(p_D^1 \wedge t(E_1)), \ldots, x_p \leftarrow \sharp(p_D^p \wedge t(E_p))]$$

where $\phi(x_1, \ldots, x_p)[x_1 \leftarrow \sharp(p_D^1 \wedge t(E_1)), \ldots, x_p \leftarrow \sharp(p_D^p \wedge t(E_p))]$ is obtained from $\phi(x_1, \ldots, x_p)$ by replacing each occurrence of x_i by $\sharp(p_D^i \wedge t(E_i))$.

New propositional variables need to be introduced and a constraint on them needs to be stated because in SL in Presburger constraints each child can count only once. It is not difficult to show that t is sound.

Lemma 9. t is a logspace reduction such that ϕ is SL satisfiable iff ϕ' is PML satisfiable.

So, SL satisfiability is in PSPACE which contrasts with the complexity of the decision procedure from [ZL06].

Proposition 1. *SL is* PSPACE-*complete.*

PSPACE-hardness is obtained by reducing modal logic K without propositional variables [Hem01].

4.3   Fixed-Point Free SSMH Logic

In this section, we recall the syntax and semantics of the fixed-point free fragment of the logic from [SSMH04]. For brevity, we call it SSMH. The SSMH formulae are inductively defined as follows:

$$\phi ::= \text{true} \mid \neg\phi \mid \phi \wedge \phi' \mid \alpha\langle\Phi(x_1, \ldots, x_p) : x_1\phi_1 \& \cdots \& x_p\phi_p\rangle \mid$$

$$\star\langle\Phi(x_1, \ldots, x_p) : x_1\phi_1 \& \cdots \& x_p\phi_p\rangle \mid \alpha\langle\mathcal{A}(\phi_1, \ldots, \phi_p)\rangle \mid \star\langle\mathcal{A}(\phi_1, \ldots, \phi_p)\rangle.$$

where α belongs to a countably infinite set TAGS of tags, $\mathcal{A}$ is a nondeterministic finite-state automaton over an p-letter alphabet and $\Phi(x_1, \ldots, x_p)$ is a Presburger formula as in SL. A model $\mathcal{M}$ for SSMH is a structure $\mathcal{M} = \langle T, R, (<_{nd})_{nd \in T}, l\rangle$ where T is a finite set of states, $\langle T, R\rangle$ is a tree and each $<_{nd}$ is a total ordering on $R(nd)$ and, $l : T \to$ TAGS is a labeling function (no datatypes here). The satisfaction relation is inductively defined below where $\mathcal{M}$ is a model for SSMH and $nd \in T$ (we omit the clauses for Boolean operators):

- $\mathcal{M}, nd \models \alpha$ iff $\alpha = l(nd)$,
- $\mathcal{M}, nd \models \alpha\langle\Phi(x_1, \ldots, x_p) : x_1\phi_1 \& \cdots \& x_p\phi_p\rangle$ iff $\alpha = l(nd)$ and $R(nd) = nd_1 < \cdots < nd_k$ and $[x_1 \leftarrow n_1, \ldots, x_p \leftarrow n_p] \models \Phi(x_1, \ldots, x_p)$ where $n_i = \text{card}(\{l \in \{1, \ldots, k\} : \mathcal{M}, nd_l \models \phi_i\})$,

- $\mathcal{M}, nd \models \star \langle \phi(x_1, \ldots, x_p) : x_1 \phi_1 \& \cdots \& x_p \phi_p \rangle$ iff $[x_1 \leftarrow n_1, \ldots, x_p \leftarrow n_p] \models \Phi(x_1, \ldots, x_p)$ where $n_i = \text{card}(\{l \in \{1, \ldots, k\} : \mathcal{M}, nd_l \models \phi_i\})$,

- $\mathcal{M}, nd \models \alpha \langle \mathcal{A}(\phi_1, \ldots, \phi_p) \rangle$ iff $\alpha = l(nd)$, $R(nd) = nd_1 < \cdots < nd_k$ and there is $i_1, \ldots, i_k$ such that for every $j \in \{1, \ldots, k\}$, $\mathcal{M}, nd_j \models \phi_{i_j}$ and $\mathbf{a}_{i_1} \cdots \mathbf{a}_{i_k} \in L(\mathcal{A})$. (analogous clause for $\star \langle \mathcal{A}(\phi_1, \ldots, \phi_p) \rangle$).

Unlike SL and like PML, a child can count more than once in Presburger constraints. Let ϕ be an SSMH formula with tags $\{\alpha_1, \ldots, \alpha_n\}$. We shall define a PML formula ϕ' built over the propositional variables $VP = \{p_{\alpha_1}, \ldots, p_{\alpha_n}\}$. Let t be a logspace reduction from SSMH formulae to PML formulae:

- t is homomorphic for Boolean operators and $t(\mathbf{true}) = \mathbf{true}$,
- $t(\alpha \langle \phi(x_1, \ldots, x_p) : x_1 \phi_1 \& \cdots \& x_p \phi_p \rangle)$ equals

$$p_\alpha \wedge \phi(x_1, \ldots, x_p)[x_1 \leftarrow \sharp t(\phi_1), \ldots, x_p \leftarrow \sharp t(\phi_p)].$$

- $t(\star \langle \phi(x_1, \ldots, x_p) : x_1 \phi_1 \& \cdots \& x_p \phi_p \rangle)$ equals

$$\phi(x_1, \ldots, x_p)[x_1 \leftarrow \sharp t(\phi_1), \ldots, x_p \leftarrow \sharp t(\phi_p)].$$

- $t(\alpha \langle \mathcal{A}(\phi_1, \ldots, \phi_p) \rangle) = p_\alpha \wedge \mathcal{A}(t(\phi_1), \ldots, t(\phi_p))$,
- $t(\star \langle \mathcal{A}(\phi_1, \ldots, \phi_p) \rangle) = \mathcal{A}(t(\phi_1), \ldots, t(\phi_p))$.

Lemma 10. t *is a logspace reduction s.t.* ϕ *is SSMH satisfiable iff* $\forall^{|\phi|} \bigvee_{p \in VP} (p \wedge \bigwedge_{q \in VP \setminus \{p\}} \neg q) \wedge t(\phi)$ *is PML satisfiable.*

The proof is similar (and indeed simpler) than the proof of Lemma 9. So, SSMH satisfiability is in PSPACE. We can do better as done for SL.

Proposition 2. *SSMH is* PSPACE-*complete.*

4.4 PDL over Finite Trees

In [ABD+05] a PDL-like logic PDL_{tree} is introduced where models are finite, labeled ordered trees and the four atomic relations are: left-sibling, right-sibling, mother-of and daughter-of. Other relations can be generated with standard "program operators" (iteration, test, union and composition). There is no (full) Presburger constraints in PDL_{tree} but regularity constraints can be stated thanks to the interplay between the program operators and the atomic relations. PDL_{tree} satisfiability is shown EXPTIME-complete in [ABD+05]. It is not difficult to show that, on the model of the undecidability proof for [ZL06, Proposition 1], adding Presburger constraints to PDL_{tree} leads to undecidability. We provide below an undecidability proof for a logic sharing features from PDL_{tree} and PML, say $\mathcal{L}$, that is a strict fragment of the logic PDL_{tree} on which are added Presburger constraints. Hence, the logic $\mathcal{L}$ contains features from both PDL_{tree} and PML while being incomparable with them since $\mathcal{L}$ satisfiability will be shown below undecidable.

Given a countably infinite set $\text{AP} = \{p_1, p_2, \ldots\}$ of propositional variables and $\Sigma = \{\downarrow, \downarrow^*, \rightarrow, \rightarrow^*, \leftarrow, \leftarrow^*, \uparrow, \uparrow^*\}$ a set of symbol relations, we define the set

of formulae and terms inductively as follows: $\phi ::= p \mid \neg\phi \mid \phi \wedge \phi \mid t \sim b$ and
$t ::= a \times \sharp^{\mathsf{R}}\phi \mid t + a \times \sharp^{\mathsf{R}}\phi$, where $p \in \mathrm{AP}$, $\mathsf{R} \in \Sigma$, $b \in \mathbb{N}$, $a \in \mathbb{Z}$, $\sim \in \{<,>,=\}$.
The programs from $\mathtt{PDL_{tree}}$ are much richer than Σ because iteration, test, union
and composition are present in $\mathtt{PDL_{tree}}$. Similarly, the Presburger constraints
from PML strictly contains those of $\mathcal{L}$. A model $\mathcal{M}$ for $\mathcal{L}$ is a structure $\mathcal{M} = \langle T, R_\downarrow, R_{\downarrow^*}, R_\rightarrow, R_{\rightarrow^*}, R_\leftarrow, R_{\leftarrow^*}, R_\uparrow, R_{\uparrow^*}, l\rangle$ where

- $\langle T, R_\downarrow, R_\rightarrow\rangle$ is a finite ordered tree with $R_\downarrow$ and $R_\rightarrow$ are child-of and right-sibling relations, respectively; $l : T \rightarrow 2^{\mathrm{AP}}$ is the valuation function,
- for every $\mathsf{R} \in \{\downarrow, \rightarrow, \leftarrow, \uparrow\}$, $R^*_\mathsf{R} = R_{\mathsf{R}^*}$ (R^*_R is the reflexive and transitive closure of R_R), $R_\rightarrow = R^{-1}_\leftarrow$ and $R_\uparrow = R^{-1}_\downarrow$,

The satisfaction relation is inductively defined as for PML except this time
the models are finite ordered trees.

Proposition 3. *The satisfiability problem for $\mathcal{L}$ is undecidable.*

The proof is by reducing the halting problem for 2-counter machines. If we modify the models by allowing infinite trees with finite-branching, satisfiability becomes Σ^1_1-hard by reducing the recurring problem for nondeterministic 2-counter
machines [AH94, Lemma 8]. The formulae built in the proof of Proposition 3
are specific since only the relation symbols from $\{\downarrow^*, \downarrow, \rightarrow^*, \leftarrow\}$ are used. The
decidability status of the following logics is still open: restriction of $\mathcal{L}$ to formulae
with no subformula of the form $\Sigma_i a_i \sharp^{\mathsf{R}_i}\phi_i$ where for some $j \neq j'$, $\mathsf{R}_j \neq \mathsf{R}_{j'}$, PML
augmented with the relation symbol $\leftarrow$.
The logic obtained by adding $\downarrow^*$ to PML is a fragment of the logic SSMH
extended with fixed-points, for which satisfiability is in EXPTIME [SSMH04].
Actually, this fragment is already EXPTIME-hard, even if we use only trivial
regularity and Presburger constraints (use the complexity result of [FL79]).

5 Concluding Remarks

We have shown that Presburger modal logic that admits in its language full Presburger and regularity constraints has a PSPACE-complete satisfiability problem,
that is the same complexity of the modal logic K. This is shown by designing a specially tailored Ladner-like algorithm that takes advantage of the constraint systems to be solved from PML formulae. This improves previous results
from [Tob00, SSMH04, ZL06] and paves the way to design querying language for
XML documents that can express Presburger and regularity constraints and for
which the underlying modal logic is only in PSPACE.

References

[ABD+05] L. Afanasiev, P. Blackburn, I. Dimitriou, B. Gaiffe, E. Goris, M. Marx, and M. de Rijke. PDL for ordered trees. *JANCL*, 15(2):115–135, 2005.
[ADdR03] N. Alechina, S. Demri, and M. de Rijke. A modal perspective on path constraints. *JLC*, 13(6):939–956, 2003.

[AH94]   R. Alur and T. Henzinger. A really temporal logic. *JACM*, 41(1):181–204, 1994.

[BC85]   M. Fattorosi Barnaba and F. De Caro. Graded modalities. *Studia Logica*, 44(2):197–221, 1985.

[BCT04]   N. Bidoit, S. Cerrito, and V. Thion. A first step towards modeling semistructured data in hybrid multimodal logic. *JANCL*, 14(4):447–475, 2004.

[BdRV01]   P. Blackburn, M. de Rijke, and Y. Venema. *Modal Logic*. Cambridge University Press, 2001.

[BP04]   P. Bonatti and A. Peron. On the undecidability of logics with converse, nominals, recursion and counting. *AI*, 158(1):75–96, 2004.

[BT05]   I. Boneva and J.M. Talbot. Automata and logics for unranked and un-ordered trees. In *RTA'05*, volume 3467 of *LNCS*, pages 500–515, 2005.

[Cer94]   C. Cerrato. Decidability by filtrations for graded normal logics (graded modalities V). *Studia Logica*, 53(1):61–73, 1994.

[CG05]   D. Calvanese and G. De Giacomo. Expressive description logics. In *De-scription Logics Handbook*, pages 178–218. Cambridge University Press, 2005.

[Dem03]   S. Demri. A polynomial space construction of tree-like models for logics with local chains of modal connectives. *TCS*, 300(1–3):235–258, 2003.

[DL06]   S. Demri and D. Lugiez. Presburger modal logic is PSPACE-complete. Technical report, LSV, ENS de Cachan, 2006.

[Fin72]   K. Fine. In so many possible worlds. *NDJFL*, 13(4):516–520, 1972.

[FL79]   M. Fischer and R. Ladner. Propositional dynamic logic of regular pro-grams. *JCSS*, 18:194–211, 1979.

[Gor99]   R. Goré. Tableaux methods for modal and temporal logics. In *Handbook of Tableaux Methods*, pages 297–396. Kluwer, 1999.

[Hem01]   E. Hemaspaandra. The complexity of poor man's logic. *JLC*, 11(4):609–622, 2001.

[HST00]   I. Horrocks, U. Sattler, and S. Tobies. Reasoning with individuals for the description logic SHIQ. In *CADE-17*, volume 1831 of *LNCS*, pages 482–496. Springer, 2000.

[KSV02]   O. Kupferman, U. Sattler, and M.Y. Vardi. The complexity of the graded μ-calculus. In *CADE'02*, volume 2392 of *LNCS*, pages 423–437, 2002.

[Lad77]   R. Ladner. The computational complexity of provability in systems of modal propositional logic. *SIAM Journal of Computing*, 6(3):467–480, 1977.

[Mar03]   M. Marx. XPath and Modal Logics of finite DAG's. In *TABLEAUX'03*, volume 2796 of *LNAI*, pages 150–164. Springer, 2003.

[MP97]   A. Montanari and A. Policriti. A set-theoretic approach to automated deduction in graded modal logics. In *IJCAI-15*, pages 196–201, 1997.

[OSH96]   H.J. Ohlbach, R. Schmidt, and U. Hustadt. Translating graded modalities into predicate logics. In H. Wansing, editor, *Proof theory of modal logic*, pages 253–291. Kluwer, 1996.

[Pap81]   Chr. Papadimitriou. On the complexity of integer programming. *JACM*, 28(4):765–768, 1981.

[Spa93]   E. Spaan. The complexity of propositional tense logics. In M. de Rijke, editor, *Diamonds and Defaults*, pages 287–309. Kluwer, 1993.

[SSMH04]   H. Seidl, Th. Schwentick, A. Muscholl, and P. Habermehl. Count-ing in trees for free. In *ICALP'04*, volume 3142 of *LNCS*, pages 1136–1149, 2004. Long version available at http://www.mathematik.uni-marburg.de/~tick/.

[Tob00]   S. Tobies. PSPACE reasoning for graded modal logics. *JLC*, 10:1–22, 2000.

[vdH92]   W. van der Hoek. On the semantics of graded modalities. *JANCL*, 2(1):81–123, 1992.

[vdHdR95]   W. van der Hoek and M. de Rijke. Counting objects. *JLC*, 5(3):325–345, 1995.

[vdHM91]   W. van der Hoek and J.-J. Meyer. Graded modalities in epistemic logic. *Logique et Analyse*, 133–134:251–270, 1991.

[VSS05]   K. N. Verma, H. Seidl, and Th. Schwentick. On the complexity of equational Horn clauses. In *CADE'05*, volume 3632 of *LNCS*, pages 337–352, 2005.

[Wol83]   P. Wolper. Temporal logic can be more expressive. *I & C*, 56:72–99, 1983.

[ZL03]   S. Dal Zilio and D. Lugiez. XML schema, tree logic and sheaves automata. In *RTA 2003*, volume 2706 of *LNCS*, pages 246–263. Springer, 2003.

[ZL06]   S. Dal Zilio and D. Lugiez. XML schema, tree logic and sheaves automata. *Applicable Algebra in Engineering, Communication and Computing (AAECC)*, 2006. To appear.

Tree Automata with Equality Constraints Modulo Equational Theories[*]

Florent Jacquemard[1], Michael Rusinowitch[2], and Laurent Vigneron[3]

[1] INRIA Futurs & LSV, UMR 8643
florent.jacquemard@inria.fr
[2] LORIA & INRIA Lorraine, UMR 7503
rusi@loria.fr
[3] LORIA & Univ. Nancy 2, UMR 7503
vigneron@loria.fr

Abstract. This paper presents new classes of tree automata combining automata with equality test and automata modulo equational theories. We believe that these classes have a good potential for application in *e.g.* software verification. These tree automata are obtained by extending the standard Horn clause representations with equational conditions and rewrite systems. We show in particular that a generalized membership problem (extending the emptiness problem) is decidable by proving that the saturation of tree automata presentations with suitable paramodulation strategies terminates. Alternatively our results can be viewed as new decidable classes of first-order formula.

1 Introduction

Combining tree automata and term rewriting systems (TRS) has been successful in domains like automated theorem proving [6] and verification of infinite state systems *e.g.* [12,18,16].

A problem with such approaches is to extend the decidability results on tree automata languages to equivalence classes of terms modulo an equational theory. Some authors, *e.g.* [25,20], have investigated the problem of emptiness decision for tree automata modulo specific equational theories, *e.g.* A, AC, ACU... Moreover, it is also shown in [20] that emptiness is decidable for any linear equational theory, and results about regularity preservation under rewriting have been established for several general classes of TRS (see *e.g.* [22] § 2.3).

Another important difficulty stems from the non linear variables (variables with multiple occurrences) in the rewrite rules, which impose in general some over-approximations of the rewrite relation. Tree automata with constraints have been proposed earlier in order to deal with non-linear rewrite systems (see [6]). They are an extension of classical tree recognizers where syntactic equality and

---

[*] This work has been partially supported by the research projects RNTL PROUVÉ (No 03 V 360) and ACI–SI SATIN and ROSSIGNOL.

U. Furbach and N. Shankar (Eds.): IJCAR 2006, LNAI 4130, pp. 557–571, 2006.

disequality tests between subterms are performed during the automata computations. The emptiness of the recognized language is undecidable without restriction, and two remarkable subclasses with decidable emptiness problem are tree automata with equality and disequality constraints restricted to brother positions of [3] and the *reduction automata* of [7]. This second class captures in particular languages of terms (ir)reducible by non linear rewrite systems.

Following [11], it is classical to represent tree automata by Horn clause sets. In this setting, a recognized language is defined as a least Herbrand model and it is possible to use classical first-order theorem proving techniques in order to establish decision results [25,13].

In this paper, we follow this approach in order to unify the two problems mentioned above: we show how techniques of basic ordered paramodulation with selection and a variant of splitting without backtracking solve some decision problems on languages of tree automata with equality constraints, transformed by rewriting. More precisely, we show that the so called *Generalized Membership Problem*, GMP (whether there exists a ground instance of a given term in a given language) is decidable by saturation with a standard calculus presented in Section 3. Note that GMP generalizes the emptiness problem. Alternatively our results can be viewed as new decidable classes of first-order formula. Both classes of standard tree automata (TA) and tree automata with equality constraints generalizing those of [7], where the equality tests are presented by arbitrary equations (TAD), are studied in these settings, as well as their respective generalisation modulo an equational theory $\mathcal{E}$ presented as a convergent term rewriting system (monadic TRS in the case of TA and restricted collapsing TRS in the case of TAD). The decision results are presented as follows in the paper:

	$\mathcal{E} = \emptyset$	$\mathcal{E}$
TA	Section 4	Section 6
TAD	Section 5	Section 7

The last result (lower right corner of the table) is to our knowledge one of the first decision results (after [14]) concerning tree automata with equality constraints modulo equational theories. We show that emptiness is undecidable for TA extended with non-linear facts, even with only one state. Unlike stated in [7,6], we prove also that this problem is undecidable for non-deterministic reduction automata (see Section 5). Therefore, we have introduced for the definition of TAD a refinement on the restriction for the automata of [7] in order to make GMP decidable. The idea is roughly to bound the number of equality tests that can be performed along a whole computation (and not only along each computation path). The representation of constrained automata as Horn clauses permits us to use state of the art first-order theorem proving techniques to provide an effective (implementable) decision procedure for GMP (hence emptiness), instead of the complicated pumping lemmas used so far which hardly lead to effective algorithms. A key-ingredient for the termination of our saturation-based decision procedure was the application of recently proposed *splitting* rules.

As illustrated by two examples of authentication protocols (one with recursion) the class of automata of Section 7 permits a sharper modeling of verification problems (avoiding approximation as it is often required with more standard tree automata). A long version of this paper, completed with the proofs in appendix and more example is available in [15].

Related work. A comparison with the reduction automata of [7] is detailed in Sections 5 and 7.

The closely related works [18,13] propose a different extension H_1 of standard TA defined as Horn clause sets for which satisfiability is decidable. In the version [13] of H_1 Horn clauses have a head whose argument is at most of height one and linear (without duplicated variables), or are purely negative (goals). None of the classes TAD and H_1 contains the other. However, H_1 becomes undecidable when allowing variable duplication in the heads. Our TAD class allows this under the previously mentioned restrictions.

2   Preliminaries

Term algebra. Let $\mathcal{F}$ be a signature of function symbols with arity, denoted by lowercase letters f, g... and let $\mathcal{X}$ be an infinite set of variables. The term algebra is denoted $T(\mathcal{F}, \mathcal{X})$, and $T(\mathcal{F})$ for ground terms. A term is called *linear* if every variable occurs at most once in it and *sublinear* if all its strict subterms are linear. We denote $vars(t)$ as the set of variables occurring in a term $t \in T(\mathcal{F}, \mathcal{X})$. A *substitution* σ is a mapping from $\mathcal{X}$ to $T(\mathcal{F}, \mathcal{X})$ such that $\{x | \sigma(x) \neq x\}$, the *support* of σ, is a finite set. The application of a substitution σ to a term t is denoted by $t\sigma$ and is equal to the term t where all variables x have been replaced by the term $\sigma(x)$. A substitution σ is *grounding* for t if $t\sigma \in T(\mathcal{F})$. The *positions* $Pos(t)$ in a term t are represented as sequence of positive integers (Λ, the empty sequence, denotes the root position). A subterm of t at position p is denoted $t|_p$, and the replacement in t of the subterm at position p by u denoted $t[u]_p$.

Rewriting. We assume standard definitions and notations for TRS [9].

Clauses. Let $\mathcal{P}$ be a finite set of predicate symbols which contains an equality predicate $=$. The other predicate symbols are denoted by uppercase letter P, Q,... and are assumed unary. We shall later use a partition $\mathcal{P} \setminus \{=\} = \mathcal{P}_0 \uplus \mathcal{P}_1$, where $\mathcal{P}_0$ and $\mathcal{P}_1$ are sets of predicate symbols. Let $\mathcal{Q}$ be a finite set of nullary predicate symbols disjoint from $\mathcal{P}$ and that we call *splitting predicates*, denoted by lowercase letters q... Constrained Horn clauses are constrained disjunctions of literals denoted $\Gamma \Rightarrow H \ [\![\theta]\!]$ where Γ is a set of negative literals called *antecedents*, H is a positive literal called *head* of the clause and the constraint θ is a set of equations between terms of $T(\mathcal{F}, \mathcal{X})$. A clause with a splitting literal as head or with no head at all is called a *goal*. The constraint is omitted when θ is empty. For the sake of notation, we shall sometimes make no distinction between the constraint and its most general solution (when it exists). When θ is satisfiable, we call the *expansion* of the above clause the unconstrained clause $\Gamma\theta \Rightarrow H\theta$.

Atoms of the form $P(s)$, resp. q, where $P \in \mathcal{P}$ and $s \in T(\mathcal{F}, \mathcal{X})$, resp. $q \in \mathcal{Q}$, are represented for uniformity as equations $P(s) = true$, resp. $q = true$, where $true$ is a distinguished function symbol (in $\mathcal{F}$). An atom of the latter form is called *non-equational* and can be denoted simply $P(s)$, resp. q. We assume in the following that predicate symbols can only occur at the root of the terms that we consider.

Orderings. We assume we are given a *precedence* ordering $\succeq$ on $\mathcal{F} \cup \mathcal{P} \cup \mathcal{Q}$, and denote by $\sim$ the relation $\preceq \cap \succeq$ and $\succ$ the relation $\succeq \setminus \sim$. We assume that $\succ$ is total on $\mathcal{P}_1$ and moreover that for all predicates $P_0, P_0' \in \mathcal{P}_0$, $P_1 \in \mathcal{P}_1$, $q \in \mathcal{Q}$ and every function symbol $f \in \mathcal{F}$, $P_0 \sim P_0'$ and $P_1 \succ P_0 \succ q \succ f$. We assume the symbol *true* to be the minimal one. Assume that $\mathcal{P}_1 = \{P_1, \ldots, P_n\}$ with $P_1 \succ \ldots \succ P_n$. We call i the *index* of P_i, denoted $ind(P_i)$, and let $ind(Q) = 0$ for all $Q \in \mathcal{P}_0$. We shall also use the constant $\infty = \max(ind(P)|P \in \mathcal{P}) + 1$, which is bigger than the index of every predicate in $\mathcal{P}_1$.

We assume a reduction ordering $\succ_{lpo}$ [9] on $\mathcal{T}(\mathcal{F} \cup \mathcal{P} \cup \mathcal{Q}, \mathcal{X})$ total on ground terms, defined as a *lexicographic path ordering*. This ordering is extended to literals as in [2], see [15], Appendix A, for complete definitions.

Tree Automata. Tree automata are finite state recognizers of ground terms. We consider here a definition à la Frühwirth et al [11] of tree automata as finite sets of Horn clauses on $\mathcal{P}$ and $\mathcal{F}$ with equality. Every non-equational predicate symbol occurring in a given tree automaton $\mathcal{A}$ is called a *state* of $\mathcal{A}$. Given a tree automaton $\mathcal{A}$ and a state $Q \in \mathcal{P}$ of $\mathcal{A}$, the language of $\mathcal{A}$ in Q, denoted by $L(\mathcal{A}, Q)$, is the set of terms $t \in \mathcal{T}(\mathcal{F})$ such that $Q(t)$ is a logical consequence of $\mathcal{A}$.

General Membership Problem (GMP). We focus on one decision problem, GMP, which generalizes many important problems concerning tree automata (in particular membership and emptiness decision). This problem has been shown decidable in [23] for standard tree automata.

INSTANCE: a tree automaton $\mathcal{A}$, a state Q of $\mathcal{A}$ and a term $t \in \mathcal{T}(\mathcal{F}, \mathcal{X})$, QUESTION: is there a substitution σ grounding for t such that $t\sigma \in L(\mathcal{A}, Q)$?

In particular, when t is a ground term, this problem is equivalent to a *membership* problem for $\mathcal{A}$: $t \in L(\mathcal{A}, Q)$? When t is a variable, it is equivalent to a *non-emptiness* problem for $\mathcal{A}$: $L(\mathcal{A}, Q) \neq \emptyset$?

Lemma 1. *GMP is satisfied by $\mathcal{A}$, Q and t iff $\mathcal{A} \cup \{Q(t) \Rightarrow \}$ is inconsistent.*

3   Basic Ordered Paramodulation with Selection

We shall establish the decidability of GMP for several classes of tree automata (with equations), using techniques of saturation under paramodulation, based on Lemma 1 and the calculus described in this section.

Basic Ordered Paramodulation with Selection. The following set of inference rules, parametrized by a reduction ordering $\succ$, which we assume total on ground terms, and a *selection function* which assigns to each clause a set of selected negative literals[1], forms a sound and refutationally complete (*i.e.*

---

[1] We shall sometimes underline literals to indicate that they are selected.

for every unsatisfiable set of clauses the inference system will generate, with a fair strategy, the empty clause) calculus for Horn clauses called *basic ordered paramodulation with selection* [2,19].

$$\frac{\Gamma \Rightarrow \ell = r \; [\![\theta]\!] \quad \Gamma' \Rightarrow u[\ell']_p = v \; [\![\theta']\!]}{\Gamma, \Gamma' \Rightarrow u[x]_p = v \; [\![\theta, \theta', \ell' = \ell, x = r]\!]} \; \text{RP}$$

if x is fresh, and (i) $\ell' \notin \mathcal{X}$, (ii) no literal is selected in Γ and Γ', (iii) and (v) hold.

$$\frac{\Gamma \Rightarrow \ell = r \; [\![\theta]\!] \quad \Gamma', u[\ell']_p = v \Rightarrow A \; [\![\theta']\!]}{\Gamma, \Gamma', u[x]_p = v \Rightarrow A \; [\![\theta, \theta', \ell' = \ell, x = r]\!]} \; \text{LP}$$

if x is fresh, (i) $\ell' \notin \mathcal{X}$, (ii) no literal is selected in Γ, (iii) holds, (iv) $u = v$ is selected or (v') holds.

$$\frac{\Gamma, s = t \Rightarrow A \; [\![\theta]\!]}{\Gamma \Rightarrow A \; [\![\theta, s = t]\!]} \; \text{Eq}$$

if (vi) $s = t$ is selected or (vii) $s\sigma \not\preceq t\sigma$ and $s\sigma = t\sigma$ is maximal in $\Gamma\sigma, s\sigma = t\sigma, A\sigma$, where σ is the mgu of $\theta, s = t$.

The conditions missing above are: (iii) $\ell\sigma \not\preceq r\sigma$ and $\ell\sigma = r\sigma$ is strictly maximal in $\Gamma\sigma, \ell\sigma = r\sigma$, (v) $u\sigma = v\sigma$ is maximal in $\Gamma'\sigma, u\sigma = v\sigma$, where σ is the most general unifier (mgu) of $\theta, \theta', \ell' = \ell, x = r$, (v') $u\sigma = v\sigma$ is maximal in $\Gamma'\sigma, u\sigma = v\sigma, A\sigma$ (σ is as in (v)).

Concerning RP and LP, we shall talk of paramodulation of the first clause (called first *premise*) into the second clause (second *premise*). The clause returned by the above inferences is called the *conclusion*. If after every step the constraints are eagerly propagated in the clauses (*i.e.* each clause is expanded) the calculus is called *ordered paramodulation with selection*.

Resolution. The application of LP at the root of non-equational atoms followed by Eq is called *basic resolution*.

$$\frac{\Gamma \Rightarrow P(\ell) = true \; [\![\theta]\!] \quad \Gamma', P(\ell') = true \Rightarrow A \; [\![\theta']\!]}{\Gamma, \Gamma' \Rightarrow A \; [\![\theta, \theta', \ell' = \ell]\!]} \; \text{R}$$

Note that the clause generated by the LP step is deleted, subsumed by the clause generated by the Eq step.

When the non-basic version of LP and Eq are used, this inference is simply called *ordered resolution*.

Note that when the unconstrained part of a clause only contains variables (no function symbols), only the resolution rule applies into this clause, and the clause obtained also contains only variables (*i.e.* every application of LP is performed at the root position of an atom). Therefore, for the sake of presentation, we shall eagerly apply the constraint when describing the application of R in this case. The application of RP to clauses whose heads are non-equational returns a tautology, and hence this case will be ignored in the following proofs.

Deletion of redundant clauses. We assume that the deletion of tautologies and subsumed clauses (these notions are considered after clause expansion) and the simplification under rewriting by orientable positive equational clauses are applied as in [2].

Splitting. We shall use ε-*splitting* [13], a variant of *splitting without backtracking* [21].

$$\frac{B, \Gamma \Rightarrow H[\![\theta]\!]}{B \Rightarrow q_B[\![\theta]\!] \quad q_B, \Gamma \Rightarrow H[\![\theta]\!]} \; \varepsilon\text{split}$$

where the literals of $\Gamma \cup H$ are not equational, $B\theta$ is an ε-*block*, *i.e.* a set of literals of the form $Q_1(x), \ldots, Q_n(x)$, with $Q_1, \ldots, Q_n \in \mathcal{P}$, x is a variable which does not occur in Γ and H, and where $q_B \in \mathcal{Q}$ is uniquely associated with B, modulo variable renaming.

Note that the above splitting rule *replaces* a clause by two split clauses. Using this rule eagerly (as soon as possible) preserves correctness and completeness of the calculus. Indeed, since every splitting predicate q_B is smaller than any predicate of $\mathcal{P}$, the original clause is redundant (wrt the general redundancy criterion of [2]) because its reduced instances are implied by smaller reduced instances of the split clauses. Another important point is that the number of splitting literals that can be introduced is bounded. We will assume that the set $\mathcal{Q}$ is large enough to cover all ε-blocks.

4   Standard Tree Automata

The transitions of standard tree automata are classically encoded into Horn clauses of the following form:

$$Q_1(x_1), \ldots, Q_n(x_n) \Rightarrow Q\big(f(x_1, \ldots, x_n)\big) \tag{s}$$

where $n \geq 0$ (when $n = 0$, by convention, the set of antecedents of the clause is empty), $x_1, \ldots, x_n$ are distinct variables and $Q_1, \ldots, Q_n, Q \in \mathcal{P}_0$.

Definition 1. *A* standard bottom-up tree automaton *(TA) is a finite set of clauses of type (s).*

The language of a TA is called a *regular* language.

Example 1. The language of the following TA in Q_1 is the set of binary trees with inner nodes labelled by f and leaves labelled by 0 or 1, such that at least a leaf is labeled by 1: $\Rightarrow Q_0(0)$, $\Rightarrow Q_1(1)$,

$$Q_0(x_1), Q_0(x_2) \Rightarrow Q_0(f(x_1, x_2)), \quad Q_1(x_1), Q_0(x_2) \Rightarrow Q_1(f(x_1, x_2)),$$
$$Q_0(x_1), Q_1(x_2) \Rightarrow Q_1(f(x_1, x_2)), \quad Q_1(x_1), Q_1(x_2) \Rightarrow Q_1(f(x_1, x_2))$$

The emptiness and membership problems for TA can be solved in deterministic time, respectively linear and quadratic. GMP for a linear term can be decided by a procedure of the same quadratic time complexity. For a non-linear term, the problem is EXPTIME-complete [10]. We sketch below a slight variation of a DEXPTIME procedure of [13] in our framework, in order to introduce the principles of the proofs in the next sections. It is based on the function sel_1 which selects in a Horn clause $\Gamma \Rightarrow H[\![\theta]\!]$: every splitting negative literal, if any, and otherwise every non-equational literal $Q(t)$ of Γ such that $t\theta$ is not a variable.

Proposition 1 ([13]). *Ordered resolution with selection and ε-splitting saturates the union of a TA and a goal clause $P(t) \Rightarrow$.*

Proof. (sketch, the complete proof may be found in [15], Appendix B). We show that the saturation of a TA $\mathcal{A}$ and the goal $P(t) \Rightarrow$ under ordered resolution wrt $\succ_{lpo}$ and the selection function sel_1, with eager application of the εsplit rule of Section 3, produce only clauses of one of the following form (**gs**), for goal-subterm, or (**gf**), for goal-flat.

$$\underline{q_1}, \ldots, \underline{q_k}, P_1(s_1), \ldots, P_m(s_m) \Rightarrow [q] \qquad \text{(gs)}$$

where $m, k \geq 0$, $s_1, \ldots, s_m$ are subterms of t, $P_1, \ldots, P_m \in \mathcal{P}_0$, and $q_1, \ldots, q_k, q$ are splitting literals (the q in the head is optional, as indicated by the square brackets).

$$P_1(y_{i_1}), \ldots, P_k(y_{i_k}), \underline{P_1'(f(y_1, \ldots, y_n))}, \ldots, P_m'(f(y_1, \ldots, y_n)) \Rightarrow [q] \qquad \text{(gf)}$$

where $k, m \geq 0$, $i_1, \ldots, i_k \leq n$, $y_1, \ldots, y_n$ are distinct variables, $P_1, \ldots, P_k, P_1', \ldots P_m' \in \mathcal{P}_0$, and q is a splitting literal (optional in the clause).

Since the number of clauses of type (**gs**) and (**gf**) is exponential, the saturation terminates and GMP is solvable in deterministic exponential time. $\quad\square$

Corollary 1. *GMP is decidable for TA.*

Undecidable extension. Let us call a *fact* a Horn clause $\Rightarrow H$ with no antecedents at all. We define a clause to be of type (s_+) if it is of type (**s**) or a fact. Note that we allow non-linear variables in facts. We can show that GMP for this slight extension of TA is undecidable [2] (even with one predicate only):

Proposition 2. *GMP for sets of clauses of type (s_+) is undecidable.*

Proof. We reduce in [15], Appendix C, the halting problem of 2 counter machines to GMP for (s_+).

5   Tree Automata with Syntactic Equational Constraints

Reduction Automata. The original reduction automata (RA) of [7] can be defined as finite sets of constrained Horn clauses of the following form:

$$Q_1(x_1), \ldots, Q_n(x_n) \Rightarrow Q(f(x_1, \ldots, x_n))[\![c]\!] \qquad \text{(red)}$$

where $n > 0$, $x_1, \ldots, x_n$ are distinct variables, c is a conjunction of constraints of the form $x_i|_p = x_{i'}|_{p'}$ (equality constraint) or $x_i|_p \neq x_{i'}|_{p'}$ (disequality constraint) for some positions p and p' (sequences of integers), Q is maximal in $\{Q, Q_1, \ldots, Q_n\}$ (here, we do not assume that the ordering on predicates is total) and it is moreover *strictly* maximal if c contains at least one equality constraint. An equality constraint as above (resp. disequality constraint) is satisfied

---

[2] GMP with linear facts can be shown decidable [6].

564   F. Jacquemard, M. Rusinowitch, and L. Vigneron

by every two ground terms $t, t' \in T(\mathcal{F})$ such that $p \in Pos(t)$, $p' \in Pos(t')$ and $t|_p = t'|_{p'}$ (resp. $p \in Pos(t)$, $p' \in Pos(t')$ and $t|_p \neq t'|_{p'}$). Given an RA $\mathcal{A}$ and a state Q of $\mathcal{A}$, the language $L(\mathcal{A}, Q)$ is defined as in page 560 (extending the definition from Horn clause to constrained Horn clauses). The definition of GMP and emptiness problems for RA follow.

We prove that the emptiness problem is undecidable for non-deterministic reduction automata, contradicting a claim in [7,6].

Proposition 3. *The emptiness problem is undecidable for non-deterministic RA.*

The proof, a variation of the proof of Proposition 2, is given in [15], Appendix D.

TAD. We propose here the definition of a new class of tree automata where the constraints are generalized (compared to [7]) to equations between arbitrary terms and where the transitions comply to stronger ordering conditions, based on the ordering $\succ$ on states, in order to obtain a decidable GMP. We call below *test predicates*[3] the elements of $\mathcal{P}_1$. The constrained transitions of our automata have the following form:

$$Q_1(x_1), \ldots, Q_n(x_n), u_1 = v_1, \ldots, u_k = v_k \Rightarrow Q^*(x) \qquad (d)$$

where $n, k \geq 0$, $x_1, \ldots, x_n, x$ are distinct variables, $u_1, v_1, \ldots, u_k, v_k \in T(\mathcal{F}, \{x_1, \ldots, x_n, x\})$, $Q_1, \ldots, Q_n, Q \in \mathcal{P}$, Q^* is a test predicate, and for all $i \leq n$, if Q_i is a test predicate then $Q^* \succ Q_i$.

The unconstrained transitions are restricted to clauses of type (s) which contain no more test predicates symbols in their antecedents than in their heads.

$$Q_1(x_1), \ldots, Q_n(x_n) \Rightarrow Q\big(f(x_1, \ldots, x_n)\big) \qquad (t)$$

where $n > 0$, $x_1, \ldots, x_n$ are distinct variables, and either $Q_1, \ldots, Q_n, Q \in \mathcal{P}_0$ or Q is a test predicate and at most one of $Q_1, \ldots, Q_n$ is equal to Q, and the others belong to $\mathcal{P}_0$.

Definition 2. *A tree automaton with equational constraints or TAD is a finite set of clauses of type (t) or (d).*

Note that every TA is a particular case of TAD (without test predicates).

Example 2. The language of the following TAD in state Q_2 is the set of stuttering lists of natural numbers build with the symbols cons and empty:

$$\Rightarrow Q_0(0) \qquad\qquad Q_0(x_1) \Rightarrow Q_0(s(x_1))$$
$$\Rightarrow Q_1(\text{empty}) \qquad\qquad Q_0(x_1), Q_1(x_2) \Rightarrow Q_1(\text{cons}(x_1, x_2))$$
$$Q_0(x_1), Q_2(x_2) \Rightarrow Q_2(\text{cons}(x_1, x_2))$$
$$Q_0(x_1), Q_1(x_2), x_2 = \text{cons}(x_1, y), x = \text{cons}(x_1, x_2) \Rightarrow Q_2(x)$$

Proposition 4. *Ordered paramodulation with selection and ε-splitting saturates the union of a TAD and a goal clause $P(t) \Rightarrow$.*

---

[3] And we shall sometimes mark a predicate Q with an asterisk like in Q^* to indicate that it is a test predicate.

Proof. (sketch) Let sel_2 be a selection function which generalizes sel_1, by selecting every equational negative literals, if any, and otherwise is defined just like sel_1. We consider saturation under ordered paramodulation wrt $\succ_{lpo}$ with selection by sel_2 and ε-splitting.

The principle of the proof of termination (detailed in [15], Appendix E) is to show that, starting with a TAD $\mathcal{A}$ and $P(t) \Rightarrow$, every step of paramodulation returns either a clause smaller than all its premises (wrt to a well founded ordering $\gg$) or a clause of type (gf). Two key points ensure this result. First, because of the selection strategy, equations in clauses of type (d) will be eliminated first, using Eq, before these clauses can be involved in resolution. The type of clauses obtained (when all equations have been eliminated) is called (d_+) and their predicates satisfy the same ordering condition as for (d). Second, thanks to the ordering conditions on predicates for (t) and (d_+) the application of such clauses in resolution makes clauses decrease (wrt $\gg$). $\qquad\qquad\square$

Corollary 2. *GMP is decidable for TAD.*

6   Tree Automata Modulo Monadic Theories

There have been many works to identify some classes of rewrite systems preserving the regularity of sets of terms, like for instance ground TRS, right-linear monadic TRS, linear semi-monadic TRS... (see [22], Section 2.3 for a summary of some recent results). These results often rely on a procedure of *completion* of TA wrt some TRS, which adds new TA transitions without adding new states. As observed in [14], such a TA completion can be simulated by saturation under paramodulation. The next results show that this method is effective (*i.e.* terminates) in the case of monadic theories.

Definition 3. *A rewrite rule $\ell \to r$ is called* sublinear *if ℓ is sublinear,* collapsing *if r is either a ground term or a variable, and* monadic *if r is either a variable occurring in ℓ or a term $g(z_1, \ldots, z_k)$ for some $g \in \mathcal{F}$, $k \geq 0$ and some distinct variables $z_1, \ldots, z_k$ occurring in ℓ.*

Example 3. The following axiom for integer equality: $\mathsf{eq}(\mathsf{s}(x), \mathsf{s}(y)) \to \mathsf{eq}(x, y)$ as well as this rule for the elimination of stuttering in lists: $\mathsf{cons}(x, \mathsf{cons}(x, y)) \to \mathsf{cons}(x, y)$ are monadic rewrite rules. Sublinear and collapsing rewrite rules permit to describe cryptographic functions [1], like decryption in a symmetric cryptosystem $\mathsf{dec}(\mathsf{enc}(x, y), y) \to x$ (the symbols enc and dec stand for encryption and decryption and the variables x and y correspond respectively to the encrypted plaintext and the encryption key), or, in the case of public (asymmetric) key cryptography: $\mathsf{adec}(\mathsf{aenc}(x, \mathsf{pub}(y)), \mathsf{inv}(\mathsf{pub}(y))) \to x$ and $\mathsf{adec}(\mathsf{aenc}(x, \mathsf{inv}(\mathsf{pub}(y))), \mathsf{pub}(y)) \to x$ where inv is an idempotent operator, following the rule $\mathsf{inv}(\mathsf{inv}(y)) \to y$, which associates to a public encryption key its corresponding private key (for decryption), and conversely. We will also consider below projections on pairs: $\mathsf{fst}(\mathsf{pair}(x, y)) \to x$ and $\mathsf{snd}(\mathsf{pair}(x, y)) \to y$.

We call an *equational theory* a set of positive clauses of the form:

$$\Rightarrow \ell = r \tag{eq}$$

An equational theory $\mathcal{E}$ is called $\succ$-*convergent* if for each clause of $\mathcal{E}$, the equation $\ell = r$ is orientable by $\succ_{lpo}$, i.e. $\ell \succ_{lpo} r$, and the rewrite system $\mathcal{R} = \{\ell \to r \mid \Rightarrow \ell = r \in \mathcal{E} \text{ and } \ell \succ_{lpo} r\}$ is confluent. Moreover, the theory $\mathcal{E}$ is called sublinear (resp. collapsing, monadic) if all the rules of $\mathcal{R}$ are sublinear (resp. collapsing, monadic).

Definition 4. *A tree automaton modulo an equational theory (TAE) is the union of an equational theory and of a finite set of clauses of type (s).*

Example 4. The language of the following simple TAE in state Q_e is the set of expressions equivalent to non-negative even integers:

$$\Rightarrow \mathsf{p}(\mathsf{s}(x)) = x \qquad \Rightarrow \mathsf{s}(\mathsf{p}(x)) = x$$
$$\Rightarrow Q_e(0) \quad Q_e(x) \Rightarrow Q_o(\mathsf{s}(x)) \qquad Q_o(x) \Rightarrow Q_e(\mathsf{s}(x))$$

If, instead of the above equational theory for successor and predecessor we consider the following monadic equational theory for a partial subtraction on natural numbers: $\mathsf{s}(x) - \mathsf{s}(y) = x - y, x - 0 = x, 0 - x = 0$, the language is the set of ground terms equivalent to non-negative even integers.

Proposition 5. *Basic ordered paramodulation with selection and ε-splitting. saturates the union of a TAE modulo a $\succ$-convergent monadic equational theory and a goal clause $P(t) \Rightarrow$.*

Proof. We show the termination of saturation of $\mathcal{A} \cup \{P(t) \Rightarrow\}$ under basic ordered paramodulation wrt the ordering $\succ_{lpo}$ and the selection function sel_1 and with eager ε-splitting.

The new situation here is that the right paramodulation RP can be applied to a clause of type (s), using an equation of the equational theory (i.e. of clause of $\mathcal{A}$ of type (eq)).

$$\frac{\Rightarrow f(\ell_1, \ldots, \ell_n) = r \quad Q_1(x_1), \ldots, Q_1(x_n) \Rightarrow Q(f(x_1, \ldots, x_n))}{Q_1(x_1), \ldots, Q_n(x_n) \Rightarrow Q(y) [\![x_1 = \ell_1, \ldots, x_n = \ell_n, y = r]\!]} \, \text{RP}$$

Also, LP with an equational clause (eq) is possible into the initial goal clause $P(t) \Rightarrow$. We introduce in [15], Appendix F, a new clause type (l) to characterize the (expansions of) clauses obtained this way, and show by a case analysis that all the clauses obtained during the saturation are of type (l) or of a type (f) which generalizes (gf) (proof of Proposition 1), allowing a head of the form $Q(r)$ where r is either a variable or a linear flat term $g(x_1, \ldots, x_n)$.

Since the number of clauses of type (l) and (f) is finite, this proves that the saturation of $\mathcal{A} \cup \{P(t) \Rightarrow\}$ under basic ordered paramodulation terminates. $\square$

Note that the expanded form of the above clause $Q_1(\ell_1), \ldots, Q_n(\ell_n) \Rightarrow Q(y)$ is related to the push clauses of two-automata [25] or *selecting theories* [24]. We will come back to this remark in Example 7 showing how the approach for protocol verification of this last paper can be carry on by TADE.

Corollary 3. *GMP is decidable for TAE modulo a $\succ$-convergent monadic equational theory.*

7 Tree Automata with Equational Constraints Modulo a Theory

It is shown in [14] that the class of languages of terms recognized by tree automata of [3], with equality constraints between brother positions is not closed under rewriting with shallow theories (rewrite systems whose left and right members of rules have depth 1). The reason is that these tree automata test syntactic equalities whereas we want to consider languages of terms modulo an equational theory. The problem is the same with the tree automata of [7]. Our definition based on Horn clauses and our saturation method solve this problem by considering a class of tree automata which combines both equality constraints like TAD and equational theories like TAE. The tree automata defined this way test equality constraints modulo an equational theory and recognize languages of terms modulo the same theory.

Definition 5. *A tree automaton with equational constraints modulo an equational theory (TADE) is the union of an equational theory and of a TAD.*

We show in [15], Appendix G, that every reduction automaton with equality constraints only is equivalent to a TADE of the same size, as long as its transitions fulfill the restrictions on predicates introduced in the definition of (t) and (d) in order to make emptiness decidable.

Example 5. We illustrate in this example how TADE can be used to characterize the behaviour of security protocols running in an insecure environment, following a model with explicit destructors [1] specified with the rewrite rules of Example 3. It is known [17] that such model with rewrite rules is more expressive than a standard model of cryptosystems based on free algebras. For instance, the attack mentioned in Example 6 cannot be captured by free algebras based approach like *e.g.* [12]. Our representation is such that a state of the protocol is reachable (from an initial state) iff it is in the TADE language. The protocol of Denning & Sacco [8] permits two agents A and B to exchange a new symmetric key using an asymmetric cryptosystem. The respective behaviour of the agents can be represented by the two following clauses of type (d)[4]:

$$Q_{0j}(x) \Rightarrow Q_{1j}(\mathsf{pair}(A, \mathsf{aenc}(\mathsf{aenc}(K, \mathsf{inv}(\mathsf{pub}(A))), \mathsf{pub}(B)))) \qquad j = 0,1$$
$$Q_{i0}(x) \Rightarrow Q_{i1}(\mathsf{enc}(S, \mathsf{adec}(\mathsf{adec}(\mathsf{snd}(x), \mathsf{inv}(\mathsf{pub}(B))), \mathsf{pub}(\mathsf{fst}(x))))) \; i = 0,1$$

The predicate Q_{ij} represent the content of the channel Q when agents A and B are in respective states i, j, which are either 0 (initial state) or 1 (final state). In the first clause, A initiates the protocol, sending B a freshly chosen symmetric key K for further secure communications (A, B, K, S are constant function symbols).

---

[4] For the sake of simplicity we denote $Q_1(x_1), x = u \Rightarrow Q(x)$ by $Q_1(x_1) \Rightarrow Q(u)$.

This key is K signed, for authentication purpose, with the secret key $\mathsf{inv}(\mathsf{pub}(A))$ of A and encrypted with the public key $\mathsf{pub}(B)$ of B. Moreover, A appends its name at the beginning of the message. In the second clause, B answers with a secret value S encrypted with K, which has been extracted from the received message (using the destructor symbols and the rules of Example 3). Note that in this setting, equations in clauses (d) permit to model conditionals for the agents of protocols.

We add some clauses of type (t) and (d) in order to model the control of an attacker over the public communication channel Q, namely the ability to read / analyze and recompose (by application of any public function f, possibly a destructor symbol) / resend messages:

$$Q_{00}(x_1), Q_{00}(x_2) \Rightarrow Q_{00}(\mathsf{f}(x_1, x_2)) \qquad Q_{00}(x_1), Q_{01}(x_2) \Rightarrow Q_{01}(\mathsf{f}(x_1, x_2))$$
$$Q_{00}(x_1), Q_{10}(x_2) \Rightarrow Q_{10}(\mathsf{f}(x_1, x_2)) \qquad Q_{00}(x_1), Q_{11}(x_2) \Rightarrow Q_{11}(\mathsf{f}(x_1, x_2))$$
$$\text{symmetric of the above clauses:} \qquad Q_{01}(x_1), Q_{00}(x_2) \Rightarrow Q_{01}(\mathsf{f}(x_1, x_2)) \ldots$$
$$Q_{01}(x_1), Q_{10}(x_2) \Rightarrow Q_{11}(\mathsf{f}(x_1, x_2)) \qquad Q_{10}(x_1), Q_{01}(x_2) \Rightarrow Q_{11}(\mathsf{f}(x_1, x_2))$$

Note that in the above clauses we allow several combinations of the agent's states in the antecedents, but not every combination. The principle is that if A (resp. B) is in state 1 in the first antecedent, it must be in state 0 in the second one (and conversely), because we assume that each agent can run only once. This way, we ensure an exact representation (as ground terms) of the executions of an instance of the protocol, whereas many other Horn clauses or tree automata models are approximating [12,18,25]. Note that these conditions fit well with the ordering restrictions on clauses of type (t) and (d). We also add some clauses (t) ensuring that some ground terms are initially known to the attacker, $e.g. \Rightarrow Q_{00}(A)$.

Proposition 6. *Basic ordered paramodulation with selection and ε-splitting saturates the union of a TADE modulo a $\succ$-convergent sublinear and collapsing equational theory and a goal clause $P(t) \Rightarrow$.*

Proof. (sketch) We consider saturation under basic ordered paramodulation wrt the ordering $\succ_{lpo}$ and the selection function sel_2 (defined in the proof of Proposition 4) and with eager ε-splitting. Following the same proof schema as for Proposition 4 (TAD) we show (in [15], Appendix H) that, starting with a TADE $\mathcal{A}$ and $P(t) \Rightarrow$, every step of paramodulation returns either a clause smaller than all its premises (wrt to a well founded ordering $\gg$) or a clause of type (gf) or (df) where this latter clause type is similar to (gf) and also contains only a finite number of clauses.

The proof is nevertheless much more complicated than in the case of TAD (see [15], Table 5). Indeed, like for TAD (Proposition 4), we obtain clauses of type (d_+) generalizing (d), in this case using basic narrowing. However, these clauses (d_+) can be combined, by resolution, with clauses of a type similar to (l) in Proposition 5. Clause decreasing, wrt $\gg$, is obtained for such resolution steps thanks to the restrictions on the equational theory considered. $\qquad \square$

Corollary 4. *GMP is decidable for TADE modulo a $\succ$-convergent sublinear and collapsing equational theory.*

Example 6. Several security properties of the Denning & Sacco's protocol may be expressed as GMP wrt the TADE of Example 5: $Q_{01}(x) \Rightarrow$ expresses for instance that B has answered to a message not originating from A (authentication flaw) and $Q_{01}(S) \Rightarrow$ that the secret is revealed (confidentiality flaw). Both instances of GMP can be solved with the method of Proposition 6, revealing a known attack, which is described in [15], Example 6.

Example 7. The *recursive authentication protocol* [4] ensures the distribution of certified session keys to a group of clients by a server which process recursively an unbounded list of requests. The automated verification of such group protocols has been studied in [16,24]. We shall follow below the presentation of [16], showing that it fits in our formalism. The server receives a sequence of requests for keys represented by a term of the form nil or[5]: $\langle \mathsf{hash}(\mathsf{m}(a), a, b, n_a, y), \langle a, b, n_a, y \rangle \rangle$, denoted below by $h_{\mathsf{m}_a}(a, b, n_a, y)$, where hash is a unary one-way function, a is the name of the principal requesting a certificate, b is the name of the principal with whom a is willing to share a key, n_a is a random number generated by a (nonce), $\mathsf{m}(a)$ is a mac key shared by the server and a and y is a subsequence of the other requests, which (if not nil) has the form $h_{\mathsf{m}_c}(c, a, n_c, y')$ (c is the name of another principal). The behaviour of the server, when receiving a request sequence, is defined by the following clauses of type (d)) (a, b, c, n_a, n_c are variables):

$$Q_0(x), x = h_{\mathsf{m}_a}(a, b, n_a, \mathsf{nil}) \Rightarrow Q_1\big(\mathsf{aenc}(\mathsf{pub}(a), \langle \mathsf{k}(a, b, n_a), b, n_a \rangle)\big)$$
$$Q_0(x), x = h_{\mathsf{m}_a}(a, b, n_a, h_{\mathsf{m}_c}(c, a, n_c, y')) \Rightarrow Q_1\big(\mathsf{aenc}(\mathsf{pub}(a), \langle \mathsf{k}(a, b, n_a), b, n_a \rangle)\big)$$
$$Q_1\big(\mathsf{aenc}(\mathsf{pub}(a), \langle \mathsf{k}(c, a, n_c), c, n_a \rangle)\big)$$

It means that the server sends to a one or two certificates encrypted with his public key, where k is a secret function used for the generation of session keys. Note the two occurrences of a in the equation of the second clause, which implicitly express an equality between the name of the requester of a query and the receiver in the next one. It is assumed that for the first element of the sequence, the receiver is actually the server himself (hence it is not necessary to send him a certificate). Moreover, we have a clause of type (t) for the enumeration of the requests by the server: $Q_0(x) \Rightarrow Q_0(\mathsf{next}(x))$, where next is an operator which pops the first element of a request's sequence, defined by the following collapsing equation (m is a variable): $\mathsf{next}(\mathsf{hash}(m, x_1, x_2, x_3, y), \langle x_1, x_2, x_3, y \rangle) = y$.

8   Conclusion and Further Works

We have introduced new classes of tree automata with constraints and shown that the General Membership Problem is decidable for them with a uniform theorem-proving technique. Potential extensions are numerous.

As future work we plan to extend the tree automata classes defined in this paper to disequality tests as in [7]. This would permit us to characterize languages of normal form wrt a TRS and is useful in particular in inductive theorem proving [6].

---

[5] We abbreviate $\mathsf{pair}(t_1, \mathsf{pair}(t_2, \ldots, \mathsf{pair}(t_{n-1}, t_n)))$ by $\langle t_1, \ldots, t_n \rangle$ ($n \geq 2$).

Equality tests between brother positions à la [3] can be easily incorporated into the Horn clauses representation of tree automata (see *e.g.* [14]). Equations are not necessary for this purpose, since multiple occurrences of a variable suffice, as in: $Q_1(x), Q_2(x) \Rightarrow Q(f(x, x))$. The combination of TA classes of [3] and [7] preserves emptiness decidability [5]. Hence the combination of the above class of TA with equality test modulo and unrestricted test between brother positions is interesting to study.

It would also be interesting to extend the above saturation results (in particular for classes modulo monadic or collapsing theories) to term algebra modulo AC, using AC-paramodulation techniques. This combination (AC + sublinear–collapsing) permits us to axiomatize primitives like the exclusive-or.

Acknowledgments. We wish to thank Stéphanie Delaune for her contribution to early phases of this work, Anne-Cécile Caron, Sophie Tison Jean Goubault-Larrecq and Christopher Lynch for their feedback.

References

1. M. Abadi and C. Fournet. Mobile values, new names, and secure communication. In *28th ACM SIGPLAN-SIGACT Symposium on Principles of Programming Languages*, pages 104–115, 2001.
2. L. Bachmair, H. Ganzinger, C. Lynch, and W. Snyder. Basic Paramodulation. *Information and Computation*, 121(2):172–192, 1995.
3. B. Bogaert and S. Tison. Equality and Disequality Constraints on Direct Subterms in Tree Automata. In *9th Symp. on Theoretical Aspects of Computer Science, STACS*, volume 577 of *LNCS*, pages 161–171. Springer, 1992.
4. J. A. Bull and D. J. Otway. The authentication protocol. Technical report, Defence Research Agency, Malvern, UK, 1997.
5. A.-C. Caron, H. Comon, J.-L. Coquidé, M. Dauchet, and F. Jacquemard. Pumping, Cleaning and Symbolic Constraints Solving. In *21st Int. Coll. on Automata, Languages and Programming, ICALP*, volume 820 of *LNCS*, pages 436–449. Springer, 1994.
6. H. Comon, M. Dauchet, R. Gilleron, F. Jacquemard, D. Lugiez, S. Tison, and M. Tommasi. *Tree Automata Techniques and Applications*. http://www.grappa.univ-lille3.fr/tata, 1997.
7. M. Dauchet, A.-C. Caron, and J.-L. Coquidé. Automata for Reduction Properties Solving. *Journal of Symbolic Computation*, 20(2):215–233, 1995.
8. D. E. Denning and G. M. Sacco. Timestamps in Key Distribution Protocols. In *Communications of the ACM*, 1981.
9. N. Dershowitz and J.-P. Jouannaud. *Rewrite systems*, chapter Handbook of Theoretical Computer Science, Volume B, pages 243–320. Elsevier, 1990.
10. P. Devienne, J.-M. Talbot, and S. Tison. Set-based analysis for logic programming and tree automata. In P. V. Hentenryck, editor, *Static Analysis, 4th International Symposium, SAS*, volume 1302 of *Lecture Notes in Computer Science*, pages 127–140. Springer, 1997.
11. T. Frühwirth, E. Shapiro, M. Vardi, and E. Yardeni. Logic programs as types for logic programs. In *Proc. of the 6th IEEE Symposium on Logic in Computer Science*, pages 300–309, 1991.

12. T. Genet and F. Klay. Rewriting for Cryptographic Protocol Verification. In *Proc. of 17th Int. Conf. on Automated Deduction, CADE*, volume 1831 of *LNCS*. Springer, 2000.

13. J. Goubault-Larrecq. Deciding $\mathcal{H}_1$ by Resolution. *Information Processing Letters*, 95(3):401–408, 2005.

14. F. Jacquemard, C. Meyer, and C. Weidenbach. Unification in Extensions of Shallow Equational Theories. In *9th Int. Conf. on Rewriting Techniques and Applications, RTA*, volume 1379 of *LNCS*, pages 76–90. Springer, 1998.

15. F. Jacquemard, M. Rusinowitch, and L. Vigneron. Tree automata with equality constraints modulo equational theories. Technical Report LSV-06-07, LSV, 2006. http://www.lsv.ens-cachan.fr/Publis.

16. R. Küsters and T. Wilke. Automata-Based Analysis of Recursive Cryptographic Protocols. In *21st Annual Symp. on Theoretical Aspects of Computer Science, STACS*, volume 2996 of *LNCS*, pages 382–393. Springer, 2004.

17. C. Lynch and C. Meadows. On the relative soundness of the free algebra model for public key encryption. *Electr. Notes Theor. Comput. Sci.*, 125(1):43–54, 2005.

18. F. Nielson, H. Riis Nielson, and H. Seidl. Normalizable Horn Clauses, Strongly Recognizable Relations, and Spi. In *Static Analysis, 9th Int. Symp., SAS*, volume 2477 of *LNCS*, pages 20–35. Springer, 2002.

19. R. Nieuwenhuis and A. Rubio. *Paramodulation-Based Theorem Proving*, chapter Handbook of Automated Reasoning, Volume I, Chapter 7. Elsevier Science and MIT Press, 2001.

20. H. Ohsaki and T. Takai. Decidability and Closure Properties of Equational Tree Languages. In *13th Int. Conf. on Rewriting Techniques and Applications, RTA*, volume 2378 of *LNCS*, pages 114–128. Springer, 2002.

21. A. Riazanov and A. Voronkov. Splitting Without Backtracking. In *Proc. of the 17th Int. Joint Conf. on Artificial Intelligence, IJCAI*, pages 611–617. Morgan Kaufmann, 2001.

22. H. Seki, T. Takai, Y. Fujinaka, and Y. Kaji. Layered Transducing Term Rewriting System and Its Recognizability Preserving Property. In *Int. Conf. on Rewriting Techniques and Applications, RTA*, volume 2378 of *LNCS*, pages 98–113. Springer, 2002.

23. S. Tison. Tree automata and term rewrite systems. Invited tutorial at the 11th Int. Conf. on Rewriting Techniques and Applications, RTA, 2000.

24. T. Truderung. Selecting theories and recursive protocols. In M. Abadi and L. de Alfaro, editors, *CONCUR*, volume 3653 of *Lecture Notes in Computer Science*, pages 217–232. Springer, 2005.

25. K. N. Verma. *Two-Way Equational Tree Automata*. PhD thesis, ENS Cachan, Sept. 2003.

CASC-J3
The 3rd IJCAR ATP System Competition

Geoff Sutcliffe

Department of Computer Science, University of Miami
geoff@cs.miami.edu

The CADE ATP System Competition (CASC) is an annual evaluation of fully automatic, first-order Automated Theorem Proving (ATP) systems - the world championship for such systems. CASC-J3 was held on 18th August 2006, as part of the 3rd International Joint Conference on Automated Reasoning[1], in Seattle, Washington. It was the eleventh competition in the CASC series.

CASC-J3 was (like all CASCs) divided into divisions according to problem and system characteristics. The competition divisions were:[2]

- The FOF division: Mixed FOF non-propositional theorems.
- The CNF division: Mixed CNF really-non-propositional theorems.
- The SAT division: Mixed CNF really-non-propositional non-theorems.
- The EPR division: CNF effectively propositional theorems and non-theorems.
- The UEQ division: Unit equality CNF really-non-propositional theorems.

The systems were ranked in each division according to the number of problems solved (just a "yes" output). The systems in the FOF, CNF, and SAT divisions were also ranked according to the number of problems solved with an acceptable proof/model output. The problems were selected from the TPTP problem library v3.2.0, which was not released until the day of the competition. The selection of problems was biased towards up to 50% new problems not previously seen by the entrants. A CPU time limit was imposed on each system's run on each problem, and a wall clock time limit was imposed to limit very high memory usage that causes swapping. The CASC-J3 WWW site provides access to all the details of the competition design, competition resources, and the systems that were entered: http://www.tptp.org/CASC/J3/

The main change in CASC-J3 since CASC-20 (the previous CASC) was the promotion of the FOF division to primary place. This change reflects the increased number of FOF contributions to the TPTP - 550 new FOF problems between TPTP v3.0.1 and TPTP v3.1.0, in contrast with only 168 new CNF problems. The contributions reflect a corresponding increased use of FOF in applications, where problems are typically generated mechanically as part of a more complex software process, e.g., proof obligations arising from software verification [DFS04], or problems that check the consistency of an ontology [RPG05].

---

[1] CADE was a constituent conference of IJCAR, hence CASC-"J3".

[2] The acronyms mean: FOF - First Order Form (with all quantifiers and connectives), CNF - Clause Normal Form, SAT - Satisfiable, EPR - Effectively propositional (with a finite Herbrand universe), UEQ - Unit equality.

U. Furbach and N. Shankar (Eds.): IJCAR 2006, LNAI 4130, pp. 572–573, 2006.
© Springer-Verlag Berlin Heidelberg 2006

The use of ATP is typically just one of many software components within such applications, whose developers are best served by ATP systems that accept problems in whatever form is naturally produced by the application, without a need for transformation to any particular form, e.g., CNF or FOF with a restricted use of connectives. In accordance with that need, the FOF problems in CASC-J3 used the full set of FOF operators defined in the TPTP language, e.g., including <= and <~>, and interpreted propositions for *true* and *false*. No standardizing preprocessing was performed.

For CASC-21 (in next CASC) a FOF satisfiability division is planned, which will require systems to establish the satisfiability of sets of FOF formulae. This division will provide a link to the QF_UF division of the SMT-COMP competition [BdMS05], where systems must establish the satisfiability of sets of ground FOF formulae with equality. In the long term it is hoped to build closer ties between the TPTP and SMT-LIB [RTRL], which may lead to corresponding links between CASC and SMT-COMP. Combining the reasoning strengths of state-of-the-art first order systems (as evaluated in CASC) with theory reasoning capabilities (as evaluated in SMT-COMP) will provide users with better reasoning tools for solving application problems.

CASC has been a catalyst for improved engineering and performance of many ATP systems, and provides stimulus and insights that can lay the basis for the development of future ATP systems [SS06]. One of the virtues of the competition, which makes it repetitive to people who are looking for new features, is the fact that changes are made conservatively: this makes the results comparable over time, and provides incremental challenges to system developers. A key to sustaining the value of CASC in the future is continued growth of the TPTP. Developers and users are strongly encouraged to contribute new problems to the TPTP, particularly problems from emerging commercial applications of ATP.

References

[BdMS05]   C. Barrett, L. de Moura, and A. Stump. SMT-COMP: Satisfiability Modulo Theories Competition. In K. Etessami and S. Rajamani, editors, *Proceedings of the 17th International Conference on Computer Aided Verification*, number 3576 in Lecture Notes in Computer Science, pages 20–23. Springer-Verlag, 2005.

[DFS04]   E. Denney, B. Fischer, and J. Schumann. Using Automated Theorem Provers to Certify Auto-generated Aerospace Software. In M. Rusinowitch and D. Basin, editors, *Proceedings of the 2nd International Joint Conference on Automated Reasoning*, LNAI 3097, pages 198–212, 2004.

[RPG05]   D. Ramachandran, Reagan P., and K. Goolsbey. First-orderized Research-Cyc: Expressiveness and Efficiency in a Common Sense Knowledge Base. In Shvaiko P., editor, *Proceedings of the Workshop on Contexts and Ontologies: Theory, Practice and Applications* , 2005.

[RTRL]   S. Ranise and C. Tinelli. The Satisfiability Modulo Theories Library (SMT-LIB). http://goedel.cs.uiowa.edu/smtlib/, URL.

[SS06]   G. Sutcliffe and C. Suttner. The State of CASC. *AI Communications*, 19(1):35–48, 2006.

Matrix Interpretations
for Proving Termination of Term Rewriting

Jörg Endrullis[1], Johannes Waldmann[2], and Hans Zantema[3]

[1] Department of Computer Science, Vrije Universiteit Amsterdam
De Boelelaan 1081, 1081 HV Amsterdam, The Netherlands
joerg@few.vu.nl
[2] Hochschule für Technik, Wirtschaft und Kultur (FH) Leipzig
Fb IMN, PF 30 11 66, D-04251 Leipzig, Germany
waldmann@imn.htwk-leipzig.de
[3] Department of Computer Science, Technische Universiteit Eindhoven
P.O. Box 513, 5600 MB Eindhoven, The Netherlands
h.zantema@tue.nl

Abstract. We present a new method for automatically proving termination of term rewriting. It is based on the well-known idea of interpretation of terms where every rewrite step causes a decrease, but instead of the usual natural numbers we use vectors of natural numbers, ordered by a particular non-total well-founded ordering. Function symbols are interpreted by linear mappings represented by matrices. This method allows to prove termination and relative termination. A modification of the latter in which strict steps are only allowed at the top, turns out to be helpful in combination with the dependency pair transformation.

By bounding the dimension and the matrix coefficients, the search problem becomes finite. Our implementation transforms it to a Boolean satisfiability problem (SAT), to be solved by a state-of-the-art SAT solver. Our implementation performs well on the Termination Problem Data Base: better than 5 out of 6 tools that participated in the 2005 termination competition in the category of term rewriting.

1 Introduction

The annual Termination Competition [2] has given a new drive to the quest for automated methods to obtain termination proofs for term rewriting.

The termination provers do apply established methods (path orderings, dependency pairs, interpretations, labellings) as well as new methods (RFC match bounds). Two insights are that general methods can be restricted to special cases, gaining efficiency without loosing too much power, and combining methods may lead to strong improvements. We present here one such phenomenon: termination proofs from interpretations into a well-founded monotone algebra. This is a well-known general theme, but our point is

- the special choice of the algebra, and
- the special implementation of how to find suitable interpretations.

U. Furbach and N. Shankar (Eds.): IJCAR 2006, LNAI 4130, pp. 574–588, 2006.

The carrier of the algebra consists of vectors of natural numbers on which we define a well-founded ordering that is not total. Each function symbol is interpreted by a suitable linear mapping. This method allows to prove termination and relative termination. It has been proposed for string rewriting by Hofbauer and Waldmann [11]. In the present paper, we discuss its extension to term rewriting and a modification that allows to prove relative top-termination, i.e., a variant of relative termination where the strict steps are only allowed on top level. The latter is very helpful when using the dependency pair transformation. In order to cover the two-sorted nature of the dependency pair transformation, our monotone algebra setting is presented many-sorted.

We have implemented the method by bounding the dimension and the matrix coefficients, resulting in a search problem with a finite but typically huge search space. This is solved by transforming this finite search problem to a SAT problem, and using the state-of-the-art SAT solver SatELiteGTI, [3]. This performs surprisingly well on the Termination Problem Data Base, see section 7.

The main part of the paper is organized as follows. We present a many-sorted monotone algebra framework for relative termination and relative top-termination in Section 3, generalizing earlier results on monotone algebras. Then we choose the matrix instance of this framework in Section 4. Later, we combine this with the Dependency Pair method in Section 5. Our implementation is described in Section 6 and its performance is discussed in Section 7.

Our methods are illustrated by examples. They are kept simple for the sake of presentation. Nevertheless none of them can be proved terminating by any of the programs that participated in the Termination Competition 2005 [2].

2 Preliminaries

Let S be a non-empty set of sorts, and let Σ be an S-sorted signature, being a set of operation symbols each having a fixed arity in $S^* \times S$. An *S-sorted set* A is defined to consist of a set A_s for every $s \in S$. For an S-sorted set $\mathcal{X}$ of variable symbols let $\mathcal{T}(\Sigma, \mathcal{X})$ be the S-sorted set of terms over Σ and $\mathcal{X}$, that is, the smallest S-sorted set satisfying

- $x_s \in \mathcal{T}(\Sigma, \mathcal{X})_s$ for all $x_s \in \mathcal{X}_s$, and
- if the arity of $f \in \Sigma$ is $((s_1, \ldots, s_n), s)$ and $t_i \in \mathcal{T}(\Sigma, \mathcal{X})_{s_i}$ for $i = 1, \ldots, n$, then $f(t_1, \ldots, t_n) \in \mathcal{T}(\Sigma, \mathcal{X})_s$.

A *term rewriting system* (TRS) R over $\Sigma, \mathcal{X}$ is a S-sorted set in which for every $s \in S$ the set R_s consists of pairs $(\ell, r) \in \mathcal{T}(\Sigma, \mathcal{X})_s \times \mathcal{T}(\Sigma, \mathcal{X})_s$, for which $\ell \notin \mathcal{X}_s$ and all variables in r occur in ℓ. Pairs (ℓ, r) are called *rewrite rules* of sort s and are usually written as $\ell \to r$.

An S-sorted relation $\to$ over an S-sorted set A is defined to be an S-sorted set for which $\to_s \subseteq A_s \times A_s$ for every $s \in S$.

A substitution $\sigma : \mathcal{X} \to \mathcal{T}(\Sigma, \mathcal{X})$ is defined by a map $\sigma_s : \mathcal{X}_s \to \mathcal{T}(\Sigma, \mathcal{X})_s$ for every $s \in S$. These extend to terms in the obvious way.

For a TRS R the (S-sorted) *top rewrite relation* $\overset{top}{\to}_R$ on $\mathcal{T}(\Sigma, \mathcal{X})$ is defined by $t \overset{top}{\to}_{R,s} u$ if and only if there is a rewrite rule $\ell \to r \in R_s$ and a substitution $\sigma : \mathcal{X} \to \mathcal{T}(\Sigma, \mathcal{X})$ such that $t = \ell\sigma$ and $u = r\sigma$. The (S-sorted) *rewrite relation* $\to_R$ is defined to be the smallest S-sorted relation satisfying

- if $t \overset{top}{\to}_R u$ then $t \to_R u$, and
- if $t_i \to_{R,s_i} u_i$ and $t_j = u_j$ for $j \neq i$, then $f(t_1, \ldots, t_n) \to_{R,s} f(u_1, \ldots, u_n)$ for every $f \in \Sigma$ of arity $((s_1, \ldots, s_n), s)$ and every $i = 1, \ldots, n$.

For S-sorted binary relations we write $\cdot$ for sort-wise relation composition, and $*$ for sort-wise transitive reflexive closure.

An S-sorted relation $\to$ is called *well-founded* or *terminating* if for no $s \in S$ an infinite sequence $t_1, t_2, t_3, \ldots$ exists such that $t_i \to_s t_{i+1}$ for all $i = 1, 2, 3, \ldots$.

A TRS R is called *terminating* if $\to_R$ is well-founded. Termination is also called *strong normalization*; therefore the property of R being terminating is written as $\mathsf{SN}(R)$.

A binary relation $\to_1$ is called *terminating relative to* a binary relation $\to_2$, written as $\mathsf{SN}(\to_1 / \to_2)$, if for no $s \in S$ an infinite sequence $t_1, t_2, t_3, \ldots$ exists such that

- $t_i \to_{1,s} t_{i+1}$ for infinitely many values of i, and
- $t_i \to_{2,s} t_{i+1}$ for all other values of i.

We use the notation $\to_1 / \to_2$ to denote $\to_2^* \cdot \to_1 \cdot \to_2^*$; it is easy to see that $\mathsf{SN}(\to_1 / \to_2)$ coincides with well-foundedness of $\to_1 / \to_2$. We write $\mathsf{SN}(R/S)$ as a shorthand for $\mathsf{SN}(\to_R / \to_S)$, and we write $\mathsf{SN}(R_{top}/S)$ as a shorthand for $\mathsf{SN}(\overset{top}{\to}_R / \to_S)$.

3   Monotone Algebras

A Σ-algebra $(A, [\cdot])$ is defined to consist of a S-sorted set A, and for every $f \in \Sigma$ a function $[f] : A_{s_1} \times \cdots \times A_{s_n} \to A_s$, where $((s_1, \ldots, s_n), s)$ is the arity of f. This function $[f]$ is called the *interpretation* of f.

Let $\alpha_s : \mathcal{X}_s \to A_s$ for every $s \in S$; this collection of maps α_s is written as $\alpha : \mathcal{X} \to A$. We define the term evaluation $[\cdot, \alpha] : \mathcal{T}(\Sigma, \mathcal{X}) \to A$ inductively by

$$[x, \alpha] = \alpha_s(x),$$
$$[f(t_1, \ldots, t_n), \alpha] = [f]([t_1, \alpha], \ldots, [t_n, \alpha])$$

for $f \in \Sigma$ and $x \in \mathcal{X}_s$.

Definition 1. *An operation* $[f] : A_{s_1} \times \cdots \times A_{s_n} \to A_s$ *is* monotone *with respect to an S-sorted binary relation* $\to$ *on A if for all $a_i, b_i \in A_{s_i}$ for $i = 1, \ldots, n$ with $a_i \to_{s_i} b_i$ for some i and $a_j = b_j$ for all $j \neq i$ we have*

$$[f](a_1, \ldots, a_n) \to_s [f](b_1, \ldots, b_n).$$

A *weakly monotone* Σ-*algebra* $(A, [\cdot], >, \gtrsim)$ *is a* Σ-*algebra* $(A, [\cdot])$ *equipped with two S-sorted relations* $>, \gtrsim$ *on A such that*

  − > *is well-founded;*

  − $> \cdot \gtrsim\ \subseteq\ >$;

  − *for every* $f \in \Sigma$ *the operation* $[f]$ *is monotone with respect to* $\gtrsim$.

An extended monotone Σ-algebra $(A, [\cdot], >, \gtrsim)$ *is a weakly monotone* Σ-*algebra* $(A, [\cdot], >, \gtrsim)$ *in which moreover for every* $f \in \Sigma$ *the operation* $[f]$ *is monotone with respect to* $>$.

The combination $>, \gtrsim$ is closely related to the notion of *reduction pair* in the dependency pair framework, e.g. in [8]. A crucial difference is that the relations in a reduction pair are relations on terms that are closed under substitutions, while in our setting they are relations on the arbitrary (many-sorted) set A.

In the sequel we often omit sort information, e.g. writing $[t, \alpha] > [u, \alpha]$ rather than $[t, \alpha] >_s [u, \alpha]$. A TRS given without sort information is assumed to be one-sorted, i.e., S consists of one element.

The one-sorted version of extended monotone algebra where $\gtrsim$ is left implicit by defining it as the union of $>$ and equality is called *well-founded monotone algebra* in [14,15]. A main theorem states that a TRS is terminating if and only if there is a well-founded monotone algebra $(A, [\cdot], >)$ such that $[\ell, \alpha] > [r, \alpha]$ for every rule $\ell \to r$ and every $\alpha : \mathcal{X} \to A$. First we show that for relative termination we have a similar characterization based on extended monotone algebras, but not on this earlier version of well-founded monotone algebras.

Theorem 1. *Let* R, S *be TRSs over a signature* Σ. *Then*

1. $\mathsf{SN}(R/S)$ *if and only if there exists an extended monotone* Σ-*algebra* $(A, [\cdot], >, \gtrsim)$ *such that* $[\ell, \alpha] > [r, \alpha]$ *for every rule* $\ell \to r$ *in* R *and* $[\ell, \alpha] \gtrsim [r, \alpha]$ *for every rule* $\ell \to r$ *in* S, *for every* $\alpha : \mathcal{X} \to A$.
2. $\mathsf{SN}(R_{top}/S)$ *if and only if there exists a weakly monotone* Σ-*algebra* $(A, [\cdot], >, \gtrsim)$ *such that* $[\ell, \alpha] > [r, \alpha]$ *for every rule* $\ell \to r$ *in* R *and* $[\ell, \alpha] \gtrsim [r, \alpha]$ *for every rule* $\ell \to r$ *in* S, *for every* $\alpha : \mathcal{X} \to A$.

Proof. For the 'if'-part of part *1* assume such an extended monotone algebra $(A, [\cdot], >, \gtrsim)$ exists; we have to prove $\mathsf{SN}(R/S)$. So assume an infinite reduction

$$t_1 \to_{R \cup S} t_2 \to_{R \cup S} t_3 \to_{R \cup S} \cdots$$

containing infinitely many R-steps. Choose $\alpha : \mathcal{X} \to A$ arbitrary. Due to monotonicity with respect to $>$ we obtain $[t_i, \alpha] > [t_{i+1}, \alpha]$ if $t_i \to_R t_{i+1}$, and due to monotonicity with respect to $\gtrsim$ we obtain $[t_i, \alpha] \gtrsim [t_{i+1}, \alpha]$ if $t_i \to_S t_{i+1}$. Since $> \cdot \gtrsim\ \subseteq\ >$ we obtain $> \cdot \gtrsim^* \subseteq\ >$, hence for $t_i \to_R t_{i+1} \to_S^* t_j$ we obtain $[t_i, \alpha] > [t_j, \alpha]$. Since there are infinitely many R-steps this gives rise to an infinite decreasing sequence with respect to $>$, contradicting well-foundedness.

The proof of the 'if'-part of part *2* is similar; now all $\to_R$-steps in the assumed infinite reduction are $\overset{top}{\to}_R$-steps, by which monotonicity with respect to $>$ is not required.

For the 'only if'-part assume $\mathsf{SN}(R/S)$, respectively $\mathsf{SN}(R_{top}/S)$, holds. Choose $A = \mathcal{T}(\Sigma, \mathcal{X})$, and $[f](t_1, \ldots, t_n) = f(t_1, \ldots, t_n)$ for all $f \in \Sigma$. Define $> = (\to_R / \to_S)^+$ and $\gtrsim = (\to_{R \cup S})^*$, respectively $> = (\overset{top}{\to}_R / \to_S)^+$ and

$\gtrsim = \to_S^*$. Then $(A, [\cdot], >, \gtrsim)$ satisfies all requirements; where well-foundedness of $>$ is concluded from the assumption $\mathsf{SN}(R/S)$, respectively $\mathsf{SN}(R_{top}/S)$.   □

For the relations $>, \gtrsim$ we typically have in mind some more properties, like transitivity of both $>$ and $\gtrsim$, reflexivity of $\gtrsim$, and $\gtrsim \cdot > \cdot \gtrsim \subseteq > \subseteq \gtrsim$. However, from the proof of Theorem 1 we see that these properties are not essential.

For this characterization of relative termination the general notion of extended monotone algebra is essential: it does not hold for the restricted case where $\gtrsim$ coincides with the union of $>$ and equality. For instance, if R consists of the rule $f(f(x)) \to f(g(f(x)))$ and S consists of the rule $f(x) \to g(f(x))$ then $\mathsf{SN}(R/S)$ holds, but no extended monotone algebra exists in which $\gtrsim$ coincides with the union of $>$ and equality and the properties of Theorem 1 hold.

Now we arrive at the theorem for extended monotone algebras as we will use it for proving (relative) termination by matrix interpretations.

Theorem 2. *Let R, S be TRSs over a signature Σ.*

1. *Let $(A, [\cdot], >, \gtrsim)$ be an extended monotone Σ-algebra such that $[\ell, \alpha] \gtrsim [r, \alpha]$ for every rule $\ell \to r$ in $R \cup S$ and every $\alpha : \mathcal{X} \to A$. Let R' consist of all rules $\ell \to r$ from $R \cup S$ satisfying $[\ell, \alpha] > [r, \alpha]$ for every $\alpha : \mathcal{X} \to A$.*
   Then $\mathsf{SN}((R \setminus R')/(S \setminus R'))$ implies $\mathsf{SN}(R/S)$.
2. *Let $(A, [\cdot], >, \gtrsim)$ be a weakly monotone Σ-algebra such that $[\ell, \alpha] \gtrsim [r, \alpha]$ for every rule $\ell \to r$ in $R \cup S$ and every $\alpha : \mathcal{X} \to A$. Let R' consist of all rules $\ell \to r$ from R satisfying $[\ell, \alpha] > [r, \alpha]$ for every $\alpha : \mathcal{X} \to A$.*
   Then $\mathsf{SN}((R \setminus R')_{top}/S)$ implies $\mathsf{SN}(R_{top}/S)$.

Proof. For part *1* assume $\mathsf{SN}((R \setminus R')/(S \setminus R'))$. Take any infinite reduction with respect to $R \cup S$. From Theorem 1 part *1* we conclude $\mathsf{SN}(R'/(R \cup S))$, so this infinite reduction contains only finitely many R'-steps. So after removing a finite initial part, this reduction only consists of $(R \cup S) \setminus R'$-steps. Since $\mathsf{SN}((R \setminus R')/(S \setminus R'))$ this remaining part contains only finitely many $R \setminus R'$-steps. So the original infinite reduction contains only finitely many R-steps. Hence we proved $\mathsf{SN}(R/S)$.

For part *2* assume $\mathsf{SN}((R \setminus R')_{top}/S)$. Take any infinite reduction with respect to $\overset{top}{\to}_R \cup \to_S$. From Theorem 1 part *2* we conclude $\mathsf{SN}(R'_{top}/(R \cup S))$, so this infinite reduction contains only finitely many $\overset{top}{\to}_{R'}$-steps. So after removing a finite initial part, this reduction only consists of $\overset{top}{\to}_{R \setminus R'}$-steps and $\to_S$-steps. Since $\mathsf{SN}((R \setminus R')_{top}/S)$ this remaining part contains only finitely many $\overset{top}{\to}_{R \setminus R'}$-steps. So the original infinite reduction contains only finitely many $\overset{top}{\to}_R$-steps, proving $\mathsf{SN}(R_{top}/S)$.   □

The basic way to apply Theorem 2 is as follows. If $\mathsf{SN}(R/S)$ (or $\mathsf{SN}(R_{top}/S)$) has to be proved then try to find an extended (or weakly) monotone Σ-algebra satisfying the conditions for which R' is not empty. Then the proof obligation is weakened to $\mathsf{SN}((R \setminus R')/(S \setminus R'))$ (or $\mathsf{SN}((R \setminus R')_{top}/S)$). For this we again apply Theorem 2 in the same way. This is repeated until $R \setminus R' = \emptyset$, for which

the remaining proof obligation $\mathsf{SN}((R \setminus R')/(S \setminus R'))$ (or $\mathsf{SN}((R \setminus R')_{top}/S))$
trivially holds. Proving termination rather than relative termination is a special
case of this approach: then S is empty in $\mathsf{SN}(R/S)$.

Application of Theorem 2 is well-known for the case where A consists of the
natural numbers, or natural numbers ≥ 2, and all functions $[f]$ are polynomials,
and $>$ and $\gtrsim$ have their usual meaning. For part 1 strict monotonicity is required,
while for part 2 weak monotonicity is sufficient. In this polynomial case $\gtrsim$ coincides with the union of $>$ and equality. In the matrix interpretations in the vector
algebras considered in this paper, this is not the case for dimensions > 1.

4   Matrix Interpretations

In this paper we focus on interpretations based on matrices. For the basic version this means that we fix a dimension d and construct a one-sorted extended
monotone algebra $(A, [\cdot], >, \gtrsim)$ in which $A = \mathbf{N}^d$. Without any complication this
extends to the many-sorted setting in which every sort has its own dimension. To
keep the presentation simple here we restrict to the one-sorted case.

The relations $>$ and $\gtrsim$ on A are defined as follows:

$$(v_1, \ldots, v_d) > (u_1, \ldots, u_d) \iff v_1 > u_1 \wedge v_i \geq u_i \text{ for } i = 2, 3, \ldots, d,$$

$$(v_1, \ldots, v_d) \gtrsim (u_1, \ldots, u_d) \iff v_i \geq u_i \text{ for } i = 1, 2, \ldots, d.$$

All requirements for $>$ and $\gtrsim$ from Definition 1 trivially hold. Note that $\gtrsim$ does
not coincide with the union of $>$ and equality.

For the interpretation $[c]$ of a symbol $c \in \Sigma$ of arity 0 we choose any element of
A. For the interpretation $[f]$ of a symbol $f \in \Sigma$ of arity $n \geq 1$ we choose n matrices
$F_1, F_2, \ldots, F_n$ over $\mathbf{N}$, each of size $d \times d$, such that the upper left elements $(F_i)_{1,1}$
are positive for all $i = 1, 2, \ldots, n$, and a vector $\boldsymbol{f} \in \mathbf{N}^d$. Now we define

$$[f](\boldsymbol{v_1}, \ldots, \boldsymbol{v_n}) = F_1 \boldsymbol{v_1} + \cdots + F_n \boldsymbol{v_n} + \boldsymbol{f}$$

for all $\boldsymbol{v_1}, \ldots, \boldsymbol{v_n} \in A$. One easily checks that f is monotonic with respect to $\gtrsim$.
Due to positiveness of the upper left matrix elements we also conclude that f is
monotonic with respect to $>$. So by choosing all $[f]$ of this shape all requirements
of an extended monotone algebra are fulfilled.

In order to apply Theorem 2, part 1, we should be able to check whether $[\ell, \alpha] \gtrsim$
$[r, \alpha]$ or $[\ell, \alpha] > [r, \alpha]$ for all $\alpha : \mathcal{X} \to A$, for given rewrite rules $\ell \to r$. Let
$x_1, \ldots, x_k$ be the variables occurring in ℓ, r. Then due to the linear shape of the
functions $[f]$ we can compute matrices $L_1, \ldots, L_k, R_1, \ldots, R_k$ and vectors $\boldsymbol{l}, \boldsymbol{r}$ such
that

$$[\ell, \alpha] = L_1 \boldsymbol{x_1} + \cdots + L_k \boldsymbol{x_k} + \boldsymbol{l}$$

and

$$[r, \alpha] = R_1 \boldsymbol{x_1} + \cdots + R_k \boldsymbol{x_k} + \boldsymbol{r}$$

where $\alpha(x_i) = \boldsymbol{x_i}$ for $i = 1, \ldots, k$.

For matrices $B, C \in \mathbf{N}^{d \times d}$ write

$$B \gtrsim C \iff \forall i, j : (B)_{i,j} \geq (C)_{i,j}.$$

The following lemma states how the conditions of Theorem 2 can be checked.

Lemma 1. *Let $L_1, \ldots, L_k, R_1, \ldots, R_k$ and l, r correspond to a rewrite rule $\ell \to r$ as described above. Then*

- *$[\ell, \alpha] \gtrsim [r, \alpha]$ for every $\alpha : \mathcal{X} \to A$ if and only if*

$$L_i \gtrsim R_i \text{ for } i = 1, \ldots, k, \text{ and } l \gtrsim r,$$

- *$[\ell, \alpha] > [r, \alpha]$ for every $\alpha : \mathcal{X} \to A$ if and only if*

$$L_i \gtrsim R_i \text{ for } i = 1, \ldots, k, \text{ and } l \gtrsim r, \text{ and } l_1 > r_1.$$

So for applying Theorem 2, part *1*, we fix a dimension d and choose matrices F_i and vectors f for all $f \in \Sigma$. Next for every rule $\ell \to r \in R \cup S$ we check whether $L_i \gtrsim R_i$ for $i = 1, \ldots, k$ and $l \gtrsim r$. If so, then we may remove all rules moreover satisfying $l_1 > r_1$. After having done so we may continue by choosing new matrices, or by any other technique for proving (relative) termination.

Note that for our matrix interpretations after choosing the interpretation checking whether a left hand side is greater (or greater or equal) than a right hand side is decidable due to Lemma 1, in contrast to non-linear polynomial interpretations.

Example 1. Consider the TRS consisting of the following rule.

$$\mathrm{h}(\mathrm{g}(\mathrm{s}(x), y), \mathrm{g}(z, u)) \to \mathrm{h}(\mathrm{g}(u, \mathrm{s}(z)), \mathrm{g}(\mathrm{s}(y), x))$$

We choose $A = \mathbf{N}^2$ together with the symbol interpretations:

$$[\mathrm{h}](\boldsymbol{x_0}, \boldsymbol{x_1}) = \begin{pmatrix} 3 & 1 \\ 1 & 0 \end{pmatrix} \cdot \boldsymbol{x_0} + \begin{pmatrix} 1 & 3 \\ 0 & 1 \end{pmatrix} \cdot \boldsymbol{x_1} + \begin{pmatrix} 0 \\ 2 \end{pmatrix}$$

$$[\mathrm{g}](\boldsymbol{x_0}, \boldsymbol{x_1}) = \begin{pmatrix} 2 & 1 \\ 1 & 0 \end{pmatrix} \cdot \boldsymbol{x_0} + \begin{pmatrix} 1 & 0 \\ 2 & 1 \end{pmatrix} \cdot \boldsymbol{x_1}$$

$$[\mathrm{s}](\boldsymbol{x_0}) = \begin{pmatrix} 1 & 0 \\ 0 & 1 \end{pmatrix} \cdot \boldsymbol{x_0} + \begin{pmatrix} 0 \\ 2 \end{pmatrix}$$

Let $\alpha : \mathcal{X} \to A$ be arbitrary; write $\alpha(x) = \boldsymbol{x}$, $\alpha(y) = \boldsymbol{y}$, $\alpha(z) = \boldsymbol{z}$ and $\alpha(u) = \boldsymbol{u}$. Then we obtain

$$[\mathrm{h}(\mathrm{g}(\mathrm{s}(x), y), \mathrm{g}(z, u)), \alpha]$$

$$=$$

$$\begin{pmatrix} 7 & 3 \\ 2 & 1 \end{pmatrix} \cdot \boldsymbol{x} + \begin{pmatrix} 5 & 1 \\ 1 & 0 \end{pmatrix} \cdot \boldsymbol{y} + \begin{pmatrix} 5 & 1 \\ 1 & 0 \end{pmatrix} \cdot \boldsymbol{z} + \begin{pmatrix} 7 & 3 \\ 2 & 1 \end{pmatrix} \cdot \boldsymbol{u} + \begin{pmatrix} 6 \\ 4 \end{pmatrix}$$

$$>$$

$$\begin{pmatrix} 7 & 3 \\ 2 & 1 \end{pmatrix} \cdot \boldsymbol{x} + \begin{pmatrix} 5 & 1 \\ 1 & 0 \end{pmatrix} \cdot \boldsymbol{y} + \begin{pmatrix} 5 & 1 \\ 1 & 0 \end{pmatrix} \cdot \boldsymbol{z} + \begin{pmatrix} 7 & 3 \\ 2 & 1 \end{pmatrix} \cdot \boldsymbol{u} + \begin{pmatrix} 4 \\ 2 \end{pmatrix}$$

$$=$$

$$[\mathrm{h}(\mathrm{g}(u, \mathrm{s}(z)), \mathrm{g}(\mathrm{s}(y), x)), \alpha].$$

By Theorem 2 we conclude that the system is terminating.

Just as in this example, in general we conclude $[\ell, \alpha] > [r, \alpha]$ for arbitrary α : $\mathcal{X} \to A$ if we have a strict decrease in the first vector coefficient, and $\geq$ for all matrix coefficients and all other vector coefficients.

We conclude this section by an example of relative termination.

Example 2. Define R, S as follows; we want to prove $\mathsf{SN}(R/S)$.

$$R = \{\ \mathsf{f}(\mathsf{a}, \mathsf{g}(y), z) \to \mathsf{f}(\mathsf{a}, y, \mathsf{g}(y)),\ \mathsf{f}(\mathsf{b}, \mathsf{g}(y), z) \to \mathsf{f}(\mathsf{a}, y, z),\ \mathsf{a} \to \mathsf{b}\ \}$$

$$S = \{\ \mathsf{f}(x, y, z) \to \mathsf{f}(x, y, \mathsf{g}(z))\ \}.$$

We choose the following symbol interpretations:

$$[\mathsf{a}] = \begin{pmatrix} 1 \\ 0 \end{pmatrix} \qquad [\mathsf{b}] = \begin{pmatrix} 0 \\ 0 \end{pmatrix}$$

$$[\mathsf{f}](x_0, x_1, x_2) = \begin{pmatrix} 1 & 0 \\ 0 & 0 \end{pmatrix} \cdot x_0 + \begin{pmatrix} 1 & 2 \\ 0 & 0 \end{pmatrix} \cdot x_1 + \begin{pmatrix} 1 & 0 \\ 0 & 0 \end{pmatrix} \cdot x_2 + \begin{pmatrix} 0 \\ 0 \end{pmatrix}$$

$$[\mathsf{g}](x) = \begin{pmatrix} 1 & 0 \\ 1 & 1 \end{pmatrix} \cdot x + \begin{pmatrix} 0 \\ 1 \end{pmatrix}$$

Thereby all rules in $R \cup S$ are weakly decreasing, i.e. all matrix coefficients in the left hand side are greater or equal to the corresponding coefficients in the right hand side. Moreover, all upper left matrix coefficients are nonzero and the rules in R are strictly decreasing in the first coefficient. Hence by Theorem 2 all rules from R may be removed proving $\mathsf{SN}(R/S)$.

5   Top Reduction and Dependency Pairs

For a one-sorted TRS R a symbol $f \in \Sigma$ is called a *defined symbol* if f is the root symbol of a left hand side of a rule of R. For every defined symbol $f \in \Sigma$ a new marked symbol $f_\#$ is added having the same arity as f. If $f(s_1, \ldots, s_n) \to C[g(t_1, \ldots, t_m)]$ is a rule in R and g is a defined symbol of R, then the rewrite rule $f_\#(s_1, \ldots, s_n) \to g_\#(t_1, \ldots, t_m)$ is called a *dependency pair* of R. The TRS consisting of all dependency pairs of R is denoted by $\mathsf{DP}(R)$. We consider these TRSs R and $\mathsf{DP}(R)$ to be S-sorted for $S = \{s, \#\}$, and every $f \in \Sigma$ has arity $((s, \ldots, s), s)$ and its marked version $f_\#$ has arity $((s, \ldots, s), \#)$.

The main theorem about dependency pairs is the following, due to Arts and Giesl, [1].

Theorem 3. *Let R be a one-sorted TRS. Then $\mathsf{SN}(R)$ if and only if $\mathsf{SN}(\mathsf{DP}(R)_{top}/R)$.*

We will use this theorem for proving $\mathsf{SN}(R)$ by proving $\mathsf{SN}(\mathsf{DP}(R)_{top}/R)$ using part *2* of Theorem 2.

For doing so by matrix interpretations we fix a dimension d as before and construct a weakly monotone algebra $(A, [\cdot], >, \gtrsim)$ in which $A_s = \mathbf{N}^d$ and $A_\# = \mathbf{N}$. The relation $\gtrsim$ on $A_s = \mathbf{N}^d$ is defined as before:

$$(v_1, \ldots, v_d) \gtrsim (u_1, \ldots, u_d) \iff v_i \gtrsim u_i \text{ for all } i = 1, 2, \ldots, d;$$

the relation $\gtrsim$ on $A_\# = \mathbf{N}$ is the usual $\geq$ on $\mathbf{N}$. However, for $>$ on $A_s = \mathbf{N}^d$ we now choose another relation as before: we choose $>$ to be the empty relation. The relation $>$ on $A_\# = \mathbf{N}$ is the usual $>$ on $\mathbf{N}$. All requirements for $>$ and $\gtrsim$ from Definition 1 trivially hold.

For the interpretation $[f]$ of a symbol $f \in \Sigma$ of arity $n \geq 0$ we define

$$[f](\boldsymbol{v_1}, \ldots, \boldsymbol{v_n}) = F_1 \boldsymbol{v_1} + \cdots + F_n \boldsymbol{v_n} + \boldsymbol{f}$$

for n matrices $F_1, F_2, \ldots, F_n$ over $\mathbf{N}$ of size $d \times d$, and a vector $\boldsymbol{f} \in \mathbf{N}^d$. Note that now we do not require any more that the upper left elements of the matrices are positive. For the interpretation $[f_\#]$ of a marked symbol $f_\#$ corresponding to f of arity $n \geq 0$ we define

$$[f_\#](\boldsymbol{v_1}, \ldots, \boldsymbol{v_n}) = \boldsymbol{f_1} \boldsymbol{v_1} + \cdots + \boldsymbol{f_n} \boldsymbol{v_n} + c_f$$

for n row vectors $\boldsymbol{f_1}, \ldots, \boldsymbol{f_n}$ over $\mathbf{N}$ of size d, and a constant $c_f \in \mathbf{N}$. Here $\boldsymbol{f_i} \boldsymbol{v_i}$ denotes the inner product, corresponding to matrix multiplication of a row vector by a column vector.

As before $[f]$ is monotonic with respect to $\gtrsim$, and monotonicity with respect to $>$ is trivial since $>$ is empty. The same holds for $f_\#$. By choosing all $[f]$ and $f_\#$ of this shape all requirements of a weakly monotone algebra are fulfilled.

In order to apply Theorem 2, part 2, for rules in R we check whether $[\ell, \alpha] \gtrsim [r, \alpha]$ for all $\alpha : \mathcal{X} \to A$ for given rewrite rules as before. Checking whether $[\ell, \alpha] > [r, \alpha]$ for all α is only required for rules $\ell \to r$ in $\mathsf{DP}(R)$ being of sort $\#$. This restriction can be written as $\boldsymbol{lx} + c_l > \boldsymbol{rx} + c_r$ for every vector $\boldsymbol{x}$ over $\mathbf{N}$, being equivalent to $\boldsymbol{l} \gtrsim \boldsymbol{r} \wedge c_l > c_r$. Similarly, for rules $\ell \to r$ in $\mathsf{DP}(R)$ the requirement $[\ell, \alpha] \gtrsim [r, \alpha]$ for all α is equivalent to $\boldsymbol{l} \gtrsim \boldsymbol{r} \wedge c_l \gtrsim c_r$.

It is also possible to keep the treatment of $\mathsf{SN}(\mathsf{DP}(R)_{top}/R)$ one-sorted on vectors of size d, choosing $>$ to be the strict part of $\gtrsim$. However, then the search space is much bigger since for every $f_\#$ n matrices of size $d \times d$ plus a vector have to be chosen, instead of n vectors of size d plus a constant, where n is the arity of f. Every termination proof in this one-sorted setting also yields a termination proof in the two-sorted setting as presented here, with the same bound on matrix- and vector elements. This can be seen as follows. If there is a proof in the one-sorted setting then for at least one dependency pair the interpretation of the lhs strictly exceeds the interpretation of the rhs. Since $>$ is the strict part of $\gtrsim$, there is at least one dimension in which strict inequality appears. Then by eliminating all other dimensions an interpretation in our two-sorted setting is found by which this particular dependency pair can be removed. By repeating the argument, the full termination proof in the one-sorted setting can be mimicked in our two-sorted setting. So the two-sorted approach is as powerful but yields much smaller search spaces, by which this two-sorted approach is preferred.

Example 3. Consider the TRS consisting of the following rule.

$$\mathsf{g}(\mathsf{g}(\mathsf{s}(x), y), \mathsf{g}(z, u)) \to \mathsf{g}(\mathsf{g}(y, z), \mathsf{g}(x, \mathsf{s}(u)))$$

Using the dependency pairs transformation we get 3 dependency pairs:

1. $g_\#(g(s(x), y), g(z, u)) \rightarrow g_\#(g(y, z), g(x, s(u)))$
2. $g_\#(g(s(x), y), g(z, u)) \rightarrow g_\#(y, z)$
3. $g_\#(g(s(x), y), g(z, u)) \rightarrow g_\#(x, s(u))$

The dependency pairs 2 and 3 can easily be removed by counting the symbols. That is using $[g_\#](x, y) = [g](x, y) = 1 + x + y$ and $[s](x) = x + 1$ as polynomial interpretation over $\mathbf{N}$. So the original rule and the first dependency pair remain. We choose the following interpretation with dimension $d = 2$ (i.e. $A_s = \mathbf{N}^2$, $A_\# = \mathbf{N}$).

$$[g_\#](\boldsymbol{x_0}, \boldsymbol{x_1}) = (1,\ 0) \cdot \boldsymbol{x_0} + (0,\ 1) \cdot \boldsymbol{x_1}$$

$$[g](\boldsymbol{x_0}, \boldsymbol{x_1}) = \begin{pmatrix} 1 & 0 \\ 1 & 0 \end{pmatrix} \cdot \boldsymbol{x_0} + \begin{pmatrix} 1 & 0 \\ 0 & 1 \end{pmatrix} \cdot \boldsymbol{x_1}$$

$$[s](\boldsymbol{x_0}) = \begin{pmatrix} 1 & 0 \\ 0 & 0 \end{pmatrix} \cdot \boldsymbol{x_0} + \begin{pmatrix} 1 \\ 0 \end{pmatrix}$$

For the original rule $g(g(s(x), y), g(z, u)) \rightarrow g(g(y, z), g(x, s(u)))$ we obtain

$$\begin{pmatrix} 1 & 0 \\ 1 & 0 \end{pmatrix} \cdot \boldsymbol{x} + \begin{pmatrix} 1 & 0 \\ 1 & 0 \end{pmatrix} \cdot \boldsymbol{y} + \begin{pmatrix} 1 & 0 \\ 1 & 0 \end{pmatrix} \cdot \boldsymbol{z} + \begin{pmatrix} 1 & 0 \\ 0 & 1 \end{pmatrix} \cdot \boldsymbol{u} + \begin{pmatrix} 1 \\ 1 \end{pmatrix}$$

$$\gtrsim$$

$$\begin{pmatrix} 1 & 0 \\ 1 & 0 \end{pmatrix} \cdot \boldsymbol{x} + \begin{pmatrix} 1 & 0 \\ 1 & 0 \end{pmatrix} \cdot \boldsymbol{y} + \begin{pmatrix} 1 & 0 \\ 1 & 0 \end{pmatrix} \cdot \boldsymbol{z} + \begin{pmatrix} 1 & 0 \\ 0 & 0 \end{pmatrix} \cdot \boldsymbol{u} + \begin{pmatrix} 1 \\ 0 \end{pmatrix}$$

and for the remaining dependency pair $g_\#(g(s(x), y), g(z, u)) \rightarrow g_\#(g(y, z), g(x, s(u)))$ we obtain

$$(1,\ 0) \cdot \boldsymbol{x} + (1,\ 0) \cdot \boldsymbol{y} + (1,\ 0) \cdot \boldsymbol{z} + (0,\ 1) \cdot \boldsymbol{u} + (1)$$

$$>$$

$$(1,\ 0) \cdot \boldsymbol{x} + (1,\ 0) \cdot \boldsymbol{y} + (1,\ 0) \cdot \boldsymbol{z} + (0,\ 0) \cdot \boldsymbol{u} + (0).$$

So all rules are weakly decreasing and the dependency pair is strictly decreasing and thus can be removed. Hence the system is terminating.

Note that the given interpretation cannot be used to prove termination directly by Lemma 1. All the upper left matrix elements are nonzero, but $(1, 1)^T \not> (1, 0)^T$. In Section 7 we will see that in experiments it often happens similarly that this dependency pair approach succeeds where the basic matrix approach from Section 4 fails.

6   Implementation

The method described in the previous sections has been implemented as follows.

The basic algorithm finds a matrix interpretation that allows to remove rules from a termination problem. It is called repeatedly until all rules have been removed.

Algorithm *Remove*:

- inputs
  - a pair of rewrite systems (R, S) over signature Σ
  - a flag $f \in \{\text{Full}, \text{Top}\}$
  - numbers d, b, b'
- outputs a matrix interpretation $[\cdot]$ such that
  - if $f = $ Full, then the interpretation fulfills the conditions of Theorem 2, part *1*, for a non-empty TRS R';
  - if $f = $ Top, then the interpretation fulfills the conditions of Theorem 2, part *2*, for a non-empty TRS R';
  - the interpretation $[\cdot]$ uses matrices of dimension $d \times d$;
  - all the coefficients in the matrices in the interpretations of operation symbols are in the range $0 \ldots 2^b - 1$;
  - all the coefficients in the in the matrices in the interpretations of rules are in the range $0 \ldots 2^{b'} - 1$.

It may be useful to choose $b < b'$. For instance, if $b = 2$ and $b' = 3$ then the algorithm searches for matrices with coefficients < 4 as the interpretations of the operation symbols, but allows coefficients up to 7 in the matrices obtained by multiplying these basic matrices guided by the shape of the rules.

As described in Sections 4 and 5 the conditions for Theorem 2 give rise to constraints on coefficients in vectors and matrices that constitute the interpretations of the rules.

The implementation of the algorithm has two stages: the first stage produces a system I of inequalities, representing these constraints. The second stage solves this constraint system I by translation to a boolean satisfiability problem F.

We stress that the constraint system I consists of inequalities between polynomials of the unknowns. The maximal degree of these polynomials is the maximal depth of a term in a rewrite rule. The number of unknowns depends linearly on the size of the alphabet and quadratically on the dimension of the vector space we use. The number of the inequalities is quadratic in the dimension and linear in the number of rules. Because of the size and the non-linearity of this system, there is no hope for a feasible exact algorithm that solves it.

By putting the bounds b, b' on the range of the variables, the problem has become finite. This finite problem is translated into propositional logic. Each variable from I is then represented by a list of b boolean variables, giving its binary representation. To represent intermediate results (partial sums and products), we need additional constraint variables (translated into bit strings of length b').

Then the formula F is transformed into conjunctive normal form, and we call a SAT solver to find a satisfying assignment. We use SatELiteGTI, [3], the winner of last year's SAT competition. But our translators are not specific to that solver since we use a system-independent data exchange format. E. g. we checked with ZChaff ([12]) and got nearly identical results. Information about the 2005 SAT competition and these tools is obtained via http://www.satcompetition.org/.

From the satisfying assignment for F a satisfying assignment for the original system I is constructed. This gives the matrices and vectors for the symbol interpretations. The rule interpretations are re-calculated to double-check that all constraints do really hold and that indeed a nonempty set R' of rules can be removed according to Theorem 2.

If the solver does not find a satisfying assignment within a given time bound, the process is repeated by either giving larger bounds for the coefficients or larger dimension for the vector space.

While this gives the general idea, quite some effort has to be invested to organize the repeated attempts in such a manner that all potentially successful parameter combinations are actually tried within the given time bound. For instance, we start with the direct matrix method using dimension one with 5 bits for coefficients, followed by dimension two with 3 bits for coefficients, both 5 seconds time-out. Afterward we do a dependency pairs transformation and use matrix interpretations of dimension one, up to dimension 4, with 2 bits for coefficients, 3 bits for intermediates, increasing the time-out stepwise.

To give an impression of this search and the size of the resulting formula, consider the TRS consisting of the following rules.

$$h(x, c(y, z)) \rightarrow h(c(s(y), x), z)$$

$$h(c(s(x), c(s(0), y)), z) \rightarrow h(y, c(s(0), c(x, z)))$$

For smaller dimensions no solution is found, but by choosing dimension $d = 3$ and 2 bits per coefficient suitable interpretations are found by which the second rule can be removed. Termination of the remaining rule is easily shown by a one-dimensional interpretation.

For the main step in this proof, i.e., removing the second rule, the translation of the constraint problem needs 8.000 boolean variables and 40.000 propositional clauses. A satisfying assignment is found by SatELiteGTI in around 5 seconds on a current personal computer.

The translation of one binary multiplication (where the arguments have 3 bits and the result has 6 bits) needs about 150 clauses. One can exchange variables for clauses, to a certain extent.

We developed two independent implementations:

– as part of Matchbox [13], by Waldmann, written in Haskell, and
– as part of Jambox, [4], by Endrullis, written in Java.

This allows to double-check our results. We each use slightly different algorithms that produce formulas of different sizes. It is not automatically the case that the smaller formula is better for the solver. In some cases, the solver will find a solution for a larger formula earlier than for a smaller one.

7 Performance Measurements

In this section we will analyze the performance of the matrix method under various setting on the TRS part of the Termination Problem Database 2005 (TPDB). This problem set was the basis of the 2005 Termination Competition and is available via [2]. It consists of 773 TRS, among which 588 could be proved to be terminating by any of the six participating tools; the rest both contains non-terminating TRSs and TRSs for which the termination behavior is unknown or only established by a human.

By *direct method* we mean pure matrix interpretations, i.e. without usage of any other termination methods like dependency pairs. Likewise the method with dependency pairs stands for the combination of matrix interpretations with the dependency pairs framework. A huge amount of methods has been developed for the dependency pairs framework. In our implementation we restrict to the most basic methods, since our goal is to analyze the strength of the matrix method. In particular, we use dependency graph approximation and the usable rules criterion [5,8], the sub-term criterion [8], and compute strongly connected components as in [9]. Finally, dependency pairs + stands for the extension by the transformation of applicative TRSs into functional form as described in [6], and rewriting of right hand sides [16]. Both techniques are non-branching syntactic transformations, to be used as preprocessing.

We want to emphasize that we did not apply any of the following techniques: recursive path order, argument filtering and semantic labelling, as they were considered sometimes to be essential for any serious termination tool.

The following table presents our results.

method	dimension d	initial bits b	result bits b'	cumulative YES score
direct	1	4	5	141
direct	2	2	3	219
direct	3	3	4	225
dependency pairs	1	4	5	433
dependency pairs	2	1	2	503
dependency pairs	2	2	3	505
dependency pairs	3	2	3	507
dependency pairs	4	2	3	509
dependency pairs +	4	2	3	538

For these results we took the time limit of 1 minute, just like in the Termination Competition. However, this time was hardly ever consumed; the average computation time for all proofs is around 1 second. The full results, including all proofs generated by Jambox, are available via

    http://joerg.endrullis.de/ijcar06/.

For the following 6 systems our approach found termination proofs where all participating tools in the 2005 competition failed: TRCSR-Ex1-2-Luc02c-GM, TRCSR-Ex14-AEGL02-C, TRCSR-Ex1-GL02a-C, TRCSR-Ex4-7-15-Bor03-C, TRCSR-Ex49-GM04-C and TRCSR-Ex6-9-Luc02c-GM. So by adding our approach the total score of 588 for all tools would increase to 594.

We also applied our approach the subcategory of relative termination in TPDB, on which the 2005 competition also run. The winner in this subcategory was TPA with a score of 23; our approach would have yielded a second place with a score of 20. Among these 20 proofs 10 are done with dimension one, 8 with dimension two and 2 with dimension three.

8 Conclusions

The idea of using matrix interpretations for termination proofs for string rewriting was developed by Hofbauer and Waldmann [11]. It allowed them to prove termination for $\{aa \to bc, bb \to ac, cc \to ab\}$. In this paper we showed how to extend this approach to term rewriting successfully. A crucial ingredient is taking linear combinations of matrix interpretations for symbols of arity > 1.

In the results on the benchmark database TPDB we see a big jump when increasing the dimension from 1 (representing linear polynomial interpretations) to 2. Increasing the dimension from 2 to higher values only yields a minor improvement, while then the sizes of the satisfiability formulas strongly increase. By adding the dependency pairs approach an enormous jump is achieved: then using only linear polynomial interpretations ($d = 1$) already reaches a score of 433 points. In the Termination Competition 2005 this would have been a remarkable third place. Finally, our highest score of 538 for dependency pairs + would have yielded a second place in this competition: still below the winning score of 576 for AProVE [7], but significantly better than the second score of 509 for TTT [10].

We like to stress that among the 538 TRSs for which termination was proved by our tool, for several (6) of them all six tools from the 2005 competition failed.

References

1. T. Arts and J. Giesl. Termination of term rewriting using dependency pairs. *Theoretical Computer Science*, 236:133–178, 2000.
2. Termination Competition. http://www.lri.fr/~marche/termination-competition/.
3. N. Eén and A. Biere. Effective preprocessing in sat through variable and clause elimination. In F. Bacchus and T. Walsh, editors, *Proc. 8th Int. Conf. Theory and Applications of Satisfiability Testing SAT 2005*, volume 3569 of *Lecture Notes in Computer Science*, pages 61–75, Berlin, 2005. Springer-Verlag.
4. J. Endrullis. Jambox: Automated termination proofs for string rewriting. http://joerg.endrullis.de/, 2005.
5. J. Giesl, R. Thiemann, and P. Schneider-Kamp. The dependency pair framework: Combining techniques for automated termination proofs. In *Proceedings of the 11th International Conference on Logic for Programming, Artificial Intelligence, and Reasoning (LPAR 2004)*, volume 3452 of *Lecture Notes in Computer Science*, pages 301–331. Springer, 2005.
6. J. Giesl, R. Thiemann, and P. Schneider-Kamp. Proving and disproving termination of higher-order functions. In *Proceedings of the 5th International Workshop on Frontiers of Combining Systems (FroCoS 2005)*, volume 3717 of *Lecture Notes in Computer Science*, pages 216–231. Springer, 2005.
7. J. Giesl, R. Thiemann, P. Schneider-Kamp, and S. Falke. Automated termination proofs with AProVE. In V. van Oostrom, editor, *Proceedings of the 15th Conference on Rewriting Techniques and Applications (RTA)*, volume 3091 of *Lecture Notes in Computer Science*, pages 210–220. Springer, 2004.

8. N. Hirokawa and A. Middeldorp. Dependency pairs revisited. In V. van Oostrom, editor, *Proceedings of the 15th Conference on Rewriting Techniques and Applications (RTA)*, volume 3091 of *Lecture Notes in Computer Science*, pages 249–268. Springer, 2004.
9. N. Hirokawa and A. Middeldorp. Automating the dependency pair method. *Information and Computation*, 199:172–199, 2005.
10. N. Hirokawa and A. Middeldorp. Tyrolean termination tool. In J. Giesl, editor, *Proceedings of the 16th Conference on Rewriting Techniques and Applications (RTA)*, volume 3467 of *Lecture Notes in Computer Science*, pages 175–184. Springer, 2005.
11. D. Hofbauer and J. Waldmann. Proving termination with matrix interpretations. In F. Pfenning, editor, *Proceedings of the 17th Conference on Rewriting Techniques and Applications (RTA)*, Lecture Notes in Computer Science. Springer, 2006.
12. M. Moskewicz, C. Madigan, Y. Zhao, L. Zhang, and S. Malik. Chaff: Engineering an efficient SAT solver. In *Proceedings of the 38th Design Automation Conference DAC 2001*, pages 530–535. ACM, 2001.
13. J. Waldmann. Matchbox: A tool for match-bounded string rewriting. In V. van Oostrom, editor, *Proceedings of the 15th Conference on Rewriting Techniques and Applications (RTA)*, pages 85–94, Berlin, 2004. Springer-Verlag.
14. H. Zantema. Termination of term rewriting: Interpretation and type elimination. *Journal of Symbolic Computation*, 17:23–50, 1994.
15. H. Zantema. Termination. In *Term Rewriting Systems, by Terese*, pages 181–259. Cambridge University Press, 2003.
16. H. Zantema. Reducing right-hand sides for termination. In A. Middeldorp, V. van Oostrom, F. van Raamsdonk, and R. de Vrijer, editors, *Processes, Terms and Cycles: Steps on the Road to Infinity:Essays Dedicated to Jan Willem Klop on the Occasion of His 60th Birthday*, volume 3838 of *Lecture Notes in Computer Science*, pages 173–197, Berlin, 2005. Springer-Verlag.

Partial Recursive Functions in Higher-Order Logic

Alexander Krauss

Technische Universität München, Institut für Informatik
http://www4.in.tum.de/~krauss

Abstract. Based on inductive definitions, we develop an automated tool for defining partial recursive functions in Higher-Order Logic and providing appropriate reasoning tools for them. Our method expresses termination in a uniform manner and includes a very general form of pattern matching, where patterns can be arbitrary expressions. Termination proofs can be deferred, restricted to subsets of arguments and are interchangeable with other proofs about the function. We show that this approach can also facilitate termination arguments for total functions, in particular for nested recursions. We implemented our tool as a definitional specification mechanism for Isabelle/HOL.

1 Introduction

Advanced specification mechanisms that introduce definitions in a natural way are essential for the practical usability of proof assistants.

In a logic of total functions, notably Higher-Order Logic (HOL), recursive function definitions usually require a termination proof. On the other hand, many interesting algorithms do not always terminate: Some examples are search in an infinite search space, semi-decision procedures or the evaluation of programs.

There are several ways to express partiality in a logic of total functions [14], but defining a function from a set of non-terminating equations is generally difficult, especially if it is not clear when the recursion terminates, or if the termination proof is nontrivial. Thus, modelling non-terminating algorithms as logic functions often requires artificial manual workarounds, which can complicate subsequent reasoning.

In order to improve this situation, we describe a general function definition principle for Isabelle/HOL [15], which is not limited to terminating recursions. From a set of recursive equations, our package defines a partial function (modeled as an underspecified total function), together with a set describing the function's domain. On the domain, the defined function coincides with the specification. The provided tools allow to reason about such a partial function as conveniently as it is common for total functions. Our package has the following key properties:

Definitional. Every definition is reduced to a simpler form that can be processed by existing means. The original specification is then *derived* from that definition by an automated proof procedure. Since all reasoning is performed within the theorem prover, this approach offers a maximum of safety without having to rely on an external soundess proof.

Generalized Pattern matching. Functions may be specified by pattern matching. Patterns are not restricted to datatype constructors, may contain guards and overlap, but must be proved to be compatible.

U. Furbach and N. Shankar (Eds.): IJCAR 2006, LNAI 4130, pp. 589–603, 2006.

Reasoning Principles. For each recursive function f, an induction principle (which we call f-*induction*) is proved, which corresponds to the recursive structure of the definition of f, and is the main tool for reasoning about it.

Deferred Termination. Termination proofs are strictly separated from function definitions. At definition time, no other input than the specification is needed. Properties of the function can be proved before its termination is established. This particularly simplifies the treatment of nested recursions.

1.1   Motivation

Partiality. As an example for partiality, we define an interpreter for a minimalistic imperative language. Such an interpreter must be partial, since the interpreted program might loop and this non-termination cannot be detected. However we would expect to be able to prove termination for certain classes of programs, for example the class of all programs without while loops.

The language is straightforward and we present it directly in Isabelle/HOL notation. For simplicitly, a shallow embedding is used for expressions, instead of modeling their syntax. The notation $f(x := y)$ denotes function update, and *iter* denotes function exponentiation.

types	*var*	= *nat*		**datatype** *com* =	
	val	= *nat*		ASSIGN *var exp*	
	env	= *var* $\Rightarrow$ *val*		| SEQ *com com*	
	exp	= *env* $\Rightarrow$ *val*		| IF *exp com com*	
consts				| WHILE *exp com*	
	exec :: *com* $\Rightarrow$ *env* $\Rightarrow$ *env*			| FOR *exp com*	

function

exec (ASSIGN v exp) e = $e(v:=exp\ e)$
exec (SEQ c_1 c_2) e = exec c_2 (exec c_1 e)
exec (IF exp c_1 c_2) e = if $exp\ e \neq 0$ then exec c_1 e else exec c_2 e
exec (FOR exp c) e = iter ($exp\ e$) (exec c) e
exec (WHILE exp c) e = if $exp\ e \neq 0$
                        then exec (WHILE exp c) (exec c e) else e

Current tools in Isabelle/HOL cannot handle the definition of *exec*. The attempt would lead to an unsolvable termination proof obligation.

As a workaround, we can always extend a partial function to a total one: If we know that the function terminates under certain conditions, this check can be added to the function body, returning a dummy value if the check fails:

$$\text{f } x = \text{if } \langle \text{guard} \rangle \; x \text{ then } \langle \text{body}_\text{f} \rangle \; x \text{ else dummy}$$

Then f can be defined as a total function. But this is unsatisfactory as a general method for two reasons: First, the termination guard must be known at definition time. If it turns out later that this condition was too restrictive, one must change the definition of the function. Second, the workaround changes the body of the function. Since the termination guard is alien to the functional specification, this is inelegant and may cause difficulties when executable code is to be extracted from the definition at a later stage.

Restricting our interpreter to programs without while loops is certainly inadequate. We would have to find a condition that covers all possible terminating programs, which is not obvious.

Our package allows to define *exec* as a partial function and later prove its termination on the sets we need.

Generalized Pattern Matching. Function definitions by pattern matching are convenient in functional programming, and the same is true for logic.

In functional languages, patterns consist only of variables and datatype constructors, so that they can be compiled into efficient tests. Some languages also allow simple invertible arithmetic expressions like $n + 2$.

Such restrictions seem inappropriate for an extensible logical framework like Isabelle/HOL. We can for example define a type for α-equated lambda terms, using a package of Urban and Berghofer (see [20]), and the need arises to define functions on such terms as well. For example, the following equations describe capture-avoiding substitution $[. ::= .]$:

$$(\text{Var } a)[b::=u] = \text{if } a=b \text{ then } u \text{ else Var } a$$
$$(\text{App } t_1 \ t_2)[b::=u] = \text{App } (t_1[b::=u]) \ (t_2[b::=u])$$
$$a\sharp(b, u) \implies (\text{Lam } [a].t)[b::=u] = \text{Lam } [a].(t[b::=u])$$

This is obviously a form of pattern matching, but different from patterns used in functional programming: First, due to α-equivalence, the constructor in the lambda case is not injective (eg. Lam $[a]$.(Var a) = Lam$[b]$.(Var b)), and second, the lambda case is conditional: It requires that a is fresh in b and u.

To be able to support such constructions, we adopt a more general notion of pattern matching, which is purely logical. Our patterns may essentially be arbitrary expressions, but we require two properties to ensure that the patterns really form a function definition:

1. Every possible argument is matched by at least one pattern. (*Completeness*)
2. If more than one pattern matches an argument, the associated right hand sides are equal. (*Compatibility*)

Pattern completeness will be needed to generate an induction rule and does not stand in the way of partial definitions, since missing patterns can easily be added by introducing trivial equations f p = f p. Compatibility ensurtes that the whole specification is consistent. Note that in contrast to functional programming, the equations do not have any associated order. Every equation will become a simplification rule on its own.

These two conditions are very natural (though undecidable), and sometimes used to justify function definitions in pen-and-paper theories. As expected, a definition with our package requires a proof of these conditions.

1.2 An Overview of Our Method

Starting from the specification of a function, our package inductively defines its graph G and its smallest recursion relation R, which captures the recursive structure of the definition. Using the definite description operator, the graph is turned into a total function f, which models the specified partial function. Its domain dom_f is defined as the accessible part of R.

Then, pattern completeness and compatibility must be proved by the user or auto-mated tools. Our package builds on these facts to prove that G actually describes a function on dom_f. Then it automatically derives the original recursion equations and an induction rule. The rules are constrained by preconditions of the form $t \in \text{dom}_f$, that is, they describe the function's behaviour *on its domain*. Despite these constraints, they allow convenient reasoning about the function, before its termination is established. To support natural termination proofs, the package provides introduction rules for dom_f and a special termination rule.

The rest of this paper is organized as follows: In §2 we introduce some logical concepts required by our package. In §3, we describe the automated definition process. In §4, we discuss how our package supports termination proofs. In §5, we show how our particular method can improve the treatment of nested recursive definitions. In §6, we briefly describe case studies, and §7 discusses related work.

2 Logical Preliminaries

We work in classical Higher-Order Logic. Derivations are expressed in the natural de-duction framework Isabelle/Pure, using universal quantification $\bigwedge$ and implication $\implies$.

2.1 Recursion Relations and Termination Conditions

The extraction of termination conditions was first introduced by Boyer and More [5] and is an important component in every implementation of general recursion in theorem provers, definitional or not.

Given a function definition, we call a relation R on the function's argument type a *recursion relation*, if the function argument decreases wrt. R in every recursive call. Consider the following function definition:

$$
\begin{aligned}
\gcd(x, 0) &= x \\
\gcd(0, y) &= y \\
\gcd(x + 1, y + 1) &= \text{if } x < y \text{ then } \gcd(x + 1, y - x) \\
&\qquad \text{else } \gcd(x - y, y + 1)
\end{aligned}
$$

Then the relation $\{((x_1, y_1), (x_2, y_2)) \mid x_1 + y_1 < x_2 + y_2\}$ is a recursion relation. Another one is the lexicographic ordering, and a third one is the universal relation where everything is smaller than everything else. Note that we do not require the relation to be wellfounded.

From a definition, we can automatically extract a set of *termination conditions*, which a recursion relation must satisfy. In our example, these conditions are:

$$
\begin{aligned}
x < y &\implies (x + 1, y - x) <_R (x + 1, y + 1) \\
\neg x < y &\implies (x - y, y + 1) <_R (x + 1, y + 1)
\end{aligned}
$$

The details of the extraction in HOL are described in Slind's thesis [18]. Abstractly, the extraction is a syntax directed search for recursive calls in the function body. For each recursive call, a condition is generated, stating that the argument in the recursive call is smaller than the original argument.

Note that this extraction must be context-aware and take the positions of recursive calls into account. In the above example, these occur inside an if-expression, which is reflected in additional premises. In general, a context consists of bound variables and premises, and is denoted by Γ. Termination conditions have the general form[1]:

$$\Gamma_k \implies r_k <_R \text{lhs}$$

This general notion of context can express Higher-Order recursion: Consider a datatype for trees and a function which maps its argument f over all leaves:

$$\begin{aligned}\text{treemap } f \text{ (Leaf } x) \quad &= \text{Leaf } (f\ x) \\ \text{treemap } f \text{ (Branch } ts) &= \text{Branch (map (treemap } f)\ ts)\end{aligned}$$

The termination condition reflects the fact that recursive calls occur only on elements of ts:

$$\bigwedge x.\ x \in \text{set } ts \implies x <_R \text{Branch } ts$$

Since the extraction process requires some knowledge about the contexts resulting for terms occuring at certain positions, the algorithm is parametrized with a set of *congruence rules*, which express this knowledge. The shape of congruence rules is not relevant for us, and can be found in Slind's thesis [18].

2.2   Accessible Part

We adopt the notion of the *accessible part* (or wellfounded part) of a relation, denoted by $\text{acc } R$. The accessible part consists of just the elements which do not occur in an infinitely descending R-chain. It is inductively defined by the following rule:

$$\frac{\forall y <_R x.\ y \in \text{acc } R}{x \in \text{acc } R} \quad \text{(ACC-INTRO)}$$

If R is wellfounded, then $\text{acc } R$ is just the universal set. In other cases, it might still contain interesting subsets. Using this notion instead of wellfoundedness is crucial to be able to support non-termination.

The accessible part comes with a very general induction principle, which we call acc-induction:

$$\frac{\forall x \in \text{acc } R.\ (\forall y <_R x.\ P\ y) \longrightarrow P\ x}{\forall x \in \text{acc } R.\ P\ x} \quad \text{(ACC-INDUCT)}$$

This rule works like wellfounded induction, but with arbitrary relations. Consequently, the inductive result is only proved for the elements of $\text{acc } R$.

---

[1] To distinguish them from logical symbols, meta-variables like contexts are printed in bold. Also note that $\Gamma \implies \phi$ is slight abuse of notation: If Γ binds variables, they are quantified over the whole implication: $\bigwedge v_1 \ldots v_n.\ \Gamma \implies \phi$.

2.3 Inductive Definitions

To define inductive relations, our tool uses an existing package [16] from Isabelle/HOL, which introduces inductive sets as least fixed-points by means of the Knaster-Tarski fixed-point theorem. Given some introduction rules for a set S, the package defines the set and returns the introduction rules as theorems. An elimination rule, expressing that S is in fact the smallest such set, is also generated automatically. The package also provides an induction rule, but we will not use it, since we rely on acc-induction.

3 The Process of Definition

We start with the recursive equations given as input by the user and which he would like to get back as simplification rules in the end:

$$C_1 \implies f \, \mathbf{lhs}_1 = \mathbf{rhs}_1$$
$$\vdots$$
$$C_n \implies f \, \mathbf{lhs}_n = \mathbf{rhs}_n$$

Each equation may contain free variables, which we collectively denote by $\mathbf{v}_i^*$.

3.1 Defining the Graph and the Recursion Relation

We transform the equations into an inductive definition of a relation G, representing the graph of the function. The first step is the termination condition extraction from §2.1, which extracts from each equation a list of m_i recursive calls and their contexts: $(\mathbf{\Gamma}_{i1}, \mathbf{r}_{i1}), \ldots, (\mathbf{\Gamma}_{im_i}, \mathbf{r}_{im_i})$. From the i-th equation we now build the following introduction rule for G:

$$C_i \quad \frac{(\mathbf{\Gamma}_{i1}^{[h/f]} \implies (\mathbf{r}_{i1}^{[h/f]}, h(\mathbf{r}_{i1}^{[h/f]})) \in G) \ldots (\mathbf{\Gamma}_{im_i}^{[h/f]} \implies (\mathbf{r}_{im_i}^{[h/f]}, h(\mathbf{r}_{im_i}^{[h/f]})) \in G)}{(\mathbf{lhs}_i, \mathbf{rhs}_i^{[h/f]}) \in G} \quad (\text{GINTRO}_i)$$

In $\mathbf{\Gamma}^{[h/f]}$ etc., the function variable h is substituted for the function symbol f.

Compared to a naive relational description, which would invent a new variable for the result of each recursive call[2], we use a single function variable h, which is constrained to the graph on all recursive calls.

The introduction rules form an inductive definition of the relation G, and we can introduce G, using the package for inductive definitions. Next, we can already define the function f, using HOL's definite description operator:

$$f \stackrel{\text{def}}{=} \lambda x. \, \text{THE} \, y. \, (x, y) \in G \qquad (\text{F-DEF})$$

The basic reasoning tool for our new function is acc-induction on a recursion relation. While other packages require the user to supply such a relation, this is not necessary, since it can be defined automatically.

The essential observation is that the termination conditions extracted from a definition (see §2.1) always have the form of introduction rules for R:

---

[2] Inventing separate variables for the recursive calls would require additional bookkeeping and lead to problems with Higher-Order recursion.

$$\mathbf{C}_i \implies \mathbf{\Gamma}_{i,1} \implies \mathbf{r}_{i,1} <_R \mathbf{lhs}_i$$
$$\vdots$$
$$\mathbf{C}_i \implies \mathbf{\Gamma}_{i,m_i} \implies \mathbf{r}_{i,m_i} <_R \mathbf{lhs}_i \qquad (\text{RINTROS}_i)$$

Collecting all the rules, one for each recursive call, we can regard them as a specification of the recursion relation, and thus define a relation R from them. For convenience, we use the package for inductive definitions again, but in fact the specification is not truly inductive: R appears only on the right hand sides.

Note that from such a definition we get the *smallest* recursion relation for our function and that smaller relations have bigger accessible parts. Since the accessible part of this relation will be the domain of our function, the smallest recursion relation is the best we can get.

3.2 Completeness and Compatibility

The following proof requires *completeness* and *compatibility* of the patterns, which were already mentioned in §1.1.

Completeness ensures that every possible input value is matched by one of the patterns. It has the following form[3]:

$$\frac{\bigwedge \mathbf{v}_1^*.\ \mathbf{C}_1 \implies x = \mathbf{lhs}_1 \implies P \quad \dots \quad \bigwedge \mathbf{v}_n^*.\ \mathbf{C}_n \implies x = \mathbf{lhs}_n \implies P}{P} \ (\text{COMPLETE})$$

Compatibility states that the set of equations are not contradictory, in the sense that they assign different values to the same argument. This is expressed by special elimination rules for G, one for each equation:

$$\frac{\mathbf{C}_i \quad (\mathbf{lhs}_i, y) \in G \quad \begin{array}{l} \bigwedge h.\ (\mathbf{\Gamma}_{i1} \implies (\mathbf{r}_{i1}, h(\mathbf{r}_{i1})) \in G) \implies \dots \\ \qquad \implies (\mathbf{\Gamma}_{im_i} \implies (\mathbf{r}_{im_i}, h(\mathbf{r}_{im_i})) \in G) \\ \qquad \implies y = \mathbf{rhs}_i[h/\mathbf{f}] \implies P \end{array}}{P} \ (\text{COMPAT}_i)$$

In many cases, compatibility can easily be proved using the definition of G. In particular, disjoint patterns, where each argument is matched by at most one pattern, are trivially compatible.

Our package generates proof obligations for completeness and compatibility which must be solved to complete the definition. For the case of disjoint constructor patterns, we provide an automated proof tactic which solves these goals. Automation of completeness proofs works as described by Slind [18], and compatibility uses the definition of G and simplification.

3.3 The Relation Is a Function

We are now prepared to prove that the relation G describes a function on acc R:

$$\forall x \in \mathrm{acc}\ R.\ \exists! y.(x, y) \in G$$

---

[3] Completeness and compatibility are existential statements, which are expressed in Isabelle/Pure by elimination rules.

The proof of this property is performed automatically by our package, when a definition is made, using only primitive inference steps and rewriting. The following informal but detailed proof sketch illustrates the structure of the derivation:

Proof. We use acc-induction on the recursion relation R. For the induction step, fix an $x \in \operatorname{acc} R$. As induction hypothesis, we can assume the property for all $z <_R x$. Splitting into existence and uniqueness, and using the fact that the unique value is denoted by f, this yields:

$$\bigwedge z. \ z <_R x \Longrightarrow (z, \mathrm{f}\, z) \in G \qquad\qquad \text{(IH-EXIST)}$$
$$\bigwedge y\, z. \ z <_R x \Longrightarrow (z, y) \in G \Longrightarrow y = \mathrm{f}\, z \qquad \text{(IH-UNIQUE)}$$

To complete the induction step, we have to prove $\exists! y.\ (x, y) \in G$. We distinguish cases and look at each of the defining equations in turn, proving existence and uniqueness separately: For the i-th equation, assume $\mathbf{C}_i$ and $x = \mathbf{lhs}_i$.

Existence: From RINTROS$_i$ and IH-EXIST get $\boldsymbol{\Gamma}_{ij} \Longrightarrow (\mathbf{r}_{ij}, \mathrm{f}\, \mathbf{r}_{ij}) \in G$ for all $j \leq m_i$. Applying GINTRO$_i$ yields $(\mathbf{lhs}_i, \mathbf{rhs}_i) \in G$.
Uniqueness: Assume $(\mathbf{lhs}_i, y) \in G$ for some y. Instantiate COMPAT$_i$ with $P := (y = \mathbf{rhs}_i)$ and apply the assumption. It remains to prove the second premise of COMPAT$_i$. For this, assume $\boldsymbol{\Gamma}_{ij} \Longrightarrow (\mathbf{r}_{ij}, h\, \mathbf{r}_{ij}) \in G$ for all $j \leq m_i$ and $y = \mathbf{rhs}_i[h/\mathrm{f}]$ for some function h. From RINTROS$_i$ and IH-UNIQUE, get $\boldsymbol{\Gamma}_{ij} \Longrightarrow h\, \mathbf{r}_{ij} = \mathrm{f}\, \mathbf{r}_{ij}$. Use these equations as contextual rewrite rules to show $\mathbf{rhs}_i[h/\mathrm{f}] = \mathbf{rhs}_i$. Thus $y = \mathbf{rhs}_i$.

Combining existence and uniqueness, we have for each equation $\mathbf{C}_i \Longrightarrow x = \mathbf{lhs}_i \Longrightarrow \exists! y.(x, y) \in G$. Using COMPLETE, these results can be combined into one, which completes the induction step. $\qquad\qquad\qquad\qquad\qquad\qquad\qquad\square$

3.4 Deriving Partial Simplification and Induction Rules

Having established that function values exist and are unique on $\operatorname{acc} R$, we introduce the abbreviation $\mathrm{dom}_\mathrm{f} \equiv \operatorname{acc} R$ and prove the original recursion equations and an induction rule. The equations are guarded by termination assumptions:

$$\mathbf{lhs}_1 \in \mathrm{dom}_\mathrm{f} \Longrightarrow \mathbf{C}_1 \Longrightarrow \mathrm{f}\, \mathbf{lhs}_1 = \mathbf{rhs}_1$$
$$\cdots$$
$$\mathbf{lhs}_n \in \mathrm{dom}_\mathrm{f} \Longrightarrow \mathbf{C}_n \Longrightarrow \mathrm{f}\, \mathbf{lhs}_n = \mathbf{rhs}_n$$

Deriving the recursion equations is simple: From uniqueness we know that $(x, y) \in G$ implies $\mathrm{f}\, x = y$, and we have already proved the required relations in the existence part of the previous proof. We can reuse them after lifting them out of the induction context, which is technical but straightforward.

The partial induction rule follows the structure of the recursion: In each case, the property may be assumed on the arguments of the recursive calls, but the inductive result is restricted to dom_f. The rule is a simple consequence of acc-induction, the definition of R and pattern completeness:

$$\bigwedge v_1^*. \; \mathbf{lhs}_1 \in \mathrm{dom}_f \implies \mathbf{C}_1$$
$$\implies (\mathbf{\Gamma}_{11} \implies P \, \mathbf{r}_{11}) \implies \ldots \implies (\mathbf{\Gamma}_{1m_1} \implies P \, \mathbf{r}_{1m_1})$$
$$\implies P \, \mathbf{lhs}_1$$

$\vdots$

$$\bigwedge v_n^*. \; \mathbf{lhs}_n \in \mathrm{dom}_f \implies \mathbf{C}_n$$
$$\implies (\mathbf{\Gamma}_{n1} \implies P \, \mathbf{r}_{n1}) \implies \ldots \implies (\mathbf{\Gamma}_{nm_n} \implies P \, \mathbf{r}_{nm3_n})$$
$$\implies P \, \mathbf{lhs}_n$$
$$\rule{8cm}{0.4pt}$$
$$a \in \mathrm{dom}_f \implies P \, a$$

(F-PINDUCT)

With the proof of the partial simplification and induction rules, the actual definition process is finished: The rules provide adequate means for reasoning about the function. In particular, we can now establish the properties we might need for a termination proof. We will see in §5 that this is extremely useful when dealing with nested recursion.

3.5 A Simple Example

Let us define the Fibonacci function:

$$\begin{aligned} \mathrm{fib} \; 0 \quad &= 1 \\ \mathrm{fib} \; 1 \quad &= 1 \\ \mathrm{fib} \; (n+2) &= \mathrm{fib} \; n + \mathrm{fib} \; (n+1) \end{aligned}$$

The graph of the function, G_{fib}, is defined by

$$(0,1) \in G_{\mathrm{fib}} \qquad (1,1) \in G_{\mathrm{fib}} \qquad \frac{(n, h(n)) \in G_{\mathrm{fib}} \quad (n+1, h(n+1)) \in G_{\mathrm{fib}}}{(n+2, h(n) + h(n+1)) \in G_{\mathrm{fib}}}$$

The termination conditions (and definition of R_{fib}) are:

$$n <_{R_{\mathrm{fib}}} n+2 \qquad\qquad n+1 <_{R_{\mathrm{fib}}} n+2$$

The proof obligation for completeness is a simple property of natural numbers, and compatibility is trivial, since the patterns are disjoint. We get the following simplification and induction rules:

$$\begin{aligned} 0 \in \mathrm{dom}_{\mathrm{fib}} &\implies \mathrm{fib} \; 0 \quad = 1 \\ 1 \in \mathrm{dom}_{\mathrm{fib}} &\implies \mathrm{fib} \; 1 \quad = 1 \\ n+2 \in \mathrm{dom}_{\mathrm{fib}} &\implies \mathrm{fib} \; (n+2) = \mathrm{fib} \; n + \mathrm{fib} \; (n+1) \end{aligned}$$

$$\frac{\begin{array}{l} 0 \in \mathrm{dom}_{\mathrm{fib}} \hspace{5cm} \implies P \, 0 \\ 1 \in \mathrm{dom}_{\mathrm{fib}} \hspace{5cm} \implies P \, 1 \\ \bigwedge n. \, n+2 \in \mathrm{dom}_{\mathrm{fib}} \implies P \, n \implies P \, (n+1) \implies P \, (n+2) \end{array}}{a \in \mathrm{dom}_{\mathrm{fib}} \implies P \, a}$$

4   Termination Proofs

All results obtained from the partial simplification and induction rules will contain termination assumptions of the form $t \in \mathrm{dom}_f$. Thus, it is desirable to know more about

dom_f, which is the objective of a termination proof. Often, our goal will be to show that a function is total and any value is element of dom_f. For partial functions, we will usually be interested in a certain subset.

While the definition process was fully automated and worked for any function definition[4], we cannot expect such automation for termination proofs. But there are powerful methods for proving termination [8,12,21], and we plan to integrate them in subsequent work. Here we concentrate on the fundamental tools for conducting interactive termination proofs in a natural and simple way. This is particularly important for the difficult cases, where automated methods fail.

4.1 Domain Introduction Rules

To show that some value belongs to the domain of a function, one can use the rule ACC-INTRO (cf. §2.2), and the definition of R. From this, general introduction rules for the domain can be derived. For fib, these rules are:

$$0 \in \text{dom}_{\text{fib}} \qquad 1 \in \text{dom}_{\text{fib}} \qquad \frac{n \in \text{dom}_{\text{fib}} \quad (n+1) \in \text{dom}_{\text{fib}}}{(n+2) \in \text{dom}_{\text{fib}}}$$

Domain introduction rules are a natural description of the termination behaviour of the function, and termination proofs with these rules are straightforward: We can show that fib is total, i.e. that $\forall x.\, x \in \text{dom}_{\text{fib}}$, by simple mathematical induction on naturals, using the domain introduction rules.

Our package proves domain introduction rules automatically. Note however that in some cases of pathological pattern overlaps, they can be weaker then one first expects, since recursive calls can be "hidden" in other equations. Consider the definition

$$\begin{aligned} \text{f } 0 &= 0 \\ \text{f } (x+1) &= \text{f } x \\ \text{f } (x+2) &= \text{f } x \end{aligned}$$

Here, the termination of f $x+2$ case not only depends on f x, but also on f $(x+1)$, since the second equation is also applicable. However, in practice such cases do not appear very frequently, and the generated domain introduction rules are generally useful.

4.2 Wellfounded Recursion Relations

Often, a function is proved total by providing a wellfounded relation and showing that it is a recursion relation. Although we do not use user-specified recursion relations for the definition itself, we can still support this approach to termination proofs: Since we used the smallest recursion relation, if any other recursion relation is wellfounded, then so is R. This argument is reflected by the following rule (again, for our fib-example).

---

[4] It is instructive to see that for the non-terminating definition $f\, x = f\, x + 1$, our algorithm defines the Graph G as the empty set and the recursion relation R as the diagonal, where each element is smaller than itself. Then the accessible part of R is the empty set, which means that the derived partial simplification and induction rules are of little use: They are instances of *ex falso quodlibet*.

$$\frac{\text{wf } R' \qquad n <_{R'} n + 2 \qquad n + 1 <_{R'} n + 2}{\forall x. x \in \text{dom}_{\text{fib}}}$$

Our package automatically provides this rule, which allows existing termination proofs to be easily "ported" to our package.

4.3 Simplification and Induction Rules Revisited

For total functions, the termination assumptions in the simplification and induction rules are actually unnecessary, and can be easily removed after the termination proof, to get unconstrained simplification and induction rules familiar from total function definitions.

For partial functions, we can replace the abstract domain dom_f by a concrete set D, for which we have proved termination. Note that in order to replace dom_f in the *premises* of the induction rule, we must also show that D is downward closed under R, since the induction principle is only valid, if calls on elements of D only recurse on elements of D[5]. In practice, this is often simple. Our package supports the removal of termination assumptions by setting up the required proof obligations, and modifying the rules after the proof.

5   Nested Recursion

Functions with nested recursive calls are notoriously difficult to define and reason about. The central problem is that the termination conditions resulting from a nested recursion contain references to the function that is to be defined. As a very simple (and prominent) example, consider the following definition of the constant zero function:

$$f\, 0 = 0$$
$$f\, (n + 1) = f\, (f\, n)$$

As a termination condition one would have to prove that $f\, n < n + 1$. Since the function is always zero, this is certainly true, but seems difficult to prove, before the function f is "properly" defined. We can identify two problems here:

(1) If the system requires the termination proof to be conducted before the function symbol f is even introduced in the logic, it is difficult to support nested recursion, since the termination goal can not even be stated. Definitional packages like ours do not have this problem, since definitions are transformed into a non-recursive form and can be introduced into the logic immediately. Observe that nested recursions do not make our definitions circular, although the definition of R may refer to f.

(2) After stating the termination goal, we need to prove it, and this requires reasoning principles for the function. But the main tool, namely f-induction, is usually not available at that point, since it depends on f's termination.

Slind's recursion package TFL [17] provides a "provisional induction rule" [19] to solve nested termination goals. This rule is basically a severely mangled f-induction

---

[5] For example, we cannot use the set of even numbers in our example fib. Although the function does terminate on all even numbers, the modified induction principle would not be true.

rule, where the unsolved termination conditions become part of the function body. With TFL's second definition principle, relationless definition, this becomes even more diffi-cult. The provisional induction rule can help with termination proofs, but this is often quite inelegant due to the structure of the rule. Slind already observes these shortcom-ings in the conclusion of [19]:

> "We regard our results on relationless definition of nested recursion as only partly satisfactory. The specified recursion equations and induction theorems are automatically derived, which is good; however, the termination proof us-ing the provisional induction theorem and recursion equations for the auxiliary function is usually clumsy and hard to explain."

As an alternative approach, Krstić and Matthews [11] proposed the notion of *induc-tive invariants* to describe properties of a function f in terms of an input-output relation, without the need to explicitly mention f. They show how such an inductive invariant can be used to prove f's termination.

But this comes at a high cost, since establishing an inductive invariant is compara-tively hard: The proof of an inductive invariant corresponds to a wellfounded induction, and to be able to apply the induction hypothesis, one has to show that the arguments in the inner recursive calls are decreasing. This means that one has to anticipate parts of the termination proof to establish the inductive invariant.

Instead, we would like to be able to use f-induction, which is generally simpler[6]. Giesl [7] shows that this approach is sound: We may prove lemmas by f-induction and then use them (in a certain way) in the termination proof of f. His argument is that anything proved by f-induction is "partially true", i.e. it holds for all x where f terminates. Then, a close look reveals that at the positions where the lemmas are needed, one can assume this, since the inner recursive calls are proved first. But since Giesl's informal proofs include statements like *"P holds for all x where f terminates"*, it was not clear how to formalize them in a logic like HOL, where "termination" has no direct correspondence.

Fortunately, our framework provides adequate tools to express such notions, since termination is modeled by membership in dom_f. We can state and prove that f returns zero, whenever it terminates:

$$x \in \text{dom}_f \implies f\, x = 0$$

The proof is just as simple as if we already knew that the function is total: Induc-tion and simplification, but using the partial induction and simplification rules. Then termination of f is equally simple, using structural induction and the domain intro-duction rules, making use of the lemma to show termination of the outer recursive call.

---

[6] To compare wellfounded induction with f-induction, it is an interesting exercise to add even more nesting to the nested-zero example by changing the second equation to $f\,(n+1) = f\,(f\,(f\,(f\,n)))$, and then trying to prove the lemma $\forall n. f\, n = 0$ once by *nat*-induction, where the property can be assumed on smaller arguments and once by f-induction, where the property can be assumed on the arguments of all recursive calls.

6 Case Studies

To test our method and implementation, we conducted several small case studies, which show that our tool is practically useful.

We defined the *partial interpreter* we presented in the motivation. It is trivial to show by structural induction that it terminates on programs without while loops. It is also simple to prove termination of a bigger class of programs,

We were able to define the *substitution function for α-equated lambda-terms*, which makes extensive use of the new pattern matching features. Showing pattern compatibility turned out to be the main challenge for this.

For nested recursion, we adopted an example from Slind [19]. *first order unification*. Before proving termination, we use the partial induction principle to prove two lemmas about the substitutions returned by the algorithm. These properties are needed in the termination proof. Compared to Slind's quite technical proof, this approach avoids a large amount of "formal noise".

For space reasons, we cannot give a presentation of the theories. Formal proof documents in human-readable Isabelle/Isar notation are available as an electronic appendix to this paper[7].

7 Related Work

Both Isabelle 2005 and HOL4 [9] include (different versions of) the recursion package TFL, a work by Slind [17,18]. In TFL, a definition is transformed into a functional, and a specialized fixed-point combinator is used to define the function. The user must specify a wellfounded recursion relation. Optionally, TFL allows deferred termination arguments, where the wellfounded relation is not given at definition time, but in later proofs. Proving termination amounts to showing that the relation is indeed a recursion relation and wellfounded. TFL generates an induction principle for each definition. Since it is based on wellfounded relations, TFL can only define total functions.

TFL allows pattern matching in the style of functional programming. Patterns are compiled to a conditional expression in a preprocessing step, while completing them and removing overlaps. This compilation is inherently limited to datatype patterns. Due to the preprocessing, the returned equations can differ from the original specification.

HOL Light [10] provides a similar mechanism, also based on a fixed-point combinator. Patterns are similar to ours, but since they are allowed to be incomplete, no induction principle can be provided. There is no general support for Higher-Order recursion.

Another approach to define certain partial functions is by tail recursion (see [13]). Since tail recursions always have a total model, they are immediately admissible without a termination proof. However, since no induction rule can be provided, the lack of reasoning principles often makes this approach harder than it sounds.

The idea of generating an explicit description of a function's domain was first presented by Dubois and Donzeau-Gouge [6] in a type theoretic setting, and later used by Bove and Capretta [4] to develop a definition principle for general recursion in type theory. In Coq [3], a recent package for general recursion [1] allows (non-nested) definitions in a manner similar to TFL.

---

[7] http://www4.in.tum.de/~krauss/partial/

A different approach for dealing with non-termination is to work in domain theory, where any computable function can easily be defined. But domain theory comes with a certain overhead which usually results in cumbersome reasoning about the functions later.

8 Conclusion

We have presented a method for recursive function definitions, based on an inductive definition of the function's graph, together with its domain as the accessible part of its recursion relation. Compared to existing approaches, we have been able to increase both the expressive power and the convenience in formal reasoning. In the future, we hope to use this as a basis for the principal tool for defining functions in Isabelle/HOL, subsuming both TFL [17] and the package for primitive recursion on datatypes [2]. The latter is just a special case of general recursion, where termination is immediate, but the user is forced into the recursion scheme of the datatype specification.

To complement this work, we intend to adapt existing techniques to automate termination proofs. The clear separation of definition and termination proofs in our design allows an easy integration of such external reasoning components.

References

1. G. Barthe, J. Forest, D. Pichardie, and V. Rusu. Defining and reasoning about recursive functions: a practical tool for the Coq proof assistant. In *Functional and Logic Programming (FLOPS'06)*, LNCS 3945. Springer, 2006. To Appear.
2. S. Berghofer and M. Wenzel. Inductive datatypes in HOL - lessons learned in formal-logic engineering. In Y. Bertot, G. Dowek, A. Hirschowitz, C. Paulin, and L. Théry, editors, *Theorem Proving in Higher Order Logics, TPHOLs '99*, LNCS 1690, pages 19–36. Springer, 1999.
3. Y. Bertot and P. Castéran. *Interactive theorem proving and program development: Coq'Art: the calculus of inductive constructions*. Texts in theoretical comp. science. Springer, 2004.
4. A. Bove and V. Capretta. Modelling general recursion in type theory. *Mathematical Structures in Computer Science*, 15(4):671–708, 2005.
5. R. S. Boyer and J. S. Moore. *A Computational Logic*. Academic Press, New York, 1979.
6. C. Dubois and V. Donzeau-Gouge. A step towards the mechanization of partial functions: domains as inductive predicates. In *CADE-15 Workshop on mechanization of partial functions*, 1998.
7. J. Giesl. Termination of nested and mutually recursive algorithms. *Journal of Automated Reasoning*, 19(1):1–29, Aug. 1997.
8. J. Giesl, R. Thiemann, and P. Schneider-Kamp. Proving and disproving termination of higher-order functions. In B. Gramlich, editor, *FroCos*, LNCS 3717, pages 216–231. Springer, 2005.
9. M. Gordon and T. Melham, editors. *Introduction to HOL: A theorem proving environment for higher order logic*. Cambridge University Press, 1993.
10. J. Harrison. The HOL Light theorem prover. http://www.cl.cam.ac.uk/users/jrh/hol-light.
11. S. Krstić and J. Matthews. Inductive invariants for nested recursion. In D. A. Basin and B. Wolff, editors, *Theorem Proving in Higher Order Logics, TPHOLs 2003*, LNCS 2758, pages 253–269. Springer, 2003.

12. C. S. Lee, N. D. Jones, and A. M. Ben-Amram. The size-change principle for program termination. In *ACM SIGPLAN-SIGACT Symposium on Principles of Programming Languages*, pages 81–92, 2001.

13. P. Manolios and J. S. Moore. Partial functions in ACL2. *J. Autom. Reasoning*, 31(2):107–127, 2003.

14. O. Müller and K. Slind. Treating partiality in a logic of total functions. *The Computer Journal*, 40(10):640–652, 1997.

15. T. Nipkow, L. C. Paulson, and M. Wenzel. *Isabelle/HOL — A Proof Assistant for Higher-Order Logic*. LNCS 2283. Springer, 2002.

16. L. C. Paulson. A fixedpoint approach to implementing (co)inductive definitions. In A. Bundy, editor, *Automated Deduction - CADE-12*, LNCS 814, pages 148–161. Springer, 1994.

17. K. Slind. Function definition in Higher-Order Logic. In J. von Wright, J. Grundy, and J. Harrison, editors, *Theorem Proving in Higher Order Logics, TPHOLs '96*, LNCS 1125, pages 381–397. Springer, 1996.

18. K. Slind. *Reasoning About Terminating Functional Programs*. PhD thesis, Institut für Informatik, TU München, 1999.

19. K. Slind. Another look at nested recursion. In M. Aagaard and J. Harrison, editors, *Theorem Proving in Higher Order Logics, TPHOLS 2000*, LNCS 1869, pages 498–518. Springer, 2000.

20. C. Urban and C. Tasson. Nominal techniques in Isabelle/HOL. In R. Nieuwenhuis, editor, *Automated Deduction - CADE-20*, LNCS 3632, pages 38–53. Springer, 2005.

21. C. Walther. On proving the termination of algorithms by machine. *Artif. Intell.*, 71(1):101–157, 1994.

On the Strength of Proof-Irrelevant Type Theories

Benjamin Werner

INRIA-Futurs and LIX, Ecole Polytechnique, France
Benjamin.Werner@inria.fr

Abstract. We present a type theory with some proof-irrelevance built into the conversion rule. We argue that this feature is particularly useful when type theory is used as the logical formalism underlying a theorem prover. We also show a close relation with the subset types of the theory of PVS. Finally we show that in these theories, because of the additional extentionality, the axiom of choice implies the decidability of equality, that is, almost classical logic.

1 Introduction

A formal proof system, or proof assistant, implements a formalism in a similar way a compiler implements a programming language. Among existing systems, dependent type systems are quite widespread. This can be related to various pleasant features; among them :

1. Proofs are objects of the formalism. The syntax is therefore smoothly uniform, and proofs can be rechecked at will. Also, only the correctness of the type-checker, a relatively small and well-identified piece of software, is critical for the reliability of the system ("de Bruijn principle").
2. The objects of the formalism are programs (typed λ-terms) and are identified modulo computation (β-conversion). This makes the formalism well-adapted for problems dealing with program correctness. But also the conversion rule allows the computation steps not to appear in the proof; for instance $2+2 = 4$ is simply proved by one reflexivity step, since this proposition is identified with $4 = 4$ by conversion. In some cases this can lead to a dramatic space gain, using the result of certified computations inside a proof; spectacular recent applications include the formal proof of the four-color theorem [11] or formal primality proofs [14].
3. Finally, type theories are naturally constructive. This makes stating decidability results much easier. Furthermore, combining this remark with the two points above, one comes to *program extraction*: taking a proof of a proposition $\forall x : A.\exists y : B.P(x,y)$, one can *erase* pieces of the λ-term in order to obtain a functional program of type $A \to B$, whose input and result are certified to be related by P. Up to now however, program extraction was more an external feature of implemented proof systems[1]: programs certified

---

[1] Except NuPRL; see related work.

U. Furbach and N. Shankar (Eds.): IJCAR 2006, LNAI 4130, pp. 604–618, 2006.
© Springer-Verlag Berlin Heidelberg 2006

by extraction are not anymore objects of the formalism and cannot be used anymore to assert facts like in the point above.

Some related formalisms only build on some of the points above. For example PVS implements a theory whose objects are functional programs, but where proofs are external to the formalism.

An important remark about (2) is that the more terms are identified by the conversion rule, the more powerful this rule is. In order to identify more terms it is therefore a tempting step to combine points (2) and (3) by integrating program extraction into the formalism so that the conversion rule does not require the *computationally irrelevant* parts of terms to be convertible.

In what follows, we present and argue in favor of a type-theory along this line. More precisely, we claim that such a feature is useful in at least two respects. For one, it gives a more comfortable type theory, especially in the way it handles equality. Furthermore it is a good starting point to build a platform for programming with dependent types, that is to use the theorem prover also as a programming environment. Finally, on a more theoretical level, we will also see that by making the theory more extensional, proof-irrelevance brings type theory closer to set-theory regarding the consequences of the axiom of choice.

The central idea of this work is certainly simple enough to be adjusted to various kinds of type theories, whether they are predicative or not, with various kinds of inductive types, more refined mechanisms to distinguish the computational parts of the proofs etc. ... In what follows we illustrate it by using a marking of the computational content which is as simple as possible. We define it precisely, but omit most meta-theoretical proofs and do not detail the model construction.

Related work. Almost surprisingly, proof-irrelevant type theories do not seem to enjoy wide use yet. In the literature, they are often not studied for themselves, but as a mean for proving properties of other systems. This is the case for the work of Altenkirch [2] and Barthe [4]. One very interesting work is Pfenning's modal type theory which involves proof-irrelevance and a sophisticated way to pinpoint which definitional equality is to be used for each part of a term; in comparision we here stick to much simpler extraction mechanism. Finally the NuPRL approach using a squash type [6] is very close to ours, but the extentional setting gives sometimes different results.

2   The Theory

2.1   The λ-Terms

The core of our theory is a Pure Type System (PTS) extended with Σ-types and some inductive type definitions. As in PTS's, the type of types are *sorts*; the set of sorts is:

$$\mathcal{S} \equiv \{\mathsf{Prop}\} \cup \{\mathsf{Type}(i) | i \in \mathbb{N}\}.$$

As one can see, we keep the sort names of Coq. As usual, Prop is the impredicative sort and the sorts Type(i) give the hierarchy of predicative universes. It comes as no surprise that the system contains the usual syntactic constructs of PTSs; however it is comfortable, both for defining the conversion rule and constructing a model to *tag* the variables indicating whether they correspond to a computational piece of code or not; in our case this means whether they live in the impredicative or a predicative level (i.e. whether the type of their type is Prop or a Type(i)). A similar tagging is done on the projections of Σ-types. Except for this detail, the backbone of the theory considered hereafter is essentially Luo's Extended Calculus of Constructions (ECC) [16].

The syntax of the ECC fragment is therefore:

$$s \quad ::= \quad \mathsf{Prop} \mid \mathsf{Type}(i) \qquad\qquad s \quad ::= \quad * \mid \diamond$$

$$t \quad ::= \quad s \mid x_{\mathsf{S}} \mid \lambda x_{\mathsf{S}} : t.t \mid (t\ t) \mid \varPi x_{\mathsf{S}} : t.t \mid \varSigma^{\mathsf{S}} x_{\mathsf{S}} : t.t \mid <t,t>_{\varSigma x:t.t}$$

$$\mid \pi_1^{\mathsf{S}}(t) \mid \pi_2^{\mathsf{S}}(t)$$

$$\varGamma \quad ::= \quad [] \mid \varGamma(x:t).$$

We will sometimes write x for x_s, $\Sigma x : A.B$ for $\Sigma^{\mathsf{S}} x : A.B$ or $\pi_2(t)$ for $\pi_2^s(t)$ omitting the tag s when it is not relevant or can be infered from the context.

The binding of variables is as usual. We write $t[x \setminus u]$ for the substitution of the free occurrences of variable x in t by u. As has become custom, we will not deal with α-conversion here, and leave open the choice between named variables and de Bruijn indices.

We also use the common practice of writing $A \to B$ (resp. $A \times B$) for $\varPi x : A.B$ (resp. $\Sigma x : A.B$) when x does not appear free in B. We also write $\varPi x, y : A.B$ (resp. $\lambda x, y : A.t$) for $\varPi x : A.\varPi y : A.B$ (resp. $\lambda x : A.\lambda y : A.t$).

2.2   Relaxed Conversion

The aim of this work is the study of a relaxed conversion rule. While the idea is to identify terms with respect to typing information, the tagging of impredicative *vs.* predicative variables is sufficient to define such a conversion in a simple syntactic way. A variable is computationally irrelevant when tagged with the $*$ mark. The tag on the Σ-type construction are there to indicate whether the second component of pairs is irrelevant or not. This leads to the following definition.

Definition 1 (Extraction). *We can simply define the extraction relation $\to_\varepsilon$ as the contextual closure of the following rewriting equations:*

$$x_* \to_\varepsilon \varepsilon \qquad\qquad \lambda x : A.\varepsilon \to_\varepsilon \varepsilon$$
$$(\varepsilon\ t) \to_\varepsilon \varepsilon \qquad\qquad \pi_2^*(t) \to_\varepsilon \varepsilon.$$

We write $\to_\varepsilon^*$ for the reflexive-transitive closure of $\to_\varepsilon$. We say that a term is of tag $*$ if $t \to_\varepsilon^* \varepsilon$ and of tag $\diamond$ if not. We write $s(t)$ for the tag of t.

Definition 2 (Reduction). *The β-reduction $\triangleright_\beta$ is defined as the contextual closure of the following equations:*

$$(\lambda x^{\mathsf{S}} : A.t\ u) \rhd_\beta t[x^{\mathsf{S}} \setminus u] \qquad if\ s(u) = \mathsf{s}$$
$$\pi_1^{\mathsf{S}}(< a, b >_{\Sigma x:A.B}) \rhd_\beta a \qquad if\ s(a) = \diamond$$
$$\pi_2^{\mathsf{S}}(< a, b >_{\Sigma x:A.B}) \rhd_\beta b \qquad if\ s(b) = \mathsf{s}.$$

The restrictions on the right-hand side are there in order to ensure that the tag is preserved by reduction. Without them $(\lambda x_\diamond : \mathsf{Prop}.x_\diamond\ \mathsf{Prop})$ can reduce either to ε or to Prop which would falsify the Church-Rosser property. Actually these restrictions later appear to be always satisfied on well-typed terms, but are necessary in order to assert the meta-theoretic properties below. While they are specific to our way of marking computational terms, other methods will probably yield similar technical difficulties.

The relaxed reduction $\rhd_\varepsilon$ is the union of $\rhd_\beta$ and $\to_\varepsilon$. We write $=_\varepsilon$ for the reflexive, symmetric and transitive closure of $\rhd_\varepsilon$ and $\rhd_\varepsilon^*$ for the transitive-reflexive closure of $\rhd_\varepsilon$.

Lemma 1 (β-postponement). *If* $t \rhd_\varepsilon^* t'$, *then there exists* t'' *such that* $t \to_\varepsilon^* t''$ *and* $t'' \rhd_\beta^* t'$.

Lemma 2 (Church-Rosser). *For* t *a raw term, if* $t \rhd_\varepsilon^* t_1$ *and* $t \rhd_\varepsilon^* t_2$, *then there exists* t_3 *such that* $t_2 \rhd_\varepsilon^* t_3$ *and* $t_2 \rhd_\varepsilon^* t_3$.

Proof. By a slight adaptation of the usual Tait–Martin-Löf method.

Furthermore, $\to_\varepsilon$ is obviously strongly normalizing. One therefore can "pre-cook" all terms by $\to_\varepsilon$ when checking relaxed convertibility:

Lemma 3 (pre-cooking of terms). *Let* t_1 *and* t_2 *be terms. Let* t_1' *and* t_2' *be their respective* $\to_\varepsilon$*-normal forms. Then,* $t_1 =_\varepsilon t_2$ *if and only if* $t_1' =_\beta t_2'$.

While this property is important for implementation, its converse is also true and semantically understandable. Computationally relevant β-reductions are never blocked by not-yet-performed ε-reductions:

Lemma 4. *Let* t_1 *be any raw term. Suppose* $t_1 \to_\varepsilon t_2 \rhd_\beta t_3$. *Then there exists* t_4 *such that* $t_1 \rhd_\beta t_4 \to_\varepsilon^* t3$.

Proof. It is easy to see that $\to_\varepsilon$ cannot create new β-redexes, nor does it duplicate existing ones.

It is a good feature to have the predicative universes to be embedded in each other. It has been observed (Pollack, McKinna, Barras...) that a smooth way to present this is to define a syntactic subtyping relation which combines this with $=_\beta$ (or here $=_\varepsilon$). Note that this notion of subtyping should not be confused with, for instance, subtyping of subset types in the style of PVS.

Definition 3 (Syntactic subtyping). *The subtyping relation is defined on raw-terms as the transitive closure of the following equations:*

$$\mathsf{Type}(i) \le \mathsf{Type}(i+1) \qquad T =_\varepsilon T' \Rightarrow T \le T'$$
$$B \le B' \Rightarrow \Pi x : A.B \le \Pi x : A.B'.$$

2.3   Functional Fragment Typing Rules

The typing rules for the kernel of our theory are given in PTS-style [3] and correspond to Luo's ECC. The differences are the use of subtyping in the conversion rule and the tagging of variables when they are "pushed" into the context.

The rules are given in figure 1. In the rule PROD, max is the maximum of two sorts for the order $\mathsf{Prop} < \mathsf{Type}(1) < \mathsf{Type}(2) < \ldots$

We sketch the basic meta-theory of the calculus defined up to here. As mentioned above, we cannot detail the proofs and the intermediate lemmas here. The proof techniques are relatively traditional, even if one has to take care of the more delicate behavior of relaxed reduction for the first lemmas (similarly to [21]).

Lemma 5 (Substitution). *If $\Gamma(x : A)\Delta \vdash t : T$ and $\Gamma \vdash a : A$ are derivable, then $\Gamma\Delta[x \setminus a] \vdash t[x \setminus a] : T[x \setminus a]$ is derivable.*

Of course, subject reduction holds only for $\triangleright_\beta$-reduction, since ε is not meant to be typable.

$$(\text{PROP})\frac{\Gamma \vdash \mathsf{wf}}{\Gamma \vdash \mathsf{Prop} : \mathsf{Type}(i)} \qquad (\text{TYPE})\frac{\Gamma \vdash \mathsf{wf}}{\Gamma \vdash \mathsf{Type}(i) : \mathsf{Type}(i+p)}$$

$$(\text{BASE})\frac{}{[] \vdash \mathsf{wf}} \qquad (\text{VAR})\frac{\Gamma \vdash \mathsf{wf}}{\Gamma \vdash x : A}\text{if } (x : A) \in \Gamma$$

$$(\text{CONT})\frac{\Gamma \vdash A : \mathsf{Type}(i)}{\Gamma(x_\diamond : A) \vdash \mathsf{wf}} \qquad (\text{CONT*})\frac{\Gamma \vdash A : \mathsf{Prop}}{\Gamma(x_* : A) \vdash \mathsf{wf}}$$

$$(\text{CONV})\frac{\Gamma \vdash t : A \qquad \Gamma \vdash B : s}{\Gamma \vdash t : B}\text{if } A \leq B$$

$$(\text{PROD})\frac{\Gamma \vdash A : s \qquad \Gamma(x_\mathsf{S} : A) \vdash B : \mathsf{Type}(i)}{\Gamma \vdash \Pi x_\mathsf{S} : A.B : \max(s, \mathsf{Type}(i))}$$

$$(\text{PROD*})\frac{\Gamma \vdash A : s \qquad \Gamma(x_\mathsf{S} : A) \vdash B : \mathsf{Prop}}{\Gamma \vdash \Pi x_\mathsf{S} : A.B : \mathsf{Prop}}$$

$$(\text{LAM})\frac{\Gamma \vdash \Pi x : A.B : s \qquad \Gamma(x : A) \vdash t : B}{\Gamma \vdash \lambda x : A.t : \Pi x : A.B} \qquad (\text{APP})\frac{\Gamma \vdash t : \Pi x : A.B \qquad \Gamma \vdash u : A}{\Gamma \vdash (t\ u) : B[x \setminus u]}$$

$$(\text{SIG})\frac{\Gamma \vdash A : \mathsf{Type}(i) \qquad \Gamma(x : A) \vdash B : \mathsf{Type}(i)}{\Gamma \vdash \Sigma^\diamond x : A.B : \mathsf{Type}(i)}$$

$$(\text{SIG*})\frac{\Gamma \vdash A : \mathsf{Type}(i) \qquad \Gamma(x : A) \vdash B : \mathsf{Prop}}{\Gamma \vdash \Sigma^* x : A.B : \mathsf{Prop}}$$

$$(\text{PAIR})\frac{\Gamma \vdash a : A \qquad \Gamma(x : A) \vdash b : B \qquad \Gamma \vdash \Sigma^\mathsf{S} x : A.B : \mathsf{Type}(i)}{\Gamma \vdash < a, b >_{\Sigma x : A.B} : \Sigma^\mathsf{S} x : A.B}$$

$$(\text{PROJ1})\frac{\Gamma \vdash t : \Sigma^\mathsf{S} x : A.B}{\Gamma \vdash \pi_1^\mathsf{S}(t) : A} \qquad (\text{PROJ2})\frac{\Gamma \vdash t : \Sigma^\mathsf{S} x : A.B}{\Gamma \vdash \pi_2^\mathsf{S}(t) : B[x \setminus \pi_1^\mathsf{S}(t)]}$$

Fig. 1. The ECC fragment

Lemma 6 (Subject reduction). *If $\Gamma \vdash t : T$ is derivable, if $t \rhd_\beta t'$ (resp. $T \rhd_\beta T'$, $\Gamma \rhd_\beta \Gamma'$) by a well-sorted reduction, then $\Gamma \vdash t' : T$ (resp. $\Gamma \vdash t : T', \Gamma' \vdash t : T$).*

Lemma 7. *If $\Gamma \vdash t : T$ is derivable, then there exists a sort s such that $\Gamma \vdash T : s$; furthermore $\Gamma \vdash T :$ Prop if and only if t is of tag $*$.*

A most important property is of course normalization. We do not claim any proof here, although we very strongly conjecture it. A smooth way to prove it is probably to build on top of a simple set-theoretical model using an interpretation of types as saturated Λ sets as first proposed by Altenkirch [1,20].

Conjecture 1 (Strong Normalization). If $\Gamma \vdash t : T$ is derivable, then t is strongly normalizing.

Stating strong normalization is important in the practice of proof-checker, since it entails decidability of type-checking and type-inference.

Corollary 1. *Given Γ, it is decidable whether $\Gamma \vdash$ wf. Given Γ and a raw term t, it is decidable whether there exists T such that $\Gamma \vdash t : T$ holds.*

The other usual side-product of normalization is a syntactic assessement of constructivity.

Corollary 2. *If $[] \vdash t : \Sigma x : A.B$, then $t \rhd_\beta^* < a, b >_{\Sigma x : A.B}$ with $[] \vdash a : A$ and $[] \vdash b : B[x \setminus a]$.*

2.4 Data Types

In order to be practical, the theory needs to be extended by inductive definitions in the style of Coq, Lego and others. We do not detail the typing rules and liberally use integers, booleans, usual functions and predicates ranging over them. We refer to the coq documentation [8,10]; for a possible more modern presentation [5] is interesting.

Two points are important though:

1. Data types live in Type. That is, for instance, nat : Type(1); thus, their elements are of tag $\diamond$.
2. There is no primary need for inductive definitions in Prop. Logical connectors and inductive properties can be encoded using impredicativity. For instance, we write:

$$A \wedge B \equiv \Pi P : \text{Prop}.(A \to B \to P) \to P.$$

2.5 Treatment of Propositional Equality

Propositional equality is a first example whose treatment changes when switching to a proof-irrelevant type theory. The definition itself is unchanged; two objects a and b of a given type A are equal if and only if they enjoy the same properties:

$$a =_A b \equiv \Pi P : A \to \text{Prop}.(P\ a) \to (P\ b).$$

It is well-known that reflexivity, symmetry and transitivity of equality can easily be proved. When seen as an inductive definition, the definition of "$=_A$" is viewed as its own elimination principle.

Let us write refl for the canonical proof of reflexivity:

$$\text{refl} \equiv \lambda A : \text{Type}(i).\lambda x : A.\lambda P : A \to \text{Prop}.\lambda p : (P\ x).p$$

In many cases, it is useful to extend this elimination over the computational levels:

$$\text{Eq\_rec}_i : \Pi A : \text{Type}(i).\Pi P : A \to \text{Type}(i).\Pi a,b : A.(P\ a) \to a =_A b \to (P\ b).$$

There is however a particularity to Eq_rec: in Coq, it is defined by case analysis and therefore comes with a computation rule. The term $(\text{Eq\_rec}\ A\ P\ a\ b\ p\ e)$ of type $(P\ b)$ reduces to p in the case where e is a canonical proof by reflexivity; in this case, a and b are convertible and thus coherence and normalization of the type theory are preserved.

As shown in the next section, such a reduction rule is useful, especially when programming with dependent types. In our proof-irrelevant theory however, we cannot rely on the information given by the equality proof e, since all equality proofs are treated as convertible. Furthermore, allowing, for any e, the reduction rule $(\text{Eq\_rec}\ A\ P\ a\ b\ p\ e) \triangleright p$ is too permissive, since it easily breaks the subject reduction property in incoherent contexts.

We therefore put the burden of checking convertibility between a and b on the reduction rule of Eq_rec by extending reduction with the following, non-linear rule:

$$(\text{Eq\_rec}\ A\ P\ a\ a\ p\ e) \triangleright p$$

or the equivalent conditional rule:

$$(\text{Eq\_rec}\ A\ P\ a\ b\ p\ e) \triangleright p . \quad \text{if } a =_\varepsilon b$$

Again, we do not detail meta-theory here, but the various lemmas of the previous section still hold when $=_\varepsilon$ is enriched with this new reduction.

3 Programming with Dependent Types

We now list some applications of the relaxed conversion rule, which all follow the slogan that proof-irrelevance makes programming with dependent types more convenient and efficient.

From now on, we will write $\{x : A|P\}$ for $\Sigma^* x : A.P$, that is for a Σ-type whose second component is non-computational.

3.1 Dependent Equality

Programming with dependent types means that terms occur in the type of computational objects (i.e. not only in propositions). The way equality is handled over such families of types is thus a crucial point which is often problematic in intensional type theories.

Let us take a simple example. Consider we have defined a data-type of arrays over some type A. If n is a natural number, (tab n) is the type of arrays of size n. That is tab : nat $\rightarrow$ Type(i).

Commutativity of addition can be proved in the theory: com : $\Pi m, p$: nat.$(m + p) = (p + m)$ is inhabited. Yet tab $(m + p)$ and tab $(p + m)$ are two distinct types with distinct inhabitants; the operator Eq_rec described above only allows to construct a translation function from one to the other:

$$tr : \Pi n : nat.(\text{tab } (m + p)) \rightarrow (\text{tab } (p + m)).$$

The problem is proving that this function indeed ultimately behaves like the identity; typically proving:

$$\Pi i : \text{nat.}\Pi x : i < p + m \rightarrow (t\ i\ x) = (tr\ n\ t\ i\ (\text{com } m\ p\ x)).$$

It is known [18,15], that to do so, one needs the reduction rule for Eq_rec together with a proof that equality proofs are unique. The latter property being generally established by a variant of what Streicher calls the "K axiom":

$$K : \Pi A : \text{Type.}\Pi a : A.\Pi P : a =_A a \rightarrow \text{Prop.}(P\ (\text{refl } a)) \rightarrow \Pi e : a =_A a.(P\ e)$$

where refl stands for the canonical proof by reflexivity.

Here since equality proofs are also irrelevant to conversion, this axiom becomes trivial. Actually, since $(P\ e)$ and $(P\ (\text{refl } a))$ are convertible, this statement does not even need to be mentioned anymore, and the associated reduction rule becomes superfluous.

In general, it should be interesting to transpose McBride's work [18] in the framework of proof-irrelevant theories.

3.2 Partial Functions and Equality over Subset Types

In the literature of type theory, subset types come in many flavors; they designate the restriction of a type to the elements verifying a certain predicate. The type $\{x : A|P\}$ can be viewed as the constructive statement "there exists an element of A verifying P", but also as the data-type A restricted to elements verifying P. In most current type theories, the latter approach is not very practical since equality is defined over it in a too narrow way. We have $< a, p > =_\beta < a', p' >$ only if $a =_\beta a'$ and $p =_\beta p'$; the problem is that one would like to get rid of the second condition. The same is true for propositional Leibniz equality and one can establish:

$$< a, p > =_{\{x:A|P\}} < a, p' > \rightarrow p =_{P[x\backslash a]} p'.$$

In general however, one is only interested in the validity of the assertion $(P\ a)$, not the way it is proved. A program awaiting an argument of type $\{x : A|P\}$ will behave identically if fed with $< a, p >$ or $< a, p' >$.

Therefore, each time a construct $\{x : A|P\}$ is used indeed as a data-type, one cannot use Leibniz equality in practice. Instead, one has to define a less restrictive equivalence relation $\simeq_{A,P}$ which simply states that the two first components of the pair are equal:

$$< a, p > \ \simeq_{A,P} \ < a', p' > \quad \equiv \quad a = a'.$$

But using $\simeq_{A,P}$ instead of $=_{\{x:A|P\}}$ quickly becomes very tedious; typically, for every function $f : \{x : A|P\} \to B$ one has to prove

$$\Pi c, c' : \{x : A|P\} \ . \ c \simeq_{A,P} c' \to (f\ c) =_B (f\ c')$$

and even more specific statements if B is itself a subset type.

In our theory one can prove without difficulties that $=_{\{x:A|P\}}$ and $\simeq_{A,P}$ are equivalent, and there is indeed no need anymore for defining $\simeq_{A,P}$. Furthermore, one has $< a, p > \ =_\varepsilon \ < a, p' >$, so the two terms are computationally identified which is stronger than Leibniz equality, avoiding the use of the deductive level and makes proofs and developments more concise.

Array Bounds. A typical example of the phenomenon above is observed when dealing with partial functions. For instance when an array t of size n is viewed as a function taking an index i as argument, together with a proof that i is less than n. That is:

$$t : (\mathsf{tab}\ n) \quad \text{with} \quad \mathsf{tab} \equiv \Pi i : \mathsf{nat}.i < n \to A.$$

In traditional type theory, this definition is cumbersome to use, since one has to state explicitly that the values $(t\ i\ p_i)$, where $p_i : i < n$ *do not depend upon* p_i. The type above is therefore not sufficient to describe an array; instead one needs the additional condition:

$$T_{irr} : \Pi i : \mathsf{nat}.\Pi p_i, p'_i : i < n.(t\ i\ p_i) =_A (t\ i\ p'_i)$$

where $=_A$ stands for the propositional Leibniz equality.

This is again verbose and cumbersome since T_{irr} has to be invoked repeatedly. In our theory, not only the condition T_{irr} becomes trivial, since for any p_i and p'_i one has $(t\ i\ p_i) =_\varepsilon (t\ i\ p'_i)$, but this last coercion is stronger than propositional equality: there is no need anymore to have recourse to the deductive level and prove this equality. The proof terms are therefore clearer and smaller.

3.3   On-the-Fly Extraction

An important point, which we can only briefly mention here is the consequence for the implementation when switching to a proof-irrelevant theory. In a proof-checker, the environment consists of a sequence of definitions or lemmas which have been type-checked. If the proof-checker implements a proof-irrelevant theory, it is reasonable to keep two versions of each constant: the full proof-term, which can be printed or re-checked, and the extracted one (that is $\to_\varepsilon$-normalized) which is used for conversion check. This would be even more natural when building on recent Coq implementations which already use a dual storing of constants, the second representation being non-printable compiled code precisely used for fast conversion check.

In other words, a proof-system built upon a theory as the one presented here would allow the user to efficiently exploit the computational behavior of a constructive proof in order to prove new facts. This makes the benefits of program extraction technology available inside the system and helps transforming proof-system into viable programming environments.

4   Relating to PVS

Subset types also form the core of PVS. In this formalism the objects of type $\{x : A|P\}$ are also of type A. This makes type checking undecidable and is thus impossible in our setting. But we show that it is possible to build explicit coercions between the corresponding types of our theory which basically behave like the identity.

The following lemma states that the construction and destruction operations of our subset types can actually be omitted when checking conversion:

Lemma 8 (Singleton simplification). *The typing relation of our theory remains unchanged if we extend the* $\rightarrow_\varepsilon$ *reduction of our theory by :*

$$< a, p >_{\Sigma^* x:A.P} \rightarrow_\varepsilon a$$
$$\pi_1^*(c) \rightarrow_\varepsilon c.$$

The following definition is directly transposed[2] from PVS [23]. We do not treat dependent types in full generality (see chapter 3 of [23]).

Definition 4 (Maximal super-type). *The maximal super-type is a partial function* μ *from terms to terms, recursively defined by the following equations. In all these equations, A and B are of type* Type(i) *in a given context.*

$$\mu(A) \equiv A \quad \text{if } A \text{ is a data-type} \qquad \mu(\{x : A|P\}) \equiv \mu(A)$$
$$\mu(A \rightarrow B) \equiv A \rightarrow \mu(B) \qquad\qquad \mu(A \times B) \equiv \mu(A) \times \mu(B).$$

Definition 5 (η-reduction). *The generalized η-reduction, written* $\triangleright_\eta$*, is the contextual closure of:*

$$\lambda x : A.(t\ x) \triangleright_\eta t \quad \text{if } x \text{ is not free in } t$$
$$< \pi_1(t), \pi_2(t) > \triangleright_\eta t.$$

We can now construct the coercion function between A and $\mu(A)$:

Lemma 9. *If* $\Gamma \vdash A :$ Type(i) *and* $\mu(A)$ *is defined, then:*

- $\Gamma \vdash \mu(A) :$ Type(i),
- *there exists a function* $\overline{\mu}(A)$ *which is of type* $A \rightarrow \mu(A)$ *in* Γ,

---

[2] A difference is that in PVS, propositions and booleans are identified; but this point is independent with this study. It is however possible to do the same in our theory by assuming a computational version of excluded-middle.

– *furthermore, when applying the singleton simplification $\mathcal{S}$ to $\overline{\mu}$ one obtains an η-expansion of the identity function; to be precise: $\mathcal{S}(\overline{\mu}) \to_{\varepsilon\eta}^* \lambda x : B.x.$*

Proof. It is almost trivial to check that $\Gamma \vdash \mu(A) : \mathsf{Type}(i)$. The two other clauses are proved by induction over the structure of A.

– If $f : A \to \mu(A)$, then $g \equiv \lambda x : \{x : A|P\}.(f\ \pi_1(x)) : \{x : A|P\} \to \mu(A)$. Furthermore $\pi_1(x)$ is here simplified to x, since $P : \mathsf{Prop}$. Since $(\mathcal{S}(f)\ x) \triangleright_{\varepsilon\eta}^* x$, $\mathcal{S}(g) \triangleright_{\varepsilon\eta}^* \lambda : x : \{x : A|P\}.x$.
– If $f : B \to \mu(B)$, then $g \equiv \lambda h : A \to B.\lambda x : A.(f\ (h\ x)) : A \to \mu(B)$. Since $(\mathcal{S}(f)\ (h\ x)) \triangleright_{\varepsilon\eta}^* (h\ x)$, we have $g \triangleright_{\varepsilon\eta}^* \lambda h : A \to B.h$.
– If $f_A : A \to \mu(A)$ and $f_B : B \to \mu(B)$, then
$g \equiv \lambda x : A \times B. < (f_A\ \pi_1(x)), (f_B\ \pi_2(x)) >_{A\times B}$ is of the expected type. Again, the induction hypotheses assure that $g \triangleright_{\varepsilon\eta}^* \lambda x : A \times B.x$.

The opposite operation, going from from $\mu(A)$ to A, can only be performed when some conditions are verified (TCC's in PVS terminology). We can also transpose this to our theory, still keeping the simple computational behavior of the coercion function. This time however, our typing is less flexible than PVS', we have to define the coercion function and its type simultaneously; furthermore, in general, this operation is well-typed only if the type-theory supports generalized η-reduction.

This unfortunate restriction is typical when defining transformations over programs with dependent types. It should however not be taken too seriously, and we believe this cosmetic imperfection can generally be tackled in practice[3].

Lemma 10 (subtype constraint). *Given $\Gamma \vdash A : \mathsf{Type}(i)$, if $\mu(A)$ is defined, then one can define $\pi(A)$ and $\overline{\pi}(A)$ such that, in the theory where conversion is extended with $\triangleright_\eta$, one has:*

$$\Gamma \vdash \pi(A) : \mu(A) \to \mathsf{Prop} \quad and \quad \Gamma \vdash \overline{\pi}(A) : \varPi x : \mu(A).(\pi(A)\ x) \to A.$$

Furthermore, $\overline{\pi}(A) \triangleright_{\varepsilon\eta}$-normalizes to $\lambda x : \mu(A).\lambda p : (\pi(A)\ x).x.$

Proof. By straightforward induction. We only detail some the case where $A = B \to C$. Then $\pi(A) \equiv \lambda f : A \to \mu(B).\forall x : A.(\pi(B)\ (f\ x))$ and $\overline{\pi}(A) \equiv \lambda f : A \to \mu(B).\lambda p : \forall x : A.(\pi(B)\ (f\ x)).\lambda x : A.(\overline{\pi}(B)\ (f\ x)\ (p\ x))$.

5   A More Extensional Theory

Especially during the 1970ies and 1980ies, there was an intense debate about the respective advantages of intensional versus extensional type theories. The latter denomination seems to cover various features like replacing conversion by propositional equality in the conversion rule or adding primitive quotient

---

[3] For one, in practical cases, η-does not seem necessary very often (only with some nested existentials). And even then, it should be possible to tackle the problem with by proving the corresponding equality on the deductive level.

types. In general, these features provide a more comfortable construction of some mathematical concepts and are closer to set-theoretical practice. But they break other desirable properties, like decidability of type-checking and strong normalization.

The theory presented here should therefore be considered as belonging to the intentional family. However, we retrieve some features usually understood as extensional.

5.1   The Axiom of Choice

Consider the usual form of the (typed) axiom of choice (AC):

$$(\forall x : A.\exists y : B.R(x,y)) \Rightarrow \exists f : A \to B.\forall x : A.R(x, f\ x).$$

When we transpose it into our type theory, we can chose to translate the existential quantifier either by a Σ-type, or the existential quantifier defined in Prop :

$$\exists x : A.P \equiv \Pi Q : \text{Prop}.(\Pi x : A.P \to Q) \to Q\ : \text{Prop}$$

If we use a Σ-type, we get a type which obviously inhabited, using the projections π_1 and π_2. However, if we read the existential quantifiers of AC as defined above, we obtain a (non-computational) proposition which is not provable in type theory.

Schematically, this propositions states that if $\Pi x : A.\exists y : B.R(x,y)$ is provable, then the corresponding function from A to B exists "in the model". This assumption is strong and allows to encode IZF set theory into type theory (see [26]).

What is new is that our proof-irrelevant type theory is extensional enough to perform the first part of Goodman and Myhill's proof based on Diaconescu's observation. Assuming AC, we can prove the decidability of equality. Consider any type A and two objects a and b of type A. We define:

$$\{a,b\} \equiv \{x : A | x = a \lor x = b\}$$

Let us write a' (resp. b') for the element of $\{a,b\}$ corresponding to a (resp. b); so $\pi_1(a') =_\varepsilon a$ and $\pi_1(b') =_\varepsilon b$. It is the easy to prove that

$$\Pi z : \{a,b\}.\exists e : \text{bool}.(e = \text{true} \land \pi_1(z) = a) \lor (e = \text{false} \land \pi_1(z) = b)$$

and from the axiom of choice we deduce:

$$\exists f : \{a,b\} \to \text{bool}.\Pi z : \{a,b\}.(f\ z = \text{true} \land \pi_1(z) = a) \lor (f\ z = \text{false} \land \pi_1(z) = b)$$

Finally given such a function f, one can compare $(f\ a')$ and $(f\ b')$, since both are booleans over which equality is decidable.

The key point is then that, thanks to proof-irrelevance, the equivalence between $a' = b'$ and $a = b$ is provable in the theory. Therefore, if $(f\ a')$ and $(f\ b')$ are different, so are a and b. On the other hand, if $(f\ a') = (f\ b') = \text{true}$ then $\pi_1(b') = a$ and so $b = a$. In the same way, $(f\ a') = (f\ b') = \text{false}$ entails $b = a$.

616   B. Werner

We thus deduce $a = b \vee a \neq b$ and by generalizing with respect to a, b and A we obtain:
$$\Pi A : \mathsf{Type}(i).\Pi a, b : A.a = b \vee a \neq b$$

which is a quite classical statement. We have formalized this proof in Coq, assuming proof-irrelevance as an axiom.

Note of course that this "decidability" is restricted to a disjunction in Prop and that it is not possible to build an actual generic decision function. Indeed, constructivity of results in the predicative fragment of the theory are preserved, even if assuming the excluded-middle in Prop.

5.2   Other Classical Non-computational Axioms

At present, we have not been able to deduce the excluded middle from the statement above[4]. We leave this theoretical question to future investigations but it seems quite clear that in most cases, when admitting AC one will also be willing to admit EM. In fact both axioms are validated by the simple set-theoretical model and give a setting where the $\mathsf{Type}(i)$'s are inhabited by computational types (i.e. from $\{x : A|P\}$ we can compute x of type A) and Prop allows classical reasoning about those programs.

Another practical statement which is validated by the set-theoretical model is the axiom that point-wise equal functions are equal :

$$\Pi A, B : \mathsf{Type}(i).\Pi f, g : A \to B.\Pi x : A.f\ x = g\ x \to f = g.$$

Note that combining this axiom with AC (and thus decidability of equality) is already enough to prove (in Prop) the existence of a function deciding whether a Turing machine halts.

5.3   Quotients and Normalized Types

Quotient sets are a typically extensional concept whose adaptation to type theory has always been problematic. Again, one has to chose between "effective" quotients and decidability of type-checking. Searching for a possible compromise, Courtieu [9] ended up with an interesting notion of *normalized type*[5]. The idea is remarkably simple: given a function $f : A \to B$, we can define $\{(f\ x)|x : A\}$ which is the subtype of B corresponding to the codomain of f. His rules are straightforwardly translated into our theory by simply taking:

$$\{f(x)|x : A\} \equiv \{y : B|\exists x : A.y = f\ x\}$$

Courtieu also gives the typing rules for functions going from A to $\{f(x)|x : A\}$, and back in the case where f is actually of type $A \to A$.

---

[4] In set theory, decidability of equality entails the excluded middle, since $\{x \in \mathbb{N}|P\}$ is equal to $\mathbb{N}$ if and only if P holds.

[5] A similar notion has been developped for NuPRL [22].

The relation with quotients being that in the case $f : A \to A$ we can understand $\{f(x)|x : A\}$ as the type A quotiented by the relation

$$x \, R \, y \quad \Longleftrightarrow \quad f \, x = f \, y$$

In practice this appears to be often the case, and Courtieu describes several applications.

6   Conclusion and Further Work

We have tried to show that a relaxed conversion rule makes type theories more practical, without necessarily giving up normalization or decidable type checking. In particular, we have shown that this approach brings together the world of PVS and type theories of the Coq family.

We also view this as a contribution to closing the gap between proof systems like Coq and safe programming environments like Dependant ML or ATS [7,27]. But this will only be assessed by practice; the first step is thus to implement such a theory.

Acknowledgements

Christine Paulin deserves special thanks, since she me gave the idea of a relaxed conversion rule long ago as well as the computation rule of paragraph 2.5. This work also benefited from discussions with Bruno Barras, Hugo Herbelin and Benjamin Grégoire. Anonymous referees gave numerous useful comments and hints.

References

1. T. Altenkirch. "Proving strong normalization for CC by modifying realizability semantics". In H. Barendregt and T. Nipkow Eds, *Types for Proofs and Programs*, LNCS 806, 1994.
2. T. Altenkirch. Extensional Equality in Intensional Type Theory. LICS, 1999.
3. H. Barendregt. Lambda Calculi with Types. Technical Report 91-19, Catholic University Nijmegen, 1991. In Handbook of Logic in Computer Science, Vol II, Elsevier, 1992.
4. G. Barthe. The relevance of proof-irrelevance. In K.G. Larsen, S. Skyum, and G. Winskel, editors, Proceedings of ICALP'98, volume 1443 of LNCS, pages 755-768. Springer-Verlag, 1998.
5. F. Blanqui. Definitions by rewriting in the Calculus of Constructions. MSCS, vol. 15(1), 2003.
6. J. Caldwell. "Moving Proofs-as-Programs into Practice", In Proceedings of the 12th IEEE International Conference on Automated Software Engineering, IEEE, 1997.
7. Chiyan Chen and Hongwei Xi, Combining Programming with Theorem Proving. ICFP'05, 2005.
8. The Coq Development Team. *The Coq Proof-Assistant User's Manual*, INRIA. On http://coq.inria.fr/

9. P. Courtieu. "Normalized Types". *Proceedings of CSL 2001*, L. Fribourg Ed., LNCS 2142, Springer, 2001.
10. E. Gimenez. "A Tutorial on Recursive Types in Coq". INRIA Technical Report. 1999.
11. G. Gonthier. A computer-checked proof of the Four Colour Theorem. Manuscript, 2005.
12. B. Grégoire and X. Leroy. "A compiled implementation of strong reduction", proceedings of ICFP, 2002.
13. Compilation des termes de preuves: un (nouveau) mariage entre Coq et Ocaml. Thèse de doctorat, Université Paris 7, 2003.
14. A computational approach to Pocklington certificates in type theory. In proceedings of FLOPS 2006, M. Hagiya and P. Wadler (Eds), LNCS, Springer-Verlag, 2006.
15. M. Hofmann and T. Streicher. "A groupoid model refutes uniqueness of identity proofs". LICS'94, Paris. 1994.
16. Z. Luo. "ECC: An Extended Calculus of Constructions." Proc. of IEEE LICS'89. 1989.
17. P. Martin-Löf. *Intuitionistic Type Theory*. Studies in Proof Theory, Bibliopolis, 1984.
18. C. McBride. "Elimination with a Motive". Proceedings of TYPES'00, 2000.
19. J. McKinna and R. Pollack. "Pure Type Systems formalized", in TLCA'93, M. Bezem and J. F. Groote Eds, LNCS 664, Springer-Verlag, Berlin, 1993.
20. P.-A. Melliès and B. Werner. "A Generic Normalization Proof for Pure Type System" in TYPES'96, E. Gimenez and C. Paulin-Mohring Eds, LNCS 1512, Springer-Verlag, Berlin, 1998.
21. A. Miquel and B. Werner. "The not so simple proof-irrelevant model of CC". In Geuvers and Wiedijk (Eds.), Proceedings of TYPES 2002, LNCS 2646, 2003.
22. A. Nogin and A. Kopilov. "Formalizing Type Operations Using the "Image" Type Constructor". To appear in WoLLIC 2006, ENTCS.
23. S. Owre and N. Shankar. "The Formal Semantics of PVS". SRI Technical Report CSL-97-2R. Revised March 1999.
24. C. Paulin-Mohring. *Extraction de Programmes dans le Calcul des Constructions*. Thèse de doctorat, Université Paris 7, 1989.
25. F. Pfenning. "Intensionality, Extensionality, and Proof Irrelevance in Modal Type Theory". Proceedings of LICS, IEEE, 2001.
26. B. Werner. "Sets in Types, Types in Sets". In, M. Abadi and T. Itoh (Eds), Theoretical Aspects of Computer Science, TACS'97, LNCS 1281, Springer-Verlag, 1997.
27. Hongwei Xi, Dependent Types in Practical Programming, Ph.D, CMU, 1998.

Consistency and Completeness of Rewriting in the Calculus of Constructions

Daria Walukiewicz-Chrząszcz and Jacek Chrząszcz*

Institute of Informatics, Warsaw University
ul. Banacha 2, 02-097 Warsaw, Poland
{daria, chrzaszcz}@mimuw.edu.pl

Abstract. Adding rewriting to a proof assistant based on the Curry-Howard isomorphism, such as Coq, may greatly improve usability of the tool. Unfortunately adding an arbitrary set of rewrite rules may render the underlying formal system undecidable and inconsistent. While ways to ensure termination and confluence, and hence decidability of type-checking, have already been studied to some extent, logical consistency has got little attention so far.

In this paper we show that consistency is a consequence of canonicity, which in turn follows from the assumption that all functions defined by rewrite rules are complete. We provide a sound and terminating, but necessarily incomplete algorithm to verify this property. The algorithm accepts all definitions that follow dependent pattern matching schemes presented by Coquand and studied by McBride in his PhD thesis. Moreover, many definitions by rewriting containing rules which depart from standard pattern matching are also accepted.

1 Introduction

Equality is ubiquitous in mathematics. Yet it turns out that proof assistants based on the Curry-Howard isomorphism, such as Coq [9] are not very good at handling equality. While proving an equality is not a problem in itself, using already established equalities is quite problematic.

Apart from equalities resulting from internal reductions (beta, iota), which can be used via the conversion rule without being recorded in the proof term, any other use of an equality requires giving all details about the context explicitly in the proof. As a result, proof terms may become extremely large, taking up memory and making type-checking time consuming: working with equations in Coq is not very convenient.

A straightforward idea for reducing the size of proof terms is to allow other equalities in the conversion, making their use transparent. This can be done by using user-defined *rewrite rules*. However, adding arbitrary rules may easily lead to logical inconsistency, making the proof environment useless. It is of course possible to put the responsibility on the user, but it is contrary to the current Coq policy to guarantee consistency of developments without axioms. It is desirable to retain this guarantee when rewriting is added to Coq. Since consistency is undecidable in presence of rewriting, one has find some decidable criteria satisfied only by rewriting systems which do not violate consistency.

---

* This work was partly supported by KBN grant 3 T11C 002 27.

U. Furbach and N. Shankar (Eds.): IJCAR 2006, LNAI 4130, pp. 619–631, 2006.

The syntactical proof of consistency of the calculus of constructions, which is the base of the formalism implemented in Coq, requires every term to have a normal form [2]. The same proof is also valid for the calculus of inductive constructions [22], which is even closer to the formalism implemented in Coq.

There exist several techniques to prove (strong) normalization of the calculus of constructions with rewriting [1,5,4,19,20], following numerous works about rewriting in the simply-typed lambda calculus. Practical criteria for ensuring other fundamental properties, like confluence, subject reduction and decidability of type-checking are addressed e.g. in [4].

Logical consistency is also studied in [4]. It is shown under an assumption that for every symbol f defined by rewriting, $f(t_1, \ldots, t_n)$ is reducible if $t_1 \ldots t_n$ are terms in normal form in the environment consisting of one type variable. Apart from an informal proof that this is the case for the two rules defining the induction predicate for natural numbers and a remark that this property resembles the completeness of definitions, satisfying the assumption of the consistency lemma is not discussed.

Practical techniques for checking completeness of definitions are known for almost 30 years for the first-order algebraic setting [12,18,13]. More recently, their adaptations to type theory appeared in [10,14] and [16]. In this paper we show how the latter algorithm can be tailored to the calculus of constructions extended with rewriting. We study a system, similar to a proof assistant reality, where the sets of available function symbols and rewrite rules are not known from the beginning but may grow as the proof development advances.

We show that logical consistency is an easy consequence of canonicity (see Def. 2 and Lemma 4), which in turn can be proved from completeness of definitions by rewriting, provided that termination and confluence are proved first. Our completeness checking algorithm closes the list of necessary procedures needed to guarantee logical consistency of developments in a proof assistant based on the calculus of constructions with rewriting. For additional examples and the proofs of all lemmas we refer the reader to the Web appendix [21].

2   Rewriting in the Calculus of Constructions

Let us briefly discuss how we imagine introducing rewriting in Coq and what problems we encounter on the way to a usable system.

From the user's perspective definitions by rewriting could be entered just as all other definitions:[1]

```
Inductive  nat : Set  := O : nat | S : nat → nat.
Symbol + : nat → nat → nat
Rules
  O + y      ⟶  y                    x + O      ⟶  x
  (S x) + y ⟶ S (x + y)              x + (S y) ⟶ S (x + y)
  x + (y + z) ⟶ (x + y) + z.
Parameter n : nat.
```

---

[1] The syntax of the definition by rewriting is inspired by the experimental "Rewriting" branch of Coq developed by Blanqui. For the sake of clarity we omit certain details, like environments of rule variables and allow the infix + in the definition.

The above fragment can be interpreted as an environment E consisting of the inductive definition of natural numbers, symmetric definition by rewriting of addition and the declaration of a variable n of type *nat*. In this environment all rules for + contribute to conversion. For instance both $\forall x.\ x + 0 = x$ and $\forall x.\ 0 + x = x$ can be proved by $\lambda x:nat.\ refl\ nat\ x$, where *refl* is the only constructor of the Leibniz equality inductive predicate. Note that the definition of + is terminating and confluent. The latter can be checked by an (automatic) examination of its critical pairs.

Rewrite rules can also be used to define higher-order and polymorphic functions, like the map function on polymorphic lists.

```
Symbol map : forall (A:Set), (A → A) → list A → list A
Rules
   map A f (nil A) ⟶ nil A
   map A f (cons A a l) ⟶ cons A (f a) (map A f l)
   map A λx.x l ⟶ l
```

Even though we consider higher-order rewriting, we choose the simple matching modulo α-conversion. Higher-order matching is useful for example to encode logical languages by higher-order abstract syntax, but it is seldom used in Coq where modeling relies rather on inductive types. Instead of higher-order matching, one needs a possibility not to specify certain arguments in left-hand sides, and hence to work with rewrite rules built from terms that may be not typable. Consider, for example the type tree of trees with size and the function rotr performing a right rotation in the root of the tree.

```
Inductive tree : nat → Set :=
   Leaf : tree 0
| Node : forall n1:nat, tree n1 → bool → forall n2:nat, tree n2
            → tree (S(n1+n2)).

Symbol rotr : forall n:nat, (tree n) → (tree n)
Rules
   rotr 0 t ⟶ t
   rotr ? (Node 0 t1 a n2 t2) ⟶ Node 0 t1 a n2 t2
   rotr ?1 (Node ?2 (Node ?3 A b ?4 C) d ?5 E)
            ⟶ Node ?3 A b (S (?4 + ?5)) (Node ?4 C d ?5 E)
```

The first argument of rotr is the size of the tree and the second is the tree itself. The first two rules cover the trees which cannot be rotated and the third one performs the rotation.

The ? marks above should be treated as different variables. The information they hide is redundant: if we take the third rule for example, the values of ?3, ?4 and ?5 must correspond to the sizes of the trees A, C and E respectively, ?2 must be equal S(?3+?4) and ?1=S(?2+?5). Note that by not writing suitable subterms we make the rule left-linear (and therefore easier to match) and avoid critical pairs with +, therefore helping the confluence proof.

This way of writing left-hand sides of rules was already used by Werner in [22] to define elimination rules for inductive types, making them orthogonal (the left-hand sides are of the form $I_{elim}\ P\ \boldsymbol{f}\ \boldsymbol{w}\ (c\ \boldsymbol{x})$, where P, $\boldsymbol{f}$, $\boldsymbol{w}$, $\boldsymbol{x}$ are distinct variables and c is a constructor of I). In [4], Blanqui gives a precise account of these omissions using them to make more rewriting rules left-linear. Later, the authors of [6] show that these redundant subterms can be completely removed from terms (in a calculus without rewriting however). In [3], a new optimized convertibility test algorithm is presented for Coq, which ignores testing equality of these redundant arguments.

In our paper we do not specify which arguments should/could be replaced by ? and do not restrict left-hand sides to be left-linear, but rely on the acceptance condition for definitions by rewriting to guarantee needed metatheoretical properties listed in the next section.

It is also interesting to note that when the first argument of rotr is a ? then we may say that it is matched modulo conversion and not syntactically.

3   Pure Type Systems with Generative Definitions

Even though most papers motivated by the development of Coq concentrate on the calculus of constructions, we present here a slightly more general formalization of a pure type system with inductive definitions and definitions by rewriting. The presentation, taken from [7,8], is quite close to the way these elements are and could possibly be implemented in Coq. The formalism is built upon a set of PTS sorts S, a binary relation A and a ternary relation R over S governing the typing rules (**Term/Ax**) and (**Term/Prod**) respectively (Fig. 1). The syntactic class of pseudoterms is defined as follows:

$$t ::= v \mid s \mid (t_1\ t_2) \mid (\lambda v{:}t_1.t_2) \mid ((v{:}t_1)t_2)$$

A pseudoterm can be a variable, a sort from S, an application, an abstraction or a product. We use Greek letters γ, δ to denote substitutions which are finite partial maps from variables to pseudo-terms. The postfix notation is used for the application of substitutions to terms.

Inductive definitions and definitions by rewriting are *generative*. They are stored in the environment and are used in terms only through names they "generate". An environment is a sequence of declarations, each of them is a variable declaration $v : t$, an inductive definition $\mathsf{Ind}(\Gamma^I := \Gamma^C)$, where Γ^I and Γ^C are environments of (possibly mutually defined) inductive types and their constructors, or a definition by rewriting $\mathsf{Rew}(\Gamma, R)$, where Γ is an environment of (possibly mutually defined) function symbols and R is a set of rewrite rules defining them. Given an environment E, inductive types, constructors and function symbols declared in E are called constants (even though syntactically they are variables). General environments are denoted by E and the environment containing only variable declarations are denoted by Γ, Δ, G, D. We assume that names of all declarations in environments are pairwise disjoint. A pair consisting of an environment E and a term e is called a sequent and denoted by $E \vdash e$. A sequent is well-typed if $E \vdash e : t$ for some t.

Definition 1. *A pure type system with generative definitions is defined by the typing rules in Fig. 1, where:*

- *The relation $\approx$ used in the rule* (**Term/Conv**) *is the smallest congruence on well typed terms, generated by $\longrightarrow$ which is the sum of beta $\longrightarrow_\beta$ and rewrite $\longrightarrow_R$ reductions.*
- *The notation $E \vdash \mathsf{Ind}(\Gamma^I := \Gamma^C)$:* correct *means that:*
  - $\Gamma^I = I_1 : t_1^I \ldots I_k : t_k^I$ *is the environment of inductive types*
  - $\Gamma^C = c_1 : t_1^C \ldots c_n : t_n^C$ *is the environment of inductive constructors*
  - *the positivity condition* $\mathsf{POS}_E(\Gamma^I := \Gamma^C)$, *as defined e.g. in [15], is satisfied.*

$$\frac{}{\epsilon \vdash \mathsf{ok}} \qquad\qquad \frac{E \vdash \mathsf{ok} \quad E \vdash t : s}{E; v : t \vdash \mathsf{ok}}$$

$$\frac{E \vdash \mathsf{ok} \quad E \vdash \mathsf{Ind}(\Gamma^I := \Gamma^C) : \mathsf{correct}}{E; \mathsf{Ind}(\Gamma^I := \Gamma^C) \vdash \mathsf{ok}} \qquad \frac{E \vdash \mathsf{ok} \quad E \vdash \mathsf{Rew}(\Gamma, R) : \mathsf{correct}}{E; \mathsf{Rew}(\Gamma, R) \vdash \mathsf{ok}}$$

$$\frac{E_1; v : t; E_2 \vdash \mathsf{ok}}{E_1; v : t; E_2 \vdash v : t}$$

$$\frac{E \vdash \mathsf{ok}}{E \vdash I_i : t_i^I} \qquad \frac{E \vdash \mathsf{ok}}{E \vdash c_i : t_i^C} \qquad \text{where} \quad \begin{cases} E = E_1; \mathsf{Ind}(\Gamma^I := \Gamma^C); E_2 \\ \Gamma^I = I_1 : t_1^I \dots I_n : t_n^I \\ \Gamma^C = c_1 : t_1^C \dots c_m : t_m^C \end{cases}$$

$$\frac{E \vdash \mathsf{ok}}{E \vdash f_i : t_i} \qquad \frac{E \vdash \mathsf{ok} \quad \delta : \Gamma_i \to E}{E \vdash l_i \delta \longrightarrow_R r_i \delta} \qquad \text{where} \quad \begin{cases} E = E_1; \mathsf{Rew}(\Gamma, R); E_2 \\ \Gamma = f_1 : t_1 \dots f_n : t_n \\ R = \{\Gamma_i \vdash l_i \longrightarrow r_i\}_{i=1\dots m} \end{cases}$$

(Term/Prod) $\qquad\qquad$ **(Term/Abs)** $\qquad\qquad$ **(Term/Ax)**

$$\frac{E \vdash t_1 : s_1 \quad E; v : t_1 \vdash t_2 : s_2}{E \vdash (v{:}t_1)t_2 : s_3} \qquad \frac{E; v : t_1 \vdash e : t_2 \quad E \vdash (v{:}t_1)t_2 : s}{E \vdash \lambda v{:}t_1.e : (v{:}t_1)t_2} \qquad \frac{E \vdash \mathsf{ok}}{E \vdash s_1 : s_2}$$
where $s_1, s_2, s_3 \in \mathcal{S}$ $\qquad\qquad\qquad\qquad\qquad\qquad\qquad\qquad\qquad$ where $(s_1, s_2) \in \mathcal{A}$

(Term/App) $\qquad\qquad\qquad\qquad$ **(Term/Conv)**

$$\frac{E \vdash e : (v{:}t_1)t_2 \quad E \vdash e' : t_1}{E \vdash e\,e' : t_2\{v \mapsto e'\}} \qquad \frac{E \vdash e : t \quad E \vdash t' : s \quad E \vdash t \approx t'}{E \vdash e : t'}$$

Fig. 1. Environment correctness, environment lookup and PTS rules

- *The notation* $E \vdash \mathsf{Rew}(\Gamma, R) : \mathsf{correct}$ *means that:*
  - $\Gamma = f_1 : t_1 \dots f_n : t_n$ *is the environment of function symbols with* $E \vdash t_i : s_i$
  - $R = \{\Gamma_i \vdash l_i \longrightarrow r_i\}_{i=1\dots n}$ *is the set of rewrite rules, where* Γ_i *is the environment of variables (including ? variables),* l_i *is the left-hand side and* r_i *is the right-hand side*
  - *for each rule,* $E; \Gamma_i \vdash \mathsf{ok}$
  - R *satisfies the acceptance condition* $\mathsf{ACC}_E(\Gamma; R)$ *(see below).*
- *The notation* $\delta : \Gamma \to E$ *means that* δ *is a* well-typed substitution, *i.e.* $E \vdash v\delta : t\delta$ *for all* $v : t \in \Gamma$.

As in [20,4], recursors and their reduction rules have no special status and they are supposed to be expressed by rewriting.

Assumptions. We assume that we are given a positivity condition **POS** and an acceptance condition **ACC** for definitions by rewriting. Together with the right choice of the PTS they must imply the following properties:

P1) subject reduction, i.e. $E \vdash e : t$, $E \vdash e \longrightarrow e'$ implies $E \vdash e' : t$

P2) uniqueness of types, i.e. $E \vdash e : t$, $E \vdash e : t'$ implies $E \vdash t \approx t'$.

P3) strong normalization, i.e. $E \vdash \mathsf{ok}$ implies that reductions of all well-typed terms in E are finite

P4) confluence, i.e. $E \vdash e : t$, $E \vdash e \longrightarrow^* e'$, $E \vdash e \longrightarrow^* e''$ implies $E \vdash e' \longrightarrow^* \hat{e}$ and $E \vdash e'' \longrightarrow^* \hat{e}$ for some $\hat{e}$.

These properties are usually true in all well-behaved type theories. They are for example all proved for the calculus of algebraic constructions [4], an extension of the calculus of constructions with rewriting where the General Schema is the ACC condition. We use the notation $t{\downarrow}$ for the unique normal form of t.

4   Towards Consistency and Completeness

Consistency of the calculus of constructions (resp. calculus of inductive constructions) can be shown by rejecting all cases of a hypothetical normalized proof c of $(x : *)x$ in a *closed* environment, i.e. empty environment (resp. an environment containing only inductive definitions and no axioms). Our goal is to extend the definition of closed environments to the calculus of constructions with rewriting, allowing also a certain class of definitions by rewriting.

Let us try to identify that class. If we reanalyze e in the new setting, the only new possible normal form of e is an application of a function symbol f, coming from a rewrite definition $\mathsf{Rew}(\Gamma, R)$, to some arguments in normal form. There is no obvious argument why such terms could not be proofs of $(x : *)x$, but we could complete the consistency proof if we knew that such terms were always reducible. Let us call $\mathsf{COMP}(\Gamma, R)$ the condition on rewrite definitions we are looking for, meaning that function symbols from Γ are completely defined by the given set of rules R.

Note that the completeness of f has to be checked much earlier than it is used: we use it in a given closed environment $E = E_1; \mathsf{Rew}(\Gamma, R); E_2$ but it has to be checked when f is added to the environment, i.e. in the environment E_1. It implies that completeness checking has to account for environment extension and can be performed only with respect to arguments of types whose set of normal forms would not change in the future. This is the case for arguments of inductive types.

The requirement that functions defined by rewriting are completely defined could very well be included in the condition ACC. On the other hand, the separation between ACC and COMP is motivated by the idea of working with abstract function symbols, equipped with some rewrite rules not defining them completely. For example if + from Sect. 2 were declared using only the third rewrite rule, one could develop a theory of an associative function over natural numbers.

In the next section we define COMP and provide an always terminating and sound algorithm checking whether a rewrite definition is complete.

5   Checking Completeness

The intuition behind the definitions given below is the following. A rewrite definition $\mathsf{Rew}(\Gamma, R)$ satisfies COMP (or is *complete*) if for all f in Γ, the goal $f(x_1, \ldots, x_n)$ is *covered* by R. A goal is covered if all its instances are *immediately covered*, i.e reducible by R at the root position. Following the discussion from the previous section we limit ourselves to *normalized canonical instances*, i.e. built from constructors wherever possible.

Definition 2 (Canonical form and canonical substitution). *Given a judgment $E \vdash e : t$ we say that the term e is in* canonical *form if and only if:*

- *if $t\downarrow$ is an inductive type then $e = c(e_1, \ldots, e_n)$ for some constructor c and terms $e_1, \ldots, e_n$ in canonical form*
- *otherwise e is arbitrary*

Let Δ be a variable environment and E a correct environment. We call $\delta : \Delta \to E$ canonical if for every variable $x \in \Delta$, the term $x\delta$ is canonical.

From now on, let E be a global environment and let $\mathsf{Rew}(\Gamma, R)$ be a rewrite definition such that $E \vdash \mathsf{Rew}(\Gamma, R) : \mathsf{correct}$. Let $f : (x_1 : t_1) \ldots (x_n : t_n)t \in \Gamma$.

Definition 3. *A goal is a well-typed sequent $E; \Gamma; \Delta \vdash f(e_1, \ldots, e_n)$.*

A *normalized canonical instance of the goal* $E; \Gamma; \Delta \vdash f(e_1, \ldots, e_n)$ *is a well-typed sequent* $E; \mathsf{Rew}(\Gamma, R); E' \vdash f(e_1\delta\downarrow, \ldots, e_n\delta\downarrow)$ *for any canonical substitution* $\delta : \Delta \to E; \mathsf{Rew}(\Gamma, R); E'$.

A *term e is* immediately covered *by R if there is a rule $G \vdash l \longrightarrow r$ in R and a substitution γ such that $l\gamma = e$. By obvious extension we can also write that a goal or a normalized canonical instance is immediately covered by R.*

A *goal is* covered *by R if all its normalized canonical instances are immediately covered.*

Note that, formally, a normalized canonical instance is not a goal. The difference is that the conversion corresponding to the environment of an instance contains reductions defined by R, while the one of a goal does not.

Definition 4 (Complete definition). *A rewrite definition $\mathsf{Rew}(\Gamma; R)$ is complete in the environment E, which is denoted by $\mathsf{COMP}_E(\Gamma; R)$, if and only if for all function symbols $f : (x_1 : t_1) \ldots (x_n : t_n)t \in \Gamma$ the goal $E; \Gamma; x_1 : t_1; \ldots; x_n : t_n \vdash f(x_1, \ldots, x_n)$ is covered by R.*

Example 1. The terms (S O), λx:nat.x and (Node O Leaf true O Leaf) are canonical, while (O + O) and (Node nA A b O Leaf) are not. Given the definition of rotr from Sect. 2 consider the following terms:

$$t_1 = \mathsf{rotr} \ (\mathsf{S} \ (\mathsf{nA} + \mathsf{nC})) \ (\mathsf{Node} \ \mathsf{nA} \ \mathsf{A} \ \mathsf{b} \ \mathsf{nC} \ \mathsf{C})$$
$$t_2 = \mathsf{rotr} \ (\mathsf{S} \ \mathsf{O}) \ (\mathsf{Node} \ \mathsf{O} \ \mathsf{Leaf} \ \mathsf{true} \ \mathsf{O} \ \mathsf{Leaf})$$

Both (with their respective environments) are goals for rotr, and t_2 (with a slightly different environment) is also a normalized canonical instance of t_1. The goal t_1 is not immediately covered, but its instance t_2 is, as it is head-reducible by the second rule defining rotr. Since other instances of t_1 are also immediately covered, the goal is covered (see Example 3).

5.1 Splitting

The algorithm that we present in Sect. 5.3 checks that a goal is covered using successive splitting, i.e. replacement of variables of inductive types by constructor patterns. In presence of dependent types not all constructors can be put in every place. Consider the first rule of the definition of rotr. It is clear that only Leaf can replace t and in order to decide so one must use unification modulo conversion.

Even though in general this problem is undecidable, we assume the existence of a partial unification algorithm Alg, which given a unification problem U, returns a substitution γ, $\perp$ or ?. If it returns a substitution γ then γ is the most general unifier of U and if it returns $\perp$, U has no unifier; ? means that the problem is too difficult for the algorithm (for the exact definitions we refer the reader to [21]). An example of such a partial unification algorithm is constructor unification, that is first-order unification with constructors and type constructors as rigid symbols, answering ? whenever one compares a non-trivial pair of terms involving non-rigid symbols.

In the definitions below, we use $Ran(\gamma)$ for the variable part of the codomain of a substitution γ.

Definition 5 (Splitting). *Let* $E; \Gamma; \Delta \vdash f(e)$ *be a goal. A variable* x *is a* splitting variable *if* $x : t \in \Delta$ *and* $t \downarrow = Iu$ *for some inductive type* $I \in E$.

A splitting operation considers all constructors c *of the inductive type* I *and for each of them constructs the following unification problem* U_c:

$$E; \Gamma, \ \Delta; \Delta_c \vdash x = c(z_1, \dots z_k) \qquad E; \Gamma, \ \Delta; \Delta_c \vdash Iu = Iw$$

where $c : (z_1 : Z_1) \dots (z_k : Z_k).Iw$ *and* $\Delta_c = z_1 : Z_1, \dots, z_k : Z_k$.

If $Alg(U_c) \neq$? *for all* c, *the splitting is successful. In that case, let* $Sp(x) = \{\sigma_c \mid \sigma_c = Alg(U_c) \land Alg(U_c) \neq \perp\}$. *The result of splitting is the set of goals* $\{E; \Gamma; Ran(\sigma_c) \vdash f(e)\sigma_c\}_{\sigma_c \in Sp(x)}$.

If $Alg(U_c) =$? *for some* c, *the splitting fails.*

Example 2. If one splits the goal `rotr n t` along the variable n, one gets two goals: `rotr O t` and `rotr (S m) t`. The first one is immediately covered by the first rule for `rotr` and if we split the second one along t, the `Leaf` case is impossible, because `tree O` does not unify with `tree (S m)` and the `Node` case gives `rotr (S (nA + nC)) (Node nA A b nC C)`.

The following lemma states the correctness of splitting, i.e. that splitting does not decrease the set of normalized canonical instances. Note that the lemma would also hold if we had a unification algorithm returning an arbitrary set of most general solutions, but in order for the coverage checking algorithm to terminate the set of goals resulting from splitting must be finite.

Lemma 1. *Let* $E; \Gamma; \Delta \vdash f(e)$ *be a coverage goal and let* $\{E; \Gamma; Ran(\sigma_c) \vdash f(e)\sigma_c\}_{\sigma_c \in Sp(x)}$ *be the result of successful splitting along* $x : Iu \in \Delta$. *Then every normalized canonical instance of* $E; \Gamma; \Delta \vdash f(e)$ *is a normalized canonical instance of* $E; \Gamma; Ran(\sigma_c) \vdash f(e)\sigma_c$ *for some* $\sigma_c \in Sp(x)$.

5.2 Preservation of Reducibility

Although one would expect that an immediately covered goal is also covered, it is not always true, even for confluent systems. In fact we need a property of critical pairs that is stronger than just joinability. Let us suppose that `or : bool` $\to$ `bool` $\to$ `bool` is defined by four rules by cases over `true` and `false` and that `if : bool` $\to$ `bool` $\to$ `bool` $\to$ `bool` is defined by two rules by cases on the first argument.

```
Inductive I : bool → Set := C : forall b:bool, I (or b b).
Symbol f:   forall b:bool, I b → bool
Rules
  f (or b b) (C b) ⟶ if b (f true (C true)) (f false (C false))
```

In the example presented above all expressions used in types and rules are in normal form, all critical pairs are joinable, the system is terminating, and splitting of f b i along i results in the only reducible goal f (or b b) (C b). In spite of that f is not completely defined, as f true (C true) is a normalized canonical instance of f (or b b) (C b) and it is not reducible. In order to know that an immediately covered goal is always covered we need one more condition on rewrite rules, called preservation of reducibility.

Definition 6. *Definition by rewriting* Rew(Γ, R) *preserves reducibility in an environment E if for every critical pair $\langle f(u), r\delta \rangle$ of a rule $G_1 \vdash f(e) \longrightarrow r$ in R with a rule $G_2 \vdash g \longrightarrow d$ coming from R or from some other rewrite definition in E, the term $f(u{\downarrow})$ is immediately covered by R.*

Note that by using ? variables in rewrite rules one can get rid of (some) critical pairs and hence make a definition by rewriting satisfy this property. In the example above one could write f ? (C b) as the left-hand side (which would make the system non-terminating, but that is another story). Of course all orthogonal rewrite systems, in particular inductive elimination schemes, as defined in [22], preserve reducibility.

Lemma 2. *Let* Rew(Γ, R) *preserve reducibility in an environment E and let $E; \Gamma; \Delta \vdash f(e)$ be a goal. If it is immediately covered then it is covered.*

5.3   Coverage Checking Algorithm

In this section we present an algorithm checking whether a set of goals is covered by the given set of rewrite rules. The algorithm is correct only for definitions that preserve reducibility. The algorithm, in a loop, picks a goal, checks whether it is immediately covered, and if not, splits the goal replacing it by the subgoals resulting from splitting. In order to ensure termination splitting is limited to *safe splitting variables*. Intuitively, a splitting variable is safe if it lies within the contour of the left-hand side of some rule when we superpose the tree representation of the left-hand side with the tree representation of the goal. The number of nodes that have to be added to the goal in order to fill the tree of the left-hand side is called a distance, and a sum of distances over all rules is called a measure. Since the measures of goals resulting from splitting are smaller than the measure of the original goal, the coverage checking algorithm terminates.

Safe splitting variables used in the algorithm are computed by the splitting matching procedure: $SV(\phi, R)$ is the set of safe splitting variables for the goal ϕ along left-hand sides of rules from R.

We refer the reader to [21] for the formal definitions of the notions mentioned above and the corresponding lemmas.

Definition 7 (Coverage checking algorithm). *Let W be a set of pairs consisting of a goal and a set of safe variables of that goal along left-hand sides of rules from R and let CE be a set of goals. The coverage checking algorithm works as follows:*

Initialize
$$W = \{(E; \Gamma; x_1 : t_1; \ldots; x_n : t_n \vdash f(x_1, \ldots, x_n), \quad SV(f(x_1, \ldots, x_n), R))\}$$
$$CE = \emptyset$$

Repeat

1. *choose a pair* (ϕ, X) *from* W,
2. *if* ϕ *is immediately covered by one of the rules from* R *then*
   $$W := W \setminus \{(\phi, X)\}$$
3. *otherwise*
   (a) *if* $X = \emptyset$ *then* $W := W \setminus \{(\phi, X)\}$, $CE := CE \cup \{\phi\}$
   (b) *otherwise choose* $x \in X$; *split* ϕ *along* x
       i. *if splitting is successful and returns* $\{\phi_1 \ldots \phi_n\}$ *then*
          $$W := W \setminus \{(\phi, X)\} \cup \{(\phi_i, SV(\phi_i, R))\}_{i=1\ldots n},$$
       ii. *otherwise* $W := W \setminus \{(\phi, X)\} \cup \{(\phi, X \setminus \{x\})\}$

until $W = \emptyset$

Lemma 3. *If* $\mathsf{Rew}(\Gamma, R)$ *preserves reducibility and the algorithm stops with* $CE = \emptyset$ *then the initial goal is covered.*

Example 3. The beginning of a possible run of the algorithm for the function `rotr` is presented already in Example 2. Both splitting operations are performed on safe variables, as required. We are left with the remaining goal `rotr (S (nA + nC))` `(Node nA A b nC C)`. Splitting along A results in:

```
rotr (S (O + nC)) (Node O Leaf b nC C)
rotr (S((S(nX+nZ))+nC)) (Node (S(nX+xZ)) (Node nX X y nZ Z) b nC C)
```

immediately covered by the second and the third rule respectively.

Since we started with the initial goal `rotr n t` and since the definition of `rotr` preserves reducibility, it is complete.

When the coverage checking algorithm stops with $CE \neq \emptyset$, we cannot deduce that R is complete. The set CE contains potential counterexamples. They can be true counterexamples, false counterexamples, or goals for which splitting failed along all safe variables, due to incompleteness of the unification algorithm. In some cases further splitting of a false counterexample may result in reducible goals or in the elimination of the goal as uninhabited, but it may also loop. Some solutions preventing looping (finitary splitting) can be found in [16].

Unfortunately splitting failure due to incompleteness of the unification may happen while checking coverage of a definition by case analysis over complex dependent inductive types (for example trees of size 2), even if rules for all constructors are given. Therefore, it is advisable to add a second phase to our algorithm, which would treat undefined output of unification as success. Using this second phase of the algorithm, one can accept all definitions by case analysis that can be written in Coq.

6   Completeness Implies Canonicity Implies Consistency

It follows that completeness of definitions by rewriting guarantees canonicity and logical consistency.

Definition 8. *An environment E is* closed *if and only if it contains only inductive definitions and complete definitions by rewriting, i.e. for each partition of E into E_1; $\mathsf{Rew}(\Gamma, R)$; E_2 the condition $\mathsf{COMP}_{E_1}(\Gamma, R)$ is satisfied.*

Lemma 4 (Canonicity). *Let E be a closed environment. If $E \vdash e : t$ and e is in normal form then e is canonical.*

Theorem 1. *Every closed environment is consistent.*

Proof. Let E be a closed environment. Suppose that $E \vdash e : (x : \star)x$. Since $E \vdash \mathsf{ok}$ and $E \vdash \mathsf{Ind}(\mathtt{False} : \star :—) : \mathsf{correct}$ we have $E' \vdash \mathsf{ok}$ where $E' = E; \mathsf{Ind}(\mathtt{False} : \star :=)$. Moreover E' is a closed environment.

Hence, we have $E' \vdash e\,\mathtt{False} : \mathtt{False}$. By Lemma 4, the normal form of $e\,\mathtt{False}$ is canonical. Since $\mathtt{False}$ has no constructors, this is impossible.

7 Conclusions and Related Work

In this paper we study consistency of the calculus of constructions with rewriting. More precisely, we propose a formal system extending an arbitrary PTS with inductive definitions and definitions by rewriting. Assuming that suitable positivity and acceptance conditions guarantee termination and confluence, we formalize the notion of complete definitions by rewriting. We show that in every environment consisting only of inductive definitions and complete definition by rewriting there is no proof of $(x : \star)x$. Moreover, we present a sound and terminating algorithm for checking completeness of definitions. It is necessarily incomplete, since in presence of dependent types emptiness of types trivially reduces to completeness and the former is undecidable.

Our coverage checking algorithm resembles the one proposed by Coquand in [10] for Martin-Löf type theory and used by McBride for his OLEG calculus [14]. In these works the procedure consisting in successive case-splittings is used to interactively built pattern matching equations, or to check that a given set of equations can be built this way. Unlike in our paper, Coquand and McBride do not have to worry whether all instances of a reducible subgoal are reducible. Indeed, in [10] pattern matching equations are meant to be applied to terms modulo conversion, and in [14] equations (or rather the order of splittings in the successful run of the coverage checking procedure) serve as a guideline to construct an OLEG term verifying the equations. Equations themselves are never used for reduction and the constructed term reduces according to existing rules.

In our paper rewrite rules are matched against terms modulo α. Rewriting has to be confluent, strongly normalizing and has to preserve reducibility. Under these assumptions we can prove completeness for all examples from [10] and for the class of pattern matching equations considered in [14]. In particular we can deal with elimination rules for inductive types and with Streicher's axiom K stating that all proofs of $(\mathtt{eq}\,A\,\mathtt{a}\,\mathtt{a})$ are equal. Moreover, we can accept definitions which depart from standard pattern matching, like $\mathtt{rotr}$ and $+$ (for the axiom K and more examples we refer the reader to [21]).

The formal presentation of our algorithm is directly inspired by the recent work of Pfenning and Schürmann [16]. A motivation for that paper was to verify that a logic program in the Twelf prover covers all possible cases. In LF, the base calculus of Twelf, there is no polymorphism, no rewriting and conversion is modulo $\beta\eta$. The authors use higher-order matching modulo $\beta\eta$, which is decidable for patterns of Miller and strict patterns. Moreover, since all types and function symbols are known in advance, the coverage is checked with respect to all available function symbols. In our paper, conversion contains rewriting and it cannot be used for matching; instead we use matching modulo α. This simplifies the algorithm searching for safe splitting variables, but on the other hand it does not fit well with instantiation and normalization. To overcome this problem we introduce the notions of normalized canonical instance and preservation of reducibility which were not present in previously mentioned papers. Finally, since the sets of function symbols and rewrite rules grow as the environment extends, coverage is checked with respect to constructors only.

Even though the worst-case complexity of the coverage checking is clearly exponential, for practical examples the algorithm should be quite efficient. It is very similar in spirit to the algorithms checking exhaustiveness of definitions by pattern matching in functional programming languages and these are known to work effectively in practice.

An important issue which is not addressed in this paper is to know how much we extend conversion. Of course it depends on the choice of conditions ACC and POS and on the unification algorithm used for coverage checking. In particular, some of the definitions by pattern matching can be encoded by recursors [11], so if ACC is strict, we may have no extension at all. In general there seems to be at least two kinds of extensions. The first are non-standard elimination rules for inductive types, but the work of McBride shows that the axiom K is sufficient to encode all other definitions by pattern matching considered by Coquand. The second are additional rules which extend a definition by pattern matching (like associativity for $+$). It is known that for first-order rewriting, these rules are inductive consequences of the pattern matching ones, i.e. all their canonical instances are satisfied as equations (Thm. 7.6.5 in [17]). Unfortunately, this is no longer true for higher-order rules over inductive types with functional arguments. Nevertheless we believe that such rules are also some sort of inductive consequences of the pattern matching part.

Our completeness condition COMP verifies closure properties defined in [7,8]. Hence, it is adequate for a smooth integration of rewriting with the module system implemented recently in Coq.

References

1. Franco Barbanera, Maribel Fernández, and Herman Geuvers. Modularity of strong normalization in the algebraic-λ-cube. *Journal of Functional Programming*, 7(6):613–660, 1997.
2. Henk Barendregt. Lambda calculi with types. In S. Abramsky, D. M. Gabbay, and T. S. E. Maibaum, editors, *Handbook of Logic in Computer Science*, vol. 2, chap. 2, pp. 117–309. Oxford University Press, 1992.
3. Bruno Barras and Benjamin Grégoire. On the role of type decorations in the calculus of inductive constructions. In C.-H. Luke Ong, editor, *Proc. of CSL'05, LNCS* 3634, pp. 151–166. Springer, 2005
4. Frédéric Blanqui. Definitions by rewriting in the Calculus of Constructions. *Mathematical Structures in Computer Science*, 15(1):37–92, 2005.

5. Frédéric Blanqui, Jean-Pierre Jouannaud, and Mitsuhiro Okada. The Calculus of Algebraic Constructions. In P. Narendran and M. Rusinowitch, editors, *Proc. of RTA'99*, *LNCS* 1631, pp. 301–316. Springer, 1999

6. Edwin Brady, Connor McBride, and James McKinna. Inductive families need not store their indices. In S. Berardi, M. Coppo, and F. Damiani, editors, *TYPES 2003, Revised Selected Papers*, *LNCS* 3085, pp. 115–129. Springer, 2004.

7. Jacek Chrząszcz. Modules in Coq are and will be correct. In S. Berardi, M. Coppo, and F. Damiani, editors, *TYPES 2003, Revised Selected Papers*, *LNCS* 3085, pp. 130–146. Springer, 2004.

8. Jacek Chrząszcz. *Modules in Type Theory with Generative Definitions*. PhD thesis, Warsaw Univerity and University of Paris-Sud, Jan 2004.

9. The Coq proof assistant. http://coq.inria.fr/.

10. Thierry Coquand. Pattern matching with dependent types. In *Proceedings of the Workshop on Types for Proofs and Programs*, pp. 71–83, Båstad, Sweden, 1992.

11. Cristina Cornes. *Conception d'un langage de haut niveau de réprésentation de preuves*. PhD thesis, Université Paris VII, 1997.

12. J. V. Guttag and J. J. Horning. The algebraic specification of abstract data types. *Acta Informatica*, 10:27–52, 1978.

13. Emmanuel Kounalis. Completeness in data type specifications. In *Proc. of EUROCAL 85*, *LNCS* 204, pp. 348–362. Springer-Verlag, 1985.

14. Conor McBride. *Dependently Typed Functional Programs and Their Proofs*. PhD thesis, University of Edinburgh, 1999.

15. Christine Paulin-Mohring. Inductive definitions in the system Coq: Rules and properties. In M. Bezem and J. F. Groote, editors, *Proc. of TLCA'93*, *LNCS* 664, pp. 328–345. Springer-Verlag, 1993

16. Carsten Schürmann and Frank Pfenning. A coverage checking algorithm for LF. In D. Basin and B. Wolff, editors, *Proc. of TPHOLs'03*, *LNCS* 2758, pp. 120–135. Springer, 2003.

17. Terese, editor. *Term Rewriting Systems*, volume 55 of *Cambridge Tracts in Theoretical Computer Science*. Cambridge University Press, 2003.

18. J.-J. Thiel. Stop loosing sleep over incomplete specifications. In *Proc. of POPL'84*, pp. 76–82. ACM Press, 1984.

19. Daria Walukiewicz-Chrząszcz. Termination of rewriting in the calculus of constructions. *Journal of Functional Programming*, 13(2):339–414, 2003.

20. Daria Walukiewicz-Chrząszcz. *Termination of Rewriting in the Calculus of Constructions*. PhD thesis, Warsaw University and University Paris XI, 2003.

21. Daria Walukiewicz-Chrząszcz and Jacek Chrząszcz. Consistency and completeness of rewriting in the calculus of constructions. Available for download at http://www.mimuw.edu.pl/~chrzaszcz/papers/.

22. Benjamin Werner. *Méta-théorie du Calcul des Constructions Inductives*. PhD thesis, Université Paris 7, 1994.

Specifying and Reasoning About
Dynamic Access-Control Policies

Daniel J. Dougherty[1], Kathi Fisler[1], and Shriram Krishnamurthi[2]

[1] Department of Computer Science, WPI
[2] Computer Science Department, Brown University
dd@cs.wpi.edu, kfisler@cs.wpi.edu, sk@cs.brown.edu

Abstract. Access-control policies have grown from simple matrices to non-trivial specifications written in sophisticated languages. The increasing complexity of these policies demands correspondingly strong automated reasoning techniques for understanding and debugging them. The need for these techniques is even more pressing given the rich and dynamic nature of the environments in which these policies evaluate. We define a framework to represent the behavior of access-control policies in a dynamic environment. We then specify several interesting, decidable analyses using first-order temporal logic. Our work illustrates the subtle interplay between logical and state-based methods, particularly in the presence of three-valued policies. We also define a notion of policy equivalence that is especially useful for modular reasoning.

1 Introduction

Access control is an important component of system security. Access-control policies capture rules that govern access to data or program operations. In the classical framework [28], a policy maps each user, resource and action to a decision. The policy is then consulted whenever a particular user wants to perform an action on a resource. The information that defines this user, resource, and action forms an access *request*.

Modern applications increasingly express policies in domain-specific languages, such as the industrially popular language XACML [33], and consult them through a policy-enforcement engine. Separating the policy from the program in this manner has several important consequences: it allows the same policy to be used with multiple applications, it enables non-programmers to develop and maintain policies, and it fosters rich mechanisms for combining policy modules [9,33] derived from different, even geographically distributed, entities. (In XACML, a typical combiner is "a decision by one module to deny overrides decisions by all other modules".) A university administration can, for example, author a common policy for campus building ID-card locks; each department can individually author a policy covering its unique situations (such as after-hours access for undergraduate research assistants); and an appropriate policy combiner can mediate the decisions of the two sub-policies.

Access-control policies are hard to get right. Our appreciation for the difficulty of authoring policies stems from our experience maintaining and debugging the policies from a highly-configurable commercial conference paper manager called CONTINUE [27]. Almost all interesting bugs in CONTINUE have related to access control in some form.

U. Furbach and N. Shankar (Eds.): IJCAR 2006, LNAI 4130, pp. 632–646, 2006.

1. During the submission phase, an author may submit a paper
2. During the review phase, reviewer r may submit a review for paper p if r is assigned to review p
3. During the meeting phase, reviewer r can read the scores for paper p if r has submitted a review for p
4. Authors may never read scores

1. During the submission phase, an author may submit a paper
2. During the review phase, reviewer r may submit a review for paper p if r is not conflicted with p
3. During the meeting phase, reviewer r can read the scores for paper p if r has submitted a review for p and r is not conflicted with p
4. Authors may never read scores

Fig. 1. Two candidate policies for controlling access to review scores

Many sources of complexity make policies difficult to author. Combiners are one natural cause of difficulty. Size is another factor: policies in realistic applications can govern hundreds of actions, resources, and classes of users (called roles). Perhaps most significantly, decisions depend on more than just the information in the access request. Consider the policy governing PC member access to conference paper reviews: a reviewer assigned to a paper may be required to submit his own review before being allowed to read those of others. The conference manager software maintains the information about which reviewers have submitted reviews for which papers; the policy engine must be able to consult that information when responding to an access request. Such information forms the *environment* of the policy. As this simple example shows, environment data may be highly dynamic and affected by user actions.

What is the impact of the environment? Figure 1 shows two candidate policies governing access to review scores for papers in a conference manager. Which policy should we choose? The policies differ syntactically only in rules 2 and 3 but, if the application allows conflict-of-interest to change after paper assignment, the *semantic* change is considerable. Imagine a reviewer who is initially assigned a paper and submits a review, but the PC chair later learns that the reviewer was conflicted with the paper. By the policy on the left, the reviewer can read the scores for the conflicted paper.

As the example shows, such leaks are not evident from the policy document alone: they require consideration of the dynamic environment. Fixing these, however, requires edits to the *policy*, not the program. This suggests that analysis should focus on the policy, but treat information from the program as part of the policy's environment.

Whereas existing work on reasoning about access-control policies models the environment only lightly, if at all, this paper presents formal analyses for access-control policies in their dynamic environments. We propose a new mathematical model of policies, their environments, and the interactions between them. We then propose analyses that handle many common scenarios, focusing on two core problems: *goal reachability* and *contextual policy containment*. Such analyses require a combination of relational reasoning (to handle interesting policies) and temporal reasoning (for the environments). In addition, the analyses must support realistic development scenarios for policies, such as modular policy authoring and upgrading. A recurring theme in this work is the interplay between techniques for defining these analyses originating from formal verification and from databases.

Permit(a, submit-paper, p) :– author(a) , paper(p) , phase(submission)
Permit(r, submit-review, p) :– reviewer(r) , paper(p), assigned(r, p) , phase(review)
Permit(r, read-scores, p) :– reviewer(r) , paper(p), has-reviewed(r, p) , phase(meeting)
Deny(a, read-scores, p) :– author(a) , paper(p)

Fig. 2. Formal model of policy on left in Figure 1

2 Modeling Policies and Their Dynamic Environments

The sample policies in Figure 1 require information such as the assignment of papers to reviewers and conflicts of interest between reviewers and papers. Policies are declarative statements over data from requests and over relations that capture information gathered by the application (such as conflict-of-interest data). Following many other policy models [5,12,23,29,30], we capture policies as Datalog programs.

A Datalog rule is an expression of the form

$$R_0(\vec{u}_0) :\!- R_1(\vec{u}_1), \ldots, R_n(\vec{u}_n)$$

where the R_i are relation names, or *predicates*, and the $\vec{u}_i$ are (possibly empty) tuples of variables and constants. The *head* of the rule is $R_0(\vec{u}_0)$, and the sequence of formulas on the right hand side is the *body* of the rule. Given a set of Datalog rules, a predicate occurring only in the bodies of rules is called *extensional* and a predicate occurring in the head of some rule is called *intentional*. For a set of rules P, $edb(P)$ and $idb(P)$ denote the extensional and intentional predicates of P, respectively. A policy is *recursive* if some idb appears in a rule body. The *signature* of P, Σ_P, is $edb(P) \cup idb(P)$. A set of *facts* is a set of closed atomic formulas over a signature Σ.

Definition 1. Let Subjects, Actions, and Resources each be sorts. Let Σ be a first-order relational signature including at least the two distinguished ternary predicates Permit and Deny of type Subjects $\times$ Actions $\times$ Resources.[1] A *policy rule* over Σ is a Datalog rule over Σ whose head is either Permit or Deny. A *policy* over Σ is a set of policy rules over Σ.

That is, a policy is a set of Datalog rules whose idb predicates are amongst Permit and Deny. We use an explicit Deny relation following the XACML policy language [33], rather than interpret deny as the negation of permit, to allow a policy to not apply to some requests. The distinction between denial and non-applicability is useful for decomposing policies into sub-policies that only cover pertinent requests, as in the university example of the Introduction. (Bertino *et al.* discuss implications of supporting negated decisions [8].) We point out the consequences of this decision on our models and analyses as they arise in the paper.

Figure 2 shows a sample policy. The policy governs the use of the actions submit-paper, submit-review, and read-scores based on information from the environment.

---

[1] Subjects, Actions, and Resources could have more structure, such as tuples to model resources with attributes or sets of Subjects to model joint actions. Such changes do not affect our theoretical foundations, so we use the atomic versions to simplify the presentation.

What is an environment? A principal source of environment information is the program (e.g., which reviewers have submitted papers). Some information comes from end-users (such as credentials). The run-time system also provides information (such as the current time), and some information comes from the policy framework itself (in role-based access control, for example, policies operate under assignments of users to roles and under hierarchies of permission inheritance among roles). These diverse sources suggest that (i) the environment must be a transition system, to model the program's execution and the passage of time, and (ii) each state must consist of an instance of the edb relations referred to by the policy. This model is therefore in the family of recent work on representing programs as transitions over relations [2,13,41,44]. Because our model is general enough to handle most forms of environment information, we focus on the general model and ignore finer distinctions in the rest of this paper.

Concretely, consider the policy in Figure 2. The predicate has-reviewed tracks which reviewers have submitted reviews for which papers. When a reviewer r submits a review for paper p, the tuple $\langle r, p \rangle$ is added to has-reviewed in the policy environment. The phase predicate tracks the current phase of the reviewing process. When the PC chair ends the review phase and starts the program committee meeting, the fact phase(review) is removed from the set of current facts and phase(meeting) is added.

Semantically, at any given time the set $\mathbf{E}$ of facts in the environment relevant to the policy rules constitute an instance over the edb relations of P. Evaluation of access requests, such as Permit(s,a,r), can thus be viewed as asking for the truth of the sentence Permit(s,a,r) in this structure. More constructively, it is well-known that a set P of Datalog rules defines a monotone operator on the instances over Σ_P. In this vein, P inductively defines instances of idb names in terms of $\mathbf{E}$, as follows. Treat $\mathbf{E}$ as an instance over Σ_P by adding empty relations for the idb names, and take the least fixedpoint of the operator determined by P starting with $\mathbf{E}$. The idb relations in the resulting instance are the defined relations. We call the generated idb facts the *access tables* of P with respect to $\mathbf{E}$ (denoted $P(\mathbf{E})$). Negation can be introduced into the framework with some conceptual and computational cost [1].

Transitions in the policy's environment are triggered by various conditions. Some arise from the passage of time (such as the passing of the submission deadline moving the conference into the review phase). Others arise from user or program actions (once an author submits a review, for example, he can read other reviews for the same paper). We use the generic term *event* for all of these conditions, and assume a signature of events that can label transitions in the environment:

Definition 2. Given an event signature Σ_{EV}, an *event* is a closed instance of one predicate or constant in Σ_{EV}. An *environment model* over a signature Σ relative to event signature Σ_{EV} is a state machine $\mathcal{V}$ whose states are relational structures over Σ and whose transitions are labeled with events from Σ_{EV}.

A policy interacts with its dynamic environment by consulting facts in the environment and potentially constraining certain actions in the environment. The latter captures the influence of policy decisions on an application that uses it (recall that the policy's environment includes the model of the application). We model such interactions through events that share the same names as actions in policy requests. For example, a transition labeled submit-review(Alice,paper1) would correspond to a request sent to the policy.

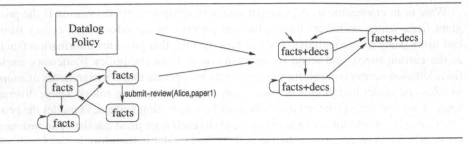

Fig. 3. Combining an environment model and a policy into a dynamic access model

Not all events need to be governed by the policy. To avoid ambiguity, we require that all predicates that appear in both Σ_{EV} and the Actions sort of the policy have the type Subjects $\times$ Resources in Σ_{EV}.

A policy and an environment model for the policy's dynamic environment combine to form a state machine over access tables, as shown in figure 3 (where "decs" is short for "decisions"). Intuitively, the access tables arise from applying the policy to the facts at each state of the environment model. The transitions are a subset of those in the environment model. Transitions whose event labels are policy actions are kept if the request defined by that event yields **Permit** in the source state of the transition, and removed if the request yields **Deny**. Some transitions may be labeled with policy actions for which their source state yields neither **Permit** nor **Deny**. Applications must determine whether to permit or deny such actions. Rather than fix an interpretation, we assume that an application specifies which transitions should be treated as denied in the absence of a policy decision. This expectation is reasonable because an application queries the policy engine for decisions and acts on the responses. We use the term *policy context* for a pair containing an environment model and a subset of its transitions, denoted $C = \langle \mathcal{V}, \mathcal{E} \rangle$, where $\mathcal{E}$ is the set of transitions that the application treats as defaulting to deny.

Definition 3. Let P be a policy, $\mathcal{V}$ be an environment model over Σ_P and $C = \langle \mathcal{V}, \mathcal{E} \rangle$ be a policy context. The *dynamic access model* for P, $\mathcal{V}$, and $\mathcal{E}$ is the state machine $\mathcal{D}$ obtained by

- augmenting each state q of $\mathcal{V}$ with the access tables from evaluating P at q; then
- eliminating transitions t that are labeled with policy actions such that (i) P does not yield **Permit**, and (ii) either P yields **Deny** or t is in $\mathcal{E}$, and
- eliminating unreachable states.

We use the term (C, P)-*accessible* for states in $\mathcal{D}$. We say "accessible" rather than "reachable" to connote the influence of the policy: states in $\mathcal{D}$ are reached only by securing the permission of the <u>access</u>-control policy.

Dynamic access models satisfy the definition of environment models. This allows incremental construction of dynamic access models from a series of policy modules. The definition assumes that the policy will not yield both **Permit** and **Deny** for any request considered in the second clause. If this assumption is violated, we say the policy has no model. The subsequent results in this paper assume that policies have models.

The following remark will be useful later.

Remark 4. Let $C = \langle \mathcal{V}, \emptyset \rangle$ be a policy context with an empty set of default-deny transitions and let P and P' be policies. Then any state which is $(C, P \cup P')$-accessible is (C, P)-accessible.

Ideally, environment models would be at least partially derived from applications. Standard techniques such as abstract interpretation [11] address this problem. Such techniques are commonly used in software verification, and are not discussed further in this paper. In general, we expect that finite models over-approximate their original infinite models, so that all sets of facts reachable in the original model remain reachable in the abstracted model.

3 Analyzing and Comparing Policies

Formal analyses can answer many useful questions about policies. Two fundamental analyses are *safety* (does a policy prohibit users from doing something undesirable) and *availability* (does a policy permit a user to do something that they are allowed to do). Both of these depend on the dynamic environment and resemble properties common to model checking.

   Policy authors also need the ability to compare policies in the absence of formal properties. Policies require upgrades and revisions just as programs do. Authors need to know that their policies implement expected changes, but more importantly, that the change did not yield *unanticipated* changes to decisions. Property-based verification is of limited use for this problem as it would require the policy author to write properties expressing the unanticipated changes. Analyses that compare policies and provide insights into the requests on which they yield different decisions are therefore crucial. This section formalizes analyses both on single-policies and for comparing policies.

3.1 Goal Reachability

The analyses for safety and availability (a form of liveness) share a similar structure: they ask whether there is some accessible state in the dynamic access model which satisfies some boolean expression over policy facts. Checking whether a policy allows authors to read review scores, for example, amounts to finding an accessible state satisfying the formula

$$\exists x_1 x_2.(\mathsf{Permit}(x_1, \text{read-scores}, x_2) \wedge \mathsf{author}(x_1) \wedge \mathsf{paper}(x_2)).$$

We use the term *goal reachability* for this common analysis problem, where a goal is formally defined as follows:

Definition 5. An *n-ary goal* is a sentence of the form $\exists x_1 \ldots x_n . A$, where A is a Boolean combination of atomic formulas over Σ_P. A goal is *conjunctive* if A is a conjunction of edbs. A goal is (C, P)-*reachable* if it is satisfied in a (C, P)-accessible state.

The formulas that capture goals do not interleave quantifiers and temporal operators. When formulas do interleave these, the logic gets complicated if the domains of the structures at different states are allowed to vary (this phenomenon is familiar from predicate modal logic). For problems that require such formulas, FO-LTL is a sublanguage of linear predicate temporal logic that avoids the difficulty with varying-domain models, yet is rich enough to express many properties of interest [13,41].

Goal reachability combines database query evaluation and reachability analysis. The body of a goal is precisely a database query: to evaluate the goal at a particular state in a model is to evaluate the associated Boolean query on the database of facts at that state. Model checking algorithms for first-order temporal logics subsume this problem [13,41]. Given that goal reachability is a very useful and special case of first-order model checking, however, it is worth understanding the complexity of goal checking. Although checking the truth of an arbitrary first-order sentence in a finite model is PSPACE-complete, the result of any fixed Datalog query can be computed in polynomial time in the size of the database, and the result of any fixed *conjunctive* query over a database Q can be computed in space $O(\log |Q|)$ [42]. Strategies for efficient evaluation of Datalog queries have been much-studied [1], particularly in the case of of conjunctive queries, resulting in many fast evaluation techniques [16].

The following theorem records an upper bound on the asymptotic complexity of deciding goal reachability in models with fixed domains.

Theorem 6. *Let $\mathcal{D}$ be a finite dynamic access model with n states, each of which has the same finite domain of size d. Reachability in $\mathcal{D}$ of a fixed goal G can be checked in time polynomial in n and d. If G is a conjunctive goal then reachability can be checked in nondeterministic logspace in the size of $\mathcal{D}$.*

Proof. Each state q of $\mathcal{D}$ can be considered as a database Q over the schema given by the signature of the policy. For a fixed signature the size of Q is bounded by a polynomial in d. Hence the satisfiability of a goal formula at a given state can be computed in polynomial time in d. We then use the fact that reachability between nodes in a directed graph is in NLOGSPACE [24] and so requires time polynomial in n. When the goal is conjunctive, we require NLOGSPACE to check satisfiability of a goal formula at a given state. Hence, the entire goal reachability test can be done in NLOGSPACE.   □

3.2 Contextual Policy Containment

Intuitively, policy containment asks whether one policy is more permissive than another. For example, we could say that policy P_2 subsumes the decisions of policy P_1 if every permitted request under P_1 is permitted under P_2 and every denied request under P_2 is denied under P_1. Whether a request is permitted or denied in a policy, though, depends on the set of facts that might support the request. We can exploit our environment model to restrict attention to those sets of facts that are accessible in the environment. This gives rise to the following formal definition of contextual policy containment:

Definition 7. Let $P(Q)(\text{Permit})$ denote the Permit table defined by policy P over a set of facts Q (and similarly for $P(Q)(\text{Deny})$). P_2 *contains* P_1 *in context* C, written $P_1 \preceq^C P_2$, if for all instances Q of edb and idb facts in (C, P_1)-accessible states,

$$P_1(Q)(\text{Permit}) \subseteq P_2(Q)(\text{Permit}) \quad \text{and} \quad P_2(Q)(\text{Deny}) \subseteq P_1(Q)(\text{Deny}).$$

P_1 and P_2 are *contextually equivalent* if $P_1 \preceq^C P_2$ and $P_2 \preceq^C P_1$.

A subtlety in comparing the semantics of two polices arises due to the fact that changing policies can result in a change in the accessibility relation in a dynamic access model: which states should we examine? The following lemma justifies the choice made in Definition 7.

Lemma 8. *If $P_1 \leq^C P_2$, then every (C, P_1)-accessible state is (C, P_2)-accessible.*

Proof. We induct over the length of a shortest path from the start state to a given (C, P_1)-accessible state. It suffices to show that at any such state the set of actions enabled under P_1 is a subset of those enabled under P_2. But this is clear from an examination of Definition 3. □

Ideally, we would like to use contextual containment to reason about relationships between *fragments* of policies, as well as entire policies. Reasoning about the relationships between policy fragments is critical for policies authored across multiple entities (as in our university example in the Introduction). Modular policy reasoning is subtle, however, in the presence of requests to which the policy does not apply. In our model, the context determines how such requests are handled. If a new policy fragment permits a request that defaulted to Deny in the context, new states could become accessible; these states would have not been tested for containment, thus rendering policy reasoning unsound.

Modular reasoning is sound, however, if policy combination cannot make additional states accessible. If the containment check between two fragments occurs in a context in which all non-applicables default to Permit, for example, policy containment and accessibility lift to modular policy reasoning, as we now show.

Lemma 9. *Let $C = \langle \mathcal{V}, \emptyset \rangle$ be a policy context with an empty set of default-deny transitions. If $P_1 \leq^C P_2$ then for all policies P, $(P \cup P_1) \leq^C (P \cup P_2)$.*

Proof. Let q be a state which is $(C, P \cup P_1)$-accessible and let $\mathbf{Q}$ be the associated database of edb and idb facts at q. By Remark 4, q is (C, P_1)-accessible, so the inclusions in the definition of $P_1 \leq^C P_2$ apply at $\mathbf{Q}$. Letting T denote the operator constructing the idb relations for a Datalog program, note that the fixed point of $T_{P \cup P_i}$ is the same as that of $T_{P_i} \circ T_P$. By hypothesis, at each iteration n of the fixpoint construction starting with $\mathbf{Q}$, we have $(T_{P_1} \circ T_P)^n(\mathbf{Q}) \subseteq (T_{P_2} \circ T_P)^n(\mathbf{Q})$. The lemma follows. □

Contextual containment under an empty set of default Deny transitions is analogous to uniform containment as defined for Datalog programs [10,35] (which is itself a generalization of the standard homomorphism-based characterization of containment for conjunctive queries). Correspondingly, we use the term *uniform contextual containment* for this scenario. Such preservation under context is also the key feature of observational equivalence in programming language theory. For the same reasons that observational equivalence is the canonical notion of equality between programming language expressions, we feel that uniform contextual equivalence should be vjewed as a fundamental notion of policy equivalence.

Uniform contextual containment supports the following analyses, none of which require a policy author to write formal properties:

- A new policy P neither removes any permissions nor adds any denials if and only if the new *fragment* of P uniformly contextually contains the fragment it replaced. If the replaced fragment also contains the new fragment, the two policies yield precisely the same decisions.
- A new policy P' adds a specific set of permissions I to an old policy P if $P \cup I$ (where I is a set of idb facts) is uniformly contextually equivalent to P'.

Lemma 9 over-approximates the set of accessible states by setting $\mathcal{E}$ to $\emptyset$. Such over-approximation is inherent to an open system setting, where we cannot make assumptions about the behavior of other modules. Naturally, this can result in irrelevant failures to prove containment. This effect can be mitigated: the degree of over-approximation is controlled entirely by the value of $\mathcal{E}$, which is a parameter to the containment check.

3.3   Checking Contextual Policy Containment

We now discuss how to implement a test for contextual policy containment. The most straightforward approach is to rename the predicates in the two policies so they are disjoint (we use subscripts in the formula below), take the union of the two policies, and use model checking to verify the temporal logic sentence

$$\text{AG } \forall x_1 x_2 x_3 . ((\text{Permit}_1(x_1, x_2, x_3) \rightarrow \text{Permit}_2(x_1, x_2, x_3))$$
$$\wedge (\text{Deny}_2(x_1, x_2, x_3) \rightarrow \text{Deny}_1(x_1, x_2, x_3))).$$

The universal quantification over requests makes this approach potentially expensive to evaluate at each state of the dynamic access model.

We can improve the situation by focusing on the relationship between policies and single rules. Roughly speaking we will reduce the policy containment question to consideration of whether individual rules are contained in (whole) policies. It is natural to consider a single rule as a policy in its own right. But the notion of accessibility is different depending on whether a rule is considered in isolation or as part of a larger policy. We will thus want to explore containment between a rule ρ from policy P_1 and a whole policy P_2 but restricting attention to states accessible under all of policy P_1. This motivates the following refinement of contextual containment.

Definition 10. Let P_1 and P_2 be policies and let ρ be a rule. Then $\rho \leq^C_{P_1} P_2$ if for all instances $\mathbf{Q}$ of edb and idb facts in (C, P_1)-accessible states, $\rho(\mathbf{Q})(R) \subseteq P_2(\mathbf{Q})(R)$, where R is the predicate at the head of ρ.

Analyzing contextual containment in terms of individual rules will be sound assuming a rather natural constraint on rules: that no Permit rule has the Deny predicate occurring in its body and no Deny rule has the Permit predicate occurring in its body. We will call such polices *separated*. This restriction is naturally satisfied in most policies. Furthermore, note that if only one kind of violation occurs, for example if some Permit rules depend on Deny but not vice versa, then the policy can be rewritten to be separated simply by expanding the offending occurrences of Deny by their definitions.

Lemma 11. *Let P_1 and P_2 be separated policies and let C be a policy context. Then $P_1 \leq^C P_2$ if and only if for each Permit rule ρ_1 of P_1, $\rho_1 \leq^C_{P_1} P_2$, and for each Deny rule ρ_2 of P_2, $\rho_2 \leq^C_{P_1} P_1$.*

Proof. Suppose $P_1 \leq^C P_2$, and let ρ_1 be a Permit-rule of P_1. Since P_1 is separated, at any state q with associated database $\mathbf{Q}$, $\rho_1(\mathbf{Q})(\mathsf{Permit}) \subseteq P_1(\mathbf{Q})(\mathsf{Permit})$; it follows that $\rho_1 \leq^C_{P_1} P_2$. A similar argument shows that $\rho_2 \leq^C_{P_2} P_1$ for each Deny-rule ρ_2 from P_2.

For the converse we consider without loss of generality a fact $\mathsf{Permit}(\vec{u})$ in $P_1(\mathbf{Q})$ for $\mathbf{Q}$ associated with a (C, P_1)-accessible state q and argue that $\mathsf{Permit}(\vec{u})$ is in $P_2(\mathbf{Q})$ by induction on the number of stages in the Datalog computation of this fact under P_1. Since P_1 is separated this computation relies only on edb facts from q and Permit-facts generated in fewer steps by P_1, so the result follows. $\qquad\square$

We now focus on the problem of testing containments of the form $\rho_1 \leq^C_{P_1} P_2$ (from Definition 10). While it is tempting to treat this as a purely logical problem, this is insufficient because it might miss relationships among the edb relations being maintained in the dynamic access model. Consider an example in which a policy author wants to replace the following rule ρ_1 for reviewers' access to paper reviews with rule ρ_2:

ρ_1: $\mathsf{Permit}(r, \mathsf{read\text{-}scores}, p)$:– $\mathsf{reviewer}(r)$, $\mathsf{has\text{-}reviewed}(r,p)$, $\mathsf{phase}(\mathsf{meeting})$
ρ_2: $\mathsf{Permit}(r, \mathsf{read\text{-}scores}, p)$:– $\mathsf{reviewer}(r)$, $\mathsf{assigned}(r,p)$, $\mathsf{phase}(\mathsf{meeting})$

Suppose the the dynamic access model maintains an invariant that reviews have only been submitted by reviewers who were assigned to a paper. Then $\rho_1 \leq^C \rho_2$ as single-rule policies since at every state, $\mathsf{has\text{-}reviewed}(r,p)$ implies $\mathsf{assigned}(r,p)$.

A related semantic phenomenon is the following. If every Subject (for example) in a model's domain were named by a constant, it could happen that the effect of a given rule was subsumed by finitely many rules of a policy in a "non-uniform" way.

Such examples illustrate why syntactic analysis is in general insufficient for checking contextual containment. The following algorithm works directly with the policy context C to check containment.

Algorithm 12. Let C be a policy context, P_1 and P_2 be policies, and $\rho \equiv R_0(\vec{u}_0)$:– $R_1(\vec{u}_1), \ldots, R_n(\vec{u}_n)$ be a rule from P_1. To test whether $\rho \leq^C_{P_1} P_2$:

For each (C, P_1)-accessible state q and for each valuation η mapping the variables of ρ into q which makes each $R_i(\eta\vec{u}_i)$ true, let $\mathbf{Q}^*$ be the database whose edb facts are those of q and whose idb facts are those $R_i(\eta\vec{u}_i)$ where R_i is an idb predicate from ρ. If $\eta\vec{u}_0 \in P_2(\mathbf{Q}^*)(R_0)$ for each such $\mathbf{Q}^*$, return success; if this fails for some $\mathbf{Q}^*$, fail.

Lemma 13. *Algorithm 12 is sound and complete for testing $\rho \leq^C_{P_1} P_2$.*

Proof. Suppose $\rho \leq^C_{P_1} P_2$ holds. Let q be a (C, P_1)-accessible state, let $\mathbf{Q}$ be the associated database instance and suppose $R(\vec{a})$ is in $\rho(\mathbf{Q})$, where R is the predicate at the head of ρ; we want to show that $R(\vec{a})$ is in $P_2(\mathbf{Q})$. The fact that $R(\vec{a})$ is in $\rho(\mathbf{Q})$ is witnessed by an instantiation of the body of ρ with elements from q that comprise edb facts from q and idb facts derived from evaluating ρ as a policy over q. But those latter idb facts are part of the instance $\mathbf{Q}^*$ as constructed in Algorithm 12, as are the edb facts from q. So the algorithm will report success. The argument that the algorithm correctly reports failures is similar. $\qquad\square$

The effect of a rule will often be captured by a policy in the sense of logical entailment, without appealing to the semantics of the application in question. Such relationships can be uncovered by purely symbolic computation: this is essentially the notion of uniform containment between Datalog programs. In our setting this takes the following form. First note that a collection B of atomic formulas can be considered as a database of facts by viewing the variables as values and the formulas as defining tables.

Definition 14. Let P be a policy, $\rho \equiv R_0(u_0) :- R_1(u_1), \ldots, R_n(u_n)$ be a rule, and B be the database instance derived from the body of ρ. P *simulates* ρ if $u_0 \in P(B)(R_0)$.

Lemma 15. *Let C be a policy context, let P_1 and P_2 be policies, and let ρ_1 be a rule from P_1. If P_2 simulates rule ρ_1 then $\rho_1 \leq^C_{P_1} P$.*

Proof. It is easy to see that when P_2 simulates ρ_1, the computation in Algorithm 12 will succeed at any state q.   □

Checking rule simulation requires time polynomial in ρ when the schema Σ is considered fixed: the complexity is $O(d^k)$ where k is the maximum arity of a predicate in Σ and d is the number of distinct variables in B.

The following algorithm summarizes how we can combine rule simulation and direct checking of a policy context to test contextual containment.

Algorithm 16 (Improved containment checking). Let C be a policy context and let P_1 and P_2 be separated policies. To test whether $P_1 \leq^C P_2$:

(i) Consider each **Permit** rule ρ_1 of P_1:
   Test whether P_2 simulates ρ_1. If so continue with the next rule. If not, use Algorithm 12 to directly test whether $\rho_1 \leq^C_{P_1} P_2$. If so continue with the next rule; if not halt and return failure.
(ii) Proceed similarly with each **Deny** rule of P_2.
(iii) If no failure is reported above, return success.

Theorem 17. *Algorithm 16 is sound and complete for testing $P_1 \leq^C P_2$.*

Proof. This follows from Lemmas 11, 13, and 15.   □

Algorithm 16 can produce counterexamples when the containment check fails. The check in Algorithm 12 identifies both a request that violates containment (formed from the head of the rule causing failure) and a path through the dynamic access model to a set of facts that fail to support the request. Counterexamples are important for creating useful analyses, as experience with model checking has shown.

Ideally, however, we would like to go beyond mere containment. A policy author would benefit from knowing the *semantic difference* between two policies, given as the set of all requests whose decisions changed from one policy to the other. Furthermore, these differences should be first-class objects, amenable to querying and verification just as policies are. The ability to analyze differences matters because authors can often state precise expectations of changes even if they cannot state global system properties, as Fisler *et al.* [14] discuss. This is therefore an important problem for future work.

4 Related Work

Using state transition systems to model programs guarded by access control policies goes back to Bell and LaPadula [6] and Harrison et al. [18]. More recent works support state transitions over richer models of access control and properties beyond safety [3,17,25,31,32,36]. Our model is unique in separating the static policy from its dynamic environment. This enables us to consider analyses such as semantic differencing that can meaningfully be applied to the policy alone. This separation also reflects the growing practice of writing policies in a different (domain-specific) language from applications.

Role-based access control (RBAC) [37] offers one form of support for a dynamic environment. The role abstraction allows users to change roles without having to modify the policy. In that sense it does illustrate the principle of a dynamic environment, but it is simply not rich enough to model the multitude of sources of change.

Bertino et al.'s TRBAC model captures time-sensitive, role-based access control policies [7]. TRBAC views time in concrete units such as hours and days and supports rule enabling and disabling based on concrete times (such as "give the night nurse permission to check charts at 5pm"). This concrete-time model explicitly elides other aspects of the dynamic environment, such as the passage of time induced by program events, and is thus unsuitable for reasoning about interactions between programs and policies.

Guelev et al. reduce access control policies to state machines over propositions by encoding each first-order relational term as a separate proposition [17]. They provide propositional temporal logic verification, but do not consider policy comparison. Abiteboul et al. verify FO-LTL properties against web services modeled as graphs over relational facts [2,13]. Our work includes a model of the facts over time whereas theirs assumes that the facts are arbitrary (within a given schema). Spielmann's work on verifying e-commerce systems has similar limitations relative to our project [41].

Alloy [22] supports reasoning about relational data. Several researchers, including the authors, have tried building policy analysis tools atop Alloy [14,21,39], but these all assume non-dynamic environments. Alloy's support for temporal reasoning is limited to properties of small bounded-length paths. Frias et al.'s DynAlloy tool extends Alloy to handle dynamic specifications [15], but retains Alloy's bounded path restrictions.

Datalog is the foundation for many access-control and related frameworks [5,12,23,29,30,34]. These works support only non-temporal query evaluation, while we are targeting richer analyses. Our use of uniform containment is inspired by results in the database literature. Shmueli [40] showed that simple containment of Datalog programs is undecidable while Sagiv [35] showed that uniform containment of programs is decidable, building on ideas of Cosmadakis and Kanellakis [10].

Several researchers have also built access-control reasoning tools atop Prolog [17,26,38], but their work does not address policy comparison. Weissman and Halpern model policies using the full power of first-order logic [43]. Their criticisms of Datalog-based models for capturing request denial do not apply to our model with an explicit Deny predicate. Verifying a property against a static policy in their model reduces to checking validity of first-order logic formulas; policy comparison would reduce to computing the set of first-order models that satisfy one formula but not another. We thus believe our model provides a better foundation for building usable verification tools.

Given that our model involves both relational terms and a transition system, our analyses require logics that integrate predicate logic and temporal operators. Hodkinson *et al.* have shown [19,20] that such logics have very bad decidability properties, even when the first-order components are restricted to decidable fragments. For example, the monadic fragment of first-order linear temporal logic is undecidable, even restricted to the 2-variable case. (The one-variable fragment is decidable.) For branching-time logics, even the one-variable monadic fragment is undecidable. These results suggest that checking validity or satisfiability (conventional theorem-proving tasks) to reason about first-order properties of dynamic policies would face severe difficulties. This paper uses models of policy environments to yield decidable analysis questions.

Backes *et al.* [4] propose refinement relations as a means for determining whether one policy contains another, but their work focuses solely on policies and does not account for the impact of the dynamic environment. Fisler *et al.* [14] have implemented both verification and semantic differencing for role-based policies, but their work handles only weaker (propositional rather than relational) policy models and ignores the impact of the dynamic environment.

5 Perspective

This work has demonstrated the importance of analyzing access-control policies in the dynamic context in which they evaluate requests. A great deal of the subtlety in this work arises because policies are are not two-valued (i.e., they may respond with "not-applicable"), but as we explain in the Introduction, this complexity is crucial to enable policies to be modular and to properly separate concerns and spheres of influence. This paper routinely employs results and insights from both the database and computer-aided verification literature, and thus highlight synergies between the two; however, the definitions and lemmas relating policy containment and accessibility under policies and contexts demonstrate the subtle ways in which these results interact within a common model. We believe that the notions of uniform contextual containment and equivalence defined in this paper are fundamental concepts for a theory of policies. The work in this paper can be used to analyze any situation where a program's execution is governed by a logical policy, but we have not explored applications other than access control.

Acknowledgements. The authors thank Moshe Vardi for a question that inspired many clarifications in the formalization. This work is partially supported by NSF grants.

References

1. S. Abiteboul, R. Hull, and V. Vianu. *Foundations of Databases*. Addison-Wesley, 1995.
2. S. Abiteboul, V. Vianu, B. S. Fordham, and Y. Yesha. Relational transducers for electronic commerce. *Journal of Computer and System Sciences*, 61(2):236–269, 2000.
3. T. Ahmed and A. R. Tripathi. Static verification of security requirements in role based CSCW systems. In *Symposium on Access Control Models and Technologies*, pages 196–203, 2003.
4. M. Backes, G. Karjoth, W. Bagga, and M. Schunter. Efficient comparison of enterprise privacy policies. In *Symposium on Applied Computing*, pages 375–382, 2004.

5. M. Y. Becker and P. Sewell. Cassandra: Flexible trust management, applied to electronic health records. In *IEEE Computer Security Foundations Workshop*, 2004.
6. D. Bell and L. J. LaPadula. Secure computer systems: Mathematical foundations and model. Technical Report M74-244, The Mitre Corporation, 1976.
7. E. Bertino, P. A. Bonatti, and E. Ferrari. TRBAC: A temporal role-based access control model. *ACM Transactions on Information and Systems Security*, 4(3):191–233, 2001.
8. E. Bertino, P. Samarati, and S. Jajodia. Authorizations in relational database management systems. In *ACM Conference on Computer and Communications Security*, pages 130–139, 1993.
9. P. Bonatti, S. D. C. di Vimercati, and P. Samarati. An algebra for composing access control policies. *ACM Transactions on Information and Systems Security*, 5(1):1–35, 2002.
10. S. Cosmadakis and P. Kanellakis. Functional and inclusion dependencies: A graph theoretic approach. In P. Kanellakis and F. Preparata, editors, *Advances in Computing Research*, volume 3: Theory of Databases, pages 163–185. JAI Press, 1986.
11. P. Cousot and R. Cousot. Abstract interpretation: A unified lattice model for static analysis of programs by construction or approximation of fixpoints. In *ACM Symposium on Principles of Programming Languages*, pages 238–252, 1977.
12. J. DeTreville. Binder: a logic-based security language. In *IEEE Symposium on Security and Privacy*, pages 95–103, 2002.
13. A. Deutsch, L. Sui, and V. Vianu. Specification and verification of data-driven web services. In *ACM Symposium on Principles of Database Systems*, pages 71–82, 2004.
14. K. Fisler, S. Krishnamurthi, L. A. Meyerovich, and M. C. Tschantz. Verification and change-impact analysis of access-control policies. In *International Conference on Software Engineering*, pages 196–205, May 2005.
15. M. F. Frias, J. P. Galeotti, C. G. L. Pombo, and N. M. Aguirre. DynAlloy: upgrading Alloy with actions. In *International Conference on Software Engineering*, pages 442–451. ACM Press, 2005.
16. G. Gottlob, N. Leone, and F. Scarcello. The complexity of acyclic conjunctive queries. *J. ACM*, 48(3):431–498, 2001.
17. D. P. Guelev, M. D. Ryan, and P.-Y. Schobbens. Model-checking access control policies. In *Information Security Conference*, number 3225 in Lecture Notes in Computer Science. Springer-Verlag, 2004.
18. M. A. Harrison, W. L. Ruzzo, and J. D. Ullman. Protection in operating systems. *Communications of the ACM*, 19(8):461–471, Aug. 1976.
19. I. Hodkinson, F. Wolter, and M. Zakharyaschev. Decidable fragments of first-order temporal logics. *Annals of Pure and Applied Logic*, 106:85–134, 2000.
20. I. Hodkinson, F. Wolter, and M. Zakharyaschev. Decidable and undecidable fragments of first-order branching temporal logics. In *IEEE Symposium on Logic in Computer Science*, pages 393–402, 2002.
21. G. Hughes and T. Bultan. Automated verification of access control policies. Technical Report 2004-22, University of California, Santa Barbara, 2004.
22. D. Jackson. Automating first-order relational logic. In *ACM SIGSOFT International Symposium on the Foundations of Software Engineering*, Nov. 2000.
23. T. Jim. SD3: A trust management system with certified evaluation. In *IEEE Symposium on Security and Privacy*, pages 106–115, 2001.
24. N. D. Jones. Space-bounded reducibility among combinatorial problems. *Journal of Computer and System Sciences*, 11(1):68–85, 1975.
25. M. Koch, L. V. Mancini, and F. Parisi-Presicce. Decidability of safety in graph-based models for access control. In *European Symposium on Research in Computer Security*, pages 299–243, 2002.

26. G. Kolaczek. Specification and verification of constraints in role based access control for enterprise security system. In *International Workshop on Enabling Technologies: Infrastructure for Collaborative Enterprises*, pages 190–195, 2003.
27. S. Krishnamurthi. The CONTINUE server. In *Symposium on the Practical Aspects of Declarative Languages*, number 2562 in Springer Lecture Notes in Computer Science, pages 2–16, January 2003.
28. B. W. Lampson. Protection. *ACM Operating Systems Review*, 8(1):18–24, Jan. 1974.
29. N. Li, B. N. Grosof, and J. Feigenbaum. Delegation logic: A logic-based approach to distributed authorization. *ACM Transactions on Information and Systems Security*, 6(1):128–171, 2003.
30. N. Li and J. C. Mitchell. Datalog with constraints: A foundation for trust management languages. In *Symposium on the Practical Aspects of Declarative Languages*, pages 58–73, 2003.
31. N. Li, J. C. Mitchell, and W. H. Winsborough. Beyond proof-of-compliance: Security analysis in trust management. *Journal of the ACM*, 52(3):474–514, May 2005.
32. N. Li and M. V. Tripunitara. Security analysis in role-based access control. In *ACM Symposium on Access Control Models and Technologies*, 2004.
33. T. Moses. eXtensible Access Control Markup Language (XACML) version 1.0. Technical report, OASIS, Feb. 2003.
34. A. Pimlott and O. Kiselyov. Soutei, a logic-based trust-management system. In *Functional and Logic Programming*, pages 130–145, 2006.
35. Y. Sagiv. Optimizing datalog programs. In *Foundations of Deductive Databases and Logic Programming*, pages 659–698. Morgan Kaufmann, 1988.
36. R. Sandhu. The schematic protection model: its definition and analysis for acyclic attenuating systems. *Journal of the ACM*, 35(2):404–432, 1988.
37. R. S. Sandhu, E. J. Coyne, H. L. Feinstein, and C. E. Youman. Role-based access control models. *IEEE Computer*, 29(2):38–47, 1996.
38. B. Sarna-Starosta and S. D. Stoller. Policy analysis for security-enhanced Linux. In *Proceedings of the 2004 Workshop on Issues in the Theory of Security*, pages 1–12, April 2004.
39. A. Schaad and J. D. Moffett. A lightweight approach to specification and analysis of role-based access control extensions. In *Symposium on Access Control Models and Technologies*, pages 13–22, 2002.
40. O. Shmueli. Decidability and expressiveness aspects of logic queries. In *ACM Symposium on Principles of Database Systems*, pages 237–249, 1987.
41. M. Spielmann. Verification of relational transducers for electronic commerce. In *ACM Symposium on Principles of Database Systems*, pages 92–103. ACM Press, 2000.
42. M. Y. Vardi. The complexity of relational query languages (extended abstract). In *Symposium on the Theory of Computing*, pages 137–146. ACM, 1982.
43. V. Weissman and J. Halpern. Using first-order logic to reason about policies. In *IEEE Computer Security Foundations Workshop*, pages 187–201, 2003.
44. E. Yahav, T. Reps, M. Sagiv, and R. Wilhelm. Verifying temporal heap properties specified via evolution logic. In P. Degano, editor, *European Symposium on Programming*, volume 2618 of *Lecture Notes in Computer Science*, pages 204–222. Springer-Verlag, 2003.

On Keys and Functional Dependencies as First-Class Citizens in Description Logics

David Toman and Grant Weddell

David R. Cheriton School of Computer Science
University of Waterloo, Canada
{david, gweddell}@uwaterloo.ca

Abstract. We investigate whether *identification constraints* such as keys and functional dependencies can be granted full status as a concept constructor in a Boolean-complete description logic. In particular, we show that surprisingly simple forms of such constraints lead to undecidability of the associated logical implication problem if they are allowed within the scope of a negation or on the left-hand-side of inclusion dependencies. We then show that allowing a very general form of identification constraints to occur in the scope of *monotone* concept constructors on the right-hand-side of inclusion dependencies still leads to decidable implication problems. Finally, we consider the relationship between certain classes of identification constraints and nominals.

1 Introduction

To date, description logics (DLs) have incorporated keys or functional dependencies in one of two ways. The first adds a separate family of terminological constraints to inclusion dependencies, e.g., in the form of a *key box* [5,7,13,14], while the second avoids this by adding a new concept constructor called a *path-functional dependency* (PFD) [11,18,19]. However, the latter approach still falls short of a full integration of keys or functional dependencies since there are syntactic restrictions on occurrences of PFDs and on the syntax of the PFD constructor itself. In particular, all earlier work has required that any occurrence of this constructor appears only at the top level on the right hand side of inclusion dependencies, and that the left hand sides of PFDs themselves are nonempty. Note that an ordinary functional dependency of the form "{} → A" has an empty left hand side and consequently enforces a fixed A value. In this paper, we investigate whether such syntactic restrictions are necessary—unfortunately, it turns out that this is indeed the case—and study the limits of decidability in such a setting. Our main contributions are as follows.

- We show that allowing PFDs on the left hand side of inclusion dependencies, or in the scope of a containing negation on the right hand side, leads to undecidability. Notably, this remains true when PFDs are limited to very simple forms of relational keys or functional dependencies.

U. Furbach and N. Shankar (Eds.): IJCAR 2006, LNAI 4130, pp. 647–661, 2006.

- Conversely, we show that allowing PFDs within the scope of *monotone* concept constructors on the right hand side of inclusion dependencies, still leads to decidable implication problems.
- We show that allowing left hand sides of PFDs to be empty also leads to undecidability. This entails first showing that the introduction of an ABox to previously decidable PFD dialects already makes logical implication undecidable. The result follows by showing that such PFDs can simulate nominals.

DLs have become an important part of the semantic web. Indeed, OWL, the current standard for capturing semantic web ontologies, is largely based on a DL dialect. They have also been used as a lingua franca for a large variety of languages for capturing metadata: UML class diagrams, ER models, relational schema, object-oriented schema, DTDs for XML and XML itself are all examples [6,15].

1.1   Identification Is Important

Identification constraints are fundamentally tied to issues of equality, and as web services with query languages such as SWRL that are based on OWL are introduced, important questions such as *how can one reliably identify resources* and *whether there is at most one kind of web service* inevitably surface when finding execution strategies for services and when communicating results of such services. With the addition of the PFD concept constructor along the lines considered in this paper, it becomes possible to express, e.g., that *among all possible clients, social security numbers are a reliable way of identifying those that are registered.* In particular, this can be captured by the following inclusion dependency.

$$\text{Client} \sqsubseteq \neg\text{Registered} \sqcup \text{Client} : SIN \rightarrow Id$$

To paraphrase: *If a client is registered, then no other client will share his or her social insurance number.* Note that social insurance numbers may not be a reliable way of identifying an arbitrary unregistered client in general.

There are a number of additional applications and capabilities that become possible after removing syntactic restrictions on PFDs, beyond the fact that a simple and elegant presentation of the associated DL would ensue. For example, to say that *all information about clients is located at a single site*, one can add the dependency

$$\text{Client} \sqsubseteq \text{Client} :\rightarrow LocationOfData$$

Again to paraphrase: *For any pair of clients, both will agree on the location of available data.*

As we shall see, relaxing existing restrictions to accommodate the first example is possible since disjunction is a monotone concept constructor, but is not possible for the second example without the introduction of alternative restrictions on the use of PFDs or syntax of the PFD constructor itself.

1.2   Background and Related Work

PFDs were introduced and studied in the context of object-oriented data models [9,23]. An FD concept constructor was proposed and incorporated in Classic [4], an early DL with a PTIME reasoning procedure, without changing the complexity of its implication problem. The generalization of this constructor to PFDs alone leads to EXPTIME completeness of the implication problem [11]; this complexity remains unchanged in the presence of additional concept constructors common in rich DLs [18,19]. Note that all earlier work has assumed the above syntactic restrictions on occurrences of the PFD concept constructor in inclusion dependencies.

In [5], the authors consider a DL with functional dependencies and a general form of keys added as additional varieties of dependencies, called a *key box*. They show that their dialect is undecidable for DLs with inverse roles, but becomes decidable when unary functional dependencies are disallowed. This line of investigation is continued in the context of PFDs and inverse features, with analogous results [17]. We therefore disallow inverse features in this paper to exclude an already known cause for undecidability.

A form of key dependency with left hand side feature paths has been considered for a DL coupled with various concrete domains [14,13]. In this case, the authors explore how the complexity of satisfaction is influenced by the selection of a concrete domain together with various syntactic restrictions on the key dependencies themselves.

PFDs have also been used in a number of applications in object-oriented schema diagnosis and synthesis [2,3], in query optimization [8,10] and in the selection of indexing for a database [16]. The results reported in this paper are an expansion of earlier preliminary work in [20].

The remainder of the paper is organized as follows. The definition of $\mathcal{DLFD}$, a Boolean complete DL based on attributes or features that includes the PFD concept constructor is given next. In Section 3, we show that the interaction of this constructor with negation leads to undecidability for a variety of simple cases of PFDs. Section 4 then shows how decidability can be regained while still allowing PFDs in the scope of monotone concept constructors on the right hand sides of inclusion dependencies, most significantly in the scope of concept union and attribute restriction. In Section 5, we consider relaxing the requirement that PFDs have non-empty left hand sides, showing that both this and a (weaker) alternative of admitting an ABox leads to undecidability. Our summary comments follow in Section 6.

2 Definitions

Our investigations are based on the following dialect of description logic called $\mathcal{DLFD}$. To simplify the presentation, the dialect is based on *attributes* or *features* instead of the more common case of roles. Note that $\mathcal{ALCN}$ with a suitable PFD construct can simulate our dialect. Conversely, $\mathcal{DLFD}$ can simulate $\mathcal{ALCQI}$ [21].

Definition 1 (Description Logic $\mathcal{DLFD}$). *Let* F *and* C *be sets of attribute names and primitive concept names, respectively. A path expression is defined by the grammar* "Pf ::= f. Pf | *Id* " *for* $f \in$ F. *We define derived concept descriptions*

| SYNTAX | SEMANTICS: DEFN OF "$(\cdot)^{\mathcal{I}}$" |

$D, E ::= C$ $(C)^{\mathcal{I}} \subseteq \Delta$

$\quad |\quad D_1 \sqcap D_2$ $(D_1)^{\mathcal{I}} \cap (D_2)^{\mathcal{I}}$

$\quad |\quad D_1 \sqcup D_2$ $(D_1)^{\mathcal{I}} \cup (D_2)^{\mathcal{I}}$

$\quad |\quad \forall f.D$ $\{x : (f)^{\mathcal{I}}(x) \in (D)^{\mathcal{I}}\}$

$\quad |\quad \neg D$ $\Delta \setminus (D)^{\mathcal{I}}$

$\quad |\quad D : \mathsf{Pf}_1, ..., \mathsf{Pf}_k \to \mathsf{Pf}$ $\{x : \forall y \in (D)^{\mathcal{I}}.$
$\bigwedge_{i=1}^{k}(\mathsf{Pf}_i)^{\mathcal{I}}(x) = (\mathsf{Pf}_i)^{\mathcal{I}}(y) \Rightarrow (\mathsf{Pf})^{\mathcal{I}}(x) = (\mathsf{Pf})^{\mathcal{I}}(y)\}$

Fig. 1. Syntax and Semantics of $\mathcal{DLFD}$

by the grammar on the left-hand-side of Figure 1. A concept description obtained by using the fourth production of this grammar is called an attribute value restriction. A concept description obtained by using the final production is called a path functional dependency (PFD). Note that we assume for this production that $k > 0$, that the left hand side of a PFD is non-empty. In addition, a PFD is called: (1) unary when $k = 1$, (2) key when the right hand side is Id, and (3) simple when there is no path expression with more than a single attribute name.

An inclusion dependency $\mathcal{C}$ is an expression of the form $D \sqsubseteq E$. A terminology $\mathcal{T}$ consists of a finite set of inclusion dependencies.

The semantics of expressions is defined with respect to a structure $(\Delta, \cdot^{\mathcal{I}})$, where Δ is a domain of "objects" and $(.)^{\mathcal{I}}$ an interpretation function that fixes the interpretation of primitive concepts C to be subsets of Δ and primitive attributes f to be total functions $(f)^{\mathcal{I}} : \Delta \to \Delta$. The interpretation is extended to path expressions, $(Id)^{\mathcal{I}} = \lambda x.x$, $(f.\mathsf{Pf})^{\mathcal{I}} = (\mathsf{Pf})^{\mathcal{I}} \circ (f)^{\mathcal{I}}$ and derived concept descriptions D and E as defined on the right-hand-side of Figure 1.

An interpretation satisfies an inclusion dependency $D \sqsubseteq E$ if $(D)^{\mathcal{I}} \subseteq (E)^{\mathcal{I}}$. The logical implication problem asks if $\mathcal{T} \models D \sqsubseteq E$ holds; that is, for a posed question $D \sqsubseteq E$, if $(D)^{\mathcal{I}} \subseteq (E)^{\mathcal{I}}$ for all interpretations that satisfy all inclusion dependencies in $\mathcal{T}$.

3   Undecidability

It turns out that allowing arbitrary use of very simple varieties of the PFD concept constructor lead to undecidable implication problems. This is true for three *boundary* cases in particular:

1. when all PFDs are simple and key,
2. when all PFDs are simple and unary, and
3. when all PFDs are simple and non-key.

In the first case, a PFD resembles $C : f_1, \ldots, f_k \to Id$, which captures the standard notion of *relational keys*, while in the second, a PFD has either the form $C : f \to g$ or the form $C : f \to id$. The standard notion of a (relational) *functional dependency* (FD) is captured by the final third case in which a PFD resembles $C : f_1, \ldots, f_k \to f$.

Observe that the three cases are exhaustive in the sense that the only possibility not covered happens when all PFDs have the form $C : f \rightarrow Id$ (i.e., are simple, unary, and key). However, it is a straightforward exercise in this case to map logical implication problems to alternative formulations in decidable DL dialects with inverses and number restrictions. In the rest of this section, we elaborate on the first two of these cases. Notably, our reductions make no use of attribute value restrictions; they rely solely on PFDs and the standard Boolean constructors. The reduction for the last case is similar and will be given in an extended version of the paper.

Our undecidability results are all based on a reduction of the unrestricted tiling problem to the $\mathcal{DLFD}$ implication problem. An instance U of this problem is a triple (T, H, V) where T is a finite set of tile types and $H, V \subseteq T \times T$ two binary relations. A *solution* to T is a mapping $t : \mathbf{N} \times \mathbf{N} \rightarrow T$ such that $(t(i, j), t(i+1, j)) \in H$ and $(t(i, j), t(i, j + 1)) \in V$ for all $i \in \mathbf{N}$. This problem is Π_0^0-complete [1,22].

3.1   PFDs That Are Simple and Key (Relational Keys)

The reduction constructs a terminology for a given tiling problem $U = (T, H, V)$, denoted $\mathcal{T}_U^1$, by first establishing an *integer grid* in three steps.

1. Begin by introducing primitive concepts A, B, C and D to serve as possible grid points.

$$A \sqcap B \sqsubseteq \bot \ \ A \sqcap C \sqsubseteq \bot \ \ A \sqcap D \sqsubseteq \bot \ \ B \sqcap C \sqsubseteq \bot \ \ B \sqcap D \sqsubseteq \bot \ \ C \sqcap D \sqsubseteq \bot$$

2. Then create an "infinitely branching" tree of squares. Such a tree can be rooted at a hypothetical top-left with, e.g., an A object.

$$A \sqsubseteq \neg(B : g, k \rightarrow Id) \sqcap \neg(C : f, g \rightarrow Id)$$
$$B \sqsubseteq \neg(A : f, h \rightarrow Id) \sqcap \neg(D : f, g \rightarrow Id)$$
$$C \sqsubseteq \neg(A : h, k \rightarrow Id) \sqcap \neg(D : g, k \rightarrow Id)$$
$$D \sqsubseteq \neg(B : h, k \rightarrow Id) \sqcap \neg(C : f, h \rightarrow Id)$$

3. And finally, flatten and align the tree into an integer grid using keys.

$$A \sqsubseteq A : h \rightarrow Id \quad B \sqsubseteq B : k \rightarrow Id \quad C \sqsubseteq C : f \rightarrow Id \quad D \sqsubseteq D : g \rightarrow Id$$

The accumulated effect of these inclusion dependencies on an interpretation is illustrated in Figure 2. Note that the *thick edges* indicate places where flattening of the infinitely branching tree of squares happens.

We model the tiling problem U using primitive concepts T_i for each tile type $t_i \in T$, asserting that $T_i \sqcap T_j \sqsubseteq \bot$ for all $i < j$. The tiles are placed on the grid points using the assertion $(A \sqcup B \sqcup C \sqcup D) \sqsubseteq \bigsqcup_{t_i \in T} T_i$. The adjacency rules for the instance U of the tiling problem can now be captured as follows:

- for $(t_i, t_j) \notin H$:

$$A \sqcap T_i \sqsubseteq (B \sqcap T_j) : g \rightarrow Id \quad B \sqcap T_i \sqsubseteq (A \sqcap T_j) : f \rightarrow Id$$
$$C \sqcap T_i \sqsubseteq (D \sqcap T_j) : k \rightarrow Id \quad D \sqcap T_i \sqsubseteq (C \sqcap T_j) : h \rightarrow Id$$

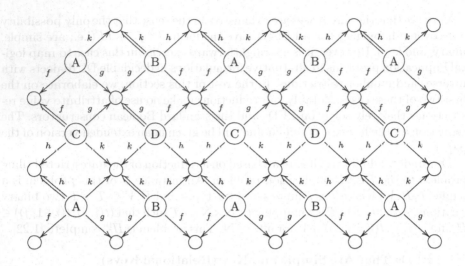

Fig. 2. Defining a Grid

– for $(t_i, t_j) \notin V$:

$$A \sqcap T_i \sqsubseteq (C \sqcap T_j) : f \rightarrow Id \qquad C \sqcap T_i \sqsubseteq (A \sqcap T_j) : h \rightarrow Id$$
$$B \sqcap T_i \sqsubseteq (D \sqcap T_j) : g \rightarrow Id \qquad D \sqcap T_i \sqsubseteq (B \sqcap T_j) : k \rightarrow Id$$

where T_i corresponds to tile type $t_i \in T$. The above constraints form a terminology $\mathcal{T}_U^1$ associated with an unrestricted tiling problem U that immediately yields the following result:

Theorem 2. *An instance $U = (T, H, V)$ of the infinite tiling problem admits a solution if and only if*

$$\mathcal{T}_U^1 \not\models A \sqsubseteq \bot.$$

Corollary 3. *The logical implication problem for $\mathcal{DLFD}$ with PFDs that are simple and key is undecidable. This remains true in the absence of attribute values restrictions.*

3.2   PFDs That Are Simple and Unary

Again, the reduction constructs a terminology for a given tiling problem $U = (T, H, V)$, denoted this time as $\mathcal{T}_U^2$, by first establishing an integer grid. For this case, an extra step is needed.

1. As before, introduce primitive concepts A, B, C and D to serve as possible grid points.

$$A \sqcap B \sqsubseteq \bot \quad A \sqcap C \sqsubseteq \bot \quad A \sqcap D \sqsubseteq \bot \quad B \sqcap C \sqsubseteq \bot \quad B \sqcap D \sqsubseteq \bot \quad C \sqcap D \sqsubseteq \bot$$

2. To create an analogous infinitely branching tree of squares, first create "raw material" consisting of the necessary chains.

$$A \sqsubseteq \neg(B : k \rightarrow Id) \sqcap \neg(C : f \rightarrow Id) \quad B \sqsubseteq \neg(A : h \rightarrow Id) \sqcap \neg(D : g \rightarrow Id)$$
$$C \sqsubseteq \neg(A : h \rightarrow Id) \sqcap \neg(D : g \rightarrow Id) \quad D \sqsubseteq \neg(B : k \rightarrow Id) \sqcap \neg(C : f \rightarrow Id)$$

3. The chains are then shaped into squares with functional dependencies.

$$A \sqsubseteq \neg(B : k \rightarrow g) \sqcap \neg(C : f \rightarrow g) \quad B \sqsubseteq \neg(A : h \rightarrow f) \sqcap \neg(D : g \rightarrow f)$$
$$C \sqsubseteq \neg(A : h \rightarrow k) \sqcap \neg(D : g \rightarrow k) \quad D \sqsubseteq \neg(B : k \rightarrow h) \sqcap \neg(C : f \rightarrow h)$$

4. And then as before, an integer grid is obtained by flattening and aligning using keys.

$$A \sqsubseteq A : h \rightarrow Id \quad B \sqsubseteq B : k \rightarrow Id \quad C \sqsubseteq C : f \rightarrow Id \quad D \sqsubseteq D : g \rightarrow Id$$

The final accumulated effect of these inclusion dependencies on an interpretation is the same as in Figure 2, and, since a tiling problem can then be overlaid on this grid in the same manner as in the above case for PFDs that are simple and key, we have the following result:

Theorem 4. *An instance* $U = (T, H, V)$ *of the infinite tiling problem admits a solution if and only if*

$$\mathcal{T}_U^2 \not\models A \sqsubseteq \bot.$$

Corollary 5. *The logical implication problem for* $\mathcal{DLFD}$ *with PFDs that are simple and unary is undecidable. This remains true in the absence of attribute value restrictions.*

4 On Regaining Decidability

We now show that undecidability is a consequence of allowing PFDs to occur within the scope of negation. In particular, and for the remainder of the paper, we shall assume a *limited* $\mathcal{DLFD}$ in which inclusion dependencies, D $\sqsubseteq$ E, are presumed to adhere to the following less general grammar.

$$D ::= C \mid D_1 \sqcap D_2 \mid D_1 \sqcup D_2 \mid \forall f.D \mid \neg D$$
$$E ::= D \mid E_1 \sqcap E_2 \mid E_1 \sqcup E_2 \mid \forall f.E \mid D : \mathsf{Pf}_1, ..., \mathsf{Pf}_k \rightarrow \mathsf{Pf}$$

Observe that PFDs must now occur on right hand sides of inclusion dependencies at either the top level or *within the scope of monotone concept constructors*; this implies that limited $\mathcal{DLFD}$ is a strict generalization of earlier dialects. Note that allowing PFDs on left hand sides is equivalent to allowing PFDs in the scope of negation:

Example 6. $D_1 \sqsubseteq \neg(D_2 : f \rightarrow g)$ is equivalent to $D_1 \sqcap (D_2 : f \rightarrow g) \sqsubseteq \bot$.

In the following, we reduce logical implication problems in limited $\mathcal{DLFD}$ to simpler formulations for which existing decisions procedures can be applied [18].

4.1   Transformation of Terminologies

We start by showing that allowing PFDs in *monotone* concept constructors within terminologies can be avoided by a syntactic transformation.

Definition 7 (Simple Constraints and Terminologies). *An inclusion dependency* $D \sqsubseteq E \in \mathcal{T}$ *is called* simple *if it conforms to limited* $\mathcal{DLFD}$ *and if the right hand side can be parsed by the following grammar.*

$$E ::= \mathcal{D} \mid \mathcal{D} : \mathsf{Pf}_1, ..., \mathsf{Pf}_k \to \mathsf{Pf}$$

A terminology $\mathcal{T}$ *is called* simple *if all its inclusion dependencies are simple.*

For a given terminology $\mathcal{T}$, we construct a simple terminology $\mathcal{T}^{\mathrm{simp}}$ by rewriting the right hand sides of inclusion dependencies as follows:

$$
\begin{aligned}
(D \sqsubseteq D')^{\mathrm{simp}} &= \{D \sqsubseteq D'\} \\
(D \sqsubseteq E_1 \sqcap E_2)^{\mathrm{simp}} &= \{D \sqsubseteq D_1 \sqcap D_2\} \cup (D_1 \sqsubseteq E_1)^{\mathrm{simp}} \cup (D_2 \sqsubseteq E_2)^{\mathrm{simp}} \\
(D \sqsubseteq E_1 \sqcup E_2)^{\mathrm{simp}} &= \{D \sqsubseteq D_1 \sqcup D_2\} \cup (D_1 \sqsubseteq E_1)^{\mathrm{simp}} \cup (D_2 \sqsubseteq E_2)^{\mathrm{simp}} \\
(D \sqsubseteq \forall f.E_1)^{\mathrm{simp}} &= \{D \sqsubseteq \forall f.D_1\} \cup (D_1 \sqsubseteq E_1)^{\mathrm{simp}}
\end{aligned}
$$

for $D \sqsubseteq D'$ a simple inclusion dependency and D_1 and D_2 fresh primitive concept names. We define $\mathcal{T}^{\mathrm{simp}} = \bigcup_{D \sqsubseteq E \in \mathcal{T}} (D \sqsubseteq E)^{\mathrm{simp}}$.

Lemma 8.   *1. Let* $\mathcal{I} \models \mathcal{T}^{\mathrm{simp}}$. *Then* $\mathcal{I} \models \mathcal{T}$;
   2. Let $\mathcal{I} \models \mathcal{T}$. *Then there is* $\mathcal{I}'$ *such that* $\mathcal{I}$ *and* $\mathcal{I}'$ *agree on the interpretation of all symbols in* $\mathcal{T}$ *and* $\mathcal{I}' \models \mathcal{T}^{\mathrm{simp}}$.

Proof. Follows by straightforward inductions on the definition of $(\cdot)^{\mathrm{simp}}$.   □

Thus, in terminologies, the interaction of positive concept constructors with PFDs poses little difficulty and we can use existing decision procedures for the implication problem.

Theorem 9. *Let* $\mathcal{T}$ *be a terminology conforming to limited* $\mathcal{DLFD}$ *and* $\mathcal{C}$ *a simple inclusion dependency. Then* $\mathcal{T} \models \mathcal{C}$ *is decidable and complete for EXPTIME.*

Proof. The theorem is a consequence of Lemma 8 and of reductions presented in [18].   □

4.2   Transformation of Posed Questions

Now assuming, w.l.o.g., that a given terminology is simple, we exhibit a reduction of a logical implication problem with a posed question expressed in limited $\mathcal{DLFD}$. Unfortunately, allowing other than simple inclusion dependencies as posed questions leads to more complications as the following two examples illustrate.

Example 10. *A counterexample to* $D \sqsubseteq (C : f, g \to h) \sqcup (C : f, h \to g)$ *is depicted in Figure 3. Note that any such counterexample must also falsify* $C \sqsubseteq C : f \to \mathrm{Id}$ *since distinct C objects that agree on* f *will be required. Thus:*

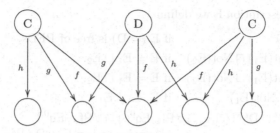

Fig. 3. Counterexample for Example 10

$$\{C \sqsubseteq C : f \to Id\} \models D \sqsubseteq (C : f, g \to h) \sqcup (C : f, h \to g).$$

Example 11. *A counterexample to* $D \sqsubseteq (C : f \to g) \sqcup \forall f.(C : f \to g)$ *is shown in Figure 4. Observe with this case that distinct C objects must occur at* different *levels when compared to a D-rooted tree.*

The examples suggest a need for multiple *root objects* in counterexample interpretations, with the roots themselves occurring at different levels. Our overall strategy is to therefore reduce a logical implication problem to a negation of a consistency problem in an alternative formulation in which objects in a satisfying counterexample *denote up to ℓ possible copies in a counterexample interpretation for the original problem*, where ℓ is the number of occurrences of PFDs in the posed question.

To encode this one-to-many mapping of objects, we require a general way to have ℓ copies of concepts occurring in a given membership problem. We therefore write D^i to denote the concept description D in which all primitive concepts C are replaced by C^i. For a simple terminology $\mathcal{T}$ we then define

$$\mathcal{T}^i = \{ \mathsf{Nd}^i \sqcap D^i \sqsubseteq E^i \mid D \sqsubseteq E \in \mathcal{T}, E \text{ a non PFD} \}, \text{ and}$$

$$\mathcal{T}^{i,j} = \{ \mathsf{Nd}^i \sqcap \mathsf{Nd}^j \sqcap D^i \sqcap E^j \sqcap (\sqcap_{1 \le n \le k} \forall \mathsf{Pf}_n . \mathsf{Eq}^{i,j}) \sqsubseteq \forall \mathsf{Pf} . \mathsf{Eq}^{i,j},$$
$$\mathsf{Nd}^i \sqcap \mathsf{Nd}^j \sqcap D^j \sqcap E^i \sqcap (\sqcap_{1 \le n \le k} \forall \mathsf{Pf}_n . \mathsf{Eq}^{i,j}) \sqsubseteq \forall \mathsf{Pf} . \mathsf{Eq}^{i,j}$$
$$\mid D \sqsubseteq E : \mathsf{Pf}_1, \dots, \mathsf{Pf}_k \to \mathsf{Pf} \in \mathcal{T} \}.$$

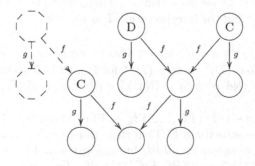

Fig. 4. Counterexample for Example 11

For a concept description E we define

$$\text{Not}(E) = \begin{cases} \neg D^0 & \text{if } E \,(= D) \text{ is free of PFDs,} \\ \text{Not}(E_1) \sqcap \text{Not}(E_2) & \text{if } E = E_1 \sqcup E_2, \\ \text{Not}(E_1) \sqcup \text{Not}(E_2) & \text{if } E = E_1 \sqcap E_2, \\ \forall f.\text{Not}(E_1) & \text{if } E = \forall f.E_1, \\ \text{Nd}^i \sqcap D^i \sqcap (\sqcap_{1 \leq i \leq k} \forall \text{Pf}_i\,.\text{Eq}^{0,i}) \sqcap \forall \text{Pf}\,.\neg \text{Eq}^{0,i} \\ \qquad\qquad \text{otherwise, when } E = D : \text{Pf}_1, \ldots, \text{Pf}_k \to \text{Pf}\,. \end{cases}$$

where i in the last equation is the index of the PFD in the original posed question.

In the above, we have introduced primitive concepts $\text{Eq}^{i,j}, 0 \leq i \neq j \leq \ell$, to express that the ith and jth object copies coincide, and $\text{Nd}^i, 0 \leq i \leq \ell$, to assert that the ith copy exists. The following auxiliary sets of constraints are therefore defined to account for the axioms of equality and for the fact that features in $\mathcal{DLFD}$ denote total functions.

$$\begin{aligned} \mathcal{E}(l) \;=\; & \{\text{Eq}^{i,j} \sqcap \text{Eq}^{j,k} \sqsubseteq \text{Eq}^{i,k} \mid 0 \leq i < j < k \leq l\} \\ & \cup\ \{\text{Eq}^{i,j} \sqsubseteq \text{Eq}^{j,i} \mid 0 \leq i < j \leq l\} \\ & \cup\ \{(\text{Eq}^{i,j} \sqcap C^i) \sqsubseteq C^j \mid 0 \leq i \neq j \leq l \text{ and } C \text{ a primitive concept}\} \\ & \cup\ \{\text{Eq}^{i,j} \sqsubseteq \forall f.\text{Eq}^{i,j} \mid 0 \leq i \neq j \leq l \text{ and } f \text{ a primitive feature}\} \\ \mathcal{N}(l) \;=\; & \{\text{Nd}^i \sqsubseteq \forall f.\text{Nd}^i \mid 0 \leq i \leq l \text{ and } f \text{ a primitive feature}\} \end{aligned}$$

Theorem 12. *Let $\mathcal{T}$ be a simple terminology and $D \sqsubseteq E$ an inclusion dependency containing l occurrences of the PFD concept constructor. Then $\mathcal{T} \models D \sqsubseteq E$ if and only if*

$$\Big(\bigcup_{0 \leq i \leq l} \mathcal{T}^i\Big) \cup \Big(\bigcup_{0 \leq i < j \leq l} \mathcal{T}^{i,j}\Big) \cup \mathcal{E}(l) \cup \mathcal{N}(l) \models (\text{Nd}^0 \sqcap D^0 \sqcap \text{Not}(E)) \sqsubseteq \bot.$$

Proof. (sketch) Given an interpretation $\mathcal{I}$ such that $\mathcal{I} \models \mathcal{T}$ and $\mathcal{I} \not\models D \sqsubseteq E$ we construct an interpretation $\mathcal{J}$ as follows. First, in the construction, we use a many-to-one map $\delta : \Delta \to \Delta^{\mathcal{J}}$ to associate objects in $\mathcal{I}$ with those in $\mathcal{J}$. The range of δ serves as the domain of the interpretation $\mathcal{J}$. For the counterexample object $o \in (D \sqcap \neg E)^{\mathcal{I}}$ we set $\delta o \in (\text{Nd}^0)^{\mathcal{J}}$. Then, for all $o \in \Delta$ and $0 \leq i \neq j \leq l$ we define the map δ and the interpretation $\mathcal{I}$ as follows:

- $\delta o \in (\text{Nd}^i)^{\mathcal{J}} \wedge (f)^{\mathcal{I}}(o) = o' \Rightarrow \delta o' \in (\text{Nd}^i)^{\mathcal{J}} \wedge (f)^{\mathcal{J}}(\delta o) = \delta o'$,
- $\delta o \in (\text{Nd}^i)^{\mathcal{J}} \wedge o \in (D)^{\mathcal{I}} \Rightarrow \delta o \in (D)^{\mathcal{J}}$ for D a PFD-free concept,
- $\delta o = \delta o' \wedge \delta o \in (\text{Nd}^i)^{\mathcal{J}} \wedge \delta o' \in (\text{Nd}^j)^{\mathcal{J}} \wedge (\text{Pf})^{\mathcal{I}}(o) = (\text{Pf})^{\mathcal{I}}(o') \Rightarrow$
  $$\delta o \in (\text{Eq}^{i,j})^{\mathcal{J}}, \text{ and}$$
- $\delta o \in (\text{Nd}^i)^{\mathcal{J}} \wedge o \in (\neg D : \text{Pf}_1, \ldots, \text{Pf}_k \to \text{Pf})^{\mathcal{I}}$ where $D : \text{Pf}_1, \ldots, \text{Pf}_k \to \text{Pf}$ is the i-th PFD constructor in E. Thus there must be $o' \in \Delta$ such that $o' \in (D)^{\mathcal{I}}$ and the pair o, o' agrees on all Pf_i but disagrees on Pf; we set $\delta o = \delta o'$ and $\delta o' \in (\text{Nd}^i \sqcap D^i \sqcap (\sqcap_{1 \leq i \leq k} \forall \text{Pf}_i\,.\text{Eq}^{0,i}) \sqcap \forall \text{Pf}\,.\neg \text{Eq}^{0,i})^{\mathcal{J}}$.

Note that, due to the syntactic restrictions imposed on the uses of PFD constructors, a negation of an PFD can be enforced only in the counterexample of the description E. Spurious occurrences of negated PFDs in the interpretation $\mathcal{I}$ are therefore ignored as the interpretation itself satisfies all PFDs in $\mathcal{T}$.

It is easy to verify THAT $\delta o \in (\mathsf{Nd}^0 \sqcap \mathsf{D}^0 \sqcap \mathsf{Not}(E))^{\mathcal{J}}$ for $o \in (\mathsf{D} \sqcap \neg E)^{\mathcal{I}}$. By inspecting all inclusion dependencies in $\mathcal{T}$ we have $\mathcal{J} \models \mathcal{T}^i$ as $\mathcal{I} \models \mathcal{T}$. Furthermore, the construction of $\mathcal{J}$ enforces $\mathcal{J} \models \mathcal{E}(l) \cup \mathcal{N}(l)$.

On the other hand, given an interpretation $\mathcal{J}$ of $(\mathsf{Nd}^0 \sqcap \mathsf{D}^0 \sqcap \mathsf{Not}(E))$ that satisfies all assertions in

$$(\bigcup_{0 \leq i \leq l} \mathcal{T}^i) \cup (\bigcup_{0 \leq i < j \leq l} \mathcal{T}^{i,j}) \cup \mathcal{E}(l) \cup \mathcal{N}(l),$$

we construct an interpretation $\mathcal{I}$ of $\mathcal{T}$ that falsifies $\mathsf{D} \sqsubseteq \mathsf{E}$ as follows:

- $\Delta^{\mathcal{I}} = \{(o, i) : o \in (\mathsf{Nd}^i)^{\mathcal{J}}, 0 \leq i \leq l \text{ and } o \notin (\mathsf{Eq}^{j,i})^{\mathcal{J}} \text{ for any } 0 \leq j < i\}$,
- $(f)^{\mathcal{I}}((o, i)) = (o', j)$ whenever $(f)^{\mathcal{J}}(o) = o'$ where j is the smallest integer such that $o \in (\mathsf{Eq}^{j,i})^{\mathcal{J}}$ if such value exists and i otherwise; and
- $(o, i) \in (\mathsf{D})^{\mathcal{I}}$ whenever $(o, i) \in \Delta^{\mathcal{J}}$ and $o \in (\mathsf{D}^i)^{\mathcal{J}}$.

It is easy to verify that $(o, 0)$ falsifies $\mathsf{D} \sqsubseteq \mathsf{E}$ whenever o belongs to $(\mathsf{Nd}^0 \sqcap \mathsf{D}^0 \sqcap \mathsf{Not}(E))$, and such an object must exist by our assumptions. Also, $\mathcal{I} \models \mathcal{T}$, as otherwise by cases analysis we get a contradiction with $\mathcal{J} \models (\bigcup_{0 \leq i \leq l} \mathcal{T}^i) \cup (\bigcup_{0 \leq i < j \leq l} \mathcal{T}^{i,j}) \cup \mathcal{E}(l) \cup \mathcal{N}(l)$. □

Corollary 13. *The implication problem for limited $\mathcal{DLFD}$ is decidable and EXPTIME-complete.*

Proof. Follows immediately from Theorems 9 and 12 above. □

5 On PFDs, Nominals and ABoxes

In this section, we explore the possibility of relaxing the non-emptiness condition for left hand sides of PFDs in limited $\mathcal{DLFD}$. Doing so is highly desirable, since, as we have hinted in our introductory comments, this would effectively endow limited $\mathcal{DLFD}$ with a capability for *nominals*. To see this, consider that our introductory *single site for client information* example can be elaborated as follows.

$$\mathsf{Site3} \sqsubseteq \mathsf{Site3} : \to Id \quad \top \sqsubseteq \forall Site3Ref.\mathsf{Site3} \quad \mathsf{Client} \sqsubseteq \forall LocationOfData.\mathsf{Site3}$$

The first pair of inclusion dependencies define an individual called Site3 in two steps: (1) establish that at most one such individual exists, and (2) that at least one exists if anything exists. The final inclusion dependency then asserts that the location of data for any given client is this individual, thus accomplishing the objectives.

Although desirable, we show in the remainder of this section that allowing PFDs with empty left hand sides leads to undecidability of the logical implication problem for limited $\mathcal{DLFD}$. To do so, we digress to consider a weaker alternative in which the problem is considered in the context of an ABox, showing for this case to begin with that the problem already becomes undecidable by presenting a reduction of the unrestricted tiling problem. However, it is possible with enough restrictions on the use of other concept constructors to re-obtain decidability [9].

An ABox consists of a finite collection of assertions $\mathcal{A}$ about individuals Ind_1, Ind_2, etc., that denote elements of the domain. An assertion establishes concept membership for individuals with the form "$D(\mathrm{Ind}_i)$", or attribute values for individuals with the form "$f(\mathrm{Ind}_i, \mathrm{Ind}_j)$". The reduction of a given tiling problem $U = (T, H, V)$ to a logical implication problem for limited $\mathcal{DLFD}$ in the context of an ABox constructs a terminology and ABox pair, denoted $\langle \mathcal{T}_U, \mathcal{A}_U \rangle$, by first establishing an integer grid in steps.

1. Begin by defining a triangle *seed* pattern by including in $\mathcal{A}_U$ the following assertions.

$$X(\mathrm{Ind}_1) \quad Y(\mathrm{Ind}_2) \quad Z(\mathrm{Ind}_3) \quad f(\mathrm{Ind}_1, \mathrm{Ind}_2) \quad g(\mathrm{Ind}_1, \mathrm{Ind}_3) \quad g(\mathrm{Ind}_2, \mathrm{Ind}_3)$$

2. Now use the triangle seed pattern to create a possibly infinite *horizontal sequence* of objects that are instances of alternating concepts A_0 and B_0. The results of this step are illustrated along the top of Figure 5.

$$X \sqsubseteq A_0 \quad Y \sqsubseteq B_0$$
$$A_0 \sqsubseteq A \sqcap (\forall f.B_0) \sqcap (B_0 : g \to fh) \quad B_0 \sqsubseteq B \sqcap (\forall f.A_0) \sqcap (A_0 : h \to fg)$$

3. And finally, extend this sequence in the vertical direction to form the integer grid. The results of this step are also illustrated in Figure 5.

$$A \sqsubseteq (\forall k.A) \sqcap (B : g \to kg) \quad B \sqsubseteq (\forall k.B) \sqcap (A : h \to kh)$$

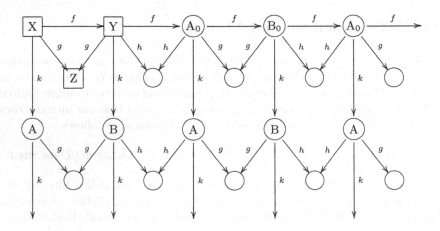

Fig. 5. Defining a Grid using an ABox

As before, the tiling problem U is modeled using primitive concepts T_i for each tile $t_i \in T$, asserting that $T_i \sqcap T_j \sqsubseteq \bot$ for all $i < j$. We place the tiles on the grid points using the assertion $(A \sqcup B) \sqsubseteq \bigsqcup_{t_i \in T} T_i$. The adjacency rules for the instance U of the tiling problem are then captured as follows:

- for $(t_i, t_j) \notin H$:

$$A \sqcap T_i \sqsubseteq (B \sqcap T_j) : g \to Id \quad B \sqcap T_i \sqsubseteq (A \sqcap T_j) : h \to Id$$

- for $(t_i, t_j) \notin V$:

$$(A \sqcap T_i) \sqcap \forall k.(A \sqcap T_j) \sqsubseteq \bot \quad (B \sqcap T_i) \sqcap \forall k.(B \sqcap T_j) \sqsubseteq \bot$$

where T_i corresponds to a tile type $t_i \in T$. The above constraints form a terminology $\mathcal{T}_U$ and ABox $\mathcal{A}_U$ associated with an unrestricted tiling problem U that immediately yields the following result:

Theorem 14. *An instance* $U = (T, H, V)$ *of the infinite tiling problem admits a solution if and only if*

$$\langle \mathcal{T}_U, \mathcal{A}_U \rangle \not\models X \sqsubseteq \bot.$$

Corollary 15. *The logical implication problem for limited* $\mathcal{DLFD}$ *in the context of an ABox is undecidable.*

Our main result in this section now follows since PFDs with empty left hand sides can simulate the above triangle seed by instead adding the following to $\mathcal{T}_U$:

$$X \sqcap Y \sqsubseteq \bot \quad X \sqsubseteq (\forall f.Y) \sqcap (\forall g.Z) \quad Y \sqsubseteq \forall g.Z \quad Z \sqsubseteq Z :\to Id$$

Corollary 16. *The logical implication problem for limited* $\mathcal{DLFD}$ *in which PFDs are permitted empty left hand sides is undecidable.*

6 Conclusions

We have shown that allowing PFDs to occur in the scope of negation or on the left hand sides of inclusion dependencies in $\mathcal{DLFD}$ leads to undecidability of its logical implication problem, and therefore that a full integration of keys and functional dependencies in expressive DLs is not in general possible. Conversely, by virtue of reductions to simpler dialects, we have shown that the complexity of this problem remains unchanged for limited $\mathcal{DLFD}$ in which PFDs are restricted to occur within the scope of monotone concept constructors on right hand sides of inclusion dependencies.

There are several ways that limited $\mathcal{DLFD}$ can be extended without changing the complexity of its logical implication problem. For example, by using reductions introduced in [18], it is straightforward to add roles, quantified number restrictions on roles and even role inversion. (Feature inversion, however, is another matter since its addition to simple $\mathcal{DLFD}$ already leads to undecidability [17,19].)

There is also a possibility of extending limited $\mathcal{DLFD}$ with *regular path functional dependencies* as defined in [21]. In this case, left and right-hand-sides of PFDs are specified as regular languages that can define infinite sets of path functions. Such constraints have applications in reasoning about equality in semistructured databases [21] and in capturing inductive data types in information integration, thus extending the work in [12].

Another direction of future research includes studying terminologies stratified with respect to the interactions of the PFD constructor and negation in an attempt to extend the applicability of the proposed approach.

References

1. R. Berger. The undecidability of the dominoe problem. *Mem. Amer. Math. Soc.*, 66:1–72, 1966.
2. Joachim Biskup and Torsten Polle. Decomposition of Database Classes under Path Functional Dependencies and Onto Constraints. In *Foundations of Information and Knowledge Systems*, pages 31–49, 2000.
3. Joachim Biskup and Torsten Polle. Adding inclusion dependencies to an object-oriented data model with uniqueness constraints. *Acta Informatica*, 39:391–449, 2003.
4. Alexander Borgida and Grant E. Weddell. Adding Uniqueness Constraints to Description Logics (Preliminary Report). In *International Conference on Deductive and Object-Oriented Databases*, pages 85–102, 1997.
5. Diego Calvanese, Giuseppe De Giacomo, and Maurizio Lenzerini. Identification Constraints and Functional Dependencies in Description Logics. In *Proc. of the 17th Int. Joint Conf. on Artificial Intelligence (IJCAI)*, pages 155–160, 2001.
6. Diego Calvanese, Giuseppe De Giacomo, and Maurizio Lenzerini. Representing and reasoning on xml documents: A description logic approach. *J. Log. Comput.*, 9(3):295–318, 1999.
7. Diego Calvanese, Maurizio Lenzerini, and Giuseppe De Giacomo. Keys for Free in Description Logics. In *Proceeding of the 2000 International Workshop on Description Logics*, pages 79–88, 2000.
8. David DeHaan, David Toman, and Grant E. Weddell. Rewriting Aggregate Queries using Description Logics. In *Description Logics 2003*, pages 103–112. CEUR-WS vol.81, 2003.
9. Minoru Ito and Grant E. Weddell. Implication Problems for Functional Constraints on Databases Supporting Complex Objects. *Journal of Computer and System Sciences*, 49(3):726–768, 1994.
10. Vitaliy L. Khizder, David Toman, and Grant E. Weddell. Reasoning about Duplicate Elimination with Description Logic. In *Rules and Objects in Databases (DOOD, part of CL'00)*, pages 1017–1032, 2000.
11. Vitaliy L. Khizder, David Toman, and Grant E. Weddell. On Decidability and Complexity of Description Logics with Uniqueness Constraints. In *International Conference on Database Theory ICDT'01*, pages 54–67, 2001.
12. Huizhu Liu, David Toman, and Grant E. Weddell. Fine Grained Information Integration with Description Logic. In *Description Logics 2002*, pages 1–12. CEUR-WS vol.53, 2002.
13. C. Lutz and M. Milicic. Description Logics with Concrete Domains and Functional Dependencies. In *Proc. European Conference on Artificial Intelligence (ECAI)*, pages 378–382, 2004.

14. Carsten Lutz, Carlos Areces, Ian Horrocks, and Ulrike Sattler. Keys, Nominals, and Concrete Domains. In *Proc. of the 18th Int. Joint Conf. on Artificial Intelligence (IJCAI)*, pages 349–354, 2003.
15. U. Sattler, D. Calvanese, and R. Molitor. Relationships with other formalisms. In *The Description Logic Handbook: Theory, Implementation, and Applications*, chapter 4, pages 137–177. Cambridge University Press, 2003.
16. Lubomir Stanchev and Grant E. Weddell. Index Selection for Embedded Control Applications using Description Logics. In *Description Logics 2003*, pages 9–18. CEUR-WS vol.81, 2003.
17. David Toman and Grant Weddell. On the Interaction between Inverse Features and Path-functional Dependencies in Description Logics. In *Proc. of the 19th Int. Joint Conf. on Artificial Intelligence (IJCAI)*, pages 603–608, 2005.
18. David Toman and Grant E. Weddell. On Attributes, Roles, and Dependencies in Description Logics and the Ackermann Case of the Decision Problem. In *Description Logics 2001*, pages 76–85. CEUR-WS vol.49, 2001.
19. David Toman and Grant E. Weddell. Attribute Inversion in Description Logics with Path Functional Dependencies. In *Description Logics 2004*, pages 178–187. CEUR-WS vol.104, 2004.
20. David Toman and Grant E. Weddell. On Path-functional Dependencies as First-class Citizens in Description Logics. In *Description Logics 2005*. CEUR-WS vol.147, 2005.
21. David Toman and Grant E. Weddell. On Reasoning about Structural Equality in XML: A Description Logic Approach. *Theoretical Computer Science*, 336:181–203, 2005. doi:10.1016/j.tcs.2004.10.036.
22. P. van Emde Boas. The convenience of tilings. In *Complexity, Logic, and Recursion Theory*, volume 187 of *Lecture notes in pure and applied mathe-matics*, pages 331–363. Marcel Dekker Inc., 1997.
23. Grant Weddell. A Theory of Functional Dependencies for Object Oriented Data Models. In *International Conference on Deductive and Object-Oriented Databases*, pages 165–184, 1989.

A Resolution-Based Decision Procedure for $\mathcal{SHOIQ}$

Yevgeny Kazakov and Boris Motik

University of Manchester, UK

Abstract. We present a resolution-based decision procedure for the description logic $\mathcal{SHOIQ}$—the logic underlying the Semantic Web ontology language OWL-DL. Our procedure is goal-oriented, and it naturally extends a similar procedure for $\mathcal{SHIQ}$, which has proven itself in practice. Applying existing techniques for deriving saturation-based decision procedures to $\mathcal{SHOIQ}$ is not straightforward due to nominals, number restrictions, and inverse roles—a combination known to cause termination problems. We overcome this difficulty by using the basic superposition calculus, extended with custom simplification rules.

1 Introduction

Description logics (DLs) are a family of knowledge representation formalisms [2] that have been applied in numerous areas of computer science, such as information integration and ontology modeling. In particular, the DL $\mathcal{SHOIQ}$ provides a logical foundation for the Web Ontology Language (OWL)—the language standardized by the W3C for building ontologies in the Semantic Web. Thus, to implement advanced Semantic Web applications based on OWL-DL, practical reasoning procedures for $\mathcal{SHOIQ}$ are required.

It is known that $\mathcal{SHOIQ}$ can be embedded into $\mathcal{C}^2$ [21]—the two-variable fragment of first-order logic with counting quantifiers. Furthermore, $\mathcal{C}^2$ is decidable in NExpTime [18] (this result was recently sharpened to allow for binary coding of numbers [19]). However, all known decision procedures for $\mathcal{C}^2$ use a rather blind "guess-and-check" approach, which is unlikely to be suitable for practical purposes. Rather, a practical algorithm should be goal-oriented, using the input problem to guide the search.

Designing such a procedure for $\mathcal{SHOIQ}$ has proved to be a nontrivial task. Namely, this logic provides for inverse roles, number restrictions, and *nominals*—concepts with a bounded number of elements. The intricate interaction between these constructs makes extending existing (tableau-based) procedures difficult. Only recently, a goal-directed tableau-based procedure was presented in [10]; it uses a nondeterministic guess on the size of nominals to ensure termination.

In this paper, we present an alternative reasoning procedure based on resolution. $\mathcal{SHOIQ}$ is a hard logic, so it is not obvious which reasoning method is most suitable for practice. Rather, comparing different methods and identifying which ones are suitable for which types of problems can give crucial insights

U. Furbach and N. Shankar (Eds.): IJCAR 2006, LNAI 4130, pp. 662–677, 2006.

into building practical reasoning systems. Furthermore, this procedure is based on the same principles as the procedure for a weaker logic $\mathcal{SHIQ}$ [11], which was implemented in a new reasoning system KAON2,[1] and has shown promising results for answering queries over large data sets.

To obtain an algorithm for $\mathcal{SHOIQ}$, we face problems analogous to those encountered in constructing the tableau algorithm from [10]. Namely, the combination of nominals, inverse roles, and number restrictions can cause resolution to derive clauses of unbounded size, thus preventing termination. We solve these problems using novel *simplification* rules, which rename complex terms with simpler ones based on their semantic meaning.

2 Preliminaries

Description Logic $\mathcal{SHOIQ}$. Given a set of role names N_R, a *role* is either some $R \in N_R$ or an *inverse role* R^- for $R \in N_R$. An *RBox* $KB_{\mathcal{R}}$ is a finite set of role inclusion axioms $R \sqsubseteq S$ and transitivity axioms $\mathsf{Trans}(R)$, for R and S roles. For $R \in N_R$, we set $\mathsf{Inv}(R) = R^-$ and $\mathsf{Inv}(R^-) = R$, and assume that $R \sqsubseteq S \in KB_{\mathcal{R}}$ ($\mathsf{Trans}(R) \in KB_{\mathcal{R}}$) implies $\mathsf{Inv}(R) \sqsubseteq \mathsf{Inv}(S) \in KB_{\mathcal{R}}$ ($\mathsf{Trans}(\mathsf{Inv}(R)) \in KB_{\mathcal{R}}$). A role R is said to be *simple* if $\mathsf{Trans}(S) \notin KB_{\mathcal{R}}$ for each $S \sqsubseteq^* R$, where $\sqsubseteq^*$ is the reflexive-transitive closure of $\sqsubseteq$.

For N_C a set of *concept names* and N_I a set of *individuals*, the set of *concepts* is the smallest set containing $\top$, $\bot$, A, $\neg C$, $C \sqcap D$, $C \sqcup D$, $\{a\}$, $\exists R.C$, $\forall R.C$, $\geqslant n\,S.C$, and $\leqslant n\,S.C$, where $A \in N_C$, C and D are concepts, R is a role, S is a simple role, a is an individual, and n is a nonnegative integer.

A TBox $KB_{\mathcal{T}}$ is a finite set of *concept inclusion axioms* $C \sqsubseteq D$. An ABox $KB_{\mathcal{A}}$ is a finite set of axioms $C(a)$, $R(a,b)$, and (in)equalities $a \approx b$ and $a \not\approx b$, for $a,b \in N_I$. A $\mathcal{SHOIQ}$ knowledge base KB is a triple $(KB_{\mathcal{R}}, KB_{\mathcal{T}}, KB_{\mathcal{A}})$. With $|KB|$ we denote the number of symbols needed to encode KB using unary coding of numbers. KB is given semantics by translating it into first-order logic using the operator π defined in Table 1. The main inference problem in $\mathcal{SHOIQ}$ is checking satisfiability of KB, or, equivalently, of $\pi(KB)$.

Basic Superposition Calculus. We assume familiarity with standard notions of resolution theorem proving [4] and term rewriting [3]. For a term t, $t|_p$ denotes the subterm of t at the position p, and $t[s]_p$ denotes the replacement of $t|_p$ in t with a term s. We encode literals $(\neg)A$ as $(\neg)A \approx \mathsf{tt}$ in a multi-sorted setting, so $\approx$ is the only predicate symbol. We do not distinguish $(\neg)s \approx t$ from $(\neg)t \approx s$. For a literal L, with $\overline{L}$ we denote a literal obtained from L by flipping its sign.

Basic superposition ($\mathcal{BS}$) [5,15] is a calculus for equational theorem proving. Its inference rules work with *closures*, which consist of (i) a *skeleton* clause C and (ii) a *substitution* σ. A closure is written as $C \cdot \sigma$ and it is semantically interpreted as the clause $C\sigma$; it is *ground* if $C\sigma$ is ground. The *empty closure* is denoted by $\square$. A closure can be conveniently represented by *marking* with $[\,]$ the terms from $C\sigma$ occurring at variable positions of C. Any position at

---

[1] http://kaon2.semanticweb.org/

Table 1. Semantics of $\mathcal{SHOIQ}$ by Mapping to FOL

Translating Concepts to FOL

$$\pi_y(\top, X) = \top$$
$$\pi_y(\bot, X) = \bot$$
$$\pi_y(A, X) = A(X)$$
$$\pi_y(\{a\}, X) = X \approx a$$
$$\pi_y(\neg C, X) = \neg\pi_y(C, X)$$
$$\pi_y(C \sqcap D, X) = \pi_y(C, X) \wedge \pi_y(D, X)$$
$$\pi_y(C \sqcup D, X) = \pi_y(C, X) \vee \pi_y(D, X)$$
$$\pi_y(\exists R.C, X) = \exists y : R(X, y) \wedge \pi_x(C, y)$$
$$\pi_y(\forall R.C, X) = \forall y : R(X, y) \rightarrow \pi_x(C, y)$$
$$\pi_y(\geqslant n\, S.C, X) = \exists y_1, \ldots, y_n : \bigwedge_{i=1}^{n} [S(X, y_i) \wedge \pi_x(C, y_i)] \wedge \bigwedge_{1 \leq i < j \leq n} y_i \not\approx y_j$$
$$\pi_y(\leqslant n\, S.C, X) = \forall y \exists y_1, \ldots, y_n : [S(X, y) \wedge \pi_x(C, y)] \rightarrow \bigvee_{i=1}^{n} y \approx y_i$$

Translating Axioms to FOL

$$\pi(C \sqsubseteq D) = \forall x : \pi_y(C, x) \rightarrow \pi_y(D, x)$$
$$\pi(R \sqsubseteq S) = \forall x, y : R(x, y) \rightarrow S(x, y)$$
$$\pi(\mathbf{Trans}(R)) = \forall x, y, z : R(x, y) \wedge R(y, z) \rightarrow R(x, z)$$
$$\pi(C(a)) = \pi_y(C, a)$$
$$\pi(R(a, b)) = R(a, b)$$
$$\pi(a \circ b) = a \circ b \text{ for } \circ \in \{\approx, \not\approx\}$$
$$\pi(KB) = \bigwedge_{R \in N_R} \forall x, y : [R(x, y) \leftrightarrow R^-(y, x)] \wedge \bigwedge_{\alpha \in KB_{\mathcal{T}} \cup KB_{\mathcal{R}} \cup KB_{\mathcal{A}}} \pi(\alpha)$$

π_x is obtained by simultaneously substituting in the definition of
π_y all $x_{(i)}$ for all $y_{(i)}$, respectively, and π_y for π_x.
X is a meta-variable and is substituted by the actual variable.

or beneath a marked position is called a *substitution position*. For example, $(P(x) \vee z \approx b) \cdot \{x \mapsto f(y), z \mapsto g(b)\}$ can be written as $P([f(y)]) \vee [g(b)] \approx b$.

The $\mathcal{BS}$ calculus is parameterized with an admissible ordering on terms and a selection function. An *admissible ordering on terms* $\succ$ is a *reduction ordering* total on ground terms. The term ordering is extended to literals by identifying a literal $s \approx t$ with a multiset $\{\{s\}, \{t\}\}$ and a literal $s \not\approx t$ with a multiset $\{\{s, t\}\}$, and by comparing these multisets by a two-fold multiset extension of the term ordering $\succ$; we denote the literal ordering also with $\succ$. A *selection function* selects an arbitrary set of negative literals in each clause.

A literal $L \cdot \sigma$ is (strictly) maximal w.r.t. a closure $C \cdot \sigma$ if $L' \sigma \succ L\sigma$ ($L' \sigma \succeq L\sigma$) for no $L' \in C$. A literal $L \cdot \sigma$ is *(strictly) eligible* in $(C \vee L) \cdot \sigma$ if either (i) no literal is selected in $(C \vee L) \cdot \sigma$ and $L \cdot \sigma$ is (strictly) maximal w.r.t. $C \cdot \sigma$, or (ii) $L \cdot \sigma$ is selected in $(C \vee L) \cdot \sigma$. The inference rules of $\mathcal{BS}$ are presented in Table 2. Note that the standard resolution and factoring inference rules can be viewed as "macros," combining negative superposition and equality factoring, respectively, with reflexivity resolution.

We next present the redundancy criteria for closures. Let $\mathcal{R}$ be a ground and convergent rewrite system, and $C \cdot \sigma$ a ground closure. A variable x in the skeleton C of $C \cdot \sigma$ is *variable irreducible w.r.t.* $\mathcal{R}$ if (i) $x\sigma$ is irreducible by $\mathcal{R}$, or (ii) x occurs in C only in literals of the form $x \approx s$ such that $x\sigma \succ s\sigma$, and $x\sigma$ is irreducible by those rules $l \Rightarrow r \in \mathcal{R}$ for which $x\sigma \approx s\sigma \succ l \approx r$. Furthermore, $C \cdot \sigma$ is *variable irreducible w.r.t.* $\mathcal{R}$ if all variables from C are variable irreducible w.r.t. $\mathcal{R}$. For $C \cdot \sigma$ a possibly nonground closure, $\mathrm{irred}_{\mathcal{R}}(C \cdot \sigma)$ is the set of all ground closures $C \cdot \sigma\tau$ that are variable irreducible w.r.t. a rewrite system $\mathcal{R}$.

Table 2. Inference Rules of the $\mathcal{BS}$ Calculus

Positive superposition: $$\frac{(C \vee s \approx t) \cdot \rho \quad (D \vee w \approx v) \cdot \rho}{(C \vee D \vee w[t]_p \approx v) \cdot \theta}$$	(i) $\sigma = \mathsf{MGU}(s\rho, w\rho\|_p)$ and $\theta = \rho\sigma$; (ii) $t\theta \not\preceq s\theta$ and $v\theta \not\preceq w\theta$; (iii) $(s \approx t) \cdot \theta$ is strictly eligible; (iv) $(w \approx v) \cdot \theta$ is strictly eligible; (v) $s\theta \approx t\theta \not\preceq w\theta \approx v\theta$; (vi) $w\|_p$ is not a variable.
Negative superposition: $$\frac{(C \vee s \approx t) \cdot \rho \quad (D \vee w \not\approx v) \cdot \rho}{(C \vee D \vee w[t]_p \not\approx v) \cdot \theta}$$	(i) $\sigma = \mathsf{MGU}(s\rho, w\rho\|_p)$ and $\theta = \rho\sigma$; (ii) $t\theta \not\preceq s\theta$ and $v\theta \not\preceq w\theta$; (iii) $(s \approx t) \cdot \theta$ is strictly eligible; (iv) $(w \not\approx v) \cdot \theta$ is eligible; (v) $w\|_p$ is not a variable.
Reflexivity resolution: $$\frac{(C \vee s \not\approx t) \cdot \rho}{C \cdot \theta}$$	(i) $\sigma = \mathsf{MGU}(s\rho, t\rho)$ and $\theta = \rho\sigma$; (ii) $(s \not\approx t) \cdot \theta$ is eligible.
Equality factoring: $$\frac{(C \vee s \approx t \vee s' \approx t') \cdot \rho}{(C \vee t \not\approx t' \vee s' \approx t') \cdot \theta}$$	(i) $\sigma = \mathsf{MGU}(s\rho, s'\rho)$ and $\theta = \rho\sigma$; (ii) $t\theta \not\preceq s\theta$ and $t'\theta \not\preceq s'\theta$; (iii) $(s \approx t) \cdot \theta$ is eligible.

A closure $C \cdot \sigma$ is *redundant w.r.t. a set of closures* N if, for all rewrite systems $\mathcal{R}$ and all ground substitutions τ, if $C \cdot \sigma\tau \in \mathsf{irred}_{\mathcal{R}}(C \cdot \sigma)$, then $\mathsf{irred}_{\mathcal{R}}(N)$ contains closures $C_1, \ldots, C_n$, such that $\{C_1, \ldots, C_n\} \models C\sigma\tau$ and $C\sigma\tau \succ C_i$, where $\succ$ is the multiset extension of the literal ordering to closures.

We extend basic superposition with several *simplification rules*, which can simplify a closure set $N \cup \{C \cdot \rho\}$ to $N \cup \{C_1 \cdot \rho, \ldots, C_n \cdot \rho\}$. Such application of a simplification rule is *sound* if it preserves satisfiability; it is *correct* if the closure $C \cdot \rho$ is redundant w.r.t. $N \cup \{C_1 \cdot \rho, \ldots, C_n \cdot \rho\}$. In [5] the authors present several sound and correct simplification rules, such as elimination of duplicate literals, tautology deletion, closure subsumption, and elimination of marked positions—that is, replacing $C \cdot \sigma$ with $C\rho \cdot \theta$ such that $\sigma = \rho\theta$.

The following two simplification rules can be used to split off ground literals in closures: *cut* nondeterministically derives $L \cdot \{\}$ or $\overline{L} \cdot \{\}$ for a ground literal L, and *ground unit resolution* simplifies a closure $C \cdot \rho \vee L \cdot \rho$ into $C \cdot \rho$ if the closure set contains a ground closure $L' \cdot \theta$ such that $\overline{L}\rho = L'\theta$.

Let N_0 be a set of closures of the form $C \cdot \{\}$, and let N_∞ be obtained by a fair saturation of N_0 by $\mathcal{BS}$ up to redundancy. Then, N_0 is unsatisfiable if and only if N_∞ contains the empty closure.

3 Preprocessing

We split our decision procedure into a *preprocessing phase*, which converts a $\mathcal{SHOIQ}$ knowledge base KB into a set of closures of a certain type, and a *saturation phase*, which checks satisfiability of the closure set using $\mathcal{BS}$. In the rest of this section, we present the preprocessing phase in detail.

Table 3. Closure Types after Preprocessing

Axiom	Closure
$R = \mathsf{Inv}(S)$	1. $\neg R(x,y) \vee S(y,x)$ and $\neg S(x,y) \vee R(y,x)$
$R \sqsubseteq S$	2. $\neg R(x,y) \vee S(x,y)$
$L_1 \sqsubseteq \geqslant n\, R.L_2$	3. $\overline{L_1(x)} \vee R(x, f_i(x))$
	4. $\overline{L_1(x)} \vee L_2(f_i(x))$
	5. $\overline{L_1(x)} \vee f_i(x) \not\approx f_j(x)$ $1 \leq i < j \leq n$
$\top \sqsubseteq \bigsqcup L_i$	6. $\bigvee L_i(x)$
$L \sqsubseteq \{c\}$	7. $L(x) \vee x \approx c$
$L_1 \sqsubseteq \leqslant n\, R.L_2$	8. $\overline{L_1(x)} \vee \neg R(x,y) \vee \overline{L_2(y)} \vee \bigvee_{i=1}^n f_i(x) \approx y$
$L(c)$	9. $L(c)$
$R(c,d)$	10. $R(c,d)$
$c \approx d$	11. $c \approx d$
$c \not\approx d$	12. $c \not\approx d$

Note: $L_{(i)}$ are of the form A or $\neg A$ for A an atomic concept. $L_1 \sqsubseteq \exists R.L_2$ and $L_1 \sqsubseteq \forall R.L_2$ are translated as $L_1 \sqsubseteq \geqslant 1\, R.L_2$ and $L_1 \sqsubseteq \leqslant 0\, R.\overline{L_2}$, respectively.

Eliminating Transitivity Axioms. It is well-known that deciding a logic with transitivity axioms by means of saturation calculi is difficult, and that it requires advanced techniques [13]. Therefore, we eliminate transitivity axioms by polynomially encoding KB into an equisatisfiable knowledge base $\Omega(KB)$ without such axioms. Roughly speaking, a transitivity axiom $\mathsf{Trans}(S)$ is replaced with axioms $\forall R.C \sqsubseteq \forall S.(\forall S.C)$, for each R with $S \sqsubseteq^* R$ and C is a "relevant" concept from KB. For more details, please see [14, Section 5.2]. (The latter result considers only $\mathcal{SHIQ}$; for $\mathcal{SHOIQ}$, the encoding is the same, and extending the correctness proof is trivial.) Similar encodings were presented in [21,20].

Translation into Closures. Next, we simplify the TBox axioms of $\Omega(KB)$ by introducing new concept names for nonatomic subconcepts. For example, we simplify the axiom $C \sqsubseteq \exists R.\exists S.A$ by introducing a new concept Q and by replacing this axiom with $C \sqsubseteq \exists R.Q$ and $Q \sqsubseteq \exists S.A$. This transformation is analogous to the *structural transformation* [17]; for details, please see [14, Section 5.3.1].

For unary coding of numbers in number restrictions, this transformation is polynomial, and it preserves satisfiability. Furthermore, it produces axioms containing at most one nonatomic concept. Such axioms are converted into closures by translating them into first-order logic using the operator π from Table 1, skolemizing the existential quantifiers, and translating the result into conjunctive normal form. We denote the resulting set of closures with $\Xi(KB)$. Table 3 shows the closures that are produced by different types of axioms.

Introduction of Guards. Using nominals, one can restrict the cardinality of the interpretation domain, which makes it possible to derive a closure of the form $x \approx a_1 \vee \cdots \vee x \approx a_n$. Such closures can cause problems, since the variable x is *unshielded* (that is, x does not occur in the closure as a proper subterm). This allows for superposition inferences from x, which are prolific since x unifies with any term. We avoid this problem using the following transformation.

Definition 1. *For a closure $C \cdot \rho$, a variable x of $C\rho$ is guarded if it occurs in $C\rho$ in a negative nonequational literal, called a guard for x. Let KB be a $\mathcal{SHOIQ}$ knowledge base and T a predicate not occurring in $\Xi(KB)$. Then, $\Gamma(KB)$ is the smallest set such that (i) for each closure $C \cdot \rho \in \Xi(KB)$, $\Gamma(KB)$ contains the closure $\neg T(x_1) \vee \cdots \vee \neg T(x_n) \vee C \cdot \rho$, where $x_1, \ldots, x_n$ are all nonguarded variables of $C\rho$; (ii) for each constant c occurring in $\Xi(KB)$, $\Gamma(KB)$ contains the closure $T(c)$ (if there are no constants, we add one); and (iii) for each function symbol f occurring in $\Xi(KB)$, $\Gamma(KB)$ contains the closure $\neg T(x) \vee T(f(x))$.*

Lemma 1. *$\Xi(KB)$ is satisfiable if and only if $\Gamma(KB)$ is satisfiable.*

Proof. ($\Rightarrow$) Let I be a model of $\Xi(KB)$, and I' an interpretation obtained by making $T(x)$ to be true for all x. Clearly, I' is a model of $\Gamma(KB)$. ($\Leftarrow$) In each Herbrand model I of $\Gamma(KB)$, $\neg T(x) \vee T(f(x))$ and $T(c)$ ensure that T holds on all elements of I. Hence, each $\neg T(x_i)$ in a closure from $\Gamma(KB)$ is false in I, so I is a model of $\Xi(KB)$. $\qquad\square$

4 Saturating Closures by Basic Superposition

After preprocessing, our algorithm continues by saturating the set of closures $\Gamma(KB)$ by basic superposition. To prove that the saturation terminates, we apply the approach used in most existing resolution-based procedures [12,6,7,16,1]. We define a class of closures $\mathcal{N}_{DL}$ and demonstrate the following properties: (i) $\mathcal{N}_{DL}$ contains the closures obtained by translating a $\mathcal{SHOIQ}$ knowledge base KB, (ii) applying an inference rule of $\mathcal{BS}$ to closures from $\mathcal{N}_{DL}$ produces a closure in $\mathcal{N}_{DL}$, and (iii) $\mathcal{N}_{DL}$ contains finitely many closures for a finite signature. For a fixed signature, Conditions (i)–(iii) ensure that $\mathcal{BS}$ produces only finitely many closures from $\mathcal{N}_{DL}$ in a saturation. However, as we discuss in the following subsection, to coerce $\mathcal{BS}$ into producing closures of a restricted syntactic structure, we introduce several novel *simplification* rules. These rules can extend the signature, so, to ensure termination, we additionally show that (iv) the signature is extended only a finite number of times in a saturation.

4.1 The Problems in Ensuring Termination for $\mathcal{SHOIQ}$

It is well-known that reasoning in $\mathcal{SHOIQ}$ is difficult due to a subtle interaction involving nominals, number restrictions, and inverse roles. This interaction makes it difficult to ensure termination of $\mathcal{BS}$ on $\Xi(KB)$. We demonstrate these problems next on an example and sketch our solution.

Let KB be a $\mathcal{SHOIQ}$ knowledge base containing axioms T1–T4 from Table 4. The preprocessing step, when applied to these axioms, produces the closures (1)–(9) shown on the far right; furthermore, saturation of (1)–(9) by basic superposition produces closures (10)–(18). Note that (18) is similar in structure

Table 4. Example of Termination Problems

Knowledge base KB and the closures obtained after preprocessing:

T1. $O \sqsubseteq \{c\}$ $\quad\Rightarrow$ $\quad\Rightarrow$ (1) $\neg O(x) \lor x \approx c$

T2. $\top \sqsubseteq \exists R_1.\top \sqcup \exists R_2.\top$ $\quad\Rightarrow \top \sqsubseteq U_1 \sqcup U_2$ $\quad\Rightarrow$ (2) $\neg \overline{T(x)} \lor U_1(x) \lor U_2(x)$

$\quad\Rightarrow U_i \sqsubseteq \exists R_i.\top, \quad i = 1,2$ $\quad\Rightarrow$ (3) $\neg \overline{U_i(x)} \lor R_i(x, f_i(x))$

T3. $\top \sqsubseteq\, \leqslant 1\, R_i^-.\top, \; i = 1,2 \Rightarrow$ $\quad\Rightarrow$ (4) $\neg R_i^-(x,y) \lor g_i(x) \approx y$

$\quad\Rightarrow$ inverses of R_i, $i = 1,2$ $\quad\Rightarrow$ (5) $\neg R_i(x,y) \lor R_i^-(y,x)$

T4. $O \sqsubseteq \forall R_i.O, \quad i = 1,2 \Rightarrow$ $\quad\Rightarrow$ (6) $\neg O(x) \lor \neg R_i(x,y) \lor O(y)$

$\qquad\qquad$ introduction of guards $\Rightarrow$ (7) $T(c)$

$\quad\Rightarrow$ (8) $\neg \overline{T(x)} \lor T(f_i(x))$

$\quad\Rightarrow$ (9) $\neg T(x) \lor \overline{T(g_i(x))}$

Saturation of (1)–(9):

[Resolving 3 with 6]: (10) $\neg U_i(x) \lor \neg O(x) \lor O([f_i(x)])$

[Resolving 10 with 1]: **(11) $\neg U_i(x) \lor \neg O(x) \lor \overline{[f_i(x)]} \approx c$**

[Superposing 11 into 3]: (12) $\neg U_i(x) \lor \neg O(x) \lor R_i(x, c)$

[Resolving 12 with 5]: (13) $\neg U_i(x) \lor \neg O(x) \lor R_i^-(c, x)$

[Resolving 13 with 4]: (14) $\neg U_i(x) \lor \neg O(x) \lor x \approx g_i(c)$

[Resolving 2 with 8]: (15) $\neg \overline{T(x)} \lor U_1([f_i(x)]) \lor U_2([f_i(x)])$

[Resolving 15 with 14]: (16) $\neg T(x) \lor \overline{U_2([f_i(x)])} \lor \neg O([f_i(x)]) \lor [f_i(x)] \approx g_1(c)$

[Resolving 16 with 14]: (17) $\neg T(x) \lor \overline{\neg O([f_i(x)])} \lor [f_i(x)] \approx g_1(c) \lor [f_i(x)] \approx g_2(c)$

[Resolving 10 with 17]: **(18) $\neg T(x) \lor \overline{\neg U_i(x)} \lor \neg O(x) \lor [f_i(x)] \approx g_1(c) \lor [f_i(x)] \approx g_2(c)$**

The result after simplifying (18) with (11):

(19) $\neg T(x) \lor \neg U_i(x) \lor \neg O(x) \lor g_1(c) \approx c \lor g_2(c) \approx c$

---

to (11): (18) just contains two literals $f_i(x) \approx g_1(c)$ and $f_i(x) \approx g_2(c)$ instead of just one literal $f_i(x) \approx c$; additionally, (18) contains $\neg T(x)$. It is easy to see that all inferences with (11) can be repeated for (18), and that this would produce even longer closures with even deeper literals $f_i(x) \approx g_1(g_1(c))$, $f_i(x) \approx g_2(g_1(c))$ and so on. This clearly prevents the saturation from terminating.

To deal with this problem, we express (18) equivalently using an additional closure (19). It is easy to see that (19) is a logical consequence of (11) and (18). Furthermore, (19) makes (18) redundant, since (18) follows from smaller closures (11) and (19). Thus, (18) can be deleted from the closure set, which eventually ensures termination of the saturation.

4.2 The Saturation Strategy for Deciding Satisfiability of $\Gamma(KB)$

We say that N is a set of *DL-closures* if every closure in N is of some form from Table 5. Unary predicate symbols in N are organized into two sets $\mathcal{A}$ and $\mathcal{B}$.

Lemma 2. *For KB a $\mathcal{SHOIQ}$ knowledge base, $\Gamma(KB)$ is a set of DL-closures.*

Proof. The set $\Xi(KB)$ contains only closures from Table 3, and, due to Definition 1, each closure in $\Gamma(KB)$ contains a guard literal for each variable. $\quad\square$

To obtain a procedure for checking satisfiability of $\Gamma(KB)$, we next choose the appropriate parameters for $\mathcal{BS}$, and extend it with certain simplification rules.

Table 5. Types of DL-Closures

1	$\alpha(x) \vee (\neg)f(x) \approx g(x)$
2	$\alpha(x) \vee (\neg)f([g(x)]) \approx x$
3	$\alpha(x) \vee (\neg)A(f(x))$
4	$\beta(x) \vee (\neg)f(x) \approx c$
5	$\beta(x) \vee \bigvee(\neg)x \approx t_i$
6	$\alpha(x) \vee \beta([f(x)]) \vee \bigvee [f(x)] \approx t_i \vee \bigvee(\neg)x \approx c_i$
	Condition (∗): if the closure contains a literal $x \approx c_i$, then the closure set
	$\quad\quad\quad$ contains $\alpha'(x) \vee g(f(x)) \approx x$ such that $\alpha(x) = \alpha'(x) \vee \alpha''(x)$.
7	$\alpha_1(x) \vee \neg R(x, y) \vee \alpha_2(y) \vee \bigvee_{i=1}^{n} f_i(x) \approx y$
8	$\neg R(x, y) \vee S(x, y)$ $\quad$ or $\quad$ $\neg R(x, y) \vee S(y, x)$
9	$\alpha(x) \vee R(x, f(x))$ $\quad$ or $\quad$ $\alpha(x) \vee R(f(x), x)$
10	$\beta(x) \vee R(x, c)$ $\quad\quad$ or $\quad$ $\beta(x) \vee R(c, x)$
11	unit closures and $\quad$ $(\neg)B(t)$ $\quad\quad$ $(\neg)t_1 \approx t_2$ $\quad\quad$ $(\neg)f(g(c)) \approx d$
	the empty closure: $\quad$ $(\neg)R(c, d)$ $\quad$ $(\neg)R(c, f(d))$ $\quad$ $(\neg)R(f(c), d)$ $\quad$ $\square$

$\mathcal{A} \subseteq \mathcal{B}$ are sets of predicate symbols; $\mathcal{A}$ contains all predicate symbols of $\Gamma(KB)$.
Each variable in each closure is guarded (see Definition 1).
$\alpha(x)$ is a disjunction $(\neg)A_1(x) \vee \cdots \vee (\neg)A_n(x)$ with $A_i \in \mathcal{A}$.
$\beta(x)$ is a disjunction $(\neg)B_1(x) \vee \cdots \vee (\neg)B_n(x)$ with $B_i \in \mathcal{B}$.
Disjunctions $\alpha(x)$, $\beta(x)$, $\beta([f(x)])$, $\bigvee(\neg)x \approx t_i$, and $\bigvee [f(x)] \approx t_i$ may be empty.
c and d are constants, and $t_{(i)}$ are ground terms of the form c or $f(c)$.

These rules can extend the signature with new predicate symbols and constants. To ensure that only finitely many new symbols are introduced into the signature, our rules reuse previously introduced symbols whenever possible. Thus, an application of a simplification rule depends not only on the current closure set, but also on the inferences applied previously.

Definition 2. *With $\mathcal{BS}_{DL}$ we denote the $\mathcal{BS}$ calculus parametrised by any admissible term ordering $\succ$ such that $f(x) \succ A(x) \succ B(x) \succ c$, $R(x, c) \succ A(x)$, $R(c, x) \succ A(x)$, and $B(f(x)) \succ g(c)$, for a binary predicate $R \in \mathcal{A}$, and unary predicates $A \in \mathcal{A}$ and $B \in \mathcal{B} \setminus \mathcal{A}$. The selection function of $\mathcal{BS}_{DL}$ selects in $C \cdot \sigma$ a literal of the form $\neg R(x, y)$, $x \not\approx c$, or $x \not\approx f(c)$; if there are no such literals and $C\sigma$ does not contain a term $f(x)$, an atom $R(x, c)$, or an atom $R(c, x)$, it selects a literal $\neg B(x)$ if there is one.*

Apart from the standard $\mathcal{BS}$ inferences, $\mathcal{BS}_{DL}$ eagerly applies the simplification rules from Table 6, elimination of duplicate literals, tautology deletion, closure subsumption, and ground unit resolution. Immediately after deriving a closure $C \cdot \rho \vee L \cdot \rho$ where $L\rho$ is ground, $\mathcal{BS}_{DL}$ applies the cut rule for $L\rho$. Marked positions are removed eagerly if this enables applying a simplification rule.

An example of an ordering suitable for $\mathcal{BS}_{DL}$ is a Knuth-Bendix ordering (KBO) [3] with $\mathsf{weight}(f) > \mathsf{weight}(R) > \mathsf{weight}(A) > \mathsf{weight}(B) > \mathsf{weight}(c) > \mathsf{weight}(\mathsf{tt})$, for each function symbol f, binary predicate symbol R, unary predicate symbols $A \in \mathcal{A}$ and $B \in \mathcal{B} \setminus \mathcal{A}$, and a constant symbol c.

Next, we demonstrate that the simplification rules of $\mathcal{BS}_{DL}$ are sound and correct, so that they do not affect soundness or completeness of $\mathcal{BS}$.

Table 6. Simplification Rules of $\mathcal{BS}_{DL}$

Decomposition 1: $$\frac{D \cdot \rho \vee L \cdot \rho}{\begin{array}{c} D \cdot \rho \vee A(x), \\ \neg A(x) \vee L \cdot \rho \end{array}}$$	(i) $L \cdot \rho$ is $(\neg)f(x) \approx g(x)$, $(\neg)f([g(x)]) \approx x$, $R(x, f(x))$, or $R(f(x), x)$; (ii) $D\rho$ contains a term $h(x)$; (iii) If Decomposition 1 has already been applied to a premise with the same $L \cdot \rho$, then A is the same as in the previous application; otherwise, $A \in \mathcal{A}$ is fresh.
Decomposition 2: $$\frac{D \cdot \rho \vee f(x) \approx c}{\begin{array}{c} D \cdot \rho \vee B(x), \\ \neg B(x) \vee f(x) \approx c \end{array}}$$	(i) $D\rho$ contains either a term $h(x)$, or a literal $(\neg)A(x)$ with $A \in \mathcal{A}$; (ii) If Decomposition 2 has already been applied to a premise with the same $f(x) \approx c$, then B is the same as in the previous application; otherwise, $B \in \mathcal{B} \setminus \mathcal{A}$ is fresh.
Nominal Generation 1: $$\frac{\alpha(x) \vee \bigvee_{i=1}^{n} [f(x)] \approx t_i}{\begin{array}{c} \alpha(x) \vee \bigvee_{i=1}^{k} f(x) \approx c_i, \\ \alpha(x) \vee \bigvee_{j=1}^{n} c_i \approx t_j \end{array}}$$ $(1 \leq i \leq k)$	(i) Some t_i is of the form $h(c)$; (ii) If Nominal Generation 1 has already been applied to some $\alpha(x) \vee \bigvee_{i=1}^{n_1} [f(x)] \approx t_i'$ (with the same $\alpha(x)$ and f), then k and c_i are the same as in this previous application; otherwise, $k = n$ and c_i are fresh.
Nominal Generation 2: $$\frac{\alpha(x) \vee \bigvee_{i=1}^{n} [f(x)] \approx t_i \vee \bigvee_{i=1}^{m} x \approx c_i}{\begin{array}{c} \alpha(x) \vee \bigvee_{i=1}^{k} B_i(x), \\ \neg B_i(x) \vee f(x) \approx e_i, \\ \neg B_i(x) \vee x \approx d_i, \\ \alpha(x) \vee \bigvee_{j=1}^{n} e_i \approx t_j \vee \bigvee_{j=1}^{m} d_i \approx c_j \end{array}}$$ $(1 \leq i \leq k)$	(i) Some t_i is of the form $h(c)$; (ii) A closure $\alpha'(x) \vee g(f(x)) \approx x$, such that $\alpha(x) = \alpha'(x) \vee \alpha''(x)$, has been derived before; (iii) If Nominal Generation 2 has been applied to some $\alpha(x) \vee \bigvee_{i=1}^{n_1} [f(x)] \approx t_i' \vee \bigvee_{i=1}^{m_1} x \approx c_i'$ (with the same $\alpha(x)$ and f), then k, d_i, e_i, and B_i are the same as in this previous application; otherwise, $k = n + m$ and d_i, e_i, and $B_i \in \mathcal{B} \setminus \mathcal{A}$ are fresh.

Lemma 3 (Soundness). *In every $\mathcal{BS}_{DL}$ saturation, each application of a simplification rule is sound.*

Proof. Let $N_0, N_1, \ldots, N_n$ be a $\mathcal{BS}_{DL}$ saturation and I_0 a model of N_0. We prove the lemma by constructing a model I_s for each N_s with $1 \leq s \leq n$ inductively. Consider all possible cases for the inference producing N_s from N_{s-1}:

(Standard $\mathcal{BS}$ inferences) $I_s := I_{s-1}$ is clearly a model of N_s.

(Decomposition 1) If the predicate symbol A is reused in the inference, we set $I_s := I_{s-1}$; otherwise, we extend I_{s-1} to I_s by interpreting $A(x)$ exactly as $L\rho$. Obviously, I_s is a model of N_s.

(Decomposition 2) Analogous to Decomposition 1.

(Nominal Generation 1) If c_i are reused in the inference, we set $I_s := I_{s-1}$. If c_i are new and $\alpha(x)$ is true for all x, we extend I_{s-1} to I_s by interpreting new symbols arbitrarily. Otherwise, $\alpha(x) \vee \bigvee_{i=1}^{n} [f(x)] \approx t_i$ ensures that, for those x for which $\alpha(x)$ is false in I_{s-1}, $f(x)$ has ℓ distinct values $o_1, \ldots, o_\ell$ in I_{s-1}, $1 \leq \ell \leq n$, so we extend I_{s-1} to I_s by interpreting c_i as o_i for $i \leq \ell$ and as o_1 for $i > \ell$.

Hence, if $\alpha(x)$ is true for all x, all conclusions are obviously true in I_s. Otherwise, c_i represent exactly those values $f(x)$ for which $\alpha(x)$ is false, so each c_i is interpreted as some t_j; therefore, all conclusions are true in I_s.

(Nominal Generation 2) If d_i, e_i, and B_i are reused in the inference, we set $I_s := I_{s-1}$. If d_i, e_i, and B_i are new and $\alpha(x)$ is true for all x, we extend I_{s-1} to I_s by interpreting d_i and e_i arbitrarily, and making B_i false everywhere. Otherwise, let x be such that $\alpha(x)$ is false in I_{s-1}. By Condition (ii), $\alpha'(x)$ is also false, so $x \approx g(f(x))$. Moreover, $\alpha(x) \vee \bigvee_{i=1}^{n} [f(x)] \approx t_i \vee \bigvee_{i=1}^{m} x \approx c_i$ ensures that either $f(x)$ is equal to one of $t_1, \ldots, t_n$, or x is equal to one of $c_1, \ldots, c_m$. These two conditions imply that x can only be equal to one of $g(t_1), \ldots, g(t_n), c_1, \ldots, c_m$, so $\alpha(x)$ is false for exactly ℓ distinct domain elements $o_1, \ldots, o_\ell$, $1 \leq \ell \leq n + m$. We extend I_{s-1} to I_s as follows: for $i \leq \ell$, we interpret d_i as o_i, e_i as $f(o_i)$, and make B_i true only for o_i; for $i > \ell$, we interpret d_i as o_1, e_i as $f(o_1)$, and make B_i true only for o_1.

Hence, if $\alpha(x)$ is true for all x, all conclusions are obviously true in I_s. Otherwise, for every x such that $\alpha(x)$ is false, i exists such that d_i is equal to x, B_i holds only on x, and e_i is equal to $f(x)$. This makes the first three conclusions true in I_s; the fourth conclusion is true in I_s because of the premise.   □

Lemma 4 (Correctness). *All $\mathcal{BS}_{DL}$ simplification rules are correct.*

Proof. For each simplification rule with the premise $C \cdot \rho$ and conclusions $C_i \cdot \rho$, $1 \leq i \leq n$, ground substitution τ, and rewrite system $\mathcal{R}$, we need to show that, if $C \cdot \rho\tau$ is variable irreducible w.r.t. $\mathcal{R}$, then (i) $C_i \cdot \rho\tau$ are variable irreducible w.r.t. $\mathcal{R}$, (ii) $C_1\rho\tau, \ldots, C_n\rho\tau \models C\rho\tau$, and (iii) $C\rho\tau \succ C_i\rho\tau$. Property (i) is trivially satisfied for all simplification rules from Table 6, since each substitution position in $C_i \cdot \rho$ corresponds to a substitution position in $C \cdot \rho$. Next, we prove properties (ii) and (iii) for each rule. Let $u = x\tau$.

(Decomposition 1) The instance $C = D\rho\tau \vee L\rho\tau$ of the premise can be obtained by resolving the instances $E_1 = \neg A(u) \vee L\rho\tau$ and $E_2 = D\rho\tau \vee A(u)$ of the conclusions on $A(u)$. Furthermore, $D\rho\tau$ contains a term $h(u)$ by Condition (ii), and $h(u) \succ A(u)$ by Definition 2, so $D\rho\tau \succ A(u)$. Similarly, $L\rho\tau$ contains a term $f(u)$ by Condition (i), so $L\rho\tau \succ \neg A(u)$. Thus, $C \succ E_1$ and $C \succ E_2$.

(Decomposition 2) By Condition (i), $D\rho$ contains either $h(x)$, but then $h(u) \succ B(u)$, or $D\rho$ contains $(\neg)A(x)$, but then $(\neg)A(u) \succ B(u)$ by Definition 2. Hence, $D\rho\tau \succ B(u)$, so the rest is analogous to Decomposition 1.

(Nominal Generation 1) The instance $C = \alpha(u) \vee \bigvee_{i=1}^{n} f(u) \approx t_i$ of the premise can be obtained by simultaneously paramodulating on each c_i from $D = \alpha(u) \vee \bigvee_{i=1}^{k} f(u) \approx c_i$ into $E_i = \alpha(u) \vee \bigvee_{j=1}^{n} c_i \approx t_j$. Furthermore, by Condition (i) of Nominal Generation 1, some $t = t_i$ is of the form $h(c)$, and, because $h(c) \succ c_i$, we have $f(u) \approx t \succ f(u) \approx c_i$, which implies $C \succ D$. Similarly, $f(u) \approx t_j \succ c_i \approx t_j$, so $C \succ E_i$.

(Nominal Generation 2) The instance $C = \alpha(u) \vee \bigvee_{i=1}^{n} f(u) \approx t_i \vee \bigvee_{i=1}^{m} u \approx c_i$ of the premise can be obtained from the conclusions as follows: first, paramodulate from $C_i = \neg B_i(u) \vee f(u) \approx e_i$ and from $D_i = \neg B_i(u) \vee u \approx d_i$ on e_i and d_i, respectively, into $E_i = \alpha(u) \vee \bigvee_{j=1}^{n} e_i \approx t_j \vee \bigvee_{j=1}^{m} d_i \approx c_j$; this produces $E_i' = \alpha(u) \vee \neg B_i(u) \vee \bigvee_{j=1}^{n} f(u) \approx t_j \vee \bigvee_{j=1}^{m} u \approx c_j$; then, resolve all E_i' with $F = \alpha(u) \vee \bigvee_{i=1}^{k} B_i(u)$ on $B_i(u)$ to obtain C. Furthermore, some $t = t_i$ is of the form $h(c)$ by Condition (i), so $h(c) \succ e_i$ implies $f(u) \approx t \succ f(u) \approx e_i$. Since

$f(u) \succ \neg B_i(u)$, so $C \succ C_i$. Similarly, $f(u) \approx t \succ u \approx d_i$, so $C \succ D_i$. Finally, $f(u) \succ e_i$ and $f(u) \succ d_i$ imply $C \succ E_i$, and $f(u) \succ B_i(u)$ implies $C \succ F$.   □

4.3   Saturation of DL-Closures by $\mathcal{BS}_{DL}$

We now show that $\mathcal{BS}_{DL}$ inferences on DL-closures always produce a DL-closure.

Lemma 5 (Preservation of DL-Closures). *Let N be a set of DL-closures to which no $\mathcal{BS}_{DL}$ simplification is applicable. Then, an application of a $\mathcal{BS}_{DL}$ inference to N followed by exhaustive simplification produces a set of DL-closures.*

Proof. Before considering all possible inferences with closures from N, we consider the types of literals that can be eligible in each closure from N. Each closure of type 1–4 contains exactly one literal containing a function symbol; this literal is then eligible since it is maximal and no literal is selected. A closure of type 5 either contains a literal $x \not\approx t$ which is selected, or it contains a guard for x which is selected. A closure of type 6 (that is not also of type 5) can contain a literal $x \not\approx c$, which is then selected. Otherwise, the closure must contain a literal $(\neg)B([f(x)])$: if this were not the case, the closure would have the form $\alpha(x) \vee \bigvee [f(x)] \approx t_i \vee \bigvee x \approx c_i$; if some t_i is of the form $h(c)$, the closure would be simplified by Nominal Generation 1 or 2 (Condition (ii) of Nominal Generation 2 is satisfied because Condition $(*)$ holds for the premise); if all t_i are constants, the closure would be simplified by Decomposition 2 (Condition (i) is satisfied by a guard for x occurring in $\alpha(x)$). Since $B(f(x)) \succ f(x)$ and $B(f(x)) \succ g(c)$ by Definition 2, a literal of this form is eligible for inferences. The cases for the remaining closures are straightforward and are summarized in Table 7.

Next, we enumerate all $\mathcal{BS}_{DL}$-inferences between DL-closures and show that they result in DL-closures. With $[c1, c2] = [s] = [r1, r2, \ldots]$ we denote an

Table 7. Eligible Literals in DL-Closures

1	$\alpha(x) \vee \boxed{(\neg)f(x) \approx g(x)}$	2	$\alpha(x) \vee \boxed{(\neg)f([g(x)]) \approx x}$
3	$\alpha(x) \vee \boxed{(\neg)A(f(x))}$	4	$\beta(x) \vee \boxed{(\neg)f(x) \approx c}$
5.1	$\beta(x) \vee \bigvee(\neg)x \approx t_i \vee \boxed{x \not\approx t}$	5.2	$\beta(x) \vee \boxed{\neg B(x)} \vee \bigvee x \approx t_i$

6.1 $\alpha(x) \vee \bigvee [f(x)] \approx t_i \vee \bigvee(\neg)x \approx c_i \vee \boxed{x \not\approx c}$

6.2 $\alpha(x) \vee \beta([f(x)]) \vee \boxed{(\neg)B([f(x)])} \vee \bigvee [f(x)] \approx t_i \vee \bigvee x \approx c_i$

7   $\alpha_1(x) \vee \boxed{\neg R(x,y)} \vee \alpha_2(y) \vee \bigvee_{i=1}^n f_i(x) \approx y$

8.1	$\boxed{\neg R(x,y)} \vee S(x,y)$	8.2	$\boxed{\neg R(x,y)} \vee S(y,x)$
9.1	$\alpha(x) \vee \boxed{R(x, f(x))}$	9.2	$\alpha(x) \vee \boxed{R(f(x), x)}$
10.1	$\beta(x) \vee \boxed{R(x, c)}$	10.2	$\beta(x) \vee \boxed{R(c, x)}$

11.1	$\boxed{(\neg)B(t)}$	11.2	$\boxed{(\neg)t_1 \approx t_2}$	11.3	$\boxed{(\neg)f(g(c)) \approx d}$
11.4	$\boxed{(\neg)R(c, d)}$	11.5	$\boxed{(\neg)R(c, f(d))}$	11.6	$\boxed{(\neg)R(f(c), d)}$

inference between closures c1 and c2 resulting in closures $r1, r2, \ldots$, possibly by applying simplification s exhaustively. Cut, ground unit resolution, and closure subsumption ensure that ground literals occur only in unit closures; we call a combination these inferences *splitting*.

Resolution inferences are possible only between closures of types 3, 5.2, 6.2, and 11.1 on unary literals; 9, 10, 11.4, 11.5, and 11.6 on positive binary literals; and 7, 8, 11.4, 11.5, and 11.6 on negative binary literals. Resolution with a premise of type 11 results in a ground closure, which is split into closures of type 11. The remaining resolution inferences are as follows: [3,3] = [5], [3,5.2] = [6], [3,6.2] = [6], [5.2,6.2] = [6], [6.2,6.2] = [6], [9.1,7] = [Decomposition 1] = [1,6], [9.2,7] = [Decomposition 1] = [2,6], [9,8] = [9], [10.1,7] = [Decomposition 2, Splitting] = [4,5,11], [10.2,7] = [Splitting] = [5,11], [10,8] = [10].

Superposition inferences are possible from a nonground closure of type 1, 2, or 4, or from a ground closure of type 11.2 or 11.3, either into a term $f(x)$ of 1, 3, 4, or 9, a term $f([g(x)])$ of 2, or a ground (sub)term of 5.1, 6.1, 10, or 11. Note that superposition into or from a ground term does not increase the term depth, so the other premise remains of the same type or becomes ground. Therefore, we do not consider types 5.1, 6.1, 10, and 11 in the following case analysis.

Superposition from 1 into 1, 3, 4, or 9 produces the closure of the latter type, since a function symbol f is just replaced by g: [1,1] = [1], [1,3] = [3], [1,4] = [4], [1,9] = [9]. Superposition from 1 into 2 produces $\alpha([g'(x)]) \lor \alpha'(x) \lor g([g'(x)]) \approx x$ which is simplified into types 2 and 6 using Decomposition 1.

Superposition from 2 into 1, 3, 4, or 9 instantiates the variable of the second premise to $[g(x)]$: [2,1] = [Decomposition 1] = [2,6], [2,3] = [6], [2,4] = [6], [2,9] = [Decomposition 1] = [9,6]. Superposition from 2 into 2 produces either a tautology, which is deleted, or a closure with a literal $x \not\approx x$, which is removed by reflexivity resolution and subsumption deletion.

Superposition from 4 into 1, 2, 3, 4, or 9 results in these inferences: [4,1] = [4], [4,2] = [6], [4,3] = [Splitting] =[5,11], [4,4] = [Splitting] = [5,11], [4,9] = [10].

Reflexivity resolution inferences can be applied only to a closure of type 1, 5.1, 6.1, or 11.2. For 1 we obtain 5; in the remaining cases, the result is ground and it is split into closures of type 11.

Factoring inferences are not applicable, because duplicate literals are eagerly eliminated and closures with multiple equality literals are eagerly decomposed.

Condition (∗). Consider an inference producing a closure of type 6 with a literal $x \approx c_i$. Such an inference is either a superposition between 2 and 4, so the premise of type 2 validates Condition (∗) of the conclusion, or it has a premise of type 6, so $x \approx c_i$ in the conclusion stems from this premise. Hence, (∗) is satisfied for all conclusions of type 6.

Guards are preserved by all inferences because each premise contains a guard, and no inference involves a negative nonequational literal from all premises.

Simplification inferences always produce DL-closures: for our custom rules, this follows from Table 6, and for the remaining standard ones this is trivial.   □

4.4   Termination and Complexity Analysis

We now show that each saturation of $\Gamma(KB)$ by $\mathcal{BS}_{DL}$ terminates. Assuming unary coding of numbers in number restrictions, the number of function symbols in $\Gamma(KB)$ is linear in $|KB|$. To the best of our knowledge, this assumption is used in all practical DL reasoning algorithms.

Lemma 6. *Let $\Gamma(KB) = N_0, N_1, \ldots, N_n$ be a $\mathcal{BS}_{DL}$ saturation. Then, the number of constants in each N_i is at most doubly exponential, and the number of clo-. sures in N_i is at most triply exponential in $|KB|$, for unary coding of numbers.*

Proof. Nominal Generation 1 and 2 introduce new constants at most once for a combination of $\alpha(x)$ and f. Other than the predicates from $\Gamma(KB)$, $\alpha(x)$ can contain the predicates A introduced by Decomposition 1, of which at most four are introduced for a pair of function symbols f and g. Hence, the number of disjunctions $\alpha(x)$ is at most exponential in $|KB|$, and so is the number of Nominal Generation inferences that introduce new constants. Furthermore, the premise of such an inference can involve all terms of the form c or $f(c)$ derived thus far, so the total number of constants can increase only by a linear factor. Thus, the number of constants in N_i can be at most doubly exponential in $|KB|$.

Decomposition 2 introduces at most one predicate B for a combination of f and c, and Nominal Generation 2 introduces at most one predicate B_i for each e_i or d_i. Hence, the number of predicates in N_i is at most doubly exponential in $|KB|$. Since each DL-closure contains at most one variable, the number of different literals is at most doubly exponential, so the number of DL-closures without repeated literals is at most triply exponential in $|KB|$.   □

Theorem 1. *$\mathcal{BS}_{DL}$ decides satisfiability of a $\mathcal{SHOIQ}$ knowledge base KB in triply exponential time, for unary coding of numbers.*

Proof. Without loss of generality we can assume that an inference between two closures is performed at most once in a saturation. By Lemmas 2 and 5, each set of closures in a $\mathcal{BS}_{DL}$ saturation contains only DL-closures, and is at most triply exponential in size by Lemma 6. Hence, all DL-closures are derived after at most triply exponential number of steps. Because simplification rules of $\mathcal{BS}_{DL}$ are sound and correct by Lemmas 3 and 4, the set of closures upon termination is saturated up to redundancy. Hence, $\Gamma(KB)$, and by Lemma 1 KB as well, is satisfiable if and only if the saturated set does not contain the empty closure.

Since $\mathcal{BS}_{DL}$ uses the cut rule, it is nondeterministic, so a straightforward complexity estimation gives us only a nondeterministic triply exponential upper bound. This can be improved to a deterministic triply exponential bound as follows. The number of unit ground closures is at most doubly exponential, so the number of cut inferences performed on each branch of the saturation is at most doubly exponential. Hence, if we implement our procedure using backtracking, the number of all inferences is triply exponential.   □

Table 8. Expressing Big Cardinality Restrictions in $\mathcal{SHOIQ}$

T1.	$\top \sqsubseteq \,\leqslant 2\,R.\top$	T2.	$\top \sqsubseteq \,\geqslant 1\,R^-.\top$
T3.	$B_0 \sqsubseteq \forall R.\neg B_0$	T4.	$B_{i+1} \sqcap B_i \sqsubseteq \forall R.((B_{i+1} \sqcap B_i) \sqcup (\neg B_{i+1} \sqcap \neg B_i))$
T5.	$\neg B_0 \sqsubseteq \forall R.B_0$	T6.	$\neg B_{i+1} \sqcap B_i \sqsubseteq \forall R.((\neg B_{i+1} \sqcap B_i) \sqcup (B_{i+1} \sqcap \neg B_i))$
T7.	$\neg B_p \sqcap \cdots \sqcap \neg B_0 \sqsubseteq \{c\}$		$i = 1 \ldots p$

T8.	$\top \sqsubseteq \,\geqslant 2\,S.\top$	T9.	$\top \sqsubseteq \,\leqslant 1\,S^-.\top$
T10.	$A_0 \sqsubseteq \forall S.\neg A_0$	T11.	$A_{i+1} \sqcap A_i \sqsubseteq \forall S.((A_{i+1} \sqcap A_i) \sqcup (\neg A_{i+1} \sqcap \neg A_i))$
T12.	$\neg A_0 \sqsubseteq \forall S.A_0$	T13.	$\neg A_{i+1} \sqcap A_i \sqsubseteq \forall S.((\neg A_{i+1} \sqcap A_i) \sqcup (A_{i+1} \sqcap \neg A_i))$
A1.	$\neg A_q \sqcap \cdots \sqcap \neg A_0(c)$		$i = 1 \ldots q$

T1—T7 express $|B_p \sqcap \cdots \sqcap B_0| \leq 2^{2^p}$; T8—T12, A1 express $|A_q \sqcap \cdots \sqcap A_0| \geq 2^{2^q}$

5   Discussion and Conclusion

In this paper, we presented a resolution-based procedure for deciding satisfiability of a $\mathcal{SHOIQ}$ knowledge base KB running in triply exponential time. The high complexity of our procedure is due to a possibly doubly exponential number of constants introduced by Nominal Generation 1 and 2. To understand the situations in which this can happen, consider the following example.

Let KB be a knowledge base from Table 8, which uses the well-known encoding of binary numbers by DL concepts. A concept B_i represents the i-th bit of a number. Thus, a number $b_p\,b_{p-1}\ldots b_0$ with $b_i \in \{0,1\}$ is represented by a concept $\mu_p(b_p) \sqcap \cdots \sqcap \mu_0(b_0)$, where $\mu_i(0) = \neg B_i$ and $\mu_i(1) = B_i$. Axioms T1 and T2 ensure that a model of KB can be embedded into a binary R-tree: every element has at most two R-successors and at least one R-predecessor. Axioms T3–T6 ensure that the numbers $b_p\,b_{p-1}\ldots b_0$ corresponding to elements connected by R-links are incremented by one. Together with axiom T7, this ensures that the number of elements in the concept at the k-th level of this tree is at most 2^k. In particular, the last level, corresponding to the concept $B_p \sqcap \cdots \sqcap B_0$, can contain at most 2^{2^p} elements. Using a dual set of axioms T8–T13 and A1, we express in a similar way that the concept $A_q \sqcap \cdots \sqcap A_0$ contains at least 2^{2^q} objects.

Now checking subsumption between $A_q \sqcap \cdots \sqcap A_0$ and $B_p \sqcap \cdots \sqcap B_0$ w.r.t. KB amounts to testing whether a set with 2^{2^q} elements can be embedded into another set with 2^{2^p} elements. Such combinatorial problems, commonly called the *pigeon hole principle*, are known to be very hard for resolution [9]. On KB, our algorithm applies the Nominal Generation rules for all possible $\alpha(x) = (\neg)B_p(x) \vee \cdots \vee (\neg)B_0(x)$ and introduces a doubly exponential number of constants, because the constraint $|B_p \sqcap \cdots \sqcap B_0| \leq 2^{2^p}$ is represented using a fresh constant for each element of the set. Although this observation does not prove that an optimal resolution-based procedure for $\mathcal{SHOIQ}$ cannot exist, it suggests that resolution alone may not suffice. In our future work, we shall investigate if it is possible to integrate algebraic reasoning directly into resolution—for example, as this was done for tableau calculi in [8].

However, worst-case complexity does not say anything about the typical case. Namely, the previous example causes problems because it succinctly encodes binary numbers. However, many applications do not require much combinatorial reasoning, so, on them, our algorithm does not introduce too many new constants. In fact, the Nominal Generation rules are triggered by terms $g(c)$, which can only result from interaction between inverse roles, number restrictions, and nominals. If these constructs are not used simultaneously, our algorithm becomes similar to the algorithm for the DL $\mathcal{SHIQ}$ presented in [11], and it runs in exponential time. Thus, our algorithm exhibits "pay-as-you-go" behavior. We shall implement our new algorithm in KAON2 to see how it behaves in practice.

References

1. A. Armando, S. Ranise, and M. Rusinowitch. Uniform Derivation of Decision Procedures by Superposition. In *Proc. CSL' 01*, volume 2142 of *LNCS*, pages 549–563, Paris, France, September 10–13 2001. Springer.
2. F. Baader, D. Calvanese, D. McGuinness, D. Nardi, and P. F. Patel-Schneider, editors. *The Description Logic Handbook: Theory, Implementation and Applications.* Cambridge University Press, January 2003.
3. F. Baader and T. Nipkow. *Term Rewriting and All That.* Cambridge University Press, 1998.
4. L. Bachmair and H. Ganzinger. Resolution Theorem Proving. In A. Robinson and A. Voronkov, editors, *Handbook of Automated Reasoning*, volume I, chapter 2, pages 19–99. Elsevier Science, 2001.
5. L. Bachmair, H. Ganzinger, C. Lynch, and W. Snyder. Basic Paramodulation. *Information and Computation*, 121(2):172–192, 1995.
6. C. Fermüller, T. Tammet, N. Zamov, and A. Leitsch. *Resolution Methods for the Decision Problem*, volume 679 of *LNAI*. Springer, 1993.
7. H. Ganzinger and H. de Nivelle. A Superposition Decision Procedure for the Guarded Fragment with Equality. In *Proc. LICS '99*, pages 295–305, Trento, Italy, July 2–5 1999. IEEE Computer Society.
8. V. Haarslev, M. Timmann, and R. Möller. Combining Tableaux and Algebraic Methods for Reasoning with Qualified Number Restrictions. In *Proc. DL 2001*, volume 49 of *CEUR Workshop Proceedings*, Stanford, CA, USA, August 1–3 2001.
9. A. Haken. The Intractability of Resolution. *Theorerical Computer Science*, 39:297–308, 1985.
10. I. Horrocks and U. Sattler. A Tableaux Decision Procedure for $\mathcal{SHOIQ}$. In *Proc. IJCAI 2005*, pages 448–453, Edinburgh, UK, July 30–August 5 2005. Morgan Kaufmann Publishers.
11. U. Hustadt, B. Motik, and U. Sattler. Reducing $\mathcal{SHIQ}^-$ Description Logic to Disjunctive Datalog Programs. In *Proc. KR 2004*, pages 152–162, Whistler, Canada, June 2–5 2004. AAAI Press.
12. W. H. Joyner Jr. Resolution Strategies as Decision Procedures. *Journal of the ACM*, 23(3):398–417, 1976.
13. Y. Kazakov and H. de Nivelle. A Resolution Decision Procedure for the Guarded Fragment with Transitive Guards. In *Proc. IJCAR 2004*, volume 3097 of *LNAI*, pages 122–136, Cork, Ireland, July 4–8 2004. Springer.
14. B. Motik. *Reasoning in Description Logics using Resolution and Deductive Databases.* PhD thesis, Univesität Karlsruhe, Germany, 2006.
15. R. Nieuwenhuis and A. Rubio. Theorem Proving with Ordering and Equality Constrained Clauses. *Journal of Symbolic Computation*, 19(4):312–351, 1995.
16. H. De Nivelle, R. A. Schmidt, and U. Hustadt. Resolution-Based Methods for Modal Logics. *Logic Journal of the IGPL*, 8(3):265–292, 2000.

17. A. Nonnengart and C. Weidenbach. Computing Small Clause Normal Forms. In A. Robinson and A. Voronkov, editors, *Handbook of Automated Reasoning*, volume I, chapter 6, pages 335–367. Elsevier Science, 2001.

18. L. Pacholski, W. Szwast, and L. Tendera. Complexity Results for First-Order Two-Variable Logic with Counting. *SIAM Journal on Computing*, 29(4):1083–1117, 2000.

19. I. Pratt-Hartmann. Complexity of the Two-Variable Fragment with Counting Quantifiers. *Journal of Logic, Language and Information*, 14(3):369–395, 2005.

20. R. A. Schmidt and U. Hustadt. A Principle for Incorporating Axioms into the First-Order Translation of Modal Formulae. In *Proc. CADE-19*, volume 2741 of *LNAI*, pages 412–426, Miami Beach, FL, USA, July 28–August 2 2003. Springer.

21. S. Tobies. *Complexity Results and Practical Algorithms for Logics in Knowledge Representation*. PhD thesis, RWTH Aachen, Germany, 2001.

Author Index

Lecture Notes in Artificial Intelligence (LNAI)

Vol. 3904: M. Baldoni, U. Endriss, A. Omicini, P. Torroni (Eds.), Declarative Agent Languages and Technologies III. XII, 245 pages. 2006.

Vol. 3900: F. Toni, P. Torroni (Eds.), Computational Logic in Multi-Agent Systems. XVII, 427 pages. 2006.

Vol. 3899: S. Frintrop, VOCUS: A Visual Attention System for Object Detection and Goal-Directed Search. XIV, 216 pages. 2006.

Vol. 3898: K. Tuyls, P.J. 't Hoen, K. Verbeeck, S. Sen (Eds.), Learning and Adaption in Multi-Agent Systems. X, 217 pages. 2006.

Vol. 3891: J.S. Sichman, L. Antunes (Eds.), Multi-Agent-Based Simulation VI. X, 191 pages. 2006.

Vol. 3890: S.G. Thompson, R. Ghanea-Hercock (Eds.), Defence Applications of Multi-Agent Systems. XII, 141 pages. 2006.

Vol. 3885: V. Torra, Y. Narukawa, A. Valls, J. Domingo-Ferrer (Eds.), Modeling Decisions for Artificial Intelligence. XII, 374 pages. 2006.

Vol. 3881: S. Gibet, N. Courty, J.-F. Kamp (Eds.), Gesture in Human-Computer Interaction and Simulation. XIII, 344 pages. 2006.

Vol. 3874: R. Missaoui, J. Schmidt (Eds.), Formal Concept Analysis. X, 309 pages. 2006.

Vol. 3873: L. Maicher, J. Park (Eds.), Charting the Topic Maps Research and Applications Landscape. VIII, 281 pages. 2006.

Vol. 3863: M. Kohlhase (Ed.), Mathematical Knowledge Management. XI, 405 pages. 2006.

Vol. 3862: R.H. Bordini, M. Dastani, J. Dix, A.E.F. Seghrouchni (Eds.), Programming Multi-Agent Systems. XIV, 267 pages. 2006.

Vol. 3849: I. Bloch, A. Petrosino, A.G.B. Tettamanzi (Eds.), Fuzzy Logic and Applications. XIV, 438 pages. 2006.

Vol. 3848: J.-F. Boulicaut, L. De Raedt, H. Mannila (Eds.), Constraint-Based Mining and Inductive Databases. X, 401 pages. 2006.

Vol. 3847: K.P. Jantke, A. Lunzer, N. Spyratos, Y. Tanaka (Eds.), Federation over the Web. X, 215 pages. 2006.

Vol. 3835: G. Sutcliffe, A. Voronkov (Eds.), Logic for Programming, Artificial Intelligence, and Reasoning. XIV, 744 pages. 2006.

Vol. 3830: D. Weyns, H. V.D. Parunak, F. Michel (Eds.), Environments for Multi-Agent Systems II. VIII, 291 pages. 2006.

Vol. 3817: M. Faundez-Zanuy, L. Janer, A. Esposito, A. Satue-Villar, J. Roure, V. Espinosa-Duro (Eds.), Nonlinear Analyses and Algorithms for Speech Processing. XII, 380 pages. 2006.

Vol. 3814: M. Maybury, O. Stock, W. Wahlster (Eds.), Intelligent Technologies for Interactive Entertainment. XV, 342 pages. 2005.

Vol. 3809: S. Zhang, R. Jarvis (Eds.), AI 2005: Advances in Artificial Intelligence. XXVII, 1344 pages. 2005.

Vol. 3808: C. Bento, A. Cardoso, G. Dias (Eds.), Progress in Artificial Intelligence. XVIII, 704 pages. 2005.

Vol. 3802: Y. Hao, J. Liu, Y.-P. Wang, Y.-m. Cheung, H. Yin, L. Jiao, J. Ma, Y.-C. Jiao (Eds.), Computational Intelligence and Security, Part II. XLII, 1166 pages. 2005.

Vol. 3801: Y. Hao, J. Liu, Y.-P. Wang, Y.-m. Cheung, H. Yin, L. Jiao, J. Ma, Y.-C. Jiao (Eds.), Computational Intelligence and Security, Part I. XLI, 1122 pages. 2005.

Vol. 3789: A. Gelbukh, Á. de Albornoz, H. Terashima-Marín (Eds.), MICAI 2005: Advances in Artificial Intelligence. XXVI, 1198 pages. 2005.

Vol. 3782: K.-D. Althoff, A. Dengel, R. Bergmann, M. Nick, T.R. Roth-Berghofer (Eds.), Professional Knowledge Management. XXIII, 739 pages. 2005.

Vol. 3763: H. Hong, D. Wang (Eds.), Automated Deduction in Geometry. X, 213 pages. 2006.

Vol. 3755: G.J. Williams, S.J. Simoff (Eds.), Data Mining. XI, 331 pages. 2006.

Vol. 3735: A. Hoffmann, H. Motoda, T. Scheffer (Eds.), Discovery Science. XVI, 400 pages. 2005.

Vol. 3734: S. Jain, H.U. Simon, E. Tomita (Eds.), Algorithmic Learning Theory. XII, 490 pages. 2005.

Vol. 3721: A.M. Jorge, L. Torgo, P.B. Brazdil, R. Camacho, J. Gama (Eds.), Knowledge Discovery in Databases: PKDD 2005. XXIII, 719 pages. 2005.

Vol. 3720: J. Gama, R. Camacho, P.B. Brazdil, A.M. Jorge, L. Torgo (Eds.), Machine Learning: ECML 2005. XXIII, 769 pages. 2005.

Vol. 3717: B. Gramlich (Ed.), Frontiers of Combining Systems. X, 321 pages. 2005.

Vol. 3702: B. Beckert (Ed.), Automated Reasoning with Analytic Tableaux and Related Methods. XIII, 343 pages. 2005.

Vol. 3698: U. Furbach (Ed.), KI 2005: Advances in Artificial Intelligence. XIII, 409 pages. 2005.

Vol. 3690: M. Pěchouček, P. Petta, L.Z. Varga (Eds.), Multi-Agent Systems and Applications IV. XVII, 667 pages. 2005.

Vol. 3684: R. Khosla, R.J. Howlett, L.C. Jain (Eds.), Knowledge-Based Intelligent Information and Engineering Systems, Part IV. LXXIX, 933 pages. 2005.

Vol. 3683: R. Khosla, R.J. Howlett, L.C. Jain (Eds.), Knowledge-Based Intelligent Information and Engineering Systems, Part III. LXXX, 1397 pages. 2005.

Vol. 3682: R. Khosla, R.J. Howlett, L.C. Jain (Eds.), Knowledge-Based Intelligent Information and Engineering Systems, Part II. LXXIX, 1371 pages. 2005.

Vol. 3681: R. Khosla, R.J. Howlett, L.C. Jain (Eds.), Knowledge-Based Intelligent Information and Engineering Systems, Part I. LXXX, 1319 pages. 2005.

Vol. 3673: S. Bandini, S. Manzoni (Eds.), AI*IA 2005: Advances in Artificial Intelligence. XIV, 614 pages. 2005.

Vol. 3662: C. Baral, G. Greco, N. Leone, G. Terracina (Eds.), Logic Programming and Nonmonotonic Reasoning. XIII, 454 pages. 2005.

Vol. 3661: T. Panayiotopoulos, J. Gratch, R. Aylett, D. Ballin, P. Olivier, T. Rist (Eds.), Intelligent Virtual Agents. XIII, 506 pages. 2005.